NEUROPSYCHOLOGY OF ALZHEIMER'S DISEASE AND OTHER DEMENTIAS

NEUROPSYCHOLOGY OF ALZHEIMER'S DISEASE AND OTHER DEMENTIAS

Edited by

Randolph W. Parks, Ph.D., Psy.D., A.B.P.D.C.

Geriatric Psychopharmacology, Laboratory of Clinical Science
National Institute of Mental Health
Department of Psychiatry
Center for Alzheimer's Disease and Related Disorders
Southern Illinois University School of Medicine

Ronald F. Zec, Ph.D., A.B.P.N.

Departments of Psychiatry and Neurology
Center for Alzheimer's Disease and Related Disorders
Southern Illinois University School of Medicine

Robert S. Wilson, Ph.D., A.B.P.P.

Rush Alzheimer's Disease Center
Department of Psychology and Social Sciences
Rush Medical College

New York   Oxford
OXFORD UNIVERSITY PRESS
1993

Oxford University Press

Oxford   New York   Toronto
Delhi   Bombay   Calcutta   Madras   Karachi
Kuala Lumpur   Singapore   Hong Kong   Tokyo
Nairobi   Dar es Salaam   Cape Town
Melbourne   Auckland   Madrid

and associated companies in
Berlin   Ibadan

Library of Congress Cataloging-in-Publication Data
Neuropsychology of Alzheimer's disease and other dementias /
[edited by] Randolph W. Parks, Ronald F. Zec, Robert S. Wilson.
    p. cm.   Includes bibliographical references and index.
ISBN 0-19-506612-X
1. Alzheimer's disease—Physiological aspects. 2. Alzheimer's
disease—Diagnosis. 3. Dementia—Physiological aspects.
4. Clinical neuropsychology.
I. Parks, Randolph W. II. Zec, Ronald F.
III. Wilson, Robert S. (Robert Smith), 1948–   .
    [DNLM: 1. Alzheimer's Disease. 2. Brain—radionuclide imaging.
3. Dementia—diagnosis. 4. Diagnosis Differential.
5. Neuropsychology.
WM 220 N4927] RC523.N485 1993 616.8′31—dc20
DNLM/DLC 92-49274

Preface

The past 25 years have witnessed an explosion of scientific interest in Alzheimer's disease in particular and in dementing illnesses in general. In part, this upsurge of interest reflects the continued growth of the older population age groups in the United States and other developed countries. It also reflects a growing appreciation of the enormous consequences of these disorders in terms of public health costs and the shattered lives of the afflicted individuals and their families.

The distinguishing feature of Alzheimer's disease and the other disorders described in this volume is dementia, or global impairment of cognitive functions. Not surprisingly, therefore, much of the recent research on Alzheimer's disease and other dementias has been neuropsychological in nature. Although many of these research efforts have traversed familiar paths, others have not. For example, because of the wide variation in the general level of cognitive impairment observed in the dementias, many new cognitive assessment tools have been developed. The assessment of neuropsychiatric manifestations among persons with dementia has also presented neuropsychologists with a relatively novel set of challenges. In addition to these neuropsychological developments, research by other neuroscientists, epidemiologists, etc., has proceeded at an equally rapid pace. As a result, clinicians who do not specialize in dementia are faced with the daunting task of staying current with a geometrically expanding body of knowledge which has dramatically altered the landscape of the field in the past decade and which promises to become increasingly relevant to clinical practice in the decades to come.

This volume is intended as a bridge connecting leading behavioral neuroscientists investigating the dementias with practitioners responsible for the diagnosis and care of those afflicted. The aim of the volume, then, is to present the most current scientific information on Alzheimer's disease and other dementias in a format that is likely to be useful to practicing neuropsychologists and other clinicians involved in caring for persons with global cognitive impairment. The volume consists of 22 chapters divided into four parts. Part I addresses the principal components of Alzheimer's disease, including chapters on its neuropsychological, behavioral, and neuroanatomic features and on the demarcation between Alzheimer's disease and normal aging. Part II details the neuropsychological features of other major dementia syndromes which may be confused with Alzheimer's disease. These chapters are intended to provide the clinical, neuropsychological, and epidemiological information pertinent to differential diagnosis. Specific issues regarding patho-

physiology and management are also addressed. Part III details recent developments in brain imaging as they relate to dementia. Part IV addresses psychosocial,
pharmacological, and legal/ethical issues pertinent to the care of persons with
Alzheimer's disease. Our hope is that this volume will prove to be a useful guide
and sourcebook for clinicians who face the considerable challenge of improving
the quality of life of those afflicted with these devastating disorders.

Springfield   RWP
Chicago   RFZ
May 1993   RSW

Contents

PART III.   BRAIN IMAGING

chapter). This history should include a review of the patient's current and past functioning in four areas: (a) cognitive, (b) medical, (c) psychosocial, and (d) emotional/psychiatric. A brief Alzheimer patient history form is published in Strub and Black (1988, pp. 143–145) and a useful history form for neuropsychological evaluations is published in Spreen and Strauss (1991, pp. 4–6).

The neuropsychologist needs to determine whether the patient's premorbid and current levels (high, average, or low) of functioning for each of the four areas mentioned above. Indicators of a high level of premorbid cognitive functioning include having been well educated, well read, successful in a cognitively demanding profession, and a leader in the community. Conversely, indicators of a low level of premorbid cognitive functioning include a poor education, poor scholastic performance, and having a low-level job. The neuropsychologist should inquire about the following manifestations of impaired cognitive functioning in daily life: forgetfulness, poor concentration, word-finding difficulty, poor judgment, impairments in problem solving, difficulty with skilled movement (praxis), and tendency to get lost easily. Information about past and current levels of cognitive functioning is essential in judging to what degree there is cognitive decline.

The neuropsychologist should also describe the past and present general health status of the patient. Has the patient been generally in excellent, average, or poor health? What specific illnesses or health problems exist currently or existed previously (e.g., high blood pressure, diabetes, thyroid dysfunction, heart attack, stroke, cancer, head injury, visual or hearing problems, etc.)? Hospitalizations and medications should be recorded. Family illnesses should also be noted.

The neuropsychologist should establish whether the patient has one or more of the three well-established risk factors for AD: advanced age, Down's syndrome, and a history of dementia in first-degree relatives (Cummings & Benson, 1992). The age of the patient is important because the prevalence rate of probable AD is very strongly correlated with age (Evans et al., 1989). The likelihood of a person having AD increases greatly from age 65 to age 90. It is important to inquire about the history of dementia in first-degree relatives, as this presents a well-established risk factor for AD (Hofman et al., 1989; Henderson, 1988). Down's syndrome is another established risk factor for AD (Henderson, 1988).

The neuropsychologist should determine the level of the person's psychosocial functioning by inquiring about school and job histories, marriage and children, social functioning, hobbies and recreation, activities of daily living, and substance abuse. The neuropsychologist should also inquire about any psychiatric problems in the patient's history such as clinical depressions, including their onset, precipitating events, severity, duration, hospitalizations, treatments, and treatment effects.

The patient's premorbid level of functioning needs to be estimated in order to judge to what degree current cognitive status represents a decline from a previously higher level. The probability of making a diagnostic error in deciding the presence or absence of a dementing disorder is appreciably greater if one does not obtain and utilize careful estimates of premorbid cognitive functioning. For example, a bright, well-educated individual may score well within normal limits and thus be diagnosed as normal when in reality this person may be several years into a dementing illness and have deteriorated cognitively (i.e., a false-negative error) (Naugle et al., 1990). Conversely, a poorly educated person with below average intelligence may score in the impaired range and be wrongly diagnosed as having a dementing disorder (i.e., a false-positive error). The neuropsychologist needs to make estimates of premorbid functioning in order to take premorbid level into consideration when interpreting test scores. Premorbid IQ can be estimated by either using a present ability measure (e.g., National Adult Reading Test [NART]) or by using a demographically based estimate in which age, sex, race, education, and occupation are put into a regression formula (Wilson, Rosenbaum, & Brown, 1979; Stebbins, Wilson, Gilley, Bernard, & Fox, 1990; Stebbins, Gilley, Wilson, Bernard, and Fox, 1990). However, research indicates that the applicability of the NART in estimating premorbid IQ in dementia is limited.

In addition to helping estimate the patient's level of premorbid functioning, a thorough history aids in determining the presence of an alternative or coexisting disorder (e.g., depression, vascular disease, Parkinson's disease, etc.).

Early Detection of AD

A typical neuropsychological profile for a person with mild to moderate AD includes recent memory impairment (both verbal and nonverbal), a reduction in overall level of intellectual functioning (including deficits in judgment and abstract reasoning), a lower Performance IQ than Verbal IQ, constructional problems, reduction in verbal fluency, and variable language deficits with naming difficulties being most common (Rosen, 1983a, 1983b; Kaszniak, 1986). Motor disorders rarely are exhibited by AD patients until the late stages, and sensory functions remain intact throughout the course of AD (Cummings, 1990). Minor extrapyramidal symptoms are seen in a subgroup of AD patients (Cummings, 1990).

Impaired intellectual functioning and the symptom triad of memory loss, dysnomia, and visuospatial deficits have been suggested as the hallmark of AD, although patients may exhibit only one or two of these symptoms in the early stages of the disorder (Rosen, 1983a). This variability in dysfunction in the early stages of AD may lead to misdiagnosis, which underscores the necessity for a thorough assessment, for caution in diagnosis, and for retesting 12 months after the initial evaluation to document significant changes. A thorough assessment need not be lengthy, however. With a carefully chosen set of tests, a screening battery taking an hour or less can provide a fairly comprehensive picture of the subject's cognitive status, including most subjects in the relatively early stages of Alzheimer's disease. A somewhat lengthier battery (approximately 2 hours) may be useful in cases suspected of cognitive decline who do not clearly display the degree or pattern of impairments typically seen in an early AD patient.

A useful guideline for the early neuropsychological presentation of AD is memory impairment plus one other area of impaired cognitive functioning (i.e., Memory + 1). In the author's experience, memory impairment is a nearly universal presenting feature, but which other area of cognitive functioning will be next impaired varies across patients. For example, the only additional area of impairment in a given patient may be (a) complex constructional praxis (CFT, clock to command), (b) confrontational naming (BNT), (c) word fluency, (d) psychomotor performance (Trails B, Digit Symbol), or (e) verbal abstraction (Similarities). Ideational praxis and ability to carry out simple multistep commands tend to be impaired later in the course of the illness.

Storandt, Botwinick, and Danzinger (1986) administered a 2-hour neuropsychological test battery three times over 2.5 years to patients with mild Alzheimer dementia and normal control subjects. The test battery included parts of the WMS (Mental Control, Logical Memory, Digit Span, Associate Learning), four WAIS subtests (Information, Comprehension, Block Design, Digit Symbol), the Benton Visual Retention Test (BVRT) (memory and copy), the BNT, Word Fluency, Trail-Making Test Part A, Bender Gestalt Test, and the Crossing-Off Test. Patients and control subjects differed significantly on all tests during the initial baseline assessment, except Digit Span forward. The patient group exhibited significant declines on all tests, whereas no significant decline was found in the control subjects over time. The authors reported that secondary memory and psychomotor speed were especially sensitive to early Alzheimer dementia.

Memory deficits are typically the first cognitive deficits to appear in AD, followed by problems with abstract reasoning and complex attention, and then by impairments in language and visuospatial abilities (Grady et al., 1988) (Figure 1.1). In particular, memory for events (episodic memory) is usually impaired early in the course of AD, and this impairment becomes increasingly severe with dementia progression (Butters, 1984; Kaszniak, 1986; Grady et al., 1988). AD patients, unlike

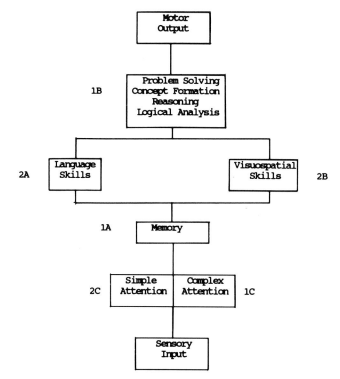

FIGURE 1.1. A brain-behavior model indicating the typical progression of Alzheimer's dementia across specific neuropsychological domains. 1 (A,B,C) usually decline before 2 (A,B,C); A, B, and C appear to decline in that order but overlap considerably; sensory and motor functions are not affected until late stage, if at all. [Adapted from Reitan & Wolfson, (1988) with modifications by R. Zec–AD sequencing and separation of attention and memory into different levels.]

normally aging individuals, forget events rapidly (Moss, Albert, Butters, & Payne, 1986). Thus, memory measures are among the most useful early detectors of AD. Tests of episodic memory, including measures of immediate recall, delayed recall, and recognition, should be included within any dementia assessment battery.

Marshall and Newcombe (1984) argued that patients with brain damage must first be studied in detail as single cases before they can be grouped in a neuropsychologically meaningful manner. Martin (1987) said this statement was especially true for patients diagnosed with AD because of the variability in the cognitive profiles of individual patients in the early and middle stages of the disease. Thus, although the course of AD usually begins with memory impairment and progresses to other cognitive problems, there have been reports of patients with AD, confirmed by biopsy or autopsy, presenting initially with a progressive right parietal lobe syndrome (Crystal, Horoupian, Katzman, & Jotkowitz, 1982) or a progressive aphasia (Kirshner, Webb, Kelly, & Wells, 1984).

The majority of AD patients initially present with memory deficits, and as the dementia progresses will also typically exhibit relatively equal impairments on measures of semantic knowledge (e.g., BNT) and visuospatial and constructional ability (e.g., Rey-Osterreith Complex Figure Test [CFT]) (Martin, 1987). However, some patients exhibit very specific deficits limited to only one of these cognitive domains even though they have relatively equal deficits in general intellectual functioning and memory (Martin, 1987). Martin (1987) reported nine patients who displayed severe word-finding difficulties but relatively intact spatial and constructional skills, and eight patients with the reverse pattern. AD patients ($n = 4$) with predominate word-finding deficits had significantly greater hypometabolism in the left temporal lobe relative to all other cortical regions, whereas patients with primarily severe constructional impairment ($n = 5$) displayed significantly greater hypometabolism in the right temporal and parietal areas. Martin (1987) concludes that this clinical evidence demonstrates that the system responsible for representing semantic knowledge is independent from the system mediating visuospatial and constructional ability.

The memory decline in the normal elderly is primarily limited to secondary memory, whereas AD patients display impairment in all stages of memory: sensory, primary (short-term memory [STM]), secondary (long-term memory [LTM]), and tertiary (remote) (Kaszniak, Poon, & Riege, 1986). A more extensive discussion of memory deficits in AD is provided in the section, Memory, later in this chapter.

Mohs, Kim, Johns, Dunn, and Davis (1986) argued that the sensitivity of a given neuropsychological test to the progressive deterioration in Alzheimer patients is a function of the patient's initial level of performance on that test. Tests on which the patient exhibits an intermediate degree of impairment are most likely to be sensitive to the progressive worsening in the coming year. Tests that are too difficult or too easy for the patient will not be sensitive to immediate subsequent cognitive declines. For example, Mohs et al. (1986) reported that although recall was more impaired on the initial evaluation, recognition memory better documented progressive worsening over 12 months. They also found that learning low-frequency paired associates (a difficult task) and naming common objects (an easy task) were both insensitive to change. On the other hand, scores on tasks of intermediate difficulty, including sentence reading and paired-associate learning, had declined at the 1-year follow-up indicating sensitivity to change (Mohs et al., 1986).

Christensen et al. (1991) did a meta-analysis on studies using psychometric tests to differentiate dementia patients from healthy elderly. Effect sizes were considerably larger for memory and orientation (2.8 and 2.6, respectively) than for language, praxis, or perception (1.9, 1.4, 1.2, respectively).

Tests of episodic memory (e.g., the Buschke Selective Reminding Test [SRT] and the WMS) were the best at discriminating AD patients versus normal controls (Christensen et al., 1991). Confrontational naming and generative naming tests also were good discriminators. The least discriminating test was the NART, which appears to be a relatively good estimator of premorbid intelligence level. Digit Span forward produced lower effect sizes than did language tasks. Mental status scales yielded higher average effect sizes than did most individual neuropsychological tests, except for the measures of episodic memory. Orientation and memory functions were more impaired than language and praxis abilities. Perception was less affected than other domains of functioning. Problem solving was only represented by one investigation in the meta-analysis and thus was not studied well enough to draw conclusions about its efficacy in discriminating normal elderly and dementia patients.

The authors noted that ceiling/floor effects and stage of dementia influenced a test's ability to discriminate demented from healthy elderly (Christensen et al., 1991). In addition, some tests were better discriminators than others at particular stages of the illness.

Christensen et al. (1991) pointed out that the major limitation of their study was that only the effect sizes for single tests were available for meta-analysis, not for combinations of tests (Christensen et al., 1991). Because neuropsychological evaluations involve the interpretation of a combination of tests, the direct applicability of these findings to the clinical context is limited. For example, although language and perceptual tasks may have lower effect sizes than memory tests, these tests may be crucial in the differentiation of AD from other dementing disorders.

Neuropsychological Test Batteries for Dementia

It has been recommended that any battery of neuropsychological tests for the evaluation of dementia needs to provide an assessment of a wide range of cognitive abilities, with special emphasis on memory (Salmon & Butters, 1992; Fuld, 1983; Rosen, 1983a, 1983b). A comprehensive cognitive assessment is necessary in order to provide a reasonably complete description of the individual's cognitive profile and to decide whether a patient has the two or more areas of cognitive impairment required to meet NINCDS-ADRDA neuropsychological criteria for AD (McKhann et al., 1984). A comprehensive assessment should consist of a set of tests that measure the several areas of cognitive decline in Alzheimer patients (such as memory, language, visuospatial functioning, and general intellectual decline). The test series need not be lengthy to assess the several major cognitive domains affected in AD. The NINCDS-ADRDA Task Force recommended tests that could be used to evaluate different domains of neuropsychological functioning in patients suspected of having Alzheimer dementia (McKhann et al., 1984). It has been pointed out, however, that there are many alternative test measures that could be used to evaluate the several areas of cognitive functioning that become impaired in patients with AD (Salmon & Butters, 1992). For example, four different test batteries for the evaluation of dementia patients are briefly discussed below. Note that each battery includes measures of intellect, memory, language, and visuospatial functioning. The test battery for dementia evaluations used at Southern Illinois University (SIU) School of Medicine is described toward the end of this chapter in the section in which two case examples of AD are discussed.

The Consortium to Establish a Registry for Alzheimer's Disease (CERAD) is a short neuropsychological battery designed to evaluate memory, language, praxis, and general intellectual functioning (Welsh, Butters, Hughes, Mohs, & Heyman, 1991, 1992; Morris et al., 1988; Morris et al., 1989). The battery has been found to have good test-retest reliability, interrater reliability, longitudinal validity, and discriminative validity. The battery includes the following test measures: Verbal Fluency ("animals"), Boston Naming (abbreviated 15-item version), MMSE, Word List Memory (10 words, three trials), Constructional Praxis (copy a circle, rhombus, overlapping rectangles, cube), Short-Delay Word List Recall, and a Short-Delay True-False Word Recognition test.

In research on the CERAD neuropsychological battery it was found that delayed recall was highly sensitive to early AD, but none of the memory measures was particularly useful in identifying the severity of dementia (Welsh et al., 1991). In a subsequent study, delayed recall was again the best discriminator for detecting early AD (Welsh et al., 1992). Among the nonmemory tests on the CERAD (i.e., fluency, naming, and praxis), only confrontation naming aided in the discrimination between patients with early AD and elderly normal controls. A combination of measures (e.g., fluency, praxis, and recognition memory) best differentiated mild dementia patients from those with moderate or severe dementia. Delayed recall was not useful for staging because of "floor effects." Thus, delayed recall is highly sensitive to AD, whereas lexical-semantic processing and visuospatial functions are better indicators of progressive decline.

Salmon and Butters (1992) recently published a complete description of the neuropsychological tests that comprise the 4-hour assessment battery used at the University of California, San Diego Alzheimer's Disease Research Center (UCSD-ADRC). The length of the battery is longer than is necessary for a reasonably comprehensive dementia evaluation because some of the tests are being used primarily for research purposes, but many of the tests listed are commonly used in dementia evaluations by neuropsychologists working elsewhere.

The UCSD-ADRC battery includes tests that measure cognitive functions that typically decline in dementing disorders; that is, attention (using Digit Span and Visual Span from the WMS-R), explicit memory (including RAVLT, Buschke-Fuld SRT, Moss Recognition Span Test, WMS Logical Memory, Russell's adaptation of the WMS Visual Reproduction Test, Number Information Test), implicit memory (Pursuit Rotor, Lexical Priming, Semantic Priming), remote memory (Remote Memory Test), language (BNT, letter and category fluency tests, Token Test, vocabulary test), abstraction and cognitive flexibility (modified Wisconsin Card Sorting Test [WCST]; WAIS-R Similarities, Trail-Making Test Parts A and B), and constructional and visuospatial abilities (Block Design from the Wechsler Intelligence Scale for Children-Revised [WISC-R], WAIS-R Digit Symbol, Clock Drawing Test, Clock Setting Test, and Copy-a-Cube Test). Several mental status examinations are also routinely administered at UCSD, including the Blessed, MMSE, and the Mattis Dementia Rating Scale (MDRS).

In the early 1980s, Fuld (1983) and Rosen (1983a, 1983b) each published a list of tests that they used in dementia evaluations. These batteries included formal assessment of mental status, memory, language, and visual-spatial functioning using tests similar to those already mentioned. These batteries also included the complete WAIS, whereas it is more common today to only use a few selected WAIS-R subtests.

At the SIU Center for Alzheimer Disease and Related Disorders we are currently using an extended version of the Alzheimer's Disease Assessment Scale (ADAS) as our initial screening test with all dementia referrals. The extended ADAS is very similar to the CERAD neuropsychological battery (Zec et al., 1992a, 1992b). If the results on the ADAS are equivocal in a suspected dementia referral (e.g., an error score of less than 15 on the original ADAS), we bring the patient back for a more comprehensive dementia assessment that incorporates many of the same tests used at UCSD-ADRC (see cases discussed at the end of this chapter and associated tables for a list of the tests we employ).

Mental Status Tests

The NINCDS-ADRDA Work Group includes in its criteria for the clinical diagnosis of *probable* Alzheimer's disease that the dementia be "established by clinical examination and documented by the Mini-Mental Status, Blessed Dementia Scale, or some similar examination, and confirmed by neuropsychological tests" (McKhann et al., 1984). Brief mental status tests, such as the Blessed Mental Status Exam (Blessed et al., 1968) and the MMSE (Folstein, Folstein, & McHugh, 1975), are reliable and valid measures of dementia in the moderate to severe range (Kaszniak, 1986). These tests are easy to administer and useful for measuring cognitive decline into the later stages of dementia. One of the well-known brief mental status tests (e.g., the MMSE or the Blessed) should be used as part of any dementia workup because it provides a universally meaningful quantitative index of dementia severity. Unfortunately, these mental status tests yield an excessively high number of false-negative errors for patients with early dementia (Pfeffer et al., 1981; Wilson & Kaszniak, 1986). Kaszniak (1986) concluded that "when employed alone they [brief mental status tests] are inadequate for assessment of mild dementia" (p. 306). Cohen, Eisdorfer, and Holm (1984) recommended that mental status tests be only one part of a comprehensive neuropsychological evaluation for dementia.

The MDRS is a relatively brief screening instrument, yet more comprehensively assesses cognitive functioning than the Blessed MSE or the Folstein MMSE (Coblentz et al., 1973; Mattis, 1976). There have been some anecdotal reports that the MDRS is useful in evaluating the mild to moderately demented AD patient (e.g., Albert, 1981). Vitaliano, Breen, Albert, Russo, and Prinz (1984) reported that MDRS scores, particularly memory recall, were statistically worse for mildly demented AD patients compared to healthy elderly. Hersch (1979) reported a significant decline in MDRS scores when subjects were retested at 6- and 12-month intervals. Unfortunately, the magnitude of the difference between the groups and the hit rates using optimal cutting scores were not reported in these two studies. Consequently, these studies do not address the clinical utility of the MDRS for detecting mild dementia.

Rosen, Mohs, and Davis (1984) developed the ADAS to evaluate the severity of AD and to comprehensively assess the multiple areas of cognitive impairment that typically characterize this disorder (see also Mohs, Rosen, Greenwald, & Davis, 1983). The ADAS is a brief, portable screening test that measures the major characteristics of AD, including both cognitive and noncognitive dysfunction. Rosen et al. (1984) reported that the ADAS was sensitive to the progressive decline in functioning in patients with AD.

Zec et al. (1992a) administered the ADAS to 61 patients with AD and 52 normal elderly controls. The AD group was subdivided into different severity levels of dementia based on scores from the Folstein MMSE: (a) very mild ($\geq$ 24), (b) mild ($\geq$ 20), (c) moderate (10–19), and (d) severe (0–9). The scores on the ADAS Cognitive subscale for the four levels of dementia (very mild = 23.1 $\pm$ 7.7, mild = 22.9 $\pm$ 8.9, moderate = 38.6 $\pm$ 9.8, severe = 54.8 $\pm$ 7.6) were statistically different from one another ($p < .0001$, except very mild vs. mild) and were significantly worse than the scores of the elderly control group (5.5 $\pm$ 2.7, $p < .0001$, paired t test) (Figure 1.2).

The ADAS Cognitive score was highly effective in discriminating individual Alzheimer patients from elderly controls. The ADAS Cognitive score correctly classified 98% of the elderly control group, 100% of the very mild AD group, 91% of the entire mild group, and 100% of the moderate and severe groups when a cutoff score of 2 standard deviations below the control group mean was used. Using a 3–standard deviation cutoff, 100% of controls, 89% of the very mild AD group, 87% of the entire mild group, and 100% of the moderate and severe groups were correctly classified.

The ADAS Cognitive score and the MMSE score were highly correlated ($r = -.76, p < .0001$). However, the ADAS was found to be considerably more sensitive

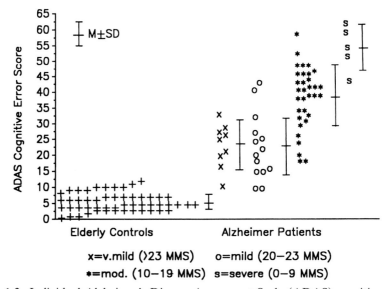

FIGURE 1.2. Individual Alzheimer's Disease Assessment Scale (ADAS) cognitive scores for each elderly control and probable Alzheimer's patient grouped according to severity of dementia (group means $\pm$ standard deviations also indicated). (Reprinted from Zec et al., 1992a.)

to mild dementia than the Folstein MMSE. All nine AD patients who had Folstein MMSE scores that were within normal limits ($\geq$ 24; i.e., < 2 *SD*) scored in the abnormal range ($\geq$ 11) on the ADAS Cognitive subscale (Figure 1.2) (please note that in contrast to the MMSE, 0 is a perfect score on the ADAS). A score of 23 on the Folstein MMSE represents the beginning of the impaired range if standardized administration is followed for this test which includes the counting backwards by 7 items. A regression analysis was conducted and the regression equation predicted that a 23 on the MMSE is equivalent to a 23.6 on the ADAS Cognitive subscale. This equivalency was also evident on the plot of the predicted regression line for ADAS Cognitive scores versus MMSE scores (Figure 1.3). A 23 on the MMSE (the beginning of the impaired range) is 2.7 standard deviations from the elderly control group mean, whereas a 23.6 on the ADAS is 6.7 standard deviations from the control mean and 12 points from the beginning of the impaired range on the ADAS. Furthermore, the percentage of correct classifications using the Folstein MMSE for the mild AD group was only 61% at the 2–standard deviation and 48% at the 3–standard deviation cutoff. These percentages are considerably lower than the 91% and 87% correct classification rate for mild AD patients using the ADAS at the 2–standard deviation or 3–standard deviation cutoff, respectively. This again clearly indicates the greater sensitivity of the ADAS to mild dementia. Zec et al. (1992a) concluded that the ADAS is a very valuable dementia screening test that has utility in both early detection and staging of AD.

Zec et al. (1992b) did a subtest analysis of the ADAS and found that all 11 ADAS Cognitive subtest scores for the mild, moderate, and severe dementia groups were statistically worse than for the elderly control group. This was also the case for the very mild group, except for scores on the Naming, Commands, Constructional Praxis, and Ideational Praxis subtests. In terms of magnitude of effect, memory and spontaneous language items were the earliest indicators on the ADAS, whereas Praxis, Commands, and Naming subtests were sensitive only later in the

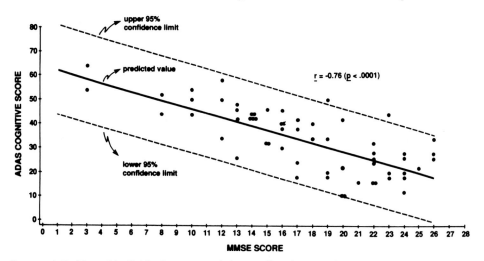

FIGURE 1.3. Plot of individual scores and the predicted regression line with upper and lower 95% confidence limits for the Alzheimer's Disease Assessment Scale (ADAS) Cognitive scores versus Folstein Mini-Mental State Examination (MMSE) scores. (Reprinted from Zec et al., 1992b.)

course of the disorder. The best single indicators of progression throughout the severity continuum of dementia (i.e., from normal to severe) were the Orientation subtest, the ADAS Cognitive score, and the ADAS Total score. Differences in educational level had no statistically significant effects on any of the ADAS subtest scores, and age differences were few and small in magnitude.

The ADAS and MDRS each take 30 minutes to administer and provide a more comprehensive assessment of cognitive functioning than either the Folstein MMSE or the Blessed Memory-Information-Concentration Test, which take only 10 minutes to administer. The ADAS Cognitive subscale consists of 11 subtests with a total error score of 70; zero is a perfect score. The ADAS was used as the primary outcome measure in the multicenter study assessing the effects of tacrine in Alzheimer patients (Davis et al., 1992). On the Folstein MMSE a perfect score is 30 and scores below 24 are considered abnormal ($> 2\ SD$ from the elderly control mean). On the MDRS a perfect score is 144 and scores below 123 are considered abnormal) ($> 2\ SD$ from the elderly control mean) (Montgomery & Costa, 1983; Mattis, 1976). The Blessed MSE consists of two sections: (a) a rating of the patient's activities of daily living (0 is perfect and 28 is maximum impairment), and (b) the Memory-Information-Concentration Test (0 is complete failure and 37 is perfect).

Somewhat different areas of cognition are emphasized in each of these four tests. Orientation is adequately measured on each of the four mental status examinations, with the Blessed being the most thorough. Semantic memory only is measured on the Blessed. Episodic memory is measured on all four scales, but the ADAS (followed by the MDRS) devotes the most points and the highest percentage of points to this assessment. Receptive and expressive language are rated only on the ADAS; whereas repetition, reading, and writing are assessed only on the Folstein MMSE. Confrontational naming is more thoroughly assessed on the ADAS than the Folstein MMSE and is not rated on the Blessed or the MDRS. There are praxis items on all the scales except the Blessed. Attention/concentration is measured on all the scales. Initiation/perseveration, generative naming, and conceptualization are measured only on the MDRS. The most difficult item for Alzheimer patients on the MMSE is recalling three words after a short delay, and the second-most-difficult item is copying the two intersecting pentagons (Teng, Chui, Schneider, & Metzger, 1987).

The error rate is low in the normal elderly on both the ADAS and the MDRS (Coblentz et al., 1973; Montgomery & Costa, 1983; Rosen, Mohs, & Davis, 1984). However, the items on the MDRS appear to be more elementary. Thus, the MDRS may be more sensitive to the later decline in AD, whereas the ADAS potentially is more sensitive to the early decline. For example, although the relative sensitivity of the ADAS and MDRS to memory impairment has not been formally studied, the ADAS measures appear to be more sensitive in detecting subtle or mild memory deficits. The ADAS devotes more points and a much higher percentage of its points to measuring episodic memory. The MDRS has measures of generative naming and conceptualization that are not included on the ADAS, whereas the ADAS has measures of confrontational naming and receptive/expressive language that are not assessed on the MDRS.

Christensen et al. (1991) published a meta-analysis of the effect sizes for a variety of mental status tests and neuropsychological tests across dementia severity levels. The effect sizes were calculated by subtracting the means of the control and

dementia groups, and dividing by the mean of the standard deviations of the two groups. Using this method for calculating effect sizes, the magnitude of the effect for the ADAS Cognitive score in the Zec et al. (1992a) study was (a) 3.5 for the entire AD group (i.e., all severity levels), (b) 5.5 for the very mild group, (c) 3.0 for the mild group, (d) 5.3 for the moderate group, and (e) 9.5 for the severe group. These effect sizes are clearly superior to those found in the meta-analysis of other mental status tests (Folstein MMSE, MDRS, Short Portable Mental Status Questionnaire, Blessed Dementia Scale) (Christensen et al., 1991). For example, the effect sizes for the Folstein MMSE for the entire AD group, and for the mild, moderate, and severe dementia groups were 2.9, 2.8, 3.0, and 3.9, respectively. The effect sizes for the ADAS Cognitive scale also were equal to or better than the best of the neuropsychological tests reported in that study. For example, the Buschke SRT had effect sizes of 3.3 for all severity levels and 3.1 for mild dementia, and the Delayed Memory for Logical Passages from the WMS had effect sizes of 2.8 for the entire AD group, 2.3 for the mild dementia group, 3.7 for the moderate dementia group, and 4.5 for the severe dementia group.

Terry, Masliah, Salmon, Butters, De Teresa, Hill, Hansen, & Katzman (1991) examined the relationships between global cognitive scores on three mental status examinations (the Blessed IMC test, the Folstein MMSE, and the Mattis DRS) and several structural and neurochemical variables (i.e., plaques, tangles, large neurons, synapse density, choline acetyltransferase, somatostatis) in three brain areas (midfrontal, inferior parietal, and rostral superior temporal). Only weak correlations were found between mental status test scores and plaques and tangles, whereas very strong correlations were found between mental status scores and the density of neocortical synapses. The density of midfrontal presynaptic boutons was clearly the highest correlate of these global cognitive tests (IMC, -0.76; MMSE, 0.73; DRS, 0.67). Multivariate analysis of stepwise regression produced a formula which included midfrontal and inferior parietal synaptic density, plus inferior parietal plaque counts with a remarkably high correlation of 0.96 with the Mattis DRS. Thus, it appears that severity of dementia as measured on mental status tests best correlates with synaptic loss, especially in the midfrontal region.

Attention

Selective attention can be evaluated using the visual letter cancellation task and the digit cancellation task. These tasks require the subject to cross out a specified target digit or letter each time it appears in an array on a printed page. Mildly demented AD patients often do not show impairments on this type of task (Vitaliano, Russo, Breen, Vitiello, & Prinz, 1986), whereas moderately demented AD patients usually do exhibit impaired performance (Allender & Kaszniak, 1985, in Bayles, Kaszniak, & Tomoeda, 1987).

Early AD is associated with impairment on tests that put strong demands on working memory and vigilance (Sahakian, Jones, Levy, Gray, & Warburton, 1989; Wesnes & Warburton, 1984), and on continuous performance tests (Baddeley, Della Salla, & Spinnler, 1991; Tariot et al., 1987). AD patients are impaired in their ability to perform 2 tasks simultaneously which is consistent with the hypothesis of a deficit in the central executive component of working memory which

directs and controls attentional resources (Baddeley, Bressi, Della Sala, Logie, and Spinnler, 1991). The time-sharing component of working memory is largely intact in normal aging. Using both a cross-sectional and longitudinal approach to study AD, Grady et al. (1988) found that memory impairment occurred first in the progression of AD and was followed by attentional impairment (Trail-Making Test B and Stroop test), and then visuospatial and linguistic dysfunction. Sahakian et al. (1990) reported that a mild AD group was not impaired on two tests of visual selective attention (one requiring an intradimensional shift, the other an extradimensional shift), whereas a more severe AD group was impaired on these attentional tasks. This could be explained by the fact that in an intradimensional shift the stimuli from the same sensory category (e.g., color, shape) continue to be relevant and reinforced, whereas in an extradimensional shift the subject must switch responding to a previously nonreinforced category when presented with new examples of compound stimuli. Although the mild AD group displayed clear impairment on tests of memory, this group was intact compared to controls on a visual search task requiring matching of stimuli on two dimensions with variable numbers of alternatives.

Sahakian et al. (1990) reported a double dissociation of memory and attentional deficits when comparing PD and AD patient groups. On the tasks used in their study, AD patients were found to have memory deficits but no problems with attentional shifting early in the course of the disease, whereas the opposite is true for PD patients. The early memory deficits in AD may be due to temporal lobe dysfunction, whereas early cognitive deficits in PD are probably related to frontal-striatal dysfunction.

General Cognitive Slowing in Aging and Alzheimer's Disease

Although general mental slowing occurs with age (Cerella, 1985; Cerella, Poon, & Williams, 1980; Salthouse, 1985), an even greater general slowing of cognitive processing is associated with Alzheimer's disease (Nebes & Madden, 1988; Nebes & Brady, 1992). A meta-analysis of RT studies demonstrated that, irrespective of the nature of the cognitive task, the difference in RT between AD patients and normals increases linearly but proportionately with increasing task complexity. When AD patients and normals are compared on conditions that differ in complexity, the group difference (in terms of absolute RT) will be larger for the more complex condition (i.e., it will tend to produce a group by condition interaction). Thus, when a group by condition interaction is found, this interaction may be reflecting general slowing of cognition, rather than indicating the presence of a specific cognitive deficit in AD. Evidence for specific cognitive deficits in AD patients is more convincingly demonstrated if the AD patients are disproportionately slow on a particular experimental condition (i.e., if RTs are far above the regression line). The size of this general slowing is not only greater in AD patients than in the normal elderly, but increases with dementia severity (Nebes & Brady, 1992).

A practical application of these findings to early detection of AD is that the more complex response time tasks may yield a better correct classification rate of early AD patients versus normal elderly because the standard deviation difference

between the two groups will tend to be larger. The standard deviation difference between AD patients and normal elderly will be larger for the more complex tasks if the mean difference between the groups is increased, whereas the standard deviation of the control groups remains relatively constant.

Problem Solving, Judgment, and Abstraction Ability

Problem solving is strongly suspected of being impaired in the relatively early stages of AD, but has not been systematically studied as thoroughly as memory, language, or visuoconstruction. The paucity of work in this area is probably due to the fact that problem solving is an ill-defined conceptual area within the field of neuropsychology. An improved understanding of problem-solving ability in AD patients could probably be attained by incorporating recent advances in the understanding and measurement of the components of problem-solving ability that have been achieved in cognitive psychology (e.g., Hayes-Roth & Hayes-Roth, 1979). What is known about this elusive but important area of impairment in AD patients will be covered in this section.

Abstract problem-solving skills decline in the elderly and show even further decline in patients with early AD. Declines in abstraction ability in the normal elderly have been shown for such diverse tasks as interpretation of proverbs (Bromley, 1957), the Category Test of the Halstead-Reitan Battery (Reed & Reitan,1963; Schludermann, Schludermann, Merryman, & Brown, 1983), the Reasoning subtest of the Primary Mental Abilities Test (Schaie, 1958), and Raven's Progressive Matrices (Botwinick, 1973). Early Alzheimer patients usually display impairment on tasks of abstraction and judgment (e.g., WAIS-R Similarities and Comprehension subtests) (Moss & Albert, 1988). Impairments on tests of memory and abstraction are often the only deficits in mild AD and are sufficient to meet the criteria for dementia requiring deficits in at least two areas of cognitive functioning. Even a well-educated, mildly impaired AD patient will typically exhibit deficits in proverb interpretation and similarities.

Abstraction deficits in AD patients are also evident on tests of card sorting and picture absurdities, which is discussed at greater length below. Impaired abstract reasoning in dementia patients has been shown for Raven's Colored Progressive Matrices (Alexander, 1973) and for Piaget's abstract problem-solving tasks (Burnand, Richard, Tissot, & de Ajuriaguerra, 1972). Mild AD patients are able to do easy visual abstractions like those on the MDRS (Mattis, 1976), but performance on this task declines over time. Judgment may be tested by posing situational problems for patients and asking them how they would resolve the difficulty. Impairment of calculation skills (i.e., addition, multiplication, division, and subtraction) appear early in AD (Cummings, 1990), although it is unclear whether these deficits are primarily due to impaired problem-solving skills or due to impairments in other neuropsychological functions (e.g., attention, semantic memory). Errors in placement of the hands and/or numbers on Clock Drawing Tests to command (e.g., "draw a clock with all the numbers on it and put the hands on the clock to make it read 10 after 11" [Goodglass & Kaplan, 1976; Salmon & Butters, 1992] or in another version of the test "make it read 2:45" [Sunderland et al., 1989]) when the same clock can be correctly copied from a model suggests that this test is sensitive to the conceptual impairments in Alzheimer patients.

Caution must be exercised in using tests of abstraction diagnostically because performance on these tests is highly correlated with age and education, and because impairment of abstraction is also found in other diagnostic groups (e.g., Pick's disease and depression [Raskin, Friedman, & DiMascio, 1982]). Abstraction deficits associated with depression will, however, tend to fluctuate with the mood disorder (LaRue, Spar, & Hill, 1986).

Proverb Interpretation

The ability to interpret proverbs was studied in AD patients in the early to middle stages of the disease and in a group of age- and education-matched controls (Andree, Hittmair, & Benke, 1992). AD patients were good at understanding the proverbs as measured in a recognition paradigm, but had difficulties explaining them. The investigators conclude that the poor ability of AD patients to explain proverbs may be caused by metalinguistic deficits rather than by impaired abstract thinking. Frequent types of errors in proverb interpretation included responses that were wrong, incomplete, circumstantial, and verbose, whereas literal and "concrete" interpretations were rarely exhibited.

Picture Absurdities Test

Shuttleworth and Huber (1989) reported that performance on the Picture Absurdities Test (Wells & Ruesch, 1972), in which the patient describes what seems out of place or absurd in a series of pictures, was found to be significantly impaired in a group of patients with early AD ($M \pm SD = 5.5 \pm 0.5$) compared to patients with dementia syndrome of depression (8.0 ± 0.6) and cerebrovascular dementia (7.8 ± 0.8), even when matched for age, education, and dementia severity (MMSE score: $M = 23$).

Performance on the Picture Absurdities subtest from the Stanford-Binet Intelligence Scale (Terman & Merrill, 1973) was significantly poorer for AD patients who would be deceased within 1 year after examination versus those who would still be alive (Kaszniak et al., 1978). Picture Absurdities scores were inversely correlated with amount of electroencephalographic (EEG) slowing in a sample of suspected dementia patients (Kaszniak, Garron, Fox, Bergen, & Huckman, 1979).

Delayed Alternation and Object Alternation

AD patients were reported to be significantly impaired on delayed alternation and object alternation compared to patients with PD, even though both groups were equated for severity of dementia (Freedman, 1990). These tasks are sensitive to orbitofrontal system dysfunction in nonhuman animals. AD patients, but not the PD patients, made a significant number of perseverative responses. The investigators concluded that the marked perseverative deficit in AD may reflect orbitofrontal system dysfunction, whereas the milder, nonperseverative deficits in PD may reflect dorsolateral frontal system involvement.

Object-Sorting Task

Flicker, Ferris, Crook, & Bartus (1986) administered a simultaneous object-sorting task and a control task to young normals, aged normals, and early AD patients and advanced AD patients. Subjects were asked to select 8 of 25 items simultaneously projected on a video screen for both the control task and the concept formation task. The subject was told the selection principle on the control task, whereas the selection principle had to be deduced by the subject on the concept formation task. The normal elderly were intact on the control task, early dementia patients were mildly to moderately impaired, and advanced dementia patients were markedly impaired. All three groups performed significantly worse on the concept formation task, but the increase in errors compared to the control task was greatest in the early dementia patients, less in the aged normals, and least in the young normals and advanced dementia patients. The performance of the severely demented participants on the concept formation task approached floor levels. The results of this study provide clear evidence of deficient abstract reasoning in both aging and senile dementia, as demonstrated on the simultaneous object-sorting task.

Awareness of Deficit

In some dementing disorders the patients typically lack awareness or insight about their impairments (i.e., they display "anosognosia for dementia") (Frederiks, 1985). Babinski (1914) coined the term "anosognosia" to describe the lack of awareness of deficit exhibited by patients with hemiplegia due to stroke, but subsequently the term has come to refer to unawareness of *any* neurological or neurocognitive impairment. Loss of insight need not be an "all or none" phenomenon, it can involve various degrees of unawareness and can fluctuate over time and across symptomatic domains.

Several studies have reported some loss of insight early in the course of AD (Mahendra, 1984; Frederiks, 1985; Joynt & Shoulson, 1985). Other studies have emphasized that AD patients have relatively intact awareness of their memory and cognitive impairments in the early "forgetfulness" stage of the disorder, but that after a certain point in the disease this awareness or insight decreases with increasing severity of dementia (Schneck, Reisberg, & Ferris, 1982; Reisberg, Gordon, McCarthy, & Ferris, 1985). However, patients did continue to display awareness of the cognitive functioning of their spouses (Schneck et al., 1982; Reisberg et al., 1985). In another study AD patients were found to greatly overestimate their memory ability on a categorized word list task when compared to the self-estimation performance of a group of control subjects (Schacter, McLachlan, Moscovitch, & Tulving, 1986). Neary et al. (1986), however, have reported considerable variability in insight among dementia patients. The lack of insight in the AD patient may in part be due to not having an enduring record of their experiences, which would seem to be necessary for having insight into one's own condition.

AD patients have been reported to significantly underestimate their cognitive problems in daily life compared with the ratings by relatives (McGlynn & Kaszniak, 1991a, 1991b). The discrepancy between the patient's self-report and the relative's report on the patient was found to increase with severity of dementia. In this same study AD patients were also found to be poor in predicting their own performance on most cognitive tasks when these predictions were compared to (a) the patient's actual performance, (b) the predictions by relatives, or (c) the patient's predictions about the performance of relatives. The authors interpreted these results in terms of a breakdown in metacognitive processes or executive functions in which patients have increasing difficulty self-monitoring and predicting their own performance.

Anosognosia for dementia has been most commonly found in the "cortical" dementias, such as AD or Pick's disease (e.g., Gustafson & Nilsson, 1982; Schneck et al., 1982; Benson, 1983; Mahendra, 1984; Reisberg et al., 1985; Neary et al., 1986). Patient's with Pick's disease actually display a greater loss of insight into illness early in the dementia than AD patients (Gustafson & Nilsson, 1982), which may be due to the more severe frontal degeneration in the early stages of Pick's disease. Lack of insight has also been reported in Huntington's disease (HD), a frontal-subcortical dementia (McHugh & Folstein, 1975; Cummings & Benson, 1984; Joynt & Shoulson, 1985; Bruyn, 1968; Wilson & Garron, 1979). Patients with PD who typically have little cortical involvement retain reasonably good insight into their illness even in the advanced stages, whereas patients with AD, atypical Parkinson's disease (AP) with signs of vascular disease, and multi-infarct dementia (MID) exhibit disturbed awareness of their deficits (Danielczyk, 1983). The AD group displayed the greatest lack of awareness into their illness, followed by the AP group, and then by the MID group (Danielczyk, 1983).

Kaszniak (1992) proposed that three types of behavioral disturbances exhibited by AD patients may be manifestations of unawareness of deficit in everyday life: (a) delusional ideation, (b) risky behavior, and (c) failure to employ compensatory strategies or aids. Lacking self-awareness of a memory deficit a person might erroneously conclude (i.e., delude themselves into thinking) that someone had stolen something they could not readily locate, whereas a person with self-awareness of their deficit would be likely to correctly infer that they forgot where they placed the object. Or an AD patient may jump to the delusional conclusion that their absent spouse is having an affair because they have forgotten that their spouse went grocery shopping and they do not consider the possibility that their spouse told them they were running an errand because they are unaware of their poor memory. Unawareness of deficit could also increase the likelihood that an impaired driver would not self-limit their risky driving due to lack of awareness of the impairment and consequently a lack of awareness of the risk inherent in engaging in this impaired behavior. Similarly, a person will not adopt strategies or aids to help compensate for adaptive impairments if they cannot accurately self-appraise their level of functioning. On the other hand, it also appears that unawareness of deficit serves a protective function in that it spares the person with a progressive dementia the pain of realizing the full extent of their cognitive decline. This may in part account for the unusually low incidence of serious depression in AD patients compared to some other serious medical conditions.

Memory in AD

Memory Failures in Everyday Life

As Alzheimer dementia gradually progresses, the frequency of memory lapses and the rate of forgetting increases in daily life. Patients with AD tend to repeatedly ask the same question and tend to frequently repeat the same statement or story.

They tend to forget people's names, telephone numbers, conversations, directions, and events of the day. They frequently forget scheduled appointments and forget to take medications as prescribed. They often leave tasks unfinished because of forgetting to return to them after an interruption (e.g., forgetting to turn off the stove or leaving the water running). Patients with AD frequently forget where they have placed objects and the reason for going into a room. They may increasingly rely on reminder notes (in the early stages), and they often need to rely on family members to compensate for their memory failures.

Family members frequently comment on what appears to them as a paradox that the Alzheimer victim in their family can better recall experiences from the very distant past (i.e., childhood, adolescence, and young adulthood) than they can from recent years or days. This is because in the early stages there is an anterograde amnesia, which impairs the encoding and storage of new information, and the retrograde amnesia is temporally graded, with relative sparing of remote (i.e., tertiary) memory.

The rate of forgetting becomes more rapid as the disease progresses. Initially, the patient with AD forgets significant events from a few days ago (i.e., something performed, said, heard, watched, or otherwise experienced). As the disease gradually advances, they forget events from the previous day, then from a few hours ago, and then from a few minutes ago. In the advanced stages, they forget events from even a few moments ago.

Similarly, AD patients display a progressive difficulty in remembering people's names. Initially, they forget names of people with whom they have less frequent contact (e.g., acquaintances and distant relatives). Then they forget the names of relatively close friends and relatives (e.g., grandchildren). In the advanced stages they may forget the names of very close relatives (i.e., spouse, siblings, children). In these late stages they may also forget very overlearned information like their birthday, occupation, schooling, or even their own name. It is the severe impairment in episodic memory (i.e., the anterograde amnesia) that interferes with the acquisition of new names of people and also disrupts the consolidation of recently acquired names. Semantic memory impairment and retrograde amnesia are responsible for failure to recall previously acquired names. Anomic aphasia and visual agnosia may also contribute to the difficulty in correctly naming people.

When should there be serious concern that the forgetfulness associated with normal aging is beginning to resemble the more severe memory difficulties associated with Alzheimer disease? A rule of thumb is that if a person frequently cannot recall information they wanted to remember even after being provided reminder cues, then a serious memory problem is indicated. On the other hand, if a person usually can recall at a later time what they momentarily have forgotten (e.g., what they went into a room to get), even if they may sometimes need a reminder cue, then this is more likely the forgetfulness associated with normal aging.

Global Amnesia

The cardinal neuropsychological feature of AD is a profound, global amnesia (Table 1.1). Memory difficulty begins insidiously, progresses gradually, and typically is the first presenting symptom. In the very early phase of the disease, memory deterioration reaches a plateau for a period of up to several years in some patients.

TABLE 1.1.   Memory in Alzheimer's Disease

Description
 Onset: early severe
 Course: progressive, but floor effects
 Severity: very severe (amnesia)
 Extent: largely global
 Reliability: consistently impaired
Learning, recall, and recognition
 Learning: flat learning curve across trials
 Delayed recall: very poor after even a short delay
  Repetitions: often displayed
  Intrusions: frequently exhibited
 Recognition memory: impaired, indicating storage problems
  Positive response bias: false-positive errors
Encoding, storage, and retrieval
 Encoding and retrieval: impaired, but overshadowed by the storage problem
 Storage (consolidation): failure to store new information
  Rate of forgetting: rapid
Amnesia
 Anterograde amnesia: evident early
 Retrograde amnesia: also early, but difficult to measure
Types of memory
 Episodic (verbal & visual): severe early
 Semantic: impaired
 Implicit (unconscious memory): typically impaired (e.g., failure to prime)[a]
 Procedural: relatively intact
 Primary: relatively intact early (e.g., digit span), impaired later
 Temporal orientation: impaired relatively early and progressive; reflects both anterograde and
  retrograde amnesia
Neuropathology
 Impaired episodic memory:
  Bilateral medial temporal: hippocampus (CA1, enthorhinal cortex, subiculum), amygdala,
   parahippocampal gyrus
  Basal forebrain: nucleus basalis, medial septal nuclei, diagonal band of Broca
 Impaired semantic and implicit memory: association neocortex
 Impaired organization, encoding, and source memory: frontal lobes
 Intact procedural memory: relatively intact basal ganglia

[a]Semantic priming is impaired, while perceptual priming appears to be intact.

Memory impairment will also show a floor effect on most available standardized tests of memory by the middle stages of AD. In the typical case, memory impairment remains a prominent and disproportionate feature of Alzheimer dementia throughout most of the course of the disorder. However, some Alzheimer cases (perhaps 2%) have atypical initial presentation of either language or visuospatial deficits and may only later become amnestic. Virtually all aspects and types of memory are severely impaired by the middle stages of the disease when there is a moderate dementia. Alzheimer patients become progressively disoriented to time, place, and then person (Ashford, Kolm, Colliver, Bekian, & Hsu, 1989).

 Alzheimer amnesia is characterized by very poor learning and retention. There is a dramatic loss of information over a brief delay (e.g., 2 to 10 minutes) (Moss et al., 1986; Hart, Kwentus, Harkins, & Taylor, 1988). This very rapid forgetting is evident not only on free recall measures, but also on sensitive measures of cued recall and recognition memory. This rapid loss of information even on measures with low retrieval demands indicates that the Alzheimer amnesia is primarily due to failure to store information in LTM, rather than merely due to a failure to efficiently encode or retrieve information.

Effects of AD on Different Types of Memory

There are multiple memory systems in the brain (Squire, 1992). The major biological dichotomy is between declarative and nondeclarative memory. Declarative (explicit) memory includes memory for facts (semantic memory) and events (episodic memory), in which the memory content can be described or declared through verbalization and/or visualization and depends on the integrity of the medial temporal lobe system (i.e., hippocampus and related structures, including entorhinal, perirhinal, and parahippocampal cortices) (Squire & Zola-Morgan, 1991). Memory impairment has been linked to the medial temporal lobe by study of cases of bilateral surgical removal, viral encephalitus, posterior cerebral artery occlusions, and Alzheimer's disease. This memory system is fast, has limited capacity, and performs a critical function during learning by establishing long-term declarative memory for facts and events presumably by virtue of its extensive and reciprocal connections with neocortex (Squire & Zola-Morgan, 1991). Its role continues after learning during a long period of reorganization and consolidation during which memories stored in neocortex gradually become independent of the medial temporal lobe system. Thus, the long-term (permanent) memory storage is gradually assumed by neocortex, which assures that the medial temporal lobe system is always available for the acquisition of new information.

Nondeclarative (implicit) memory refers to a heterogenous set of distinct learning and memory abilities that change performance without access to the experiences that caused the change, and is independent of the medial temporal lobe. In nondeclarative memory, experience alters behavior nonconsciously without providing any memory context. Types of nondeclarative memory include skills (motor, perceptual, cognitive), priming (perceptual, semantic), dispositions (operant and classical conditioning), and nonassociative memory (e.g., habituation, sensitization).

In AD, semantic and episodic types of declarative memory and semantic priming (one type of nondeclarative memory) are impaired. Perceptual priming and the acquisition of skills (procedural learning) are other types of nondeclarative memory that remain relatively intact in AD.

Other memory dichotomies discussed in the literature include: (a) anterograde and retrograde amnesia, (b) primary and secondary memory, (c) recent and remote memory, (d) STM and LTM, (e) verbal and visual memory, (f) free recall and cued recall, and (g) recall and recognition memory. These different memory dichotomies are not mutually exclusive, and some memory terms and types overlap considerably (e.g., anterograde, episodic, recent, and short-term memory). All of these memory types are severely impaired in AD, with the notable exception of procedural memory (skill learning).

Unlike the normal elderly who show declines only in secondary memory, Alzheimer dementia is associated with impairment in all stages of memory: sensory, primary, secondary, and tertiary (Kaszniak, Poon, & Riege, 1986). Primary memory, also called immediate memory span, span of apprehension, and attention span, can be measured by tests like forward digit span. The impairment of primary memory tends to be mild in early AD, but progressively worsens over time (Kaszniak et al., 1986). Some experiments suggest that the deficit in secondary memory is due to failure to encode essential aspects of to-be-learned information. Impairment of primary memory may to some extent limit the amount of information that is transferred into secondary memory. Working memory is a more complex view of primary memory in which three principal subsystems have been identified (i.e., the central executive which is an attention control system, the visuospatial scratch-pad, and the phonological loop) (Baddeley et al., 1991). As mentioned earlier, AD patients have difficulty in performing two concurrent tasks suggesting a deficit in the central executive component of working memory (Baddeley et al., 1991).

Episodic Memory

Episodic memory refers to memories that require temporal and spatial contextual cues for retrieval (Tulving, 1983). Patients with AD display a severe and progressive difficulty in learning and retaining new episodic information (i.e., an anterograde amnesia). This impairment in episodic memory is easily measured by a variety of standardized memory tests; for example, the RAVLT (Zec & Vicari, 1990; Powell, Cripe, & Dodrill, 1991), the Buschke SRT (Buschke, 1973; Buschke & Fuld, 1974; Masur et al., 1989; Masur, Fuld, Blau, Crystal, Aronson, 1990), the California Verbal Learning Test (CVLT) (Delis, Kramer, Kaplan, & Ober, 1987; Delis, Massman, Butters, et al., 1991; Delis, Massman, Kaplan, et al., 1991), the WMS-R (Butters et al., 1988; Troster, Jacobs, Butters, Cullum & Salmon, 1989), the Memory Assessment Scale (MAS) (Williams, 1991), the Fuld Object-Memory Evaluation (OM) (Fuld, 1981; Fuld, Masur, Blau, Crystal, & Aronson, 1990), the Hopkins Verbal Learning Test (Brandt, 1991) and the Delayed Recognition Span Test (Moss et al., 1986; Salmon, Granholm, McCullough, Butters, & Grant, 1989). This memory deficit can also be conceptualized as a failure to transfer information from primary memory (i.e., STM) to secondary memory (LTM).

Retrograde Amnesia

Retrograde amnesia refers to difficulty in remembering previously learned information including both public and autobiographical facts. Alzheimer patients exhibit a temporally extended, severe retrograde amnesia that is manifested relatively early in the course of the disorder (Albert et al., 1981). The retrograde amnesia in AD extends back to the early years of life, but the amnesia is temporally graded, i.e., remote memories (e.g., from childhood and adolescence) are relatively better preserved than more recent memories. The retrograde amnesia becomes flat (i.e., loses its temporally graded aspect) by the middle stages of AD.

The temporally graded aspect of retrograde amnesia in early AD is thought to be due to difficulty retrieving information from episodic memory. According to this view, newly learned information becomes independent of spatial and temporal cues for retrieval gradually over many years due to frequent rehearsal. Thus, recently learned information is more dependent upon temporal and spatial cues for retrieval and thus more inaccessible. Older, overlearned information is primarily semantic memory rather than episodic memory. The long-standing and worsening anterograde amnesia may also contribute to the graded aspect of the retrograde amnesia in two ways: (a) the increasing failure to acquire new information over recent years, and (b) the increasing failure to rehearse and further strengthen memories learned in recent years.

Semantic Memory

Semantic memory, in contrast to episodic memory, refers to overlearned information that is part of one's general fund of knowledge and is no longer dependent upon temporal and spatial contextual cues for retrieval. For example, it can be tested by asking about common geographical information, historical information, number facts, vocabulary, and the like. Tests of semantic memory include the WAIS-R Information and Vocabulary subtests, the Number Information test from the Boston approach (Goodglass & Kaplan, 1976), and word fluency tests. Although episodic memory is impaired in both amnesia and dementia, semantic memory as measured by category fluency is impaired in dementia but intact in amnesia (Butters, Granholm, Salmon, Grant, & Wolfe, 1987).

Implicit Memory

Implicit memory refers to the unconscious activation of a memory trace. This can be contrasted with explicit memory, which refers to information that is consciously learned and retrieved. Lexical (stem completion) and semantic (free associate task) priming deficits have been reported in patients with AD (Salmon, Shimamura, Butters, & Smith, 1988). Implicit memory can be measured on lexical priming tasks (e.g., stem-completion, paired associate paradigm), perceptual priming (e.g., identification of fragmented drawings of common objects), motor skill learning (pursuit-motor task), and weight-biasing skill. A double-dissociation was found for AD and HD patients on these priming tasks and skill (procedural) learning tasks in which AD patients were impaired only on the former and HD patients were impaired only on the latter (Butters, Heindel, & Salmon, 1990). The authors inferred that impaired priming in AD patients was due to damage in the association cortices, whereas impaired skill learning in HD was due to basal ganglia dysfunction. Classical conditioning of the eyeblink response has also been reported to be impaired in AD patients compared to age-matched controls (Solomon, Levine, Bein, & Pendlebury, 1991).

Verbal and Nonverbal Memory

Because memory systems in both cerebral hemispheres are typically damaged in AD, both verbal and nonverbal memory are impaired. If there is a large discrepancy between verbal and visual memory, suggesting highly lateralized cerebral involvement, then a diagnosis other than AD, such as stroke, should be considered. However, it should be remembered that a minority of Alzheimer cases present atypically with lateralized findings.

Primacy and recency effects

Primacy and recency effects, which are typically present in subjects with intact memory, refer to the relatively better recall for words or information at the beginning (primacy) and end (recency) of a list or story as compared to the middle of the list or story.

The primacy effect is due to the greater rehearsal that information at the beginning of a list or story receives and reflects information transferred to LTM.

AD patients have been reported to display a reduced primacy effect and an exaggerated recency effect. The recency effect is attributable to information at the end of a list or story still being held in a temporary STM store (Atkinson & Shiffrin, 1968). However, the presence of a reduced primacy effect and an exaggerated recency effect are not helpful in the differential diagnosis of the dementias or amnesias because all memory disorders tend to show this pattern. A disproportionate recency effect and a reduced or absent primacy effect suggests a failure to transfer information from STM to LTM. Sometimes patients with AD adopt the strategy of repeating the initial words on the list over and over again. This will result in remembering these initial few words held in working memory (primacy effect) at the expense of the final words on the list (reduced recency effect).

Pathophysiology of AD Amnesia

There is extensive and severe episodic memory impairment in mild AD patients because the three major brain regions implicated in episodic memory are damaged bilaterally (medial temporal lobe, midline diencephalon, and basal forebrain). There is also damage to the association cortex which presumably causes the breakdown of semantic knowledge.

The very rapid rate of forgetting on episodic memory tasks in AD patients is due primarily to the early and extensive bilateral damage to medial temporal lobe structures (i.e., hippocampus—especially area CA1, amygdala, entorhinal cortex, and subiculum) (see chapter 4). There are plaques, tangles, amyloid and neuronal loss in these brain areas critical to memory. Furthermore, the entorhinal cortex, which provides input to the hippocampus, and the subiculum, which supplies the output from the hippocampus, are both damaged in AD. This results in the functional isolation of the hippocampus. Nonhuman primate studies have shown that combined damage to both the hippocampus and amygdala bilaterally is necessary to produce a profound amnesia (Squire, 1992). However, bilateral damage limited to the CA1 region of the hippocampus is sufficient to produce a severe, chronic anterograde amnesia in man (Squire, 1992).

The nucleus basalis is also damaged fairly early in AD and produces an early, severe, and relatively selective cholinergic deficit in the cerebral cortex (Arendt, Bigl, Arendt, & Tennstedt, 1983). Loss of cholinergic input from the medial septal nuclei produces a cholinergic deficit in the hippocampus. Because anticholinergic drugs produce a robust amnestic effect, the cholinergic deficit in AD may contribute to the severe amnesia that characterizes Alzheimer dementia. The basal forebrain includes the nucleus basalis of Meynart in the substantia innominata, the medial septal nucleus, and the diagonal band of Broca. The cholinergic system innervating the hippocampus and the cerebral cortex originates in the basal forebrain. The basal ganglia (i.e., caudate nucleus, globus pallidus, and putamen) is the only major memory system not affected in AD. This presumably accounts for the intact procedural (i.e., skill) learning found in Alzheimer patients.

The neuropathological changes in the hippocampus and association cortex are probably sufficient to cause the global amnesia of AD. Damage to the midline diencephalic structures, temporal neocortex, and basal forebrain with consequent cholinergic deficit undoubtedly also contributes to the episodic memory impairment in AD.

Memory Assessment

Memory assessment of a suspected dementia patient begins with taking a cognitive history and includes formal testing of memory using sensitive standardized procedures. Reliable informants should be questioned carefully about the initial presenting symptoms, the time of onset, the rate of progression, and the course of the symptoms. It is important to get a specific description of the memory difficulty because lay persons often identify any cognitive impairment as a memory problem; for example, forgetting how to do certain tasks (apraxia) or forgetting the names of objects (anomia). The initial presenting symptom in AD usually is episodic memory impairment that begins insidiously and progresses gradually. If the initial deficit is not memory impairment or if the onset of memory impairment is acute and the progression rapid, a disorder other than AD should be seriously considered as a possible alternative diagnosis.

According to the DSM-III-R (American Psychiatric Association, 1987), dementia evaluations should formally evaluate difficulty in learning new information by asking the patient to remember three objects or a sentence after 5 minutes of distraction. Although this method is useful for a quick screening for memory difficulty, a more accurate assessment can be obtained using any of several psychometric tests of memory. The DSM-III-R is seriously remiss in not acknowledging the importance of formal psychometric assessment of memory impairment in cases of suspected amnestic syndromes or dementing disorders. The NINCDS-ADRDA Work Group (McKhann et al., 1984), recommends neuropsychological testing to aid in the clinical diagnosis of AD.

A meta-analysis of psychometric tests revealed that memory tests, such as the Buschke SRT and the WMS better differentiated dementia patients from normal elderly than did any other specific tests, including mental status exams and language measures (Christensen et al., 1991). Tests of verbal memory are among the most sensitive measures of impaired episodic memory in AD patients. Tests of verbal episodic memory are generally easy to administer, score, and interpret for clinical assessment purposes. The best normative values are available for these tests, although virtually all neuropsychological tests are inadequately normed in terms of one or more important demographic variables (such as age, education, gender, ethnic group, and health status). The RAVLT, CVLT, and the Buschke SRT are among the most commonly used of these measures. Other measures of episodic verbal memory assess the memory for short prose passages (such as the Logical Memory portion of the WMS or WMS-R) or evaluate paired-associate learning (e.g., from the WMS-R). Tests of visual nonverbal memory tests include the WMS-R Visual Memory index and the WMS-R visual subtests (immediate and delayed Visual Reproduction and immediate and delayed Visual Paired Associates), the BVRT, immediate and delay recall of the Rey-Osterreith CFT, and the Warrington Visual Memory Test.

Assessment of implicit memory, retrograde amnesia, and procedural learning could be potentially helpful in the differential diagnosis of Alzheimer dementia from other dementias and amnesias, but clinical tests in general use are not currently available for measuring these types of memory. Implicit memory is intact in subcortical dementias and in a variety of amnestic disorders, but is impaired in AD.

On the other hand, procedural learning is impaired in basal ganglia disorders (e.g., HD and PD), but is intact in AD. Retrograde amnesia is temporally graded and severe in early AD, but flat and mild to moderate in HD. Currently, however, there are no standardized tests available for measuring implicit memory and procedural learning. The experimental paradigms, which have been used in research studies, do not have an adequate normative base. Tests of retrograde amnesia have been developed, but these tests require local normative values, which limits the availability of these tests for clinical applications. Fortunately, there are other ways to differentiate among the dementias. For example, recognition memory (for both episodic and semantic memory tasks) and language abilities (e.g., confrontational naming) are considerably more impaired in AD than in the subcortical dementias. Also unlike AD, amnestic disorders have relatively intact semantic memory, intellectual functioning, language, and visuospatial functioning.

In general, memory measures on mental status examinations are usually not psychometrically adequate (e.g., they are typically insensitive to memory impairment clearly revealed on more demanding memory tests). Four popular standardized mental status tests are the Blessed Mental Status Exam (Blessed et al., 1968), the Folstein MMSE (Folstein et al., 1975), the MDRS, and the ADAS. These tests adequately measure orientation (the Blessed is the most thorough), but do not generally measure semantic memory. A thorough assessment of orientation should be included in any neuropsychological evaluation for dementia. Significant disorientation is virtually pathognomonic for dementia. In the meta-analysis of effect sizes, psychometric tests of orientation ($n = 14$; 2.64) and memory ($n = 22$; 2.78) were clearly greater than the effect sizes for six other categories of tests. The effect sizes for orientation were based on data from studies using the Benton Temporal Orientation Test (Benton, de S. Hamsher, Varney, & Spreen, 1983). Although episodic memory is measured on each of the four mental status scales, only the ADAS measures are reasonably sensitive. The Folstein MMSE has only a three-word brief delay recall item, whereas the Blessed has only a delayed recall for a name and address. Memory items on the MDRS mainly consist of short delay recall for two sentences and recognition memory for a few verbal and visual items. The memory tests on the ADAS include a 10-word three-trial word recall test and a 12-word three-trial word recognition test. The ADAS measures appear more sensitive in detecting subtle or mild memory deficits. However, measurement of memory on the ADAS could be improved by adding a delayed recall and a delayed recognition test because, as mentioned previously, rapid forgetting is a cardinal feature of AD (Zec et al., 1992b). This rapid forgetting over the first few minutes may to a large extent be due to a loss of information from primary memory, rather than forgetting of information recently transferred to secondary memory.

Zec and Vicari (1990) compared the performance on the RAVLT in 86 Alzheimer patients and 53 elderly controls. The elderly controls displayed a clear learning curve, good recall, and good recognition memory with minimal intrusions. The *mild* AD group displayed very little learning over trials, very poor recall, and very poor recognition memory with many intrusions on the recognition trial. The learning, recall, and recognition memory of the *moderate* and *severe* AD groups were more severely impaired than the *mild* group, but the differences between the *mild*, *moderate*, and *severe* dementia groups were relatively small in magnitude due to floor effects.

Minimum Requirements for Memory Assessment of AD Patients

Although the NINCDS-ADRDA recommendations regarding memory assessment for AD are an improvement on those given in DSM-III and DSM-III-R, more specific guidelines can be made regarding proper memory assessment of suspected Alzheimer's disease patients. For example, if a word-list learning test is employed, it should satisfy the following minimum requirements in order to be useful in the evaluation of secondary memory: (a) the list should contain at least 10 target words; (b) there should be at least three learning trials; (c) the test should include a short-delay recall test; and (d) the test should also include a short-delay recognition memory test. Any test meeting these minimum requirements and having adequate normative values should do a reasonably good job of detecting memory impairment in even the relatively early patient with AD.

In order to adequately test secondary memory using a word-list paradigm, it is necessary to administer a supraspan list of words (i.e., the list should at the minimum include 10 words) over multiple learning trials (i.e., at least three trials) followed by measures of short-delay recall and recognition memory. The word list should exceed the 7 ± 2 bits of information that people can typically hold in primary memory (i.e., STM). There should be a minimum of three learning trials in order to generate a learning curve. Multiple learning trials ensure that the subject has had an adequate opportunity to learn and store new information. These learning trials provide repeated practice that should facilitate the transfer of information from a temporary primary memory store (STM) to a more permanent secondary memory store (LTM). The three learning trials will also ensure that the subject has paid adequate attention to the to-be-remembered information and consequently poor recall after a short delay would more convincingly indicate impaired memory rather than inattention.

If primary memory were perfectly intact, a subject could remember as much as 7 ± 2 words on each learning trial without any of this information actually having been transferred and stored in secondary memory. Because primary memory usually is relatively intact in the early stages of Alzheimer's disease, the number of words recalled by an Alzheimer patient on the learning trials, especially the initial learning trials, may overlap considerably with the distribution of scores for age-matched normal elderly controls. Over multiple learning trials the difference between the mean scores of an Alzheimer group and a normal control group tends to become increasingly large as the normal controls learn and store new information in secondary memory and the Alzheimer patients do not.

Primary memory provides a limited, temporary store of information, and consequently this information will be almost immediately forgotten after active rehearsal is stopped. For this reason it is very useful to administer measures of free recall and recognition memory after a short delay following the last learning trial in order to obtain a measure of secondary memory that is not confounded by information temporarily stored in primary memory. A short-delay free recall test should be administered after 2 to 10 minutes of distraction in order to assess retention after a delay. A high savings score would indicate that information was stored in secondary memory and was readily retrieved. A low savings score would indicate rapid forgetting over the delay, but this could be either a retrieval problem or a storage problem. As mentioned previously, delayed recall is the most sensitive measure to early or mild dementia of the Alzheimer type (Welsh et al., 1991, 1992). This measure is the most sensitive of the memory measures to AD because it reflects both a failure to learn over multiple practice trials and a failure to retain over time.

If free recall is impaired, a short-delay recognition memory test would help determine whether the poor retention was mainly due to a retrieval problem or to a storage problem. Poor performance on a recognition memory test would indicate a failure to learn and store new information. Poor delayed recall in the context of good recognition memory would indicate a retrieval rather than a storage problem. Relatively early in dementia of the Alzheimer type there are severe impairments in both recall and recognition memory (if a sensitive recognition memory measure with multiple foils is used) and this fact can help in the differential diagnosis of AD versus many other memory impairing conditions that tend to predominately affect retrieval (e.g., normal aging, depression, the white matter dementias, and the subcortical dementias). Thus, whereas short-delay free recall is the measure with the greatest sensitivity to early AD, evaluations of short-delay recognition memory greatly improve the selectivity of our memory measures.

Although the prose recall of the Logical Memory subtest from the original WMS has shown some utility in the early detection of dementia of the Alzheimer type (Storandt & Hill, 1989), this memory measure lacks three of the important features described above needed to make it an optimal memory test for the early detection of AD. First, although the number of informational units presented on the prose passage exceeds the span of immediate memory (i.e., primary memory), the Logical Memory subtests from the WMS and the WMS-R do not involve multiple learning trials. This one-trial learning does not provide enough rehearsal to maximize the opportunity for information to be learned (i.e., to be transferred from primary memory to secondary memory). Second, the original WMS did not have a delayed recall measure (although the WMS-R does have a delayed recall measure), and consequently the typical immediate recall measure will reflect unknown proportions of information retrieved from primary and secondary memory stores. Finally, there is no recognition memory paradigm in either the WMS or the WMS-R and consequently it is difficult to determine to what extent memory deficits are a retrieval problem versus a storage problem.

If prose passages are used, the following testing modifications would probably increase the sensitivity of this type of memory test to early AD: (a) using three learning trials; (b) employing a short-delay recall test; and (c) using a short-delay recognition memory test. In testing recognition memory, a multiple-choice format can be used in which questions are asked about each informational unit in the prose passage and the subject is presented with four alternative answers (i.e., the correct answer and three distractors). The same recommendation may also help to improve the sensitivity and selectivity of visual reproduction measures of memory (e.g., WMS Visual Reproduction subtest).

Language

This section consists of three major subsections: (a) aphasia, (b) generative naming, and (c) confrontational naming. The subsection on aphasia describes the language disturbances of AD patients and compares them to known aphasic syndromes. The subsections on generative and confrontational naming discuss the use of these measures in the early detection and differential diagnosis of AD.

Aphasia

The information in this section on Alzheimer aphasia draws heavily on two studies: (a) Appell, Kertesz, and Fisman (1982), and (b) Cummings, Benson, Hill, and Read (1985). The methods, results, and conclusions of these two studies regarding the language disturbances of AD patients are very similar; therefore, these studies in effect cross-validate each other. Appell et al. (1982) evaluated the language performance of 25 hospitalized Alzheimer patients and 21 normal control subjects using the Western Aphasia Battery (Kertesz, 1980), a modification of the Boston Diagnostic Aphasia Examination (Goodglass & Kaplan, 1976). An additional control population of 141 stroke patients, previously described by Kertesz (1979), were used for comparison. The AD group was socially decompensated and had a large number of persons over 75 years of age. Cummings et al. (1985) administered a comprehensive aphasia evaluation (consisting of questions derived from the Boston Diagnostic Aphasia Examination (Goodglass & Kaplan, 1976) and the Western Aphasia Battery (Kertesz, 1979) to 30 patients with AD (MMSE: $M = 10.5$, moderate to severe dementia) and 70 normal controls.

Aphasia is clearly a very common diagnostic feature of AD (Appell et al., 1982; Cummings et al., 1985). Even the first described case of AD displayed an aphasia, including paraphasia, alexia, and agraphia, along with memory deficits and paranoia, but with intact motor function (Alzheimer, 1977). Clear-cut speech deficits typically become evident 1 to 3 years after onset of AD, and are clearly progressive thereafter (Sjögren, Sjögren, & Lindren, 1952). Occasionally, however, language difficulty will precede general cognitive decline (Allison, 1962).

Cummings et al. (1985) found that control subjects were intact, whereas the AD group displayed moderate to severe language impairment. Similarly, all the hospitalized AD patients in the Appell et al. (1982) study were aphasic to some degree. At least half of these institutionalized patients showed a marked to severe language impairment (Appell et al., 1982). As a group, the AD patients in the Appell et al. (1982) study differed from normals on all language variables, and from stroke patients in terms of high fluency and lower comprehension (Appell et al., 1982).

Progression of Alzheimer Aphasia

All aphasic syndromes have lexical retrieval problems (i.e., word-finding difficulty); for example, naming problems, difficulty providing personal information, and/or difficulty describing a pictured scene (Helm-Estabrooks & Albert, 1991). In order to identify the type of aphasia syndrome being displayed by a particular patient, three additional characteristics of language need to be evaluated and described: (a) speech fluency (e.g., average longest phrase length), (b) auditory comprehension, and (c) repetition (Helm-Estabrooks & Albert, 1991). The aphasia classification system most commonly used today includes the eight aphasia syndromes listed in Table 1.2.

An anomic aphasia typically is evident early in the course of AD (Kertesz,

TABLE 1.2.   Classification of Aphasia Syndromes Using Three
Language Parameters

Aphasia Syndromes	Fluency	Comprehension	Repetition
Anomic	Intact	Intact	Intact
Transcortical sensory	Intact	Impaired	Intact
Wernicke's	Intact	Impaired	Impaired
Global	Impaired	Impaired	Impaired
Conduction aphasia	Intact	Intact	Impaired
Broca's	Impaired	Intact	Impaired
Transcortical motor	Impaired	Intact	Intact
Mixed	Borderline	Borderline	Intact or Impaired

1979; Cummings et al., 1985). The anomic aphasia involves naming difficulty in the context of relatively intact speech fluency, auditory comprehension, articulation, and repetition (Kertesz, 1979; Appell et al., 1982; Cummings et al., 1985). A slowly progressive anomic aphasia may be the result of a brain tumor in either cerebral hemisphere and needs to be considered in a differential diagnosis (Mesulam, 1985). Anomic aphasia is also common after head injury and in metabolic or toxic disorders (Mesulam, 1985). The latter condition will, however, often be accompanied by some degree of confusion.

Comprehension deficits become more severe as the dementia progresses and consequently Alzheimer aphasia increasingly resembles a transcortical sensory aphasia (Cummings et al., 1985). For most of the course of AD, the language disorder is very similar to a transcortical sensory aphasia in which the patients exhibit fluent paraphasic output, impaired auditory comprehension, and a relative preservation of the ability to repeat (Cummings et al., 1985). Repetition declines in the late stages of the disease and then the language disorder more closely resembles a Wernicke's aphasia (Cummings et al., 1985). In the end-stage of the disease a global aphasia may be displayed (Appell et al., 1982).

Appell et al. (1982) found that transcortical sensory aphasia and Wernicke's aphasia were frequent in their sample of hospitalized Alzheimer patients (44% of the Alzheimer sample compared to 22% in the stroke sample), but Broca's aphasia and transcortical motor aphasia were notably absent (0% compared to 24% of the stroke sample). Alzheimer aphasia does not resemble Broca's aphasia, because grammatical structure remains relatively intact throughout most of the course of AD. Obvious syntactical difficulties tend to appear only in the late stages (Appell et al., 1982). Of the AD sample, 24% displayed global aphasia and 20% exhibited anomic aphasia (the latter probably being underrepresented, because this was an institutionalized sample). Conduction aphasia accounted for another 4% of the AD patient sample (compared to 9% in the stroke group).

Reading and writing difficulties are also similar to those found in transcortical sensory aphasia: impaired reading comprehension and impaired writing ability. However, the ability to read aloud was relatively intact (Benson, 1979). Unlike in transcortical sensory aphasia, however, AD patients showed less paraphasia, less echolalia, but more impairment in executing overlearned sequences (such as reciting the alphabet) (Cummings et al., 1985). AD patients did not exhibit the completion phenomenon in which patients will automatically complete nursery rhymes (Cummings et al., 1985), which is displayed by many patients with transcortical sensory aphasia (Goodglass & Kaplan, 1976).

Other Features of Alzheimer Aphasia

In the early and middle stages of AD the following fluency characteristics remain relatively intact: conversational speech, articulation and phenomic competence, repetition, phrase length, syntax (i.e., grammar), prosody, reading aloud (Appell et al., 1982; Cummings et al., 1985), and discrimination of speech sounds (Ernst, Dalby, & Dalby, 1970; Irigaray, 1973). AD patients have been reported to have a "lack of speech initiative" and slowness to respond (Stengel, 1964; Irigaray, 1973). Mild to moderately demented AD subjects (Clinical Dementia Rating score: $M = 1.47; 0 =$ no dementia, $3 =$ severe dementia) were found to write considerably shorter descriptive paragraphs when asked to write a story about a picture of a picnic scene than normal elderly subjects ($M = 28$ words for AD group vs. $M = 80$ words for the normal elderly) (Neils, Boller, Gerdeman, & Cole, 1989). The speech of Alzheimer patients typically has little informational content and an increasing number of paraphasias (Cummings et al., 1985). Alzheimer speech has been described as circuitous, vague, empty, and meaningless (Appell et al., 1982). Perseveration is common; for example, repetition of a word or syllable, set phrases, themes, or other complex response (Appell et al., 1982). Echolalia may occur in advanced cases, but complete mutism is uncommon (Allison, 1962).

Effects of Age at Onset of AD on Language Impairment

Bayles (1991) reported that early age of onset of AD was *not* related to greater language impairment in a large sample of Alzheimer patients after severity of dementia was controlled (Bayles, 1991). On the contrary, a statistically significant association was found between later age at onset of AD and greater language impairment. This association held for confrontation naming, auditory comprehension, and reading comprehension, but not for writing to dictation. The findings of the Bayles study disagree with some previous reports showing a relationship between early onset of AD and more severe language deficits. The contradictory findings appear to be due to the fact that in the Bayles study, the effects of dementia severity on language scores were controlled, whereas this was not done in previous studies.

Word-Finding Difficulty

Difficulty in word finding, especially naming, appears early in the course of AD (Constantinidis, Richard, & de Ajuriaguerra, 1978). Ability to name common objects is often relatively intact initially, but a deficit may be detected using naming tasks that involve low-frequency words on reaction time measures (Irigaray, 1973). Object-naming tasks are less impaired than more abstract word-finding tasks (i.e., similarities or opposites, sentence completion, or word fluency) (Allison, 1962; Gustafson, Hagberg, & Ingvar, 1978). Semantic paraphasias and circumlocutions appear relatively early in the speech of AD patients, whereas phonemic paraphasias and phonemic transpositions only appear in the late stages of the disease (Constantinidis et al., 1978; Appell et al., 1982).

Naming difficulties are typically present in aphasic syndromes and are not unique to Alzheimer dementia (Kertesz, 1979). However, the types of naming errors may have discriminative value. The spontaneous speech of AD patients contains a high incidence of circumlocutions (e.g., "horse with a horn" for unicorn) and semantic paraphasias (e.g., "plane" for helicopter), but no phonemic paraphasias (e.g., "harmotica" for harmonica) (Appell et al., 1982).

Auditory Comprehension

Comprehension of the speech of others is often impaired in AD (Appell et al., 1982), and it becomes progressively more impaired as the disease progresses. Early AD patients are able to understand simple concrete sentences (i.e., can correctly respond to simple commands and questions), but comprehension of more complex sentences may be impaired. For example, AD patients have difficulty with abstract propositions and with sentences that use comparatives or require understanding of causal relations (Allison, 1962). The patients in the Appell et al. sample also experienced severe difficulty in carrying out sequential commands.

Semantic Versus Syntactic Functions

Semantic processing and cognitive operations are impaired in Alzheimer patients, whereas phonemic and syntactive functions remain intact. Whitaker (1976) and Schwartz, Marin, & Saffran (1979) reported AD patients may have a profound loss of meaningful speech in the context of preserved grammar (e.g., correct word endings or tenses, plural endings, or negating sentences). Complex sentences will often show impaired syntax. Sentences are often left unfinished and phrases may be left hanging (Constantinidis et al., 1978).

Pragmatics of Language

Irigaray (1973) and Obler (1981) have discussed problems with the pragmatic aspects of language. The speech of Alzheimer patients tends to lack questions, commands, second-person pronouns, and qualifying terms like "perhaps." For these reasons AD patients have difficulty in sentence construction and narrative tasks. There is a breakdown of language as a tool for: (a) communicating, (b) directing actions, (c) generating concepts, and (d) testing the truth of propositions.

The language of AD patients appears to be stimulus bound or overly dependent on context (Obler, 1981). For example, AD patients who are instructed to make a sentence out of a group of stimulus words will tend to maintain the order in which the words are presented even though the sentences produced will be awkward (Irigaray, 1973).

Brain Localization

Mild anomic aphasia, an early deficit in AD, is difficult to reliably and precisely localize in the brain (Mesulam, 1985). Frontal, parietal, and temporal damage in the left hemisphere is likely. However, right hemisphere damage and subcortical lesions can cause a mild anomic aphasia (Mesulam, 1985). A severe anomic aphasia with an acute onset usually implicates the left temporoparietal junction.

It is very likely, however, that damage to the left temporal cortex is responsible for the major presentations of Alzheimer aphasia, because the four types of fluent aphasia associated with AD (i.e., anomic aphasia, transcortical sensory aphasia, Wernicke's aphasia, and global aphasia) can all be caused by focal damage to this brain region, depending on the location and extent of the lesion (Benson, 1979). Furthermore, the fact that Alzheimer patients do not display either Broca's aphasia or transcortical motor aphasia indicates that the left posterior frontal cortex is not significantly damaged in AD. Damage to the association cortex in AD patients is probably responsible for the substantial loss of semantic operations and cognitive performance that they display (Appell et al., 1982).

Stroke Versus AD

Naming was not significantly different when a group of stroke patients was compared with a group of AD patients. It is the intact speech fluency in the context of naming impairment that helps define Alzheimer aphasia (Appell et al., 1982). As a group, AD patients differed from a group of stroke patients in terms of high fluency and lower comprehension (Appell et al., 1982). Phonemic paraphasias, which are common in conduction aphasia due to stroke, are rare in Alzheimer aphasia, especially early in the course of the disease (Constantinidis et al., 1978; Appell et al., 1982).

Patients with AD tend to show more poverty of speech than aphasics with focal brain disease (Critchley, 1964). Also unlike Wernicke's aphasics, patients with AD are generally not verbose, and they do not make the very large numbers of paraphasic errors that characterize the aphasias associated with stroke (Appell et al., 1982).

Dysarthria is absent during most of the course of AD (Cummings et al., 1985). In the late stages, however, there is a progressive decline in speech pitch and intelligibility. In the end-stage, reiterative speech disturbance (e.g., echolalia) has been reported to be frequent in the verbal output of AD patients (Cummings & Benson, 1983). Early AD patients display aphasia with normal articulation, whereas MID patients often exhibit a clear-cut dysarthria along with aphasia. Severe articulatory problems with mild aphasia are present in dementias associated with extrapyramidal disorders (Cummings & Benson, 1983). Thus, the presence of dysarthria in the earlier stages of a dementing disorder suggests a diagnosis other than AD or in addition to AD.

Aphasic syndromes associated with stroke, but not AD, are often associated with a right hemisensory defect, a right hemiparesis, and a right visual field defect. Thus, aphasia in the presence of lateralized sensory and/or motor deficits strongly indicates stroke, whereas aphasia without lateralized sensory-motor deficits is compatible with a diagnosis of AD.

In summary, there are a number of ways to distinguish the language disorder associated with a typical presentation of AD from that produced by most strokes. However, the angular gyrus syndrome (AGS) discussed below poses a special problem for differential diagnosis because it is commonly misdiagnosed as AD.

Angular gyrus syndrome versus AD. Many of the clinical features of AGS (also called "focal infarct dementia"), which includes posterior aphasia, alexia with agraphia, and Gerstmann's syndrome (i.e., finger agnosia, right-left confusion, agraphia, and acalculia), overlap with those of AD, and the two conditions are easily confused (Benson, Cummings, & Tsai, 1982). In one series, 7 of 14 patients with AGS had been previously diagnosed by experienced clinicians as having AD (Benson et al., 1982). Both AGS patients and AD patients have fluent aphasias and will often display empty paraphasic output and impaired language comprehension. There are many other clinical characteristics shared by AD and AGS that lead to misdiagnosing AGS as AD. These common clinical attributes include the following: aphasia, alexia, agraphia, acalculia, right-left disorientation, finger agnosia, constructional disturbances, verbal learning problems, impaired proverb interpretation, impaired similarity and difference interpretation, decreased digit span, and difficulty maintaining a coherent stream of conversation. Focal neuro-logical signs may be absent, and standard CT scan findings may be normal for age. Mistaking AGS for AD is particularly likely if there are no focal neurological signs present to suggest a possible stroke.

There are, however, many clinical features that can be used to help distinguish AD from AGS. AD has an insidious onset and progressive course, whereas AGS has an abrupt onset and the cognitive impairment does not typically progress. Amnesia is almost always an early symptom in AD, whereas memory is intact in AGS except for verbal tests. When patients with AGS report memory problems, they are usually referring to naming difficulty (e.g., problems remembering names of people or things). Topographical orientation is impaired in AD (i.e., tendency to become lost; spatial disorientation), but it is intact in AGS. AD patients are generally unaware of their own language difficulties, whereas AGS patients are frustratingly aware of their deficit. Reading aloud and reading comprehension are usually severely impaired in AGS, whereas reading aloud may be intact long after reading compre-hension has deteriorated in AD. It is difficult to engage AD patients in conversation, whereas this is not the case with AGS patients. There are often no neurological findings in AD, whereas right-sided abnormalities may be present in AGS.

The presence of risk factors for cerebrovascular disease, particularly hyper-tension or cardiac disease, raises the possibility of a vascular disorder like AGS. Also, motor system abnormalities appear only late in the course of AD and then are bilaterally symmetrical, whereas patients with cerebral infarctions frequently have focal neurological deficits. The proper diagnosis of AGS is very important, because cognitive rehabilitation and treatment for the underlying vascular disorder can be beneficial.

Differential Diagnosis of AD Aphasia

AD patients have a fluent aphasia; therefore, their condition is not likely to be confused with nonfluent aphasias like Broca's aphasia or transcortical motor aphasia. The majority of patients with aphasia due to stroke should be easily distinguishable from those with Alzheimer aphasia (Bayles et al., 1987) because nonfluent aphasia, which is rarely seen in AD, is more common in stroke patients than is fluent aphasia (Brust, Shafer, Richter, & Bruun, 1976).

AD can be confused, however, with a fluent aphasia (i.e., Wernicke's anomic, or transcortical sensory aphasia). The memory impairments invariably associated with AD help differentiate AD from fluent aphasias resulting from other causes (e.g., stroke). The age of the patient is another characteristic that may help in this differential diagnosis, because the average age of a Wernicke's aphasia patient is 10 to 12 years younger (Harasymiw, Halper, & Sutherland, 1981; Holland, 1980; Kertesz & Sheppard, 1981; Reinvang, 1983) than the average age of patients with Broca's aphasia (nonfluent), which is 52 years old (Davis & Holland, 1981).

A medical and cognitive history, memory assessment, and performance on a repetition task can aid in differential diagnosis. The best clinical features for dif-ferentiating AD from aphasia patients are as follows: intact fluency helps distinguish AD from Broca's aphasia, good fluency and poor comprehension help distinguish AD from transcortical motor aphasia, poor memory and poor comprehension help differentiate AD from anomic aphasia, good repetition can help distinguish AD from conduction aphasia, and history can help distinguish AD from global aphasia.

In the remainder of this section, the literatures on impaired confrontational naming and impaired generative naming (word fluency) in AD are discussed. These are deficits that occur relatively early in the course of the disorder and are useful measures in assessing a person suspected of having early AD.

Confrontational Naming

As mentioned earlier, AD is associated with a progressive anomia (Hart, Smith, & Swash, 1988). Many studies have demonstrated impaired confrontational naming ability in AD patients, although mild AD patients are sometimes not significantly impaired. Table 1.3 contains a summary of the important facts about confrontational and generative naming in AD.

Hodges, Salmon, and Butters (1991) recently compared the confrontational naming performance on the BNT (Kaplan, Goodglass, & Weintrout, 1983) of a group of patients with AD, a group with HD, and a group of normal control subjects. Naming was significantly impaired in both the AD and HD groups compared to the normal control group, and the AD group was significantly more impaired than the HD group. Normal controls made predominately semantic-within-category errors and circumlocutory errors. Semantic-within-category errors are responses from the same semantic category as the target object but not visually similar (e.g., "lettuce" for asparagus). Circumlocutory errors are multiword responses in which there is an accurate identification of the object using its physical attribute (e.g., "Eskimo's snow house" for igloo), or its function or action ("used to draw circles" for compass). The HD group only was significantly worse than the normal control group in the percentage of visual naming errors. Visual naming errors are responses that are visually similar to the object but from a different semantic category ("motel" for harmonica).

The AD group, on the other hand, made significantly greater percentages of semantic-superordinate errors and semantic-associative errors even after matching an AD group and an HD group for general naming ability. Semantic-superordinate

TABLE 1.3. Language in Alzheimer's Disease

Confrontational naming (e.g., Boston Naming Test)
　Onset: impaired early, but not as early as episodic memory
　Individual differences: atypical cases with early disproportionate naming deficit; other cases with
　　later than usual onset
　Severity and course: initially mild; gradually progresses to severe impairment
　Types of errors: semantic associative errors, semantic superordinate errors, and circumlocutions
　　appear early; misperceptions appear later; semantic associative errors increase over time
　Value: dysnomia helps confirm diagnosis of Alzheimer's disease
　Neuropathology: reflects left hemisphere cortical damage
Generative naming
　Phonemic word fluency (PWF): word generation to letters (e.g., F,A,S)
　Semantic word fluency (SWF): word generation to categories (e.g., animals)
　Onset: SWF impaired relatively early, often before confrontational naming
　Severity: SWF more severely impaired than PWF throughout course
　Types of errors: perseverations and intrusions on both PWF and SWF tasks

---

errors are responses that indicate the general category to which the object belongs (e.g., "vegetable" for asparagus). Semantic-associative errors are responses in which there is a clear semantic association with the target object including statements of action or function (e.g., "painting" for easel), physical characteristics (e.g., "ice" for igloo), contextual associates ("ocean" for octopus), or specific subordinates of the target object (e.g., "Vesuvius" for volcano).

Over a 3-year period, the worsening naming ability of the AD group was accompanied by a change in the proportion of types of naming errors (e.g., the percentage of semantic associative errors and visual errors increased significantly). The authors interpret their findings as indicating that early in the course of AD there appears to be a breakdown in semantic processing. As AD progresses, semantic processing continues to deteriorate and perceptual problems increasingly contribute to naming difficulty on the BNT. Perceptual impairment is reflected in the naming performance of HD patients much earlier in the course of their dementia than in patients with AD. Phonemic (i.e., postlexical) processes remain relatively intact in both disorders. An analysis of naming errors using the categorization system described by Hodges et al. (1991) is discussed for two cases of AD at the end of this chapter. In one case the BNT was given at the beginning and end of a 3-year period and the changes in the type of naming errors for individual items is described.

Generative Naming

Generative naming or word fluency tasks are another important component of a comprehensive neuropsychological assessment of dementia (Bayles et al., 1987). Generative naming tasks, along with episodic memory tasks, are among the most sensitive measures for differentiating mild AD patients from normal elderly (Storandt, Botwinick, Danziger, Berg, & Hughes, 1984). These tests are commonly used in evaluations of patients suspected of having AD because they have proven useful in the early detection of Alzheimer dementia and because they are very brief (5–10 minutes) and easy to administer. Generative naming is a language measure and also a measure of semantic memory (Bayles et al., 1987; Bayles et al., 1989).

Tests of generative naming or word fluency require the subject to generate instances of a particular semantic category (i.e., semantic word fluency [SWF]); or words that begin with a certain letter (i.e., phonemic word fluency [PWF]). The subject is asked to generate as many words beginning with a certain letter of the alphabet (e.g., the letters FAS or PRW or CFL) or belonging to a particular category (e.g., animals, states, grocery store items) within a certain time limit (usually, 60-second trials). Early AD patients generate fewer appropriate words than normal subjects (Bayles & Tomoeda, 1983; Cummings et al., 1985; Martin & Fedio, 1983; Miller & Hague, 1975; Rosen, 1980; Weingartner et al., 1981; Butters et al., 1987; Zec et al., 1991). Generative naming has been shown to be sensitive to severity of dementia in both cross-sectional and longitudinal studies (Bayles et al., 1987, p. 87). Some studies have reported that generative naming is more sensitive to the effects of early dementia than confrontational naming (Bayles & Tomoeda, 1983; Benson, 1979; Appell et al., 1982; Bayles et al., 1987).

A meta-analysis (Christensen et al., 1991) reported that the effect sizes ($M \pm SD$) for word fluency tests in discriminating dementia and normal aging are 1.86 ± 0.7 ($n = 14$ studies) for all severity levels of dementia and 1.55 ± 0.61 for mild dementia ($n = 5$ studies). These effect sizes were considered respectable, but not as good as those reported for memory measures (2.78 ± 0.81; $n = 22$) or confrontational naming (2.13 ± 1.07, $n = 22$). Unfortunately, this meta-analysis did not distinguish between SWF and PWF tests. In the following section, literature will be reviewed that indicates that SWF may be considerably more useful than PWF tests in the differential diagnosis of AD from normal aging (see Table 1.3 for a brief summary of the important facts about generative naming in AD).

Phonemic Versus Semantic Word Fluency

Eight studies have compared the performance of Alzheimer's patients and elderly controls on both PWF and SWF tasks (Rosen, 1980; Ober, Dronkers, Koss, Delis, & Friedland, 1986; Hart et al., 1988; Weingartner et al., 1981; Butters et al., 1987; Bayles et al., 1989; Zec et al., 1990; Monsch, Bondi, Butters, Salmon, Katzman, & Thal, 1992). Four of seven studies have found SWF to be superior in differentiating patients with AD from normal elderly persons. The three studies not finding superiority for the SWF task are Rosen (1980), Ober et al. (1986), and Bayles et al. (1989). Rosen (1980) found that PWF was better than SWF at differentiating mild dementia patients from elderly controls, although no difference was found for the moderate to severe dementia group. Ober et al. (1986) found that SWF and PWF tasks were equally effective in discriminating both a group of mild AD patients and moderate to severe patients from an elderly control group. Bayles et al. (1989) also did not find that SWF (animals, fruits, vegetables) was more sensitive than PWF (FAS) to dementia. Five other studies, however, found that SWF was superior to PWF in discriminating patients with AD from elderly controls (Weingartner et al., 1981; Hart et al., 1988, Butters et al., 1987; Zec et al., 1990; Monsch et al., 1992), including mildly demented patients with AD (Monsch et al., 1992).

Butters et al. (1987) explained the greater impairment of Alzheimer's patients on SWF versus PWF tasks as reflecting the breakdown in the hierarchical structure of semantic knowledge (Martin, 1987) that interferes with the ability to generate exemplars of an abstract concept. Martin and Fedio (1983) and Ober et al. (1986) had previously suggested that the language deficits in Alzheimer's patients involve a reduction in the number of exemplars comprising an abstract category. Butters et al. (1987) argued that words can be generated on the PWF task using phonemic cues to search a very large set of exemplars (i.e., rhyming their way through the test). Butters et al. (1987) interpreted the severe generative naming deficits in the HD group as reflecting a general retrieval deficit that also interferes with recall on tests of episodic memory. Only the AD patient group showed a moderate degree of dysnomia. They concluded that the word fluency performance of Alzheimer's patients was negatively affected by both their aphasic disorder and their increased sensitivity to interference. Like some of the previous studies, this study had only a small number of subjects in each group, and only one category was used to measure SWF, whereas three different letters were used to measure PWF.

In summary, SWF may be considerably more useful than PWF in the differential diagnosis of patients with AD at all stages of dementia from normal elderly persons (Butters et al., 1987; Monsch et al., 1992). However, PWF may be useful for eliciting intrusion errors to help confirm the diagnosis of AD because AD patients tend to lose set (derailment) on the PWF task (e.g., to the letter "p," saying pears, then apples). AD patients also tend to make more repetitions and make more semantic errors (e.g., giving cities for the category "states") than normal elderly on generative naming tasks. There is little effect of age on generative naming except for a statistically significant decline in SWF for the oldest age group (age ≥ 75 years) for whom separate normative values for SWF are needed (Zec et al., 1990).

Impaired Word Generation: Pathophysiology and Differential Diagnosis

Both left and right frontal lesions result in reduced verbal fluency, but lesions in the left frontal lobe have been associated with poorer scores than lesions of the right frontal lobe (Benton, 1968; Miceli, Caltagirone, Gainotti, Masullo, & Silveri, 1981; Milner, 1964; Perret, 1974; Ramier & Hecaen, 1970). Ramier and Hecaen (1970) reported that in a small group of patients with brain tumors, those patients with right frontal lesions were second only to those with left frontal lesions in being the most impaired group on a PWF task. They hypothesized that there are two components to word fluency: (a) a fluency factor that is sensitive to lesions in either frontal lobe, and (b) a linguistic factor sensitive to the left hemisphere.

PWF is more disrupted by frontal lobe lesions than nonfrontal lesions (Milner, 1964; Benton, 1968; Ramier & Hecaen, 1970; Perret, 1974; Crockett, Bilsker, Hurwitz, & Kozak, 1986). SWF (animal naming), on the other hand, has been reported to be impaired with nonspecific left hemisphere damage (Newcombe, 1969). Very severe impairment is found on PWF, but not SWF, after lesions in the left frontal lobe anterior to Broca's area (i.e., left precentral face area) (Jones-Gotman & Milner, 1977). Patients with left frontal lesions anterior to Broca's area are not aphasic, but they do display a diminished spontaneity of speech associated with their poor performance on word-fluency tasks (Kolb & Whishaw, 1985). Lesions in the central face area and orbital frontal region produce the greatest reductions in word fluency. Jones-Gotman and Milner (1977) interpreted their finding of impaired PWF and intact SWF after left precentral face area lesions as providing indirect support for the two-factor hypothesis proposed by Ramier and Hecaen (1970). The greater sensitivity of SWF to both nonfrontal lesions and to AD is consistent with the greater posterior cortical damage in AD (i.e., especially in temporal and parietal cortex) (Brun, 1983).

Lesions in different brain regions can negatively affect word generation for different reasons. Word fluency is generally very poor in patients with HD (Butters et al., 1987). This finding has been interpreted as indicating that damage to the basal ganglia (e.g., caudate nucleus) can also produce impaired word generation (Butters et al., 1987; Heindel et al., 1989). Frontal lobe involvement has also been implicated in HD and may be contributing to the word-fluency deficit found in HD patients. The impaired word fluency in HD is thought to reflect a general retrieval problem associated with bradyphrenia. HD patients have difficulty re-trieving information from both semantic memory as in the case of word fluency, and from episodic memory as reflected on measures of free recall. The basal ganglia usually are relatively spared in AD, and so impairment of word fluency in AD cannot be ascribed to damage to this brain region.

Amnesic patients, on the other hand, usually have relatively intact word fluency. Consequently, the word-fluency deficits found in AD patients are probably not primarily due to their severely impaired episodic memory or due to the damaged brain structures responsible for the impaired episodic memory (e.g., hippocampal system, dorsal medial nucleus of the thalamus). On the other hand, damage to the brain structures essential for episodic memory is probably responsible for the repetitions and intrusion errors commonly exhibited by Alzheimer's patients on word-fluency tasks. Although HD patients have severely impaired verbal fluency, they tend to make less repetitions and intrusions than Alzheimer's patients because their ability to store episodic memory is relatively intact.

Bayles et al. (1987) interpreted the generative naming deficits in AD as reflecting impairment of the processes and contents of semantic memory and impairment of ideational capacity (i.e., ability to link concepts). Thus, the SWF deficits in Alzheimer's dementia may reflect a breakdown of the structure of semantic knowledge due to damage in the association cortices, especially left temporal and parietal cortex. Executive functioning deficits as a result of frontal lobe damage and/or general damage to the association cortex may also be contributing to the poor word fluency in Alzheimer's patients.

Design fluency, a nonverbal analog of word fluency (Jones-Gotman & Milner, 1977), has also been reported to be severely impaired in AD (Bigler et al., 1989). Jones-Gotman and Milner (1977) demonstrated that patients with nondominant right frontal lesions have the greatest difficulty in generating novel designs, whereas patients with posterior lesions did not differ from normal controls. Bigler et al., 1989 found that AD patients (n = 15) also made numerous perseverative errors. Unfortunately, we do not know whether design fluency is useful in the detection of mild or early AD, because the severity of dementia was not reported in the Bigler et al., 1989 study.

Zec et al. (1991) found selective impairments in generative naming in patients with very mild AD as compared to patients with very severe closed head injury (CHI) even though MMSE scores were equal in the two groups, and even after age effects were taken into account. The AD group was older than the CHI group (p = .0001), but education and MMSE scores were nearly identical for the two groups. The mean correct for SWF was significantly lower in the AD group (30.2 ± 10.6) compared with the CHI group (41.7 ± 15.0, p = .004). In contrast, the mean correct for PWF was *not* significantly different for the AD versus CHI groups (26.1 ± 12.7 vs. 29.5 ± 13.2). After subtracting out the small, albeit nonsignificant, differences of age on SWF and PWF, the very mild AD group still scored considerably lower than the very severe CHI group on SWF, whereas the scores on PWF were virtually identical. In the mild AD group 86% were impaired on the SWF task and 43% were impaired on the PWF task compared with only 22% of the severe CHI group impaired on each task when a cutoff score of 2 standard deviations below appropriate age-matched control groups was used. Thus, SWF but not PWF is useful in the differential diagnosis of mild AD and severe CHI.

Visuospatial Abilities

Visuospatial deficits (impairments of visuoperceptual and constructional abilities) are exhibited in most types of dementia (Cummings & Benson, 1983). Although visuospatial impairment may not always be evident in the early stages of AD, the deficits are usually displayed by the middle stages of the disorder (Cummings & Benson, 1992; Cummings & Benson, 1983; Adams & Victor, 1977; Sim & Sussman, 1962; Sim, Turner, & Smith, 1966; Sjögren et al., 1952). Because neuropathological studies (Brun & Gustafson, 1976) and brain imaging studies (see chapters 16 and 17) demonstrate disproportionate degenerative changes or dysfunction in posterior cortical areas (including the parietal lobe) relatively early in the course of AD, impairments in visuospatial functioning are expected. Visuospatial deficits can sometimes be the initial presenting cognitive deficit in AD (Crystal et al., 1982; Martin, 1987), even though it should be emphasized that this appears to be a relatively rare occurrence. Manifestation of visuospatial deficits in the everyday life of AD patients includes: (a) getting lost in familiar surroundings, (b) getting lost when driving, (c) becoming disoriented in their own homes, and (d) difficulty recognizing familiar faces (Cummings & Benson, 1992).

Tests that can be used to measure visuospatial deficits in AD patients include constructional tasks, drawing and copying tasks, judgment of line orientation tests, facial discrimination tests, mental rotation tests, map reading, maze tests, and the performance subtests of the WAIS (Cummings, 1990; Becker, Huff, Nebes, Holland, & Boller, 1988; Brouwers, Cox, Martin, Chase, & Fedio, 1984; Storandt et al., 1984). Visuospatial problem solving, as measured by the performance subtests of the WAIS or WAIS-R (e.g., Block Design) has been consistently shown to be more impaired than performance on the verbal subtests (Perez et al., 1975). This may be in part because of the visuospatial impairment, but the problem-solving component is likely to be another important contributing factor. Spatial-rotation abilities (using an accuracy response measure) decline with normal aging, but apparently do not show any further impairment in early AD patients (Flicker, Ferris, Crook, Reisberg, & Bartus, 1988).

There are quantitative and qualitative differences in the visuospatial deficits exhibited in cortical versus subcortical dementias (Cummings, 1990). Visuospatial impairment appears earlier in the course of AD than in most subcortical dementias (Cummings, 1990). AD patients were found to be significantly more impaired on complex constructional tasks such as the Rey-Osterreith CFT, than a normal control group or an HD group; the latter two groups did not differ significantly on CFT performance (Brouwers et al., 1984). The HD group was, however, found to be selectively impaired on tasks involving egocentric space (e.g., the Road Map Test) (Brouwers et al., 1984). Differences in level of dementia and degree of motor disability between groups are potential confounding factors in these comparative studies. In Table 1.4 the important facts about visual-spatial skills are summarized.

Visual-Perceptive Ability

Visual-perceptual deficits in AD appear to increase with increasing severity of dementia (Bayles et al., 1987), but again are rarely the initial presenting symptom.

TABLE 1.4.   Visual-Spatial Skills in Alzheimer's Disease

Tests: Rey-Osterreith Complex Figure Test (CFT), Block Design, Hooper Visual Organization Test, Picture Completion
Onset: impairment fairly early on more complex tasks, later on simpler tasks
Individual differences: atypical cases with early disproportionate praxis deficit; other cases with later than usual onset
Neuropathology: tends to reflect parietal cortical damage, especially right parietal
Types of errors: omissions and impoverishment reflect left hemisphere damage, whereas fragmentation and impaired spatial relations reflect right hemisphere damage

In the early stages, an Alzheimer's patient may get lost when traveling in an unfamiliar area, and in the middle and later stages may get lost in familiar places. Alzheimer's patients in the middle and later stages may lose the ability to recognize familiar faces. Technically, the poor face recognition of AD patients does not meet the criteria for proposoagnosia because there is not a preseveration of recognition through other sensory channels and because intellect is not intact.

Eslinger and Benton (1983) compared visual-perceptual ability in a group of dementia patients with mixed etiology to a group of matched normal controls. Visual-perceptual ability was evaluated with the Benton Facial Recognition Test (Benton & Van Allen, 1968) and the Benton Line Orientation Test (Benton et al., 1978). The Facial Recognition Test requires the matching of unfamiliar faces using visual discrimination. The dementia group scored significantly worse than the matched normal groups on both these visual-perceptual tests and the effect sizes were large. Both these tests are sensitive to right posterior change (Benton et al., 1983). However, the Facial Recognition Test is also sensitive to damage in the left postrolandic area that also tends to cause fluent aphasias (Hamsher, Levin, & Benton, 1979). Dissociations in performance on the two tests were common for the dementia patients but rare for the normal subjects. This suggests that the two tests are measuring different aspects of perceptual deterioration, which will vary across subjects. Normative data are available on these tests for subjects aged 65 to 84 years, grouped by 5-year intervals (Benton, Eslinger, & Damasio, 1981).

Even though three studies have demonstrated that AD patients score worse than control subjects on the Benton Line Orientation Test (Ska, Poissant, & Joanette, 1990; Eslinger & Benton, 1983; Eslinger, Damasio, Benton, & Van Allen, 1985), there was some overlap between the global scores of some controls and some AD subjects in each study. However, Ska et al. (1990) did an error analysis in their study and found that some error types were much more frequent in the AD than in the control group. A high percentage of AD patients (approximately 72%) incorrectly chose the vertical or horizontal line rather than the oblique line at least once, whereas a low percentage of control subjects made this type of error (approximately 8%–10%). Some AD subjects (approximately 9%) chose both a vertical and horizontal line for their two choices on a single trial, whereas control subjects never committed this error. An appreciable percentage of AD patients made both an interquadrant error (an error occurring between lines in the right and left quadrants) and either a vertical error (approximately 38% of the AD sample) or a horizontal error (approximately 68% of the AD sample), whereas no control ever made this combination of errors. Thus, an analysis of error types observed in the line orientation judgment task may be helpful in differentiating normal elderly from early AD.

Spatial Orientation

A considerable burden for caregivers is the tendency of some patients with AD to wander and to get lost. This spatial disorientation is often one of the first recognizable symptoms of AD because of the profound negative effect it has on daily functioning (Strub & Black, 1988). Spatial disorientation (also called geographical or topographical disorientation) is a form of visual agnosia (Luria, 1966; Branconnier & DeVitt, 1983) that is often observed in patients with AD. A patient may get lost easily in his own neighborhood or be incapable of locating familiar items at home (Alexander & Geschwind, 1984). Sjögren, Sjögren, and Lindren (1952) reported that all of their stage I AD patients had a clear impairment in the ability to orient in space, while orientation for time was still intact. A variety of disorders fall under the rubric of spatial disorientation (Mesulam, 1985): difficulty locating a public building in a city or locating one's room at home, or difficulty describing verbally or by means of a map how to get to a specific place. It is characterized by diminished ability to orient places on maps, estimate distances accurately, and find routes in both familiar and new places (Lezak, 1983). These deficits can be due to hemispatial neglect, global amnesia, or agnosia (Mesulam, 1985). Spatial disorientation may result from severe impairment of visuospatial memory in addition to visuoperceptual dysfunction per se (Flicker et al., 1988). Patients with spatial disorientation appear to have difficulty retrieving the stored memories needed to determine their location and to plan their route to a specific destination.

Spatial disorientation might be an inevitable consequence of disease progression or it may be due to a specific, severe deficit in spatial relations, like that caused by damage to the right inferior parietal lobule. Henderson, Mack, and Williams (1989) have found an association between spatial disorientation and memory. When memory is impaired, the tendency of some AD patients to wander or to get lost appears to be determined by the degree of visuospatial impairment (i.e., by the severity of dysfunction of right parietal cortex (Henderson et al., 1989). Wandering and getting lost are unusual among patients with focal lesions who exhibit only constructional deficits or only memory problems. Thus, it appears to be the combination of these two neuropsychological deficits that are necessary for spatial disorientation to occur.

De Leon, Potegal, and Gurland (1984) reported that wandering in AD patients better correlates with certain parietal signs than global disease severity, but both left and right inferior parietal impairment was implicated in that study. Mesulum (1985) argued that the operators involved in spatial orientation are complex and probably involve a variety of structures in both inferior and superior visual association cortices, with an essential contribution from the right occipitoparietal region.

Constructional Ability

Disturbances of constructional ability can be evaluated using the Block Design subtest of the WAIS-R or WISC-R or by a variety of drawing and copying tasks. Block Design is usually impaired in moderate to severe dementia patients (Miller, 1977), and has also been shown to be impaired in mildly demented AD patients (Storandt et al., 1984). Block Design performance in AD patients shows progressive deterioration over the course of the disease (Berg et al., 1984).

Strub and Black (1988) recommend that every patient being evaluated for AD be asked to draw and copy a series of line drawings because drawing deficits are commonly observed in Alzheimer's patients (Bayles et al., 1987; Cummings & Benson, 1983; Field, 1960; Grossi & Orsini, 1978; Grossi, Orsini, & Michele, 1978; Pearce & Miller, 1973; Storandt et al., 1984; Eslinger, Pepin, & Benton, 1988; Moore & Wyke, 1984). Drawing ability is impaired in dementia in proportion to the overall severity of dementia (De Ajuriaguerra & Tissot, 1968) and deteriorates as the disease progresses (Berg et al., 1984; Sjögren, Sjögren, & Lindren, 1952;

Strub & Black, 1986). Drawings to command (also referred to as spontaneous drawings or drawings from memory) may be considerably more sensitive than reproduction drawings early in the course of the disorder (Strub & Black, 1988). AD patients usually have considerable difficulty copying three-dimensional figures and often will also have difficulty copying two-dimensional figures (Henderson et al., 1989; Moore & Wyke, 1984; Pan, Stern, Sano, & Mayeux, 1989). My colleagues and I at SIU School of Medicine have observed that an impaired copy of complex geometrical designs (e.g., the Rey-Osterreith CFT) will appear long before impairment is evident in copying less complex designs, including the Greek cross or intersecting pentagons. In the two AD cases discussed at the end of this chapter, severe constructional dyspraxia was evident on the CFT, whereas copies of less complex geometrical forms were generally intact.

Mildly demented AD patients show significantly more errors than age-matched control subjects in copying the Bender Gestalt (Bender, 1938) or other geometric forms (Storandt et al., 1984). Drawing tests that have been used to assess constructional abilities in AD patients include the Clock Drawing Test (the subject is first asked to draw a clock with numbers and set the hands to show "10 past 11," then asked to copy a model of a clock set at 10 past 11), the Clock Setting Test (the subject is asked to draw the hour and minute hands on four clocks for certain hand settings), and the Copy-a-Cube Test (Goodglass & Kaplan, 1976; Salmon & Butters, 1992). In another version of the Clock Drawing Test that proved to be sensitive to dementia severity in Alzheimer's disease, subjects were asked to draw the face of a clock reading the time of 2:45 (Sunderland et al., 1989). Clock drawings to command, in our experience, are more sensitive to mild Alzheimer's dementia than copying a clock from a model. The misplacement of hands and/or numbers on the clock drawings to command in patients who can copy from a model suggest that this task is primarily sensitive to the conceptual difficulties of the patients rather than to visuospatial abilities.

Constructional disturbance strongly suggests parietal lobe dysfunction (Mesulam, 1985, p. 282). Most studies have found that posterior lesions such as those involving the parietal, temporal, and/or occipital cortices produce greater impairment in drawing than anterior lesions (Benson & Barton, 1970; Benton, 1985; Black & Strub, 1976). Visuoconstructive impairment is more frequent, more severe, and qualitatively different following unilateral damage to the right hemisphere as compared to unilateral left hemisphere damage (Arigoni & De Renzi, 1964; Benton, 1967; Benton & Fogel, 1962; De Renzi & Faglioni, 1967; Hannay, Varney, & Benton, 1976; Piercy & Smyth, 1962; Mesulam, 1985, p. 281).

Most AD patients have severe hypometabolism as measured by PET scans bilaterally in the temporoparietal cortex (Frackowiak, Pozzilli, Legg, & DuBoulay, 1981; Friedland et al., 1983; Foster et al., 1984). Foster et al. (1983) reported that AD patients with moderate to severe dementia and with prominent and disproportionate visuoconstructional deficits exhibited large decreases in glucose utilization in the *right* temporal and parietal lobes. Two other studies have found that early AD patients with relatively greater right than left hemisphere hypometabolism showed greater impairment on visuospatial functions as compared to language functions, and vice versa (Haxby, Duara, Grady, Cutler, & Rapoport, 1985; Koss, Friedland, Ober, & Jagust, 1985).

On the other hand, in a recent study (Ober, Jagust, Koss, Delis, & Friedland,

1991), drawing measures were found to be significantly correlated with regional glucose metabolism in *both* left and right occipital and/or temporoparietal regions. Furthermore, no dissociation was found between performance on configural versus detailed aspects of drawing and metabolic activity in the right versus left hemisphere in AD. Ober et al. (1991) speculated that this is due to the fact that there is bilateral damage in AD and there is probably an interdependence of residual functioning in each hemisphere.

Qualitative Analysis of the Drawings of AD Patients

The drawings of AD patients share similarities with the drawings of patients with both left hemisphere lesions (i.e., very impoverished drawings with major parts omitted) and right hemisphere lesions (i.e., fragmentation and impaired spatial relations) (Moore & Wyke, 1984; Ober et al., 1991). Studies of drawing ability in patients with focal brain lesions have shown that left versus right hemisphere damage produces qualitatively different kinds of impaired drawings (i.e., the types of errors are different) (Warrington, 1969; McFie & Zangwill, 1960). The spontaneous drawings of patients with right hemisphere lesions are scattered and fragmented and display a loss of spatial relations, faulty orientation, and the addition of lines to try to make the drawing correct. Patients with right-sided lesions did not perform any better when they could copy a drawing. Several neuropsychological studies have confirmed that the drawings of right hemisphere–damaged patients are impaired in the overall configuration and in spatial relationships among its parts, whereas the drawings of left hemisphere–damaged patients are impoverished due to the omission of details (Delis, Kiefner, & Fridlund, 1988; Delis, Robertson, & Efron, 1986; Gainotti, Messerlie, & Tissot, 1972; Milberg, Hebben, & Kaplan, 1986; Warrington, James, & Kinsbourne, 1966).

Two studies also reported that AD patients do *not* display left-sided neglect in their drawings (left hemispacial neglect is common after right hemisphere lesions) (Moore & Wyke, 1984; Ober et al., 1991). A third study (Freedman & Dexter, 1991), however, reported an equal incidence and severity of neglect in a right hemisphere stroke group and a dementia group except that whereas neglect in the right hemisphere group was always to the left hemispace, 50% of dementia patients exhibited right hemispacial neglect.

In addition to more omission errors, AD patients make more confabulatory errors (i.e., irrelevant responses) and perseverations than control subjects (Brantjes & Bouma, 1991). Perseverations were common in the drawings of AD patients. Three types of perseveration were observed only in the AD group: (a) perseveration of activity (i.e., inability of the drawer to switch from one cognitive mode to another), (b) perseveration of features (e.g., a fish is drawn with the legs of a bird that was drawn previously), and (c) hyperkinesia-like motor perseveration (i.e., inability to terminate individual movements). These error types were displayed in the drawing-from-memory task and in the copying task, but not in the tracing task. It appears that perseverations are not exhibited in highly structured situations, like the tracing task. Goldberg and Tucker (1979) suggested that each type of perseveration reflects a breakdown of cognitive processing at different levels of executive functions. Perseverations are frequently found in patients with frontal-lobe lesions, in aphasic patients with left hemisphere lesions, and in patients with subcortical involvement (Sandson & Albert, 1984).

AD patients also tend to display the "closing-in" phenomenon in copying geometrical figures and the tendency to give globalistic and odd responses on the Raven's Colored Matrices (Gianotti, Parlato, Monteleone, & Carlomagno, 1992). Closing-in refers to the tendency to trace over the lines of the model or to trace lines from the model to the surrounding space rather than drawing a freestanding figure. Globalistic errors on the Raven's Colored Matrices are response choices that are reduced duplicates of the whole shape of the model rather than the missing piece. Odd responses are completely different from the missing piece or the overall form of the model.

The drawings of AD patients also are affected by the general impairment of intellect, memory, and attention (Ober et al., 1991). Drawing deficits correlate with dementia severity (Moore & Wyke, 1984).

Skilled Movement (Praxis)

Apraxia is defined as a disorder of skilled movement not caused by more elementary sensory or motor deficits, nor caused by intellectual deterioration, poor comprehension, or uncooperativeness (Heilman & Gonzalez Rothi, 1985). Thus, the presence of dementia is a confounding factor that makes it difficult to study praxis in AD. Nonetheless, considerable research that has been done on how well AD patients perform praxis items and these studies will be reviewed in this section.

Nonsymbolic motor functions were studied in 12 subjects with mild to moderate AD, 12 aphasics, and 12 normal controls by use of a movement imitation task requiring subjects to copy single and sequential oral movements, hand positions, and hand movements (Benke, 1992). Aphasics who had lesions including the lateral precentral cortex performed poorly on all four tasks. Alzheimer's patients had deficits in imitating hand positions, hand movements, and sequential orofacial movements, but performed adequately on single oral movements. Thus, frontal motor systems responsible for the production of single orofacial movements seem to remain intact in early AD, whereas parietal motor systems are damaged.

Disturbance of skilled movement (apraxia)—specifically, forgetting the use of objects—was noted in Alzheimer's initial report on a patient with a progressive dementia (Alzheimer, 1977). Pick (1905) and Liepmann (1920) also reported incorrect use of objects and other abnormalities of skilled movement such as ideational and ideomotor apraxia in patients with senile dementia. De Ajuriaguerra and Tissot (1963, 1968) categorized the apraxias of senile dementia as follows: (a) constructional apraxia, (b) ideomotor apraxia, and (c) ideational apraxia. Ideomotor and ideational apraxia occur in the later stages of Alzheimer's disease, after memory and language impairments have usually become severe (Cummings & Benson, 1983; Della Sala, Lucchelli, & Spinnler, 1987). Limb transitive movements are especially impaired, whereas limb intransitive, buccofacial, and axial movements are better preserved (Rapcsak, Croswell, & Rubens, 1989). Difficulty with dressing is common in the middle phases of the disease (Cummings & Benson, 1992, p. 50).

Ideomotor apraxia is an inability to execute a motor activity in response to a verbal command that is easily performed spontaneously (Mesulam, 1985). Ideational apraxia, on the other hand, was originally described by Liepmann (1920) as an inability to carry out a serial act (i.e., a sequence of related activities such as filling and lighting a pipe), even though each separate activity could be successfully performed. Difficulty successfully executing a serial act can be demonstrated in AD and in confusional states (Mesulam, 1985). Strub and Black (1988, p. 152) gave the example of an Alzheimer's patient who carefully unwrapped a sugar cube for her coffee, hesitated about what to do next, and then put the paper in her coffee and discarded the sugar cube. Ideational apraxia later came to refer to an inability to handle concrete objects (tool use) when correct pantomined use of the object could be demonstrated (Ochipa, Rothi, Heilman, 1989; Mesulam, 1985). This type of ideational apraxia is also observed in AD patients.

Rapcsak et al. (1989) concluded that the disorders of skilled movement observed in their group of AD patients were qualitatively similar to the apraxic syndromes that have been described in patients with left parietal damage. The left hemisphere is known to play an essential role in the regulation of skilled movements to both verbal command and imitation (Liepmann, 1920; Geschwind, 1975). Heilman (1979) hypothesized that the visuokinesthetic motor engrams that are prerequisite for skilled movement are contained in the left inferior parietal lobe.

When pantomiming limb transitive movements, AD patients made frequent errors in which the body part (typically the hand) was concretely used as the target object (e.g., using one's fingers as a toothbrush or comb) and also spatial errors (e.g., not gripping the imagined toothbrush, or holding it too far from one's mouth) (Rapcsak et al., 1989). The body-part-as-object errors occurred even though all subjects were instructed to act as if they were holding and using the real object. Normal controls also occasionally make the error of using the body part as an object. However, normal controls will correct their mistake when reminded of the instructions, whereas apraxics will usually not be able to correct their mistake (Rapcsak & Ochipa, 1990). The AD patients performed considerably better when using actual objects than when performing on verbal command or imitation—the latter two conditions were not statistically different. Ideomotor apraxia is often associated with aphasia, but the two symptoms can be dissociated as was the case with some of the AD patients in the Rapcsak study. AD patients, like other apraxics, are generally not aware of their errors (anosognosia).

Alzheimer's disease is the most common cause of ideational apraxia (Rapcsak & Ochipa, 1990). Sometimes the AD patients were able to correctly perform the individual movements on the tasks requiring serial use of objects but not in the correct sequence, whereas other times even individual movements were not correctly executed (Rapcsak et al., 1989). Ideational apraxia was strongly correlated with ideomotor apraxia (Rapcsak et al., 1989). However, whereas ideational apraxia was always associated with ideomotor apraxia, 10 AD patients had ideomotor apraxia without ideational apraxia (Rapcsak et al., 1989). Somewhat at odds with these findings are the results of a recent study demonstrating that both ideational apraxia and ideomotor apraxia can occur in isolation, thus demonstrating that the two types of apraxia can be independent of each other (Lopez, Lucchelli, Faglioni, & Boller, 1992).

Ideomotor apraxia appears to be a disruption of a production system, whereas ideational apraxia appears to be due to a disruption of a conceptual system (Rapcsak & Ochipa, 1990). Difficulty with using tools is an essential attribute of ideational apraxia because it can be observed even in patients whose ability to carry out commands is intact (Rapcsak & Ochipa, 1990). Ideational apraxia, like ideomotor apraxia, is highly associated with posterior left hemisphere lesions (Rapcsak et al., 1989). Ideomotor apraxia after focal damage is often associated with aphasia, but can occur in the absence of aphasia. Ideational apraxia following focal damage (e.g., due to a stroke) usually is associated with aphasia. Similar findings were reported for the AD patients in the Rapcsak study. Some AD patients with ideomotor apraxia had intact auditory comprehension, whereas severe ideational apraxia was primarily found in AD patients with poor comprehension.

Ideomotor apraxia does not have a major impact on everday functioning because performance improves when the object is present, as in the home (Rapcsak & Ochipa, 1990). Ideational apraxia, on the other hand, involves impaired tool use and thus can have a definite adverse effect on functioning in the home and consequently can be a serious management issue (Rapcsak & Ochipa, 1990).

In summary, the findings of the Rapcsak et al. (1989) study indicated that the apraxic syndrome in AD is qualitatively similar to the disorders of skilled movement following posterior left hemispheric lesions. Rapcsak et al. (1989) recommended apraxia testing (particularly for limb transitive movements) in the neuropsychological evaluation of suspected AD patients. Ideomotor and ideational apraxias are obviously not useful, however, in the early detection of AD because these deficits do not typically appear until the later stages of the illness. Apraxia assessment may prove useful in the differential diagnosis of later stage Alzheimer's disease from other dementing disorders, but direct comparative studies directly comparing praxis in different dementias have not yet been conducted.

Case Examples

A case of definite AD in the early stages is discussed first in this section to illustrate the typical cognitive profile of very mild Alzheimer's dementia, which was described earlier in this chapter. This case example also gives an indication of the differential sensitivity of various psychometric tests to very mild AD.

Case 1: An Example of a Typical Neuropsychological Profile of Early Alzheimer's Dementia (Autopsy Confirmed)

The patient is a 76-year-old, right-handed female who completed 8 years of education. She is a housewife and a former bookkeeper for a family business. Her family noticed a clear cognitive decline over the past 6 to 8 months. A 3-hour test battery measuring a variety of cognitive functions was administered to the patient. The results of this patient's cognitive evaluation are presented in Table 1.5.

The patient's neuropsychological test results are consistent with DSM-III-R diagnostic criteria for dementia and NINCDS-ADRDA criteria for probable Alzheimer's disease because the patient has severe impairments in two or more cognitive domains. The patient displays the triad of deficits characteristic of Alzheimer's disease: severe memory impairment, language deficits, and visuospatial impairment in the context of general intellectual decline and problem-solving difficulty. Possible alternative causes or contributing factors to her cog-

TABLE 1.5.   Cognitive Test Results on an Early Definite AD Patient[a] (Case 1)

	Score	SD Difference[b]
Mental status		
Folstein Mini-Mental State Examination (correct)	26 (30)	−0.2
Original Alzheimer Disease Assessment Scale (errors)	11 (70)	−2.0
Extended Alzheimer Disease Assessment Scale (errors)	70.5 (170)	
SIU Orientation and Information Test (correct)	21.5 (30)	
Memory		
Rey Auditory Verbal Learning Test (15-word list)		
Learning trials (8 trials)		
Trial 1 (correct)	1	−2.5
Trials 3–7 (correct)	2,4,3,4,2,5	
Trial 8 (correct)	3	−4.2
Intrusion errors (total)	5	
List B (correct)	2	
Short Delay Recall (correct)	1	−3.2
Short Delay Recognition		
Correct	11	
False-positive errors	7	
Correct minus false-positive errors	4	−9.8
Long Delay Recall		
Correct	1	
Intrusion errors	2	
Rey-Osterreith Complex Figure Test		
Immediate Memory (points)	2.5 (36)	−1.9
Delayed Memory (points)	1.0 (36)	−2.2
Language		
Boston Naming Test (correct)	42 (60)	−2.1
FAS Word Fluency (total for the 3 trials)	6	−3.2
Category Word Fluency (total for the 3 trials)	30	−2.4
Visual-spatial skills		
Rey-Osterreith Complex Figure Test (copy) (points)	22.5 (36)	−1.4
Hooper Visual Organization Test (correct)	22 (30)	−0.5
Raven's Colored Matrices (correct)	25 (36)	−0.7
Performance subtests from the WAIS-R		
Picture Completion (age-equivalent scaled score)	7	−1.0
Block Design (age-equivalent scaled score)	10	0
Digit Symbol (age-equivalent scaled score)	6	−1.3
Trails A: time (seconds)	121	−7.0
Errors	1	
Trails B: time (seconds)	328	−5.1
Errors	2	
Verbal abstraction		
WAIS-R Similarities (age-equivalent scaled score)	10	0
Attention/information processing speed		
Stroop Test		
Reading (seconds)	41	−3.9
Naming (seconds)	72	−7.6
Color-Word (correct items within 2 minutes)	27 (50)	

[a]Patient was a 76-year-old female with 8 years of education.
[b]We classify severity of cognitive impairment according to the number of standard deviations from the mean of an age-appropriate control group (local norms except for WAIS-R): within normal limits $\leq$ −0.06 SD, mild = −0.7 to −1.3 SD, moderate = −1.4 to −1.6 SD, severe = −1.7 to −3.0 SD, very severe $\geq$ −3.1 SD.

nitive impairment need to be considered and ruled out. A reevaluation in 12 months or whenever there is a suspicion of an appreciable change in her cognitive status is recommended in order to determine if there was actually a change compared to the baseline assessment. If this patient does have AD, then a gradually progressive decline in cognitive functioning would be expected over time.

This case illustrates some noteworthy points about the relative sensitivity of a variety of psychometric tests to early AD. The MMSE was insensitive in this case of early AD. However, forgetting two out of three words at one minute suggested that there may be a memory problem. Her performance on the ADAS was impaired and thus proved to be more sensitive than the MMSE in this case of early AD. The errors on the ADAS were, however, again limited to the memory measures and thus not sufficient to meet either the DSM-III-R criteria for dementia or NINCDS-ADRDA criteria for probable Alzheimer's disease, which require impairment in two or more domains of cognitive functioning. The extended ADAS more clearly demonstrated both memory problems and other cognitive difficulties. However, it was the more comprehensive battery of cognitive tests for dementia that most convincingly demonstrated the triad of memory, language, and visuospatial deficits, and thereby best satisfied diagnostic criteria for Alzheimer's dementia.

The BNT revealed a clear dysnomia that was undetected on the ADAS Naming Objects and Fingers subtests. The patient's responses on the BNT were categorized using the system described by Hodges, Salmon, and Butters (1991). The patient made three superordinate category errors (17% of total errors; e.g., "bird" for pelican), five semantic associative errors (28%; "ancient days" for sphinx), one semantic-category errors (6%; i.e., "plane" for helicopter), four circumlocutory errors (22%; e.g., "horse with a cone" for unicorn), two visual errors (11%; e.g., "snake" for pretzel), three ambiguous visual/semantic category errors (17%; e.g., "rat" for beaver).

The SIU Orientation and Information Test revealed a deficit that was not evident on the Orientation subtest of the ADAS. The Rey-Osterreith CFT was more sensitive to graphomotor praxis difficulty than a variety of other figures including the overlapping pentagons from the MMSE, the Greek Cross from the Halstead-Reitan Battery, and the complex cube from the ADAS (Figures 1.4 and 1.5). In addition to the MMSE and the original ADAS subtests, except the two memory subtests, several other test scores were within normal limits: the Hooper Visual Organization Test (visuointegrative ability), the WAIS-R Block Design (visuoconstructional problem solving), and the WAIS-R Similarities (verbal abstraction). The patient's performance on Raven's Colored Progressive Matrices (simple visuospatial problem solving) was only at the beginning of the impaired range.

Discussion

This patient was selected for discussion because her test results represent the typical case of a patient that we would currently classify as having early AD. Although the patient scored well within normal limits on the MMSE, she clearly displayed severely to very severely impaired recent memory, severely impaired confrontational naming, severely to very severely impaired generative naming, and moderately impaired graphomotor praxis. Thus, the more sensitive cognitive test measures demonstrate that this patient has severe impairments in several domains of

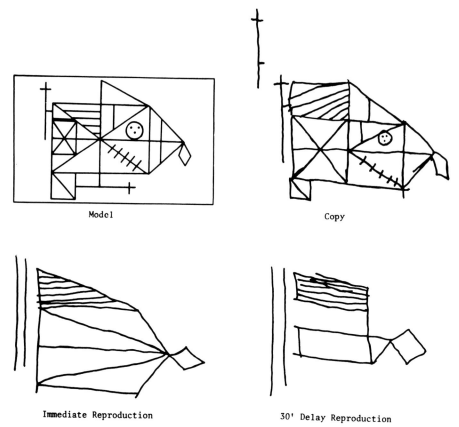

Model   Copy

Immediate Reproduction   30' Delay Reproduction

FIGURE 1.4. The performance of Case 1 with early definite Alzheimer's disease (AD) on the Rey-Osterreith Complex Figure Test: moderately impaired direct copy, very severely impaired immediate reproduction, and very severely impaired 30-minute delay reproduction (figures were reduced in size for publication).

cognitive functioning and is well beyond the incipient stages of AD. Therefore, the description of this patient as having early or mild AD based on the intact MMSE is misleading. Given the severe to very severe cognitive impairments displayed by this patient with a MMSE score of 26, this set of sensitive psychometric tests probably would have been capable of detecting signs of a dementing illness several years earlier in her course.

Memory impairment is usually the first presenting symptom in AD. As was the case with the patient presented in this section, poor performance on both recall and recognition memory tests is typically found relatively early in the course of Alzheimer's dementia. Because the memory deficits associated with many other neurological and psychiatric disorders consist of impaired free recall in the context of relatively intact recognition memory, deficits in recognition memory, as previously discussed, are helpful in the differential diagnosis of Alzheimer's disease from many other disorders producing memory impairment (e.g., depression, PD, frontal lobe dementias, multiple sclerosis, acquired immunodeficiency syndrome [AIDS]).

However, a cautionary note needs to be made because in our experience

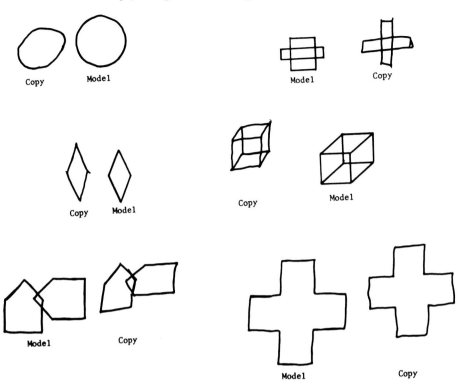

FIGURE 1.5. Intact copies of six geometrical forms by Case 1 with early definite Alzheimer's disease (AD) (figures were reduced in size for publication).

impaired recall with relatively intact recognition memory can occur in very early AD. Free recall memory measures, not recognition memory measures, appear to be especially sensitive to very early Alzheimer's disease. It follows then that the differential diagnosis of Alzheimer's disease versus other disorders causing cognitive impairment will be more difficult during the very early stages. Follow-up assessments demonstrating progressive cognitive decline and an emerging cognitive profile characteristic of Alzheimer's dementia would increase confidence in a diagnosis of AD. The severe impairments on both recall and recognition memory measures of the patient discussed in this section are another indication that this patient was well beyond the incipient stages of AD.

Periodic reassessments are helpful not only in confirming a preclinical impression of AD, but also in confirming the diagnosis of AD in those patients who initially present atypically. There are individual differences in the presenting neuropsychological profile of Alzheimer's patients during the early stages. For example, some patients with AD may begin with language or visuospatial deficits rather than memory deficits. In addition, some patients may present with a disproportionate language deficit in the context of relatively intact visuospatial functioning, whereas other patients may exhibit the opposite pattern (i.e., severe visuospatial deficits in the context of relatively intact language functioning). Over time, however, the characteristic pattern of deficits usually emerges; therefore, follow-up evaluations can help confirm the diagnosis of Alzheimer's dementia in cases with atypical initial presentations.

Case 2: The Cognitive Course of an Alzheimer's Disease Patient with a Plateau Period (Autopsy Confirmed)

The patient is an 86-year-old, right-handed female who completed 12 years of education and a few college courses. She had worked part-time in her husband's insurance company. She was initially referred for a neuropsychological evaluation because she had a 2-year history of memory problems and a suspicion of AD. She received three cognitive evaluations over a 4-year period. On the initial assessment, recent memory, confrontational naming, and word fluency were clearly impaired, but intellectual functioning and visuospatial skills were relatively intact. These test results are generally consistent with the typical neuropsychological profile of an early AD patient. On the second assessment 14 months later, there was little further decline in cognitive functions, indicating a "plateau" period. Large declines in most of her test scores were, however, evident at the third assessment 18 months later (32 months after the initial baseline assessment), thus demonstrating progression of her dementia.

Baseline

On the initial baseline assessment in 1988, the following cognitive functions were clearly impaired: (a) memory (RAVLT), (b) confrontational naming (BNT), (c) generative naming, (d) psychomotor ability (Trails A and B), (e) color naming speed (Stroop Color Naming Test), and (f) the ability to inhibit dominant responses (Color-Word Test) (Table 1.6). On the other hand, the patient's scores on six WAIS-R subtests were not clearly impaired compared to local age norms. In addition, the patient scored within normal limits on a test of visuointegrative ability (Hooper VOT) and on a test of constructional praxis (Rey-Osterreith CFT).

Second Assessment

The second assessment was performed 14 months after the initial baseline evaluation, but test scores did not show the expected decline (Table 1.6). Memory scores were still poor, but did not decline any further. Confrontational naming actually improved to some extent. The three WAIS-R performance subtests that were readministered tended to decline, but scores on the three verbal subtests remained relatively stable. Reading speed on the Stroop test was somewhat slower, but color-naming speed was somewhat faster. Thus, there was no clear evidence of further cognitive decline over 14 months, (i.e., there was a plateau in the deterioration of cognitive functions over this period). The ADAS was administered for the first time during this second assessment and the patient scored clearly in the impaired range.

Third Assessment

The patient's performance at the third assessment (32 months after baseline) revealed very large declines in most scores compared to the second evaluation performed 18 months earlier (see Table 1.6). Memory scores declined, but the true magnitude of the deterioration could not be determined due to floor effects on this memory test. There was a dramatic decline in performance on the four WAIS-R subtests that were administered. The following test measures worsened

TABLE 1.6. Cognitive Test Results on a Definite AD Patient Tested Three Times Over 32 Months (Case 2)

	Norm[a]	9/29/88 Baseline	11/20/89 14 months	5/15/91 32 months	
Mental status					
SIU Orientation & Information Test				11	(30 maximum correct)
Folstein MMSE				17	points (30 maximum)
ADAS[b]	7		28	44	error score
Memory					
RAVLT Trials					
1	5.5	3	3	0	correct (15 maximum)
2	7.8	3	3	0	
3	9.4	3	3	2	
4	10.5	7	3	1	
5	11.4	4	5	2	
B	6.0	2	2	0	
Recall	8.2	1	2	0	
Recognition	14.1	14	8	4	
Intrusions	0.8	12	20	12	
Difference	13.3	2	− 12	− 8	
Benton VRT		6			
Language					
Boston Naming	51.4	33	39	20	correct (60 maximum)
Phonemic WF	35	19		8	words correct
Semantic WF	51	37		10	words correct
WAIS-R subtests					
Information	19.7	20	19		raw scores
Digit Span	14.5	11	13		
Similarities	18.5	21	19	0	
Picture Completion	13.6	16	12	2	
Block Design	22.9	15	13	0	
Digit Symbol	35.9	28	18	5	
Visuospatial skills					
Trails A	49	156 (1 error)		313	seconds
Trails B	133	321 (1 error)		CND	seconds
Hooper VOT	29	27		16.5	correct
Rey-Osterreith CFT		30		1.5	points
Raven's Colored Matrices				11	(36 possible)
Attention/information processing speed					
Stroop Test					
Reading	24	28	32	53	seconds
Color Naming	34	46	40	83	seconds
Color-Word Test	50[c]	29	34	14	items/120 sec

[a]normative values are based on local mean normative values for her age group
[b]Alzheimer Disease Assessment Scale
[c]In 89 seconds.
Note: AD = Alzheimer's disease; SIU = Southern Illinois University; MMSE = Mini-Mental State Examination; ADAS = Alzheimer's Disease Assessment Scale; RAVLT = Rey Auditory Verbal Learning Test; WF = Word Fluency; VOT = Visual Organization Test; CFT = Complex Figure Test.

considerably: performance on the BNT (a measure of confrontational naming), reading and color naming speeds on the Stroop test, performance on the Stroop Color-Word test, and performance on the ADAS. Compared to the initial baseline assessment, there were large declines in the following test scores: phonemic and semantic word fluency, Trails A and B (psychomotor ability), and the Hooper VOT (visuointegrative ability). The MMSE exam score, which was administered for the first time, was in the moderately impaired range. The SIU Orientation and Information Test, also administered for the first time, indicated severe impairment.

The patient accurately copied 11 of 12 geometrical figures (Figures 1.6 and 1.7) at the 32-months assessment, but did not properly overlap the pentagons in her copy of the intersecting pentagons. In contrast to her generally good copies of these other geometrical figures, her copy of the Rey-Osterreith CFT, which was within normal limits at the baseline assessment, was very severely impaired at 32 months (Figure 1.8).

Discussion

Thus, the data from both Cases 1 and 2 suggest that the Rey-Osterreith CFT is considerably more sensitive to constructional praxis deficits than copying tests using less complex geometrical figures. The less complex figures, however, are valuable in assessing the depth of the constructional praxis impairment. The finding that these patients could accurately copy a variety of less complex figures indicates that their constructional praxis difficulty is limited to more complex constructional tasks.

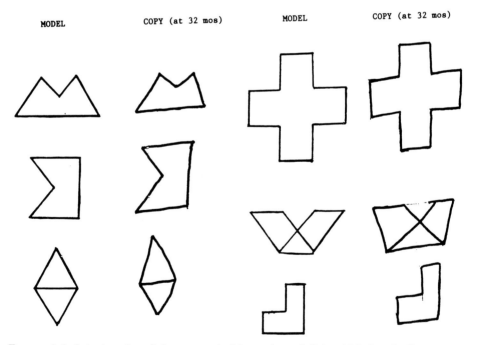

FIGURE 1.6. Intact copies of six geometrical forms by a definite Alzheimer's disease (AD) patient (Case 2) 32 months after a baseline cognitive evaluation that did not include these particular figures (figures were reduced in size for publication).

MODEL   COPY (at 32 mos)   MODEL   COPY (at 32 mos)

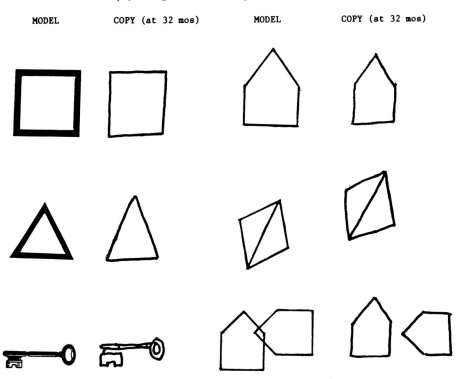

FIGURE 1.7. Intact copies of five of six more geometrical forms (except for pentagons that did not overlap as in the model) by a definite Alzheimer's disease (AD) patient (Case 2) 32 months after a baseline cognitive evaluation that did not include these particular figures (figures were reduced in size for publication).

Error Analysis of Responses on the BNT

The patient displayed severely impaired confrontational naming ability (BNT) in 1988 and even greater impairment in 1991 (Table 1.6). The patient's errors were classified using the categorization system for naming errors described by Hodges et al. (1991). In Table 1.7 the percentages of different error types are given for Case 1 (previously discussed) and for Case 2 (1988 and 1991 assessments). Also in Table 1.7 are the error percentages reported by Hodges et al. (1991) for three groups: (a) patients with AD, (b) normal elderly controls, and (c) patients with HD.

Semantic circumlocutory errors and semantic associative errors were the most frequent error type in the first assessment for Case 2. Over the course of 3 years there was a very large decrease in circumlocutory errors and a corresponding increase in semantic associative errors. Examining the changes in responses to individual items, the following three major observations were made about the performance of this patient at baseline and then at 32 months: (a) many semantic associative errors remained semantic associative errors (e.g., cactus—"you see on the desert," 1988; "beautiful," 1991); (b) many correct answers changed into semantic associative errors (e.g., mask—"for fun," 1991); and (c) many semantic circumlocutory errors also changed to semantic associative errors (e.g., noose— "a twisted rope they hang you with," 1988; "rope," 1991).

MODEL

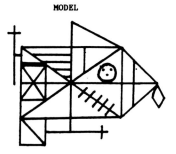

COPY (at baseline)

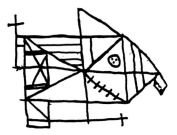

COPY (at 32 mos)

FIGURE 1.8. The performance of a patient with definite Alzheimer's disease (AD) (Case 2) on the Rey-Osterreith Complex Figure Test at baseline and again at 32 months after the baseline evaluation (figures were reduced in size for publication).

TABLE 1.7.   Percentages of Different Error Types on the Boston Naming Test for Case 1 (One Assessment) and for Case 2 at Baseline (1988) and 32 Months Later (1991)

		Case 2		Hodges et al.		
Error Types	Case 1	1988	1991	AD	NC	HD
Visual	11%	1%	6%	11%	4%	18%
Visual-semantic	17	4	0	12	19	19
Semantic within-category errors	6	19	19	11	30	
Semantic superordinate	17	0	0	20	12	12
Semantic associative	28	31	56	16	5	4
Semantic circumlocutory	22	38	9	18	20	
Unrelated	0	0	9			
No response	0	0 (60)	2 (60)			

Note: AD = Alzheimer's disease; NC = controls; HD = Huntington's disease.

Conclusions

A neuropsychological evaluation of the cognitive functioning of a patient suspected of having AD is necessary to objectively describe the severity, extent, and pattern of the cognitive and memory impairments. A comprehensive description of the patient's cognitive impairments is important both to the differential diagnosis of the patient's disorder and to the care and treatment planning for the patient (McKhann et al., 1984). It can provide a baseline against which future assessments can be compared. Comparison with a baseline evaluation is necessary to accomplish the following: (a) to objectively measure the course of the disorder, (b) to confirm the diagnosis, and (c) to evaluate treatments. There are many different causes for the syndrome of dementia, including reversible causes, and this underscores the need for an accurate differential diagnosis.

Alzheimer's disease is the leading cause of amnesia in the elderly. Memory impairment begins insidiously, is gradually progressive, and is usually the first presenting deficit. In the very early stages, there appears to be a fair degree of variability in the pattern of cognitive dysfunction beyond the almost universal presence of severe memory impairment. A typical neuropsychological profile for a person with mild to moderate AD includes impairment of recent memory, a reduction in general intellectual functioning, visuoconstructional problems, reduction in verbal fluency, and impaired confrontational naming. Basic sensory and motor functions remain relatively intact through most of the course of AD. Alzheimer's dementia is gradually progressive; therefore, serial neuropsychological testing is strongly recommended to document this defining feature of the disease and help confirm the diagnosis. However, it should be kept in mind that Alzheimer's dementia as measured by neuropsychological tests can plateau for periods of up to several years.

Although neuropsychological tests have the potential to reliably detect early AD, the currently published normative values are generally inadequate. The NINCDS-ADRDA task force (McKhann et al., 1984) operationally defined impairment in a domain of functioning as a score below the fifth percentile level compared to appropriate normative data controlling for age, gender, and education. However, this task force also pointed out that there are no normative values for many of the tests that they recommended. The lack of precise normative data makes it very difficult to reliably judge whether a score is abnormal or not for a particular individual. Stratified neuropsychological normative data are needed for important demographic variables. Normative studies are currently being conducted in a number of laboratories (see chapter 2 in this volume). Studies are also needed to determine which tests are sensitive to the progressive worsening of the disorder, because tests that are most sensitive to early dementia are usually the least sensitive to monitoring change over time.

Future research should also determine the ability of neuropsychological tests to detect *very* early AD. It may be that mild to moderate impairment on one or more specific neuropsychological tests (i.e., between 1 and 2 *SD* below the mean of an appropriate control group) is an indication that the patient is "at risk" for AD (i.e., in the preclinical stages). Some have proposed this predementia designation for patients with cognitive impairments that have not yet met the NINCDS criteria of severe impairments (> 2 *SD* below an appropriate control group). Longitudinal prospective studies need to determine the probability of developing AD in patients with mild to moderate cognitive impairments on sensitive neuropsychological tests compared to those without these deficits.

Several studies indicate that cognitive impairment measured by sensitive psychometric tests precedes impairments in functioning in everyday life as measured by rating scales and clinical interview (Grady et al., 1988; LaRue & Jarvik, 1987). This is especially true in the retired elderly, who are less likely to be engaged in cognitive demanding tasks in which job performance is periodically evaluated. Cerebral metabolic changes may, however, even precede the cognitive changes (Grady et al., 1988). According to the "threshold" model, neurological changes in the brains of Alzheimer's patients (e.g., plaques, tangles, cell loss, cholinergic deficiency, and other neurotransmitter deficits) must reach a certain critical level or threshold before performance on demanding psychometric tests or everyday functioning is affected (Grady et al., 1988). Thus, although sensitive neuropsychological tests have the potential of detecting early and maybe even very early Alzheimer's *dementia*, AD presumably begins some time before subtle cognitive impairment is manifested. Theoretically, biological markers should exist that precede even subtle cognitive impairment.

Dementia is a manifestation of the progressive damage to the brains of patients with AD; therefore, neuropsychological assessment is an indirect measure of the underlying neurological changes. On the other hand, neuropsychological assessment is a direct measure of Alzheimer's *dementia* and therefore central to the clinical work-up of patients with AD. Thus, assessment of Alzheimer's dementia in contrast to Alzheimer's disease will remain primarily the domain of the neuropsychologist.

Future Research

Some important areas for future research on the neuropsychology of AD include the following: (a) early detection (sensitivity), (b) presentation and evolution of AD, (c) differential diagnosis (selectivity), (d) severity and progression, (e), aging (of the brain and senses), (f) biological correlates (brain-behavior relationships), (g) behavioral correlates and case management (ecological validity and modification), and (h) evaluation of treatment efficacy. Further work is needed to improve our ability to make early and accurate diagnostic and prognostic statements. Neuropsychology's contribution to early detection will permit the early study of the disease, including the incipient biological changes, which will increase the likelihood of finding etiological factors. Early intervention (e.g., with psychopharmacological treatment) and the study of the effectiveness of early interventions presupposes early detection. Furthermore, neuropsychological tests are usually the major measure of efficacy or outcome in drug trials to treat AD. More work needs to be done on the sensitivity of these neuropsychological efficacy measures to psychopharmacological treatment. One goal of drug treatments of AD is to retard the progression of the disease. Consequently, more work is also needed on rates and profiles of cognitive decline so that we can better determine the effects of psychopharmacological treatment on the progression of AD.

References

Adams, R. D., & Victor, M. (1977). *Principles of neurology*. New York: McGraw-Hill.

Albert, M. S. (1981). Geriatric neuropsychology. *Journal of Consulting and Clinical Psychology, 49*, 835–850.

Albert, M. S., Butters, N., & Brandt, J. (1981). Patterns of remote memory in amnestic and demented patients. *Archives of Neurology, 38*, 495–500.

Albert, M. S., & Moss, M. B. (1988). *Geriatric neuropsychology*. New York: Guilford Press.

Alexander, D. A. (1973). Some tests of intelligence and learning for elderly psychiatric patients: A validation study. *British Journal of Social and Clinical Psychology, 12*, 188–193.

Alexander, M. P., & Geschwind, N. (1984). Dementia in the elderly. In M. L. Albert (Ed.), *Clinical neurology of aging* (pp. 254–276). New York: Oxford University Press.

Allender, J., & Kaszniak, A. W. (1985). *Processing of emotional cues and personality change in dementia of the Alzheimer type*. Paper presented at the Annual meeting of the International Neuropsychology Society, San Diego, CA.

Allison, R. S. (1962). *The senile brain*. London: Edward Arnold.

Alzheimer, A. (1977). A unique illness involving the cerebral cortex. In D. A. Rottenbert & F. H. Hochberg (Eds.), Hochberg C. N. & Hochberg F. H. (trans.), *Neurological classics in modern translation* (pp. 41–43). New York: Haffner Press.

American Psychiatric Association. (1987). *Diagnostic and statistical manual of mental disorders* (3rd ed., rev.). Washington, DC: Author.

Andree, B., Hittmair, M., & Benke, T. H. (1992). Recognition and explanation of proverbs in Alzheimer's disease. *Journal of Clinical and Experimental Neuropsychology, 14*, 372.

Appell, J., Kertesz, A., & Fisman, M. (1982). A study of language functioning in Alzheimer's patients. *Brain and Language, 17*, 73–91.

Arendt, T., Bigl, V., Arendt, A., & Tennstedt, A. (1983). Loss of neurons in the nucleus basalis of Meynert in Alzheimer's disease. *Acta Neuropathologica, 61*, 101–108.

Arigoni, G., & De Renzi, E. (1964). Constructional apraxia and hemispheric locus of lesion. *Cortex (Milano), 1*, 170–197.

Arriagada, P. V., Marzloff, K., & Hyman, B. T. (1992). Distribution of Alzheimer-type pathologic changes in nondemented elderly individuals matches the pattern in Alzheimer's disease. *Neurology, 42*, 1681–1688.

Ashford, J. W., Kolm, P., Colliver, J. A., Bekian, C., & Hsu, L. H. (1989). Alzheimer patient evaluation and the Mini-Mental State: Item characteristic curve analysis. *Journal of Gerontology: Psychological Sciences, 44*, 139–146.

Atkinson, R. C., & Shiffrin, R. M. (1968). Human memory: A proposed system and its control process. In K. W. Spence & J. T. Spence (Eds.), *The psychology of learning and motivation: Advances in research and theory* (Vol. 2). New York: Academic Press.

Babinski, M. J. (1914). Contribution a l'etude des troubles mentaux dans l'hemiplegie organique cerebrale (anosognosie). [Contribution to the study of mental disturbance in organic cerbral hemiplegia (anosoagnosia)]. *Review of Neurology (Paris), 12*, 845–848.

Baddeley, A. D., Bressi, S., Della Sala, S., Logie, R., & Spinnler, H. (1991). The decline of working memory in Alzheimer's disease: A longitudinal study. *Brain, 114*, 2521–2542.

Baddeley, A., Della Sala, S., & Spinnler, H. (1991). The two-component hypothesis of memory deficit in Alzheimer's disease. *Journal of Clinical and Experimental Neuropsychology*, *13*(2), 372–380.

Bayles, K. A. (1991). Age at onset of Alzheimer's disease: Relation to language dysfunction. *Archives of Neurology*, *48*, 155–159.

Bayles, K. A., Kaszniak, A. W., & Tomoeda, C. K. (1987). *Communication and cognition in normal aging and dementia.* Boston: College Hill Little, Brown & Company.

Bayles, K. A., Salmon, D. P., Tomoeda, C. K., Jacobs, D., Caffrey, J. T., Kaszniak, A. W., & Troster, A. I. (1989). Semantic and letter category naming in Alzheimer's patients: A predictable difference. *Developmental Neuropsychology*, *5*, 335–347.

Bayles, K. A., & Tomoeda, C. K. (1983). Confrontational and generative naming abilities of dementia patients. In R. H. Brookshire (Ed.), *Proceedings of the clinical aphasiology conference* (pp. 304–315). Minneapolis, MN: BRK Publishers.

Becker, J. T., Huff, F. J., Nebes, R. D., Holland, A., & Boller, F. (1988). Neuropsychological function in Alzheimer's disease. *Archives of Neurology*, *45*, 263–268.

Bender, L. A. (1938). *A visual-motor gestalt test and its clinical use.* New York: American Orthopsychiatric Association.

Benke, T. H. (1992). Structural apraxia in AD. *Journal of Clinical and Experimental Neuropsychology*, *14*, 50.

Benson, D. F. (1979). *Aphasia, alexia, and agraphia.* New York: Churchill Livingstone.

Benson, D. F. (1983). Subcortical dementia: A clinical approach. In R. Mayeux & W. G. Rosen (Eds.), *The dementias* (pp. 185–193). New York: Raven Press.

Benson, D. F., & Barton, M. I. (1970). Disturbances in constructional ability. *Cortex*, *6*, 19–46.

Benson, D. F., Cummings, J. L., & Tsai, S. Y. (1982). Angular gyrus syndrome simulating Alzheimer disease. *Archives of Neurology*, *39*, 616–620.

Benton, A. L. (1967). Constructional apraxia and the minor hemisphere. *Confinia Neurologica*, *29*, 1–16.

Benton, A. L. (1968). Differential behavioral effects in frontal lobe disease. *Neuropsychologia*, *6*, 53–60.

Benton, A. (1985). Visuoperceptual, visuospatial, and visuoconstructive disorders. In K. M. Heilman & E. Valenstein (Eds.), *Clinical neuropsychology*, (2nd ed., pp. 151–186). New York: Oxford University Press.

Benton, A., Eslinger, P. J., & Damasio, A. R. (1981). Normative observations on neuropsychological test performances in old age. *Journal of Clinical Neuropsychology*, *3*, 33–42.

Benton, A. L., & Fogel, M. L. (1962). Three dimensional constructional praxis. *Archives of Neurology*, *7*, 347–354.

Benton, A. L., de S. Hamsher, K., Varney, N. R., & Spreen, O. (1983). *Contributions to neuropsychological assessment: A clinical manual.* New York: Oxford University Press.

Benton, A. L., & Van Allen, M. W. (1968). Impairment in facial recognition in patients with cerebral disease. *Cortex*, *4*, 344–358.

Benton, A. L., Varney, N. R., & de S. Hamsher, K. (1978). Visuospatial judgment. *Archives of Neurology*, *35*, 364–367.

Berg, L., Danziger, W. L., Storandt, M., Coben, L. A., Gado, M., Hughes, C. P., Knesevich, J. W., and Botwinick, J. (1984). Predictive features in mild senile dementia of the Alzheimer type. *Neurology* (Cleveland), *34*, 563–569.

Bigler, E. D., Schultz, R., Grant, M., Knight, G., Lucas, J., Roman, M., Hall, S., & Sullivan, M. (1989). Design fluency in dementia of the Alzheimer type: Preliminary findings. *Neuropsychology*, *2*, 127–133.

Birren, J. E., & Botwinick, J. (1955). Age differences in finger, jaw, and foot reaction time to auditory stimuli. *Journal of Gerontology*, *10*, 429–432.

Birren, J. E., & Morrison, D. F. (1961). Analysis of WAIS subtests in relation to age and education. *Journal of Gerontology, 16*, 363–369.

Black, F. W., & Strub, R. L. (1976). Constructional apraxia in patients with discrete missile wounds of the brain. *Cortex, 12*, 212–220.

Bleecker, M. L., Bolla-Wilson, K., Kawas, J., & Agnes, D. A. (1988). Age-specific norms for the Mini-Mental State Exam. *Neurology, 38*, 1565–1568.

Blessed, G., Tomlinson, B. E., & Roth, M. (1968). The association between quantitative measures of dementia and senile change in the cerebral gray matter of elderly subjects. *Journal of Psychiatry, 114*, 797–811.

Botwinick, J. (1967). *Cognitive processes in maturity and old age*. New York: Springer.

Botwinick, J. (1971). Sensory set factors in age differences in reaction time. *Journal of General Psychology, 119*, 241–249.

Botwinick, J. (1973). *Aging and Behavior*. New York: Springer.

Botwinick, J., Brinley, J. F., & Birren, J. E. (1957). Set in relation to age. *Journal of Gerontology, 12*, 300–305.

Botwinick J., & Thompson, L. W. (1966). Components of reaction time in relation to age and sex. *Journal of General Psychology, 108*, 175–183.

Branconnier, R. J., & DeVitt, D. R. (1983). Early detection of incipient Alzheimer's disease: Some methodological considerations on computerized diagnosis. In B. Reisberg (Ed.), *Alzheimer's disease: The standard reference*. (pp. 214–227). New York: The Free Press.

Brandt, J. (1991). The Hopkins Verbal Learning Test: Development of a New Memory Test with six equivalent forms. *The Clinical Neuropsychologist, 5*(2), 125–142.

Brantjes, M., & Bouma, A. (1991). Qualitative analysis of the drawings of Alzheimer patients. *The Clinical Neuropsychologist, 5*(1), 41–52.

Bromley, D. B. (1957). Some effects of age on the quality of intellectual output. *Journal of Gerontology, 12*, 318–323.

Brouwers, P., Cox, C., Martin, A., Chase, T., & Fedio, P. (1984). Differential perceptual-spatial impairment in Huntington's and Alzheimer's dementia. *Archives of Neurology, 41*, 1073–1076.

Brun, A. (1983). An overview of light and electron microscopic changes. In B. Reisberg (Ed.), *Alzheimer disease* (pp. 37–47). New York: The Free Press.

Brun, A., & Gustafson, L. (1976). Distribution of cerebral degeneration in Alzheimer's disease. *Archiv fur Psychiatrie und Nervenkrankheiten, 223*, 15–33.

Brust, J. C. M., Shafer, S. Q., Richter, R. W., and Bruun, B. (1976). Aphasia in acute stroke. *Stroke, 7*, 167–174.

Bruyn, G. W. (1968). A historical, clinical and laboratory synopsis. In P. Vinken & G. W. Bruyn (Eds.). *Handbook of clinical neurology* (pp. 298–378). Amsterdam: North Holland.

Burnand, T., Richard, J., Tissot, R., & de Ajuriaguerra, J. (1972). Nature of the operational deficit in the aged afflicted with degenerative dementia. *Encephale, 61*, 5–31.

Buschke, H. (1973). Selective reminding for analysis of memory and learning. *Journal of Verbal Learning and Verbal Behavior, 12*, 543–550.

Buschke, H., & Fuld, P. A. (1974). Evaluating storage, retention, and retrieval in disordered memory and learning. *Neurology, 24*, 1019–1025.

Butters, N. (1984). The clinical aspects of memory disorders: Contributions from experimental studies of amnesia and dementia. *Journal of Clinical Neuropsychology, 6*, 17–36.

Butters, N., Granholm, E., Salmon, D. P., Grant, I., & Wolfe, J. (1987). Episodic and semantic memory: A comparison of amnestic and dementia patients. *Journal of Clinical and Experimental Neuropsychology, 9*, 479–497.

Butters, N., Heindel, W. C., Salmon, D. P. (1990). Dissociation of implicit memory in dementia: Neurological implications. *Bulletin of the Psychonomic Society*, *28*(4), 359–366.

Butters, N., Salmon, D. P., Munro Cullum, C., Cairns, P., Troster, A. I., Jacobs, D., Moss, M., & Cermak, L. S. (1988). Differentiation of amnestic and demented patients with the Wechsler Memory Scale—Revised. *The Clinial Neuropsychologist*, *2*, 133–148.

Cattell, R. B. (1943). The measurement of adult intelligence. *Psychological Bulletin*, *3*, 153–193.

Cerella, J. (1985). Information processing rates in the elderly. *Psychological Bulletin*, *98*, 67–83.

Cerella, J., Poon, L. W., & Williams, D. M. (1980). Age and the complexity hypothesis. In L. W. Poon (Ed.), *Aging in the 1980's: Psychological issues* (pp. 332–340). Washington, DC: American Psychological Association.

Christensen, H., Hadzi-Pavlovic, D., & Jacomb, P. (1991). The psychometric differentiation of dementia from normal aging: A meta-analysis. *Journal of Consulting and Clinical Psychology*, *3*, 147–155.

Coblentz, J. M., Mattis, S., Zingesser, L. H., Kassoff, S. S., Wisniewski, H. M., & Katzman, R. (1973). Presenile dementia: Clinical evaluation of cerebral spinal fluid dynamics. *Archives of Neurology*, *29*, 299–308.

Cohen, D., Eisdorfer, C., & Holm, C. L. (1984). Mental status examinations in aging. In M. L. Albert (Ed.), *Clinical neurology of aging* (pp. 219–230). New York: Oxford University Press.

Constantinidis, J., Richard, J., & de Ajuriaguerra, J. (1978). Dementias with senile plaques and neurofibrillary changes. In A. Isaacs & F. Post (Eds.), *Studies in geriatric psychiatry*. Toronto: Wiley.

Critchley, M. (1964). The neurology of psychotic speech. *British Journal of Psychiatry*, *40*, 353.

Crockett, B., Bilsker, D., Hurwitz, T., & Kozak, J. (1986). Clinical utility of three measures of frontal lobe dysfunction in neuropsychiatric samples. *International Journal of Neuroscience*, *30*, 241–248.

Crystal, H. A., Horoupian, D. S., Katzman, R., & Jotkowitz, S. (1982). Biopsy-proven Alzheimer disease presenting as a right parietal lobe syndrome. *Annals of Neurology*, *12*, 186–188.

Cummings, J. L. (1990). Clinical diagnosis of Alzheimer's disease. In J. L. Cummings & B. L. Miller (Eds.), *Alzheimer's disease: Treatment and long-term management* (pp. 3–22). New York: Marcel Dekker.

Cummings, J. L., & Benson, D. F. (1983). *Dementia: A clinical approach*. Boston: Butterworth's.

Cummings, J. L., & Benson, D. F. (1984). Subcortical dementia. *Archives of Neurology*, *41*, 874–879.

Cummings, J. L., & Benson, D. F. (1992). *Dementia: A clinical approach*. Boston: Butterworth's.

Cummings, J. L., Benson, D. F., Hill, M., & Read, S. (1985). Aphasia in dementia of the Alzheimer type. *Neurology*, *35*, 394–397.

Cunningham, W. R., Clayton, V., & Overton, W. (1975). Fluid and crystallized intelligence in young adulthood and old age. *Journal of Gerontology*, *30*, 53–55.

Danielczyk, W. (1983). Various mental behavioral disorders in Parkinson's disease, primary degenerative senile dementia, and multiple infarction dementia. *Journal of Neural Transmission*, *56*, 161–176.

Davis, G. A., & Holland, A. L. (1981). Age in understanding and treating aphasia. In D. S. Beasley & G. A. Davis (Eds.), *Aging: Communication processes and disorders* (pp. 207–228). New York: Grune & Stratton.

Davis, K. L., Thal, L. J., Gamzu, E. R., Davis, C. S., Woolson, R. F., Gracon, S., Drachman, D. A.,Schneider, L. S., Whitehouse, P. J., Hoover, T. M., Morris, J. C., Kawas, C. H., Knopman, D. S., Earl, N. L., Kumar, V., Doody, R. S., & the Tacrine Collaborative Study Group. (1992). A double-blind, placebo-controlled multicenter study of tacrine for Alzheimer's disease. *New England Journal of Medicine, 327*(18), 1253–1259.

De Ajuriaguerra, J., & Tissot, R. (1963). The apraxias. In P. J. Vinkin & G. W. Bruyn (Eds.), *Handbook of clinical neurology* (pp. 48–66). Amsterdam: North Holland.

De Ajuriaguerra, J., & Tissot, R. (1968). Some aspects of psycho-neurologic disintegration in senile dementia. In C. Muller & L. Ciompi (Eds.), *Senile dementia: Clinical and therapeutic aspects* (pp. 69–84). Bern, Switzerland: Hans Huber.

De Leon, M. J., Potegal, M., & Gurland, B. (1984). Wandering and parietal signs in senile dementia of Alzheimer's type. *Neuropsychobiology, 11*, 155–157.

Delis, D. C., Kiefner, M. G., & Fridlund, A. J. (1988). Visuospatial dysfunction following unilateral brain damage: Dissociations in hierarchical and hemispatial analysis. *Journal of Clinical and Experimental Neuropsychology, 10*, 421–431.

Delis, D. C., Kramer, J. H., Kaplan, E., & Ober, B. A. (1987). *The California Verbal Learning Test* (research ed.). New York: The Psychological Corporation.

Delis, D. C., Massman, P. J., Butters, N., Salmon, D. P., Cermak, L. S., & Kramer, J. H. (1991). Profiles of demented and amnesic patients on the California Verbal Learning Test: Implications for the assessment of memory disorders. *Psychological Assessment: A Journal of Consulting and Clinical Psychology, 3*(1), 19–26.

Delis, D. C., Massman, P. J., Kaplan, E., McKee, R., Kramer, J. H., & Gettman, D. (1991). Alternate form of the California Verbal Learning Test: Development and reliability. *The Clinical Neuropsychologist, 5*(2), 154–162.

Delis, D. C., Robertson, L. C., & Efron, R. (1986). Hemispheric specialization of memory for visual hierarchical stimuli. *Neuropsychologia, 24*, 205–214.

Della Sala, S., Lucchelli, F., & Spinnler, H. (1987). Ideomotor apraxia in patients with dementia of Alzheimer type. *Journal of Neurology, 234*, 91–93.

De Renzi, E., & Faglioni, P. (1967). The relationship between visuospatial impairment and constructional apraxia. *Cortex, 3*, 327–342.

Ernst, B., Dalby, M. A., & Dalby, A. (1970). Aphasic disturbances in presenile dementia. *Acta Neurologica Scandinavica, 46* (Suppl. 43), 99–100.

Eslinger, P. J., & Benton, A. L. (1983). Visuoperceptual performances in aging and dementia: Clinical and theoretical implications. *Journal of Clinical Neuropsychology, 5*, 213–220.

Eslinger, P. J., Damasio, A. R., Benton, A. L., & Van Allen, M. (1985). Neuropsychologic detection of abnormal mental decline in older persons. *Journal of the American Medical Association, 253*, 670–674.

Eslinger, P. J., Pepin, L., & Benton, A. L. (1988). Different patterns of visual memory errors occur with aging and dementia. *Journal of Clinical and Experimental Neuropsychology, 10*, 60–61.

Evans, D. A., Funkenstein, H. H., Albert, M. S., Scherr, P. A., Cook, N. R., Chown, M. J., Herbert, L. E., Hennekens, C. H., & Taylor, J. O. (1989). Prevalence of Alzheimer's disease in a community population of older persons: Higher than previously reported. *Journal of the American Medical Association, 262*, 2551–2556.

Evans, D. A., Scherr, P. A., Cook, N. R., Albert, M. S., Funkenstein, H. H., Smith, L. A., Hebert, L. E., Wetle, T. T., Branch, L. G., Chown, M., Hennekens, C. H., & Taylor, J. O. (1990). Estimated prevalence of Alzheimer's disease in the United States. *Milbank Quarterly, 68*, 267–289.

Field, J. G. (1960). Some factors affecting the drawing of abstract designs by elderly "organic" and "functional" psychiatric patients. *Acta Psychologica, 17*, 260–272.

Flicker, C., Ferris, S. H., Crook, T., & Bartus, R. T. (1986). The effects of aging and dementia on concept formation as measured on an object-sorting task. *Developmental Neuropsychology*, *2*, 65–72.

Flicker, C., Ferris, S. H., Crook, T., Reisberg, B., & Bartus, R. T. (1988). Equivalent spatial-rotation deficits in normal aging and Alzheimer's disease. *Journal of Clinical and Experimental Neuropsychology*, *10*(4), 387–399.

Folstein, M. F., Folstein, S. E., & McHugh, P. R. (1975). Mini-Mental State: A practical method for grading the cognitive state of the patient for the clinician. *Journal of Psychiatric Research*, *12*, 189–198.

Foster, N. L., Chase, T. N., Fedio, P., Patronas, N. J., Brooks, R. A., & Chiro, G. D. (1983). Alzheimer's disease: Focal cortical changes shown by positron emission tomography. *Neurology*, *33*, 961–965.

Foster, N. L., Chase, T. N., Mansi, L., Brooks, R., Fedio, P., Patronas, N. J., & DiChiro, G. (1984). Cortical abnormalities in Alzheimer's disease. *Annals of Neurology*, *16*, 649–654.

Frackowiak, R. S. J., Pozzilli, C., Legg, N. J., & DuBoulay, G. H. (1981). Regional cerebral oxygen supply and utilization in dementia. A clinical and physiological study with oxygen-15 and positron tomography. *Brain*, *104*, 753–778.

Frederiks, J. A. M. (1985). The neurology of aging and dementia. In J. A. M. Frederiks (Ed.), *Handbook of clinical neurology* (pp. 199–219). Amsterdam: Elsevier.

Freedman, L. & Dexter, L. E. (1991). Visuospatial ability in cortical dementia. *Journal of Clinical and Experimental Neuropsychology*, *13*, 677–690.

Freedman, M. (1990). Object alternation and orbitofrontal system dysfunction in Alzheimer's and Parkinson's disease. *Brain and Cognition*, *14*, 134–143.

Friedland, R. P., Budinger, T. F., Ganz, E., Yano, Y., Mathis, C. A., Koss, B., Ober, B. A., Huesman, R. H., & Derenzo, S. E. (1983). Regional cerebral metabolic alternations in dementia of the Alzheimer type: Positron emission tomography with [18F] fluorodeoxyglucose. *Journal of Computer Assisted Tomography*, *7*, 590–598.

Fuld, P. A. (1981). *The Fuld Object-Memory Test*. Chicago, IL: The Stoelting Instrument Company.

Fuld, P. A. (1983). Psychometric differentiation of the dementias: An overview. In B. Reisberg (Ed.), *Alzheimer's disease: The standard reference* (pp. 201–213). New York: The Free Press.

Fuld, P. A., Masur, D. M., Blau, A. D., Crystal, H., & Aronson, M. K. (1990). Object-memory evaluation for prospective detection of dementia in normal-functioning elderly: Predictive and normative data. *Journal of Clinical and Experimental Neuropsychology*, *12*, 520–528.

Gainotti, G., Messerlie, P., & Tissot, R. (1972). Qualitative analysis of unilateral spatial neglect in relation to laterality of cerebral lesion. *Journal of Neurology, Neurosurgery and Psychiatry*, *35*, 545–550.

Gainotti, G., Parlato, V., Monteleone, D., & Carlomagno, S. (1992). Neuropsychological markers of dementia on visual-spatial tasks: a comparison between Alzheimer type and vascular forms of dementia. *Journal of Clinical and Experimental Neuropsychology*, *14*, 239–252.

Geffen, G., Moan, K. J., O'Hanlon, A. P., Clark, C. R., & Geffen, L. B. (1990). Performance measures of 16- to 86-year old males and females on the Auditory Verbal Learning Test. *The Clinical Neuropsychologist*, *4*, 45–63.

Geschwind, N. (1975). The apraxias: Neural mechanisms of disorders of learned movement. *American Scientist*, *63*, 188–195.

Goldberg, E., & Tucker, D. (1979). Motor perseverations and long-term memory for visual forms. *Journal of Clinical Neuropsychology*, *1*, 273–288.

Goodglass, H., & Kaplan, E. (1976). *Assessment of aphasia and related disorders.* Philadelphia: Lea & Febiger.

Grady, C. L., Haxby, J. V., Horwitz, B., Sundaram, M., Berg, G., Schapiro, M., Friedland, R. P., & Rapoport, S. I. (1988). Longitudinal study of the early neuropsychological and cerebral metabolic changes in dementia of the Alzheimer type. *Journal of Clinical and Experimental Neuropsychology, 10,* 576–596.

Grossi, D., & Orsini, A. (1978). The visual crosses in dementia: An experimental study of 110 subjects. *Acta Neurologica, 33,* 170–174.

Grossi, D., Orsini, A., & Michele, G. (1978). The copying of geometric drawings in dementia. *Acta Neurologica, 33,* 355–360.

Gustafson, L., Hagberg, B., & Ingvar, D. H. (1978). Speech disturbances in presenile dementia related to local cerebral blood flow abnormalities in the dominant hemisphere. *Brain and Language, 5,* 103–118.

Gustafson, I., & Nilsson, L. (1982). Differential diagnosis of presenile dementia on clinical grounds. *Acta Psychiatrica Scandinavica, 65,* 194–207.

Hamsher, K., Levin, H. S., & Benton, A. L. (1979). Facial recognition in patients with focal brain lesions. *Archives of Neurology, 36,* 837–839.

Hannay, H. J., Varney, H. R., & Benton, A. L. (1976). Visual localization in patients with unilateral brain disease. *Journal of Neurology, Neurosurgery and Psychiatry, 39,* 307–313.

Harasymiw, S. J., Halper, A., & Sutherland, B. (1981). Sex, age, and aphasia type. *Brain and Language, 12,* 190–198.

Hart, R. P., Kwentus, J. A., Harkins, S. W., & Taylor, J. R. (1988). Rate of forgetting in mild Alzheimer's-type dementia. *Brain and Cognition, 7,* 31–38.

Hart, S., & Semple, J. M. (1990). *Neuropsychology and the dementias.* London: Taylor and Francis.

Hart, S., Smith, C. M., & Swash, M. (1988). Word fluency in patients with early dementia of Alzheimer type. *British Journal of Clinical Psychology, 27,* 115–124.

Haxby, J. V., Duara, R., Grady, C. L., Cutler, N. R., & Rapoport, S. I. (1985). Relations between neuropsychological and cerebral metabolic asymmetries in early Alzheimer's disease. *Journal of Cerebral Blood Flow and Metabolism, 5,* 193–200.

Hayes-Roth, B., & Hayes-Roth, F. (1979). A cognitive model of planning. *Cognitive Science, 3,* 275–310.

Heaton, R. K., Grant, I., & Matthews, C. G. (1986). Differences in neuropsychological test performance associated with age, education, and sex. In I. Grant & K. M. Adams (Eds.), *Neuropsychological assessment of neuropsychiatric disorders.* New York: Oxford University Press.

Heilman, K. M. (1979). Apraxia. In K. M. Heilman & E. Valenstein (Eds.), *Clinical neuropsychology* (pp. 159–185). New York: Oxford University Press.

Heilman, K. M., & Gonzalez Rothi, L. J. (1985). Apraxia. In K. M. Heilman & E. Valenstein (Eds.), *Clinical neuropsychology* (pp. 131–150). New York: Oxford University Press.

Heindel, W. C., Salmon, D. P., & Butters, N. (1990). Neuropsychological differentiation of memory impairments in dementia. In G. C. Gilmore, P. J. Whitehouse, & M. L. Wykle (Eds.), *Memory, aging, and dementia: Theory, assessment, and treatment* (pp. 112–139). New York: Springer.

Heindel, W. C., Salmon, D. P., Shults, C. W., Walicke, P. A., & Butters, N. (1989). Neuropsychological evidence for multiple implicit memory systems: A comparison of Alzheimer's, Huntington's, and Parkinson's disease patients. *Journal of Neuroscience, 9,* 582–587.

Helm-Estabrooks, N., & Albert, M. L. (1991). *Manual of aphasia therapy.* Austin: Proed.

Henderson, A. S. (1988). The risk factors for Alzheimer's disease: a review and a hypothesis. *Acta Psychiatrica Scandinavica*, *78*, 257–275.

Henderson, V. W., Mack, W., & Williams, B. W. (1989). Spatial disorientation in Alzheimer disease. *Archives of Neurology*, *46*, 391–394.

Hersch, E. L. (1979). Development and application for the extended scale for dementia. *Journal of the American Geriatrics Society*, *27*, 348–354.

Hodges, J. R., Salmon, D. P., & Butters, N. (1991). The nature of the naming deficit in Alzheimer's and Huntington's disease. *Brain*, *114*, 1547–1558.

Hofman, A., Schulte, W., Tanja, T. A., van Duijn, C. M., Haaxma, R., Lameris, A. J., Otten, V. M., & Saan, R. J. (1989). History of dementia and Parkinson's disease in 1st-degree relatives of patients with Alzheimer's disease. *Neurology*, *39*(12), 1589–1592.

Holland, A. L. (1980). *Communicative abilities in daily living*. Baltimore: University Park Press.

Hooper, H. E. (1958). *The Hooper Visual Organization Test manual*. Los Angeles: Western Psychological Services.

Husen, T. (1951). The influence of schooling upon IQ. *Theorique*, *17*, 61–88.

Irigaray, L. (1973). *Le langage des dements*. The Hague: Mouton.

Ivnik, R. J., Malec, J. F., Tangalos, E. R., Peterson, R. C., Kokmen, E., & Kurland, L. T. (1990). The Auditory-Verbal Learning Test (AVLT): Norms for ages 55 years and older. *Psychological Assessment: A Journal of Consulting and Clinical Psychology*, *2*, 304–312.

Ivnik, R. J., Malec, J. F., Smith, G. E., Tangalos, E. G., Petersen, R. C., Kokmen, E., & Kurland, L. T. (1991a). Mayo's older americans normative studies: WAIS-R norms for ages 56 to 97. *The Clinical Neuropsychologist*, *6*(Suppl.), 1–30.

Ivnik, R. J., Malec, J. F., Smith, G. E., Tangalos, E. G., Petersen, R. C., Kokmen, E., & Kurland, L. T. (1991b). Mayo's older americans normative studies: WMS-R norms for ages 56 to 94. *The Clinical Neuropsychologist*, *6* (Suppl.), 49–82.

Ivnik, R. J., Malec, J. F., Smith, G. E., Tangalos, E. G., Petersen, R. C., Kokmen, E., & Kurland, L. T. (1991c). Updated AVLT norms for ages 56 to 97. *The Clinical Neuropsychologist*, *6* (Suppl.), 83–104.

Ivnik, R. J., Malec, J. F., Smith, G. E., Tangalos, E. G., Petersen, R. C., Kokmen, E., & Kurland, L. T. (1991d). Wechsler Memory Scale (WMS): I.Q. dependent norms for persons age 65 to 97. *Psychological Assessment: A Journal of Consulting and Clinical Psychology*, *3*, 156–161.

Jones-Gotman, M., & Milner, B. (1977). Design fluency: The invention of nonsense drawings after focal cortical lesions. *Neuropsychologia*, *15*, 653–674.

Joynt, R. J., & Shoulson, I. (1985). Dementia. In K. M. Heilman & E. Valenstein (Eds.), *Clinical neuropsychology* (2nd ed., pp. 453–479). New York: Oxford University Press.

Kaplan, E., Goodglass, H., & Weintrout, S. (1983). *Boston Naming Test manual*. Philadelphia: Lea & Febiger.

Kaszniak, A. W. (1986). The neuropsychology of dementia. In I. Grant & K. M. Adams (Eds.), *Neuropsychological assessment of neuropsychiatric disorders* (pp. 172–220). New York: Oxford University Press.

Kaszniak, A. W. (1991, August). *Neuropsychological assessment of dementias*. Paper presented at the American Psychological Association convention, San Francisco, CA.

Kaszniak, A. W. (1992). *Awareness of cognitive and behavioral deficit in Alzheimer's dementia*. Paper presented at the American Psychological Association Meeting, Washington, DC.

Kaszniak, A. W., Fox, J., Gandell, D. L., Garron, D. C., Huckman, M. S., & Ramsey,

R. G. (1978). Prediction of mortality in presenile and senile dementia. *Annals of Neurology*, *3*, 246–252.

Kaszniak, A. W., Garron, D., Fox, J., Bergen, D., & Huckman, M. (1979). Cerebral atrophy, EEG slowing, age, education, and cognitive functioning in suspected dementia. *Neurology*, *29*, 1273–1279.

Kaszniak, A. W., Poon, L. W., & Riege, W. (1986). Assessing memory deficits: an information-processing approach. In L. W. Poon (Ed.), *Clinical memory assessment of older adults* (pp. 277–284). Washington, DC: American Psychological Association.

Katzman, R. (1976). The prevalence and malignancy of Alzheimer disease: A major killer. *Archives of Neurology*, *33*, 217–218.

Katzman, R., Terry, R. D., DeTeresa, R., Brown, L. T., Davies, P., Fuld, P., Renbing, X., & Peck, A. (1988). Clinical pathological and neurochemical changes in dementia: A subgroup with preserved mental status and numerous neocortical plaques. *Annals of Neurology*, *23*, 53–59.

Kertesz, A. (1979). *Aphasia and associated disorders*. New York: Grune & Stratton.

Kertesz, A. (1980). *Western Aphasia Battery*. London, Canada: University of Western Ontario.

Kertesz, A., & Sheppard, A. (1981). The epidemiology of cognitive and aphasic impairment in stroke. *Brain*, *104*, 117–128.

Khachaturian, Z. S. (1985). Diagnosis of Alzheimer's disease. *Archives of Neurology*, *42*, 1097–1105.

Kirshner, H. S., Webb, W. G., Kelly, M. P., & Wells, C. E. (1984). Language disturbance: An initial symptom of cortical degenerations and dementia. *Archives of Neurology*, *41*, 491–496.

Kolb, B., & Whishaw, I. Q. (1985). *Fundamentals of human neuropsychology* (2nd ed.). New York: W. H. Freeman.

Koss, E., Friedland, R. P., Ober, B. A., & Jagust, W. J. (1985). Differences in lateral hemispheric asymmetries of glucose utilization between early- and late-onset Alzheimer type dementia. *American Journal of Psychiatry*, *142*, 638–640.

LaRue, A. (1982). Memory loss and aging: Distinguishing dementia from benign senescent forgetfulness and depressive pseudodementia. *Psychiatric Clinics of North America*, *5*, 89–103.

LaRue, A. (1992). *Aging and neuropsychological assessment*. New York: Plenum Press.

LaRue, A., & Jarvik, L. (1987). Cognitive function and prediction of dementia in old age. *International Journal of Aging and Human Development*, *25*, 79–89.

LaRue, A., Spar, J., & Hill, C. D. (1986). Cognitive impairment in late-life depression: Clinical correlates and treatment implications. *Journal of Affective Disorders*, *11*(3), 179–184.

Lezak, M. D. (1983). *Neuropsychological assessment* (2nd ed.). New York: Oxford University Press.

Liepmann, H. (1920). Apraxie. *Ergebnisse der gesamte Medizin*, *1*, 516–543.

Lopez, O. L., Lucchelli, F., Faglioni, P., & Boller, F. (1992). Ideational apraxia in AD. *Journal of Clinical and Experimental Neuropsychology*, *14*, 50.

Luria, A. R. (1966). *Higher cortical functions in man*. New York: Basic Books.

Mahendra, B. (1984). *Dementia*. Lancaster: MTP Press.

Marshall, J. C., & Newcombe, F. (1984). Putative problems and pure progress in neuropsychological single-case studies. *Journal of Clinical Neuropsychology*, *6*(1), 65–70.

Martin, A. (1987). Representation of semantic and spatial knowledge in Alzheimer's patients: Implications for models of persevered learning in amnesia. *Journal of Clinical and Experimental Neuropsychology*, *9*, 191–224.

Martin, A., & Fedio, P. (1983). Word production and comprehension in Alzheimer's disease: The breakdown of semantic knowledge. *Brain and Language*, *19*, 124–141.

Masur, D. M., Fuld, P. A., Blau, A. D., Thal, L. J., Levin, H. S., & Aronson, M. K.

(1989). Distinguishing normal and demented elderly with the Selective Reminding Test. *Journal of Clinical and Experimental Neuropsychology*, *11*, 615–630.

Masur, D. M., Fuld, P. A., Blau, A. D., Crystal, H., & Aronson, M. K. (1990). Predicting development of dementia in the elderly with the Selective Reminding test. *Journal of Clinical and Experimental Neuropsychology*, *12*, 529–538.

Matarazzo, J. D. (1972). *Wechsler's measurement and appraisal of adult intelligence* (5th ed.). Baltimore: Williams & Wilkins.

Mattis, S. (1976). Mental status examination of organic mental syndrome in the elderly patient. In L. Bellack & T. B. Karasu (Eds.), *Geriatric psychiatry* (pp. 77–121). New York: Grune & Stratton.

McFie, J., & Zangwill, O. L. (1960). Visual constructive disabilities associated with lesions of the left cerebral hemisphere. *Brain*, *83*, 243–260.

McGlynn, S. M., & Kaszniak, A. W. (1991a). Unawareness of deficits in dementia and schizophrenia. In G. P. Prigatano & D. L. Schacter (Eds.), *Awareness of deficit after brain injury: Clinical and theoretical issues* (pp. 84–110). New York: Oxford University Press.

McGlynn, S. M., & Kaszniak, A. W. (1991b). When metacognition fails: Impaired awareness of deficit in Alzheimer disease. *Journal of Cognitive Neuroscience*, *3*, 183–189.

McHugh, P. R., & Folstein, M. F. (1975). Psychiatric syndromes of Huntington's chorea: A clinical and phenomenologic study. In D. F. Benson & D. Blumer (Eds.), *Psychiatric aspects of neurologic disease* (pp. 267–285). Orlando, FL: Grune & Stratton.

McKhann, G., Drachman, D., Folstein, M., Katzman, R., Price, D., & Stadlin, E. M. (1984). Clinical diagnosis of Alzheimer's disease: Report of the NINCDS-ADRDA work group under the auspices of the Department of Health and Human Services Task Force on Alzheimer's Disease. *Neurology*, *34*, 939–944.

Mesulam, M-M. (1985). *Principles of behavioral neurology*. Philadelphia: F.A. Davis Company.

Miceli, G., Caltagirone, C., Gainotti, G., Masullo, C., & Silveri, M. C. (1981). Neuropsychological correlates of localized cerebral lesions in non-aphasic brain damaged patients. *Journal of Clinical Neuropsychology*, *3*, 53–63.

Milberg, W. P., Hebben, N., & Kaplan, E. (1986). The Boston process approach to neuropsychological assessment. In I. Grant & K. M. Adams (Eds.), *Neuropsychological assessment of neuropsychiatric disorders* (pp. 65–86). New York: Oxford University Press.

Miller, E. (1977). *Abnormal aging: The psychology of senile and presenile dementia*. London: John Wiley & Sons.

Miller, E., & Hague, F. (1975). Some characteristics of verbal behavior in presenile dementia. *Psychological Medicine*, *5*, 255–259.

Milner, B. (1964). Some effects of frontal lobotomy in man. In J. M. Warren, & K. Akert (Eds.). *The frontal granular cortex and behavior* (pp. 313–334). New York: McGraw-Hill.

Mohs, R. C., Kim, Y., Johns, C. A., Dunn, D. D., & Davis, K. L. (1986). Assessing changes in Alzheimer's disease: Memory and language. In L. W. Poon (Ed.), *Clinical memory assessment of older adults* (pp. 149–155). Washington, DC: American Psychological Association.

Mohs, R. C., Rosen, W. G., Greenwald, B. S., & Davis, K. L. (1983). Neuropathologically validated scales for Alzheimer's disease. In T. Crook, S. Ferris, & R. Bartus (Eds.), *Assessment in geriatric psychopharmacology* (pp. 37–45). New Canaan, CT: Mark Powley Associates.

Monsch, A. U., Bondi, M. W., Butters, N., Salmon, D. P., Katzman, R., & Thal, L. J. (1992). Comparisons of verbal fluency tasks in the detection of dementia of the Alzheimer type. *Archives of Neurology*, *49*, 1253–1258.

Montgomery, K., & Costa, L. (1983). *Neuropsychological test performance of a normal elderly sample.* Paper presented at the annual meeting of the International Neuropsychological Society, Mexico City, Mexico.

Moore, V., & Wyke, M. A. (1984). Drawing disability in patients with senile dementia. *Psychological Medicine, 14,* 97–105.

Morris, J. C., Heyman, A., Mohs, R. C., Hughes, J. P., van Belle, G., Fillenbaum, G., Mellits, E. D., Clark, C., & The CERAD Investigators. (1989). The Consortium to Establish a Registry for Alzheimer's Disease (CERAD), I: Clinical and neuropsychological assessment for Alzheimer's disease. *Neurology, 39,* 1159–1165.

Morris, J. C., Mohs, R. C., Rogers, H., Fillenbaum, G., Heyman, A., et al. (1988). CERAD clinical and neuropsychological assessment of Alzheimer's disease. *Psychopharmacological Bulletin, 24,* 641–651.

Moss, M., & Albert, M. (1988). Alzheimer's disease and other dementing disorders. In M. S. Albert & M. B. Moss (Eds.), *Geriatric neuropsychology* (pp. 145–178). New York: The Guilford Press.

Moss, M. B., Albert, M. S., Butters, N., & Payne, M. (1986). Differential patterns of memory loss among patients with Alzheimer disease, Huntington's disease, and Alcoholic Korsakoff's syndrome. *Archives of Neurology, 43,* 239–246.

Naugle, R. I. (1990). Evaluation of intellectual and memory function among dementia patients who were intellectually superior. *The Clinical Neuropsychologist, 4,* 355–374.

Naugle, R. I., Cullum, C. M., & Bigler, E. D. (1990). Evaluation of intellectual and memory function among dementia patients who were intellectually superior. *The Clinical Neuropsychologist, 4*(4), 355–374.

Neary, D., Snowden, J. S., Bowen, D. M., Sims, N. R., Mann, D. M. A., Benton, J. S., Northen, B., Yates, P. O., & Davison, A. N. (1986). Neuropsychological syndromes in presenile dementia due to cerebral atrophy. *Journal of Neurology, Neurosurgery and Psychiatry, 49,* 163–174.

Nebes, R. D., & Brady, C. B. (1992). Generalized cognitive slowing and severity of dementia in Alzheimer's disease: Implications for the interpretation of response-time data. *Journal of Clinical and Experimental Neuropsychology, 14,* 317–326.

Nebes, R. D., & Madden, D. J. (1988). Different patterns of cognitive slowing produced by Alzheimer's disease and normal aging. *Psychology and Aging, 3,* 102–104.

Neils, J., Boller, F., Gerdeman, B., & Cole, M. (1989). Descriptive writing abilities in Alzheimer disease. *Journal of Clinical and Experimental Neuropsychology, 11,* 692–698.

Newcombe, F. (1969). *Missile wounds of the brain.* London: Oxford University Press.

Ober, B. A., Dronkers, N. F., Koss, E., Delis, D. C., & Friedland, R. P. (1986). Retrieval from semantic memory in Alzheimer-type dementia. *Journal of Clinical and Experimental Neuropsychology, 8,* 75–92.

Ober, B. A., Jagust, W. J., Koss, E., Delis, D. C., & Friedland, R. P. (1991). Visuoconstructive performance and regional cerebral glucose metabolism in Alzheimer disease. *Journal of Clinical and Experimental Neuropsychology, 13,* 752–772.

Obler, L. (1981). Review of le langage des dements, by L. Irigarary, 1973. The Hague: Mouton. *Brain and Language, 12,* 375–386.

Ochipa, C., Rothi, L. J. G., Heilman, K. M. (1989). Ideational apraxia: A deficit in tool selection and use. *Annals of Neurology, 25,* 190–193.

Owens, W. A. (1966). Age and mental abilities: A second adult follow-up. *Journal of Educational Psychology, 57,* 311–325.

Pan, G. D., Stern, Y., Sano, M., & Mayeux, R. (1989). Clock-drawing in neurological disorders. *Behavioral Neurology, 2,* 39–48.

Parsons, O. A., & Prigatano, G. P. (1978). Methodological considerations in clinical neuropsychological research. *Journal of Consulting and Clinical Psychology*, *46*, 609–619.

Pearce, J., & Miller, E. (1973). *Clinical aspects of dementia.* London: Bailliere.

Perez, F. I., Rivera, V. M., Meyer, J. S., Gay, J. R. A., Taylor, R. L., & Mather, N. T. (1975). Analysis of intellectual and cognitive performance in patients with multi-infarct dementia, vertebro-basilar insufficiency with dementia and Alzheimer's disease. *Journal of Neurology, Neurosurgery and Psychiatry*, *38*, 533–540.

Perret, E. (1974). The left frontal lobe of man and the suppression of habitual responses in verbal categorical behavior. *Neuropsychologia*, *12*, 323–330.

Pfeffer, R. I., Kurosaki, T. T., Harrah, C. H., Chance, J. M., Bates, D., Detels, R., Filos, S., & Butzke, C. (1981). A survey diagnostic tool for senile dementia. *American Journal of Epidemiology*, *114*, 515–527.

Pick, A. (1905). *Studien uber motorische apraxia und ihre mahestenhende Erscheinungen.* Leipzig, Germany: Deuticke.

Piercy, M., & Smyth, V. O. G. (1962). Right hemisphere dominance for certain nonverbal intellectual skills. *Brain*, *85*, 775–790.

Poon, L. W., Crook, T., Davis, K., Eisdorfer, C., Gurland, B., Kaszniak, A. W., & Thompson, L. (Eds.). (1986). *Handbook for clinical memory assessment of older adults.* Washington, DC: American Psychological Association.

Powell, J. B., Cripe, L. I., & Dodrill, C. B. (1991). Assessment of brain impairment with the Rey Auditory Verbal Learning Test: A comparison with other neuropsychological measures. *Archives of Clinical Neuropsychology*, *6*, 241–249.

Rabitt, P. M. A. (1965). An age decrement in the ability to ignore irrelevant information. *Journal of Gerontology*, *20*, 233–238.

Ramier, A. M., & Hecaen, H. (1970). Role respectif des atteintes frontales et de la lateralisation lesionnelle dans les deficits de la "fluence verbale." *Revue Neurologique*, *123*, 17–22.

Rapcsak, S. Z., Croswell, S. C., & Rubens, A. B. (1989). Apraxia in Alzheimer's disease. *Neurology*, *39*, 664–668.

Rapcsak, S. Z., & Ochipa, C. (1990). *The apraxias: Neuropsychological mechanisms, clinical assessment, and differential diagnosis.* Paper presented at the 10th annual conference of the National Academy of Neuropsychology, Reno, NV.

Raskin, A., Friedman, A. S., & DiMascio, A. (1982). Cognitive and performance deficits in depression. *Psychopharmacology Bulletin*, *18*(4), 196–202.

Read, D. E. (1987). Neuropsychological assessment of the memory in the elderly. *Canadian Journal of Psychology*, *41*, 158–174.

Reed, H. B. C., & Reitan, R. M. (1963). A comparison of the effects of the normal aging process with the effects of organic brain damage on adaptive abilities. *Journal of Gerontology*, *18*, 177–179.

Reinvang, I. (1983). *Aphasia and brain organization.* Oslo: University of Oslo.

Reisberg, B., Gordon, B., McCarthy, M., & Ferris, S. H. (1985). Clinical symptoms accompanying progressive cognitive decline and Alzheimer's disease. In V. L. Melnick & N. N. Dubler (Eds.), *Alzheimer's dementia* (pp. 19–39). Clifton, NJ: Humana Press.

Rosen, W. G. (1980). Verbal fluency in aging and dementia. *Journal of Clinical Neuropsychology*, *2*, 135–146.

Rosen, W. G. (1983a). Clinical and neuropsychological assessment of Alzheimer disease. In R. Mayeux & W. G. Rosen (Eds.), *The dementias* (pp. 51–64). New York: Raven Press.

Rosen, W. G. (1983b). Neuropsychological investigation of memory, visuoconstructional, visuoperceptual, and language abilities in senile dementia of the Alzheimer type. In

R. Mayeux & W. G. Rosen (Eds.), *The dementias* (pp. 51–64). New York: Raven Press.

Rosen, W. G., Mohs, R. C., & Davis, K. L. (1984). A new rating scale for Alzheimer disease. *American Journal of Psychiatry, 141*(11), 1356–1364.

Roth, M. (1955). The natural history of mental disorder in old age. *Journal of Mental Science, 101*, 281–301.

Sahakian, B. J., Downes, J. J., Eagger, S., Evenden, J. L., Levy, R., Philpot, M. P., Roberts, A. C., & Robbins, T. W. (1990). Sparing of attentional relative to mnemonic function in a subgroup of patients with dementia of the Alzheimer type. *Neuropsychologia, 28*, 1197–1213.

Sahakian, B. J., Jones, G., Levy, R., Gray, J., & Warburton, D. (1989). The effects of nicotine on attention, information processing, and short-term memory in patients with dementia of the Alzheimer type. *British Journal of Psychiatry, 154*, 797–800.

Salmon, D. P., & Butters, N. M. (1992). Neuropsychologic assessment of dementia in the elderly. In R. Katzman & J. W. Rowe (Eds.), *Principles of geriatric neurology* (pp. 144–163). Philadelphia: F.A. Davis Company.

Salmon, D. P., Granholm, E., McCullough, D., Butters, N., & Grant, I. (1989). Recognition memory span in mildly and moderately demented patients with Alzheimer disease. *Journal of Clinical and Experimental Neuropsychology, 11*, 429–443.

Salmon, D. P., Shimamura, A. P., Butters, N., & Smith, S. (1988). Lexical and semantic priming deficits in patients with Alzheimer disease. *Journal of Clinical and Experimental Neuropsychology, 10*, 477–494.

Salthouse, T. A. (1985). Speed of behavior and its implications for cognition. In J. E. Birren & K. W. Schaie (Eds.), *Handbook of the psychology of aging* (2nd ed., pp. 400–426). New York: Van Nostrand Reinhold Co.

Sandson, T., & Albert, M. (1984). Varieties in perseverations. *Neuropsychologia, 22*, 715–732.

Savage, R. D. (1973). Old age. In H. J. Eysenck (Ed.), *Handbook of abnormal psychology* (2nd ed.). London: Pitman.

Schacter, D. L., McLachlan, D. R., Moscovitch, M., & Tulving, E. (1986). Monitoring of recall performance by memory-disordered patients. *Journal of Clinical and Experimental Neuropsychology, 8*, 130.

Schaie, K. W. (1958). Rigidity-flexibility and intelligence: A cross-sectional study of the adult life span from 20 to 70 years. *Psychological Monographs, 72* (462, Whole No. 9).

Schaie, K. W. (1983). The Seattle Longitudinal Study: A 21-year exploration of psychometric intelligence in adulthood. In K. W. Schaie (Ed.), *Longitudinal studies of adult psychological development* (pp. 64–135). New York: Guilford.

Schaie, K. W., & Gribbin, K. (1975). Adult development and aging. *Annual Review of Psychology, 26*, 65–96.

Schaie, K. W., & Strother, C. R. (1968a). The effect of time and cohort differences upon age changes in cognitive behavior. *Multivariate Behavioral Research, 3*, 259–294.

Schaie, K. W., & Strother, C. R. (1968b). A cross-sectional study of age changes in cognitive behavior. *Psychological Bulletin, 70*, 671–680.

Schludermann, E. H., Schludermann, S. M., Merryman, P. W., & Brown, B. W. (1983). Halstead's studies in the neuropsychology of aging. *Archives of Gerontology and Geriatrics, 2*, 49–172.

Schneck, M. K., Reisberg, B., & Ferris, S. H. (1982). An overview of current concepts of Alzheimer's disease. *American Journal of Psychiatry, 139*, 165–173.

Schwartz, M. F., Marin, O. S. M., & Saffran, E. M. (1979). Dissociations of language function in dementia: A case study. *Brain and Language, 7*, 277–306.

Shuttleworth, E. C., & Huber, S. J. (1989). The Picture Absurdities Test in the evaluation of dementia. *Brain and Cognition, 11*, 50–59.

Sim, M., & Sussman, I. (1962). Alzheimer's disease: Its natural history and differential diagnosis. *Journal of Nervous and Mental Disease, 135*, 489–499.

Sim, M., Turner, E., & Smith, W. T. (1966). Cerebral biopsy in the investigation of presenile dementia. I. Clinical aspects. *British Journal of Psychiatry, 112*, 119–125.

Sjögren, T., Sjögren, H., & Lindren, A. G. H. (1952). Morbus Alzheimer and morbus Pick, genetic, clinical and patho-anatomical study. *Acta Psychiatrica Scandinavica 82* (Suppl.), 611–617.

Ska, B., Poissant, A., & Joanette, Y. (1990). Line orientation judgment in normal elderly and subjects with dementia of Alzheimer's type. *Journal of Clinical and Experimental Neuropsychology, 12* (5), 695–702.

Solomon, P. R., Levine, E., Bein, T., & Pendlebury, W. W. (1991). Disruption of classical conditioning in patients with Alzheimer's disease. *Neurobiology of Aging, 12*, 283–287.

Spinnler, H., & Della Sala, S. (1988). The role of clinical neuropsychology in the neurological diagnosis of Alzheimer's disease. *Journal of Neurology, 235*, 258–271.

Spreen, O., & Strauss, E. (1991). *A compendium of neuropsychological tests: Administration, norms, and commentary.* New York: Oxford University Press.

Squire, L. R. (1992). Memory and the hippocampus: A synthesis from findings with rats, monkeys, and humans. *Psychological Review, 99* (2), 195–231.

Squire, L. R., & Zola-Morgan, S. (1991). The medial temporal lobe memory system. *Science, 253*, 1380–1385.

Stebbins, G. T., Gilley, D. W., Wilson, R. S., Bernard, B. A., & Fox, J. H. (1990). Effects of language disturbance on premorbid estimates of IQ in mild dementia. *The Clinical Neuropsychologist, 4*(1), 64–68.

Stebbins, G. T., Wilson, R. S., Gilley, D. W., Bernard, B. A., & Fox, J. H. (1990). Use of the National Adult Reading Test to estimate premorbid IQ in dementia. *The Clinical Neuropsychologist, 4*(1), 18–24.

Stengel, E. (1964). Psychopathology of dementia. *Proceedings of the Royal Society of Medicine, 57*, 911–914.

Storandt, M., Botwinick, J., & Danzinger, W. L. (1986). Longitudinal changes: Patients with mild SAD and matched healthy controls. In L. W. Poon (Ed.), *Clinical memory assessment of older adults* (pp. 277–284). Washington, DC: American Psychological Association.

Storandt, M., Botwinick, J., Danziger, W. L., Berg, L., & Hughes, C. P. (1984). Psychometric differentiation of mild senile dementia of the Alzheimer's type. *Archives of Neurology, 41*, 497–499.

Storandt, M., & Hill, R. D. (1989). Very mild senile dementia of the Alzheimer type: II. Psychometric test performance. *Archives of Neurology, 46*, 383–386.

Strub, R. L., & Black, F. W. (1986). The clinical diagnosis of Alzheimer's disease: Relative sensitivity of various mental status and neurological examination test items. *Annals of Neurology, 20*, 129.

Strub, R. L., & Black, F. W. (1988). *Neurobehavioral disorders: A clinical approach.* Philadelphia: F.A. Davis Company.

Sunderland, T., Hill, J. L., Mellow, A. M., Lawlor, B. A., Gundersheimer, J., Newhouse, P. A., & Grafman, J. H. (1989). Clock drawing in Alzheimer's disease; a novel measure of dementia severity. *Journal of the American Geriatric Assocation, 37*, 725–729.

Tariot, P. N., Sunderland, T., Weingarten, H., Murphy, D. L., Welkowitz, J. A., Thompson, K., & Cohen, R. M. (1987). Cognitive effects of L-deprenyl in Alzheimer's disease. *Psychopharmacology, 91*(4), 489–495.

Teng, E. L., Chui, H. C., Schneider, L. S., & Metzger, L. E. (1987). Alzheimer's dementia: Performance on the Mini-Mental State Examination. *Journal of Consulting and Clinical Psychology*, 55(1), 96–100.

Terman, L. M., & Merrill, M. A. (1973). *The Stanford-Binet Intelligence Scale*. Boston: Houghton Mifflin.

Terry, R., & Katzman, R. (1992). Alzheimer disease and cognitive loss. In R. Katzman & J. W. Rowe (Eds.), *Principles of geriatric neurology* (pp. 207–265). Philadelphia: F. A. Davis Company.

Terry, R. D., Masliah, E., Salmon, D. P., Butters, N., DeTeresa, R., Hill, R., Hansen, L. S., & Katzman, R. (1991). Physical basis of cognitive alterations in Alzheimer's disease: Synapse loss is the major correlate of cognitive impairment. *Annals of Neurology*, 30(4), 572–580.

Troster, A. I., Jacobs, D., Butters, N., Cullum, C., & Salmon, D. P. (1989). Differentiating Alzheimer's disease from Huntington's disease with the Wechsler Memory Scale-Revised. *New Developments in Neuropsychological Evaluation*, 5, 611–632.

Tulving, E. (1983). *Elements of episodic memory*. New York: Oxford University Press.

U.S. Congress Office of Technology Assessment. (1987). *Losing a million minds: Confronting the tragedy of Alzheimer's disease and other dementias* (OTA-BA-323). Washington, DC: U.S. Government Printing Office.

Van Gorp, W. G., Satz, P., Kiersch, M. E., & Henry, R. (1986). Normative data on the Boston Naming Test for a group of normal older adults. *Journal of Clinical and Experimental Neuropsychology*, 8, 702–705.

Vitaliano, P. P., Breen, A. R., Alberts, M. S., Russo, J., & Prinz, P. N. (1984). Memory, attention, and functional status in community-residing Alzheimer type dementia patients and optimally healthy aged individuals. *Journal of Gerontology*, 39(1), 58–64.

Vitaliano, P. P., Russo, J., Breen, A. R., Vitiello, M. V., & Prinz, P. N. (1986). Functional decline in the early stages of Alzheimer's disease. *Journal of Psychology and Aging*, 1, 41–46.

Warrington, E. K. (1969). Constructional apraxia. In P. J. Vinken & G. W. Bruyn (Eds.), *Handbook of clinical neurology* (vol. 4). New-Holland: Amsterdam.

Warrington, E. K., James, M., & Kinsbourne, M. (1966). Drawing disability in relation to laterality of lesion. *Brain*, 89, 53–82.

Wechsler, D. (1981). *Wechsler Adult Intelligence Scale-Revised*. New York: The Psychological Corporation; Harcourt Brace Jovanovich, Inc.

Wechsler, D. (1987). *Wechsler Memory Scale-Revised*. New York: The Psychological Corporation; Harcourt Brace Jovanovich, Inc.

Weingartner, H., Kaye, W., Smallberg, S. A., Ebert, M. H., Gillin, J. C., & Sitaram, B. (1981). Memory failures in progressive idiopathic dementia. *Journal of Abnormal Psychology*, 90, 187–196.

Wells, F. L., & Ruesch, J. (1972). *Mental examiner's handbook*. New York: The Psychological Corporation.

Welsh, K., Butters, N., Hughes, J., Mohs, R., & Heyman, A. (1991). Detection of abnormal memory decline in mild cases of Alzheimer's disease using CERAD neuropsychological measures. *Archives of Neurology*, 48, 278–281.

Welsh, K. A., Butters, B., Hughes, J. P., Mohs, R. C., & Heyman, A. (1992). Detection and staging of dementia of Alzheimer's disease: Use of the neuropsychological measures developed for the Consortium to Establish a Registry for Alzheimer's Disease. *Archives of Neurology*, 49, 448–452.

Wesnes, K., & Warburton, D. (1984). Effects of scopolamine and nicotine on human information processing performance. *Psychopharmacology*, 82, 147–150.

Whitaker, H. (1976). A case of isolation of the language function. In H. Whitaker & H. A. Whitaker (Eds.), *Studies in neurolinguistics* (vol. 2). New York: Academic Press.

Wilkie, F., & Eisdorfer, C. (1971). Intelligence and blood pressure in the aged. *Science*, *172*, 959–962.

Williams, J. M. (1991). *Memory Assessment Scale professional manual*. Odessa, FL: Psychological Assessment Resources, Inc.

Wilson, R. S., & Garron, D. C. (1979). Cognitive and affective aspects of Huntington's disease. *Advances in Neurology*, *23*, 193–201.

Wilson, R. S., & Kaszniak, A. W. (1986). Longitudinal changes: Progressive idiopathic dementia. In L. W. Poon, B. J. Gurland, C. Eisdorfer, T. Crook, L. W. Thomas, A. W. Kaszniak, & K. Davis (Eds.), *The handbook of clinical memory assessment of older adults* (pp. 285–293). Washington, DC: American Psychological Association.

Wilson, R. S., Rosenbaum, G., & Brown, G. (1979). The problem of premorbid intelligence in neuropsychological assessment. *Journal of Clinical Neuropsychology*, *1*, 49–53.

Zec, R. F. (1990). Neuropsychology: Normal aging versus early AD. In R. E. Becker & E. Giacobini (Eds.), *Alzheimer disease: Current research in early diagnosis* (pp. 105–117). New York: Taylor and Francis.

Zec, R. F., Andrise, A. B., Vicari, S., Feldman, E., Belman, J., Landreth, E., & Markwell, S. (1990). A comparison of phonemic and semantic word fluency in Alzheimer patients and elderly controls. *Journal of Clinical and Experimental Neuropsychology*, *12*, 18.

Zec, R. F., Landreth, E. S., Vicari, S. K., Feldman, E., Belman, J., Andrise, A., Robbs, R., Kumar, V., & Becker, R. (1992a). Alzheimer Disease Assessment Scale: Useful for both early detection and staging of dementia of the Alzheimer type. *Alzheimer Disease and Related Disorders—An International Journal*, *6*(2), 89–102.

Zec, R. F., Landreth, E. S., Vicari, S. K., Belman, J., Feldman, E., Andrise, A., Robbs, R., Becker, R., & Kumar, V. (1992b). Alzheimer Disease Assessment Scale: A subtest analysis. *Alzheimer Disease and Related Disorders—An International Journal*, *6*(3), 1–19.

Zec, R. F., & Vicari, S. (1990). Rey Auditory Verbal Learning Test: Utility in dementia evaluations. *The Clinical Neuropsychologist*, *4*, 281.

Zec, R. F., Vicari, S., Andrise, A., Landreth, E., Belman, J., Ferneau, D., Miller, J., Zellers, D., Matthews, J., Kocis, M., Robbs, R., & Verhulst, S. (1991). *Confrontational and generative naming in very mild DAT vs very severe CHI*. Paper presented at the eleventh annual meeting of the National Academy of Neuropsychology, Dallas, TX.

2

Neuropsychology and Normal Aging: The Clinician's Perspective

JAMES F. MALEC, ROBERT J. IVNIK, and GLENN E. SMITH

A large number of studies have examined the relationship between various cognitive functions and increasing chronological age. This prior literature may be characterized as *studies of normal aging*. In contrast, this chapter will focus on *normative studies and aging*. In other words, unlike much of the prior scientific literature, we will not attempt to define what is normal for the elderly population. Instead, we will address issues related to the development of psychometric normative data that are maximally useful in identifying abnormal cognitive functioning in the elderly. We will present data on intellectual and memory test performances of normal elderly samples that may be of use to the practicing clinical psychologist or neuropsychologist in considering diagnoses of dementia.

With this stated focus, the chapter is not an attempt at an exhaustive review of studies of normal aging. Consequently, reference to secondary sources appears appropriate. Several important reference volumes, *Handbook of the Psychology of Aging*, 1st through 3rd editions (Birren & Schaie, 1977, 1985, 1990); *New Directions in Memory and Aging* (Poon, Fozard, Cermak, Arenberg, & Thompson, 1980); and *Aging in the 1980's* (Poon, 1980), contain multiple chapters reviewing the nearly universal findings of diminished capacity to process new or unfamiliar information with advancing age in the presence of retention of the capacity to utilize remotely learned information. Prior research has described the contrast between good performance among the elderly on measures of crystallized intelligence (e.g., Wechsler Adult Intelligence Scale-Revised [WAIS-R] [Wechsler, 1981] Verbal IQ), and poorer performance on measures of fluid intelligence (e.g., WAIS-R Performance IQ), which assess the capacity to solve novel problems (Botwinick, 1977; Albert & Heaton, 1988; Perlmutter & Nyquist, 1990; Wechsler, 1981). Performance on measures of abstract reasoning that require novel problem solving also predictably declines with advancing age (Albert, Wolfe, & Lafleche, 1990; Cornelius, 1984; Mack & Carlson, 1978).

In the area of memory, three major findings have appeared consistently in the literature (Cullum, Butters, Troster, & Salmon, 1990; Labouvie-Vief & Schell, 1982; Perlmutter & Nyquist, 1990; Poon, 1985; Salthouse, 1982). First, the ability to access remotely learned information is relatively preserved across the adult lifespan. Second, the capacity to attend to or register new information does not decline with age. Third, the subsequent process of learning and retention of new information does become more limited with advancing age. Declines in new learning with normal aging, however, may become prominent only as the Biblical expected lifespan of "three score and ten" is approached (Schaie & Parham, 1977).

Controversy remains regarding factors underlying this well-documented age-related decline in abilities involved in processing novel information. Hypothetical factors identified fall into three major groups: intellectual endowment, biological processes, and motivation. In research, intellectual endowment has most frequently been estimated by vocabulary knowledge because this is an element of intelligence testing that is both highly representative of general intellectual abilities and relatively resistant to age effects. The capacity to learn novel information appears to be more resistant to age effects among individuals with larger vocabularies (Bowles & Poon, 1982; Taub, 1979).

Perhaps best known among biological hypotheses is Birren's suggestion of a generalized slowing of neural events underlying cognition with normal aging (Birren, 1964, 1970, 1974). Although Birren has not conjectured regarding specific mechanisms, the implication is of a generalized erosion of fundamental neural capacities. Under the heading of biological factors also falls well-known brain diseases that create cognitive impairments (i.e., Alzheimer's disease, cerebrovascular disease, and other dementias), which are discussed in detail elsewhere in this volume. Cognitive decline, possibly affecting abstract reasoning more than memory abilities (Willis, Yeo, Thomas, & Garry, 1988), has also been found associated with systemic diseases that are not primary to the central nervous system (Albert, 1981; Benton & Sivan, 1984; Siegler & Costa, 1985). What is often not underscored is the extent to which the elderly population suffers from one or more medical illnesses. Fozard, Metter, and Brant (1990) have described a curvilinearly accelerating relationship between number of medical diagnoses and age. Our own data (reported later) also show that the "normal" elderly population is a frequently ill population. Although illnesses and associated medical treatments may have a negative impact on cognitive status in some cases, our analyses have failed to confirm a statistically reliable relationship between health status and intellectual or memory abilities.

Biological sex does not appear to have a direct effect on the maintenance of cognitive abilities with aging; women at various ages show about the same capacities as men for new learning (Offenbach, 1974; Sanders, Sterns, Smith, & Sanders, 1975; Sanders, Sanders, Mayes, & Sielski, 1976; Trahan & Quintana, 1990) and reasoning (Reese & Rodeheaver, 1985).

Finally, several researchers and theoreticians (Labouvie-Vief & Blanchard-Fields, 1982; Poon, 1985; Reese & Rodeheaver, 1985) have raised the possibility that differences in performance between elderly and younger subjects may reflect a different style or a different set of values in approaching tests, rather than a difference in basic competencies required to perform well on a test. For instance, the elderly may perform more poorly than younger subjects on laboratory tests of cognition because they place less value on doing well on these tests or because the tests have no practical utility or apparent relevance to the daily life of most elderly people. In an assessment format that does not penalize incorrect guessing, the elderly may do less well than younger subjects because they tend to approach novel tasks more cautiously in a way that reduces the risk of failure, but also reduces the chance of correct guessing. Motivational factors may in themselves be patho-logical. Pseudodementia (discussed more comprehensively elsewhere in this text) provides an example of diminished acquisition (but usually without diminished retention) of new information due to diminished motivation associated with a depressive disorder.

Consideration of the possibility of motivational factors affecting test perform-ance raises an important concern for the practicing clinician in the assessment of competence versus performance. True competence deficits on cognitive tasks are believed to be associated with pathological cerebral function. However, in the elderly, performance deficits on psychological tests may reflect motivational factors rather than true competence deficits.

Even if the relative prominence of neurological versus motivational factors in poor test performance can be identified in a specific case, the question remains whether the identified impairment affects the patient's everyday functioning and capacity to live independently. Ideally, assessments of competence would be ref-erenced to particular tasks performed by the patient in particular settings. It is important, for instance, to know if an elderly patient can prepare a meal in their own home or will remember to take needed medications. Answering such specific questions challenges the predictive capacities of a neuropsychometric evaluation. Although severely deficient performance on neuropsychological tests may accu-rately identify individuals who would be at definite risk in an unstructured envi-ronment, generally, neuropsychological test performances correlate only moder-ately with performances on tasks of everyday living (Chelune & Moehle, 1986; Heaton & Pendleton, 1981; Searight, Dunn, Grisso, Margolis, & Gibbons, 1989).

The extensive literature on normal aging has identified parameters of cognition that change with advancing age and potential factors that may modulate such change, but has offered little of practical use to the clinician in answering challenging questions regarding patient competence. Studies of normal aging have resulted in few new tests or evaluation protocols with demonstrated ecological or diagnostic validity. If the cognitive debilitation of old age is the "dragon" we are attempting to engage, then academic geriatric neuropsychology has apparently become so fascinated with arriving at an increasingly detailed description of the dragon, that the necessity of forging swords to fight it has been forgotten.

The testing industry has been unresponsive to the needs of geriatric neuro-psychological practice for valid measures appropriate for use with an elderly pop-ulation. Despite the fact that the effects of aging on cognition are most apparent after age 70, most commonly used psychometric measures have no published norms beyond age 74 (cf. manuals for WAIS-R and Wechsler Memory Scale-Revised [WMS-R] [Wechsler, 1981, 1987]).

As might be expected in the absence of even basic normative data, more sophisticated treatment of psychometric test data is lacking. As this brief overview indicates, performance declines in the elderly appear to be multifactorial. In the individual case, cognitive performance may be affected by health status, intellectual endowment, motivational state, and other more longstanding motivational factors such as values and problem-solving style, in addition to basic cognitive competen-cies. Because of the multifactorial nature of performance declines in the elderly, normative data among this group may be expected to be more variable and perhaps non-normally distributed as compared to similar data for younger individuals. Eventually, the field of clinical geriatric neuropsychology must address such statistical concerns as well as other more technically advanced challenges of test construction, such as ecological validity. Ultimately, the psychological armamentarium against the ravages of increasing age will include not only better assessment tools, but also behavioral interventions that facilitate the maintenance of satisfying lifestyles by elderly individuals with specified cognitive disabilities.

What follows in this chapter is a description of a single-center effort to develop normative data for an elderly population, and some of the unique features of such a data set and the population from which it was derived. This work extends normative data to life's oldest ages and highlights issues related to normative research, especially among the elderly. At this point in time, the "sword" we are trying to forge still looks much like a club. Although our subject recruitment procedures have resulted in adequate numbers even into very elderly age ranges, the applicability of the data set in other geographical or cultural settings (e.g., nonwhite, inner city urban) is limited, as other studies have been, by population features of the sample. The study design does not address issues of ecological validity, and studies of the validity of the normative data in terms of identifying brain pathology have not been completed at the time of this writing. Nonetheless, data presented here do offer some interesting and, it is hoped, practical information about features of performance on traditional psychometric measures by a normal elderly population.

Effects of Normal Aging on Cognition: Data from Olmsted County, Minnesota

Study Methods

Defining "Normal" Elderly

We have collected population-based, cognitive test norms on persons above age 54 in two independent, but similarly designed, research projects. The first project, the Community Project, was designed to obtain age-specific norms for traditional and experimental cognitive tests. The second project is a component of the Mayo Clinic's on-going National Institutes of Health/National Institute on Aging (NIH/NIA)-funded Alzheimer's Disease Patient Registry (ADPR). The ADPR attempts to identify, enroll, and follow all newly diagnosed demented persons (without regard to etiology) who have presented to Mayo's Community Internal Medicine facility. Every such person is age- and sex-matched to a normal control selected at random. Data from these controls contribute to our normal data pool. Both projects employ the same definition of "normal" and randomly solicit volunteers from a complete geographic region (i.e., Olmsted County, MN). Together with other research projects at Mayo, these studies define our general interest in normative neuropsychological investigations, which we have collectively labeled Mayo's Older Americans Normative Studies (MOANS).

Definitions of normal vary widely. The definition we use is influenced by the goals of our research. In establishing norms for tests that will be applied to individuals with a range of clinical problems, the definition of normal selected should be comprehensive and representative of the complete elderly population. Experimental geropsychology frequently excludes persons with any illness or disease from being accepted as normal in order to study the purest influences of age on cognition. However, completely healthy persons do not represent the majority of the elderly. Normal aging requires adaptation to many physical and psychological problems.

In our work, persons are considered normal if they are cognitively capable of independent functioning in their environment. Our *normal* volunteers (a) consider themselves normal and (b) are considered cognitively normal by their personal physician, who recently examined them. They also meet the following criteria:

> 1. No *active* central nervous system or psychiatric conditions that would adversely affect cognition.
> 2. No complaint of cognitive difficulty during the history-taking and systems-review components of their medical examination, and no examination findings indicating cognitive compromise.
> 3. No psychoactive medication use in amounts expected to compromise cognition.
> 4. Prior histories of disorders potentially affecting cognition (e.g., head injury, substance abuse) may be present provided it is clear the condition is no longer active and there is no residual cognitive deficit.
> 5. Chronic medical illness (e.g., diabetes, hypertension, cardiac problems) may be present provided the examining physician has not reported that the condition is associated with compromised cognition.

We believe that this definition of normal results in a representative sample of the elderly population. This definition excludes persons with apparent cognitive impairment while recognizing that the elderly population has many medical problems.

Although data regarding past neurological/psychiatric problems do not automatically exclude a person from serving as a *normal* in MOANS, such data are obtained on each *normal* volunteer via medical record review and self-reports. All medications used at the time of testing are also recorded. Thus, necessary data regarding prior neurological/psychiatric diagnoses are available to further subcategorize our *normals* in order to examine more restrictive definitions of normal than the one used in our research. To assess implications of our definition of normal as compared to alternative definitions, we constructed several such *normal* subgroups.

Based on medical record review of health history (without reference to self-report information) and current medication use, a sample of 403 persons from MOANS was divided into two subsamples. The first subsample, Medical Record–Possibly Abnormal ($n = 238$), were those with any prior neurological or psychiatric disorder or any current possibly psychoactive medicine (e.g., barbiturates, minor tranquilizers, narcotic analgesics) use in any amount for any reason. (Individuals identified as "possibly abnormal" based on medication use were few because those taking psychoactive medications in amounts that would clearly be expected to impair cognition were not admitted to the study.) The second subsample, Medical Record–Fully Normal ($n = 165$), were those with no record of prior neurological or psychiatric disorder or current psychoactive medication use. Two similar groups were formed based on self-report health history and medication data without reference to the medical record information: Self-Report–Fully Normal (SR-FN) ($n = 273$), and Self-Report–Possibly Abnormal (SR-PA) ($n = 130$). Although many persons were identified by both procedures, there was not complete agreement between self-report and the medical record. Lastly, a Super Normal subgroup was composed by excluding from the original sample any person identified as possibly abnormal by either the medical record or self-report processes described previously.

Mean cognitive profiles, corrected for age, were compared for each of the Fully Normal versus Possibly Abnormal dyads. Table 2.1 presents WAIS-R and WMS-R data, referenced to the Mayo norms for ages 56 to 97, for these subsamples. Statistical analyses of these data support the conclusions that are obvious upon simple visual inspection: *there are essentially no differences between groups*. The only comparisons that did attain statistical significance (Bonferroni criterion for multiple comparison: $p < .004$) occurred when the Medical Record–Fully Normal and Medical Record–Possibly Abnormal groups were compared on the Mayo Performance IQ ($p = .003$) for the WAIS-R and Mayo Visual Memory Index ($p = .003$) for the WMS-R. However, ω^2 values (representing Percent of Variance Explained) for each of these comparisons equalled .02, suggesting minimal clinical relevance.

Even though the null hypothesis cannot be proven, these results make it attractive. The data suggest that cognitive test variance occurring within the elderly population is minimally influenced by past neurological and psychiatric histories for persons who are functionally independent, who live in the general population, and who appear normal not only to themselves but also to their personal physicians.

TABLE 2.1.   WAIS-R and WMS-R Mean Summary Scores for Subsamples Meeting Different *Normal* Criteria

		Fully Normal			Possibly Abnormal	
	Total Sample	Medical Record	Self-Report	Super-Normal	Medical Record	Self-Report
Sample size	403	238	273	192	165	130
Female:male ratio	237:166	135:103	155:118	106:86	102:63	82:48
Means						
Age	70.5	70.5	70.4	71.0	70.6	70.7
Education	13.2	13.3	13.2	13.2	13.1	13.3
Number of medications	1.9	1.6	1.8	1.7	2.4	2.2
Number of diagnoses	3.0	2.9	3.0	3.0	3.1	3.0
Mayo IQs for WAIS-R						
VIQ	105	106	105	105	105	106
PIQ	107	109	107	107	105	108
FSIQ	106	107	106	106	105	107
Mayo indices for WMS-R						
Verbal Memory	107	107	107	107	106	107
Visual Memory	112	113	112	113	109	111
General Memory	110	111	110	111	108	110
Attention/Concentration	103	103	103	103	103	102
Delayed Recall	110	111	110	111	109	111
% Retention	110	111	110	110	109	110

Note: VIQ = Verbal IQ; PIQ = Performance IQ; FSIQ = Full Scale IQ.

Solicitation and Accrual

Research considerations that are not always addressed in normative projects include solicitation procedures and accrual success. Research design theory requires that estimates of population characteristics be based upon samples drawn at random from that population. In nonrandom samples, the influence of selection biases must be considered. Although some psychological tests present norms with predetermined characteristics (e.g., race, geographic region, and occupation composition of the WAIS-R normative sample reflects U.S. Census data), few normative projects, if any, have randomly solicited volunteers. Indeed, solicitation and sampling procedures are often simply not described. Even when sampling procedures are reported, accrual rates (i.e., the percentage of people asked who agree to participate) are not.

Procedures for unbiased solicitation and accrual rates for MOANS are completely described in Ivnik et al. (1990). Over 1,500 persons were asked to volunteer; 1,219 persons for the Community Project and 361 persons for the ADPR. Of these, 540 persons volunteered (404 in the Community Project and 136 in the ADPR); 527 persons were actually tested and provided data judged valid. Thirteen volunteers were not validly tested; several could not be scheduled within project time constraints, several were incorrectly contacted due to clerical errors, and a very few who kept their appointments withdrew once testing began, stating that they would not have volunteered if they had fully appreciated what was involved (i.e., completing tests of intellect, learning, and memory). Only data from subjects who were cooperative were included in statistical analyses.

Even with random sampling, the value of the resultant norms is diminished if a large percentage of potential subjects are not willing to be tested. Perfect accrual to any project is unrealistic. Project requirements (e.g., age, sex, health status), study demands (e.g., duration, remuneration, organization, perceived difficulty), and non-project-related issues (e.g., distance to the project site, weather, institutional reputation, "word of mouth") impact upon the best-designed research with human volunteers. Projects such as these that use elderly volunteers; provide no remuneration for time, effort, and inconvenience; study the sensitive issue of cognition at older ages; and require several hours of the volunteers' time ask much of their participants. Solicitation methods also impact accrual success. Accrual rates are consistently better for the ADPR (37.7% overall)—in which invitations to participate are extended by the volunteers' personal physicians—than for the Community Project (33.1% overall), in which mailed solicitations were used. Apparently, the simplest of considerations, such as the manner in which someone is asked to volunteer, can impact accrual success. In this context we believe that our 34.2% overall accrual rate is quite acceptable.

Sample Characteristics

Demographics. Descriptive demographic data for this normative sample are presented in Table 2.2. Figure 2.1 shows percentages of men and women of various ages who participated in the study compared to percentages of these age-by-sex groups in the Olmsted County population according to U.S. Census data.

TABLE 2.2.   Demographic Characteristics by Age Groupings

	55–59	60–64	65–69	70–74	75–79	80–84	85 +	Totals
Sex								
Males	31	32	41	34	38	12	18	206
Females	38	40	40	42	58	56	47	321
Total	69	72	81	76	96	68	65	527
Handedness								
Right	64	68	75	73	88	64	64	496
Left	4	2	4	1	4	2	1	18
Both	1	2	2	2	4	2	0	13
Marital status								
Single	5	3	5	6	15	13	17	64
Married	62	61	62	49	51	25	15	325
Separated/ divorced	2	3	0	2	3	2	0	12
Widowed	0	5	14	19	27	28	33	126
Education								
<8	0	0	0	1	1	2	3	7
8–11	3	6	12	8	18	15	21	83
12–15	39	53	56	51	49	35	21	304
16–17	17	7	7	8	17	14	12	82
>17	10	6	6	8	11	2	8	51

Health Status. As noted previously, elderly persons live with many medical problems. For many, to be elderly is to be sick to some degree. Health problems are normal at older ages and are common among individuals participating in MOANS, as Tables 2.3 and 2.4 show. Counting the number of medical diagnoses assigned at the time of their recent examinations yields the distribution enumerated in Table 2.3. There is an average of 3.0 diagnoses assigned per participant. The standard deviation is 1.6 diagnoses, with a range of 0 to 10. Very few persons, about 5%,

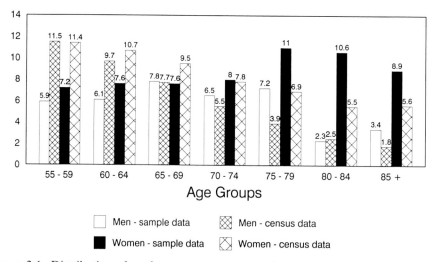

FIGURE 2.1. Distribution of sex by age groups expressed as percentage of population over age 54; obtained results versus census expectation.

TABLE 2.3.   Active Medical Diagnoses: Number of Diagnoses per Individual

Number of Diagnoses	Number of Individuals	%
None	25	4.7
One	63	12.0
Two	119	22.6
Three	138	26.2
Four	97	18.4
Five	56	10.6
Six	16	3.0
Over six	13	2.5
Totals	527	100.0

TABLE 2.4.   Medication Use

Number of Medications Used	Number of Individuals	%
None	153	29.0
One	108	20.5
Two	83	15.7
Three	97	18.4
Four	51	9.7
Five	20	3.8
Six	11	2.1
Over six	4	.8
Totals	527	100.0

have no diagnosed medical condition. Only 6% are given more than five diagnoses. Forty-four percent of all diagnoses assigned are either cardiovascular (25%) or musculoskeletal (19%). Diagnoses in other systems are much less common (< 8% per diagnosis).

Finally, again as might be expected, these volunteers are taking a reasonably wide range of medications (see Table 2.4). Remember that persons were excluded if they used medicines with definite psychoactive potential; therefore, such medicines are not frequently encountered. Table 2.4 and data analyses related to number of medications used, as reported in this section, include all prescription and over-the-counter medications listed in the patient's medical record. On average, our participants take 1.8 medications; the range is 0 to 8.

Thus, our data yield three indices of current health: the number of diagnoses assigned, the number of physical systems involved, and the number of medicines used. We divided the distributions of each of these three indices into three groups: the *best* one-third, the *common* one-third, and the *worst* one-third. Each Mayo summary score from the WAIS-R and WMS-R was then examined using an analysis of variance (ANOVA) to test for the cognitive effects of each health variable. Linear correlations were also computed between the health measures and each cognitive summary score. These data are presented in Tables 2.5, 2.6, and 2.7.

The data on the number of diagnoses assigned contain the only instances where possible associations with cognitive performance were found. Specifically, number

TABLE 2.5.   Summary IQ and Memory Scores by Number of Medical Diagnoses

	Best	Common	Worst	r	F	p
Number of diagnoses	0–2	3	4–10			
Sample size	197	135	181			
Mayo IQs for WAIS-R						
VIQ	106	104	105	−.03	1.15	.32
PIQ	109	106	105	−.13	4.57	.01
FSIQ	107	105	105	−.08	2.58	.07
Mayo indices for WMS-R						
Verbal Memory	108	107	106	−.06	1.00	.37
Visual Memory	113	112	110	−.12	2.97	.05
General Memory	111	110	108	−.10	2.19	.11
Attention/Concentration	103	103	103	−.02	.13	.88
Delayed Recall	112	109	110	−.09	2.14	.12

Note: VIQ = Verbal IQ; PIQ = Performance IQ; FSIQ = Full Scale IQ.

of diagnoses related very slightly to the Mayo Performance IQ and the Mayo Visual Memory Index. These two associations are statistically significant primarily due to our sample size; their practical significance is questionable because neither association explains more than 2% of test variance. Neither the number of physical systems involved nor the number of medications taken show any association with overall intellectual or memory ability.

These findings suggest that although our subjects have many of the medical conditions common among the elderly, we have no evidence that their cognitive status is adversely influenced by their health problems.

Study Results

Wechsler Adult Intelligence Scale-Revised (WAIS-R)

We began our inspection of the effects of aging on cognitive test performance by analyzing standard measures of intelligence included in the WAIS-R with a series

TABLE 2.6.   Summary IQ and Memory Scores by Number of Physical Systems Involved in Diagnosed Illness

	Best	Common	Worst	r	F	p
Number of diagnoses	0–1	2–3	4–7			
Sample size	105	294	114			
Mayo IQs for WAIS-R						
VIQ	105	105	105	−.01	.01	.99
PIQ	108	107	105	−.09	1.83	.16
FSIQ	106	106	105	−.04	.25	.78
Mayo indices for WMS-R						
Verbal Memory	106	107	106	−.02	.62	.54
Visual Memory	114	112	110	−.09	2.37	.10
General Memory	111	110	108	−.06	.83	.44
Attention/Concentration	104	102	103	−.01	.59	.55
Delayed Recall	112	111	109	−.05	.64	.53

Note: VIQ = Verbal IQ; PIQ = Performance IQ; FSIQ = Full Scale IQ.

TABLE 2.7.   Summary IQ and Memory Scores by Number of Medications Used

	Best	*Common*	*Worst*	*r*	*F*	*p*
Number of diagnoses	0–1	2–3	4–7			
Sample size	147	186	180			
Mayo IQs for WAIS-R						
VIQ	105	105	105	−.01	.04	.97
PIQ	108	107	106	−.08	.62	.54
FSIQ	106	106	106	−.03	.05	.95
Mayo indices for WMS-R						
Verbal Memory	108	106	107	.01	.52	.59
Visual Memory	112	112	111	−.02	.25	.78
General Memory	111	110	110	.00	.31	.73
Attention/Concentration	104	102	103	.01	.36	.70
Delayed Recall	111	110	111	.04	.32	.73

Note: VIQ = Verbal IQ; PIQ = Performance IQ; FSIQ = Full Scale IQ.

of multiple regression analyses. We examined the influence of age, sex, and education on raw scores for each WAIS-R subtest. We also examined the relationship of age, sex, and education to raw sums of subtest scaled scores (uncorrected for age) for the Verbal subtests and the Performance subtests. In initial analyses, we included terms for the interactions among the three predictor variables. However, no interactions accounted for significant variance in any analysis. Consequently, we present multiple regression analyses based on a general linear model that employs only three variables: age and education (as continuous variables), and sex (as a categorical variable).

Sex and Percent of Total Variance Explained.   Table 2.8 shows the Percent of Total

TABLE 2.8.   Percent of Variance Explained on WAIS-R Measures by Sex, Age, and Education[a]

Measure	*Sex (%)*	*Age (%)*	*Education (%)*
Verbal Sum of Scaled Scores	*1.48*	*8.44*	*26.73*
Performance Sum of Scaled Scores	0.01	*42.12*	*4.87*
Vocabulary	0.06	*1.90*	*25.78*
Comprehension	2.16	*3.98*	*15.86*
Information	2.92	*4.99*	*31.30*
Digit Span	0.00	*5.07*	7.82
Arithmetic	7.36	*6.21*	6.83
Similarities	0.11	*10.30*	*17.60*
Picture Completion	*1.90*	*23.38*	4.59
Object Assembly	0.04	*23.66*	0.14
Picture Arrangement	0.46	*27.45*	6.96
Block Design	0.04	*28.73*	2.82
Digit Symbol	*4.74*	*37.12*	5.99
Verbal-Comprehension	0.82	*3.25*	*32.98*
Perceptual-Organization	0.01	*32.48*	1.20
Freedom-from-Distractibility	*3.23*	7.71	*9.31*

[a]Italicized percentages are significant at $p < .001$.

Variance Explained by the three predictor variables for each WAIS-R variable. Examination of Percent of Total Variance Explained is more informative than simply considering tests of significance. Because of our large sample size, many relationships in the analyses were statistically significant (see Table 2.8), but did not contribute to the prediction of performance to a degree that would be clinically useful.

To illustrate this point: the relationship of sex to Digit Symbol score in the context of a multiple regression equation that included age and education was statistically significant at $p<.001$. As can be seen in Table 2.8, however, sex accounts for only 4.74% of the total variance on Digit Symbol. In practical terms, the predicted Digit Symbol raw score for a male, age 67, with 12 years of education without the inclusion of sex in the equation is 42.1:

$$42.1 = 82.5 - 0.8 (67) + 1.1 (12). \tag{1}$$

Including sex in the equation results in a predicted raw score of 42.4:

$$42.4 = 77.0 - 0.8 (67) + 1.1 (12) + 5.8 (1). \tag{2}$$

Obviously, including the gender variable would not influence our clinical expectation in this case.

To further illuminate the clinical limitations of the small but significant Percent of Total Variance Explained of sex, consider its beta weight in Equation 2 (the regression equation), above. Our entire sample had a Digit Symbol mean score of 42.0 with a standard deviation of 12.9. Values for sex are 0 and 1. The change in expected score that the variable sex can maximally create is only 5.8 points (i.e., the value of the beta weight). This is less than $\frac{1}{2}$ a standard deviation. A $\frac{1}{2}$ standard deviation difference is not likely to change interpretation of an individual's Digit Symbol score. Thus there appears to be little clinical value in developing norms stratified by sex for a measure like Digit Symbol.

Contrast the effect of sex with the effect of age on Digit Symbol ($M = 42.0$; $SD = 12.9$). Age accounts for 37.12% of variance on Digit Symbol. The beta weight for age in predicting Digit Symbol is -0.8. An age difference of 16 years is sufficient to change the expected score by 1 standard deviation. Even in this age-restricted sample of 55- to 97-year olds, the variation in age is great enough to influence Digit Symbol performance significantly. Obviously, norms for Digit Symbol should be stratified by age.

At what point does Percent of Total Variance Explained reach a level of clinical relevance? Table 2.8 shows that, for Similarities, age explains 10.3% of the variance and education accounts for 17.6%. The regression equation describing the prediction of Similarities raw score by age and education is:

$$\hat{Y} = 19.5 - 0.2 (\text{Age}) + 0.8 (\text{Education}). \tag{3}$$

For the entire sample the mean Similarities raw score is 17 and the standard deviation is 5.4. A difference of 7 years in education would produce a difference of 1 standard deviation in the expected value for the student. Age requires a change of more than 25 years to produce a difference of 1 standard deviation in expectation for Similarities. In both of these cases the raw score difference required to make a clinically significant shift in expectation is fairly large. In each case, however, it

is within the range of the pertinent variable, even within the age-restricted normative sample studied here. It is clear that these variables should be included in developing norms for Similarities.

Based on these types of analyses, we concluded that instances in which age, sex, or education represent 10% or more of Percent of Total Variance Explained indicate relationships with test performances that should be considered in clinical interpretations. Sex can be dismissed as a factor in clinical interpretation of WAIS-R scores among the elderly population. Albert and Heaton (1988) and Reynolds, Chastain, Kaufman, & McLean (1987) reached a similar conclusion in their analyses of normative data for the WAIS-R and the unrevised Wechsler Adult Intelligence Scale (WAIS). Kaufman, McLean, and Reynolds (1988) reported statistically significant sex differences on some WAIS-R subtests, but these differences were of about the same magnitude as our own ($\frac{1}{4}$ to $\frac{1}{3}$ SD). Trahan and Quintana (1990) reported a statistically significant difference between males and females for immediate, but not delayed, recall on the Visual Reproduction Test of the original WMS. The actual mean difference, however, was less than 1 point.

This, of course, does not mean that statistically significant effects for sex on intelligence test performance are not of scientific interest. Males scored higher than females on the Verbal Sum of Scaled Scores overall ($p < .0003$), and on Information, Comprehension, Arithmetic ($p < .001$), and Picture Completion ($p < .001$). Females outperformed males on Digit Symbol ($p < .001$). Kaufman et al. (1988) reported male superiority on Information, Arithmetic, Comprehension, Picture Completion, Picture Arrangement, Block Design, and Object Assembly at some age levels. Consistent with our findings, Kaufman et al. (1988) found the females consistently outperformed males on Digit Symbol. Such performance differences between the sexes merit further discussion, but in another context. In this context, we will focus the remainder of our discussion of intelligence test scores on relationships of age and education to performance on these measures.

Age and Education. Further examination of Table 2.8 reveals that age does not have a consistent effect on performance on all intelligence subtests. The effects of age on individual WAIS-R subtests is graphically depicted in Figure 2.2. Age effects are most obvious on the Performance subtests, and relatively minimal on the Verbal subtests. The opposite is true for education. Education contributes to performance on many of the Verbal subtests, but only minimally to Performance measures. Effects of age and education on Verbal Sum of Scaled Scores compared to the effects of these variables on Performance Sum of Scaled Scores shows this rather dramatically. Age accounts for 42.1% of the variance on Performance Sum of Scaled Scores, but only 8.4% of the variance on Verbal Sum of Scaled Scores. Conversely, education accounts for 26.7% of the variance on Verbal Sum of Scaled Scores, but only 4.9% of the variance on Performance Sum of Scaled Scores.

These findings should not surprise those who are familiar with the literature on cognitive changes among the elderly. Albert and Heaton (1988) have documented a similar pattern of relationships among verbal and nonverbal intelligence, age, and education. Reynolds et al. (1987) showed consistently higher correlations of education with WAIS-R Verbal IQ than with Performance IQ across age contingents, and reported summary correlations of .60 between Verbal IQ and education and .44 between Performance IQ and education. Kaufman et al. (1988)

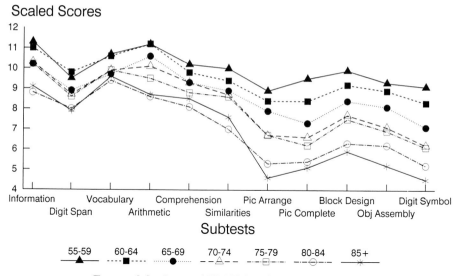

FIGURE 2.2. Age and WAIS-R subtest scaled scores.

reported generally stronger relationships of education to WAIS-R Verbal subtests than to Performance subtests. In their study, education was most highly correlated with Vocabulary and Information. Kaufman et al. (1988) did find that education accounted for 15% to 24% of the variance on most Performance subtests in some age groups.

Aging has its most significant effect on the capacity to manage novel problems and information. WAIS-R Performance subtests pose many problems that use unfamiliar stimuli or require the use of familiar stimuli in unfamiliar ways. Aging also has a deleterious effect on cognitive speed. The Performance measures are timed, whereas the Verbal measures are not. On the other hand, access to remotely learned information (remote memory) is relatively resistant to the effects of aging. The WAIS-R Verbal subtests depend heavily on recall of information that is usually acquired during schooling and socialization. Thus, age is not expected to impact performance on those Verbal subtests that depend highly on remote memory. Indeed, our results show minimal effects of age on the WAIS-R measure of Vocabulary and Information.

There is also significant variation in the contributions of age and education to subtests within both the Verbal and Performance domains. Among Verbal subtests, Vocabulary is highly related to education and minimally related to age. The Similarities subtest, which depends both on remote memory for categorical relationships and the capacity for abstraction, is affected both by age and education. Measures of focused attention and registration memory, like Digit Span, are not strongly related to either age or education in our data.

The WAIS-R Factors. We were interested in how these relationships of age and education to intelligence subtests might parallel the factor structure of the WAIS-R. Traditionally, three major factors have been identified in factor analyses of the WAIS-R (Kaufman, 1990; Parker, 1983): (a) Verbal-Comprehension, composed of Vocabulary, Information, Similarities, and Comprehension; (b) Perceptual-

Organization, represented by Block Design and Object Assembly; and (c) Freedom-from-Distractability, represented by Digit Span and Arithmetic. In fact, subtests contributing to Perceptual-Organization (Block Design and Object Assembly) appear highly related to age and minimally to education (see Table 2.8). Subtests contributing to Freedom-from-Distractibility (Arithmetic, Digit Span) are not highly related to either age or education. The four subtests contributing to Verbal-Comprehension vary in their relationships to age and education. However, if we choose only Vocabulary and Information to represent Verbal-Comprehension, we have a factor that represents remote verbal memory and is minimally related to age, but highly related to education. Use of such factor scores has the added appeal to clinicians of providing measures that, because of the increased item numbers and variety, should be more stable and reliable than individual subtest scores.

In all analyses reported in this chapter, we have defined the WAIS-R factors as the sum of non-age-corrected scaled scores for the following subtest pairs:

> Verbal-Comprehension = Vocabulary + Information,
> Perceptual-Organization = Block Design + Object Assembly,
> Freedom-from-Distractibility = Digit Span + Arithmetic.

Relationships of sex, age, and education to these three factors are shown in Table 2.8. These relationships demonstrate the need to norm Verbal-Comprehension scores in terms of education and Perceptual-Organization by chronological age. Of course, because of the significant correlations between verbal and nonverbal WAIS-R measures, any corrections for age and education must be applied to all WAIS-R measures to preserve expected relationships among these measures.

The import of these analyses is further illustrated in Figures 2.3 and 2.4. Figure 2.3 shows mean performances on the three factor scores across seven hemidecade age contingents after these scores have been corrected for the effects of education. As can be seen, correcting for education produces a relatively flat relationship of Verbal-Comprehension to progressive age. The same correction, however, does not

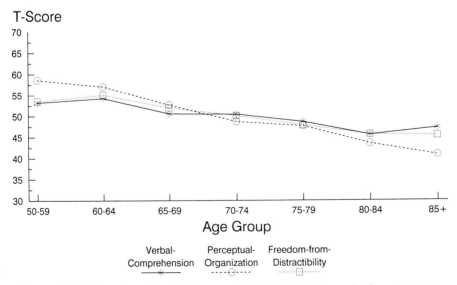

FIGURE 2.3. Education-adjusted T-scores for WAIS-R factor scales by age group.

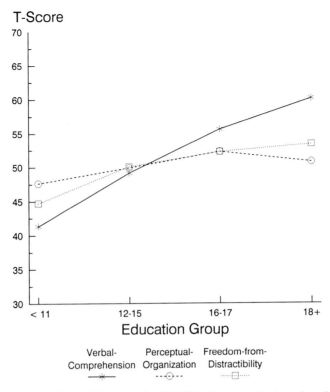

FIGURE 2.4. Age-adjusted T-scores for WAIS-R factor scales by education group.

change the negative linear relationship of Perceptual-Organization to age. We can also look at Perceptual-Organization and Verbal-Comprehension with age influences controlled. Figure 2.4 shows the factor scores grouped in contingents of educational accomplishment after these scores have been statistically corrected for age. In this illustration, correcting for age flattens the curve for Perceptual-Organization, which is minimally related to education. However, Verbal-Comprehension remains positively and linearly related to education despite the age correction.

In both illustrations, Freedom-from-Distractibility, which represents attention/ registration memory, is minimally affected by either age or education. These marginal relationships of Freedom-from-Distractibility to age and education probably are due to the novelty of some aspects of the task and the more challenging aspects of the mental arithmetic tests. Although the marginal degree of variance explained on Freedom-from-Distractibility by age and education probably will not be meaningful in clinical settings, we prefer to use a combination of Mental Control and Digit Span from the WMS-R as a measure of focused attention and registration memory because it is even less related to age or education (see Table 2.9). We have labeled this index the Registration-Attention Index.

A drawback to the use of Perceptual-Organization in clinical practice is that it begins to show a floor effect in the upper age ranges. As can be seen in Figure 2.2, mean scaled scores for Block Design and Object Assembly are below 6 in the upper age ranges. In fact, 25% of the group above age 84 obtained a *raw* score

less than 9 on Block Design; 10% obtain a raw score less than 7. In the 80 to 84 age group, 25% scored less than 10; 10%, less than 8. For Object Assembly, 25% scored less than 13 and 10% scored less than 10 in the over 84 group. In the 80 to 84 group, 25% score less than 18; 10%, less than 15.

Normality and Homogeneity of Variance. Stratifying normative tables by age or education is required for some WAIS-R measures, given the above discussion. However, after a measure has been appropriately stratified, the question remains whether data within these groups is normally distributed.

Verbal-Comprehension, Perceptual-Organization, and Freedom-from-Distractibility do show significant deviations from normality ($p<.05$) in one or both of the oldest age groups (80–84, 85 +) by the Shapiro-Wilk Test (Royston, 1982). Verbal-Comprehension shows significant deviations from normality within three of four education groups (Ws = .956, .976, and .966, for ≤11, 12–15, and 18 + -years-of-education groups, respectively; each $p<.05$). Tests of normality for individual WAIS-R subtests also show occasional deviations from normality within some age groups for most subtests. Because of these differences from normality within relevant normative groups, we recommend that normative data be presented in tabular percentile format (i.e., that tables giving specific percentile ranks for raw scores be developed for each WAIS-R variable).

The question also remains whether distributions for the Verbal-Comprehension and Perceptual-Organization remain normal and are of equivalent variance once corrections are made for age and education. *Age-corrected* scores for Perceptual-Organization show normal distributions in each of the four categories of educational attainment. However, variance at the highest level of educational attainment (18 + years) is almost twice as large (s^2 = 17.0) as in the other three education groups with variances equal to 10.4, 11.5, and 8.8 for groups with less than 11 years, 12 to 15 years, and 16 to 17 years, respectively. This marked change in variance for the highest educational group recommends that age-referenced norms for Perceptual-Organization be provided by separate education groups. *Education-corrected* scores for Verbal-Comprehension show a possible non-normal distribution in the 70 to 74 age group (W = .946, $p<.06$), again suggesting the appropriateness of presenting norms in a tabular percentile format. Additionally, a significant increase in variance occurs in the oldest age group. Variances for education-corrected scores for Verbal-Comprehension by age group are as follows:

$$55–59, s^2 = 9.1$$
$$60–64, s^2 = 12.4$$
$$65–69, s^2 = 9.5$$
$$70–74, s^2 = 11.2$$
$$75–79, s^2 = 10.7$$
$$80–84, s^2 = 8.9$$
$$85 +, s^2 = 16.7$$

Because of the marked increase in variance above age 84, norms for Verbal-Comprehension that are referenced to education should also be divided into groups that are less than and greater than 85 years of age.

Wechsler Memory Scale-Revised (WMS-R)

Attention and New Learning. Table 2.9 shows Percent of Total Variance Explained for WMS-R indices and subtests. Among measures of focused attention/registration memory, Mental Control and Digit Span are the purest measures, with only weak relationships to age and education. Probably because of the novelty of the task, Visual Memory Span, which also contributes the WMS-R Attention-Concentration Index, shows a stronger relationship to age. We have constructed an alternative to the Attention-Concentration Index that consists of the unweighted sum of raw scores for Mental Control and Digit Span. This index, the Registration-Attention Index, is only weakly related to either age or education (see Table 2.9). As such, the Registration-Attention Index provides a clearer measure of the capacity to focus attention and register new information, functions that the scientific literature suggests should not be related to age or education.

Among measures of new learning, most show only weak relationships to sex and education, but stronger relationships to age. The exception is the Visual Paired Associate subtest, which also shows a marginal relationship to sex. Figure 2.5 illustrates the more substantial effects of normal aging on the major indices of new learning (General Memory Index, Verbal Memory Index, Visual Memory Index) than on the indices of attention/registration memory (Attention-Concentration Index, Registration-Attention Index).

Factor Analytic Studies. Factor analyses (Smith, et al., 1992; Smith, Malec, & Ivnik, 1992) of intelligence and memory test data from this sample indicate a factor for attention/registration represented by tests like digit span and mental control. Factors for Verbal-Comprehension and Perceptual-Organization consistently emerged in our analyses. A single factor for learning and immediate memory and another

TABLE 2.9.   Percent of Variance Explained on WMS-R Measures by Sex, Age, and Education[a]

Measure	Sex (%)	Age (%)	Education (%)
Verbal Memory	0.01	*19.47*	*4.12*
Visual Memory	*3.09*	*39.63*	*3.39*
General Memory	0.71	*32.28*	*4.87*
Attention-Concentration	0.07	*12.40*	*4.56*
Registration-Attention	0.15	*6.70*	*7.40*
Mental Control	0.02	*3.70*	2.23
Digit Span	0.16	*4.82*	6.83
Figural Memory	0.01	7.99	.22
Visual Memory Span	0.87	*14.72*	.49
Logical Memory I	0.37	*15.62*	3.21
Verbal Paired Associates I	*6.07*	*16.86*	3.93
Visual Paired Associates I	*11.30*	*26.61*	1.69
Visual Reproduction I	0.07	*31.58*	3.61
Logical Memory % Retention	0.73	*7.18*	2.18
Visual Reproduction % Retention	0.41	*19.60*	0.80

[a]Italicized percentages are significant at $p < .001$.

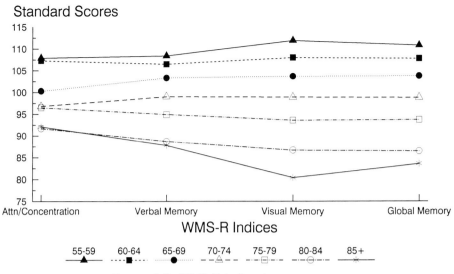

FIGURE 2.5. WMS-R indices by age groups.

factor for percent retention of initial learning after a time delay have also been identified in our factor studies. Although Bornstein and Chelune (1988) found separate verbal and nonverbal memory factors, most other studies have found only a single immediate memory factor (Larrabee, Kane, Schuck, & Francis, 1985; Roid, Prifitera, & Ledbetter, 1988). Roth, Conboy, Reeder, and Boll (1990) found a delayed recall factor in addition to factors for attention/registration and immediate recall in their analysis of the WMS-R data for a group of head-injured patients. In our studies, all factors were at least moderately correlated with each other.

Because factor analyses suggest that immediate recall on most memory tests appears to represent a single cognitive domain, and because of the increased stability of index scores based on large item pools, our discussion here will focus on the major indices of the WMS-R, particularly the General Memory Index.

It has been a common clinical practice to compare the Memory Quotient from the original Wechsler Memory Scale (Wechsler, 1945) to WAIS or WAIS-R Full Scale IQ and to interpret a markedly lower Memory Quotient (MQ) as a sign of cognitive deterioration, even though the MQ has come under much criticism as a memory measure (Prigatano, 1978). Our factor analyses do raise a question about the viability of comparing IQ measures with the General Memory Index because these variables constitute separate factors. Nonetheless, these factors are not completely orthogonal. The possibility that a measure of new learning (General Memory Index) may be related to a measure of remote memory (Verbal-Comprehension) in a normal sample has intriguing possibilities for clinical practice. Results of regression analyses presented in Table 2.10 indicate that substantial variance on the General Memory Index is explained by Verbal-Comprehension in addition to variance accounted for by age. Significant discrepancies between the capacity to acquire new information as indicated by the General Memory Index and the capacity to retrieve remotely learned information (Verbal-Comprehension) may indeed indicate cognitive deterioration.

TABLE 2.10.   Percent of Variance Explained on WMS-R Indices and Percent Retention Scores by Age and Verbal-Comprehension[a]

Measure	Age (%)	Verbal-Comprehension (%)
Verbal Memory	*11.20*	*16.96*
Visual Memory	*29.43*	*8.48*
General Memory	*21.40*	*16.65*
Attention-Concentration	*7.25*	*13.65*
Logical Memory % Retention	*4.06*	*5.88*
Visual Reproduction % Retention	*16.58*	1.13

[a]Italicized percentages are significant at $p < .001$.

Retention. We question the utility of the Delayed Memory Index. This index is based on raw scores from four measures (Logical Memory, Visual Reproduction, Verbal Paired Associates, and Visual Paired Associates) after a half-hour delay. In fact, our correlational analyses have shown that, in a normal population, these delayed measures are almost redundant with their immediate recall counterparts, correlating at .85 and greater. Measures based on percent retention of original learning have traditionally been considered to be of greater value in clinical settings, and this is also our impression. Our factor analytic studies of this sample identified a percent retention factor, but not a standard delayed memory factor. With these considerations in mind, we present percent retention data for delayed recall of WMS-R Logical Memory and Visual Reproduction stimuli.

Tables 2.9 and 2.10 show that percent retention measures have their strongest relationships with age and only weak or nil relationships with education, sex, and Verbal-Comprehension. Logical Memory Percent Retention did have a statistically significant but weak relationship with age in our investigation. Haaland, Linn, Hunt, and Goodwin (1983) have found that Logical Memory Percent Retention varies with age. However, Cullum et al. (1990) did not find a statistical difference for average Logical Memory Percent Retention between a group age 50 to 70 and a group age 75 to 95. Age does account for substantial variance on Visual Reproduction Percent Retention and this is consistent with results obtained by both Haaland et al. (1983) and Cullum et al. (1990).

Because of the percent conversion, Logical Memory Percent Retention and Visual Reproduction Percent Retention would not be expected to be normally distributed. Thus, relationships with age may be most appropriately examined in the context of percentile ranks. Figures 2.6 and 2.7 show 75th, median, 25th, and 10th percentile scores for Logical Memory Percent Retention and Visual Reproduction Percent Retention, respectively. Although decline is apparent with increasing age, Logical Memory Percent Retention does not show marked deterioration with aging. Among those 85 and older, 90% of the sample retains at least 50% of the paragraph information originally learned. On the other hand, Visual Reproduction Percent Retention shows rather marked deterioration, with an apparent floor effect in the highest age group. Among those 85 years and older, 25% recalled only 40% of the design information learned previously, and 10% of our *normal* sample was unable to recall any of the design information accurately after the delay.

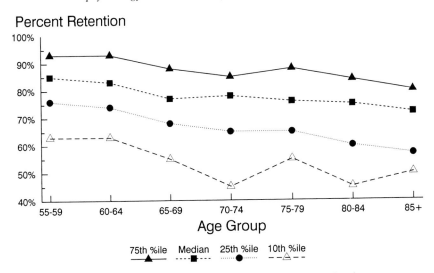

FIGURE 2.6. WMS-R logical memory delayed percent retention by age group.

Normality. Distributions of the Attention-Concentration Index were not significantly different from normal within each of the seven age groups on the Shapiro-Wilk Test ($p > .05$). However, the distributions of the General Memory Index and the Verbal Memory Index show significant deviations from normality in the 65 to 69 year age group ($p < .001$). The distribution of the Visual Memory Index deviates from normality in the 60 to 64, the 65 to 69, and the 75 to 79 year age groups ($p < .05$). These findings suggest that norms for most WMS-R indices are best communicated in a tabular percentile format rather than a parametric standard score format. As mentioned previously, percent retention scores are expected to be non-normally distributed. Thus, norms for these should be referenced to percentile ranks.

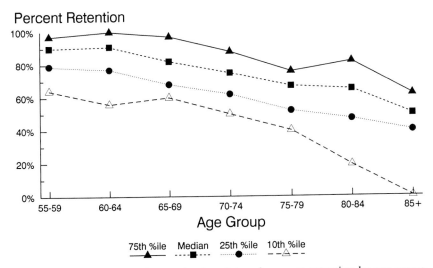

FIGURE 2.7. WMS-R visual reproduction delayed percent retention by age group.

Available Wechsler Norms for the Elderly

Normative data based on the work presented here are available in the 1992 Supplement issue of *The Clinical Neuropsychologist*. We have presented data that use nonparametric procedures for correcting the WAIS-R measures for individuals' ages from age 56 through 97 (Ivnik et al., 1992a). In a subsequent study, we offer additional conversion tables for correcting WAIS-R measures for the effects of education (Malec et al., 1992). Normative data from the same group of elderly persons are provided for the WMS-R (Ivnik et al., 1992b). WMS-R norms are corrected for age, but not for education, because of the negligible Percent of Total Variance Explained on WMS-R measures by education. This supplement issue also contains age-corrected norms for the Auditory Verbal Learning Test (Rey, 1964) from the same elderly sample (Ivnik et al., 1992c).

Other normative studies on the Wechsler measures among the elderly have been few. These few studies are limited, as perhaps all single-center normative studies including our own are, by sample selection. Ryan, Paolo, and Brungardt (1990) have presented norms for the WAIS-R for two groups of elderly: one group age 75 to 79 ($n = 60$) and a second group over age 80 ($n = 70$). Although this study includes fewer subjects over age 75 than our own, the sample represents a more urban population (90% urban; 92% white; 8% black). Ryan, Paolo, and Findley (1991) have presented tables based on the WAIS-R standardization sample that allow correction of WAIS-R IQs for education for the "young" elderly (ie., those < age 75). Heaton, Grant, and Matthews (1991) have presented normative tables that provide corrections for age, sex, and education for measures obtained from the unrevised WAIS through age 80.

Cullum et al. (1990) have provided preliminary norms for the WMS-R, including percent retention on delayed measures, for small groups of subjects ages 50 to 70 ($n = 47$) and ages 75 to 95 ($n = 32$). Spreen and Strauss (1991) provided age-corrected norms for the original WMS based on several studies of WMS performance among the elderly (Abikoff et al., 1987; Haaland et al., 1983; Hulicka, 1966; Klonoff & Kennedy, 1966; Trahan, Quintana, Willingham, & Goethe, 1988). Although combining data as Spreen and Strauss did may have resulted in a more generally applicable normative base, most of the individual studies have used relatively select samples. For instance, Klonoff and Kennedy (1966) studied only veterans. Haaland et al. (1983) reported on a group of apparently superior functioning elderly with no chronic medical illnesses. Our group has presented norms for the original WMS that are age-corrected and referenced to WAIS-R IQ (Ivnik, Smith, et al., 1991). Our WMS norms are based on a sample that is smaller, but otherwise similar to the one we have described here.

Age-Associated Memory Impairment

The differential effects of aging on cognition and cognitive test performance produces the need to carefully explore the impact of age on each component of tests for which norms are being presented. The cognitive changes associated with aging also create the need for special care in assignment of clinical labels. The effect of aging on memory, as distinct from memory impairment due to dementia-producing neurological disease, provides the clearest case in point. Over 30 years ago, Kral (1958) identified a subgroup of older persons with poor memory but generally preserved global intellectual functioning and a survival rate consonant with that of other normal older persons and distinct from demented patients. He coined the terms *benign* and *malignant* senescent forgetfulness to distinguish deteriorating dementia patients from forgetful but otherwise cognitively stable older persons. More recently, a National Institute of Mental Health (NIMH) workgroup (Crook et al., 1986), in an effort to better operationalize the concept of memory loss with age and stimulate research and clinical discussion on its effects, has offered diagnostic criteria for Age-Associated Memory Impairment.

The NIMH workgroup offers Age-Associated Memory Impairment as a diagnostic term for older persons with subjective memory complaint, absence of memory-impairing medical conditions, and scores on memory testing that are greater than 1 standard deviation below the mean for young adults. Blackford and LaRue (1989) offered several revisions to these criteria. The most salient revision is their distinction within Age-Associated Memory Impairment of two subgroups: Group 1, those with age-consistent memory scores (Age-Consistent Memory Impairment), and Group 2, those with memory scores that are both impaired relative to young adults and in the borderline range relative to age-matched peers (Late-Life Forgetfulness).

Our large sample of normal older adults provided an opportunity to evaluate the cognitive criteria of Age-Associated Memory Impairment, Age-Consistent Memory Impairment, and Late-Life Forgetfulness among community-dwelling normal elderly who did *not* complain of memory problems (Smith, Ivnik, Petersen, et al., 1991). Two groups were created. Group 1 included 99 subjects from the ADPR project described previously in this chapter. The data set for this group included the WAIS-R, WMS, Auditory Verbal Learning Test (AVLT), Hachinski Ischemia, Mini-Mental State, and depression measures. The NIMH criteria could be applied to the letter to this group. Group 2 ($n = 424$) was composed of nearly 400 subjects from the Community Project, with the remainder coming from the ADPR studies. Everyone in the second group had received the WAIS-R, WMS-R, and AVLT. The ischemia and mental status scores were not available on these subjects.

The NIMH Age-Associated Memory Impairment scheme requires one memory test to fall at least 1 standard deviation below the mean for young adults. Following exclusion for reasons unrelated to memory function, 98% of 66 remaining Group 1 subjects and 77% of 338 remaining Group 2 subjects met memory criteria on at least one memory measure in the respective batteries. AVLT Total Learning was among the most inclusive measures (96% of Group 1 and 58% of Group 2 members met memory criteria on this test), whereas Logical Memory was the least inclusive (20% in Group 1 and 11% in Group 2). The Blackford and LaRue cognitive criteria would diagnose as Age-Associated Memory Impairment (but function 1 *SD* or greater than age-appropriate means) in 31% of Group 1 members and 8% of Group 2 members. Fifty-two percent of Group 1 and 30% of Group 2 members met Age-Consistent Memory Impairment criteria. Late-Life Forgetfulness cognitive criteria were met by no Group 1 members, but 31% of Group 2 members.

It is apparent that these diagnostic criteria as presently defined lack specificity. Crook (1989) has argued that this lack of specificity is not a concern. He believes Age-Associated Memory Impairment to be a highly prevalent and, in fact, a normative condition in the elderly. However, as presently conceptualized, Age-Associated Memory Impairment nosology and criteria imply deficiency or impairment, not normality.

It should be noted that a major component of both the NIMH and the Blackford and LaRue criteria is the presence of subjective memory complaint. For the purposes of our evaluation, we purposely ignored this criterion. In fact, as noted above, all of the subjects in the MOANS are specifically selected for the absence of any spontaneous complaint of cognitive impairment, including memory problems. Our decision to ignore the subjective complaint criterion was based on our goal of determining the specificity of the *cognitive* criteria for diagnoses that connote cognitive deficits. The application of the cognitive criteria to our sample reveals that the cognitive criteria, as presently described, can be so inclusive that a subjective complaint virtually guarantees a diagnosis of indicating impairment.

This would not be a problem if all variance in subjective complaints were accounted for by cognitive dysfunction. However, a number of other factors contribute to subjective complaints of memory problems in the elderly including the degree of demand placed on them by the environment, personality traits such as anxiety or self-criticalness, and sensitivity to societal beliefs about memory change.

Several clinical concerns are illustrated in this application of Age-Associated Memory Impairment criteria to our normal sample. The most specific of these concerns may be the need to revise operationalization of Age-Associated Memory Impairment criteria to improve the reliability of this diagnosis. This unreliability arises from the variable sensitivity of given measures to age effects. The need to consider this variable sensitivity of measures is a more global concern that is also pertinent to the discussion of appropriate norms above.

The most global concern arising from this discussion of Age-Associated Memory Impairment pertains to defining "impaired" for older persons. A number of models present themselves. The NIMH group criteria explicitly reference normality in older persons to the functioning of younger persons. As a substitute for longitudinal serial assessments of the same individual, the NIMH approach suggests that memory performance of an elderly adult that is significantly lower than the average young adult is evidence of age-associated memory decline. Blackford and LaRue (1989) argue that impairment should reference deviation from age-matched peers. Another approach might define "impairment" with reference to the person's ability to perform adequately in their current or desired environment. It would seem that before diagnostic models proceed and diagnostic labels are applied, additional consensus in the definitions of normal and impairment as they apply to older persons are needed.

Summary and Implications

Our analyses of WAIS-R and WMS-R data from over 500 *normal* elderly subjects demonstrates that five major areas of cognitive functioning are represented by indicators derived from these well-known tests. A Verbal-Comprehension factor from the WAIS-R represents remote memory. WAIS-R Perceptual-Organization represents novel visuospatial problem-solving. An attention/registration memory index (Registration-Attention Index) from the WMS-R provides an indicator of the capacity to focus attention and register new information. The General Memory Index offers an index of the capacity to acquire new information. Percent retention scores for the Logical Memory and Visual Reproduction subtests of the WMS-R indicate the ability to retain this new information.

Consistent with the experimental literature on cognition and aging, remote memory (Verbal-Comprehension) and attention/registration (Registration-Attention Index) do not show strong correlations with age. Indicators of new learning (General Memory Index) and problem-solving (Perceptual-Organization) do show strong relationships with age, and clinical use of these measures requires age correction. The measure of remote memory (Verbal-Comprehension) is highly associated with educational attainment, and clinical use of this measure is enhanced by use of norms referenced to educational level.

Verbal-Comprehension shows a significant increase in variance in the oldest age range (85 +), and separate norms for this age group in addition to education-referenced norms are needed. Perceptual-Organization appears to require separate norms for those with very advanced education in addition to age-referenced norms. Most major indicators (Verbal-Comprehension, Perceptual-Organization, General Memory Index) show occasional deviations at some age ranges from normal distribution. Percent retention indicators are not normally distributed. Thus, reference to percentile ranks (rather than parametric standard scores) is appropriate for normative presentation of most WAIS-R and WMS-R data. We recommend use of major indicators because individual subtest scores are less stable. Because of occasional deviations from normality, normative data for all subtests should probably be presented as percentile ranks or standard scores referenced to percentile ranks rather than as parametric standard scores.

Whereas remote verbal memory (as indicated by performance on the WAIS-R Information and Vocabulary subtests) appears to remain relatively stable even into the oldest ages, the capacities involved in novel visuospatial problem solving and memory show dramatic reductions with increasing age. In the older age ranges, measures of these constructs (Perceptual-Organization, Visual Reproduction Percent Retention) show a floor effect. In fact, 10% of our *normal* elderly sample over the age of 84 was unable to accurately recall a single feature of the WMS-R designs after a half-hour delay. In clinical evaluation, such a performance would typically be interpreted as a clear sign of cognitive impairment. Our studies suggest, to the contrary, that such a performance does not indicate cognitive impairment of a degree that would interfere with independent living. (Recall that all individuals in our study were living independently in the community and had recently presented to a physician with no evidence of significant cognitive problems).

Of course, independence can have many different meanings. We have no information on how much help this lowest 10% of our eldest sample was actually getting from spouses, friends, children, and others. Nonetheless, our findings suggest a need for conservatism in diagnosing pathology in the oldest age ranges. Diagnostic conservatism is also recommended by our evaluation of Age-Associated Memory Impairment criteria in our sample of community-dwelling elderly individuals. A large percentage of our normal sample met various criteria for Age-

Associated Memory Impairment, Age-Consistent Memory Impairment, and Late-Life Forgetfulness. Percentages meeting these criteria varied widely with the memory measure used. Until criteria with acceptable specificity and reliability have been adapted, diagnoses of Age-Associated Memory Impairment, Age-Consistent Memory Impairment, and Late-Life Forgetfulness should be applied with caution, if at all.

Some indicators (Registration-Attention Index, Logical Memory Percent Retention) appear to be relatively resilient in the face of advancing age. Thus, impaired or declining performances on these measures may signify cerebral pathology. However, the relationships among cerebral pathology, psychometric measures, and everyday functioning remain imperfectly understood. Extensive analyses of psychometric evaluation procedures reveal not only the utility, but also the limitations of these procedures, and underscore the need for measures of everyday functioning, especially in the oldest age ranges. Adequate evidence of significant cognitive impairment in individuals over age 84 may need to include a measure of independence in community functioning.

Implicit in much of our data analysis and discussion is the notion that normative psychometric data can be developed and analyzed much more thoroughly than has typically been the case in presentations in test manuals. Manuals for the major psychometric instruments constitute rather minimal efforts at presentation of normative data that, at best, offer some attempt to obtain a representative sample and norms referenced to age. Our initial analyses of our normative data set suggest that some measures must be referenced to other demographic variables, most notably education. Some measures are not appropriately converted to parametric standard scores because of non-normal distributions. Predictable relationships among measures that may be of clinical utility (e.g., the relationship of Verbal-Comprehension to General Memory Index) and equations specifying these relationships within different normative groups should be routinely presented in test manuals.

Other demographic variables, in addition to the basic variables of age, sex, and education, merit investigation. Because we have found that a majority of the elderly population is in less than perfect health, we have felt that it is inappropriate to base norms for the elderly only on individuals who are in perfect health. On the one hand, such normative data might be appropriate only for the relatively small group of "super-elderly" whose constitution has allowed them to escape physiological problems that are common among persons of advanced age. On the other hand, however, we have been unable to demonstrate that the general health of the individual and current use of medications are variables that generally or consistently affect psychometric test performances.

Cultural experience is another variable that may significantly affect psychometric test performance. Different norms are likely needed for individuals of different cultural backgrounds. Because of the area of the country in which we are located, our norms do not include people from diverse cultural and ethnic backgrounds. Our normative data may have application to large segments of the American population, but are clearly not applicable to all. Reynolds et al. (1987) found no differences in performance between urban and rural dwellers, but did identify race as a significant factor in intelligence test performance. Kaufman et al. (1988) corroborated the significance of race to WAIS-R performances for various age groups, and also showed geographic regional variations in WAIS-R subtest performances for most age contingents.

Dealing with the issue of cultural effects on psychometric test performance is a complex matter that is not entirely addressed simply by norming traditional measures to an identified cultural group (Anastasi, 1988). New measurement techniques are probably required to offer adequate assessment of individuals who live outside of the dominant American culture for which most psychometric measures have been developed. With the increasingly proprietary stance of psychometric test publishers, it is clear that the responsibility for development, more thorough analysis, and more complete presentation of useful tests and clinically useful normative data falls on test publishers.

In this chapter, we have tried to focus on changes in cognitive capacities with advancing age that are clinically meaningful. Our data also show many more subtle changes in cognition with age and subtle cognitive differences related to other variables, such as sex and education, that may be of scientific interest. The field of clinical geropsychology is in need of more extensive, applied research to support it. Nonetheless, this need for clinical geriatric research must be supported by the ongoing basic research in cognition and aging that has provided the foundation for current clinical practice and will always constitute the most fundamental support of the practice of clinical psychology.

Acknowledgments

Preparation of this manuscript was supported by grants from the Mayo Foundation and the National Institute on Aging (Alzheimer's Disease Patient Registry, AG06786-04).

We gratefully acknowledge the assistance of the Psychometrists in Mayo's Psychological Assessment Laboratory for their professionalism in test administration and data management. We are especially grateful to Martha Mandarino, who served as the research assistant for the Mayo's Older Americans Normative Studies. Similarly, we are particularly grateful to Mary Beard, R.N., Gayle Ness, R.N., Linda Linbo, R.N., and Mary Severson, R.N. for their assistance on the Alzheimer's Disease Patient Registry.

References

Abikoff, H., Alvir, J., Hong, G., Sukoff, R., Orazio, J., Solomon, S., & Saravay, S. (1987). Logical Memory subtest of the Wechsler memory Scale: Age and education norms and alternate-form reliability of two scoring systems. *Journal of Clinical and Experimental Neuropsychology, 9,* 435–448.

Albert, M. S. (1981). Geriatric neuropsychology. *Journal of Consulting and Clinical Psychology, 49,* 835–850.

Albert, M. S., & Heaton, R. K. (1988). Intelligence testing. In M. S. Albert & M. B. Moss (Eds.), *Geriatric Neuropsychology* (pp. 13–32). New York: Guilford.

Albert, M. S., Wolfe, J., & Lafleche, G. (1990). Differences in abstraction ability with age. *Psychology and Aging, 5,* 94–100.

Anastasi, A. (1988). *Psychological Testing* (6th ed.). New York: Macmillan.

Benton, A. L., & Sivan, A. B. (1984). Problems and conceptual issues in neuropsychological research in aging and dementia. *Journal of Clinical Neuropsychology, 6,* 57–63.

Birren, J. E. (1964). *The psychology of aging.* Englewood Cliffs, NJ: Prentice-Hall.

Birren, J. E. (1970). Toward an experimental psychology of aging. *American Psychologist,* *25,* 124–135.

Birren, J. E. (1974). Translations in gerontology—from lab to life: Psychophysiology and the speed of response. *American Psychologist, 29,* 808–815.

Birren, J. E., & Schaie, K. W. (Eds.). (1977). *Handbook of the psychology of aging.* New York: Van Nostrand.

Birren, J. E., & Schaie, K. W. (Eds.). (1985). *Handbook of the psychology of aging.* (2nd ed.). New York: Van Nostrand.

Birren, J. E., & Schaie, K. W. (Eds.). (1990). *Handbook of the psychology of aging.* (3rd ed.). San Diego: Academic Press.

Blackford, R. C., & LaRue, A. (1989). Criteria for diagnosing Age-Associated Memory Impairment: Proposed improvements from the field. *Developmental Neuropsychology, 5,* 295–306.

Bornstein, R. A., & Chelune, G. J. (1988). Factor structure of the Wechsler Memory Scale-Revised. *The Clinical Neuropsychologist, 2,* 107–115.

Botwinick, J. (1977). Intellectual abilities. In J. E. Birren & K. W. Schaie (Eds.), *Handbook of the psychology of aging.* New York: Van Nostrand.

Bowles, N. L., & Poon, L. W. (1982). An analysis of the effect of aging on memory. *Journal of Gerontology, 37,* 212–219.

Chelune, G. J., & Moehle, K. A. (1986). Neuropsychological assessment of everyday functioning. In D. Wedding, A. M. Horton, Jr., & J. Webster (Eds.), *The neuropsychology handbook: Behavioral and clinical perspectives.* New York: Springer.

Cornelius, S. W. (1984). Classic pattern of intellectual aging: Test familiarity, difficulty, and performance. *Journal of Gerontology, 39,* 201–206.

Crook, T. (1989). Diagnosis and treatment of normal and pathological memory impairment in later life. *Seminars in Neurology, 9,* 20–30.

Crook, T., Bartus, R. T., Ferris, S. H., Whitehouse, P., Cohen, G. D., & Gershon, S. (1986). Age-Associated Memory Impairment: Proposed diagnostic criteria and measures of clinical change—report of a National Institute of Mental Health work group. *Developmental Neuropsychology, 2,* 261–276.

Cullum, C. M., Butters, N., Troster, A. I., & Salmon, D. P. (1990). Normal aging and forgetting rates on the Wechsler Memory Scale-Revised. *Archives of Clinical Neuropsychology, 5,* 23–30.

Fozard, J. L., Metter, J., & Brant, L. J. (1990). Next steps in describing aging and disease in longitudinal studies. *Journal of Gerontology: Psychological Sciences, 45,* 116–127.

Haaland, K. Y., Linn, R. T., Hunt, W. C., & Goodwin, J. S. (1983). A normative study of Russell's variant of the Wechsler Memory Scale in a healthy elderly population. *Journal of Consulting and Clinical Psychology, 51,* 878–881.

Heaton, R. K., Grant, I., & Matthews, C. G. (1991). *Comprehensive norms for an expanded Halstead-Reitan Battery: Demographic corrections, research findings, and clinical applications.* Odessa, FL: Psychological Assessment Resources.

Heaton, R. K., & Pendleton, M. G. (1981). Use of neuropsychological tests to predict adult patients' everyday functioning. *Journal of Consulting and Clinical Psychology, 49,* 807–821.

Hulicka, I. M. (1966). Age differences in Wechsler Memory Scale scores. *Journal of Genetic Psychology, 109,* 135–145.

Ivnik, R. J., Malec, J. F., Tangalos, E. R., Petersen, R. C., Kokmen, E., & Kurland, L. T. (1990). The Auditory-Verbal Learning Test (AVLT): Norms for ages 55 years and older. *Psychological Assessment: A Journal of Consulting and Clinical Psychology, 2,* 304–312.

Ivnik, R. J., Malec, J. F., Smith, G. E., Tangalos, E. G., Petersen, R. C., Kokmen, E., & Kurland, L. T. (1992a). Mayo's Older Americans Normative Studies: WAIS-R norms for ages 56 to 97. *The Clinical Neuropsychologist, 6* (Suppl.), 1–30.

Ivnik, R. J., Malec, J. F., Smith, G. E., Tangalos, E. G., Petersen, R. C., Kokmen, E., & Kurland, L. T. (1992b). Mayo's Older Americans Normative Studies: WMS-R norms for ages 56 to 97. *The Clinical Neuropsychologist, 6* (Suppl.), 49–82.

Ivnik, R. J., Malec, J. F., Smith, G. E., Tangalos, E. G., Petersen, R. C., Kokmen, E., & Kurland, L. T. (1992c). Mayo's Older Americans Normative Studies: Updated AVLT norms for ages 56 to 97. *The Clinical Neuropsychologist, 6* (Suppl.), 83–104.

Ivnik, R. J., Smith, G. E., Tangalos, E. G., Petersen, R. C., Kokmen, E., & Kurland, L. T. (1991). Wechsler Memory Scale (WMS): I.Q. dependent norms for persons age 65 to 97. *Psychological Assessment: A Journal of Consulting and Clinical Psychology, 3*, 156–161.

Kaufman, A. S. (1990). *Assessing adolescent and adult intelligence.* Boston: Allyn & Bacon.

Kaufman, A. S., McLean, J. E., & Reynolds, C. R. (1988). Sex, race, residence, region, and education differences on the 11 WAIS-R subtests. *Journal of Clinical Psychology, 2*, 231–248.

Klonoff, H., & Kennedy, M. (1966). A comparative study of cognitive functioning in old age. *Journal of Gerontology, 21*, 239–243.

Kral, V. C. (1958). Neuro-psychiatric observations in an old peoples home. *Journal of Gerontology, 13*, 169–176.

Labouvie-Vief, G., & Schell, D. A. (1982). Learning and memory in later life. In B. B. Welman (Ed.), *Handbook of developmental psychology.* Englewood Cliffs, NJ: Prentice-Hall.

Labouvie-Vief, G., & Blanchard-Fields, F. (1982). Cognitive ageing and psychological growth. *Ageing and Society, 2 (Pt. 2)*, 183–209.

Larrabee, G. J., Kane, R. L., Schuck, J. R., & Francis, D. J. (1985). Construct validity of various memory testing procedures. *Journal of Clinical and Experimental Neuropsychology, 7*, 239–250.

Mack, J. L., & Carlson, N. J. (1978). Conceptual deficits and aging: The category test. *Perceptual and Motor Skills, 46*, 123–128.

Malec, J. F., Ivnik, R. J., Smith, G. E., Tangalos, E. G., Petersen, R. C., Kokmen, E., & Kurland, L. T. (1992). Mayo's Older Americans Normative Studies: Utility of corrections for age and education for the WAIS-R. *The Clinical Neuropsychologist, 6* (Suppl.), 31–48.

Offenbach, S. I. (1974). A developmental study of hypothesis testing and cue selection strategies. *Developmental Psychology, 10*, 484–490.

Parker, K. C. H. (1983). Factor analysis of the WAIS-R at nine age levels between 16 and 74 years. *Journal of Consulting and Clinical Psychology, 51*, 302–308.

Perlmutter, M., & Nyquist, L. (1990). Relationships between self-reported physical and mental health and intelligence performance across adulthood. *Journal of Gerontology: Psychological Sciences, 45*, 145–155.

Poon, L. W., Fozard, J. L., Cermak, L. S., Arenberg, D., & Thompson, L. W. (Eds.). (1980). *New directions in memory and aging: Proceedings of the George A. Talland memorial conference.* Hillsdale, NJ: Lawrence Erlbaum.

Poon, L. W. (Ed.). (1980). *Aging in the 1980's.* Washington, DC: American Psychological Association.

Poon, L. W. (1985). Differences in human memory with aging: Nature, causes, and clinical implications. In J. E. Birren & K. W. Schaie (Eds.), *Handbook of the psychology of aging* (2nd ed.). New York: Van Nostrand.

Prigatano, G. P. (1978). Wechsler Memory Scale: A selective review of the literature. *Journal of Clinical Psychology, 34*, 816–832.

Reese, H. W., & Rodeheaver, D. (1985). Problem solving and complex decision making. In J. E. Birren & K. W. Schaie (Eds.), *Handbook of the psychology of aging* (2nd ed.). New York: Van Nostrand.

Rey, A. (1964). *L'examen clinique en pscyhologie*. Paris: Presses Universitaires de France.

Reynolds, C. R., Chastain, R. L., Kaufman, A. S., & McLean, J. E. (1987). Demographic characteristics and IQ among adults: Analysis of the WAIS-R standardization sample as a function of the stratification variables. *Journal of School Psychology, 25*, 223–242.

Roid, G. H., Prifitera, A., & Ledbetter, M. (1988). Confirmatory analysis of the factor structure of the Wechsler Memory Scale-Revised. *The Clinical Neuropsychologist, 2*, 116–120.

Roth, D. L., Conboy, T. J., Reeder, K. P., & Boll, T. J. (1990). Confirmatory factor analysis of the Wechsler Memory Scale-Revised in a sample of head-injured patients. *Journal of Clinical and Experimental Neuropsychology, 12*, 834–842.

Royston, J. P. (1982). An extension of Shapiro and Wilk's W test for normality to large samples. *Applied Statistics, 31*, 115–124.

Ryan, J. J., Paolo, A. M., & Brungardt, T. M. (1990). Standardization of the Wechsler Adult Intelligence Scale-Revised for persons 75 years and older. *Psychological Assessment, 2*, 404–411.

Ryan, J. J., Paolo, A. M., & Findley, P. G. (1991). Percentile rank conversion tables for WAIS-R IQs at six educational levels. *Journal of Clinical Psychology, 47*, 104–107.

Salthouse, T. A. (1982). *Adult cognition: An experimental psychology of human aging*. New York: Springer.

Sanders, J. A. C., Sterns, H. L., Smith, M., & Sanders, R. E. (1975). Modification of concept identification performance in older adults. *Developmental Psychology, 11*, 824–829.

Sanders, R. E., Sanders, J. A. C., Mayes, G. J., & Sielski, K. A. (1976). Enhancement of conjunctive concept attainment in older adults. *Developmental Psychology, 12*, 485–486.

Schaie, K. W., & Parham, I. A. (1977). Cohort-sequential analysis of adult intellectual development. *Developmental Psychology, 13*, 649–653.

Searight, H. R., Dunn, E. J., Grisso, T., Margolis, R. B., & Gibbons, J. L. (1989). The relation of the Halstead-Reitan neuropsychological battery to ratings of everyday functioning in a geriatric sample. *Neuropsychology, 3*, 135–145.

Siegler, I. C., & Costa, P. (1985). Health behavior relationships. In J. E. Birren & K. W. Schaie (Eds.), *Handbook of the psychology of aging* (2nd ed.). New York: Van Nostrand.

Smith, G. E., Ivnik, R. J., Malec, J. F., Petersen, R. C., Tangalos, E. G., & Kurland, L. T. (1992). Mayo's Older American Normative Studies (MOANS): Factor structure of a core battery. *Psychological Assessment, 4*, 382–390.

Smith, G. E., Malec, J. F., & Ivnik, R. J. (1992), Validity of the construct of nonverbal memory: A factor analytic study in a normal elderly sample. *Journal of Clinical and Experimental Neuropsychology, 14*, 211–221.

Smith, G. E., Ivnik, R. J., Petersen, R. C., Malec, J. F., Kokmen, E., & Tangalos, E. (1991). Age-Associated Memory Impairment diagnoses: Problems of reliability and concerns for terminology. *Psychology and Aging, 6*, 551–558.

Spreen, O., & Strauss, E. (1991). *A compendium of neuropsychological tests: Administration, norms, and commentary*. New York: Oxford.

Taub, H. A. (1979). Comprehension and memory of prose materials by young and old adults. *Experimental Aging Research, 5*, 3–13.

Trahan, D. E., & Quintana, J. W. (1990). Analysis of gender effects upon verbal and visual memory performance in adults. *Archives of Clinical Neuropsychology, 5*, 325–334.

Trahan, D. E., Quintana, J., Willingham, A. C., & Goethe, K. D. (1988). The visual reproduction subtest: Standardization and clinical validation of a delayed recall procedure. *Archives of Clinical Neuropsychology, 2*, 29–39.

Wechsler, D. (1945). A standardized memory scale for clinical use. *Journal of Psychology, 19*, 87–95.

Wechsler, D. A. (1981). *Wechsler Adult Intelligence Scale-Revised*. New York: Psychological Corporation.

Wechsler, D. A. (1987). *Wechsler Memory Scale-Revised*. New York: Psychological Corporation.

Willis, L., Yeo, R. A., Thomas, P., & Garry, P. J. (1988). Differential declines in cognitive functioning with aging: The possible role of health status. *Developmental Neuropsychology, 4*, 23–28.

3

Behavioral and Affective Disturbances in Alzheimer's Disease

David W. Gilley

Neuropsychological studies of Alzheimer's disease (AD) have primarily focused on cognition, particularly memory and language disorders. Although complex disturbances of emotion and behavior have been recognized as part of the syndrome since Alzheimer's original case report in 1907, these disturbances have only recently been systematically investigated. A number of factors probably contributed to this broadening of horizons. Noncognitive disturbances are common presenting complaints (Rabins, Mace, & Lucas, 1982) and may impact decisions for institutionalization (Knopman, Kitto, Deinard, & Heiring, 1988; Steele, Rovner, Chase, & Folstein, 1990). Unlike cognitive dysfunction, these disturbances may also respond to existing pharmacological treatments (Schneider, Pollock, & Lyness, 1990). Finally, clinicopathological studies can shed light on the biological substrate of these phenomena (e.g., Palmer, Stratmann, Procter, & Bowen, 1988; Zweig et al., 1988) with implications for understanding symptoms associated with psychiatric disorders.

This area of inquiry, however, is not for the faint of heart. A host of nebulous concepts float over murky measurement waters. With the exception of psychiatric symptoms, there is no inherited body of theoretical concepts or experimental paradigms comparable to those used to study cognition in AD. The principal data are largely derived from observations by caregiver informants who must contend with the disruptive influences of these behaviors on a daily basis. Furthermore, the study populations are not random samples of affected individuals with AD; rather, the behavioral disturbances of interest are frequently the same features that bring these individuals to medical attention (Rabins et al., 1982). The natural history of noncognitive behavioral disturbances cannot be studied free from potential interference by pharmacological interventions. Thus, this area of inquiry requires some willing suspension of disbelief, and there is considerable temptation for the rigid empiricist to dismiss the data out of hand.

This review will first address the problem of measurement. Second, salient research in three broad areas of noncognitive disturbances in AD will be reviewed: depression, psychotic symptoms, and other behavioral abnormalities. Within each area, a primary focus will be the relationship between these disturbances and cognitive dysfunction, because most research to date has examined this question.

Only a very sparse mosaic of the correlates with other patient and clinical variables, care-related outcomes, and neurophysiological variables can be provided. The focus will be primarily limited to AD because there is not sufficient data to address differential patterns of disturbance across diagnostic lines.

The Problem of Measurement

The greatest obstacle to the systematic study of behavioral and affective disturbances in AD and other dementia syndromes is measurement. Widely accepted, standardized instrumentation for these disturbances does not currently exist. This development is crucial to clinical applications and scientific study. The problems of measurement of these noncognitive disturbances go well beyond the traditional lack of rigorous psychometric data on neuropsychological measures of cognition. The fundamental issues center around sampling of behavioral content, time, and sources of information; scaling severity; and metric standards of reliability and validity.

Sampling Issues

Behavioral Content

One central problem has been an inadequate specification of the domain of behavioral disturbances in dementia. Previous studies have included behaviors pertaining to "functional status" or activities of daily living (e.g., changes in personal hygiene, dressing) (Swearer, Drachman, O'Donnell, & Mitchell, 1988; Teri, Hughes, & Larson, 1990; Zarit, Reever, & Bach-Peterson, 1980), behavioral manifestations of cognitive dysfunction (e.g., failure to recognize familiar faces, incoherent speech) (Penn, Martin, Wilson, Fox, & Savoy, 1988; Zarit et al., 1980), vegetative disturbances (e.g., sleep disturbances, change in eating patterns) (Reisberg et al., 1987; Swearer et al., 1988), psychiatric symptoms (e.g., depression, delusions, hallucinations) (Cummings, Miller, Hill, & Neshkes, 1987; Merriam, Aronson, Gaston, Wey, & Katz, 1988; Reisberg et al., 1987; Rovner, Broadhead, Spencer, Carson, & Folstein, 1989; Teri, Larson, & Reifler, 1988; Swearer et al., 1988), and subtle alterations of "personality" (Petry, Cummings, Hill, & Shapira, 1988; Rubin, Morris, Storandt, & Berg, 1987a). The lack of clear conceptual boundaries probably reflects an implicit assumption that these diverse disturbances stem from the same underlying disease processes and may, in fact, be collinear. Unidimensionality may eventually be demonstrated in AD among the domains of cognition, physical function, behavior, and emotion. At present, however, the weight of the evidence is to the contrary (Gilley, Wilson, Bennett, Bernard, & Fox, 1991a; Teri, Borson, Kiyak, & Yamagishi, 1989).

Excluding obvious manifestations of cognition and physical function, six general categories of behavioral disturbance are consistently reported in AD patients: depression, psychotic symptoms (hallucinations, delusions), agitation, apathy, irritable affect/aggressiveness, and inappropriate actions. Disorders of emotion are classified as behavioral disturbances because emotional states are inferred from behavior. There is general consensus on the defining features of depression and psychotic symptoms. However, inconsistent or conflicting definitions of target behaviors plague the remaining areas.

The domain of agitation provides a case in point. In a review of agitation, Cohen-Mansfield and Billig (1986) defined agitation as "inappropriate verbal, vocal, or motor activity that is not explained by needs or confusion" (p. 712). This broad categorization would encompass most forms of behavior disturbance described in dementia patients. Others have treated agitation, wandering, and restlessness as separable, distinct dimensions (Teri et al., 1988), or adopted a covariance structure that defines agitation as a hybridization of irritability, wandering, and sexual misdemeanor (Rubin et al., 1987a).

Observation Period

The probability of detecting a target behavior and estimates of relative frequency of occurrence depend on the length of an observation period. For example, a sporadic behavior pattern with mean occurrence of once per week will be easily captured in retrospective recall of the past 6 months, but may not be recorded during a 24-hour observation period. No consistent observation period has been utilized in previous studies of behavioral disturbances in AD. With the endpoint fixed at the time of data collection, the range of observation periods include the entire disease course, the period from first evaluation, the period from previous evaluation, a fixed interval (e.g., 4 weeks, 24 hours), and not specified.

Source

The study of abnormal patterns of thought, emotion, and behavior is hardly unique to dementia syndromes. Numerous self-report and psychiatric rating scales have been developed for these areas. However, these instruments typically rely heavily on the patient to describe the range, intensity, and duration of symptoms. This strategy is both valuable and defensible in the individuals with grossly intact cognitive function. In dementia syndromes, where cognitive dysfunction is a defining feature, the accuracy of patient report is suspect, particularly at more severe levels of impairment.

The potential limitation of self-report instrumentation is illustrated in a recent study of the validity of the Geriatric Depression Scale (GDS) in AD (Burke, Houston, Boust, & Roccaforte, 1989). This study compared sensitivity and specificity for the spectrum of possible scores on the GDS referenced against the clinical diagnosis of major depressive disorder. In 70 cognitively intact elderly outpatients (15 with major depression), optimal cutoff scores ranging from 14 to 16 correctly classified approximately 80% of sample. In 72 AD patients (10 cases of depression) with mild cognitive impairment (mean Mini-Mental State Examination [MMSE] score of 18.5), no GDS cutoff score exceeded chance levels of classification. Although sample size is small, these data suggest some fundamental distortion of expected response patterns on the GDS in AD patients with relatively mild cognitive impairment.

Patient report has largely been abandoned in the study of affective and behavioral disturbances in dementia syndromes. Most recent studies of depression in AD have relied on surrogate informants, typically the patient's primary caregiver (Knesevich, Martin, & Berg, 1983; Merriam et al., 1988), chart review (Rovner et al., 1989), or both sources (Cummings et al., 1987). Structured interview methods for depression using informant report have begun to appear (Alexopoulos, Abrams, Young, & Shamoian, 1988; Sunderland et al., 1988). Recent information on behavioral disturbances in AD has also been derived from these sources (*surrogates*: Gilley et al., 1991a; Rubin et al., 1987a; Rubin, Morris, & Berg, 1987b; Teri et al., 1989; *chart review*: Reisberg et al., 1987; *combined surrogates/chart review*: Cummings et al., 1987; Teri et al., 1988).

Informant methods make it possible to bypass patient report to monitor the patient over the course of the disease, and assess target behavior within a naturalistic setting, thereby ensuring at least modest ecologically valid inferences. However, this approach constrains information collected to specific, readily observable behaviors. Furthermore, the utility depends on reliable abstraction techniques.

Scaling Severity

A variety of schemes have been employed to scale the severity of behavioral disturbances. Simple summation of target behaviors present during an observation period provides a logical index of behavior "load" (Penn et al., 1988; Teri et al., 1989). One advantage of this approach is that there is no added complexity of informant decisions beyond the presence-absence dichotomy. Summary scores across behavioral domains, however, may be difficult to interpret unless behavior disturbance in AD is unidimensional. Frequency estimation requires a more complex judgment by informants, possibly at the expense of reliability, and is only defensible for relatively discrete events. Ranks, reflecting different categories of event frequency, have been adopted in previous applications (Gilley et al., 1991a; Zarit et al., 1980) in lieu of absolute counts. Well-defined anchors for frequency ranks are needed to generate a meaningful metric.

Grading intensity requires comparative judgment of behaviors and existing data on behavioral disturbances are not sufficient for empirical derivation of intensity dimensions. As an alternative, one study (Reisberg et al., 1987) scaled intensity using correlative behavioral features (e.g., violence toward others as a result of persecutory ideation) or responses to the behaviors by caregivers (e.g., restraint for purposeless activity). Nonanchored intensity ratings have also been used (Swearer et al., 1988).

Duration, a viable alternative to scaling continuously expressed behavior patterns, has rarely been applied. Gilley et al. (1991a) attempted to scale manifestations of apathy using an estimation of the proportion of time that a given behavior pattern was expressed. At best, this represents a crude approximation of duration.

Each of these approaches to scaling severity may have some utility in differentiating levels of disturbance across patients and time. The available applications, however, have not been empirically driven. Furthermore, the longer the retrospective observation period, the more difficult many of these discriminations will become for informants. The apparent contribution of severity ratings to the short-term instability of measures of physical function in one recent study (Smith et al., 1990) serves as a useful reminder of the potential cost of complexity.

Psychometric Standards

Reliability

Measurement error is inextricably tied to the data source. Unreliability in self-report measures in AD patients was previously discussed. Circumvention of the patient, however, introduces additional sources of error. First, reproducible data necessitates the application of consistent abstraction techniques whether from patient records or interview with informants. Information on reliability from chart review studies is sparse other than implied consensus among two independent reviewers. Consistency in the original recording of information into charts is unknown, particularly in the absence of standard forms. Similar issues apply to the use of interviewers for informant-report methods. Cross-training procedures and frequent reliability checks should be minimum standards.

The second major source of error concerns informants. The uncontrolled nature of observations by informants, typically caregivers of the patient, may limit temporal stability. Temporal stability is influenced by random error and changes in the underlying disease processes. In measures of cognition, the random error component is limited by holding stimulus factors constant. By contrast, the stimulus situations affecting the expression of behavioral disturbances cannot be fixed. Likewise, the length and timing of observations is determined by patient contact rather than a structured protocol. These factors will inflate random error and increase the probability of Type II inferential error in cross-sectional and longitudinal research. Unfortunately, there are no data on the short-term stability of measures of behavioral disturbances in AD.

In addition to the random error component, there may also be systematic recall biases associated with informant report. Recall bias has been documented for surrogate informants in epidemiological studies of psychiatric symptomatology (Thompson, Orvaschel, Prusoff, & Kidd, 1982; Weissman, Kidd, & Prusoff, 1982) and other medical disorders (Pickle, Brown, & Blot, 1983). Similar bias may also exist for informant report of noncognitive symptomatology in AD. Gilley and Wilson (1991) found small but statistically significant differences between spouse and child informants in the reported severity of several types of noncognitive symptomatology.

Validity

The study of behavior disturbances in AD using informant report has been launched without any attempt to demonstrate the validity of inferences based on a given measurement. On the one hand, few independent criteria have been identified to serve as suitable "gold standards" for dimensions of behavior. However, Goldfried (1977) has eloquently described the process by which assessment procedures develop a life of their own in the absence of an identified gold standard. Previous use, correlation with similar measures, comparison against "expert" judgment, and covariance structure analyses are all useful to perpetuate the myth of adequacy.

At a minimum, the reproducibility of the ordinal scaling of particular behavioral attributes generated from uncontrolled observation methods needs to be established. Direct observation measures as standards of comparison are also readily available for a number of behavioral areas. For example, ambulatory recording devices (e.g., Redmond & Hegge, 1985) provide quantifiable and relatively un-obtrusive recording of patient activity levels over a continuous period.

Depression

The relationship between depression and Alzheimer's disease is complicated by the potential role of depression as a competing source of cognitive impairment in the elderly. Although the term *pseudodementia* has fallen from favor (Reifler, 1986), the choice between *dementia syndrome of depression* (DSD) (Folstein & McHugh, 1978) and *AD with depression* remains problematic because the two conditions share clinical features, including cognitive impairment. Nonetheless, attempts to draw rigid, exclusive boundaries between these conditions may not be productive.

The dementia syndrome of depression is potentially reversible (Folstein & McHugh, 1978; Rabins, Merchant, Nestadt, 1984) compared to the progressive deterioration of cognition in AD. Evidence of significant diagnostic confusion between DSD and AD is largely derived from inpatient psychiatric settings. In two seminal studies (Nott & Fleminger, 1975; Ron, Toone, Garralda, & Lishman, 1979), depression and other psychiatric disorders were common in patients diag-nosed as having organic brain syndrome without clear-cut neuropsychological evi-dence of progressive decline.

The diagnostic conundrum associated with the comorbidity of depression and dementia has less frequently been encountered in noninstitutional settings. In ter-tiary diagnostic centers, depression is typically identified as the probable basis for dementia in less than 5% of cases (Clarfield, 1988). In one of the few prospective studies of patients with the clinical diagnosis of dementia, Larson, Reifler, Feath-erstone, and English (1984) found evidence of depression in only 1 of 107 outpa-tients. Finally, in a recent community-based epidemiological study of dementia (Evans et al., 1989), DSD also accounted for less than 1% of cases.

Irrespective of the base rates of misclassification with respect to AD, clinically significant alterations of cognition in conjunction with depression in late life may not be benign. Evidence of cerebral atrophy (Nott & Fleminger, 1975; Ron et al., 1979) and abnormal patterns of electrophysiological activity (Ron et al., 1979) are common in DSD cases. Furthermore, increased brain ventricular size in late-life depression relative to that seen in aged controls has consistently been reported in computed tomography (CT) studies (see Pearlson et al., 1989). Leukoariosis on CT (Coffey et al., 1988) and high-signal white matter lesions on magnetic resonance imaging (MRI) (Zubenko et al., 1990) may also be more common in late-life depression. Finally, depressive disorders are common in diverse diseases of the central nervous system such as cerebrovascular disease (Robinson, Kubos, Starr, Rao, & Price, 1984; see also Chapter 14), Parkinson's disease (Mayeux, Stern, Rosen, & Levanthal, 1981; see also Chapter 11), Huntington's disease (Folstein, Folstein, & McHugh, 1975a), multiple sclerosis (Devins & Seland, 1987), pro-gressive supranuclear palsy (Albert, Feldman, & Willis, 1974), and normal pressure hydrocephalus (Price & Tucker, 1977).

Finally, there are several lines of evidence suggesting that depression may be associated with increased risk for the subsequent development of AD. Depression has been identified as a common presenting complaint in AD patients (Liston, 1977). Furthermore, the frequency of premorbid depressive disorders has been shown to be elevated in AD patients relative to nondemented controls (Agbayewa, 1986), particularly in the 10-year period prior to the onset of dementia (Broe et al., 1990; Reding, Haycox, & Blass, 1985). Finally, Kral, and Emery (1989) have reported the eventual development of AD in 39 of 44 elderly patients with reversible cognitive deficits associated with depression after 4 to 18 years of follow-up.

Taken together, the available evidence does not unequivocally support any strong position on the pathological significance of late-life depression and associated cognitive deficits. Suspicion of comorbid AD or other neurological disease in no way precludes aggressive treatment of depression. Likewise, it is also prudent to recognize that cognitive deficits do not lose clinical significance in association with depression. There is no logical or empirical basis to assume that depression provides any protection against AD or other neurological disorders.

Depression in AD

Symptoms of depression are common in patients with the clinical diagnosis of AD (Burke, Rubin, Morris, & Berg, 1988; Lazarus, Newton, Cohler, Lesser, & Schweon, 1987; Merriam et al., 1988). With the exception of suicidal ideation, the point prevalent rate of most symptoms exceeds 10%. Apart from manifestations of cognitive dysfunction, symptoms with the highest base rate of occurrence are changes in activity patterns (increased gross motor activity, decreased spontaneous participation in complex activities), sleep and diurnal cycle alterations, and mood disturbances (dysphoria or irritability).

There is little consensus, however, regarding the frequency of depressive disorders in AD. The range of estimates reported in 20 available studies (see Table 3.1) is vast (0%–86%), although most fall within the 10% to 50% range. There is no apparent relationship to time of study despite significant shifts in methodology over the 50-year period covered by this research. Prior to 1980, most studies were reporting retrospective chart review data on patients drawn from inpatient settings. The diagnosis of AD was primarily restricted to patients with presenile onset (<age 65) during this period. By contrast, studies appearing after 1980 assessed concurrent depressive features through direct evaluation of the patient or through informant report, applied standard criteria for the diagnosis of depressive disorders (American Psychiatric Association, 1980, 1987) and AD (American Psychiatric Association, 1980; McKhann et al., 1984), and generally used samples drawn from outpatient cohorts.

All of the available evidence on the frequency of depressive disorders in AD has come from "samples of convenience," which are subject to unknown referral biases. There is sufficient evidence to assume that significant depression may occur in patients with clinically typical AD, but the prevalence and incidence of depression is unknown.

Evidence of a systematic relationship between the severity of cognitive impairment and the presence of clinically significant depression was reported by Reifler, Larson, and Hanley (1982). In this cross-sectional study of diagnostically heterogeneous outpatients, depression was more common in mildly impaired patients (33%) than among severely impaired patients (10%). Subsequent studies of depres-

TABLE 3.1. Frequency of Depression in Alzheimer's Disease

Study	Sample Size	Cases with Depression (%)	Patient Source	Data Source[a]
Rothschild (1941)	31[b]	0 (0.0)	Inpatient, psychiatry	CT
Goodman (1953)	23[b]	5 (21.7)	Inpatient, psychiatry	CT
Ziegler (1954)	40	6 (15.0)	Inpatient, general	CT
Sim & Susman (1962)	22[b]	12 (54.5)	Inpatient, psychiatry	CT
Rosenstock (1970)	11	4 (36.4)	Inpatient, psychiatry	CT
Birkett (1972)	10[b]	1 (10.0)	Inpatient, psychiatry	PT
Gustafson (1975)	57	17 (30.0)	Outpatient, dementia referrals	PT
Nott & Fleminger (1975)	15	6 (40.0)	Inpatient, psychiatry	CT
Liston (1977)	50	8 (16.0)	Inpatient, psychiatry	CT
Ron et al. (1979)	33	10 (30.0)	Inpatient, psychiatry	CT
Bucht & Adolfsson (1983)	18	2 (11.1)	Outpatient, dementia referrals	PT
Kral (1983)	40	6 (15.0)	Inpatient, psychiatry	CT/PT
Knesevich et al. (1983)	30	0 (0.0)	Outpatient, dementia referrals	PT
Reding et al. (1985)	99	19 (19.2)	Outpatient, dementia referrals	PT
Reifler et al. (1986)	131	41 (31.3)	Outpatient, dementia referrals	PT
Cummings et al. (1987)	30	5 (16.6)	Outpatient, dementia referrals	PT/SO/CT
Lazarus et al. (1987)	42	17 (40.4)	Outpatient, study referrals	PT
Merriam et al. (1988)	175	150 (85.9)	Outpatient, dementia referrals	SO
Rovner et al. (1989)	144	24 (16.6)	Outpatient, dementia referrals	CT
Mackenzie et al. (1989)	36	18 (50.0)	Outpatient, dementia referrals	SO
Totals	1,037	351 (33.8)		
Mean frequency		27.0		
Median frequency		20.5		

[a]CT = chart; PT = patient; SO = significant other.
[b]Postmortem diagnosis of Alzheimer's disease.

sion in AD, however, have failed to replicate this finding of an inverse relationship between dementia severity and depression (Lazarus et al., 1987; Merriam et al., 1988; Reifler, Larson, Teri, & Poulson, 1986; Rovner et al., 1989). Furthermore, cognitive function was unchanged after resolution of depressive symptomatology in several reports (Reifler et al., 1986, Reifler et al., 1989). These data provide no compelling evidence that the presence of depression exacerbates cognitive dysfunction in AD. Likewise, the presence of severe cognitive impairment does not apparently alter the probability of expression of depressive symptomatology.

No difference in the rate of cognitive progression for depressed and nondepressed AD patients has been reported. Lopez, Boller, Becker, Miller, and Reynolds (1990) found no difference on any measure in an extensive battery of neuropsychological tests at 12-month retest for 10 depressed and 10 nondepressed patients matched on initial mental status. Similar findings were reported by Reifler et al. (1986) with a longer follow-up observation period (average interval of 18 months). These data fail to replicate the principal findings of Nott and Fleminger (1975) and Ron et al. (1979) on the lack of cognitive progression in patients with comorbid depression. However, an important difference in the recent studies is the application of specific diagnostic criteria for AD. Evidence of impaired recent memory performance has been treated as a necessary, albeit not sufficient, condition for the diagnosis of AD (e.g., McKhann et al., 1984). Differences in retention may facilitate the separation of AD with depression from the dementia syndrome of depression (Hart, Kwentus, Taylor, & Hamer, 1987a; Hart, Kwentus, Taylor, & Harkins, 1987b).

One important question regarding depression in AD is the functional equivalence to the psychiatric variant uncomplicated by dementia. Anecdotal reports suggest that depressive symptomatology, in particular the dominant expression of mood, may be highly variable (Merriam et al., 1988). Complementary data has been reported by Reifler et al. (1989). In this double-blind comparison of imipramine and placebo in AD, parallel resolution of depressive symptomatology was observed at the end of 8 weeks for drug and placebo conditions. The only other study of the course of depression in AD, however, found minimal change in symptom severity at the end of 12 months (Lopez et al., 1990).

The influence of premorbid function on the heterogeneity of clinical expression in AD has not received much empirical scrutiny. Premorbid psychiatric history, particularly depression, may increase the probability that depression will develop during the course of AD. Rovner et al. (1989) reported that approximately one third of their AD patients with depression had a premorbid psychiatric history, a threefold increase over the rate for nondepressed patients. Furthermore, the rate of family history of psychiatric disorders is also reportedly elevated in depressed AD patients (Pearlson et al., 1990).

Premorbid factors may predispose some AD patients to develop depressive symptomatology after the onset of dementia. However, the majority of cases with depression have no remarkable premorbid historical features. Preliminary data (Gilley, Bennett, Grosse, & Wilson, 1990) suggest that the idiopathic development of depression in AD may be associated with early age at onset. In a case-control study, 26 AD patients were identified with coexistent major depressive disorder and matched to 26 AD without depression. Only cases with clinically typical AD with psychometric evidence of progressive cognitive decline on multiple evaluations were selected. Cases and controls were matched on global cognitive function using Mini-Mental State Examination (Folstein, Folstein, & McHugh, 1975b) scores. Of dimensions putatively related to clinical heterogeneity in AD, only dementia onset prior to age 65 was differentially related to depression (see Table 3.2). This relationship has not been reported in other studies of depression in AD, but prior research has not excluded patients with a premorbid history of psychiatric disorders. An association between depression and age at onset, if replicated, is noteworthy because of morphologic and neurochemical alterations associated with age at onset in AD (Crow et at., 1984; Brane et al., 1989; Zubenko et al., 1989).

Degenerative changes within subcortical aminergic nuclei have been suggested as one possible factor in the development of depression in AD (Liston, Jarvik, & Gerson, 1987). Zweig et al. (1988) evaluated this hypothesis in 21 AD patients, eight of whom had documented evidence of major depression during the course of the disease. The presence of depression was associated with significantly greater

TABLE 3.2.   Results of Case-Control Study of Possible Associations Between Major Depressive Disorder and Risk Factors in AD

Risk Factors	Discordant Pairs + −	Discordant Pairs − +	Concordant Pairs + +	Concordant Pairs − −	Matched Pairs, Odds Ratio	χ^2_{mh}[a]	p
Onset < 65	11	2	4	9	5.5	4.9	.027
Extrapyramidal signs	6	1	5	14	6.0	3.2	.074
White matter lesions on MRI[b]	4	6	2	14	.7	.1	.752
Family history of dementia	4	7	5	10	.6	.4	.527

[a]Mantel-Haenszel chi-square (χ^2) procedure with 1 degree of freedom (*df*).
[b]MRI = magnetic resonance imaging.

neuronal loss at the midlevel of the locus ceruleus and the rostral section of the central superior nucleus of the raphe. The specificity of these differences is unknown and there was a trend toward greater neuronal loss in patients with depression at other levels of the locus ceruleus and the dorsal raphe in this study. Zubenko and Moossy (1988) failed to demonstrate any association between depression and cell loss in the locus ceruleus, but these results are difficult to interpret because the sample included non-AD patients and used only a five-point ranking of neuronal loss as opposed to the more direct estimation procedure of Zweig et al. (1988). However, independent support for the role of the locus ceruleus in depression comes from a study of patients with Parkinson's disease. Chan-Palay and Asan (1989) reported greater neuronal loss at the rostral level and midlevel of the locus ceruleus in patients with depression. The rostral locus ceruleus is the source of primary noradrenergic projections to the neocortex and hippocampus, and the raphe is the source of primary serotonergic projections. At this point, the data seem to support the hypothesis that depletion of these cell populations during the course of AD may be associated with the development of depression.

Psychotic Symptoms

Persecutory ideation and possible auditory hallucinations were described in the original case report by Alzheimer (1907). Numerous studies subsequently documented the presence of delusions and hallucinations in AD (Cummings, 1985; Cummings et al., 1987; Goodman, 1953; Sim & Susman, 1962). Delusions in AD are typically simple persecutory ideas reflected in accusations of theft or malicious intent (Cummings, 1985). More complex, systematized thought disturbances have been reported (e.g., Cummings et al., 1987; Drevets & Rubin, 1989), but are rare. Hallucinations indirectly manifest themselves as verbal reports of sensory experiences not corroborated by others present.

Several recent reports link the psychotic symptoms of hallucinations and delusions to dementia severity and rate of progression in AD. Cross-sectional studies generally report higher rates of these symptoms in patients with greater cognitive impairment (Drevets & Rubin, 1989; Gilley, Whalen, Wilson, & Bennett, 1991b;

Mayeux, Stern, & Spanton, 1985; Merriam et al., 1988; Stern, Mayeux, Sano, Hauser, & Bush, 1987), although contradictory evidence exists (Cummings et al., 1987; Teri et al., 1988). However, the form of the relationship to cognitive impairment may differ for hallucinations and delusions. For hallucinations, the prevalence appears to increase with greater levels of cognitive impairment in approximately linear fashion (Drevets & Rubin, 1989; Gilley et al., 1991b; Teri et al., 1988). By contrast, a curvilinear pattern has been identified for delusions (Drevets & Rubin, 1989; Swearer et al., 1988).

The complex relationship between psychotic symptoms and cognitive impairment can be illustrated using data from 230 outpatients with probable AD (McKhann et al., 1984), 21 of whom had postmortem confirmation of the clinical diagnosis. In addition to the clinical diagnosis of AD, these patients were not currently receiving psychotropic medications and lived with the primary caregiver. A detailed description of sample selection, diagnostic evaluation, and subject characteristics may be found in Gilley et al. (1991b). The presence of delusions and hallucinations in the preceding 4 weeks was assessed using a structured interview with the primary caregiver. Figure 3.1 presents the proportion of the sample exhibiting hallucinations (HALL), delusions (DEL), and either symptom (ANY SX) at five score levels on the MMSE: 0–5 (n = 53), 6–10 (n = 51), 11–15 (n = 48), 16–20 (n = 39), and 21–25 (n = 39). Despite apparent asymptote in the probability of hallucinations in the severe dementia ranges (MMSE ≤ 10), a linear logit regression model (3.41 + .49 × MMSE Severity Level) adequately fit the observed data (Likelihood Ratio = 1.8, df = 3, p = .62). By contrast, the linear logit model for delusions (4.57 − .05 × MMSE Severity Level) fit the data poorly (Likelihood Ratio = 7.7, df = 3, p = .05) with a sharp decrement in the frequency of delusions at the most severe range (MMSE ≤ 5). Finally, a linear logit model (4.37 + .18 × MMSE Severity Level) marginally fit the data for the presence of any psychotic symptoms (Likelihood Ratio = 3.9, df = 3, p = .27).

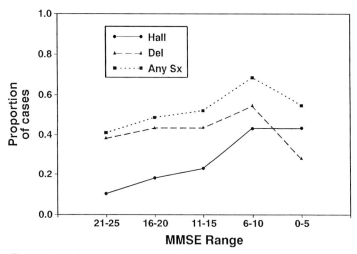

FIGURE 3.1. Proportion of cases reporting hallucinations (HALL), delusions (DEL), or any perceptual abnormality at different levels of dementia severity on the Mini-Mental State Examination (MMSE).

The correlation between psychotic symptoms and cognitive impairment in cross-sectional studies suggests some link to the disease process, but a more direct effect of cognition on symptom ascertainment cannot be ruled out. Delusions and hallucinations are largely reflected in verbalizations by the patient. The semantic integrity of these verbalizations as reliable expressions of experiential phenomena is uncertain in the context of progressive deterioration of diverse cognitive processes.

Available longitudinal data, however, suggest that the relationship between psychotic symptoms and cognitive impairment may not be entirely artifact. Independent studies have demonstrated more rapid decline in cognition among AD patients with psychotic symptoms early in the course of the disease (Drevets & Rubin, 1989; Stern et al., 1987). The same pattern was observed in another study (Teri et al., 1990), but was not statistically significant. Specific alterations in neural substrate that might account for these observations have not been identified.

Beyond cognition, psychotic symptoms have only been associated with two other clinical features. Mayeux (Mayeux et al., 1985; Stern et al., 1987) reported a higher frequency of psychotic symptoms in AD patients with extrapyramidal signs (EPS). Subsequent studies have replicated this finding (Gilley et al., 1991a; Gilley et al., 1991b) and demonstrated an association between psychotic symptoms and the severity of other behavioral symptoms (Gilley et al., 1991b; Lopez et al., 1991), particularly indices of irritable affect.

Several studies have examined neuropathological and neurochemical correlates of psychotic symptoms in AD. In a study of aminergic nuclei in AD, Zweig et al. (1988) reported that the presence of hallucinations was not related to the density of neuritic plaques or neurofibrillary tangles in the locus ceruleus or medial raphe. Alzheimer's disease patients with psychotic symptoms were, however, found to have more neuritic plaques in the subicular subfield of the hippocampus and a decrement in serotonergic metabolites in multiple brain regions in another recent study (Zubenko et al., 1991). These studies stratified patients on the basis of the presence of psychotic symptoms at any time during the disease course to evaluate pathophysiological correlates. Our group (Bennett, Gilley, Cochran, Wilson, & Mufson, 1992) took a different approach in evaluating the possible role of the substantia nigra in the covariance between EPS and psychotic symptoms reported in previous work. This study compared behavioral disturbances at initial clinical examination in nine patients with pathologically verified AD and nine patients with pathologically verified AD and Parkinson's disease (PD), matched in age and dementia severity. Postmortem diagnosis of PD required cell loss, gliosis, and Lewy bodies in the substantia nigra. Psychotic symptoms (specifically, hallucinations) were more frequent in AD/PD patients; pathological differences between these groups were confined to degenerative changes in the substantia nigra and locus ceruleus. Taken together, these studies support a role of aminergic systems in the generation of psychotic symptoms in AD, but fail to provide convergent evidence for pathogenesis of these behaviors.

Other Behavioral Disturbances

Apathy

Kleist (1934) identified two mirror-image syndromes in patients with frontal lobe damage. The *apathetico-akinetico-abulic* syndrome described patients with decreased awareness of internal and external sources of stimulation, decreased emotional and behavioral responsiveness to environmental stimuli, and decreased spontaneous initiation of activity. The apposing hyperkinetic-impulsive syndrome covered a similarly wide spectrum: increased and poorly modulated patterns of emotion, motor activity, and behavior. The anatomical correlates suggested by Kleist—prefrontal convexity for apathy-hypokinesis and orbital region for impulsivity-hyperkinesis—have undergone subsequent revision and elaboration (Lhermitte, 1986; Luria, 1965; Stuss & Benson, 1984). Similar behavior patterns may also emerge following lesions in the striatum and basal ganglia, which receive projections from the frontal cortex (Cummings, 1986).

The relevance of apathy-hypokinesis to AD is that the prefrontal cortex (Pearson, Esiri, Hiorns, Wilcock, & Powell, 1985) and basal ganglia (Rudelli, Ambler, & Wisniewski, 1985) are involved, particularly in the later stages of this disease. The problem is one of measurement. Unlike other behavioral and affective manifestations, apathy and hypokinesis refer to the diminution of behavior. The informant must, therefore, assess a pattern of diminished response and apparent effort across situations as opposed to the occurrence of discrete events. This is a complex judgment. One further complication is the problem of separating reduced participation in activities due to cognitive impairment from reduced response to stimulation and spontaneous activity patterns. Feedback from caregiver informants and trained interviewers alike at our center invariably suggests some confusion regarding this behavioral domain.

A discernible reduction in initiative and responsiveness commensurate with apathy appears to be ubiquitous in AD (Merriam et al., 1988; Rubin et al., 1987a). In Rubin et al. (1987a), 70% of AD cases with mild cognitive impairment exhibited symptoms of apathy. This figure increased to 93% for cases with severe impairment. Despite this minimal fluctuation in frequency, symptom severity appears to be highly correlated with dementia severity (Gilley et al., 1991a). Nearly 50% of the variance of a composite apathy score was accounted for by measures of cognitive function and physical self-maintenance in this study.

The presence of EPS in AD also appears to be associated with the expression of apathy in AD. In a cross-sectional study of 146 AD patients, Gilley et al. (1991a) reported higher apathy scores in the subgroup with EPS. This relationship was replicated in a second sample stratified by level of cognitive impairment. The potential significance of this observation is that EPS is typically related to degenerative changes in the substantia nigra (e.g., Ditter & Mirra, 1987).

Agitation

The boundaries of the concept of agitation are indistinct (see Cohen-Mansfield & Billig, 1986). There is no consensus in target behaviors, no empirical or theoretical justification for a priori behavioral constellations, and a long-standing connotative equivalence to any disruptive behavior in cognitively impaired elderly. Nonetheless, some conceptual label is needed as a referent for increased levels of gross motor movement in AD (Merriam et al., 1988; Reisberg et al., 1987; Rubin et al., 1987a; Teri et al., 1988). As a label of convenience, psychomotor agitation denotes increased levels of motor activity irrespective of dominant affective state.

Indices of psychomotor agitation in AD range from subtle increases in body position during periods of minimal external stimulation, to gross excesses of movement (e.g., pacing the floor). References to "wandering" are common in the literature (Reisberg et al., 1987; Rubin et al., 1987a; Teri et al., 1988; Teri et al., 1989; Zarit et al., 1980). Wandering logically falls within the spectrum of psychomotor agitation, but behavioral definition has often been contaminated with possible consequences such as getting lost. Increased verbal output, reflecting frequency of engagement rather than fluency, is another relevant dimension. Unfortunately, verbal output is difficult to scale independently of aphasia.

Assessment is further complicated by the continuity of motoric activity. For the observer, the task of rating the behavioral components of motoric activity is tantamount to the detection of phase shifts from a moving baseline. The task has been simplified in some rating scales (e.g., Hamilton Rating Scale for depression [Hamilton, 1960]) as an estimate of intensity of activity during a time-limited observation period. This simplification limits generality, as it is unlikely that motor activity is free of situational constraints.

Ambulatory recording devices (e.g., Redmond & Hegge, 1985) are an attractive alternative to the use of indirect measures to record patient activity levels. These devices provide quantifiable and relatively unobtrusive recording over a continuous period. Previous clinical applications in hyperactive children (Porrino et al., 1983), bipolar affective disorder (Weiss, Foster, Reynolds, & Kupfer, 1974), and sleep disorders (Mullaney, Kripke, & Messin, 1980) have been reported. Lieberman, Wurtman, and Teicher (1989) found age and circadian cycle differences in activity patterns recorded in a laboratory environment. Although the use of these monitors is not feasible in routine clinical practice, there are several obvious applications in AD: validation of informant report measures; monitoring pharmacological effects; and testing specific hypotheses regarding circadian cycle, sleep, and activity patterns throughout the disease course.

Data from informant reports indicate some discernible increase in activity levels in 40% to 60% of outpatient AD samples (Merriam et al., 1988; Teri et al., 1988) with no apparent relationship to level of cognitive impairment. By contrast, more severe activity disturbances (pacing, wandering) are less common (Reisberg et al., 1987; Teri et al., 1988; Teri et al., 1989) and modestly associated with greater cognitive impairment (Teri et al., 1988).

An inverse relationship between psychomotor agitation and age/age at onset has been reported in AD (Gilley et al., 1991a). That is, higher levels of motor activity were reported by caregiver informants for younger patients. Reduced activity levels in conjunction with the aging process have been demonstrated (Lieberman et al., 1989). However, it is unclear whether a mean difference of only 10 years could account for detectable differences in levels of activity in Gilley et al. (1991a). A competing explanation for the finding might be differences in the distribution of neuropathological features associated with age at onset (Bondareff et al., 1987; Zubenko et al., 1989).

Irritable Affect

Verbal and physical manifestations of irritable affect are common in AD (Knopman et al., 1988; Kumar, Koss, Metzler, Moore, & Friedland, 1988; Reisberg et al., 1987). The relative frequency of individual behaviors is uncertain given the lack of consistent definitions and assessment techniques. For example, indices of irritable affect were subsumed under the broad category of *agitation* in some studies (Rubin et al., 1987a; Teri et al., 1988). Within the domain of irritable affect, specification ranged from the broad categorization of verbal or physical abuse by the patient (Knopman et al., 1988; Kumar et al., 1988) to specific behavioral referents (Ryden, 1988).

The incidence of the superordinate categories of verbal and physical aggressive behavior in studies of community-dwelling patients with dementia syndromes is summarized in Table 3.3. These studies provide retrospective estimates of the frequency of target behaviors since disease onset. There is surprising consensus on verbal behaviors, but disparity in the estimates for episodes of physical aggression. Diagnostic composition does not appear to be a factor, as the effect for diagnosis within studies was consistently negative (Hamel et al., 1990; Ryden, 1988; Swearer et al., 1988). The low yield of physical aggression in the study with mild AD patients (Kumar et al., 1988) and discrepancy among studies using identical measurement procedures (Hamel et al., 1990; Ryden, 1988) suggest the influence of sample selection factors.

The presence of behavioral indices of irritable affect is modestly correlated with greater cognitive impairment in AD (Gilley et al., 1991a; Knopman et al., 1988) and heterogeneous dementia (Hamel et al., 1990; Ryden, 1988; Swearer et al., 1988) patients. This relationship, however, may hold only for physical aggression (Ryden, 1988; Swearer et al., 1988). This differential association along with evidence of limited correlation between verbal and physical behaviors (Ryden, 1988) challenge the presumed homogeneity of these disturbances.

One facet of the relationship between irritable affect and cognitive impairment is noteworthy. With one exception (Gilley et al., 1991a), most studies report rates of verbal and physical markers of irritable affect that are based on the entire period since disease onset. There are several possible explanations for the relationship between these frequency estimates and current status measures in cross-sectional studies. The presence of significant irritable affect may be related to faster progression similar to the pattern observed for hallucinations. In fact, hallucinations and irritable affect may be closely linked (Gilley et al., 1991b). Second, the behavioral manifestations of irritable affect may not appear until relatively late in the course of the disease. Finally, there may be recency effects in retrospective estimation.

Gilley et al. (1991a) reported an interaction between level of cognitive im-

TABLE 3.3.   Frequency of Verbal and Physical Manifestations of Irritable Affect Since Disease Onset in Dementia Outpatients

Study	N	Verbal	Physical	Diagnosis[a]
Knopman et al. (1985)	88	—	19.3%	Mixed
Reisberg et al. (1987)	57	14.0%	17.5%	AD
Kumar et al. (1988)	28	60.7%	7.1%	AD
Ryden (1988)	183	49.7%	46.4%	Mixed/69% AD
Swearer et al. (1988)	126	50.8%	21.4%	Mixed/45% AD
Hamel et al. (1990)	213	51.0%	34.1%	Mixed/82% AD

[a]AD = Alzheimer's disease. Mixed = heterogeneous diagnosis; percentage with AD is noted if reported.

pairment and age at onset in the expression of irritable affect in AD. Specifically, the behavioral manifestations of irritable affect were more frequent in patients with severe cognitive impairment and early onset of symptoms (≤ 62 years of age). Given the difficulties of precisely establishing onset in AD, this study excluded patients in the border zone surrounding the traditional cutoff of age 65 (i.e., onset between ages 63 and 67).

Apart from cognitive impairment, the only other patient variable associated with irritable affect is premorbid aggressive episodes (Hamel et al., 1990; Ryden, 1988). Unfortunately, there was limited specification of the assessment of pre-morbid aggression and the magnitude of relative risk associated with this variable was not addressed in these studies. The role of situational factors has also been examined. Situations necessitating patient compliance with specific requests is a common thread in anecdotal reports (Hamel et al., 1990; Ryden, 1988). In addition, a disproportionate number of aggressive episodes may be directed at specific in-dividuals (Ryden, 1988). Finally, a higher probability of irritable behaviors at a specific time of day, particularly late evening, has also been noted (Ryden, 1988).

The component behaviors of irritable affect are complex phenomena with multiple potential determinants. With this caution in mind, there are preliminary data suggesting that aggressive behaviors in AD may be associated with region-specific reductions in serotonin. Palmer et al. (1988) reported evidence of sero-tonergic deficit in AD relative to age-matched controls in several areas of frontal (Brodmann area 9) and temporal (Brodmann areas 21, 22, and 38) cortex. In addition, four AD patients with retrospective evidence of aggressive episodes had a significant reduction in serotonin in the orbital frontal region (Brodmann area 11) relative to other AD patients and controls. These observations are interesting in light of the putative role of serotonin in behavioral inhibition and emotional dyscontrol (van Praag, Plutchik, & Comte, 1986). However, there is extensive involvement of many structures in AD that utilize serotonin, including the raphe nuclei (Wilcock, Esiri, Bowen, & Hughes, 1988), amygdala (Brady & Mufson, 1990), and hippocampal formation (Cross et al., 1984). Further work is clearly needed to explore specific topographic differences associated with the control and expression of emotion in this disease.

Higher subjective reports of "burden" (Hamel et al., 1990) and higher rates of aggressive responses to the patient (Hamel et al., 1990; Ryden et al., 1988) by caregivers attest to the clinical significance of irritable affect. In addition, the presence of irritable affect may impact caregiver decisions regarding institution-alization. A higher rate of planned institutionalization was found for patients with irritable affect in Hamel et al. (1990). The presence of irritable affect was associated with higher rates of institutionalization over a 3-year period (Knopman et al., 1988). Finally, Steele et al. (1990) reported higher rates of behavioral symptomatology, including irritability, at entry into a nursing home relative to community-dwelling controls matched for dementia severity. Although none of this evidence is com-pelling in isolation, taken together these studies provide convergent data despite vastly different methodological approaches.

Inappropriate Patterns of Activity

Inappropriate actions is a broad taxonomy covering repetitive, purposeless behav-iors (carphologia, collecting objects, buttoning/unbuttoning clothing), and deviations from socially prescribed conduct (inappropriate sexual activity, eating with fingers). Less than 25% of outpatients with AD exhibit some inappropriate or "bizarre" behavior patterns (Reisberg et al., 1987; Swearer et al., 1988; Teri et al., 1989). Level of cognitive impairment only weakly predicts the presence (Swearer et al., 1988) and frequency (Gilley et al., 1991a) of these behaviors. No other variables have been linked with these disturbances.

Repetitive behaviors are the most intriguing facets of this broad category. These actions range from stereotypic simple motor sequences to complex patterns such as storing away small objects in pockets, drawers, and/or purses. Relative to the most obviously disruptive behavioral sequelae of AD and other dementia syndromes, these repetitive behaviors are intuitively less obvious targets of investigations. However, there is some superficial similarity in these stereotypic behaviors to compulsive rituals in psychiatric syndromes.

There is convergent evidence implicating the basal ganglia in the development of repetitive behavior patterns in infrahuman mammals (e.g., Kolb, 1977) and obsessive-compulsive disorders in humans (e.g., Laplane et al., 1989). It has been speculated that the production of these behavioral features may be related to the regulation of firing patterns within a frontothalamic feedback loop through connections with the caudate and lentiform nuclei (Modell, Mountz, Curtis, & Greden, 1989). These basal ganglia structures are thought to provide inhibitory modulation within the frontothalamic loop that may be diminished by focal lesions, pharmacological manipulations, or other disruptive influences. Thus, it is possible that the stereotypic behavior patterns evident in some AD patients may be related to specific patterns of degenerative involvement of the caudate and striatopallidothalamic projection tracts (Rudelli et al., 1985).

Summary

Description of the frequency of diverse behavioral disturbances in AD has been one common denominator of previous studies. A number of methodological problems, however, cloud the interpretation of these data. Although measurement issues were considered at length in this review, other problems were only briefly mentioned. Virtually all work in this area has been subject to potential selection biases. Behavioral disturbances are prominently mentioned as reasons for referral to tertiary care services (Rabins et al., 1982) and for institutionalization (Steele et al., 1990). Thus, behavioral disturbances may increase the probability of entering a tertiary care cohort and accelerate departure from this cohort to an institutional end point. Samples of convenience from caregiver support groups are similarly problematic.

Psychotropic medication and source of informant data are frequently neglected in previous work. Most studies fail to report the proportion of patients on psychotropic medications despite the potential impact of these agents on behavior, cognition, and other clinical features. For example, neuroleptic agents have been shown to precipitate or exacerbate EPS (Salzman, 1982) and have a deleterious impact on cognition (Devanand, Sackeim, Brown, & Mayeux, 1989) in AD. Disproportionate use of these medications in patients with psychotic symptoms (Mayeux et al., 1985) could thus alter the covariance of these clinical features. Informant characteristics pertinent to understanding the source of data and amount of contact with the patient are also rarely provided.

Few hypotheses have been tested thus far regarding behavioral disturbances in AD. With respect to antecedent conditions, there is limited support for a possible role of premorbid behavior patterns in the development of depression and aggressive behaviors after disease onset. In contrast to these distal effects, the role of proximal situational factors is unknown.

A number of clinical covariates have been examined. The available evidence suggests that overall level of cognitive impairment provides limited prediction of the presence and severity of psychomotor agitation, apathy, hallucinations, and physical aggression. The form of this relationship appears linear in terms of expected values with marked variability in expression at a given level of impairment. Differences in behavioral disturbances among clinical subtype features, such as age at onset and EPS, have been reported. These relationships are potentially important in prediction and generating testable hypotheses regarding biological bases. Finally, specific correlations between behavior patterns and neuropathology have been reported for depression and physical aggression, but meaningful integration of such findings into large-scale neural network models has not been accomplished.

The impact of behavioral disturbances on care-related outcomes has primarily been evaluated at the level of correlations between global indices of patient behavior and measures of caregiver affective and behavioral responses (see Chapter 20). This undifferentiated treatment of behavioral disturbance limits meaningful interpretation of these findings. However, convergent data relating aggressive behaviors to institutionalization and other significant outcomes may pave the way for more sophisticated outcome studies in the future.

Future Directions

Noncognitive disturbances in AD have long been recognized as part of the dementia syndrome, but have been typically viewed as secondary symptoms. The volume of systematic studies appearing after 1986 attests to the widespread recognition of the potential importance of these features. Continued progress, however, depends upon the development of appropriate instrumentation. The existing "paradigm" for evaluating alterations of behavior and emotion provides only crude characterization of the range, frequency, duration, and constellation of potential responses. The observational methodology is uncontrolled and thus prone to many sources of measurement error. Accumulation of a reproducible body of knowledge will be slow without progress on these measurement problems.

The apparent heterogeneity among AD patients in the expression of behavioral and affective disturbances is noteworthy. This lack of uniformity raises the possibility of identifying relatively unique pathophysiological correlates. The preponderance of many behavioral disturbances in conjunction with severe cognitive impairment should enhance postmortem clinicopathological correlations given the predominance of advanced patients in these studies. Tantalizing preliminary observations have already been reported for depression (Zweig et al., 1988), psychotic symptoms (Bennett et al., 1992; Zubenko et al., 1991), and aggression (Palmer et al., 1988).

Rubin (1990) suggested that pathological changes in the frontal lobes may be responsible for many behavior disturbances in AD. Supporting evidence is largely circumstantial. The heteromodal association areas of frontal cortex with extensive corticocortico connections are preferentially involved in AD (Pearson et al., 1985). The progression of changes in these areas appears to parallel changes in other heteromodal association areas in the neocortex as well as cognitive decline (Mann, Marcyniuk, Yates, Neary, & Snowden, 1988). Many behavioral disturbances in AD are at least superficially similar to disturbances seen after prefrontal and or-bitofrontal lesions. Topographically specific differences in the distribution of ser-otonin concentration in the frontal cortex have been related to aggression (Palmer et al., 1988). However, frontal heteromodal association areas are connected with many basal ganglia and limbic structures (see Alexander, Crutcher, & DeLong, 1990), making the demonstration of specific brain-behavior relationships particu-larly challenging.

Environmental factors, on the other hand, have been neglected except in anecdotal reports in studies of aggression. Most target behaviors are not contin-uously expressed. Unless these "responses" are inherently random, chaotic expres-sions, the role of specific stimulus conditions cannot be excluded. Alterations of neural substrate may provide the predisposition and situational factors may supply the catalyst.

The relationship between behavioral disturbances and cognitive deficits in AD has not been extensively explored. Studies to date have used the severity of global cognitive dysfunction as a simple marker of disease severity in relation to behavioral disturbances. A more detailed examination may be fruitful. For example, is the pattern of excess generalized cognitive slowing in AD (Nebes & Madden, 1988) tied to behavioral manifestations of apathy-hypokinesis? Could context-specific information processing deficits in AD (e.g., Mendez, Mendez, Martin, Smyth, & Whitehouse, 1990) be contributing to hallucinations?

Formulation of rational and effective treatment modalities is logically de-pendent on understanding neural and environmental factors. There is a wealth of reports on the use of psychotropic medications in the management of behavioral and affective symptomatology in dementia patients. The choice among agents has largely been based on effectiveness in uncomplicated psychiatric disorders and minimization of side effects (e.g., EPS, anticholinergic effects), rather than specific neurochemical targets. Likewise, the development of nonpharmacological ap-proaches may benefit from knowledge of environmental factors that elicit or sustain problematic behavioral patterns.

References

Agbayewa, M. O. (1986). Earlier psychiatric morbidity in patients with Alzheimer's disease. *Journal of the American Geriatric Society, 34*, 561–564.

Albert, M. L., Feldman, R. G., & Willis, A. L. (1974). The "subcortical dementia" of progressive supranuclear palsy. *Journal of Neurology, Neurosurgery and Psychiatry, 37*, 121–130.

Alexander, G. E., Crutcher, M. D., & DeLong, M. R. (1990). Basal ganglia-thalamocortical circuits: Parallel substrates for motor, oculomotor, "prefrontal" and "limbic" func-tions. *Progress in Brain Research, 85*, 119–146.

Alexopoulos, G. S., Abrams, R. C., Young, R. C., Shamoian, C. A. (1988). Cornell Scale for depression in dementia. *Biological Psychiatry, 23*, 271–284.

Alzheimer, A. (1907/1987). A characteristic disease of the cerebral cortex (original title: Uber eine eigenartige Erkrankung der Hirnrinde). In A. Schultze & O. Snell (Eds.), *Allgemeine zeitschrift fur psychiatrie und psychisch-gerichtliche medizin*, Vol. LXIV (pp. 146–148). Berlin: Georg Relmer. Reprinted (1987) In K. Bick, L. Amaducci, & G. Pepeu (Eds.), *The early story of Alzheimer's disease* (pp. 1–3). New York: Raven Press.

American Psychiatric Association. (1980). *Diagnostic and statistical manual of mental disorders* (3rd ed.). Washington, DC: Author.

American Psychiatric Association. (1987). *Diagnostic and statistical manual of mental disorders* (3rd ed., rev.). Washington, DC: Author.

Bennett, D. A., Gilley, D. W., Cochran, E., Wilson, R. S., & Mufson, E. (1992, July). *Aminergic pathology and psychotic features in Alzheimer's disease.* Presented at the Third International Conference on Alzheimer's Disease and Related Disorders, Padova, Italy.

Birkett, D. P. (1972). The psychiatric differentiation of senility and arteriosclerosis. *British Journal of Psychiatry, 12*, 321–325.

Bondareff, W., Mountjoy, C. Q., Roth, M., Rossor, M. N., Iversen, L. L., & Reynolds, G. P. (1987). Age and histopathologic heterogeneity in Alzheimer's disease. *Archives of General Psychiatry, 44*, 412–417.

Brady, D. R., & Mufson, E. J. (1990). Amygdaloid pathology in Alzheimer's disease: Qualitative and quantitative analysis. *Dementia, 1*, 5–17.

Brane, G., Gottfries, C. G., Blennow, K., Karlsson, I., Lekman, A., Parnetti, L., Svennerholm, L., & Wallin, A. (1989). Monoamine metabolites in cerebrospinal fluid and behavioral ratings in patients with early and late onset of Alzheimer dementia. *Alzheimer Disease and Associated Disorders, 3*, 148–156.

Broe, G. A., Henderson, A. S., Creasey, H., McCusker, E., Korten, A. E., Jorm, A. F., Longley, W., & Anthony, J. C. (1990). A case-control study of Alzheimer's disease in Australia. *Neurology, 40*, 1698–1707.

Bucht, G., & Adolfsson, R. (1983). The comprehensive psychopathological rating scale in patients with dementia of the Alzheimer type and multi-infarct dementia. *Acta Psychiatrica Scandinavica, 68*, 263–270.

Burke, W. J., Houston, M. J., Boust, S. J., & Roccaforte, W. H. (1989). Use of the Geriatric Depression Scale in dementia of the Alzheimer type. *Journal of the American Geriatrics Society, 37*, 856–860.

Burke, W. J., Rubin, E. H., Morris, J., & Berg, L. (1988). Symptoms of "depression" in senile dementia of the Alzheimer type. *Alzheimer Disease and Associated Disorders, 2*, 356–362.

Chan-Palay, V., & Asan, E. (1989). Alterations in catecholamine neurons of the locus coeruleus in senile dementia of the Alzheimer type and in Parkinson's disease with and without dementia and depression. *Journal of Comparative Neurology, 287*, 373–392.

Clarfield, A. M. (1988). The reversible dementias: Do they reverse? *Annals of Internal Medicine, 109*, 476–486.

Coffey, C. E., Figiel, G. S., Djang, W. T., Cress, M., Saunders, W. B., & Weiner, R. D. (1988). Leukoencephalopathy in elderly depressed patients referred for ECT. *Biological Psychiatry, 24*, 143–161.

Cohen-Mansfield, J., & Billig, N. (1986). Agitated behaviors in the elderly: A conceptual review and preliminary results in the cognitively deteriorated. *Journal of the American Geriatrics Society, 34*, 711–721.

Cross, A. J., Crow, T. J., Johnson, J. A., Perry, E. K., Perry, R. H., Blessed, G., &

Tomlinson, B. E. (1984). Studies on neurotransmitter receptor systems in neocortex and hippocampus in senile dementia of the Alzheimer type. *Journal of Neurological Sciences, 64*, 109–117.

Crow, T. J., Cross, A. J., Cooper, S. J., Deakin, J. F. W., Ferrier, I. N., Johnson, J. A., Joseph, M. H., Owen, F., Poulter, M., Lofthouse, R., Corsellis, J. A. N., Chambers, D.R., Blessed, G., Perry, E. K., Perry, R. H., & Tomlinson, B. E. (1984). Neurotransmitter receptors and monoamine metabolites in the brains of patients with Alzheimer-type dementia and depression, and suicides. *Neuropharmacology, 23* (128), 1561–1569.

Cummings, J. L. (1985). Organic delusions: Phenomenology, anatomical correlations, and review. *British Journal of Psychiatry, 146*, 184–197.

Cummings, J. L. (1986). Subcortical dementia—neuropsychology, neuropsychiatry, and pathophysiology. *British Journal of Psychiatry, 149*, 682–697.

Cummings, J. L., Miller, B., Hill, M. A., & Neshkes, R. (1987). Neuropsychiatric aspects of multi-infarct dementia and dementia of the Alzheimer type. *Archives of Neurology, 44*, 389–393.

Devanand, D. P., Sackeim, H. A., Brown, R. P., & Mayeux, R. (1989). A pilot study of haloperidol treatment of psychosis and behavioral disturbances in Alzheimer's disease. *Archives of Neurology, 46*, 854–857.

Devins, G. M., & Seland, T. P. (1987). Emotional impact of multiple sclerosis: Recent findings and suggestions for future research. *Psychological Bulletin, 101*, 363–375.

Ditter, S. M., & Mirra, S. S. (1987). Neuropathologic and clinical features of Parkinson's disease in Alzheimer's disease patients. *Neurology, 37*, 754–760.

Drevets, W. C., & Rubin, E. H. (1989). Psychotic symptoms and the longitudinal course of senile dementia of the Alzheimer type. *Biological Psychiatry, 25*, 39–48.

Evans, D. A., Funkenstein, H. H., Albert, M. S., Scherr, P. A., Cook, N. R., Chown, M. J., Hebert, L. E., Hennekens, C. H., & Taylor, J. O. (1989). Prevalence of Alzheimer's disease in a community population of older persons: Higher than previously reported. *Journal of the American Medical Association, 262*, 2551–2556.

Folstein, S. E., Folstein, M. F., & McHugh, P. R. (1975a). Psychiatric syndromes in Huntington's disease. *Advances in Neurology, 23*, 281–289.

Folstein, M. F., Folstein, S. E., & McHugh, P. R. (1975b). "Mini-Mental State": A practical method for grading the mental state of patients for the clinician. *Journal of Psychiatric Research, 12*, 189–198.

Folstein, M. F., & McHugh, P. R. (1978). Dementia syndrome of depression. In R. Katzman, R. D. Terry, & K. L. Bick (Eds.), *Alzheimer's disease: Senile dementia and related disorders* (pp. 87–93). New York: Raven Press.

Gilley, D. W., Bennett, D. A., Grosse, D. A., & Wilson, R. S. (1990). Risk factors and clinical features associated with depression in Alzheimer's disease. *Neurology, 40* (Suppl. 1), 447.

Gilley, D. W., Whalen, M. E., Wilson, R. S., & Bennett, D. A. (1991b). Hallucinations and associated factors in Alzheimer's disease. *Journal of Neuropsychiatry and Clinical Neurosciences, 3*, 371–376.

Gilley, D. W., & Wilson, R. S. (1991). Nuisance parameters in the assessment of noncognitive manifestations of dementia. *Psychology and Aging, 6*, 528–532.

Gilley, D. W., Wilson, R. S., Bennett, D. A., Bernard, B. A., & Fox, J. H. (1991a). Prediction of behavioral disturbances in Alzheimer's disease. *Journal of Gerontology: Psychological Sciences, 46*, P362–371.

Goodman, L. (1953). Alzheimer's disease: A clinico-pathological analysis of 23 cases with a theory on causation. *Journal of Nervous and Mental Disorders, 101*, 97–130.

Goldfried, M. R. (1977). Behavioral assessment in perspective. In J. D. Cone & R. P.

Hawkins (Eds.), *Behavioral assessment: New directions in clinical psychology*. New York: Academic Press.

Gustafson, L. (1975). Psychiatric symptoms in dementia with onset in the presenile period. *Acta Psychiatrica Scandinavica, 257*, 8–35.

Hamel, M., Gold, D. P., Andres, D., Reis, M., Dastoor, D., Grauer, H., & Bergman, H. (1990). *Gerontologist, 30*, 206–211.

Hamilton, M. (1960). A rating scale for depression. *Journal of Neurology, Neurosurgery and Psychiatry, 23*, 56–62.

Hart, R. P., Kwentus, J. A., Taylor, J. R., & Hamer, R. M. (1987a). Selective reminding procedure in depression and dementia. *Psychology and Aging, 2*, 111–115.

Hart, R. P., Kwentus, J. A., Taylor, J. R., & Harkins, S. W. (1987b). Rate of forgetting in dementia and depression. *Journal of Consulting and Clinical Psychology, 55*, 101–105.

Kleist, K. (1934). *Kriegverletzungen des gehirns in ihrer bedeutung fur hirnlokalisation and hirnpathologie*. Leipzig: Barth.

Knesevich, J. W., Martin, R. L., & Berg, L. (1983). Preliminary report on affective symptoms in the early stages of senile dementia of the Alzheimer type. *American Journal of Psychiatry, 140*, 233–235.

Knopman, D. S., Deinard, S., Kitto, J., Hartman, M., & Mackenzie, T. (1985). A clinic for dementia. Two years' experience. *Minnesota Medicine, 68*, 687–692.

Knopman, D. S., Kitto, J., Deinard, S., & Heiring, J. (1988). Longitudinal study of death and institutionalization in patients with primary degenerative dementia. *Journal of the American Geriatrics Society, 36*, 108–112.

Kolb, B. (1977). Studies on the caudate-putamen and the dorsomedial thalamic nucleus of the rat: Implications for mammalian frontal lobe functions. *Physiology and Behavior, 18*, 237–244.

Kral, V. A. (1983). The relationship between senile dementia (Alzheimer type) and depression. *Canadian Journal of Psychiatry, 28*, 304–306.

Kral, V. A., & Emery, O. B. (1989). Long-term follow-up of depressive pseudodementia of the aged. *Canadian Journal of Psychiatry, 34*, 445–446.

Kumar, A., Koss, E., Metzler, D., Moore, A., & Friedland, R. P. (1988). Behavioral symptomatology in dementia of the Alzheimer type. *Alzheimer Disease and Associated Disorders, 2* (4), 363–365.

Laplane, D., Levasseur, M., Pillon, B., Dubois, B., Baulac, M., Mazoyer, B., Tran Dinh, S., Sette, G., Danze, F., & Baron, J. C. (1989). Obsessive-compulsive and other behavioral changes with bilateral basal ganglia lesions—a neuropsychological, magnetic resonance imaging and positron tomography study. *Brain, 112*, 699–725.

Larson, E. G., Reifler, B. V., Featherstone, H. J., & English, D. R. (1984). Dementia in elderly outpatients: A prospective study. *Annals of Internal Medicine, 100*, 417–423.

Lazarus, L., Newton, N., Cohler, B., Lesser, J., & Schweon, C. (1987). Frequency and presentation of depressive symptoms to patients with primary degenerative dementia. *American Journal of Psychiatry, 144*, 41–45.

Lhermitte, F. (1986). Human autonomy and the frontal lobes. II. Patient behavior in complex and social situations. The "environmental dependency syndrome." *Annals of Neurology, 19*, 335–343.

Lieberman, H. R., Wurtman, J. J., & Teicher, M. H. (1989). Circadian rhythms of activity in healthy young and elderly humans. *Neurobiology of Aging, 10*, 259–265.

Liston, E. H. (1977). Occult presentile dementia. *Journal of Nervous and Mental Disease, 164*, 263–267.

Liston, E. H., Jarvik, L. F., & Gerson, S. (1987). Depression in Alzheimer's disease: An overview of adrenergic and cholinergic mechanisms. *Comprehensive Psychiatry, 28* (5), 444–457.

Lopez, O. L., Becker, J. T., Brenner, R. P., Rosen, J., Bajulaiye, O. I., & Reynolds,

C. F., III. (1991). Alzheimer's disease with delusions and hallucinations: Neuropsychological and electroencephalographic correlates. *Neurology, 41,* 906–912.

Lopez, O. L., Boller, F., Becker, J. T., Miller, M., & Reynolds, C. F., III. (1990). Alzheimer's disease and depression: Neuropsychological impairment and progression of the illness. *American Journal of Psychiatry, 147,* 855–860.

Luria, A. R. (1965). Two kinds of motor perseveration in massive injuries of the frontal lobes. *Brain, 88,* 1–10.

Mackenzie, T. B., Robiner, W. N., & Knopman, D. S. (1989). Differences between patient and family assessments of depression in Alzheimer's disease. *American Journal of Psychiatry, 146,* 1174–1178.

Mann, D. M. A., Marcyniuk, B., Yates, P. O., Neary, D., & Snowden, J. S. (1988). The progression of the pathological changes of Alzheimer's disease in frontal and temporal neocortex examined both at biopsy and at autopsy. *Neuropathology and Applied Neurobiology, 14,* 177–195.

Mayeux, R., Stern, Y., Rosen, J., & Levanthal, J. (1981). Depression, intellectual impairment, and Parkinson disease. *Neurology, 31,* 645–650.

Mayeux, R., Stern, Y., & Spanton, S. (1985). Heterogeneity in dementia of the Alzheimer type: Evidence of subgroups. *Neurology, 35,* 453–461.

McKhann, G., Drachman, D., Folstein, M., Katzman, R., Price, D., & Stadlan, E. (1984). Clinical diagnosis of Alzheimer's disease: Report of the NINCDS-ADRDA work group. *Neurology, 34,* 939–944.

Mendez, M. F., Mendez, M. A., Martin, R. N., Smyth, K. A., & Whitehouse, P. J. (1990). Complex visual disturbances in Alzheimer's disease. *Neurology, 40,* 439–443.

Merriam, A. E., Aronson, M. K., Gaston, P., Wey, S. L., & Katz, I. (1988). The psychiatric symptoms of Alzheimer's disease. *Journal of the American Geriatrics Society, 36,* 7–12.

Modell, J. G., Mountz, J. M., Curtis, G. C., & Greden, J. F. (1989). Neurophysiologic dysfunction in basal ganglia/limbic striatal and thalamocortical circuits as a pathogenetic mechanism of obsessive-compulsive disorder. *Journal of Neuropsychiatry and Clinical Neurosciences, 1,* 27–36.

Mullaney, D. J., Kripke, D. F., & Messin, S. (1980). Wrist actigraphic estimation of sleep time. *Sleep, 3,* 82–91.

Nebes, R. D., & Madden, D. J. (1988). Different patterns of cognitive slowing produced by Alzheimer's disease and normal aging. *Psychology and Aging, 3,* 102–104.

Nott, P. N., & Fleminger, J. J. (1975). Presenile dementia: The difficulties of early diagnosis. *Acta Psychiatrica Scandinavica, 51,* 210–217.

Palmer, A. M., Stratmann, G. C., Procter, A. W., & Bowen, D. M. (1988). Possible neurotransmitter basis of behavioral changes in Alzheimer's disease. *Annals of Neurology, 23,* 616–200.

Pearlson, G. D., Rabins, P. V., Kim, W. S., Speedie, L. J., Moberg, P. J., Burns, A., & Bascom, M. (1989). Structural brain CT changes and cognitive deficits in elderly depressives with and without reversible dementia ('pseudodementia'). *Psychological Medicine, 19,* 573–584.

Pearlson, G. D., Ross, C. A., Lohr, W. D., Rovner, B. W., Chase, G. A., & Folstein, M. F. (1990). Association between family history of affective disorder and the depressive syndrome of Alzheimer's disease. *American Journal of Psychiatry, 147,* 452–456.

Pearson, R. C. A., Esiri, M. M., Hiorns, R. W., Wilcock, G. K., & Powell, T. P. S. (1985). Anatomical correlates of the distribution of the pathological changes in the neocortex in Alzheimer's disease. *Proceedings of the National Academy of Sciences of the United States of America, 82,* 4531–4534.

Penn, R. D., Martin, E. M., Wilson, R. S., Fox, J. H., & Savoy, S. M. (1988). Intraventricular bethanechol infusion for Alzheimer's disease: Results of double-blind and escalating dose trials. *Neurology, 38,* 219–222.

Petry, S., Cummings, J. L., Hill, M. A., & Shapira, J. (1988). Personality alterations in dementia of the Alzheimer type. *Archives of Neurology, 45,* 1187–1190.

Pickle, L. W., Brown, L. M., & Blot, W. J. (1983). Information available from surrogate respondents in case-control interview studies. *American Journal of Epidemiology, 118,* 99–108.

Porrino, L. J., Rapoport, J. L., Behar, D., Sceery, W., Ismond, D. R., & Bunney, W. E. (1983). A naturalistic assessment of the motor activity of hyperactive boys: I. Comparison with normal controls. *Archives of General Psychiatry, 40,* 681–687.

Price, T. R. P., & Tucker, G. J. (1977). Psychiatric and behavioral manifestations of normal pressure hydrocephalus. *Journal of Nervous and Mental Disease, 164,* 51–55.

Rabins, P. V., Mace, N. L., & Lucas, J. (1982). The impact of dementia on the family. *Journal of the American Medical Association, 248,* 333–335.

Rabins, P. V., Merchant, A., & Nestadt, G. (1984). Criteria for diagnosing reversible dementia caused by depression: Validation by 2-year follow-up. *British Journal of Psychiatry, 144,* 488–493.

Reding, M., Haycox, J., & Blass, J. (1985). Depression in patients referred to a dementia clinic. *Archives of Neurology, 42,* 894–898.

Redmond, D. P., & Hegge, F. W. (1985). Observations on the design and specification of a wrist-worn human activity monitoring system. *Behavioral Research Methods: Instrumentation and Computation, 17* (6), 659–669.

Reifler, B. V. (1986). Arguments for abandoning the term pseudodementia. *Journal of the American Geriatrics Society, 30,* 665–668.

Reifler, B. V., Larson, E., & Hanley, R. (1982). Coexistence of cognitive impairment and depression in geriatric outpatients. *American Journal of Psychiatry, 139,* 623–626.

Reifler, B. V., Larson, E., Teri, L., & Poulson, M. (1986). Dementia of the Alzheimer's type and depression. *Journal of the American Geriatrics Society, 34,* 855–859.

Reifler, B. V., Teri, L., Raskind, M., Veith, R., Barnes, R., White, E., & McLean, P. (1989). Double-blind trial of imipramine in Alzheimer's disease patients with and without depression. *American Journal of Psychiatry, 146,* 45–49.

Reisberg, B., Borenstein, B., Salob, S. P., Ferris, S. H., Franssen, E., & Georgotos, A. (1987). Behavioral symptoms in Alzheimer's disease: Phenomenology and treatment. *Journal of Clinical Psychiatry, 48* (Suppl.), 9–15.

Robinson, R. G., Kubos, K. L., Starr, L. B., Rao, K., & Price, T. R. (1984). Mood disorders in stroke patients: Importance of location of lesion. *Brain, 107,* 81–93.

Ron, M. A., Toone, B. K., Garralda, M. E., & Lishman, W. A. (1979). Diagnostic accuracy in presenile dementia. *British Journal of Psychiatry, 134,* 161–168.

Rosenstock, H. A. (1970). Alzheimer's presenile dementia. *Diseases of the Nervous System, 31,* 826–829.

Rothschild, D. (1941). The clinical differentiation of senile and arteriosclerotic psychoses. *American Journal of Psychiatry, 98,* 324–33.

Rovner, B. W., Broadhead, J., Spencer, M., Carson, K., & Folstein, M. F. (1989). Depression and Alzheimer's disease. *American Journal of Psychiatry, 146,* 350–353.

Rubin, E. H. (1990). Psychopathology of senile dementia of the Alzheimer type. In R. J. Wurtman, S. Corkin, J. Growden, & E. Ritter-Walker (Eds.), *Advances in neurology: Vol. 51: Alzheimer's disease* (pp. 53–59). New York: Raven Press.

Rubin, E. H., Morris, J. C., Storandt, M., & Berg, L. (1987a). Behavioral changes in patients with mild senile dementia of the Alzheimer's type. *Psychiatry Research, 21,* 55–62.

Rubin, E. H., Morris, J. C., & Berg, L. (1987b). The progression of personality changes in senile dementia of the Alzheimer's type. *Journal of the American Geriatrics Society,* *35*, 721–725.

Rudelli, R. D., Ambler, M. W., & Wisniewski, H. M. (1985). Morphology and distribution of Alzheimer neuritic (senile) and amyloid plaques in striatum and diencephalon. *Acta Neuropathologica, 64*, 273–281.

Ryden, M. B. (1988). Aggressive behavior in persons with dementia who live in the community. *Alzheimer Disease and Associated Disorders, 2*, 342–355.

Salzman, C. (1982). A primer on geriatric psychopharmacology. *American Journal of Psychiatry, 139*, 67–74.

Schneider, L. S., Pollock, V. E., & Lyness, S. A. (1990). A metaanalysis of controlled trials of neuroleptic treatment in dementia. *Journal of the American Geriatrics Society, 38*, 553–563.

Sim, M., & Sussman, I. (1962). Alzheimer's disease: Its natural history and differential diagnosis. *Journal of Nervous and Mental Disorders, 135*, 489–499.

Smith, L. A., Branch, L. G., Scherr, P. A., Wetle, T., Evans, D. A., Hebert, L., & Taylor, J. O. (1990). Short-term variability of measures of physical function in older people. *Journal of the American Geriatrics Society, 38*, 992–998.

Steele, C., Rovner, B., Chase, G. A., & Folstein, M. (1990). Psychiatric symptoms and nursing home placement of patients with Alzheimer's disease. *American Journal of Psychiatry, 147*, 1049–1051.

Stern, Y., Mayeux, R., Sano, M., Hauser, W. A., & Bush, T. (1987). Predictors of disease course in patients with probable Alzheimer's disease. *Neurology, 37*, 1649–1653.

Stuss, D. T., & Benson, D. F. (1984). Neuropsychological studies on the frontal lobes. *Psychological Bulletin, 95* (1), 3–28.

Sunderland, T. S., Yount, D., Hill, J. L., Tariot, P. N., Newhouse, P. A., Mueller, E. A., Mellow, A. M., & Cohen, R. M. (1988). A new scale for the assessment of depressed mood in dementia patients. *American Journal of Psychiatry, 145*, 955–959.

Swearer, J. M., Drachman, D. A., O'Donnell, B. F., & Mitchell, A. L. (1988). Troublesome and disruptive behaviors in dementia. Relationships to diagnosis and disease severity. *Journal of the American Geriatrics Society, 36*, 784–790.

Teri, L., Borson, S., Kiyak, H. A., & Yamagishi, M. (1989). Behavioral disturbance, cognitive dysfunction, and functional skill. Prevalence and relationship in Alzheimer's disease. *Journal of the American Geriatrics Society, 37*, 109–116.

Teri, L., Hughes, J. P., & Larson, E. B. (1990). Cognitive deterioration in Alzheimer's disease: Behavioral and health factors. *Journal of Gerontology: Psychological Sciences, 45*, 58–63.

Teri, L., Larson, E. B., & Reifler, B. V. (1988). Behavioral disturbance in dementia of the Alzheimer's type. *Journal of the American Geriatrics Society, 36*, 1–6.

Thompson, W. D., Orvaschel, H., Prusoff, B. A., & Kidd, K. K. (1982). An evaluation of the family history method of ascertaining psychiatric disorders. *Archives of General Psychiatry, 39*, 53–58.

van Praag, H. M., Plutchik, R., & Comte, H. (1986). The serotonin hypothesis of (auto) aggression. *Annals of the New York Academy of Sciences, 487*, 150–167.

Weiss, B. L., Foster, F. G., Reynolds, C. F., & Kupfer, D. J. (1974). Psychomotor activity in mania. *Archives of General Psychiatry, 31*, 379–383.

Weissman, M. M., Kidd, K. K., & Prusoff, B. A. (1982). Variability in the rates of affective disorders in relatives of depressed and normal probans. *Archives of General Psychiatry, 39*, 1397–1403.

Wilcock, G. K., Esiri, M. M., Bowen, D. M., & Hughes, A. O. (1988). The differential involvement of subcortical nuclei in senile dementia of Alzheimer's type. *Journal of Neurology, Neurosurgery and Psychiatry, 51*, 842–849.

Zarit, S. H., Reever, K. E., & Bach-Peterson, J. (1980). Relatives of the impaired elderly: Correlates of feelings of burden. *Gerontologist, 20*, 649–654.

Ziegler, D. K. (1954). Cerebral atrophy in psychiatric patients. *American Journal of Psychiatry, 111*, 454–458.

Zubenko, G. S., & Moossy, J. (1988). Major depression in primary dementia: Clinical and neuropathological correlates. *Archives of Neurology, 45*, 1182–1186.

Zubenko, G. S., Moossy, J., Martinez, A. J., Rao, G., Claassen, D., Rosen, J., & Kopp, U. (1991). Neuropathologic and neurochemical correlates of psychosis in primary dementia. *Archives of Neurology, 48*, 619–624.

Zubenko, G. S., Moossy, J., Martinez, A. J., Rao, G. R., Kopp, U., & Hanin, I. (1989). A brain regional analysis of morphologic and cholinergic abnormalities in Alzheimer's disease. *Archives of Neurology, 46*, 634–638.

Zubenko, G. S., Sullivan, S., Nelson, J. P., Belle, S. H., Huff, J., & Wolf, G. L. (1990). Brain imaging abnormalities in mental disorders of late life. *Archives of Neurology, 47*, 1107–1111.

Zweig, R. M., Ross, C. A., Hedreen, J. C., Steele, C., Cardillo, S. E., Whitehouse, P. J., Folstein, M. F., & Price, D. L. (1988). The neuropathology of aminergic nuclei in Alzheimer's disease. *Annals of Neurology, 24*, 233–242.

4

Memory Impairment in Alzheimer's Disease: An Anatomical Perspective

Bradley T. Hyman, Paulina V. Arriagada, Gary W. Van Hoesen, and Antonio R. Damasio

Neuropsychological Aspects of Memory Impairment in Alzheimer's Disease

For the majority of patients with Alzheimer's disease (AD), memory impairment is not only the cardinal sign of the disease, but is also a central and dominant feature of the illness throughout its course. At the initial visit to the physician, families frequently report that there had been a gradual evolution of memory impairment over several years. This may begin with an excessive "where did I leave my car keys?" sort of absent mindedness that is ignored at the time, and recognized only in retrospect. Slowly there is forgetting of day-to-day events or a tendency toward repeating conversations, forgetting items at the store, and some word-finding difficulties. Appointments may be forgotten, and questions may be asked again and again.

These first memory changes occur primarily relative to learning new information and retrieving recently learned information. Recollection of youth and early adulthood remains intact, and retrieval of both personal and general information is unimpaired. For example, it is common for a patient to be able to give a detailed account of intricate family relationships or of their personal activities during World War II, but at the same time be unable to recall a single item from a name and address presented to them 5 minutes previously.

In time, even long-term memory becomes impaired. The patient becomes unable to find their way home over a familiar route, or even becomes "lost" within their own home. Voices on the telephone can no longer be identified. Individuals who are well known to them become strangers. Ultimately, family and friends cannot be securely recognized, and even knowledge of themselves, their immediate environment and their relationship to it (autobiographical update memory) fails.

In spite of the fact that some Alzheimer's patients do begin the disease process with some other prominent symptom (e.g., visuospatial disorientation or paranoid ideation), it is certainly fair to say that memory impairment is one of the core clinical features of Alzheimer's disease (Moss, Albert, Butters, & Payne, 1986).

As the disease progresses, not only does the deficit worsen, but the type of deficit changes. An initial problem with recent learning (an anterograde defect) gradually grows to encompass what was learned in the past (a retrograde defect). Unique attributes of stimuli no longer evoke the pertinently related information necessary for recognition, resulting in agnosia. Word-finding difficulties progress to become an anomic aphasia. At the same time, there can be a remarkable preservation of certain other memory functions. For example, AD patients learn and recall a pursuit rotor task in a manner comparable to controls (Eslinger & Damasio, 1986; Corkin et al., 1986; Heindel, Salmon, Shutts, Walicke, & Butters, 1989). Of interest, patients with amnesia due to focal lesions of the temporal lobe have the same dissociation between profound impairments of verbal or visual memory on the one hand, and demonstrable savings of skill learning on the other (Corkin, 1968; Cohen, Eichenbaum, Deacedo, & Corkin, 1985; Damasio, Eslinger, Damasio, Van Hoesen, & Cornell, 1985).

Pepin and Eslinger (1989) recently used a serial-position function of an immediate free recall task in AD patients to examine the effect of severity of disease on primacy and recency effects. In "mild" AD patients, both primacy and recency effects were intact. There was loss of primacy effect with preservation of recency effect in "moderate" patients. Both primacy and recency were lost in individuals in whom the overall dementia syndrome was most advanced. Thus the exact type of memory impairment is dependent on the stage of the disease.

The Anatomical Basis of a Memory-Related Neural System

Bilateral damage to the hippocampal formation in the human leads to a profound amnesia (Scoville & Milner, 1957; Corkin, 1968; Damasio, 1984; Damasio et al., 1985; Damasio, Travel, & Damasio, 1989; Zola-Morgan, Squire & Amarel, 1986). Experimental work in the nonhuman primate also documents substantial memory impairments after lesions to the hippocampus and closely related structures (Mishkin, 1982; Squire & Zola-Morgan, 1983, 1988). The hippocampus is just one of a set of forebrain structures that has been implicated as playing a role in the neural substrate of memory (Figure 4.1). Based on the available behavioral evidence in humans and animals, and experimental anatomical studies, a list of structures whose integrity is essential for normal memory function can be outlined (Van Hoesen,

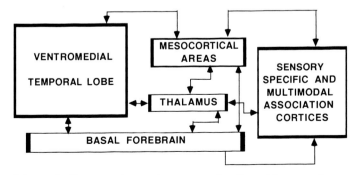

FIGURE 4.1. Schematic diagram of neural structures implicated in normal memory function. Arrows indicate the anatomical connections referred to in the text.

1985; Amaral, 1987). The major additional components of such a list include the parahippocampal gyrus, the perirhinal cortex, the amygdala, the limbic association cortices; and subcortical structures such as the cholinergic basal forebrain; the mammillary bodies; and the anterior, dorsomedial, and midline thalamic nuclei. The anatomical interrelationships among these structures form the basis of a neural system related to learning.

It is important to include in this conceptualization of the neural basis of memory the relationship of this learning system to a series of cortical regions interlocked by feedforward and feedback projections. Those cortical regions encompass a variety of association cortices for several sensory modalities that are in a position to receive information about the environment from the primary sensory cortices, and are instrumental in the perception and recording of such information. The conceptualization of the architecture and operation of the neural systems in which the information would be recorded is a subject of great interest. Elsewhere, one of us (ARD) has articulated a proposal for such an architecture, based on the known feedforward and feedback projections among these hierarchically disposed cortical fields. The proposal posits that feedforward projections are directed at *convergence zones* from which reciprocating feedback projections originate. The role of the neuron ensembles that constitute these convergence zones is to embody the code for simultaneous activity in the cortices feeding toward them, and to fire back simultaneously (when fired upon), via the feedback projections, so as to reactivate in synchronous manner a variety of cortical regions located in different areas. In short, the convergence zones in the association cortices would provide the substrate for *retroactivation* of the neural activities that took place during previous perception and thought processing, so as to form the basis of the apparent seamless content of recall (Damasio, 1989; Damasio et al., 1989; Damasio, 1990).

Hippocampal Anatomy

The principal connections from the association cortices to the hippocampal formation are via the entorhinal cortex. The entorhinal cortex receives projections from widespread cortical areas, the amygdala and midline thalamus, and is therefore in a position to provide highly refined polymodal association information to the hippocampus (Figure 4.2). The projection from entorhinal to the hippocampal formation is called the perforant pathway. Because of the convergence of projections on entorhinal cortex, the perforant pathway is a common final projection in a series linking association cortices and the hippocampus. The perforant pathway arises primarily from neurons in entorhinal layers II and III, and terminates in a discrete zone in the outer portion of the molecular layer of the dentate gyrus and on the distal dendrites of the subicular and CA1 fields. The perforant pathway is the first step of a multisynaptic pathway, and initiates a largely unidirectional chain of intrinsic connections within the Ammonic subfields. The granule cells project to CA3 pyramids via the mossy fiber system. CA3 neurons project to CA1 via the Schaffer collaterals. The ammonic-subicular projection (CA1 to subiculum) completes the series of intrinsic projections.

The efferent projections of the hippocampal formation are derived primarily from a limited set of neurons. The subiculum and the CA1 pyramids project via the fornix to the septum, and the subiculum provides the major source of projections to the anterior thalamus and mammillary bodies. The subicular cortices and the CA1 zone also give rise to the majority of hippocampal-cortical projections. Strong projections to the amygdala, to periallocortical areas including entorhinal cortex, and to proisocortical areas such as the perirhinal cortex, the temporal pole, and posterior parahippocampal gyrus have been demonstrated. These areas are major staging areas for further projections to multimodal and sensory-specific association cortices, indirectly reciprocating the inputs to entorhinal cortex. For example, layer IV of entorhinal cortex receives a strong projection from the subiculum, and, in turn, gives rise to widespread projections to limbic and association cortices (Van Hoesen, 1982; Kosel, Van Hoesen, & Rosene, 1982; see Rosene & Van Hoesen, 1987, for review).

Cell-Specific Pathology in the Hippocampal Formation in Alzheimer's Disease

The major neuropathological changes in Alzheimer's disease are neurofibrillary tangles (NFT) and senile plaques (SP). The former are intraneuronal lesions that consist, at least in part, of a mass of insoluble cytoskeletal proteins. Figure 4.3 illustrates the subiculum from a case of AD in which nearly all the neurons contain NFT. Senile plaques are a complex neuropil alteration consisting of a deposition of β/A4 amyloid protein, often accompanied by glial cells and dystrophic neurites. The technological advance of immunohistochemical techniques using antibodies directed against β/A4 have revealed a wide morphologic spectrum of amyloid deposits. In addition to tightly compact, densely stained deposits (classical amyloid cores), small granular deposits of β/A4 and "diffuse" plaques that consist of light β/A4 staining over a large area have been described. Figure 4.4 illustrates an example of tightly compact plaque "cores" in the molecular layer of the dentate gyrus.

Although the early literature implied that NFT and SP occur more or less randomly throughout the cortex, the predisposition of the hippocampal formation to both tangle and plaque formation has been well documented (Hirano & Zimmerman, 1962; Ball, 1976; Kemper, 1978). Understanding the details of hippocampal circuitry using modern neuroanatomic methods (e.g., see Van Hoesen, 1982) provided the basis for a further analysis of the patterns of Alzheimer pathology. In terms of NFT, an analysis of the hippocampal formation revealed a stereotyped pattern of vulnerable neurons that were largely restricted to certain cytoarchitectural fields and even to lamina within those fields (Hyman, Damasio, Van Hoesen, & Barnes, 1984; Hyman, Van Hoesen, Kromer, & Damasio, 1986; Hyman, Van Hoesen, & Damasio, 1990). Moreover, it was apparent that those neurons most important for both afferents and efferents of the hippocampus were the most severely affected. Layer II of entorhinal cortex, the neurons that receive widespread projections from limbic and association cortices and give rise to a major component of the perforant pathway, are severely affected by NFT in every case of AD we have examined.

We recently carried out a semiquantitative study of the patterns of tangles and plaques in the hippocampal formation (Hyman & Van Hoesen, 1990). Using

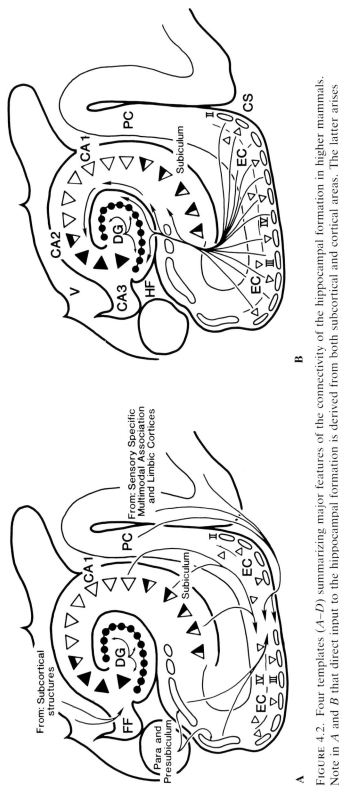

A

B

FIGURE 4.2. Four templates (A–D) summarizing major features of the connectivity of the hippocampal formation in higher mammals. Note in A and B that direct input to the hippocampal formation is derived from both subcortical and cortical areas. The latter arises almost exclusively from the entorhinal cortex, which gives rise to the perforant pathway, the major link between the association and limbic cortices and the hippocampal formation. Template C summarizes the major intrinsic hippocampal connections; the mossy fiber system from the dentate gyrus granule cell to the CA3 zone of the hippocampus, the Schaeffer collaterals that arise from CA3 neurons, and an unnamed pathway from CA1 neurons to the subiculum. As shown in D, all

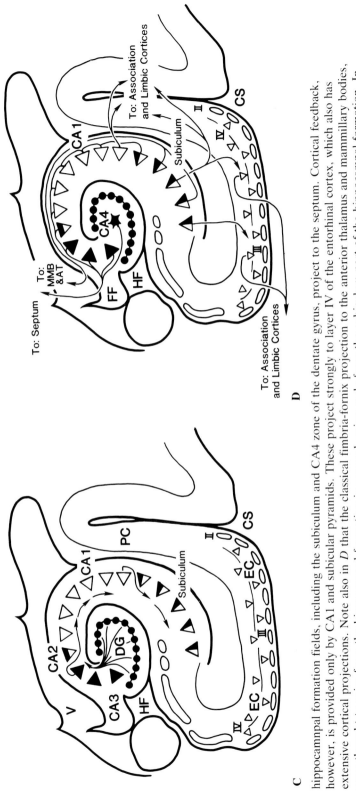

C

D

hippocampal formation fields, including the subiculum and CA4 zone of the dentate gyrus, project to the septum. Cortical feedback, however, is provided only by CA1 and subicular pyramids. These project strongly to layer IV of the entorhinal cortex, which also has extensive cortical projections. Note also in *D* that the classical fimbria-fornix projection to the anterior thalamus and mammillary bodies, once thought to arise from the hippocampal formation in general, arises only from the subiculum part of the hippocampal formation. In summary, the entorhinal cortex is a vital link for cortical association input to the hippocampal formation, and the CA1 and subicular pyramids are vital links for reciprocal hippocampocortical projections.

FIGURE 4.3. Thioflavine-S-stained section from the subiculum of a 72-year-old individual with Alzheimer's disease. Innumerable flame-shaped neurofibrillary tangles (NFT) invest these neurons. Some senile plaques (SP), visible especially in the molecular layer, can also be seen.

thioflavine-S-stained sections, we graded the degree of pathological changes using a 0 to + + + + scale (per 10 × objective field) as follows:

    0 = No NFT (or SP)
    + = 1–10 NFT (or SP)
    + + = 10–25 NFT (or SP)
    + + + = 26–50 NFT (or SP)
    + + + + = >50 NFT (or SP)

Given the configuration of the microscope in this study, this was a 3.0-mm^2 field. The method is essentially the same as used in our study of the amygdala and is described therein (Kromer-Vogt, Hyman, Van Hoesen, & Damasio, 1990). One hundred percent of a series of 22 cases had more than 50 NFT/3.0-mm^2 field in layer II of entorhinal cortex and nearly 90% had this substantial degree of NFT in layer IV, whereas layer III (45%), and layers V plus IV (14%) were much less affected. Layer IV receives the projection from the subiculum and projects back to widespread limbic and association cortices. Thus in entorhinal cortex, a consistent pattern of NFT accumulate specifically in layers II and IV, in neurons responsible for cortical-hippocampal and hippocampal-cortical connections (Figure 4.5).

A similarly restricted pattern of NFT involvement was seen in hippocampus. The CA1 and subicular areas contained >50 NFT/3.0-mm^2 field in approximately 90% of the cases, whereas the presubiculum, dentate gyrus, CA4, and CA3 reached this level of involvement less than 5% of the time (Figure 4.6). The CA1/subiculum area gives rise to the majority of cortical (and subcortical) projections, and so again

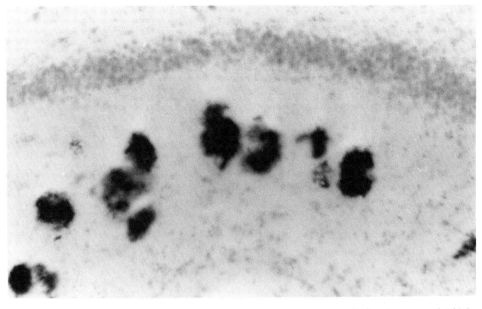

FIGURE 4.4. Immunohistochemical visualization of senile plaques (SP) using an anti-β/A4 monoclonal antibody (Hyman, Tanzi, Marzloff, Barbour & Schenk, 1992) reveals the amyloid cores of senile plaques. These plaques are located in a characteristic position in the outer portion of the molecular layer of the dentate gyrus, in the perforant pathway terminal zone.

this pattern of pathology would specifically disrupt communication between the hippocampal formation and its targets.

The distribution of SP is not as closely linked to cytoarchitectural fields or lamina as are NFT, but there are nonetheless certain areas that consistently accumulates SP, and others that do not. Senile plaque counts in entorhinal cortex showed that layer III was most frequently involved, and had >25 SP/3.0-mm² field in 55% of the cases. No other layer had this many SP in more than 9% of the series (Figure 4.5). In hippocampus, the subiculum had >25 SP/3.0-mm² field in approximately two thirds of the cases, whereas CA3, CA4, or presubiculum contained this number in less than 5% of the cases (Figure 4.6). The dentate gyrus granule cell layer infrequently had SP or NFT, but the molecular layer of the dentate gyrus, especially the outer two thirds of the molecular layer, consistently contained SP (Hyman et al., 1986; Hyman, Van Hoesen, & Damasio, 1988). This region is the terminal zone of the perforant pathway projection from entorhinal cortex, and disruption of the terminal zone by SP undoubtedly leads to further dysfunction of the perforant pathway system.

Hippocampal Pathology in Relationship to Other Forebrain Regions

We have described anatomical changes in the hippocampal formation that specifically dissect and destroy the major projection neurons of this structure. These neurons subserve hippocampal connections with the other cortical and subcortical

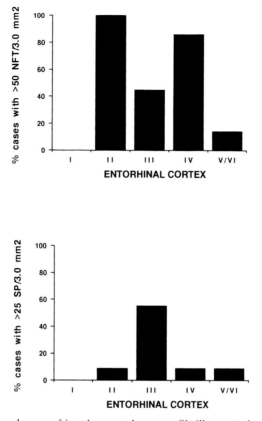

FIGURE 4.5. Relative degree of involvement by neurofibrillary tangles (NFT) and senile plaques (SP) of the lamina of the entorhinal cortex is shown by graphing the percentage of total cases (of 22 total) that contained a substantial degree of pathology. The criteria used were >50 NFT/3.0-mm² field or >25 SP/3.0-mm² field, respectively (see text for details).

areas that make up the memory-related neural system. We believe that these lesions contribute strongly to the memory impairment of AD.

Our recent studies of nondemented elderly (Arriagada & Hyman, 1990) and of Down's syndrome individuals of various ages (Hyman & Mann, 1991) suggest that the neurons of layer II of entorhinal cortex and the CA1/subicular area of hippocampus are among the first neurons in the brain to develop NFT in aging and during the first stages of AD. It is possible that these lesions in the hippocampal formation contribute most to the initial memory changes of AD; namely, a predominantly anterograde impairment characterized by poor recent learning and memory. As the disease progresses to agnosias, retrograde memory losses, and so forth, we predict an increasing degree of change in association areas. In a detailed study of individuals with AD who had been studied clinically within 1 year of death, we found a significant correlation between score on a memory-concentration battery (the Blessed Dementia Scale) and number of NFT in association cortex (Arriagada, Growdon, Hedley-White, & Hyman, 1991). Patients with relatively more NFT in association cortices had a significantly worse Blessed score. We also found a trend

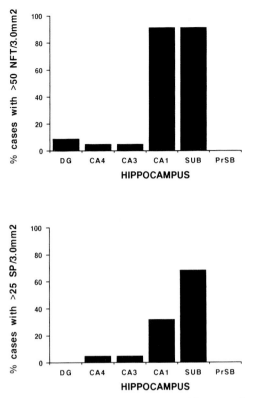

FIGURE 4.6. Relative degree of involvement by neurofibrillary tangles (NFT) and senile plaques (SP) of various cytoarchitectural areas in the hippocampus. These plots represent the percentage of total cases that contained substantial pathology in each of the cytoarchitectural fields, using the same criteria as noted in Figure 4.5.

toward individuals with shorter duration of disease having a higher percentage of total NFT in limbic areas. These data are consistent with the notion that NFT occur initially in medial temporal lobe structures, and that NFT accumulate in association cortices as the clinical severity increases.

Anatomical studies of the topography of forebrain lesions in AD highlight involvement of structures whose integrity is important for normal memory, including the amygdala (Brashear, Godec, & Carlsen, 1988; Kromer-Vogt et al., 1990; Hyman et al., 1990), the nucleus basalis of Meynert (Whitehouse, Price, Clark, Coyle, & DeLong, 1981) and the association cortices (Van Hoesen & Damasio, 1987; Lewis, Campbell, Terry, & Morrison, 1987; Arnold, Hyman, Flory, Damasio, & Van Hoesen, 1991). In each instance it appears that a major target of the disease is the population of projection neurons important for feed-forward/feedback projections among the association cortices and the limbic system. There is likely a great deal of anatomical and functional redundancy within this neural system. However, we suggest that the slow accumulation of pathology specifically affecting neurons crucial for normal cortical-limbic projections ultimately overwhelms this reserve, and more substantial memory impairments are expressed. It is possible that detailed evaluation of the Alzheimer brain, in combination with modern neuropsychological evaluation, will provide a further window on the organization of the neural substrates of memory.

Acknowledgments

This work was supported by National Institutes of Health Grants AG08487, NS 14944, PO NS19632, and grants from the Kiwanis International (Illinois-Eastern Iowa District), Spastic Paralysis Research Foundation, Fraternal Order of Eagles, and the Brookdale Foundation. We thank Dr. H. Damasio for review of this manuscript. We thank S. Melanson for assistance with the manuscript.

References

Amaral, D. G. (1987). Memory: Anatomical organization of candidate brain regions. In V. B. Mountcastle, F. Plum, S. R. Geiger (Eds.), *Handbook of physiology* (Vol. 5, pp. 211–294). Bethesda, MD: American Physiological Society.

Arnold, S. E., Hyman, B. T., Flory, J., Damasio, A. R., & Van Hoesen, G. W. (1991). The topographical and neuroanatomical distribution of neuroflexibility tangles and neuritic plaques in the cerebral cortex of patients in Alzheimer's disease. *Cerebral Cortex* (in press).

Arriagada, P., & Hyman, B. T. (1990). Topographic distribution of Alzheimer's neuronal changes in normal aging brains [Abstract]. *Journal of Neuropathology and Experimental Neurology*, *49*, 226.

Arriagada, P. V., Growdon, J. H., Hedley-Whyte, E. T., & Hyman, B. T. (1991). Clinical pathological correlations in Alzheimer's disease [Abstract]. *Neurology* (in press).

Ball, M. J. (1976). Neurofibrillary tangles and the pathogenesis of dementia: A quantitative study. *Neuropathology and Applied Neurobiology*, *2*, 395–410.

Brashear, H. R., Godec, M. S., & Carlsen, J. (1988). The distribution of neuritic plaques and acetylcholinesterase staining in the amygdala in Alzheimer's disease. *Neurology*, *38*, 1694–1699.

Cohen, N. J., Eichenbaum, H., Deacedo, B. S., & Corkin, S. (1985). Different memory systems underlying acquisition of procedural and declarative knowledge. *Annals of the New York Academy of Sciences*, *444*, 54–71.

Corkin, S. (1968). Acquisition of motor skill after bilateral medial temporal lobe excision. *Neuropsychologia*, *6*, 255–265.

Corkin, S., Gabrielli, J. D. E., Stranger, B. Z., et al. (1986). Skill learning and priming in Alzheimer's disease [Abstract]. *Neurology*, *36* (Suppl. 1), 296.

Damasio, A. R., Eslinger, P. J., Damasio, H., Van Hoesen, G. W., & Cornell, S. (1985). Multimodal amnesia syndrome following bilateral temporal and basal forebrain damage. *Archives of Neurology*, *42*, 252–259.

Damasio, A. (1984). The anatomic basis of memory disorders. *Seminars in Neurology*, *4*, 223–225.

Damasio, A. (1989). Time locked multiregional retroactivation: A system level proposal for the neural substrates of recall and recognition. *Cognition*, *33*, 25–62.

Damasio, A., Travel, D., & Damasio, H. (1989). Amnesia caused by herpes simplex encephalities, infarctions in basal forebrain, Alzheimer's disease, and anoxia. In L. Squire (Ed.), *Handbook of physiology* (Vol. 3, pp. 495–166). Amsterdam: Elsevier.

Damasio, A. R. (1990). Synchronous activation in multiple cortical regions: A mechanism for recall. *Seminars in Neuroscience*, *2*, 287–296.

Eslinger, P. J., & Damasio, A. R. (1986). Preserved motor learning in Alzheimer's disease. *Journal of Neuroscience*, *6*, 3006–3009.

Heindel, W. C., Salmon, D. P., Shults, C. W., Walicke, P. A., & Butters, N. (1989). Neuropsychological evidence for multiple implicit memory systems: A comparison of Alzheimer's, Huntington's and Parkinson's disease. *Journal of Neuroscience, 9,* 582–587.

Hirano, A., & Zimmerman, H. M. (1962). Alzheimer's neurofibrillary changes. *Archives of Neurology, 7,* 73–88.

Hyman, B. T. , & Mann, D. M. A. (1991). Neurofibrillary pathology in Down's syndrome individuals of various ages. In K. Iqbal, D. R. C. McLachlan, B. Winblad, & H. M. Wisniewski (Eds.), *Alzheimer's disease: Basic mechanisms, diagnosis and therapeutic strategies* (pp. 105–113). New York: Wiley.

Hyman, B. T., Damasio, A. R., Van Hoesen, G. W., & Barnes, C. L. (1984). Alzheimer's disease: Cell-specific pathology isolates the hippocampal formation. *Science, 298,* 83–95.

Hyman, B. T., & Van Hoesen, G. W. (1990). Hierarchical vulnerability of the entorhinal cortex and the hippocampal formation to Alzheimer neuropathological changes: A semiquantitative study [Abstract]. *Neurology, 40,* 403.

Hyman, B. T., Van Hoesen, G. W., & Damasio, A. R. (1988). A direct demonstration of the perforant pathway terminal zone in Alzheimer's disease using the monoclonal antibody Alz-50. *Brain Research, 450,* 392–397.

Hyman, B. T., Van Hoesen, G. W., & Damasio, A. R. (1990). Memory-related neural systems in Alzheimer's disease. *Neurology, 40,* 1729–1730.

Hyman, B. T., Van Hoesen, G. W., Kromer, L. J., & Damasio, A. R. (1986). Perforant pathway changes and the memory impairment of Alzheimer's disease. *Annals of Neurology, 20,* 472–481.

Hyman, B. T., Tanzi, R. E., Marzloff, K. M., Barbour, R., & Schenk, D. (1992). Kunitz protease inhibitor containing amyloid precursor protein immunoreactivity in Alzheimer's disease: A quantitative study. *Journal of Neuropathology and Experimental Neurology, 51,* 76–83.

Kemper, T. L. (1978). Senile dementia: A focal disease in the temporal lobe. In K. Nandy (Ed.). *Senile dementia: A biomedical approach* (pp. 105–113). Amsterdam: Elsevier.

Kosel, K. C., Van Hoesen, G. W., & Rosene, D. L. (1982). Nonhippocampal cortical projections from the entorhinal cortex in the rat and rhesus monkey. *Brain Research, 244,* 201–214.

Kromer-Vogt, L. J., Hyman, B. T., Van Hoesen, G. W., & Damasio, A. R. (1990). Pathological alterations in the amygdala in Alzheimer's disease. *Neuroscience, 37,* 377–385.

Lewis, D. A., Campbell, M. J., Terry, R. D., & Morrison, J. H. (1987). Laminar and regional distributions of neurofibrillary tangles and neuritic plaques in Alzheimer's disease: A quantitative study of visual and auditory cortices. *Journal of Neuroscience, 7,* 1799–1808.

Mishkin, M. (1982). A memory system in the monkey. *Philosophical Transactions of the Royal Society of London. Series B: Biological Sciences (London), 298,* 83–95.

Moss, M. B., Albert, M. S., Butters, N. & Payne, M. (1986). Differential patterns of memory loss among patients with Alzheimer's disease, Huntington's disease, and alcoholic Korsakoff's syndrome. *Archives of Neurology, 43,* 239–246.

Pepin, E. P., & Eslinger, P. J. (1989). Verbal memory decline in Alzheimer's disease. *Neurology, 39,* 1477–1482.

Rosene, D. L., & Van Hoesen, G. W. (1987). The hippocampal formation of the primate brain. In E. G. Jones & A. Peters (Eds.), *Cerebral cortex* (Vol. 6, pp. 345–356). New York: Plenum Press.

Scoville, W. B., & Milner, B. (1957). Loss of recent memory after bilateral hippocampal lesions. *Journal of Neurology, Neurosurgery and Psychiatry, 20,* 11–21.

Squire, L. R., & Zola-Morgan, S. (1983). The neurology of memory: The case for correspondence between the findings for human and nonhuman primate. In J. A. Deutsch
(Ed.). *The physiological basis of memory* (pp. 200–268). New York: Academic Press.

Squire, L. R., & Zola-Morgan, S. (1988). Memory: Brain systems and behavior. *Trends in
Neuroscience*, *11*, 170–175.

Van Hoesen, G. W. (1982). The parahippocampal gyrus. New observations regarding its
cortical connections in the monkey. *Trends in Neuroscience*, *5*, 345–350.

Van Hoesen, G. W. (1985). Neural systems of the non-human primate forebrain implicated
in memory. *Annals of the New York Academy of Sciences*, *444*, 97–112.

Van Hoesen, G. W., Damasio, A. R. (1987). Neural correlates of cognitive impairment in
Alzheimer's disease. In V. B. Mountcastle, F. Plum, & S. R. Geiger (Eds.), *Hand-
book of physiology* (Vol. 5, pp. 871–898). Bethesda, MD: American Physiological
Society.

Whitehouse, P. J., Price, D. L., Clark, A. W., Coyle, J. T., & DeLong, M. R. (1981).
Alzheimer's disease: Evidence for selective loss of cholinergic neurons in the nucleus
basalis. *Annals of Neurology*, *10*, 122–126.

Zola-Morgan, S., Squire, L. R., & Amaral, D. G. (1986). Human amnesia and the medial
temporal lobe region: Enduring memory impairment following a bilateral lesion limited to field CA1 of the hippocampus. *Journal of Neuroscience*, *6*, 2950–2967.

PART II

DIFFERENTIATING ALZHEIMER'S DISEASE FROM OTHER DEMENTIAS

5

Neuropsychological Findings in HIV Infection, Encephalopathy, and Dementia

WILFRED G. VAN GORP, CHARLES HINKIN, PAUL SATZ,
ERIC MILLER, and LOUIS F. D'ELIA

Overview of Central Nervous System Involvement
Secondary to HIV Infection

Soon after the initial case reports of patients with unexplained immune deficiency and rare opportunistic infections appeared (Gottlieb et al., 1981), observations of altered mental status in these patients began to emerge in the literature (e.g., Snider et al., 1983). Initially, these alterations were termed *subacute encephalitis*, *encephalopathy*, or simply *altered mental status* and were thought to result from opportunistic infections involving the central nervous system (CNS) such as cytomegalovirus infection or other secondary processes. Four years after the initial case reports of acquired immunodeficiency syndrome (AIDS) were published, it was determined that human immunodeficiency virus (HIV) could be isolated in the brains of infected patients with dementia (Ho et al., 1985) and in the cerebrospinal fluid (CSF) of infected individuals (Resnick et al., 1985; Resnick, Berger, Shapshak, & Tourtellotte, 1988). In several seminal papers, Navia, Jordan, and Price (1986a) and Navia, Cho, Petito, and Price (1986b) reported the presence of mental status changes and subsequent neuropathological findings in a sample of 70 patients with AIDS, 46 (66%) of whom had evidence of progressive cognitive or motor disturbance prior to death. Widespread neuropathological changes were found, with diffuse changes most prominent in the subcortical white matter. This led Navia and colleagues to conclude that HIV can affect the CNS in the absence of other discernable secondary etiologies, producing a subcortical dementia with prominent cognitive, behavioral, and motor features, a syndrome they termed the *AIDS dementia complex* (ADC).

This chapter will focus on the neuropsychological changes associated with HIV encephalopathy in adults. In addition, we will briefly review the clinicopathological changes associated with HIV encephalopathy as well as findings from both structural (magnetic resonance imaging [MRI], computed tomography [CT]) and functional (positron emission tomography [PET], single photon emission computed tomography [SPECT], electroencephalogram [EEG]) neuroimaging studies. We will also briefly discuss secondary processes often found in HIV-infected individuals that can cause mental status abnormalities. Finally, we will highlight important clinical issues in the neuropsychological assessment, interpretation, and management considerations specific to this population.

It is also important to note that HIV infection can cause severe neurological disease in children as well. However, it is beyond the scope of this chapter to survey the increasing literature on neuropsychological changes associated with HIV encephalopathy in children, a subject of its own. As such, we will limit our discussion to adults, who account for the majority of cases of HIV infection to date.

A Note on Terminology and Diagnostic Nomenclature

Remarkable confusion and controversy currently exists over which term(s) should be applied to describe the constellation of cognitive, behavioral, and motor abnormalities associated with HIV infection. Navia et al. (1986a) first proposed the term *AIDS dementia complex* to describe the constellation of neuropsychological, neuropsychiatric, and motor abnormalities associated with HIV infection. However, this definition was purely descriptive and was not operationally defined. Additionally, this definition did not specify the breadth or severity of symptoms necessary to objectively diagnose a patient as demented (i.e., would an individual with discernable but mild neuropsychological compromise affecting only psychomotor speed be labeled with a dementia?). Nevertheless, this term has gained acceptance and is perhaps the term most commonly used for this condition. To stage the severity of the dementia complex, this group (Sidtis & Price, 1990) has developed a staging scheme shown in Table 5.1 to be applied once the diagnosis of ADC is warranted.

One year after the Navia et al. (1986a) description, the Centers for Disease Control (CDC) included the diagnosis of HIV encephalopathy among those qualifying an otherwise HIV-seropositive but asymptomatic individual for a diagnosis of full-blown AIDS. The CDC defines HIV encephalopathy as:

> Clinical findings of disabling cognitive and/or motor dysfunction interfering with occupation or activities of daily living, or loss of behavioral developmental milestones affecting a child, progressing over weeks to months, in the absence of a concurrent illness or other condition than HIV infection that could explain the findings. Methods to rule out such concurrent illness and conditions must include cerebrospinal fluid examination and either brain imaging (computed tomography or magnetic resonance) or autopsy. (Centers for Disease Control, 1987)

This definition is also limited because of the lack of specific operational criteria. For example, how are *clinical findings* defined? Can only motor abnormalities qualify an individual for a diagnosis of HIV encephalopathy if they lead to poor work performance? If they are not progressive over *weeks to months*, can the diagnosis still be applied?

Because of the confusion over specific diagnostic criteria, whether the term *dementia* should be used, and how to stage the severity of the illness, the American

TABLE 5.1. Severity Staging Criteria for AIDS Dementia Complex

ADC Stage	Characteristics
Stage 0. Normal	Normal mental and motor function.
Stage 0.5. Equivocal/subclinical	Either minimal or equivocal symptoms of cognitive or motor dysfunction characteristic of ADC, or mild signs (snout response, slowed extremity movements), but without impairment of work or capacity to perform activities of daily living (ADL); gait and strength are normal.
Stage 1. Mild	Unequivocal evidence (symptoms, signs, neuropsychological test performance) of functional intellectual or motor impairment characteristic of ADC, but able to perform all but the more demanding aspects of work of ADL; can walk without assistance.
Stage 2. Moderate	Cannot work or maintain the more demanding aspects of daily life, able to perform basic activities of self-care ambulatory, but may require a single prop.
Stage 3. Severe	Major intellectual incapacity (cannot follow news or personal events, cannot sustain complex conversation, considerable slowing of all output), or motor disability (cannot walk unassisted, requiring walker or personal support, usually with slowing and clumsiness of arms as well).
Stage 4. End stage	Nearly vegetative; intellectual and social comprehension and responses are at a rudimentary level; nearly or absolutely mute; paraparetic or paraplegic with double incontinence.

Note: The ADC stage is applied only after establishing a clinical diagnosis of ADC, which requires the presence of documented HIV-1 infection, evidence of an acquired neurological deficit, and exclusion of other neurological or psychiatric disorders explaining this deficit. It also requires the presence of characteristic clinical abnormalities in cognitive, motor, or behavioral functions. In the cognitive sphere, this may include early symptoms of impaired concentration and slowed thinking. Complaints of forgetfullness are common, but early in ADC formal memory testing may reveal normal function. Cognitive changes may then evolve to significant impairments in abstraction, profound slowing, failures in concentration and memory, and later, to global dementia. In the motor sphere, characteristic ADC changes include early slowing of rapid extremity movements, which may evolve to clumsiness and ataxia of gait and impaired hand coordination, and later to paraplegia, with incontinence in the most severe cases. Behavioral dysfunction has somewhat less diagnostic precision, but characteristic abnormalities include early personality change and apathy without dysphoria, which may progress hand in hand with one psychomotor retardation to the point of near or full mutism; a subgroup of patients may exhibit psychosis, agitation, or even frank mania. Laboratory studies of ancillary value include neuropsychological assessments in which the characteristic profile demonstrates psychomotor slowing and poor performance on tasks of attention and concentration, with relative sparing of language and memory skills early in the course computed tomography (CT) or magnetic resonance imaging (MRI) showing brain atrophy and, in some white matter or basal ganglion abnormalities; and elevated cerebrospinal fluid (CSF) β-microglobulin or neopterin in the absence of other causes.
Source: From Sidtis & Price, 1990. Reprinted by permission.

Academy of Neurology AIDS Task Force has recently proposed the term *HIV-associated cognitive/motor complex* rather than ADC or the more general term, HIV encephalopathy (American Academy of Neurology AIDS Task Force, 1991). As Table 5.2 indicates, HIV-associated cognitive/motor complex can be subclassified as minor, or if sufficiently severe, the term *HIV-associated dementia complex* can be given.

It remains unclear which term(s) or diagnostic criteria will ultimately be uniformly adopted by clinicians and researchers in this field. Because of the current state of using differing nomenclature with differing implications, we will use the term *HIV encephalopathy* to refer to cases in which neuropsychological abnor-

TABLE 5.2.   American Academy of Neurology Diagnostic Criteria for HIV-Associated
Cognitive/Motor Complex

I. Consistent with diagnosis of AIDS
  A. *HIV-1-Associated Dementia Complex*
    Probable (Must have each of the following):
    1. Laboratory evidence for systemic HIV-1 infection (ELISA test confirmed by Western
       blot; or polymerase chain reaction [PRCR]; or culture).
    2. Acquired impairment in at least two of the following cognitive abilities (present for at
       least 1 month): attention/concentration, speed of processing information, abstraction/
       reasoning, visuospatial skills, memory/learning, and speech/language. The decline
       should be verified by reliable history and mental status examination. In all cases, when
       possible, history should be obtained from an informant and examination should be
       supplemented by neuropsychological testing.
    Cognitive dysfunction causes impairment of work or activities of daily living[a] (objectively
    verifiable or by report of a key informant). This impairment should not be attributable
    solely to severe systemic illness.
    3. At least one of the following:
      a. Acquired abnormality in motor function or performance verified by clinical
         examination (e.g., slowed rapid movements, abnormal gait, limb incoordination,
         hyperreflexia, hypertonia, or weakness) and/or neuropsychological tests (e.g., fine
         motor speed, manual dexterity, perceptual motor skills).
      b. Decline in motivation or emotional control or change in social behavior. This may be
         characterized by any of the following: change in personality with apathy, inertia,
         irritability, emotional lability, or new onset of impaired judgment characterized by
         socially inappropriate behavior or disinhibition.
    4. Absence of clouding of consciousness during a period long enough to establish the
       presence of #2.
    5. Evidence of another etiology, including active central nervous system opportunistic
       infection of malignancy, psychiatric disorders such as depressive disorder, active alcohol
       or substance use or acute or chronic substance withdrawal must be sought from history,
       physical and psychiatric examination, and appropriate laboratory and radiologic
       investigation (e.g., lumbar puncture, neuroimaging). However, if another potential
       etiology (e.g., major depression) is present, it is *not* the cause of the above cognitive,
       motor, or behavioral symptoms and signs.
  A. *Other Potential Etiology Present*
    Possible (must have each of the following):
    1. As above #1, 2, 3, 4.
    5. Other potential etiology is present but the cause of #2 is uncertain.
  B. *Incomplete Clinical Evaluation*
    (must have each of the following):
    1. As above #1, 2, 3, 4.
    5. Etiology cannot be determined (appropriate laboratory or radiologic investigations not
       performed).

Continued

---

malities secondary to HIV are present but in which the severity of impairment is
either mild or unspecified. We will reserve the use of the term *AIDS dementia
complex* for cases that appear to represent moderate to severe cognitive impairment, affecting three or more cognitive domains (Cummings & Benson, 1983), and
affecting a person's ability to perform their usual activities of daily living (ADL).

Other Secondary Processes that Can Cause Neuropsychological Dysfunction

This chapter will focus on the effects of HIV upon the nervous system independent
of other secondary processes that can often cause focal neuropsychological deficits.

B. *HIV-1-Associated Myelopathy*

Probable (must have each of the following):

1. Laboratory evidence for systemic HIV-1 infection (ELISA test confirmed by Western blot; or PCR; or culture)
2. Acquired abnormality in lower extremity neurological function out of proportion to upper extremity abnormality verified by reliable history (lower extremity weakness, incoordination, and/or urinary incontinence) and neurological examination (paraparesis, lower extremity spasticity, hyperreflexia, or the presence of Babinski signs, with or without sensory loss).
3. Disturbance in #2 is severe enough[b] to require constant unilateral support for walking.
4. Although mild cognitive impairment may be present, criteria for HIV-1-associated dementia complex are not fulfilled.
5. Evidence of another etiology including neoplasm, compressive lesion, or multiple sclerosis must be sought from history, physical examination and appropriate laboratory and radiologic investigation (e.g., lumbar puncture, neuroimaging, myelography). However, if another potential etiology is present, it is *not* the cause of the myelopathy. This diagnosis cannot be made in a patient infected with both HIV-1 and HTLV-1; such a patient should be classified as having possible HIV-1-associated myelopathy.

A. *Other Potential Etiology Present*

Possible (must have each of the following):

1. As above #1, 2, 3, 4.
5. Other potential etiology is present but the cause of the myelopathy is uncertain.

B. *Incomplete Clinical Evaluation*

(must have each of the following):

1. As above #1, 2, 3, 4.
5. Etiology cannot be determined (appropriate laboratory or radiologic investigations not performed).

II. Not consistent with diagnosis of AIDS

A. *HIV-1-Associated Minor Cognitive/Motor Disorder*

Probable (must have each of the following):

1. Laboratory evidence for systemic HIV-1 infection (ELISA test confirmed by Western blot; or PCR; or culture).
2. Cognitive/Motor/Behavioral Abnormalities (must have each of the following):
   a. At least two of the following acquired cognitive, motor, or behavioral symptoms (present for at least 1 month), verified by reliable history, when possible, from an informant:
      1. Impaired attention or concentration
      2. Mental slowing
      3. Impaired memory
      4. Slowed movements
      5. Incoordination
      6. Personality change or irritability or emotional lability
   b. Acquired cognitive/motor abnormality verified by clinical neurological examination or neuropsychological testing (e.g., fine motor speed, manual dexterity, perceptual motor skills, attention/concentration, speed of processing information, abstraction/reasoning, visuospatial skills, memory/learning, or speech/language).
3. Disturbance in #2 causes mild impairment of work or activities of daily living[c] (objectively verifiable or by report of a key informant).
4. Does not meet criteria for HIV-1-associated dementia complex or HIV-1-associated myelopathy.
5. No evidence of another etiology, including active central nervous system opportunistic infection or malignancy, or severe systemic illness determined by appropriate history, physical examination and laboratory and radiologic investigation (e.g., lumbar puncture, neuroimaging). The above features should not be attributable solely to the effects of active alcohol or substance use, acute or chronic substance withdrawal, adjustment disorder, or other psychiatric disorder.

Continued

TABLE 5.2.   (*Continued*)

A. *Other Potential Etiology Present*
   Possible (must have each of the following):
   1. As above #1, 2, 3, 4.
   5. Other potential etiology is present but the cause of the cognitive/motor/behavior abnormalities is uncertain.
B. *Incomplete Clinical Evaluation*
   (must have each of the following):
   1. As above #1, 2, 3, 4.
   2. Etiology cannot be determined (appropriate laboratory of radiologic investigations not performed).

---

[a]The level of impairment due to cognitive dysfunction should be assessed as follows:

Mild   Decline in performance at work, including work in the home, that is conspicuous to others. Cannot work at usual job, although may be able to work at a less demanding job. Activities of daily living or social activities are impaired but not to a degree making the person dependent on others. More complicated daily tasks or recreational activities cannot be undertaken. Capable of basic self-care such as feeding self, dressing, and maintaining personal hygiene, but activities such as handling money, shopping, using public transportation, driving a car, or keeping track of appointments or medications is impaired.

Moderate   Unable to work, including work in the home. Unable to function without some assistance of another in daily living, including dressing, maintaining personal hygiene, eating, shopping, handling money, and walking.

Severe   Unable to perform any activities of daily living without assistance of others. Requires continual supervision. Unable to maintain personal hygiene, nearly or absolutely mute.

[b]The severity of HIV-1-associated myelopathy should be graded as follows:

Mild   Ambulatory but requires constant unilateral support (e.g., cane) for walking.
Moderate   Requires constant bilateral support (e.g., walker) for walking.
Severe   Unable to walk even with assistance, confined to bed or wheelchair.

[c]Able to perform all but the more demanding aspects of work or activities of daily living. Performance at work is mildly impaired but able to maintain usual job; social activities may be mildly impaired but not to the degree making the person dependent on others. Only the most demanding aspects of work on activities of daily living cannot be undertaken. Can feed self, dress, and maintain personal hygiene, handle money, shop, use public transportation, or drive a car, but complex daily tasks such as keeping track of appointments or medications may be occasionally impaired.

Source: From American Academy of Neurology AIDS Task Force (1991). Reprinted by permission.

Because these secondary processes also typically result in compromise to cognitive functions, clinicians and researchers must first rule out their presence before a diagnosis of an HIV-related dementia can be considered.

The most frequent and treatable secondary CNS process in HIV-infected individuals is cerebral toxoplasmosis, a parasitic infection caused by *toxoplasma gondii*. This condition, often appearing as focal intensities on MRI and ring-enhancing lesions on CT scans, results in one or more focal lesions, with corresponding cognitive dysfunction dependent on specific site of the lesion(s). Following medical treatment for these parasite-induced lesions, the patient's cognitive status may often improve. Primary CNS lymphomas are perhaps the second most common secondary CNS-related neurological disturbance in HIV-infected individuals. Because of the focal nature of the neoplastic process, the neuropsychological deficits will often be similar to those seen in toxoplasmosis. Another secondary process not uncommon in HIV is progressive multifocal leukoencephalopathy (PML), an opportunistic viral infection produced by the papova virus, causing white matter changes and focal neuropsychological deficits. The course of this condition is often rapid and brain biopsy may be warranted to confirm the diagnosis. Although few reports of neuropsychological findings in PML have appeared, at least one paper

(Stenquist et al., 1990) has documented various focal neuropsychological abnormalities in a series of four patients with PML. There are other, less common, focal CNS diseases (cf. Rosenblum, Levy, & Bredesen, 1988) that can affect the mental status in HIV-infected individuals. For the neuropsychologist, whenever an HIV-infected patient presents with isolated or focal neuropsychological deficits, such as an aphasia or marked visuospatial disturbance in a nondemented individual, one of these secondary CNS processes should be considered and a prompt referral for neurological evaluation including neuroimaging and lumbar puncture should be made.

Clinicopathological Correlates of HIV Infection Involving the Central Nervous System

Neuropathological abnormalities are present in approximately 70% to 90% of the brains of individuals diagnosed with AIDS (Vinters, Tomiyasu, & Anders, 1989; Ho, Bredesen, Vinters, & Daar, 1989). As noted above, Navia et al. (1986b) found neuropathological abnormalities primarily in the subcortical white matter with relative sparing of the cortex. Diffuse pallor of the white matter was the most common abnormality. Curiously, these investigators noted that in approximately one third of their demented cases, the neuropathological abnormalities were remarkably bland, whereas mild neuropathological abnormalities were found in many of the nondemented patients. Unfortunately, no quantitative neuropsychological testing was obtained prior to death on these individuals, which could have helped to reconcile the inconsistent findings between bedside mental status observations and degree of neuropathology on autopsy. In contrast to the largely subcortical findings of Navia and colleagues, de la Monte, Ho, Schooley, Hirsch, and Richardson (1987) found gliosis of the cortex and white matter in most of their sample, as well as small foci of tissue necrosis, microglial nodules, demyelination, and multinucleated giant cells in 20% of the sample. Lesions were most common in the white matter and cortex, although the amygdala, basal ganglia, and hippocampus were also affected. Gabuzda and Hirsch (1987) reported that the white matter and basal ganglia appeared most severely affected. Several investigators have noted ventricular dilation and mild cortical atrophy (e.g., Brew, Sidtis, Petito, & Price, 1988).

More recently, two autopsy series have reported the presence of neocortical damage. Ketzler, Weis, Huag, and Budka (1990) reported the presence of neuronal loss confined to the frontal lobes, whereas Wiley et al. (1991), in their series of 18 autopsied brains, reported thinning of the neocortical ribbon predominantly in the parietal and temporal lobes, diminished synaptic density, and vacuolation of dendritic processes.

Imaging Studies

Both structural (CT, MRI) and functional (PET, SPECT, EEG) measures of the brain have been conducted in patients with HIV-spectrum disease. A review of CT scans performed on 443 HIV-infected individuals (De La Paz & Enzmann, 1988) found intraaxial lesions in 38% of the scans and atrophy in 33%, whereas normal results were found in the remaining 29% based on clinical reading. De La Paz and Enzmann note that in nonfocal HIV-related neurological disease (such as HIV encephalopathy, cytomegalovirus infection, viral encephalitis, and meningitis), CT findings have generally been read as normal or mild atrophy even in proven cases. Post et al. (1988), however, found that of 21 patients with AIDS, 20 evidenced cortical atrophy on CT, whereas 13 were judged to evidence ventriculated enlargement.

Studies using MRI in HIV-related disease have begun to accumulate. Grant et al. (1987) reported a high frequency of MRI abnormalities in a relatively small sample of patients with AIDS ($N = 13$) and ARC ($N = 10$). MRI findings were rated as abnormal in 9 of the 13 patients with AIDS and 5 of 10 patients with ARC. The most common findings were sulcal and ventricular enlargement and bilateral patchy areas of high signal intensity in the white matter. The findings of Grant et al. are difficult to fully interpret because no seronegative controls were included. McArthur et al. (1989) analyzed MRI findings (based on clinical neuroradiological ratings) for a group of 35 asymptomatic HIV-seropositive and 25 seronegative gay or bisexual men enrolled in the Multicenter AIDS Cohort Study (MACS). The most common findings were either normal appearance or diffuse sulcal prominence and focal areas of high signal intensity in the white matter. Surprisingly, the proportion or type of MRI abnormalities did not differ between the seropositive and seronegative groups, and no association was found between the presence of MRI findings and other clinical abnormalities. A follow-up study by the MACS group (McArthur et al., 1990) obtained very similar results, with 24% of seronegatives, 26% of asymptomatic seropositives, and 17% of symptomatic seropositives demonstrating focal white matter hyperintensities. Similarly, Koralnik et al. (1990) reported that their seronegative and seropositive cohorts did not differ on MRI. Olsen, Longo, Mills, and Norman (1988) reviewed the results of MRI scans in a series of 365 patients with AIDS who were scanned at four San Francisco hospitals between 1985 and 1987. Of the 365 scans reviewed, 112 (31%) had signal abnormalities confined to the white matter. Olsen et al. (1988) reported the most common findings to be: (1) diffuse, widespread involvement; (2) poorly defined patchy abnormalities; (3) clearly defined focal involvement; and (4) punctate abnormalities with small foci smaller than 1 cm^2. When the cases for which a known secondary disease process (such as PML) were excluded, white matter abnormalities were most commonly observed. Unfortunately, as with the Grant et al. study, no seronegative control group was included. White matter hyperintensity on MRI has also been reported by Chrysikopoulos, Press, Grafe, Hesselenik, and Wiley (1990) and by Elovaara et al. (1990). Levin et al. (1990) reported the presence of small (<1 cm in all but two cases) focal lesions in 25% of their seropositive sample (CDC Groups II-IV) as well as the presence of atrophy, particularly among their CDC IV subjects. While the presence of focal lesions was not found by Levin et al. to correlate with neurobehavioral change, a significant relationship was found between atrophy and psychomotor slowness.

Based on these studies, the nature and frequency of HIV-related nonfocal CT/MRI abnormalities cannot be stated with certainty, although studies on larger clinical samples suggest that one third or more of symptomatic patients may show abnormalities including atrophy or white matter intensities. Although structural imaging approaches are useful in detecting atrophy and focal CNS processes, their sensitivity in detecting mild to moderate HIV encephalopathy is inadequate to make them diagnostically useful except as exclusionary measures.

In contrast to *structural* imaging approaches, physiologic imaging measures of brain *function* have begun to appear. Rottenberg et al. (1987) studied the resting cerebral metabolic function of 12 HIV-seropositive patients diagnosed with ADC and 18 normal control subjects with PET using [18F]flurodeoxyglucose (FDG) as the tracer. Compared with controls, Rottenberg and colleagues found increased metabolic activity in the thalamus and basal ganglia in the patients with mild HIV encephalopathy, but decreased cortical and subcortical metabolism in the remaining patients with more advanced dementia. In the only other reported controlled study to date of PET in AIDS, van Gorp, Mandelkern et al. (1992) studied 17 AIDS patients with and without dementia and 14 seronegative controls. Subjects were studied with FDG and PET in a resting state paradigm, similar to the Rottenberg et al. study. All subjects in the clinical group were rated for severity of dementia using the AIDS Dementia Rating Scale developed by Sidtis and Price (1990) and regional metabolic values were quantitated using the ratio of regional metabolic activity (corrected for pixel count) to subjects' whole brain metabolic activity.

Of the 17 AIDS patients, 7 were rated as 0 (normal, $n = 3$) or 0.5 (equivocal, $n = 4$) and 10 were rated as either 1 (mild, $n = 6$) or 2 (moderate, $n = 4$). As Figure 5.1 illustrates, only the regional activity of the thalamus and basal ganglia differed significantly between controls and the AIDS group. As was found in the Rottenberg et al. study, there was relative regional hypermetabolism in these subcortical regions. As Figure 5.2 indicates, a stepwise multiple regression analysis was performed to predict severity of dementia (using dementia severity scores) using PET regional values for the subjects with AIDS. In this analysis, only temporal lobe activity was significantly associated with dementia rating (multiple $R = .50$). The finding of lowered activity in the temporal lobe as dementia severity worsens is interesting in light of the neuropsychological findings (see below), which have found memory and psychomotor speeded tasks to be differentially affected in AIDS. Brunetti et al. (1989) also employed PET-FDG in a study of four patients

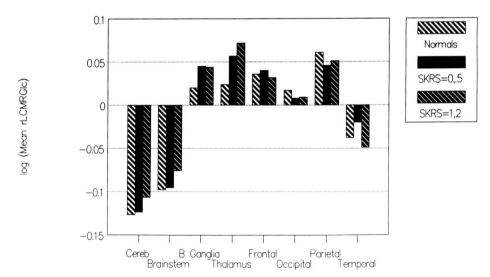

FIGURE 5.1. Normalized regional cerebral metabolic values (in log units) for eight cerebral regions of interest. Ratio scores of region to whole brain metabolic activity are used for each region.

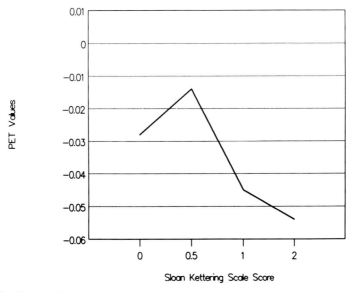

FIGURE 5.2. The relationship between dementia severity and cerebral metabolic activity for the temporal lobe in the AIDS group.

before and after institution of an azido thymidine (AZT) regimen and found the use of AZT to result in an overall increase in cortical glucose metabolic rate.

Single photon emission computerized tomography has also been used to image brain function in HIV-related disease. LaFrance et al. (1988), using I-123-IMP SPECT, studied seven mildly demented HIV-infected men without evidence of focal CNS disease, six cognitively normal HIV-seropositive men, and five sero-negative controls. Five of the seven demented subjects and five of six seropositive but nondemented subjects had blood flow values 2 or more standard deviations from the control group mean. Pohl, Vogl, Fill, Rossler, and Zangerle (1988) used SPECT to study blood flow in 12 HIV-infected patients with subacute encephalopathy. All 12 patients demonstrated either multiple or focal perfusion defects. Unfortunately, this study is also weakened by the absence of a control group as well as the quantitative assessment of neuropsychological function, limiting the conclusions that may be drawn from it.

Kramer and Sanger (1990) did employ a control group (though inclusion/exclusion criteria were not specified) in their study of 30 HIV-seropositive and eight sero-negative subjects using SPECT with I-123-IMP. They concluded that their SPECT findings suggest a progression of the ADC from subcortical asymmetry to cortical abnormality to more globally affected cerebral perfusion.

Brain electrical activity or EEG measures have been reported as a useful adjunctive diagnostic technique in advanced HIV-related CNS disease (Gazbuda, Levy, & Chiappa, 1988). Leuchter, Newton, van Gorp, and Miller (1989) studied computer-analyzed quantitative EEG function in a group of 28 patients with AIDS and 56 seronegative controls. Electroencephalogram coherence was the primary variable chosen for study. Relative to seronegative controls, subjects with AIDS demonstrated significantly increased coherence values in the 6 to 10-Hz band. The most robust differences were in coherence values between distant cerebral regions.

Parisi et al. (1989) reported that 25% of their CDC Group II and 30% of their CDC Group III subjects evidence EEG abnormalities, the most common abnormality being theta slowing of the frontal and frontotemporal lobes. Koralnik et al. (1990) also report the presence of anterior theta rhythm abnormalities in their asymptomatic cohort. Ollo, Johnson, and Grafman (1991) have recently reported that AIDS/ARC patients, relative to seronegative controls, evidence reduced P300 amplitudes and increased P300 latencies in response to both auditory and visual stimuli, whereas asymptomatics evidenced such abnormalities only for visual stimuli. Delayed P2 latency in response to auditory stimuli was also observed among their AIDS/ARC patients.

What conclusions can be drawn for the preceding imaging studies? Structural and functional imaging studies in nonfocal HIV-related CNS disease suggest that the greatest changes in HIV-related disease occur in the subcortical white matter and to the thalamus and basal ganglia, with increased metabolic activity in these subcortical regions in response to viral perturbation. As the dementia worsens, the frontal and temporal lobes may become selectively dysfunctional, followed by global cortical and subcortical involvement. However, caution is still recommended in the interpretation of these results because of small sample sizes, lack of quantitative indices in many studies, and often, the absence of a seronegative control group.

Incidence/Prevalence of Neuropsychological Impairment in the Spectrum of HIV-Related Disease

As discussed earlier, there is general consensus that HIV penetrates the blood-brain barrier shortly following initial infection in most individuals. While some individuals exhibit an initial acute encephalopathic or meningitis-like pattern (see below), most individuals show no outward signs of brain infection in the early stages of the disease. There is also a general consensus that a subsample of patients with AIDS will demonstrate crippling cognitive impairments commonly labeled ADC, although there is still dispute about the prevalence of this disorder as well as the natural history of HIV infection of the nervous system between the time of initial infection and the onset of medical symptoms. During the period when an individual is medically asymptomatic but infected with HIV, are there any changes occurring in the CNS? And, if so, are these changes of functional relevance; that is, do they affect the individual's self-perception or ability to perform normally in activities of daily living?

In an influential early study of neuropsychological functioning in HIV-infected individuals, Grant et al. (1987) reported a significant trend toward greater neuropsychological impairment with increasing severity of HIV disease. Although the sample size was small, the pattern of results initially appeared quite persuasive, with impairment (as judged by clinical impression) in 1 of 11 (9%) seronegative controls, 7 of 16 (44%) asymptomatic seropositive subjects, 7 of 13 (54%) ARC patients, and 13 of 15 (87%) AIDS patients. The actual mean level of performance in the asymptomatic seropositive group was not significantly lower than that found in the seronegative control group (the only statistically significant differences were between the seronegative and AIDS groups), however.

Since the time of this initial report, there have been several additional studies of ASP subjects reported in the literature. These studies continue to find differing results as to whether or not subtle cognitive changes occur prior to the onset of medical symptoms of AIDS. Janssen et al. (1988) reported that 9 of 18 patients with lymphadenopathy syndrome had abnormal neuropsychological test results, with the majority scoring in the mildly impaired range. The authors later clarified (Saykin et al., 1988) that most of the subjects classified as impaired actually showed symptoms of constitutional disease (CDC Group IVa). Tross et al. (1988) found no evidence of significant cognitive impairment in asymptomatic seropositive men (n = 16). Similarly, Koralnik et al. (1990) also reported that their cohort of 29 asymptomatic subjects did not differ from 33 seronegative subjects on a series of neuropsychological and neurological measures. Goethe et al. (1989) found no differences in performance between a group of 83 neurologically intact HIV-seropositive men and seronegative controls on a detailed battery of neuropsychological tests, although this study suffered from an inappropriate control group of men referred on the basis of past history of head injury. In contrast, Perry, Belsky-Barr, Barr, and Jacobsberg (1989) studied a group of 20 asymptomatic HIV-seropositive homosexual men and a well-matched control group of 20 seronegative controls and found that the HIV-infected group exhibited lower mean scores on 17 of 20 neuropsychological measures and the HIV-seropositive subjects were significantly more likely to be classified as impaired than the matched seronegative controls. Wilkie, Eisdorfer, Morgan, Loewenstein, and Szapocznik (1990) studied 46 asymptomatic seropositive subjects and found that they performed significantly worse than seronegative controls on several measures of verbal memory and reaction time. Unfortunately, their seronegative control sample included only 13 subjects. A thorough review of this published literature and a number of recent conference abstracts are reviewed more extensively in an excellent paper by Perry (1990).

Most of these early studies are limited either by small sample sizes, inadequate specification of subject groups and sampling procedures, or a lack of population-specific normative data. A recent study by Janssen et al. (1989), however, overcomes many of these limitations. Janssen et al. studied 74 asymptomatic seropositive subjects and 157 seronegative controls drawn from the 6,000 men in the San Francisco City Clinic Cohort. This sample was initially recruited prior to the discovery of the cause of AIDS, thus reducing the chances of selection bias. Janssen et al. found no significant differences between their seronegative controls and asymptomatic seropositive subjects on a brief neuropsychological screening battery, regardless of whether they assessed differences on the basis of mean test scores or frequency of cases judged to reflect impairment. In addition to their work with this large sample, Janssen et al. administered a comprehensive neuropsychological battery to a subsample of 41 seronegative and 28 asymptomatic seropositive subjects. Again, they found no differences between the subject groups, this time using clinical judgments for assessing neuropsychological impairment.

The largest project in this area of research comes from the MACS. In three reports from this project, McArthur et al. (1989), Miller et al. (1990), and Selnes et al. (1990) present perhaps the most persuasive evidence to date that asymptomatic HIV-infected individuals as a group are no more likely than seronegative controls to show clinically significant cognitive impairment. Miller et al. adminis-

tered a screening battery of standardized neuropsychological measures to 769 seronegative and 727 medically asymptomatic HIV-seropositive gay men, all of whom were participating in a longitudinal epidemiological study of the natural history of HIV infection. Unlike earlier studies, the MACS sample includes a broad cross-section of homosexual and bisexual men drawn from four regional centers (Baltimore, Chicago, Pittsburgh, Los Angeles), each city representing different stages in the AIDS epidemic. Subjects were initially recruited before the discovery of the cause of AIDS and the development of HIV antibody testing, thus reducing a major source of selection bias affecting most other studies. Furthermore, the researchers controlled for the effects of age, education, and depression on neuropsychological test results. Using these procedures, the MACS investigators found that the frequency of neuropsychological abnormalities in asymptomatic HIV-infected seropositive men was low, and did not differ significantly from the frequency of abnormalities found in seronegative controls. McArthur et al. (1989) administered a more comprehensive neuropsychological test battery to a subsample of 68 asymptomatic seropositive men and 39 seronegative controls drawn from the MACS. Using this more extensive test protocol, McArthur et al. again found no differences in cognitive functioning between asymptomatic seropositive subjects and seronegative controls. Finally, Selnes et al. (1990) conducted the first study of neuropsychological changes over time using a subsample of 238 asymptomatic seropositive and 170 seronegative subjects from the MACS. Selnes et al. found no evidence of cognitive decline over a $1\frac{1}{2}$ year period among asymptomatic seropositive subjects.

The greatest limitation of the data from the MACS is that the mean educational level for these subjects is quite high, averaging 16 years. This suggests the possibility that among such a well-functioning group of individuals, cognitive impairments might be masked because of ceiling effects or insufficient test sensitivity. Recently, Satz et al. (in press) have re-analyzed data from the MACS, looking specifically at subjects with 12 years of education or less. For the 173 asymptomatic seropositive and seronegative subjects meeting this criterion, Satz et al. found a threefold increase in the percentage of neuropsychological "outliers" in the asymptomatic seropositive group relative to the seronegative controls in only the low-education group. This study raises the possibility that, whereas mild cognitive deficits may occur during the asymptomatic stages of infection, conventional neuropsychological procedures may lack sufficient sensitivity to detect cognitive changes among better educated individuals. These findings suggest the possible risk effects of low eduction on neuropsychological impairment in a subset of the population of ASP individuals.

In sum, the bulk of evidence to date suggests that HIV-related neuropsychological abnormalities among asymptomatic HIV-seropositive individuals are rare, and, in most cases, no more frequent than the abnormalities seen among seronegative controls. Although there have been several well-designed and well-controlled studies that have reported an increased frequency of mild neuropsychological abnormalities among some asymptomatic seropositive individuals, there has been no suggestion that this small subsample of individuals has neuropsychological impairment to a degree producing functional impairment in their day-to-day activities. However, some individuals may be at greater risk (such as those with limited educational attainment), and hence, have a lower threshold for overt neuropsychological impairment. Thus, the current body of research still largely agrees with the World Health Organization's 1988 conclusion that "there is no evidence that

otherwise healthy HIV infected individuals are more likely to be functionally impaired than persons not infected with HIV." (World Health Organization (WHO), 1988, p. 16).

Neuropsychological Findings in HIV Infection

One might ask if there is a pattern of neuropsychological changes characteristic of HIV infection, given that certain cerebral regions (thalamus, basal ganglia, and perhaps some cortical regions such as the temporal lobes) seem to be sites of predilection by the virus. Below, we discuss the findings of the published studies to date in HIV-infected individuals. We must include the caveat, however, that a simple comparison across studies is difficult and potentially misleading, because of differences in inclusion/exclusion criteria, types of control groups, as well as differences in individuals at various stages of HIV-related illness. Additionally, no study thus far has studied a sample composed solely of patients diagnosed with ADC or HIV encephalopathy. It is important for the reader to keep this in mind before drawing firm conclusions about the specific pattern of HIV-related neuropsychological compromise when reading the following section. As an aid, we have specified whether subjects in each study were asymptomatic seropositive (ASP) or symptomatic seropositives (SxSP).

Recently, a National Institute of Mental Health (NIMH) workshop on neuropsychological assessment approaches (Butters et al., 1990) recommended a brief and expanded neuropsychological test battery for HIV-infected individuals. Recommended assessment measures include many standard approaches (e.g., Vocabulary subtest from the Wechsler Adult Intelligence Scale-Revised [WAIS-R], California Verbal Learning Test [CVLT], Grooved Pegboard Test) as well as other experimentally based measures (e.g., Sternberg Search Task, simple and choice reaction times measures). Though most studies described below were completed before the recommendations of this group were published, most of the neuropsychological tests were administered by at least some research groups.

Attention

The majority of investigations have not found differences between HIV-seropositive versus seronegative subjects on measures of attention and concentration. Though Stern et al. (1991) report their sample of HIV-seropositive subjects (composed of both ASP and mildly symptomatic men) performed worse on digit span backwards than did seronegative controls, no other study that reported digit span performance found differences between SxSP and seronegative groups (Grant et al., 1987; Miller et al., 1990; Ollo & Pass, 1988; Ollo et al., 1991; Saykin et al., 1988; Tross et al., 1988; van Gorp, Miller, Satz, & Visscher, 1989). Both van Gorp et al. (1989) and Ollo and Pass (1988) failed to find significant differences between SxSP versus seronegative controls on the Mental Control subtest of the Wecshler Memory Scale (WMS) although Perry et al. (1989), who employed an extended Mental Control test, found their ASP subjects to perform worse than seronegative controls.

Similarly, studies that have assessed sustained concentration have largely failed to find significant differences between seropositive versus seronegative subjects.

Symptomatic seropositive subjects, relative to seronegative controls, performed as well on the Arithmetic subtest of the WAIS-R (Franzblau et al., 1991; Poutiainen, Livanainen, Elovaara, Valle, & Lahdevirta, 1988; van Gorp, Miller, Satz, & Visscher, 1989) and the color- and word-naming conditions of the Stroop Color-Word Interference Test (Stern, Sano, Williams, & Gorman, 1989). Also, ASP subjects, compared to seronegative controls, performed equally well on the Stroop (Stern et al., 1991; Ollo et al., 1991), the Seashore Rhythm Test of the Halstead-Reitan Battery (Claypoole et al., 1990), and on letter (Perry et al., 1989) and number cancellation tasks (Rubinow, Benettini, Brouwers, & Lane, 1988). On this latter task, however, Rubinow's group found SxSP subjects to perform lower than their seronegative controls.

Divided attention, in contrast, has been underassessed. Using the Paced Auditory Serial Addition Test (PASAT) to assess sustained concentration and divided attention, Grant et al. (1987) found subjects with AIDS to perform worse on this task than seronegative controls though the performance of subjects with ARC did not differ from that by controls. Similarly, studies of ASP subjects' performance on the PASAT have failed to find group differences when compared to controls (Claypoole et al., 1990; Goethe et al., 1989; Perry et al., 1989).

In summary, neuropsychological investigations of basic attention/concentration have generally found SxSP individuals not to evidence lowered performance in this domain relative to seronegative controls. Divided and sustained attention may be affected, however, in the symptomatic group. It should be noted that assessment of patients who are experiencing an acute exacerbation of systemic physical illness or who are in the latter stages of an ADC, and thus possibly obtunded, would likely reveal significant impairment of attention and concentration. While a decrement in concentration is frequently reported by SxSP individuals relatively early in the course of their illness (e.g., trouble concentrating while reading), it appears this may be secondary to fatigue or affective disturbance rather than impaired concentration per se.

Language

Investigations of language function among HIV-seropositive individuals have generally demonstrated normal language abilities. Confrontational naming, as assessed by performance on the Boston Naming Test (BNT), has been found in most studies to be unimpaired in SxSP subjects relative to seronegative subjects (Janssen et al., 1989; Stern et al., 1989; Tross et al., 1988; van Gorp et al., 1989), although Saykin et al. (1988) reported significantly lower performance in their HIV-related lymphadenopathy syndrome (LAS) cohort relative to seronegative controls. Similarly, Stern et al. (1991) also found their seropositive cohort to perform significantly worse on the BNT than did controls. Studies of verbal fluency, as measured by word list generation tasks (e.g., FAS), have also found SxSP subjects to generally perform as well as seronegative subjects (Goethe et al., 1989; Miller et al., 1990; Ollo & Pass, 1988; Ollo et al., 1991; Stern et al., 1989; Tross et al., 1988; van Gorp et al., 1989). Again, Saykin et al. (1988) found SxSP subjects to generate fewer words than seronegative subjects. Two studies that examined the performance of ASP subjects on word generation tasks have also reported similar results (Claypoole et al., 1990; Wilkie et al., 1990) although Perry et al. (1989) and Stern et al. (1991) reported their ASP subjects to produce significantly fewer words than seronegative controls. WAIS-R Vocabulary was found to be unimpaired among SxSP subjects by van Gorp et al. (1989), Grant et al. (1987), Saykin et al. (1988), and Tross et al. (1988) and also unaffected in ASP individuals by Wilkie et al. (1990) and Claypoole et al. (1990). Rubinow et al. (1988), however, reported their SxSP group to have performed worse on the Vocabulary subtest of the WAIS-R than their seronegative control group.

Thus, with the exception of the data reported by Saykin et al. (1988), the majority of studies have found language abilities to remain largely unimpaired even in the symptomatic stages of HIV infection.

Visuospatial Function

The investigations that have examined visuoconstructive and visuoperceptive abilities have reported somewhat conflicting results. Symptomatic seropositive subjects have been found to perform as well as seronegative subjects on the Rey-Osterreith Complex Figure Drawing (Poutiainen et al., 1988; van Gorp et al., 1989), although Poutiainen et al. reported impaired cube drawing in their SxSP group. Block Design was reported to be unimpaired among SxSP subjects by Poutiainen et al. (1988), Saykin et al. (1988), and Stern et al. (1989) as well as among ASP individuals (Stern et al., 1991), whereas van Gorp et al. (1989) and Tross et al. (1988) found SxSP individuals, relative to seronegative controls, to show lower performance. No differences were observed between SxSP and seronegative groups on the Object Assembly (van Gorp et al., 1989) and Picture Completion (Poutiainen et al., 1988) subtests of the WAIS-R, nor were group differences found on the Benton Line Orientation Test (Stern et al., 1989) or the Tactile Performance Test (TPT) (Saykin et al., 1988). Wilkie et al. (1990) found ASP subjects to perform as well as controls on a mental rotation test.

Taken together, the majority of investigations suggest that as a group, SxSP individuals do not demonstrate impaired visuospatial abilities. Whereas van Gorp et al. (1989) and Tross et al. (1988) found group differences on Block Design (because this is a timed test), it may well be that psychomotor slowing contributed to the lowered performance among the SxSP groups.

Verbal Memory

Mixed results have been reported for this functional domain. Studies that have used various subtests of the WMS have generally failed to find differences between seropositive and seronegative groups. On the Logical Prose subtest, SxSP subjects were found to perform as well as seronegative subjects (Grant et al., 1987; Ollo & Pass, 1988; Poutiainen et al., 1988; Tross et al., 1988; van Gorp et al., 1989). Of the studies reviewed that utilized the Logical Prose subtest, only Janssen et al. (1989) and Saykin et al. (1988) found SxSP subjects to perform worse than seronegative controls. Among ASP subjects, Wilkie et al. (1990) and Claypoole et al. (1990) failed to find differences between their ASP and seronegative groups on the immediate recall condition. Delayed recall of the passages was unimpaired among the Claypoole et al. ASP cohort, but was found to be significantly lower by Wilkie et al. (1990). On the Paired Associates subtest of the WMS, all studies reviewed failed to find differences between SxSP subjects and seronegative controls.

Several researchers have also reported group differences on supraspan word learning tasks. On verbal learning tasks (i.e., RAVLT or CVLT), both van Gorp et al. (1989) and Ollo and Pass (1988) failed to find differences between SxSP and seronegative subjects on Trial 5. Similarly, Miller et al. (1990) found SxSP subjects to recall as many words as seronegative subjects on Trial 5 of the RAVLT, although the SxSP group recalled significantly fewer words when Trials 1 through 5 were summed (a variable not used in the van Gorp or Ollo and Pass studies). Stern et al. (1989), using the Buschke Selective Reminding Test (SRT), found SxSP individuals to perform significantly worse than seronegative controls. Wilkie et al. (1990) and Stern et al. (1991) also found ASP subjects to perform worse than controls on the SRT, Although Goethe et al. (1989) and Claypoole et al. (1990) failed to find group differences between ASP subjects and seronegatives. Serial digit learning was found by Franzblau et al. (1991) to be unimpaired among both ASP and SxSP subjects.

In sum, studies of verbal learning and memory ability among SxSP individuals have found conflicting results with studies utilizing unstructured list learning tasks generally reporting less learning to occur over trials in symptomatic subjects.

Visual Nonverbal Memory

Approximately one half of the investigations that have examined nonverbal memory have found SxSP subjects to show impairment relative to seronegative controls. On the Visual Reproductions subtest of the WMS, Poutiainen et al. (1988), Grant et al. (1987), Saykin et al. (1988), and Tross et al. (1988) all found SxSP subjects to perform similarly to seronegative controls. In contrast, van Gorp et al. (1989) and Ollo and Pass (1988) found SxSP individuals to recall significantly less on this measure. Symptomatic seropositive subjects were also found to perform worse than controls on the delayed recall of the Rey Osterreith figure (van Gorp et al., 1989) and on recall of Digit-Symbol pairings (Janssen et al., 1989). Stern et al. (1989) report SxSP subjects and seronegative controls to perform equally well on the Benton Visual Retention Test and Saykin et al. (1988) report SxSP to evidence normal incidental learning on the TPT. None of the reviewed studies found ASP subjects to demonstrate deficits in nonverbal memory.

Thus, it appears that SxSP subjects, compared to seronegative controls, may well exhibit lowered performance in nonverbal visual memory. Supporting this contention is the reported sparing of visuospatial ability in HIV-related disease. With visuoconstruction retained, subsequent deficits in nonverbal memory can most likely be attributed to impaired memory function.

Motor Speed

Conflicting findings have been reported on measures of motor speed. Finger tapping speed was found to be unimpaired among SxSP and ASP subjects by Claypoole et al. (1990), Franzblau et al. (1991), and Ollo et al. (1991) and was also found to be normal among ASP subjects by Goethe et al. (1989). Saykin et al. (1988) found SxSP subjects to be slower with the nondominant, but not the dominant, hand. In contrast, on the Grooved Pegboard Test, lower performance relative to controls was observed among SxSP subjects by Miller et al. (1990) and Tross et al. (1988) but not by Franzblau et al. (1991) or Ollo et al. (1991). No differences were found between SxSP and seronegative subjects on the Purdue Pegboard (Stern et al. 1989) nor between ASP and seronegative subjects (Stern et al., 1991).

Given that Navia et al., (1986a) considered motoric abnormalities to be one of the three hallmarks (along with behavioral and cognitive deficits) of ADC, the failure of several studies to document such deficits bears further scrutiny. Generally, as HIV-related disease progresses and patients become increasingly ill, motor speed and strength significantly decreases. Because most studies have excluded more acutely ill and nonambulatory patients, it is possible that an ascertainment bias exists against the inclusion of subjects with pronounced motoric deficits. Such an explanation could explain the null findings reported above.

Psychomotor Speed/Speed of Information Processing

Of all the functional neuropsychological domains, SxSP individuals have shown greatest impairment on measures of psychomotor speed. On Trails A, most studies have failed to find a difference between SxSP and seronegative subjects (Grant et al., 1987; Janssen et al., 1989; Miller et al., 1990; Tross et al., 1988). Stern's group (1989) reported their SxSP subjects to make more errors on this task than controls, although time to completion did not differ. Van Gorp et al. (1989) and Saykin et al. (1988) found a significant difference between SxSP and seronegative subjects on Trails A, and Claypoole et al. (1990) reported their ASP group to be slower than seronegative controls. In contrast, approximately 50% of studies have found SxSP subjects to perform worse than seronegative controls on Trails B (Miller et al., 1990; Rubinow et al., 1988; Saykin et al., 1988; Tross et al., 1988; van Gorp et al., 1989), with the remainder failing to find group differences on this measure (Grant et al., 1987; Janssen et al., 1989; Ollo et al., 1991; Poutiainen et al., 1988; Stern et al., 1989). Janssen et al. (1989), Poutiainen et al. (1988), van Gorp et al. (1989), and Miller et al. (1990) have also reported SxSP subjects to perform worse on the Digit Symbol or Symbol Digit tasks or both. Ollo and Pass (1988) found SxSP subjects to be slower on the written, but not oral, version of the Symbol-Digit test. In contrast, SxSP and seronegative groups performed equally well on digit-symbol substitution tasks in studies performed by Franzblau et al. (1991), Grant et al. (1987), Ollo et al. (1991), Saykin et al. (1988), Stern et al. (1989), and Tross et al. (1988), although Tross et al. did find significant slowing when only college-educated subjects were included in their analyses.

Some investigators have employed computer-assisted methods for assessing reaction time and speed of information processing in symptomatic individuals. Perdices and Cooper (1989) found choice reaction time, but not simple reaction time, to be slower among SxSP subjects relative to seronegative controls. Miller et al. (1990) reported SxSP subjects to perform significantly slower on one third of trials of a simple reaction time measure and to also react significantly slower on both a choice and a sequential reaction time measure. Speed of information processing and reaction time have also been studied in ASP individuals. Symptomatic seropositive, ASP, and seronegative controls were found by Franzblau et al. (1991) to not significantly differ on the CPT. Although Miller et al. (1990) found no differences between their ASP and seronegative groups on any of their simple or complex reaction time measures, Wilkie et al. (1990) found ASP subjects to perform significantly slower than controls on the Posner Letter Matching test with equivocal results on a measure of simple reaction time. Asymptomatic seropositive and sero-negative subjects did not differ on the Wilkie et al. measures of choice reaction time. In an effort to distinguish between motoric and cognitive slowing in their ASP cohort, Wilkie and colleagues also employed the Sternberg paradigm. They found ASP and seronegative groups to evidence an equivalent slope (i.e., increase in response latency under increased cognitive load), although the ASP group's *y* intercept was significantly higher (i.e., response time under minimal cognitive load).

In sum, the weight of evidence thus far suggests that many SxSP subjects experience psychomotor slowing. This slowing cannot be attributed solely to motoric factors, but instead appears to also reflect a slowing of cognition. This slowing of psychomotor functions, where thought is wedded to action, may be the cardinal feature of HIV encephalopathy. Asymptomatic seropositive individuals may also demonstrate subtle slowing of information processing, though this remains to be fully established.

Executive/Frontal Systems Functions

Most studies have failed to find significant group differences on measures of executive functions. Performance of SxSP subjects on the Wisconsin Card Sorting Test (WCST) was found by Stern et al. (1989) not to differ from serongetaive controls. Claypoole et al. (1990) found SxSP subjects to make significantly more errors on the WCST than controls, but not to differ on number of perseverative errors. Stern et al. (1989) further report an equivocal pattern on the Odd-Man Out test, a category/concept shifting task similar to the WCST. On the Odd-Man Out, SxSP subjects performed worse than seronegative controls on Trial 1, but did not differ on Trials 2 through 4, a finding that Stern and colleagues contend may reflect a difficulty getting into set. In a subsequent study, Stern et al. (1991) continued to find seropositive subjects to perform worse on this task than seronegative controls. Three studies have reported on SxSP subjects' performance on the Category Test, one that found differences compared to controls (Grant et al., 1987) and two that did not (Rubinow et al., 1988; Saykin et al., 1988). Verbal abstraction (e.g., WAIS-R Similarities) has been reported by most to be unaffected (Poutiainen et al., 1988; Rubinow et al., 1988; Stern et al., 1989; Tross et al., 1988), although van Gorp et al. (1989) did find SxSP subjects to perform worse than controls, whereas Stern et al. (1991) reported that their ASP cohort performed significantly worse than controls on an analogies test. Judgment, as reflected by the Comprehension subtest of the WAIS-R, has also been reported to be unimpaired among SxSP subjects (Poutiainen et al., 1988; van Gorp et al., 1989). Symptomatic seropositive and seronegative groups have been found not to differ on response inhibition tasks such as a Go-No Go task and the Stroop C (Stern et al., 1989). Saykin et al. (1988), however, report their LAS cohort to have performed worse on the Stroop C than did seronegative controls. As noted in the discussion on language, verbal fluency has been generally reported to be spared among SxSP subjects, as has design fluency. In contrast, as reviewed above, approximately 50% of studies that have employed the PASAT and Trails B have found seronegative controls to outperform SxSP subjects.

In summary, SxSP subjects do not as a group evidence dramatic impairment on most measures of executive function. There is evidence that hypothesis formation and nonverbal problem solving may be deficient relative to seronegative controls, although this not conclusive. Also, to the degree that Trails B and the PASAT reflect executive function, additional support accrues for the contention advanced HIV-related cognitive impairment can result in impaired frontal systems function.

Global Cognitive Functioning/Intelligence

Interpretation of the results of intelligence testing among HIV-seropositive subjects is difficult due to the sensitivity of measures of intelligence to any premorbid differences between subject groups. While this potential confound applies to other neuropsychological domains as well, it can be expected to be most pronounced here. Mindful of this caveat, several studies that have assessed intelligence can be reviewed. Van Gorp et al. (1989) and Rubinow et al. (1988) report their SxSP subjects to evidence lower WAIS-R Full Scale and Verbal IQs than seronegative controls. Poutiainen et al. (1988) and van Gorp et al. (1989), but not Rubinow et al. (1988), also found SxSP subjects to score lower as a group on Performance IQ. Saykin and his associates (1988) report significant differences between SxSP and seronegative groups on both the information subtest of the WAIS-R and the Vocabulary section of the Shipley Hartford. No difference was reported between SxSP and seronegative groups on the Raven Progressive Matrices (Stern et al., 1989) nor between ASP and seronegative subjects (Stern et al., 1991). Ollo et al. (1991) also report that their SxSP group did not differ from seronegative controls on the Mattis Dementia Rating Scale.

Thus, of those studies that have reported the performance of SxSP subjects on measures of intelligence, most have found differences on WAIS-R Full Scale, Verbal, and Performance IQ. Again, whether this reflects premorbid differences, increased slowing (especially salient on Performance IQ measures), or actual CNS effects of HIV is unclear.

The Mini-Mental State Examination (MMSE) has generally not been found to distinguish SxSP or ASP subjects from seronegative controls (Stern et al., 1989; Stern et al., 1991; van Gorp et al., 1989). Wilkie et al. (1990) report their ASP subjects to have performed statistically worse on the MMSE than did seronegative controls, though examination of group means (27.9 vs. 29.2) reveals both groups to be functioning well within the normal range.

Mood

Most studies assessing affective status among seropositive subjects have focused on depression and anxiety. Using the Beck Depression Inventory (BDI), van Gorp et al. (1989) and Ollo and Pass (1988) failed to find differences between SxSP subjects and seronegative controls. Whereas Poutiainen et al. (1988) did find statistically significant group differences on the BDI, both SxSP and seronegative subjects scored within the normal range (7 vs. 2). In contrast, in our series of 39 clinically referred SxSP patients (van Gorp et al., 1990), significant statistical and clinical differences were observed between SxSP individuals and seronegative controls on both the BDI (18 vs. 4) and scale 2 of the MMPI-168 (mean T scores of 83 vs. 58). On the Center for Epidemiological Studies Depression Scale (CES-D), Perdices and Cooper (1989) report SxSP subjects not to differ from seronegative controls, whereas Miller et al. (1990) did find significant group differences. Curiously, Satz et al. (1988) found seronegative subjects to score higher on the CES-D than ASP subjects. Janssen et al. (1989) reported SxSP and seronegative groups not to differ on the Zung Depression Scale, whereas Franzblau et al. (1991) found their SxSP, ASP, and seronegative cohorts not to significantly differ on the Profile of Mood States. Levels of state anxiety were found by Perdices and Cooper (1989) not to differ between SxSP and seronegative individuals, although Janssen et al. (1989) did report SxSP subjects to be more anxious. On the MMPI-168, our clinically referred SxSP subjects scored markedly higher than seronegative controls on scale 7 (mean T scores of 77 vs. 50). They also scored higher on scales F, 1, 2, 3, 4, 8, and 0 (van Gorp et al., 1990).

Thus, with the exception of one series of patients referred for clinical evaluation because of reported or observed cognitive or affective changes, most studies have failed to find significant group differences on measures of depression and anxiety. Given that complaints of affective symptomatology are not uncommon in HIV-infected individuals, this negative finding is puzzling. One possible explanation would argue that an ascertainment bias exists and that investigators may have eliminated dysphoric subjects from their samples to avoid confounding measures of cognition. Second, subjects who are depressed or anxious or both may simply avoid volunteering for these studies. Therefore, despite the null findings described in several of the above-cited studies, it is our clinical experience that, not surprisingly, many SxSP subjects demonstrate changes in mood, affect, or personality.

However, the presence of significant affective distress, including depression, is not necessarily correlated with increased cognitive impairment. Using the BDI, Hinkin et al. (1992) divided their clinically referred, largely SxSP cohort into depressed (mean BDI = 29) and nondepressed (mean BDI = 6) groups. They then compared their performance on an extensive battery of neuropsychological tests and found the two groups to differ only on the Grooved Pegboard Test. Accordingly, whereas depression may exert a deleterious effect on cognition in the elderly (cf. Caine, 1981), among relatively young HIV-seropositive individuals the presence of even marked elevations in depressed mood appears not to unduly affect cognitive functioning.

Major Psychiatric Disorder

Although there is yet no consensus as to whether seropositive subjects, as a group, evidence depressed or anxious mood or both, a number of clinical reports have noted that seropositive subjects may present with acute psychiatric disorder, occasionally as the sole and initial manifestation of HIV disease. Several authors have reported on the occurrence of psychosis in seropositive patients (Halstead, Riccio, Harlow, Oretti, & Thompson, 1988; Kermani, Drob, & Alpert, 1984; Nurnberg, Prudic, Fiori, & Freedman, 1984; Perry & Jacobson, 1986; Thomas &

Szabadi, 1987). Boccelari, Dilley, and Shore (1988) examined the frequency of psychiatric symptomatology in a clinical series of 33 SxSP patients. They found 76% to evidence depressed mood; 64%, anxious mood; 30%, secondary mania; 29%, delusional thinking; 23%, paranoia; 27%, visual hallucinations; and 13%, auditory hallucinations.

Adjustment disorders and major depressive episode are common in SxSP subjects and are believed to be elevated in risk groups for HIV infection. The prevalence of acute, and generally brief, dysphoria is highest immediately before and after serostatus evaluation. For example, the WHO (1988) has found an acute stress reaction to be present in 90% of such patients. In large part this is fueled by the discovery that one has contracted a potentially terminal disease. For many, however, the resultant familial and societal reaction attendant to the diagnosis is at least equally stress inducing. Fortunately, this acute reaction resolves for most individuals, although a significant percentage will develop an adjustment disorder or major depressive episode. Point prevalence of rates of major depression offered by Dilley, Ochitill, Perl, and Volberding (1985) (15%) and by Perry and Tross (1984) (17%) can be considered to be reasonable initial estimations.

What remains to be established is the etiological basis for the major psychiatric disorders evidenced by these individuals. Several theories can be entertained. One is that the occurrence of psychiatric disorder in an HIV-seropositive individual is simply coincidental. However, because the epidemiological base rates for these disorders in the population at large do not approach the rates reported in HIV-seropositive individuals, this explanation is insufficient. Psychiatric disorder as a reaction to one's diagnosis (e.g., reactive or exogenous depression) is a tenable explanation. Also, it is possible that HIV may be directly affecting the CNS in such a fashion as to cause both cognitive and affective symptomatology. Such a dual pronged manifestation is common in many dementing diseases such as Huntington's disease, Parkinson's disease, and stroke. In that the virus has been shown to exercise a predilection for subcortical structures, this hypothesis is intriguing.

The overlap between symptomatology characteristic of depression, that seen in subcortical dementia, and that typical in severe systemic illness such as AIDS can give rise to diagnostic uncertainty. For example, a patient presenting with diminished interest, weight loss, sleep disturbance, anergia, somatic preoccupation, diminished libido, and diminished motivation could appear depressed to all but the most astute observer. Such symptomatology, however, is common in many severe physical illnesses (e.g., cancer) and is certainly common in SxSP subjects. Conversely, forgetfulness, difficulty concentrating, slowed thought and action, hypophonic speech, and apathetic or depressed mood can be present in both depression and subcortical dementia. Accordingly, the medical and neuropsychological workup of the SxSP patient who evidences cognitive and affective disturbance requires exacting attention. Should diagnostic uncertainty persist, one can opt to treat the depression and follow with repeat neuropsychological evaluation.

Awareness of Neuropsychological Deficits

Few studies have compared subjects' subjective sense of their level of cognitive functioning with objective neuropsychological data. The few papers that have been presented at conferences thus far that have included some assessment of subjective perception of performance have reported few correlations between subjects' own perceptions of their level of neuropsychological function and objective measures (cf. Perry, 1990). In data from the MACS, subjects enrolled in two study sites of the Multicenter AIDS Cohort Study ($N = 479$; 233 asymptomatic seropositives and 256 seronegatives) completed the Cognitive Failures Questionnaire (CFQ) (Broadbent, Cooper, Fitzgerald, & Parkes, 1982) along with a brief neuropsychological screening battery. The CFQ is a 25-item self-report questionnaire in which subjects rate themselves about cognitive failures in everyday life, such as absentmindedness, forgetting of appointments, conversations, directions, and so forth (e.g., "Do you find you forget appointments?"; "Do you find you can't quite remember something even though it's on the tip of your tongue?"). Subjects rate their degree of difficulty on each item using a scale ranging from 0 (no difficulty) to 4 (very often), yielding a summary score ranging from 0 to 100. We (van Gorp, Hinkin, et al., 1992) found that the asymptomatic seropositive and seronegative groups did not differ on the number or severity of reported cognitive failures (see Table 5.3). However, we did find a positive correlation between CFQ score and a measure of depression using the CES-D (multiple $r = -.37, p < .01$). Hence, although the degree of complaints of everyday failures in the MACS ASP sample is low (and similar to seronegative controls), when present, they seem to be primarily associated with level of depression. These results are particularly relevant to clinicians and researchers who rate (or stage severity of) subjects for possible ADC based largely on the patient's own self-report. Similar results have recently been reported by Wilkins et al. (1991), who found a relationship between cognitive complaints and psychiatric, but not neuropsychological, symptomatology. In contrast, they did find a significant relationship between complaints of motoric dysfunction and actual motoric deficit. These data and those reviewed by Perry (1990) suggest that, at least in nondemented asymptomatic seropositives, self-reported complaints of cognitive failures may be more related to an individual's current affective state rather than to objective neuropsychological difficulties. Hence, it is important to pair an individual's own report of cognitive difficulty with objective neuropsychological and affective measures before making a diagnosis of ADC or

TABLE 5.3.   Demographic Characteristics of Asymptomatic Seropositive and Seronegative Groups

Measure	Seronegative (n = 256)	Asymptomatic Seropositive (n = 223)
Mean age (SD)	40.53 (8.31)	40.18 (6.78)[a]
Mean years of education (SD)	16.35 (2.39)	15.94 (2.54)[a]
Mean CES-D score	9.42 (10.01)	9.53 (8.78)[a]
Mean CFQ score	31.21 (13.73)	30.25 (12.78)[a]
CD4 cells/mm (SD)	790.27 (390.75)	532.82 (315.71)*
CD8 cells/mm (SD)	37.64 (11.06)	26.47 (11.62)**

[a]Nonsignificant.

*$p < .00001$; **$p < .00001$.

Source: From van Gorp, Satz, Hinkin, Selnes, Miller, McArthur, Cohen, Paz, & the MACS. 1991. p. 814. Reprinted with permission.

HIV encephalopathy in order to avoid the serious error of overdiagnosing HIV encephalopathy.

Relationship Between Immunosuppression and ADC

Price and colleagues have proposed a general model (Figure 5.3) to account for the timing and course of invasion of the CNS by HIV (Price et al., 1988, p. 587). As the figure illustrates, HIV enters the nervous system early, shortly after infection. After an initial meningitis-like syndrome that some patients experience, the individual enters a latent period of infection in which CNS "integrity," as defined by intact cognitive function, is maintained. As the immune system is further diminished, however, a threshold of immunocompetence is reached. As this threshold is crossed, the CNS effects of the virus are increased, overt neuropsychological integrity is lost, and an encephalopathy may result. There is support for the Price et al. model, through the study of the CD4 T-helper cell and the relationship of this "marker" of immune system function with the onset of constitutional symptoms. Epidemiological studies have found an association between reduced serum CD4 levels and the development of AIDS-defining illnesses (Detels et al., 1987;

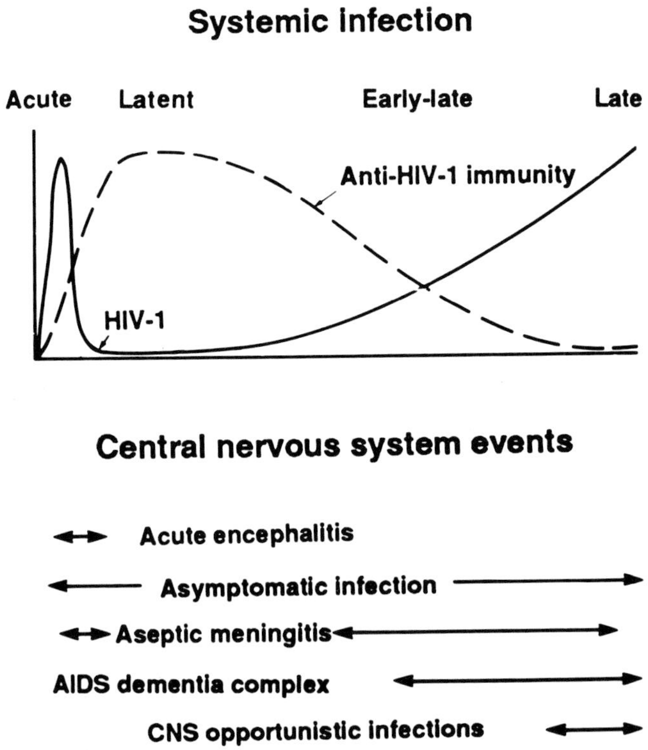

FIGURE 5.3. The hypothesized relationship between immune status and neurological symptoms. (From Price et al., 1988, p. 587. Reprinted by permission. Copyright 1988 by the AAAS.)

Taylor, Fahey, Detels, & Giorgi, 1989). Consistent with Price and colleagues' model, Goethe et al. (1989) have noted clinically that "[w]e have not seen significant cognitive decline before the T-helper cell count has fallen below 400/mm^3" (p. 133).

There have been several attempts to empirically study this issue from a neuropsychological perspective. Janssen et al. (1989) studied 100 HIV-seropositive patients, and of the 19 whose CD4 counts were below 200, only 2 (11%) evidenced clinically abnormal neuropsychological test results. Perry et al. (1989) divided their seropositive subjects into two groups: those with neuropsychological performance above the mean on all tests and one with performance 2 standard deviations below the mean on at least 1 test. Perry and colleagues report a nonsignificant trend toward lower CD4 levels in the low-neuropsychological group (CD4 means of 737 vs. 516, p = .06). However, they failed to find an association between low-neuropsychological performance and CD4 level when a more conservative definition of low-neuropsychological performance was employed (≥ 2 tests at ≥ 2 SD).

The MACS has also examined this issue. Miller et al. (1990) performed four analyses using CD4 cutting scores of 250 and 500 and examined group differences on the neuropsychological measures as well as the number of individual neuropsychological outliers at each CD4 cutoff. Despite a large sample size, they failed to find a significant relationship between CD4 levels and neuropsychological functioning. Because their study was composed of mostly asymptomatic individuals in which the base rate of neuropsychologically deficient performance is low, this may have contributed to their inability to find differences. Schmitt et al. (1988) reported several low but significant correlations between CD4 counts and measures of mood and cognition (Pearson r values $\geq$ .16) though following correction for multiple comparisons, no significant correlations remained. Finally, Hinkin et al. (1990) studied an HIV-infected sample referred from a large, private medical group for clinical evaluation. Fifty-six seropositive and 23 seronegative controls were compared. Of the 56 seropositives, 25 (45%) had absolute CD4 T-helper counts less than 200/mm^3, with 31 above 200/mm^3. They found that subjects in the low-CD4 grouping had an increase in both the number and severity of neuropsychological deficits relative to seropositive subjects with higher CD4 counts. In fact, the number of neuropsychological "outliers" was twice as great (52%) in the low-CD4 group as in the higher CD4 group (26%).

Thus, studies that have examined mostly symptomatic patients and that have used lower CD4 cutoff scores ($<$200/mm^3) have tended to find greater neuropsychological deficits, whereas studies with mostly asymptomatic individuals or with higher CD4 cutoff scores have not found as great an association with neuropsychological impairment. These data support Price and colleagues' contention that the onset of significant neuropsychological deficits occurs in the presence of greatest immunosuppression. It may well be that reliance upon quantitative indices of immune status (CD4 number, percentage, and CD4:CD8 ratio) may eventually be shown to be a better predictor of ADC risk status than merely *symptomatic* or *asymptomatic* classifications.

Comparison of AIDS Dementia Complex with Other Dementias

Navia et al. (1986a,b) first described the ADC as a "prototypic" subcortical dementia. Brouwers, Mohr, Hendricks, and Baron (1988) performed a discriminant function analysis to examine the pattern of neuropsychological test performance among three patient groups: HIV-infected individuals, patients with Huntington's disease (HD), and patients with Alzheimer's disease (AD). They found the HIV group to be more similar to the HD patients than those with AD. Similarly, our group (van Gorp et al., 1989; Hinkin et al., 1990) compared the neuropsychological performance of relatively young patients with HIV encephalopathy (M = 37.5 years) to young seronegatives (M = 35.86 years), and normal elderly individuals with a mean age of 70.14 years. Based on the work of Hicks and Birren (1970), Albert and Kaplan (1980), and Veroff (1980), it was hypothesized that normal aging has its greatest impact upon the frontal-subcortical axis of brain function. As such, the HIV encephalopathy patients should resemble the normal elderly more than the young seronegatives of the elderly subjects with AD. A discriminant function analysis, a procedure that differentially weights selected variables in order to maximally differentiate among groups, was performed. The resultant discriminant equation can then be used to classify subjects and predict group membership. In the analysis on the variables depicted in Figure 5.4 (in order to compare performance across tests, data were converted to Z scores), the discriminant function equation correctly classified all of the AIDS subjects and all but one of the young normal subjects into their respective groups. This classification function was then applied to the normal elderly subjects to determine if their pattern of performance

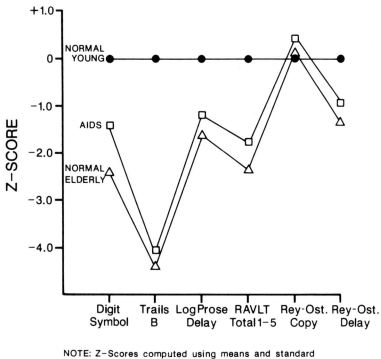

NOTE: Z–Scores computed using means and standard
deviations obtained from young normals.

FIGURE 5.4. Performance on neuropsychological tests in three subject groups: normal elderly, younger HIV encephalopathy subjects, and young controls. (From Hinkin, Cummings, van Gorp, & Mitrushina, 1990. Reprinted by permission.)

was more similar to the ADC group or the normal younger individuals. Following jackknifing, this classification function placed all 14 of the normal elderly with the younger AIDS patients.

Hence, these data support the contention that the neuropsychological profile of the ADC is similar to the subcortical presentation seen in HD, and to the neuropsychological changes associated with normal aging.

Practical Psychosocial Implications

Because patients with HIV-related cognitive impairment still may retain many functional capacities, it is important to consider various compensatory cognitive and environmental strategies that the patient and their family might employ to lessen the impact of this disability. Table 5.4 describes a number of strategies that we recommended in a previous paper (Buckingham & van Gorp, 1988). It is also important to note that many family members and friends, angry over the devastating impact of the illness upon the patient and themselves, may tend to blame the patient and view these memory and other cognitive problems as willful manipulation by the patient ("He could do better if he wanted to—he should just try harder").

TABLE 5.4.   Practical Considerations and Recommendations for Persons with AIDS Dementia Complex

Forgetfullness
1. Use calendars and appointment books
2. Place Post-It notes in conspicuous places
3. Make lists (questions for your physician, groceries, etc.)
4. Develop list for important things to check when leaving the house (gas, stove, lights, etc.)
5. Use alarm clock as a reminder for medication
6. Keep a log or journal for complex projects
7. Maintain a telephone log and keep important telephone numbers near the telephone
8. Maintain a medication log
9. Use a cassette tape recorder to dictate thoughts and questions
10. Purchase a noise-activated key chain

Slowed Speech
1. Allow more time for conversations
2. Don't hurry; give yourself permission to take your time

Visuospatial problems
1. Don't drive if unable to do so
2. If able to drive, plan routes in advance, allow plenty of time, and take a friend along when you can

Depression and social withdrawal
1. Plan recreational activities
2. Be an active participant
3. Rekindle interest in hobbies and activities

Concentration problems, inattentiveness, distractibility
1. Limit distractions (e.g., turn off television when talking)
2. Meet with people one at a time
3. Break large tasks into smaller, more manageable tasks
4. Don't drive in heavy traffic

Problems with sequential reasoning or multistep tasks
1. Don't take on new or unfamiliar job responsibilities
2. Avoid tasks for which speed of performance is important
3. Don't drive in heavy traffic
4. Simplify activities (e.g., don't plan a seven-course meal, use prepared foods)
5. Plan activities at the time of day when you are at your best

Source: From Buckingham & van Gorp, 1988. Reprinted by permission.

Reassurance and education may be very helpful to reduce the patient's anxiety and feelings of fear and anger by family members, significant others, and friends.

Summary

Considerable progress has been made in research on the neurological and neuro-psychological sequelae of HIV infection since the initial case reports of AIDS in 1981. From the available evidence, it appears that the CNS, a site of viral predi-lection, is involved early in the course of infection. Careful longitudinal studies will help clarify the natural history of HIV-related neuropsychological involvement, although it appears that loss of neuropsychological integrity is not apparent in most subjects until the onset of constitutional symptoms or significant immune system impairment. HIV-associated motor/cognitive complex appears to most resemble a subcortical dementia, with consequent psychomotor slowing. Timed psychomotor tests and complex and choice reaction time measures may be most sensitive to the early features of this disease.

Acknowledgment

This manuscript was supported by the Department of Veteran's Affairs Medical Research Service in the form of a Merit Review Grant to Wilfred G. van Gorp.

References

Albert, M. S., & Kaplan, E. (1980). Organic implications of neuropsychological deficits in the elderly. In L. W. Poon, J. L. Fozard, L. S. Cermak, D. Arenberg, & L. W. Thompson (Eds.), *New directions in memory and aging: Proceedings of the George A. Talland Memorial Conference.* Hillsdale, NJ: Lawrence Erlbaum Associates.

American Academy of Neurology AIDS Task Force. (1991). Nomenclature and research case definitions for neurologic manifestations of human immunodeficiency virus-type 1 (HIV-1) infection. *Neurology, 41,* 778–785.

Boccellari, A., Dilley, J. W., & Shore, M. D. (1988). Neuropsychiatric aspects of AIDS dementia complex: A report on a clinical series. *Neurotoxicology, 9,* 381–390.

Brew, B. J., Sidtis, J. J., Petito, C. K., & Price, R. W. (1988). The neurologic complications of AIDS and human immunodeficiency virus infection. In F. Plum (Ed.), *Advances in contemporary neurology.* Philadelphia: F. A. Davis.

Broadbent, D. E., Cooper, P. F., Fitzgerald, P., & Parkes, K. R. (1982). The Cognitive Failures Questionnaire (CFQ) and its correlates. *British Journal of Clinical Psychology, 21,* 1–16.

Brouwers, P., Mohr, E., Hendricks, M., & Baron, I. (1988, June 12–16). *The use of discriminant analysis to differentiate the neuropsychological profile of HIV patients.* Paper presented at the fourth annual AIDS conference, Stockholm, Sweden.

Brunetti, A., Berg, G., Di Chiro, G., Cohen, R. M., Yarchoan, R., Pizzo, P. A., Broder, S., Eddy, J., Fulham, M. J., Finn, R. D., & Larson, S. M. (1989). Reversal of brain metabolic abnormalities following treatment of AIDS dementia complex with 3′-azido-2′,3′-dideoxythymidine (AZT, Zidovudine): A PET-FDG study. *Journal of Nuclear Medicine, 30,* 581–590.

Buckingham, S., & van Gorp, W. (1988). AIDS-dementia complex: Implications for practice. *Social Casework: The Journal of Contemporary Social Work, 69*, 371–375.

Butters, N., Grant, I., Haxby, J., Judd, L., Martin, A., McClelland, J., Pequegnat, W., Schacter, D., & Stover, E. (1990). Assessment of aids-related cognitive changes: Recommendations of this NIMH workshop on neuropsychological assessment approaches. *Journal of Clinical and Experimental Neuropsychology, 12*, 963–978.

Caine, E. D. (1981). Pseudodementia: Current concepts and future directions. *Archives of General Psychiatry, 38*, 1359–1364.

Centers for Disease Control. (1987). Revision of the CDC surveillance case definition for acquired immunodeficiency syndrome. *Morbity and Mortality Weekly Report* (Suppl. 1S), 3–15.

Chrysikopoulos, H. S., Press, G. A., Grafe, M. R., Hesselenik, J. R., & Wiley, C. A. (1990). Encephalitis caused by human immunodeficiency virus: CT and MR imaging manifestation with clinical and pathological correlation. *Radiology, 175*, 185–191.

Claypoole, K., Townes, B., Collier, A., Combs, R., Longstreth, W., Cohen, W., Marra, C., Gerlach, R., Maravilla, K., Bahls, F., White, D., Murphy, V., Maxwell, C., & Handsfield, H. (1990). *Neuropsychological aspects of early HIV infection.* Presented at the eighteenth annual International Neuropsychological Society Conference, Orlando, FL.

Cummings, J. L., & Benson, D. F. (1983). *Dementia: A clinical approach.* Boston: Butterworth's.

De La Paz, R., & Enzmann, D. (1988). Neuroradiology of acquired immunodeficiency syndrome. In M. L. Rosenblum, R. S. Levy, & D. Bredesen (Eds.), *AIDS and the nervous system* (pp. 121–123). New York: Raven Press.

de la Monte, S. M., Ho, D. D., Schooley, R. T., Hirsch, M. S., & Richardson, E. P. (1987). Subacute encephalomyelitis of AIDS and its relation to HTLV-III infection. *Neurology, 37*, 562–569.

Detels, R., Visscher, B. R., Fahey, J. L., Sever, J., Gravell, M., Madden, D., Schwartz, K., Dudley, J., English, P., Powers, H., Clark, V. A., & Gottlieb, M. S. (1987). Predictors of clinical AIDS in young homosexual men in a high risk area. *International Journal of Epidemiology, 26*, 271–276.

Dilley, J. W., Ochitill, H. N., Perl, M., & Volberding, P. (1985). Findings in psychiatric consultation with patients with acquired immune deficiency syndrome. *American Journal of Psychiatry, 142*, 82–86.

Elovaara, I., Poutiainen, E., Raininko, R., Valanne, L., Virta, A., Valle, S., Lahdevirta, J., & Iivanainen, M. (1990). Mild brain atrophy in early HIV infection: The lack of association with cognitive deficits and HIV-specific intrathecal immune response. *Journal of the Neurological Sciences, 99*, 121–136.

Franzblau, A., Letz, R., Hershman, D., Mason, P., Wallace, J. I., & Bekesi, G. (1991). Quantitative neurologic and neurobehavioral testing of persons infected with human immunofdeficiency virus type 1. *Archives of Neurology, 48*, 263–268.

Gabuzda, D. H., & Hirsch, M. S. (1987). Neurologic manifestations of infection with human immunodeficiency virus. *Annals of Internal Medicine, 107*, 383–391.

Gabuzda, D. H., Ho, D. D., De la Monte, S. M., Hirsch, M. S., Rota, T. R., & Sobel, R. A. (1986). Immunohistochemical identification of human T lymphotropic virus type III antigen in brains of patients with acquired immune deficiency syndrome. *Annals of Neurology, 20*, 290–295.

Gabuzda, D. H., Levy, S. R., & Chiappa, K. H. (1988). Electroencephalography in AIDS and AIDS-related complex. *Clinical Electroencephalography, 19*, 1–6.

Goethe, K. E., Mitchell, J. E., Marshall, D. W., Brey, R. L., Cahill, W. T., Leger, D., Hay, L. S., & Boswell, R. N. (1989). Neuropsychological and neurological function of human immunodeficiency virus seropositive asymptomatic individuals. *Archives of Neurology, 46,* 129–133.

Gottlieb, M., Schroff, R., Schanker, H., Weisman, J., Fan, P., Wolf, R., & Saxon, A. (1981). *Pneumocystis carinii* pneumonia and mucosal candidiasis in previously healthy homosexual men: Evidence of a newly acquired cellular immunodeficiency. *New England Journal of Medicine, 305,* 1425–1430.

Grant, I., Atkinson, J., Hesselink, J., Kennedy, C., Richman, D., Spector, S., & McCutchan, J. (1987). Evidence for early central nervous system involvement in the acquired immunodeficiency syndrome (AIDS) and other human immunodeficiency virus (HIV) infections. *Annals of Internal Medicine, 107,* 828–836.

Halstead, S., Riccio, M., Harlow, P., Oretti, R., & Thompson, C. (1988). Psychosis associated with HIV infection. *British Journal of Psychiatry, 153,* 618–623.

Hicks, L., & Birren, J. (1970). Aging, brain damage, and psychomotor slowing. *Psychological Bulletin, 74,* 377–396.

Hinkin, C., Cummings, J. L., van Gorp, W. G., & Mitrushina, M. (1990). Frontal/subcortical features of normal aging: An empirical analysis. *Canadian Journal of Aging, 9,* 104–119.

Hinkin, C., van Gorp, W., Satz, P., Weisman, J., Freeman, D., Rogolsky, E., Hitt, R., & Buckingham, S. (1990). *Relationship between CD4 levels and neuropsychological impairment among HIV-1 seropositive individuals.* Presented at the conference on neurological and neuropsychological complications of HIV infection: A satellite conference to the VI international AIDS conference, Monterey, CA.

Hinkin, C., van Gorp, W., Satz, P., Weisman, J., Thommes, J., & Buckingham, S. (1992). Depressed mood and its relationship to neuropsychological test performance in HIV-1 seropositive individuals. *Journal of Clinical and Experimental Neuropsychology, 14,* 289–297.

Ho, D., Bredesen, D., Vinters, H., & Daar, E. (1989). The acquired immunodeficiency syndrome (AIDS) dementia complex. *Annals of Internal Medicine, 111,* 400–410.

Ho, D., Rota, D., Schooley, R., Kaplan, J., Allan, J., Groopman, J., Resnick, L., Felenstein, D., Andrews, C., & Hirsch, M. (1985). Isolation of HTLV-III from cerebrospinal fluid and neural tissue of patients with neurologic syndromes related to the acquired immunodeficiency syndrome. *New England Journal of Medicine, 313,* 1493–1497.

Janssen, R., Saykin, A., Kaplan, J., Spira, T., Pinsky, P., Sprehn, G., Hoffman, J., Mayer, W., & Schonberger, L. (1988). Neurological complications of human immunodeficiency virus infection in patients with lymphadenopathy syndrome. *Annals of Neurology, 23,* 49–55.

Janssen, R., Saykin, J., Cannon, L., Campbell, J., Pinsky, P., Hessol, N., O'Malley, P., Lifson, A., Doll, L., Rutherford, G., & Kaplan, J. (1989). Neurologic and neuropsychologic manifestations of human immunodeficiency virus (HIV-1) infection: Association with AIDS-related complex but not asymptomatic HIV-1 infection. *Annals of Neurology, 26,* 592–600.

Kermani, E. J., Drob, S., & Alpert, M. (1984). Organic brain syndrome in three cases of acquired immune deficiency syndrome. *Comprehensive Psychiatry, 25,* 294–297.

Ketzler, S., Weis, S., Huag, H., & Budka, H. (1990). Loss of neurons in the frontal cortex in AIDS brains. *Acta Neuropathologica, 80,* 92–94.

Koralnik, I. J., Beaumanoir, A., Hausler, R., Kohler, A., Safran, A. B., Delacoux, R., Vibert, D., Mayer, E., Burkhard, P., Nahory, A., Magistris, M. R., Sanches, J., Myers, P., Paccolat, F., Quoex, F., Gabriel, V., Perrin, L., Mermillod, B., Gauthier, G., Waldvogel, F. A., & Hirschel, B. (1990). A controlled study of early neurologic abnormalities in men with asymptomatic human immunodeficiency virus infection. *New England Journal of Medicine, 323,* 864–870.

Kramer, E. L., & Sanger, J. J. (1990). Brain imaging in acquired immunodeficiency syndrome dementia complex. *Seminars in Nuclear Medicine, 20*, 353–363.

LaFrance, N., Pearlson, G., Schaerf, F., McArthur, J., Polk, B., Links, J., Bascom, M., Knowles, M., & Galen, S. (1988). I-123 IMP-SPECT in HIV-related dementia. *Advances in Functional Neuroimaging, Fall*, 9–15.

Leuchter, A., Newton, T., van Gorp, W., & Miller, E. (1989). *Early detection of HIV effects on brain function*. Paper presented at the 142nd annual meeting of the American Psychiatric Association, San Francisco, CA.

Levin, H. S., Williams, D. H., Borucki, M. J., Hillman, G. R., Williams, M. B., Guinto, F. C., Amparo, E. G., Crow, W. N., & Pollard, R. B. (1990). Magnetic resonance imaging and neuropsychological findings in human immunodeficiency virus infection. *Journal of Acquired Immune Deficiency Syndrome, 3*, 757–762.

McArthur, J., Cohen, B., Selnes, O., Kumar, A., Cooper, K., McArthur, J., Coucy, G., Cornblath, D., Chmiel, J., Want, M-C., Starkey, D., Ginzburg, H., Ostrow, D., Johnson, R., Phair, J., & Polk, B. (1989). Low prevalence of neurological and neuropsychological abnormalities in otherwise healthy HIV-1 infected individuals: Results of the Multicenter AIDS Cohort Study. *Annals of Neurology, 26*, 601–611.

McArthur, J., Kumar, A., Johnson, D., Selnes, O., Becker, J., Herman, C., Cohen, B., & Saah, A. (1990). Incidental white matter hyperintensities on magnetic resonance imaging in HIV-1 infection. *Journal of Acquired Immune Deficiency Syndrome, 3*, 252–259.

Miller, E., Selnes, O., McArthur, J., Satz, P., Becker, J., Cohen, B., Sheridan, K., Machado, A., van Gorp, W., & Visscher, B. (1990). Neuropsychological performance in HIV-1 infected homosexual men: The Multicenter AIDS Cohort Study (MACS). *Neurology, 40*, 197–203.

Navia, B., Jordan, B., & Price, R. (1986a). The AIDS dementia complex: I. Clinical features. *Annals of Neurology, 19*, 517–524.

Navia, B., Cho, E-S., Petito, C., & Price, R. (1986b). The AIDS dementia complex: II. Neuropathology. *Annals of Neurology, 19*, 525–535.

Nurnberg, H., Prudic, J., Fiori, M., & Freedman, E. P. (1984). Psychopathology complicating acquired immune deficiency syndrome (AIDS). *American Journal of Psychiatry, 141*, 95–96.

Ollo, C., Johnson, R., & Grafman, J. (1991). Signs of cognitive change in HIV disease: An event-related brain potential study. *Neurology, 41*, 209–215.

Ollo, C., & Pass, H. (1988). *Neuropsychological performance in HIV disease: Effect of depression and chronic CNS infection*. Presented at the sixteenth annual meeting of the International Neuropsychological Society, New Orleans, LA.

Olsen, W., Longo, F., Mills, C., & Norman, D. (1988). White matter disease in AIDS: Findings at MR imaging. *Radiology, 169*, 445–448.

Parisi, A., Strosselli, M., Di Perri, S., Minoli, L., Bono, G., Moglia, A., & Nappi, G. (1989). Electroencephalography in the early diagnosis of HIV-related subacute encephalitis: Analysis of 185 patients. *Clinical Electroencephalography, 20*, 1–5.

Perdices, M., & Cooper, D. (1989). Simple and choice reaction time in patients with human immunodeficiency virus infection. *Annals of Neurology, 25*, 460–467.

Perry, S., & Tross, S. (1984). Psychiatric problems of AIDS patients at the New York Hospital: preliminary report. *Public Health Reports, 39*, 200–205.

Perry, S., & Jacobsen, P. (1986). Neuropsychiatric manifestations of AIDS-spectrum disorders. *Hospital and Community Psychiatry, 37*, 135–142.

Perry, S., Belsky-Barr, D., Barr, W., & Jacobsberg, L. (1989). Neuropsychological performance in physically asymptomatic, HIV seropositive men. *Journal of Neuropsychiatry, 1*, 296–302.

Perry, S. (1990). Organic mental disorders caused by HIV: Update on early diagnosis and treatment. *American Journal of Psychiatry, 147*, 696–710.

Pohl, P., Vogl, G., Fill, H., Rossler, H., & Zangerle, R. (1988). Single photon emission computed tomography in AIDS dementia complex. *The Journal of Nuclear Medicine, 29*, 1382–1386.

Post, M., Tate, L., Quencer, R., Hensley, G., Berger, J., Sheremata, W., & Maul, G. (1988). CT, MR, and pathology in HIV encephalitis and meningitis. *American Journal of Radiology, 151*, 373–380.

Poutiainen, E., Iivanainen, M., Elovaara, I., Valle, S., & Lahdevirta, J. (1988). Cognitive changes as early signs of HIV infection. *Acta Neurologica Scandinavica, 78*, 49–52.

Price, R., Brew, B., Sidtis, J., Rosenblum, M., Scheck, A. C., & Clearly, P. (1988). *Science, 239*, 586–592.

Resnick, L., Berger, J. R., Shapshak, P., & Tourtellotte, W. W. (1988). Early penetration of the blood-brain-barrier by HIV. *Neurology, 38*, 9–14.

Resnick, L., diMarzio-Veronese, F., Schüpbach, J., Tourtellotte, W., Ho, D., Müller, F., Shapshak, P., Vogt, M., Groopman, J., Markham, P., & Gallo, R. (1985). Intra-blood-brain-barrier synthesis of HTLV-III specific IgG in patients with neurological symptoms associated with AIDS or ARC. *New England Journal of Medicine, 313*, 1498–1504.

Rosenblum, M., Levy, R., & Bredesen, D. (1988). *AIDS and the nervous system*. New York: Raven Press.

Rottenberg, D., Moeller, J., Strother, S., Sidtis, J., Navia, B., Dhawan, V., Ginos, Z., & Price, R. (1987). The metabolic pathology of the AIDS dementia complex. *Annals of Neurology, 22*, 700–706.

Rubinow, D., Berettini, C., Brouwers, P., & Lane, H. (1988). Neuropsychiatric consequences of AIDS. *Annals of Neurology, 23* (Suppl.), S24–S26.

Satz, P., Miller, E., Visscher, B., van Gorp, W., D'Elia, L., & Dudley, J. (1988, June 12–16). Changes in mood as a function of HIV serostatus: A 3-year longitudinal study. *Proceedings of the Fourth International Conference on AIDS*. Stockholm, Sweden.

Satz, P., Morgenstern, H., Miller, E. N., D'Elia, L. F., van Gorp, W., & Visscher, B. (in press). Low education as a possible risk factor for cognitive abnormalities in HIV-1: Findings from the Multicenter AIDS Cohort Study (MACS). *Journal of Acquired Immune and Deficiency Syndrome*.

Saykin, A., Janssen, R., Sprehn, G., Kaplan, J., Spira, T., & Weller, P. (1988). Neuropsychological dysfunction in HIV-infection: Characterization in a lymphadenopathy cohort. *International Journal of Clinical Neuropsychology, 10*, 81–95.

Schmitt, F., Bigley, J., McKinnis, R., Logue, P., Evans, R., & Drucker, J. (1988). Neuropsychological outcome of zidovudine (AZT) treatment of patients with AIDS and AIDS-related complex. *New England Journal of Medicine, 319*, 1573–1578.

Selnes, O., Miller, E., McArthur, J., Gordon, B., Munoz, A., Sheridan, K., Fox, R., & Saah, A. J. (1990). HIV-1 infection: No evidence of cognitive decline during the asymptomatic stages. *Neurology, 40*, 204–208.

Sidtis, J., & Price, R. (1990). Early HIV-1 infection and the AIDS dementia complex. *Neurology, 40*, 323–326.

Snider, W., Simpson, D., Nielsen, S., Gold, J., Metroka, C., & Posner, J. (1983). Neurological complications of acquired immune deficiency syndrome: Analysis of 50 patients. *Annals of Neurology, 14*, 403–418.

Stenquist, P. K., Feraru, E. R., Aronow, H. A., van Gorp, W. G., Lawner, P., & Berger, J. (1990). *Neuropsychological testing in progressive multifocal leukoencephalopathy*. Presented at the conference on Neurological and Neuropsychological Complications of HIV: A satellite conference to the VI international AIDS conference, Monterey, CA.

Stern, Y., Marder, K., Bell, K., Chen, J., Dooneief, G., Goldstein, S., Mindry, D., Richards, M., Sano, M., Williams, J., Gorman, J., Ehrhardt, A., & Mayeux, R. (1991). Multidisciplinary baseline assessment of homosexual men with and without human immunodeficiency virus infection. III. Neurologic and neuropsychological findings. *Archives of General Psychiatry, 48*, 131–138.

Stern, Y., Sano, M., Williams, J., & Gorman, J. (1989). Neuropsychological consequences of HIV infection. *Journal of Clinical and Experimental Neuropsychology, 11*, 78.

Taylor, J., Fahey, J., Detels, R., & Giorgi, J. (1989). CD4 percentage, CD4 number, and CD4:CD8 ratio in HIV infection: Which to choose and how to use. *Journal of Acquired Immune Deficiency Syndrome, 2*, 114–124.

Thomas, C., & Szabadi, E. (1987). Paranoid psychosis as the first presentation of fulminating lethal case of AIDS. *British Journal of Psychiatry, 151*, 693–695.

Tross, S., Price, R., Navia, B., Thaler, H., Gold, J., & Sidtis, J. (1988). Neuropsychological characterization of the AIDS dementia complex: A preliminary report. *AIDS, 2*, 81–88.

Van Gorp, W., Hinkin, C., Freeman, D., Satz, P., Weisman, J., Rothman, P., Scarsella, A., & Buckingham, S. (1990). *Depressed vs. non-depressed mood and its effect on neuropsychological test performance among HIV-1 seropositive individuals.* Presented at the conference on neurological and neuropsychological complications of HIV infection: A satellite conference to the VI international AIDS conference, Monterey, CA.

Van Gorp, W., Hinkin, C., Satz, P., Weisman, J., & Buckingham, S. (1992). The relationship between degree of HIV-related immunosuppression and neuropsychological test performance. Manuscript submitted for publication.

Van Gorp, W., Mandelkern, M., Gee, M., Hinkin, C., Stern, C., Paz, D., Dixon, W., Evans, G., Flynn, F., Frederick, C., Ropchan, J., & Bland, W. (1992). Cerebral metabolic dysfunction in AIDS: Findings in an AIDS sample with and without dementia. *Journal of Neuropsychiatry and Clinical Neurosciences.*

Van Gorp, W., Miller, E. N., Satz, P., & Visscher, B. (1989). Neuropsychological performance in HIV-1 immunocompromised patients: A preliminary report. *Journal of Clinical and Experimental Neuropsychology, 11*, 763–773.

Van Gorp, W., Satz, P., Hinkin, C., Selnes, O., Miller, N., McArthur, J., Cohen, B., & Paz, D. (1991). Metacognition in HIV-1 seropositive asymptomatic individuals: Self-ratings versus objective neuropsychological performance. *Journal of Clinical and Experimental Neuropsychology, 13*, 812–819.

Veroff, A. (1980). The neuropsychology of aging. *Psychological Research, 41*, 259–268.

Vinters, H. V., Tomiyasu, U., & Anders, K. H. (1989). Neuropathologic complications of infection with the human immunodeficiency virus (HIV). *Progress in AIDS Pathology, 1*, 101–130.

Wiley, C. A., Masliah, E., Morey, M., Lemere, C., DeTeresa, R., Grafe, M., Hansen, L., & Terry, R. (1991). Neocortical damage during HIV infection. *Annals of Neurology, 29*, 651–657.

Wilkie, F., Eisdorfer, C., Morgan, R., Loewenstein, D., & Szapocznik, J. (1990). Cognition in early HIV infection. *Archives of Neurology, 47*, 433–440.

Wilkins, J., Robertson, K., Snyder, C., Robertson, W., van der Horst, C., & Hall, C. (1991). Implications of self-reported cognitive and motor dysfunction in HIV-positive patients. *American Journal of Psychiatry, 148*, 641–643.

World Health Organization. (1988). *Report of the consultation on the neuropsychiatric aspects of HIV infection*, Geneva, 17 March. Author.

6

Alcoholic Dementia and Related Disorders

DAVID P. SALMON, NELSON BUTTERS, AND WILLIAM C. HEINDEL

It is well known that long-term chronic alcoholism may result in impairment of intellectual abilities. The nature and severity of this cognitive deterioration may vary from extremely subtle, and possibly reversible, deficits in memory, problem solving, and visuoperceptual abilities to a frank dementia syndrome characterized by profound and global cognitive decline. Two chronic and severe neurological disorders that may arise as a consequence of heavy and prolonged alcoholism and the nutritional deficiency that often accompanies alcoholic behavior are the Wernicke-Korsakoff syndrome and alcoholic dementia. These disorders are related conditions that result in profound and largely irreversible cognitive impairment that includes severe amnesia, and in the case of alcoholic dementia, general intellectual decline.

This chapter reviews the neuropsychological, neurological, and epidemiological characteristics of the Wernicke-Korsakoff syndrome and alcoholic dementia, and describes the etiological and neuropathological factors underlying their occurrence. In addition, the implications of recent neuropathological findings for the management and treatment of these debilitating disorders will be discussed. Because these new neuropathological findings suggest that brain lesions associated with Wernicke-Korsakoff disease may occur at a subclinical level in non-Korsakoff alcoholics, and indicate a possible direct neurotoxic effect of alcohol upon the cerebral cortex, it may be useful to briefly review the cognitive and neuroradiological deficits that are found in neurologically normal chronic alcoholics before embarking on a discussion of the Wernicke-Korsakoff syndrome and alcoholic dementia.

A number of mild cognitive deficits have been shown to persist in neurologically normal chronic alcoholics who have been abstinent for more than 3 weeks. The nature and extent of these deficits has been thoroughly described in several recent reviews (see Loberg, 1986; Parsons, Butters, & Nathan, 1987; Ryan & Butters, 1986; Tarter & Ryan, 1986) and will only be summarized here. Briefly, three areas of cognitive function appear to be affected in these chronic alcoholic patients. First, alcoholics perform significantly worse than nonalcoholic control subjects on difficult memory tasks, particularly when patterned visual stimuli must be remembered

(Cutting, 1978a; Miglioli, Buchtel, Campanini, & DeRisio, 1979; Ryan, Brandt, Bayog, & Butters, 1980; Ryan & Butters, 1980a, 1980b). Second, problem solving, abstraction, and concept formation abilities are impaired in chronic alcoholics (Goldman, 1983; Parsons & Leber, 1981; Parsons & Farr, 1981; Ryan & Butters, 1983; Tarter & Parsons, 1971), and recent evidence suggests that other so-called frontal functions, such as the ability to make accurate temporal-order or frequency-of-occurrence judgments, are also deficient (Salmon, Butters, & Schuckit, 1986). Third, deficits have been noted in alcoholics' performance of visuoperceptual and visuospatial tasks that require detailed pattern analysis (e.g., the Embedded Figures Test) (Bertera & Parsons, 1978; Glosser, Butters, & Kaplan, 1977; Kapur & Butters, 1977).

The cognitive deficits that are observed in detoxified chronic alcoholics occur in conjunction with brain abnormalities revealed by neuroimaging. Pneumoencephalography, computed tomography (CT) and magnetic resonance imaging (MRI) studies have consistently shown that neurologically normal alcoholics, with or without mild cognitive impairment, often have indices of cerebral atrophy, such as ventricular enlargement and sulcal widening, and atrophy of the cerebellum (Bergman, 1987; Bergman, Borg, Hindmarsh, Idestrom, & Mutzell, 1980; Brewer & Perret, 1971; Cala & Mastaglia, 1981; Carlen et al., 1981; Gebhardt, Naeser, & Butters, 1984; Jernigan, Schafer, Butters, & Cermak, 1991; Jernigan et al., 1982; Ron, Acker, & Lishman, 1980; Wilkinson, 1982). Although some investigators have found performance on certain memory tests to be related to specific CT measures of third-ventricle dilatation (Gebhardt et al., 1984), no clear association has been firmly established between degree of neuropsychological impairment and the various radiological indices of cortical atrophy. In a recent MRI study of 28 detoxified alcoholics, Jernigan, Butters, et al. (1991) did note significant correlations between neuropsychological measures and ventricular and sulcal cerebrospinal fluid (CSF) volumes, but they failed to find any consistent relationships between cognition and either cortical or subcortical grey matter volumes. This lack of correlation seemed especially surprising given that the alcoholics evidenced marked volume losses in the diencephalon, caudate nuclei, dorsolateral and parietal cortex, and mesial temporal lobe structures.

Longitudinal examinations of neurologically normal chronic alcoholics have revealed that the mild cognitive and neuroradiological abnormalities exhibited by these patients may be reversible with continued abstinence. Several studies have shown improved performance by alcoholics on tests of memory, concept formation, and visuoperceptual processing following 1 to 5 years of continuous abstinence (Brandt, Butters, Ryan, & Bayog, 1983; Fabian & Parsons, 1983; Grant, Adams, & Reed, 1986; Ryan et al., 1980). Similarly, periodically repeated CT scans in long-term alcoholics have revealed that continued abstinence leads to reductions in ventricular enlargement and sulcal widening (Artmann, Gall, Hacker, & Herrlich, 1981; Carlen, Wortzman, Holgate, Wilkinson, & Rankin, 1978; Carlen et al., 1986; Ron, 1983; Ron et al. 1982). This morphological "recovery" has led some investigators to suggest that the cerebral changes noted in radiological studies are a reflection of brain "shrinkage" rather than due to true tissue atrophy (Harper & Krill, 1985, 1986; Bowden, 1990). The mild and reversible nature of the neuropsychological and neuropathological deficits associated with chronic alcoholism distinguishes them from the severe and permanent impairments of the Wernicke-Korsakoff syndrome and alcoholic dementia.

The Wernicke-Korsakoff Syndrome

The Wernicke-Korsakoff syndrome is a neurological disorder that consists of an acute phase of potentially reversible cognitive and motor abnormalities related to an encephalopathy, and a chronic phase with long-lasting cognitive changes associated with permanent structural lesions in the brain. The syndrome is believed to result from thiamine deficiency and is most often observed in long-term alcoholics who have failed to maintain an adequate nutritional status (Victor, Adams, & Collins, 1989).

The initial stage of the disorder, the Wernicke phase, is characterized by abnormal eye movements (e.g., ophthalmoplegia, nystagmus), gait ataxia, and a global confusional state that are attributable to inflammatory disease (i.e., encephalopathy) affecting subcortical and brainstem structures. Clinical studies over the last 25 years have demonstrated that these neurological symptoms are progressive, and that if the patient with Wernicke's encephalopathy is not treated with large doses of thiamine, fatal midbrain hemorrhages may occur after approximately 5 weeks. However, if proper vitamin therapy is initiated the global confusional state will quickly clear and the ophthalmoplegia and ataxia will show marked improvement within 2 to 4 weeks.

Once the patient has recovered from the acute effects of Wernicke's encephalopathy, they usually enter the chronic Korsakoff state (i.e., alcoholic Korsakoff syndrome). The alcoholic Korsakoff (AK) syndrome is marked by a severe and permanent amnesic condition, and often by dramatic changes in personality in which impulsivity, aggression, and severe alcohol abuse are replaced at the onset of the syndrome by apathy, passivity, and a virtual disinterest in alcohol (Butters, 1984; Butters & Cermak, 1980; Cutting, 1985; Heindel, Salmon, & Butters, 1991). The AK patient evidences great difficulty in formulating, organizing, and initiating a series of plans, and behaves in a passive and indifferent manner. Very few patients (<25%) who survive Wernicke's encephalopathy show a complete return to their premorbid intellectual or personality state, particularly if their medical history includes long-term alcoholism (Victor et al., 1989).

The nature and extent of the cognitive impairment associated with the AK syndrome has been the focus of considerable clinical and experimental investigation. The cardinal feature of the syndrome is a severe inability to learn and retain new information (i.e., anterograde amnesia) or to remember events that occurred prior to the onset of the disorder (i.e., retrograde amnesia). The AK patient is often unable to learn the name of their physician and nurse, or the location of their hospital bed, even after several weeks of constant repetition. Despite this severe amnesia, the AK patient's general intellectual abilities remain relatively well preserved. Indeed, the clinical and psychometric hallmark of the AK syndrome has been the scatter between the patient's normal IQ score (Wechsler Adult Intelligence Scales [WAIS or WAIS-R]) (Wechsler, 1955, 1981) and their severely impaired MQ (memory quotient) score (Wechsler Memory Scale [WMS]) (Wechsler, 1945). A 20- to 30-point scatter between the IQ and MQ scores (e.g., IQ =

100, MQ = 75) of AK patients has been reported (Butters & Cermak, 1980), and even this disparity may underestimate the true difference between these patients' intellectual and memory abilities. In its original form the WMS includes attention and concentration tasks (e.g., Digit Span, Mental Control) that are usually un-impaired in amnesia, and does not include highly sensitive measures of delayed recall for verbal or nonverbal materials. The severe memory problems of AK patients are more accurately estimated by the recently revised version of the WMS (WMS-R) (Wechsler, 1987), which provides five separate memory indices (i.e., Attention/Concentration, Verbal Memory, Visual Memory, General Memory, and Delayed Memory). Butters et al. (1988) recently demonstrated that AK patients achieve WMS-R General and Delayed Memory indices of 65 and 57, respectively, in contrast to MQs on the WMS in the 70- to 80-point range.

In addition to anterograde amnesia, temporally graded retrograde amnesia is also a distinct and consistent feature of the AK syndrome (Albert, Butters, & Levin, 1979; Cohen & Squire, 1981; Kopelman, 1989, 1991; Marslen-Wilson & Teuber, 1975; Seltzer & Benson, 1974). The AK patient is usually severely impaired in their ability to retrieve from long-term memory information about events that occurred in the 20-year period prior to the onset of their illness. However, infor-mation about events that occurred in the more distant past are retrieved relatively well. Although retrograde and anterograde amnesia usually co-occur in the Wernicke-Korsakoff syndrome, the available evidence suggests that these forms of memory impairment are independent (Parkin, 1991). For example, in a recent study, Ko-pelman (1991) found no significant correlation between severity of retrograde and anterograde amnesia in a group consisting of 16 AK patients and 16 patients with dementia of the Alzheimer type (DAT). However, the severity of retrograde, but not anterograde, amnesia in this group was significantly correlated with perform-ance on tests sensitive to frontal lobe dysfunction.

In contrast to the striking remote memory loss of the AK patient, there is little evidence to suggest that retrograde amnesia occurs in non-Korsakoff alcoholics (Albert, Butters, & Brandt, 1980). The relatively intact remote memory of chronic alcoholics suggests that the retrograde amnesia of the AK patient cannot be at-tributed to a failure to learn new materials during their decades of alcohol abuse, but must be due to the abrupt loss of remote memory at the onset of the syndrome. Additional evidence in support of this notion is provided in a case report of a chronic alcoholic patient (case P.Z.) who at the onset of the Wernicke-Korsakoff syndrome suffered a sudden loss of personal memories that he had previously remembered sufficiently to include in his autobiography (Butters & Cermak, 1986).

Another common clinical feature associated with the AK patient's severe memory impairment is the tendency to confabulate (Kopelman, 1987; Lishman, 1987; Victor et al., 1989). When faced with questions they cannot answer, the AK patient is likely to "fill in" a gap in memory with appropriate, but incorrect, information. For example, the AK patient may describe a trip or sporting event that occurred many years ago when asked about the previous day's activities. The tendency to confabulate is not a constant or necessarily permanent characteristic of the patient, but is most apparent during the acute phase of the disorder and less noticeable or nonexistent in the later, chronic stages (Butters, 1984).

In addition to these clinical indices, the memory disorder of the AK syndrome has been more fully characterized through extensive experimental study. The experimental studies have focused, for the most part, on the severity and extent of the AK patient's memory impairment, on the processes underlying their memory disorder, and on the relative impairment or preservation of different forms of memory. Generally, these studies have demonstrated that whereas some aspects of memory are severely impaired in AK patients, other aspects remain relatively intact.

The profound amnesia exhibited by AK patients can be conceptualized as a deficit in episodic memory. Episodic memory refers to memory for specific events or episodes that are dependent upon temporal or spatial cues for their retrieval (Tulving, 1983). For example, the ability to remember yesterday morning's breakfast, the names of newly introduced people, or the score of last week's football game are all examples of episodic memory. Experimentally, tasks requiring the learning and retention of lists of words, lists of figures or faces, or short narrative paragraphs are most often used to assess episodic memory. Using such procedures, episodic memory deficits have been clearly demonstrated in AK patients. For example, AK patients were shown to be deficient in learning short lists of five or six paired-associates (Ryan & Butters, 1980a; Winocur & Weiskrantz, 1976) and in retaining three words or consonants in working (i.e., short-term) memory for more than 9 seconds if a demanding distractor activity intervenes between presentation and recall (DeLuca, Cermak, & Butters, 1975). An indication of the severity of the AK patients' episodic memory impairment is provided in a recent study in which they were as severely impaired as patients with DAT on a difficult list-learning task, the California Verbal Learning Test (CVLT) (Delis et al., 1991).

One process that may partially underlie the impaired performance of AK patients on episodic memory tests is an increased sensitivity to interference. A number of investigators have shown that these patients are often unable to acquire new information because of interference from previously learned material (i.e., proactive interference) (for review, see Parkin, 1987). The AK patient tends to perseverate responses (i.e., intralist intrusions) on free recall tasks, to intrude items from one recall task into another (i.e., interlist intrusions), and to demonstrate improved recall performance when conditions are structured to reduce proactive interference (Butters & Cermak, 1980; Fuld, 1976; Meudell, Butters, & Montgomery, 1978; Winocur, Kinsbourne, & Moscovitch, 1981).

In contrast to their severe impairment on episodic memory tests, some aspects of the AK patient's memory is preserved. For example, AK patients perform relatively well on tests of semantic memory. Semantic memory refers to knowledge of general principles, associations and rules that are independent of the context in which they were learned (e.g., arithmetical operations, the alphabet, vocabulary) (Tulving, 1983). The intact semantic memory of AK patients is demonstrated by their normal performance on tests of verbal fluency (Weingartner, Grafman, Boutelle, Kaye, & Martin, 1983), and their preserved knowledge of the meaning of words, rules of syntax, and basic arithmetical skills (Kinsbourne & Wood, 1975).

Alcoholic Korsakoff patients also demonstrate intact performance on a variety of priming tasks, despite their severe anterograde and retrograde memory impairments. Priming is defined as the temporary (and unconscious) facilitation of performance by prior exposure to specific stimuli (Schacter, 1985; Shimamura, 1986). For example, AK patients and intact control subjects have a strong tendency (relative to chance) to complete three-letter word stems (e.g., MOT) with previously presented words (e.g., MOTEL) despite the failure of the AK patients to recall or recognize these words on standard memory tests (Graf, Squire, & Mandler, 1984). Normal facilitation of the AK patient's performance by prior exposure to stimuli has been observed in tasks requiring the generation of exemplars from a particular semantic category (Gardner, Boller, Moreines, & Butters, 1973; Shimamura & Squire, 1984), the identification of briefly flashed words (Cermak, Talbot, Chandler, & Wolbarst, 1985; Jacoby & Dallas, 1981), and the identification of incomplete (i.e., fragmented) line drawings of animate and inanimate objects (Warrington & Weiskrantz, 1968, 1970). In addition, AK patients demonstrate a normal ability to acquire and retain motor and cognitive skills such as mirror tracing, reading mirror-reversed words, and pursuit rotor performance (Brooks & Baddeley, 1976; Cermak, Lewis, Butters, & Goodglass, 1973; Cohen & Squire, 1980; Martone, Butters, Payne, Becker, & Sax, 1984).

Comparisons of the Cognitive Deficits of Korsakoff and Non-Korsakoff Alcoholics

The severe anterograde and retrograde amnesia of the AK syndrome is both quantitatively and qualitatively different from the subtle memory impairment associated with chronic, long-term alcohol abuse. The memory disorder of the non-Korsakoff alcoholic is relatively mild, may be limited to the visual modality, and is not characterized by an increased susceptibility to proactive interference (Salmon & Butters, 1987a). Furthermore, little evidence of retrograde amnesia in non-Korsakoff alcoholics has been noted (Albert, Butters, & Brandt, 1980). In contrast to these differences, AK and non-Korsakoff alcoholics both demonstrate preserved semantic memory and priming ability.

Although there are a number of quantitative and qualitative differences in the memory dysfunction exhibited by AK patients and non-Korsakoff long-term alcoholics, these groups demonstrate qualitatively similar deficits in visuospatial processing and problem-solving abilities. Despite attaining IQ scores well within the normal range, both AK and neurologically intact alcoholics are impaired on tests that require visuoperceptual processing such as digit-symbol substitution (Glosser et al., 1977) or embedded figures (Kapur & Butters, 1977) tasks. For example, Kapur and Butters (1977) found that both Korsakoff and non-Korsakoff alcoholics were impaired relative to nonalcoholic controls on a digit-symbol association task, and that the impairment appeared to be related to a deficiency in analyzing the geometric forms used in the task as well as to some retardation in learning specific digit-symbol associations. The Korsakoff and non-Korsakoff alcoholics' degree of impairment on this task correlated highly with the amount of difficulty they encountered in locating specific geometric figures embedded within random unrelated lines, and in performing a rapid visual search.

In addition to their impairments on visuospatial tasks, both AK patients and non-Korsakoff long-term alcoholics are impaired on tests that require the learning and shifting of problem-solving strategies. For example, both groups have been shown to perform poorly on difficult problem-solving tasks such as the Wisconsin Card Sorting Test (WCST) and Reitan's Category Test (Jones & Parsons, 1971; Moscovitch, 1982; Squire, 1982; Talland, 1965; Tarter, 1973; Tarter & Parsons,

1971). Several studies have directly compared the performances of AK patients and long-term alcoholics on problem-solving tasks. Oscar-Berman (1973) administered a series of two-choice visual discrimination problems to AK patients, non-Korsakoff long-term alcoholics, patients with aphasic symptoms, and normal control subjects. The subject's task was to discover the particular stimulus dimension (e.g., color, size, form, position) the examiner had chosen to reinforce. Hypothesis formation, development of strategies to solve the problem, and focusing behavior of the subject was evaluated. The results indicated that AK patients could formulate and use hypotheses, but that their strategies were inefficient and insensitive to the feedback provided by the examiner. The performance of the long-term alcoholics fell between those of the AK patients and control subjects, and resembled that of the AK patients in that they did not efficiently use the examiners feedback to guide their problem-solving strategies.

Similarities in the problem-solving deficits of AK and long-term alcoholic patients have also been demonstrated with a task developed as a modification of the parlor game "20 Questions" (Becker, Butters, Rivoira, & Miliotis, 1986; Laine & Butters, 1982). In one version of this task, the subject was shown a presentation card with 42 stimuli (e.g., outline drawings of common objects) arranged in a 6×7 matrix and then asked to figure out which object the examiner was thinking of at that time. The subject could ask any question as long as the examiner could answer it with a yes or no response. The subject's goal was to identify the preselected object in as few questions as possible. Becker et al. (1986) found that control subjects usually adopted the efficient strategy of first asking constraint-seeking questions that reduced by as much as 50% the number of possible alternatives (objects) regardless of a yes or no response from the examiner (e.g., "Is it a tool?", "Is it in the first three columns?"). Only when two or three alternatives remained did a control subject ask a hypothesis-scanning question that referred to a single object (e.g., "Is it the saw?"). In contrast, both the AK and non-Korsakoff long-term alcoholics quickly abandoned this efficient use of constraint-seeking questions and shifted to hypothesis-scanning and even pseudoconstraint-seeking questions that superficially seemed to be general questions but actually referred to only one object on the card (e.g., the question "Is it something to tell time with?" is only relevant to a drawing of a clock and not to any other alternative).

The results of the studies by Becker et al. (1986) and by Oscar-Berman (1973) demonstrate that long-term alcoholics have not only a quantitatively similar but also an approach to problem solving that is qualitatively similar to that of alcoholics with Korsakoff's syndrome. Both groups seem unable to plan, initiate, or consistently apply an optimal problem-solving strategy. Such deficiencies in planning and problem solving have often been attributed to damage to the frontal association cortex (Stuss & Benson, 1986).

Alcoholic Korsakoff patients have been shown to demonstrate another form of cognitive impairment that is often associated with damage to the frontal lobes, the inability to accurately judge temporal order and event frequency (Squire, 1982; Weingartner et al., 1983). To determine if AK and non-Korsakoff long-term alcoholics also share this aspect of frontal lobe dysfunction, Salmon et al., (1986) examined whether non-Korsakoff alcoholics were deficient in incidental encoding of temporal order or event frequency information during a memory task. In the temporal order judgment task, alcoholics and a matched nonalcoholic control group were asked to remember two lists of words (or complex geometric figures) that were presented 5 minutes apart. Following exposure to the second list, a recognition test was administered that was composed of words (or figures) from the two presented lists and distractor items that were not presented. The subject was asked to indicate whether or not each item had or had not appeared on one of the two previous lists. When a subject correctly identified an item as having been previously presented, they were then asked to indicate (i.e., judge) on which of the two lists the stimulus had appeared. Although the alcoholics performed normally on the recognition aspect of the verbal task and were only mildly deficient in recognizing the geometric stimuli, they were significantly impaired in judging the temporal recency of both words and geometric patterns they had correctly recognized.

In the frequency judgment task, alcoholics and matched nonalcoholic controls were asked to view and remember 32 different stimuli (words, complex geometric patterns), each of which were presented in the list at one of eight frequencies (1, 2, 3, 4, 5, 7, 9, and 11 presentations). At the completion of the presentation list, the 32 items from the list, and 32 distractor stimuli, were shown in a quasi-random order and the subject was asked to indicate (i.e., judge) the number of times each item had been presented. The subject was to indicate zero if the item had not been presented previously. Although the alcoholics' judgments of frequency of occurrence were as accurate as the controls' when words were employed, they demonstrated a significant deficit in judging the frequency with which geometric patterns were presented.

In summary, neuropsychological investigations comparing neurologically normal chronic alcoholics and patients with the AK syndrome indicate that these groups demonstrate qualitatively similar deficits on tests of visuoperceptual ability and on cognitive tasks that are dependent on the integrity of the frontal lobes (e.g., conceptualization, problem solving). This continuity in deficits of higher cortical functions contrasts with the qualitative and quantitative difference in these patients' memory deficits. This pattern of results suggests that the visuoperceptual, conceptual, and problem-solving deficits of Korsakoff and non-Korsakoff alcoholics may have a common neuropathological basis, whereas a distinct neuropathological event may contribute to the severe amnesia of the AK patient. Neuropathological evidence in support of this notion will be further discussed in a subsequent section.

Alcoholic Dementia

In contrast to the relatively circumscribed memory defect of the AK patient, some chronic alcoholics develop a global dementia characterized by severe memory and general intellectual impairment (Cutting, 1978b; Goldstein, 1985; Horvath, 1975; Jacobson & Lishman, 1987; Lishman, 1981; Lishman, 1990; Victor & Adams, 1985). The cognitive deficits of the patient with alcoholic dementia are sufficiently severe to interfere with work and usual social activities. Although the disorder occurs in the presence of a long history of alcoholism, the global and severe intellectual deficits persist after at least 3 weeks of abstinence and usually remain largely unabated over the patient's lifetime.

Patients with alcoholic dementia exhibit amnesia that is as severe as that of patients with the AK syndrome (Longmore & Knight, 1988; Martin, Adinoff,

Weingartner, Mukherjee, & Eckardt, 1986; Strub & Black, 1981). In a recent study, Longmore and Knight (1988) compared the performance of AK patients, patients with alcoholic dementia, and nonamnesic alcoholic control subjects on tests of verbal recall, short-term retention, release from proactive interference, and stem-completion priming. The AK patients and patients with alcoholic dementia demonstrated significantly faster forgetting than control subjects on the short-term retention test, and the degree of memory impairment was equivalent in these two brain-damaged groups. The patients with the AK syndrome and alcoholic dementia were also equally impaired, relative to the control subjects, on the verbal recall test, and in terms of sensitivity to and release from proactive interference. In contrast to these episodic memory deficits, both AK and alcoholic dementia patients demonstrated normal performance on the stem-completion priming task. The preserved priming ability exhibited by the alcoholic dementia patients differs from the reported deficits in stem-completion priming of patients with DAT (Shimamura, Salmon, Squire & Butters, 1987; Salmon, Shimamura, Butters, & Smith, 1988) and may be useful for differentiating between these two dementing disorders. The results of the study by Longmore and Knight (1988) demonstrate that AK and alcoholic dementia patients evidence equivalently severe memory deficits and exhibit similar patterns of impaired and preserved memory processes.

In contrast to patients with the AK syndrome, the memory defect of patients with alcoholic dementia is *not* more prominent than their impairment in other cognitive spheres (Cutting, 1978b; Horvath, 1975; Lishman, 1981, 1986, 1990; Martin et al., 1986; Seltzer & Sherwin, 1978; Strub & Black, 1981). In addition to amnesia, alcoholic dementia patients typically suffer severe deficits in conceptual and problem-solving abilities (Martin et al., 1986; Strub & Black, 1981), and often exhibit pronounced deficiencies on visuospatial or visuoconstructional tasks, particularly those that require visuoperceptual analysis (Seltzer & Sherwin, 1978; Strub & Black, 1981). Despite these visuospatial deficits, the ability to copy simple geometric designs often remains relatively intact. Severe language dysfunction is usually not evident in alcoholic dementia (Martin et al., 1986; Seltzer & Sherwin, 1978), although a mild language disorder was reported as a presenting symptom in a recent case study (Everall, 1988). It should be noted, however, that the language disorder in this case was primarily one of disordered and muddled speech, rather than a form of dysnomia, aphasia, or dysarthria that is often associated with other forms of dementia such as DAT or Huntington's disease.

In addition to these cognitive manifestations, alcoholic dementia is also characterized by marked behavioral changes. As observed in patients with the AK syndrome, the alcoholic dementia patient is apathetic and unconcerned about ongoing environmental events, and there is often a total lack of concern about personal care and appearance. This apathetic behavior is usually accompanied by impaired judgment and a general slowness in thought processes (Goldstein, 1985; Horvath, 1975; Lishman, 1990; Martin et al., 1986).

As the above review attests, alcoholic dementia and the AK syndrome share a number of clinical and neuropsychological characteristics and cannot always be clearly distinguished. Indeed, the ambiguity in the distinction between the two disorders was highlighted in a study by Cutting (1978b) that compared patients with acute-onset Korsakoff syndrome, gradual-onset Korsakoff syndrome, and alcoholic dementia. Cutting found that while the acute-onset AK patients displayed the neuropsychological profile typical of the syndrome, the gradual-onset AK patients suffered not only memory impairment, but also a global intellectual deterioration that was equivalent to that of the alcoholic dementia patients. In addition, the gradual-onset Korsakoff and alcoholic dementia patients shared a number of other clinical features including gradual onset, similar age and sex distributions, and longer drinking histories than the acute-onset Korsakoff patients. Based on these results, Cutting suggested that the term alcoholic Korsakoff syndrome be applied only to those patients who demonstrate a relatively circumscribed memory disorder of acute onset, and that patients with a gradual development of more global symptoms should be considered to have alcoholic dementia.

An alternative position is adopted by Victor, Adams, and Collins (1989), who conclude that there is little justification for distinguishing between patients with the AK syndrome and alcoholic dementia, primarily because of the lack of a clear morphological basis for the distinction. According to these investigators, a common neuropathological change (i.e., diencephalic hemorrhagic lesions) underlies the clinical and neuropsychological manifestations of acute-onset Korsakoff syndrome, gradual-onset Korsakoff syndrome, and alcoholic dementia. Alcoholic dementia, in this view, may simply represent "burned-out" Wernicke-Korsakoff's disease rather than a distinct clinical and neuropathological entity (Victor et al., 1989).

Prevalence

Because of the noted difficulty in distinguishing patients with alcoholic dementia from those with the AK syndrome, and because of the general lack of prospective neuropathological studies in which AK and alcoholic dementia patients were clinically and psychometrically evaluated prior to death, the prevalence of alcoholic dementia remains unclear. Wilkinson, Kornaczewski, Rankin, and Santamaria (1971) reported on 1,000 alcoholic patients (825 men and 175 women) who were examined while voluntarily attending an alcoholism clinic in Melbourne, Australia. Alcoholic dementia (or chronic brain syndrome) was evident in 63 of the men (7.6%) and 25 of the women (14.3%), for an overall prevalence of 8.8% in these chronic alcoholics. These demented patients were reported to have "a continuing memory defect, and obvious intellectual impairment" (p. 1220). No attempt was made by these authors to distinguish between alcoholic dementia and chronic AK syndrome.

In a more recent study, Torvik, Lindboe, and Rogde (1982) completed neuropathological examination of the brains of 8,735 individuals who died during a 5-year period in Oslo, Norway. Of these individuals, clinical records indicated that 713 (8.2%) had suspected or verified alcoholism. Neuropathological examination performed on approximately 75% of the 713 alcoholic patients revealed that 70 (or about 12.5%) had pathological changes associated with Wernicke-Korsakoff disease: 22 (3.9%) with active (e.g., swelling of the vascular endothelium, signs of neuropil destruction with macrophage response and astrocytic reaction, perivascular hemorrhages) and 48 (8.6%) with inactive or chronic Wernicke's encephalopathy (e.g., destruction of neuropil with tissue sponginess and gliosis in the mammillary bodies and medial parts of the thalamus, no vascular swelling).

Clinical records were available on 20 of Torvik et al.'s patients with inactive, chronic Wernicke's encephalopathy. A selective memory deficit typical of Korsakoff's syndrome was reported in five of the cases, whereas the remaining 15 evidenced global dementia in addition to severe memory impairment. Of these 15 globally demented patients, two received a neuropathological diagnosis of Alzheimer's disease and one of multi-infarct dementia. The remaining 12 of the 20 patients (60%) were considered to have alcoholic dementia.

Neuropathological Considerations

Recent neuropathological studies with neurologically normal chronic alcoholics and patients with the Wernicke-Korsakoff syndrome suggest that the deficits in higher cortical functions (e.g., problem solving and visuoperceptual abilities) that are present in both of these alcoholic groups may have a common neuropathological basis; namely, a direct toxic effect of alcohol on the association cortex. As mentioned previously, numerous radiological studies have demonstrated that chronic alcoholics, as well as patients with alcoholic Korsakoff syndrome, have indices of cortical atrophy or "shrinkage" such as ventricular enlargement and sulcal widening (Bergman, 1987; Bergman et al., 1980; Brewer & Perret, 1971; Cala & Mastaglia, 1981; Carlen et al., 1981; Jernigan et al., 1982; Ron et al., 1980; Wilkinson, 1982). Additional evidence of cortical abnormalities related to chronic alcoholism is provided in several neuropathological studies with animals and humans. Walker, Hunter, and Abraham (1981) observed a loss and shrinkage of hippocampal pyramidal neurons in chronic ethanol-consuming rats. Harper, Kril, and Daly (1987) reported that chronic human alcoholics suffered an 18% reduction in neurons in the anterior frontal cortex (i.e., superior frontal gyrus) relative to matched nonalcoholic control subjects. Harper and colleagues speculated that such neuron loss and subsequent degeneration of axons may be the cause of the cerebral shrinkage, particularly of the white matter, noted in chronic alcoholics by many investigators. Freund and colleagues suggest that chronic alcoholism may result in the destruction of many synaptic receptors before gross histological changes and atrophy, or severe cognitive changes, become evident. Freund and Ballinger (1989) examined the brains of 26 chronic alcohol abusers who were free of liver disease, neuropathological indices of Wernicke-Korsakoff disease, or dementia severe enough to require hospitalization prior to death. Muscarinic cholinergic receptors were reduced by 40% in the temporal cortex of these patients relative to 26 matched nonalcoholic controls. Similar reductions in cholinergic receptors were noted in the frontal cortex of alcoholic subjects.

Although such cortical dysfunction may underlie the qualitatively and quantitatively similar problem-solving and visuoperceptual deficits in both Korsakoff and non-Korsakoff alcoholics, the qualitative differences in the memory impairment of these two groups suggests that the truly amnesic condition of the AK patient cannot be achieved without some acute insult combining with the detrimental effects of ethanol. The sudden appearance of the amnesic symptoms of the AK syndrome has been attributed to the development of small hemorrhagic lesions in the midline diencephalic region following thiamine deprivation (Victor et al., 1989). The dorsomedial nucleus of the thalamus and the mammillary bodies of the hypothalamus are the specific structures most often associated with the amnesia of the AK patient (for review, see Victor et al., 1989; Markowitsch, 1982; Markowitsch & Pritzel, 1985).

Damage to the mammillary bodies has been found in a number of studies to contribute importantly to the development of amnesia in the AK patient. In an early study of the brains of 16 AK patients, Gamper (1928) observed extensive atrophy of the mammillary bodies in all 16 cases. Riggs and Boles (1944) examined the brains of 29 patients who had Wernicke's disease due to various causes and noted that the mammillary bodies were affected in 21 of 23 cases, the dorsomedial nucleus of the thalamus in 23 of 27 cases, and the pulvinar nucleus of the thalamus in 10 of 14 cases. In another neuropathological series, Delay, Brion, and Elissalde (1958a, 1958b) observed that atrophy of the mammillary bodies was common to eight brains of AK patients who exhibited anterograde and retrograde amnesia, whereas significant thalamic involvement was noted in only one of these brains.

A significant role of thalamic lesions in producing the amnesic symptoms of AK patients has been supported by several more recent neuropathological studies. Adams, Collins, and Victor (1962) found that the severe amnesia of 54 AK patients was related to the presence of lesions in several thalamic nuclei including the dorsomedial, anterior, and pulvinar, as well as the mammillary bodies. In their postmortem study of 82 alcoholic Korsakoff brains, Victor et al. (1989) examined the medial diencephalic region in 43 cases. Atrophy of the mammillary bodies was observed in all 43 cases, and extensive atrophy of the dorsomedial nucleus of the thalamus was also noted in 38 of the 43 brains. Because the five brains without atrophy of the dorsomedial nucleus represented cases without lasting memory impairments, Victor et al. concluded that the dorsomedial nucleus of the thalamus is the critical structure for the amnesic syndrome. It should be noted, however, that the findings of Victor et al. can also be interpreted as demonstrating that damage to both the dorsomedial nucleus of the thalamus and the mammillary bodies is necessary for the appearance of severe memory disorders (Butters, 1981).

The importance of these diencephalic structures in the memory disorder of the AK syndrome receives additional support from recent neuroradiological studies (Charness & De La Paz, 1987; Kitaguchi, Kobayashi, Tobimatus, Goto, & Kuriowa, 1987; Shimamura, Jernigan, & Squire, 1988). For example, Shimamura et al. (1988) examined neuropathological changes in seven AK patients, seven detoxified non-Korsakoff alcoholics, and seven non-alcoholic control subjects using computer-generated measures derived from CT scans. The Korsakoff subjects were found to have lower density values in the region of the thalamus and greater fluid volumes in the third ventricle than did the alcoholic and control subjects. Signs of anterior cortical atrophy (e.g., increased sulcal size) were noted in both the Korsakoff and non-Korsakoff alcoholics. Indices of memory functioning correlated with thalamic density measures and with fluid volume in the region of the frontal lobes in the Korsakoff subjects.

Despite the evidence reviewed above, the unique role of thalamic and mammillary body damage in producing the severe amnesia of the AK syndrome has been recently challenged by the results of several studies by Harper and his colleagues. These studies were designed to examine the prevalence of the neuropathological changes of the Wernicke-Korsakoff syndrome in a large series of autopsies performed in Western Australia (Harper, 1979; Harper, 1983; Harper, Giles, & Finlay-Jones, 1986; Harper, Gold, Rodriguez, & Perdices, 1989). Using mammillary body atrophy and abnormal periventricular (third ventricle) tissue and periaqueductal structures as defining neuropathological characteristics, Harper (1979) identified 51 cases of Wernicke's encephalopathy from among 2,891 brains examined during a 4-year period at the Perth City Coroner's Office and the Department of Neuropathology of the Royal Perth Hospital. A follow-up study encompassing a 9-year period revealed neuropathologically diagnosed Wernicke's encephalopathy in 131 of 4,677 examined brains (2.8%) (Harper, 1983).

In addition to the relatively high prevalence of Wernicke's encephalopathy, one of the most surprising aspects of Harper's studies was the large discrepancy that was observed between the number of neuropathologically identified cases of Wernicke's encephalopathy and the number of cases clinically diagnosed with the Wernicke-Korsakoff syndrome during life. In his initial study, only 7 of the 51 (i.e., 14%) pathologically diagnosed cases of Wernicke-Korsakoff syndrome had been clinically diagnosed. Similarly, a clinical diagnosis of either Wernicke's encephalopathy, Wernicke-Korsakoff syndrome, or Korsakoff's psychosis had been made in only 26 of the 131 cases (20%) that were identified in the larger autopsy series. These low rates of concordance between clinical and pathological diagnoses were obtained despite the fact that the majority of patients had been seen in a major hospital during the latter part of their lives (Harper, 1983). In summarizing the results of his own and previously published neuropathological studies, Harper and colleagues (Harper, Giles, & Finlay-Jones, 1986) found the classic triad of clinical symptoms of the Wernicke-Korsakoff syndrome (i.e., ophthalmoplegia/nystagmus, ataxia, and abnormal mental state) to be present in only 10% of the neuropathologically diagnosed patients. Individual symptoms of gait ataxia, ophthalmoplegia/nystagmus, and abnormal mental state had been observed in 23%, 29%, and 82% of these patients, respectively.

The failure of a large number of patients with the neuropathological changes of Wernicke's encephalopathy to be identified clinically during life has led Harper and others to postulate that chronic alcoholics may suffer repeated subclinical bouts of Wernicke's encephalopathy associated with periodic thiamine deficiency. Although these subclinical bouts result in neuropathological changes associated with Wernicke-Korsakoff syndrome, the damage remains below some threshold level required for the full manifestation of the usual neurological and neuropsychological deficits of the disorder. Only until the threshold of diencephalic damage is exceeded, either acutely or gradually, is the full Wernicke-Korsakoff syndrome exhibited. In light of these findings, Bowden (1990) has suggested that the full range of cognitive impairment associated with chronic alcohol abuse, from very mild cognitive impairment to alcoholic dementia, may be due simply to different degrees of Wernicke-Korsakoff neuropathology (i.e., atrophy of the mammillary bodies, hemorrhagic lesions of the thalamus, dilatation of the third ventricle). Arguing that psychometrically artificial distinctions have been made in the past between non-Korsakoff alcoholics, alcoholics with Korsakoff syndrome, and alcoholic dementia patients, Bowden suggests that a continuum of severity in cognitive impairment due to chronic alcoholism is mediated by a continuum in the severity of Wernicke-Korsakoff neuropathology.

It should be noted that the extremely high rate of subclinical Wernicke-Korsakoff disease reported by Harper and colleagues may overestimate the true prevalence of this condition. As Victor et al. (1989) point out, Harper's clinical data were derived solely from retrospective examination of hospital charts for recorded signs of the Wernicke-Korsakoff syndrome. It is possible that clinical signs may have been present in these patients but gone unreported. If this is indeed the case, then Harper's retrospective analysis may have resulted in an inflated estimate of subclinical disease. A more definitive answer to this question awaits the results of a neuropathological study of long-term alcoholics who have been assessed during life and are known to be free of the clinical manifestations of the Wernicke-Korsakoff syndrome.

The fact that large numbers of chronic alcoholics who do not manifest clinical symptoms of the Wernicke-Korsakoff syndrome have significant thalamic and mammillary body damage suggests that the severe memory disorder of the AK patient, and the global and severe cognitive deficits of alcoholic dementia, may not arise until neuropathological changes occur in brain regions beyond these midline diencephalic structures. A brain region that has recently been implicated in the cognitive deficits of AK patients and patients with alcoholic dementia is the basal forebrain, the major source of cholinergic input to the cerebral cortex and hippocampus (Butters, 1985; Lishman, 1986). Damage to the basal forebrain has been shown to produce severe memory deficits in both humans and animals (for review, see Salmon & Butters, 1987a), and is thought to mediate, at least in part, the global dementia of Alzheimer's disease (Whitehouse et al., 1982).

Several studies support the notion that basal forebrain damage may play an important role in the AK syndrome and in alcoholic dementia. In a recent study by Jernigan, Schafer, et al. (1991), MRI scans of eight patients with AK syndrome were compared to those of 13 age-matched normal control subjects and 12 non-amnesic alcoholic control subjects. Quantitative image-analytic measurements of volume were obtained for ventricular and cortical CSF, as well as for cortical and subcortical grey matter structures. Both the Korsakoff and non-Korsakoff alcoholic subjects demonstrated a significant reduction in overall diencephalic grey matter volume relative to age-matched nonalcoholic controls, but the two alcoholic groups did not differ from each other. Separate analysis of the anterior and posterior portions of the diencephalon revealed that the two alcoholic groups did not differ in the reduction of volume in the posterior portion that consists primarily of thalamic structures, such as the dorsomedial nucleus, and the mammillary bodies. In contrast, AK patients had a significantly greater volume reduction than the nonamnesic alcoholics in the structures of the anterior region of the diencephalon including the septal nuclei (i.e., basal forebrain) and hypothalamic grey matter. In addition, alcoholic Korsakoff patients had a significant reduction in grey matter volume in the mesial temporal lobe region, and the region of the orbitofrontal cortex, relative to both nonamnesic alcoholic and nonalcoholic control subjects. Finally, consistent with numerous reports, both alcoholic groups demonstrated significant sulci and ventricular enlargement which is indicative of increased CSF volume.

The results of this study are consistent with a recent report by Hata et al. (1987) that blood flow is significantly reduced in the hypothalamus, septum, and temporal limbic structures of AK patients. These studies suggest the amnesic symptoms of the AK patient that are usually attributed to thalamic or mammillary body damage may be mediated to some degree by hypothalamic and septal nuclei comprising the anterior diencephalic region, and possibly by mesial temporal lobe structures.

Additional support for the notion that the basal forebrain nuclei are critically involved in the AK syndrome is provided in an anatomical study by Arendt, Bigl, Arendt, and Tennstedt (1983). Arendt et al. derived total neuron counts and indices of maximum neuronal population density in the three subdivisions of the basal forebrain and in portions of the globus pallidus in several patient groups. Of 72 cases studied, 14 were control cases, 3 were cases of AK syndrome, 5 were cases of chronic alcoholism without dementia, 14 were cases of Alzheimer's disease, 9 were cases of Huntington's disease, and 3 were cases of schizophrenia. The major finding of the study was that the number of neurons in the basal forebrain of the Alzheimer's disease and AK patients was reduced by 70% and 47%, respectively. No significant loss of neurons in the basal forebrain was noted for the chronic alcoholics, schizophrenic, and Huntington's disease cases.

The encroachment of the neuropathological changes associated with Wernicke's encephalopathy (i.e., small hemorrhagic lesions) on critical basal forebrain nuclei has also been proposed as a possible mechanism underlying the global cognitive impairment of alcoholic dementia (Lishman, 1986, 1990). According to Lishman (1986), the degree and extent of involvement of the cholinergic basal forebrain nuclei may determine the scope of the cognitive dysfunction, ranging from the relatively circumscribed amnesia of the AK syndrome to the more widespread cognitive deficits of alcoholic dementia. In suppport of this notion, Lishman points out that the three cases of AK syndrome studied by Arendt et al. (1983) were not clinically described, so the scope and degree of their cognitive impairment during life cannot be ascertained. It may be that these cases suffered a global dementia rather than the relatively circumscribed amnesia of Korsakoff's syndrome. Using a more carefully defined subject population, Akai and Akai (1989) compared neuron counts in the nucleus basalis of Meynert (nbM) in nine cases of alcoholic dementia and in three nondemented alcoholic controls. The demented subjects in this study were selected on the basis of a clinical evaluation prior to death or a retrospective chart review that indicated irreversible general decline in mental activities that prevented the subject from returning to society and functioning in a generally accepted manner. Although only a small number of subjects were examined, a significant reduction in nbM neurons was observed in the alcoholic dementia cases.

In accordance with Lishman's hypothesis (Lishman, 1986, 1990), it may be the case that individuals with a particular vulnerability to the neurotoxic effects of alcohol are those who develop alcoholic dementia rather than the classic AK syndrome. Such vulnerability may lead to greater cortical damage in these individuals, and possibly to more widespread involvement of the basal forebrain cholinergic system than is typically found in the chronic alcoholic or the patient with the AK syndrome. A significant depletion in cholinergic projections to hippocampal and neocortical regions that are already highly compromised due to a direct toxic effect of alcohol may result in a global and profound dementia rather than a relatively circumscribed memory impairment.

Implications for Treatment and Management

The treatment and management of severe neurological and cognitive complications of chronic alcoholism has received little research attention in the past (Martin &

Eckardt, 1985). This neglect may have occurred in part because of the belief that most structural and functional changes attributable to alcohol abuse were reversible with continued abstinence. However, the etiological and neuropathological findings described above indicate that irreversible changes may occur not only in the brains of patients with Wernicke-Korsakoff syndrome or alcoholic dementia, but also, at a subclinical level, in neurologically normal chronic alcoholics. These findings highlight the importance of prevention of alcohol-related brain damage through abstinence or moderation in alcohol use and indicate the need to broadly encourage vitamin supplementation in all alcoholics.

Once irreversible brain damage sufficient to produce the AK syndrome or alcoholic dementia has occurred, little can be done on a behavioral level to ameliorate the cognitive dysfunction. Memory rehabilitation efforts have been attempted with AK patients in the past, but have resulted in little success (for review, see O'Connor & Cermak, 1987). The inability of amnesic and demented patients to employ complex mnemonic strategies to overcome their deficits has been described numerous times, and may be at least partially due to concomitant loss of other cognitive capacities such as the ability to generalize from one situation to another or to easily elaborate on "to-be-remembered" information (Salmon & Butters, 1987b). A potentially fruitful behavioral rehabilitation strategy that has only recently been attempted with amnesic patients is to build on those learning and memory capacities that are preserved (Glisky & Schacter, 1988; Glisky, Schacter, & Tulving, 1986). Although priming, skill learning, and other forms of procedural memory have so far proven to be of only limited use in the cognitive retraining of amnesic patients, this is clearly an area that deserves further investigation.

The possible role of damage to the basal forebrain cholinergic system in the cognitive deficits of alcoholic Korsakoff syndrome and alcoholic dementia suggests that pharmacological interventions may prove useful in the treatment of these disorders. Following the model established for the treatment of Alzheimer's disease, another dementing disorder involving damage to the cholinergic system, drugs that enhance acetylcholine either by mimicking its action or preventing its breakdown may prove useful in enhancing the cognitive performance of these amnesic and demented patients.

Although this pharmacological approach to the treatment of the AK syndrome and alcoholic dementia may have some merit, it should be noted that both disorders involve relatively extensive neurobiological and cognitive deficits that undoubtedly extend beyond the cholinergic system. Indeed, some investigators have suggested that AK patients' anterograde memory deficits may be associated with a deficiency in norepinephrine (McEntee & Mair, 1978, 1980; Mair & McEntee, 1986) or serotonin (Martin et al., 1989). Given the diverse neurochemical and neuropathological changes associated with the AK syndrome and alcoholic dementia, a simplistic pharmacological approach in which a single neurotransmitter system is manipulated will most likely be unsuccessful in ameliorating the severe cognitive deficits associated with these disorders.

Acknowledgments

Preparation of this manuscript was supported in part by National Institute on Aging Grants AG05131 and AG08204 to the University of California at San Diego, by funds from the

Medical Research Service of the Department of Veterans Affairs, and by NIAAA Grant AA00187 to Boston University.

References

Adams, R. D., Collins, G. H., & Victor, M. (1962). Troubles de la memoire et de l'apprentissage chez l'homme; leurs relations avec des lesions des lobes temporaux et du diencephale. In *Physiologie de l'Hippocampe*. Paris: Centre National de la Recherche Scientifique.

Akai, J., & Akai, K. (1989). Neuropathological study of the nucleus basalis of Meynert in alcoholic dementia. *Japanese Journal of Alcohol and Drug Dependence, 24,* 80–88.

Albert, M. S., Butters, N., & Brandt, J. (1980). Memory for remote events in alcoholics. *Journal of Studies on Alcohol, 41,* 1071–1081.

Albert, M. S., Butters, N., & Levin, J. (1979). Temporal gradients in the retrograde amnesia of patients with alcoholic Korsakoff disease. *Archives of Neurology, 36,* 211–216.

Arendt, T., Bigl, V., Arendt, A., & Tennstedt, A. (1983). Loss of neurons in the nucleus basalis of Meynert in Alzheimer's disease, paralysis agitans and Korsakoff's disease. *Acta Neuropathologica, 61,* 101–108.

Artmann, H., Gall, M. V., Hacker, H., & Herrlich, J. (1981). Reversible enlargement of cerebral spinal fluid spaces in chronic alcoholics. *American Journal of Neuroradiology, 2,* 23–27.

Becker, J., Butters, N., Rivoira, P., & Miliotis, P. (1986). Asking the right questions: Problem solving in male alcoholics and male alcoholics with Korsakoff syndrome. *Alcoholism: Clinical and Experimental Research, 10,* 641–646.

Bergman, H. (1987). Brain dysfunction related to alcoholism: Some results from the KAR-TAD project. In O. A. Parsons, N. Butters, & P. E. Nathan (Eds.), *Neuropsychology of alcoholism: Implications for diagnosis and treatment* (pp. 21–45). New York: Guilford Press.

Bergman, H., Borg, S., Hindmarsh, T., Idestrom, C. M., & Mutzell, S. (1980). Computed tomography of the brain and neuropsychological assessment of male alcoholic patients and a random sample from the general male population. *Acta Psychiatrica Scandinavica, 62* (Suppl. 286), 77–88.

Bertera, J. H., & Parsons, O. A. (1978). Impaired visual search in alcoholics. *Alcoholism: Clinical and Experimental Research, 2,* 9–14.

Bowden, S. C. (1990). Separating cognitive impairment in neurologically asymptomatic alcoholism from Wernicke-Korsakoff syndrome: Is the neuropsychological distinction justified? *Psychological Bulletin, 107,* 355–366.

Brandt, J., Butters, N., Ryan, C., & Bayog, R. (1983). Cognitive loss and recovery in long-term alcohol abusers. *Archives of General Psychiatry, 40,* 435–442.

Brewer, C., & Perrett, L. (1971). Brain damage due to alcohol consumption: An air-encephalographic, psychometric and electroencephalographic study. *British Journal of Addiction, 66,* 170–182.

Brooks, D. N., & Baddeley, A. D. (1976). What can amnesic patients learn? *Neuropsychologia, 14,* 111–122.

Butters, N. (1981). The Wernicke-Korsakoff syndrome: A review of psychological, neuropathological and etiological factors. In M. Galanter (Ed.), *Currents in alcoholism* (Vol. 3, pp. 205–232). New York: Grune & Stratton.

Butters, N. (1984). Alcoholic Korsakoff's syndrome: An update. *Seminars in Neurology, 4,* 226–244.

Butters, N. (1985). Alcoholic Korsakoff's syndrome: Some unresolved issues concerning etiology, neuropathology, and cognitive deficits. *Journal of Clinical and Experimental Neuropsychology, 7,* 181–210.

Butters, N., & Cermak, L. S. (1980). *Alcoholic Korsakoff's syndrome.* New York: Academic Press.

Butters, N., & Cermak, L. S. (1986). A case study of the forgetting of autobiographical knowledge: Implications for the study of retrograde amnesia. In D. Rubin (Ed.), *Autobiographical memory* (pp. 253–272). New York: Cambridge University Press.

Butters, N., Salmon, D. P., Cullum, C. M., Cairns, P., Troster, A. I., Jacobs, D., Moss, M., & Cermak, L. S. (1988). Differentiation of amnesic and demented patients with the Wechsler Memory Scale-Revised. *The Clinical Neuropsychologist, 2,* 133–148.

Cala, L. A., & Mastaglia, F. L. (1981). Computerized tomography in chronic alcoholics. *Alcoholism: Clinical and Experimental Research, 5,* 283–294.

Carlen, P. L., Penn, R. D., Fornazzari, L., Bennet, J., Wilkinson, D. A., & Wortzman, G. (1986). Computerized tomographic scan assessment of alcoholic brain damage and its potential reversibility. *Alcoholism: Clinical and Experimental Research, 10,* 226–232.

Carlen, P. L., Wilkinson, D. A., Wortzman, G., Holgate, R., Cordingly, J., Lee, M. A., Huszar, L., Moddel, G., Singh, R., Kiraly, L., & Rankin, J. G. (1981). Cerebral atrophy and functional deficits in alcoholics without clinically apparent liver disease. *Neurology, 31,* 377–385.

Carlen, P. L., Wortzman, G., Holgate, R. C., Wilkinson, D. A., & Rankin, J. G. (1978). Reversible cerebral atrophy in recently abstinent chronic alcoholics measured by computed tomography scans. *Science, 200,* 1076–1078.

Cermak, L. S., Lewis, R., Butters, N., & Goodglass, H. (1973). Role of verbal mediation in performance of motor tasks by Korsakoff patients. *Perceptual and Motor Skills, 37,* 259–262.

Cermak, L. S., Talbot, N., Chandler, K., & Wolbarst, L. R. (1985). The perceptual priming phenomenon in amnesia. *Neuropsychologia, 23,* 615–622.

Charness, M. E., & De La Paz, R. L. (1987). Mammillary body atrophy in Wernicke's encephalopathy: Antemortem identification using magnetic resonance imaging. *Annals of Neurology, 22,* 595–600.

Cohen, N., & Squire, L. R. (1980). Preserved learning and retention of pattern analyzing skills in amnesia: Dissociation of knowing how and knowing that. *Science, 210,* 207–210.

Cohen, N., & Squire, L. R. (1981). Retrograde amnesia and remote memory impairment. *Neuropsychologia, 19,* 337–356.

Cutting, J. (1978a). Specific psychological deficits in alcoholism. *British Journal of Psychiatry, 133,* 119–122.

Cutting, J. (1978b). The relationship between Korsakoff's syndrome and alcoholic dementia. *British Journal of Psychiatry, 132,* 240–251.

Cutting, J. (1985). Korsakoff's syndrome. In J. A. M. Fredericks (Ed.), *Handbook of clinical neurology, Vol. 1 (45): Clinical neuropsychology* (pp. 193–204). New York: Elsevier Press.

Delis, D. C., Massman, P. J., Butters, N., Salmon, D. P., Cermak, L. S., & Kramer, J. H. (1991). Profiles of demented and amnesic patients on the California Verbal Learning Test: Implications for the assessment of memory disorders. *Psychological Assessment, 3,* 19–26.

Delay, J., Brion, S., & Elissalde, B. (1958a). Corps mamillaires et syndrome Korsakoff. Etude anatomique de huit cas de syndrome de Korsakoff d'origine alcoolique sans alterations significative du cortex cerebral. I. Etude anatomo-clinique. *La Presse Medicale, 66,* 1849–1852.

Delay, J., Brion, S., & Elissalde, B. (1958b). Corps mamillaires et syndrome Korsakoff.

Etude anatomique de huit cas de syndrome de Korsakoff d'origine alcoolique sans alterations significative du cortex cerebral. II. Tubercules mammillaires et mecanisme de la memoire. *La Presse Medicale, 66*, 1965–1968.

DeLuca, D., Cermak, L. S., & Butters, N. (1975). An analysis of Korsakoff patients' recall following varying types of distractor activity. *Neuropsychologia, 13*, 271–279.

Everall, I. P. (1988). Language disorder: A presenting symptom of alcoholic dementia. *British Journal of Addiction, 83*, 433–436.

Fabian, M. S., & Parsons, O. A. (1983). Differential improvements of cognitive functions in recovering alcoholic women. *Journal of Abnormal Psychology, 92*, 81–95.

Freund, G., & Ballinger, W. E. (1989). Loss of muscarinic cholinergic receptors from the temporal cortex of alcohol abusers. *Metabolic Brain Disease, 4*, 121–141.

Fuld, P. A. (1976). Storage, retention and retrieval in Korsakoff's syndrome. *Neuropsychologia, 14*, 225–236.

Gamper, E. (1928). Zur frage der polioencephalitis haemorrhagic der chronischen alcoholiker. Anatomische befunde beim alkoholischen Korsakov undihre Beziehungen zum klinischen bild. *Deutsche Zeitschrift fur Nervenheilkunde, 102*, 122–129.

Gardner, H., Boller, F., Moreines, J., & Butters, N. (1973). Retrieving information from Korsakoff patients: Effects of categorical cues and reference to the task. *Cortex, 9*, 165–175.

Gebhardt, G., Naeser, M. A., & Butters, N. (1984). Computerized measures of CT scans of alcoholics. *Alcohol, 1*, 133–140.

Glisky, E. L., & Schacter, D. L. (1988). Long-term retention of computer learning by patients with memory disorders. *Neuropsychologia, 26*, 173–178.

Glisky, E. L., Schacter, D. L., & Tulving, E. (1986). Computer learning by memory-impaired patients: Acquisition and retention of complex knowledge. *Neuropsychologia, 24*, 313–328.

Glosser, G., Butters, N., & Kaplan, E. (1977). Visuoperceptual processes in brain-damaged patients on the digit-symbol substitution tests. *International Journal of Neuroscience, 7*, 59–66.

Goldman, M. S. (1983). Cognitive impairment in chronic alcoholics. *American Psychologist, 38*, 1045–1054.

Goldstein, G. (1985). Dementia associated with alcoholism. In R. E. Tarter & D. H. Van Thiel (Eds.), *Alcohol and the brain: Chronic effects* (pp. 283–294). New York: Plenum Press.

Graf, P., Squire, L. R., & Mandler, G. (1984). The information that amnesics do not forget. *Journal of Experimental Psychology: Learning, Memory and Cognition, 10*, 164–178.

Grant, I., Adams, K. M., & Reed, R. (1986). Intermediate-duration (subacute) organic mental disorder of alcoholism. In I. Grant (Ed.), *Neuropsychiatric correlates of alcoholism* (pp. 38–60). Washington, DC: American Psychiatric Press.

Harper, C. (1979). Wernicke's encephalopathy: A more common disease than realized. *Journal of Neurology, Neurosurgery and Psychiatry, 42*, 226–231.

Harper, C. (1983). The incidence of Wernicke's encephalopathy in Australia—a neuropathological study of 131 cases. *Journal of Neurology, Neurosurgery and Psychiatry, 46*, 593–598.

Harper, C., Giles, M., & Finlay-Jones, R. (1986). Clinical signs in the Wernicke-Korsakoff complex: A retrospective analysis of 131 cases diagnosed at necropsy. *Journal of Neurology, Neurosurgery and Psychiatry, 49*, 341–345.

Harper, C., Gold, J., Rodriguez, M., & Perdices, M. (1989). The prevalence of the Wernicke-Korsakoff syndrome in Sydney, Australia: A prospective necropsy study. *Journal of Neurology, Neurosurgery and Psychiatry, 52*, 282–285.

Harper, C., & Krill, J. (1985). Brain atrophy in chronic alcoholic patients: A quantitative pathological study. *Journal of Neurology, Neurosurgery and Psychiatry, 48*, 211–217.

Harper, C., & Krill, J. (1986). Pathological changes in alcoholic brain shrinkage. *Medical Journal of Australia, 144,* 3–4.

Harper, C., Krill, J., & Daly, J. (1987). Are we drinking our neurons away? *British Medical Journal, 294,* 534–536.

Hata, T., Meyer, J. S., Tanahashi, N., Ishikawa, Y., Imai, A., Shinohara, T., Velez, M., Fann, W. E., Kandula, P., & Sakai, F. (1987). Three-dimensional mapping of local cerebral perfusion in alcoholic encephalopathy with and without Wernicke-Korsakoff syndrome. *Journal of Cerebral Blood Flow and Metabolism, 7,* 35–44.

Heindel, W. C., Salmon, D. P., & Butters, N. (1991). Alcoholic Korsakoff's syndrome. In T. Yanagihara & R. C. Petersen (Eds.), *Memory disorders* (pp. 227–253). New York: Marcel Dekker.

Horvath, T. B. (1975). Clinical spectrum and epidemiological features of alcoholic dementia. In J. Rankin (Ed.), *Alcohol, drugs and brain damage* (pp. 1–16). Toronto: Addiction Research Foundation.

Jacobson, R. R., & Lishman, W. A. (1987). Selective memory loss and global intellectual deficits in alcoholic Korsakoff syndrome. *Psychological Medicine, 17,* 649–655.

Jacoby, L. L., & Dallas, M. (1981). On the relationship between autobiographical memory and perceptual learning. *Journal of Experimental Psychology: General, 3,* 306–340.

Jernigan, T. L., Butters, N., DiTraglia, G., Schafer, K., Smith, T., Irwin, M., Grant, I., Schuckit, M., & Cermak, L. (1991). Reduced cerebral grey matter observed in alcoholics using magnetic resonance imaging. *Alcoholism: Clinical and Experimental Research, 15,* 418–427.

Jernigan, T. L., Schafer, K., Butters, N., & Cermak, L. S. (1991). Magnetic resonance imaging of alcoholic Korsakoff patients. *Neuropsychopharmacology, 4,* 175–186.

Jernigan, T. L., Zatz, L. M., Ahumada, A. J., Pfefferbaum, A., Moses, J. A., & Tinklenberg, J. (1982). CT measures of cerebrospinal fluid volume in alcoholics and normal volunteers. *Psychiatry Research, 7,* 9–17.

Jones, B. M., & Parsons, O. A. (1971). Impaired abstracting ability in chronic alcoholics. *Archives of General Psychiatry, 24,* 71–75.

Kapur, N., & Butters, N. (1977). Visuoperceptive deficits in long-term alcoholics with Korsakoff's psychosis. *Journal of Studies on Alcohol, 38,* 2025–2035.

Kinsbourne, M., & Wood, F. (1975). Short-term memory processes and the amnesic syndrome. In D. Deutsch & J. A. Deutsch (Eds.), *Short term memory* (pp. 258–291). New York, Academic Press.

Kitaguchi, T. M., Kobayashi, T., Tobimatsu, S., Goto, I., & Kuriowa, Y. (1987). Computed tomography and magnetic resonance imaging in a young patient with Wernicke's encephalopathy. *Journal of Neurology, 234,* 449–450.

Kopelman, M. (1987). Two types of confabulation. *Journal of Neurology, Neurosurgery and Psychiatry, 50,* 1482–1487.

Kopelman, M. (1989). Remote and autobiographical memory, temporal context memory and frontal atrophy in Korsakoff and Alzheimer patients. *Neuropsychologia, 27,* 437–460.

Kopelman, M. (1991). Frontal dysfunction and memory deficits in the alcoholic Korsakoff syndrome and Alzheimer-type dementia. *Brain, 114,* 117–137.

Laine, M., & Butters, N. (1982). A preliminary study of the problem solving strategies of detoxified long-term alcoholics. *Drug and Alcohol Dependence, 10,* 235–242.

Lishman, W. A. (1981). Cerebral disorder in alcoholism: Syndromes of impairment. *Brain, 104,* 1–20.

Lishman, W. A. (1986). Alcoholic dementia: A hypothesis. *Lancet, 1,* 1184–1185.

Lishman, W. A. (1987). *Organic psychiatry* (2nd ed.). London: Blackwell Scientific Publications.

Lishman, W. A. (1990). Alcohol and the brain. *British Journal of Psychiatry, 156,* 635–644.

Loberg, T. (1986). Neuropsychological findings in the early and middle phases of alcoholism. In I. Grant & K. M. Adams (Eds.), *Neuropsychological assessment of neuropsychiatric disorders* (pp. 415–440). New York: Oxford University Press.

Longmore, B. E., & Knight, R. G. (1988). The effect of intellectual deterioration on retention deficits in amnesic alcoholics. *Journal of Abnormal Psychology, 97*, 448–454.

Mair, R. G., & McEntee, W. J. (1986). Cognitive enhancement in Korsakoff's psychosis by clonidine: A comparison with L-dopa and ephedrine. *Psychopharmacology, 88*, 374–380.

Markowitsch, H. J. (1982). Thalamic mediodorsal nucleus and memory: A critical evaluation of studies in animals and man. *Neuroscience and Biobehavioral Reviews, 6*, 351–380.

Markowitsch, H. J., & Pritzel, M. (1985). The neuropathology of amnesia. *Progress in Neurobiology, 25*, 189–287.

Marslen-Wilson, W. D., & Teuber, H. L. (1975). Memory for remote events in anterograde amnesia: Recognition of public figures from news photographs. *Neuropsychologia, 13*, 347–352.

Martin, P.R., Adinoff, B., Eckardt, M. J., Stapleton, J. M., Bone, G. A. H., Rubinow, D. R., Lane, E. A., & Linnoila, M. (1989). Effective pharmacotherapy of alcoholic amnesic disorder with fluvoxamine: Preliminary findings. *Archives of General Psychiatry, 46*, 617–621.

Martin, P. R., Adinoff, B., Weingartner, H., Mukherjee, A. B., & Eckardt, M. J. (1986). Alcoholic organic brain disease: Nosology and pathophysiologic mechanisms. *Progress in Neuropsychopharmacology and Biological Psychiatry, 10*, 147–164.

Martin, P. R., & Eckardt, M. J. (1985). Pharmacological interventions in chronic organic brain syndromes associated with alcoholism. In C. A. Naranjo & E. M. Sellers (Eds.), *Research advances in new psychopharmacological treatments of alcoholism* (pp. 257–272). Amsterdam: Elsevier/North Holland Biomedical Press.

Martone, M., Butters, N., Payne, M., Becker, J., & Sax, D. S. (1984). Dissociations between skill learning and verbal recognition in amnesia and dementia. *Archives of Neurology, 41*, 965–970.

McEntee, W. J., & Mair, R. G. (1978). Memory impairments in Korsakoff's psychosis: A correlation with brain noradrenergic activity. *Science, 202*, 905–907.

McEntee, W. J., & Mair, R. G. (1980). Memory enhancement in Korsakoff's psychosis by clonidine: Further evidence for a noradrenergic deficit. *Annals of Neurology, 7*, 466–470.

Meudell, P. R., Butters, N., & Montgomery, K. (1978). Role of rehearsal in the short-term memory performance of patients with Korsakoff's and Huntington's disease. *Neuropsychologia, 16*, 507–510.

Miglioli, M., Buchtel, H. A., Campanini, T., & DeRisio, C. (1979). Cerebral hemispheric lateralization of cognitive deficits due to alcoholism. *Journal of Nervous and Mental Disease, 167*, 212–217.

Moscovitch, M. (1982). Multiple dissociations of function in amnesia. In L. S. Cermak (Ed.), *Human memory and amnesia* (pp. 337–370). Hillsdale, NJ: Lawrence Erlbaum Associates.

O'Connor, M., & Cermak, L. S. (1987). Rehabilitation of organic memory disorders. In M. Meier, A. L. Benton, & L. Diller (Eds.), *Neuropsychological rehabilitation* (pp. 260–279). New York: Churchill Livingstone.

Oscar-Berman, M. (1973). Hypothesis testing and focusing behavior during concept formation by amnesic Korsakoff patients. *Neuropsychologia, 11*, 191–198.

Parkin, A. J. (1987). *Memory and amnesia: An introduction.* Oxford: Blackwell.

Parkin, A. J. (1991). The relationship between anterograde and retrograde amnesia in alcoholic Wernicke-Korsakoff syndrome. *Psychological Medicine, 21*, 11–14.

Parsons, O. A., Butters, N., & Nathan, P. E. (Eds.). (1987). *Neuropsychology of alcoholism: Implications for diagnosis and treatment.* New York: Guilford Press.

Parsons, O. A., & Farr, S. P. (1981). The neuropsychology of alcohol and drug abuse. In S. B. Filskov & T. J. Bolls (Eds.), *Handbook of clinical neuropsychology* (pp. 320–365). New York: John Wiley & Sons.

Parsons, O. A., & Leber, W. R. (1981). The relationship between cognitive dysfunction and brain damage in alcoholics: Causal, interactive or epiphenomenal? *Alcohol: Clinical and Experimental Research, 5,* 326–343.

Riggs, H., & Boles, H. S. (1944). Wernicke's disease: A clinical and pathological study of 42 cases. *Quarterly Journal of Studies on Alcohol, 5,* 361–370.

Ron, M. A. (1983). The alcoholic brain: CT scan and psychological findings. *Psychological Medicine Monograph,* Suppl. 3.

Ron, M. A., Acker, W., & Lishman, W. A. (1980). Morphological abnormalities in the brains of chronic alcoholics: A clinical, psychological and computerized axial tomographic study. *Acta Psychiatrica Scandinavica, 62* (Suppl. 286), 31–40.

Ron, M. A., Acker, W., Shaw, G. K., & Lishman, W. A. (1982). Computerized tomography of the brain in chronic alcoholism: A survey and follow-up study. *Brain, 105,* 497–514.

Ryan, C., Brandt, J., Bayog, R., & Butters, N. (1980). The persistence of neuropsychological impairment in male alcoholics despite five years of sobriety. *Alcoholism: Clinical and Experimental Research, 4,* 227.

Ryan, C., & Butters, N. (1980a). Learning and memory impairments in young and old alcoholics: Evidence for the premature aging hypothesis. *Alcoholism: Clinical and Experimental Research, 4,* 288–293.

Ryan, C., & Butters, N. (1980b). Further evidence for a continuum-of-impairment encompassing male alcoholic Korsakoff patients and chronic alcoholic men. *Alcoholism: Clinical and Experimental Research, 4,* 190–198.

Ryan, C., & Butters, N. (1983). Cognitive deficits in alcoholics. In B. Kissin & H. Begleiter (Eds.), *Biology of alcoholism* (Vol. 7, pp. 485–538). New York: Plenum Press.

Ryan, C., & Butters, N. (1986). The neuropsychology of alcoholism. In D. Wedding, A. M. Horton, & J. Webster (Eds.), *The neuropsychology handbook: Behavioral and clinical perspectives* (pp. 376–409). New York: Springer.

Salmon, D. P., & Butters, N. (1987a). The etiology and neuropathology of alcoholic Korsakoff's syndrome: Some evidence for the role of the basal forebrain. In M. Galanter (Ed.), *Recent developments in alcoholism* (pp. 27–58). New York: Plenum Press.

Salmon, D. P., & Butters, N. (1987b). Recent developments in learning and memory: Implications for the rehabilitation of the amnesic patient. In M. Meier, A. L. Benton, & L. Diller (Eds.), *Neuropsychological rehabilitation* (pp. 280–293). New York: Churchill-Livingstone.

Salmon, D. P., Butters, N., & Schuckit, M. (1986). Memory for temporal order and frequency of occurrence in detoxified alcoholics. *Alcohol, 3,* 323–329.

Salmon, D. P., Shimamura, A. P., Butters, N., & Smith, S. (1988). Lexical and semantic priming deficits in patients with Alzheimer's disease. *Journal of Clinical and Experimental Neuropsychology, 10,* 477–494.

Schacter, D. L. (1985). Multiple forms of memory in humans and animals. In N. Weinberger, J. McGaugh, & G. Lynch (Eds.), *Memory systems of the brain* (pp. 351–379). New York: Guilford Press.

Seltzer, B., & Benson, D. F. (1974). The temporal pattern of retrograde amnesia in Korsakoff's disease. *Neurology, 24,* 527–530.

Seltzer, B., & Sherwin, I. (1978). Organic brain syndromes: An empirical study and critical review. *American Journal of Psychiatry, 135,* 13–21.

Shimamura, A. P. (1986). Priming effects in amnesia: Evidence for a dissociable memory function. *Quarterly Journal of Psychology [A]*, *38*, 619–644.

Shimamura, A. P., Jernigan, T. L., & Squire, L. R. (1988). Korsakoff's syndrome: Radiological (CT) findings and neuropsychological correlates. *Journal of Neuroscience*, *8*, 4400–4410.

Shimamura, A. P., Salmon, D. P., Squire, L. R., & Butters, N. (1987). Memory dysfunction and word priming in dementia and amnesia. *Behavioral Neuroscience*, *101*, 347–351.

Shimamura, A. P., & Squire, L. R. (1984). Paired-associate learning and priming effects in amnesia: A neuropsychological study. *Journal of Experimental Psychology: General*, *113*, 556–570.

Squire, L. R. (1982). Comparisons between forms of amnesia: Some deficits are unique to Korsakoff's syndrome. *Journal of Experimental Psychology: Learning, Memory and Cognition*, *8*, 560–571.

Strub, R. L., & Black, F. W. (1981). *Organic brain syndromes: An introduction to neurobehavioral disorders*. Philadelphia: F. A. Davis Company.

Stuss, D. T., & Benson, D. F. (1986). *The frontal lobes*. New York: Raven Press.

Talland, G. (1965). *Deranged memory*. New York: Academic Press.

Tarter, R. E. (1973). An analysis of cognitive deficits in chronic alcoholics: A review. *Journal of Nervous and Mental Diseases*, *157*, 138–147.

Tarter, R. E., & Parsons, O. A. (1971). Conceptual shifting in chronic alcoholics. *Journal of Abnormal Psychology*, *77*, 71–75.

Tarter, R. E., & Ryan, C. M. (1986). Neuropsychology of alcoholism: Etiology, phenomenology, process and outcome. *Recent Developments in Alcoholism*, *1*, 449–469.

Torvik, A., Lindboe, C. F., & Rogde, S. (1982). Brain lesions in alcoholics. *Journal of the Neurological Sciences*, *56*, 233–248.

Tulving, E. (1983). *Elements of episodic memory*. New York: Oxford University Press.

Victor, M., & Adams, R. D. (1985). The alcoholic dementias. In J. A. M. Fredericks (Ed.), *Handbook of clinical neurology, Vol. 2 (46): Neurobehavioral disorders* (pp. 335–352). New York: Elsevier Press.

Victor, M., Adams, R. D., & Collins, G. H. (1989). *The Wernicke-Korsakoff syndrome*. Philadelphia: F. A. Davis Company.

Walker, D. W., Hunter, B. E., & Abraham, C. W. (1981). Neuroanatomical and functional deficits subsequent to chronic ethanol administration in animals. *Alcoholism: Clinical and Experimental Research*, *5*, 267–282.

Warrington, E. K., & Weiskrantz, L. (1968). New method of testing long-term retention with special reference to amnesic patients. *Nature*, *217*, 972–974.

Warrington, E. K., & Weiskrantz, L. (1970). Amnesic syndrome: Consolidation or retrieval? *Nature*, *228*, 628–630.

Wechsler, D. (1945). A standardized memory scale for clinical use. *Journal of Psychology*, *19*, 87–95.

Wechsler, D. (1955). *Wechsler Adult Intelligence Scale Manual*. New York: Psychological Corporation.

Wechsler, D. (1981). *Wechsler Adult Intelligence Scale-Revised*. New York: Psychological Corporation.

Wechsler, D. (1987). *Wechsler Memory Scale-Revised*. New York: Psychological Corporation.

Weingartner, H., Grafman, J., Boutelle, W., Kaye, W., & Martin, P. R. (1983). Forms of memory failure. *Science*, *221*, 380–382.

Whitehouse, P. J., Price, D. L., Struble, R. G., Clark, A. W., Coyle, J. T., & DeLong, M. R. (1982). Alzheimer's disease and senile dementia: Loss of neurons in basal forebrain. *Science*, *215*, 1237–1239.

Wilkinson, D. A. (1982). Examination of alcoholics by computed tomographic (CT) scans: A critical review. *Alcoholism: Clinical and Experimental Research*, *6*, 31–45.

Wilkinson, P., Kornaczewski, A., Rankin, J. G., & Santamaria, J. N. (1971). Physical disease in alcoholism: Initial survey of 1,000 patients. *Medical Journal of Australia, 1*, 1217–1223.

Winocur, G., Kinsbourne, M., & Moscovitch, M. (1981). The effect of cuing on release from proactive interference in Korsakoff amnesic patients. *Journal of Experimental Psychology: Human Learning and Memory, 7*, 56–65.

Winocur, G., & Weiskrantz, L. (1976). An investigation of paired-associate learning in amnesic patients. *Neuropsychologia, 14*, 97–110.

7

Brain Tumors and Dementia

Jim Hom

Among the approximately 60 known organic disorders causing dementia (Haase, 1977), intracranial tumors are among the dementing disorders most readily identifiable by the medical profession. Medical differential diagnosis is significantly aided by the use of computed tomography (CT) and magnetic resonance imaging (MRI) along with electroencephalography (EEG) and angiography. With the neurological diagnostic procedures currently available, errors in diagnosis of intracranial tumors are relatively uncommon.

In contrast to the relative ease of identification of the existence of an intracranial tumor by the medical profession, an understanding of the cognitive and behavioral effects of cerebral tumors is more difficult. Complex interactions exist among neurological variables, such as tumor type, location, extent, and distribution of the lesion; and neuropsychological and psychological variables, such as age and education, which affect the brain-behavior expression of cerebral neoplasms. Nonetheless, a distinct and definite neuropsychological pattern of brain dysfunction can frequently be identified that allows for differentiation of tumor-based dementia from other neurological and dementing disorders and from normal brain function. In fact, such a pattern of neuropsychological dysfunction may help in the early identification of cognitive changes and provide important information in the prognosis and treatment of the patient with a cerebral tumor.

Most neuropsychologists are unlikely to see many patients with cerebral neoplasms in their clinical practice. Such patients are usually seen by the medical professional or in specialized neuropsychological settings. Nonetheless, such patients provide neuropsychological profiles that illustrate many of the important aspects of brain-behavior relationships and which provide an understanding of the neuropsychological function of patients with other dementing and neurological diseases. The goal of this chapter is to discuss the neuropsychological correlates of intrinsic cerebral neoplasms and to identify patterns of cognitive and intellectual function that may aid in differential behavioral diagnosis. These brain-behavior relationships will be presented in a neuropsychological framework based on the Halstead-Reitan neuropsychological conceptualization and methodology. In addition, a brief review of the epidemiology and clinical symptomatology associated with cerebral tumors will be presented. Finally, where appropriate, comparisons of neuropsychological function in intrinsic cerebral tumors and Alzheimer's disease

(AD) will be made. A comprehensive review of the neurological and neuropathological aspects of intracranial tumors is beyond the scope of this chapter. However, the reader may wish to refer to the reviews of intracranial tumors presented by Adams and Victor (1989b), Rowland (1989), Reitan and Wolfson (1985a), or Youmans (1982).

Classification

Tumors are primarily classified according to the cell type from which they originate (Bailey & Cushing, 1926). However, factors such as location and malignancy of the tumor are also considered. The term *intracranial tumor* refers to all neoplasms arising from the cranial cavity.

The World Health Organization (WHO) has developed classification systems for tumors of the central nervous system, *Manual of Tumor Nomenclature* and the *International Classification of Diseases for Oncology* (WHO, 1977; Zulch, 1980), which are based on cell type, location, and malignancy of the tumor. Fetell and Stein (1989) present a nine-division classification of intracranial tumors that includes:

1. Tumors of the skull and cranial nerves.
2. Tumors of the meninges.
3. Tumors of the supportive tissue.
4. Tumors of the pineal region.
5. Tumors of the pituitary gland.
6. Congenital tumors.
7. Blood vessel tumors.
8. Metastatic tumors and granulomas.
9. Multiple tumors of the cranial nerves.

In addition to the above classification systems, more general classification schemes have used tumor origination or location. For example, intracranial tumors may be considered primary tumors when they arise from within the cranium. Metastatic tumors arise from sites outside the cranium and include primary sites such as the lungs, gastrointestinal tract, breasts, and kidneys. Brain tumors have also been classified as intrinsic or extrinsic. Intrinsic brain tumors refer to tumors that develop from tissues within the brain. Extrinsic brain tumors arise from tissues outside the brain but within the cranium, such as the meninges.

Classification of intracranial tumors is also based on their degree of malignancy, particularly for gliomas. Kernohan, Maben, Svien, and Adson (1949) proposed a system of classification based on degree of anaplasia (cell differentiation). The more anaplastic the neoplasm, the more malignant the tumor. In this system, astrocytomas are graded from I to IV with greater malignancy being assigned a higher number.

A more detailed description of the various tumor types is available in Cushing (1932), Adams and Victor (1989b), Rowland (1989), Reitan and Wolfson (1985a,b), and Youmans (1982). The classification systems are more thoroughly described in Bailey and Cushing (1926), Kernohan et al. (1949), Youmans (1982), and Zulch (1980).

Epidemiology of Intracranial Neoplasms

The incidence rate of intracranial tumors varies according to factors such as type of tumor, age group, and gender. Using estimates from a U.S. probability sample from the 2-year period of 1973 to 1974, Walker, Robins, and Weinfeld (1985) found approximately 8.2/100,000 population incidence rate for primary intracranial neoplasms. In this same sample, an estimated incidence rate of 8.3/100,000 U.S. population was found for secondary intracranial tumors; that is, for metastases from systemic neoplasms to the intracranial cavity. However, reported incidence rates for primary brain tumors have ranged from 4/100,000 in Iowa (Haenszel, Marcus, & Zimmerer, 1956) to 15/100,000 population in Rochester, Minnesota (Kurland, Schoenberg, Anneger, Okazaki, & Molgaard, 1982).

Variations in incidence rates are likely due to artifactual problems, such as the definition of tumor type and identification of cases, along with differences in methods used for case inclusion and verification. Furthermore, many of the reported population-based surveys, such as the Walker et al. (1985) study, pre-date the availability of CT and MRI imaging. It is quite possible that the earlier clinically based diagnoses of brain tumor resulted in biased or overly conservative rates.

Despite the artifactual problems, the Walker et al. (1985) and other population-based surveys (Schoenberg, Christine, & Whisnant, 1978) generally indicate a high frequency rate of primary brain tumors in children with a slight decrease in the teens, followed by a steady rise in frequency to a peak in the sixth decade. A general decline in incidence is then found after age 70. This pattern has been shown for both men and women.

More recently, Greig, Ries, Yancik, and Rapoport (1990) reported significantly increased incidence rates between 1974 and 1985 for brain tumors in the elderly, particularly for individuals aged 80 years or older. Increases of 394% and 501% in incidence rates for individuals between the ages of 80 and 84 years, and 85 years and older, respectively, were found compared to the 1973 to 1974 rates. For age groups 30 to 34 and 75 to 79 years, increases of 179% and 187%, respectively, were also reported. However, incidence rates for other age groups were found to be relatively stable over this period. An average annual rise in incidence of brain tumors was demonstrated in the elderly of up to 23.4%, which is much greater than the total cancer incidence rate increase (0.9%) in the age-adjusted population over the same period. These dramatic changes in incidence are partly attributable to the availability of more advanced imaging techniques; however, other unidentified factors may also be contributing to the increases.

The most frequent type of tumor across the age ranges is glioma. Cerebellar astrocytomas, medulloblastomas, and other posterior fossa tumors are primarily found in children and young adults. Glioblastomas and astrocytomas, meningiomas, neurinomas, and metastatic tumors are strongly associated with advancing age.

Gender differences in incidence rates have been reported that indicate a higher rate of brain tumors among males than females. Males tend to have greater susceptibility to gliomas and neurinomas, whereas females have higher rates of meningiomas and pituitary adenomas.

Brain Tumor and Dementia

Cummings and Benson (1983) have summarized the prevalence rates of tumor-based dementia in comparison to other dementia etiologies. Based on seven studies of groups of demented patients (Benson, Cummings, & Tsai, 1982; Freemon, 1976; Hutton, 1981; Maletta, Pirozzolo, Thompson, & Mortimer, 1982; Marsden & Harrison, 1972; Smith & Kiloh, 1981; Victoratos, Lenman, & Herzberg, 1977) totaling 708 patients, a cumulative prevalence rate of 3% was found for neoplasms among these demented patients. Prevalence rates for neoplastic etiologies of dementia varied from 1% in the Smith and Kiloh (1981) sample, to 8% in the Marsden and Harrison (1972) and Victoratos et al. (1977) groups.

In comparison, Cummings and Benson (1983) found the prevalence rates for Alzheimer's disease in the seven studies varied from 22% to 57% of all dementia etiologies, for an overall prevalence rate of 39%. Clearly, the frequency of dementia associated with intracranial tumors is significantly lower compared to dementia of the Alzheimer type. However, in this set of studies, neoplastic etiologies for dementia were found to be more common than infections, toxic conditions, post-trauma, postanoxia, subdural hematoma, and Huntington's or Parkinson's diseases.

It should be noted that in this series of patients, the majority of diagnoses were based upon pre-CT and pre-MRI imaging methods. Artifactual problems similar to those mentioned above in the population-based survey studies for incidence rates of intracranial neoplasms also apply to these studies of frequency rates of tumor-based dementia.

Because of the medically compelling nature of brain tumor, neuropsychological exploration of tumors is only infrequently done. More frequently, the diagnosis of tumor-based dementia has primarily been part of the medical domain. However, from a neuropsychological standpoint, the current models and methodologies for assessment of dementia are of limited conceptual and clinical usefulness in providing an understanding and identification of tumor-based dementia. The current definitions of dementia inadequately address neuropsychological issues of behavioral and cognitive dysfunctions in brain tumors compared to other neurological processes and dementias such as AD. Furthermore, these definitions of dementia may in fact be contributing to underdiagnosis of dementia associated with tumors.

In this section, the definition of dementia will be briefly reviewed and its applicability for understanding brain tumors will be discussed. A neuropsychological conceptual framework will be presented that will allow for better differential behavioral diagnosis of cerebral tumors compared to other etiologies.

According to Wells (1977), "Dementia is a word that has successfully defied attempts to limit its meaning and to fix its definition" (p. 1). Frequently, each researcher or clinician determines their own definition according to their needs. Furthermore, disciplines also develop their own idiosyncratic definitions. Nonetheless, the definition of dementia posed by the American Psychiatric Association's (APA) *Diagnostic and Statistical Manual of Mental Disorders III-Revised* (DSM-III-R) (APA, 1987) provides the basis for most definitions in the literature and clinical practice. DSM-III-R classifies dementia as an organic mental syndrome or, when the underlying organic etiology is known, as an organic mental disorder. In general, the definition is based on a constellation of behavioral symptoms that requires demonstrable evidence of memory dysfunction, both short- and long-term, and impairment in one of the following areas: abstract thinking, judgment, or other higher cortical function (e.g., aphasia or apraxia); or change in personality. Before dementia can be diagnosed, the changes in mental function must be sufficiently severe to interfere with social or vocational functioning. Evidence of a specific organic etiology is necessary, which may be established by history, physical examination, or laboratory tests. However, in the absence of a specific organic etiology, dementia may be diagnosed by exclusion if the cognitive/behavioral impairments cannot be etiologically linked to a nonorganic mental disorder. Other definitions of dementia also exist in the literature and in clinical practice, some of which are more specific or focus on a particular feature of dementia (e.g., Adams & Victor, 1989a; Cummings & Benson, 1983; Katzman, 1989).

On the whole, the current definitions of dementia reflect a medical orientation. The primary focus is on the identification of the etiology of the dementia. Issues paramount to this orientation include onset, duration, progression, reversibility, location, distribution, and pathophysiology of the lesion. The clinical emphasis is to determine whether the dementia is medically treatable. Significant limitations of this orientation include overly simplified conceptions of the behavioral complexities of brain-behavior function. This frequently leads to the development of diagnostic criteria that are nonspecific. For example, as defined by the DSM-III-R, primary degenerative dementia of the Alzheimer's type and multi-infarct dementia differ in terms of their clinical and pathological presentations but not in their behavioral presentation. Similarly, a dementia associated with a brain tumor is seen as being diagnostically different from other dementias only because of its etiology.

The current dementia classification schemes are primarily based on the clinical syndrome conceptual model. This model primarily uses the pathognomonic sign inferential approach, which relies upon the identification of signs and symptoms thought to be associated with a syndrome or pathology. Although this model has been used relatively successfully in medicine and can aid the clinician in identifying and classifying symptoms associated with a given etiology, it clearly suffers when used to understand the behavioral ramifications of neurological disease. Davison (1974) and Rourke and Brown (1986) have aptly identified and described limitations of this model for behavioral neurology. These investigators have noted limitations in validity, reliability, base rates, flexibility, and procedural considerations with medicine in general and with behavioral neurology in particular. For example, behavioral neurology primarily relies on the qualitative analytical approach for the understanding of neurobehavioral disorder. However, the qualitative approach tends to classify into broad categories without significant consideration of the subtle individual differences within a category. Similar problems are applicable to the current definitions of dementia. Furthermore, issues regarding the nature of behavioral and cognitive disorder cannot be adequately addressed by a methodology that is based on a dichotomous classification scheme of presence or absence of a symptom.

In contrast to the clinical syndrome model, the clinical neuropsychological model uses a multifaceted inferential approach. The clinical neuropsychological model includes the pathognomonic sign approach as well as the concepts of clinical

syndromes into its methodology. In addition, however, it uses other methods of inference, including level of performance, differential scores, pattern analysis, and intraindividual differences. Primary focus in this model is placed on continuously distributed psychological variables in a psychometric tradition in elucidating brain-behavior relationships associated with brain pathology. This allows a more comprehensive and systematic understanding of brain pathology and its effect on the adaptive functioning of the individual. Cerebral functioning is viewed as a consequence of a complex interaction of a number of different factors, including anatomical organization, physiological function, genetic potential, and experiences of the individual. Furthermore, these factors are seen to interact in a sequential, parallel, and hierarchical manner, and impairment of any of these factors may lead to significant disruption of the cognitive abilities of the individual. For example, a glioblastoma multiforme involving the left temporal-parietal region of the cerebral cortex may cause right-sided sensory-perceptual deficits as well as various aphasic and apraxis symptoms. However, in addition, cognitive and intellectual abilities, such as abstract reasoning, problem solving, attention/concentration, and memory, may also be significantly impaired. The neuropsychological deficits are viewed in terms of degree and nature of impairment as well as in terms of how they relate to the type of lesion, location, and pathology.

A significant body of clinical research clearly demonstrates the validity of the clinical neuropsychological model. Issues concerning various aspects of brain-behavior relationships have been formally and scientifically addressed, including identification of cerebral damage, effects of lesion location, and differentiation of lesion types and neurological etiologies. In addition, the behavioral and cognitive concomitants of brain pathology have been vigorously investigated. Review of these issues and research studies are available in Filskov and Boll (1981, 1986), Grant and Adams (1986), and Reitan and Davison (1974).

Given the established validity of the clinical neuropsychological model for the investigation of brain-behavior relationships, this model is quite applicable to the study of brain tumors and their neuropsychological correlates. The neuropsychological approach that best exemplifies the clinical neuropsychological model and has direct application to the study and understanding of cerebral tumors is the conceptual and methodological framework underlying the Halstead-Reitan Neuropsychological Test Battery (HRB) (Reitan & Wolfson, 1985b, 1988). The HRB framework provides an approach that is comprehensive and systematic; a full range of behavioral functions subserved by the brain are evaluated, reflecting both general and specific cerebral functions. Significant emphasis is placed on the central processing aspects of higher level cortical function in the context of sensory input and motor output aspects of brain functioning. A multi-inferential evaluative process is utilized that integrates the various behavioral correlates of cerebral function. This provides a valid understanding of the neuropsychological manifestations of brain pathology and prediction of the neurological status. The HRB is probably the most thoroughly researched methodology in the clinical neuropsychological literature. Issues concerning presence or absence of cerebral damage, localization, lesion type, duration of lesion, and acuteness or chronicity, as well as neuropsychological correlates of neurological pathology have been studied in detail. Detailed reviews of the HRB model and the scientific research associated with it are available from a number of excellent sources including Boll (1981), Reitan (1966a, 1966b,

1986), Reitan and Davison (1974), and Reitan and Wolfson (1988). In this chapter, the effect of brain tumors on cerebral function will be presented using the HRB model.

Clinical Neurological Symptoms of Brain Tumors

Although patients with brain tumors may present with significant changes that mimic many aspects of dementia, such as slow and progressive changes in mental functions, the clinical symptoms of brain tumor are the result of focal pathology. However, unlike the diagnostic clinical symptom constellations found with other focal neurological diseases such as stroke, the signs and symptoms found with intracranial tumors are more variable. In fact, there is no symptom constellation that is pathognomonic for intracranial tumor. However, the triad of symptoms commonly considered characteristic of intracranial tumors consists of headache, vomiting, and papilledema. These symptoms may occur early in the development of the tumor, at the terminal stages of the tumor growth, or not at all. Furthermore, all three symptoms may never appear together. Other symptoms and signs of intracranial tumors are seizures, altered states of consciousness, sensory and motor deficits, personality changes, and changes in mental state and function, including clinical manifestations of dementia.

Headaches are an early symptom in approximately 20% to 33% of brain tumor patients, and their frequency has been reported to be as high as 90%. The headaches are variable in nature and are not differentially diagnostic of intracranial tumors as opposed to other causes of headache. Furthermore, the mechanism of the headaches is not fully understood, and they are not directly related to the level of intracranial pressure. Obviously, a patient presenting with severe recurrent headaches without a previous history of headaches requires a thorough medical/neurological evaluation. Absence of headache, however, does not preclude the existence of an intracranial tumor. Reported common features of headache associated with intracranial tumor include nocturnal occurrence or presence on awakening, localization in the frontal or occipital region, variable onset and duration, worsening by change of posture, coughing or straining, and a deep nonpulsatile quality.

Nausea and vomiting are less frequent than headache in brain tumors, but may occur in as many as one third of patients (Adams & Victor, 1989b). These symptoms often accompany headache. Vomiting may be more prominent on awakening and is more frequent with tumors of the posterior fossa.

A common sign of increased intracranial pressure associated with the growth of the tumor is papilledema (swelling of the optic nerve head), although absence of changes in the optic nerve does not preclude the diagnosis. It is estimated that between 50% and 90% of tumor cases demonstrate evidence of papilledema during the course of the disease. Factors such as location, nature, and stage of the tumor are important in the development of papilledema. Papilledema more likely appears when the tumor interferes with the circulation of cerebrospinal fluid (CSF) as will occur with tumors involving the occlusion of the third ventricle, cerebral aqueduct, or fourth ventricle. A highly destructive tumor involving the cerebral cortex may not produce papilledema until it interferes with the flow of CSF.

In addition to the triad of tumor symptoms, adult-onset seizures are commonly

considered by neurologists and neurosurgeons to be suggestive of brain tumor unless proven otherwise. Seizures may occur in 20% to 50% of all patients with cerebral tumors, and are frequently the first symptom of a growing tumor. They may for many years be the predominant or only symptom of slow-growing tumors. Seizures tend to be more common in tumors involving the cerebral hemispheres compared to tumors of the posterior fossa or brain stem (Fetell & Stein, 1989). The seizures may be focal or generalized and do not differ from seizures due to other neurological etiologies.

Due to the growth of intracranial tumors and the restricted volume of the cranial cavity, tumors result in brain edema and brain herniations. These two factors are considered the major pathophysiological changes associated with intracranial neoplasms. Adams and Victor (1989b) attribute many of the clinical symptoms of intracranial tumors to the mechanical changes of brain edema and herniations, along with intracranial pressure and tissue displacement, compared to the direct invasion of tumor into the neurological structures.

Behavioral/Psychiatric Symptoms of Brain Tumors

Accompanying the neurological symptoms of cerebral tumors are various behavioral and cognitive symptoms. As in the neurological symptoms, the expression of the behavioral and cognitive symptoms is also dependent on features such as tumor type, location, and growth characteristics. Slowly growing tumors may exist for years without any significant behavioral symptoms, whereas rapidly growing tumors may within a very short time produce acute confusional states. Furthermore, symptoms may fluctuate and vary considerably during the course of tumor growth. Tumors involving the left cerebral hemisphere may produce language-oriented deficits, whereas right hemisphere tumors may produce visual-spatial deficits. In this section, the behavioral-psychiatric manifestations of cerebral tumors will be presented. Cognitive and neuropsychological aspects of cerebral tumors will be presented subsequently.

As with the neurological symptoms, no specific syndrome of behavioral/psychiatric symptoms is typical of brain tumors. Many of these symptoms are similar regardless of the location of the tumor. However, tumors involving the frontal and temporal regions of the brain are more likely to produce the behavioral/psychiatric symptoms (Kanakaratnam & Direkze, 1976; Keschner, Bender, & Strauss, 1938a, 1938b; Levin, 1949; Malamud, 1967; Remington & Rubert, 1962; Soniat, 1951; Strauss & Keschner, 1935). Moreover, Malamud (1967) suggests that involvement of the limbic system is necessary for behavioral/psychiatric symptoms to be produced.

In the largest studies of cases of verified intracranial neoplasms, Keschner and colleagues (Keschner, Bender, & Strauss, 1938a, 1938b; Strauss & Keschner, 1935) reported mental symptoms to be present in 94% of cases with temporal lobe tumors and 90% of cases with frontal lobe tumors. In addition, mental symptoms were found to be twice as frequent in patients with supratentorial as compared to patients with infratentorial neoplasms. These investigators observed various mental symptoms associated with intracranial tumors involving the frontal or temporal lobes that included;

1. Disturbances of the sensorium (manifestations of impaired consciousness such as confusion or somnolence).

2. Hallucinations (visual, auditory, olfactory, gustatory, haptic, visceral, or kinesthetic).

3. Changes in personality.

4. Disturbances in affect (depression, irritability, mania, euphoria).

5. Disturbances in memory and orientation.

6. Disturbances in intellect and higher cognitive functions.

In this series of verified tumor cases, it was found that mental symptoms had little or no value in localizing the tumor. The appearance of the mental symptoms varied considerably; however, they were more frequent, severe, and apt to appear early in the disease process in patients with supratentorial tumors compared to infratentorial tumors. Finally, the mental symptoms depended upon tumor factors such as extent and rapidity of growth, intracranial pressure, presence of aphasia, and previous personality structure.

Clinical Neuropsychological Symptoms of Brain Tumors

Neuropsychological symptoms of cerebral tumors, similar to the neurological and psychiatric symptoms, are quite variable. However, the pathological features of the tumor process strongly influence the expression of the neuropsychological symptoms. Compared to other etiologies of dementia (Haase, 1977), brain tumors produce neuropsychological manifestations that are highly influenced by the type, location, size, and growth characteristics of the pathology. Tumors may show highly focal and discrete neuropsychological effects in some cases, whereas in others, effects involving relatively large areas of brain as well as bilateral focal effects may be seen. Nonetheless, relatively distinctive and differential patterns of neuropsychological impairment may be recognized, especially when a comprehensive and systematic neuropsychological approach is used. In the following sections, clinical neuropsychological and intellectual findings associated with cerebral tumors will be detailed. However, it should be noted that a paucity of quantitative neuropsychological research exists for cerebral tumors, especially when considered in a clinical neuropsychological conceptual framework. This is clearly illustrated in a summary of the literature by Farr, Greene, and Fisher-White (1986). They found only five studies in the literature concerning intellectual function (Wechsler Adult Intelligence Scale [WAIS]) and neuropsychological function (HRB) of cerebral tumors. Furthermore, since the time of the Farr et al. review, only a few additional research studies of the neuropsychological nature of brain tumors have been conducted.

Although brain tumors are focal lesions, they frequently present with diffuse as well as focal neurological symptoms. Similarly, brain tumors often demonstrate a neuropsychological pattern of symptoms that involves both general and specific deficits. The importance of the general as well as the specific functions of the brain has been emphasized by Goodglass and Kaplan (1979) and Reitan and Wolfson (1985b). Whereas neuropsychological measures of specific functions provide information concerning brain function that are dependent on specific sites or areas of the brain, measures of general function reflect the overall status of brain functioning and are relatively independent of a particular location of impairment. As

a result, even relatively focal lesions can produce both specific and nonspecific ("general") neuropsychological deficits. The pattern of these general and specific neuropsychological symptoms allows for differential diagnosis and understanding of the behavioral ramifications of brain pathology (Reitan, 1964). In the following sections, neuropsychological and intellectual function in cerebral tumors will be compared with Alzheimer's disease, considered the prototypical model of dementia. It is believed that this comparison using the HRB framework will help elucidate the differences in neuropsychological function between these neurological disease processes, and will also demonstrate the usefulness of a comprehensive neuropsychological approach for understanding brain-behavior relations.

Comparisons of intellectual and neuropsychological function in brain tumors versus AD will be based on a study conducted by Hom (1992), which evaluated an AD group of 35 patients (12 men and 23 women) ranging from 57 to 79 years of age, with a mean age of 69.31 years (SD = 6.44). Mean educational level was 13.71 years (SD = 2.56). The AD subjects were diagnosed by a board-certified neurologist according to the NINCDS-ADRDA medical criteria for "probable" Alzheimer's disease (McKhann et al., 1984). Based on the criteria outlined by Reisberg, Ferris, de Leon, and Crook (1982), the AD subjects were considered to be in an earlier stage of the disease and demonstrated clinical symptoms consistent with Global Deterioration Scale (GDS) stages 4 to 5. Each subject was given a battery of neuropsychological tests that included the complete Halstead-Reitan Neuropsychological Test Battery for Adults (Reitan & Wolfson, 1985b), and WAIS (Wechsler, 1955).

Intellectual Abilities

Surprisingly few studies exist in the research literature that investigate intellectual function associated with cerebral tumors. Furthermore, existing studies are conceptually limited in that important pathological features of tumors are not considered in the research design. For example, tumor type, location, growth characteristics, and size have not been systematically investigated. In addition, the effects on intellectual function of medical aspects of tumor treatment, such as surgery, radiation, or chemotherapy, alone or in combination, have not been adequately addressed.

Intellectual performances on Wechsler intelligence scales (e.g., WAIS, 1955, or Wechsler-Bellevue Intelligence Scale [W-B], 1944) have been reported by a number of investigators. When considered as a group, reported mean Full Scale IQ (FSIQ) performances of patients with cerebral tumors have varied from the high 80s to high 90s (Boll, 1974; Farr et al., 1986; Haaland & Delaney, 1981; Hom & Reitan, 1984; Smith, 1966a, 1966b). Furthermore, Verbal IQ (VIQ) and Performance IQ (PIQ) abilities range from the 80s to 100. Overall, these performances represent below average to average intellectual abilities and suggest that cerebral tumors have mild or no significant clinical effects on measured intellectual abilities, especially when age and education of the samples are considered.

Regardless of the location of the tumor, similar FSIQ performances have been demonstrated. Smith (1966a) compared the intellectual functions in patients with lateralized frontal tumors and found the mean FSIQ of frontal neoplasms to be similar to the performances of the nonfrontal neoplasms (95.55 and 91.46, respectively).

In contrast, differential VIQs and PIQs have been reported in relation to the lateralization of the cerebral tumor. Andersen (1950, 1951) was the first to report differential intellectual performances of lateralized brain lesions; he found greater impairment of VIQ following left hemisphere lesions and greater impairment of PIQ with right hemisphere lesions. Reitan and his colleagues have provided a significant body of research evidence confirming the systematic differential effects of lateralized brain lesions on the two IQ domains of the Wechsler scale (see Klove, 1974, for review). Hom and Reitan (1984) demonstrated this differential relationship for cerebral neoplasms. In a group of 92 adult patients with lateralized intrinsic cerebral tumors, significant interhemispheric differences were found, indicating greater impairment of VIQ than PIQ with left cerebral hemisphere neoplasms. Conversely, greater impairment of PIQ than VIQ was found with right cerebral hemisphere tumors. No significant difference was found for FSIQ between the lateralized tumor groups.

However, some researchers have not found this interhemispheric relationship for the two WAIS scales (Haaland & Delaney, 1981). Smith (1966b) also failed to find the lateralized relationship between VIQ and PIQ abilities reported by others. Inspection of the group performances in the Smith (1966b) study, however, does reveal significant differential intellectual performance in the expected direction with the right tumor group. Interestingly, Smith (1966a) found the expected poorer verbal intellectual performance for a group of left frontal tumors but not the expected poorer nonverbal intellectual performance for a right frontal tumor group. Smith also reported poorer FSIQ for the left frontal tumor group compared to the right frontal tumor group.

The variability in the findings for intellectual performance in cerebral tumors may partially be due to the heterogeneity of tumor type and tumor growth characteristics of the studied patient samples. The majority of the reported studies have used patient samples that included both extrinsic and intrinsic tumors. Furthermore, the growth characteristics of the tumors have not been fully considered. Hom and Reitan (1984) considered both of these two factors in their study of cerebral tumor. They found that the differential relationship between VIQ and PIQ was confirmed in lateralized rapidly growing intrinsic cerebral tumors. In addition, they reported poorer verbal and nonverbal IQ abilities for patients with rapidly growing intrinsic cerebral neoplasms compared to those with slowly growing intrinsic cerebral neoplasms.

Although these findings highlight the complex interaction of neurological and psychological variables, other important factors play a role in the variance found, including age, education, and validity or differential sensitivity of the variable (Reitan, 1966b; Smith, 1962; Yates, 1966). For example, Hom and Reitan (1984) found striking differential sensitivity of the psychological measures in identifying the effect of tumor growth characteristics. Highly significant and consistent differentiation of the rapidly growing versus the slowly growing intrinsic tumor groups was found for the neuropsychological measures, whereas only moderate and variable differentiation was demonstrated for the intellectual measures.

Comparing the IQs of tumor patients with those of patients in the earlier stages of the Alzheimer's disease process (Hom, 1992), the mean IQs of tumor patients are only mildly poorer than those of AD patients (see Table 7.1). However, the AD group was found to demonstrate clear deterioration of intellectual function. These results suggest equivocal clinical differentiation of tumor from AD on intellectual measures, possibly due to the relative insensitivity of IQ to the effects of cerebral lesions.

General Neuropsychological Functions

Classification of HRB variables into functional groupings associated with general and specific neuropsychological function has been formulated by Hom (1992) for AD and by Hom (1991) and Hom and Reitan (1984, 1990) for cerebral neoplasms and cerebrovascular disease. The functional groupings are based on the neuropsychological function measured by each variable; they have been supported by principal component analyses indicating single principal components for each grouping accounting for percentages of variance ranging from 59% to 88% (Hom, 1992).

Overall Brain Function

The Halstead Impairment Index (HII) has been demonstrated to be a very sensitive indicator of overall brain impairment (Reitan, 1955; Vega & Parsons, 1967). The HII is a summary value based on the proportion of impaired performances on the Halstead tests of the HRB. This index is basically a consistency-of-impairment value that represents the number of brain-sensitive measures that are in the brain-damaged range (Reitan & Wolfson, 1985b). The HII values range from 0.0 to 1.0, with 0.0 to 0.3 typically indicating normal brain functioning, 0.4 indicating borderline range, and 0.5 to 1.0 indicating brain impairment.

Haaland and Delaney (1981) reported mean HII values of 0.6 (SD = 0.3) and 0.7 (SD = 0.3) for groups of patients with right and left cerebral tumors, respectively. In contrast, poorer HII values were reported by Hom and Reitan (1984) for patients with lateralized intrinsic tumors. Patients with rapidly growing intrinsic tumors earned mean HIIs of 0.89 (SD = 0.19), and those with slowly growing intrinsic tumors earned mean HIIs of 0.76 (SD = 0.25). However, patients with

TABLE 7.1. Intellectual Performances of Patients with Lateralized Rapidly or Slowly Growing Intrinsic Cerebral Tumors and Patients with Alzheimer's Disease

Measure of Intelligence		Intrinsic Tumor[a]				AD[b]
		Rapid	Slow	Left	Right	
FSIQ	M	90.11	91.00	87.83	93.28	99.14
	SD	18.73	18.63	20.48	16.24	13.96
VIQ	M	92.00	93.59	86.39	99.20	101.94
	SD	20.24	16.87	19.69	14.96	14.31
PIQ	M	93.50	90.67	93.65	90.52	95.46
	SD	18.18	19.92	20.29	17.75	16.32

[a]Hom & Reitan, 1984.
[b]Hom, 1992.
Notes: FSIQ = Full Scale IQ; VIQ = Verbal IQ; PIQ = Performance IQ.

right versus left intrinsic tumors obtained equivalent mean HII values ($\overline{X}$ = 0.84, SD = 0.21 and $\overline{X}$ = 0.81, SD = 0.25, respectively). The differences in HII values between the two studies are likely due to differences in patient samples, tumor type, and tumor growth characteristics. The patient sample in the Haaland and Delaney study included mixed tumor types (intrinsic and extrinsic), and tumor growth characteristics were not taken into account. In contrast, the Hom and Reitan (1984) study investigated both of these tumor characteristics, and their slowly growing intrinsic tumor group more likely approximated the Haaland and Delaney sample. Nonetheless, these results indicate moderate to severe brain impairment in patients with cerebral tumors. The HII values indicate that a significant number of general neuropsychological functions are impaired.

Rapidly growing intrinsic tumors may result in HII values that are equivalent to those found in AD (Table 7.2). These tumor patients manifest significant and

TABLE 7.2.   General Neuropsychological Performances of Patients with Lateralized Rapidly or Slowly Growing Intrinsic Cerebral Tumors and Patients with Alzheimer's Disease

Measure		Intrinsic Tumor[a]				AD[b]
		Rapid	Slow	Left	Right	
Overall brain function						
Impairment Index	M	0.89	0.76	0.81	0.84	0.89
	SD	0.19	0.25	0.25	0.21	0.14
Abstraction and problem solving						
Category Test	M	112.94	81.49	89.52	104.89	101.03
	SD	51.09	42.51	40.97	55.89	20.18
TPT Total	M	0.66	1.13	1.02	0.78	0.53
Blocks/Minute	SD	0.75	0.74	0.70	0.84	0.49
Trail Making B	M	455.94	219.46	289.98	385.41	252.77
	SD	780.02	157.72	177.07	791.13	89.12
Digit Symbol	M	3.78	5.72	4.76	4.73	3.97
	SD	3.16	2.97	3.09	3.34	2.78
Incidental memory						
TPT Memory	M	3.26	4.87	4.13	4.00	2.91
	SD	2.65	2.40	2.69	2.62	2.08
TPT Localization	M	0.83	1.39	1.41	0.96	0.37
	SD	1.39	1.47	1.50	1.41	0.49
Attention/concentration						
Seashore Rhythm	M	15.11	18.22	15.85	17.48	18.21
	SD	9.58	8.56	10.57	7.52	6.69
Speech-sounds Perception	M	26.61	15.43	21.98	20.07	14.23
	SD	18.03	15.12	17.76	17.32	7.87
Trail Making A	M	123.54	76.13	86.87	112.80	69.06
	SD	88.16	49.64	52.41	91.07	41.24
Digit Span	M	5.00	6.63	4.83	6.80	7.71
	SD	3.96	3.40	4.00	3.26	2.88
Arithmetic	M	5.20	6.09	4.65	6.63	7.17
	SD	4.59	4.57	4.70	4.28	3.00

[a]Hom & Reitan, 1984.
[b]Hom, 1992.
Notes: TPT = Tactual Performance Test.

severe limitations in immediate adaptive function. Less overall brain impairment is found for slower growing tumors compared to AD. Nonetheless, the patients with slower growing tumors are still likely to be experiencing significant impairment of cognitive function. These results indicate the difficulty in differentiating the cognitive impairments of the tumor patient from those of the earlier stage AD patient.

Abstract Reasoning and Problem Solving

Measures best representative of abstraction and problem solving in the HRB model include the Halstead Category Test, Tactual Performance Test–Total Time, Trail Making Test–Part B, and Digit Symbol from the Wechsler scales. As a single principal component, these measures have been shown to account for 80.1% of the variance in a sample of AD patients (Hom, 1992). These measures reflect neuropsychological functions that require observing and integrating information into principles and ideas, modifying ideas and hypotheses, learning and solving problems in complex novel environments, and maintaining and utilizing competing information in a productive manner.

These neuropsychological functions have been shown to be significantly impaired in patients with cerebral neoplasms. Hom and Reitan (1984) demonstrated significant impairment in abstract reasoning and problem-solving abilities among patients with intrinsic cerebral tumors. Furthermore, rapidly growing intrinsic tumors resulted in significantly worse dysfunction in these abilities when compared to slower growing tumors. However, equivalent levels of impairment were found with intrinsic tumors lateralized to the right versus left cerebral hemisphere. Similar findings for cerebral tumor have been reported by other investigators (Boll, 1974; Farr et al., 1986; Hochberg & Slotnick, 1980).

When rapidly growing intrinsic tumors are compared to early stage AD, equivalent and significant levels of impairment are found in abstraction and problem-solving abilities (Hom & Reitan, 1984; Hom, 1992) (see Table 7.2). However, when compared to early stage AD, slowly growing tumors tend to result in less dysfunction of these abilities, although the level of performance is still poorer than expected as compared to normative performances.

Incidental Memory

Significant impairment of the ability to acquire information incidentally during the completion of a task has been demonstrated for brain tumors. However, the level of impairment varies with the complexity of the material. In the HRB model, measures of incidental memory include the Memory and Localization components of the Tactual Performance Test. Hom and Reitan (1984) reported significant dysfunction for both incidental memory variables in rapidly growing intrinsic tumors. However, less significant dysfunction was demonstrated for slower growing intrinsic tumors. No significant differential impairment was found for right versus left tumors. Other investigators have found relatively adequate abilities on the Memory component but impairment of Localization similar to that reported by Hom and Reitan (Farr et al., 1986; Hochberg & Slotnick, 1980). Differences in findings may be partially due to the tumor types used in the various studies.

Patients with AD demonstrate greater impairment of incidental memory than do those with cerebral neoplasms (see Table 7.2). Greater impairment of incidental memory is evidenced for AD even when compared to rapidly growing intrinsic tumors.

Attention/Concentration

Measures representative of attention and concentration on the HRB include the Seashore Rhythm Test, Speech-Sounds Perception Test, Trail Making Test–Part A, and the Digit Span and Arithmetic subtests from the Wechsler scales. Various neuropsychological studies of patients with cerebral tumors have shown them to perform significantly poorly on all attention/concentration variables (Boll, 1974; Farr et al., 1986; Hom & Reitan, 1984). However, adequate Speech-Sounds Perception Test performances were found in the Farr et al. study. Greater impairment of attention/concentration is found with rapidly growing intrinsic tumors as compared to slowly growing tumors. However, no differential performance in attention/concentration is associated with lateralized tumor damage (Hom & Reitan, 1984).

Similarly significant levels of impairment of attention/concentration have been shown for early-stage AD. Compared to the AD group, patients with rapidly growing intrinsic tumors show poorer performances on these variables, whereas those with slowly growing tumors demonstrate performance levels similar to AD (see Table 7.2).

In summary, although cerebral tumors are considered focal lesions, their effects on brain function include impairment of general neuropsychological functioning that is somewhat independent of site or location of the lesion and which requires overall intact cerebral function. Impairments in intellectual functions, abstraction and problem solving, overall brain function, incidental memory, and attention/concentration are evidenced among patients with cerebral tumors. The degree and nature of the higher cognitive deficits vary with the tumor pathology. More malignant and progressive intrinsic tumors result in greater general neuropsychological impairment. However, slower growing intrinsic tumors also result in definite and consistent impairments. Whereas lateralized cerebral tumors may result in differential intellectual impairments, they do not result in differential generalized neuropsychological impairment. Compared to measures of intellectual function, neuropsychological measures are significantly more sensitive to the effects of cerebral tumors.

As compared to early-stage AD, cerebral tumors have similar effects on higher cognitive functions. In general, the more malignant tumors manifest levels of impairment that are similar to those found in AD, making it difficult to differentiate the two pathological neurological processes when only general neuropsychological functioning is considered. The extent and degree of general neuropsychological impairment in cerebral tumors extends beyond the focal nature of the lesion and mimics many of the impairments typically found in AD, a diffuse degenerative neuronal disease.

Specific Neuropsychological Function

In addition to the general neuropsychological deficits associated with brain tumors, impairments are usually evident in neuropsychological function more dependent on the focal nature of the pathology. Significant specific neuropsychological dysfunctions are often demonstrated, including impairment of motor abilities, sensory-perceptual function, and language or visuoconstructive deficits. The pattern of deficits allows for the identification of the location and distribution of the lesion. It is the focal and/or lateralized pattern of these specific neuropsychological impairments that permits the differential diagnosis of cerebral tumor from AD.

Motor Abilities

Primary motor skills are assessed in the HRB model using the Halstead Finger Oscillation Test and the Grip Strength Test. These two measures provide information concerning motor abilities, including the relative abilities of each side of the body. This allows a comparision of the integrity of the contralateral cerebral hemisphere, particularly the posterior frontal regions. In evaluating the patient's motor abilities and sensory-perceptual abilities (which are described in the next section), the patient serves as their own control, thus permitting intraindividual performance comparisons that provide important and sometimes very essential information concerning specific areas of brain involvement.

A number of studies have investigated motor skills in patients with brain tumors. These studies have generally yielded the expected finding of greater motor impairment contralateral to the cerebral tumor (Haaland & Delaney, 1981; Hom & Reitan, 1982, 1984). Relative to controls, tumor patients demonstrate significantly poorer motor function. However, compared to cerebrovascular lesions, patients with cerebral tumors demonstrate a milder degree of motor impairment (Haaland & Delaney, 1981; Hom, 1991; Hom & Reitan, 1982, 1990). Whereas motor abilities are frequently impaired in patients with tumors, the same motor abilities in AD are relatively preserved and unaffected (see Table 7.3). Hom (1992) reported no differences in primary motor function in patients with early-stage AD when compared to matched normally aging controls. Furthermore, AD patients did not demonstrate asymmetrical motor performances as typically found with cerebral tumors or cerebrovascular lesions. This pattern of contralateral motor impairment can help in diagnostic differentiation between AD and tumors.

Sensory-Perceptual Abilities

As found with motor functioning, the sensory-perceptual abilities of patients with brain tumors are significantly affected by the focal nature of tumors. Comprehensive evaluation of sensory-perceptual abilities using the Reitan-Klove Sensory Perceptual Examination has revealed significant deficits across various sensory modalities in patients with brain tumors (Hom & Reitan, 1982). Furthermore, greater sensory-perceptual impairment is found contralateral to the lesion. This pattern permits differential identification of the location of the tumor.

This pattern of significant sensory-perceptual deficits along with differential performance of the left and right sides of the body in cerebral tumors is clearly different than the pattern found with AD (see Table 7.3). On the whole, AD patients do not demonstrate a significant level of sensory-perceptual impairment as compared to matched normally aging controls (Hom, 1992). Furthermore, no

TABLE 7.3. Specific Neuropsychological Performances of Patients with Lateralized Rapidly or Slowly Growing Intrinsic Cerebral Tumors and Patients with Alzheimer's Disease

Measure		Intrinsic Tumor[a]		AD[b]
		Left	Right	
Motor abilities				
Finger Tapping, Dominant	M	33.33	42.72	44.43
	SD	18.25	10.44	7.58
Finger Tapping, Nondominant	M	37.58	27.00	40.74
	SD	11.53	16.19	5.69
Grip Strength, Dominant	M	28.00	32.36	31.54
	SD	15.87	10.61	10.52
Grip Strength, Nondominant	M	32.16	17.66	28.12
	SD	11.48	13.39	9.77
Sensory-perceptual abilities				
Tactile, Right	M	2.12	0.88	0.88
	SD	3.35	1.62	1.61
Tactile, Left	M	0.20	3.32	0.41
	SD	0.50	4.10	0.74
Auditory, Right	M	0.16	0.24	0.56
	SD	0.62	0.60	0.99
Auditory, Left	M	0.12	1.44	0.94
	SD	0.44	1.50	1.21
Visual, Right	M	2.00	0.56	0.17
	SD	4.08	2.40	0.71
Visual, Left	M	0.00	4.60	0.20
	SD	0.00	5.20	0.47
Finger Agnosia, Right	M	4.20	2.88	1.17
	SD	4.38	2.74	2.29
Finger Agnosia, Left	M	3.16	7.68	1.51
	SD	4.75	5.60	2.25
Fingertip Number Writing, Right	M	5.32	6.32	4.63
	SD	5.56	4.69	3.47
Fingertip Number Writing, Left	M	4.16	9.60	4.11
	SD	5.00	6.44	3.76
TFR Errors, Right	M	1.92	0.08	0.37
	SD	3.03	0.40	1.24
TFR Errors, Left	M	0.40	2.36	0.34
	SD	1.63	3.41	0.97

[a]Hom & Reitan, 1982.
[b]Hom, 1992.
Note: TFR = Tactile Form Recognition Test.

differential pattern of deficits is found that relates to a focal pathology as is found in cerebral tumors.

Language Function and Constructional Abilities

The Reitan-Indiana Aphasia Screening Examination permits assessment of basic language and communication function and visual-construction abilities. Wheeler and Reitan (1962) demonstrated the usefulness of this brief examination in determining various aphasic and apraxic symptoms related to brain damage. In general, lesions of the left cerebral hemisphere result in various language impairments, whereas lesions of the right affect visual construction. Differential performances on this examination are related to the nature and extent of the neurological process. Although no specific pattern of aphasic or apraxic deficits can be defined specifically for cerebral tumors, distinct and definite significance can be attributed to positive findings on this examination permitting the identification of the impaired cerebral hemisphere. The focal nature of tumors usually implicate one cerebral hemisphere as opposed to the other. In contrast, AD usually presents with significant symptoms involving both language and visual constructive abilities as a result of the diffuse and bilateral nature of the disease (Hom, 1992).

Management, Treatment, and Rehabilitation

From the preceding discussion, it is clear that cerebral tumors result in various neuropsychological and behavioral changes. The identification of these changes may provide important clinical information regarding diagnosis and prognosis. In addition, such information can aid in the treatment of the tumor patient. Although typically the primary concern regarding treatment of tumor patients is medical, the clinical neuropsychologist can contribute relevant information concerning the effects of the neoplasm on the immediate adaptive abilities of the individual. This information can aid the neurosurgeon or neurologist with management and treatment decisions regarding the tumor patient with respect to issues of independent living, and vocational and psychosocial adjustment. In addition, serially obtained neuropsychological information will allow for the determination of the efficacy of treatment as it impacts the functioning of the patient. For a small segment of the tumor population, patients with more "benign" or relatively stable tumors, neuropsychological information is quite relevant for effective cognitive and behavioral rehabilitation of the patient.

Until quite recently, the prognosis of patients with intrinsic intracranial neoplasms was poor. Recently, more optimistic prognoses are the result of advances in various therapies. However, considerable debate and skepticism exists concerning the long-term efficacy of these therapies. Nonetheless, for the clinical neuropsychologist to make relevant clinical contributions to the management of the tumor patient, thorough awareness is required of the various neurosurgical and neurological issues, the current methods of treatment and management, as well as knowledge of the neuropsychological and psychological abilities of the patient. For example, the clinical implications of a patient's general and specific neuropsychological abilities requires specific knowledge about the neuropathology of the tumor; specific management and treatment methods for the type of tumor; morbidity and mortality associated with the tumor; and treatment procedures, psychosocial repercussions, and so forth. Clearly, a recommendation of cognitive rehabilitation for a patient with a glioblastoma multiforme would be of no relevance or value because of the very poor prognosis and dramatically decreased survival associated with this type of tumor. A more relevant clinical contribution in such cases would involve issues of survivorship, anticipatory grieving, and family counseling.

Medical management and treatment of patients with cerebral tumors is very complex and beyond the scope of this chapter. More detailed description of these issues and therapeutic modalities is available in standard neurological and neuro-surgical texts, such as Adams and Victor (1989b), Rowland (1989), and Youmans (1982). Additional references include Thomas and Graham (1980) and Kornblith and Walker (1988). In general, the modern therapies available for cerebral tumors include surgery, radiotherapy, chemotherapy, immunotherapy, and various combinations of these approaches. General principles of management include pathological diagnosis, relief of distressing symptoms, and improvement of quality of life and survival. However, factors such as tumor type, localization, duration and growth, morbidity and mortality, and patient characteristics pose significant limitations to medical management and treatment of the patient. For example, although almost all brain tumors may be imaged and visualized, not many tumors are easily treated or result in successful long-term survival for the patient.

With advances in neurosurgical techniques, imaging, and neuroanesthesia, benign tumors of the brain have been successfully treated and for the most part have become curable entities. In contrast, treatment of malignant brain tumors has not enjoyed similar success. Neurosurgery alone can frequently remove significant portions of malignant tumors but rarely can effect a cure. Radiation therapy has been found to increase the survival of brain tumor patients. The effectiveness of chemotherapy on malignant tumors is clearly less dramatic as compared to its role in other human cancers. Yet some difference in survival has been shown for certain compounds (nitrosourea compounds). Immunotherapy with interleukin-2 and other substances offer some exciting promise in the future treatment of brain tumors.

Despite the advances in neuro-oncology, the overall picture for malignant brain tumors remains relatively poor. In such cases, whereas neuropsychological information may contribute to diagnosis, prognosis, and assessment of the effectiveness of therapy, the contribution of neuropsychology is typically minimal. Clearly, of greater importance are the psychosocial and clinical repercussions of the malignancy for the patient and family. In contrast, for the small number of patients with benign or more stable tumors, neuropsychological information is essential for planning cognitive rehabilitation of the patient. Identification of general and specific neuropsychological deficits and strengths in individual patients of this population can be the basis for comprehensive neuropsychological rehabilitation. A neuropsychological rehabilitation model that makes use of identified general and specific neuropsychological dysfunction is the Reitan Evaluation of Hemispheric Abilities and Brain Improvement Training (REHABIT) program proposed by Reitan and Wolfson (1988).

The REHABIT program is an extension of the HRB framework previously described. Initially, a comprehensive evaluation of the patient's neuropsychological function is conducted. The identified neuropsychological deficits provide the prescription for the remediation program. Specific training of the areas of deficit is effected by utilizing rehabilitation materials from five tracks representing general and specific neuropsychological functioning. The REHABIT program includes the following tracks: A, development and remediation of fundamental verbal, language, and academic abilities; B, training of higher cognitive aspects of Track A including abstraction and reasoning, logical analysis, and organization; C, development of higher cognitive function such as abstract reasoning, planning, and organization which are not dependent on any particular content area; D, training of abilities that require visual-spatial, sequential, and manipulatory oriented abstraction and reasoning components; and *E*, remediation of fundamental components of visual-spatial and manipulatory abilities.

Although other rehabilitation programs exist, the REHABIT program is the only known program that is based on the HRB conceptual model of brain-behavior relations. Rather than using a "shotgun" approach, REHABIT requires a comprehensive evaluation of the patient's neuropsychological function and utilizes the resultant information as the basis of the remediation program. Therefore, a highly individualized prescription for retraining is formulated that is directly related to the patient's ability structure. For example, the REHABIT program would be applicable for a patient who has successfully undergone removal of a meningioma involving the left sylvian region. Such an individual may present with some mild neuropsychological dysfunctions involving abstract reasoning, attention/concentration, memory, and language/communication. After identification of the specific pattern of neuropsychological deficits, the patient may be prescribed a REHABIT program involving elements of Tracks A, B, and C. Comprehensive remediation of the patient's deficits using materials from these tracks should alleviate these specific dysfunctions and serve to "rebalance" the ability structure of the patient. However, REHABIT is fairly new, and additional outcome studies are needed to document its effectiveness. A more thorough description of the REHABIT program is found in Reitan and Wolfson (1988).

For the specific population of patients with benign or stable tumors, neuropsychological remediation is a useful adjunct to medical management and treatment. Effective remediation will lead to more successful reintegration of the tumor patient back to a productive life. Furthermore, identification of neuropsychological function in this population may allow for appropriate and necessary environmental, familial, or societal adjustments.

Concluding Remarks

With the advent of CT and MRI, identification of brain tumors has been greatly facilitated, resulting in a reduction in inaccuracies of neurological diagnosis. In contrast, neurological and behavioral symptoms still remain difficult to diagnose and are often nonspecific to the disease. The diagnosis and understanding of neuropsychological impairment in patients with brain tumors has been hampered by the medical necessity of treating the tumor; such understanding has been hampered in patients with dementia by current conceptual diagnostic orientations. Moreover, the understanding of tumor-based dementia is further complicated by the relative infrequency of occurrence and by overreliance on pathognomonic sign approaches in clinical assessment.

Issues discussed in this chapter highlight some of the limitations of current classification schemes in understanding dementia. A more productive understanding of dementia would be obtained by determining the neuropsychological concomitants of a particular dementing process, rather than using a syndrome-based technique. Differential neuropsychological patterns may be discovered that may aid in the diagnosis, treatment, and future research of dementia and other neurological diseases.

A pattern of both general and specific neuropsychological dysfunctions is found with cerebral neoplasms. A broad range of cognitive functions is simultaneously impaired that may include intelligence, abstract reasoning/problem-solving, attention/concentration, incidental memory, language/visuospatial abilities, and sensorimotor function. The extent and nature of the neuropsychological impairments are not completely explicable by the focal pathological features of the tumor, neurological symptomology, or psychiatric state of the patient. Furthermore, as reported by Hochberg and Slotnik (1980), these neuropsychological impairments help to explain the failure of many tumor patients to return to premorbid levels of psychosocial function.

By using a clinical neuropsychological framework that includes measurement of both general and specific neuropsychological function, the differential neuropsychological patterns associated with brain tumors versus dementia can be better understood. Although many neuropsychological features are similar in cerebral tumors and dementia of the Alzheimer's type, brain tumors are usually associated with a pattern of relatively lateralized and even focal neuropsychological dysfunction along with the significant generalized neuropsychological impairment. In contrast, dementia of the AD type presents a pattern of significant generalized and specific neuropsychological impairment involving both cerebral hemispheres with relatively retained sensorimotor function and few signs of lateralization.

Finally, the material discussed in this chapter provides information regarding the contribution of the HRB conceptual model of neuropsychological function in determining clinical differentiation of neuropsychological impairments associated with neurological disease. Use of this model of neuropsychological investigation in conjunction with existing neurological knowledge will result in a more comprehensive understanding of brain-behavior relations in neurological diseases and dementias and may allow for effective neuropsychological intervention in certain cases such as patients with benign or stable tumors. For this specific tumor population, the REHABIT program allows for comprehensive neuropsychological remediation based on identified general and specific neuropsychological dysfunction. This program is a direct and practical extension of the HRB conceptual model and affords the tumor patient retraining of impaired brain functions associated with the neoplasm. It is hoped that such neuropsychological rehabilitation will increase the potential of the patient to return to a productive life.

References

Adams, R. D., & Victor, M. (1989a). Dementia and the amnesic (Korsakoff) syndrome. In R. D. Adams & M. Victor (Eds.), *Principles of neurology* (pp. 334–346). New York: McGraw-Hill.

Adams, R. D., & Victor, M. (1989b). Intracranial neoplasms. In R. D. Adams & M. Victor (Eds.)., *Principles of neurology* (pp. 516–553). New York: McGraw-Hill.

American Psychiatric Association. (1987). *Diagnostic and statistical manual of mental disorders* (3rd ed., rev.). Washington, DC: Author.

Andersen, A. L. (1950). The effect of laterality localization of brain damage on Wechsler-Bellevue indices of deterioration. *Journal of Clinical Psychology, 6,* 191–194.

Andersen, A. L. (1951). The effect of laterality localization of focal brain lesions on the Wechsler-Bellevue subtests. *Journal of Clinical Psychology, 7,* 149–153.

Bailey, P., & Cushing, H. (1926). *A classification of the tumors of the glioma group on histogenetic basis with a correlated study of prognosis.* Philadelphia: J.B. Lippincott.

Benson, D. F., Cummings, J. L., & Tsai, S. Y. (1982). Angular gyrus syndrome simulating Alzheimer's disease. *Archives of Neurology, 39,* 616–620.

Boll, T. J. (1974). Psychological differentiation of patients with schizophrenia versus lateralized cerebrovascular, neoplastic, or traumatic brain damage. *Journal of Abnormal Psychology, 83,* 456–458.

Boll, T. J. (1981). The Halstead-Reitan neuropsychological battery. In S. B. Filskov & T. J. Boll (Eds.), *Handbook of clinical neuropsychology* (pp. 577–607). New York: John Wiley & Sons.

Cummings, J. L., & Benson, D. F. (1983). *Dementia: A clinical approach.* Boston: Butterworth's.

Cushing, H. (1932). *Intracranial tumors.* Springfield, IL: Charles C. Thomas.

Davison, L. A. (1974). Introduction. In R. M. Reitan & L. A. Davison (Eds.), *Clinical neuropsychology: Current status and applications* (pp. 1–18). Washington, DC: V.H. Winston & Sons.

Farr, S. P., Greene, R. L., & Fisher-White, S. P. (1986). Disease process, onset, and course and their relationship to neuropsychological performance. In S. B. Filskov & T. J. Boll (Eds.), *Handbook of clinical neuropsychology* (Vol. 2, pp. 213–253). New York: John Wiley & Sons.

Fetell, M. R., & Stein, B. M. (1989). General considerations. In L. P. Rowland (Ed.), *Merritt's textbook of neurology* (pp. 275–285). Philadelphia: Lea & Febiger.

Filskov, S. B., & Boll, T. J. (Eds.). (1981). *Handbook of clinical neuropsychology.* New York: John Wiley & Sons.

Filskov, S. B., & Boll, T. J. (Eds.). (1986). *Handbook of clinical neuropsychology* (Vol. 2). New York: John Wiley & Sons.

Freemon, F. R. (1976). Evaluation of patients with progressive intellectual deterioration. *Archives of Neurology, 33,* 658–659.

Goodglass, H., & Kaplan, E. (1979). Assessment of cognitive deficit in the brain-injured patient. In M. S. Gazzaniga (Ed.), *Handbook of behavioral neurobiology: Vol. 2 Neuropsychology* (pp. 3–22). New York: Plenum Press.

Grant, I., & Adams, K. M. (Eds.). (1986). *Neuropsychological assessment of neuropsychiatric disorders.* New York: Oxford University Press.

Greig, N. H., Ries, L. G., Yancik, R., & Rapoport, S. I. (1990). Increasing annual incidence of primary malignant brain tumors in the elderly. *Journal of the National Cancer Institute, 82,* 1621–1624.

Haaland, K. Y., & Delaney, H. D. (1981). Motor deficit after left or right hemisphere damage due to stroke or tumor. *Neuropsychologica, 19,* 17–27.

Haase, G. R. (1977). Diseases presenting as dementia. In C. E. Wells (Ed.), *Dementia* (pp. 27–67). Philadelphia: F. A. Davis Company.

Haenszel, W., Marcus, S. C., & Zimmerer, E. G. (1956). *Cancer morbidity in urban and rural Iowa.* (U.S. Dept. of Public Health Monograph No. 37). Washington, DC: U.S. Government Printing Office.

Hochberg, F. H., & Slotnick, B. (1980). Neuropsychologic impairment in astrocytoma survivors. *Neurology, 30,* 172–177.

Hom, J. (1991). Contributions of the Halstead-Reitan Battery in the neuropsychological investigation of stroke. In R. A. Bornstein & G. G. Brown (Eds.), *Neurobehavioral aspects of cerebrovascular disease* (pp. 165–181). New York: Oxford University Press.

Hom, J. (1992). General and specific cognitive dysfunctions in patients with Alzheimer's disease. *Archives of Clinical Neuropsychology, 7,* 121–133.

Hom, J., & Reitan, R. M. (1982). Effects of lateralized cerebral damage upon contralateral and ipsilateral sensorimotor performances. *Journal of Clinical Neuropsychology, 4,* 249–268.

Hom, J., & Reitan, R. M. (1984). Neuropsychological correlates of rapidly vs. slowly growing intrinsic cerebral neoplasms. *Journal of Clinical Neuropsychology, 6,* 309–324.

Hom, J., & Reitan, R. M. (1990). Generalized cognitive function after stroke. *Journal of Experimental and Clinical Neuropsychology, 12,* 644–654.

Hutton, J. T. (1981). Results of clinical assessment for the dementia syndrome: Implications for epidemiological studies. In J. A. Mortimer & L. M. Schuman (Eds.), *The epidemiology of dementia* (pp. 62–69). New York: Oxford University Press.

Kanakaratnam, G., & Direkze, M. (1976). Aspects of primary tumours of the frontal lobe. *British Journal of Clinical Practice, 30,* 220–221.

Katzman, R. (1989). Delirium and dementia. In L. P. Rowland (Ed.), *Merritt's textbook of neurology* (pp. 3–9). Philadelphia: Lea & Febiger.

Kernohan, J. W., Maben, R. F., Svien, H. J., & Adson, A. W. (1949). A simplified classification of the gliomas. *Proceedings of the Staff Meetings of the Mayo Clinic, 24,* 71–75.

Keschner, M., Bender, M. B., & Strauss, I. (1938a). Mental symptoms in cases of tumor of the temporal lobe. *Archives of Neurology and Psychiatry, 110,* 572–596.

Keschner, M., Bender, M. B., & Strauss, I. (1938b). Mental symptoms associated with brain tumor. *Journal of the American Medical Association, 110,* 714–718.

Klove, H. (1974). Validational studies in adult clinical neuropsychology. In R. M. Reitan & L. A. Davison (Eds.), *Clinical neuropsychology: Current status and applications* (pp. 211–235). Washington, DC: V. H. Winston & Sons.

Kornblith, P. L., & Walker, M. D. (Eds.). (1988). *Advances in neuro-oncology.* New York: Futura.

Kurland, L. T., Schoenberg, B. S., Anneger, J. F., Okazaki, H., & Molgaard, C. A. (1982). The incidence of primary intracranial neoplasms in Rochester, Minnesota, 1935–1977. *Annals of the New York Academy of Sciences, 381,* 6–16.

Levin, S. (1949). Brain tumors in mental hospital patients. *American Journal of Psychiatry, 105,* 897–900.

Malamud, N. (1967). Psychiatric disorder with intracranial tumors of limbic system. *Archives of Neurology, 17,* 113–123.

Maletta, G. J., Pirozzolo, F. T., Thompson, G., & Mortimer, J. A. (1982). Organic mental disorders in a geriatric outpatient population. *American Journal of Psychiatry, 139,* 521–523.

Marsden, C. D., & Harrison, M. J. G. (1972). Outcome of investigation of patients with presenile dementia. *British Medical Journal, 2,* 249–252.

McKhann, G., Drachman, D., Folstein, M., Katzman, R., Price, D., & Stadlan, E. M. (1984). Clinical diagnosis of Alzheimer's disease: Report of the NINCDS-ADRDA work group under the auspices of Department of Health and Human Services Task Force on Alzheimer's disease. *Neurology, 34,* 939–944.

Reisberg, B., Ferris, S. H., de Leon, M. J., & Crook, T. (1982). The Global Deterioration Scale (GDS): An instrument for the assessment of primary degenerative dementia (PDD). *American Journal of Psychiatry, 139,* 1136–1139.

Reitan, R. M. (1955). An investigation of the validity of Halstead's measures of biological intelligence. *Archives of Neurology and Psychiatry, 73,* 28–35.

Reitan, R. M. (1964). Psychological deficits resulting from cerebral lesions in man. In J. M. Warren & K. A. Akert (Eds.), *The frontal granular cortex and behavior* (pp. 295–312). New York: McGraw-Hill.

Reitan, R. M. (1966a). A research program on the psychological effects of brain lesions in human beings. In N. R. Ellis (Ed.), *International review of research in mental retardation* (Vol. I, pp. 153–218). New York: Academic Press.

Reitan, R. M. (1966b). Problems and prospects in studying the psychological correlates of brain lesions. *Cortex, 2*, 127–154.

Reitan, R. M. (1986). Theoretical and methodological bases of the Halstead-Reitan neuropsychological test battery. In I. Grant & K. M. Adams (Eds.), *Neuropsychological assessment of neuropsychiatric disorders* (pp. 3–30). New York: Oxford University Press.

Reitan, R. M., & Davison, L. A. (Eds.). (1974). *Clinical neuropsychology: Current status and applications* (pp. 1–18). Washington, DC: V. H. Winston & Sons.

Reitan, R. M., & Wolfson, D. (1985a). *Neuroanatomy and neuropathology: A clinical guide for neuropsychologists.* Tucson: Neuropsychology Press.

Reitan, R. M., & Wolfson, D. (1985b). *The Halstead-Reitan neuropsychological test battery.* Tucson: Neuropsychology Press.

Reitan, R. M., & Wolfson, D. (1988). *Traumatic brain injury. Vol. II: Recovery and rehabilitation.* Tucson: Neuropsychology Press.

Remington, F. B., & Rubert, S. L. (1962). Why patients with brain tumors come to a psychiatric hospital: A thirty-year survey. *American Journal of Psychiatry, 119*, 256–257.

Rourke, B. P., & Brown, G. G. (1986). Clinical neuropsychology and behavioral neurology: Similarities and differences. In S. B. Filskov & T. J. Boll (Eds.), *Handbook of clinical neuropsychology* (pp. 3–18). New York: John Wiley & Sons.

Rowland, L. P. (1989). *Merritt's textbook of neurology.* Philadelphia: Lea & Febiger.

Schoenberg, B. S., Christine, B. W., & Whisnant, J. P. (1976). The descriptive epidemiology of primary intracranial neoplasms: The Connecticut experience. *American Journal of Epidemiology, 104*, 499–510.

Schoenberg, B. S., Christine, B. W., & Whisnant, J. P. (1978). The resolution of discrepancies in the reported incidence of primary brain tumors. *Neurology, 28*, 817–823.

Smith, A. (1962). Ambiguities in concepts and studies of "brain damage" and "organicity." *Journal of Nervous and Mental Disease, 135*, 311–326.

Smith, A. (1966a). Intellectual functions in patients with lateralized frontal tumors. *Journal of Neurology, Neurosurgery and Psychiatry, 29*, 52–59.

Smith, A. (1966b). Verbal and nonverbal test performances of patients with "acute" lateralized brain lesions (tumors). *Journal of Nervous and Mental Disease, 141*, 517–523.

Smith, J. S., & Kiloh, L. G. (1981). The investigation of dementia: Results in 200 consecutive admissions. *Lancet, i*, 824–827.

Soniat, T. L. L. (1951). Psychiatric symptoms associated with intracranial neoplasms. *American Journal of Psychiatry, 108*, 19–22.

Strauss, I., & Keschner, M. (1935). Mental symptoms in cases of tumor of the frontal lobe. *Archives of Neurology and Psychiatry, 33*, 986–1007.

Thomas, D. G. T., & Graham, D. I. (Eds.). (1980). *Brain tumours.* London: Butterworth's.

Vega, A., & Parsons, O. A. (1967). Cross-validation of the Halstead-Reitan tests for brain damage. *Journal of Consulting Psychology, 31*, 619–625.

Victoratos, G. C., Lenman, J. A. R., & Herzberg, L. (1977). Neurological investigation of dementia. *British Journal of Psychiatry, 130*, 131–133.

Walker, A. E., Robins, M., & Weinfeld, F. D. (1985). Epidemiology of brain tumors: The national survey of intracranial neoplasms. *Neurology, 35*, 219–226.

Wechsler, D. (1944). *The measurement of adult intelligence* (3rd ed.). Baltimore: Williams & Wilkins.

Wechsler, D. (1955). *Wechsler Adult Intelligence Scale Manual.* New York: The Psychological Corporation.

Wells, C. E. (1977). Dementia: Definition and description. In C. E. Wells (Ed.), *Dementia* (pp. 1–14). Philadelphia: F. A. Davis Company.

Wheeler, L., & Reitan, R. M. (1962). The presence and laterality of brain damage predicted from responses to a short aphasia screening test. *Perceptual and Motor Skills, 15,* 783–799.

World Health Organization. (1977). *Manual of the international statistical classification of diseases, injuries and causes of death* (1975 rev.). Geneva: Author.

Yates, A. B. (1966). Psychological deficit. *Annual Review of Psychology, 17,* 111–144.

Youmans, J. R. (1982). *Neurological Surgery: Tumors.* (Vol. 5, 2nd ed.). Philadelphia: W. B. Saunders Company.

Zulch, K. J. (1980). Principles of the New World Health Organization (WHO) classification of brain tumors. *Neuroradiology, 19,* 59–66.

8

Dementia and the Frontal Lobes

PAUL SUNGAILA AND DAVID J. CROCKETT

In this chapter we shall describe behavioral and cognitive sequelae of impairment following injury or degeneration of the frontal lobes, particularly prefrontal cortex. The term *dementia* is generally used in two senses. The first is the more general DSM-III-R definition (American Psychiatric Association, 1987). The second is a more restricted definition, referring to symptoms of a group of degenerative neuropathological processes. First, we shall review evidence for the existence of dementing conditions that affect the frontal lobes preferentially and are distinct from Alzheimer's disease (AD) and other recognized degenerative diseases. Because frontal dementia represents a new diagnostic entity, clinicians should be made more aware of this condition. Second, we review frontal lobe deficits and theories of frontal function more generally. This section emphasizes that frontal functions should be routinely assessed in any type of suspected dementia. Finally, we offer a brief review and some of our observations on the clinical assessment of frontal systems.

The more general, DSM-III-R definition of dementia requires the presence of two types of signs. The first is "impairment in short-term and long-term memory." The second is impairment in abstract thinking, judgment, "higher cortical functions" (e.g., aphasia, apraxia, agnosia), or personality change. In addition, the impairment must be significant enough to impair social or vocational functioning, must not occur solely in the course of delirium, and must be attributable to a demonstrated or presumed organic etiology. By this definition, dementia refers to cognitive and behavioral sequelae of virtually any neurological condition. As such, it is not particularly useful, either descriptively or prognostically. The chapters of this volume attest to the diversity of behavioral sequelae in various neurological conditions. Many of the conditions discussed may produce amnesia, aphasia, agnosia, apraxia, and personality change, and thus satisfy the DSM-III-R criteria for dementia. However, the obtained patterns of cognitive deficit may be entirely different. Although the DSM-III-R definition of dementia may be widely used for administrative purposes, it is not particularly helpful in the clinical description of cognitive and behavioral changes accompanying brain dysfunction. Nowhere is this more apparent than in describing deficits accompanying damage to the frontal lobes. Particularly in the early stages of frontal dementia, neither of the two major DSM-III-R criteria need be present; memory and higher cortical functions are frequently intact. Stuss and Benson's (1987) claim that "it is now widely accepted that frontal lobe damage, unless massive and involving other brain areas, does not result in a 'dementia'" (p. 151) is based on this more general, DSM-III-R definition of dementia.

A second use of the term dementia is less clearly defined, but has emerged in response to the clinical realities of neuropsychological assessment. It refers to cognitive and behavioral sequelae of progressive neurodegenerative conditions. Typical referral questions in neuropsychological assessment, particularly in older patient populations, are to differentiate depression and dementia, assess the effects of head injury, or rule out dementia. The referring psychiatrists and psychologists use the term *dementia* to indicate a progressive, degenerative condition distinct from more "functional" psychoses (which, by DSM-III-R definition, must not be due to any organic mental disorder). This latter definition is more etiologically based and may be more useful in predictive statements about the course and treatment of these conditions. It is this latter definition of the term *dementia* that we have in mind when we describe the syndrome of frontal dementia.

Anatomy and Physiology of the Frontal Lobes

The functions of the frontal lobes, particularly the prefrontal areas, are among neuropsychology's greatest mysteries. The frontal lobes comprise one half of the cerebrum (Damasio, 1991), and prefrontal cortex alone comprises over 25% of the entire cortex (Goldman-Rakic, 1987). Prefrontal cortex is the nervous system's most recent evolutionary development. It is also the last central nervous system structure to be completed in the course of human development. Prefrontal areas have no direct sensory or motor functions. Nonetheless, they are connected directly or indirectly to every other region of the brain. Undoubtedly, the frontal lobes are among the most interesting of neuropsychology's mysteries, as their study may shed light on psychology's age-old dilemmas of self-awareness and personal identity.

Our knowledge of the frontal lobes is limited by several factors. They have no simple behavioral function. Animal models are limited. Finally, we have few satisfactory conceptual models of the function of these areas of the brain. We shall limit ourselves to a brief overview of anatomy and physiology.

The frontal lobes comprise the primary motor area or motor strip, premotor areas, and prefrontal areas. The functional specificity of these areas decreases as one moves anteriorly from the central (rolandic) sulcus. The *primary motor area* has a distinctive cell structure and specific somatotopic organization. *Premotor* areas are less specific in function. They include Broca's area, supplementary motor area (SMA), and frontal eye fields. Least specific of all are *prefrontal* areas, which are the main subject of this chapter. Table 8.1 summarizes the main divisions of the frontal lobes. The major divisions of the frontal lobes may also be classified by their thalamic connections. Primary motor cortex receives projections primarily from ventral lateral thalamic nuclei, premotor cortex from ventral anterior thalamic nuclei, and prefrontal cortex from medial dorsal thalamic nuclei.

Perhaps the most distinctive feature of the frontal lobes is the richness of their interconnections with other parts of the brain. Connections with other cortical areas include projections to and from the homologous cortex in the other hemi-

TABLE 8.1. Major Divisions and Subdivisions of the Frontal Lobes

Main Division	Subdivision	Brodmann Area[a]	Histology	Thalamic Connections[b]
Primary motor		4	Agranular	VL
Premotor		6, 8	Dysgranular	VL
	Supplementary motor area	6, 8	Dysgranular	VA, VL
	Frontal eye fields	8, 9	Dysgranular	VA
	Broca's area	44, 45	Dysgranular	VA
Prefrontal	Dorsolateral	9, 10, 12, 46	Granular	MD
	Orbital	11, 47	Granular	MD
	Medial	10-12, 24, 32	Granular	MD

[a]Relation between Brodmann and functional areas is approximate.
[b]VA = ventral anterior nucleus; VL = ventral lateral nucleus; MD = medial dorsal nucleus.

sphere via corpus callosum, as well as connections with temporal, parietal, and occipital cortex. There are prominent prefrontal-caudate and premotor-cerebellar connections (Wise & Strick, 1984). Finally, widespread connections with limbic structures play a critical role in emotions and memory. In fact, the anterior frontal cortex is so intimately related to the limbic system that it has been referred to as an association area for these systems (Pribram, 1981).

Primary motor and premotor areas are involved in the planning, production, and modulation of motor functions. They are intimately involved with circuits incorporating cerebellum, basal ganglia, and spinal motor tracts. Some authors (e.g., Milner, 1982) subdivide the prefrontal cortex into two functional areas, dorsolateral and orbital. Others (e.g., Kolb & Whishaw, 1990) subdivide it into three areas: dorsolateral, orbital, and medial. Still others (e.g., Stuss & Benson, 1984) identify basal-medial, dorsolateral, mesial, and orbital areas.

At a still finer level, the frontal cortex is arranged in a modular columnar structure. Columns are similar across species (Goldman-Rakic, 1987). Contralateral callosal fibers interdigitate with association fibers, providing a basis for interhemispheric integration. This arrangement of continual separation of higher order inputs "could also permit combination and recombination among these inputs that would constitute a highly adaptive and plastic mechanism" (Goldman-Rakic, 1984, p. 424). More detailed reviews of the anatomy and physiology of frontal functions are provided in Kolb and Whishaw (1990), Stuss and Benson (1984, 1986), and Damasio (1991). It is apparent from our brief overview of the complexity of frontal and prefrontal functions that: first, the subdivisions are somewhat arbitrary, but still complete enough to serve as the basis for models of more complex behaviors; and second, that simple functional models are inappropriate.

Degenerative Frontal Lobe Dementia

Frontal Lobe Involvement in Alzheimer's and Pick's Disease

Since frontal lobes comprise such a large part of the brain, the chances are high that they will be involved in any diffuse pathological process. A number of dementias have been known for some time to affect the frontal lobes preferentially. These include Jakob-Creutzfeldt disease and Pick's disease (Adams & Victor, 1990). Pick's disease is a relatively rare condition, but is probably the best-recognized dementia that preferentially affects frontal (and temporal) lobes. It is defined by characteristic argyrophilic "Pick's bodies" in frontal and temporal lobes.

It has become clear over the last decade that Alzheimer's disease also affects the frontal lobes. Histopathological studies (Kemper, 1984) suggest that in normal aging, Brodmann area 10 loses 28% of its neurons. This increases to 42% of neurons in patients with AD. Similarly, area 38 loses 12% of its neurons in normal aging, but 50% in AD. Many of the neurotransmitter changes in AD occur either in frontal lobes or along frontal projection routes. Coyle, Price, and DeLong (1983) demonstrated that AD involves selective degeneration of cholinergic cells in nucleus basalis of Meynert in basal forebrain. These cholinergic neurons innervate widespread regions of frontal cortex and play an important role in cognitive functions, especially memory. Chu, Penney, and Young (1987) reported a loss of over 50% of gamma-aminobutyric acid (GABA) in layers II, III, V in superior frontal gyrus. Monoamine neurotransmitters are prominent in frontal lobe activity. Palmer et al. (1987) compared monoaminergic changes in the brains of AD subjects with those of age-matched controls. Noradrenaline and serotonin were reduced in frontal and temporal cortex of Alzheimer patients as compared with controls. Moreover, in the Alzheimer subjects an inverse relationship was found between serotonin concentrations and the presence of neurofibrillary tangles, a primary pathological change in AD.

Patients with AD show metabolic deficiencies primarily in temporal and parietal cortex (e.g., Duara et al., 1986), leading to deficits in memory and other higher cortical functions. Neuropsychologically, patients with AD may present with a range of deficits (Martin, 1991), including impairment on tests of frontal function. For example, Kopelman (1991) compared Korsakoff alcoholics and AD patients on a range of "frontal" tests including the Wisconsin Card Sorting Test (WCST), Weigl card sorting, word fluency, and cognitive estimation (Milner, Petrides, & Smith, 1985; Shallice & Evans, 1978), and found significant impairment on all tests in the AD group.

Chase, Burrows, and Mohr (1987) compared cortical glucose utilization patterns (positron emission tomography [PET] scans) in patients with anterior, posterior, and mixed dementia. "Posterior" patients were selected on the basis of showing aphasia, apraxia, or agnosia. "Anterior" patients had primarily personality changes. The "mixed" group showed signs of both types. Positron emission scans demonstrated clear differences in the groups. Patients with aphasia, apraxia, and agnosia showed glucose metabolism levels of 20% below those of neurologically normal controls in posterior parietal and temporal lobes (Brodmann areas 37 and 39). Patients with deficits in personality and social behavior showed glucose metabolism levels 29% below those of controls in prefrontal cortex (Brodmann areas 10 and 46). Left-right hemisphere differences were minimal, and both groups showed relative sparing of primary motor and sensory areas. It should be noted that the two groups were not doubly dissociated; two of the five "anterior" patients showed posterior as well as anterior hypofunction, and two of five "posterior" patients also showed anterior hypofunction. Nonetheless, Chase et al. (1987) propose that an anterior-posterior axis is a useful dimension for classification of dementia, particularly in its early stages. A posterior cortical dementia as a clinically distinct entity has been described by Freedman et al. (1991).

Evidence for a Specific Frontal Dementia

There is some recent evidence for a degenerative dementia that is specific to the frontal lobes and is not histologically similar to either Alzheimer's or Pick's diseases. Although it may be too early to definitively establish this condition as a diagnostic entity, there is certainly enough evidence that clinicians should recognize this as a possibility.

The most extensive evidence comes from a prospective study of dementia in Sweden, now in its 20th year (Brun, 1987; Gustafson, Brun, & Risberg, 1990). Psychiatric, neuropsychological, cerebral blood flow, and electroencephalographic (EEG) studies were carried out on most patients. Neuropathological studies have been carried out on 80% of the deceased patients, a group which now comprises 158 cases. Of these, 45% had AD, 19% had vascular dementia, and an additional 10% had a combination of AD and cerebrovascular pathology. These figures are consistent with general prevalence estimates. Of the 158 brains, 26 had primarily frontal impairment. On detailed neuropathological examination, four of these were found to have Pick's disease, two had AD, three had Jakob-Creutzfeldt disease, and one had a bilateral thalamic infarction. Sixteen cases (10% of the entire sample) were found to have none of the neuropathological features of AD (senile plaques, neurofibrillary tangles) or Pick's disease. This group was termed *frontal lobe dementia (FLD) of the non-Alzheimer type*. Neuropathology involved neuronal loss, gliosis, and spongiosis. All involved white matter as well as cortical degeneration. These changes occurred in frontal convexities in all FLD cases; basal frontal cortex was also involved in 3 of the 16. The insula and anterior cingulate were also commonly involved. There was little or no involvement of sensorimotor cortex, postcentral cortex, amygdala, hippocampus, nucleus basalis, or striate. Regional cerebral blood flow studies (Risberg, 1987) were available on nine of the FLD cases and showed reduced flow in prefrontal areas. These patterns were markedly different from the AD cases in the same study, which showed temporoparietal blood flow reductions. The mean age of onset for FLD cases was 56, with average duration of illness (i.e., ending in death) of 8.1 years. The FLD patients had slightly earlier onset and shorter duration than a reference group of 21 AD cases from the same study. The onset of disease in the 16 FLD patients was characterized by disinhibition, restlessness, poor judgment, and emotional lability ranging from euphoria to depression to unconcern. Personality changes were of the "pseudo-psychopathic" rather than the "pseudodepressed" type (Blumer & Benson, 1975). Gustafson (1987) provides some guidelines for the differential diagnosis of this condition. Euphoria and restlessness may be mistaken for a manic or hypomanic state, and apathy and reduced speech may be misdiagnosed as depression. In the FLD group, depressive episodes were typically brief, and tended to be accompanied by agitation. Premorbid personality disorders were absent in the 16 FLD cases. After onset, they were generally described as emotionally cold, and in some cases, hostile. Six had frank psychotic episodes, typically paranoid, with hallucinations, and in several cases, accompanied by severe violence. Extreme compulsive behavior was noted in four cases. Language disorders were apparent in all cases of FLD and Pick's disease, and were characterized mainly by deficits in expression, with asponteneity, use of stereotyped phrases, occasional confabulation, and echolalia. Both FLD and Pick's cases also showed hyperorality, including excessive smoking, drinking, and eating. This may lead to misdiagnosis of alcoholism. Electroence- phalographic studies were carried out in most patients. The FLD and Pick's patients had almost universally normal EEGs, which contrasted sharply with AD, in which normal EEGs were rare.

A second line of work supporting the notion of a specific frontal dementia is that of Knopman, Mastri, Frey, Sung, and Rustan (1990) in Minnesota. These workers studied the brains of 460 dementing patients. Of these, a *dementia lacking distinctive histology (DLDH)* was found in 14 cases (3% of the entire sample). Of the younger patients, DLDH appeared in 10% of cases. Cortical degeneration was found mostly in frontal and parietal cortex. No neurofibrillary tangles were found. Unlike the Swedish studies, hippocampal degeneration was found in most of these cases (10 of the 14). As in the Swedish studies, dopamine deficiencies were found together with an absence of cholinergic deficiencies. Clinically, personality changes were prominent. Five of the 14 patients had formal neuropsychological evaluations. Memory impairment was less prominent in DLDH patients than in a comparable AD sample. Four of the five DLDH patients had executive function deficits, as assessed by such measures as the Trail-Making Test and word fluency.

A third line of work supporting the notion of a frontal dementia is that of Neary, Snowden, Northen, and Goulding (1988; Neary & Snowden, 1991) in Man- chester. Over a 5-year period, Neary et al. identified 26 cases of dementia with primarily frontal presentations. Of these, selective anterior abnormalities were confirmed by single photon emission computed tomography (SPECT) in 15 pa- tients. Neary et al. (1988) termed the condition *dementia of frontal lobe type (DFT)*and described the clinical presentations of seven cases in detail: early per- sonality changes, social breakdown, normal EEG, and a striking lack of deficits in spatial and memory functions. Neary et al. (1988) maintain that because it has not been a recognized diagnostic entity, the prevalence of DFT has been underesti- mated and may in fact comprise 25% of dementias.

More recent evidence also supports the notion that a clinical presentation of deterioration in personality or adaptive behavior with little or no cognitive loss may indicate frontal degeneration. Miller et al. (1991) studied eight patients with FLD. Social and behavioral problems typically preceded the onset of cognitive loss by several years. When cognitive deficits did appear, these typically involved tasks of mental flexibility and memory. Blood flow studies revealed frontal and temporal hypoperfusion. Frontal dementia may start at an even younger age. Ferrer, Roig, Espino, Peiro, & Guiu (1991) outlined the neuropathology in a 38-year-old man with atrophy, neuronal loss, and gliosis in frontal cortex. Orrell and Sahakian (1991) compared the clinical presentation of early DFT with the so-called Diogenes syn- drome, or senile self-neglect. They emphasize that

> Early diagnosis of FLD should improve management and prevent some of the most serious consequences to the family such as divorce, economic problems, and suicide. These outcomes might be avoided if the family and health profes- sionals understood that the patient suffers from a dementing illness and not merely an unruly personality. (p. 555)

Consequences of Frontal Lobe Damage

The history of models of frontal lobe function reflects the localization–mass action debate. Prior to systematic anatomic studies, the major theory of behavioral-brain relations was phrenology. Paul Broca's classic studies of language deficits following left frontal damage beginning in 1861 placed localization of function on firm empirical ground. Between 1861 and 1900 (see Caplan, 1987 for references) Wernicke and Lichtheim extended this method to a classification of aphasias, and outlined connections among various centers that might account for the clinical subtypes of aphasia. By 1900 Dejerine had extended this method to acallosal syndromes; and Liepmann, to apraxias. Current models of distributed function continue to build on the early work demonstrating the existence of specialized brain centers related to specific psychological functions.

Theorists who were a priori uncommitted to a localizationist approach, such as Freud and Henry Head, described cases that did not fit the Wernicke-Lichtheim models. The major theoretical approach of this competing school was that of Hughlings Jackson (1874; see Caplan, 1987, p. 89). Jackson argued that a patient's behavior after brain injury is not a partial performance with a component missing, but is rather the product of an integrated organism whose balance is fundamentally altered. Jackson proposed a hierarchical view in which higher centers modulate the performance of lower centers by means of inhibition. Most relevant to our discussion, dementia due to diffuse or degenerative processes was thought to affect performance hierarchically. According to Jackson, higher, inhibitory centers should be impaired earliest, leaving the organism with only more stimulus-bound, automatic, stereotyped behavior. Kurt Goldstein (1944) extended the Jacksonian view that any type of brain injury is expressed as an adaptation of the entire organism to the injury. Goldstein proposed that mental changes frequently take the form of abnormal exaggeration of premorbid personality. Particularly in the case of frontal lobe damage, impairment should be seen as the positive action of an abnormal area rather than the negative effect of its absence.

The early 20th century produced a body of evidence suggesting that frontal injuries have global rather than specific behavioral and cognitive effects (Halstead, 1947). The study of patients with tumors (e.g., Ackerly, 1935; Hebb, 1939; Kahn & Schlesinger, 1951) found changes not in specific cognitive functions, but rather in the patients' approach to problems. Irritability, euphoria, and inertia were common. Feuchtwanger (1923; see Teuber, 1964) studied 400 cases of missile injury from World War I, half with frontal damage. Few deficits in intellect or memory were noted in these patients. Rather, "the more pervasive changes were those of mood and attitude, ranging from euphoria, or, less frequently, depression, to a curious form of 'other-directedness' on the patients' part—an incapacity for making plans" (Teuber, 1964, p. 416). Teuber (1964; Teuber, Battersby, & Bender, 1951) studied World War II patients up to 7 years after penetrating missile injuries. One hundred thirty-one patients with either frontal, intermediate, or posterior damage were assessed on various perceptual and motor tasks, including hidden figures and card sorting tasks. Teuber found no pattern of impairment that was specific to frontal damage. Reitan (1964) studied 112 patients, half with diffuse and half with focal injuries of various etiologies, including tumors, vascular lesions, and head injuries. Neuropsychological measures were found to have little relation to the anatomical site of injury.

In much of this research, lesions were diffuse and difficult to specify. More precise lesion localization was possible, however, following surgical excisions of epileptic foci, and prefrontal leukotomy for schizophrenia. Milner (1964) studied patients with lateralized excisions, and found hemispheric differences in behavioral effects. Left dorsolateral lesions resulted in card sorting deficiencies; right frontal lesions affected maze learning. Benton (1968) found similar, lateralized effects; in this study, patients with left frontal lesions showed deficits in word fluency and paired associate learning, whereas patients with right frontal lesions showed deficits in block construction and figure copying tasks. Prefrontal leukotomy studies have yielded less clear-cut findings (Stuss & Benson, 1986). Interestingly, patients with the largest lesions showed the greatest reduction in psychiatric symptoms.

This earlier work demonstrated that damage to frontal lobes results in complex changes in cognition, emotions, and personality. More recent work has focused on the integration of these systems. We will review some of the constructs used to interpret changes in emotions and cognition following insult to the frontal lobes. *Emotional* changes may result from the disruption of cognitive-motivational linkages. Cognitive impairments have been characterized in terms of constructs such as *perseveration, autonomy* from the environment, *executive* control, cognitive control of *memory*, and *self-awareness*.

Emotions

Developing knowledge of prefrontal cortex-limbic systems may provide a basis for understanding motivational changes following frontal lesions. There is general agreement that brainstem and thalamic systems provide arousal, limbic systems control emotional tone and its expression in autonomic arousal (via hypothalamus), and cortical systems produce the cognitive set required to interpret complex inputs.

Based on anatomical and behavioral research with monkeys, Nauta (1971) outlined a model of frontal function in terms of the integration of cognition and motivation. In this model, connections between neocortical (sensory) and visceral inputs from the limbic system and hypothalamus serve as cognitive-motivational links that maintain the influence of reward and punishment on behavior. Disruption of these links results in *interoceptive agnosia*, a form of distractibility attributed to lack of control of rewards over behavior. Nonaffective components such as novelty seeking are disinhibited. In macaques, separate neural systems have been found for memories of motor responses (basal ganglia) and memories of reinforcement values of events (limbic system-hippocampus and amygdala) (Mishkin, 1982).

Damasio (1979) has proposed a similar account of prefrontal cortex in the *gating* of diencephalic activity. In this model, the hypothalamic reinforcement system evaluates the motivational relevance and hedonic value of stimuli. Gating is controlled by both the current motivational state and past experience.

> Frontal lobe structures mediate the cognition necessary to harmonize internal and external pressures by modulating primitive forms of response. In simple terms, frontal lobe disease would downgrade the quality of "gate" mechanisms

and allow less elaborate responses to complex environmental situations to take place. (p. 371)

Blumer and Benson (1975) proposed a *pseudodepressed/psychopathic* axis for prefrontal emotional changes. They described clinical syndromes in which orbitofrontal lesions (Brodmann area 11) produce disinhibited, pseudopsychopathic emotional changes, and poor word fluency, but not perseveration. Dorsolateral lesions (Brodmann area 9) cause an inhibited, pseudodepressed syndrome accompanied by poor conceptual shifting on the Wisconsin Card Sorting Test. Grafman, Vance, Weingartner, Salazar, and Amin (1986) studied patients with lateralized frontal lesions, and reported that right orbitofrontal lesions produced anxiety and depression, whereas left orbitofrontal lesions were associated with anger and hostility.

Disorders of Flexibility: Perseveration

Flexibility refers to the ability to switch lines of thought. It is essential for adaptation to novelty. Perseveration may be seen as the converse of flexibility, and is a primary manifestation of many types of cerebral damage. Two competing views of perseveration have emerged. One is that perseveration is a deficit in a unitary integrative mechanism. Goldberg (1986; Goldberg & Tucker, 1979) holds to this classical view that frontal lobes serve to integrate and control all other cerebral activity. In this model, perseveration following prefrontal injury may affect any cerebral activity, at whatever level of the "neurocognitive hierarchy" that activity operates. Goldberg's descriptive taxonomy comprises perseveration of features or elements, motor perseveration, and perseveration of activities.

The competing view is that perseveration of language, motor, and conceptual set are fundamentally different mechanisms (Sandson & Albert, 1984, 1987). At a neurobehavioral level, these forms of perseveration are similar to Goldberg's (1986) perseveration of features, motor perseveration, and perseveration of activities. Sandson and Albert (1984) refer to these types as recurrent, continuous, and stuck-in-set, respectively. In order to validate this reclassification, Sandson and Albert (1987) compared 18 aphasics with left hemisphere damage, 13 patients with exclusively right hemisphere damage, and 11 Parkinson's disease patients (the "frontal" group). Left hemisphere patients showed perseveration on Boston Naming and fluency tests (word and design). This *recurrent* perseveration was thought to be caused by a deficit in access to semantic memory. Right hemisphere patients showed perseveration in *continuous* motor activities such as drawing a series of loops or alternating cursive MNs (Luria, 1980) and alternation in naming series of letter names. The underlying deficit was thought to be in attention, specifically, in disengaging attention from the current focus. Patients with Parkinson's disease showed perseveration in tasks of drawing alternating figures in response to conflicting verbal labels. A dissociation of intentions and actions was thought to underlie this type of perseveration.

Autonomy from the Environment

Luria (1980) maintained that a primary result of prefrontal lesions was the inability of the patient to separate him- or herself from the environment, and to maintain a smooth flow of planning and control of behavior in the face of potential distractions. The *dominant program*, or the highest level of control for Luria was the internalized speech act. Subsequent work has shown that behavioral programs may also be nonverbally based (e.g., Milner & Petrides, 1984). However, the notion of fragmentation of the control of behavior is central.

Lhermitte, Pillon, and Serdaru (1986) coined the term *environmental dependency syndrome* to describe a particularly striking deficit following frontal damage. This is the apparent inability of patients to resist acting upon stimuli presented to them or to resist copying the actions of other persons. Lhermitte's patients entered the examiner's office in which everyday objects such as a candle and a comb were available. Frontal patients almost invariably combed their hair and lit the candle, even when explicitly asked not to do so. Alternatively, the examiner demonstrated a series of actions such as kneeling in prayer, ostensibly as a test of memory. Patients were again specifically asked not to repeat the actions. Despite this warning, frontal patients frequently did copy the examiner. Two variants of this syndrome were noted: acting upon objects in the environment (*utilization* behavior), and copying another person's actions (*imitative* behavior). When utilization behavior was present, imitative behavior was also present, although imitative behavior was occasionally found in isolation. Imitative behavior, or social dependence, was seen as an early stage of utilization behavior, or overly strong dependence of behavior on the physical environment. Lhermitte (1986) proposed that frontal damage reduces the patient's separation from the environment. The proposed mechanism involves a balance of frontal and parietal activity. Frontal and parietal lobes are richly interconnected via the superior longitudinal fasciculus and numerous other pathways. Since parietal lobes are primarily concerned with processing environmental information, their overall effect in this model is to draw the organism closer to the external environment. Frontal lobes, on the other hand, interpose processing between input and output, which tends to increase the distance between the organism and environment. Patients with damage to prefrontal areas are missing the distancing component, and are thus unable to disengage themselves from their immediate environment to evaluate the appropriateness of any given action toward achieving a larger goal.

Lhermitte's (1986) model is based on the notion that frontal lobes interpose an evaluative component between input and output. A similar theme has been mentioned in the context of integration of thought and "emotion." We have already mentioned the rich interconnections of the frontal lobes and limbic system. Damasio (1979) proposed that frontal lobes maintain an equilibrium between limbic/arousal and sensory/motor systems by acting as a "comparator," with which "the nervous system has achieved the maximal separation between stimulus and response" (p. 369).

Impairment in separating oneself from the environment may underlie the deficits in sustained attention commonly found in frontal patients. Wilkins, Shallice, and McCarthy (1987) found that patients with right frontal damage were poor at counting stimuli occurring at a 1/sec rate, but were identical with controls when stimuli were presented at a rate of 7/sec.

Disorders of Planning and Executive Functions

Frontal patients frequently have intact sensory, motor, and reasoning abilities required to perform tasks, but fail to correct their own actions in response to ongoing feedback. They may perseverate on an incorrect response and be unable to correct themselves even with external verbal guidance. They typically fail on problems that lack a simple algorithm. Frontal patients also demonstrate deficits in response preparation and inhibition, deficits which may to some extent be lateralized. Heilman has long been a proponent of a primary role for the right hemisphere in attention and arousal (e.g., Heilman & Van Den Abell, 1979). Verfaille and Heilman (1987) studied two patients with chronic unilateral medial frontal lesions (one left, one right) in tasks of response preparation and inhibition. In the preparation task, subjects responded to a dim light with the right hand and a bright light with the left. Subjects were given valid warning stimuli on 80% of trials. The inhibition task was one of reversal: when the right hand was touched, subjects were to raise their left hand, and vice versa. The patient with the left unilateral lesion benefitted as much as normals from information prior to the preparation task and was also normal on the inhibition task. The right-lesion patient was deficient in both tasks.

Planning behavior is generally seen as a component of *executive* function (e.g., Lezak, 1983). Models of information processing typically posit an executive or supervisory system that handles higher level or effortful tasks requiring flexibility and fluency, whereas lower level processing is thought to be automatized. For example, Duncan (1986) has characterized frontal lobe disorganization as fragmentation of action sequences or highly automatized routines. When executive control is lost, action behavior comes under the control of random environmental events, which may be a form of Lhermitte's utilization behavior. Shallice (1982, 1988) outlined a theory of executive functions in which routine behaviors are controlled at low levels, and follow default patterns driven by concurrently activated schemas or frames. Nonroutine, novel behaviors, or responses to unexpected events are controlled by a *Supervisory Attention System (SAS)*. Tasks thought to require an intact SAS include cognitive estimation of the sizes or speeds of everyday objects (e.g., "How tall is a telephone pole?"; "How fast does a racehorse gallop?") and abstract problem-solving tasks such as the Tower of Hanoi. Frontal patients were inferior to patients with posterior lesions on both tasks (Shallice, 1982; Shallice & Evans, 1978). In a task developed by Shallice and Burgess (1991), subjects were required to perform six simple tasks such as arithmetic and naming pictures in 15 minutes. The scoring system rewarded subjects for spending only a short time on each task, and attempting some items from all six tasks in 15 minutes. Frontal patients were found to be inefficient at scheduling the best use of the time available.

The research described in this section suggests that the core deficit in executive functions is a failure to utilize environmental cues to guide behavior. This includes failure to benefit from preparatory information as well as ongoing feedback regarding the adequacy of the behavior. Goal-directed behavior may become fragmented due to a lack of hierarchical organization. Thus, in some cases, what may seem like inertia or lack of motivation may in fact be the frontal patient's inability to prioritize activities.

Memory Deficits

Frontal damage produces memory deficits unlike those found in classic organic amnesias. Frontal deficits affect memory through poor organization, inability to use effective strategies, and susceptibility to interference (Mayes, 1988). In the Northampton V.A. study, Stuss et al. (1982) studied memory deficits in 16 schizophrenics 25 years following prefrontal leukotomy. Large bilateral orbitofrontal lesions did not result in classic recall or recognition deficits, but patients demonstrated increased susceptibility to interference, for example, in the Brown-Peterson task. They concluded that one important role of the frontal lobes in memory is to maintain directed attention.

Release from proactive interference (PI) may be impaired in frontal damage. In this task, the subject learns and recalls up to four lists of words drawn from a single semantic category. A final list from a different semantic category is presented. In normal subjects, performance decreases over the same-category lists, but increases when the semantic category is changed. Moscovitch (1982) and Freedman and Cermak (1986) evaluated the extent to which patients with temporal and frontal lesions showed release from PI on a verbal learning task. Temporal lesions were associated with poor recall, but a normal release from PI. Frontal patients showed no release. Their failure to benefit from the semantic shift was taken to indicate that they did not encode the semantic characteristics of the words. Significantly, the patients showing the least release also performed most poorly on the WISC. This effect has not been found consistently, however. Shimamura, Janowski, and Squire (1991) compared the performance of seven "pure" frontal patients with that of 12 amnesics, seven with Korsakoff syndrome. Frontal patients showed normal release from PI, whereas the Korsakoff patients failed to show normal release. Korsakoff syndrome is known to involve both frontal and diencephalic lesions (Jacobson, 1989; Moscovitch, 1982; Shimamura, Jernigan, & Squire, 1988). Their failure to show release from PI may illustrate that memory depends on the interaction of diverse functional systems within the brain.

In the Shimamura et al. (1991) study, frontal and Korsakoff patients showed equally impaired card sorting performance, though other differences between frontal patients and amnesics were found. On the Wechsler Memory Scale - Revised (WMS-R) (Wechsler, 1987) the performance of frontal patients was doubly dissociated from that of the two amnesic groups. Frontal patients were impaired on the WMS-R attention-concentration index but not the delayed memory index. Korsakoff and other amnesics showed the opposite pattern; they were impaired on delayed memory but were intact on attention-concentration.

Thus, memory deficits following frontal damage may be characterized more by disorganization and loss of cognitive control than the delayed memory deficits of classic amnesic syndromes. The pattern of deficits in Korsakoff syndrome patients illustrates the important point that the anatomic unity of frontal lobes does not indicate functional unity of frontal systems. Other memory constructs that may be related to frontal systems include memory for the temporal ordering of events, prospective memory, and feeling of knowing.

Confabulation

The reporting of memories of events that in fact never occurred often accompanies psychiatric conditions, delirium, and brain injury. When it occurs following brain injury, it is generally referred to as *confabulation*. Confabulation has been subdivided into two types (Berlyne, 1972). In *fantastic* confabulation, the patient spontaneously produces fictitious constructions; whereas in *momentary* confabulation, the constructions are distortions of actual events. Kapur and Coughlan (1980) studied a patient with a subarachnoid hemorrhage in the medial left frontal lobe who showed marked confabulation, but whose performance on memory tests was not typically amnesic. This patient's improvement over several months as assessed on a number of neuropsychological tests was associated with a decrease in confabulation, particularly of the fantastic type.

Confabulation is often thought of as an attempt to fill in memory gaps using memory construction processes similar to those used in normal memory. Joseph (1986) outlined a model in which right hemisphere and frontal damage result in the fragmentation of arousal and attention, causing the experience of gaps in memory. These are filled in with fragments of memories that are exaggerated through frontal disinhibition, resulting in fantastic and grandiose associations. In Johnson's (1991) multiple-entry model of memory (discussed in more detail below), confabulation is seen as a deficit in reality monitoring, or an incorrect attribution of a memory to a perceptual record rather than an internally generated image or reconstruction. On this view, confabulation may be more similar to deficient self-awareness than to memory loss.

Confabulation may also be similar to loss of autonomy from the environment, in Lhermitte's sense. Muller (1985) defines confabulation as one aspect of impaired reality testing. In Muller's model, impaired reality testing represents the dissolution of the highest brain functions in the jacksonian hierarchy, which may occur in any type of diffuse damage. Evidence that frontal patients have deficits in delayed memory tasks suggests that prefrontal cortex "allows remoteness of input and output." When this separation is disrupted, impaired reality testing is the result.

Disorders of Self-Awareness

The recognition that one is making an error and the ability to self-correct have been mentioned in our discussion of executive functions. Self-correction or error utilization also requires an ability to view one's own behavior from an "outside," or "objective" standpoint. Developmentalists such as Piaget have long held that decentering, or the loss of egocentrism, is a major milestone in cognitive development. Frontal damage may also be manifested as a loss in self-awareness (Schacter, 1991). The dissociation of error recognition and error utilization may be one expression of such impairment. Konow and Pribram (1970) described a 69-year-old patient with Hodgkin's disease with left frontal metastasis, confusion, expressive aphasia, and right hemiparesis who could describe her own errors in carrying out complex instructions (as well as errors made by others) but could not self-correct. In a study of Picture Arrangement performance in 143 patients with focal lateralized lesions, McFie and Thompson (1972) noted that patients with right hemisphere lesions, particularly right frontal lesions, frequently left the stimulus cards in the original, incorrect sequence. McFie and Thompson surmised that "this tendency to leave pictures in the presented order reflects a specific inability to correct a response in spite of evidence that it is wrong, which is maximal with right frontal lesions" (p. 551).

The self-other distinction may be related to the constructs of egocentric and allocentric space. It is well known that parietal damage, particularly in the nondominant hemisphere, affects spatial functions such as navigating with a map or reconstructing spatial relations in external objects. This is referred to as *allocentric* space. In contrast, patients with frontal impairment show impaired *egocentric* spatial orientation. They have difficulty pointing out their own body parts, but they can use a map to navigate around a building (Kolb & Whishaw, 1990). Patients with parietal injury show the opposite pattern. Deficient egocentric spatial orientation may be seen as a rudimentary impairment in perception of self.

In an earlier section of this chapter we described autonomy from the environment as a useful construct for understanding impairment to frontal lobes. We also mentioned Muller's (1985) model of reality testing, which was based on separation between input and output. A further model of the self-other distinction based on cognitive representations of internal versus external events has been proposed by Johnson (1981, 1991; Johnson & Raye, 1981). This *Multiple-Entry* model posits two classes of mental representation: *perceptual*, or records based on external inputs; and *reflective*, or those based on internal cues. The key construct for our purposes is that of *reality monitoring*, which underlies the discrimination of intentions from actions. One may have intended to make a telephone call yesterday, but have difficulty in recalling whether the phone call was actually made or if one simply imagined it. Deficits such as confabulation, anosognosia, error utilization, and time estimation may be the result of disrupted reality monitoring. According to this model, confabulation may arise from fragmentary records and a failure to discriminate between perceptual and reflective representations. Thus, a confabulated memory may be experienced as the recollection of an actual event.

In summary, disturbances of self-awareness encountered in frontal patients may include deficits in error recognition and utilization, impaired egocentric spatial orientation, and confusion of internal and external memories resulting in confabulation. These disturbances interact with the executive function deficits discussed above.

Models of Distributed Function

Clearly, neither a narrow localizationist nor a global mass-action perspective can account for clinical findings from patients with frontal lesions. The solution that has emerged is that of *distributed* models of function. In this class of models, complex behaviors are thought to be the result of the interaction of numerous subcomponents, each making a unique contribution to one or more distributed systems. Subcomponents of a single system may be located in widely dispersed areas of the brain. These models may offer a solution to the twin dilemmas that: first, patients with lesions in widely disparate brain areas may display similar behavioral deficits (e.g., unilateral neglect, perseveration); and second, focal lesions (particularly in frontal lobes) may result in a variety of behavioral deficits.

Luria

The most important model to emerge from the clinical findings of the first half of the 20th century was that of Alexander Luria (1980). Luria's method followed a clinical hypothesis-testing rather than a psychometric approach. That is, inherent in any analysis of behavior is a task analysis of components rather than an absolute scaling in comparison with norms. Luria proposed a distributed model in which various parts of the brain contribute some aspect of function to virtually every discrete behavior. The model posits three functional units or blocks. Each block is thought to be hierarchically organized, from primary projection areas that handle the input and output functions of the block, to secondary association areas where higher level processing and integration occurs, to tertiary or overlapping areas. Block I is responsible for maintaining an optimal level of cortical tone. This block integrates the internal drives and metabolic state of the organism, orients to stimuli arriving from the outside world, and regulates the level of arousal with respect to the intentions and plans of the organism. Impairment of this block results in disturbances of consciousness and basic orientation to stimuli. Luria included the reticular activating system and much of the limbic system in this functional unit. Block II receives, analyzes, and stores information. Comprising the posterior cortex, this block shows clear hierarchical organization in primary projection areas, secondary association areas, and multimodal tertiary areas. Block III programs, regulates, and verifies activity. This block is distributed through frontal cortex. Hierarchical organization is also evident in the relation between primary motor, premotor, and prefrontal areas. Luria described numerous simple clinical tasks that have been adopted in many neuropsychological assessment batteries.

Distributed Neurocognitive Networks

Recent models of distributed functioning may be seen as extensions of Luria's approach. Mesulam (1990) outlined a model of distributed processing that rejects Luria's hierarchical principle, in the sense of a cognitive agency which plans or forms intentions which are then passed down to lower centers to be implemented in a step-by-step fashion. Rather, the organism satisfies multiple constraints using an iterative, or "best-fit" approach. Mesulam distinguishes between anatomical *vectors* that transfer information, or the "content" of experience; and more diffuse *matrices*, or neurochemical systems that determine the "color" of experience. Five such matrices are described: cholinergic, dopaminergic, histaminergic, serotonergic, and noradrenergic. Information processing vectors are handled within distributed systems for attention, language, and integration of other networks, each with its own "hubs" and subsidiary structures.

Attention is controlled by a network involving three primary hubs: frontal eye fields, area parahippocampal gyrus (PG) in temporoparietal association cortex, and anterior cingulate. Each contributes a unique set of inputs to the system. Frontal eye fields control orientation and movement, PG contributes a map of extrapersonal space, and cingulate regulates the motivational value of the objects of attention via limbic system. Language is handled similarly through a network incorporating two main hubs, the classical Broca's and Wernicke's areas. Both are involved in all language tasks. This model also incorporates processing areas within which all the other networks can "play out different scenarios, the most successful of which may then dominate the landscape of neural activity" (p. 608). The major hubs of this network are prefrontal cortex, and its two major subcortical connections: the head of the caudate and medial dorsal thalamic nuclei.

Metabolic Subdivision of Prefrontal Cortex

The notion of distributed functional systems is supported by recent studies of in vivo cerebral metabolic activity. This work suggests that coactivation of multiple brain areas occurs in virtually every behavior. Roland (1984) identifies no fewer than 17 distinct frontal areas that are distinguished both in terms of the behavioral tasks in which they are activated and which other cortical areas are coactivated with them.

Findings from the anterior prefrontal area may be considered as an example of the level of detail possible (see Table 8.2). Four subareas have been identified. The *superior* division is activated when the brain initiates behavior according to prior instructions or when tasks involve multiple steps; Roland (1984) suggests that this division is most active when other brain areas must be recruited and organized. When a subject expects somatosensory stimulation, somatic areas are activated even if the stimulation does not actually occur. The *midfrontal* division is activated in response to patterned sensory stimuli and is coactivated with parietal zones. The *intermediate* division is involved with complex visual and auditory tasks, but is not consistently coactivated in other cortical areas. Finally, the *inferior* division is coactivated with temporal cortex, and is activated in complex visual and auditory tasks.

This line of work provides important support for multiple-pathway, distributed models of function. Behavior is controlled by networks involving many interacting subcomponents. The demonstration of coactivation among brain areas suggests that the concept of localization of function should be reconceptualized as localization within a network of interconnected systems rather than to a single brain area.

Time-Locked Regional Retroactivation

Another recent model of distributed functioning is Damasio's (1989) "time-locked regional retroactivation" model of memory. This model is somewhat more hierarchical than Mesulam's, but retains the notion of distributed storage of information. Perceptual records, or "feature fragments," of events are thought to be stored in the primary sensory or motor areas in which they were originally processed. Local convergence zones then store amodal records of features that were coactivated during the processing ("synchronous combinatorial arrangements").

TABLE 8.2. Subdivisions of the Anterior Prefrontal Area Found in Metabolic Studies

Subdivision	Activation	Coactivated Regions
Superior	Acting on prior instructions When other multiple areas are recruited	Task specific
Midfrontal	Patterned sensory information	Intraparietal sulcus
Intermediate	Anterior-auditory discrimination Posterior-visual discrimination	? ?
Inferior	Anterior-visual analysis Posterior-auditory analysis	Posterior inferior temporal mid-temporal

Source: After Roland, 1984.

Still higher convergence zones integrate those records with feed-forward and feed-back projections from wider systems. Recall occurs when neurons storing original feature fragments are once again activated together. Similar systems may underlie category-specific anomias, in which one is unable to recognize items of certain categories but recognizes others without difficulty.

Damage to systems underlying the motivational or emotional relevance of stimuli may lead to social dysfunction. Eslinger and Damasio (1985) described a patient (EVR) who exhibited profound personality changes after bilateral ablation of ventromedial frontal cortex for meningioma. This patient had intact cognitive and intellectual functions, but could not function in his professional or personal life, a syndrome referred to as *acquired sociopathy*. This was thought to result from impairment in activation of *somatic markers*. In this model, somatic markers represent the appetitive or inhibitory emotional states accompanying various environmental events. Since ventromedial frontal areas have extensive connections with hippocampus and amygdala, these areas are thought to contain records of somatic states that accompany memories of events. To examine this concept further, Damasio, Tranel, and Damasio (1991) compared skin conductance responses (SCRs) of five bifrontal ventromedial patients and control patients while viewing emotionally arousing pictures. Patients with ventromedial lesions had normal SCRs in simple orienting situations, but their SCRs were smaller than those of controls in response to scenes of disaster, mutilation, and nudity. These authors proposed that SCR reductions in ventromedial patients were caused by a failure of activation of somatic markers. They further propose that this model may explain aspects of many psychiatric disorders in addition to the social impairment found in frontal patients.

Clinical Assessment of Frontal Systems

We have emphasized the range of cognitive and behavioral deficits that can be seen following frontal lobe damage. It is evident from our review that these deficits are not easily defined, let alone quantified. Thus, neuropsychological assessment of frontal impairment is complex. Earlier work on neuropsychological assessment of frontal functions has focused on structured tests of attention, flexibility, and planning. Much of this work has focused on determining the effects of laterlized lesions (e.g., Benton, 1968; Milner, 1964). More recent work on distributed systems suggests that quantitative, norm-based psychometric testing of frontal systems may be of limited value because behavior is pervasively impaired, and may result in an altered approach to *all* tests. The highly controlled interpersonal situation of the individual assessment may "serve as the patient's frontal lobes" and have the result of obscuring rather than revealing frontal system deficits altogether. Thus, when one suspects damage to frontal systems, the assessment must not be limited only to structured tests; it is essential to assess the patient's behavior in minimally structured tasks such as writing an open-ended short story, responding to ambiguous pictures (e.g., Thematic Apperception Test), free drawing, and carrying on a conversation (on a topic that is of interest to the patient).

A number of general process-oriented approaches to neuropsychological assessment have been described. As noted above, Luria (1980) outlined a hierarchical, distributed model for brain-behavior relations, and described a hypothesis-testing approach to assessment. Goldberg and Costa (1986) extended Luria's approach and applied the hypothesis-testing method to executive function deficits following prefrontal lesions. An analytical approach, focusing on subdividing complex skills into components and assessing these components individually, has been described by McKenna and Warrington (1986). The Boston Process Approach (Milberg, Hebben, & Kaplan, 1986) combines description with quantification of performance, first, by gathering norm-referenced data by means of a core set of tests, and second, by extending and modifying standardized procedures in order to assess the reason for a patient's failure on a given task. In a similar vein, Kaplan, Fein, Morris, and Delis (1991) have recently provided guidelines for interpretation of Wechsler Adult Intelligence Scale-Revised (WAIS-R) (Wechsler, 1981) errors and have developed norms for WAIS-R scatter scores.

Earlier in this chapter we reviewed some of the cognitive deficits and personality changes which may accompany FLD. In this final section we shall examine some standardized tests that are thought to assess "frontal lobe" functions, and comment on the qualitative analysis of behavior during these tests. We will not review the basics of administration and scoring; these are better left to the test manuals and to specialized texts such as Lezak (1983) and Spreen and Strauss (1991). We shall organize our comments in terms of the forms of deficit reviewed above—namely, emotions, perseveration, autonomy, executive functions, memory, and self-awareness. The behavioral expression of these deficits and their assessment are summarized in Table 8.3. Neuropsychological and personality changes in FLD have also been reviewed by Johanson and Hagberg (1989), and Neary and Snowden (1991). Many of Lezak's (1989) comments on deficits in executive functions and emotional changes following head injury may also apply here.

Assessing Emotions: Alertness, Motivation, and Affect

As our brief historical review has pointed out, frontal damage was initially construed primarily as personality change. More recent theories of emotional changes have focused on disruption of cognitive-motivational links that maintain the influence of reward and punishment on behavior. Emotions as defined here include a range of behaviors including, at the most basic level, arousal and alertness. A patient's level of consciousness and alertness must be adequate before any other structured testing can be undertaken (Strub & Black, 1985). While attention is not typically thought of as an emotional function, simple measures of attention may be useful in assessing level of consciousness, arousal, and alertness. If a patient cannot repeat at least five digits forward, it is unlikely that reliable patterns of impairment will be found in more extensive neuropsychological testing.

Our review of FLD suggests that deterioration in emotions, personality, and social behavior may represent the earliest clinical presentation of this condition. For example, the 16 FLD cases in the Swedish series (Gustafson et al., 1990) showed prominent disinhibition, restlessness, and emotional lability. In Miller's et al. (1991) series of eight FLD cases, social and behavioral problems preceded cognitive loss by up to several years. Orrell and Sahakian (1991) describe early FLD presenting as "senile self-neglect." Given the widespread cortical and subcortical neuronal degeneration found in this condition (Brun, 1987; Ferrer et al., 1991; Knopman et al., 1990), it is unlikely that a specific pattern of emotional or

TABLE 8.3. Clinical Assessment of Frontal Systems

Function	Deficit	Behavior	Assessment
Emotions	Reduced alertness, arousal, span of attention, disrupted motivational relevance of stimuli	Impulsivity, rage, lethargy, depression, unconcern, inappropriate dress, crude humor, sexual advances	Level of consciousness, digit span, ward behavior, nurse or family reports, questionnaires
Flexibility	Poor selective and alternating attention, perseveration	Rigid, stereotyped behavior	Trail-Making Test, WCST, alternating figures
Autonomy	Stimulus-boundedness, poor vigilance, sustained attention, fluency	Distractibility, utilization behavior, lack of initiation, dissociation between intent and action	Digit span, vigilance tasks, PASAT, Brown-Peterson task, fluency tests, go-no go, free drawing
Planning/ executive functions	Poor self-regulation, inability to take abstract attitude, disruption of priorities	Impaired problem solving and judgment, concreteness, sequence of steps disrupted, lack of error correction	WAIS-R Comprehension, Similarities, Block Design, Tinker Toy test, cognitive estimation, WCST, mazes
Memory	Disorganization, loss of temporal context	Intrusions, source amnesia, confabulation	List learning (CVLT), paired associate learning, everyday memory
Self-awareness	Anosognosia, confusion of internal and external records	Lack of error correction, denial of deficits, poor hygiene, inappropriate dress, confabulation	Interview, adaptive behavior questionnaires

Note: WCST = Wisconsin Card Sorting Test; PASAT = Paced Auditory Serial Addition Test; WAIS-R = Wechsler Adult Intelligence Scale-Revised; CVLT = California Verbal Learning Test.

personality change will be found in FLD. Specific behavioral patterns will vary greatly from patient to patient.

Emotional functions should be constantly observed and documented throughout the assessment. Some of the changes seen in frontal patients in general, and which we would also expect in FLD patients, would be crude and stereotyped humor, inappropriate sexual advances, and low frustration tolerance in structured tests. Ward and home behavior are of critical importance; reports from nursing staff and relatives are often the best indicators of the patient's behavior in unstructured situations. As Lezak (1989) points out, one of the most important questions that can be asked is "What does the patient do when there's nothing to do?"

Structured behavioral inventories to be completed by clinical staff or relatives may be helpful in documenting emotional and behavioral changes. Such inventories have been developed for use with head injuries (e.g., Portland Adaptability Inventory; Lezak, 1989), Alzheimer's disease (e.g., the Columbia University Scale; Devanand et al., 1991), and for the assessment of functional behavior in the elderly (e.g., Functional Rating Scale, Present Functioning Questionnaire; Tuokko & Crockett, 1991). These scales may be useful in the quantification of behavioral changes in FLD.

Assessing Mental Flexibility

We have discussed mental flexibility in the context of models of perseveration. Mental flexibility is similar to, but more extensive than alternating attention. Deficits in mental flexibility may be elicited through simple procedures such as the "go–no go" reversal procedure, learning a three-step hand sequence, and drawing alternating figures such as cursive MNs and loops (Luria, 1980). Perseveration may appear even in simple tasks such as digit span in the form of repetition of digit sequences from trial to trial (i.e., perseveration across trials) or persistent lapsing into automatized sequences (e.g., 5,6,7) within a trial.

A classic test of flexibility is the Trail-Making Test. The test is useful because the two parts (part A, joining dots in a simple number sequence: A,B,C..., and part B, joining dots in an alternating number-letter sequence: 1,A,2,B,...) partial out the effects of motor speed, visual scanning, and mental flexibility. Norms vary widely. The most conservative are those of Davies (1968; see Lezak, 1983, p. 558; or revision by Spreen & Strauss, 1991). Stuss et al.'s (1987, Table 6, p. 148) comparison of norms from eight independent studies illustrates that there is considerable discrepancy among norms, particularly for older patients. This discrepancy is unfortunate, because geriatric patients are the very population for which the test may be most useful. For example, a 75-year-old male with Grade 9 education who completes Trails B in 3 minutes (180 seconds) would fall in the middle of the average range according to the Davies norms, but at least 2 standard deviations below the mean according to any other norms. Our own solution is to virtually disregard the norms and compare the patient's performance on Trails A and Trails B. If the former is completed quickly and efficiently, and the time on the latter is relatively slow, then the deficit is likely in mental flexibility. As a final check, the patient can be asked to produce the alternating number and letter series orally. If they can do this without difficulty, then the deficit is more likely in visual scanning or visual attention, and not in flexibility.

Two of the most widely used standardized tests assessing the ability to shift set are the WCST (Heaton, 1981) and Halstead's Category Test (HCT) (Reitan, 1979; Reitan & Wolfson, 1985). Short forms and alternate versions of both are available (see Lezak, 1983; Spreen & Strauss, 1991). Despite their popularity, the WCST and HCT have a number of limitations. First, in both the WCST and the HCT the subject is told whether their response on each trial is correct or incorrect. Thus, more impaired patients may hear the examiner say "incorrect" 20, 30, or more consecutive times. This may elicit frustration or rage in the patient, or at the very least, may initiate a vicious circle of poor performance, perseveration, frustration, and even greater difficulty in abstracting and flexibility. Second, although the WCST and HCT both appear to be measuring mental flexibility or shifting set, the convergent validity of this underlying construct is questionable. The intercorrelation of the two tests is only .3 to .6 (Donders & Kirsch, 1991; Pendleton & Heaton, 1982). This may reflect differences either in the administration formats or in the underlying constructs being assessed. A third problem is that the sensitivity

(Heck & Bryer, 1986) and specificity (Anderson, Damasio, Jones, & Tranel, 1991; Hermann, Wyler, & Richey, 1988) of these measures to prefrontal lesions is imperfect.

Assessing Autonomy

The ability to separate oneself from the environment is required to maintain attention to a given task. Vigilance may be assessed by simple tasks such as asking the patient to tap the desk each time they hear the letter A, while the examiner reads a string of 40 or 50 letters (see also Lezak, 1983; Strub & Black, 1985). Impaired sustained attention in patients with right frontal damage was found by Wilkins et al. (1987); their patients could not count stimuli occurring slowly (1/sec) but were intact in counting small stimuli that occurred at a faster, 7/sec rate. A deficit in sustained attention may present as distractibility or "stimulus-boundedness." This may be a version of Lhermitte's (1986) environmental dependency syndrome, or inability to interpose thought between an external stimulus and a response.

Patients with prefrontal damage frequently demonstrate a normal span of attention as assessed by forward Digit Span. The more complex backward Digit Span may produce confusion or inability to maintain the digit sequence in working or short-term memory long enough to reverse the sequence. Lezak (1983) maintains that a marked discrepancy between performance on Digit Span forward and backward is characteristic of early dementia, and this is our experience as well.

Continuous attention may be measured in tasks such as the Paced Auditory Serial Addition Test (PASAT) and the Brown-Peterson task. The Brown-Peterson task has been used in experimental cognition since the 1950s, and is just finding its way into clinical neuropsychological assessment of early dementing conditions. The PASAT is also a recent addition. Norms and descriptions for both can be found in Stuss, Stethem, and Poirier (1987) and in Stuss, Stethem, and Pelchat (1988). Stuss, Stethem, Hugenholtz, and Richard (1989) describe the application of these tests in the assessment of recovery following head trauma.

Autonomy from the environment is also required in the production of fluent behavior. *Fluency* may be defined as the ability to integrate behavior into a connected or goal-directed flow, and involves goal formulation and error correction. Fluency may be assessed at various levels. Perhaps the simplest assessment of fluency is in the patient's conversation, both in discussing personal topics and producing connected speech during WAIS-R Verbal subtests. A number of standardized measures of word fluency have been developed. The traditional measure has been the Thurstone Word Fluency test, in which the subject writes words under various constraints; for example, words beginning with a given letter or containing four letters and starting with a given letter. A commonly used version is the Controlled Oral Word Association test (e.g., Lezak, 1983), in which the patient says as many words as possible beginning with a letter given by the examiner. Three 1-minute trials are given, with either the letters F, A, S or the letters C, F, L. The frontal patient may provide a few words in the first few seconds of each trial, then simply stop. Word fluency productions may be limited to objects visible in the testing room. Alternatively, patients may run-on with repetitive productions (for example, in producing *S* words, one patient said "so, soft, she, so, soft, she, silly, silly, silly").

Verbal fluency may also be assessed in the written modality by having the patient write a short story. This may be on a topic of the patient's choice, or a standard stimulus such as the "cookie theft" picture from the Boston Diagnostic Aphasia Examination (Goodglass & Kaplan, 1987). Design Fluency is a nonverbal compliment to measures of verbal fluency. Jones-Gotman and Milner (1977) first described a test requiring the patient to draw as many figures as possible under various constraints. Ruff, Light, and Evans (1987) further standardized the test and provided norms from a large sample of normal adults.

Assessing Planning/Executive Functions

We have described planning and executive function deficits as involving poor judgment and abstraction, disruption in the sequences of steps in complex tasks, and inability to correct oneself in response to ongoing feedback. A basic factor underlying the integration of cognitive functions is the ability to shift mental set between the concrete (perceptual) and abstract (conceptual) aspects of a task in an appropriate, goal-related fashion. The ability to take an abstract attitude is routinely assessed in many psychological tests. For example, verbal abstraction is assessed in a number of WAIS-R subtests, particularly the Similarities subtest and in the proverbs of the Comprehension subtest. Proverbs have long been regarded as a measure of the ability to think metaphorically, and thus, abstractly. Specific tests of proverb interpretation are Gorham's Proverbs Test (Gorham, 1956) and the California Proverb Test. It should be noted that proverb interpretation may be deficient due to limited experience of verbal social conventions. One way to circumvent this type of deficiency is to ask the subject to recall a proverb and then interpret it. If the subject can relate one or more proverbs with reasonably abstract interpretations, then a poor performance on a standard set of proverbs is unlikely to reflect limited relevant experience.

Planning and executive functions may be assessed in unstructured construction and drawing tasks. Lezak (1983) describes the use of Tinker Toy construction pieces to assess a combination of fluency and reasoning. The patient is given 50 pieces and is told to assemble whatever they wish within a limited time (typically, 5 minutes). Mendez and Ashla-Mendez (1991) found that patients with multi-infarct dementia, a prototypic frontal-subcortical dementia, produced fewer constructional assemblages on this unstructured task than did AD patients.

Assessing Memory

We have discussed memory impairment in frontal damage as being manifested not so much in recall or recognition deficits, but as impaired organization, disruption of cognitive control, and the loss of temporal context and source (Mayes, 1988). We have reviewed evidence (e.g., Shimamura et al., 1991) that frontal patients may do well on delayed recall (tasks on which AD patients do very poorly), but fail on attention-concentration tasks. Often, everyday memory will appear superficially intact. Frontal patients may well have intact mechanisms for consolidation and retention of information, but they do not use their memory efficiently. This may appear as a relatively greater decrement with increased task complexity. For example, frontal patients may learn easy paired associates at normal rate, but may not learn difficult paired associates at all. List learning tests such as the California Verbal Learning Test (CVLT) (Delis, Kramer, Kaplan, & Ober, 1987) and the Hopkins Verbal Learning Test (HVLT) (Brandt, 1991) are useful in assessing the processes underlying impaired memory. A poor learning curve, for example, may be attributable to perseveration, intrusions, or distractibility when the examiner is reading the list. Poor recall may be attributable to list intrusions (recalling words from the interfering list when asked for the original list).

Assessing Self-Awareness

A number of recent models were described above that emphasize the importance of frontal systems in self-awareness (Johnson, 1991). In clinical assessment, the patient's self-awareness may be noted at a number of levels. First, the ability to observe one's own progress toward a goal and to detect and self-correct errors may be directly assessed through such tasks as Porteus Mazes, and indirectly, through observing the patient's approach to constructional tasks such as the WAIS-R Block Design or the Rey Complex Figure (Lezak, 1983). The patient's awareness of his or her own deficits should be assessed. This may be done though an unstructured interview. Impaired awareness of deficits may be seen as unconcern, euphoria, confabulation, or angry denial that a problem is present. Alternatively, patients may show intense but short-lived depressions. A standardized interview procedure for awareness of deficits has been developed by Anderson and Tranel (1989).

Summary

In this chapter we have described research on the behavioral and cognitive sequelae of damage to neurobehavioral systems distributed throughout frontal lobes. The greatest emphasis was given to prefrontal areas, which have projections not only to other areas of cortex but also to subcortical and limbic structures as well. Perhaps the most challenging feature of frontal systems is their structural diversity combined with their rich interconnections with other parts of the brain. The diversity of interconnections allows prefrontal areas to be intimately involved in the planning, production, and modulation of behavior. Psychological descriptions of behaviors such as environmental autonomy, flexibility and its converse (perseveration), error utilization, and self-concept are only loosely connected with anatomic loci. Similarly, neuropathological processes affecting prefrontal areas have diverse behavioral sequelae. This has led to a reconceptualization away from the localization–mass action dimension toward distributed systems models. In distributed systems, complex behavior emerges from the simultaneous activation of numerous anatomically distributed subcomponents of more basic functions. The smooth integration of inputs, outputs, and functions of the subcomponents is the primary responsibility of prefrontal areas. While rejecting hierarchical principles of cortical organization, these models hypothesize systems that underlie higher order cognitive functions such as attention, mental set, problem solving, memory, and emotional processing. Each of these systems may operate independently but also shares subcomponents with other systems. Different systems gain temporary dominance in various forms of complex behavior. It is this dynamic balance between competing systems that differentiates the distributed approach from the earlier, hierarchical approaches.

Imaging studies support the notion of distributed systems, but the real basis for this approach is the clinical evidence. From early studies based on penetrating war injuries, clinicians have shown that no specific pattern of deficits accompanies frontal damage. The most frequent description of these patients is in terms of difficulty in mental flexibility, poor planning and sequencing of problem-solving behavior, an inability to maintain balance between internal and external demands, and changes in the emotional control of behavior, with both disinhibition and apathy being common.

The study of functions attributed to frontal systems points out a need to integrate psychogenic, psychiatric, and organic descriptions of deficits. We believe that analysis is only hampered by attempts to distinguish between functional and organic deficits. The terms *functional* and *organic* should be used only to refer to levels of explanation, and not to competing accounts of complex neurobehavioral phenomena. We submit that the DSM-III-R definition of *dementia* is too broad to be useful in the analysis of frontal-type deficits. We suggest that the simpler term *cognitive deficits* be used in its place (preliminary indications suggest that this may in fact occur in DSM-IV). The term *frontal lobe dementia* was used in this chapter to refer specifically to a progressive degenerative condition affecting primarily the frontal lobes. Particularly in the early stages of FLD, a pattern of clinical changes can be identified that, while sharing many features in common with other degenerative conditions, stands alone and offers both clinicians and researchers a viable diagnostic alternative.

References

Ackerly, S. (1935). Instinctive, emotional, and mental changes following prefrontal lobe extirpation. *American Journal of Psychiatry, 92*, 717–729.

Adams, R. D., & Victor, M. (1990). *Principles of neurology* (4th ed.). New York: McGraw-Hill.

American Psychiatric Association. (1987). *Diagnostic and statistical manual of mental disorders* (3rd ed., rev.). Washington, DC: Author.

Anderson, S. W., Damasio, H., Jones, R. D., & Tranel, D. (1991). Wisconsin Card Sorting performance as a measure of frontal lobe damage. *Journal of Clinical and Experimental Neuropsychology, 13*, 909–922.

Anderson, S. W., & Tranel, D. (1989). Awareness of disease states following cerebral infarction, dementia, and head trauma: Standardized assessment. *The Clinical Neuropsychologist, 3*, 327–339.

Benton, A. L. (1968). Differential behavioral effects in frontal lobe disease. *Neuropsychologia, 6*, 53–60.

Berlyne, N. (1972). Confabulation. *British Journal of Psychiatry, 120*, 31–39.

Blumer, D., & Benson, D. F. (1975). Personality changes with frontal and temporal lesions. In D. F. Benson & D. Blumer (Eds.), *Psychiatric aspects of neurological disease*. New York: Grune & Stratton.

Brandt, J. (1991). Hopkins Verbal Learning Test: Development of a new memory test with six equivalent forms. *The Clinical Neuropsychologist, 5*, 125–142.

Brun, A. (1987). Frontal lobe degeneration of non-Alzheimer type. I. Neuropathology. *Archives of Gerontology and Geriatrics, 6*, 193–208.

Caplan, D. (1987). *Neurolinguistics and linguistic aphasiology*. Cambridge, MA: Cambridge University Press.

Chase, T. N., Burrows, G. H., & Mohr, E. (1987). Cortical glucose utilization patterns in primary degenerative dementias of the anterior and posterior types. *Archives of Gerontology and Geriatrics, 6*, 289–297.

Chu, D. C., Penney, J. B., & Young, A. B. (1987). Cortical GABAb and GABAa receptors in Alzheimer's disease: A quantitative autoradiographic study. *Neurology, 37*, 1454–1459.

Coyle, J. T., Price, D. L., & DeLong, M. R. (1983). Alzheimer's disease: A disorder of cortical cholinergic innervation. *Science, 219*, 1184–1190.

Damasio, A. R. (1979). The frontal lobes. In K. M. Heilman & E. Valenstein (Eds.), *Clinical neuropsychology* (pp. 360–412). New York: Oxford University Press.

Damasio, A. R. (1989). Time-locked regional retroactivation: A systems-level proposal for the neural substrates of recall and recognition. *Cognition, 33*, 25–62.

Damasio, A. R., Tranel, D., & Damasio, H. C. (1991). Somatic markers and the guidance of behavior: Theory and preliminary testing. In H. S. Levin, H. M. Eisenberg, & A. L. Benton (Eds.), *Frontal lobe function and dysfunction* (pp. 125–138). New York: Oxford University Press.

Damasio, H. C. (1991). Neuroanatomy of frontal lobe in vivo: A comment on methodology. In H. S. Levin, H. M. Eisenberg, & A. L. Benton (Eds.), *Frontal lobe function and dsyfunction* (pp. 92–121). New York: Oxford University Press.

Delis, D. C., Kramer, J. M., Kaplan, E., & Ober, B. A. (1987). *California Verbal Learning Test, Adult Version: Manual*. San Antonio: The Psychological Corporation.

Devanand, D. P., Miller, L., Richards, M., Marder, K., Bell, K., Mayeux, R., & Stern, Y. (1992). The Columbia University Scale for Psychopathology in Alzheimer's disease. *Archives of Neurology, 49*, 371–376.

Donders, J., & Kirsch, N. (1991). Nature and implications of selective impairment on the Booklet Category Test and the Wisconsin Card Sorting Test. *The Clinical Neuropsychologist, 5*, 78–82.

Duara, R., Grady, C., Haxby, J., Sundarem, N., Cutler, N. R., Heston, L., Moore, A. M., Schlageter, N. L., Larson, S., & Rapoport, S. I. (1986). Positron emission tomography in Alzheimer's disease. *Neurology, 36*, 879–887.

Duncan, J. (1986). Disorganization of behavior after frontal lobe damage. *Cognitive Neuropsychology, 3*, 271–290.

Eslinger, P. J., & Damasio, A. R. (1985). Severe disturbance of higher cognition after bilateral frontal lobe ablation: Patient EVR. *Neurology, 35*, 1731–1741.

Ferrer, I., Roig, C., Espino, A., Peiro, G., & Guiu, X. M. (1991). Dementia of the frontal lobe type and motor neuron disease. A Golgi study of the frontal cortex. *Journal of Neurology, Neurosurgery and Psychiatry, 54*, 932–934.

Freedman, M., & Cermak, L. S. (1986). Semantic encoding deficits in frontal lobe disease and amnesia. *Brain and Cognition, 5*, 108–114.

Freedman, L., Selchen, D. H., Black, S. E., Kaplan, R., Garnett, E. S., & Nahmias, C. (1991). Posterior cortical dementia with alexia: Neurobehavioral, MRI, and PET findings. *Journal of Neurology, Neurosurgery and Psychiatry, 54*, 443–448.

Goldberg, E. (1986). Varieties of perseveration: A comparison of two taxonomies. *Journal of Clinical and Experimental Neuropsychology, 8*, 710–726.

Goldberg, E., & Costa, L. D. (1986). Qualitative indices in neuropsychological assessment: An extension of Luria's approach to executive deficit following prefrontal lesions. In I. Grant & K. M. Adams (Eds.), *Neuropsychological assessment of neuropsychiatric disorders* (pp. 48–64). New York: Oxford University Press.

Goldberg, E., & Tucker, D. (1979). Motor perseveration and long-term memory for visual forms. *Journal of Clinical Neuropsychology, 1*, 273–288.

Goldman-Rakic, P. S. (1984). Modular organization of prefrontal cortex. *Trends in Neurosciences, 7*, 419–424.

Goldman-Rakic, P. S. (1987). Circuitry of the frontal association cortex and its relevance to dementia. *Archives of Gerontology and Geriatrics, 6*, 299–309.

Goldstein, K. (1944). Mental changes due to frontal lobe damage. *Journal of Psychology, 17*, 187–210.

Goodglass, H., & Kaplan, E. (1987). *The assessment of aphasia and related disorders* (2nd ed.). Philadelphia: Lea & Febiger.

Gorham, D. R. (1956). A proverbs test for clinical and experimental use. *Psychological Reports, 1*, 1–12.

Grafman, J., Vance, S. C., Weingartner, H., Salazar, A. M., & Amin, D. (1986). The effects of lateralized frontal lesions on mood regulation. *Brain, 109*, 1127–1148.

Gustafson, L. (1987). Frontal lobe degeneration of non-Alzheimer type. II. Clinical picture and differential diagnosis. *Archives of Gerontology and Geriatrics, 6*, 209–223.

Gustafson, L., Brun, A., & Risberg, J. (1990). Frontal lobe dementia of the non-Alzheimer type. In R. J. Wurtman (Ed.), *Advances in neurology. Vol. 51: Alzheimer's disease.* New York: Raven Press.

Halstead, W. C. (1947). *Brain and intelligence: A qualitative study of the frontal lobes.* Chicago: University of Chicago Press.

Hasher, L., & Zacks, R. T. (1979). Automatic and effortful processes in memory. *Journal of Experimental Psychology: General, 108*, 356–388.

Heaton, R. K. (1981). *Wisconsin Card Sorting Test Manual.* Odessa, FL: Psychological Assessment Resources.

Hebb, D. O. (1939). Intelligence in man after large removals of cerebral tissue: Report of four left frontal lobe cases. *Journal of General Psychology, 21*, 73–89.

Heck, E. T., & Bryer, J. B. (1986). Superior sorting and categorizing ability in a case of bilateral frontal atrophy: An exception to the rule. *Journal of Clinical and Experimental Neuropsychology, 8*, 313–316.

Heilman, K. M., & Van Den Abell, T. (1979). Right hemisphere dominance for mediating cerebral activation. *Neuropsychologia, 17*, 315–321.

Hermann, B. P., Wyler, A. R., & Richey, E. T. (1988). Wisconsin Card Sorting Test performance in patients with complex partial seizures of temporal-lobe origin. *Journal of Clinical and Experimental Neuropsychology, 10*, 467–476.

Jacobson, R. R. (1989). Alcoholism, Korsakoff's Syndrome, and the frontal lobes. *Behavioural Neurology, 2*, 25–38.

Johanson, A., & Hagberg, B. (1989). Psychometric characteristics in patients with frontal lobe degeneration of non-Alzheimer type. *Archives of Gerontology and Geriatrics, 8*, 129–137.

Johnson, M. K. (1991). Reality monitoring: Evidence from confabulation in organic brain disease patients. In G. P. Prigatano & D. L. Schacter (Eds.), *Awareness of deficit after brain injury: Clinical and theoretical issues* (pp. 176–197). New York: Oxford University Press.

Johnson, M. K., & Raye, C. L. (1981). Reality monitoring. *Psychological Review, 88*, 67–85.

Jones-Gotman, M., & Milner, B. (1977). Design Fluency: The invention of nonsense drawings after focal cortical lesions. *Neuropsychologia, 15*, 653–674.

Joseph, R. (1986). Confabulation and delusional denial: Frontal lobe and lateralized influences. *Journal of Clinical Psychology, 42*, 507–520.

Kahn, R. L., & Schlesinger, B. (1951). Preoperative and postoperative personality changes accompanying frontal lobe meningioma. *Journal of Nervous and Mental Disease, 114*, 492–509.

Kaplan, E., Fein, D., Morris, R., & Delis, D. C. (1991). *The WAIS-R as a neuropsychological instrument*. San Antonio: Psychological Corporation.

Kapur, N., & Coughlan, A.K. (1980). Confabulation and frontal lobe dysfunction. *Journal of Neurology, Neurosurgery and Psychiatry, 43*, 461–463.

Kemper, T. (1984). Neuroanatomical and neuropathological changes in normal aging and dementia. In M. L. Albert (Ed.), *Clinical neurology of aging* (pp. 9–25). New York: Oxford University Press.

Kirkpatrick, B., & Buchanan, R. W. (1990). The neural basis of the deficit syndrome in schizophrenia. *Journal of Nervous and Mental Disease, 178*, 545–555.

Knopman, D. S., Mastri, A. R., Frey, W. H., Sung, J. H., & Rustan, T. (1990). Dementia lacking distinctive histologic features: A common non-Alzheimer degenerative dementia. *Neurology, 40*, 251–256.

Kolb, B., & Whishaw, I. Q. (1990). *Fundamentals of human neuropsychology* (3rd ed.). New York: Freeman.

Konow, A., & Pribram, K. H. (1970). Error recognition and utilization produced by injury to the frontal cortex in man. *Neuropsychologia, 8*, 489–491.

Kopelman, M. D. (1991). Frontal dysfunction and memory deficits in the alcoholic Korsakoff syndrome and in Alzheimer-type dementia. *Brain, 114*, 117–137.

Lezak, M. D. (1983). *Neuropsychological assessment* (2nd ed.). New York: Oxford University Press.

Lezak, M. D. (1989). Assessment of psychosocial dysfunctions resulting from head trauma. In M. D. Lezak (Ed.), *Assessment of the behavioral consequences of head trauma* (pp. 113–143). New York: Alan R. Liss.

Lhermitte, F. (1986). Human autonomy and the frontal lobes: Part II: Patient behavior in complex and social situations: The "environmental dependency syndrome". *Annals of Neurology, 19*, 335–343.

Lhermitte, F., Pillon, B., & Serdaru, M. (1986). Human autonomy and the frontal lobes: Part I: Imitation and utilization behavior: A neuropsychological study of 75 patients. *Annals of Neurology, 19*, 326–334.

Luria, A. R. (1980). *Higher cortical functions in man* (2nd ed.). New York: Basic Books.

Martin, A. (1991). Neuropsychology of Alzheimer's disease: The case for subgroups. In M. F. Schwartz (Ed.), *Modular deficits in Alzheimer-type dementia* (pp. 143–175). Cambridge, MA: Bradford Books.

Mayes, A. E. (1988). The memory problems caused by frontal lobe lesions. In *Human organic memory disorders* (pp. 102–123). Cambridge: Cambridge University Press.

McFie, J., & Thompson, J. A. (1972). Picture Arrangement: A measure of frontal lobe function? *British Journal of Psychiatry, 121*, 547–552.

McKenna, P., & Warrington, E. K. (1986). The analytical approach to neuropsychological assessment. In I. Grant & K. M. Adams (Eds.), *Neuropsychological assessment of neuropsychiatric disorders* (pp. 31–47). New York: Oxford University Press.

Mendez, M. F., & Ashla-Mendez, M. (1991). Differences between multi-infarct dementia and Alzheimer's disease on unstructured neuropsychological tasks. *Journal of Clinical and Experimental Neuropsychology, 13*, 923–932.

Mesulam, M.-M. (1990). Large-scale neurocognitive networks and distributed processing for attention, language, and memory. *Annals of Neurology, 28*, 597–613.

Milberg, W. P., Hebben, N., & Kaplan, E. (1986). The Boston Process Approach to neuropsychological assessment. In I. Grant & K. M. Adams (Eds.), *Neuropsychological assessment of neuropsychiatric disorders* (pp. 65–86). New York: Oxford University Press.

Miller, B. L., Cummings, J. L., Villaneuve-Meyer, J., Boone, K., Mehringer, C. M., Lesser,

I. M., & Mena, I. (1991). Frontal lobe degeneration: Clinical neuropsychological, and SPECT characteristics. *Neurology, 41*, 1374–1382.

Milner, B. (1964). Some effects of prefrontal lobectomy in man. In J.M. Warren & K. Ackert (Eds.), *The frontal granular cortex and behavior* (pp. 313–331). New York: McGraw-Hill.

Milner, B. (1982). Some cognitive effects of frontal-lobe lesions in man. *Philosophical Transactions of the Royal Society of London, B298*, 211–226.

Milner, B., & Petrides, M. (1984). Behavioural effects of frontal-lobe lesions in man. *Trends in Neurosciences, 7*, 403–407.

Milner, B., Petrides, M., & Smith, M. L. (1985). Frontal lobes and the temporal organization of memory. *Human Neurobiology, 4*, 137–142.

Mishkin, M. (1982). A memory system in the monkey. In D. E. Broadbent & L. Weiskrantz (Eds.), *The neuropsychology of cognitive function*. London: The Royal Society.

Moscovitch, M. (1982). Multiple dissociations of function in amnesia. In L. S. Cermak (Ed.), *Human memory and amnesia*. Hillsdale, NJ: Erlbaum.

Muller, H. F. (1985). Prefrontal cortex dysfunction as a common factor in psychosis. *Acta Psychiatrica Scandinavica, 71*, 431–440.

Nauta, W. (1971). The problem of the frontal lobe: A reinterpretation. *Journal of Psychiatric Research, 8*, 167–187.

Neary, D., Snowden, J. S., Northen, B., & Goulding, P. (1988). Dementia of the frontal lobe type. *Journal of Neurology, Neurosurgery and Psychiatry, 51*, 353–361.

Neary, D., & Snowden, J. S. (1991). Dementia of the frontal lobe type. In H. S. Levin, H. M. Eisenberg, & A. L. Benton (Eds.), *Frontal lobe function and dysfunction* (pp. 304–317). New York: Oxford University Press.

Orrell, M. W., & Sahakian, B. J. (1991). Dementia of the frontal lobe type. *Psychological Medicine, 21*, 553–556.

Palmer, A.M., Wilcock, G.K., Esiri, M.M., Francis, P.T., & Bowen, D. M. (1987). Monoaminergic innervation of the frontal and temporal lobes in Alzheimer's disease. *Brain Research, 401*, 231–238.

Pendleton, M. G., & Heaton, R. K. (1982). A comparison of the Wisconsin Card Sorting Test and the Category Test. *Journal of Clinical Psychology, 38*, 392–396.

Pribram, K. H. (1981). Emotions. In S. B. Filskov & T. J. Boll (Eds.), *Handbook of clinical neuropsychology* (pp. 102–134). New York: Wiley.

Reitan, R. M. (1964). Psychological deficits resulting from cerebral lesions in man. In J. M. Warren & K. Ackert (Eds.), *The frontal granular cortex and behavior*. New York: McGraw-Hill.

Reitan, R. M. (1979). *Manual for the administration of neuropsychological test batteries for adults and children*. Indianapolis: Author.

Reitan, R. M., & Wolfson, D. (1985). *The Halstead-Reitan neuropsychological test battery: Theory and clinical interpretation*. Tucson: Neuropsychology Press.

Risberg, J. (1987). Frontal lobe degeneration of non-Alzheimer type. III. Regional cerebral blood flow. *Archives of Gerontology and Geriatrics, 6*, 225–233.

Roland, P. E. (1984). Metabolic measurements of the working frontal cortex in man. *Trends in Neurosciences, 7*, 430–435.

Ruff, R. M., Light, R. H., & Evans, R. W. (1987). The Ruff Figural Fluency Test: A normative study with adults. *Developmental Neuropsychology, 3*, 37–51.

Sandson, J., & Albert, M. (1984). Varieties of perseveration. *Neuropsychologia, 22*, 715–732.

Sandson, J., & Albert, M. L. (1987). Perseveration in behavioral neurology. *Neurology, 37*, 1736–1741.

Schacter, D. L. (1991). Unawareness of deficit and unawareness of knowledge in patients with memory disorders. In G. P. Prigatano & D. L. Schacter (Eds.), *Awareness of deficit after brain injury: Clinical and theoretical issues* (pp. 127–151). New York: Oxford University Press.

Shallice, T. (1982). Specific impairments in planning. *Philosophical Transactions of the Royal Society of London (Biology), 298*, 199–209.

Shallice, T. (1988). *From neuropsychology to mental structure.* Cambridge: Cambridge University Press.

Shallice, T., & Burgess, P. (1991). Higher-order cognitive impairments and frontal lobe lesions. In H. S. Levin, H. M. Eisenberg, & A. L. Benton (Eds.), *Frontal lobe function and dysfunction* (pp. 125–138). New York: Oxford University Press.

Shallice, T., & Evans M. E. (1978). The involvement of the frontal lobes in cognitive estimation. *Cortex, 4,* 294–303.

Shimamura, A. P., Janowski, J. S., & Squire, L. R. (1991). What is the role of frontal lobe damage in memory disorders? In H. S. Levin, H. M. Eisenberg, & A. L. Benton (Eds.), *Frontal lobe function and dysfunction* (pp. 173–195). New York: Oxford University Press.

Shimamura, A. P., Jernigan, T. L., & Squire, L. R. (1988). Korsakoff syndrome: Radiological (CT) findings and neuropsychological correlates. *Journal of Neuroscience, 8,* 4400–4410.

Spreen, O., & Strauss, E. (1991). *A compendium of neuropsychological tests: Administration, norms, and commentary.* New York: Oxford University Press.

Strub, R. L., & Black, F. W. (1985). *The mental status examination in neurology* (2nd ed.). Philadelphia: F. A. Davis Company.

Stuss, D. T., & Benson, D. F. (1984). Neuropsychological studies of the frontal lobes. *Psychological Bulletin, 95,* 3–28.

Stuss, D. T., & Benson, D. F. (1986). *The frontal lobes.* New York: Raven Press.

Stuss, D. T., & Benson, D. F. (1987). The frontal lobes and control of cognition and memory. In E. Perecman (Ed.), *The frontal lobes revisited* (pp. 141–158). New York: The IRBN Press.

Stuss, D. T., Kaplan, E. F., Benson, D. F., Weir, W. S., Chiulli, S., & Sarazin, F. F. (1982). Evidence for the involvement of orbitofrontal cortex in memory functions: An interference effect. *Journal of Comparative and Physiological Psychology, 96,* 913–925.

Stuss, D. T., Kaplan, E. F., Benson, D. F., Weir, W. S., Naeser, M. A., & Levine, H. L. (1981). The long-term effects of prefrontal leukotomy—an overview of the neuropsychologic residuals. *Journal of Clinical Neuropsychology, 3,* 13–32.

Stuss, D. T., Stethem, L. L., Hugenholtz, H., & Richard, M. T. (1989). Traumatic brain injury: A comparison of three clinical tests, and analysis of recovery. *The Clinical Neuropsychologist, 3,* 145–156.

Stuss, D. T., Stethem, L. L., & Pelchat, G. (1988). Three tests of attention and rapid information processing: An extension. *The Clinical Neuropsychologist, 2,* 246–250.

Stuss, D. T., Stethem, L. L., & Poirier, C. A. (1987). Comparison of three tests of attention and rapid information processing across six age groups. *The Clinical Neuropsychologist, 1,* 139–152.

Teuber, H.-L. (1964). The riddle of frontal lobe function in man. In J.M. Warren & K. Ackert (Eds.), *The frontal granular cortex and behavior* (pp. 410–444). New York: McGraw-Hill.

Teuber, H.-L., Battersby, W. S., & Bender, M. B. (1951). Performance of complex visual tasks after cerebral lesions. *Journal of Nervous and Mental Disease, 114,* 413–427.

Tuokko, H. A., & Crockett, D. (1991). Assessment of everyday functioning in normal and malignant memory disordered elderly. In D. E. Tupper & K. D. Cicerone (Eds.), *The neuropsychology of everyday life: Issues in development and rehabilitation* (pp. 135–182). Boston: Kluwer Academic.

Verfaille, M., & Heilman, K. M. (1987). Response preparation and response inhibition after lesions of the medial frontal lobe. *Archives of Neurology, 44,* 1265–1271.

Wechsler, D. (1981). *WAIS-R manual.* New York: The Psychological Corporation.

Wechsler, D. (1987). Wechsler Memory Scale Revisited. New York: The Psychological Corporation.

Wilkins, A. J., Shallice, T., & McCarthy, R. (1987). Frontal lesions and sustained attention. *Neuropsychologia, 25,* 359–365.

Wise, S. P., & Strick, P. L. (1984). Anatomical and physiological organization of the non-primary motor cortex. *Trends in Neurosciences, 7,* 442–446.

9

The Dementia of Huntington's Disease

JASON A. BRANDT AND FREDERICK W. BYLSMA

In 1872, a Long Island (NY) physician named George Huntington delivered an address to a medical society in which he described the essential features of "the hereditary chorea." In his brief, eloquent report, Huntington noted the similarity of this disease to common (Sydenham's) chorea, but noted three marked peculiarities: (a) "its hereditary nature"; (b) "a tendency to insanity and suicide"; and (c) "its manifesting itself as a grave disease only in adult life" (Huntington, 1872). Of note for the present volume, Huntington said, "As the disease progresses the mind becomes more or less impaired, in many amounting to insanity, while in others mind and body both gradually fail until death relieves them of their sufferings."

The next century saw relatively little progress in our understanding of Huntington's disease (HD) or its associated dementia syndrome. In 1972, largely through the strong determination and will of Marjorie Guthrie (the widow of folksinger Woodie Guthrie, a victim of HD), the first scientific symposium devoted to HD was held. Three years later, the U.S. Congress created the Commission for the Control of Huntington's Disease and its Consequences. Scientific workshops and conferences were convened, a national registry of HD families was established in 1979, and two national centers for HD research were funded by the National Institutes of Health in 1980. In 1983, the chromosomal locus of HD was established, making a systematic hunt for the gene and a presymptomatic test for the illness possible. Thus, most of what we know about the neurobiology, neuropsychology, and molecular genetics of HD has been acquired in the past 20 years.

Clinical, Genetic, and Neuropathological Features of Huntington's Disease

Huntington's disease is an uncurable neurodegenerative disorder with an estimated prevalence of 5 to 10 cases per 100,000 (Conneally, 1984; Folstein, 1989). It is inherited as an autosomal dominant genetic trait with full lifetime penetrance. This means that each offspring of an affected individual has a 50% risk of inheriting the gene, and everyone who inherits the gene will eventually develop the disease (if he or she lives long enough). Onset of HD is insidious, with subtle involuntary movements and cognitive difficulties typically noticed between 35 and 45 years of age (Bell, 1934; Heathfield & McKenzie, 1971; Folstein, 1989). In a 1980 survey of HD patients in Maryland, age of onset was found to range from 3 to 77 years of age, with an average of 40 years (Folstein, Chase, Wahl, McDonnell, & Folstein, 1987). After onset, the disease is slowly progressive, with increasing motor and cognitive impairment. Patients become severely demented, motorically dilapidated, unable to care for themselves, and eventually bedridden. Death results an average of 16 to 17 years after onset, usually from aspiration pneumonia or cardiopulmonary failure.

Emotional disturbance, primarily depression and less often mania or bipolar disorder, has been noted in a large proportion of HD patients (Folstein, Abbott, Chase, Jensen, & Folstein, 1983; Mindham, Steele, Folstein, & Lucas, 1985; Shoulson, 1990). In some patients, affective disorder may antedate the onset of observable motor abnormalities by several years, suggesting that affective disturbance is part of the neuropsychiatric symptom-complex and not an understandable psychological response to the illness (McHugh, 1989). Suicide is the cause of death in up to 6% of individuals with HD (Farrer, 1986). Other psychiatric symptoms, including irritability, apathy, sexual disturbance, conduct disorders, substance abuse, and schizophreniform thought disorder, are also observed in HD, but less frequently (Dewhurst, Oliver, & McKnight, 1970; Folstein, Franz, Jensen, Chase, & Folstein, 1983; McHugh & Folstein, 1975; Folstein, Brandt, & Folstein, 1990; Shoulson, 1990).

The neuropathology of HD is relatively specific. Macroscopically, the most significant feature is atrophy of the head of the caudate nucleus bilaterally. Microscopic analysis in the earliest stages of disease reveals loss of small, spiny neurons in the dorsomedial aspects of the head of the caudate nucleus. As the disease progresses, the entire caudate and putamen become involved (Vonsattel et al., 1985). Often, marked cortical atrophy is noted in HD brains at autopsy. Whether cortical atrophy is a primary neuropathological feature of the disease, or is a reaction to loss of striatal neurons that project to the cortex, remains unknown.

The pathophysiology of HD remains incompletely understood. One likely mechanism involves a defect in the N-methyl-D-aspartate (NMDA) subtype of glutamate receptors on striatal neurons (Coyle & Schwarz, 1976; McGeer & McGeer, 1976; Young et al., 1988). Glutamate and aspartate are the primary excitatory neurotransmitter in the brain and are abundant in striatum. Animal research has shown that injections of quinolinic, ibotenic, or kainic acid (analogues of glutamate) result in a pattern of striatal pathology that closely mimics that observed in autopsied HD patients (Coyle and Schwarz, 1976; Hantraye, Riche, Maziere, & Isacson, 1990; McGeer & McGeer, 1976). It is believed that glutamate and its analogues have their toxic effect by prolonged excessive excitation of neurons that ultimately results in cell death (Albin et al., 1990).

The gene defect responsible for HD has been localized by linkage analysis to the terminal cytogenetic band of the short arm of chromosome 4 (Gusella et al., 1983). The discovery of a recombinant deoxyribonucleic acid (DNA) marker for HD has led to the development of a genetic test that can identify at-risk individuals who have a very high probability of developing the illness (Meissen et al., 1988; Brandt et al., 1989). To date, however, the gene itself has not been identified, and the faulty gene product remains undiscovered.

Neuropsychological Features of Huntington's Disease

Typical complaints of HD patients early in the disease are of difficulty with attention and concentration, inability to organize or plan activities, and memory problems. The validity of these complaints has been demonstrated in many studies of cognitive functioning in early HD (Butters, Sax, Montgomery, & Tarlow, 1978; Brandt et al., 1984; Josiassen, Curry, & Mancall, 1983). Impairments in other areas of cognition become evident as the disease progresses. Selective defects in certain aspects of procedural learning, visuospatial cognition, and language abilities have recently been demonstrated, with preserved abilities in other aspects of these same functions (Brandt, 1991).

General Mental Status

Cognitive screening tests, such as the Mini-Mental State Examination (MMSE) (Folstein, Folstein, & McHugh, 1975) and the Dementia Rating Scale (DRS) (Mattis, 1976) are often useful in quantifying the severity of dementia when time or resources do not permit a thorough neuropsychological exam. Brandt, Folstein, and Folstein (1988) have demonstrated that certain MMSE items are more sensitive to the dementia of HD than are others. The resulting MMSE "profile" is relatively stable across severity of illness and may differentiate HD from other dementias. A comparison of groups of HD and Alzheimer's disease (AD) patients, stratified by severity of dementia and matched for years of education, revealed a double dissociation on two items: serial sevens from 100 and recall of three words after 1 minute. At all dementia severities, HD patients were more impaired than AD patients on serial sevens, but less impaired than AD patients on recall. Using a linear combination of six MMSE items in a discriminant function analysis, Brandt and colleagues (1988) were able to correctly classify 84% of HD patients and 83% of AD patients. The discriminant function replicated in a cross-validation sample. In a similar study, Salmon, Kwo-on-Yuen, Heindel, Butters, and Thal (1989) found that a combination of subscale scores from the DRS produced a comparable level of discrimination between HD and AD patients. These findings indicate that patterns of performance on cognitive screening tests may be helpful in illuminating relatively impaired and spared functions and might be helpful in differential diagnosis. It is important to note, however, that both these studies involved retrospective classifications of unambiguously diagnosed cases. It remains to be determined whether these discriminant functions can distinguish equally well among competing etiologies for individual cases as they present to the clinic for diagnosis.

Attention and Concentration

Difficulty maintaining concentration is a frequent complaint of HD patients early in the disease. There are few, if any, psychometric tests that assess attention in isolation, yet attentional difficulties can be inferred from poor performance on standard tests. It has consistently been demonstrated, for example, that HD patients perform most poorly on subtests of the Wechsler Adult Intelligence Scale (WAIS) and WAIS-R (Revised) that comprise a concentration and *freedom-from-distraction* factor (Arithmetic, Digit Span, and Digit Symbol) (Boll, Heaton, & Reitan, 1974; Fedio, Cox, Neophytides, Canal-Frederick, & Chase, 1979; Josiassen et al., 1983; Brandt et al., 1984; Strauss & Brandt, 1986). Several research teams have commented on the severe difficulty HD patients have on tests of arithmetic computation (Brandt et al., 1988; Caine, Bamford, Schiffer, Shoulson, & Levy, 1979), a finding that may implicate attentional dysregulation.

Speech and Language

Despite the progressive nature of the dementia of HD, clinically significant aphasia is rarely seen. The absence of aphasia in HD stands in marked contrast to the dementia of AD, and may serve as a distinguishing feature of the cortical and subcortical dementias more generally (Cummings, 1990; Folstein et al., 1990). However, particular speech and language impairments are observed in HD. Dysarthria and dysprosody are most common, affecting approximately 50% of early patients. These speech disorders become more pronounced as the disease progresses, often precluding intelligible communication late in the disease (Gordon & Illes, 1987; Ludlow, Connor, & Bassich, 1987; Wallesch & Fehrenbach, 1988; Podoll, Caspary, Lange, & Noth, 1988; Illes, 1989). Speedie, Brake, Folstein, Bowers, & Heilman (1990) recently reported that HD patients are also impaired in the comprehension of both affective and propositional prosody.

Expressive language of HD patients undergoes marked change over the course of the disease. Like patients with frontal lobe lesions (Alexander, Benson, & Stuss, 1988), HD patients initiate verbal communication less often, and participate little in ongoing conversations. The HD patients tend to have an increased response latency to questions and longer intervals between phrases, resulting in conversation that is interspersed with long gaps of silence. Syntactic complexity of both spoken and written sentences becomes reduced, and phrase length is progressively restricted. In advanced HD, spoken language consists of single words or short phrases that often do not constitute complete sentences. In contrast with the marked reduction in complexity, syntactic *structure* remains correct and speech *content* is usually appropriate until very advanced illness (Gordon & Illes, 1987; Podoll et al., 1988; Illes, 1989).

Early in the disease, word-finding difficulties and reduced output are common and are evident on verbal fluency tests such as the Controlled Oral Word Association Test (FAS Test) (Borkowski, Benton, & Spreen, 1967) and category fluency tasks (e.g., naming foods or animals) (Butters et al., 1978; Butters, Wolfe, Granholm, & Martone, 1986). Furthermore, the words generated by HD patients on fluency tests may be qualitatively different from that of other brain-disordered patients. Butters et al. (1986) showed that HD patients make many fewer perseverative responses than do patients with alcoholic Korsakoff's syndrome (KS). Intrusion errors, which permeate AD patients' performance on verbal fluency tests (Fuld, Katzman, Davies, & Terry, 1982), are rarer in HD patients. On category fluency tasks, mild HD patients, like healthy subjects, tend to report category exemplars (e.g., meat, beef, pork), whereas AD patients tend to produce higher order category labels (e.g., meat, vegetables, fruit), but lose the fine-structure of category membership (Martin & Fedio, 1983). Tröster, Salmon, McCullough, and

Butters (1989) recently reported that in more advanced HD patients, the ratio of items reported to categories sampled can be reduced to the level of AD patients. These data are among the first to suggest a disruption in the semantic system of HD patients. Smith, Butters, White, Lyon, and Granholm, (1988) reached a similar conclusion based on a semantic priming study.

Confrontation naming is also affected in HD. Performance on the Boston Naming Test (Kaplan, Goodglass, & Weintraub, 1978) and similar tests becomes poorer as the disease progresses. Errors are rarely paraphasic in nature until the advanced stages. More often, patients misperceive the stimulus drawings or give responses based on a portion of the stimuli (Butters et al., 1978; Bayles & Tomoeda, 1983; Podoll et al., 1988).

Spatial Cognition

Deficits in visuomotor performance are evident in even mild HD patients, although true constructional apraxia is rarely noted. Patients early in the disease take significantly longer than age- and education-matched controls to copy the Rey-Osterrieth Complex Figure and typically produce a less-than-adequate rendition (Brouwers, Cox, Martin, Chase, & Fedio, 1984). Deficits are also noted on the Block Design and Object Assembly subtests of the WAIS-R, assessing visuomotor and visuoconstructional abilities.

Visuospatial difficulties in HD are not fully attributable to chorea, as they often appear prior to clinically significant movement disorders (Josiassen et al., 1983). In addition, deficits on visuospatial tests that do not require motor responses are also observed. Using the untimed, motor-free Mosaic Comparisons Tests, for example, Fedio and co-workers (1979) found HD patients to be less efficient than normal controls in identifying differences between checkerboard-like grids.

A major visuospatial defect noted in HD involves the mental manipulation of personal, or egocentric, space (Brouwers et al., 1984). Huntington's disease patients perform particularly poorly on tasks such as the Standardized Road Map Test of Directional Sense (Money, 1976). This task requires subjects to trace a route winding through the map of a city. The route leads away from the subject for the first half, and toward the subject for the second half. Subjects must imagine they are the traveller, and indicate the turn direction (right or left) at each turning point. Huntington's disease patients perform this task more poorly than either normal controls or AD patients matched for education and WAIS full-scale IQ (Fedio et al., 1979). In addition, they show most marked deficits on the "toward" portion of the test where mental rotation is required (Brouwers et al., 1984). Patients show similar performance deficits on related tasks where actual rotation or movement is required. Potegal (1971) blindfolded HD patients and healthy controls, and had them point to a visual target whose location was previously viewed. The patients were as accurate as controls in localizing the target when standing in front of it. Unlike controls, however, they became significantly less accurate after moving one step to the left or right. Potegal interpreted this finding as indicating that the caudate pathology of HD interferes with the process of adjusting the cognitive representation of position in space after self-initiated movements.

Whereas ideomotor apraxia (a disorder in the performance of skilled, learned movements) is classically considered a "cortical" sign, Shelton and Knopman (1991) recently reported significant apraxia that could not be ascribed to other movement abnormalities in one third of the HD patients studied. The authors speculated on the role of subcortical motor nuclei in motor programming.

Memory

Capacity for new learning and memory in HD has been the focus of much neuropsychological research in recent years, and distinct patterns of memory dysfunction have been recognized. Many studies have contrasted the memory performance of HD patients with that of patients with alcoholic KS or patients with AD.

Standardized memory batteries, such as the original Wechsler Memory Scale (WMS), typically reveal mild to moderate deficits in early-stage HD patients (Butters et al., 1978; Brandt et al., 1984). However, the WMS Memory Quotient (MQ) is often equivalent in HD, AD, and KS, making this test of little value in the qualitative analysis of memory. The 1987 revision of the Wechsler Memory Scale (WMS-R) (Wechsler, 1987) does permit a differentiation of patterns of memory dysfunction in different amnesic and demented populations (Butters, Salmon, & Cullum, 1988; Tröster, Jacobs, Butters, Cullum, & Salmon, 1989). Relative to their Global Memory Index, HD patients have been shown to have a lower mean Attention/Concentration Index than equivalently demented AD patients. On the other hand, the AD patients had a lower Delayed Memory Index than predicted by their General Memory Index. This was not the case in the HD patients.

More focused assessments using specialized tasks have revealed particular breakdowns in encoding and retrieval, some of which may distinguish the memory defect of HD from that of other patient groups. Early studies of verbal learning in HD patients indicated poor recall after short delays (Caine, Ebert, & Weingartner, 1977; Wilson et al., 1987). Huntington's disease patients were found to use inadequate elaboration strategies during encoding, resulting in poor storage and subsequent recall of new information (Weingartner, Caine, & Ebert, 1979). However, subsequent research has demonstrated that the encoding deficits of HD patients are not as significant as those of KS or AD patients. Huntington's disease patients, but not KS or AD patients, benefit from verbal mediation strategies for enhancing memory (Butters et al., 1983; Granholm & Butters, 1988). On the other hand, KS but not HD or AD patients benefit from longer rehearsal times and restricting the amount of interference during the learning-recall interval (Butters, 1984). These data indicate that the memory deficits experienced by HD patients are not entirely attributable to encoding difficulties (see also Wilson et al., 1987).

Recent research has demonstrated relatively preserved recognition of newly presented material, despite marked deficits in explicit recall. Investigators using various paradigms (e.g., free recall of word lists, selective reminding tasks, paired associate learning) have reported that on-demand recall of new material is often as impaired in HD patients as in KS and AD patients (Caine, Ebert, & Weingartner, 1977; Butters et al., 1978; Granholm & Butters, 1988). However, HD patients show significantly better memory for the same information, often approaching that of healthy controls, when recognition paradigms are used (Butters, Wolfe, Martone, Granholm, & Cermak, 1985; Butters et al., 1986; Caine, Hunt, Weingartner, & Ebert, 1978). These demonstrations of near-normal recognition of material that cannot be recalled explicitly has led to the hypothesis that inefficient memory retrieval is the major source of poor memory performance in HD (Butters, 1984; Butters et al., 1978; Caine et al., 1978).[1] Brandt (1985) employed a "feeling-of-knowing" paradigm to test this hypothesis directly. Patients were first asked questions of general information (e.g., "What is the largest planet in the solar system?"). For questions answered incorrectly, they then rated their confidence that they could recognize the correct answer from among eight alternatives. The HD patients were as accurate as healthy control subjects in predicting what they would or would not recognize. However, whereas a strong feeling of "knowing for a fact" was associated with an increased response latency in the normal controls, this was not the case in the patients. That is, the HD patients spent no more time searching for information they thought they knew than for information they thought they didn't know. These results were interpreted as implicating defective metamemorial control processes that direct memory search and retrieval.

Certain aspects of implicit memory (the ability to learn general rules, or acquire skills and procedures) may be differentially impaired in HD. Martone and colleagues (1984) compared HD and KS patients on the acquisition of mirror reading skill (an implicit memory task), as well as on explicit recognition of the words read. On 3 consecutive days, patients were presented with word triads printed in mirror-image and were required to read them aloud. Some word triads were repeated across sessions and the remaining triads were unique. Skill learning was inferred from reductions in reading latency. Immediately after the last test session, patients were given a test of recognition of the words used in the skill-acquisition task. The KS patients demonstrated skill learning equal to that of normal controls, but were later unable to recognize the words they read. The HD patients showed deficient skill learning, but demonstrated both a significant reduction in reading latency for repeated triads over unique triads (a form of repetition priming) and normal recognition of the words. These findings compliment the demonstrations of normal verbal recognition and the previous finding that HD patients show abnormalities in motor skill acquisition (Fedio et al., 1979).

Several recent studies have focused on the selectivity of deficits in skill learning in HD (Heindel, Butters, & Salmon, 1988; Heindel, Salmon, Shults, Walicke, & Butters, 1989; Saint-Cyr, Taylor, & Lang, 1988). Bylsma, Brandt, and Strauss (1990) assessed mildly affected HD patients on a computerized version of the "bolt-head" maze, using three different routes. One maze route contained a predictable, repetitive pattern (e.g., UP, LEFT, DOWN, LEFT, UP, LEFT, DOWN, LEFT, etc.), and two routes were unpredictable. Patients produced learning curves equal to those of healthy control subjects for the unpredictable routes. Unlike control subjects, however, HD patients were unable to take advantage of the patterned route to learn the patterned maze in fewer trials. Furthermore, they showed no transfer of training across the three mazes. These results suggest that different aspects of procedural memory are differentially affected in HD. Recent demonstrations that semantic priming (another aspect of implicit memory) is preserved in HD while motor skill learning is deficient lend further support to this assertion (Shimamura, Salmon, Squire, & Butters, 1987; Smith et al., 1988; Heindel et al., 1989).

Few studies have examined visuospatial memory in HD. Moss and co-workers (1986) assessed visual recognition of spatial positions, colors, patterns, faces, and words in normal controls, HD, AD, and KS patients. The HD patients performed significantly worse than normal controls for all types of memoranda except words, again reinforcing the relative preservation of verbal recognition in HD. Jacobs and colleagues (Jacobs, Salmon, Tröster, & Butters, 1990; Jacobs, Tröster, Butters, Salmon, & Cermak, 1990) found immediate visual memory to be only mildly affected in early HD patients. On the Visual Reproductions subtest of the WMS-R, HD patients recalled and reproduced as many line drawings as controls, and significantly more than AD patients matched for level of dementia. Both HD and AD patients produced more prior-figure intrusion errors than controls, but these errors were significantly more frequent in AD than HD.

Assessment of remote memory, or memory for events preceding onset of illness, has revealed qualitative differences among patients with HD, AD, and KS. Albert, Butters, and Brandt (1981a, 1981b) reported that while HD and KS patients both show poor recall of newsworthy events and people, only the KS group displayed a temporal gradient. That is, the KS patients remembered more events from the distant past than from recent times, whereas the HD patients displayed poor memory for all decades assessed. Beatty and colleagues (1988) found that AD patients, like KS patients, produce a temporal gradient on an updated version of the same task, but the HD patients produced a "flat" profile. The lack of temporal gradient in the retrograde amnesia of HD patients is evident in both early and more advanced stages of the disease (Albert et al., 1981b). It is thought that the same retrieval deficit that results in poor performance on anterograde memory tasks affects performance on this task. If explicit recall deficits are due to inefficient retrieval strategies, then HD patients would be expected to find it equally difficult to recall events from all time periods.

Executive Functions

The pattern of neuropsychological impairment of HD is similar in many ways to that seen in individuals with prefrontal cortical lesions. These parallels are not entirely unexpected, given the reciprocal connection between the frontal cortex and the basal ganglia. At least five functionally specific, anatomically discrete pathways connecting the frontal lobes to the striatum have been described; three of them involve the caudate nucleus (Alexander, Delong, & Strick, 1986). Many early stage HD patients describe difficulties with planning, organizing, and scheduling day-to-day activities. Spouses and family members report that patients are less adaptable, behaviorally rigid, and get "stuck" on an idea or task. In early HD, impairment of daily functioning is more likely to result from these cognitive deficits than from motor impairment (Bamford, Caine, Kido, Plassche, & Shoulson, 1989). Similarities between HD and frontal lobe pathology are also reflected on neuropsychological tests. Both types of patients display decreased verbal fluency, poor performance on maze-learning tasks, difficulty compensating for postural adjustments, inability to switch cognitive sets, difficulties with abstraction, and a tendency to perseverate (Potegal, 1971; Butters et al., 1978; Fedio et al., 1979; Josiassen et al., 1983; Alexander et al., 1988).

Neuroimaging Studies in Huntington's Disease

Several lines of evidence suggest that the disorders of complex cognition seen in HD result directly from degeneration of the caudate nucleus, not from retrograde degeneration of the prefrontal cortex. First, patients with circumscribed lesions of the caudate nucleus display cognitive deficits strikingly similar to those noted in HD: difficulty with planning, sequencing, and attention; impaired verbal recall with relatively better recognition; and language abnormalities (Caplan et al., 1990; Mendez, Adams, & Skoog-Lewandowski, 1989). Second, measures of caudate atrophy on the computed tomography (CT) scans of HD patients correlate strongly with many cognitive measures, including several subtests of the WAIS and WMS (Sax et al., 1983) and "complex psychomotor" tasks, including the Trail-Making Test and the Stroop Color-Word Test (Bamford et al., 1989). Starkstein et al. (1988) found significant correlations between the bicaudate ratio (a measure of caudate atrophy) and performance on the Symbol Digit Modalities Test, and parts A and B of the Trail-Making Test. Impairment in everyday functioning, as indexed by the Total Functional Capacity (TFC) score (Shoulson & Fahn, 1979) or the Huntington's Disease Activities of Daily Living Scale (HDADL) (Brandt et al., 1984) is also related to caudate atrophy (Shoulson, Plassche, & Odoroff, 1982; Sax et al., 1983; Starkstein et al., 1988). In a very recent study, Starkstein et al. (1992) performed neuropsychological tests on 50 HD patients on whom brain magnetic resonance imaging (MRI) scans were also performed. Measurements of specific cortical and subcortical regions were differentially correlated with cognitive performance deficits. Tests requiring memory and rapid information processing were most highly correlated with atrophy of the caudate (but not putamen or thalamus) and frontal cortex.

The third line of research implicating the caudate nucleus in the dementia of HD comes from studies of cerebral metabolism. Positron emission tomography (PET) and single photon emission computed tomography (SPECT) studies of early HD patients indicate abnormalities in blood flow (Reid et al., 1988) and glucose metabolism (Hayden et al., 1987; Mazziotta et al., 1987; Berent et al., 1988) in the caudate, but not in the frontal cortex. Abnormalities of caudate glucose metabolism are correlated with lower Total Functional Capacity scores (Young et al., 1986) and performance deficits on the Verbal Paired Associates subtest of the WMS (Berent et al., 1988). Weinberger and colleagues (1988) found that the poor performance of HD patients on a computerized version of the Wisconsin Card Sorting Test (WCST) was not associated with hypoperfusion of cortex as it often is in patients with schizophrenia. This suggests that the disorders of complex cognition seen in HD are not attributable to intrinsic cortical pathology, but are more likely reflections of the primary neostriatal degeneration.

Treatment and Management of Huntington's Disease

There is currently no treatment to arrest or slow the progression of HD. There have been several experimental trials of putative therapeutic agents, but none has demonstrated a significant effect. An early strategy was to replace striatal gamma-aminobutyric acid (GABA), a neurotransmitter that is progressively depleted as striatal neurons die, with agonists. No ameliorative effects were noted (Shoulson, Goldblatt, Charlton, & Joynt, 1978; Foster, Chase, Denaro, Hare, & Tamminga, 1983). An alternate approach was to reduce levels of brain dopamine, because increased levels of striatal dopamine are noted at autopsy (Sanberg & Coyle, 1984). Dopamine antagonists tend to reduce involuntary motor symptoms, but have no effect on disease progression (Folstein, 1989). More recent trials have attempted to prevent or slow striatal cell death. Because administration of excitatory neurotransmitter glutamate (or its agonists) results in striatal pathology that closely approximates that noted in autopsied brains of HD patients (Coyle & Schwarcz, 1976; McGeer & McGeer, 1976), Shoulson and colleagues (1989) administered baclofen, a glutamatergic antagonist, to HD patients in a 3-year double-blind, placebo-controlled trial. They found no greater reduction in rate of progression in the baclofen-treated patients than in the placebo-treated group. Despite these findings, compounds with more specific effects on the glutamate system are under investigation, with the hope of finding an effective therapeutic agent.

Although it is not currently possible to slow the progression of HD, many of the disease's symptoms are responsive to therapeutic intervention, particularly when patients are earlier in the course of the illness. Chorea, but not the voluntary motor disorder, is often reduced by low doses of neuroleptic medicines (e.g., haloperidol, fluphenazine). Emotional disturbance and psychiatric symptoms are also responsive to pharmacological treatments: irritability is reduced by neuroleptics, anxiety by benzodiazapines, depression by tricyclic antidepressants, and hallucinations and delusions by neuroleptics. In addition, environmental and behavioral interventions can often reduce some symptoms. Modifying the patient's environment or daily routine to be less complex and more consistent, and removing potential irritants and anxiety-inducing stimuli, often results in reduced irritability and anxiety.

A major component of any treatment program for HD is genetic counseling. Persons afflicted with HD need to appreciate that each child they have has a 50% chance of inheriting the illness. Those who already have children often need assistance in deciding when and how to convey this information to their children. The recent development of a genetic screening test for HD (Meissen et al., 1988; Brandt et al., 1989) allows individuals at risk for HD to determine whether they carry the genetic marker that segregates with the disease in their family. Knowing that one does or does not have a high probability of developing HD allows the at-risk person to make more-informed decisions about marriage, childbearing, careers, and future care needs prior to the onset of symptoms. Also, awareness of the potential for depression, irritability, and anxiety may facilitate seeking treatment for these symptoms.

Neuropsychological Studies of At-Risk Individuals

Determining which healthy at-risk individuals carry the HD gene and will eventually go on to develop the disease has been a research goal for many years. First, a safe and reliable predictive tests would be very useful in genetic counseling. Surveys have indicated that the majority of people at risk for HD would want to take such a test in order to better plan their futures and to alleviate the anxiety of being at risk (Schoenfeld, Meyers, Berkman, & Clark, 1984; Tyler & Harper, 1983; Kessler, Field, Worth, & Mosbarger, 1987; Markel, Young, & Penney, 1987; but cf. Quaid, Brandt, & Folstein, 1987). Second, such a test would be of great scientific value, in that it would enable us to determine whether the gene responsible for the illness has subtle neurobehavioral effects prior to onset of clinical illness.

Past attempts at presymptomatic identification have examined physiological parameters (electromyography [EMG] and electroencephalography [EEG]), the effects of biochemical challenges, and PET imaging of glucose metabolism in the caudate (Petejan, Jarcho, & Thurman, 1979; Klawans, Goetz, & Perlik, 1980; Kuhl et al., 1982). However, these measures were found not to be adequately sensitive or specific (e.g., Young et al., 1987). Similarly, performance on neuropsychological tests has not provided an adequate preclinical indicator of HD (Lyle & Gottesman, 1977, 1979; Fedio et al., 1979; Strauss & Brandt, 1986).

Recently, a presymptomatic test for HD using a polymorphic DNA marker has been developed (Gusella et al., 1983). In many cases, this test can indicate, with greater than 95% certainty, whether an individual does or does not carry the HD gene (Meissen et al., 1988; Brandt et al., 1989). Individual reactions to learning that one probably carries the gene and will develop the disease have varied. However, severe depressive reactions have been rare, and most individuals appear to cope well with the information (Brandt et al., 1989).

The identification of groups of at-risk individuals who do and do not carry the genetic marker affords the opportunity to investigate the premorbid characteristics of these individuals. One recent study reported significant neuropsychological impairment in healthy "marker-positive" individuals. Jason et al. (1988) reported that at-risk individuals who carry the gene marker perform more poorly on the Visual Reproductions subtest of the WMS, delayed recall of the Rey-Osterrieth Complex Figure, the Wisconsin Card Sorting Test, and on two-point sensory discrimination. While potentially of great importance, this study has been criticized on methodological and statistical grounds by Strauss and Brandt (1990). In a larger sample of clinically well but marker-positive subjects, Strauss and Brandt could not detect any cognitive or emotional abnormalities associated with the HD marker. They suggested that neurocognitive deficits in HD are detectable only after clinical onset of the illness.

The ability to determine who at risk for HD carries the gene affords the unique opportunity to examine the evolution of a dementia syndrome. Longitudinal study of marker-positive at-risk individuals, presymptomatically and as the disease begins its relentless course, will allow a fine-grain analysis of the dementia of HD. Such knowledge will undoubtedly add much to our understanding of cognitive impairments associated with degeneration of basal ganglia.

Acknowledgments

This work was supported by grants NS16375 and MH46034. The authors thank Drs. Marshal Folstein, Susan Folstein, and Milton Strauss for their fruitful collaboration. Drs. Brandt and Bylsma are investigators in the Baltimore Huntington's Disease Center at the Johns Hopkins University School of Medicine. Dr. Brandt is also an investigator in the Johns Hopkins

Alzheimer's Disease Research Center and directs the Cortical Function Laboratory and Medical Psychology Clinic at the Johns Hopkins Hospital.

Notes

1. Several recent studies comparing HD patients to AD patients, matched for recall performance, have *not* found preserved recognition in the HD group (Kramer et al., 1988; Brandt, Corwin, & Krafft, 1992). In addition, Caine et al. (1986) found that verbal recognition memory was worse in HD patients than in equivalently disabled multiple sclerosis patients. Differences in methods of group matching and particular test characteristics may underlie some of the apparent discrepancies.

References

Albert, M. S., Butters, N., & Brandt, J. (1981a). Patterns of remote memory in amnesic and demented patients. *Archives of Neurology, 38*, 495–500.

Albert, M. S., Butters, N., & Brandt, J. (1981b). Development of remote memory loss in patients with Huntington's disease. *Journal of Clinical Neuropsychology, 3*, 1–12.

Albin, R. L., Young, A. B., Penney, J. B., Handelin, B., Balfour, R., Anderson, K. D., Markel, D. S., Tourtellotte, W. W., & Reiner, A. (1990). Abnormalities of striatal projection neurons and *N*-methyl-*D*-aspartate receptors in presymptomatic Huntington's disease. *New England Journal of Medicine, 322*, 1293–1298.

Alexander, G. E., Delong, M. R., & Strick, P. L. (1986). Parallel organization of functionally segregated circuits linking basal ganglia and cortex. *Annual Review of Neuroscience, 9*, 357–381.

Alexander, M. P., Benson, D. F., & Stuss, D. T. (1988). Frontal lobes and language. *Brain and Language, 37*, 656–691.

Bamford, K. A., Caine, E. D., Kido, D. K., Plassche, W. M., & Shoulson, I. (1989). Clinical-pathological correlation in Huntington's disease: A neuropsychological and computed tomography study. *Neurology, 39*, 796–801.

Bayles, K. A., & Tomoeda, C. K. (1983). Confrontation naming in dementia. *Brain and Language, 19*, 98–114.

Beatty, W. W., Salmon, D. P., Butters, N., Heindel, W. C., & Granholm, E. (1988). Retrograde amnesia in patients with Alzheimer's disease and Huntington's disease. *Neurobiology of Aging, 9*, 181–186.

Bell, J. (1934). Huntington's chorea. In R. A. Fisher (Ed.), *The treasury of human genetics* (Vol. 4, pp. 1–29). London: Cambridge University Press.

Berent, S., Giordani, B., Lehtinen, S., Markel, D., Penney, J. B., Buchtel, H. A., Starosta-Rubenstein, S., Hichwa, R., & Young, A. B. (1988). Positron emission tomographic scan investigations of Huntington's disease: Cerebral metabolic correlates of cognitive function. *Annals of Neurology, 23*, 541–546.

Boll, T. J., Heaton, R., & Reitan, R. (1974). Neuropsychological and emotional correlates of Huntington's disease. *Journal of Nervous and Mental Disorders, 158*, 61–69.

Borkowski, J. G., Benton, A. L., & Spreen O. (1967). Word fluency and brain damage. *Neuropsychologia, 5*, 135–140.

Brandt, J. (1985). Access to knowledge in the dementia of Huntington's disease. *Developmental Neuropsychology, 1*, 335–348.

Brandt, J. (1991). Cognitive impairments in Huntington's disease: Insights into the neuropsychology of the striatum. In F. Boller and J. Grafman (Eds.), *Handbook of neuropsychology* (Vol. 5, pp. 241–264). Amsterdam: Elsevier.

Brandt, J., Corwin, J., & Krafft, L. (1992). Is verbal recognition memory really different in Alzheimer's and Huntington's disease? *Journal of Clinical Neuropsychology, 12,* 773–784.

Brandt, J., Folstein, S. E., & Folstein, M. F. (1988). Differential cognitive impairment in Alzheimer's disease and Huntington's disease. *Annals of Neurology, 23,* 555–561.

Brandt, J., Quaid, K. A., Folstein, S. E., Garber, P., Maestri, N. E., Abbott, M. H., Slavney, P. R., Franz, M. L., Kasch, L., & Kazazian, H. H. (1989). Presymptomatic diagnosis of delayed-onset disease with linked DNA markers: The experience in Huntington's disease. *Journal of the American Medical Association, 26,* 3108–3114.

Brandt, J., Strauss, M. E., Larus, J., Jensen, B., Folstein, S. E., & Folstein, M. F. (1984). Clinical correlates of dementia and disability in Huntington's disease. *Journal of Clinical Neuropsychology, 6,* 401–412.

Brouwers, P., Cox, C., Martin, A., Chase, T., & Fedio, P. (1984). Differential perceptual-spatial impairment in Huntington's and Alzheimer's dementias. *Archives of Neurology, 41,* 1073–1076.

Butters, N. (1984). The clinical aspects of memory disorders: Contributions from experimental studies of amnesia and dementia. *Journal of Clinical Neuropsychology, 6,* 17–36.

Butters, N., Albert, M. S., Sax, D. S., Miliotis, P., Nagode, J., & Sterste, A. (1983). The effect of verbal mediators on pictorial memory in brain-damaged patients. *Neuropsychologia, 21,* 307–323.

Butters, N., Salmon, D. P., & Cullum, C. M. (1988). Differentiation of amnesic and demented patients with the Wechsler Memory Scale-Revised. *The Clinical Neuropsychologist, 2,* 133–148.

Butters, N., Sax, D. S., Montgomery, K., & Tarlow, S. (1978). Comparison of neuropsychological deficits associated with early and advanced Huntington's disease. *Archives of Neurology, 35,* 585–589.

Butters, N., Wolfe, J., Granholm, E., & Martone, M. (1986). An assessment of verbal recall, recognition and fluency abilities in patients with Huntington's disease. *Cortex, 22,* 11–32.

Butters, N., Wolfe, J., Martone, M., Granholm, E., & Cermak, L. S. (1985). Memory disorders associated with Huntington's disease: Verbal recall, verbal recognition, and procedural memory. *Neuropsychologia, 23,* 729–743.

Bylsma, F. W., Brandt, J., & Strauss, M. E. (1990). Aspects of procedural memory are differentially impaired in Huntington's disease. *Archives of Clinical Neuropsychology, 5,* 287–297.

Caine, E. D., Bamford, K. A., Shiffer, R. B., Shoulson, I., & Levy, S. (1986). A controlled neuropsychological comparison of Huntington's disease and multiple sclerosis. *Archives of Neurology, 43,* 249–254.

Caine, E. D., Ebert, M. H., & Weingartner, H. (1977). An outline for the analysis of dementia. *Neurology, 27,* 1087–1092.

Caine, E. D., Hunt, R. D., Weingartner, H., & Ebert, M. H. (1978). Huntington's dementia: Clinical and neuropsychological features. *Archives of General Psychiatry, 35,* 378–384.

Caplan, L. R., Schmahmann, J. D., Kase, C. S., Feldman, E., Baquis, G., Greenberg, J. P., Gorelick, P. B., Helgason, C., & Hier, D. B. (1990). Caudate infarcts. *Archives of Neurology, 47,* 133–143.

Conneally, P. M. (1984). Huntington's disease: Genetics and epidemiology. *American Journal of Human Genetics, 36,* 506–526.

Coyle, J. T., & Schwarz, R. (1976). Lesions of striatal neurons with kainic acid provides a model for Huntington's disease. *Nature, 263,* 244–246.

Cummings, J. L. (Ed.). (1990). *Subcortical dementia.* New York: Oxford University Press.

Dewhurst, K., Oliver, J. E., & McKnight, A. L. (1970). Socio-psychiatric consequences of Huntington's disease. *British Journal of Psychiatry, 116*, 255–258.

Farrer, L. A. (1986). Suicide and attempted suicide in Huntington's disease: Implications for preclinical testing of persons at risk. *American Journal of Medical Genetics, 24*, 305–311.

Fedio, P., Cox, C. S., Neophytides, A., Canal-Frederick, G., & Chase, T. N. (1979). Neuropsychological profile of Huntington's disease. *Advances in Neurology, 23*, 239–255.

Folstein, S. E. (1989). *Huntington's disease: A disorder of familes.* Baltimore: Johns Hopkins University Press.

Folstein, S. E., Abbott, M. H., Chase, G. A., Jensen, B. A., & Folstein, M. F. (1983). The association of affective disorder with Huntington's disease in a case series and in families. *Psychological Medicine, 13*, 537–542.

Folstein, S. E., Brandt, J., & Folstein, M. F. (1990). Huntington's disease. In J. L. Cummings (Ed.), *Subcortical dementia* (pp. 87–107). New York: Oxford University Press.

Folstein, S. E., Chase, G. A., Wahl, W. E., McDonnell, A. M., & Folstein, M. F. (1987). Huntington's disease in Maryland: Clinical aspects of racial variation. *American Journal of Human Genetics, 41*, 168–179.

Folstein, S. E., Franz, M. L., Jensen, B., Chase, G. A., & Folstein, M. F. (1983). Conduct disorder and affective disorder among the offspring of patients with Huntington's disease. In S. B. Guze, F. J. Earls, & J. E. Barrett (Eds.), *Childhood psychopathology and development* (pp. 231–245). New York: Raven Press.

Folstein, M. F., Folstein, S. E., & McHugh, P. R. (1975). 'Mini-Mental State': A practical method for grading the cognitive state of patients for the clinician. *Journal of Psychiatric Research, 12*, 189–198.

Foster, N. L., Chase, T. N., Denaro, A., Hare, T. A., & Tamminga, C. A. (1983). THIP treatment of Huntington's disease. *Neurology, 33*, 637–639.

Fuld, P. A., Katzman, R., Davies, P., & Terry, R. D. (1982). Intrusions as a sign of Alzheimer's dementia: Chemical and pathological verification. *Annals of Neurology, 11*, 155–159.

Gordon, W. P., & Illes, J. (1987). Neurolinguistic characteristics of language production in Huntington's disease: A preliminary report. *Brain and Language, 31*, 1–10.

Granholm, E., & Butters, N. (1988). Associative encoding and retrieval in Alzheimer's and Huntington's disease. *Brain and Cognition, 7*, 335–347.

Gusella, J. F., Wexler, N. S., Conneally, P. M., Naylor, S. L., Anderson, M. A., Tanzi, R. E., Watkins, P. C., Ottina, K., Wallace, M. R., Sakaguchi, A. Y., Young, A. B., Shoulson, I., Bonilla, E., & Martin, J. B. (1983). A polymorphic DNA marker genetically linked to Huntington's disease. *Nature, 306*, 234–238.

Hantraye, P., Riche, D., Maziere, M., & Isacson, O. (1990). A primate model of Huntington's disease: Behavioral and anatomical studies of unilateral excitotoxic lesions of the caudate-putamen in the baboon. *Experimental Neurology, 108*, 91–104.

Hayden, M. R., Hewitt, J., Stoessl, A. J., Clark, C., Ammann, W., & Martin, W. R. W. (1987). The combined use of positron emission tomography and DNA polymorphisms for preclinical detection of Huntington's disease. *Neurology, 37*, 1441–1447.

Heathfield, K. W. G., & McKenzie, I. C. (1971). Huntington's chorea in Bedfordshire, England. *Guy's Hospital Report, 120*, 295–309.

Heindel, W. C., Butters, N., & Salmon, D. P. (1988). Impaired learning of motor skill in patients with Huntington's disease. *Behavioral Neuroscience, 102*, 141–147.

Heindel, W. C., Salmon, D. P., Shults, C. W., Walicke, P. A., & Butters, N. (1989). Neuropsychological evidence for multiple implicit memory systems: A comparison of Alzheimer's, Huntington's, and Parkinson's disease patients. *Journal of Neuroscience, 9*, 582–587.

Huntington, G. (1872). On chorea. *Advances in Neurology, 1*, 33–35.

Illes, J. (1989). Neurolinguistic features of spontaneous language production dissociate three forms of neurodegenerative disease: Alzheimer's, Huntington's, and Parkinson's. *Brain and Language, 37*, 628–642.

Jacobs, D., Salmon, D. P., Tröster, A. I., & Butters, N. (1990). Intrusion errors in the figural memory of patients with Alzheimer's and Huntington's disease. *Archives of Clinical Neuropsychology, 5*, 49–57.

Jacobs, D. Tröster, A. I., Butters, N., Salmon, D. P., & Cermak, L. S. (1990). Intrusion errors on the visual reproduction test of the Weschler Memory Scale and the Weschler Memory Scale-Revised: An analysis of demented and amnesic patients. *The Clinical Neuropsychologist, 4*, 177–191.

Jason, G. W., Pajurkova, E. M., Suchowersky, O., Hewitt, J., Hillbert, C., Reed, J. & Hayden, M. (1988). Presymptomatic neuropsychological impairment in Huntington's disease. *Archives of Neurology, 45*, 769–773.

Josiassen, R. C., Curry, L. M., & Mancall, E. L. (1983). Development of neuropsychological deficits in Huntington's disease. *Archives of Neurology, 40*, 791–796.

Kaplan, E., Goodglass, H., & Weintraub, S. (1978). *The Boston Naming Test*. E. Kaplan & H. Goodglass, Boston.

Kessler, S., Field, T., Worth, L., & Mosbarger, H. (1987). Attitudes of persons at risk for Huntington disease towards predictive testing. *American Journal of Medical Genetics, 26*, 259–270.

Klawans, H. L., Goetz, C. G., & Perlik, S. (1980). Presymptomatic and early detection in Huntington's disease. *Annals of Neurology, 8*, 343–347.

Kramer, J. H., Delis, D. C., Blusewicz, M. J., Brandt, J., Ober, B. A., & Strauss, M. (1988). Verbal memory errors in Alzheimer's and Huntington's dementias. *Developmental Neuropsychology, 4*, 1–15.

Kuhl, D. E., Phelps, M. E., Markham, C. H., Metter, E. J., Reige, W. H., & Winter, J. (1982). Cerebral metabolism and atrophy in Huntington's disease determined by [16]FDG and computed tomographic scan. *Annals of Neurology, 12*, 425–434.

Ludlow, C. L., Connor, N. P., & Bassich, C. J. (1987). Speech timing in Parkinson's and Huntington's disease. *Brain and Language, 32*, 195–214.

Lyle, O. C., & Gottesman, I. I. (1977). Premorbid psychometric indicators of the gene for Huntington's disease. *Journal of Clinical and Consulting Psychology, 45*, 1011–1022.

Lyle, O. C., & Gottesman, I. I. (1979). Subtle cognitive deficits as 15- to 20-year precursors of Huntington's disease. In T. N. Chase, N. S. Wexler, & A. Barbeau (Eds.), *Advances in Neurology* (Vol. 23, pp. 227–237). New York: Raven Press.

Markel, D. S., Young, A. B., & Penney, J. B. (1987). At risk persons' attitudes towards presymptomatic and prenatal testing of Huntington disease in Michigan. *American Journal of Medical Genetics, 26*, 295–305.

Martin, A., & Fedio, P. (1983). Word production and comprehension in Alzheimer's disease: The breakdown of semantic knowledge. *Brain and Language, 19*, 124–141.

Martone, M., Butters, N., Payne, M., Becker, J., & Sax, D. S. (1984). Dissociations between skill learning and verbal recognition in amnesia and dementia. *Archives of Neurology, 41*, 965–970.

Mattis, S. (1976). Mental status examination for organic mental syndrome in the elderly patient. In L. Bellak & T. B. Karasu (Eds.) *Geriatric psychiatry: A handbook for psychiatrists and primary care physicians* (pp. 77–121). New York: Grune & Stratton.

Mazziotta, J., Phelps, M., Pahl, J. J., Huang, S., Baxter, L., Reige, W., Hoffman, J., Kuhl, D., Lanto, D., Wapenski, J., & Markham, C. (1987). Reduced cerebral glucose metabolism in asymptomatic subjects at risk for Huntington's disease. *New England Journal of Medicine, 316*, 357–362.

McGeer, E. G., & McGeer, P. L. (1976). Duplication of biochemical changes of Huntington's chorea. In A. Barbeau & T. R. Brunette (Eds.), *Progress in neurogenetics* (pp. 645–650). Amsterdam: Excerpta Medic Foundation.

McHugh, P. R. (1989). The neuropsychiatry of basal ganglia disorders: A triadic syndrome and its explanation. *Neuropsychiatry, Neuropsychology, and Behavioral Neurology, 2*, 239–246.

McHugh, P., & Folstein, M. F. (1975). Psychiatric syndromes of Huntington's chorea: A clinical and phenomenologic study. In D. F. Benson & D. Blumer (Eds.), *Psychiatric aspects of neurologic disease*. New York: Grune & Stratton.

Meissen, G. J., Meyers, R. H., Mastromauro, C. A., Koroshetz, W. J., Klinger, K. W., Farrea, L. A., Watkins, P. A., Gusella, J. F., Bird, E. D., & Martin, J. B. (1988). Predictive testing for Huntington's disease with use of a linked DNA marker. *New England Journal of Medicine, 318*, 535–542.

Mendez, M. F., Adams, N. L., & Skoog-Lewandowski, K. (1989). Neurobehavioral changes associated with caudate lesions. *Neurology, 39*, 349–354.

Mindham, R. H. S., Steele, C., Folstein, M. F., & Lucas, J. (1985). A comparison of the frequency of major affective disorder in Huntington's disease. *Journal of Neurology, Neurosurgery and Psychiatry, 48*, 1172–1174.

Money, J. (1976). *A standardized road map test of directional sense*. San Rafael: Academic Therapy Publications.

Moss, M. B., Albert, M. S., Butters, N., & Payne, M. (1986). Differential patterns of memory loss among patients with Alzheimer's disease, Huntington's disease, and alcoholic Korsakoff's syndrome. *Archives of Neurology, 43*, 239–246.

Petejan, J. H., Jarcho, L. W., & Thurman, D. J. (1979). Motor unit control in Huntington's disease: A possible presymptomatic test. In T. N. Chase, N. S. Wexler, & A. Barbeau (Eds.), *Advances in neurology* (Vol. 23, pp. 163–175). New York: Raven Press.

Podoll, K., Caspary, P., Lange, H. W., & Noth, J. (1988). Language functions in Huntington's disease. *Brain, 111*, 1475–1503.

Potegal, M. (1971). A note on spatial motor deficits in patients with Huntington's disease: A test of a hypothesis. *Neuropsychologia, 9*, 233–235.

Quaid, K. A., Brandt, J., & Folstein, S. E. (1987). The decision to be tested for Huntington's disease [Letter]. *Journal of the American Medical Association, 257*, 3362.

Reid, I. C., Besson, J. A. O., Best, P. V., Sharp, P. F., Gemmell, H. G., & Smith, F. W. (1988). Imaging of cerebral blood flow markers in Huntington's disease using single photon emission computed tomography. *Journal of Neurology, Neurosurgery and Psychiatry, 51*, 1264–1268.

Saint-Cyr, J. A., Taylor, A. E., & Lang, A. E. (1988). Procedural learning and neostriatal dysfunction in man. *Brain, 111*, 941–959.

Salmon, D. P., Kwo-on-Yuen, P. F., Heindel, W. C., Butters, N., & Thal, L. J. (1989). Differentiation of Alzheimer's disease and Huntington's disease with the Dementia Rating Scale. *Archives of Neurology, 46*, 1204–1208.

Sanberg, J. H., & Coyle, J. T. (1984). Scientific approaches to Huntington's disease. *Critical Reviews in Clinical Neurobiology, 1*, 1–44.

Sax, D. S., O'Donnell, B., Butters, N., Menzer, L., Montgomery, K., & Kayne, H. L. (1983). Computed tomographic, neurologic, and neuropsychologic correlates of Huntington's disease. *International Journal of Neuroscience, 18*, 21–36.

Schoenfeld, M., Meyers, R. H., Berkman, B., & Clark, E. (1984). Potential impact of a predictive test on the gene frequency of Huntington's disease. *American Journal of Medical Genetics, 18*, 423–429.

Shelton, P. A., & Knopman, D. S. (1991). Ideomotor apraxia in Huntington's disease. *Archives of Neurology, 48*, 35–41.

Shimamura, A. P., Salmon, D. P., Squire, L. R., & Butters, N. (1987). Memory dysfunction and word priming in dementia and amnesia. *Behavioral Neuroscience, 101*, 347–351.

Shoulson, I. (1990). Huntington's disease: Cognitive and psychiatric features. *Neuropsychiatry, Neuropsychology, and Behavioral Neurology, 3*, 15–22.

Shoulson, I., & Fahn, S. (1979). Huntington's disease: Clinical care and evaluation. *Neurology, 29*, 1–3.

Shoulson, I., Goldblatt, D., Charlton, M., & Joynt, R. J. (1978). Huntington's disease: Treatment with muscimal, a GABA-mimetic drug. *Annals of Neurology, 4*, 279–284.

Shoulson, I., Odoroff, C., Oakes, D., Behr, J., Goldblatt, D., Caine, E., Kennedy, J., Miller, C., Bamford, K., Rubin, A., Plumb, S., & Kurlan, R. (1989). A controlled clinical trial of baclofen as protective therapy in early Huntington's disease. *Annals of Neurology, 25*, 252–259.

Shoulson, I., Plassche, W., & Odoroff, C. (1982). Huntington disease: Caudate atrophy parallels functional impairment. *Neurology, 32*, A143.

Smith, S., Butters, N., White, R., Lyon, L., & Granholm, E. (1988). Priming semantic relations in patients with Huntington's disease. *Brain and Language, 33*, 27–40.

Speedie, L. J., Brake, N., Folstein, S. E., Bowers, D., & Heilman, K. M. (1990). Comprehension of prosody in Huntington's disease. *Journal of Neurology, Neurosurgery and Psychiatry, 53*, 607–610.

Starkstein, S. E., Brandt, J., Bylsma, F., Peyser, C., Folstein, M., & Folstein, S. E. (1992). Neuropsychological correlates of brain atrophy in Huntington's disease: A magnetic resonance imaging study. *Neuroradiology, 34*, 487–489.

Starkstein, S., Brandt, J., Folstein, S. E., Strauss, M. E., Berthier, M. L., Pearlson, G. D., Wong, D., McDonnell, A., & Folstein, M. (1988). Neuropsychological and neuroradiological correlates in Huntington's disease. *Journal of Neurology, Neurosurgery and Psychiatry, 51*, 1259–1263.

Strauss, M. E., & Brandt, J. (1986). An attempt at presymptomatic identification of Huntington's disease with the WAIS. *Journal of Clinical and Experimental Neuropsychology, 8*, 210–218.

Strauss, M. E., & Brandt, J. (1990). Are there neuropsychological manifestations of the gene for Huntington's disease in asymptomatic, at-risk individuals? *Archives of Neurology, 47*, 905–908.

Tröster, A. I., Jacobs, D., Butters, N., Cullum, C. M., & Salmon, D. P. (1989). Differentiating Alzheimer's disease from Huntington's disease with the Wechsler Memory Scale-Revised. *Clinics in Geriatric Medicine, 5*, 611–632.

Tröster, A. I., Salmon, D. P., McCullough, D., & Butters, N. (1989). A comparison of the category fluency deficits associated with Alzheimer's and Huntington's disease. *Brain and Language, 37*, 500–513.

Tyler, A., & Harper, P. S. (1983). Attitudes of subjects at risk and their relatives towards genetic counseling in Huntington's chorea. *Journal of Medical Genetics, 20*, 179–188.

Vonsattel, J. P., Myers, R. H., Stevens, T. J., Ferrante, R. J., Bird, E. D., & Richardson, E. P., Jr. (1985). Neuropathological classification of Huntington's disease. *Journal of Neuropathology and Experimental Neurology, 44*, 559–577.

Wallesch, C. W., & Fehrenbach, R. A. (1988). On the neurolinguistic nature of language abnormalities in Huntington's disease. *Journal of Neurology, Neurosurgery and Psychiatry, 51*, 367–373.

Wechsler, D. (1987). *Wechsler Memory Scale-Revised*. New York: Psychological Corporation.

Weinberger, D., Berman, K. F., Iadarola, M., Driesen, A., & Zec, R. F. (1988). Prefrontal cortical blood flow and cognitive function in Huntington's disease. *Journal of Neurology, Neurosurgery and Psychiatry, 51*, 94–104.

Weingartner, H., Caine, E. D., & Ebert, M. H. (1979). Encoding processes, learning, and recall in Huntington's disease. In T. N. Chase, N. S. Wexler, & A. Barbeau (Eds.), *Advances in neurology* (Vol. 23, pp. 215–226). New York: Raven Press.

Wilson, R. S., Como, P. G., Garron, D. C., Klawans, H. L., Barr, A., & Klawans, D. (1987). Memory failure in Huntington's disease. *Journal of Clinical and Experimental Neurology, 9*, 147–154.

Young, A. B., Greenamyre, J. T., Hollingsworth, Z., Albin, R., D'Amato, C., Shoulson, I., & Penney, J. (1988). NMDA receptor losses in putamen from patients with Huntington's disease (HD). *Science, 241*, 981–983.

Young, A. B., Penney, J. B., Starosta-Rubenstein, S., Markel, D. S., Berent, S., Giordani, B., Ehrenkaufer, R., Jewett, D., & Hichwa, R. (1986). PET scan investigations of Huntington's disease: Cerebral metabolic correlates of neurological features and functional decline. *Annals of Neurology, 20*, 296–303.

Young, A. B., Penney, J. B., Starosta-Rubenstein, S., Markel, D., Berent, S., Rothley, J., Betley, A., & Hichwa, R. (1987). Normal caudate glucose metabolism in persons at risk for Huntington's disease. *Archives of Neurology, 44*, 254–257.

10

Communicating (Normal-Pressure) Hydrocephalus

Michael Stambrook, Daryl D. Gill, Erico R. Cardoso, and Allan D. Moore

Normal-pressure hydrocephalus (NPH) has been traditionally recognized on clinical grounds by a triad of symptoms—gait and balance disturbance, bladder incontinence, and cognitive symptoms resembling dementia—as well as radiographic evidence of ventricular dilatation. This potentially treatable syndrome was first identified by Adams, Fisher, Hakim, Ojemann, and Sweet (1965) and Hakim and Adams (1965), with Adams et al. (1965) stating that "the importance of recognizing this condition lies in the opportunity it affords of rescuing from oblivion at least a few of the vast number of middle age or elderly patients now labelled as having senile dementia or 'cerebral arteriosclerosis' " (p. 117).

Whereas those sentiments, expressed approximately 25 years ago, are quite dramatic, particularly given the potential reversibility of the syndrome, the initial potential and "widespread interest and in some instances great enthusiasm for the surgical treatment of large numbers of patients with dementia" (Fishman, 1985, p. 1255) has failed to be realized by the subsequent surgical outcome literature. However, as dementia is rapidly becoming a pervasive significant clinical problem in our society with increasing lifespan across all ages, and the increased numbers of individuals over the age of 65 with the known risk of dementia increasing with decade of age (Strub & Black, 1988), attention remains focused on identifying situations where any particular patient's dementia is potentially reversible. Strub and Black (1988) review data indicating that, potentially, 6% to 12% of all presenting dementia may have hydrocephalic etiology. Hence, a working knowledge of the clinical features, the pathophysiology, the diagnostic workup, and the potential reversibility of the symptom complex is important for those who work with aging populations.

The study of NPH has presented neuroscientists with a number of ironies since its emergence as a clinical entity. Listing these not only assists in introducing this topic but also highlights and introduces some of the points to be made later in this chapter. In the first case, *normal-pressure* hydrocephalus may be, to some degree, a misnomer, because the intracranial pressure (ICP) was assumed to have been initially elevated (Adams et al., 1965; Fisher, 1977) and recent work has demon-

283

strated episodic elevations in ICP (Cardoso, Piatek, Del Bigio, Stambrook, & Sutherland, 1989). Second, NPH's potential reversibility distinguishes it from other dementing processes. Here, the initial excitement and hopes for treatment success have not been demonstrated in the literature. Whereas the current success rates for treating NPH have not fulfilled these initial hopes, research has, however, endowed the neurosciences with at least two lasting benefits: an increasingly sophisticated neurological workup for patients who present with accelerating cognitive deficits; and a Zeitgeist amongst neuroscientists to continue to search for treatments, in a field previously felt to be without much hope. Third, as shall be noted, NPH is not necessarily a dementia when it is first diagnosable. The cognitive deficits are generally mild when compared to the more pronounced physical symptoms of gait disturbance and balance problems that frequently are the earliest signs of NPH. Thus, whereas many are aware of the *classic* triad of NPH—dementia, gait disturbance, and incontinence—it needs to be emphasized that physical symptoms de novo in the context of mild changes in cognitive functioning should raise suspicions, with NPH one of the potential differential diagnoses. This fact is also important in distinguishing NPH from other dementias. Finally, whereas much has been learned regarding the hydrodynamics of cerebrospinal fluid (CSF) production, movement, and absorption, NPH may not be, by itself, in all instances the primary etiology of the patient's dementia. It frequently occurs secondary to other processes such as subarachnoid hemorrhage, intraventricular hemorrhage, meningeal inflammation, or head injury. As a result, the clinician must be aware of the potential multiple determinants of the presentation of NPH. As will be discussed below, there is vigorous debate in the literature on the appropriate diagnosis for hydrocephalic patients, their selection for treatment, and over an understanding of the pathophysiology of the disorder and its clinical features.

Central Nervous System Hydrodynamics

Hydrocephalus is a term referring to ventriculomegaly resulting from impaired CSF absorption. In the normal state, the craniospinal ventricular system is a closed system, filled with CSF, consisting of the cerebral ventricles, the central canal of the spinal cord, and the subarachnoid spaces that surround the brain and spinal cord (Jeffreys, 1987; Schmidley & Maas, 1990; Wood, 1980). Cerebrospinal fluid is produced in the choroid plexus within all the ventricles. It circulates through the lateral ventricles, the foramina of Monro, the third ventricle, the aqueduct of Sylvius, the fourth ventricle, and then exits through the subarachnoid space via the foramina of Luschka and Magendie. The CSF circulates through the subarachnoid space and then is reabsorbed into the venous blood system through the arachnoid granulations of the cranial venous sinuses and the epidural veins along the spinal nerve roots (Schmidley & Maas, 1990; Wood, 1980).

Hydrocephalus results when there is a disruption in this flow, and/or when there is an imbalance between production and absorption of CSF (Jeffreys, 1987; Sklar & Linder, 1984). This in turn decreases the compliance of the craniospinal space. The CSF pulsations generated by respiration and cardiac pulsations are magnified, producing dilatation of the lateral, third, and/or fourth ventricles (Cardoso, Rowan, & Galbraith, 1983).

As the dilatation occurs, there is a stretching to corticospinal axons and other nerve fibers as they arch around the increasingly distended ventricular system as well as, potentially, compromised blood flow due to similar stretching of the anterior cerebral artery and capillaries that provide blood flow to the frontal lobes. In addition, ventricular CSF seeps into the periventricular white matter, creating periventricular edema and loss of myelin. The clinical changes seen in NPH result then from the reduction in the arterial supply to brain tissue, the direct effects of compression, and edema of the periventricular white matter. The effects of the ventricular enlargement with the stretching of corticospinal fibers from the vertex, ischemia from arterial stretching and compression, and periventricular white matter injury may account for the frontal lobe–like (subcortical) dementia as well as gait disturbance and incontinence (Fishman, 1985).

Subtypes of Hydrocephalus

Hydrocephalus may be classified as *nonobstructive* or *obstructive*. *Nonobstructive hydrocephalus* or *communicating hydrocephalus* refers to an expansion of the ventricular system originating from an imbalance between production and absorption of CSF. This is also known as *normal-pressure hydrocephalus*. In contrast, in obstructive hydrocephalus, there is a blockage of movement of CSF on an intraventricular level from the lateral ventricles to the third ventricle, from the third ventricle to the fourth ventricle, or from an obstruction of the ventricular outlet foramina. These blockages prevent the flow of CSF from where it is produced to where it can be reabsorbed. With the advent of computed tomographic (CT) and magnetic resonance imaging (MRI) scanning, the diagnosis of obstructive hydrocephalus is less contentious as is the need for surgical intervention to remove the obstruction, if appropriate, or to divert the CSF. The previously used term *hydrocephalus ex vacuo* referred to ventriculomegaly as compensation for loss of brain cells secondary either to a degenerative brain condition such as Alzheimer's disease (AD) or through blunt head trauma. This is currently regarded as atrophy, rather than a true hydrocephalus, which involves CSF flow abnormalities.

Normal-Pressure Hydrocephalus Pathophysiology

In communicating (normal-pressure) hydrocephalus, ventricular dilatation is thought to result from abnormalities in the production or absorption of CSF, with some presumed abnormality within the subarachnoid space itself. Although communicating hydrocephalus is also referred to as NPH, unfortunately, this label of "normal-pressure" has, in some situations, been misunderstood to mean that the intraventricular pressure was always normal. However, as early work suggests (Fisher, 1977), the terminology was not meant "in any way to suggest that a ventricular enlargement developed under conditions of normal pressure, and from the beginning we assumed that initially the pressure had been elevated" (p. 271). In fact, recent work indicates that while the mean ICP for a sample of patients undergoing corrective surgery for NPH was within normal limits, all patients who improved demonstrated pathological intermittent elevations of ICP, manifested as B waves that occur most frequently in rapid eye movement (REM) sleep during continuous ICP monitoring (Cardoso et al., 1989). The B waves, in turn, might be produced by cyclic respiratory abnormalities (Unger & Cardoso, 1989).

The typical presentation of a patient suffering from hydrocephalus is the so-called clinical triad consisting of gait disturbance, urinary incontinence, and dementia. Many cases, however, do not present the complete "typical" triad. The central issue in the neurodiagnosis of these patients and their subsequent treatment is in appropriately determining that the symptoms are attributable to ventricular enlargement, not to non-neurological disease, or to neurological disease for which the prognosis is bleak, such as the case with AD. This is of critical importance and has been a subject of vigorous research focusing on developing greater accuracy in identifying: (a) clinical correlates of ventricular enlargement, (b) those clinical signs and symptoms that are attributable to ventriculomegaly as distinct from those potentially attributable to the disease process causing the ventriculomegaly, (c) the relative validity of imaging and diagnostic tests for hydrocephalus that maximize prognostic information while minimizing risks for the patient, and (d) developing ways to select those patients who have ventricular enlargement into groups who may differentially respond to surgical treatment. This is important because prognosis following shunting is better early in the course of disease progression (Cardoso et al., 1989). Thus, early diagnosis is desirable, before the full triad is manifested.

In understanding the clinical presentation, course, and potential surgical treatment effect, it is vital to understand the nature of the diagnostic entity causing the ventricular expansion, and to have an understanding of the pathophysiological processes that lead to the ventricular enlargement. There are a variety of causes of NPH that include severe head trauma, central nervous system infection leading to postinflammatory fibrosis and adhesions, and subarachnoid hemorrhage (Jeffreys, 1987; Ojemann & Black, 1982). In contrast, congenital malformations and neoplastic obstructions are potential causes of obstructive hydrocephalus. All of these processes involve either obstruction of CSF pathways, overproduction of CSF, or defective absorption of CSF (Fishman, 1980).

In NPH, it is thought that there is impairment or blockage in the subarachnoid space over the cerebral hemisphere convexities that hinders circulation and absorption of the CSF (cf. Fishman, 1980). The initial view (e.g., Hakim, 1972) was that there was initial high intraventricular pressure that caused the ventricular enlargement. As indicated previously, more recent work has demonstrated that on intracranial pressure monitoring, there are episodic spike waves of high pressure that have been labeled pathological B waves (e.g., Cardoso et al., 1989). It was classically believed that these B waves originate from episodic cerebrovascular dilatation caused by retention of respiratory carbon dioxide. However, recent work suggests that B waves are the result of retrograde transmission of abnormal respiratory rhythm into the craniospinal space (Unger & Cardoso, 1989). Figure 10.1 illustrates typical ICP monitoring with pathological B waves present.

As the ventricles expand, there is reduced blood flow to periventricular white matter (Pickard, 1982) and other surrounding areas due to the distention of the ventricles (Jeffreys, 1987). Mathew, Meyer, Hartman, and Oh (1975) have demonstrated decreased cerebral blood flow and cerebral volume in the territory of the anterior cerebral artery in hydrocephalic patients, which is absent in patients with other forms of dementia. Vorstrup et al., (1987) have also demonstrated preoperative

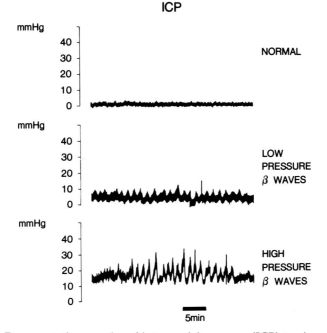

FIGURE 10.1. Representative samples of intracranial pressure (ICP) tracings in normal (top), and abnormal (middle and bottom) ICP samples. (From "Quantification of Abnormal Intracranial Pressure Waves and Isotope Cisternography for Diagnosis of Occult Communication Hydrocephalus" by E.R. Cardoso, D. Piatek, M. Del Bigio, M. Stambrook, and J. Sutherland, 1989, *Surgical Neurology, 31*, p. 22. Copyright 1989 by Elsevier Science Publishing Co., Inc. Reprinted by permission.)

abnormalities in cerebral blood flow corresponding to enlarged ventricles with increased flow, for some patients, following surgery. Permanent tissue damage was hypothesized where blood flow abnormalities persisted postsurgically. Following procedures that reduce intraventricular volume (such as lumbar puncture with CSF removal and CSF diversion shunt procedures), cerebral blood flow and cerebral blood volume increase, and these are correlated with clinical improvement (see also Mamo et al., 1987). The suggestion is that the changes in cerebral blood flow may be one of the mechanisms responsible for the improvement (Meyer, et al., 1985b). Grubb, Raichle, Gado, Eichling, and Hughes (1977) and others have also indicated that the anterior horn of the lateral ventricle undergoes the largest changes, with greatest compression of tissue due to the expanding ventricle in the frontal central white matter and in the corpus callosum (e.g., Jeffreys, 1987). Hence, there may be a pathophysiological basis for the disturbance of subcortical white matter functioning primarily in deep frontal lobe territory that is related to the clinical presentation and associated features.

Clinical Presentation

Normal-pressure hydrocephalus was first described as a clinical entity by Adams, Fisher, Hakim, Ojemann, and Sweet (1965) in the *New England Journal of Med-*

icine. Their case reports are instructive in describing the chronology of evolution of clinical signs and the reversal of symptoms following surgical treatment. One of their cases involves a 63-year-old woman who had slow onset of gait disturbance followed by months of cognitive slowness, concentration difficulties, memory lapses, and a more recent onset of urinary incontinence. A pneumoencephalogram demonstrated enlarged ventricles. A subsequent ventriculoatrial shunt resulted in significant improvement. However, following shunting the patient fell and fractured her hip, subsequently becoming lethargic, inert, and drowsy. During surgery, it was noted that the fall presumably had damaged the patency of the CSF drainage system and following repair, there was again substantial improvement in the woman's cognitive status. This woman's clinical course variability was felt to be a powerful demonstration of the progressive symptoms of communicating hydrocephalus, their initial reversal following shunting, the subsequent worsening as this shunt became ineffective, and subsequent reversal when the shunt was repaired. This initial presentation is noteworthy not only for the demonstration of treatment effectiveness, but also for the insight given into the evolution of the clinical presentation. Adams et al. (1965) state that "the cardinal early features of 'normal pressure hydrocephalus' in our patients were a mild impairment of memory, slowness and paucity of thought and action, unsteadiness of gait and unwitting urinary incontinence" (p. 122).

Physical Symptoms

Fisher (1977) has further elaborated on the development of the physical presentation in an analysis of 30 NPH patients. The clinical picture presented is consistent with other clinical descriptions that appear in the literature in addition to our clinical experience. Sixteen of the 30 patients demonstrated what was termed "definite improvements" following shunting and these cases were used to outline the specific deficits presumably attributable "solely" to hydrocephalus and to gain an understanding of the evolution of symptoms over time. In all 16 patients who improved, a gait disorder was apparent, and in 12 of these 16 cases, this symptom was the first to emerge. In contrast, of the 11 patients who showed no improvement following shunting, 9 demonstrated cognitive signs as the initial symptom.

The disturbance of gait has been described as having both pyramidal and extrapyramidal qualities and has been variously labeled gait ataxia, gait apraxia, frontal gait disorder, or magnetic gait. In the patients described by Fisher (1977), it was a specific difficulty with balance and a "slowness in correcting potential instability" (p. 274), with gait examination demonstrating short steps, wide-base, and unsteadiness. This is useful clinical knowledge in discriminating NPH from AD, for example, as patients with the latter disease often have significant dementia without gait abnormality (Fishman, 1985). Some patients demonstrate increased reflexes and extensor plantar responses and some may have frontal release signs such as tonic foot response, grasping, pouting, and rooting (Fishman, 1985). A number of patients demonstrated parkinsonian-type symptoms such as bradykinesia, cogwheeling, and rigidity (Jacobs, Conti, Kinkel, & Manning, 1976). This gait disorder must be differentiated from gait disturbances caused by other disease processes by both clinical analysis and exclusion (Fisher, 1982; Fishman, 1985; Rasker, Jansen, Haan, & Oostrom, 1985). Gait abnormalities can occur following,

for example, cerebral vascular accidents, Parkinson's disease, cerebellar degeneration, vestibular disorders, supranuclear palsy, myopathy, neuropathy, and rheumatoid arthritis. Gait abnormalities have also been noted following whole brain irradiation used in the treatment of cancer (Delattne & Posner, 1989). Thus, the clinical triad of NPH—mental deterioration, gait disturbance, and sphincter incontinence—needs to be examined in the context of other diseases generally and in terms of specific potential neurologically disabling diseases that could, by their action, lead to ventricular enlargement.

Urinary incontinence has been identified as one of the three cardinal signs of NPH in the review by Fisher (1977). He indicates that NPH incontinence is not usually characterized by urgency, but more so by what is described as a frontal lobe incontinence with diminished or no appropriate concern, an absence of awareness, and lack of embarrassment. Incontinence, it was felt, was frequently a late sign of NPH, occurring after gait disturbance and cognitive deterioration, and by itself is not a good prognostic sign for a positive surgical outcome. Others, however, have indicated that urinary frequency or urgency may be more readily apparent earlier in the disease progression (e.g., Strub & Black, 1988). Table 10.1 provides a summary of the clinical features of NPH.

Neurobehavioral Symptoms

One of the most typical features of NPH patients, at least in more advanced stages, is very notable deficits in initiation and behavioral and cognitive spontaneity. Pa-

TABLE 10.1.   Clinical Features of Normal-Pressure Hydrocephalus

Age at onset
Greatest incidence in sixth to seventh decade. Although idiopathic normal-pressure hydrocephalus occurs predominantly in the elderly, it may occur at any age after trauma, infection, subarachnoid hemorrhage, craniotomy, or tumor growth.

Duration
Can develop within days following traumatic or spontaneous subarachnoid hemorrhage or months following head injury.

Prevalence
6% to 12% of patients diagnosed with a dementia have hydrocephalus.

Course of illness
Usually progresses over a period of days or weeks following subarachnoid hemorrhage and weeks to months following traumatic brain injury in general or in ideopathic normal-pressure hydrocephalus. Intermittent periods of stability may occur.

Notable features of disease course
In contrast to Alzheimer's disease, a gait disturbance and, frequently, balance problems are initial symptoms, with only mild initial cognitive changes. Primitive frontal reflexes may be present, with urinary incontinence developing after the gait disturbance and mild initial cognitive deficits. Deteriorates into general akinesis, including mutism.

Other considerations
Risk factors for hydrocephalus include subarachnoid or intraventricular hemorrhage, head injury, meningeal inflammation, and craniotomy.

Pathophysiology
Symptoms are from stretching of arteries, capillaries, and fiber tracts; compression of tissue, as anterior horns of the lateral ventricles expand; and periventricular edema.

tients can be described as akinetic, apathetic, or inert. However, apart from these characteristic behavioral responses, a range of mood disturbances have also been reported (e.g., Price & Tucker, 1977; Pujol, Leal, Fluvia, & Conde, 1989). One of the most frequent of these is "depressive" reactions accompanying the incontinence and gait disturbances. Depression has been reported in 20% of NPH patients (Philippon, Ancri, & Pertuiset, 1971), which is substantively lower than the 60% rate reported for multi-infarct patients (Cummings, Miller, Hill, & Neshkes, 1987). At present, it is unclear whether these nominally depressive symptoms are distinct from the organic inertia or, whether these symptoms are a mild form of it prior to an apathetic or akinetic state. Similarly, it is unclear whether the depressive symptoms are organically based or secondary to the patient's observations of deterioration over time (e.g., Rosen & Swigar, 1976).

In contrast to the inert presentation, agitation has also been reported in a number of patients, although this seems more frequent in NPH patients following head injury. These include case reports by Crowell, Tew, and Mark (1973), Bowen, Verma, Bajwa, and Kusmirek (1990), Lying-Tunel (1979), Price and Tucker (1977), and Rice and Gendelman (1973). Typically, this aggression and hostility significantly improves after shunting. Since agitation is a consistent feature following coma that lasts longer than 24 hours (Gill, Sparadeo, & Parziale, 1988), there may be an interaction between the original traumatic injury-based sequelae and that attributable to the subsequent NPH. A case of chronic "sociopathic" behavior has also been reported in which the patient's social functioning stabilized after shunting (Peter, 1979).

Lastly, a few case reports have appeared with presumed psychotic symptoms such as delusions, visual hallucinations, and ideas of reference being associated with NPH (Lying-Tunel, 1979; Price & Tucker, 1977; Rice & Gendelman, 1973). However, as with agitation, it is unclear whether the symptoms are partially secondary to other factors. Because some of the patients described had psychiatric histories ranging up to 20 years, certain symptoms may have had premorbid origin and/or been influenced by cognitive deficits that restrict ongoing reality testing.

Neuropsychological Features

In outlining the neuropsychological profile of hydrocephalus, at least three considerations must be emphasized. First, regardless of the specific type of hydrocephalus studied, all patients potentially have deficits not only due to the hydrocephalus, but also due to its primary cause, such as a traumatic or spontaneous subarachnoid hemorrhage or traumatic brain injury. Second, in contrast with other neurological syndromes discussed in this text, hydrocephalus does not have as yet a widely recognized, well-documented, and clearly defined set of neuropsychological features. It is not possible to assess the stage in the disease course that patients are in when reviewing studies; hence, findings from different ends of the progression and severity continuum are combined into single samples. Third, and also in contrast with other dementing syndromes, cognitive findings are generally relatively minimal early on in the evolution of the disorder in comparison to other portions of the presenting triad of gait disturbance, incontinence, and potential reflex abnormalities, and later-appearing incontinence (see Strub & Black, 1988).

In general, based in analysis of the qualitative descriptions of the neurobehavioral presentation of patients suffering from hydrocephalus, the prototypical description is of primarily "frontal" deficits or subcortical deficits (Whitehouse, 1986), with problems in mental tracking, slowness in mental functioning, easy distractibility, and loss of initiative and spontaneity (Berglund, Gustafson, & Hagberg, 1979; Caltagirone, Gainotti, Masullo, & Villa, 1982; Stambrook et al., 1988).

In contrast to patients with, for example, AD or alcoholic dementia, NPH patients have received minimal systematic or comprehensive neuropsychological study. This need has been highlighted by Stambrook et al. (1988), who not only documented the presurgical neuropsychological profile of NPH patients, but also presented a standardized and quantitative assessment of presurgical-postsurgical change. As is demonstrated in Table 10.2, this group demonstrated diffuse neuropsychological impairments, most likely stemming from the clinically observed lethargy, inertness, and apathy. Also, despite postsurgical improvement being found in many mental functions (as well as gait and balance and bladder functioning), "cognitive functioning does not necessarily return to what could be considered normal, a fact that both patients and families, and the health care team, need to consider in deliberations regarding the costs and/or benefits of the anticipated surgery" (Stambrook et al., 1988, p. 329).

More specific deficits in cognitive functions can be outlined as follows:

TABLE 10.2. Presurgical and Postsurgical Neurophychological and Computed Tomographic Scan Data

Variable	Presurgery		Postsurgery		t (correlated sample)
	M	SD	M	SD	
Tapping (dominant)	23.33	(17.55)	22.00	(18.69)	0.45
Tapping (nondominant)	25.00	(10.86)	27.00	(12.46)	−0.56
Digit Span (age-scaled)	6.50	(3.16)	9.25	(4.02)	−3.05***
Arithmetic (age-scaled)	5.13	(2.42)	6.75	(4.06)	−1.64*
Immediate Semantic Memory	6.57	(5.60)	17.57	(9.31)	−3.94***
Delayed Semantic Memory	2.14	(1.68)	12.71	(9.55)	−2.64**
Proportion Retained-Semantic	41.86	(36.40)	64.86	(17.86)	−1.16
Immediate Figural Memory	2.14	(2.27)	4.43	(3.55)	−3.06**
Delayed Figural Memory	0.71	(0.95)	3.43	(3.66)	−2.61**
Proportion Retained-Figural	26.14	(38.31)	71.86	(30.45)	−3.74***
Trails A (seconds)	151.67	(69.91)	135.33	(80.03)	0.73
Trails B (seconds)	402.00	(89.31)	419.25	(30.70)	−0.09
Aphasia (rating)	3.00	(1.26)	2.33	(1.63)	3.16**
Spatial (rating)	2.83	(0.75)	1.67	(0.82)	7.00***
Mini-Mental State Examination	15.20	(7.51)	19.80	(8.23)	−1.94**
Total Cognitive (Mental State, Semantic Memory, Figural Memory)	35.67	(23.63)	57.56	(31.24)	−2.44**
Ventricle: Brain Ratio	18.45	(5.61)	15.92	(5.80)	−3.99**
Temporal Horn Width (mm)	9.57	(3.23)	7.14	(3.70)	−5.67***

* $p < .10$ one-tailed test.
** $p < .05$ one-tailed test.
***$p < .01$ one-tailed test.
Source: From Stambrook et al. (1988), with permission.

Attention/Concentration

Attentional deficits appear to be the most frequently cited and most prevalent of all neuropsychological findings in the literature. These include decreases in auditory attention span, ability to sustain attention, "mental tracking," ability to maintain "set," and resistance to distraction. Frequently, attentional deficits arise as low scores in digit span, arithmetic, or serial processing tasks (e.g., Lezak, 1983).

Memory

In specific contrast to patients with an Alzheimer's type of dementia, anterograde memory deficits in hydrocephalic patients are not prominent in the early stages: they appear to develop later as the condition progresses, after ataxia and incontinence are observed (Adams, 1980; Ogden, 1986; Torack, 1978; Wood & Jeffries, 1978). It is as yet unclear as to whether the memory deficits are initially simply secondary to attentional deficits alone (e.g., Lezak, 1983), or in fact constitute a "core" symptom of the disease. Fisher (1977) noted that approximately 50% of his patients with cognitive deficits had their impairments mainly in memory, although the level of severity ranged between slight to moderate. Apart from a loss of information over time (e.g., Black, 1982; Briggs, Castleden, & Alvarez, 1981), there have also been reports of confabulation in association with memory deficits (e.g., Berglund, Gustafson, & Hagberg, 1979; Gustafson & Hagberg, 1978). Deficits in attentional processes often accompany the memory deficits, although primary memory deficits have also been found in the context of average to above average attention (e.g., in case reports, Ogden, 1986). Similar to the majority of other dementing processes, remote memory appears relatively preserved unless the patient's disease is advanced to the stage of disorientation or other neurological disease processes are present that have neurobehavioral implications. In a comparison of patients with Alzheimer's disease and multi-infarct dementia, hydrocephalic patients have been found to be less impaired than the Alzheimer's disease patients in memory functions, but more impaired than the multi-infarct patients (Cooke, 1981).

Language

Essentially all basic language functions are preserved in patients with NPH, including speech, comprehension, reading/writing, and naming. Although, several exceptions have been reported, these appear secondary to other processes. First, there have been reports of decreased word fluency when this has been tested along with other frontal functions (Caltagirone et al., 1982). Second, patients with a severe form of hydrocephalus have at times presented with akinetic mutism (Fisher, 1977). Lastly, the prosody, initiation, and spontaneity of patients' speech may be consistently decreased within the context of more global behavioral changes that include apathy and lack of initiation. Regardless of whether these changes represent primary or secondary deficits, there are consistent reports of relatively preserved verbal functions at least early in the disease course (e.g., Verbal IQ on the Wechsler Adult Intelligence Scale [WAIS], Fisher, 1977) compared to lower Performance IQs (Botez et al., 1977; Fisher, 1977; Hartwig, 1983).

Visuospatial/Visuoconstructional Abilities

Spatial deficits appear to be the most debated type of impairment within the hydrocephalic population. Reports fall into three categories:

1. Initial absence of spatial deficits.
2. Spatial deficits that are secondary to more general decreases in speed of processing (e.g., Lezak, 1983).
3. Primary spatial difficulties such as those evident on the block design tests (e.g., Botez, Ethier, Leveille, & Botez-Marquard, 1977; Thomsen, Borgesen, Bruhn, & Gjerris, 1986).

Abstraction and Insight

In the early stages of hydrocephalus, abstraction abilities appear relatively preserved, apart from deficits that may be expected from decreases in attention and psychomotor speed (e.g., Lezak, 1983). In particular, the patient's awareness of his physical and mental deficits often appears good initially, and this has been regarded as the possible basis of the depression that is subsequently seen in many of these patients. However, exceptions have been reported by Gustafson and Hagberg (1978), who have documented patients with a lack of awareness or neglect.

Motor Functions

The majority of reports comment on decreases in psychomotor speed. Bimanual coordination also appears to be potentially affected, with at least one reported patient performing no better with two hands than with one (Botez et al., 1977). Psychomotor retardation and slow response speed were certainly prominent features of the condition previously outlined by Adams et al. (1965), and more recent studies have found that the greatest improvement, from before to after surgery, was found in the continuous reaction-time test (Thomsen et al., 1986).

"Frontal" Functions

Whereas we have emphasized the diversity of neuropsychological findings, there is mounting evidence of a core set of symptoms in normal-pressure hydrocephalus that can be very generally termed *frontal dysfunction*. This point has been previously emphasized by Berglund et al. (1979), Caltagirone et al. (1982), and Stambrook et al. (1988). These entail deficits in behavior (including apathy, lethargy, and inertness), cognition (including mental slowing, specific "frontal" deficits, and reports of perseveration) and general physical findings (such as a frontal form of incontinence, gait disturbance, and frontal-release signs). From a pathophysiological perspective, these frontal findings may be associated with the tissue damage that is possible with dilatation of the frontal horns of the lateral ventricles.

Other Neuropsychological Considerations

In light of the variability of symptoms noted above, it must be emphasized again that the neuropsychological profile alone is insufficient to derive a diagnosis of hydrocephalus. In each individual case, however, precise delineation of the patient's neuropsychological functioning may be vital in calling attention to potential mild forms of deterioration that, combined with subtle changes in ambulation, may portend an impending surgically treatable dementia. Neuropsychological findings are nonspecific to subcortical frontal pathology and must be embedded within the neurobehavioral presentation—generally, the neurological examination; the history of evolution of problems; the associated other medical findings; the psychiatric and neuropsychological history; and the diagnostic workup that includes both static imaging and dynamic studies such as cisternograms, blood flow studies, and intracranial pressure monitoring.

The incidence of severe dementia in patients over 65 is estimated to be between 4% and 5%, whereas an additional 10% of individuals have at least a mild form of dementia (Mortimer, Shuman, & French, 1981). Similarly, the incidence of incontinence amongst individuals over 65 is high: 11% in men, 17% in women (Yarnell & St. Leger, 1979). Thus, even when armed with obvious physical symptoms, as well as neuropsychological profiles, a variety of other general medical and neurobehavioral syndromes have to be ruled out. The neuropsychologist should therefore function as a member of a multidisciplinary team and be knowledgeable about clinical features and base rates of the range of disorders that can compromise physical, cognitive, and emotional functioning in the aging population. Table 10.3 presents a summary of the neuropsychological profile in NPH.

Diagnosis

Due to the substantial variability in results from the surgical treatment of hydrocephalus, careful attention has to be given to the diagnostic workup of patients suspected of having ventriculomegaly. Specific clinical attention and thought has

TABLE 10.3.   Neuropsychological Profile of Normal-Pressure Hydrocephalus

Attention/Concentration
  One of the primary deficits. Generally impaired in all patients early in illness. Specific impairments in auditory attention span, sustained attention, and "mental tracking," with occasional perseverative responding, especially later in the disease.

Memory
  Appears to be impaired later in course of illness. Debate on whether it is secondary to attentional deficits. Mild to moderate in severity, with rare instances of confabulation.

Language
  Generally preserved. Any deficits likely secondary to decreased initiation (e.g., akinetic mutism) or attentional deficits, or specific left hemispheric disease.

Visuospatial/Visuoconstructional Abilities
  Frequently but not consistently impaired. Deficits may be secondary to psychomotor slowing.

Problem Solving/Abstraction/Concept Formation
  Verbal IQ relatively preserved. Performance IQ frequently lower than visual IQ, partly due to slow psychomotor speed. Insight frequently adequate in early stages.

Affective/Behavioral Change
  Loss of initiation and spontaneity is a cardinal symptom. Frequently appears depressed. May see occasional psychosis or agitation—particularly when normal-pressure hydrocephalus is secondary to traumatic brain injury.

Other neuropsychological considerations
  Many deficits generally regarded as frontal in nature for both behavioral changes (e.g., apathy) and cognitive changes (e.g., low attention span, mental tracking, and reduced word fluency).

to be given to the selection of patients for surgical treatment. This entails weighing and evaluating the patient's clinical presentation, the general health of the patient, and other clinical factors against the reported general risks of mortality and morbidity inherent in major surgery in the elderly, and the specific risks associated with CSF diversion shunting (e.g., shunt malfunction, CNS infection, subdural fluid collections and, rarely, seizures).

There are specific clinical investigations that have to be conducted in terms of a general review of organ systems, followed by a general neurological examination with particular attention to mental functioning, neurobehavioral status, strength, sensation, reflexes, potential signs of intracranial pressure elevations, and focal neurological signs. In contrast to many of the other potentially dementing processes, a gait disturbance and incontinence should raise suspicion in the context of negative findings on a review of other systems. In situations like this, cognitive signs may be minimal, but nevertheless are noteworthy, completing the clinical triad of NPH. This is of some importance because the presentation of the full clinical triad has been associated with higher potential recovery of function post-surgically (e.g., Laws & Mokri, 1977). In rare instances, NPH shows an aberrant clinical presentation with episodic "drop" attacks and behavioral abnormalities. Frequently, patients such as these have been previously treated for Parkinson's disease (e.g., Jacobs et al., 1976). A high degree of clinical caution is thus required and the diagnostic tests acquire paramount importance, particularly in differentiating potentially treatable NPH in a patient with some degree of cortical atrophy from a similar patient who has AD.

In terms of laboratory investigations, these can be divided into two major groups: (a) those providing more static examinations of ventricular size such as the previously used pneumoencephalography and the currently used CT scanning and MRI scanning; and (b) dynamic studies such as continuous ICP monitoring and CSF flow studies. The essential issues with imaging studies have to do with the relative size of the ventricular system in relation to cerebral matter in general, and to the potential presence of mass lesions or periventricular lucencies. On these imaging studies, cerebral atrophy secondary to other dementing illness will present with ventricular enlargement that is in proportion to enlargement of cerebral sulci and sylvian fissure (see Fitz, 1988). It has been demonstrated that a high degree of association between dilatation of the temporal horn of the lateral ventricles in hydrocephalic patients and positive surgical outcome exists, which may be a useful measurement to take on CT scanning (Cardoso et al., 1989; Sjaastad, Skalpe, & Engeset, 1969; Stambrook et al., 1988; Svendson & Duru, 1981). Whereas the amount of cerebral atrophy is correlated with patient age, dilatation of the temporal horn is not, and may be a more specific marker of surgically treatable hydrocephalus (Stambrook et al., 1988). Figure 10.2 demonstrates CT scan findings of marked ventriculomegaly in the absence of cortical atrophy as well as the infiltration of CSF into periventricular white matter.

Normal-pressure hydrocephalus is marked by ventricular enlargement in the absence of substantive cerebral atrophy. This latter point may lead to difficult diagnostic issues, as atrophy increases with age and the essential discrimination would be based on whether or not the cerebral atrophy is out of keeping with the patient's age. The fact that the anterior portion of the lateral ventricles has been

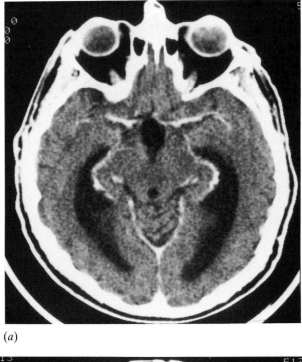

(a)

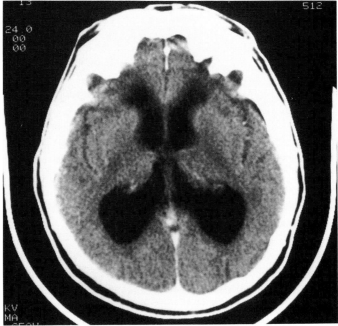

(b)

FIGURE 10.2. Hydrocephalic patient with characteristic computed tomographic (CT) scan findings. (*a*) Contrast-enhanced CT scan of a normal-pressure hydrocephalus (NPH) patient demonstrating pronounced dilatation of temporal horns of both lateral ventricles. (*b* and *c*) Marked ventriculomegaly in the absence of cortical atrophy surrounding the Sylvian fissures. Note the infiltration of cerebrospinal fluid into the periventricular white matter surrounding the anterior horns of the lateral ventricles. *Figure continues.*

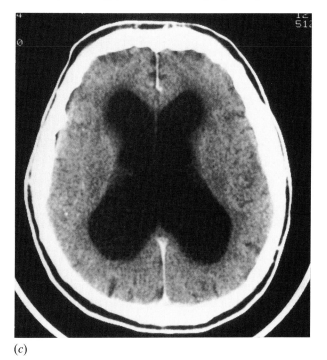

(c)

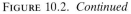

FIGURE 10.2. *Continued*

seen to be more distended than posterior portions in hydrocephalic patients may be useful in aiding this discrimination (LeMay & Hochberg, 1979).

Strub and Black (1988) indicate that for obstructive, noncommunicating hydrocephalus patients should, if medically able, be referred for surgery to divert CSF. For those patients who have communicating hydrocephalus (i.e., NPH), further investigations using more dynamic measurements are important. Here, there has been a wide range of evaluations used, from various measures of ICP, to CSF dynamic studies. The reason for the use of these other techniques is to increase the precision of the diagnosis and accuracy in the evaluation of potential treatment success. At times, lumbar puncture has been used, where 20 to 40 mL of CSF are removed to evaluate whether there are transitory changes in mental status and functioning, with improved functioning related to having potential benefits from surgery (Ahlberg, Norlen, Blomstrand, & Wikkelso, 1988; Fisher, 1982; Wikkelso, Andersson, Blomstrand, & Lindqvist, 1982). Also, radioisotope cisternography is frequently used. With this method, radioiodinated serum albumin is introduced by lumbar puncture, with sequential scanning undertaken over the next several hours, to 48 to 72 hours postinjection. The essential investigation here is an examination of the diffusion of the radiolabeled isotope through the ventricular system and over the hemispheric convexities. Abnormal diffusion exists when the ventricles are filled within 6 hours, there is a failure of the radiolabeled material to circulate out of the ventricles, or where it fails to circulate over the convexity of the hemispheres. These findings indicate an abnormality in the circulation and then absorption of CSF.

Intracranial pressure monitoring has demonstrated usefulness in determining the absolute level of ICP and in giving a longitudinal and dynamic picture of potential ICP changes. Research has demonstrated that patients with communicating hydrocephalus often have episodic periods in which their ICP spikes. In these patients, overnight recording is frequently useful. In a recent study by Cardoso et al. (1989), all patients showed abnormal intermittent elevations of ICP, and all patients improved after shunting, despite the fact that the mean ICP for patients was within normal limits. As Cardoso et al. (1989) indicate, "there is widespread agreement that ICP monitoring is the most practical and reliable investigation for the diagnosis of occult communicating hydrocephalus" (p. 25). The presence of B waves, regardless of size or number, is suggestive of potentially satisfactory response to surgery. However, in this study, isotope cisternography was not useful as a correlate of clinical improvement following surgery. Others have indicated that actual measurements of CSF circulation outflow resistance is useful in predicting potential surgical success (Editorial, 1990).

There is also some evidence that hydrocephalic patients may have optic nerve dysfunction. Alani (1985) has reported evoked potential abnormalities with postoperative improvement, suggesting that visual system fibers are potentially vulnerable for interference as the ventricles expand.

There is no single test used in the determination of potential surgery suitability (Ojemann & Black, 1982). The diagnostic task is a complex clinical one, integrating and collating many levels of data and placing them in a historical and humane context with each patient and family in determining whether the benefits and risks of surgery outweigh the risks of the natural progression of the disease process.

Surgical Treatment

Whereas there has been some interest at times in the pharmacological treatment of hydrocephalus aimed at changing parameters of CSF production and absorption, the primary methodology of treatment is surgical (Jeffreys, 1987). The purpose of surgical treatment is to divert (or shunt) CSF and allow it to be absorbed by the body more efficiently, without the attendant dysfunction and possible destruction of CNS tissue (Ojemann & Black, 1982). Shunt surgery was first attempted in the later parts of the 19th century, with significant attention being paid to the more rigorous evaluation of subject selection and surgical outcome following Adams et al.'s (1965) presentation of "Occult Symptomatic Normal Pressure Hydrocephalus". There is a wide range of success rates published in the literature regarding surgical outcome. These studies have been summarized by Caltagirone et al. (1982) earlier with surgical outcome ranging from 26% to 64% of patients improved. The literature is quite consistent in demonstrating that the opportunities for surgical successes are higher when the clinical triad is present, when there is, for the most part, recent onset and acute progression of symptoms and, as some report, a nonidiopathic causation. The following is a selective review of the literature highlighting both the emergent points and, unfortunately, the lack of clarity that is in some areas also present.

Shenkin, Greenberg, Bouzarth, Gutterman, and Morales (1973) found that 64% of NPH patients had a good response to shunting with gait disturbance being specifically associated with improvement. Isotope cisternography was not found to be useful in predicting success in surgery. Patients with cognitive findings as a predominant feature also had poor postsurgical outcome. Stein and Langfitt (1974) demonstrated that 80% of patients for whom the etiology of hydrocephalus was known showed surgical benefits whereas only 64% of idiopathic hydrocephalus improved. In this idiopathic group, no significant association could be found between postsurgical improvement and a variety of preoperative clinical features such as presence of the clinical triad, responses to isotope cisternography, or findings on the then-used pneumoencephalography. Jacobs et al. (1976) also demonstrated the significant relationship between gait disturbance and extrapyramidal signs and outcome in NPH patients, with shorter duration of symptoms having better outcome than patients with long duration of symptoms. Cisternography findings again had no relationship to surgical outcome. For the whole sample, 24% made complete recovery, 48% incomplete recovery, and 28% had no improvement. Black (1980) reported on 62 patients with NPH with 46% of patients with idiopathic normal-pressure hydrocephalus demonstrating an improvement, whereas 27% demonstrated "virtually complete recovery." He demonstrated that the strongest clinical predictor of good outcome was the presence of the complete clinical triad, with 61% of patients with this constellation of symptoms improving. Also, cranial CT scan evidence of ventriculomegaly with minimal atrophy predicted improvement. This study demonstrated, however, that there is a significant morbidity rate with the surgery, with 35.4% of patients having complications, with subdural collections, shunt malfunctions, and postoperative seizures being the most frequent types of complications. Black (1980) did not find that severity of disability was a factor in outcome. He did note, however, that the presence of incontinence was important in the clinical triad as, without it, only 31% of his sample did improve.

Meyer et al. (1985a) examined the time course of recovery following surgery noting that patients demonstrated improvements in activities of daily living within 2 months following CSF shunting (with change continuing up through the 7 months of followup). In contrast to this, improvements in mental functioning were delayed until 3 to 7 months following the procedure. In terms of gait dysfunction and sphincter dysfunction, all patients were noted to experience significant improvements and urinary continence returned within 2 months following surgery. These researchers noted that clinical recovery correlated with increased cerebral blood flow postsurgically. Laws and Mokri (1977) also demonstrated the substantial association between the clinical triad being present and surgical improvement, demonstrating that 74% of patients with the triad made gains following surgery. Meyer et al. (1985a) noted that the duration of symptoms was a potentially limiting factor on the improvement following surgery, as was extreme ventricular dilatation. This study also demonstrated that increases in cerebral blood flow correlated with clinical recovery.

Based on a follow-up of up to 157 months, Peterson, Mokri, and Laws (1985) demonstrated that 75% of the patients improved "at some time" following surgery and 40% of the patients experienced "continuous improvement." They again implicate the duration of symptoms as an important factor, stating that symptoms present for less than 24 months are associated with a more favorable surgical outcome than symptoms with a duration of greater than 24 months. A clinical presentation that includes a complete triad of symptoms was also important in determining outcome, with motor systems the most likely to improve following surgery. They were not able to document associations between ventricular size, periventricular lucencies, or cortical atrophy and clinical recovery and outcome, and found that discussions regarding improvement needed to be tempered with the observed 31% rate of morbidity for complications postsurgically. These complications included subdural fluid collections, seizures, infections, and hemiparesis, with no deaths being associated with complications in this series of patients. A further discussion of this issue pertaining to shunt malfunctioning can be found in Sekhar, Moody, and Guthkeich (1982).

The association of the primary gait disturbance with outcome was also documented in Black, Ojemann, & Tzouras (1985), with 77% of patients with a primary gait disturbance recovering, whereas only 42% of those for whom gait disturbance was not a primary presenting problem making gains. Interestingly, in this study, improvement was noted even for those patients who did have cortical atrophy documented on CT scanning. Temporal horn dilation in the context of large ventricles was also noted as associated with clinical improvement. Black et al. (1985) state that reasonable success rates following surgical treatment of hydrocephalus can be attained by selecting patients for whom gait disturbance is a major clinical factor, where patients have very large ventricles and pathological B-wave activity on ICP long-term recording, and by not operating on patients where dementia appears alone. They also state that evidence of cerebral vascular disease does not necessarily rule out a potential good surgical response. The importance of the gait disturbance occurring prior to the onset of dementia in being a predictor of positive surgical outcome has also been highlighted by Graff-Radford and Godersky (1986).

Thomsen et al., (1986) report that the duration of symptoms was important in subject selection and that patients with known causes of NPH had better treatment outcome than those that had idiopathic NPH. This study is noteworthy in that Thomsen et al. (1986) attempted to grade recovery not on subjective indices used by neurosurgeons or other collaborators, but on neuropsychological assessment data. They demonstrated that a known cause, a short history, the presence of periventricular hypodensities, the absence of atrophy, and a measurement of conductance-to-outflow of CSF can be used collectively to improve subject selection for surgery. Benzel, Pelletier, and Levy (1990) reported that CT scan findings such as ventricular enlargement, an absence of both cortical atrophy and Sylvian fissure enlargement, and the presence of the clinical triad all contributed to the diagnosis of surgically correctable hydrocephalus. Based on a sample of 37 patients, 70% were found to improve following surgery, with 75% who had the clinical triad improving. Improvement was evident in 67% of those who only had one or two elements of the triad. Urinary incontinence was stronger as a single predictor of outcome than gait disturbance or dementia.

Behavioral and Environmental Interventions

Whereas neuropsychological assessment is an important tool in the multisystem workup of patients suspected of suffering from NPH, it is also an important source of neurobehavioral data to assist in the development of individually tailored non-invasive behavioral and environmental interventions. Although for carefully selected patients surgical intervention can result in moderate to significant improvement in gait, urinary control, and cognitive functioning, there are patients who may not be candidates for surgery or who may demonstrate little or no recovery following surgery. Skilled nursing, home management, and/or self-control techniques are required to manage the long-term consequences of difficulties in mobility, urinary continence, and cognition.

Gait Disturbance

There are many potential contributing causes to gait disturbance, particularly in the elderly (e.g., sensory, vestibular, proprioceptive, musculoskeletal, hypotensive and other cardiovascular, psychiatric, and medications; Tinnetti, 1989), and the neuropsychologist plays an important role in uncovering other contributing factors through assessment of, for example, potential deficits in visuospatial, perceptual-organizational, attention and concentration resources, psychomotor integration, motor and ideational planning, and emotional functioning domains. In addition, the neuropsychologist may be involved in both environmental assessment and intervention. Tideiksaar (1986) lists simple preventative environmental strategies to reduce falls, such as attending to stability of chairs and tables, appropriate walking aids, adaptive footwear, seating, and washroom adaptations. Assessment checklists (Tideiksaar, 1986) that target potential home hazards may be administered to caregivers and relatives. Also, the neuropsychologist can assist physical therapists in selecting optimal training methods for gait retraining, transferring, positioning, and seating based on a knowledge of the patient's cognitive strengths and weaknesses.

Urinary Incontinence

Urinary incontinence is a significant cause of dependency and psychological distress among the elderly. Patients find their incontinence to be embarrassing, distressing, and inconvenient, and it is associated with increased nursing and physical care requirements (Ouslander & Abelson, 1990). Also, incontinence is associated with skin irritation and urinary tract infection. The neuropsychologist can provide interventions at both the patient and treatment team levels to ameliorate this problem. Schnelle, Newman, and Fogarty (1990) point out that whereas potential treatments for incontinence may be more time consuming than changing patients (i.e., toileting), there are compelling medical and psychological reasons to implement intervention programs. The neuropsychologist, contributing to the diagnostic workup for incontinence and in determining appropriate treatment direction, will need to attend to the neurobehavioral status of the patient in terms of precursors of incontinence, as well as the patient's ability to profit from different treatment options. By virtue of behavioral training, the neuropsychologist is in a good position to provide a behavioral assessment of the incontinence, as well as to potentially shape both the patient's and the treatment team's behavior. Potential treatments following general medical, urodynamic, and neuropsychological assessment may include what has been termed *habit training* (voiding schedule adjusted to meet needs of patient), *bladder training* (voiding schedule is gradually lengthened to break the habit of frequent voiding), contingency management (reinforcing on continent behaviors [toileting, appropriate hygiene]), and biofeedback (Burgio & Engel, 1987). Unfortunately, for seriously compromised patients, habit training would be the method of choice.

Cognition

Whereas there is a generally consistent neuropsychological/neurobehavioral pattern of symptoms associated with NPH, there may be wide variability in symptom severity and symptom profile over patients given individual variability in the underlying neurological etiology of the disorder and functional neuropsychological localization. Given this variability, there can be no single prescriptive cognitive rehabilitation approach. Each patient's unique set of strengths and weaknesses must be carefully gauged, and ecologically valid treatments put in place that focus on real-life attainable goals. For example, for patients with *frontal-lobe* impairments with concomitant mental tracking deficits, intact verbal processing can be used to remediate difficulties in attention, concentration, and planning through mental and visual prompting, checklists, schedule planners, and a concrete, predictable environment that provides structure. Unfortunately, there is a lack of a substantive literature providing guidelines for practitioners working in geriatric cognitive rehabilitation and, specifically, with hydrocephalic dementia, keeping in mind the unique issues in implementing relationship-based psychotherapeutic interventions with the elderly (Carstensen & Edelstein, 1987).

Conclusions

Cumulatively, the results from surgical outcome studies demonstrate that selected patients who are well diagnosed can benefit substantially from technically correct shunting procedures to divert CSF around blockages to cavities that can absorb it without damage. The central features that seem important are the demonstration of ventriculomegaly with minimal cortical atrophy; specific dilatation of the temporal horns of the lateral ventricles; the presence of pathological ICP spikes (B waves) seen in continuous ICP monitoring; and the presence of the complete clinical triad including frontal lobe-like neurobehavioral signs, a short duration, and with the initial presentation being of gait disturbance and mild cognitive deficits. Also, nonidiopathic hydrocephalic patients seem to have greater potential to benefit from surgery. Table 10.4 outlines prognostic factors useful in identifying potentially surgically treatable NPH patients. There is a balance needed here in the workup of hydrocephalic patients in terms of the invasiveness of diagnostic procedures used that are part of the assessment of hydrocephalus and in terms of the less than 1:1 relationship between diagnostic results and surgical outcome.

The literature on NPH, unfortunately, is replete with studies with small samples, a relative absence of reported statistical tests demonstrating the robustness of findings, multiple statistical tests in the absence of corrections for Type-1 error rate, and the use of a variety of qualitative, unstandardized ratings and reports that do not have demonstrated reliability or validity. Vanneste and Van Acker (1990) have also recently made this point, stating that unfortunately the "proliferation of research and clinical articles further increased the complexity of the puzzle, without clarifying the problem on how patients with uncertain NPH should

TABLE 10.4. Prognostic Factors in Shunt Surgery

Positive Prognostic Variables
  Short history of complaints
  Cause secondary to known etiology (i.e., infection,
    subarachnoid hemorrhage, trauma)
  Predominance of gait impairment
  Mild cognitive impairment
  Complete triad of symptoms
  No (or minimal) cerebral atrophy
  Dilated temporal horns of lateral ventricles
  Presence of pathological B waves on ICP monitoring

Variables Not Contributing to Positive Prognosis
  Periventricular lucencies
  Size of ventricles
  Abnormal isotope cisternography
  Predominance of dementia

Note: ICP = intracranial pressure.

be managed" (p. 567). Whereas there are earnest attempts to examine improvement following surgery, given the absence of a high success rate, and in understanding the evolution of the clinical picture in NPH, these are substantive factors that must be addressed in future research. These issues require further study focused on greater specification of sample composition, and examination and separation of coexistent psychiatric, addictive, and general medical disorders, all of which can impact on both quality of life and neuropsychological functioning. Ideally, future research on these aspects of NPH will include replicatable, quantifiable, and stand-ardized indices of both presurgical patient status and postsurgical outcome meas-ures.

The central issue in the appropriate management of patients with presumed hydrocephalus concerns accurately identifying patients for whom surgical inter-vention has an effect in ameliorating patient complaints, patient morbidity, and/or the family burden or, at least, arrest what may be the projected decline in functioning as the ventriculomegaly increases. In those patients for whom the hydrocephalus is secondary to another disease process, these factors must be eval-uated more specifically to disentangle the specific effects of hydrocephalus from what may be the more specific effects of other neurologically potent diagnoses that also impact on adaptive functioning, cognitive functioning, and quality of life. Neuropsychologists are in a unique position to provide valuable input to assist in the diagnostic workup of patients, to provide measurement of changes in neuro-behavioral functioning and quality of life, to collaborate in developing a broader understanding of the brain-behavior relationships in NPH, and in assisting treat-ment teams and families in providing optimal and humane care for patients who have long-term residual deficits in functioning.

References

Adams, R. D. (1980). Altered cerebrospinal fluid dynamics in relation to dementia and aging. In L. Amaducci, A. N. Davison, & P. Antuono (Eds.), *Aging of the brain and dementia*. New York: Raven Press.

Adams, R. D., Fisher, C. M., Hakim, S., Ojemann, R. G., & Sweet, W. H. (1965). Symptomatic occult hydrocephalus with "normal" cerebrospinal fluid pressure. *New England Journal of Medicine, 273* (3), 117–126.

Ahlberg, J., Norlen, L., Blomstrand, C., & Wikkelso, C. (1988). Outcome of shunt operation on urinary incontinence in normal pressure hydrocephalus predicted by lumbar puncture. *Journal of Neurology, Neurosurgery and Psychiatry, 51*, 105–108.

Alani, S. M. (1985). Pattern-reveral visual evoked potentials in patients with hydrocephalus. *Journal of Neurosurgery, 62*, 234–237.

Benzel, E., Pelletier, A., & Levy, P. (1990). Communicating hydrocephalus in adults: Prediction of outcome after ventricular shunting procedures. *Neurosurgery, 26*(4), 655–660.

Berglund, M., Gustafson, L., & Hagberg, B. (1979). Amnestic-confabulatory syndrome in hydrocephalic dementia and Korsakoff's psychosis in alcoholism. *Acta Psychiatrica Scandinavica, 60*, 323–333.

Black, P. (1980). Idiopathic normal-pressure hydrocephalus. Results of shunting in 62 patients. *Journal of Neurosurgery, 52*, 371–377.

Black, P. (1982). Normal pressure hydrocephalus: Current understanding of diagnostic tests and shunting. *Postgraduate Education, 71*(2), 57–67.

Black, P., Ojemann, R., & Tzouras, A. (1985). CSF shunts for dementia, incontinence, and gait disturbance. *Clinical Neurosurgery, 32*, 632–656.

Botez, M. I., Ethier, R., & Leveille, J., & Botez-Marquard, T. A. (1977). A syndrome of early recognition of occult hydrocephalus and cerebral atrophy. *Quarterly Journal of Medicine, 46*(183), 365–380.

Bowen, M., Verma, A., Bajwa, S., & Kusmirek, L. (1990). Pseudopsychopathic syndrome in hydrocephalus: A case report and review. *Neurosurgery, 26*(4), 661–663.

Briggs, R. S., Castleden, C. M., & Alvarez, A. S. (1981). Normal pressure hydrocephalus in the elderly: A treatable cause of dementia? *Age and Ageing, 10*, 254–258.

Burgio, K. L., & Engel, B. T. (1987). Urinary incontinence: Behavioral assessment and treatment. In L. L. Carstensen & B. A. Edelstein (Eds.), *Handbook of clinical gerontology* (pp. 252–266). New York: Pergamon Press.

Caltagirone, C., Gainotti, G., Masullo, C., & Villa, E. (1982). Neurophysiological study of normal pressure hydrocephalus. *Acta Psychiatrica Scandinavica, 63*, 93–100.

Carstensen, L. L., & Edelstein, B. A. (Eds.). (1987). *Handbook of clinical gerontology.* New York: Pergamon Press.

Cardoso, E. R., Piatek, P., Del Bigio, M., Stambrook, M., & Sutherland, J. (1989). Quantification of abnormal intracranial pressure waves and isotope cisternography for diagnosis of occult communicating hydrocephalus. *Surgical Neurology, 31*, 20–27.

Cardoso, E. R., Rowan, J., & Galbraith, S. (1983). Analysis of the cerebrospinal fluid pulse wave in intracranial pressure. *Journal of Neurosurgery, 59*, 817–812.

Cooke, N. A. (1981). Neuropsychological performance in adults with normal pressure hydrocephalus. *Dissertation Abstracts International, 42*(3), 1146-B.

Crowell, R. M., Tew, J. M., & Mark, V. H. (1973). Aggressive dementia associated with normal pressure hydrocephalus. *Neurology, 23*, 461–464.

Cummings, J. L., Miller, B., Hill, M. A., & Neshkes, R. (1987). Neuropsychiatric aspects of multi-infarct dementia and dementia of the Alzheimer type. *Archives of Neurology, 44*, 389–393.

Delattne, J., & Posner, J. B. (1989). Neurological complications of chemotherapy and radiation therapy. In M. J. Aminoff (Ed.), *Neurology and general medicine.* New York: Churchill Livingstone.

Editorial. (1990). Normal pressure hydrocephalus. *Lancet, 335*(8680), 22.

Fisher, C. M. (1977). The clinical picture in occult hydrocephalus. *Clinical Neurosurgery, 24*, 270–284.

Fisher, C. M. (1982). Hydrocephalus as a cause of disturbances of gait in the elderly. *Neurology, 32*, 1358–1363.

Fishman, R. A. (1980). *Cerebrospinal fluid in diseases of the nervous system.* Philadelphia: W. B. Saunders Company.

Fishman, R. (1985). Normal-pressure hydrocephalus and arthritis. *New England Journal of Medicine, 312*(19), 1255–1256.

Fitz, C. R. (1988). Disorders of ventricles and CSF spaces. *Seminars in Ultrasound, CT, and MR, 9*(3), 216–230.

Gill, D. D., Sparadeo, F., & Parziale, J. (1988). Agitation and acute head injury rehabilitation. *Archives of Physical Medicine and Rehabilitation, 69*, 722.

Graff-Radford, N., & Godersky, J. (1986). Normal-pressure hydrocephalus. *Archives of Neurology, 43*, 940–942.

Grubb, R. L., Raichle, M., Gado, M. H., Eichling, J., & Hughes, C. P. (1977). Cerebral blood flow, oxygen utilization, and blood volume in dementia. *Neurology, 27*, 905–910.

Gustafson, L., & Hagberg, B. (1978). Recovery in hydrocephalic dementia after shunt operation. *Journal of Neurology, Neurosurgery and Psychiatry, 41*, 940–947.

Hakim, S. (1972). Biomechanics of hydrocephalus. In J. C. Harbert (Eds.), *Cisternography and hydrocephalus* (pp. 25–56). Springfield, IL: Charles Thomas.

Hakim, S., & Adams, R. D. (1965). The special clinical problem of symptomatic hydrocephalus with normal cerebrospinal fluid pressure. *Journal of Neurological Science, 2*, 307–327.

Hartwig, W. (1983). Neuropsychological assessment of normal pressure hydrocephalus: Onset of gait abnormality before dementia predicts good surgical outcome. *Clinical Neuropsychology, 5*(2), 88–92.

Jacobs, L., Conti, D., Kinkel, W., Manning, J. (1976). "Normal pressure" hydrocephalus. *Journal of the American Medical Association, 235*(5), 510–512.

Jeffreys, R. V. (1987). Hydrocephalus. In J. D. Millder (Ed.), *Northfield's surgery of the central nervous system* (pp. 543–573). Edinburgh: Blackwell.

Laws, E., & Mokri, R. (1977). Occult hydrocephalus: Results of shunting correlated with diagnostic tests. *Clinical Neurosurgery, 24*, 316–333.

LeMay, M., & Hochberg, F. H. (1979). Ventricular differences between hydrostatic hydrocephalus and hydrocephalus ex vacuo by computed tomography. *Neuroradiology, 17*, 191–195.

Lezak, M. D. (1983). *Neuropsychological assessment* (2nd ed.). New York: Oxford University Press.

Lying-Tunel, U. (1979). Psychotic symptoms in normal-pressure hydrocephalus. *Acta Psychiatrica Scandinavica, 59*, 415–419.

Mamo, H. L., Meric, P. C., Ponsin, J. C., Rey, A. C., Luft, A. G., & Seylaz, J. A. (1987). Cerebral blood flow in normal pressure hydrocephalus. *Stroke, 18*, 1074–1080.

Mathew, N. T., Meyer, J. S., Hartman, A., & Oh, E. O. (1975). Abnormal cerebrospinal fluid-blood flow dynamics. *Archives of Neurology, 32*, 657–664.

Meyer, J. S., Kitagawa, Y., Tanahashi, N., Tachibana, H., Kandula, P., Cech, D., Clifton, G., & Rose, J., & Grossman, R. G. (1985a). Evaluation of treatment of normal-pressure hydrocephalus. *Journal of Neurosurgery, 62*, 513–521.

Meyer, J. S., Kitagawa, Y., Tanashashi, N., Tachibana, H., Kandula, P., Cech, D. A., Rose, J. E., & Grossman, R. G. (1985b). Pathogenesis of normal-pressure hydrocephalus—preliminary observations. *Surgical Neurology, 23*, 121–133.

Mortimer, J. A., Shumon, L. D., & French, L. R. (1981). Epidemiology of dementing illness. In J. A. Mortimer & L. N. Shumon (Eds.), *The epidemiology of dementia.* New York: Oxford University Press.

Ogden, J. A. (1986). Neuropsychological and psychological sequelae of shunt surgery in young adults with hydrocephalus. *Journal of Clinical and Experimental Neuropsychology, 8*, 657–659.

Ojemann, R. G., & Black, P. M. (1982). Hydrocephalus in adults. In J. R. Youmans (Ed.), *Neurological surgery* (Vol. 3, 2nd ed., pp. 1423–1435). Philadelphia: W. B. Saunders Company.

Ouslander, J. G., & Abelson, S. (1990). Perceptions of urinary incontinence among elderly outpatients. *Gerontologist, 30*, 369–372.

Peter, K. (1979). The problem of hydrocephalic psychopathy. *Schweizer Archives of Neurology, Neurochirurgica, and Psychiatry, 1*, 89–101.

Petersen, R., Mokri, B., & Laws, E. (1985). Surgical treatment of idiopathic hydrocephalus in elderly patients. *Neurology, 35*, 307–311.

Philippon, J., Ancri, D., & Pertuiset, B. (1971). Hydrocephalie a pression normale. *Revue Neurologique, 125*, 347–358.

Pickard, J. D. (1982). Adult communicating hydrocephalus. *British Journal of Hospital Medicine, 27*, 35–44.

Price, T. R. P., & Tucker, G. J. (1977). Psychiatric and behavioral manifestations of normal pressure hydrocephalus. *Journal of Nervous and Mental Disease, 164*(1), 51–55.

Pujol, J., Leal, S., Fluvia, X., & Conde, C. (1989). Psychiatric aspects of normal pressure hydrocephalus: A report of 5 cases. *British Journal of Psychiatry, 154*(4), 77–80.

Rasker, J., Jansen, E., Haan, J., & Oostrom, J. (1985). Normal-pressure hydrocephalus in pheumatic patients. *New England Journal of Medicine, 312*(19), 1239–1241.

Rice, E., & Gendelman, S. (1973). Psychiatric aspects of normal pressure hydrocephalus. *Journal of the American Medical Association, 223*(4), 409–412.

Rosen, H., & Swigar, M. E. (1976). Depression and normal pressure hydrocephalus. *Journal of Nervous and Mental Disease, 163*, 35–40.

Schmidley, J. W., & Maas, E. F. (1990). Cerebral fluid, blood-brain barrier, and brain edema. In Pearlman, A. L. & Collins, R. C. (Eds.), *Neurobiology of disease* (pp. 380–398). New York: Oxford University Press.

Schnelle, J. F., Newman, D. R., & Fogarty, T. (1990). Management of patient continence in long-term care nursing facilities. *Gerontologist, 30*, 373–376.

Sekhar, L. N., Moody, J., & Guthkeich, A. N. (1982). Malfunctioning ventriculoperitoneal shunts: Clinical and pathological features. *Journal of Neurosurgery, 56*, 411–416.

Shenkin, H., Greenberg, J., Bouzarth, W., Gutterman, P., & Morales, J. (1973). Ventricular shunting for relief of senile symptoms. *Journal of the American Medical Association, 225*(12), 1486–1489.

Sjaastad, O., Skalpe, I. O., & Engeset, A. (1969). The width of the temporal horn in the differential diagnosis between pressure hydrocephalus and hydrocephalus ex vacuo. *Neurology, 19*, 1087–1093.

Sklar, F., & Linder, M. (1984). The role of the pressure-volume relationship of brain elasticity in the mechanics and treatment of hydrocephalus. In K. Shapiro, A. Marmarou, & H. Portney (Eds.), *Hydrocephalus,* (pp. 323–336). New York: Raven Press.

Stambrook, M., Cardoso, E. R., Hawryluk, G. A., Erikson, P., Piatek, D., & Sicz, G. (1988). Neuropsychological changes following the neurosurgical treatment of normal pressure hydrocephalus. *Archives of Clinical Neuropsychology, 3*, 323–330.

Stein, S. C., & Langfitt, T. W. (1974). Normal-pressure hydrocephalus: Predicting the results of cerebrospinal fluid shunting. *Journal of Neurosurgery, 41*, 463–470.

Strub, R. C., & Black, F. W. (1988). *Neurobehavioural disorders: A clinical approach.* Philadelphia: F. A. Davis Company.

Svendsen, P., & Duru, O. (1981). Visibility of the temporal horns on computed tomography. *Neuroradiology, 21*, 139–144.

Thomsen, A. M., Borgesen, S. E., Bruhn, P., & Gjerris, F. (1986). Prognosis of dementia in normal pressure hydrocephalus after a shunt operation. *Annals of Neurology, 20*(3), 304–310.

Tideiksaar, R. (1986). Preventing falls: Home hazard checklists to help older patients protect themselves. *Geriatrics, 41*, 26–28.

Tinetti, M. E. (1989). Instability and falling in elderly patients. *Seminars in Neurology, 9*, 39–45.

Torack, R. M. (1978). *The pathologic physiology of dementia.* New York: Springer-Verlag.

Unger, B., & Cardoso, E. R. (1989). Intracranial and venous pressures: Part II. Extracranial source of B-waves. In J. T. Hoff & A. L. Betz (Eds.), *Intracranial pressure VII* (pp. 206–208). Berlin: Springer-Verlag.

Vanneste, J., & Van Acker, R. (1990). Normal pressure hydrocephalus: Did publications alter management? *Journal of Neurology, Neurosurgery and Psychiatry, 53*, 564–568.

Vorstrup, S., Christensen, J., Gjerris, F., Sorensen, P., Thomsen, A., & Pulson, O. B. (1987). Cerebral blood flow in patients with normal-pressure hydrocephalus before and after shunting. *Journal of Neurosurgery, 66*, 379–387.

Whitehouse, P. J. (1986). The concept of subcortical and cortical dementia: Another look. *Annals of Neurology, 19*, 1–6.

Wikkelso, C., Andersson, H., Blomstrand, C., & Lindqvist, G. (1982). The clinical effect of lumbar puncture in normal pressure hydrocephalus. *Journal of Neurology, Neurosurgery and Psychiatry, 45*, 64–69.

Wood, J. H. (1980). Physiology, pharmacology, and dynamics of cerebrospinal fluid. In J. H. Wood (Ed.), *Neurology of cerebrospinal fluid* (Vol. I, pp. 1–16). New York: Plenum Press.

Wood, M. M., & Jeffries, R. V. (1978). Cognitive changes in the treatment of adult hydrocephalus. *Brain impairment. Proceedings of the 1978 Brain Impairment Conference* (pp. 5–9). Melbourne: University Press.

Yarnell, J. W., & St. Leger, A. S. (1979). The prevalence, severity, and factors associated with urinary incontinence in a nonrandom sample of the elderly. *Age and Ageing, 8*, 81–85.

11

Cognition in Parkinson's Disease and Related Disorders

RODERICK K. MAHURIN, EDWARD P. FEHER, MATTHEW L. NANCE,
JOEL K. LEVY, AND FRANCIS J. PIROZZOLO

Although Parkinson's disease (PD) is principally characterized by physical symptoms, cognitive deficits commonly are associated with the disorder. Reports regarding the degree of cognitive impairment range from minimal generalized deficits to dementia (Mohr, Litvan, Williams, Fedio, & Chase, 1990; Taylor, Saint-Cyr, & Lang, 1988). Impairments in motor control, including the programming, initiation, termination, and switching of motor plans, are a prominent feature of the disease (Gotham, Brown, & Marsden, 1988; Marsden, 1982). Other cognitive domains most often implicated include memory, spatial abilities, and information processing speed (Marsden, 1990). Further impairments are seen in supraordinate executive control systems, affecting performance of specific cognitive tasks (Brown & Marsden, 1990; DeLong, Georgopoulos, & Crutcher, 1983). Depression is common in PD, and appears related to subcortical mechanisms (Mayberg et al., 1990; Mayeux, 1981). Neuroanatomically, the primary dopaminergic deficit in PD involves pathways connecting the substantia nigra and striatum (which in turn project via the globus pallidus to thalamic and cortical areas) (Young & Penney, 1988). In addition, connections with other cortical associative and prefrontal regions are implicated in the cognitive changes (Alexander, DeLong, & Strick, 1986; Taylor, Saint-Cyr, & Lang, 1986). Other neurotransmitter systems are critically involved in addition to dopamine, including acetylcholine, serotonin, glutamate, gamma-aminobutyric acid (GABA), and various neuropetides (Agid, 1991). However, the contribution of these neurochemical abnormalities to cognitive deficits in PD is largely unknown. Since PD is primarily a disorder of the elderly, observed deficits must be compared with neurocognitive effects of normal aging (El-Awar, Becker, Hammond, Nebes, & Boller, 1987) as well as with other age-related neurodegenerative diseases, including Alzheimer's disease (AD), progressive supranuclear palsy (PSP), olivocerebellopontine atrophy (OPCA), and multisystem atrophy (Cummings & Benson, 1992; Pirozzolo, Mahurin, & Swihart, 1991). Finally, the medications used in treatment of PD may, in themselves, affect cognitive performance (Marder, Flood, Cote, & Mayeux, 1990) and should be accounted for in neuropsychological assessment.

Clinical and Pathological Characteristics

PD is the third most common neurological disease in the elderly, with a prevalence approaching 1% in the population aged 60 years and older (Schoenberg, 1987). It is characterized by cardinal signs of bradykinesia, resting tremor, and cogwheel-type rigidity. Although not universal, stooped posture, poverty of spontaneous facial and limb movement, micrographia, hypophonia, and postural instability are common features. Gait is typically festinating, small-stepped, shuffling, and slow. Age of onset is variable, with initial symptoms usually appearing in the fifth or sixth decade. However, young-onset disease (between 20 and 40 years) accounts for 5% to 10% of cases (Giovannini et al., 1991; Golbe, 1991). The disease course is slowly progressive, but rate of decline may vary greatly among patients (Mortimer, 1988a).

Parkinsonism is associated with a variety of etiologies, including viral encephalitis, neuroleptic usage, manganese toxicity, carbon monoxide poisoning, and multiple cerebral infarcts (Gray, Poirier, & Scaravilli, 1991). 10% to 15% of PD patients have a first-degree relative with the disease, suggesting a genetic component in a subgroup of patients (Golbe, Di Iorio, Bonavita, Miller, & Duvoisin, 1990; Johnson, 1991). Recognition in the mid-1980s of parkinsonism resulting from exposure to the dopamine-specific neurotoxin 1-methyl-4-phenyl-1,2,3,6-tetrahydropyridine (MPTP) (Langston, 1988) opened new avenues of research into possible causative mechanisms. However, approximately 80% to 85% of cases of PD are of unknown etiology and are classified as "idiopathic" (Jankovic & Marsden, 1988). In these cases, there is no compelling evidence that gender, occupation, socioeconomic status, infectious agent, diet, or environmental pollutants are primary causative factors.

Neuropathological features in PD include degeneration of pigmented brainstem nuclei, predominantly the pars compacta of the substantia nigra, but also the locus ceruleus, dorsal vagal nucleus, ventral tegmentum, and sympathetic ganglia (Agid, 1991; Albin, Young, & Penney, 1989; Goldman-Rakic & Selemon, 1990; Jellinger, 1987; Sawle, Brooks, Marsden, & Frackowiak, 1991). Histopathological appearance of intracellular Lewy bodies confirms the degenerative changes in these areas (Dubois, Pillon, Sternic, Lhermitte, & Agid, 1990; Forno, 1982; Gibb, Scott, & Lees, 1991). These brainstem nuclei primarily project to the striatal complex of the basal ganglia, which in turn are reciprocally connected (via the thalamus) to motor and premotor regions of the cortex (Alexander et al., 1986; Marsden, 1982). Additional pathways that may subserve cognition consist of basal ganglia-thalamocortical connections to associative and prefrontal regions (Alexander et al., 1986). Cerebral imaging studies in PD using radioactively tagged [18F]fluoro-L-dopa allow for in vitro visualization and quantification of dopamine depletion in humans. These studies implicate decreased contralateral striatal dopamine in hemiparkinsonism and bilateral reductions in bilateral parkinsonism, with greatest reductions in the region of the putamen (Garnett, Nahmias, & Firnau, 1984; Leenders et al., 1986; Martin et al., 1986). Dopamine reductions may be evident even in preclinical stages of the disease (Brooks, 1991). Studies of patients with MPTP-induced parkinsonism also reveal decreased dopaminergic concentrations in nigrostriatal pathways (Calne et al., 1985).

Although other neurotransmitters are implicated in PD, motor impairment primarily results from decreased dopamine and the resultant disruption of its modulatory effects on motor control pathways. The neuronal count and dopamine levels of the substantia nigra diminish throughout the adult lifespan (McGeer, McGeer, & Suzuki, 1977). Nevertheless, overt physical signs of PD do not occur until there is approximately 80% depletion of dopamine reserves (Riederer & Wuketich, 1976). This association of PD with the normal aging process suggests that if individuals at risk for PD could be identified prior to the onset of symptoms, early replacement therapy may slow disease onset and possibly extend the disease-free period (Jankovic & Marsden, 1988).

Recent findings reveal a more complicated picture of neurotransmitter interaction than previously considered (Sawle et al., 1991; Young & Penney, 1988). For example, Uhl, Hackney, Torchia, et al. (1986) report that, in addition to modest decreases in dopamine receptors, there is autoradiographic evidence for significant reductions in neuropeptide receptors within the substantia nigra. This suggests involvement of neuropeptide modulatory activity that affects dopamine-related cognitive and motor activity. Additional studies have revealed disruption of other biochemical subsystems in PD involving cholinergic, serotonergic, and GABAergic pathways (Agid, 1991; Cash, Ruberg, Raisman, & Agid, 1984; Epelbaum et al., 1983; Hornykiewicz, 1982; Perry et al., 1984; Perry et al., 1983; Ruberg, Ploska, Javoy-Agid, & Agid, 1982). However, the specific association between these neurotransmitters and cognitive dysfunction remains to be clarified.

Dementia in PD

In his original monograph on the "shaking palsy," James Parkinson characterized PD as primarily physical in presentation, with "the senses and intellect being uninjured" (Parkinson, 1817). Nevertheless, cognitive impairment consistently has been reported in PD. Estimates of the prevalence of dementia in PD populations vary, with the majority of studies reporting between 15% and 50% (Boller, Mizutani, Roessmann, & Gambetti, 1980; Brown & Marsden, 1984; Girotti, Soliveri, Carella, Piccolo, & Caggarra, 1988; Growdon & Corkin, 1986; Lieberman et al., 1979; Marttila & Rinne, 1976; Mindham, Ahmed, & Clough, 1982; Rajput, Offord, Beard, & Kurland, 1984).

In a representative study, Celesia and Wanamaker (1972) examined 170 patients with parkinsonian symptoms and excluded those with postencephalitic, arteriosclerotic, and toxic forms of PD. Sixty-one of the remaining 153 patients (40%) with idiopathic PD showed dementia. Lieberman et al. (1979) found 32% of their outpatient population ($n = 520$) to exhibit symptoms of dementia, a 10-fold greater incidence than among controls. Boller et al. (1980) found the occurrence of dementia in idiopathic PD to be six times greater than that of an age-matched sample. More recently, Cummings (1988) found dementia in 40% of a sample of PD patients, with some degree of mental status change evident in almost all subjects in the study. Using conservative criteria for dementia, Brown and Marsden (1984) reviewed published studies and suggested that 15% to 20% may be a more accurate estimate of the prevalence of dementia in PD. Other recent investigations using strict criteria and large sample sizes have reported prevalences of between 10% and 15%, again lower than previous reports (Mayeux et al., 1988a; Taylor et al., 1988).

Pirozzolo, Hansch, Mortimer, Webster, and Kuskowski (1982) compared neuropsychological performance of 60 PD patients with age-, sex-, and education-matched controls and found poorer performance by the PD patients on 20 of the 23 tests used; 93% of the PD patients performed more poorly than their individually matched controls. In addition, 83% of the PD patients performed at a lower level than their counterparts when tests requiring motor coordination and speed were excluded from the analysis. Deficits were found across a broad spectrum of cognitive functioning, including visual discrimination, spatial orientation, verbal and nonverbal memory, and psychomotor speed. Performance of the PD subjects ranged along a continuum from virtually intact intellectual operations to severe generalized impairment. The lack of bimodality in the distribution of scores did not allow a clear-cut division into "demented" and "nondemented" subgroups, indicating a "limited usefulness in attaching a prevalence estimate to the occurrence of dementia in PD" (p. 79).

Discrepancies in estimates of the prevalence of dementia in PD may result from several factors. There are variations in diagnostic criteria for dementia: studies have used bedside mental status evaluation, retrospective review of medical records, and psychometric testing to establish the diagnosis. Differences in sample selection and failure to exclude patients with parkinsonian symptoms resulting from other pathologies (e.g., multi-infarct dementia) may also account for discrepant findings. Additionally, the clinical definition of "dementia" is often difficult to operationalize. Both DSM-III-R and NINCDS definitions require presence of memory loss, one or more specific cognitive deficits (e.g., language, visuoperception, abstract reasoning), and personality change. These symptoms must be of sufficient severity to disrupt normal social and occupational functioning (American Psychiatric Association, 1987; McKhann et al., 1986). However, these criteria were developed in the diagnostic context of AD, and may not adequately characterize "subcortical" dementias. Furthermore, in PD it is often difficult to determine whether physical impairments themselves are interfering with normal functioning.

As noted by several authors (Brown & Marsden, 1984; Growdon & Corkin, 1986), earlier studies often failed to distinguish between generalized cognitive impairment and specific cognitive deficits seen in PD patients without diffuse intellectual decline. Studies comparing PD with other dementias (e.g., AD) often use brief mental status tests, such as the Mini-Mental State (MMSE) Examination (Folstein, Folstein, & McHugh, 1975), to equate subjects in severity of dementia. However, such screening tests are biased toward memory and orientation questions, and other items (e.g., language) are relatively insensitive to cognitive deficits as measured by more extensive neuropsychological testing. Therefore it is questionable whether they adequately measure a broad enough spectrum of cognitive abilities to accurately describe dementia (Feher et al., 1992). Similarly, current diagnostic criteria for dementia may overlook fundamental cognitive impairments such as executive dyscontrol that appear to differentially characterize cortical and subcortical disorders (Pillon, Dubois, Lhermitte, & Agid, 1986; Royall, Mahurin, & Gray, 1992).

Cognitive-Motor Correlates

Several studies have found an association between severity of parkinsonism and the degree of cognitive dysfunction. For example, Wolfe et al. (1990) compared neuropsychological test scores with physical impairment and levels of homovanillic acid (HVA), a dopamine metabolite, in cerebrospinal fluid (CSF) of patients with PD, AD, and depressive disorder. They found significant associations between HVA levels, information processing speed, and verbal fluency in all groups. Patients with low HVA had more extrapyramidal signs and were more depressed.

More specific relationships between physical symptoms, such as bradykinesia and tremor, and the nature of cognitive deficits have also been found. Zetusky, Jankovic, and Pirozzolo (1985) examined records from a large sample (n = 334) of patients with idiopathic PD, and found a significant positive association of cognitive decline with bradykinesia, postural instability, and gait difficulty, but a negative association between cognitive decline and tremor. Mortimer, Pirozzolo, Hansch, and Webster (1982) found that quantified measurement of bradykinesia, rigidity, and tremor were not significantly intercorrelated, suggesting their relative independence. However, there were negative correlations between the severity of bradykinesia and scores on tasks measuring visual-spatial performance (both timed and untimed), spatial-orientation memory, and psychomotor speed. Tremor, in contrast, positively correlated with spatial-orientation memory scores. Degree of rigidity did not significantly correlate with any of the neuropsychological measures. These relationships were not significantly changed when age, age of disease onset, or degree of depression were statistically controlled. The authors suggested the possibility of two subgroups of PD: one form characterized by "predominant tremor and relatively intact intellectual function, and the other with more marked bra-dykinesia and neuropsychological impairment" (p. 136). Similar findings have been reported by other investigators who found dementia and cognitive impairment were associated with bradykinesia and rigidity, but not with tremor (Ebmeier et al., 1991; Huber, Christy, & Paulson, 1991).

Other studies have failed to find a relationship between cognitive impairment and the severity of motor symptoms (Globus, Mildworf, & Melamed, 1985; Growdon & Corkin, 1986; Halgrin, Riklan, & Misiak, 1977; Tweedy, Langer, & McDowell, 1982). For example, Cooper, Sagar, Jordan, Harvey, and Sullivan (1991) investigated the relationship between cognitive impairment and motor disability in early untreated PD. They found that motor disability correlated strongly with severity of depression but weakly with cognitive impairment. The authors suggested that cognitive dysfunction may largely be independent of the frontostriatal dopamine deficiency postulated to underlie motor disability. Rafal, Posner, Walker, and Friedrich (1984) also failed to find an association between slowed information processing speed and bradykinesia, suggesting that slowed cognition in PD may not be directly related to dopaminergic-related motor symptoms.

Although there are exceptions (Globus et al., 1985), most studies find that dementia occurs more frequently in patients who are older at the time of symptom onset (Ebmeier et al., 1990; Hietanen & Teravainen, 1988b; Marder, Leung, Tang, Bell et al., 1991; Reid et al., 1989). Quinn, Critchley, and Marsden (1987) examined idiopathic PD patients with onset before 40 years of age and found a "negligible" incidence of dementia. Horiguchi, Nishimatsu, Inami, Sukegawa, and Shoda (1991) compared PD patients with older and younger ages of onset. The older group had more rapid cognitive deterioration, more psychiatric complications, and electroencephalographic (EEG) abnormalities. Motor disability did not differ between the groups. Giovannini et al. (1991) evaluated 120 early (ages 20–40 years) and late-onset (> 40 years) PD patients matched for length of illness. Later onset was characterized by greater cognitive impairment, more rapid disease progression, and less effective dopamine therapy. Lieberman et al. (1979) also found PD patients with dementia to be older at time of disease onset. The authors hypothesized the existence of two types of PD: (a) younger with motor, but not cognitive, disability; and (b) older, with a combined motor-cognitive disorder. Mayeux et al. (1988a) found characteristics of PD patients with dementia to include (a) older age, (b) later age of motor symptom onset, (c) more rapid progression of physical disability, and (d) poorer response and more adverse side effects from L-dopa therapy. Mayeux et al. (1988a) and Marder et al. (1990) reported that the cumulative incidence of dementia in PD increases with age. By age 85 years, over 65% of the surviving PD cohort members in their sample were demented. Overall, these findings suggest that in older PD patients dementia is more common than in the general population and is associated with severity and type of physical symptoms.

Subcortical Dementia in PD

The concept of subcortical dementia has generated a great deal of discussion since its introduction in the mid-1970s (Albert, Feldman, & Willis, 1974). Although originally described with reference to PSP, the pattern of cognitive impairment has since been associated with PD, Huntington's disease (HD), multiple sclerosis, Wilson's disease, and other brainstem and cerebellar degenerative diseases (Albert, 1978; Cummings & Benson, 1992; Mayeux, Stern, Rosen, & Benson, 1981a). Although motor dysfunction predominates in these disorders, accompanying cognitive deficits are postulated to result from disruption of reciprocal pathways between subcortical and frontal cortical regions (Cummings & Benson, 1984). These findings are consistent with a broad literature on animal and human studies demonstrating the role of subcortical structures in cognitive, motor, and perceptual operations (Cummings & Benson, 1988; Marsden, 1982).

Clinical features of the subcortical dementias have been reported to include impaired recall, slowness of thought process (bradyphrenia), impaired ability to manipulate acquired knowledge, visuospatial disturbance, impaired executive function, apathy, and depression (Albert, 1978; Cummings & Benson, 1992). "Instrumental" deficits of aphasia, apraxia, and agnosia are usually absent in subcortical dementia. In contrast, cortical syndromes such as AD are characterized by impaired memory encoding associated with recall and recognition deficits, perceptual disorders, and marked language impairment. Depression is rarely reported as a significant feature of the cortical dementias, with patient indifference to deficits more frequently described (Cummings & Benson, 1992; Feher, Mahurin, Inbody, Crook, & Pirozzolo, 1991).

Findings of distinct patterns of cognitive performance in PD and AD lend support to the cortical-subcortical distinction. Significant differences between AD and PD have been found in areas of visuospatial function (Mohr et al., 1990), implicit and explicit memory (Bondi & Kaszniak, 1991), language (Illes, 1989), visual learning (Freedman & Oscar-Berman, 1989), episodic and semantic memory (Helkala, Laulumaa, Soininen, & Riekkinen, 1989), sequencing (Sullivan & Sagar, 1989), naming ability (Como & Caine, 1987), and word fluency (Rogers, Lees, Smith, Trimble, & Stern, 1987). In addition, although PD and AD are both progressive disorders, PD patients show modest and variable cognitive decline on a year-to-year basis (Mortimer, 1988a), unlike AD patients, who often demonstrate significant decrement in functioning over the same time period (Growdon & Corkin, 1986; Portin & Rinne, 1980; Portin & Rinne, 1986).

Huber, Shuttleworth, and Freidenberg (1989a) examined neuropsychological differences between AD and PD patients, and found that AD patients displayed apraxia and more severe memory, language, and orientation deficits. PD patients, in contrast, showed impaired information processing speed and greater mood disturbance. This pattern of neuropsychological results was consistent with a cortical-subcortical distinction. Pillon et al. (1986) examined the cognitive abilities of patients with several subcortical disorders including PD, Parkinson's disease with dementia (PDD), HD, and PSP. Distinct patterns of performance were observed, suggesting that differences in cognitive impairment in subcortical dementia can be divided into specific, disease-related subtypes of cognitive impairment.

However, the distinction between cortical and subcortical dementia has been questioned on several grounds. First, clinical features of the two types of disorders frequently overlap. For example, characteristic "subcortical" motor signs, including rigidity, bradykinesia, and gait impairment, are frequently present in predominantly cortical dementias (e.g., AD, Pick's disease, Jakob-Creutzfeldt disease, multi-infarct dementia, and traumatic brain injury [Bakchine, Lacomblez, Palisson, Laurent, & Derouesne, 1989; Matison, Mayeux, Rosen, & Fahn, 1982; Whitehouse, 1986]). Second, imaging and neuropathological studies show that many patients with subcortical disorders have signs of cortical pathology, and those with cortical disorders frequently show subcortical neuronal abnormalities (Jernigan, Salmon, Butters, Shults, & Hesselink, 1990; Whitehouse, Hedreen, White, & Price, 1983). Third, when attempts are made to equate overall dementia severity, comparative cognitive mental status testing of PD, HD, and AD subjects has often failed to reveal distinct patterns of neuropsychological performance (Marschall et al., 1991; Mayeux, Stern, Rosen, & Benson, 1983; Stern, Mayeux, & Rosen, 1984). Fourth, a lack of precision in terms describing cognitive changes in the subcortical dementias makes comparisons difficult. For example, subcortical symptoms have been reported to include "dilapidation of cognition," "slowness in the rate of information processing," and "forgetfulness," all of which are difficult to distinguish from deficits typically seen in AD (Cummings & Benson, 1988a). Much of the current controversy results from the use of the anatomical terms "cortical" and "subcortical" to describe behavioral and cognitive differences. A more fruitful approach may be to describe these syndromes in terms of neuropsychological profiles, avoiding the problems of attempting to precisely localize comparative deficits (Butters, 1991).

Relationship of Parkinson's Disease to Alzheimer's Disease

There is strong evidence that AD and PD share common neuropathological and neurochemical mechanisms, including senile plaques (SPs), neurofibrillary tangles (NFTs), and granulovacuolar degeneration (Boller et al., 1980; Hakim & Mathieson, 1979; Whitehouse et al., 1983). Yoshimura (1988) examined 56 patients with Lewy body PD. They found evidence of dementia in 66% of cases. Of the demented group, 65% showed AD-like cortical changes, 22% did not show AD-like changes, and 13% showed combined senile-vascular changes. The findings suggested that dementia in PD and AD are both related to pathology in the cholinergic basal nucleus, noradrenergic locus ceruleus, and dopaminergic mesocortical systems. McGeer, Itagaki, Boyes, and McGeer (1988) found Lewy bodies and free melanin in the substantia nigra of a majority of PD patients and in 66% of AD patients. Additionally, they found significant plaque and tangle counts in hippocampal regions of both groups, suggesting coexistence of PD and AD-type pathology. Mastaglia, Masters, Beyreuther, and Kakulas (1989) compared cortical deposits of the AD A4 amyloid protein in PD and control patients and found that many PD patients had associated AD-type changes that appeared severe enough to account for the presence of dementia. De la Monte, Wells, Hedley-Whyte, and Growdon (1989) examined PD patients with and without dementia and found mainly subcortical neuropathological changes in uncomplicated PD, but both cortical and subcortical changes in patients with features of dementia. Boller et al. (1980) found clinical documentation of severe dementia in about one third of a group of 29 parkinsonian patients, all of whom had histologic changes (SPs and NFTs) suggestive of AD. Jellinger (1987) carried out a large autopsy study and also found a high incidence of cortical and hippocampal SPs and NFTs in PD patients with dementia.

Doty et al. (1991) investigated odor detection and identification deficits in PD and AD patients. Previous research had shown dementia-related elevated olfactory thresholds in patients with AD, presumptively associated with early degeneration of olfactory tracts and medial temporal regions (Murphy, Gilmore, Seery, Salmon, & Lasker, 1990). Doty et al. found equally severe impairments on olfactory testing in the PD and AD groups, even after controlling for overall degree of cognitive deficit. The results suggest that although olfactory testing alone cannot reliably distinguish the two diseases, pathology of underlying olfactory regions may be a common feature in PD and AD.

Further support for similarities between dementia in AD and PD comes from cerebral metabolic and neuroimaging studies. Spampinato et al. (1991) evaluated regional cerebral perfusion using single photon emission computed tomography (SPECT) in AD, PD, and PDD patients and found a reduction in regional metabolism for both PDD and AD patients in parietal, temporal, and occipital cortices. Kuhl, Metter, Benson, et al. (1985) used positron emission tomography (PET) imaging and reported similar reductions in temporal and parietal cerebral glucose metabolism in both AD patients and PD patients with dementia. Nakamura, Fukuda, Hara, Fukuyama, and Kameyama (1988) found that PD patients with dementia displayed decreased regional cerebral blood flow (rCBF) in both cortical and deep gray matter, while patients without dementia showed decreased flow in deep gray matter, but not in cerebral cortex. Peppard et al. (1990) demonstrated with PET that PDD patients had a metabolic pattern similar to that found in AD, but different from that of PD patients with normal cognition. Several investigators have reported greater loss of neurons to be associated with higher probability of dementia in PD (Gaspar & Gray, 1984; Jellinger, 1987), but imaging studies have shown that PDD is not associated with any specific pattern of magnetic resonance imaging (MRI) abnormality (Huber et al., 1989a).

Neurochemical changes typically associated with AD, particularly those of the cholinergic system, have been correlated with cognitive decline in PD (Agid, Ruberg, Dubois, & Javoy-Agid, 1984). For example, Xuereb, Perry, Candy, Bonham, and Perry (1990) measured nicotinic and muscarinic cholinergic receptors in PD, AD, and senile dementia of the Lewy body type (SDLT). They found reduced nicotinic, but not muscarinic, receptor binding in AD, PDD, and SDLT, that was associated with cortical cholinergic deficits. Whitehouse et al. (1988) used receptor autoradiography to map distribution of cortical nicotinic (3H) acetylcholine binding sites in AD and PD. They found significant loss of nicotinic receptors in all cortical layers (especially the deepest ones) in both diseases. Rinne, Myllykyla, Lonnberg, and Marjamaki (1991) examined nicotinic receptors in PD and AD and found receptor declines in frontal and temporal cortex, hippocampus, and caudate nucleus. The authors reported negative correlations between the degree of dementia in PD and the number of nicotinic receptors in the frontal cortex. Aubert et al. (1992) found similar decreases in cholinergic markers (nicotinic and muscarinic) in both PD and AD in frontal and temporal cortex. Subcortical nicotinic sites were decreased in PD and PDD, but not AD. Reduced levels of cortical choline acetyltransferase ChAT (a marker enzyme for acetylcholine) have also been demonstrated in brains of PD patients, with greater decreases associated with more severe cognitive impairment (Dubois, Ruberg, Javoy-Agid, Ploska, & Agid, 1983; McGeer et al., 1988; Perry et al., 1983; Ruberg et al., 1982). There are also consistent findings of cholinergic neuronal loss in the nucleus basalis of Meynert in PD patients, approaching the degree of involvement seen in patients with AD, and associated with degree of dementia (Chan-Palay, 1988; Chui et al., 1986; Gaspar & Gray, 1984; Jellinger, 1987; Perry et al., 1983; Whitehouse et al., 1983). In contrast, other investigators have found little or no support for an association between AD-type lesions and PDD (Ball, 1984; Chui et al., 1986; Heston, 1980; Mann & Yates, 1983; Perry et al., 1983).

Summary

Although estimates of the occurrence of dementia in PD vary considerably, most studies suggest that a subgroup of patients with PD will develop clinical and neuropathological features similar to AD. The prevalence of these findings is greater than would be expected in age-matched controls. Given the inconsistency of the data and the ambiguity surrounding definitions of dementia, the clinical neuropsychologist may decide to choose a conservative course of carefully describing and quantifying cognitive deficits elicited in the neuropsychological assessment rather than simply labeling a particular PD patient as "demented" or "nondemented."

Neuropsychological Assessment

Neuropsychological assessment contributes important information to the clinical evaluation of PD, including profiling cognitive strengths and deficits, monitoring treatment and disease progression, assessing for rehabilitative potential, offering psychological counseling, assessing the effects of depression, and describing the effects of specific cognitive impairments on everyday functioning. The assessment should be based on age-normed tests, timed and untimed measures of related abilities, and, when possible, repeat testing over several occasions. A subgroup of patients with PD may present with dementia that can be quantified by conventional testing and rating scales. In contrast, other patients may show little or no cognitive impairment on conventional neuropsychological testing. More commonly, characteristic patterns of cognitive impairment will be apparent in the absence of generalized dementia. When depressed mood is controlled for, increased prevalence of cognitive impairment is still present when PD patients are compared with normal control subjects matched in age, sex, and estimated premorbid intelligence (Boyd et al., 1991). Such deficits have been demonstrated even in individuals with PD who are functioning at high social and occupational levels, and who show limited disease progression (Mohr et al., 1990). The following sections will review frequently reported impairments in PD within the framework of commonly assessed neuropsychological domains of functioning.

Motor Control

PD patients exhibit well-documented difficulty in the initiation, sequencing, termination, and shifting of motor programs (Marsden, 1982). For example, patients often have difficulty carrying out two simultaneous tasks, although they can perform each individual task successfully (Flowers, 1976; Schwab, Chafetz, & Walker, 1954). Benecke, Rothwell, Dick, Day, and Marsden (1987) found that although PD patients were slower than normal controls on independent execution of two single movements, they had disproportionately greater slowing when the movements were performed sequentially. Harrington & Haaland (1991) showed that PD patients are impaired in the ability to rapidly switch between motor programs, although the higher order motor plan may remain intact. These studies indicate that motor dysfunction in PD is primarily a deficit in the programming and integration of complex goal-directed movements. These deficits are linked to dysfunction of frontal-basal ganglia regions and associated projection areas that control the execution of previously learned motor programs (Marsden, 1982). Additionally, motor planning deficits may be associated with deficient processing of the central "corollary discharge" representing efferent activity (Growdon & Corkin, 1986; Mahurin & Inbody, 1989).

Other investigators have reported specific sequencing deficits in PD. Beatty and Monson (1990) found that PD patients were impaired on an untimed test of picture sequencing and a three-step test of motor execution. The severity of the deficit was related to global mental status and to Wisconsin Card Sorting Test (WCST) scores, but was not related to neurological measures of disease severity.

Sullivan and Sagar (1989) compared PD and AD patients on the Wechsler Adult Intelligence Scale-Revised (WAIS-R) and found PD patients to be impaired on the Picture Arrangement subtest, but normal on the Vocabulary subtest, whereas AD patients performed poorly on both subtests. Many of the Picture Arrangement errors by the PD patients consisted of leaving the pictures in the order presented by the examiner, consistent either with avolitional behavior or impairment in set formation prerequisite to sequence formation.

Mahurin, Pirozzolo, and Appel (1989) demonstrated that both PD and AD patients were able to perform simple motor tasks within normal age-adjusted limits. However, as the tasks became more complex and required greater perceptual-motor control (e.g., Grooved Pegboard, Symbol-Digit Coding, Trail-Making Test), performance of both groups became significantly impaired relative to age- and education-matched controls. These findings indicate hierarchical dysfunction of motor control in PD, most evident on tasks that require greater perceptual-motor and cognitive demands.

Clinically evaluated praxis (i.e., the intact production of simple movements and gestures to command or imitation) has also been studied in PD. Although Pirozzolo et al. (Pirozzolo et al., 1982) failed to find evidence for apraxia in their sample of PD patients, the small number and relative ease of items may have created a ceiling effect, obscuring possible deficits. Other investigators have also failed to find deficits in apraxia when measured in the traditional clinical manner (Huber, Shuttleworth, & Paulson, 1986). In contrast, Goldenberg, Wimmer, Auff, and Schnaberth (1986) found impairments in apraxia and visuospatial function in medicated idiopathic PD patients with mild to severe bilateral motor symptoms. These patients were administered an extensive apraxia examination and four tests of visuospatial abilities. Total apraxia scores, imitation of finger and hand positions, and movement sequences were correlated with figure assembly and line orientation (after controlling for intellectual decline and age). Failures on apraxia tests could not be attributed to akinesia, hypomotility, or tremor, nor were they correlated with tests of mental rotation.

Summary

PD is characterized by well-documented motor slowing and impairments in the programming and execution of complex movement patterns. Difficulties are also present in the sequencing and simultaneous production of simple motor actions. Clinical screening for apraxia is generally negative, but more in-depth testing may reveal problems in the initiation and execution of complex skilled movements.

Attention and Information Processing

Performance on digit-span tasks, a measure of short-term memory and verbal-auditory attention, is generally intact in PD (Huber et al., 1989a; Lees & Smith, 1983; Pillon et al., 1986; Portin & Rinne, 1980). Timed cancellation tasks (visually searching for occurrences of a target letter or symbol within a random matrix of distractors) have been used as measures of sustained and selective visual attention. PD patients are slower and make more errors on these tasks than do normal controls; however, their performance does not disproportionately worsen with increased task complexity. This suggests slowed perceptual motor speed, but not impaired primary attentional abilities (De Lancey Horne, 1973; Talland & Schwab, 1964). In contrast, studies of complex attentional processes, such as measures of the internal allocation of attentional resources, have revealed deficits in "higher order" executive control of attention in PD (Girotti et al., 1986; Gotham et al., 1988).

Bradyphrenia, or cognitive slowing, is a primary feature of PD (Rogers, 1986; Rogers, Lees, Trimble, & Stern, 1986). PD patients are slower on a memory scanning task compared with age-matched normal controls (Wilson, Kaszniak, Klawans, & Garron, 1980). Although many reaction time (RT) studies have found generalized slowing in PD subjects (Daum & Quinn, 1991; Flowers, 1976; Montgomery, Nuessen, Nuessen, & Douglas, 1991), other investigators have failed to find significant impairments (Evarts, Teravainen, & Calne, 1981). Warning signals prior to signal onset do not differentially aid PD subjects over controls in obtaining a faster reaction time, a finding that argues against a deficit of endogenous arousal systems (Heilman, Bowers, Watson, & Greer, 1976).

There is also evidence that, relative to age-matched controls, PD patients are not subject to disproportionate slowing in the decision-making segment of choice RT, arguing against a hypothesis of nonspecific cognitive slowing (Evarts et al., 1981). These findings contrast with disproportionate slowing of choice RT in many other neurological disorders (Mahurin & Pirozzolo, 1986; van Zomeren, 1981). However, there may be a differential contribution of specific motor symptoms to RT performance. If bradykinesia is related to slowed information processing, then a relationship may exist between RT performance and bradykinesia, but not with other symptoms of PD such as tremor. Mahurin and Pirozzolo (1985) examined simple and choice RT in PD patients, and found such a relationship. Compared with controls, PD patients were slower in RT. Bradykinesia, but not tremor, was significantly correlated with response times.

An additional method of investigating information processing speed in PD involves the use of event-related potentials (ERPs). Prasher and Findley (1991) used ERPs and RT to examine cognitive and motor processing in PD patients before and after L-dopa treatment. They found normal P3 latency and prolonged RT before treatment, in contrast to prolonged P3 latency but improved RT performance after treatment. These results suggested a possible dopamine-induced dissociation between cognitive speed and motor performance. Goodin and Aminoff (1986) also found slowing in mid- and long-latency auditory evoked potentials (N1, N2, and P3) in PD patients. Starkstein, Esteguy, Berthier, Garcia, and Leiguarda (1989) found a decrement in P3 latency and movement time during the off-medication phase of PD, but no differences between on and off phases on RT and neuropsychological tests.

Summary

Although primary attentional processes appear grossly intact in PD, more complex attentional function can be impaired. Investigations of information processing speed show slowing in memory scanning, ERPs, and simple RT, but are inconclusive with regard to slowing of choice RT. Although response slowing has been observed, potential interactions with symptom presentation have not been fully clarified.

Memory

Memory studies in PD have examined conventional dichotomies of episodic and semantic, recall and recognition, automatic and effortful, recent and remote, and procedural and declarative abilities (Della Sala, Di Lorenzo, Giordano, & Spinnler, 1986; Gotham et al., 1988; Halgrin et al., 1977; Mohr, Fabbrini, Williams, et al., 1989; Pirozzolo et al., 1982; Tweedy et al., 1982; Weingartner, Burns, Diebel, & Le Witt, 1984). The majority of investigations indicate deficits in both verbal and nonverbal episodic memory. Many of these studies have contrasted the memory performance of PD patients with that of patients with AD. Although some authors have reported equal impairment in recent memory for PD and AD (Gainotti, Caltagirone, Massullo, & Miceli, 1980; Huber et al., 1989a; Pillon et al., 1986), the majority of studies find less impairment in PD when the two groups are matched for age and overall level of cognitive functioning.

Helkala, Laulumaa, Soininen, and Riekkinen (1988) tested AD and PD patients with a verbal selective-reminding task. They found no difference in immediate recall, but superior delayed recognition for PD patients. In delayed story recall, PD patients also benefited more from rehearsal and cues than did AD patients. The findings suggested better encoding of material in PD, which the authors associated with relative preservation of entorhinal and hippocampal cortex.

Massman, Delis, Butters, Levin, and Salmon (1990) found that PD and HD patients showed similar patterns of memory deficits on the California Verbal Learning Test (CVLT), including mild encoding difficulties, relatively intact storage, and impairment in the utilization of efficient retrieval strategies. A follow-up study (Massman, Levin, Delis, Butters, & Shear, 1992) compared memory performance of PD, HD, AD, and normal control subjects. A discriminant function model for the best three predictors from the CVLT (developed on data from the non-PD groups) showed that 23% of PD patients were similar to the age-matched controls. Classification of the remaining PD patients crossed the other diagnostic categories, indicating a heterogeneity in patterns of memory dysfunction.

Sagar (1987) and Sagar, Sullivan, Gabrieli, Corkin, and Growdon (1988a) compared PD and AD patients on word list learning and found PD patients to be more impaired in recency discrimination than in content recognition. The authors suggested that recency discrimination and short-term memory in PD are impaired secondary to subcortical deafferentation of frontal lobes and may be associated with slowed information processing. Other investigators have found superior recognition memory in PD compared with AD (Snodgrass & Corwin, 1988). Data from several studies have suggested that PD patients are slower than normal controls in acquiring new material and in organizing retrieval strategies, but retain relatively intact recognition abilities (Flowers, Pearce, & Pearce, 1984; Stern, Groves, Sano, & Hoover, 1992).

Bradley, Welch, and Dick (1989) examined working memory in PD patients and age-matched controls. They found the PD group to perform worse on a visuospatial task, but not on a verbal task. Sahakian et al. (1988) found that AD and PD patients were both impaired on several spatial memory tasks, including delayed matching to sample and visual pattern recognition memory. However, the groups showed different patterns of errors. Whereas the AD group showed a delay-dependent deficit, the PD patients showed a delay-independent deficit. Delayed response task scores were significantly associated with clinical ratings and disease duration in the PD patients. Au, Moss, White, Saint-Hilaire, and Feldman (1992) also found early-stage PD patients to be selectively impaired on a visual-delay recognition span test, with relatively spared performance on a verbal span condition.

Huber et al. (Huber et al., 1989b) reported impaired remote memory in PD, although not as severe as for AD patients matched in dementia severity on a mental status screening test. Sagar et al. (1985) and Sagar, Cohen, Sullivan, Corkin, and Growdon (1988b) compared PD and AD patients on recall and recognition of personal (Personal Remote Memory Test) and public (e.g., Famous Scenes Test) remote events. PD patients showed selective impairment in recall of dates, while AD patients were impaired in recognition of both content and dates of events. Deficits in PD patients were independent of degree of dementia. The study also found a temporal gradient in PD, with better recall of more remote events. In contrast, Freedman, Rivoira, Butters, Sax, and Robert (1984) did not find a temporal gradient in PD patients on remote memory testing. However, this study used a different test of remote memory (the Famous Faces Test), raising the possibility that differences from previous studies may be material specific.

Helkala et al. (1989) analyzed episodic and semantic memory in PD and AD patients, and in age-matched controls. The authors found more prior-story intrusions in PD and AD patients, and more extra-list intrusions in AD. The findings suggested different patterns of memory dysfunction in PD (sensitivity to proactive interference) and AD (sensitivity to interference and inability to inhibit irrelevant information). Other studies, however, have failed to show an undue sensitivity to proactive interference in PD (Massman et al., 1990). This is in contrast to the performance of AD patients, in which verbal recall is characteristically marked by intrusions from prior learned material (Butters, Granholm, Salmon, Gjrant, & Wolfe, 1987; Fuld, Katzman, Davies, & Terry, 1982).

Saint-Cyr, Taylor, and Lang (1988) tested PD patients on repeated presentations of a test of rule learning (the Tower of Hanoi test), and found impaired procedural memory (operationally defined as the ability to acquire specific skills based upon rules). Eslinger and Damasio (1986) also reported impaired procedural learning in PD on a perceptual-motor task (pursuit rotor), in contrast to relatively intact learning in AD. Harrington et al. (1990) found that PD patients were not impaired relative to controls on learning a visual-perceptual mirror reading task. More severely impaired patients, however, showed impairment on learning a pursuit rotor task. Bondi and Kaszniak (1991) examined implicit and explicit memory in AD, PD, and control subjects. They found PD patients performed better than AD patients on explicit memory tasks, but were selectively impaired on a skill-learning task (fragmented pictures), suggesting a dissociation between the groups in implicit and explicit memory domains. Kaszniak, Trosset, Bondi, and Bayles (1992) also found PD patients to be impaired on a procedural learning task based on serial RT and shifting of an established response set.

Summary

A consistent pattern of memory impairment has emerged from studies of PD. Patients generally do not have difficulty with immediate memory, such as digit span recall. Both verbal and visual recent (episodic) memory are moderately impaired, with particular difficulties evident in visuospatial working memory. These deficits are not as severe as memory impairment in AD, but it is difficult to adequately match subjects on level of cognitive decline. The memory deficit in PD appears to be associated with inefficient retrieval strategies, rather than impaired storage and consolidation as seen in AD. Compared with AD, there is little loss of learned material over a delay period (intact "savings"), and tests of recognition memory and prompted recall confirm relatively intact storage of new learning. In contrast to AD patients, PD patients have been shown to be impaired in procedural (implicit) skill learning. Additionally, PD patients appear to be impaired in the temporal ordering of recalled information. Overall, these findings indicate that although memory problems are frequently seen in PD, the difficulties are associated with impairment of control and retrieval strategies rather than deficits in new learning per se.

Language

Although speech production is often impaired in PD, language abilities are relatively spared and show only gradual decline with disease progression (Gainotti et al., 1980; Levin & Tomer, 1992; Mendez, Cummings, Darkins, Hill, & Benson, 1987). Findings of mild or no naming deficits in PD have been supported by several studies (El-Awar et al., 1987; Huber et al., 1986). For example, Bayles and Tomoeda (1983) examined naming ability in PD and AD patients equated on a mental status screening exam. PD patients performed within the normal range, but AD patients showed significant deficits. Pirozzolo et al. (1982) also failed to find naming errors for PD subjects on an abbreviated form of the Boston Naming Test, although the short form of the test may have missed possible errors on low-frequency words. Similarly, Pillon et al. (1986) failed to find naming impairments in PD patients matched for impairment with AD patients on subtests of the WAIS-R and Raven's Matrices. Chui et al. (1986) found that significant comprehension or paraphasic disturbances occurred very rarely in PD, and then usually in the context of PDD.

In contrast, Cummings, Darkins, Mendez, Hill, and Benson (1988) found PDD patients to have mild deficits in naming and writing when compared with nondemented PD patients. Other investigators have also confirmed mild naming deficits in PD (Freedman et al., 1984; Globus et al., 1985). Matison et al. (1982) examined the "tip of the tongue" phenomenon reported by PD patients, and found mild impairments in visual confrontation naming. However, performance improved substantially with either semantic or phonetic cueing. Beatty and Monson (1989) compared lexical processing in PD and multiple sclerosis patients, and found naming deficits in both groups.

Matison et al. (1982) found that PD patients performed better on a test of phonological verbal fluency (generating words beginning with a specific letter) than on a measure of semantic verbal fluency (generating words from a specific category), suggesting problems in the organized retrieval of semantic information. Fisher, Gatterer, and Danielczyk (1988) found tasks of semantic memory (naming and word fluency) were impaired in patients with AD and PDD, but were intact for controls and PD patients without dementia. Verbal fluency deficits have been demonstrated early in the course of PD, which suggests specific frontal-subcortical impairments associated with uncomplicated PD, and not related to the dementia seen in patients in more advanced stages of the disease (Taylor et al., 1986; Huber et al., 1991; Lees & Smith, 1983).

Cummings et al. (1988) compared PD, PDD, and AD patients on items from the Boston Diagnostic Aphasia Examination and the Western Aphasia Battery. PDD and AD patients were equated on a mental status test. Compared with AD patients, PDD patients showed greater deficits in motoric speech, including speech prosody, phrase length, and dysarthria. They found that PD patients showed hypophonia and dysarthria, neither of which was seen in AD. Darkins, Fromkin, and Benson (1988) confirmed the loss of prosody in PD patients, but not loss of linguistic knowledge, suggesting that dysprosody in PD is secondary to impaired motor control at the basal ganglia level. Caekebeke, Jennekens-Schinkel, var der Linden, Buruma, and Roos (1991) examined expressive and receptive prosody in PD patients, and confirmed dysprosody in expressive speech but not impairment on receptive language tasks. The authors concluded that dysprosody in PD is not a disorder of processing emotional information, but one of speech output.

Illes (1989) investigated spontaneous language production in patients with PD, AD, and HD. AD and HD patients showed temporal interruptions, verbal paraphasias, and "closed class" phrases, while PD patients showed long-duration, silent hesitations, and "open class" phrases. The results suggested that the pathology of the neostriatum in PD disrupts syntactic organization, and adaptive coping strategies lose effectiveness with increased severity of the disease. In contrast to studies that failed to find receptive impairment in PD, Grossman, Carvell, Gollomp, Stern, et al. (1991) examined the ability of nondemented PD patients to interpret grammatical aspects of sentences and found impairment in some patients on tests of sentence comprehension. This deficit was found to be correlated with reduced mesial frontal lobe glucose metabolism (as measured by PET imaging), suggesting a possible association with frontal-lobe attentional mechanisms.

Summary

PD patients frequently show impairment in motor aspects of speech, including dysprosody, hypoponia, reduced phrase length, and dysarthria. Patients may demonstrate mild impairments in naming and more significant impairment in word generation (verbal fluency). Paraphasic errors are rarely noted. Comprehension in PD, although grossly intact, may be affected by frontal-lobe-mediated attentional deficits, or may appear in conjunction with generalized dementia. However, investigators have not found the generalized breakdown of semantic language that characterizes AD.

Visuospatial Abilities

Many studies have noted poor visuospatial performance in PD. However, these findings have been disputed, and the nature and underlying mechanisms of spatial dysfunction in PD are not well understood. Evidence for visuospatial impairment comes from comparisons of Verbal and Performance scores of intellectual functioning on the WAIS or WAIS-R (Matthews & York-Haaland, 1979). Performance IQ of PD patients has been found to be up to 20 points below that of Verbal IQ (Loranger, Goodell, McDowell, Lee, & Sweet, 1972; Mohr et al., 1990). However, this evidence is offset by the probable effects of speed and motor dysfunction that directly influence timed Performance IQ scores. PD patients also have difficulty on tasks involving visual construction and copying of designs (e.g., the Rey Complex Figure) (Carvell, Peltzer, & Grossman, 1992; Richards, Cote, Groves, & Stern, 1992a; Stern et al., 1984). However, such visuoconstructive tests require planning and production of a complex motor sequence, and the results do not directly implicate an isolated deficit in visuoperceptual abilities.

Specific visuospatial deficits that have been reported in PD include impaired horizontal and vertical orientation (Danta & Hilton, 1975; Proctor, Riklan, Cooper, & Teuver, 1964), poor map-guided route walking (Bowen, Hoehn, & Yahr, 1972), and problems in mapping of external markers relative to proprioceptive space (Bowen, Burns, Brady, & Yahr, 1976). Bowen et al. (1976) found PD patients performed normally when asked to match points on their own bodies to markers on a dorsal view of a full body diagram (i.e., the task did not require mental rotation of the figure). The patients performed significantly worse than controls, however, when asked to match points on a ventral diagram of the body, a task that does require mental rotation.

PD patients have also been shown to be impaired on tests of visual matching, figure-ground discrimination, shape constancy, and spatial relationships (Portin & Rinne, 1980; Sahakian et al., 1988; Villardita, Smirni, Le Pira, Zappala, & Nicoletti, 1982). Rashkin et al. (1990) tested visual perception, discrimination, and spatial orientation, and found varying degrees of deficit that correlated with age, duration of disease, and degree of generalized dementia. Other investigators have reported deficits in visual perception, and spatial reasoning in PD (Regan & Maxner, 1987; Taylor et al., 1986). Hutton, Morris, Elias, Varma, et al. (1991) found reduced contrast sensitivity in patients with moderate physical impairment. Although Mortimer et al. (1982) failed to find deficits in simultaneous matching of line orientation or angle, they did find a deficit in these tasks with the interpolation of a delay period. Levin et al. (1991) reported on visuospatial performance of 183 idiopathic PD patients in various stages of disease progression. The authors found deteriorated visuospatial performance (compared with age- and education-matched control subjects) in five of six measures, with the severity of deficit related to both disease duration and presence or absence of dementia.

Hovestadt et al. (1987) administered PD patients the Verbal subtests of the WAIS and three tests of visuospatial function: (a) visual and tactile versions of the rod orientation test, (b) a line orientation test, and (c) a facial recognition test. Performance was impaired in both visual and tactile conditions of the rod orientation test, but not on the line orientation test or the facial recognition test. It was concluded that the PD patients demonstrated supramodal (visual and tactile) disturbances in spatial orientation. Pirozzolo et al. (1982) identified impaired visuospatial function in a large sample of PD patients. Discriminant analysis of tests not involving motor speed or accuracy showed that motor impairment was not sufficient to account for the deficits on visuospatial tests.

Mohr et al. (1990) compared visuospatial function in PD and AD, and found that PD patients were more impaired on tasks of visuospatial abstraction and reasoning. AD patients were more impaired on memory-associated visuospatial tasks, suggesting differences in underlying pathogenic mechanisms. Freedman and Oscar-Berman (1989) examined spatial and visual learning deficits in PD and AD, and found that PDD patients were less impaired on visual learning tasks than were

AD patients. Other investigators have confirmed PD patients to be less impaired than AD patients on tests of visuospatial reasoning (e.g., Raven's Matrices) (Gainotti et al., 1980; Huber et al., 1989a). Pan, Stern, Sano, and Mayeux (1989) investigated clock-drawing abilities in PD, PDD, and AD patients. AD and PDD patients had gross impairments in clock-drawing, including insertions and distortions, but nondemented PD patients showed restricted deficits in the spatial organization of clock numbers.

Other studies have failed to confirm findings of spatial impairment in PD. Della Sala et al. (1986) administered tests of visuospatial abilities, general cognitive abilities, and fine-motor coordination to PD patients with only mild cognitive involvement. The visuospatial tasks required the patients to judge where an inclined stimulus line would intercept a baseline at the bottom of the screen under several conditions. Minimal motor skills were required to respond. The PD patients were slower than controls on fine-motor testing, but no group differences were found on the visuospatial tasks. Boller et al. (1984) administered a battery of visuoperceptual and visuomotor tasks to mildly and moderately impaired PD patients. Visuospatial impairment was demonstrated on a visual matching task and on tasks requiring a complex motor response. However, PD patients were not impaired relative to controls on tests of spatial location, spatial reasoning, or spatial recognition memory.

Brown and Marsden (1986) compared PD patients with age-, sex-, and education-matched controls on a computer-generated visuospatial task requiring mental rotation of the stimulus cues. PD subjects were slower than controls on all tasks, but did not perform disproportionately worse as the stimulus conditions became more complex. Similar findings (i.e., no disproportionate slowing on more complex spatial tasks) have been reported on a spatial RT procedure comparing PD patients with and sex- and education-matched controls (Daum & Quinn, 1991).

In a review of visuospatial function in PD, Brown and Marsden (1986) conclude that the available evidence is not strong enough to unequivocally indicate an isolated visuospatial deficit. Rather, they suggest that the critical mental operation in many visuospatial tests is a shift in perceptual set. A deficit in shifting of response set is postulated to be associated with frontal-system involvement, and includes problems with set-shifting and impaired cognitive sequencing in the absence of extrapersonal cues (Brown & Marsden, 1986; Stern & Mayeux, 1986).

Summary

Although deficits on visuospatial tasks such as figural matching, spatial orientation, and spatial reasoning are frequently reported in PD, evidence for an isolated visuospatial impairment is not well established. Problems with perceptual-motor function, cognitive set-shifting, visual memory, and utilization of internal cues all make interpretation of the findings difficult. In particular, involvement of frontal-subcortical control functions may contribute to the results by affecting the organization and execution of visuospatial and visuomotor strategies.

Executive Control

Neuroanatomical studies suggest the presence of multiple parallel basal ganglia-thalamocortical circuits in the human and primate cerebrum, involving the striatum, ventrolateral and dorsal medial nuclei of the thalamus, frontal eye fields, cortical motor areas (supplementary motor and premotor), and granular association areas of the frontal lobes (DeLong et al., 1983; Goldman-Rakic & Friedman, 1991). Two of these pathways, the "motor" loop and the "oculomotor" loop are implicated in the programming and execution of complex motor actions. Additional pathways, including a "dorsolateral prefrontal" loop, a "lateral orbitofrontal" loop, and an "anterior cingulate" loop are postulated to underlie other cognitive "executive" abilities, including spatial memory, switching of mental set, and attentional control (Alexander et al., 1986).

Impaired abilities in PD such as motor planning and sequencing, memory retrieval, temporal ordering, verbal fluency, and visuospatial function have also been documented in subjects with frontal lobe lesions (Fuster, 1991; Goldman-Rakic & Friedman, 1991; Grafman, 1989; Shallice, 1988). Such frontal system involvement is postulated to underlie executive functions, including the planning, maintenance, and sequencing of actions; shifting of response set; delayed spatial memory; and control of attentional strategies (Cools, Van Den Bercken, Hostink, Van Spaendonck, & Berger, 1984; Pillon et al., 1986; Stern & Mayeux, 1986; Taylor et al., 1988; Taylor et al., 1986).

Several lines of evidence suggest the involvement of frontal system dysfunction in PD. Reduced dopamine in nigrostriatal pathways is thought to result in functional deafferentation of frontal regions from portions of the striatum involved in cognition (Bernheimer, Birkmayer, Hornykiewicz, Jellinger, & Seitelberger, 1973; Hornykiewicz, 1982; Kish, Shannak, & Hornykiewicz, 1988). Stern, Herman, Rosen, and Mayeux (1985) demonstrated that patients with parkinsonism secondary to MPTP exposure (which exerts a neurotoxic effect on the nigrostriatal system) showed frontal-cognitive deficits similar to those seen in idiopathic PD. Even MPTP patients with minimal parkinsonian signs showed executive deficits. Flurodopamine-labeled PET imaging showed these same patients to have lowered striatal dopamine levels, implicating frontal-striatal influences on executive cognitive functions (Stern, Tetrud, Martin, Kutner, & Langston, 1990). Other PET imaging studies have implicated reduced activation of frontal-subcortical structures associated with cognitive impairment in nondemented PD patients (Goldenberg, Podreka, Muller, & Deecke, 1989; Snow, 1992; Wolfson, Leenders, Brown, & Jones, 1985).

Piccirilli, D'Alessandro, Finali, and Piccinin (1989) divided PD patients without general intellectual impairment into subgroups with and without frontal motor deficits (impaired motor control). Patients were reexamined after a mean period of 4 years, at which time early frontal motor dysfunction was found to be a significant predictor of later intellectual decline. Litvan, Mohr, Williams, Gomez, & Chase (1991) confirmed greater deficits on tasks of executive function in early PD than in early AD patients, with AD patients more impaired on semantic and episodic memory tasks. Poor temporal ordering and deficits on delayed matching to sample tasks in PD also suggest involvement of dorsolateral frontal lobe regions (Goldman & Rosvold, 1970; Milner, Corsi, & Leonard, 1991). In this regard, Brown and Marsden (1990) suggest that memory problems in PD are specifically associated with frontal-subcortical deficits, which disturb executive control of working memory and attentional systems.

The WCST has been the focus of several studies in PD. Although use of the WCST as a specific marker for frontal lobe dysfunction has been challenged (Anderson, Damasio, Jones, & Tranel, 1991), investigations of PD patients have consistently shown impairments in their ability to establish, maintain, and shift mental set on this test (Bowen, Kamienny, Burns, & Yahr, 1975; Cools et al., 1984; Flowers, 1982; Flowers & Robertson, 1985; Lees & Smith, 1983; Taylor et al., 1986; Vance, Kaszniak, Bayles, & Bondi, 1991). Poor performance on the WCST has been found in PD patients early in the disease course who have not developed significant dementia (Lees & Smith, 1983). PD patients have also been shown to be impaired on the WCST relative to AD patients, when matched for severity of dementia (Pillon et al., 1986). Caltagirone, Carlesimo, Nocentini, and Vicari (1989) used a neuropsychological battery to subgroup PD patients into those with "diffuse mental deterioration" and those without. Nondemented PD patients scored worse than controls on the WCST, but obtained similar scores on tests of memory, visual-construction, and language. These findings suggest that deficits in tasks of concept formation and set shifting are independent of general dementia in PD. Nondemented PD patients have also been shown to perform poorly on other tasks that require central executive control, including delayed recognition, the Stroop interference paradigm, and perceptual set-shifting (Brown & Marsden, 1988; Flowers & Robertson, 1985; Henik, Singh, Beckley, & Rafal, 1992; Richards, Cote, & Stjern, 1992b).

Studies by Freedman et al. (Freedman, 1990; Freedman & Oscar-Berman, 1986) have compared performance of PD and AD patients on tests of delayed alternation (DA) and delayed response (DR), both of which are associated with integrity of prefrontal regions (Goldman, Rosvold, Vest, & Galkin, 1971; Mishkin, 1957; Mishkin, 1964). Both groups were found to be impaired on DR, suggesting involvement of dorsolateral frontal cortex or its projection systems. However, only AD patients were impaired on DA, suggesting orbitofrontal system involvement in AD but not PD. A follow-up study (Freedman, 1990) compared PDD and AD patients on an object alternation task (OA). Although both dementia groups were impaired relative to normal controls, AD patients made significantly more errors of response perseveration, suggesting greater orbitofrontal deficit in AD, and greater dorsolateral involvement in PD.

Summary

Neuroanatomical and neuroimaging studies implicate involvement of frontal-subcortical systems in the cognitive deficits of PD. Executive dyscontrol may account for specific cognitive impairments, even when there is not generalized dementia. Affected neuropsychological domains may include motor planning and sequencing, memory retrieval, temporal ordering, verbal fluency, visuospatial function, maintenance and shifting of response set, delayed response performance, control of attentional strategies, and efficient use of working memory.

Affective and Psychiatric Features

Depression is a common feature in PD, with estimates of its prevalence ranging from 30% to 70% (Levin, Llabre, & Weiner, 1988; Matison et al., 1982). Mayeux, Stern, Rosen, and Leventhal (1981b) reported significant depression, as defined by DSM-III criteria, in 47% of a group of PD patients, as compared with 12% in a control group matched for age, education, and socioeconomic background. A positive correlation was found between the intensity of depression and the degree of intellectual loss, including deficits in attention, calculation, and verbal recall. Mayeux et al. (1983) reported that PD patients were more depressed than AD patients with a similar degree of cognitive impairment. Other investigators have reported higher depression scores in PD patients than in AD patients or normal controls (Huber, Paulson, & Shuttleworth, 1988; Huber et al., 1989a; Mortimer, 1988b).

The underlying neurochemistry of depression in PD remains unclear. Primary hypotheses implicate disruption of mesolimbic dopamine projection pathways (Mayberg et al., 1990; Santamaria et al., 1986). An association has also been postulated between depression, bradyphrenia and dopamine dysfunction in PD (Rogers et al., 1987; Rogers et al., 1986). Several investigators have found reduced cerebrospinal 5-HIAA, a metabolite of serotonin, in depressed PD patients compared with nondepressed patients and normal controls (Mayeux, Stern, Sano, Williams, & Cote, 1988b; Sano et al., 1989). PD patients who showed both dementia and depression had the lowest values, suggesting an interaction between serotonin levels, cognitive impairment, and depressive features. Depressed PD patients are similar to patients with uncomplicated major depression in frequently showing nonsuppression on the dexamethasone suppression test, implicating dysfunction of the hypothalamic-pituitary-adrenal axis (Frochtengarten, Villares, Maluf, & Carlini, 1987; Pfeiffer et al., 1986).

Depression in PD patients has been reported to antedate the onset of overt physical symptoms and to parallel the severity of cognitive symptoms, lending support to a hypothesis of an endogenous rather than reactive basis for the affective disturbance (Mayeux et al., 1981b; Mindham, 1970). Studies have shown that PD patients are depressed more frequently than patients with equally severe physical disabilities (Dakof & Mendelsohn, 1986). Ehmann, Beninger, Gawel, and Riopelle (1990) assessed depressive symptoms in 45 PD patients and 24 disabled controls who were equated for functional disability. The PD patients obtained significantly higher total scores on the Beck Depression Inventory.

Guze and Barrio (1991) suggested that there may be two forms of PD, one with rapid cognitive decline and depression, the other with more gradual decline and no depression. Huber et al. (1988) reported significantly more rigidity and akinesia in depressed than in nondepressed PD patients. Tomer and Levin (1992) compared depressed and nondepressed PD subjects and found a symptom-by-depression interaction, in which the two groups did not differ except on memory tests, which were performed worse by depressed patients with physical signs of rigidity. Mayberg et al. (1990) studied depressed PD patients using PET imaging, and found significant correlations between depression and decreased metabolism in the orbital-inferior area of the frontal lobe, suggesting involvement of frontal-caudate pathways in affective dysfunction. Starkstein et al. (1989) and Mayberg et al. (1990) examined cognitive impairments and depression in PD and stroke patients, and found major depression to be significantly associated with cognitive deficits in both groups. The nature of cognitive deficits in these groups was similar to deficits found in patients with primary major depression, who also have been shown to have basal ganglia hypometabolism in PET imaging studies (Mayberg, 1993).

Other studies have failed to find consistent correlations between depressive symptoms in PD and severity of illness, age, sex, or mode of treatment (Huber et al., 1988; Robbins, 1976). Bieliauskas and Glantz (1989) found depression in 70% of a sample of PD patients. However, they found nonsignificant correlations between scores on the Depression subscale of the Minnesota Multiphasic Personality Inventory (MMPI) and presence of dementia, disease stage, memory and attention scores, or frontal lobe measures, suggesting that depression in PD is of a reactive nature and is independent of intellectual deficits. Other investigators have noted that the clinical presentation of depression in PD resembles a reactive rather than endogenous form of affective disorder (Taylor et al., 1988). Gotham et al. (Gotham, Brown, & Marsden, 1986) found that although significantly higher self-rated depression scores were obtained for PD patients than normal controls, this difference was equal to that of a matched group of patients with chronic arthritis, again suggesting that reactive mechanisms may partially account for depressive features in PD.

With regard to other psychiatric features, psychotic symptoms such as hallucinations and delusions are rare in PD, and usually are related to dopamine side-effects. Friedman et al. (1991) examined psychotic complications of L-dopa in PD patients, and found that patients with older age of onset were at greater risk for complications than were younger patients. Sandyk and Kay (1990) examined the overlap between parkinsonism and negative symptoms of schizophrenia, including apathy, alogia, and anhedonia. The findings suggested that negative symptoms are primary in PD and may reflect basal ganglia dysfunction.

Summary

Most investigators concur regarding the increased incidence of depression in PD, although the nature of depressive features and their relationship to cognition is unclear. Whatever the mechanism underlying depression in PD, antidepressant therapy and counseling should always be considered where indicated. The neuropsychologist must also take into account the effects of depression on test performance, and consider re-testing a depressed patient once a course of treatment has been instituted. When present, psychotic features in PD are usually related to medication side-effects.

Treatment

Treatment of parkinsonism before the 1960s was limited, involving either partial thalamotomy or medication with anticholinergic agents. These methods partially alleviated tremor, but had little effect on the more disabling symptoms of bradykinesia and rigidity (Jankovic & Marsden, 1988). The demonstration of dopaminergic nigrostriatal pathways and of severely reduced dopaminergic levels in the substantia nigra (Hornykiewicz, 1966; Hornykiewicz, 1982), led to the introduction of L-dopa as the primary pharmacologic treatment (Cotzias, Papavasiliou, & Gellen, 1969). The combination of carbidopa (a decarboxylase inhibitor that does not cross the blood-brain barrier) with L-dopa prevents conversion of L-dopa to dopamine outside the CNS. This decreases peripheral side effects and allows for greater concentrations of L-dopa in cerebral circulation (Papavasiliou, Cotzias, Duby, et al., 1972).

Although L-dopa often provides dramatic relief of hypokinesia and rigidity, it has little effect on tremor and does not stop the basic disease progression (Yahr, 1990). L-dopa appears to have maximum effectiveness in the first few years of administration. Since there is no evidence that it slows disease progression and side-effects are frequent (nausea, choreic movements, cardiac dysrhythmias, hallucinations, orthostatic hypotension), L-dopa treatment often is delayed until absolutely essential. Alternative pharmacological therapies are frequently used, including amantadine (an antiviral agent that acts to release dopamine from intact neurons) and, more recently, postsynaptic dopaminergic agonists (bromocriptine, pergolide, and lisuride) (Jankovic, 1985; Marsden, 1990). Additionally, anticholinergic drugs are used to reduce the effects of heightened cholinergic activity resulting from disruptions of the cerebral dopamine-acetylcholine balance. These agents include atropine, scopolamine, benztropine, and trihexyphenidyl. It is important to recognize that, to that extent memory deficits are associated with decreased cholinergic activity in PD, anticholinergic medications may compound memory loss.

Psychotic symptoms may occur as a side effect of dopamine therapy. Friedman et al. (1991) discuss management of L-dopa-induced psychosis in PD. They suggest reduction in parkinsonian medications for patients with nondepressive psychoses, or treatment with antipsychotic drugs, preferably clozapine, in patients who cannot tolerate worsening of parkinsonian symptoms. Kahn et al. (1991) studied long-term efficacy of clozapine in PD patients with psychotic complications and found significant improvement in symptoms.

Although the motor symptoms of PD improve with L-dopa therapy, beneficial effects on cognition have not been established (Botez & Barbeau, 1975; Halgrin et al., 1977; Hamel & Riklan, 1975; Riklan, Whelihan, & Cullinan, 1976; Sweet, McDowell, Feigenson, Loranger, & Goodell, 1976). To address this issue researchers have compared patients during "on" periods of L-dopa treatment (when motor symptom control is maximal due to optimal plasma drug levels) and during "off" periods (when motor symptom control is minimal due to suboptimal plasma drug levels). Pillon et al. (1989) tested patients with a timed overlapping figures test, and reported that cognitive slowing failed to respond to treatment with L-dopa. Gotham et al. (1988) obtained a more complicated pattern of results. Subjects were impaired on a test of verbal fluency only when off L-dopa, but showed deficits on tests of associative conditional learning and subject-ordered pointing only when *on* L-dopa. Pullman, Watts, Juncos, Chase, and Sanes (1988) examined simple and choice reaction time while controlling intravenous L-dopa infusion. Simple reaction time was slow (compared with normal subjects) at all infusion drug levels. Choice reaction time was normal at high L-dopa infusion levels, but became prolonged at low plasma levels.

Rafal et al. (1984) administered several chronometric tasks to separate the effects of treatment on motor slowing and cognitive slowing. One group of subjects was studied before and following L-dopa treatment. A second group was studied while receiving L-dopa treatment but under two separate on and off treatment conditions. The overall results suggested that motor-related task components, but not cognitive-related task components, were affected by drug treatment. Horiguchi et al. (1991) studied 89 patients with PD and found that intellectual deterioration did not correlate with amount of L-dopa treatment. Hietanen and Teravainen (1988a) failed to find differences between L-dopa-treated and untreated young PD patients. Treated older patients performed worse than untreated patients on memory tests and intellectual tests (Wechsler Memory Scale [WMS] and WAIS). However, the duration of L-dopa treatment did not correlate with degree of cognitive deficits, suggesting a possible independence of mechanisms.

Two new treatment approaches for PD have generated much clinical interest. Transplantation of dopamine producing cells (from the adrenal gland or fetal brain tissue) to the basal ganglia has been performed, and results have now appeared in many research publications (Allen, Burns, Tulipan, & Parker, 1989; Freed et al., 1990; Goetz et al., 1991; Lindvall et al., 1990; Madrazo, Drucker-Colin, V., et al., 1987; Peterson, Price, & Small, 1989; Waters, Apuzzo, Neal, & Weiner, 1992). Although selected patients have shown modest improvement with adrenal transplants, the overall degree of success has been disappointing. Studies with fetal transplants show more promising results, and this treatment approach promises future benefits as techniques are further refined (Thompson, 1992).

The second new treatment modality is the use of selegiline (L-deprenyl), a monoamine oxidase type B (MAO-B) inhibitor. MAO-B promotes the breakdown of dopamine and is also involved in metabolic pathways yielding free radicals, substances believed to cause cell damage. Vitamin E (tocopherol) is another agent that decreases free radical activity and some recent studies have used tocopherol in combination with selegiline. There is preliminary evidence that selegiline, unlike L-dopa, may actually slow disease progression (Fahn & Group, 1991; Kofman, 1991; Myllyla, Sotaniemi, Vuorinen, & Heinonen, 1992).

In addition to pharmacological agents for treatment of motor symptoms, a PD patient can be offered physical therapy to reduce stiffness and pain resulting from rigidity and muscle cramps. Occupational therapy can be employed to teach the patient how to compensate for movement restrictions, and how to use adaptive devices for everyday activities. Psychoactive medications, particularly tricyclic antidepressants and derivatives are frequently used for treatment of depression, although the patient must be carefully monitored for presence of psychotic symptoms and adverse physical side effects. Supportive therapy (for depression, adjustment to disability; and family, occupational, and interpersonal difficulties) is frequently indicated. Patients with progressive neurological disease usually respond well to being informed of the nature of symptoms, course of illness, length of time for productive activity, and a realistic appraisal of new treatments being developed.

Related Disorders

Progressive Supranuclear Palsy

Progressive supranuclear palsy (PSP) is frequently misdiagnosed as PD, particularly in early disease stages (Golbe & Davis, 1988). However, PSP is a less common disorder and differs from PD in several important respects. Tremor is less conspicuous in PSP than in PD, and the facial expression in PSP is usually described as "grimacing," in contrast to the "masked" face of PD. The axial rigidity of PSP affects the neck most prominently, causing an erect posture rather than the stooped posture of PD. Eye movement disorders (especially of down gaze) are more prominent in PSP.

The neuropathology of PSP overlaps with that of PD, but important differences are present. Degeneration occurs in a number of brainstem nuclei, including the periaqueductal grey matter, subthalamic nucleus, substantia nigra, globus pallidus, caudate, and putamen. Neurofibrillary tangles, rather than the Lewy bodies of PD, are consistently found. Recent PET scan studies have reported frontal hypometabolism in PSP (Goffinet et al., 1989; Leenders, Frackowiak, & Lees, 1988).

Cognitive decline has been associated with PSP since the disorder was first described by Steele, Richardson, and Olszewski (1964). Several researchers, however, have made the observation that test performance is often normal if test administration and choice of tests takes into account the characteristic eye movement disorder in PSP (Kimura, Barnett, & Burkhart, 1981; Pirozzolo, Swihart, Rey, Jankovic, & Mortimer, 1988). Nonetheless, recent studies have documented impaired performance on tests sensitive to frontal lobe dysfunction (Maher, Smith, & Lees, 1985; Milberg & Albert, 1989; Pillon, Dubois, Ploska, & Agid, 1991; Pillon et al., 1986). Treatment of PSP is much less effective than treatment of PD. Dopamine agonists and L-dopa have been used, but with only marginal results.

Multisystem Atrophy

"Multisystem atrophy" refers to a disease or spectrum of diseases in which degeneration occurs in the basal ganglia, but also occurs to a marked extent outside the extrapyramidal system (Quinn, 1989). Cell loss and gliosis occurs in various structures including the substantia nigra, caudate, putamen, globus pallidus, inferior olives, pontine nuclei, cerebellar Purkinje cells, intermediolateral cell columns of the spinal cord, and Onuf's nucleus. Patients may have autonomic nervous system dysfunction (orthostatic hypotension, impotence, incontinence) or prominent cerebellar symptoms. Dementia is present in some patients, but the percentage of patients so affected is unknown, partially because of confusion of nomenclature and diagnostic uncertainty. Some writers classify striatonigral degeneration, OPCA, and Shy-Drager syndrome under the rubric of "multisystem atrophy." The inconsistent nomenclature adds uncertainty to identification of the symptom complex (Quinn, 1989).

Olivopontocerebellar Atrophy

In addition to classic cerebellar features of gait ataxia, incoordination, hypotonia, and dysarthria, OPCA is characterized by extracerebellar signs of ophthalmoplegia and pyramidal tract involvement. Onset of this slowly progressive disease is usually between the ages of 30 and 50 years. OPCA can be either sporadic (unknown etiology) or genetic in origin (Adams & Victor, 1989; Berciano, 1988).

OPCA is one of the few multisystem disorders for which neuropsychological data are available. Neuropsychological test performance of 14 patients with dominantly inherited OPCA was compared to performance of subjects equated for age, educational status, and gender (Kish et al., 1988). Nonmotor tests of intellectual ability, memory, attention, naming, visuospatial function, and frontal system function were administered. Impairment in performance on verbal and nonverbal intellectual ability, verbal memory, visuospatial organization, and frontal system function (concept formation, shifting conceptual set, and sorting into classes according to concepts) was found in the OPCA patients relative to controls. Although deficits were for the most part mild, test results positively correlated with severity of cerebellar ataxia.

This finding is in contrast to results of an extensive neuropsychological test battery administered to 39 patients with OPCA who were compared with 25 normal controls of similar age (Berent et al., 1990). After controlling for differences in education and motor performance, no differences in intellectual or cognitive abilities were revealed. Scores on two instruments of personality function and subjective complaints revealed that the patients rated themselves as more depressed, anxious, and in greater distress than normal controls. Patient scores, however, were within normal limits using published normative data. The authors concluded that differences in motor ability and educational achievement accounted for apparent differences in intellectual and cognitive ability, and that impairment in motor ability and the presence of depressed mood may lead one to believe that patients with OPCA have greater cognitive impairment than is actually the case. However, they acknowledged that impaired cognition may be variable in the disease and may reflect involvement above the level of the cerebellum.

Diffuse Lewy Body Disease

Diffuse Lewy body disease has been examined in several recent publications. Lewy bodies are neuropathological cellular inclusions found both cortically and subcortically in various neurologic disorders (Armstrong et al., 1991; Burkhardt et al., 1988; Byrne, Lennox, Lowe, & Godwin-Austen, 1989; Dickson et al., 1991; Gibb, Esiri, & Lees, 1985; Gibb, Luthert, Janota, & Lantos, 1989; Hansen et al., 1990). Parkinsonian motor symptoms are common in diffuse Lewy body disease, and dementia has been reported in a high frequency of cases. However, there is limited systematic study of cognitive changes. Some writers classify diffuse Lewy body disease as a variant of PD; others consider it a variant of Alzheimer's disease. Diagnosis is invariably made at autopsy; the disorder is thus of theoretical interest but of lesser significance to the clinician.

Corticobasal Degeneration

Corticobasal degeneration is a progressive neurodegenerative disease that presents with an asymmetric-akinetic rigid syndrome and combinations of supranuclear gaze palsy, myoclonus, and dementia. Characteristic pathological features include swollen, achromatic neurons and degeneration of the cerebral cortex and substantia nigra. Neuropathological changes similar to those of Pick's disease have been found on autopsy (Gibb et al., 1989; Riley et al., 1990; Sawle et al., 1991). The cognitive deficits have not been well described, but apraxia is frequently mentioned.

Summary

In general, the nature, course, and neuropathological correlates of cognitive impairments in PD-related disorders are inadequately defined because of uncertainties and inconsistencies in clinical and pathological features. Improved clinical characterization of the disorders and more widespread application of formal neuropsychological testing should aid in further determination of disease-specific cognitive profiles.

References

Adams, R. D., & Victor, M. (1989). *Principles of neurology* (4th ed.). New York: McGraw-Hill.

Agid, Y. (1991). Parkinson's disease: Pathophysiology. *Lancet, 337,* 1321–1324.

Agid, Y., Ruberg, M., Dubois, B., & Javoy-Agid, F. (1984). Biochemical substrates of mental disturbances in Parkinson's disease. *Advances in Neurology, 40,* 211–218.

Albert, M. L. (1978). Subcortical dementia. In R. Katzman, R. Terry, & K. Bick (Eds.), *Alzheimer's disease: Senile dementia and related disorders* (pp. 173–196). New York: Raven Press.

Albert, M. L., Feldman, R. G., & Willis, A. (1974). The "subcortical dementia" of progressive supranuclear palsy. *Journal of Neurology, Neurosurgery and Psychiatry, 37,* 121–130.

Albin, R. L., Young, A. B., & Penney, J. B. (1989). The functional anatomy of basal ganglia disorders. *Trends in Neuroscience, 12,* 366–375.

Alexander, G. E., DeLong, M. R., & Strick, P. L. (1986). Parallel organization of functionally segregated circuits linking basal ganglia and cortex. *Annual Review of Neuroscience, 9,* 357–381.

Allen, G. S., Burns, S., Tulipan, N. B., & Parker, R. A. (1989). Adrenal medullary transplantation to the caudate nucleus in Parkinson's disease: Initial clinical results in 18 patients. *Archives of Neurology, 46,* 487–491.

Anderson, S. W., Damasio, H., Jones, R. D., & Tranel, D. (1991). Wisconsin Card Sorting Test performance as a measure of frontal lobe damage. *Journal of Clinical and Experimental Neuropsychology, 13,* 909–922.

Armstrong, T. P., Hansen, L. A., Salmon, D. P., Masliah, E., Pay, M., Kunin, J. M., & Katzman, R. (1991). Rapidly progressive dementia in a patient with Lewy body variant of Alzheimer's disease. *Neurology, 41,* 1178–1180.

American Psychiatric Association. (1987). *Diagnostic and statistical manual of mental disorders.* Washington, DC: Author.

Au, R., Moss, M. B., White, R. F., Saint-Hilaire, M., & Feldman, R. G. (1992). Recognition memory in patients with Parkinson's disease. *Journal of Clinical and Experimental Neuropsychology, 14,* 51.

Aubert, I., Araujo, D. M., Cecyre, D., Robitaille, Y., Gauthier, S., & Quirion, R. (1992). Comparative alterations of nicotinic and muscarinic binding sites in Alzheimer's and Parkinson's diseases. *Journal of Neurochemistry, 58,* 529–541.

Bakchine, S., Locamblez, L., Palisson, E., Laurent, M., & Derouesne, C. (1989). Relationship between primitive reflexes, extra-pyramidal signs, reflective apraxia, and severity of cognitive impairment in dementia of the Alzheimer type. *Acta Neurologica Scandinavica, 79,* 38–46.

Ball, M. J. (1984). The morphological basis of dementia in Parkinson's disease. *Canadian Journal of Neurological Sciences, 11,* 180–184.

Bayles, K. A., & Tomoeda, C. K. (1983). Confrontation naming impairment in dementia. *Brain and Language, 19,* 98–114.

Beatty, W. W., & Monson, N. (1989). Lexical processing in Parkinson's disease and multiple sclerosis. *Journal of Geriatric Psychiatry and Neurology, 2,* 145–152.

Beatty, W. W., & Monson, N. (1990). Picture and motor sequencing in Parkinson's disease. *Journal of Geriatric Psychiatry and Neurology*, *3*, 192–197.

Benecke, R., Rothwell, J. C., Dick, J. P. R., Day, B. L., & Marsden, C. D. (1987). Disturbance of sequential movements in patients with Parkinson's disease. *Brain*, *110*, 361–379.

Berciano, J. (1988). Olivopontocerebellar atrophy. In J. Jankovic & E. Tolosa (Eds.), *Parkinson's disease and movement disorders* (pp. 131–151). Baltimore: Urban & Schwarzenberg.

Berent, S., Giordani, B., Gilman, S., Junck, L., Lehtinen, S., Markel, D. S., Boivin, M., Kluin, K. J., Parks, R., & Koeppe, R. A. (1990). Neuropsychological changes in olivopontocerebellar atrophy. *Archives of Neurology*, *47*, 997–1001.

Bernheimer, H., Birkmayer, W., Hornykiewicz, O., Jellinger, K., & Seitelberger, F. (1973). Brain dopamine and the syndromes of Parkinson, Huntington. Clinical, morphological and neurochemical correlations. *Journal of Neuroscience*, *20*, 415–455.

Bieliauskas, L. A., & Glantz, R. H. (1989). Depression type in Parkinson disease. *Journal of Clinical and Experimental Neuropsychology*, *11*, 597–604.

Boller, F., Mizutani, T., Roessmann, U., & Gambetti, P. (1980). Parkinson disease, dementia, and Alzheimer disease: Clinicopathological correlations. *Annals of Neurology*, *7*, 329–335.

Boller, F., Passafiume, D., Keefe, N. C., Rogers, K., Morrow, L., & Kim, Y. (1984). Visuospatial impairments in Parkinson's disease: Role of perceptual and motor factors. *Archives of Neurology*, *41*, 485–490.

Bondi, M. W., & Kaszniak, A. W. (1991). Implicit and explicit memory in Alzheimer's disease and Parkinson's disease. *Journal of Clinical and Experimental Neuropsychology*, *13*, 339–358.

Botez, M. I., & Barbeau, A. (1975). Neuropsychological findings in Parkinson's disease: A comparison between various tests during long-term levodopa therapy. *International Journal of Neurology*, *10*, 222–232.

Bowen, F. P., Burns, M. M., Brady, E. M., & Yahr, M. D. (1976). A note on alterations of personal orientation in Parkinsonism. *Neuropsychologia*, *14*, 425–429.

Bowen, F. P., Hoehn, M. M., & Yahr, M. D. (1972). Parkinsonism: Alterations and spatial orientation as determined by a route-walking test. *Neuropsychologia*, *10*, 355–361.

Bowen, F. P., Kamienny, R. S., Burns, M. M., & Yahr, M. D. (1975). Parkinsonism: Effects of levodopa treatment on concept formation. *Neurology*, *25*, 701–704.

Boyd, J. L., Cruickshank, C. A., Kenn, C. W., Madeley, P., Mindham, R. H., Oswald, A. G., Smith, R. J., & Spokes, E. G. (1991). Cognitive impairment and dementia in Parkinson's disease: A controlled study. *Psychological Medicine*, *21*, 911–921.

Bradley, V. A., Welch, J. L., & Dick, D. J. (1989). Visuospatial working memory in Parkinson's disease. *Journal of Neurology, Neurosurgery and Psychiatry*, *52*, 1228–1235.

Brooks, D. J. (1991). Detection of preclinical Parkinson's disease with PET. *Neurology*, *41*, 24–27.

Brown, R. G., & Marsden, C. D. (1990). Cognitive function in Parkinson's disease: From description to theory. *Trends in Neuroscience*, *13*, 21–29.

Brown, R. G., & Marsden, C. D. (1984). How common is dementia in Parkinson's disease? *Lancet*, *2*(8414), 1262–1265.

Brown, R. G., & Marsden, C. D. (1986). Visuospatial function in Parkinson's disease. *Brain*, *109*, 987–1002.

Brown, R. G., & Marsden, C. D. (1988). Internal versus external cues and the control of attention in Parkinson's disease. *Brain*, *111*, 323–345.

Burkhardt, C. R., Filley, C. M., Kleinschmidt-DeMasters, B. K., De la Monte, S., Norenberg, M. D., & Schneck, S. A. (1988). Diffuse Lewy body disease and progressive dementia. *Neurology, 38*, 1520–1528.

Butters, N. (1991). Subcortical dementia: A valid neuropsychological construct? *Journal of Clinical and Experimental Neuropsychology, 13*, 93.

Butters, N., Granholm, E., Salmon, D. P., Gjrant, I., & Wolfe, J. (1987). Episodic and semantic memory: A comparison of amnesic and demented patients. *Journal of Clinical and Experimental Neuropsychology, 9*, 479–497.

Byrne, E. J., Lennox, G., Lowe, J., & Godwin-Austen, R. B. (1989). Diffuse Lewy body disease: Clinical features in 15 cases. *Journal of Neurology, Neurosurgery and Psychiatry, 52*, 709–717.

Caekebeke, J. F., Jennekens-Schinkel, A., van der Linden, M. E., Buruma, O. J., & Roos, R. A. (1991). The interpretation of dysprosody in patients with Parkinson's disease. *Journal of Neurology, Neurosurgery and Psychiatry, 54*, 145–148.

Calne, D. B., Langston, J. W., Martin, W. R. W., Stoessl, A. S., Ruth, T. J., Adam, M. J., Pate, B. D., & Schulzer, M. (1985). Positron emission tomography after MPTP: Observations relating to the cause of Parkinson's disease. *Nature, 317*, 246–248.

Caltagirone, C., Carlesimo, A., Nocentini, U., & Vicari, S. (1989). Defective concept formation in parkinsonians is independent from mental deterioration. *Journal of Neurology, Neurosurgery and Psychiatry, 52*, 334–337.

Carvell, S., Peltzer, L., & Grossman, M. (1992). Visuo-constructional processing deficits in Parkinson's disease. *Journal of Clinical and Experimental Neuropsychology, 14*, 82.

Cash, R., Ruberg, M., Raisman, R., & Agid, Y. (1984). Adrenergic receptors in Parkinson's disease. *Brain Research, 322*, 269–275.

Celesia, G. G., & Wanamaker, W. M. (1972). Psychiatric disturbances in Parkinson's disease. *Diseases of the Nervous System, 33*, 577–583.

Chan-Palay, V. (1988). Galanin hyperinnervates surviving neurons of the human basal nucleus of Meynert in dementias of Alzheimer's and Parkinson's disease: A hypothesis for the role of galanin in accentuating cholinergic dysfunction in dementia. *Journal of Comparative Neurology, 273*, 543–557.

Chui, H. C., Mortimer, J. A., Slager, U., Zarow, C., Bondareff, W., & Webster, D. D. (1986). Pathologic correlates of dementia in Parkinson's disease. *Archives of Neurology, 43*, 991–995.

Clevens, R. A., & Beal, M. F. (1989). Substance P-like immunoreactivity in brains with pathological features of Parkinson's and Alzheimer's diseases. *Brain Research, 486*, 387–390.

Como, P. G., & Caine, E. D. (1987). A comparative neuropsychological study of AD and PD. *Journal of Clinical and Experimental Neuropsychology, 9*, 74.

Cools, A. R., Van Den Bercken, J. H. L., Hostink, M. W. I., Van Spaendonck, K. P. M., & Berger, J. H. C. (1984). Cognitive and motor shifting aptitude disorder in Parkinson's disease. *Journal of Neurology, Neurosurgery and Psychiatry, 47*, 443–453.

Cooper, J. A., Sagar, H. J., Jordan, N., Harvey, N. S., & Sullivan, E. V. (1991). Cognitive impairment in early, untreated Parkinson's disease and its relationship to motor disability. *Brain, 114*, 2095–2122.

Cotzias, G. C., Papavasiliou, P. S., & Gellen, R. (1969). Modification of parkinsonism—chronic treatment with L-dopa. *New England Journal of Medicine, 280*, 337–345.

Cummings, J. L. (1988). The dementia of Parkinson disease: Prevalence, characteristics, neurobiology, and comparison with dementia of the Alzheimer type. *European Neurology, 28*:(Suppl. 1), 15–23.

Cummings, J. L., & Benson, D. F. (1984). Subcortical dementia. Review of an emerging concept. *Archives of Neurology, 41*, 874–879.

Cummings, J. L., & Benson, D. F. (1988). Psychological dysfunction accompanying subcortical dementias. *Annual Review of Medicine*, *39*, 53–61.

Cummings, J. L., & Benson, D. F. (1992). *Dementia: A clinical approach* (2nd ed.). Boston: Butterworth-Heinemann.

Cummings, J. L., Darkins, A., Mendez, M., Hill, M. A., & Benson, D. F. (1988). Alzheimer's disease and Parkinson's disease: Comparison of speech and language alterations. *Neurology*, *38*, 1556–1561.

Dakof, G. A., & Mendelsohn, G. A. (1986). Parkinson's disease: The psychological aspects of a chronic illness. *Psychological Bulletin*, *99*, 375–397.

Danta, G., & Hilton, R. C. (1975). Judgment of the visual vertical and horizontal in patients with Parkinsonism. *Neurology*, *25*, 43–47.

Darkins, A. W., Fromkin, V. A., & Benson, D. F. (1988). A characterization of the prosodic loss in Parkinson's disease. *Brain and Language*, *34*, 315–327.

Daum, I., & Quinn, N. (1991). Reaction times and visuospatial processing in Parkinson's disease. *Journal of Clinical and Experimental Neuropsychology*, *13*, 972–982.

de la Monte, S. M., Wells, S. E., Hedley-Whyte, T., & Growdon, J. H. (1989). Neuropathological distinction between Parkinson's plus Alzheimer's disease. *Annals of Neurology*, *26*, 309–320.

De Lancey Horne, D. (1973). Sensorimotor control in parkinsonism. *Journal of Neurology, Neurosurgery and Psychiatry*, *36*, 742–746.

Della Sala, S., Di Lorenzo, G., Giordano, A., & Spinnler, H. (1986). Is there a specific visuo-spatial impairment in parkinsonians? *Journal of Neurology, Neurosurgery and Psychiatry*, *49*, 1258–1265.

DeLong, M. R., Georgopoulos, A. P., & Crutcher, M. D. (1983). Cortico-basal ganglia relations and coding of motor performance. *Experimental Brain Research*, (Suppl. 7), 30–40.

Dickson, D. W., Ruan, D., Crystal, H., Mark, M. H., Davies, P., Kress, Y., & Yen, S. H. (1991). Hippocampal degeneration differentiates diffuse Lewy body disease (DLBD) from Alzheimer's disease. *Neurology*, *41*, 1402–1409.

Doty, R. L., Perl, D. P., Steele, J. C., Chen, K. M., Pierce, J. D. J., Reyes, P., & Kurland, L. T. (1991). Odor identification deficit of the parkinsonism-dementia complex of Guam: Equivalence to that of Alzheimer's and idiopathic Parkinson's disease. *Neurology*, *41*, 77–80.

Dubois, B., Pillon, B., Sternic, N., Lhermitte, F., & Agid, Y. (1990). Age-induced cognitive disturbances in Parkinson's disease. *Neurology*, *40*, 38–41.

Dubois, B., Ruberg, M., Javoy-Agid, F., Ploska, A., & Agid, Y. (1983). A subcortical-cortical cholinergic system is affected in Parkinson's disease. *Brain Research*, *288*, 213–218.

Ebmeier, K. P., Calder, S. A., Crawford, J. R., Stewart, L., Besson, J. A., & Mutch, W. J. (1990). Clinical features predicting dementia in idiopathic Parkinson's disease: A follow-up study. *Neurology*, *40*, 1222–1224.

Ebmeier, K. P., Calder, S. A., Crawford, J. R., Stewart, L., Cochrane, R. H., & Besson, J. A. (1991). Dementia in idiopathic Parkinson's disease: Prevalence and relationship with symptoms and signs of parkinsonism. *Psychological Medicine*, *21*, 69–76.

Ehmann, T. S., Beninger, R. J., Gawel, M. J., & Riopelle, R. J. (1990). Depressive symptoms in Parkinson's disease: A comparison with disabled control subjects. *Journal of Geriatric Psychiatry and Neurology*, *3*, 3–9.

El-Awar, M., Becker, J. T., Hammond, K. M., Nebes, R. D., & Boller, F. (1987). Learning deficit in Parkinson's disease. Comparison with Alzheimer's disease and normal aging. *Archives of Neurology*, *44*, 180–184.

Epelbaum, J., Ruberg, M., Moyse, E., Javoy-Agid, F., Dubois, B., & Agid, Y. (1983). Somatostatin and dementia in Parkinson disease. *Brain Research*, *278*, 376–379.

Eslinger, J., & Damasio, A. R. (1986). Preserved motor learning in Alzheimer's disease: Implications for anatomy and behavior. *Journal of Neuroscience, 6*, 3006–3009.

Evarts, E. V., Teravainen, H., & Calne, D. B. (1981). Reaction time in Parkinson's disease. *Brain, 104*, 167–186.

Fahn, S., & Group, P. S. (1991). DATATOP and clinical neuromythology. *Neurology, 41*, 771–773.

Feher, E. P., Mahurin, R. K., Inbody, S. B., Crook, T. H., & Pirozzolo, F. J. (1991). Anosognosia in Alzheimer's disease. *Neuropsychiatry, Neuropsychology, and Behavioral Neurology, 4*, 136–146.

Feher, E. P., Mahurin, R. K., Doody, R. S., Cooke, N., Sims, J., & Pirozzolo, F. J. (1992). Establishing the limits of the Mini-Mental State: Examination of MMS "subtests." *Archives of Neurology, 49*, 87–92.

Fisher, P., Gatterer, G., & Danielczyk, W. (1988). Semantic memory in DAT, MID, and parkinsonism. *Functional Neurology, 3*, 301–307.

Flowers, K. A. (1976). Visual 'closed-loop' and 'open-loop' characteristics of voluntary movement in patients with parkinsonism and intention tremor. *Brain, 99*, 269–310.

Flowers, K. A. (1982). Frontal lobe signs as a component of Parkinsonism. *Neurobehavioral Brain Research, 5*, 100–101.

Flowers, K. A., Pearce, I., & Pearce, J. M. S. (1984). Recognition memory in Parkinson's disease. *Journal of Neurology, Neurosurgery and Psychiatry, 47*, 1174–1181.

Flowers, K. A., & Robertson, C. (1985). The effects of Parkinson's disease on the ability to maintain a mental set. *Journal of Neurology, Neurosurgery and Psychiatry, 48*, 517–529.

Folstein, M., Folstein, S., & McHugh, P. R. (1975). 'Mini-Mental State': A practical method for grading the cognitive state of patients for the clinician. *Psychiatric Research, 12*, 189–198.

Forno, L. S. (1982). Pathology of Parkinson's disease. In C.D. Marsden & S. Fahn (Eds.), *Neurology 2: Movement disorders* (pp. 25–40). Boston: Butterworth's.

Freed, C. R., Breeze, R. E., Rosenberg, N. L., Schneck, S. A., Wells, T. H., Barrett, J. N., Grafton, S. T., Huang, S. C., Eidelberg, D., & Rottenberg, D. A. (1990). Transplantation of human fetal dopamine cells for Parkinson's disease: Results at one year. *Archives of Neurology, 47*, 505–512.

Freedman, M. (1990). Object alternation and orbitofrontal system dysfunction in Alzheimer's and Parkinson's disease. *Brain and Cognition, 14*, 134–143.

Freedman, M., & Oscar-Berman, M. (1986). Selective delayed response deficits in Alzheimer's and Parkinson's disease. *Archives of Neurology, 43*, 886–890.

Freedman, M., & Oscar-Berman, M. (1989). Spatial and visual learning deficits in Alzheimer's and Parkinson's disease. *Brain and Cognition, 11*, 114–126.

Freedman, M., Rivoira, P., Butters, N., Sax, D. S., & Robert, G. (1984). Retrograde amnesia in Parkinson's disease. *Canadian Journal of Neurological Sciences, 11*, 297–301.

Friedman, A., & Sienkiewicz, J. (1991). Psychotic complications of long-term levodopa treatment of Parkinson's disease. *Acta Neurologica Scandinavica, 84*, 111–113.

Friedman, J. H. (1991). The management of the levodopa psychoses. *Clinical Neuropharmacology, 14*, 283–295.

Frochtengarten, M. L., Villares, J. C. B., Maluf, E., & Carlini, E. A. (1987). Depressive symptoms and the dexamethasone suppression test in Parkinsonian patients. *Biological Psychiatry, 22*, 386–389.

Fuld, P., Katzman, R., Davies, P., & Terry, R. D. (1982). Intrusions as a sign of Alzheimer dementia: Chemical and pathological verification. *Annals of Neurology, 11*, 155–159.

Fuster, J. M. (1991). Role of prefrontal cortex in delay tasks: Evidence from reversible lesion and unit recording in the monkey. In H. S. Levin, H. M. Eisenberg, & A. L. Benton (Eds.), *Frontal lobe function and dysfunction.* New York: Oxford University Press.

Gainotti, G., Caltagirone, C., Massullo, C., & Miceli, G. (1980). Patterns of neuropsychologic impairment in various diagnostic groups of dementia. In L. Amaducci, A. N. Davison, & P. Antvono (Eds.), *Aging of brain and dementia* (pp. 245–250). New York: Raven Press.

Garnett, E. S., Nahmias, C., & Firnau, G. (1984). Central dopaminergic pathways in hemiparkinsonism examined by positron emission tomography. *Canadian Journal of Neurological Sciences, 11,* 174–179.

Gaspar, P., & Gray, F. (1984). Dementia in idiopathic Parkinson's disease. *Acta Neuropathologica, 64,* 43–52.

Gibb, W. R. G., Esiri, M. M., & Lees, A. J. (1985). Clinical and pathological features of diffuse cortical Lewy body disease (Lewy body dementia). *Brain, 110,* 1131–1153.

Gibb, W. R. G., Luthert, P. J., Janota, I., & Lantos, P. L. (1989). Cortical Lewy body dementia: Clinical features and classification. *Journal of Neurology, Neurosurgery and Psychiatry, 52,* 185–192.

Gibb, W. R. G., Scott, T., & Lees, A. J. (1991). Neuronal inclusions of Parkinson's disease. *Movement Disorders, 6,* 2–11.

Giovannini, P., Piccolo, I., Genitrini, S., Soliveri, P., Girotti, F., Geminiani, G., Scigliano, G., & Caraceni, T. (1991). Early-onset Parkinson's disease. *Movement Disorders, 6,* 36–42.

Girotti, F., Grassi, M. P., Carella, F., Soliveri, P., Musicco, M., Lamperti, E., & Caraceni, T. (1986). Possible involvement of attention processes in Parkinson's disease. In M.D. Yahr & K. J. Bergmann (Eds.), *Advances in neurology* (pp. 425–429). New York: Raven Press.

Girotti, F., Soliveri, P., Carella, F., Piccolo, I., & Caggarra, P. (1988). Dementia and cognitive impairment in Parkinson's disease. *Journal of Neurology, Neurosurgery and Psychiatry, 51,* 1498–1502.

Globus, M., Mildworf, B., & Melamed, E. (1985). Cerebral blood flow and cognitive impairment in Parkinson's disease. *Neurology, 35,* 1135–1139.

Goetz, C. G., Stebbins, G. T., Klawans, H. L., Koller, W. C., Grossman, M. D., Bakay, R. A. E., & Penn, R. D. (1991). United Parkinson Foundation Neurotransplantation Registry on adrenal medullary transplants: Presurgical and 1- and 2-year follow-up. *Neurology, 41,* 1719–1722.

Goffinet, A. M., De Volder, A. G., Gillian, C., Rectem, D., Bol, A., Michel, C., Cogneau, M., Labar, D., & Laterre, C. (1989). Positron tomography demonstrates frontal lobe hypometabolism in progressive supranuclear palsy. *Annals of Neurology, 25,* 131–139.

Golbe, L. I. (1991). Young-onset Parkinson's disease: A clinical review. *Neurology, 41,* 168–173.

Golbe, L. I., & Davis, P. H. (1988). Progressive supranuclear palsy: Recent advances. In J. Jancovic & E. Tolosa (Eds.), *Parkinson's disease and movement disorders* (pp. 121–130). Baltimore: Urban & Schwarzenberg.

Golbe, L. I., Di Iorio, G., Bonavita, V., Miller, D. C., & Duvoisin, R. C. (1990). A large kindred with autosomal dominant Parkinson's disease. *Annals of Neurology, 27,* 276–282.

Goldenberg, G., Podreka, I., Muller, C., & Deecke, L. (1989). The relationship between cognitive deficits and frontal lobe function in patients with Parkinson's disease: An emission computerized tomography study. *Archives of General Psychiatry, 2,* 79–87.

Goldenberg, G., Wimmer, A., Auff, E., & Schnaberth, G. (1986). Impairment of motor planning in patients with Parkinson's disease: Evidence from ideomotor apraxia testing. *Journal of Neurology, Neurosurgery and Psychiatry, 49*, 1266–1272.

Goldman, P. S., & Rosvold, H. E. (1970). Localization of function within the dorsolateral prefrontal cortex of the rhesus monkey. *Experimental Neurology, 27*, 291–304.

Goldman, P. S., Rosvold, H. E., Vest, B., & Galkin, T. W. (1971). Analysis of delayed alternation deficits produced by dorsolateral prefrontal lesions in the rhesus monkey. *Journal of Comparative Neurology, 77*, 212–220.

Goldman-Rakic, P. S., & Friedman, H. R. (1991). The circuitry of working memory revealed by anatomy and metabolic imaging. In H.S. Levin, H.M. Eisenberg, & A.L. Benton (Eds.), *Frontal lobe function and dysfunction.* New York: Oxford University Press.

Goldman-Rakic, P. S., & Selemon, L. D. (1990). New frontiers in basal ganglia research. *Trends in Neuroscience, 13*, 241–244.

Goodin, D. S., & Aminoff, M. J. (1986). Electrophysiologic differences between subtypes of dementia. *Brain, 109*, 1103–1113.

Gotham, A. M., Brown, R. G., & Marsden, C. D. (1986). Depression in Parkinson's disease: A quantitative and qualitative analysis. *Journal of Neurology, Neurosurgery and Psychiatry, 49*, 381–389.

Gotham, A. M., Brown, R. G., & Marsden, C. D. (1988). 'Frontal' cognitive function in patients with Parkinson's disease 'on' and 'off' levodopa. *Brain, 111*, 299–231.

Grafman, J. (1989). Plans, actions, and mental sets: Managerial knowledge units in the frontal lobes. In E. Perecman (Ed.), *Integrating theory and practice in clinical neuropsychology* (pp. 93–138). Hillsdale, NJ: Lawrence Erlbaum.

Gray, F., Poirier, J., & Scaravilli, F. (1991). Parkinson's disease and parkinsonian syndromes. In S. Duckett (Ed.), *The pathology of the aging human nervous system* (pp. 179–199). Philadelphia: Lea & Febiger.

Grossman, M., Carvell, S., Gollomp, S., Stern, M. B., Vernon, G., & Hurtig, H. J. (1991). Sentence comprehension and praxis deficits in Parkinson's disease. *Neurology, 41*, 1620–1626.

Growdon, J. H., & Corkin, S. (1986). Cognitive impairments in Parkinson's disease. In M. D. Yahr & K. J. Bergmann (Eds.), *Advances in Neurology* (pp. 383–392). New York: Raven Press.

Guze, B. H., & Barrio, J. C. (1991). The etiology of depression in Parkinson's disease. *Psychosomatics, 32*, 390–395.

Hakim, A. M., & Mathieson, G. (1979). Dementia in Parkinson disease: A neuropathologic study. *Neurology, 29*, 1209–1214.

Halgrin, R., Riklan, M., & Misiak, H. (1977). Levodopa, parkinsonism and recent memory. *Journal of Nervous and Mental Disease, 164*, 268–272.

Hamel, A. R., & Riklan, M. (1975). Cognitive and perceptual effects of long-range L-dopa therapy in Parkinsonism. *Journal of Clinical Psychology, 31*, 321–323.

Hansen, L., Salmon, D., Galasko, M., Masliah, E., Katzman, R., DeTeresa, R., Thal, L., Pay, M. M., Hofstetter, R., Klauber, M., Rice, V., Butters, N., & Alford, M. (1990). The Lewy body variant of Alzheimer's disease: A clinical and pathologic entity. *Neurology, 40*, 1–8.

Harrington, D. L., & Haaland, K. Y. (1991). Sequencing in Parkinson's disease: Abnormalities in programming and controlling movements. *Brain, 114*, 99–115.

Harrington, D. L., Haaland, K. Y., Yeo, R. A., & Marder, E. (1990). Procedural memory in Parkinson's disease: Impaired motor but not visuospatial learning. *Journal of Clinical and Experimental Neuropsychology, 12*, 323–339.

Heilman, K. M., Bowers, D., Watson, R. T., & Greer, M. (1976). Reaction times in Parkinson's disease. *Archives of Neurology, 33*, 139–140.

Helkala, E. L., Laulumaa, V., Soininen, H., & Riekkinen, P. J. (1988). Recall and recognition memory in patients with Alzheimer's and Parkinson's diseases. *Annals of Neurology, 24*, 214–217.

Helkala, E. L., Laulumaa, V., Soininen, H., & Riekkinen, P. J. (1989). Different error pattern of episodic and semantic memory in Alzheimer's disease and Parkinson's disease with dementia. *Neuropsychologia, 27*, 1241–1248.

Henik, A., Singh, J., Beckley, D. J., & Rafal, R. D. (1992). Stroop effects in patients with early and late onset Parkinson's disease. *Journal of Clinical and Experimental Neuropsychology, 14*, 81.

Heston, L. L. (1980). Dementia associated with Parkinson's disease: A genetic study. *Journal of Neurology, Neurosurgery and Psychiatry, 43*, 846–848.

Hietanen, M., & Teravainen, H. (1988a). Dementia and treatment with L-dopa in Parkinson's disease. *Movement Disorders, 3*, 263–270.

Hietanen, M., & Teravainen, H. (1988b). The effect of age of disease onset on neuropsychological performance in Parkinson's disease. *Journal of Neurology, Neurosurgery and Psychiatry, 51*, 244–249.

Horiguchi, J., Nishimatsu, O., Inami, Y., Sukegawa, T., & Shoda, T. (1991). A clinical study on intellectual impairment in parkinsonian patients during long-term treatment. *Japanese Journal of Psychiatry and Neurology, 45*, 13–18.

Hornykiewicz, O. (1966). Dopamine (3-hydroxytyramine) and brain function. *Pharmacological Review, 18*, 925–962.

Hornykiewicz, O. (1982). Brain neurotransmitter changes in Parkinson's disease. In C.D. Marsden & S. Fahn (Eds.), *Movement disorders* (pp. 41–58). Boston: Butterworth's.

Hovestadt, A., de Jong, G. J., & Meerwaldt, J. D. (1987). Spatial disorientation as an early symptom of Parkinson's disease. *Neurology, 37*, 485–487.

Huber, S. J., Christy, J. A., & Paulson, G. W. (1991). Cognitive heterogeneity associated with clinical subtypes of Parkinson's disease. *Neuropsychiatry, Neuropsychology and Behavioral Neurology, 4*, 147–157.

Huber, S. J., Paulson, G. W., & Shuttleworth, E. C. (1988). Relationship of motor symptoms, intellectual impairment, and depression in Parkinson's disease. *Journal of Neurology, Neurosurgery and Psychiatry, 51*, 855–858.

Huber, S. J., Shuttleworth, E. C., Christy, J. A., Chakeres, D. W., Curtin, A., & Paulson, G. W. (1989a). Magnetic resonance imaging in dementia of Parkinson's disease. *Journal of Neurology, Neurosurgery and Psychiatry, 52*, 1221–1227.

Huber, S. J., Shuttleworth, E. C., & Freidenberg, D. L. (1989b). Neuropsychological differences between the dementias of Alzheimer's and Parkinson's diseases. *Archives of Neurology, 46*, 1287–1291.

Huber, S. J., Shuttleworth, E. C., & Paulson, G. W. (1986). Dementia in Parkinson's disease. *Archives of Neurology, 43*, 987–990.

Hutton, J. T., Morris, J. L., Elias, J. W., Varma, R., & Poston, J. N. (1991). Spatial contrast sensitivity is reduced in bilateral Parkinson's disease. *Neurology, 41*, 1200–1202.

Illes, J. (1989). Neurolinguistic features of spontaneous language production dissociate three forms of neurodegenerative disease: Alzheimer's, Huntington's, and Parkinson's. *Brain and Language, 37*, 628–642.

Jankovic, J. (1985). Long-term use of dopamine agonists in Parkinson's disease. *Clinical Neuropharmacology, 8*, 131–140.

Jankovic, J., & Marsden, C. D. (1988). Therapeutic strategies in Parkinson's disease. In J. Jankovic & E. Tolosa (Eds.), *Parkinson's disease and movement disorders* (pp. 95–119). Baltimore: Urban & Schwarzenberg.

Jellinger, K. (1987). The pathology of parkinsonism. In C. D. Marsden & S. Fahn (Eds.), *Movement disorders 2* (pp. 124–165). London: Butterworth's.

Jernigan, T. L., Salmon, D. P., Butters, N., Shults, C. W., & Hesselink, J. R. (1990).

Specificity of brain-structural changes in Alzheimer's, Huntington's, and Parkinson's diseases. *Journal of Clinical and Experimental Neuropsychology, 12*, 410.

Johnson, W. G. (1991). Genetic susceptibility to Parkinson's disease. *Neurology, 41*, 82–87.

Kahn, N., Freeman, A., Juncos, J. L., et al. (1991). Clozapine is beneficial for psychosis in Parkinson's disease. *Neurology, 41*, 1699–1700.

Kaszniak, A. W., Trosset, M. W., Bondi, M. W., & Bayles, K. A. (1992). Procedural learning of Parkinson's disease patients in a serial reaction time task. *Journal of Clinical and Experimental Neuropsychology, 14*, 51.

Kimura, D., Barnett, H. J. M., & Burkhart, G. (1981). The psychological test pattern in progressive supranuclear palsy. *Neuropsychologia, 19*, 301–306.

Kish, S. J., El-Awar, M., Schut, I., Leach, L., Oscar-Berman, M., & Freedman, M. (1988). Cognitive deficits in olivopontocerebellar atrophy: Implications for the cholinergic hypothesis of Alzheimer's dementia. *Annals of Neurology, 24*, 200–206.

Kish, S. J., Shannak, K., & Hornykiewicz, O. (1988). Uneven pattern of dopamine loss in the striatum of patients with idiopathic Parkinson's disease: Pathophysiologic and clinical implications. *New England Journal of Medicine, 318*, 876–880.

Kofman, O. S. (1991). Deprenyl: Protective vs. symptomatic effect. *Canadian Journal of Neurological Sciences, 18*, 83–85.

Kuhl, D. E., Metter, E. J., Benson, D. F., et al. (1985). Similarities of cerebral glucose metabolism in Alzheimer's and parkinsonian dementia. *Journal of Cerebral Blood Flow and Metabolism, 5*(Suppl. 1), S169.

Langston, J. W. (1988). The etiology of Parkinson's disease. In J. Jankovic & E. Tolosa (Eds.), *Parkinson's disease and movement disorders* (pp. 75–86). Baltimore: Urban & Schwarzenberg.

Leenders, K. L., Frackowiak, R. S. J., & Lees, A. J. (1988). Steele-Richardson-Olszewski syndrome: Brain energy metabolism, blood flow and flurodopa uptake measured by positron emission tomography. *Brain, 111*, 615–630.

Leenders, K. L., Palmer, A. J., Quinn, N., Clark, J. C., Firnau, G., Garnett, E. S., Nahmias, C., Jones, T., & Marsden, C. D. (1986). Brain dopamine metabolism in patients with Parkinson's disease measured with PET. *Journal of Neurology, Neurosurgery and Psychiatry, 49*, 855–860.

Lees, A. J., & Smith, E. (1983). Cognitive deficits in the early stages of Parkinson's disease. *Brain, 106*, 257–270.

Levin, B. E., & Tomer, R. (1992). A prospective study of language abilities in Parkinson's disease. *Journal of Clinical and Experimental Neuropsychology, 14*, 34.

Levin, B. E., Llabre, M. M., Reisman, S., Weiner, W. J., Sanchez-Ramos, J., Singer, C., & Brown, M. C. (1991). Visuospatial impairment in Parkinson's disease. *Neurology, 41*, 365–369.

Levin, B. E., Llabre, M. M., & Weiner, W. J. (1988). Parkinson's disease and depression: Psychometric properties of the Beck Depression Inventory. *Journal of Neurology, Neurosurgery and Psychiatry, 51*, 1401–1404.

Lieberman, A., Dziatolowski, M., Kupersmith, M., Serby, M., Goodgold, A., Korein, J., & Goldstein, M. (1979). Dementia in Parkinson disease. *Annals of Neurology, 6*, 355–359.

Lindvall, O., Brundin, P., Widner, H., Rehncrona, S., Gustavii, B., Frackowiak, R., Leenders, K. L., Sawle, G., Rothwell, J. C., Marsden, C. D., & Bjorklund, A. (1990). Grafts of fetal dopamine neurons survive and improve motor function in Parkinson's disease. *Science, 247*, 574–577.

Litvan, I., Mohr, E., Williams, J., Gomez, C., & Chase, T. N. (1991). Differential memory and executive functions in demented patients with Parkinson's and Alzheimer's disease. *Journal of Neurology, Neurosurgery and Psychiatry, 54*, 25–29.

Loranger, A. W., Goodell, H., McDowell, F. H., Lee, J. H., & Sweet, R. D. (1972). Intellectual impairment in Parkinson's syndrome. *Brain, 95*, 405–412.

Madrazo, I., Drucker-Colin, R., Diaz, V., Martinez-Mata, J., Torres, C., & Becerril, J. (1987). Open microsurgical autograft of adrenal medulla to the right caudate nucleus in two patients with intractable Parkinson's disease. *New England Journal of Medicine, 316*, 831–834.

Maher, E. R., Smith, E. M., & Lees, A. J. (1985). Cognitive deficits in the Steele-Richardson-Olszewski syndrome (progressive supranuclear palsy). *Journal of Neurology, Neurosurgery and Psychiatry, 48*, 1234–1239.

Mahurin, R. K., & Inbody, S. B. (1989). Psychomotor assessment of the older patient. *Clinics in Geriatric Medicine, 5*, 499–518.

Mahurin, R. K., & Pirozzolo, F. J. (1984). Relative contribution of motor and cognitive demands to psychomotor performance: An analysis of bradykinetic parkinsonian patients. *The INS Bulletin, 4*, 42.

Mahurin, R. K., & Pirozzolo, F. J. (1986). Chronometric analysis: Clinical applications in aging and dementia. *Developmental Neuropsychology, 2*, 345–362.

Mahurin, R. K., Pirozzolo, F. J., & Appel, S. H. (1989). Motor control deficits in Alzheimer's disease. *Journal of Clinical and Experimental Neuropsychology, 11*, 86.

Mann, D. M. A., & Yates, P. O. (1983). Pathological basis for neurotransmitter changes in Parkinson's disease. *Neuropathology and Applied Neurobiology, 9*, 3–19.

Marder, K., Flood, P., Cote, L., & Mayeux, R. (1990). A pilot study of risk factors for dementia in Parkinson's disease. *Movement Disorders, 5*, 156–161.

Marder, K., Leung, D., Tang, M., Bell, K., et al., (1991). Are demented patients with Parkinson's disease accurately reflected in prevalence surveys? A survival analysis. *Neurology, 41*, 1240–1243.

Marschall, I., Dal-Bianco, P., Maly, J., Auff, E., Hufgard, J., Mraz, M., & Deecke, L. (1991). Clinical comparison of dementia in Parkinson's and Alzheimer's disease. *Journal of Neural Transmission, 33*(Suppl.), 81–92.

Marsden, C. D. (1982). The mysterious motor function of the basal ganglia: The Robert Wartenberg lecture. *Neurology, 32*, 514–539.

Marsden, C. D. (1990). Parkinson's disease. *Lancet, 335*, 948–952.

Marttila, R. J., & Rinne, U. K. (1976). Dementia in Parkinson's disease. *Acta Neurologica Scandinavica, 54*, 431–441.

Martin, W. W., Adam, M. J., Bergstrom, M., Ammann, W., Harrop, R., Laihinen, A., Rogers, J., Ruth, T., Sayre, C., Stoessl, J., Pate, B. D., & Calne, D. B. (1986). In vivo study of DOPA metabolism in Parkinson's disease. In S. Fahn, C. D. Marsden, P. Jenner, & P. Teychenne (Eds.), *Recent developments in Parkinson's disease* (pp. 97–102). New York: Raven Press.

Massman, P. J., Levin, B. E., Delis, D. C., Butters, N., & Shear, P. K. (1992). Heterogeneity of memory impairment in Parkinson's disease: Evidence for three major profile subtypes. *Journal of Clinical and Experimental Neuropsychology, 14*, 81.

Massman, P. J., Delis, D. C., Butters, N., Levin, B. E., & Salmon, D. P. (1990). Are all subcortical dementias alike? Verbal learning and memory in Parkinson's and Huntington's disease patients. *Journal of Clinical and Experimental Neuropsychology, 12*, 729–744.

Mastaglia, F. L., Masters, C. L., Beyreuther, K., & Kakulas, B. A. (1989). Deposition of Alzheimer's disease amyloid (A4) protein in the cerebral cortex in Parkinson's disease. *Progress in Clinical Biological Research, 317*, 475–484.

Matison, R., Mayeux, R., Rosen, J., & Fahn, S. (1982). "Tip-of-the-tongue" phenomenon in Parkinson's disease. *Neurology, 32*, 567–570.

Matthews, C. G., & York-Haaland, K. Y. (1979). The effect of symptom duration on cognitive and motor performance in parkinsonism. *Neurology, 29*, 951–956.

Mayberg, H. S. (1993). Neuroimaging studies of depression in neurologic disease. In S. E. Starkstein & R. G. Robinson (Eds.), *Depression in neurologic disease* (pp. 186–216). Baltimore: Johns Hopkins University Press.

Mayberg, H. S., Starkstein, S. E., Sadzot, B., Preziosi, T., Andrezejewski, P. L., Dannals, R. F., Wagner, H. N. J., & Robinson, R. G. (1990). Selective hypometabolism in the inferior frontal lobe in depressed patients with Parkinson's disease. *Annals of Neurology, 28*, 57–64.

Mayeux, R., Stern, Y., Rosen, J., & Benson, D. F. (1981a). Subcortical dementia: A recognizable clinical syndrome. *Annals of Neurology, 10*, 100–101.

Mayeux, R., Stern, Y., Rosen, J., & Benson, D. F. (1983). Is "subcortical dementia" a recognizable clinical entity? *Annals of Neurology, 12*, 278–283.

Mayeux, R., Stern, Y., Rosen, J., & Leventhal, J. (1981b). Depression, intellectual impairment and Parkinson's disease. *Neurology, 31*, 645–650.

Mayeux, R., Stern, Y., Rosenstein, R., Marder, K., Hauser, A., Cote, L., & Fahn, S. (1988a). An estimate of the prevalence of dementia in idiopathic Parkinson's disease. *Archives of Neurology, 45*, 260–262.

Mayeux, R., Stern, Y., Sano, M., Williams, J. B., & Cote, L. J. (1988b). The relationship of serotonin to depression in Parkinson's disease. *Movement Disorders, 3*, 237–244.

McGeer, P. L., Itagaki, S., Boyes, B. E., & McGeer, E. G. (1988). Reactive microglia are positive for HLA-DR in the substantia nigra of Parkinson's and Alzheimer's disease patients. *Neurology, 38*, 1285–1291.

McGeer, P. L., McGeer, E. G., & Suzuki, J. S. (1977). Aging and extrapyramidal function. *Archives of Neurology, 34*, 33–35.

McKhann, G., Drachman, D., Folstein, M., Katzman, R., Price, D., & Stadlan, E. M. (1986). Clinical diagnosis of Alzheimer's disease: Report of the NINCDS-ADRDA Work Group, Department of Health and Human Services Task Force on Alzheimer's Disease. *Neurology, 34*, 939–944.

Mendez, M., Cummings, J. L., Darkins, A. W., Hill, M. A., & Benson, D. F. (1987). Alzheimer's disease and Parkinson's disease: Comparison of speech and language alterations. *Neurology, 37*(Suppl. 1), 227.

Milberg, W., & Albert M. (1989). Cognitive differences between patients with progressive supranuclear palsy and Alzheimer's disease. *Journal of Clinical and Experimental Neuropsychology, 11*, 605–614.

Milner, B., Corsi, P., & Leonard, G. (1991). Frontal-lobe contribution to recency judgments. *Neuropsychologia, 29*, 601–618.

Mindham, R. H., Ahmed, S. W., & Clough, C. G. (1982). A controlled study of dementia in Parkinson's disease. *Journal of Neurology, Neurosurgery and Psychiatry, 45*, 969–974.

Mindham, R. H. S. (1970). Psychiatric symptoms in parkinsonism. *Journal of Neurology, Neurosurgery and Psychiatry, 33*, 181–191.

Mishkin, M. (1957). Effects of small frontal lesions on delayed alternation in monkeys. *Journal of Neurophysiology, 20*, 615–622.

Mishkin, M. (1964). Perseveration of central sets after frontal lesions in monkeys. In J. M. Warren & K. Akert (Eds.), *The frontal granular cortex and behavior* (pp. 219–241). New York: McGraw-Hill.

Mohr, E., Fabbrini, G., Williams, J., et al. (1989). Dopamine and memory function in Parkinson's disease. *Movement Disorders, 4*, 113–120.

Mohr, E., Litvan, I., Williams, J., Fedio, P., & Chase, T. N. (1990). Selective deficits in Alzheimer and parkinsonian dementia: Visuospatial function. *Canadian Journal of Neurological Sciences, 17*, 292–297.

Montgomery, E. B., Nuessen, J., Nuessen, G., & Douglas, S. (1991). Reaction time and movement velocity abnormalities in Parkinson's disease under different task conditions. *Neurology, 41,* 1476–1481.

Mortimer, J. A. (1988a). Human motor behavior and aging. In J. A. Joseph (Eds.), *Central determinants of age-related declines in motor function* (pp. 54–65). New York: New York Academy of Sciences.

Mortimer, J. A. (1988b). The dementia of Parkinson's disease. In G. J. Maletta (Eds.), *Treatment considerations for Alzheimer's disease and related dementing illnesses* (pp. 785–797). Philadelphia: W. B. Saunders Company.

Mortimer, J. A., Pirozzolo, F. J., Hansch, E. C., & Webster, D. D. (1982). Relationship of motor symptoms to intellectual deficits in Parkinson disease. *Neurology, 32,* 133–137.

Murphy, C., Gilmore, M. M., Seery, C. S., Salmon, D. P., & Lasker, B. R. (1990). Olfactory thresholds are associated with degree of dementia in Alzheimer's disease. *Neurobiology of Aging, 11,* 465–469.

Myllyla, V. V., Sotaniemi, K. A., Vuorinen, J. A., & Heinonen, E. H. (1992). Selegiline as initial treatment in de novo parkinsonian patients. *Neurology, 42,* 339–343.

Nakamura, S., Fukuda, H., Hara, K., Fukuyama, H., & Kameyama, M. (1988). Biochemical aspects of Parkinson-dementia complex. *European Neurology, 28,* (Suppl. 1), 24, 2.

Pan, G. D., Stern, Y., Sano, M., & Mayeux, R. (1989). Clock-drawing in neurological disorders. *Behavioural Neurology, 2,* 39–48.

Papavasiliou, P. S., Cotzias, G. C., Duby, S. E., et al. (1972). Levodopa in parkinsonism: Potentiation of central effects with a peripheral inhibitor. *New England Journal of Medicine, 286,* 8–14.

Parkinson, J. (1817). *An essay on the shaking palsy.* London: Sherwood, Nely, and Jones.

Peppard, R. F., Martin, W. R., Clark, C. M., Carr, G. D., McGeer, P. L., & Calne, D. B. (1990). Cortical glucose metabolism in Parkinson's and Alzheimer's disease. *Journal of Neuroscience Research, 27,* 561–568.

Perry, E. K., Perry, R. H., Candy, J. M., Fairbairn, A. F., Blessed, G., Dick, D. J., & Tomlinson, B. E. (1984). Cortical serotonin-S2 receptor binding abnormalities in patients with Alzheimer's disease: Comparisons with Parkinson's disease. *Neuroscience Letters, 51,* 353–357.

Perry, R. H., Tomlinson, B. E., Candy, J. M., Blessed, G., Foster, J. F., Bloxham, C. A., & Perry, E. R. (1983). Cortical cholinergic deficit in mentally impaired parkinsonian patients. *Lancet, 2,* 789–790.

Peterson, D. I., Price, M. L., & Small, C. S. (1989). Autopsy findings in a patient who had an adrenal-to-brain transplant for Parkinson's disease. *Neurology, 39,* 235–238.

Pfeiffer, R. F., Hudson, H. H., Diercks, M. J., Glaeske, C., Jefferson, A., & Cheng, S. (1986). Dexamethasone suppression test in Parkinson's disease. In M. D. Yahr & K. J. Bergmann (Eds.), *Advances in neurology* (pp. 439–442). New York: Raven Press.

Piccirilli, M., D'Alessandro, P., Finali, G., & Piccinin, G. L. (1989). Frontal lobe dysfunction in Parkinson's disease: Prognostic value for dementia? *European Neurology, 29,* 71–76.

Pillon, B., Dubois, B., Ploska, A., & Agid, Y. (1991). Severity and specificity of cognitive impairment in Alzheimer's, Huntington's, and Parkinson's diseases and progressive supranuclear palsy. *Neurology, 41,* 634–643.

Pillon, B., Dubois, B., Bonnett, A.-M., Esteguy, M., Guimaraes, J., Vigouret, J.-M., Lhermitte, F., & Agid, Y. (1989). Cognitive slowing in Parkinson's disease fails to respond to levodopa treatment: The 15-objects test. *Neurology, 39,* 762–768.

Pillon, B., Dubois, B., Lhermitte, F., & Agid, Y. (1986). Heterogeneity of cognitive impairment in progressive supranuclear palsy. Parkinson's disease, and Alzheimer's disease. *Neurology, 36,* 1179–1185.

Pirozzolo, F. J., Hansch, E. C., Mortimer, J. A., Webster, D. D., & Kuskowski, M. A. (1982). Dementia in Parkinson disease: A neuropsychological analysis. *Brain and Cognition, 1*, 71–83.

Pirozzolo, F. J., Mahurin, R. K., & Swihart, A. A. (1991). Motor function in aging and neurodegenerative disease. In F. Boller & J. Grafman (Eds.), *Handbook of neuropsychology* (pp. 167–194). Amsterdam: Elsevier Science Publishers.

Pirozzolo, F. J., Swihart, A. A., Rey, G., Jankovic, J., & Mortimer, J. A. (1988). Cognitive impairments associated with Parkinson's disease and other movement disorders. In J. Jankovic & E. Tolosa (Eds.), *Parkinson's disease and movement disorders* (pp. 425–439). Baltimore: Urban & Schwarzenberg.

Portin, R., & Rinne, U. K. (1980). Neuropsychological responses of parkinsonian patients to long-term levodopa treatment. In U. K. Rinne, M. Klinger, & G. Stamm (Eds.), *Parkinson's disease—current progress, problems and management* (pp. 271–304). Amsterdam: Elsevier/North Holland.

Portin, R., & Rinne, U. K. (1986). Predictive factors for cognitive deterioration and dementia in Parkinson's disease. In M. D. Yahr & K. L. Bergmann (Eds.), *Parkinson's disease* (pp. 413–416). New York: Raven Press.

Prasher, D., & Findley L. (1991). Dopaminergic induced changes in cognitive and motor processing in Parkinson's disease: An electrophysiological investigation. *Journal of Neurology, Neurosurgery and Psychiatry, 54*, 603–609.

Proctor, F., Riklan, M., Cooper, I. S., & Teuver, H. L. (1964). Judgment of visual and postural vertical by parkinsonian patients. *Neurology, 14*, 287–293.

Pullman, S. L., Watts, R. L., Juncos, J. L., Chase, T. N., & Sanes, J. N. (1988). Dopaminergic effects on simple and choice reaction time performance in Parkinson's disease. *Neurology, 38*, 249–254.

Quinn, N. (1989). Multiple system atrophy: The nature of the beast. *Journal of Neurology, Neurosurgery and Psychiatry,* (Suppl.), 78–79.

Quinn, N., Critchley, P., & Marsden, C. D. (1987). Young onset Parkinson's disease. *Movement Disorders, 2*, 73–91.

Rafal, R. D., Posner, M. I., Walker, J. A., & Friedrich, F. J. (1984). Cognition and the basal ganglia. Separating mental and motor components of performance in Parkinson's disease. *Brain, 107*, 1083–1094.

Rajput, A. H., Offord, K., Beard, C. M., & Kurland, L. T. (1984). Epidemiological survey of dementia in parkinsonism and control population. *Advances in Neurology, 40*, 229–234.

Rashkin, S. A., Borod, J. C., Wasserstein, J., Bodis-Wollner, I., Coscia, L., & Yahr, M. D. (1990). Visuospatial orientation in Parkinson's disease. *International Journal of Neuroscience, 51*, 9–18.

Regan, D., & Maxner, C. (1987). Orientation-selection visual loss in patients with Parkinson's disease. *Brain, 110*, 415–432.

Reid, W. G., Broe, G. A., Hely, M. A., Morris, J. G., Williamson, P. M., O'Sullivan, D. J., Rail, D., Genge, S., & Moss, N. G. (1989). The neuropsychology of de novo patients with idiopathic Parkinson's disease: The effects of age of onset. *International Journal of Neuroscience, 48*, 205–217.

Richards, M., Cote, L. J., Groves, M., & Stern, Y. (1992a). Impaired visuomotor function with preserved visuospatial ability in Parkinson's disease. *Journal of Clinical and Experimental Neuropsychology, 14*, 81.

Richards, M., Cote, L. J., & Stjern, Y. (1992b). The Odd-Man Out Test is a sensitive measure of fronto-striatal function in Parkinson's disease. *Journal of Clinical and Experimental Neuropsychology, 14*, 81.

Riederer, P., & Wuketich, S. (1976). Time course of nigrostriatal degeneration in Parkinson's disease. *Journal of Neural Transmissions, 38*, 277–301.

Riklan, M., Whelihan, W., & Cullinan, T. (1976). Levodopa and psychometric test performance in parkinsonism—5 years later. *Neurology, 26*, 173–179.

Riley, D. E., Lang, A. E., Lewis, A., Resch, L., Ashby, P., Hornykiewicz, O., & Black, S. (1990). Cortical-basal ganglionic degeneration. *Neurology, 40*, 1203–1212.

Rinne, J. O., Myllykyla, T., Lonnberg, P., & Marjamaki, P. (1991). A postmortem study of brain nicotinic receptors in Parkinson's and Alzheimer's disease. *Brain Research, 547*, 167–170.

Robbins, A. H. (1976). Depression in patients with parkinsonism. *British Journal of Psychiatry, 128*, 141–145.

Rogers, D. (1986). Bradyphrenia in parkinsonism: A historical review. *Psychological Medicine, 16*, 257–265.

Rogers, D., Lees, A. J., Smith, E., Trimble, M., & Stern, G. M. (1987). Bradyphrenia in Parkinson's disease and psychomotor retardation in depressive illness. *Brain, 110*, 761–776.

Rogers, D., Lees, A. J., Trimble, M., & Stern, G. M. (1986). Concept of bradyphrenia: A neuropsychiatric approach. In M. D. Yahr & K. J. Bergmann (Eds.), *Advances in neurology* (pp. 447–450). New York: Raven Press.

Royall, D. R., Mahurin, R. K., & Gray, K. F. (1992). Bedside assessment of executive cognitive impairment: The Executive Interview. *Journal of the American Geriatrics Society, 40*, 1221–1226.

Ruberg, M., Ploska, A., Javoy-Agid, F., & Agid, Y. (1982). Muscarinic binding and choline acetlytransferase activity in Parkinsonian subjects with reference to dementia. *Brain Research, 232*, 129–139.

Sagar, H. J. (1987). Clinical similarities and differences between Alzheimer's disease and Parkinson's disease. In R. J. Wurtman, S. H. Corkin, & J. H. Growdon (Eds.), *Alzheimer's disease: Advances in basic research and therapies* (pp. 91–107). Cambridge, MA: Center for Brain Sciences and Metabolism Charitable Trust.

Sagar, H. J., Cohen, N. J., Sullivan, E. V., Corkin, S., & Growdon, J. H. (1988b). Remote memory function in Alzheimer's disease and Parkinson's disease. *Brain, 111*, 185–206.

Sagar, H. J., Sullivan, E. V., Cohne, N. J., Gabrielli, J. D. E., Corkin, S., & Growdon, J. (1985). Specific cognitive deficits in Parkinson's disease. *Journal of Clinical and Experimental Neuropsychology, 7*, 158.

Sagar, H. J., Sullivan, E. V., Gabrieli, J. D., Corkin, S., & Growdon, J. H. (1988a). Temporal ordering and short-term memory deficits in Parkinson's disease. *Brain, 111*, 525–539.

Sahakian, B. J., Morris, R. G., Evenden, J. L., Heald, A., Levy, R., Philpot, M., & Robbins, T. W. (1988). A comparative study of visuospatial memory and learning in Alzheimer-type dementia and Parkinson's disease. *Brain, 111*, 695–718.

Saint-Cyr, J. A., Taylor, A. E., & Lang, A. E. (1988). Procedural learning and neostriatal dysfunction in man. *Brain, 111*, 941–959.

Sandyk, R., & Kay, S. R. (1990). The relationship of negative schizophrenia to parkinsonism. *International Journal of Neuroscience, 55*, 1–59.

Sano, M., Stern, Y., Williams, J., Cote, L., Rosenstein, R., & Mayeux, R. (1989). Coexisting dementia and depression in Parkinson's disease. *Archives of Neurology, 46*, 1284–1286.

Santamaria, J., Tolosa, E. S., Valles, A., Bayes, A., Blesa, R., & Masana, J. (1986). Mental depression in untreated Parkinson's disease of recent onset. In M. D. Yahr & K. J. Bergmann (Eds.), *Advances in neurology* (pp. 443–446). New York: Raven Press.

Sawle, G. V., Brooks, D. J., Marsden, C. D., & Frackowiak, R. S. J. (1991). Corticobasal degeneration. *Brain, 114*, 541–556.

Schoenberg, B. S. (1987). Epidemiology of movement disorders. In C. D. Marsden & S. Fahn (Eds.), *Movement disorders 2* (pp. 17–32). Boston: Butterworth's.

Schwab, R. S., Chafetz, M. E., & Walker, S. (1954). Control of simultaneous voluntary motor acts in normals and in parkinsonism. *Archives of Neurology and Psychiatry, 75*, 591–598.

Shallice, T. (1988). *From neuropsychology to mental structure.* New York: Cambridge University Press.

Snodgrass, J. G., & Corwin, J. (1988). Pragmatics of measuring recognition memory: Applications to dementia and amnesia. *Journal of Experimental Psychology, 117*, 34–50.

Snow, B. J. (1992). Positron emission tomography in Parkinson's disease. *Canadian Journal of Neurological Sciences, 19*, 138–141.

Spampinato, U., Habert, M. O., Mas, J. L., Bourdel, M. C., Ziegler, M., de Recondo, J., Askienazy, S., & Rondot, P. (1991). (99mTc)-HM-PAO SPECT and cognitive impairment in Parkinson's disease: A comparison with dementia of the Alzheimer type. *Journal of Neurology, Neurosurgery and Psychiatry, 54*, 787–792.

Starkstein, S. E., Esteguy, M., Berthier, M. L., Garcia, H., & Leiguarda, R. (1989). Evoked potentials, reaction time and cognitive performance in on and off phases of Parkinson's disease. *Journal of Neurology, Neurosurgery and Psychiatry, 52*, 338–340.

Steele, J. C., Richardson, J. C., & Olszewski, J. (1964). Progressive supranuclear palsy. *Archives of Neurology, 10*, 333–359.

Stern, Y., Groves, M., Sano, M., & Hoover, K. (1992). Decreased consistency of recall of verbal lists in Parkinson's disease. *Journal of Clinical and Experimental Neuropsychology, 14*, 81.

Stern, Y., & Mayeux, R. (1986). Intellectual impairment in Parkinson's disease. In M. D. Yahr & K. J. Bergmann (Eds.), *Parkinson's disease* (pp. 405–408). New York: Raven Press.

Stern, Y., Mayeux, R., & Rosen, J. (1984). Contribution of perceptual motor dysfunction to construction and tracing disturbances in Parkinson's disease. *Journal of Neurology, Neurosurgery and Psychiatry, 47*, 983–989.

Stern, Y., Tetrud, J. W., Martin, W. R., Kutner, S. J., & Langston, J. W. (1990). Cognitive change following MPTP exposure. *Neurology, 40*, 261–264.

Sullivan, E. V., & Sagar, H. J. (1989). Nonverbal recognition and recency discrimination deficits in Parkinson's disease and Alzheimer's disease. *Brain, 112*, 1503–1517.

Sweet, R. D., McDowell, H. J., Feigenson, J. S., Loranger, A. W., & Goodell, H. (1976). Mental symptoms in Parkinson's disease during chronic treatment with levodopa. *Neurology, 26*, 305–310.

Talland, G. A., & Schwab, R. S. (1964). performance with multiple sets in Parkinson's disease. *Neuropsychologia, 2*, 45–53.

Taylor, A. E., Saint-Cyr, J. A., & Lang, A. E. (1988). Idiopathic Parkinson's disease: Revised concepts of cognitive and affective status. *Canadian Journal of Neurological Sciences, 15*, 106–113.

Taylor, A. E., Saint-Cyr, J. A., & Lang, A. E. (1986). Frontal lobe dysfunction in Parkinson's disease: The cortical focus of neostriatal flow. *Brain, 109*, 845–883.

Taylor, A. E., Saint-Cyr, J. A., & Lang, A. E. (1990). Subcognitive processing in the frontocaudate "complex loop": The role of the striatum. *Alzheimer's Disease and Associated Disorders, 4*, 150–160.

Thompson, L. (1992). Fetal transplants show promise. *Science, 257*, 868–870.

Tomer, R., & Levin, B. E. (1992). Cognition in Parkinson's disease: A complex interaction between motor disability and depression. *Journal of Clinical and Experimental Neuropsychology, 14*, 50.

Tweedy, J. R., Langer, K. G., & McDowell, F. H. (1982). The effects of semantic relations

on the memory deficit associated with Parkinson's disease. *Journal of Clinical Neuropsychology, 4*, 235–247.

Uhl, G. R., Hackney, G. O., Torchia, M., & al, e. (1986). Parkinson's disease: Nigral receptor changes support peptidergic role in nigrostriatal modulation. *Annals of Neurology, 20*, 194–203.

van Zomeren, A. H. (1981). *Reaction time and attention after closed head injury.* Lisse, The Netherlands: Swets & Zeitlinger BV.

Vance, K. T., Kaszniak, A. W., Bayles, K. A., & Bondi, M. W. (1991). Performance of Parkinson's disease patients on two abstract reasoning tests. *The Clinical Neuropsychologist, 5*, 264.

Villardita, C., Smirni, P., Le Pira, F., Zappala, G., & Nicoletti, F. (1982). Mental deterioration, visuoperceptive disabilities and constructional apraxia in Parkinson's disease. *Acta Neurologica Scandinavica, 66*, 112–120.

Waters, C. H., Apuzzo, M. L. J., Neal, J. H., & Weiner, L. P. (1992). Long-term follow-up of adrenal medullary transplantation for Parkinson's disease. *Journal of Geriatric Psychiatry and Neurology, 5*, 35–39.

Weingartner, H., Burns, S., Diebel, R., & Le Witt, P. A. (1984). Cognitive impairment in Parkinson's disease: Distinguishing between effort-demanding and automatic cognitive processes. *Psychiatry Research, 11*, 223–235.

Whitehouse, P. J. (1986). The concept of subcortical dementia: Another look. *Annals of Neurology, 19*, 1–6.

Whitehouse, P. J., Hedreen, J. C., White, C. L., & Price, D. L. (1983). Basal forebrain neurons in the dementia of Parkinson disease. *Annals of Neurology, 13*, 243–248.

Whitehouse, P. J., Martino, A. M., Wagster, M. V., Price, D. L., Mayeux, R., Atack, J. R., & Keller, K. J. (1988). Reductions in [3H]nicotinic acetylcholine binding in Alzheimer's disease and Parkinson's disease: An autoradiographic study. *Neurology, 38*, 720–723.

Whitford, C., Candy, J., Edwardson, J., & Perry, R. (1988). Cortical somatostatinergic system not affected in Alzheimer's and Parkinson's diseases. *Journal of Neurological Sciences, 86*, 13–18.

Wilson, R. S., Kaszniak, A. W., Klawans, H. L., & Garron, D. C. (1980). High speed memory scanning in parkinsonism. *Cortex, 16*, 67–72.

Wolfe, N., Katz, D. I., Albert, M. L., Almozlino, A., Durso, R., Smith, M. C., & Volicer, L. (1990). Neuropsychological profile linked to low dopamine: In Alzheimer's disease, major depression, and Parkinson's disease. *Journal of Neurology, Neurosurgery and Psychiatry, 53*, 915–917.

Wolfson, L. I., Leenders, K. L., Brown, L. L., & Jones T. (1985). Alterations of regional cerebral blood flow and oxygen metabolism in Parkinson's disease. *Neurology, 35*, 1399–1405.

Xuereb, J. H., Perry, E. K., Candy, J. M., Bonham, J. R., & Perry, R. H. (1990). Parameters of cholinergic neurotransmission in the thalamus in Parkinson's disease and Alzheimer's disease. *Journal of Neurological Sciences, 99*, 185–197.

Yahr, M. D. (1990). Principles of medical treatment. In G. M. Stern (Eds.), *Parkinson's disease* (pp. 495–508). Baltimore: Johns Hopkins University Press.

Yoshimura, M. (1988). Pathological basis for dementia in elderly patients with idiopathic Parkinson's disease. *European Neurology, 28*(Suppl. 1), 29–35.

Young, A. B., & Penney, J. B. (1988). Biochemical and functional organization of the basal ganglia. In J. Jankovic & E. Tolosa (Eds.), *Parkinson's disease and movement disorders* (pp. 1–11). Baltimore: Urban & Schwarzenberg.

Zetusky, W. J., Jankovic, J., & Pirozzolo, F. J. (1985). The heterogeneity of Parkinson's disease: Clinical and prognostic implications. *Neurology, 35*, 522–526.

12

Solvent Encephalopathy

ROBERTA FIRNHABER WHITE AND SUSAN P. PROCTOR

This chapter addresses the neuropsychological effects of exposure to industrial solvents. It is divided into three sections. The first provides background information on the field of behavioral neurotoxicology, including a description of the field, definitions of nomenclature used, general information about solvents, and review of exposure variables that must be considered when studying patients or subjects who have been exposed to solvents. The second section of the chapter reviews research literature on the central nervous system (CNS) effects of industrial solvent exposure, and the third discusses assessment issues germane to the clinical assessment of solvent-exposed patients.

Behavioral Neurotoxicology

The study of the effects of exposure to neurotoxicants on behavior (behavioral neurotoxicology) has expanded enormously in the last half of this century. Early studies relied heavily on neurological evaluations, CNS symptom checklists, mental status examination techniques (Grandjean et al., 1955), or even electroencephalography (EEG) (Seppalainen & Haltia, 1980; Seppalainen & Antii-Poika, 1983). However, even in its early stages, advancement of the field was expedited considerably through the use of clinical psychological testing techniques such as those employed by Helena Hanninen (Hanninen, 1971) and through the use of psychophysiological measures (e.g., Salvini, 1971; Stewart, Gay, Shafer, Early, & Rowe, 1969). These measures carried all of the advantages inherent in psychometric methodology, including standardization of test instructions, availability of concrete and reliable numerical outcome measures (scores, response latencies), and test validation (White, 1986; White & Feldman, 1987).

The use of neuropsychological expertise and of test batteries considered to be primarily neuropsychological has been more recent. A paper published in 1977 used the term *neuropsychological* in its title (Tsushima & Towne, 1977), for example, and other studies carried out in the 1970s and 1980s employed neuropsychological test procedures such as the Halstead-Reitan battery (Peters, Levine, Matthews, Sauter, & Rankin, 1982; Peters, Levine, Matthews, & Chapman, 1988; Matthews, Chapman & Woodard, 1990) and Boston process tasks (Baker et al.,

1984, 1985). These test batteries have the obvious advantage of having met "gold standard" validation as measures of CNS function: they have been used extensively in studies of subjects with known brain damage and in studies of subjects for whom cerebral localization of damage or neuropathological disorders are documented and well defined. They are thus clearly valid as indicators of cerebral function and can provide clues as to likely sites of toxicant-induced brain damage or neuropathological processes caused by specific types of exposure (White and Feldman, 1987). This property of neuropsychological instruments is especially important because different neurotoxicants produce different neuropathological abnormalities (White, Proctor, Feldman, in press).

Another recent trend in the field has been the development of computerized versions of traditional neuropsychological tasks, some of which have been specifically aimed at neurobehavioral toxicological investigations (Letz & Baker, 1986; Letz, 1990). These measures are easy to administer in epidemiological field settings and thus have powerful potential utility in the field of behavioral neurotoxicology. However, they have yet to be validated as measures of CNS function or as indicators of specific types of neuropathology (White, Feldman & Travers, 1990b): this limits the investigator's ability to interpret results based on computerized assessment and renders the tasks relatively useless clinically until more is known about them. In our own research studies we use computerized tasks in conjunction with traditional neuropsychological tests; we are also conducting validation studies in which the computerized batteries are administered to well-defined neurological groups. However, the computerized tasks are not used in clinical assessment and diagnosis.

There are a number of recent papers that review the field of neurobehavioral toxicology from the standpoint of assessment, including primarily historical descriptions (Gamberale, 1985; Hanninen, 1985; Weiss, 1990), test-oriented summaries (Anger, 1990), functional descriptions of behavioral deficits (White et al., 1992), and toxicant-specific summaries (White et al., 1990b). Two recent books published in the public health literature are also valuable sources of historical information in the field of behavioral neurotoxicology (Johnson, 1987, 1990).

Nomenclature

The CNS effects of exposure to neurotoxicants have been described in a number of ways. In general neurological terminology, the effects of neurotoxicant exposure may constitute an intoxication and may produce an acute reversible encephalopathy or a chronic encephalopathy. The encephalopathy resulting from toxicant exposure may be generally referred to as a toxic encephalopathy or may be specifically denoted by the responsible neurotoxicant. Using this system, encephalopathy resulting from exposure to perchloroethylene may be termed a *solvent encephalopathy* or *perchloroethylene encephalopathy*.

Early in the history of behavior neurotoxicology, the term *psycho-organic syndrome* was adopted from Blueler's terminology (1944 reference in Grandjean et al., 1955; Hanninen, 1988) and used to label the behavioral syndrome seen following exposure, particularly to solvents. This syndrome was defined operationally in terms of cognitive and mood symptoms (Grandjean et al., 1955) and test results (Hanninen, 1971, 1988).

Hanninen, in a study of carbon disulfide–exposed rayon workers, noted that the psycho-organic syndrome could be observed in the absence of findings on medical examination and in the absence of obvious physical disease. Because the phenomenon of toxicant-induced behavioral change has been observed repeatedly in the absence of obvious psychosocial disease, the term *subclinical toxic enceph-alopathy* is sometimes used to identify this phenomenon.

A clinical diagnostic system integrating reversibility of findings and type of dysfunction with DSM-III terminology has been defined (Baker & White, 1985) and recently revised (White et al., 1992). In this system, diagnosis may range from acute reversible encephalopathy to severe residual chronic encephalopathy. The diagnostic system with neuropsychological symptomatology, course, and usual etio-logical agents has been summarized elsewhere (White et al., 1992).

Solvents

The term *solvents* encompasses a number of organic chemicals that differ widely in chemical structure. There are 11 general classes of organic solvents (U.S. Congress, Office of Technology Assessment, 1990):

1. Aliphatic hydrocarbons (e.g., *n*-hexane).
2. Halogenated hydrocarbons (e.g., perchloroethylene, trichloroethylene [TCE]).
3. Alcohols (e.g., methanol).
4. Cyclic hydrocarbons (e.g., cyclohexane).
5. Esters (e.g., ethyl acetate).
6. Ethers (e.g., ethyl ether).
7. Nitrohydrocarbons (e.g., ethyl nitrate).
8. Ketone (e.g., methyl-ethyl-ketone).
9. Glycols (e.g., ethylene glycol).
10. Aromatic hydrocarbons (e.g., benzene).
11. Aldehydes (e.g., acetaldehyde).

There are also individual solvents, such as carbon disulfide, that do not fit into these classes. In addition, many common solvents exist as mixtures. For example, Stoddard solvent and thinners are components of numerous products, including paints, varnishes, adhesives, glues, coatings, degreasing and cleaning agents, dyes and printing inks, floor and shoe polishes, waxes, agricultural products, and fuels.

All types of organic solvents are volatile liquids at room temperature and are lipophilic (Grasso, Sharratt, Davies, & Irvine, 1984; U.S. Department of Health and Human Services/National Institute of Occupational Safety and Health [USDHHS/NIOSH], 1987). Thus, the major routes of exposure are through inhalation and dermal contact. Following absorption, solvents may be exhaled unchanged, bio-transformed, and then excreted; and/or they may bioaccumulate in lipid-rich tissue such as brain, myelin, and adipose tissue. The human toxicity of individual solvents depends on the mechanism of action (which is usually guided by structure) and on the amount or dose of exposure. Exposure dosage depends on a number of factors in addition to route of exposure, including the concentration of solvent in the air, the solubility of solvent in the blood, and the amount of physical work the individual is doing at the time of exposure (U.S. Congress, OTA, 1990). Often, solvents are present in mixtures that may lead to additivity, synergism, or potentiation of toxic effects (Andrews & Snyder, 1986).

Because of the large number of organic solvents and their increasing use in newer technologies, there are many different occupations in which workers can be exposed to organic solvents. According to NIOSH, about 9.8 million workers are exposed to solvents every day (USDHHS/NIOSH, 1987). However, solvent exposure occurs environmentally as well as occupationally. Domestic exposure may occur through contact with cleaning agents, paints or thinners, or during home car repair. Some hobbies involve solvent use (paints, paint removers, glues, degreasers). Contaminated water supplies containing solvents are another source of exposure, particularly when wells exist near manufacturing areas or toxic dump sites. Finally, self-administration of solvents includes the common consumption of ethanol as well as abusive inhalation of toluene and gasoline (U.S. Congress, OTA, 1990).

Exposure Variables

When evaluating the behavioral effects of exposure to neurotoxicants, a number of exposure variables must be considered. These variables, and the methods for assessing and measuring them, have been described in detail elsewhere (White et al., 1992) but will be reviewed briefly here.

As mentioned earlier in this chapter, the dosage of exposure is important and can be estimated through air monitoring, soil or water sampling, or hypothetical representation through careful assessment of occupational history. Factors that affect dosage include route of entry (oral, dermal, respiratory), protective gear used during exposure (respirators, gloves, protective clothing), activities that may enhance exposure (eating or smoking during exposure, wearing contaminated clothing after leaving the exposure site, failing to clean exposed skin), and duration of exposure (per episode and over prolonged periods of time). When assessing the effects of exposure to one toxicant, it is important to assess whether multiple exposures have occurred to chemicals in the home or workplace (including contaminants of the known exposure agent), to medications, or to substances of abuse such as alcohol. There is some evidence that suggests, for example, that the neurotoxicity of solvents such as TCE may be enhanced by the use of alcohol (Sato, Nakajima, Koyama, 1981). The specific agent of exposure must also be considered. The effects of solvents are different in some ways from those of other neurotoxicants such as lead (White et al., 1990b) and even within the class of solvents neurotoxicity varies by chemical.

Chronicity of exposure is another important variable to consider. Brief exposures to high levels of a solvent may cause an acute encephalopathy with or without permanent residual encephalopathy (Feldman & Lessell, 1969; Feldman, White, Currie, Travers, & Lessell, 1985). However, exposure to solvents at much lower levels may also produce permanent residual brain damage (Bernad, Newell, & Spyker, 1987). We are finding, for example, that exposure over many years to environmental solvents occurring at levels considered to be safe by current occupational standards may produce permanent encephalopathy. It is clear that far more work needs to be done before accurate standards are developed for safe levels of exposure to well-known solvents and before all of the potential neuro-toxicants have been identified and their levels of neurotoxicity defined.

Another variable that should be considered is assessing degree of exposure. In occupational settings, exposure is often easier to estimate than in environmental settings. If an individual has been exposed to chemicals through well water, for example, it is often difficult to determine the concentration of the chemical in well water over time. In addition, the extent of one's exposure may depend on their eating, drinking, and bathing habits. Determination of the individual's degree of exposure should then be estimated based on a review of the individual's daily habits over time (Brown, Bishop, & Rowan, 1984; Andelman, 1985).

Research Findings on Solvent Toxicity

The behavioral effects of exposure to solvents have been described in varying degrees of completeness and detail. Many solvents are identified as being neurotoxic (see USDHH/PHS/CDD, 1990, for a list of solvents and other chemicals that includes chemical and common names, chemical structure, occupational recommendations, and physiological sites of toxicity). However, the behavioral toxicology of individual organic solvents is generally not as well described as the toxicology of certain metals (especially lead and mercury). Of the organic solvents, the most information has accrued on carbon disulfide, a neurotoxicant to which workers in the grain and rayon industries were in the past exposed over long periods of time as their single major hazardous exposure. The incomplete accumulation of information on other specific solvents may be due to the usual circumstances surrounding solvent exposure. Occupational and environmental solvent exposures tend to occur in mixtures of solvents or solvents and other neurotoxicants (Johnson, 1987). For example, car mechanics may be exposed to both TCE degreasing agents and carbon monoxide, painters and roofers are exposed to solvent mixtures, and some artists or artisans are exposed to both solvents and metals. It is thus more difficult to identify naturally occurring subject groups with relatively pure solvent exposures than it is to locate subject groups with primary exposure to lead or mercury. It is especially difficult to identify subject groups in which developmental exposure has occurred among children. In addition, solvents can be biodegraded into other substances that produce toxic effects, complicating the study of solvent toxicology. Finally, there are many individual solvents and solvent combinations that must each be studied and described. It will take many years to develop a complete description of all possible effects under many different types of circumstances, especially because new solvent products will most likely be produced in the future. For these reasons, when the effects of a specific solvent are being considered, it is often necessary to reason by analogy to another solvent. For example, when studying the effects of Stoddard exposure in a group of subjects with occupational exposure, we based our behavioral predictions and assessment battery on findings from studies in which exposure occurred to the chemically similar petroleum distillate white spirits (Robins et al., 1989).

The following review will summarize selected literature on the behavioral neurotoxicology of organic solvents, emphasizing the chemicals in which we have been particularly interested. Review of every toxicological report on solvents would go well beyond the scope of this chapter. We will provide a summary of some of the animal literature in this area, a description of research methods and findings from human studies, and a review of a few in-depth case studies.

Animal Studies

The use of animal models to explore the mechanisms and sites of CNS action of specific solvents is a powerful source of information in behavioral neurotoxicology. Using such models, the behavioral effects of exposure can be assessed, exposure can be systematically controlled and varied, metabolites can be investigated, and end-point organ systems can be studied anatomically and histologically. The CNS effects of solvents in humans are often only revealed after such intense exposure that the patient dies and is autopsied or develops sufficient clinical illness that pathological changes can be observed through electrophysiological or imaging measures or peripheral nervous system biopsy. Physiological abnormalities occurring at preclinical levels, when disease is present but not obvious, can be measured by behavioral tests, but it is rarely possible to examine the relationship between behavioral abnormalities and neuropathological processes in humans manifesting subclinical disease.

The effects of TCE on CNS function have been investigated in both rats and dogs. Using the rat as a model, Grandjean and colleagues conducted a series of experiments in which rats were systematically exposed to TCE vapors at various dosages over different periods of time. At exposures of 200 to 800 parts per million (ppm), behavioral performances were enhanced on some measures and impaired on others, though 800 ppm appeared to be a critical dose producing impairment. When rats were exposed to 800 ppm of TCE for 10 months, swimming rates were adversely affected, exploratory behavior was stimulated on a maze test, and learning on the Hebb test was not affected (Battig & Grandjean, 1963). In a previous paper, Grandjean described disinhibitory behavior on a rope climbing task in rats following TCE exposure (Grandjean, 1960). A series of studies on the clinicopathological correlates of TCE exposure in dogs revealed that chronic exposure to 3,000 ppm TCE over 60 hours was associated with destruction of the Purkinje layer in the cerebellum and with mild changes in the cerebral hemispheres consisting of swollen pyknotic neurons and mild focal swelling of myelin in white matter (Baker, 1958). In another fascinating series of studies, exposure to TCE was found to be associated with hippocampal damage in the rat following intrauterine and adult exposure (Isaacson & Taylor, 1989; Isaacson, Spohler, & Taylor, 1990).

Animal exposure to benzene has been described as fetotoxic (Green, Leong, & Laskin, 1978) or teratogenic (Watanabe & Yoshida, 1970). A study of developmental exposure to benzene injected in rat pups 9 to 13 days postpartum revealed long-standing changes in motor activity identifiable 45 to 100 days following exposure when the animals were administered dextro-amphetamine. These results were interpreted as suggesting a long-term benzene-induced change in catecholaminergic function (Tilson, Squibb, Meyer, & Sparber, 1980). In another study on the behavioral effects of benzene, adult mice were exposed over 6-hour intervals to 300 to 900 ppm benzene and evaluated on seven behavioral measures in their home cages. Increases in eating and grooming behaviors were identified along with a decrease in sleeping (Evans, Dempster, & Snyder, 1981).

A study of EEG changes in cats exposed to extraordinarily high levels of benzene and toluene (12,000–52,000 ppm) revealed an initial response of restless and hypersynchronous amygdaloid activity, followed by epileptiform discharges with repeated inhalations, finally resulting in diffuse slowing with repeated high exposures (Contreras, Gonzalez-Estrada, Zrabozo, & Fernandez-Guardiolo, 1979). When comparing the effects of exposure to toluene and acetone in mice, Bruckner and Peterson (1981a, 1981b), found toluene to be a faster acting narcotic than acetone, but the effects of acetone were more long lasting. Daily exposure over several weeks did not produce permanent effects on brain tissue examined histologically.

Human Studies

Experimental and quasi-experimental studies on the behavioral effects of solvent exposure generally follow one of four paradigms: acute exposure studies, case-control studies of neuropsychiatric outcome in exposed subject groups, retrospective studies of groups of subjects with well-defined occupational or environmental exposures, or prospective assessment of the relationship between exposure variables and behavioral outcome in groups of subjects experiencing specific neurotoxicant exposures. In addition, there are a number of illuminating case reports.

Acute Exposure Studies

In these studies, the subject is usually exposed to neurotoxicants by inhaling vapors in an exposure chamber. Behavioral testing is carried out at intervals following exposure. There are obvious limitations to the amount of information that can be acquired from such studies: there are restrictions on the upper levels of exposure that can be applied and it is difficult to model the long-term chronic low-level exposure which is problematic in both occupational and environmental settings. Hence, the negative findings of many of these studies are not surprising. We will review a few of these studies here. For an excellent review of the advantages, problems, and procedures that must be considered using this methodology and a concise description of acute exposure studies using solvents, the reader is referred to Johnson's book on neurotoxic illness (1987, chap. 3).

Acute exposure studies on the effects of TCE have produced conflicting results. Although Salvini (1971) identified significant impairment in performance on a battery of memory, motor, and sensory tasks at levels of 110 ppm over two 4-hour periods, exposures of 300 ppm over 2.5 to 2.75 hours showed behavioral effects in one study (Stopps & McLaughlin, 1967) but not another (Ettema et al., 1975a, 1975b; Windemuller & Ettema, 1978). Levels of 1,000 ppm produced associated impairments in two studies (Kylin, Axell, Samuel, & Lindborg, 1967; Vernon & Ferguson, 1969). Johnson (1987), in a review of these studies, concluded that 300-ppm exposure was required to document behavioral effects in acute exposure studies.

Other investigations have assessed the acute exposure effects of methyl chloroform (1,1,1-trichloromethane), with negative findings in an early study (Stewart et al., 1969), but interesting findings in another investigation reporting enhancement of performance on the Stroop test and no effect in performance on a syntactic reasoning test (Mckay et al., 1987). Acute exposure studies have also assessed the effects of tetrachloroethylene (perchloroethylene, a dry cleaning fluid), finding little effect at levels of 100 ppm or lower (Stewart, Baretta, & Torkelson, 1970). Other acute exposure studies have examined the effects of a single solvent such as methyl chloride and the interaction between methyl chloride and valium (Putz-Anderson, Seltzer, Croxton, & Phipps, 1981), and the effects of ethanol (Eche-verria, 1987). Summaries of acute exposure studies on other solvents, including methylene chloride, toluene, white spirits, and xylene can be found in Johnson (1987).

Case-Control Studies

Several case control studies have compared the occurrence of neuropsychiatric disorders in groups of workers at high risk of solvent exposure to control workers from occupations at low risk of solvent exposure. Studies of recipients of disability pensions in Sweden (Axelson, Hane, & Hogstedt, 1976), construction workers receiving disability pensions in Finland (Lindstrom, Riihimaki, & Hanninen, 1984), Danish Carpenters and Cabinet Makers Union members (Olsen & Sabroe, 1980), Dutch painters and construction workers (van Vliet et al., 1987, 1989, 1990), Norwegian chemical tank workers (Riise & Moen, 1990), and U.S. Social Security recipients (Brackbill, Maizlish, & Fishbach, 1990) found significant relationships between the diagnosis of neuropsychiatric illness and solvent exposure in at least some of the diagnostic categories used. A study comparing Danish painters (solvent-exposed group) and control bricklayers found the exposed group to be at greater risk of developing neuropsychiatric disorders (Mikkelson, 1980), but a similar in-vestigation comparing Swiss painters and electricians did not produce strikingly positive results, and the occurrence of alcoholism among the painters was a sig-nificant confounder (Guberan et al., 1989).

Three studies focused on dementia as an outcome diagnosis, one of which reported a significant solvent-associated risk (Rasmussen, Olsen, & Lauritsen, 1985) and two of which had nonsignificant findings overall (O'Flynn, Monkman, & Waldron, 1987; Shalat, Seltzer, & Baker, 1988).

Group Studies

When reviewing retrospective or prospective studies of neurobehavioral function in groups of exposed subjects, it is necessary to critically consider a number of factors in evaluating the validity of study outcomes. First, neurobehavioral test batteries differ among investigators and studies: batteries that are classically neu-ropsychological contain different tests, tasks drawn from cognitive and physiological methodology are employed, and novel computerized and noncomputerized tasks for which there is no information on validity or reliability are used. Negative results from one study may simply reflect limitations of the battery. We have described existing test batteries that have been designed for use in behavioral neurotoxico-logical studies and have delineated appropriate criteria for epidemiological battery selection elsewhere, emphasizing the point that it is often inappropriate to use clinical and epidemiological batteries interchangeably and the need to validate behavioral tests neuropsychologically in regard to identification of brain-behavior relationships (Proctor & White, 1990).

Second, it is vital that subject characteristics not be confused with exposure effects in a study. When comparing exposed subjects to controls, it may be important to secure norms specific to the exposed group on the tests used (Ryan et al., 1987) or, even more importantly, to control for native intelligence. In a recent report comparing solvent-exposed workers to controls, for example, the investigators found that the significant differences in test performance between cases and controls were reduced when findings were adjusted for estimated intelligence and that the difference disappeared when a "more appropriate" control group was used (Cherry, Hutchins, Pace, & Waldron, 1985; interestingly, symptomatic complaints still differentiated the groups significantly).

A related problem is that of cutoff scores used to conclude that impairment exists. When subjects are rated clinically as impaired versus not impaired, especially if no control groups are used, false conclusions about exposure-induced deficits may be drawn. For example, early conclusions on CNS dysfunction in painters based on interpretation of nonstandardized clinical tests by a group of Danish investigators (Arlien-Soborg, Bruhn, Gyldensted, & Melgaard, 1979; Bruhn, Arlien-Soberg, Gyldensted, & Christensen, 1981) were later disavowed by the investigators when they compared their cases to controls, adjusting for age, education, and intelligence (Gade, Mortensen, & Bruhn, 1988).

Finally, exposure must be well characterized, including identification of each known or potential neurotoxicant and dosage and duration of exposure.

Retrospective Comparisons of Exposed Groups. There are numerous papers in the field of behavioral neurotoxicology that compare the test performance of groups of subjects with known histories of neurotoxicant exposure (usually occupational) to control groups. One of the most extensively studied occupational groups is that of painters. Although findings by a Danish group of CNS dysfunction among painters were later called into question (Gade et al., 1988, see above), Hane et al. (1977), in a well-controlled study comparing Swedish house painters to controls, found poorer performance among the painters on tasks assessing visual-logical ability, psychomotor coordination, choice reaction time, and visual memory. These findings are important because the investigators had access to preexposure IQ testing done in the Swedish armed forces that allowed them to equate the groups for premorbid IQ. A later study in Sweden of car and industrial spray painters found no detrimental effects relative to controls on verbal, spatial, or reasoning tests. However, the painters performed more poorly on tasks assessing reaction time, perceptual speed, manual dexterity, short-term memory, and on peripheral nervous system measures (Elofsson et al., 1980). Car painters studied in Finland were found to perform more poorly than controls on Wechsler Adult Intelligence Scale (WAIS) Similarities, Digit Span, and Block Design, Wechsler Memory Scale (WMS) Logical Memories and Associate Learning, and Finger Tapping (left) as well as a number of measures of emotional and personality function. This study is important because careful controls of premorbid IQ were available (Hanninen, Eskelinen, Husman, & Nurminen, 1976). Other evaluations on the same subject group revealed some evidence of peripheral nervous system dysfunction but no differences between exposed subjects and controls on EEG (Seppalainen, Husman, & Martenson, 1978). An American study of shipyard painters working in three different shipyards and exposed to many different solvents showed deficits relative to controls on three visuomotor tasks. Although the groups were matched for age, race, gender, and education, this study did not control for estimated native intelligence (Valciukas, Lilis, Singer, Glickman, & Nicholson, 1985). A study carried out in Germany, in contrast, failed to identify a toxic encephalopathy among German house painters, although personality change and decreased mental efficiency were reported among the painters (Triebig et al., 1988).

The exposure of painters is somewhat unsatisfying to study because painters are exposed to a mixture of solvents and it is difficult to identify specific agents as culprits when carrying out these studies: they confirm the hazards associated with belonging to an occupational group but are not specifically informative. There are a number of other studies with this same limitation, confirming the risk associated with solvent exposure but restricting generalizations concerning specific solvents. These studies focus on groups of workers loosely identified as having "mixed solvent exposure." One of these, for whom exposure was characterized only as "documented history of exposure to organic solvents," was compared to a control group on a battery of neuropsychological tests and found to show significant relative impairments on WMS Visual Reproductions (immediate and delayed recall) and Trails A and B. In addition, a syndrome of symptoms labeled *cacosmia* (nausea, headaches, subjective distress) was found to be significantly related to performance deficits. The findings were interpreted to suggest that solvents specifically affect limbic lobe function (Ryan, Morrow, & Hodgson, 1988). A Finnish study reported by Lindstrom (1980) compared subjects with mixed solvent exposure (mainly TCE, perchloroethylene, other halogenated hydrocarbons, aromatic hydrocarbons, aliphatic hydrocarbons, paint solvents, or alcohol), subjects exposed primarily to styrene (in boat laminating), and controls. The mixed-solvent group was found to be more impaired than either of the other two groups across several measures; the styrene-exposed group showed few impairments in these comparisons. In another report from the same laboratory, styrene exposure was found to be associated with disturbances in visuomotor accuracy and psychomotor performance when plastic workers were compared to concrete reinforcement workers on test performance (Lindstrom, Harkonen, & Hernberg, 1976). Estimated level of native intelligence does not appear to have been considered in either of these studies as a control variable.

Trichloroethylene was the agent studied in one of the earliest papers evaluating solvent effects on an occupational group. In a paper published in 1955, Grandjean described cognitive changes occurring in mechanical engineers at exposure levels well below the then-recommended occupational standard, although these were not linked to neuropsychological tests. Although TCE has been recognized as a neurotoxicant since at least the early part of this century (Smith, 1966), it has not been extensively studied epidemiologically, possibly because exposure to TCE so frequently occurs in conjunction with exposure to other neurotoxicants.

Toluene has been identified as a neurotoxicant and addressed in occasional occupational studies (e.g., Struwe & Wennberg, 1983). However, it has also been of interest as a substance of abuse through glue sniffing. One study (Tsushima & Towne, 1977) compared the performance of glue sniffers to controls on 13 test measures, finding relative impairments among the sniffers on 11 of the measures and a positive relationship between duration of sniffing and impaired performance. However, their data suggest that there may have been a selection bias affecting the group differences as the sniffers performed at significantly lower levels on the Peabody Picture Vocabulary Test, which is thought to be a robust measure of premorbid intelligence and relatively insensitive to toxic effects in adults (mean Peabody IQ among sniffers was 71.6; among controls, 93.2).

Carbon disulfide has a long and illustrious history as the topic of group retrospective epidemiological studies in behavioral toxicology. In 1971, Hanninen compared carbon disulfide workers divided into two groups (those thought to be healthy and those thought to be suffering from carbon disulfide poisoning) to controls, reporting several tests that differentiated both groups from the controls (her conclusions about latent carbon disulfide poisoning have been described above) (Hanninen, 1971; Hanninen, Nurminen, Tolonen, & Martelin, 1978). These behavioral abnormalities were also accompanied by neurophysiological abnormalities on nerve conduction measures and EEG (Seppalainen & Tolonen, 1974). In addition, neuropsychological deficits associated with a parkinsonian syndrome seen following carbon disulfide exposure have been described in grain workers (Peters et al., 1982, 1988; Matthews et al., 1990).

Prospective Group Studies. Prospective epidemiological studies of solvent-exposed subject groups—in which the group is identified and behavioral testing is done in conjunction with exposure assessment—are more rarely encountered in the behavioral neurotoxicology literature than retrospective studies. In one of these, Olsen & Sabroe (1980) examined workers with exposure to a variety of solvents before and after a work day. Compared to controls, the solvent-exposed workers performed more poorly on tasks assessing short-term memory, simple reaction time, and perceptual speed. The score differences were primarily explainable by the performance of persons carrying out cleaning procedures, who had the highest exposures. Results were thought to reflect acute exposure effects. In another study, solvent-exposed workers underwent neurological and neuropsychological assessment and estimate of exposure dosage. Dose-effect relationships were identified between severity of exposure and test impairment (Gregerson et al., 1984). We have recently carried out prospective field studies documenting relationships between exposure to perchloroethylene (Echeverria et al., 1990), mixed silk screening solvents (White, Feldman, Echeverria, & Schweikert, 1990) and Stoddard solvent (Robins et al., 1989), and neuropsychological impairment.

Clinical Case Descriptions. Clinical case descriptions of individuals or small groups of individuals with solvent exposure have contributed importantly to the literature on nervous system effects of solvents by providing information on especially serious exposures and by providing data from extraordinary procedures that would not be carried out in an experimental setting. A few examples of these reports will be provided here.

There are a number of case descriptions of patients with TCE exposure. In one case report a patient is described who experienced occupational exposure to TCE degreasing metals 3 to 4 hours per day for 1 year, when she became symptomatic. Initial examination revealed EEG abnormalities and abnormal performance on psychomotor tasks. At follow-up 1, 2, and 10 months later, psychomotor performance had improved but EEG abnormalities persisted. The authors of this study felt that it confirmed the utility of follow-up evaluations in documenting the course of acute intoxication and recovery in several realms of nervous system function (Stracciari, Gallasi, Ciardulli, & Coccagna, 1985). In another report,

McCunney (1988) described three cases of TCE encephalopathy in patients exposed well below the occupational standard. Unfortunately, neuropsychological testing was not included in the report. A patient from the Boston University Medical Center Occupational Neurology Clinic with ophthalmological and neuropsychological symptoms, including attentional, visuospatial, and memory deficits and depression, has been described immediately after acute TCE intoxication and at follow-up 16 years later (Feldman & Lessell, 1969; Feldman, Mayer, & Taub, 1970; Feldman et al., 1985). Consistent with these case studies of CNS effects secondary to occupational exposure is a report based on 22 persons exposed to TCE in well water for 5 to 20 years at levels of 5 to 14 ppm. Neurological examination abnormalities were observed in many of the adults, and 9 of 12 children exhibited behavioral and learning difficulties (Bernad et al., 1987). These findings are similar to those we are observing at Boston University in evaluations of a number of patients with well-water exposures to TCE. Subjects exposed to TCE plus other solvents have also been reported to have pneumoencephalographic abnormalities suggestive of cerebral atrophy (Juntunen, Hupli, Hernberg, & Luisto, 1980) and to have psychometric and EEG abnormalities (Seppalainen et al., 1980; Seppalainen & Antii-Poika, 1983).

A description of 19 sewage treatment workers employed at the same plant who had exposure to a variety of solvents including toluene, benzene, and other organic solvents showed that 74% had CNS symptoms that were more prominent among workers who had spent more than 1 year at the plant and which remitted following transfer from the plant (Kraut et al., 1988). In another case report on workers with occupational toluene exposure, computed tomographic (CT) scans carried out on 14 printers with histories of at least 20 years of toluene exposure showed that the widths of the temporal and occipital sulci and the supravermian cisterns were greater among the printers than among age-matched controls. However, the CT findings in the exposed subjects were considered to be in the normal range (Juntunen, Matikainen, Antii-Poika, Suoranta, & Valle, 1985). A report on the CT scans of 11 persons exposed to toluene through glue sniffing described cortical atrophy in six individuals, two of whom also evidenced cerebellar atrophy (Schikler, Seitz, Rice, & Strader, 1982). The findings of impairment in neuropsychological function, cerebellar symptoms, and CT scan–identified prominent cerebellar sulci and cortical and ventricular abnormalities were also described in a report on 24 toluene abusers (Fornazzari, Wilkinson, Kapur, & Carlen, 1983). Recently, several related reports on magnetic resonance imaging (MRI) findings from toluene abusers have documented diffuse cerebellar, cerebral, and brainstem atrophy; increased periventricular white matter signal intensity on T2 weighted images; and diminished differentiation between gray and white matter (Rosenberg et al., 1988; Rosenberg, Spitz, Filley, Davis, & Schaumberg, 1988). In addition, degree of white matter abnormality was found to be significantly correlated with neuropsychological impairment (Filley, Heaton, & Rosenberg, 1990).

There are also a number of case descriptions of patients with carbon disulfide poisoning, including neuropsychological and motor deficits observed in pesticide-exposed grain workers (Peters et al., 1982, 1988). In addition, abnormal clinical neurological examinations, CT scans showing cerebral atrophy, and abnormal neuropsychological examinations were reported in the majority of 16 men with carbon disulfide exposure over 10 years or more (Aaserud et al., 1988). Exposure to carbon disulfide has also been associated with the development of cerebrovascular disease, which cannot be easily discriminated from idiopathic cerebrovascular disease (Johnson, 1987, p. 7).

CLINICAL ASSESSMENT OF SOLVENT ENCEPHALOPATHY

Nonneuropsychological Assessment Procedures

Exposure Assessment

When completing clinical assessments of patients with possible solvent encephalopathy, it is important to characterize the patient's exposure as clearly as possible. The specific solvents involved, duration of exposure, dosage of exposure, routes of entry, and environmental or occupational conditions under which exposure occurred should be understood as clearly as possible. Sometimes this is difficult due to factors such as a delay before anyone realized that exposure might have caused the patient's symptomatic complaints (in which case the conditions of exposure may no longer be available), the occurrence of a sudden accidental acute exposure in which exposure conditions cannot be replicated, or lack of accurate information about occupational or environmental circumstances of exposure (the latter can especially occur in environmental exposures to toxic dump sites involving multiple neurotoxicants) (Buffler, Crane, & Key, 1985). However, often there are industrial hygiene data available on typical dosages of exposure at a site and other information that can be used to model individual exposures. We have described some of the self-report and industrial hygiene methods that can be useful in exposure assessment elsewhere (White et al., 1992). Exposure assessment is important to the neuropsychologist because severity of exposure may affect neuropsychological outcome.

In addition to evaluating the occupational/environmental variables affecting an exposure, it is sometimes possible to obtain biological indicators of exposure in individual patients by measuring levels of a solvent (or its metabolites) in blood, urine, or fat. Unfortunately, such measurement often does not occur in hospitals or emergency rooms treating patients with acute exposure (due mostly to lack of knowledge about the availability of such measures), leaving a void in the information available about upper levels of intake of solvents in individual patients. The lack of a finding of significant levels of solvent or metabolites in patients who have been exposure-free for some time does not preclude the possibility of historical exposure with significant health effects. In some such cases fat biopsies are informative, because solvents are lipophilic (see above).

Neurological and Neurophysiological Assessment. Because solvents affect both the CNS and peripheral nervous system (PNS), neurological evaluation is often a valuable adjunct to neuropsychological testing when treating solvent-exposed patients. Trichloroethylene, for example, affects the trigeminal nerve and the PNS as well as the brain (Agency for Toxic Substances and Disease Registry [ATSDR], 1989; Feldman, Chirico-Post, & Proctor, 1988; Feldman, 1990). In addition to PNS dysfunction measurable on nerve conduction testing (which in our experience sometimes occurs independently of as well as in conjunction with an encephalopathy), nervous system effects of solvents can sometimes be observed on EEG (Seppalainen & Haltia, 1980; Seppalainen & Antii-Poika, 1983), CT (Schikler et al., 1982; Fornazzari et al., 1983), MRI (Rosenberg et al., 1988; Rosenberg, Spitz et al., 1988; White, Moss, Proctor, & Feldman, 1989), or eye blink measures (Feldman, 1990). These findings, with a clinical explanation of PNS/nerve conduction findings, are discussed in detail elsewhere (White et al., 1992).

Neuropsychological Assessment Techniques

In some ways, the epidemiological bias in the field of behavioral neurotoxicology has adversely affected neurobehavioral assessment of exposed patients in clinical settings. Perhaps because of a historical tendency to use clinical batteries in epidemiological studies (e.g., those of Hanninen, 1971; Hanninen et al., 1978; Hanninen et al., 1976), there has been a reversed tendency to apply epidemiological batteries to clinical assessment. Unfortunately, this has generally resulted in overly limited test results that do not allow a full description of behavioral and cognitive deficits and which do not provide a reasonable basis for carrying out accurate differential diagnosis concerning the etiology of impairments that are observed. The differences between epidemiological and clinical battery requirements have been delineated in some detail (Proctor & White, 1990) and we have recently defined criteria useful in developing and evaluating clinical batteries (White & Proctor, 1992). Briefly, the test battery should include tests that are specifically sensitive to the neurotoxicant(s) at issue, allow estimation of native ability patterns, be appropriate to the patient's age, allow differential diagnosis of etiology of observed cognitive deficits, and be a reasonably comprehensive description of the degree and types of cognitive strengths and weaknesses of patients. It should be noted that the majority of the test batteries that have been developed for both epidemiological and clinical assessment of solvent exposures have been aimed at adults, not children. Perhaps this is due to the relative recency of discovery that children are exposed to solvents environmentally; metals have in the past been identified as especially important in studying developmental exposure to neurotoxicants. However, the ATSDR recently convened a workshop for which a major focus has been the determination of test batteries appropriate for assessment of infants and children exposed to solvents and other neurotoxicants environmentally (ATSDR, 1991).

Adult Batteries

In addition to the standard clinical neuropsychological test battery used by the clinician, specific tests may be necessary to diagnose or fully document the existence of a solvent encephalopathy, especially if it is mild. These include sensitive measures of mood, executive function, visuospatial abilities, and sensorimotor capacity. Short-term memory testing should be detailed enough to allow an examination of components of learning and memory, especially acquisition and retention rates. In addition, retrograde memory testing may be informative, especially if the exposure has been chronic over a number of years (White, 1987). We typically use an extensive process-oriented battery with auxiliary tests evaluating the aforementioned functions in greater detail. Lists of these tests (White et al., 1990b) and the rationales for their inclusion can be found in prior papers by the authors (White et al., 1990b; White & Proctor, 1992; White et al., 1992).

For the purpose of carrying out differential diagnosis and for assessing motivational contributions to test results, adult batteries should include tasks assessing language processing, academic skills, and psychiatric status. In addition, careful review of non-exposure-related medical, academic, familial, and social history is essential to the task of differential diagnosis.

Child Batteries

There is very little literature that specifically addresses the problem of developmental exposure of children to solvents (see below). Our own clinical experience assessing children exposed to solvents such as TCE or PCE suggests that the effects are similar to those seen following lead exposure and can involve a wide spectrum of deficits affecting academic, cognitive processing, and affective/personality function (see below). Therefore, assessment methods in children should include sensitive tasks evaluating attention, language, visuospatial, motor, memory, academic, and emotional function. Because of the problem of familially transmitted cognitive processing deficit patterns, it is sometimes helpful to test parents or review parental school and testing records when carrying out differential diagnosis of etiology of test results in children.

Neuropsychological Impairments

Exposure to neurotoxicants can produce a number of conditions that affect neuropsychological test results, including acute metabolic disturbances with secondary acute confusional state, primary hypoxia with permanent secondary brain damage, epilepsy or convulsions with focal cerebral deficit, and disorders such as leukemia or other cancers that may result in brain tumors or may affect brain function through toxic effects of radiation treatment or chemotherapy. This discussion will focus on cognitive changes occurring in the absence of these conditions and disorders. The effect of peripheral neuropathy may be difficult to tease out on fine manual motor tasks, but peripheral neuropathy can co-exist with the following impairment patterns.

Adults

The pattern of neuropsychological deficits seen in adults with solvent exposure will depend on the severity of the exposure and the type of solvent to which exposure occurred. In its mildest form, solvent encephalopathy presents as a reversible or permanent disruption of executive function and attention, with or without affective complaints. More severe presentations of solvent encephalopathy, particularly in the chronic residual form following severe acute exposure or significant chronic exposure, are characterized by executive and attentional dysfunction (including impaired reasoning), problems with visuospatial organization (and at times even visuoperceptual analysis), fine manual motor slowing and/or incoordination, and deficits in learning and retention of new information. Mood is often depressed, anxious, and irritable, and homicidal or suicidal ideation can be seen, especially in the initial weeks or months following the presentation of acute symptoms. While word list generation is sometimes affected, language skills such as naming are generally intact as are measures of crystallized intelligence such as WAIS-R Information, multiple choice vocabulary performance (such as that assessed by Peabody Picture Vocabulary Test), and academic skills such as reading and spelling. (For a lengthy and detailed explication of specific processing deficits related to performance on neuropsychological tests, see White et al., 1992).

Solvent-specific and individual-specific sites of cerebral dysfunction may be observed in solvent encephalopathy. Thus, many organic solvents appear to affect frontal-limbic function (Ryan et al., 1988; White & Feldman, 1987). However, lesions in the cerebral white matter have also been reported to be associated with carbon disulfide exposure resulting in a vascular dementia (Johnson, 1987) or following other exposures such as toluene (Filley et al., 1990) and other solvents (White et al., 1989). Carbon disulfide appears to have primary effects on the basal ganglia (Peters et al., 1982, 1988) and toluene and other solvents affect the cerebellum (Filley et al., 1990). Although most patients with solvent encephalopathy have intact retrograde memory or retrograde memory deficits extending only to the time of exposure (presumably the effect of impaired learning and forgetting in the face of exposure), patients in rare cases show a Korsakoff's syndrome similar to that seen following ethanol abuse; this suggests that industrial solvents may also affect the mamillary bodies and thalamus (Brandt & Butters, 1986). Whatever site or combination of sites are observed in individual patients, the consistently "subcortical" (Albert, 1978) nature of the deficits repeatedly observed is of importance given the possible neuropathological localizations that we have just outlined.

The significant variables that determine lesion sites in individual cases cannot be determined given the current state of knowledge in the field. However, it seems likely that they represent a combination of factors, including responsible neurotoxicant, dosage, specific metabolites that appear systemically following individual exposures, routes of entry, general health, interactions between multiple neurotoxicants or neurotoxicants and hormones or neurotransmitters, and even individual sensitivity (Schottenfeld & Cullen, 1985; Schottenfeld, 1987). We have clinically seen widely divergent severity of encephalopathy in different patients following apparently similar severity of exposure to the same neurotoxicant.

Children

Developmental exposure of children to industrial solvents has received very little attention in the literature. The hypothetical possibility that developmental exposure is a special situation with differential neuropathological and neuropsychological sequelae has been preferred (Petit, 1990), and there have been some suggestions that maternal low-level occupational exposures to solvents (Holmberg & Nurminen, 1980) or toluene inhalation (Hersh, Podruch, Rogers, & Weisskopf, 1985; Toutant & Lippmann, 1979) are associated with CNS abnormalities in offspring. These were not confirmed in a study of the children of American workers with low-level solvent exposure, though the authors noted that their CNS measures may have been too gross to detect subtle effects (Eskenazi et al., 1988). Likewise, maternal ethanol ingestion is known to be fetotoxic (Jones & Smith, 1973; Landesman-Dwyer, Keller, & Streissguth, 1978; Streissguth, Landesman-Dwyer, & Smith, 1980). Certainly, exposure to substances known to be neurotoxic in adults, such as lead and mercury, have also been reported to have neurotoxic effects secondary to in utero exposure (Dietrich & Bellinger, 1991).

Research in the field is far from providing a coherent characterization of solvent encephalopathy over the developmental course. Our clinical experience testing children with in utero and childhood solvent exposure suggests that the functional deficits seen secondary to solvent exposure are similar to those observed in developmental lead exposure (Feldman & White, 1990). There is no pattern of typical deficits such as can be seen in adult exposure. Children may show deficits in attention and executive function, motor coordination, language processing, visuoperceptual skills, memory, emotional adjustment, or any combination of these. Impaired acquisition of academic skills (including reading, spelling, and arithmetic) is common. Interestingly, we have observed these deficits in solvent-exposed children whose parents were also tested and showed no evidence of learning or academic skills disability. We have also been surprised at the duration of susceptibility to solvents during childhood. Exposure onset as late as ages 8 to 10 years appears to be associated with a wide range of intellectual deficits, and the functional deficits that appear are not related to critical developmental stages at the time of exposure. Such a relationship has been hypothesized in regard to lead (Shaheen, 1984), although our own clinical observations on lead-exposed children have revealed a more diffuse pattern such as that seen in developmental solvent exposure (Feldman & White, 1990). We have tested a number of children with chronic low-level exposure to TCE. Many have serious adjustment and vocational problems in addition to their cognitive/academic impairments.

Differential Diagnosis

Adults

Differential diagnosis regarding etiology of observed cognitive impairment in patients with histories of solvent exposure can be quite difficult. The problems, especially when the exposure or resulting encephalopathy is mild, are similar to those seen in mild traumatic brain injury. Distinctions must be made between toxic effects and (a) familial, congenital or perinatal disorders of cognition, (b) psychiatric conditions, (c) motivational factors, and (d) other neurological disorders (including effects of exposure to toxic medications, substances of abuse, and incidental chemical use). In a recent paper, we have provided a detailed summary of the factors that must be considered in each of these four types of differential diagnosis (White et al., 1992). A brief summary will be provided here.

The familial or preexposure conditions of most direct interest include birth trauma (secondary to injury and in utero exposure to toxicants such as alcohol), below average premorbid intelligence, attention deficit disorder (ADD), and learning disabilities (LD). Obviously, careful assessments must include interview questions providing appropriate historical information on these possibilities and inclusion of neuropsychological tests that allow assessment of them. In our experience, a common diagnostic error is the attribution of a toxic etiology to cognitive deficits that are almost certainly long-standing (especially ADD and LD).

Psychiatric and quasi-psychiatric disorders seen frequently in patients referred with histories of solvent exposure include somatoform disorders, multiple chemical sensitivity in patients with no history of significant neurotoxicant exposure, and chronic fatigue syndrome with no viral or other identified etiology. Also seen are patients with major affective disorder, paranoia, anxiety states, or schizophrenia with somatization or somatic delusions.

Motivational factors also affect differential diagnosis. Ganser's syndrome embellishment of symptoms when there are significant issues of secondary gain and outright malingering are also seen, especially in patients with personality disorders. Often the cognitive test results are highly uneven or universally impaired, which can make differential diagnosis confusing and difficult. The issues critical to such diagnosis have been described in detail elsewhere (White et al., 1992).

Neurological disorders that we have seen on referral for possible toxic encephalopathy have included Alzheimer's disease, Parkinson's disease, frontal dementias, metabolic encephalopathy, cerebrovascular disease, and closed head injury.

Children

Because the neuropsychological outcomes of solvent exposure are less specific in children, differential diagnosis can be more difficult and may (in some cases) reflect a process of elimination of all other possible explanations of observed cognitive deficits except exposure. Estimation of native cognitive abilities can be especially problematic if exposure began at conception, in utero, or during infancy or early childhood. In some cases it is helpful to evaluate parents neuropsychologically or to review their school records when attempting to rule out familial cognitive deficits.

Forensic Issues

Because compensation for health injuries (occupational or environmental) in this country so often involves the legal system, neuropsychologists frequently become involved as expert witnesses in cases of solvent exposure. Recently, the American Psychological Association sponsored the writing of an *amicus curiae* brief that was filed with the State of Georgia Court of a lower court decision that neuropsychologists were not qualified to provide a diagnosis of encephalopathy secondary to exposure to a pesticide. The brief, which describes neuropsychological expertise specifically in reference to toxic exposures, resulted in a reversal of the lower court decision (Ogden & Misicka, 1990) which was later overturned.

References

Aaserud, O., Gjerstad, L., Nakstad, P., Nyberg-Hansen, R., Hommeren, O. J., Tvedt, B., Russell, D., & Rootwelt, K. (1988). Neurological examination, computerized tomography, cerebral blood flow and neuropsychological examination in workers with long-term exposure to carbon disulfide. *Toxicology, 49*, 277–282.

Agency for Toxic Substances and Disease Registry (ATSDR). (1989, October). *Toxicological profile for trichloroethylene.*

Agency for Toxic Substances and Disease Registry (ATSDR). (1991, September). *Workshop for the Development of a Standardized Neurobehavioral Testing Battery for Use in Environmental Health Field Studies.* Atlanta, GA.

Albert, M. L. (1978). Subcortical dementia. In R. Katzman, R. D. Terry, K. L. Bick (Eds.), *Alzheimer's disease, senile dementia and related disorders (Aging, Vol. 7)* New York: Raven Press.

Andelman, J. B. (1985). Inhalation exposure in the home to volatile organic contaminants of drinking water. *Science of the Total Environment, 47*, 443–460.

Andrews, L. S., & Snyder, R. (1986). Chapter 20. Toxic effects of solvents and vapors. In C. D. Klaassen, M. O. Amdur, & J. Doull (Eds.), *Casarett and Doull's toxicology* (3rd ed., p. 636). New York: Macmillan.

Anger, W. K. (1990). Worksite behavioral research: Results, sensitive methods, test batteries, and the transition from laboratory data to human health. *Neurotoxicology, 11*, 629–719.

Arlien-Soberg, P., Bruhn, P., Gyldensted, C., & Melgaard, B. (1979). Chronic painters' syndrome. *Acta Neurologica Scandinavica, 60*, 149–156.

Axelson, O., Hane, M., & Hogstedt, C. (1976). A case referent study of neuropsychiatric disorders among workers exposed to solvents. *Scandinavian Journal of Work, Environment and Health, 2*, 14–20.

Baker, A. B. (1958). The nervous system in trichloroethylene. An experimental study. *Journal of Neuropathology and Experimental Medicine, 17*, 649–655.

Baker, E. L., Feldman, R. G., White, R. F., Harley, J. P., Niles, C., Dinse, G., & Berkey, K. (1984). Occupational lead neurotoxicity, a behavioral and electrophysiologic evaluation: I. Study design and year one results. *British Journal of Industrial Medicine, 41*, 352–361.

Baker, E. L., White, R. F., Pothier, L. J., Berkey, C. S., Dinse, G. E., Travers, P. H., Harley, J. P., & Feldman, R. G. (1985). Occupational: II. Improvement in behavioral effects following exposure reduction. *British Journal of Industrial Medicine, 42*, 507–516.

Baker, E. L., & White, R. F. (1985). *Chronic effects of organic solvents on the central nervous system and diagnostic criteria*. World Health Organization (Copenhagen) and Nordic Council of Ministers (Oslo). Printed by the U.S. Department of Health and Human Services, Public Health Service.

Battig, K., & Grandjean, E. (1963). Chronic effects of trichloroethylene on rat behavior. *Archives of Environmental Health, 7*, 694–699.

Bernad, P. G., Newell, S., & Spyker, D. (1987). Neurotoxicity and behavior abnormalities in a cohort chronically exposed to TCE [Abstract]. *Veterinary and Human Toxicology, 29*(6), 475.

Bleuler, M. (1944). Grundsatzliches uber psychische giftschaden am beispiel einer quecksilber-und einer schwefelkohlestoff-vergiftung. *Schweizerische Medizinische Wochenschrift 74*, 923–928. (Referenced in Grandjean, 1955; Hanninen 1988).

Brackbill, R., Maizlish, N., & Fishbach, T. (1990). Risk of neuropsychiatric disability among painters in the United States. *Scandinavian Journal of Work, Environment and Health, 16*, 182–188.

Brandt, J., & Butters, N. (1986). The alcoholic Wernicke-Korsakoff syndrome and its relationship to long-term alcohol use. In I. Grant, & K. Adams (Eds.), *Neuropsychological assessment of neuropsychiatric disorders* (pp. 441–447). New York: Oxford University Press.

Brown, H. S., Bishop, D. R., & Rowan, C. A. (1984). The role of skin absorption as a route of exposure to volatile organic compounds (VOCs) in drinking water. *American Journal of Public Health, 74*, 479–484.

Bruckner, J. V., & Peterson, R. G. (1981a). Evaluation of toluene and acetone inhalant abuse: 1. Pharmacology and pharmacodynamics. *Toxicology and Applied Pharmacology, 61*, 27–38.

Bruckner, J. V., & Peterson, R. G. (1981b). Evaluation of toluene and acetone inhalant abuse: 2. Model development and toxicology. *Toxicology and Applied Pharmacology, 61*, 302–312.

Bruhn, P., Arlien-Soberg, P., Gyldensted, C., & Christensen, E. L. (1981). Prognosis in chronic toxic encephalopathy—a 2 year follow-up study in 26 house painters with occupational encephalopathy. *Acta Neurologica Scandinavica, 64,* 259–272.

Buffler, P. A., Crane, M., & Key, M. M. (1985). Possibilities of detecting health effects by studies of populations exposed to chemicals from waste disposal sites. *Environmental Health Perspectives, 62,* 423–456.

Cherry, N., Hutchins, H., Pace, T., & Waldron, H. A. (1985). Neurobehavioral effects of repeated occupational exposure to toluene and paints. *British Journal of Industrial Medicine, 42,* 291–300.

Contreras, C. M., Gonzalez-Estrada, T., Zrabozo, C., & Fernandez-Guardiolo, A. (1979). Petit mal and grand mal seizures produced by toluene or benzene intoxication in cats. *Electromyography and Clinical Neurophysiology, 46,* 290–301.

Dietrich, K. N., & Bellinger, D. (1991, September). *Assessment of neurobehavioral development in studies of the effects of fetal exposures to environmental agents.* Prepared for the Agency for Toxic Substances and Disease Registry (ATSDR) Workshop for the Development of a Standardized Neurobehavioral Testing Battery for Use in Environmental Health Field Studies. Atlanta, GA.

Echeverria, D. (1987). *Acute behavioral effects of toluene and ethanol in humans.* Unpublished doctoral dissertation, University of Michigan, Ann Arbor, MI.

Echeverria, D., White, R. F., & Sampao, C. (1990, October). *A neurobehavioral evaluation of PCE exposure in patients and dry cleaners: A possible relationship between clinical and preclinical effects.* Paper presented at the Eighth International Neurotoxicology Conference, Little Rock, AR.

Elofsson, S. A., Gamberale, F., Hindmarsh, T., et al. (1980). Exposure to organic solvents: A cross-sectional epidemiologic investigation on occupationally exposed car and industrial spray painters with special reference to the nervous system. *Scandinavian Journal of Work, Environment and Health, 6,* 239–273.

Eskenazi, B., Gaylord, L., Bracken, M. B., & Brown, D. (1988). In utero exposure to organic solvents and human neurodevelopment. *Developmental Medicine and Child Neurology, 30,* 492–450.

Ettema, J., et al. (1975a). Study of mental stress during short-term inhalation of trichloroethylene. *Staub-Reinh Luft, 35,* 409–410.

Ettema, J. H., Zielhuis, R. L., Burer, E., Meier, H. A., Kleerekoper, L., deGraef, A. (1975b). Effects of alcohol, carbon monoxide, and trichloroethylene on mental capacity. *International Archives of Occupational and Environmental Health, 35,* 117–132.

Evans, H. L., Dempster, A. M., & Snyder, C. A. (1981). Behavioral changes in mice following benzene inhalation. *Neurobehavioral Toxicology and Teratology, 3,* 481–485.

Feldman, R. G., & Lessell, S. (1969). Neuro-ophthalmologic aspects of trichloroethylene intoxication. In J. Burnett & A. Barbeau (Eds.), *Progress in Neuro-ophthalmology* (pp. 281–282). Amsterdam: Excerpta Medica.

Feldman, R. G., Mayer, R. M., & Taub, A. (1970). Evidence for peripheral neurotoxic effect of trichloroethylene. *Neurology, 20,* 599–606.

Feldman, R. G., White, R. F., Currie, J. N., Travers, P. H., & Lessell, S. (1985). Long-term follow-up after single exposure to trichloroethylene. *American Journal of Industrial Medicine, 8,* 119–126.

Feldman, R. G., Chirico-Post, J., & Proctor, S. P. (1988). Blink reflex latency after exposure to trichloroethylene in well water. *Archives of Environmental Health, 43*(2), 143–148.

Feldman, R. G. (1990). Neurotoxicologic effects of exposure to metals, solvents and pesticides. *Neurology and Neurosurgery Update Series, 8,* 2–11.

Feldman, R. G., & White, R. F. (1990, October). *Lead neurotoxicity and learning problems.*

Sixth Annual Norman Geshwind Lecture at Boston Floating Hospital, Tufts New England Medical Center.

Filley, C. M., Heaton, R. K., & Rosenberg, N. L. (1990). White matter dementia in chronic toluene abuse. *Neurology, 40*, 532–534.

Fornazzari, L., Wilkinson, D. A., Kapur, B. M., & Carlen, P. L. (1983). Cerebellar and functional impairment in toluene abusers. *Acta Neurologica Scandinavica, 67*, 319–329.

Gade, A., Mortensen, E. L., & Bruhn, P. (1988). "Chronic painter's syndrome." A reanalysis of psychological test data in a group of diagnosed cases, based on comparisons with matched controls. *Acta Neurologica Scandinavica, 77*, 293–306.

Gamberale, F. (1985). Use of behavioral performance tests in the assessment of solvent toxicity. *Scandinavian Journal of Work, Environment and Health, 11*(Supp. 1), 65–74.

Grandjean, E., Munchinger, R., Turrian, V., Haas, P. A., Knoepfel, H. K., & Rosenmund, H. (1955). Investigations into the effects of exposure to trichloroethylene in mechanical engineering. *British Journal of Industrial Medicine, 12*, 131–142.

Grandjean, E. (1960). Trichloroethylene effects on animal behavior. *Archives of Environmental Health, 1*, 106–108.

Grasso, P., Sharratt, M., Davies, D. M., & Irvine, D. (1984). Neuropsychological and psychological disorders and occupational exposure to organic solvents. *Foundations in Chemical Toxicology, 22*(10), 819–852.

Green, G. D., Leong, B. K. J., & Laskin, S. (1978). Inhaled benzene fetotoxicity in rats. *Toxicology and Applied Pharmacology, 46*, 9–18.

Gregerson, P., Angelso, B., Nielson, T. E., et al. (1984). Neurotoxic effects of organic solvents in exposed workers—an occupational neuropsychological and neurological investigation. *American Journal of Industrial Medicine, 5*, 201–225.

Guberan, E., Usel, M., Raymond, L., et al. (1989). Disability, mortality and evidence of cancer among Geneva painters and electricians: A historical prospective study. *British Journal of Industrial Medicine, 46*, 16–23.

Hane, M., Axelson, O., Blume, J., Hogstedt, C., Sundell, L., & Ydreborg, B. (1977). Psychological function changes among house painters. *Scandinavian Journal of Work, Environment and Health, 3*, 91–99.

Hanninen, H. (1971). Psychological picture of manifest and latent carbon disulfide poisoning. *British Journal of Industrial Medicine, 28*, 374–381.

Hanninen, H., Eskelinen, L., Husman, K., & Nurminen, M. (1976). Behavioral effects of long-term exposure to a mixture of organic solvents. *Scandinavian Journal of Work, Environment and Health, 2*, 240–255.

Hanninen, H., Nurminen, M., Tolonen, M., & Martelin, T. (1978). Psychological tests as indicators of excessive exposure to carbon disulfide. *Scandinavian Journal of Psychology, 19*, 163–174.

Hanninen, H. (1985). Twenty-five years of behavioral toxicology within occupational medicine: A personal account. *American Journal of Industrial Medicine, 7*, 19–30.

Hanninen, H. (1988). The psychological performance profile in occupational intoxications. *Neurotoxicology and Teratology, 10*, 485–488.

Hersh, J. H., Podruch, P. E., Rogers, G., & Weisskopf, B. (1985). Toluene embryopathy. *Journal of Pediatrics, 106*, 922–927.

Holmberg, P. C., & Nurminen, M. (1980). Congenital defects of central nervous system and occupational factors during pregnancy—a case-referent study. *American Journal of Industrial Medicine, 1*, 167–176.

Isaacson, L. G., & Taylor, D. H. (1989). Maternal exposure to 1,1,2- trichloroethylene affects myelin in the hippocampal formation of the developing rat. *Brain Research, 488*, 403–407.

Isaacson, L. G., Spohler, S. A., & Taylor, D. H. (1990). Trichloroethylene affects learning and decreases myelin in the rat hippocampus. *Neurotoxicology and Teratology, 12*, 375–381.

Johnson, B. L. (Ed). (1987). *Prevention of neurotoxic illness in working populations* (pp. 3–104). New York: Wiley.

Johnson, B.L. (Ed). (1990). *Advances in neurobehavioral toxicology*. Chelsea, MI: Lewis Publishers.

Jones, K. L., & Smith, D. W. (1973). Recognition of fetal alcohol syndrome in early infancy. *Lancet, 2*, 999–1001.

Juntunen, J., Hupli, V., Hernberg, S., & Luisto, M. (1980). Neurologic picture of organic solvent poisoning. *International Archives of Occupational and Environmental Health, 46*, 219–231.

Juntunen, J., Matikainen, E., Antii-Poika, M., Suoranta, H., & Valle, M. (1985). Nervous system effects of long-term occupational exposure to toluene. *Acta Neurologica Scandinavica, 7*, 157–168.

Kraut, A., Lilis, R., Marcus, M., Valciukas, J. A., Wolff, M. S., & Landrigan, P. J. (1988). Neurotoxic effects of solvent exposure on sewage treatment workers. *Archives of Environmental Health, 43*(4), 263–268.

Kylin, B., Axell, K., Samuel, H., & Lindborg, A. (1967). Effect of inhaled trichloroethylene on the CNS. *Archives of Environmental Health, 15*, 48–52.

Landesman-Dwyer, S., Keller, L. S., & Streissguth, A. P. (1978). Naturalistic observations of newborns—effects of maternal alcohol intake. *Alcoholism: Clinical and Experimental Research, 2*, 171–177.

Letz, R., & Baker, E. L. (1986). Computer-administered neurobehavioral testing in occupational health. *Seminars in Occupational Medicine, 1*, 197–203.

Letz, R. (1990). The neurobehavioral evaluation system—an international effort. In B. L. Johnson (Ed.), *Advances in neurobehavioral toxicology*. Chelsea, MI: Lewis Publishers.

Lindstrom, K., Harkonen, H., & Hernberg, S. (1976). Disturbances in psychological functions of workers occupationally exposed to styrene. *Scandinavian Journal of Work, Environment and Health, 3*, 129–139.

Lindstrom, K. (1980). Changes in psychological performances of solvent-poisoned and solvent-exposed workers. *American Journal of Industrial Medicine, 1*, 69–84.

Lindstrom, K., Riihimaki, H., & Hanninen, K. (1984). Occupational solvent exposure and neuropsychiatric disorders. *Scandinavian Journal of Work, Environment and Health, 19*, 321–323.

Matthews, C. G., Chapman, L. J., & Woodard, A. R. (1990). Differential neuropsychologic profiles in idiopathic versus pesticide-induced Parkinsonism. In B. L. Johnson (Ed.), *Advances in neurobehavioral toxicology* (pp. 323–330). Chelsea, MI: Lewis Publishers.

McCunney, R. (1988). Diverse manifestations of trichloroethylene. *British Journal of Industrial Medicine, 45*, 122–126.

Mckay, C. J., Campbell, L., Samuel, A. M., Alderman, K. J., Idzikowski, C., Wilson, H. K., & Gompertz, D. (1987). Behavioral changes during exposure to 1,1,1-trichloroethane: Time-course and relationship to blood solvent levels. *American Journal of Industrial Medicine, 11*, 223–239.

Mikkelson, S. (1980). A cohort study of disability pension and death among workers exposed to solvents in the Danish wood and furniture industry. *Scandinavian Journal of Social Medicine, 16*(Suppl.), 44–49.

O'Flynn, R. R., Monkman, S. M., & Waldron, H. A. (1987). Organic solvents and presenile dementia: A case-referent study using death certificates. *British Journal of Industrial Medicine, 44*, 259–262.

Ogden, D. W., & Misicka, C. (1990). Motion for leave to file a brief of *amicus curiae* and brief of the American Psychological Association as *amicus curiae*. *Morris et al. v. Chandler et al.*, (Georgia Court of Appeals No. A91A0400).

Olsen, J., & Sabroe, S. (1980). A case-referent study of neuropsychiatric disorders among workers exposed to solvents in the Danish wood and furniture industry. *Scandinavian Journal of Social Medicine, 16*, 44–49.

Peters, H. A., Levine, R. L., Matthews, C. G., Sauter, S. L., & Rankin, J. H. (1982). Carbon disulfide-induced neuropsychiatric changes in grain storage workers. *American Journal of Industrial Medicine, 3*, 373–391.

Peters, H. A., Levine R. L., Matthews, C. G., & Chapman, L. J. (1988). Extrapyramidal and other neurologic manifestations associated with carbon disulfide fumigant exposure. *Archives of Neurology, 45*, 537–540.

Petit, T. L. (1990). Memory, synaptic plasticity and neurotoxins. *Neurotoxicology, 11*, 323–332.

Proctor, S. P., & White, R. F. (1990). Psychoneurological criteria for the development of neurobehavioral test batteries. In B.L. Johnson (Ed.), *Advances in behavioral neurotoxicology* (pp. 273–281). Chelsea, MI: Lewis Publishers.

Putz-Anderson, V., Seltzer, J. V., Croxton, J. S., & Phipps, F. C. (1981). Methyl chloride and diazepam effects on performance. *Scandinavian Journal of Work, Environment and Health, 7*, 8–13.

Rasmussen, H., Olsen, J., & Lauritsen, J. (1985). Risk of encephalopathia among retired solvent-exposed workers. *Journal of Occupational Medicine, 27*, 561–566.

Riise, T., & Moen, B. E. (1990). A nested case-control study of disability among seamen with special reference to psychiatric disorder and exposure to solvents. *Neuroepidemiology, 9*, 88–94.

Robins, T. G., White, R. F., Echeverria, D., Proctor, S. P., Rocskay, A., & Seixas, N. (1989, October). *Relationship of neuropsychological and renal function measures to current and past exposure to petroleum naphthas.* Abstract presented at American Public Health Association Annual Meeting, Chicago, IL.

Rosenberg, N. L., Kleinschmidt-DeMasters, B. K., Davis, K. A., Dreisbach, J. N., Hormes, J. T., & Filley, C. M. (1988). Toluene abuse causes diffuse central nervous system white matter changes. *Annals of Neurology, 23*, 611–614.

Rosenberg, N. L., Spitz, M. C., Filley, C. M., Davis, K. A., & Schaumberg, H. H. (1988). Central nervous system effects of chronic toluene abuse—clinical, brain stem evoked response and magnetic resonance imaging studies. *Neurotoxicology and Teratology, 10*, 489–495.

Ryan, C. M., Morrow, L., Bromet, D. J., et al. (1987). Assessment of neuropsychological dysfunction in the workplace—normative data from the Pittsburgh Occupational Exposures Test Battery. *Journal of Clinical Neuropsychology, 9*, 665–679.

Ryan, C. M., Morrow, L. A., & Hodgson, M. (1988). Cacosmia and neurobehavioral dysfunction associated with occupational exposures to mixtures of solvents. *American Journal of Psychiatry, 145*, 1442–1445.

Salvini, M. (1971). Evaluation of the psychophysiological functions in humans exposed to trichloroethylene. *British Journal of Industrial Medicine, 28*, 293–295.

Sato, A., Nakajima, T., & Koyama, Y. (1981). Dose-related effects of a single dose of ethanol on the metabolism in rat liver of some aromatic and chlorinated hydrocarbons. *Toxicology and Applied Pharmacology, 60*, 8–15.

Schikler, K. N., Seitz, K., Rice, J. F., & Strader, T. (1982). Solvent abuse-associated cortical atrophy. *Journal of Adolescent Health Care, 9*, 37–39.

Schottenfeld, R. S. (1987). Workers with multiple chemical sensitivities: A psychometric approach to diagnosis and treatment. *Occupational Medicine: State of the Art Reviews, 2*, 739–753.

Schottenfeld, R. S., & Cullen, M. (1985). Occupation-induced post traumatic stress disorders. *American Journal of Psychiatry*, *142*, 198–202.

Seppalainen, A. M., & Tolonen, M. (1974). Neurotoxicity of long-term exposure to carbon disulfide in the viscose rayon industry—a neurophysiological study. *Scandinavian Journal of Work Environment and Health*, *11*, 145–153.

Seppalainen, A. M., Husman, K., & Martenson, C. (1978). Neurophysiological effects of long-term exposure to a mixture of organic solvents. *Scandinavian Journal of Work, Environment and Health*, *4*, 304–314.

Seppalainen, A. M., & Haltia, M. (1980). Carbon disulfide. In P.S. Spencer & H.H. Schaumberg (Eds.), *Experimental and clinical neurotoxicology* (pp. 356–373). Baltimore: Williams & Wilkins.

Seppalainen, A. M., & Antii-Poika, M. (1983). Time course of electrophysiological findings for patients with solvent poisoning. *Scandinavian Journal of Work, Environment and Health*, *9*, 15–24.

Shaheen, S. (1984). Neuromaturation and behavior development: The case of childhood lead poisoning. *Developmental Psychology*, *20*, 542–550.

Shalat, S. L., Seltzer, B., & Baker, E. L. (1988). Occupational risk factors and Alzheimer's disease: A case-control study. *Journal of Occupational Medicine*, *30*, 934–936.

Smith, G. F. (1966). Trichloroethylene—a review. *British Journal of Industrial Medicine*, *23*, 249–262.

Stewart, R. D., Gay, H. H., Shafer, A. W., Early, D. S., & Rowe, V. K. (1969). Experimental human exposure to methyl chloroform vapor. *Archives of Environmental Health*, *19*, 467–472.

Stewart, R. D., Baretta, E. D., & Torkelson, T. R. (1970). Experimental human exposure to tetrachloroethylene. *Archives of Environmental Health*, *20*, 225–229.

Stopps, G. J., & McLaughlin, M. (1967). Psychological testing of human subjects exposed to solvent vapors. *American Industrial Hygiene Association Journal*, *28*, 43.

Stracciari, A., Gallasi, R., Ciardulli, C., & Coccagna, G. (1985). Neuropsychological and EEG evaluation in exposure to trichloroethylene. *Journal of Neurology*, *232*, 120–122.

Streissguth, A. P., Landesman-Dwyer, S., & Smith, D. S. (1980). Teratological effects of alcohol in humans and lab animals. *Science*, *209*, 353–361.

Struwe, G., & Wennberg, A. (1983). Psychiatric and neurological symptoms in workers occupationally exposed to organic solvents—results of a differential epidemiological study. *Acta Psychologica Scandinavica*, *67*(Suppl. 303), 68–80.

Tilson, H. A., Squibb, R. E., Meyer, O. A., & Sparber, S. B. (1980). Postnatal exposure to benzene alters the neuropsychological functioning in rats when tested in adulthood. *Neurobehavioral Toxicology*, *2*, 101–106.

Toutant, C., & Lippmann, S. (1979). Fetal solvent syndrome. *Lancet*, *1*, 1356.

Triebig, G., Claus, D., Csuzda, I., et al. (1988). Cross-sectional epidemiological study on neurotoxicity of solvents in paints and lacquers. *International Archives on Occupational and Environmental Medicine*, *60*, 233–241.

Tsushima, W. T., & Towne, W. S. (1977). Effects of paint sniffing on neuropsychological test performance. *Journal of Abnormal Psychology*, *86*, 402–407.

U.S. Congress, Office of Technology Assessment. (1990). *Neurotoxicity: Identifying and controlling poisons of the nervous system* (OTA-BA-436). Washington, D.C.: U.S. Government Printing Office.

U.S. Department of Health and Human Services/National Institute of Occupational Safety and Health. (1987). *Organic solvent neurotoxicity*. (Current Intelligence Bulletin #48).

U.S. Department of Health and Human Services/Public Health Service/Centers for Disease Control. (1990, June). *The NIOSH pocket guide to chemical hazards* (#90–117).

Valciukas, J. A., Lilis, R., Singer, R. M., Glickman, L., & Nicholson, W. J. (1985).

Neurobehavioral changes among shipyard painters exposed to solvents. *Archives of Environmental Health*, *40*, 47–52.

van Vliet, C., Swaen, G. M. H., Slangen, X. Y., et al. (1987). The organic solvent syndrome. A comparison of cases with neuropsychiatric disorders among painters and construction workers. *International Archives of Occupational and Environmental Health*, *59*, 493–501.

van Vliet, C., Swaen, G. M. H., Volovics, A., et al. (1989). Exposure-outcome relationships between organic solvent exposure and neuropsychiatric disorders: Results from a Dutch case-control study. *American Journal of Industrial Medicine*, *16*, 707–718.

van Vliet, C., Swaen, G., Volovics, A., et al. (1990). Neuropsychiatric disorders among solvent-exposed workers. *International Archives of Occupational and Environmental Health*, *62*, 127–132.

Vernon, R. J., & Ferguson, R. K. (1969). Effects of trichloroethylene on visual-motor performance. *Archives of Environmental Health*, *18*, 894–900.

Watanabe, G., & Yoshida, S. (1970). The teratological effects of benzene in pregnant rats. *Acta Medica Biologica*, *17*, 285–291.

Weiss, B. (1990). Risk assessment: The insidious nature of neurotoxicity and the aging brain. *Neurotoxicology*, *11*, 305–314.

White, R. F. (1986). The role of the neuropsychologist in the evaluation of toxic central nervous system disorders. *Seminars in Occupational Medicine*, *1*, 191–196.

White, R. F., & Feldman, R. G. (1987). Neuropsychological assessment of toxic encephalopathy. *American Journal of Industrial Medicine*, *11*, 395–398.

White, R. F. (1987). Differential diagnosis of probable Alzheimer's disease and solvent encephalopathy in older workers. *The Clinical Neuropsychologist*, *1*, 153–160.

White, R. F., Moss, M. B., Proctor, S. P., & Feldman, R. G. (1989, August). *MRI-detected white matter pathology in two cases of toxic encephalopathy*. Presented at American Psychological Association, New Orleans, LA.

White, R. F., Feldman, R. G., Echeverria, D. E., & Schweikert, J. (1990a). *Neuropsychological effects of chronic solvent exposure*. Report to NIOSH on Grant #5K01 OH0028-03.

White, R. F., Feldman, R. G., & Travers, P. H. (1990b). Neurobehavioral effects of toxicity due to metals, solvents and insecticides. *Clinical Neuropharmacology*, *13*, 392–412.

White, R. F., Proctor, S. P. (1992). Research and clinical criteria for the development of neurobehavioral test batteries. *Journal of Occupational Medicine, 34*, 140–148.

White, R. F., Proctor, S. P., & Feldman, R. G. (1992). Behavioral neurotoxicology. In R. F. White (Ed.) *Clinical syndromes in adult neuropsychology*. Amsterdam: Elsevier.

Windemuller, F. J. B., & Ettema, J. H. (1978). Effects of combined exposure to trichloroethylene and alcohol on mental capacity. *International Archives of Occupational and Environmental Health*, *41*, 77–85.

13

Acute Confusional States in Toxic and Metabolic Disorders

GREGORY P. LEE and DAVID W. LORING

Toxic and metabolic disorders are among the most common forms of medical illness that may produce transient alterations of mental status. These cognitive and emotional changes are usually called either acute confusional states or delirium. The close association between toxicometabolic disorders and confusional states is illustrated by a brief listing of terms by which acute confusional states have been known, such as toxic psychosis, exogenous psychosis, metabolic encephalopathy, acute organic brain syndrome, delirium, and reversible dementia. Toxic disorders generally refer to intoxication or withdrawal from drugs or alcohol and poisoning. Metabolic disorders or encephalopathies are systemic disorders of metabolism from etiologies such as organ failure, oxygen deficiency, or electrolyte imbalances that only secondarily affect the brain. Although toxic and metabolic disorders are the most common medical conditions causing acute confusional states among the elderly, infections, nutritional deficiencies, vascular disease, hydrocephalus, head trauma, intracranial inflammatory disease, and sleep deprivation also may give rise to acute confusional states.

Acute confusional states are usually transient alterations of cognition and emotional behavior lasting days or weeks. Proper treatment of the underlying medical cause of the confusional state typically results in a return of the altered mental state to normal, or at least baseline, levels. Given these characteristics of acute confusional states, why should toxicometabolic disorders be considered in a book devoted to varieties of dementia? Justification for including a chapter on toxic and metabolic conditions is twofold. First, many physicians and neuropsychologists fail to appreciate the diagnostic distinction between confusional states and dementia, and this may result in dire consequences for the patient. Second, if a reversible medical disorder underlying a confusional state is not adequately treated, it may evolve into irreversible dementia or death. Therefore, this chapter will familiarize the reader with acute confusional states, their underlying medical causes, and the results of neuropsychological assessment in these patients. Also, because an understanding of the distinction between dementia and acute confusional states is important in neuropsychological practice, the differentiating features will be discussed.

This chapter initially will present diagnostic issues and definitions regarding confusional states. What is known about the clinical features including age of onset, prevalence, course of illness, risk factors, and pathophysiology will then be addressed. A brief overview of the major toxic agents and metabolic conditions causing confusional states will follow. The major classes of drugs causing confusional states also will be covered among the toxic disorders. Environmental toxins and alcohol, covered elsewhere in this volume, will not be included in this discussion. We then summarize the primary neuropsychological results among the toxicometabolic disorders, classified by major cognitive area such as attention or language, and conclude with comments on clinical management.

Terminology

The psychiatric literature refers to the transient alternations of mental status secondary to toxic or metabolic disorders as delirium, whereas neurology labels these conditions as acute confusional states. *Delirium* and *confusion* have had different and often idiosyncratic meanings for various authors. In general medical practice, psychiatry is more likely to be asked to consult on deliria cases involving hyperactivity, because these patients appear acutely psychotic and may require antipsychotic medication. Historically, the term delirium has been used exclusively to mean acute confusion only of the hyperactive, agitated type (Adams & Victor, 1983). Although imprecisely defined in medical literature, *confusion* has generally been used to imply incoherent thinking, difficulty in grasping the meaning of environmental stimuli, bewilderment, perplexity, and disorientation. In the past, acute confusion has been used to refer exclusively to the hypoactive type of confusional state. However, in recent years both *delirium* and *acute confusion* have been used interchangeably to refer to both the hyperactive and hypoactive forms of the syndrome.

Acute Confusional States (Delirium)

Definition

The core behavioral features of confusional states are alterations in level of arousal, disturbances of attention, and impairment in the logical stream of thought (Geschwind, 1982). Other common associated features include disturbance of the sleep-wake cycle, disorientation to time and place, rambling or incoherent speech, illusions, hallucinations, and either increased or decreased psychomotor behavior (Liston, 1982; Lipowski, 1983). Reduction in the clarity of awareness, selective attention, or arousal resulting in impairments of perceiving, thinking, and remembering have been termed *clouding of consciousness*, considered a defining feature of acute confusional states in older nosologies (Lipowski, 1967). However, because clouding of consciousness simultaneously refers to the idea of consciousness as wakefulness and to multiple cognitive processes, it has been a difficult concept to grasp and is no longer routinely used.

Alertness, attentional capacity, speech coherence, disorientation, and propensity for perceptual misidentification tend to fluctuate in intensity over the course of a day and are often worse at night (Lipowski, 1984; Evans, 1987). In addition, most diagnostic criteria require that symptoms be of acute onset and some require a relatively brief duration of symptoms (American Psychiatric Association, 1987; Lipowski, 1990). Finally, some authors (e.g., Lipowski, 1990, p. 55) require that laboratory evidence of widespread cerebral dysfunction, such as diffuse electroencephalographic (EEG) changes (slowing or fast activity) of background activity, be present before a diagnosis of confusional state or delirium can be made.

The American Psychiatric Association offers the following diagnostic criteria for delirium (acute confusional state) in the DSM-III-R (1987):

A. Reduced ability to maintain attention to external stimuli (e.g., questions must be repeated because attention wanders) and to appropriately shift attention to the new external stimuli (e.g., perseverates answer to previous question).
B. Disorganized thinking, as indicated by rambling, irrelevant, or incoherent speech.
C. At least two of the following:
   (1) Reduced level of consciousness (e.g., difficulty keeping awake during examination).
   (2) Perceptual disturbances: misinterpretations, illusions, or hallucinations.
   (3) Disturbance of the sleep-wake cycle with insomnia or daytime sleepiness.
   (4) Increased or decreased psychomotor activity.
   (5) Disorientation to time, place, or person.
   (6) Memory impairment (e.g., inability to learn new material, such as the names of several unrelated objects after 5 minutes, or to remember past events, such as history of current episode of illness).
D. Clinical features develop over a short period of time (usually hours to days) and tend to fluctuate over the course of a day.
E. Either (1) or (2):
   (1) Evidence from the history, physical examination, or laboratory tests of a specific organic factor (or factors) judged to be etiologically related to the disturbance.
   (2) In the absence of such evidence, an etiologic organic factor can be presumed if the disturbance cannot be accounted for by a nonorganic mental disorder (e.g., Manic Episode accounting for agitation and sleep disorder).

Clinical Subtypes

Many authors have described two major subtypes of acute confusional states, one characterized by increased activity, overarousal, and agitation; and the other by reduced arousal, underactivity, and stupor (Morse & Litin, 1971; Steinhart, 1979). Lipowski (1990) described three clinical variants that he termed *hyperactive-hyperalert*, *hypoactive-hypoalert*, and *mixed*. The hyperactive-hyperalert form of acute confusion is characterized by psychomotor overactivity and abnormally increased responsiveness to environmental stimuli. Patients are typically restless, excitable, and distractable. Acute confusional states secondary to alcohol withdrawal (delirium tremens) are a classic example of the hyperactive-hyperalert type. The hypoactive-hypoalert type of acute confusional state shows a reduced level of psychomotor activity and alertness. Lipowski (1990) describes these patients as quiet and listless, speaking very little, responding slowly to stimuli, and having a tendency to drift off into sleep even when talking with others. The mixed type of acute confusion reveals features of both the over- and underactive types according to Lipowski (1990). Psychomotor activity and arousal may alternate between restlessness and excitability, and lethargy and listlessness.

Differential Diagnosis

Acute confusional states among the elderly most often require differentiation from dementia, amnesia, organic hallucinosis, organic delusional syndrome, organic affective syndrome, organic personality syndrome, and functional psychosis. The chief differentiating feature between these illnesses and acute confusion is an alteration in the level of arousal, consciousness, or awareness that is present in confusion but not in the other syndromes (American Psychiatric Association, 1987; Liston, 1982; Lipowski, 1990).

Distinguishing acute confusional states from dementia can be a difficult diagnostic task, because there is a global impairment of cognition in both neurobehavioral syndromes. This is further complicated by the frequent co-occurrence of acute confusion and dementia among the elderly. Nevertheless a diagnostic distinction between confusional states and dementia is vital because acute confusion suggests a potentially reversible underlying medical disorder that if not adequately investigated and treated may progress into irreversible dementia or, not infrequently, death (Lipowski, 1990).

From a clinical perspective, acute confusion may be distinguished from dementia by knowledge of the history of development. Acute confusion often develops abruptly, whereas the onset of the cognitive impairments in dementia is more slow and insidious (with exceptions such as after head trauma or sustained anoxia). The date or even the exact time of onset of confusional symptoms may be precisely known upon questioning a relative. Because the onset of dementia is usually gradual, pinpointing the time of onset is typically difficult. Confusional symptoms fluctuate over the course of a day. Lucid intervals are frequently seen during the daytime, especially the morning hours, and symptoms often become worse at night. In contrast, the cognitive/emotional deficits in dementia do not show obvious changes over a 24-hour period, although it is not uncommon for family members to report some diurnal fluctuation. Acute confusion usually persists for hours to days, and according to the DSM-III-R, rarely endures for more than a month, whereas dementia lasts much longer. Finally, the core defining features of acute confusional states—namely, alterations of alertness and diminished awareness—may help the clinician to distinguish acute confusional states from dementia. The clinical features helpful in the differential diagnosis of dementia versus delirium have been detailed elsewhere (Levkoff, Besdine, & Wetle, 1986; Lipowski, 1990) and are summarized in Table 13.1.

Age of Onset

Acute confusional states are more common among the very young and the very old, because these are the individuals whose central nervous systems are most vulnerable to the effects of medical insults. Confusional states in pediatric age

TABLE 13.1. Clinical Differential Diagnosis—Acute Confusional State
Versus Dementia

Feature	Acute Confusional State	Dementia
Onset	Abrupt, acute	Slow, insidious
Known onset time	Often, yes	No
Course	Fluctuating	Stable
Duration	Usually brief	Usually long-standing
Alertness	Abnormal	Usually normal
Awareness	Reduced	Clear

groups have not been extensively studied, and much of our information rests on anecdotal reports and clinical lore. Although the prevalence of acute confusion in childhood is not known, it is apparently common, especially in infancy and early childhood (Amit, 1988).

In adults, the occurrence of acute confusional states becomes more frequent with increasing age (Morse & Litin, 1969; Rockwood, 1989). The prevalence has been reported to be four times higher in individuals more than 40 years old (Doty, 1946). Furthermore, it is approximately twice as frequent among patients 75 years of age and older than for patients 65 to 74 years old (Kay, 1972). This linear trend appears to continue into the oldest age groups. For example, in one sample of 279 hospitalized patients aged 70 or more years, approximately 15% of patients between the ages of 70 and 74 were diagnosed with acute confusion. However, among those 85 or more years old, the frequency of confusion more than doubled to approximately 38% (Warshaw et al., 1982).

Prevalence

Although acute confusion is apparently common among medical patients, exact figures are difficult to establish with certainty. This state of affairs exists for several reasons. First, almost all studies examining the incidence and prevalence of acute confusional states have focused on elderly patients. For example, we were unable to discover even one study reporting the frequency of confusional states among children in our literature search. Among investigations of the elderly, methodological differences exist among studies, making comparability problematic. Methodological difficulties include the use of inconsistent diagnostic criteria, different bases for patient selection, disparate patient samples, and conducting the research in noncomparable settings (e.g., general hospital, psychiatric hospital) with diverse medical populations (e.g., internal medicine, geriatric medicine, neurology). Further contributing to the confusion over diagnostic criteria, the definition of acute confusional states has changed over time. Recent studies have tended to use similar diagnostic criteria, such as DSM-III-R (American Psychiatric Association, 1987), and, therefore, may provide more reliable prevalence estimates.

Recent studies of acute confusion among elderly patients upon admission to the hospital have produced prevalence estimates between 7% and 16%. Of 172 patients over the age of 70 who were admitted to an internal medicine service of a general hospital, only 12 (7%) were delirious at the time of hospital admission (Johnson et al., 1987). In a prospective study of 80 elderly patients, age 65 to 91, admitted to a general medical service of two acute care hospitals, acute confusional states were seen in 13 of 80 (16%) cases at the time of admission (Rockwood, 1989). Similarly, Seymour, Henschke, Cape, and Campbell (1980) prospectively examined 68 patients over the age of 70 who were admitted as emergencies to a general medical unit and found 11 (16%) met acute confusion criteria on a 10-item mental status questionnaire at admission. Examination of 2,000 consecutive patients aged 55 years and older admitted to a department of medicine in a university hospital revealed that, at admission, 301 (15.1%) cases met diagnostic criteria for delirium similar to those found in DSM-III (Erkinjuntti, Wikstrom, Palo, & Autio, 1986). Thus, a reasonable estimate of the prevalence of confusion among the elderly upon admission to a general hospital would be approximately 15%.

Estimates of the number of elderly patients who develop confusion during their hospital stay are higher than those involving patients who are confused at the time of admission. Prevalence estimates generally range from 25% to 55%. During their stay on the general medical services of two tertiary care hospitals, 20 of 80 patients aged 65 to 91 developed confusion at some point during hospitalization, yielding a prevalence estimate of 25% (Rockwood, 1989). Using a broad definition of acute confusion (score of < 24 on the Mini-Mental State Examination [Folstein, Folstein & McHugh, 1975] and one or more psychomotor behaviors associated with confusion), Foreman (1989) found 27 of 71 (38%) patients over the age of 60 on a general medical unit developed confusion during their hospitalization. Gillick, Serrell, and Gillick (1982) reported 30% of prospectively studied hospitalized patients over age 70 exhibited confusion. A large study with poorly defined acute confusional state criteria found one half of 279 hospitalized patients aged 70 or more years showed some form of confusion: 19% were considered mildly confused, and 31% were classified moderately or severely confused (Warshaw et al., 1982). Unfortunately, the operational definition for delirium was not specified in this study other than being "clinical assessed" (p. 848). Finally, when studying patients over age 60 from general medical and surgical wards in a general hospital, Chisholm, Doniston, Igrisan, and Barbus (1982) found 55.5% of patients experienced acute confusion at some point during hospitalization. The higher prevalence estimate in this study probably resulted from the inclusion of surgical patients in the sample. These recent investigations suggest the actual prevalence of acute confusion among the hospitalized elderly may be as high as 30% to 50%.

Acute confusional states have been reported in 10% to 52% of cases drawn from coronary, surgical, and medical intensive care units and specialized geriatric or surgical care units (e.g., Parker & Hodge, 1967; Wilson, 1972). In a study of 21 geriatric departments in England, Hodkinson (1973) found 35% of 144 patients, 65 years and older, were acutely confused sometime during their hospital stay. Examination of 258 elderly patients on a general surgical ward revealed acute confusion in 10% of patients despite the type of surgery (Seymour & Pringle, 1983). Focusing on a single surgery type (hip-fracture surgery), over half (51.5%) of the 170 postsurgical elderly (mean age = 78.8) patients examined showed some confusion during the first 5 postoperative days (Williams et al., 1985).

Thus, the prevalence estimates of acute confusional states among the elderly vary considerably depending upon the medical population studied. Current estimates suggest that about 15% are confused upon admission to the hospital, and approximately one third to one half may become acutely confused sometime during hospitalization. When considering all types of medical specialty inpatient units, acute confusional states are generally more common among surgical and intensive care patients than in patients from geriatric and general medical wards.

Course

Acute confusional states usually develop over a period of hours to days following the medical insult or deficiency. The period of development may depend upon the nature of the medical illness. Acute confusion after trauma during emergence from coma or following major surgery usually develops soon after the event, whereas confusion secondary to metabolic disorders or infection often has a more gradual onset (Lipowski, 1990). Although confusional states have been most thoroughly studied in the elderly, the symptoms and course of acute confusion appear to be similar despite the age of the afflicted individual.

When an acute confusional state develops slowly, the early symptoms that signal its impending arrival may include concentration difficulty, problems with thinking clearly, restlessness, irritability, fatigue, insomnia, drowsiness, or over-sensitivity to environmental stimuli such as light and sound (Adams & Victor, 1983; Lipowski, 1990). The patient may remain in this subacute state for some time or progress along the continuum of confusional severity. If the confusional state progresses, the patient will move toward either restless irritability (hyperactive-hyperalert type) or drowsiness and lethargy (hypoactive-hypoalert type). Concurrent with both confusional state types, the patient becomes inattentive and has difficulty in thinking coherently and grasping the meaning of interpersonal situations (Lipowski, 1985; Levkoff et al., 1986).

As the confusion deepens, the patient may become unaware of the time, unable to sleep at night, experience nightmares, and have difficulty distinguishing reality. Disorders of perception are common, resulting in the misinterpretation of voices, common objects, familiar places, and the intentions and actions of others (Lipowski, 1980). In addition to such illusions, visual and auditory hallucinations may occur. Affective disturbances (e.g., fear, anxiety, depression, euphoria, rage, and apathy), paranoid delusions, and a variety of general physical and neurological signs and symptoms (e.g., tremor, asterixis, impairment of coordination, urinary incontinence, focal neurological signs, and autonomic nervous system dysfunction such as dilated pupils and tachycardia) have also been described as associated features of acute confusion (Liston, 1982). These symptoms may intensify or unexpectedly dissipate over the course of hours or days. This fluctuation in level of arousal and awareness is common in acute confusional states and may even help to distinguish them from other neurobehavioral conditions, such as most dementing illnesses. As the underlying medical disorder causing acute confusion is treated and recovery follows, the first signs of recovery are often short periods of normal sleep. Henry and Mann (1965) report the final emergence from delirium is usually preceded by a long period of natural sleep.

Risk Factors

Most research studies suggest patients at risk for the development of an acute confusional state are likely to be older, to suffer some form of existing brain disease, to be more physically ill, and to have poorer visual and auditory acuity than controls (Morse & Litin, 1969; Lipowski, 1983; Hodkinson, 1973). Hodkinson (1973) found that advanced age, preexisting dementia, defective hearing and vision, and more severe physical illness were statistically significant predisposing factors of confusional states in 144 patients aged 65 and older admitted to geriatric departments. Pneumonia, cardiac failure, urinary infection, carcinomatosis, and hypokalemia were statistically significant conditions associated with confusional states. Among 170 elderly surgical patients, Williams et al. (1985) reported the significant predictors of postoperative confusional states included age (older), number of errors on a mental status examination, preinjury activity level, urinary elimination problems, degree of pain, amount of narcotic administered, and lack of postsurgical mobility.

These important risk factors have been subsequently confirmed. Rockwood (1989) reported that the confusional patients admitted to general medical services tended to be older, more ill, and more likely to have chronic cognitive impairment. In patients admitted with acute confusion, infection and congestive heart failure predominated, whereas iatrogenic diseases were more frequent among patients who developed confusion after hospitalization. Purdie, Honigman, & Rosen (1981) found the most common etiological factors producing delirium superimposed upon a preexisting dementia were infections (23%) and environmental changes (17%). In contrast, the most common cause of de novo delirium was drug related. Examining the physiological and other contributory variables associated with the onset of acute confusion, Foreman (1989) developed the following profile of the elderly confused patient. Confusional patients were hypernatremic, hypokalemic, hyperglycemic, hypotensive, had elevated blood levels of creatinine and urea nitrogen, received more medications, and had fewer interactions with significant others. Confirming the predisposing role of structural brain diseases (e.g., primary degenerative and multi-infarct dementias, parkinsonism) in the genesis of delirium, Koponen, Hurri, Stenback, and Riekkinen (1987) found a significant excess of low-attenuation areas and more parenchymal atrophy when comparing the computed tomographic (CT) scans of delirium patients and controls.

Making the differential diagnosis between acute confusion and dementia even more difficult is the co-occurrence of the two conditions. In a retrospective review of 100 general hospital patients with admitting diagnoses of acute organic brain syndrome (delirium), Purdie et al. (1981) found 44% of patients were simultaneously suffering from a chronic organic brain syndrome (dementia). Similarly, of 2,000 consecutive patients aged 55 and older admitted to a university hospital, 301 (15%) were diagnosed as delirious. Seventy-five (25%) of the delirious patients later proved to meet DSM-III-type criteria for dementia, and of the 106 patients who were demented upon admission, 41.4% were simultaneously delirious (Erkinjuntti et al., 1986). These studies suggest that confusion may be superimposed upon dementia in nearly one half of elderly demented patients admitted to hospitals.

Nocturnal confusion (sundown syndrome) is the appearance or exacerbation of symptoms of confusion during the late afternoon or early evening hours. Sundowning is similar to acute confusional states except that it is often not as transient and may last for an extended period. Evans (1987) studied 59 demented and 30 nondemented nursing home residents age 60 years and older to determine the prevalence of the sundown syndrome and factors related to its occurrence. The prevalence among this nursing home sample was 12.5%. Sundowners were more likely to be demented, had more diseases affecting the brain, were often dehydrated, awakened frequently during the evening for nursing care, were more recently admitted to the nursing home, and had been in their present room for less than 1 month. The similarities between risk factors and diagnostic features of the sundown syndrome and delirium suggest that the sundown syndrome should probably be considered a subtype of acute confusional states.

Pathophysiology

Knowledge of the neural basis of confusional states is generally incomplete. Much of what is presumed about these states is inferred from their neurobehavioral symptoms. Because these symptoms usually resolve when the underlying medical disorder is reversed, it is assumed that the responsible metabolic lesions are also reversible. It is also generally assumed that the responsible biochemical insults secondarily affect the entire brain because the symptoms usually suggest bilateral and diffuse cerebral dysfunction. The medical illnesses that result in acute confusional states disrupt the extracellular environment of the central nervous system. This is usually in the form of an alteration in the biochemical constitution of the blood or a reduction in its supply. This, in turn, alters intracellular cerebral metabolism, which is thought to be the basic pathogenic mechanism in all confusional states. Such events may help to create deficient synthesis, blockade, or imbalances among various neurotransmitters or disrupt synaptic transmission (Lipowski, 1985, 1990).

Blass, Gibson, Duffy, and Plum (1981) have hypothesized that a reduction in the rate of cerebral oxygen metabolism causes deficient acetylcholine synthesis that, in turn, is the common underlying cause of toxic and metabolic confusional states. The important role of acetylcholine in creating and sustaining acute confusional states has also been shown by Itil and Fink (1966), who speculated that anticholinergics stimulate the inhibitory portion of the medial ascending reticular formation and simultaneously the medial thalamic diffuse projection system (intramedullary lamina) that has an activating influence on cortex. They suggested the degree to which each of these two systems predominate will determine whether psychomotor activity in acute confusion will be decreased (hypoactive-hypoalert type) or increased (hyperactive-hyperalert type) and if the preponderance of abnormal EEG background activity will be slow or fast. However, because a core behavioral feature of acute confusional states involves degree of arousal or wakefulness and because disruption of the sleep-wake cycle is typically present in acute confusion, other neurotransmitter systems important in mediating sleep, such as serotonergic and noradrenergic systems are probably also involved in the pathophysiology of confusion (Morgane, 1982; Gaillard, 1985; Hobson, Lydic, & Baghodoyan, 1986).

Etiology

Drug intoxication is the single most common and important cause of acute confusional states in the elderly (Hurwitz, 1969; Learoyd, 1972; Caranasos, Stewart, & Cluff, 1974; Lipowski, 1990). Geriatric patients have more diseases (and more chronic disease) than younger patients, and therefore, are prescribed more medicines over longer periods of time than those in younger age groups. In one study, 81% of patients admitted to geriatric medicine units were taking prescription drugs at the time of admission and about 25% were receiving four to six drugs simultaneously (Williamson & Chopin, 1980). Furthermore, age-related changes in the metabolism, distribution, and excretion of drugs undoubtedly contribute to the increased prevalence of adverse drug reactions in the elderly (Vestal, 1978). In Table 13.2, some of the more common toxic causes of acute confusional states are given (Davison, 1978; Williamson, 1978; Liston, 1982; Williamson & Chopin, 1980; Wells, 1985; Lipowski, 1985, 1990). For a more complete review of the effects of these toxic agents, the interested reader is referred to Lipowski (1990) and Levenson (1979).

Metabolic diseases are systemic disorders of metabolism resulting in secondary effects on the brain and are among the most common causes of acute confusional states in all age groups. Common metabolic diseases that may cause confusion are shown in Table 13.3 and have been reviewed by Wells (1985), Adams and Victor (1989), and Lipowski (1990), and include organ failure (e.g., liver, kidney, pancreas, and glands including thyroid, pituitary, adrenal, and parathyroid); other systemic diseases (e.g., cancer, porphyria, Wilson's disease); deficiency of oxygen

TABLE 13.2. Toxic Causes of Acute Confusional States

Medical drugs
  Anticholinergic agents
    Antidepressants
    Antipsychotics
    Antihistamines
    Antiemetics
  Antibiotics
  Antiparkinsonian agents
  Cardiovascular drugs
    Antiarrhythmic agents
    Antihypertensive drugs
    Digitalis derivatives
  Sedative-hypnotics
  Antineoplastic drugs
  Cimetidine
  Lithium
Alcohol
Solvent-inhalants
  Gasoline
  Glue
  Aerosol propellants
Industrial Poisons
  Carbon monoxide
  Carbon disulfide
  Organic solvents
  Heavy metals
  Methyl chloride
Alcohol withdrawal
Drug withdrawal
  Sedative-hypnotics

TABLE 13.3. Metabolic Causes of Acute Confusional States

Organ failure
  Hepatic (liver) disease
  Renal (kidney) disease
    Uremia and dialysis disequilibrium
  Hypercapnia (pulmonary, respiratory)
  Pancreatic insufficiency
  Endocrine disorders
    Hypopituitarism
    Hypothyroidism
    Hyperthyroidism
    Hypoparathyroidism
    Hyperparathyroidism
    Hypoadrenalism (Addison's disease)
    Hyperadrenalism (Cushing's disease)
    Diabetic acidosis
Deficiency of oxygen or substrate for cerebral metabolism
  Hypoxia
  Hypoglycemia
Other systemic diseases
  Cancer
  Carcinoid syndrome
  Porphyria
  Wilson's disease
Disorders of fluid, electrolyte, and acid-base balance
  Hyponatremia (sodium)
  Hypernatremia
  Hypokalemia (potassium)
  Hyperkalemia
  Hypocalcemia (calcium)
  Hypercalcemia
  Hypomagnesemia
  Hypermagnesemia
  Hypophosphatemia
  Acidosis
  Alkalosis
Vitamin deficiency or excess
Temperature regulation disorders
  Hypothermia
  Hyperthermia (heat stroke)

or substrates for cerebral metabolism (e.g., hypoxia, hypoglycemia); disorders of fluid, electrolyte, and acid-base balance (e.g., sodium, potassium, calcium, magnesium, acidosis, and alkalosis); vitamin deficiency or excess; and disorders of temperature regulation. When a systemic disorder affects the brain, as evidenced by either abnormal mental status or EEG, the term *metabolic encephalopathy* is applied. The metabolic encephalopathies have been thoroughly reviewed by Lipowski (1990).

Outcome

Acute confusional states may terminate in complete physical and neurobehavioral recovery, progress to an irreversible cognitive/emotional state such as dementia or a focal syndrome (e.g., frontal-lobe syndrome), or lead to death. The issue of reversibility of acute confusion is controversial. Lipowski (1990) proposed that the syndrome of mental impairment seen in confusion must be transient to meet criteria for the diagnosis of delirium. However, acute confusional states have been reported to persist for "many months" in cases of hyperparathyroidism (Gatewood, Organ, & Mead, 1975) and for more than 1 year in three cases of confusion following cerebral infarction (Mullally, Ronthal, Huff, & Geschwind, 1989). Furthermore, DSM-III-R (American Psychiatry Association, 1987) makes no mention of duration or reversibility of delirium in its diagnostic criteria. It appears that acute confusional states may continue for many months, and perhaps for as long as 1 year in a mild, subacute form.

The outcome of acute confusion depends on several factors. The type of illness causing the confusional state and the patient's age and general physical health are important considerations. Furthermore, the timeliness and effectiveness of treating the underlying medical disorder is a factor influencing outcome (Lipowski, 1990). Early investigations reported very high mortality rates in elderly, confused patients. For example, Flint and Richards (1956) reported a 76% mortality rate among 242 elderly patients who were confused upon admission to a general medical unit at a geriatric hospital, in contrast to a rate of 50% for demographically similar patients without confusion. Roth (1955) found that 40% of acutely confused patients admitted to a mental hospital were dead 6 months following admission; 50% had been discharged, and 10% remained hospitalized.

Summarizing results of earlier investigations, Kral (1975) reported that approximately 25% of acutely confused patients admitted to hospitals died within 1 year, another 25% developed dementia, and the remaining 50% recovered fully. Hodkinson (1973) found a 25% mortality rate within 1 month of hospital admission among 186 inpatients with toxic confusional states. Because of differences in the definition of acute confusional states used in these early studies, the accuracy of these data concerning mortality, recovery, and conversion to dementia should not be accepted without reservation. Many patients classified as acutely confused in these early studies would be classified as demented or as confusion superimposed upon dementia by more modern criteria. Furthermore, medical advances in diagnostic techniques and treatment regimens in recent years have improved the prognosis for acute confusional states.

More recent investigations of elderly hospitalized confused patients provide a more optimistic prognosis. In a retrospective review of patients admitted to a general hospital with diagnoses of acute organic brain syndrome, only 2 of 56 (3.5%) died during their hospital stay. Longer follow-up periods provide a more realistic depiction of outcome. Simon and Cahan (1963) found that 17% of acutely confused patients admitted to a psychiatric unit of a general hospital died within 1 month of admission. This study obtained a similar mortality rate of 16% for patients with confusion superimposed upon chronic dementia. In another study of 133 patients with organic mental disorder diagnoses who had been referred for psychiatric consultation, patients with delirium had the highest mortality rate—namely, 25% within 6 months of evaluation (Trzepacz, Teague, & Lipowski, 1985). Rockwood (1989) reported that 15% (3 of 20) of acutely confused cased died at some point during the 6-month study period.

A similar mortality rate for a poorly defined, mixed delirium-dementia group of 28 patients was observed by Seymour et al. (1980): 18% of patients died, 10% required institutionalization for the first time, and 72% were classified as successes (patients either went home or returned to their previous institution). In Purdie et al.'s (1981) retrospective survey of 100 patients admitted to a general hospital with diagnoses of acute organic brain syndromes, 30 of 44 (68%) patients with confusion superimposed upon dementia required institutionalization or custodial care at the time of discharge. The remaining 14 (32%) were able to return home, although many required extensive support for continued independent living.

In summary, most recent investigations indicate between 15% and 25% of elderly patients with acute confusional states will die sometime within the ensuing 6 months. Approximately 25% of confused patients may go on to develop dementia and many of these will require institutionalization. Perhaps the most important figure to emphasize is the estimate that 50% to 60% of acutely confused elderly patients will recovery fully and be able to live independently. None of these figures is definitive, however, given the methodological complexities and evolution of clinical research in this area.

Neuropsychological Findings in Toxic and Metabolic Disorders

Acute confusional states may be thought of as occupying several positions across a continuum of severity. On the hypokinetic end, symptoms of acute confusion may stretch from mild inattention and drowsiness to coma, whereas it may range between mild anxiety, hyperarousal, and hypervigilance to severe maniacal excitement on the hyperkinetic end of the continuum (Henry & Mann, 1965). Of course, both the mild (e.g., inattention) and most severe (e.g., coma) symptoms are not generally called acute confusion or delirium. However, the symptoms that fall beyond the diagnostic boundaries of confusion may nevertheless be either a precursor or prodromal stage (e.g., inattention) or an endstage (e.g., coma) of acute confusion.

As may be seen in Tables 13.2 or 13.3, acute confusional states are caused by many different agents or processes that include almost every known drug, toxin, and acute or chronic illness that interfere with brain function. It is important to realize that each toxic or metabolic cause does not result in a different set of symptoms specific to each etiology (Henry & Mann, 1965). Although there have been suggestions that metabolic encephalopathies tend to be of the hypoactive-hypoalert type, and alcohol or sedative-hypnotic withdrawal tend to be of the hyperactive-hyperalert type (Lipowski, 1990), the essential clinical features of acute confusional states are independent of etiology. As will be discussed, the same holds true for the neuropsychological results. Thus, review of the neuropsychological results in toxicometabolic disorders below will be organized by cognitive domain, not by medical agent or illness.

Because this chapter is concerned with acute confusional states, many neuropsychological studies of toxic and metabolic disorders where it was not possible to decide whether an alteration of mental status existed have been excluded. It was difficult, if not impossible in some cases, to determine accurately when investigations of various toxicometabolic disorders included acutely confused cases. Furthermore, the scientific rigor with which these investigations were conducted varied considerably. Despite this, no study was excluded from review if there was at least some indication that some patients suffered from an acute confusional state secondary to a toxic or metabolic disorder.

The review of neuropsychological results among toxicometabolic disorders below necessarily includes, for the most part, only patients with mild acute confusional states. Patients with moderate or severe acute confusional states are typically unable to cooperate with lengthy psychometric assessment due to their inability to maintain attention or a consistent level of alertness necessary to obtain valid results. Therefore, the review of neuropsychological results below is generalizable only to mild toxicometabolic confusional states.

Although there is no lack of published accounts of alterations of normal cognition or emotional tone secondary to medication toxicity, most articles consist of either descriptive case studies (e.g., Carney, 1971; Sagel & Matisonn, 1972; Adler, 1974; Knee & Razani, 1974; Ambrosetto, Tassinari, Baruzzi, & Lugaresi, 1977; Zatuchni & Hong, 1981; Tilzey, Heptonstall, & Hamblin, 1981; Van Sweden, 1985; Mandal, 1986; Molloy, 1987; Hersch & Billings, 1988), normal volunteers on various doses of drug (e.g., Itil & Fink, 1966; Liljequist, Linnoila, & Mattila, 1974; Wolkowitz et al., 1987), or various patient groups on nontoxic medication levels (e.g., Legg & Stiff, 1976; Squire, Judd, Janowsky, & Huey, 1980; Perlick, Stastny, Katz, Mayer, & Mattis, 1986). However, studies dealing with the cognitive and emotional changes due to acute medication toxicity among neurological patients are rare, and those concerned with neuropsychological measurement are almost nonexistent. Therefore, much of the empirical documentation detailed below will necessarily deal with cognitive alternations secondary to metabolic disorders.

Attention and Concentration

Attention refers to the ability to focus and direct mental processes in an immediate or sustained fashion toward both internal and external stimuli. Alertness is one aspect of attention that is closely allied to wakefulness and involves readiness to receive and respond to stimuli (Lipowski, 1984). Alertness or wakefulness is a necessary precondition for adequate attention. Concentration generally refers to attention that requires greater mental effort over a longer period and, because of these characteristics, has also been called complex mental tracking (Lezak, 1983, p. 550). Vigilance involves the capacity to maintain attention and respond to a specific set of signals over time. These constructs (alertness, attention, concentration, vigilance) have been measured by a variety of psychological instruments. Among the most common are Wechsler Adult Intelligence Scale-Revised (WAIS-R) Digit Span and Arithmetic subtests, Seashore Rhythm Test (Reitan & Wolfson, 1989), Speech-Sounds Perception Test (Reitan & Wolfson, 1990), serial subtraction, cancellation tasks, Trail-Making Test, continuous performance tasks, and reaction time measures (e.g., simple, choice, auditory, visual).

Because an impairment of attention is a core defining feature of acute confusional states, it should come as no surprise that investigations of most toxic and metabolic disorders have found deficits on psychometric tests of alertness, attention, concentration, vigilance, and reaction time. For example, attention and concentration impairment secondary to mild toxic encephalopathy was documented by Brooker, Wiens, and Wiens (1984) in a single case study followed for 1.5 years.

A 53-year-old Ph.D. was admitted to the hospital for a syndrome that had gradually worsened over the previous year consisting of increasing confusion with nystagmus, episodes of slurred speech, and cerebellar ataxia that were subsequently found to be due to meprobamate (Milltown) and diazepam intoxication. One month before hospital admission, scaled scores on WAIS-R Digit Span and Arithmetic were 9 in distinction to scaled scores on Information, 13; Comprehension, 11; Similarities, 12; and Vocabulary, 14. Other attention-concentration test results included Seashore Rhythm Test, 9 errors; Speech-Sounds Perception Test, 12 errors; Trail-Making Test-part A, 72 seconds; and part B, 225 seconds. Follow-up examination 1.5 years later, meprobamate and diazepam having been discontinued for 6 months, showed significant improvement on attention-concentration tests including Digit Span, 11; Arithmetic, 16; Rhythm, 0 errors; Trails A, 36 seconds; and Trails B, 74 seconds.

A review of studies investigating neuropsychological performance in mild to moderate confusional states secondary to toxic and metabolic disorders is given in Table 13.4. Perusal of Table 13.4 reveals that attention is generally impaired in all its aspects despite the underlying medical disorder. These investigations also show that the more severe the illness, and concomitant degree of encephalopathy, the greater the attention-concentration deficit. Attention-concentration deficits have been reported in steroid (Varney, Alexander, & MacIndoe, 1984), antianxiety (Brooker et al., 1984), and anticonvulsant (Thompson & Trimble, 1983) toxicity; alcoholic and nonalcoholic liver disease patients (e.g., Schomerus et al., 1981; Rehnstrom, Simert, Hansson, Hohnson, & Vang, 1977); renal failure and hemodialysis patients (Ryan, Souheaver, & DeWolfe, 1981; Alexander, Hightower, Anderson, & Snow, 1980); thyroid disease (Whybrow, Prange, & Treadway, 1969), hydrocephalus (Thomsen, Borgesen, Bruhn, & Gjerris, 1986); cerebrovascular inflammatory disease (Cochran, Fox, & Kelly, 1978); and mixed groups of confused patients including delirium tremens and diabetic ketoacidosis (Lee & Hamsher, 1988) and patients recovering from electroconvulsive therapy (Chedru & Geschwind, 1972a). Furthermore, among the longitudinal studies where either the drug toxicity or underlying medical condition is successfully treated, attention and concentration improve and typically return to expected baseline levels of performance.

None of the subtypes of attention deficit are spared. Thus, alertness, attention, concentration, vigilance, and reaction time have all been shown to be deficient even in patients with mild encephalopathy. These results have been reported with most psychometric measures requiring some degree of attention, such as Digit Span, serial sevens, mental arithmetic, serial subtraction, Trail-Making Test, Rhythm Test, Speech-Sounds Perception Test, Stroop Test, Digit Symbol, cancellation tasks, continuous performance tests, and simple and choice reaction time measures.

In summary, deficits of attention, concentration, vigilance, and reaction time are almost invariably present in toxic and metabolic disorders. Indeed, these deficits are among the first signs to herald the onset of an acute confusional state. Patients and family members may spontaneously complain of inattentiveness or concentration difficulties as a prodrome of acute confusion. Attention is generally impaired in all its aspects regardless of the underlying medical condition, and the more severe the illness, the greater the attention-concentration deficit. When the underlying medical condition has been successfully treated, measures of attention typically return to premorbid levels.

TABLE 13.4.   Attention and Concentration Test Results For Patients with
Toxicometabolic Disorders

Source	Subjects/Disorders
Alexander et al. (1980)	28 renal failure patients on dialysis vs. 28 age- and sex-matched controls.
Brooker et al. (1984)	Case study of meprobamate & diazepam intoxication
Chedru & Geschwind (1972)	24 patients with acute confusion of varying etiologies
Cochran et al. (1978)	Case study before and after temporal arteritis
Elithorn, Lunzer, & Weinman (1975)	7 chronic hepatic encephalopathy, vs. 7 cirrhotics without encephalopathy, vs. 7 hospital controls
Elsass, Lund, & Rankek (1978)	30 cirrhotics with encephalopathy vs. test norms
Ginn (1975)	Renal failure (unspecified N) serum creatinine levels
Hart et al. (1983)	24 dialysands, vs. 18 nondialyzed renal failure, vs. 20 chronic physical disability controls
Lee & Hamsher (1988)	12 acute confusion (mixed etiology) & 12 controls
Lewis et al. (1980)	6 maintenance dialysis patients
McKee et al. (1982)	5 end-stage renal failure predialysis and postdialysis, vs. 14 treated less than, and 15 treated more than, 1 year
Medalia et al. (1988)	19 Wilson's disease with neurological signs, vs. 15 asymptomatic Wilson's disease, vs. 15 healthy controls.
Rehnstrom et al. (1977)	41 chronic cirrhotics with encephalopathy divided into 3 groups based upon degree of EEG slowing
Ryan et al. (1981)	16 renal failure, vs. 16 dialysis, vs. 16 medical/psychological controls
Schomerus et al. (1981)	15 alcoholic cirrhotics (Group 1), vs. 15 nonalcoholic cirrhotics (Group 2), vs. 10 cirrhotics with EEG slowing (Group 3), vs. 12 alcoholics with pancreatitis (Group 4)
Starkman & Schteingart (1981)	35 patients with Cushing's syndrome
Summerskill et al. (1956)	17 acutely confused nonalcoholic cirrhotics
Tarter et al. (1987)	123 cirrhotics (some with "mild encephalopathy") vs. 14 chronic disease (Crohn's) controls
Teschan et al. (1979)	132 renal failures divided in 4 groups based upon disease severity vs. 45 healthy controls

Test(s)	Results
CPT	Dialysands showed significantly slowed RTs, but no differences on correct detections or false alarms.
WAIS Digit Span & Arithmetic, Rhythm Test, Speech-Sounds Perception, & Trails A & B	Improvement followed detoxication on all tests, except Speech-Sounds
Digit Span & Vigilance (brief auditory CPT)	Digit span impaired in 67% & CPT impaired in 79% of patients.
WMS: Mental Control & Digit Span subtests	Both mildly improved following successful treatment
Digit Span, auditory 2-choice RT, Visual 10-choice RT, Coding	Cirrhotics with encephalopathy significantly worse than others on Visual RT & Coding
Serial subtraction (100-7), WAIS Digit Span	These tests worse than hidden patterns, visual gestalts, story recall, and picture recognition
Trails B & Auditory short-term memory	Significant correlation between creatinine & Trails B & mean response time increases with more severe renal failure
Digit Span, WMS Mental Control, Trails A & B, Digit Vigilance, & WAIS Digit Symbol	Nondialyzed impaired on Digit Vigilance & Trails A & B relative to other groups & on Digit Symbol relative to controls only
WAIS-R: Digit Span & Arithmetic	Confused patients performed significantly below controls
Digit Span & Visual Choice RT	No difference on digits 1, 24, 42, or 66 hours after dialysis; RT was most efficient 24-hours after dialysis
WAIS Digit Span & Digit Symbol, & Trails A & B	Group 1 improved on Digit Span, Group 2 on Digit Symbol & Trails A & B, Group 3 showed no change over time
Trails A & B	Neurologically impaired Wilson's disease significantly worse than controls
Simple & choice RT & Stroop test	Severe EEG-slowed group worse than normal EEGs on both RT measures whereas mild EEG-slowed group worse than normals on simple RT & Stroop
Trails A & B, Rhythm Test, & Speech-Sounds perception test	Three groups worse than controls on Trails B, Rhythm & Speech-Sounds, whereas renal failures worse than dialysands & controls on Trails A
Vigilance-cancellation tasks, Trails A & B, Auditory & Visual RT	Vigilance & Trails A impaired in Groups 2 & 4 only; Group 4 slowest RTs
Serial 7 subtraction	51% of patients clinically judged impaired
Digit Span, Mental subtraction	Judged clinically impaired among confused patients up to 6 years
WAIS Digit Span, WMS Mental Control	Cirrhotics impaired compared to controls on both tests
Auditory short-term memory, Trails B, Visual Choice RT, & CPT	High azotemics impaired on memory & Trails; normals had shorter RTs & fewer incorrect CPT responses than patient groups; higher creatinine levels correlated with poorer performances

TABLE 13.4.   (*Continued*)

Source	Subjects/Disorders
Thompson & Trimble (1983)	28 epileptics; high & low anticonvulsant levels
Thomsen et al. (1986)	8 normal-pressure hydrocephalics who improved after shunting
Trieschmann & Sand (1971)	83 renal failure patients untreated with dialysis
Trzepacz et al. (1986)	40 liver transplant candidates (30% with delirium)
Varney et al. (1984)	6 steroid-induced, reversible dementia patients who were not overtly toxic
Whybrow et al. (1969)	10 hyperthyroidism patients vs. 7 hypothyroid patients

Note: CPT = Continuous Performance Test; RTs = reaction times; WAIS = Wechsler Adult Intelligence Scale; WMS = Wechsler Memory Scale; EEG = electroencephalography.

Memory

The ability to maintain knowledge about the temporal, spatial, and personal contexts in which one resides is probably dependent upon memory. Incorrect orientation concerning time, place, or personal information is common in acute confusional states, especially in acute and severe confusion, regardless of the underlying etiology (American Psychiatric Association, 1987; Lipowski, 1990). Disorientation is not present in every patient with acute confusion. For example, among 12 mixed-etiology acute confusional patients, Lee and Hamsher (1988) found only four (33%) were disoriented to time and eight (67%) to personal information and place. Daniel, Crovitz, and Weiner (1987) reported 25 of 32 (78%) patients showed some degree of disorientation when serially examined 15 minutes to 48 hours after two electroconvulsive treatments. Thus, even in mild cases of confusion where patients are able to sit for neuropsychological testing, the majority display some form of disorientation.

Among acute confusional patients who are disoriented, their responses to questions concerning age and current year are usually displaced backward in years from the correct response. As the confusional state clears, these backwardly displaced responses tend to decrease in years of remoteness in a pattern reminiscent of shrinking retrograde amnesia following head injury (Daniel, Crovitz, & Weiner, 1987).

Most patients with acute confusion show deficits of new learning that are materially nonspecific (i.e., impairment for both verbal and visuospatial materials). As with the other mental status changes in acute confusional states, these deficits are the same despite the underlying medical cause and have been documented in renal failure (Teschan et al., 1979; Spehr et al., 1977), patients on maintenance hemodialysis for renal disease (Hart, Pederson, Czerwinski, & Adams, 1983), encephalopathy secondary to liver disease (Rehnstrom et al., 1977; Tarter, Hegedus, Van Thiel, Edwards, & Schade, 1987), normal-pressure hydrocephalus (Thomsen et al., 1986), temporal arteritis (Cochran et al., 1978), steroid dementia

Test(s)	Results
Digit cancellation with & without distractor, Stroop test	High anticonvulsant levels performed worse on cancellation with distractor
Visual RT & Digit Span	Dramatic improvements on all test measures 6 months after shunting
WAIS Digit Span & Arithmetic	Mean of these tests (9) below mean (11) of other WAIS verbal subtests
Trails A & B	Test performances correlated with delirium
WAIS Digit Span & Arithmetic	Scores improved following detoxification
Trails B	Both groups impaired, but hypothyroidism significantly more impaired

(Varney et al., 1984), and in epileptics with high serum levels of antiepileptic drugs (Thompson & Trimble, 1983).

A summary of memory test results in toxic and metabolic disorders taken from recent investigations is given in Table 13.5. Examination of Table 13.5 generally reveals that the more severe the acute confusional state, the worse the performance on memory tests. For example, Lewis, O'Neill, Dustman, & Beck (1980) obtained no differences on Wechsler Memory Scale (WMS) Paired Associate Learning among six maintenance hemodialysis patients examined at 1, 24, 42, or 66 hours after treatment, although performance on two tests of visuomotor speed and accuracy was best 24 hours after dialysis. However, when McKee, Burnett, Raft, Batten, & Bain (1982) longitudinally examined five end-stage renal patients before dialysis and compared them with 14 short-term and 15 long-term dialysis patients, the end-stage renal patients improved on WMS Logical Memory relative to the other two groups, whose memory test performance did not change significantly. Similarly, Hagberg (1974) tested 23 chronic renal failure patients before dialysis and at 6 and 12 months after onset of treatment and found improvement on Paired Associate Learning and the Benton Visual Retention Test. Ginn (1975) found that response time on immediate recall of word lists was significantly correlated with serum creatinine levels in renal disease patients. Hart et al. (1983) also obtained modest negative correlations between biologic fluids and a facial recognition memory task (BUN, $r = -.23$, $p = .20$; creatinine, $r = -.35$, $p = .09$). Serum creatinine and BUN are measures of kidney functioning, and generally, the higher their serum concentration, the worse the memory performance. Further supporting the notion that increased severity of disease causes increased memory impairment, studies that examined EEG have consistently reported the poorest memory test performances are obtained in patients with the most EEG slowing (Rehnstrom et al., 1977; Schomerus et al., 1981).

In summary, the learning of new information is generally impaired in acute confusional states secondary to toxic or metabolic disorders. Memory impairment among these patients may be caused by disruption of the process of perception and analysis of stimuli, inability to sufficiently attend to the stimuli, problems in the organization of the material to be learned, breakdown in the creation of a stable intention to remember, or through disruption of the normal physiological

TABLE 13.5.   Memory Test Results for Patients with Toxicometabolic
Disorders

Source	Subjects/Disorders
Chedru & Geschwind (1972)	24 acutely confused patients with mixed etiologies
Cochran et al. (1978)	Case study before and after temporal arteritis
Hagberg (1974)	23 chronic renal failures tested before, 6 months after ($N = 21$), & 12 months after dialysis
Hart et al. (1983)	24 dialysands, vs. 18 nondialyzed renal failure, vs. 20 chronic physical disability controls
Lee & Hamsher (1988)	12 mixed etiology acute confusional states, 10 RHD, & 12 controls
Lewis et al. (1980)	6 maintenance dialysis patients
McKee et al. (1982)	5 end-stage renal failure predialysis and postdialysis, vs. 14 treated less than, and 15 treated more than, 1 year
Medalia et al. (1988)	19 Wilson's disease with neurological signs, vs. 15 asymptomatic Wilson's disease, vs. 15 healthy controls
Rehnstrom et al. (1977)	41 chronic cirrhotics with encephalopathy divided into 3 groups based upon degree of EEG slowing
Schomerus et al. (1981)	15 alcoholic cirrhotics (Group 1), vs. 15 nonalcoholic cirrhotics (Group 2), vs. 10 cirrhotics with EEG slowing (Group 3), vs. 12 alcoholics with pancreatitis (Group 4)
Spehr et al. (1977)	20 renal failure patients with encephalopathy
Starkman & Schteingart (1981)	35 patients with Cushing's syndrome
Summerskill et al. (1956)	17 acutely confused nonalcoholic cirrhotics
Tarter et al. (1987)	123 cirrhotics (some with "mild encephalopathy") vs. 14 chronic disease (Crohn's) controls
Teschan et al. (1979)	132 renal failure patients divided in 4 groups based on disease severity vs. 45 healthy controls
Thompson & Trimble (1983)	28 high- & low-serum anticonvulsant epileptics
Thomsen et al. (1986)	8 normal-pressure hydrocephalics who improved with shunting
Varney et al. (1984)	6 patients with reversible steroid dementia

Note: EEG = electroencephalography; WMS = Wechsler Memory Scale; MQ = memory quotient; VIQ = Verbal IQ; BVRT = Benton Visual Retention Test; RHD = right-hemisphere disease.

Test(s)	Results
Recall 3 words after 10 minutes	54% of mild to moderately confused performed abnormally (clinically judged)
WMS: Logical Memory, Paired-Associates, Visual Reproduction, and MQ	Visual reproduction improved after successful treatment; no other significant test score changes after treatment
Paired-Associates, BVRT & Memory-for-Designs	Paired-Associates & BVRT significantly below VIQ before; Paired-Associates performance increased postdialysis; BVRT consistent improvement trend 6 & 12 months after
WMS: Logical Memory & Visual Reproduction, & on Word List Learning, Facial Memory, Symbol-Digit Paired Associates	Nondialyzed impaired on Facial Memory relative to other groups Logical memory & Visual Reproduction relative to controls only
Orientation to time, personal information & place, Presidents Test, Digit Supraspan, & BVRT	Confusional patients were more disoriented & had a higher rate of failure on all memory tests than RHD & controls
WMS: Paired-Associate learning	No differences 1, 24, 42, or 66 hours after dialysis
WMS	Group 1 improved on Logical Memory-Delay; otherwise no significant results
WMS	Significantly lower MQs in neurologically impaired Wilson's disease than other groups; no group differences on Logical Memory, Paired-Associates, or Visual Reproduction
Paired-Associates, Memory-for-Designs, BVRT	Severe EEG-slowed group worse than normal EEGs on all tests; mildly slowed EEGs worse than normal EEGs on Memory-for-Designs
BVRT	Groups 1 & 3 performed worse than the other groups
Visual memory (tachystoscopic numbers)	Significant improvement from before to after dialysis
Recall of recent presidents, recall of 3 cities after 15 minutes	46% clinically judged impaired for presidents recall; 31% clinically judged impaired for city recall
3-minute retention & remote events recall	3-minute retention clinically judged impaired lasting up to 6 years; remote memory was normal
Abbreviated WMS Logical Memory, Visual Reproduction, & Paired Associates (all immediate & delay) and Supraspan	Significantly more alcoholic cirrhotics failed these tests than controls; no differences among cirrhotics with other etiologies
Continuous auditory-verbal memory task	High azotemics & dialysands performed significantly more poorly than controls
Recognition of 20 words & 20 pictures at 1 minute and 1 hour	High anticonvulsant levels significantly worse on both tests at 1-minute recognition, but not at 1-hour delay
Immediate & delayed recall of both 4 geometric designs & paired-associates	All tests & conditions showed improvement 6 months after shunting
WMS: Logical Memory & Paired-Associates, Digit Supraspan Learning, & BVRT	Substantial improvements following detoxification on all memory tests

functions of the mesial temporal lobe structures underlying memory consolidation. New learning is typically defective in acute confusional states despite the type of underlying medical disorder, and it appears that the more severe the illness, the greater the memory impairment.

Intellectual Functions

In keeping with the multifactorial nature of the WAIS, investigations of testable toxic and metabolic patients have found a pattern of differential decline on the various WAIS factors (Matarazzo, 1978; Hamsher, 1984). Studies have consistently reported deficits on the Performance subtests, including both the perceptual-constructional and graphomotor speed factors, with relative preservation among the Verbal IQ (VIQ) subtests. However, when impairment has been reported on the Verbal subtests, it has typically been on Digit Span and Arithmetic (attention-concentration factor) with normal or close to expected levels of performance on Information, Comprehension, Similarities, and Vocabulary (verbal-conceptual factor). These findings may be seen in Table 13.6, which presents recent investigations of intellectual functioning among patients with toxic or metabolic disorders.

In one representative study, Trieschmann and Sand (1971) examined 83 renal failure patients untreated with dialysis and found Performance IQ (PIQ) was statistically below VIQ to a significant degree. Furthermore, every mean Performance subtest scaled score was less than 10, whereas the only Verbal scaled score means below 10 were on Digit Span and Arithmetic. Similarly, Ryan et al. (1981) compared 24 end-stage uremic (kidney failure) patients with 24 patients with mixed neurological disorders and 24 with medical-psychiatric illnesses on the WAIS. There were no significant differences among the three groups on VIQ. Patients with uremia and mixed neurological diagnoses had statistically significant worse PIQs than medical-psychiatric controls. Uremic patients had large VIQ/PIQ splits, and their PIQs were lower than the other two groups. Concerning performance on specific WAIS subtests, uremic patients had significantly higher scaled scores on Information, Comprehension, and Vocabulary, and significantly lower scores on Block Design and Object Assembly, relative to their scaled score means, than the other two groups.

Because many acutely confused patients were clinically observed to show a selective impairment in spatial thinking similar to that seen with right-hemisphere lesions, Lee and Hamsher (1988) compared both types of neurological patients on the various WAIS-R factors (among other tests). Both confused and right-hemisphere disease patients displayed preserved verbal intellectual functioning, but were impaired relative to controls on the attention-concentration (Digit Span and Arithmetic) and perceptual-constructional (Block Design and Picture Arrangement) measures.

Although the toxic causes of mild acute confusion listed in Table 13.6 are all single case studies, the results appear to be similar, if not identical, to the WAIS performance deficits secondary to metabolic etiologies. The three single case studies were examined during and after intoxication due to meprobamate and diazepam, steroids, and propranolol (antihypertensive), and IQ scores showed improvement in all cases after the intoxication resolved. The IQ improvement following toxicity was most apparent on the PIQ scores. Across the three investigations, the VIQ

TABLE 13.6. Intellectual Functioning in Patients with Toxicometabolic Disorders

Source	Subject/Disorders	Test(s)	Results
Blatt & Tsushima (1966)	17 uremic dialysis candidates	WAIS	All performed better on VIQ (M = 112) than PIQ (M = 97). Selected means: Information = 12.7, Comprehension = 13.6, Block Design = 8.4, Digit Symbol = 8.4
Brooker et al. (1984)	Single case of meprobamate & diazepam intoxication	WAIS	Gained 18 VIQ and 32 PIQ standard score points following detoxification
Cummings et al. (1980)	Single case of propranolol (antihypertensive) intoxication	WAIS	Gained 11 VIQ and 22 PIQ standard score points following detoxification
Hagberg (1974)	23 chronic renal failure patients tested before, & 6 and 12 months after, beginning dialysis	Multiple choice similarities, opposites & synonyms, & Wechsler-Bellvue Block Design	No significant change on any verbal test; significant improvement at 6 months on Block Design
Lee & Hamsher (1988)	12 mixed etiology acute confusional states, 10 RHD, & 12 controls	WAIS-R	Both disease groups showed preserved Verbal DQs and were inferior to controls on Attention & Performance DQs, but did not differ from each other
Medalia et al. (1988)	19 Wilson's disease with neurological signs, vs. 15 asymptomatic Wilson's disease, vs. 15 healthy controls	WAIS-R, Dementia Rating Scale	PIQ significantly lower among neurologically impaired Wilson's disease; no differences on PIQ and VIQ; Dementia Rating Scale significantly lower among neurologically impaired Wilson's disease

Ryan et al. (1981)	24 each of end-stage uremia, vs. mixed neurological, vs. medical/psychiatric controls	WAIS	No difference among groups on VIQ; uremics had significantly larger VIQ/PIQ splits with PIQ lower than the other two groups
Schomerus et al. (1981)	15 alcoholic cirrhotics (Group 1), vs. 15 nonalcoholic cirrhotics (Group 2), vs. 10 cirrhotics with EEG slowing (Group 3), vs. 12 alcoholics with pancreatitis (Group 4)	WAIS	No difference among groups on VIQ; PIQ significantly lower in Groups 1 & 3, poorest performances were on Block Design & Digit Symbol
Smith & Smith (1977)	20 alcoholic cirrhotics, vs. 20 alcoholics, vs. 20 hospital controls	WAIS	No difference among groups on information or Vocabulary; significant group differences on Block Design, Object Assembly, & Digit Symbol (Group 1 < Group 2 < Group 3)
Trieschmann & Sand (1971)	83 renal failure patients untreated with dialysis	WAIS	PIQ (M = 97.7) significantly below VIQ (M = 103.8); every mean Performance subtest was < 10 while only Verbal scores < 10 were Digit Span & Arithmetic
Varney et al. (1984)	6 patients with reversible steroid dementia	WAIS	Greater improvement in PIQ (+14.5) than VIQ (+8) after detoxification

Note: WAIS = Wechsler Adult Intelligence Scale; VIQ = verbal intelligence quotient; PIQ = Performance intelligence quotient; RHD = right-hemisphere disease; EEG = electroencephalography.

score improvement ranged from 8 to 18 IQ points (M = 12.3), whereas PIQ score improvements ranged from 14.5 to 32 IQ points (M = 22.8). In conjunction with the methodologically better controlled WAIS studies dealing with metabolic derangement, these case examples clearly show the greater vulnerability of the WAIS Performance subtests, relative to the Verbal subtests, to the effects of toxicometabolic disorders.

As with the other areas of neurobehavioral functioning such as attention and memory, disruption of the perceptual-constructional (Performance) subtests of the WAIS seems to be greater as the severity of the medical disorder increases. This was shown in the Schomerus et al. (1981) investigation where PIQ was significantly lower (especially Block Design and Digit Symbol) among cirrhotics with abnormally slowed EEGs and alcoholic cirrhotics as compared to nonalcoholic cirrhotics and patients with alcoholic pancreatitis. Similarly, Hagberg (1974) examined 21 chronic renal failure patients before and 6 months after beginning hemodialysis. Results indicated a consistent trend among all tests toward better performance as treatment progressed and a significant increase in performance on Wechsler-Bellevue Block Design.

The severity of the metabolic disorder is also related to the degree of impairment on WAIS Attention-Concentration and Performance subtests. Modest correlations have been reported between BUN and serum creatinine (biologic fluid measures of kidney function) and Digit Span forwards (BUN, $r = -.45, p = .05$; creatinine, $r = -.18, p = .25$) and Digit Symbol (BUN, $r = -.56, p$ .02; creatinine, $r = -.41, p = .06$) among 18 nondialyzed renal outpatients (Hart et al., 1983).

In summary, investigations of general intellectual functioning (WAIS) in acute confusional states due to toxic or metabolic disorders consistently show a pattern of impairment on the Performance subtests, poor performances on Digit Span and Arithmetic, and normal performance on the remaining Verbal subtests (i.e., Information, Comprehension, Similarities, and Vocabulary). This pattern of WAIS performance has been reported across a variety of medical disorders, including drug intoxication, alcoholic and nonalcoholic cirrhosis, chronic renal failure, neurologically impaired patients with Wilson's disease, thyroid disease, and normal-pressure hydrocephalus. Furthermore, the WAIS performance pattern tends to vary directly with the severity of medical disorder.

Language

Little research has examined speech and language disturbances in toxic and metabolic disorders. Recent investigations that have explicitly examined speech and language among patients with acute confusional states are given in Table 13.7, and as can be seen, results have been disparate. This is likely due to inconsistent methods used in the various studies including such problems as the use of different dependent measures, noncomparable or no control groups, and varying severity levels of the medical condition under consideration.

With these caveats in mind, speech and language functions are normal, for the most part, in patients with mild encephalopathies and mild medication toxicity. This is particularly true for fluency of spontaneous speech, visual confrontational naming, and repetition, and reports of paraphasias in running speech are rare if

TABLE 13.7. Speech and Language Test Results in Patients with Toxicometabolic Disorders

Source	Subjects/Disorders	Test(s)	Results
Chedru & Geschwind (1972)	24 patients with acute confusion of varying etiologies	Spontaneous Speech, Object Naming, Spelling, Comprehension, Repetition, Reading, Writing, and Animal Fluency	Percentage abnormal performance (judged clinically): spontaneous Speech (0%), Naming (50%), Spelling (37%), Comprehension (12%), Repetition (46%), Reading (75%), Writing (92%), Animal Fluency (92%)
Lee & Hamsher (1988)	12 mixed etiology acute confusional states, vs. 10 RHD, vs. 12 controls	MAE: Visual Naming, Word Fluency, Token Test	Acutely confused patients showed high rate of failure on Token Test with relatively normal performance on the other language tests
Medalia et al. (1988)	19 Wilson's disease with neurological signs, vs. 15 asymptomatic Wilson's disease, vs. 15 healthy controls	Boston Naming Test, Animal Fluency (90 seconds)	No significant differences among groups for either test
Ryan et al. (1981)	16 renal failure, vs. 16 dialysis, vs. 15 medical/psychiatric controls	Aphasia Screening Test from the Halstead-Reitan battery	Both patient groups performed significantly worse than controls but did not differ statistically from each other
Tarter et al. (1987)	123 cirrhotics (some with "mild encephalopathy") vs. 14 chronic disease (Crohn's) controls	Fluency, Confrontational Naming, Descriptive Naming (from BDAE) & Token Test	No difference between cirrhosis of various etiologies and controls on any language test
Varney et al. (1984)	6 patients with reversible steroid dementia	MAE: Word Fluency	Substantial improvement from toxic (score = 6) to nontoxic (score = 12.5) state

Note: RHD = right-hemisphere disease; MAE = Multilingual Aphasia Examination; BDAE = Boston Diagnostic Aphasia Examination.

not nonexistent. These results are in keeping with the relative preservation of verbal-conceptual abilities on the WAIS found among acutely confused patients. However, deficits of aural comprehension (following complex commands), verbal and semantic fluency, and reading and writing have been more consistently, although not invariably, reported among the mild toxicometabolic disorders.

Chedru and Geschwind (1972b) examined the writing samples of 34 acute confusional patients of various etiologies (delirium tremens, 10 cases; hepatic encephalopathy, 6; Wernicke's encephalopathy, 4; acute alcohol intoxication, 1; barbiturate intoxication, 1; immediately following electroconvulsive therapy, 10; and due to administration of intravenous barbiturates, 2) and found a clinically judged impairment of writing in 33 of the 34 patients. The writing disorder involved the motor and spatial aspects of writing as well as spelling and syntax. Agraphia is a transient phenomenon that disappears when the acute confusional state has cleared. In a related study, Chedru and Geschwind (1972a) examined a subset ($n = 24$) of the 34 patients who were the subject of the above report and determined through clinical judgment that 92% of patients showed abnormal performances on the motor and spatial aspects of writing and on animal fluency. In addition, these authors reported the following percentages of abnormal language test performance: Spontaneous Speech, 0%; Naming, 50%; Oral Spelling, 37%; Comprehension, 12%; Repetition, 46%; and Reading, 75%.

Using the word fluency, confrontational naming, and responsive naming measures from the Boston Diagnostic Aphasia Examination (BDAE) and an unspecified version of the Token Test, Tarter et al. (1987) found no differences among cirrhotic patients with different etiologies of liver disease on any measure. Linguistic functions were generally preserved in comparison with psychometric measures of concentration, spatial reasoning, perceptual-motor and learning and memory. However, 31% to 38% of the two groups with greatest disease severity—namely, sober alcoholics with Laënnec's cirrhosis and postnecrotic (viral) cirrhosis—showed abnormal performances that were particular to the Token Test and word fluency and that were well below the other patient groups.

Lee and Hamsher (1988) examined 12 patients with confusional states due to toxicometabolic encephalopathies on the Visual Naming, Token Test, and Word Fluency subtests of the Multilingual Aphasia Examination (MAE). In comparison with right-hemisphere disease and control patients, 89% of the toxicometabolic patients performed at or below the fourth percentile on the Token Test, whereas no patient in either of the other groups failed on the Token Test. A small minority of toxicometabolic patients performed below normative expectations on the MAE Visual Naming (25% failure) and Associative Word Fluency (10% failure), demonstrating that a specific deficit in following complex commands is an important psychometric sign of confusion.

In summary, investigators have examined the important dimensions of linguistic functioning among toxicometabolic confusional state patients. The few studies that specifically addressed language in relation to other areas of cognitive function generally agree that linguistic functions are relatively well preserved, especially in comparison with concentration, learning and memory, and visuo-spatial problem solving. Although aphasic disorders are absent in acute confusional states secondary to toxic or metabolic disorders, impairments in following complex commands on such tests as the Token Test and in the motor and spatial aspects of writing have been documented. Results concerning associative word fluency vary and may depend upon such factors as severity of illness or degree of diffuse cerebral dysfunction.

Visuospatial, Visuoperceptual, and Constructional Performance

In comparison with attention, learning and memory, and intellectual functioning, there have been few studies explicitly measuring visuoperception, spatial reasoning, and constructional performance. Some of these investigations are presented in Table 13.8. Many WAIS Performance subtests measure these constructs, and results of investigations concerning how patients with toxicometabolic disorders perform on WAIS Performance subtests were presented in Table 13.6.

Examination of Tables 13.6 and 13.8 show that toxicometabolic patients with acute confusion consistently demonstrate impairments on tasks measuring visuo-spatial functioning and constructional performance. Spatial impairment and constructional difficulties have been reported in patients with liver disease (Rehnstrom et al., 1977; Tarter et al., 1987), renal failure (Ryan et al., 1981; Spehr et al., 1977), normal-pressure hydrocephalus (Thomsen et al., 1986), and among patients with acute confusional states from a variety of metabolic disorders and toxic disturbances (Chedru & Geschwind, 1972a; Lee & Hamsher, 1988). However, results have been inconsistent concerning deficits in visuoperception. The results obtained appear to depend upon the method of measurement employed and illness severity of the patients under investigation.

For example, Rehnstrom et al. (1977) administered a block design test (with bonus points for rapid performances) and a visual discrimination task to 41 cirrhotic patients with encephalopathy who were divided into one of three groups based upon degree of EEG slowing. The visual discrimination task required the patient to choose one out of five geometric figures that differed from the other four. On both block design and visual discrimination, the severely slowed EEG group performed significantly below the mildly slowed EEG group who, in turn, performed significantly more poorly than controls. On the visuoperceptive task, both abnormal EEG groups performed significantly more poorly than normals. Thus, among liver disease patients with mild to moderate encephalopathy, Rehnstrom et al. (1977) suggest there are deficits involving spatial thinking, constructional performance, and visuoperception. Similarly, Spehr et al. (1977) found improvement after the onset of dialysis in 20 renal failure patients with "moderate" encephalopathy on a visual discrimination task measured by tachistoscopic presentation of numbers.

Using different visuoperceptive tasks, other investigations have suggested that visual discrimination abilities are intact among confused toxicometabolic patients. A dissociation between spatial and visuoperceptive performances is reported by Chedru and Geschwind (1972a) and Lee and Hamsher (1988). The majority (71%) of acutely confused patients performed abnormally when asked to copy a Necker cube and two Bender-Gestalt figures. In contrast to these constructional difficulties, only 10 of 24 patients showed mild deficits during the visuoperceptive task— namely, recognition of Poppelreuter's hidden figures (Chedru & Geschwind, 1972a). These authors stated that although 10 patients performed poorly, the accurate description of the pictures used in this test showed that visual recognition was not a problem.

TABLE 13.8. Visuoperceptive, Visuoconstructive, and Visuospatial Functioning in Patients with Toxicometabolic Disorders

Source	Subjects/Disorders	Test(s)	Results
Chedru & Geschwind (1972)	24 patients with acute confusion of varying etiologies	Copying a cube & 2 Bender-Gestalt designs and recognition of hidden figures (Poppelreuter Test)	71% of patients performed abnormally (clinically judged) on copying, whereas patients had only "mild difficulties" with hidden figures
Lee & Hamsher (1988)	12 mixed etiology acute confusional states, vs. 10 RHD, vs. 12 controls	Judgment of Line Orientation, 3-Dimensional Constructional Praxis, Line Cancellation Test & Facial Recognition Test	Both confused & RHD patients performed below controls, but did not differ from each other on 3-Dimensional Constructional Praxis, Judgment of Line Orientation, & Line Cancellation Test; only RHD patients differed from controls on Facial Recognition Test
Rehnstrom et al. (1977)	41 chronic cirrhotics with encephalopathy divided into 3 groups based upon degree of EEG slowing.	Block Design, Visual Discrimination Task	Severely slowed EEGs performed worse than mildly slowed EEGs who in turn performed worse than the normal EEG group on both tasks
Ryan et al. (1981)	16 renal failure, vs. 16 dialysis, vs. 16 medical/psychiatric controls	Spatial Relations Test of Russell, Neuringer & Goldstein	Renal failures performed significantly worse than dialysis & control patients who did not differ from one another
Spehr et al. (1977)	20 renal failure patients most with "moderate" encephalopathy	Visual discrimination measured by tachistoscopic presentation of numbers	Significant improvement from before to after dialysis
Tarter et al. (1987)	123 cirrhotics (some with "mild encephalopathy") vs. 14 chronic disease (Crohn's) controls	Star-Tracing, WAIS Block Design, Tactual Performance Test, Trails A & B	Alcoholic & postnecrotic cirrhotics significantly impaired compared with controls
Thomsen et al. (1986)	8 normal-pressure hydrocephalics who improved after shunting	9 Block Designs	Patients improved by 34 mean T-score points (greater than 3 SD), 6 months after shunting

Note: RHD = right-hemisphere disease; EEG = electroencephalography; WAIS = Wechsler Adult Intelligence Scale; SD = standard deviations.

Lee and Hamsher (1988) report similar results among 12 toxicometabolic patients with acute confusion. Acute confusional patients performed significantly more poorly than controls on tests of construction, spatial judgment, and on a cancellation task, but did not differ from controls on a test of visuoperception (Facial Recognition Test [Hamsher, Levin, & Benton, 1979]). Only 11% of toxicometabolic patients performed at or below the 4th percentile as compared, for example, to Judgment of Line Orientation, where 57% of patients performed below normative expectations.

Summarizing these results, impairments of spatial thinking and constructional praxis have been clearly established as a common cognitive defect in acutely confused patients secondary to toxic or metabolic disturbances. The issue of whether deficits in visuoperception exist among these patients continues to be debated. One confounding factor is that patients with severe medical illnesses resulting in severe confusional states show greater disruption of attention and concentration. Because most tests of visuoperception require sustained attention, patients with severe confusion will most likely perform poorly on perceptual tests for other than perceptual reasons. Studies that reported normal visuoperception examined patients whose confusion was caused by many different medical illnesses. In contrast, investigations that found a visuoperceptive impairment studied homogeneous groups of liver or kidney disease patients. Thus, the results suggesting little or no visuoperceptive deficit are probably more representative, and hence, more likely to be valid.

Abstraction, Complex Problem Solving, and Concept Formation

The so-called higher cognitive functions, also referred to as *executive* functions, include such processes as abstraction, complex problem solving, concept formation, reasoning, planning, organization, and the use of feedback to guide ongoing performance. Because tests designed to measure executive functions depend upon many subcomponent cognitive functions (such as attention-concentration, vigilance, and language and visuo-spatial functions), it should not be surprising that patients with toxic or metabolic encephalopathy have been reported to perform deficiently on these tests. Probably due to this confounding difficulty in test interpretation, few studies of acute confusional states have specifically examined these higher cognitive functions. Table 13.9 briefly reviews several investigations of tests of higher cognitive functions among toxic or metabolic disordered patients.

Although these studies vary widely concerning type of measurement and degree of methodological rigor, the fact that all but one found deficits among higher cognitive function tests suggests a robust result. Again, the cognitive reasons for these test failures are undoubtedly multiple and, therefore, these results should not be simply interpreted as representing focal involvement of the frontal lobes. As with the cognitive domains discussed earlier, impairment on tests of abstraction, complex problem solving, and concept formation among toxicometabolic patients with confusion appears regardless of the type of underlying medical condition. Furthermore, deficits tend to be greater as the severity of the disease increases. Using six WAIS-type similarity questions, five Gorham Proverbs Test items, and the number of animals spontaneously generated in 60 seconds as measures of abstract thought, Chedru and Geschwind (1972a) clinically judged 20% of 24 acute

TABLE 13.9. Problem Solving, Abstraction, and Concept Formation in Patients with Toxicometabolic Disorders

Source	Subjects/Disorders	Test(s)	Results
Brooker et al. (1984)	Case study of meprobamate & diazepam intoxication	Category Test of Halstead-Reitan battery	Improved from 121 errors during intoxication to 26 errors (normal performance) following detoxification
Chedru & Geschwind (1972)	24 acute confusional patients of varying etiologies	"Abstract thought" measured by 6 WAIS Similarities-type & 5 Gorham Proverb test items; Animal Fluency (60 seconds)	Percentage judged abnormal; Similarities, 20%; Proverbs, 20%; Fluency, 92%
Cochran et al. (1978)	Case study during temporal arteritis	Stanford-Binet: Picture Absurdities	Performance was "extremely poor"
McDaniel (1971)	17 intermittent dialysands, vs. 10 postrenal transplants, vs. 32 healthy controls	Modified WCST	Intermittent dialysands had significantly greater error rates & greater number of sorts required for each solution; creatinine & potassium correlated ($r = .75$) with poor WCST performance
Medalia et al. (1988)	19 Wilson's disease with neurological signs, vs. 15 asymptomatic Wilson's disease, vs. 15 controls	WCST and Animal Fluency (90 seconds)	No significant differences between groups on either test
Rehnstrom et al. (1977)	41 chronic cirrhotics with encephalopathy divided into 3 groups based upon degree of EEG slowing.	Stroop Color-Word Test: interference trial	Both EEG-slowed groups differed from controls but not from each other
Ryan et al. (1981)	16 renal failure, vs. 16 dialysis, vs. 16 medical/psychiatric controls	Category Test	Uremic & dialysis performed significantly below controls, but did not differ significantly from each other
Starkman & Schteingart (1981)	35 patients with Cushing's syndrome	Proverb interpretation	46% of patients clinically judged impaired
Thomsen et al. (1986)	8 normal-pressure hydrocephalics who improved with shunting	Interpretation of 6 proverbs	Improved by 20 mean T-score points (2 SD) 6 months after shunting

Note: WAIS = Wechsler Adult Intelligence Scale; WCST = Wisconsin Card Sorting Test; EEG = electroencephalography; SD = standard deviation.

confusional patients to be abnormal on Similarities and Proverbs and 92% as performing abnormally on Animal Fluency. Starkman and Schteingart (1981) found abnormal proverb interpretation among 35 patients with Cushing's syndrome, clinically judging 46% of them to be impaired. Thomsen et al. (1986) reported eight normal-pressure hydrocephalus patients improved on interpreting six proverbs by 20 T-score points (2 SD) 6 months after shunting. Reports of difficulties in proverb interpretation are probably closely related to the disorganized thinking or impairment in the logical stream of thought that is a defining feature of acute confusional states.

Ryan et al. (1981) administered the Category Test to patients with renal failure, patients on kidney dialysis, and medical/psychiatric controls. The renal failure and dialysis patients performed significantly below controls but did not differ from each other. Similarly, Brooker et al. (1984) reported a patient with meprobamate and diazepam intoxication made 121 errors on the Category Test. When this patient was reexamined after meprobamate and diazepam had been discontinued for 6 months, the patient performed normally (26 errors) on the Category Test. Impaired attention and concentration, visuospatial reasoning, and organization of thinking may contribute to the difficulties in concept formation and abstraction ability as measured in the Category Test. However, concept formation and abstraction ability may be directly impaired as well.

The establishment, maintenance, and switching of mental sets as measured by the Wisconsin Card Sorting Test (WCST) have been inconsistently reported to be impaired in patients with toxic and metabolic disorders. Using a modified WCST (must match a 0.5-second stimulus from a multiple choice array of like stimuli and switch without warning from color to form, for example, after 10 consecutive correct matches) to examine 17 intermittent dialysis, 10 after renal transplant, and 32 healthy control patients, McDaniel (1971) reported that the intermittent dialysis patients had significantly higher error rates and required significantly greater number of sorts for each solution than controls while no differences were obtained between the transplant and control patients. Further, biological fluid measures of disease severity (serum creatinine and potassium levels) were significantly correlated ($r = .75$) with poor WCST performance (McDaniel, 1971). Medalia et al. (1988) found no differences on a standard WCST and animal fluency task among 19 neurologically impaired Wilson's disease patients, 12 asymptomatic Wilson's disease patients, and 15 normal controls. The divergent findings in these two studies can most likely be accounted for by the relatively mild mental impairment among the Wilson's disease patients and the greater difficulty level caused by rapid (0.5-second) stimulus exposure times and measurement of response latencies on the modified card sorting test used by McDaniel (1971).

The influence of a rapid response rate requirement on perceptual and cognitive complexity also may be seen on the Stroop Color-Word Test, where the patient is to name the color of a color word that is printed in a color incongruous with the word (e.g., RED printed in the color green). Besides the rapid visual perceptual processing, attention, and vigilance requirements of this task, it also demands that the patient inhibit an overlearned response tendency—namely, to read the printed word. Stroop interference effects are perhaps most sensitive to left-hemisphere injuries, especially among patients with anterior (frontal) injuries (Perret, 1974). Rehnstrom et al. (1977) reported that patients with hepatic encephalopathy were

significantly slower to read the color of the color words on the Stroop than were cirrhotic patients without encephalopathy.

In summary, patients with mild acute confusional states secondary to toxic or metabolic disorders have consistently been found to perform abnormally on tests of abstraction, complex problem solving, and concept formation. Although higher cognitive functions may be affected directly by cellular disruption of the entire brain, including the frontal lobes, deficits of executive functions also may be explained by a failure of the subcomponent cognitive requirements of the task. Many of these executive tasks demand adequate attention, concentration, vigilance, learning and memory, and visuospatial reasoning for successful performance. Since these "lower" supportive cognitive functions are commonly impaired in the toxicometabolic disorders, deficits in these cognitive domains may be partially responsible for abnormal performances on executive function tests. However much these supportive cognitive abilities contribute to executive function test failures, they probably do not fully explain these test failures. The fact that disorganized thinking, or impairment in the logical stream of thought, is a defining feature of acute confusional states would suggest there are (in addition to impairments of the more basic functions such as attention) primary deficits of higher cognitive functions.

Disorders of Emotion and Mood

Emotional disturbances are commonly observed in patients with acute confusional states secondary to toxic and metabolic disorders. Emotional reactions tend to vary in quality and intensity throughout the day and during a single episode of acute confusion (Lipowski, 1990). An early investigation noted anxiety, apprehension, and fear in all patients to some extent, but also related that depression was observed in most cases (Wolff & Curran, 1935). Farber (1959) found depression to be the most common emotional disturbance in delirium (40% of cases), although apathy was also common, being observed in 30% of patients. In the face of frightening stimuli, such as visual hallucinations or being in an unfamiliar setting like an intensive care unit, anxiety and fear may give way to panic. Similarly, minor frustration and anger may intensify into agitation and rage. Thus, the continuum of disturbances of emotion and mood may range from apathy to panic, rage, or elation (Lipowski, 1990).

Recent investigators have reiterated that depression is the most common psychiatric problem encountered among patients with toxicometabolic disorders. Stewart and Stewart (1979) have stated depression is the most common emotional disorder in those with chronic renal disease. Kaplan-DeNour and Czaczkes (1974) found one third of renal dialysis treatment patients showed mild to moderate depression and anxiety. Furthermore, Abram, Moore, and Westervelt (1971) reported that suicide is 100 times greater for dialysis patients than for the average population. Some of these dialysis patients, however, probably would not meet diagnostic criteria for an acute confusional state. A high prevalence of depression also has been reported among patients with acute confusional states due to medical illnesses other than renal disease (e.g., Engel & Romano, 1959). Thus, the type of emotional reaction is probably not particular to any specific disease state producing an acute confusional state. Because there are many more medical conditions causing confusion than consequent emotional disturbances, the alterations of mood and emotion may be viewed as a final common pathway for many different medical diseases.

Although there is very little evidence that the type of emotional reaction is particular to any specific disease state producing an acute confusional state, this issue has not been well studied. As Lipowski (1967) has pointed out, there are preliminary data that certain neurotoxins or diseases predispose patients toward certain gross categories of behavior, such as overresponsiveness or underresponsiveness. For example, the anticholinergic agent, trihexyphenidyl (Artane), may tend to produce hyperactivity (Stephens, 1967). Delirium tremens has been associated with hyperactivity and overalertness, and anxiety and fearfulness are the most likely emotions to dominate the clinical picture (Cutshall, 1965). Additionally, in patients with hepatic encephalopathy, depression and euphoria are the most common moods, whereas anxiety is unusual (Davidson & Solomon, 1958). Thus, in a very general sense, some neurotoxins and medical illnesses may predispose patients toward certain types of emotional disturbance as part of an acute confusional state.

Lipowski (1990) reported that the more intense emotions, such as fear and anger, tend to accompany the hyperactive-hyperalert variant of acute confusional states and are frequently associated with hallucinations, delusions, and signs of autonomic hyperactivity including dilated pupils, pallor or flushing of the face, sweating, tachycardia, and elevated blood pressure. Conversely, the hypoactive-hypoalert patient is more likely to be apathetic or depressed and to not hallucinate, according to Lipowski (1990).

The cause of the specific emotional disturbances in acute confusional states is unknown. However, most of the probable determinants have been discussed by other authors (e.g., Lipowski, 1990). These include release or exaggeration of premorbid personality traits, psychological stress of suffering from a severe, life-threatening, or perhaps terminal medical illness, the situational and environmental context in which the delirium occurs, and perhaps the direct effects of the disease on the limbic system itself (Lipowski, 1967). Few experimental data exist in support of these various possible determinants.

In summary, disorders of emotion and mood are common in acute confusional states secondary to toxic or metabolic disorders. The alterations of emotion and mood most often observed include depression, elation, anxiety, fear, anger, apathy, and indifference. In the face of frightening stimuli such as visual hallucinations or frustrating circumstances such as physical restraint, these basic moods or emotions may intensify into panic, agitation, or rage. Although there is little evidence that the type of emotional disturbance is particular to any specific disease state producing an acute confusional state, preliminary data suggest certain neurotoxins or diseases may predispose patients toward certain gross categories of behavior, such as overresponsiveness or underresponsiveness. The cause of specific emotional reactions is unknown, but authors have suggested premorbid personality, psychological stress associated with the medical illness, physical and emotional context in which the delirium occurs, and perhaps the direct effects of the disease of the limbic system itself.

Management of Acute Confusional States

Because only those patients who have mild acute confusional states can cooperate with extended psychometric testing, neuropsychologists are most likely to encounter these patients when they are either entering delirium or recovering from the medical insult. However, in the inpatient setting neuropsychologists may be asked to assess moderate to severely confused patients who are restless, agitated, and who show florid psychotic features such as those often seen immediately following traumatic head injury or in delirium tremens. Of course, formal neuropsychological assessment would be superfluous in such cases, but the neuropsychologist may nevertheless provide a brief bedside evaluation designed to determine such things as the degree of disorientation and what, if anything, the patient is able to comprehend linguistically. Additionally, many supportive recommendations detailed below would be applicable whether the acute confusional state is considered severe or mild.

The primary consideration in all acute confusional states is the necessity to find the underlying medical cause and correct it. This is essentially the physician's responsibility, although the neuropsychologist may contribute by taking a thorough history (especially of recent exposure to medicines, alcohol, or other toxins) from the patient or a family member. The underlying medical causative factor may not be identified in 10% to 20% of elderly delirious patients (Flint & Richards, 1956, cited in Lipowski, 1984).

When it has been determined that the patient's neurobehavioral condition is an acute confusional state and not dementia or confusion superimposed upon dementia, this should be communicated to the patient and family. This can reassure them that the condition will not be permanent and that return of normal and baseline cognitive and personality functioning may be expected. General supportive and protective measures also should be undertaken and have been detailed elsewhere (e.g., Lipowski, 1980, 1984, 1985, 1990; Adams & Victor, 1983; Wells, 1985). The physical environment should be neither overstimulating nor understimulating. A quiet, well-lighted room shielded from extraneous, loud, or sudden noises is desirable. Avoidance of a completely darkened room at night by using dimmed light may help to prevent hallucinations, disorientation to place and time, and anxiety and fear. Because unfamiliarity can breed fear and confusion, creating an environment where trusted friends or family are often present and where the patient is surrounded with familiar things, such as photographs brought from home, can help to relax and reassure the patient.

Playing soft music or certain television shows that the patient knows and enjoys may have a soothing effect. Quiet conversation can preserve important social stimulation and also may help to calm the patient. Calendars and clocks should be prominently displayed and nursing staff and family members should be instructed to frequently orient the patient to time, place, and medical circumstances.

The patient should be closely monitored because the medical condition may worsen, and immediate medical attention may be necessary. Monitoring also may be important because the patient could inadvertently place themselves in potentially hazardous circumstances or wander off and become lost. Assurance of adequate nutrition, fluid intake, rest and sleep, as well as compliance with medical treatment is important. Sleep disturbance is common in acute confusional states and may help prolong the alterations of mental status. Finally, an altered mental status may continue even after the offending underlying medical condition has been identified and effectively treated, especially in the elderly. This should not be interpreted to mean that the patient will necessarily be left with permanent cognitive impairments.

Older patients may take many weeks after successful treatment to recover fully; therefore, followup evaluations are an important part of case management.

Acknowledgments

The authors are grateful to and wish to acknowledge the contribution of Dr. Kerry deS. Hamsher for many of the ideas contained in the chapter. We thank Patricia A. Downs for her help with manuscript preparation.

References

Abram, H. A., Moore, G. L., & Westervelt, F. W. (1971). Suicidal behavior in chronic dialysis patients. *American Journal of Psychiatry*, *127*, 1199–1204.

Adams, R. D., & Victor, M. (1983). Delirium and other confusional states. In R. G. Petersdorf, R. D. Adams, E. Braunwald, K. J. Isselbacher, J. B. Martin, and J. D. Wilson (Eds.), *Harrison's principles of internal medicine* (10th ed., pp. 131–136). New York: McGraw-Hill.

Adams, R. D., & Victor, M. (1989). *Principles of neurology* (4th ed., pp. 323–333). New York: McGraw-Hill.

Adler, S. (1974). Methyldopa-induced decreased in mental activity. *Journal of the American Medical Association*, *230*, 1428–1429.

Alexander, L., Hightower, M. G., Anderson, R. P., & Snow, N. E. (1980). Suitability of vigilance test data as a neurobehavioral measure of uremic status. *Perceptual and Motor Skills*, *50*, 131–135.

Ambrosetto, G., Tassinari, C. A., Baruzzi, A., & Lugaresi, E. (1977). Phenytoin encephalopathy as probable idiosyncratic reaction: Case report. *Epilepsia*, *18*, 405–408.

American Psychiatric Association. (1987). *Diagnostic and statistical manual of mental disorders* (3rd ed., rev.). Washington, DC: Author.

Amit, R. (1988). Acute confusional state in childhood. *Child's Nervous System*, *4*, 255–258.

Blass, J. P., Gibson, G. E., Duffy, T. E., & Plum, F. (1981). Cholinergic dysfunction: A common denominator in metabolic encephalopathies. In G. Pepeu & H. Ladinsky (Eds.), *Cholinergic mechanisms* (pp. 921–928). New York: Plenum Press.

Blatt, B., & Tsushima, W. T. (1966). A psychological survey of uremic patients being considered for the chronic hemodialysis program: Intellectual and emotional patterns in uremic patients. *Nephron*, *3*, 206–208.

Brooker, A. E., Wiens, A. N., & Wiens, D. A. (1984). Impaired brain functions due to diazepam and meprobamate abuse in a 53 year old male. *Journal of Nervous and Mental Disease*, *172*, 498–501.

Caranasos, G. J., Stewart, R. B., & Cluff, L. E. (1974). Drug-induced illness leading to hospitalization. *Journal of the American Medical Association*, *228*, 713–717.

Carney, M. W. P. (1971). Five cases of bromism. *Lancet*, *2*, 523–524.

Chedru, F., & Geschwind, N. (1972a). Disorders of higher cortical functions in acute confusional states. *Cortex*, *10*, 395–411.

Chedru, F., & Geschwind, N. (1972b). Writing disturbances in acute confusional states. *Neuropsychologia*, *10*, 343–353.

Chisholm, S. E., Doniston, O. L., Igrisan, R. M., & Barbus, A. J. (1982). Prevalence of confusion in elderly hospitalized patients. *Gerontological Nursing*, *8*, 87–96.

Cochran, J. W., Fox, J. H., & Kelly, M. P. (1978). Reversible mental symptoms in temporal arteritis. *Journal of Nervous and Mental Disease*, *166*, 446–447.

Cummings, J. L., Hebben, N. A., Obler, L., & Leonard, P. (1980). Nonaphasic misnaming and other neurobehavior features of an unusual toxic encephalopathy: Case study. *Cortex, 16,* 315–323.

Cutshall, B. J. (1965). The Saunders-Sutton syndrome: An analysis of delirium tremens. *Quarterly Journal of Studies on Alcohol, 26,* 423–448.

Daniel, W. F., Crovitz, H. F., & Weiner, R. D. (1987). Neuropsychological aspects of disorientation. *Cortex, 23,* 169–187.

Davidson, E. A., & Solomon, P. (1958). The differentiation of delirium tremens from impending hepatic coma. *Journal of Mental Science, 104,* 326–333.

Davison, W. (1978). Neurological and mental disturbances due to drugs. *Age and Ageing, 7,* (Suppl.), 119–130.

Doty, E. J. (1946). The incidence and treatment of delirious reactions in later life. *Geriatrics, 1,* 21–26.

Elithorn, A., Lunzer, M., & Weinman, J. (1975). Cognitive deficits associated with chronic hepatic encephalopathy and their response to levodopa. *Journal of Neurology, Neurosurgery and Psychiatry, 38,* 794–798.

Elsass, P., Lund, Y., & Rankek, L. (1978). Encephalopathy in patients with cirrhosis of the liver. A neuropsychological study. *Scandinavian Journal of Gastroenterology, 13,* 241–247.

Engel, G. L., & Romano, J. (1959). Delirium, a syndrome of cerebral insufficiency. *Journal of Chronic Disease, 9,* 260–277.

Erkinjuntti, R., Wikstrom, J., Palo, J., & Autio, L. (1986). Dementia among medical inpatients: Evaluation of 2000 consecutive admissions. *Archives of Internal Medicine, 146,* 1923–1926.

Evans, L. K. (1987). Sundown syndrome in institutionalized elderly. *Journal of the American Geriatrics Society, 35,* 101–108.

Farber, I. J. (1959). Acute brain syndrome. *Diseases of the Nervous System, 20,* 296–299.

Flint, F. J. & Richards, S. M. (1956). Organic basis of confusional states in the elderly. *British Medical Journal, 2,* 1537–1539.

Folstein, M. F., Folstein, S. C., & McHugh, P. R. (1975). Mini-mental state: A practical guide for grading the cognitive state of patients for clinicians. *Journal of Psychiatric Research, 12,* 189–198.

Foreman, M. D. (1989). Confusion in the hospitalized elderly: Incidence, onset and associated factors. *Research in Nursing and Health, 12,* 21–29.

Gaillard, J. M. (1985). Neurochemical regulation of the states of alertness. *Annals of Clinical Research, 17,* 175–184.

Gatewood, J. W., Organ, C. H., Jr., & Mead, B. T. (1975). Mental changes associated with hyperparathyroidism. *American Journal of Psychiatry, 132,* 129–132.

Geschwind, N. (1982). Disorders of attention. A frontier in neuropsychology. *Philosophical Transactions of the Royal Society of London, B298,* 173–185.

Gillick, M. R., Serrell, N. A., & Gillick, L. S. (1982). Adverse consequences of hospitalization in the elderly. *Social Science and Medicine, 16,* 1033–1038.

Ginn, H. E. (1975). Neurobehavioral dysfunction in uremia. *Kidney International, 2,* S217–S221.

Hagberg, B. (1974). A prospective study of patients in chronic hemodialysis-III. Predictive value of intelligence, cognitive deficit and ego defense structures in rehabilitation. *Journal of Psychosomatic Research, 18,* 151–160.

Hamsher, K.deS. (1984). Specialized neuropsychological assessment methods. In G. Goldstein & M. Hersen (Eds.), *Handbook of psychological assessment* (pp. 235–256). New York: Pergamon Press.

Hamsher, K.deS., Levin, H. S., & Benton, A. L. (1979). Facial recognition in patients with focal brain lesions. *Archives of Neurology, 36,* 837–839.

Hart, R. P., Pederson, J. A., Czerwinski, A. W., & Adams, R. L. (1983). Chronic renal failure, dialysis, and neuropsychological function. *Journal of Clinical Neuropsychology*, *4*, 301–312.

Henry, W. D., & Mann, A. M. (1965). Diagnosis and treatment of delirium. *Canadian Medical Association Journal*, *93*, 1156–1166.

Hersch, E. L., & Billings, R. F. (1988). Acute confusional state with status petit mal as a withdrawal syndrome—and five year follow-up. *Canadian Journal of Psychiatry*, *33*, 157–159.

Hobson, J. A., Lydic, R., & Baghodoyan, H. A. (1986). Evolving concepts of sleep cycle generation: From brain centers to neuronal populations. *Behavioral and Brain Science*, *9*, 371–448.

Hodkinson, H. M. (1973). Mental impairment in the elderly. *Journal of the Royal College of Physicians of London*, *7*, 305–317.

Hurwitz, N. (1969). Predisposing factors in adverse reactions to drugs. *British Medical Journal*, *1*, 536–539.

Itil, L., & Fink, M. (1966). Anticholinergic drug-induced delirium: Experimental modification, quantitative EEG, and behavioral correlations. *Journal of Nervous and Mental Disease*, *143*, 492–507.

Johnson, J., Sullivan, E., Gottlieb, G., Forciea, M. A., Hogue, C., Sims, R., & Kinosian, B. (1987). Delirium in elderly patients on internal medicine services. *Journal of the American Geriatrics Society*, *35*, 972.

Kaplan-DeNour, A., & Czaczkes, J. W. (1974). Adjustment to chronic hemodialysis. *Israli Journal of Medical Science*, *10*, 498–503.

Kay, D. W. K. (1972). Epidemiological aspects of organic brain disease in the aged. In C. M. Gaitz (Ed.), *Aging and the brain* (pp. 15–27). New York: Plenum Press.

Knee, S. T., & Razani, J. (1974). Acute organic brain syndrome: A complication of disulfiram therapy. *American Journal of Psychiatry*, *131*, 1281–1282.

Koponen, H., Hurri, L., Stenback, U., & Riekkinen, P. J. (1987). Acute confusional states in the elderly: A radiological evaluation. *Acta Psychiatrica Scandinavica*, *76*, 726–731.

Kral, V. A. (1975). Confusional states: Description and management. In J. G. Howells (Ed.), *Perspectives in the psychiatry of old age* (pp. 356–362). New York: Brunner/Mazel.

Learoyd, B. M. (1972). Psychotropic drugs and the elderly patient. *The Medical Journal of Australia*, *1*, 1131–1133.

Lee, G. P., & Hamsher, K.deS. (1988). Neuropsychological findings in toxicometabolic confusional states. *Journal of Clinical and Experimental Neuropsychology*, *10*, 769–778.

Legg, J. F., & Stiff, M. P. (1976). Drug-related test patterns of depressed patients. *Psychopharmacology*, *50*, 205–210.

Levenson, A. J. (Ed.). (1979). *Neuropsychiatric side effects of drugs in the elderly*. New York: Raven Press.

Levkoff, S. E., Besdine, R. W., & Wetle, T. (1986). Acute confusional states (delirium) in the hospitalized elderly. *Annual Review of Gerontology and Geriatrics*, *6*, 1–26.

Lewis, E. G., O'Neill, W. M., Dustman, R. E., & Beck, E. C. (1980). Temporal effects of hemodialysis on measures of neural efficiency. *Kidney International*, *17*, 357–363.

Lezak, M. (1983). *Neuropsychological assessment* (2nd ed.). New York: Oxford University Press.

Liljequist, R., Linnoila, M., & Mattila, M. J. (1974). Effect of two weeks' treatment with chlorimipramine and nortriptyline, alone or in combination with alcohol, on learning and memory. *Psychopharmacologia*, *39*, 181–186.

Lipowski, Z. J. (1967). Delirium, clouding of consciousness and confusion. *Journal of Nervous and Mental Disease*, *145*, 227–255.

Lipowski, Z. J. (1980). Organic mental disorders: Introduction and review of syndromes. In H. I. Kaplan, A. M. Freedman, & B. J. Sadock (Eds.), *Comprehensive textbook of psychiatry*, (3rd ed., pp. 1359–1392). Baltimore: Williams & Wilkins.

Lipowski, Z. J. (1983). Transient cognitive disorders (delirium, acute confusional states) in the elderly. *American Journal of Psychiatry*, *140*, 1426–1436.

Lipowski, Z. J. (1984). Acute confusional states (delirium) in the elderly. In M. L. Albert (Ed.), *Clinical neurology of aging* (pp. 277–297). New York: Oxford University Press.

Lipowski, Z. J. (1985). Delirium (acute confusional state). In J. A. M. Frederiks (Ed.), *Handbook of clinical neurology*, Vol. 2 (*No. 46*), *neurobehavioral disorders* (pp. 523–559). Amsterdam: Elsevier.

Lipowski, Z. J. (1990). *Delirium: Acute confusional states*. New York: Oxford University Press.

Liston E. H. (1982). Delirium in the elderly. *Psychiatric Clinics of North America*, *5*, 49–66.

Mandal, S. K. (1986). Psychiatric side effects of ranitidine. *British Journal of Clinical Practice*, *40*, 260.

Matarazzo, J. D. (1978). *Wechsler's measurement and appraisal of adult intelligence* (5th ed.). New York: Oxford University Press.

McDaniel, J. W. (1971). Metabolic and CNS correlates of cognitive dysfunction with renal failure. *Psychophysiology*, *8*, 704–713.

McKee, D. C., Burnett, G. B., Raft, D. D., Batten, P. G., & Bain, K. P. (1982). Longitudinal study of neuropsychological functioning in patients on chronic hemodialysis: A preliminary report. *Journal of Psychosomatic Research*, *26*, 511–518.

Medalia, A., Isaacs-Glaberman, K., & Scheinberg, I. H. (1988). Neuropsychological impairment in Wilson's disease. *Archives of Neurology*, *45*, 502–504.

Molloy, D. W. (1987). Memory loss, confusion, and disorientation in an elderly woman taking meclizine. *Journal of the American Geriatrics Society*, *35*, 454–456.

Morgane, P. F. (1982). Amine pathways and sleep regulation. *Brain Research Bulletin*, *9*, 743–749.

Morse, R. M., & Litin, E. M. (1969). Postoperative delirium: A study of etiologic factors. *American Journal of Psychiatry*, *126*, 388–395.

Morse, R. M., & Litin, E. M. (1971). The anatomy of delirium. *American Journal of Psychiatry*, *128*, 111–116.

Mullally, W. J., Ronthal, M., Huff, K., & Geschwind, N. (1989). Chronic confusional state. *New Jersey Medicine*, *86*, 541–544.

Parker, D. L., & Hodge, J. R. (1967). Delirium in a coronary care unit. *Journal of the American Medical Association*, *201*, 702–703.

Perlick, D., Stastny, P., Katz, I., Mayer, M., & Mattis, S. (1986). Memory deficits and anticholinergic levels in chronic schizophrenia. *American Journal of Psychiatry*, *143*, 230–232.

Perret, E. (1974). The left frontal lobe of man and the suppression of habitual responses in verbal categorical behavior. *Neuropsychologia*, *12*, 323–330.

Purdie, F. R., Honigman, B., & Rosen, P. (1981). Acute organic brain syndrome: A review of 100 cases. *Annals of Emergency Medicine*, *10*, 455–461.

Rehnstrom, S., Simert, G., Hansson, J., Hohnson, G., & Vang, J. (1977). Chronic hepatic encephalopathy. A psychometric study. *Scandinavian Journal of Gastroenterology*, *12*, 305–311.

Reitan, R. M., & Wolfson, D. (1989). The Seashore Rhythm Test and brain functions. *The Clinical Neuropsychologist*, *3*, 70–78.

Reitan, R. M., & Wolfson, D. (1990). The significance of the Speech-Sounds Perception Test for cerebral functions. *Archives of Clinical Neuropsychology*, *5*, 265–272.

Rockwood, K. (1989). Acute confusion in elderly medical patients. *Journal of the American Geriatrics Society*, *37*, 150–154.

Roth, M. (1955). The natural history of mental disorder in old age. *Journal of Mental Science*, *101*, 281–301.

Ryan, J. J., Souheaver, G. T., & DeWolfe, A. S. (1981). Halstead-Reintan test results in chronic hemodialysis. *Journal of Nervous and Mental Disease*, *169*, 311–314.

Sagel, J., & Matisonn, R. (1972). Neuropsychiatric disturbance as the initial manifestation of digitalis toxicity. *South African Medical Journal*, *46*, 512–514.

Schomerus, H., Hamster, W., Blunck, H., Reinhard, U., Mayer, K., & Dole, W. (1981). Latent portasystemic encephalopathy. 1. Nature of cerebral functional defects and their effect on fitness to drive. *Digestive Diseases and Sciences*, *26*, 622–630.

Seymour, D. G., Henschke, P. J., Cape, R. D. T., & Campbell, A. J. (1980). Acute confusional states and dementia in the elderly: The role of dehydration/volume depletion, physical illness and age. *Age and Ageing*, *9*, 137–146.

Seymour, D. G., & Pringle, R. (1983). Post-operative complications in the elderly surgical patient. *Gerontology*, *29*, 262–270.

Simon, A., & Cahan, R. B. (1963). The acute brain syndrome in geriatric patients. *Psychiatric Research*, *16*, 8–21.

Smith, J., & Smith, L. (1977). WAIS functioning of cirrhotic and noncirrhotic alcoholics. *Journal of Clinical Psychology*, *33*, 309–313.

Spehr, W., Sartorius, H., Berglund, K., Hjorth, B., Kablitz, C., Plog, U., Wiedenman, P. H., & Zapf, K. (1977). EEG and hemodialysis. A structural survey of EEG spectral analysis, Hjorth's EEG descriptors, blood variables and psychological data. *Electroencephalography and Clinical Neurophysiology*, *43*, 787–797.

Squire, L. R., Judd, L. L., Janowsky, D. S., & Huey, L. Y. (1980). Effects of lithium carbonate on memory and other cognitive functions. *American Journal of Psychiatry*, *137*, 1042–1046.

Starkman, M. N., & Schteingart, D. E. (1981). Neuropsychiatric manifestations of patients with Cushing's syndrome. *Archives of Internal Medicine*, *141*, 215–219.

Steinhart, M. J. (1979). Treatment of delirium: A reappraisal. *International Journal of Psychiatric Medicine*, *9*, 191–197.

Stephens, D. A. (1967). Psychotoxic effects of benzhexol hydrochloride (Artane). *British Journal of Psychiatry*, *113*, 213–218.

Stewart, R. S., & Stewart, R. M. (1979). Neuropsychiatric aspects of chronic renal disease. *Psychosomatics*, *20*, 524–531.

Summerskill, W., Davidson, E., Sherlock, S., & Steiner, R. (1956). The neuropsychiatric syndrome associated with hepatic cirrhosis and an extensive portal collateral circulation. *Quarterly Journal of Medicine*, *25*, 245–266.

Tarter, R., Hegedus, A., Van Thiel, D., Edwards, N., & Schade, R. (1987). Neurobehavioral correlates of cholestatic and hepatocellular disease: Differentiation according to disease specific characteristics and severity of the identified cerebral dysfunction. *International Journal of Neuroscience*, *32*, 901–910.

Teschan, P. E., Ginn, H. E., Bourne, J. R., Ward, J. W., Baruch, H., Nunnally, J. C., Musso, M., & Vaughn, V. K. (1979). Quantitative indices of clinical uremia. *Kidney International*, *15*, 676–697.

Thompson, P. J., & Trimble, M. R. (1983). Anticonvulsant serum levels: Relationship to impairments of cognitive function. *Journal of Neurology, Neurosurgery and Psychiatry*, *46*, 227–233.

Thomsen, A. M., Borgesen, S. E., Bruhn, P., & Gjerris, F. (1986). Prognosis of dementia in normal-pressure hydrocephalus after a shunt operation. *Annals of Neurology*, *20*, 304–310.

Tilzey, A., Heptonstall, J., & Hamblin, T. (1981). Toxic confusional state and choreiform movements after treatment with anabolic steroids. *British Medical Journal, 283*, 349–350.

Trieschmann, R. B., & Sand, P. L. (1971). WAIS and MMPI correlates of increasing renal failure in adult medical patients. *Psychological Reports, 29*, 1251–1262.

Trzepacz, P. T., Teague, G. B., & Lipowski, Z. J. (1985). Delirium and other organic mental disorders in a general hospital. *General Hospital Psychiatry, 7*, 101–106.

Trzepacz, P. T., Maue, F. R., & Coffman, G. (1986). Neuropsychiatric assessment of liver transplantation candidates: Delirium and other psychiatric disorders. *International Journal of Psychiatric Medicine, 16*, 101–111.

Van Sweden, B. (1985). Toxic "ictal" confusion in middle age: Treatment with benzodiazepines. *Journal of Neurology, Neurosurgery and Psychiatry, 48*, 472–476.

Varney, N. R., Alexander, B., & MacIndoe, J. H. (1984). Reversible steroid dementia in patients without steroid psychosis. *American Journal of Psychiatry, 141*, 369–372.

Vestal, R. E. (1978). Drug use in elderly: A review of problems and special considerations. *Drugs, 16*, 358–382.

Warshaw, G. A., Moore, J. T., Friedman, W., Currie, C. T., Kennie, D. C., Kane, W. J., & Mears, P. A. (1982). Functional disability in hospitalized elderly. *Journal of the American Medical Association, 248*, 847–850.

Wells, C. E. (1985). Organic syndromes: Delirium. In H. I. Kaplan & B. J. Sadock (Eds.), *Comprehensive textbook of psychiatry* (4th ed., pp. 838–851). Baltimore: Williams & Wilkins.

Whybrow, P. C., Prange, A. J., Jr., & Treadway, C. R. (1969). Mental changes accompanying thyroid gland dysfunction. *Archives of General Psychiatry, 20*, 48–63.

Williams, M. A., Campbell, E. B., Raynor, W. J., Jr., Musholt, M. A., Mlynarczyk, S. M., & Crane, L. F. (1985). Predictors of acute confusional states in hospitalized elderly patients. *Research in Nursing and Health, 8*, 31–40.

Williamson, J. (1978). Prescribing problems in the elderly. *Practitioner, 220*, 749–755.

Williamson, J., & Chopin, J. M. (1980). Adverse reactions to prescribed drugs in the elderly: A multicentre investigation. *Age and Ageing, 9*, 73–80.

Wilson, L. M. (1972). Intensive care delirium. *Archives of Internal Medicine, 130*, 225–226.

Wolff, H. G., & Curran, D. (1935). Nature of delirium and complex and electrolyte disturbance. *Archives of Neurology and Psychiatry, 33*, 1175–1215.

Wolkowitz, O. M., Weingartner, H., Thompson, K., Pickar, D., Paul, S. M., & Hommer, D. W. (1987). Diazepam-induced amnesia: A neuropharmacological model of an "organic amnestic syndrome." *American Journal of Psychiatry, 144*, 25–29.

Zatuchni, J., & Hong, K. (1981). Methyl bromide poisoning seen initially as psychosis. *Archives of Neurology, 38*, 529–530.

14

Vascular Dementias

E. Jeffrey Metter and Robert S. Wilson

Vascular dementias are the second most frequent group of dementing disorders after Alzheimer's disease (AD). These dementias result from the pathological changes that occur in the circulatory system that supplies the brain and spinal cord and the resulting consequences within the nervous system. The high prevalence of cerebrovascular diseases (CVD) with increasing age lays the groundwork for the appearance of dementia in association with all varieties of strokes. The term *stroke* means the acute onset of a focal neurological deficit that is caused by thrombosis, embolus, hemorrhage, or damage to the cerebral vascular system. Stroke is the third leading cause of death in the United States after heart disease and cancer. There are between 500,000 and 600,000 strokes per year in the United States, and the prevalence is more than 2 million individuals who have had at least one stroke (American Heart Association, 1988). The good news is that the incidence of stroke has been on the decline since the early years of the 20th century (Garraway et al., 1979).

The most frequent vascular dementia is multi-infarct dementia (MID), a term that was introduced by Hachinski, Lassen, and Marshall (1974). The term implies that vascular dementia results from multiple brain infarctions and not athero-sclerotic changes in the blood vessels. In the past it was felt that most vascular dementia resulted from chronic hypoxia secondary to cerebral atherosclerosis; this condition was referred to as *arteriosclerotic dementia*. No evidence has been brought to bear to support this position (Haase, 1977; Liston & LaRue, 1983). Rather, it is the occurrence of multiple cerebral infarctions and hemorrhages (Hachinski et al., 1974) that is responsible.

A fundamental problem in both research and clinical work on vascular dementia is the lack of generally accepted clinical or pathological diagnostic criteria. This problem stems in large part from the heterogeneity within the vascular dementias. Fortunately, there have been two recent attempts to provide comprehensive classification systems for the vascular dementias, systems that recognize the clinical and neuropathological heterogeneity within the vascular dementias, incorporate recent radiological advances, and identify specific clinical findings that may support the diagnosis (Chui et al., 1992; Roman et al., in press). The value of these classification systems remains to be demonstrated, but at minimum they represent an advance over the two systems most widely used to date: DSM-III-R

416

(American Psychiatric Association, 1987) and the Ischemia Scale (IS) (Hachinski et al., 1974). The former system has proven difficult to operationalize and has never been pathologically validated. The IS, which is shown in Table 14.1, consists of a mixture of risk factors, clinical signs, and historical variables. Although it has received some support in clinicopathological research (Molsa, Paljarvi, Rinne, Rinne, & Sako, 1985; Rosen, Terry, Fuld, Katzman, & Peck, 1980), the results have been mixed, operationalization of items has been variable, and sensitivity to subcortical vascular dementia has been limited (Bennett, Wilson, Gilley, & Fox, 1990). Both of the new classification systems rank order diagnostic certainty and incorporate radiological findings. In the system of Chui et al. (1992), probable ischemic vascular dementia requires dementia, radiological evidence of at least one supratentorial lesion, and evidence of (a) two or more strokes or (b) a single stroke that can be temporally linked to dementia onset. In the NINDS-AIREN system (Roman et al., in press), probable vascular dementia requires dementia, clinical and radiological evidence of cerebrovascular disease, and a plausible temporal relationship between the cognitive dysfunction and cerebrovascular disease. In all likelihood, during the next decade these systems will guide case definition in longitudinal clinicopathological research that is needed to sort out the vascular dementias.

In light of the lack of accepted clinical and pathological diagnostic criteria, it should not be surprising that neither the incidence nor prevalence of vascular dementia is known. Prevalence estimates vary with age and gender and within geographic regions and racial subgroups (Tatemichi, 1991). Community surveys in the United States and Europe suggest that vascular disease accounts for between 9% and 46% of dementia cases in elderly persons (Folstein, Anthony, Parhad, Duffy, & Gruenberg, 1985; Kase, Wolf, Bachman, Linn, & Cupples, 1989; Molsa, Marttila, & Rinne, 1982). The lowest prevalence estimate comes from the Fra-

TABLE 14.1.   The Hachinski Ischemic Score (IS)

Feature	Original IS[a]	Modified IS[b]
Abrupt onset	2	2
Stepwise deterioration	1	1
Fluctuating course	2	NA
Nocturnal confusion	1	NA
Relative preservation of personality	1	NA
Depression	1	NA
Somatic complaints	1	1
Emotional incontinence	1	1
History or presence of hypertension	1	1
History of strokes	2	2
Evidence of associated atherosclerosis	1	NA
Focal neurological syndromes	2	2
Focal neurological signs	2	2
AD	0–4	0–2
MID, Mixed AD/MID	> 6	4–10

[a]Original IS is based on Hachinski et al. (1975).
[b]Modified IS is based on Rosen et al. (1980).
Note: AD = Alzheimer's disease; MID = multi-infarct dementia.

mingham study (Kase et al., 1989) and deserves particular credence because of the strict diagnostic criteria used and the longitudinal research design. Interestingly, the upper estimate came from a survey in East Baltimore with a high proportion of black participants (Folstein et al., 1985). Vascular dementia appears to be more common among men than women, and prevalence increases with age. Prevalence estimates from Japan and China are considerably increased relative to the West (Tatemichi, 1991). Finally, estimates derived from pathological or clinical series tend to exceed those derived from community surveys. Thus, autopsy studies suggest that 25% to 33% of persons who die with dementia have vascular disease as a sole or contributing cause (Chui, 1989; Katzman, 1983; O'Brien, 1988; Tatemichi, 1991).

The development of vascular dementias is related to the location(s) and the amount of brain damage. Dementia is a "localizing" sign of the underlying pathology, much as fluent aphasia is localizing to the left perisylvian region. Lesions that disrupt the organization and operation of multiple brain functions may result in a dementia. To understand vascular dementias, therefore, is to understand the neuropsychological consequences of focal and diffuse brain lesions. For many patients, stroke syndromes become the underlying model to understand the observed behavior.

A second factor in understanding MID is the underlying pathology causing the dementia. Atherosclerosis and hypertension are the most common underlying processes that lead to cerebral infarction and intercerebral hemorrhage. Other processes may explain some cases. Subacute hypoxic encephalopathy (Ginsberg, Hedley-Whyte, & Richardson, 1976) can cause a diffuse white matter disorder and has been suggested as the cause of Binswanger's disease. Carbon monoxide poisoning may result in a hypoxic state and dementia. Similarly, the occurrence of congoloid angiopathy may result in a dementia. This chapter will focus primarily on the consequences of atherosclerosis and hypertension. Finally, it should be noted that the probability of developing dementia following stroke appears to increase with increasing age, prior stroke, and cerebral atrophy (Tatemichi et al., 1990), although much work remains to be done on risk factors for vascular dementia.

The advent of magnetic resonance imaging (MRI), with its increased sensitivity to pathology in the periventricular region, has led to the radiological identification of white matter lesions in this area in a large percentage of elderly persons. The lesions are high-intensity signals on T2 weighted images in white matter and are particularly common in the periventricular regions. These lesions are more prevalent with increasing age and hypertension. Some researchers argue that they may be associated with subacute hypoxic encephalopathy. They are also commonly seen in AD (Bennett, Charletta, Gilley, Cochran, & Hayes, 1991; Brun & Englund, 1986). Pathological studies indicate that these radiological "lesions" are not exclusively vascular; rather, they represent a range of phenomena, and, at present, their clinical implications are uncertain. The complexity of the issues associated with white matter lesions and dementia has led to the proposal for a more general term to accommodate the problem of white matter pathology. Hachinski, Potter, and Merskey (1987) have thus proposed the term *leuko-araiosis* to describe these phenomena. A major debate is now in progress as to the clinical importance of these white matter lesions found in many elderly individuals. Chapter 15 provides a discussion of this work. For the purposes of this chapter, it is important to keep in mind that not all of these lesions are vascular and that their presence in a patient with dementia should not be taken as evidence that the dementia has a vascular basis.

The remainder of this chapter will review the pathological basis of vascular dementia, the clinical neurology of the major vascular dementia syndromes, the role of brain imaging in diagnostic evaluations, neuropsychological features of the vascular dementias, treatment approaches, and current knowledge about the course of vascular dementias.

Pathology of Vascular Disease

Cerebral vascular disease results from either the occlusion of blood vessels with the resulting infarction of brain tissue exclusively supplied by the artery or drained by the vein, or by hemorrhage into or around the brain. Infarction is typically a result of occlusion of the blood vessel by either thrombosis or embolism. Thrombosis is the process whereby the blood clots. It may be related to the presence of atherosclerosis with narrowing in the size of the artery (referred to as stenosis) or with alterations or injuries in the endothelial lining of the artery, making it susceptible to clot formation. Atherosclerosis typically will form in large- and medium-sized arteries located on the surface of the brain or at the bifurcation of large branches that penetrate into the brain. The major sites for the development of atherosclerotic lesions are in the internal carotid sinus in the neck and in the internal carotid artery as it leaves the cavernous sinus before reaching the surface of the brain. In the vertebrobasilar system the lesion develops at the origin of the vertebral artery and along the basilar artery. The effect of complete occlusion of the artery will depend on the presence of collateral circulation from other arteries. For example, complete occlusion of the left internal carotid artery at the bifurcation of the common carotid artery in the neck need not result in infarction or clinical consequences when adjacent arterial systems, including the left extracranial carotid artery on the side of the occlusion, the right carotid system, and/or the vertebrobasilar circulations, are able to compensate for the loss with adequate collateral flow. If these collateral circulations are unable to compensate for the occlusion, an infarction will occur in the part of the internal carotid circulation that is inadequately perfused with blood.

Smaller arteries can also develop pathology rendering them susceptible to thrombosis or hemorrhage. In hypertension, the medium-sized arteries undergo lipohyalinosis with loss of the muscular layer of the artery. This pathology can result in lacunes, which are small infarctions or hemorrhages that are less than 1 cm in diameter. Lacunes are characteristically located in the basal ganglia, thalamus, and periventricular white matter.

Cerebral blood flow (CBF) and metabolic changes have been noted to differ between MID and AD. Alzheimer's disease (AD) typically involves a more uniform reduction in CBF and metabolism, whereas MID is characterized by patchy areas of decreased flow and metabolism. The changes in MID occur early, and in one study, hemispheric blood flow changes preceded the clinical onset of symptoms by 2 years (Rogers, Meyer, Mortel, Mahurin, & Judd, 1986). These findings suggest that large-vessel disease with some degree of stenosis may be a warning of more generalized problems. In fact, longitudinal changes in cognitive ability, as measured using the Cognitive Capacity Screening Examination (CCSE) (Jacobs, Bernhard, Delgado, & Strain, 1977), have been reported to correlate with changes in mean grey matter blood flow in patients with MID (Meyer, Rogers, Judd, Mortel, & Sims, 1988).

Hemorrhage can be considered as intracerebral or extracerebral. Intracerebral hemorrhages result from degenerative changes in the artery, primarily lipohyalinosis. On the basis of its bulk, the hemorrhage will destroy tissue in the area of the bleed. Extracerebral hemorrhages consist of subdural hematomas that are associated with head trauma and subarachnoid hemorrhages associated with aneurysms. Persistent cognitive deficits can be seen with either form of extracerebral hemorrhage, resulting from secondary damage to the brain itself by pressure or from interference with cerebral circulation and secondary infarction.

Although much is known about the neurobehavioral consequences of single strokes, there is surprisingly little agreement about the pathological basis of vascular dementia. In a landmark study, Tomlinson, Blessed, and Roth (1970) concluded that destruction of at least 100 ml of brain tissue, predominantly cortical, was required to produce dementia; volumes between 50 and 100 ml were said to variably produce dementia. Unfortunately, this "mass action" approach has not been borne out by subsequent research, and there are numerous cases in the literature of apparent vascular dementia with less than 50 to 100 ml tissue loss (e.g., Erkinjuntti, 1987; Loeb, Gandolfo, & Bino, 1988). Neither of the new diagnostic systems specify a minimal volume of tissue loss for a pathological diagnosis (Chui et al., 1992; Roman et al., in press). Indeed, the pathological basis of vascular dementias appears considerably more complex. Tatemichi (1991) proposes that the location, volume, and number of lesions must be considered in addition to the co-occurrence of AD. Although this literature is currently in a state of flux, at least two points should be kept in mind. First, small but well-placed infarcts, particularly those involving the thalamus or cortical association areas or pathways, can produce dementia (e.g., Ladurner, Iliff, & Lechner, 1982). Second, stroke and AD commonly co-occur (e.g., Ulrich, Probst, & Wuest, 1986; O'Brien, 1988) and may not be independent; thus, it is vital that the diagnostician establish the temporal association between the patient's cognitive impairment and stroke. In the NINDS-AIREN system (Roman et al., in press), onset of dementia within 3 months of a stroke or a course of cognitive decline that begins abruptly or is fluctuating or stepwise is required to establish a link between dementia and cerebrovascular disease.

Brain Imaging

Brain imaging has advanced considerably in the past 20 years and now represents an important and at times critical adjunct for the diagnosis of dementias in general and the vascular dementias in particular. The major currently available imaging techniques are based on the use of computers to produce tomographic images of the brain. Four techniques are now in usage: computed tomography (CT), MRI, single photon emission computed tomography (SPECT), and positron emission tomography (PET). Detailed discussion of these procedures can be found in chapters 16, 17, and 19. These imaging procedures are a critical part of the differentiation of MID from AD. Both CT and MRI are able to show larger brain infarctions, although they are less sensitive with small lacunes. It is important to distinguish these lesions from the white matter lucencies on MRI and leuko-araiosis (Hachinski, Potter, & Merskey, 1987) on CT. As noted above and discussed in chapter 15, these white matter lucencies are by no means exclusively vascular, and their clinical significance is uncertain at the present time. SPECT and PET demonstrate patchy areas of abnormalities in the brain that do not necessarily correlate with the presence of infarcts. This patchiness differs from the tomographs typically seen in AD, in which there are uniform declines in cerebral blood flow and metabolism that are found in the parietal regions early in the disease course, and, as the disease progresses, involve most of the associative cortex (Benson et al., 1983; Kuhl, Metter, & Riege, 1985; Jagust, Budinger, & Reed, 1987). Comparison of CT, PET, and brain section are demonstrated in Figure 14.1 from a patient with mild MID.

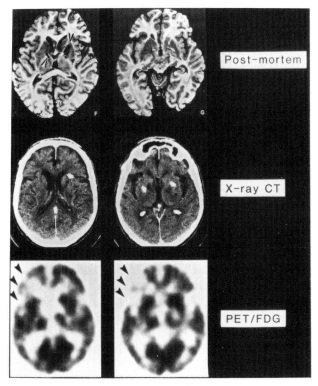

FIGURE 14.1. Positron emission tomography (PET) with fluorodeoxyglucose (FDG), computed tomography (CT), and gross pathology at postmortem from a 69-year-old man with multiple brain infarctions who was studied 1 month after a stroke with a left hemiparesis. He died 10 days later from a gastrointestinal hemorrhage. The brain section demonstrates multiple small subcortical lacunar infarctions, including a lacune that destroys the anterior limb of the left internal capsule. The middle figure is the corresponding CT scans that show the same areas of infarction. The bottom section is the FDG PET that shows the brain's utilization of glucose, which is its main source of energy. The blacker a region on the scan the greater is the utilization of glucose. (Reprinted with permission from Metter et al., 1985)

What is most striking is that the left frontal region has a much lower uptake of glucose than the right frontal region. This implies that the left frontal region is not as functionally active as the right, in a region that has no obvious structural damage by CT or pathology. The loss of functional activity appears to result from the destruction of the internal capsule which carries axons to and from the frontal regions. The left prefrontal region has lost major communications with other brain regions as reflected by changes in glucose utilization. The study demonstrates the different type of information that is obtainable from structural studies such as CT and function studies such as PET and single photon emission computed tomography (SPECT) (Metter et al., 1985).

Multi-infarct Dementia

The clinical description of vascular dementias is based on the presence of vascular disease and dementia. The clinical features reflect typical characteristics of cerebral vascular events: rapid and abrupt onset, focal neurological signs and symptoms, stepwise progression with a fluctuating course, the presence of other vascular disease, and hypertension. On physical examination there are typically focal signs including paresis, abnormalities in gait, incontinence, and bradykinesia. The appearance of gait abnormalities and incontinence, particularly when dementia is not severe, appears to be characteristic (Chui et al., 1992; Thal, Grundman, & Klauber, 1988). The dementia has been characterized as being "subcortical" in contrast to the "cortical" dementia of AD (Cummings & Benson, 1983).

To aid in the diagnosis, Hachinski and his colleagues (1975) developed the IS to separate primary degenerative dementias from vascular dementias and mixed dementias that include a vascular component (see Table 14.1). Scores greater than 6 are taken as evidence of vascular or mixed dementia, whereas scores less than 4 are consistent with AD. Two clinicopathological studies have examined the validity of the IS (Molsa et al., 1985; Rosen et al., 1980). The IS did not differentiate MID from mixed AD/MID in either study. Moreover, the contribution of individual items to the differential diagnosis was variable in the two studies. The widely used modification of the IS by Rosen et al. (1980) is also shown in Table 14.1. Both Molsa et al. (1985) and Rosen et al. (1980) found focal neurological symptoms and a history of stroke to be particularly helpful in the differential diagnosis of AD from MID.

Subgroups of MID have been described. Currently, there are attempts to divide MID into cortical and subcortical forms. The distinction reflects the differences in pathological processes that cause the dementia as well as the differing clinical outcomes associated with these processes. The cortical forms are felt to result primarily from infarctions caused by large-vessel atherosclerosis. The subcortical forms are caused by damage to medium-sized and small penetrating arteries that result from atherosclerosis or lipohyalinosis. The subcortical form of MID is strongly associated with the lacunar state and the subcortical leukoencephalopathy of Binswanger's disease (BD).

Clinical differences have been noted between cortical and subcortical forms of MID (Erkinjuntti, 1987). In subcortical MID dysarthria, pure motor hemiparesis, depression, emotional lability, and bulbar signs were said to be more common.

More striking than the differences, however, was the large overlap of findings (Erkinjuntti, 1987). The overlap argues that these two forms of MID are relatively similar, and that if different underlying pathologies are accounting for the strokes and dementia, then these pathologies frequently co-occur. The distinctions may be useful in some patients regarding the underlying pathology and subsequent treatments, but many patients in the cortical group will also have subcortical (lacunar) pathology.

Cortical Forms of MID

The appearance of dementia with stroke syndromes is dependent on the size and location of the structural damage. The clinical characteristics of cortical forms of MID are an acute onset with a stepwise progression and focal neurological signs and symptoms. The specific neurological findings depend on the location of the lesion(s) and will typically include one or more of the following: plegia or paresis, sensory loss, anopsia, aphasia, apraxia, agnosia, visuospatial problems, and neglect. A number of clinical syndromes have been described based on lesion localization or by the specific arterial distribution that has been disrupted. Some of the localized behaviors associated with specific brain regions will be briefly reviewed because such behaviors are commonly seen in vascular dementia syndromes.

The frontal lobes are responsible for the executive functions of the brain. They are critically involved in decision making, planning, and allocation of attentional resources (Fuster, 1980; Stuss & Benson, 1986; see also Chapter 8). The lateral aspects of the frontal lobe are associated with defects in sequencing information and spatial ordering. The ventrolateral and orbital frontal lobes are associated with discrimination and attention. With more mesial lesions, patients are frequently abulic; that is, there is a lack of the drive to respond and to act with spontaneity. Abnormalities in motor performance and strength are frequent. Movements may be slow in initiation and execution or there may be an apraxia. Language abnormalities may exist with an adynamic quality (Luria & Hutton, 1977); that is, there is a lack of verbal responsiveness, but when speech occurs, it may be normal in character. With more posterior frontal lesions involving Broca's area and deeper structures, an agrammatic form of aphasia or aphemia may develop. Memory is frequently subtly impaired, particularly when a premium is placed on organization and sequence.

Structural damage to dominant temporal and parietal regions frequently results in an aphasia (Benson, 1979; Luria & Hutton, 1977). The nature and severity of the aphasia are dependent on a number of factors, particularly the size and location of the lesion. Associated with the aphasia can be amnesia, visuospatial problems, acalculia, agnosia, and apraxia. The language disorder observed following damage to the temporoparietal region is typically of the fluent variety. It may include an abnormality in the use of semantic structure, in retrieval of words from the lexicon, or with syntactical structure. A related syndrome that can cause confusion with dementia is the angular gyrus syndrome (Benson, Cummings, & Tsai, 1982). This syndrome consists of aphasia, alexia, agraphia, the Gerstmann syndrome (right-left disorientation, finger agnosia, acalculia, agraphia), and constructional problems. Memory is spared except for the word-finding difficulties associated with the aphasia. The pathological lesion is typically infarction to the dominant angular gyrus.

Damage to the nondominant temporoparietal region may result in visuospatial problems including constructional apraxias, problems with depth of field, geographical disorientation, proposagnosia, and so forth. These disorders have to do with the localization of the body in space and spatial schema. Also, neglect is often seen with lesions in the nondominant temporoparietal region of the contralateral world. The neglect is most apparent for vision but can occur for other senses. A related phenomenon is anosagnosia, in which the patient is unaware of the presence or extent of a deficit.

Occipital lobe damage will result in problems with visual fields including hemianopsias. Bilateral occipital infarctions may cause Anton's syndrome, which consists of cortical blindness that is paradoxically denied by the patient.

Bilateral damage to the hippocampi and adjacent structures in the medial temporal region results in a profound anterograde amnesia. Unilateral temporal lobe lesions also result in memory impairments that are typically stimulus specific, affecting retention of verbal or nonverbal material depending on whether the dominant or nondominant temporal lobe is involved.

Subcortical Forms of MID

The most frequent form of subcortical MID is associated with the lacunar state. Fisher (1982) has described a number of clinical syndromes associated with these small, deep infarcts (Table 14.2). These syndromes are generally the result of single events. Dementia tends to occur when multiple lacunes are present. The earliest description of the lacunar state was by Marie (1901). The syndrome was one of chronic progression marked by one or more strokelike episodes leading to disability. However, not all patients with multiple lacunes exhibit cognitive impairment. There is disagreement as to whether subcortical infarctions cause dementia, and under what circumstances, and by what definition of dementia (Joynt, 1988; Kase, 1986). Fisher (1982) noted that he seldom encountered the clinical presentation described by Marie (1901). Indeed, the only lacunar dementia described by Fisher is that seen with thalamic lesions.

The subcortical forms of MID are associated with a number of clinical findings. Gait disturbances are common, with the most characteristic form being a small-steppage gait (*marche à petits pas*) or shuffling with the lower extremities slightly flexed in conjunction with poor balance. Bradykinesia, slow movement responses with limited excursions, is common and may give a parkinsonian appearance. Patients are often slow in responding to questions and in their thinking, which is referred to as bradyphrenia. They frequently appear apathetic or depressed. Many will have problems with incontinence. These patients may present with evidence of mild hemiparesis, which may be characterized as clumsiness and loss of fine motor coordination. Bilateral pyramidal tract findings (increased reflexes, Babinski signs, increased tone, and spasticity) are found. Pseudobulbar palsy may also be observed. Emotional lability, in the form of an exaggerated response to a normal stimulus, is not uncommon (Roman, 1985). A severe dysarthria may be present and is characterized by a harsh, strained, strangled voice that includes hyperphonation, poor articulation, and abnormalities in prosody, symptoms which fit the clinical features of a spastic dysarthria (Metter, 1985). At times patients will present

TABLE 14.2.   Lacunar Syndromes

Pure Sensory
Pure motor hemiparesis
   With sparing the face
   With "motor aphasia"
   With horizontal gaze palsy
   With crossed third-nerve palsy
   With crossed sixth-nerve palsy
   With confusion
Ataxic hemiparesis
Dysarthria-clumsy hand
Mesencephalothalamic syndrome
Thalamic dementia
Cerebellar ataxia with crossed third-nerve palsy
Sensorimotor stroke
Hemiballism
Lower basilar branch syndrome: dizziness, diplopia, gaze palsy, dysarthria, cerebellar ataxia,
   trigeminal numbness
Lateral medullary syndrome
Loss of memory
Locked-in syndrome
Miscellaneous
   Weakness of one leg with ease of falling
   Pure dysarthria
   Acute dystonia of thalamic origin

Source: Fisher (1982).

with the triad of gait disturbance, dementia, and incontinence that can result in clinical confusion with normal-pressure hydrocephalus (see chapter 10). Both subcortical MID and normal-pressure hydrocephalus may present with enlarged ventricles on CT or MRI. The presence of lacunar infarcts in these patients helps to confirm MID but does not rule out hydrocephalus.

Binswanger's Disease

Binswanger (1894) introduced the entity that he called "encephalitis subcorticalis chronica progressive" based on clinicopathological descriptions of eight patients. Pathologically, he noted the presence of markedly enlarged ventricles with diffuse subcortical white matter lesions. He attributed the white matter changes to severe atheromatous changes of the cerebral circulation. Alzheimer (1902) actually coined the term *Binswanger's disease* (Roman, 1987) and reported the first histopathology. He noted that the deep white matter was either absent or poorly stained, whereas the short association fibers (the U fibers) were preserved. This, then, is the characteristic histopathological description of BD: the presence of prominent demyelination of the white matter with the sparing of the U fibers. Much debate has developed over why some fibers are selectively spared if the condition represents the result of atherosclerotic disease. DeReuck, Crevitis, Deconster, Sieben, and Vander Becken (1980) have argued that the U fibers receive their blood supply from the cortical penetrating arteries, whereas the deeper white matter receives its circulation from long penetrating arteries that supply the basal ganglia and parts of the brainstem. Huang, Wu, and Luo (1985) argue that the circulation to the white matter is organized in a different manner, with the zone of demarcation between circulations lying deep in the periventricular region. They argue that the white matter changes are the result of hypoxic ischemia, with hypotension or acidosis as a secondary phenomena, and that the dementia results from lacunar infarctions. Other investigators have concurred that the dementia observed in BD is secondary to multiple lacunar infarctions (Roman, 1985).

Clinical features vary greatly in BD. Kinkel, Jacobs, Polachine, Bates, and Heffner (1985) reviewed 1,633 CT scans to identify 28 subjects with evidence of extensive white matter damage, and 23 were studied with MRI and clinical evaluation of mental status using the approach of Strub and Black (1977). No consistent pattern of association emerged between the degree of leukoencephalopathy and mental status change. Subjects who had no neurological or mental status abnormalities were found to have mild to severe leukoencephalopathy. A second group had motor deficits but no evidence of dementia. Five individuals with slowly evolving dementia, motor deficits, and incontinence had severe leukoencephalopathy. The last group had three patients whose presentation was of a progressively evolving dementia.

The observations of Kinkel et al. (1985) are not unrepresentative of the literature on BD. At one end of the spectrum are subjects with the leukoencephalopathy but without evidence of neurological or mental disabilities. These patients may be at higher risk of developing cerebrovascular events or dementia (Roman, 1987). At the other end of the spectrum are subjects who have a dementia (Babikian & Ropper, 1987). Retrospective reports suggest that this dementia can be of slow onset and gradually progress, but prospective research is lacking. It may be accompanied by motor weakness and pseudobulbar palsy (weakness of the perioral structures, with exaggerated gag reflex, jaw jerk, and emotional lability). Gait disturbances are common due either to hemiparesis or to gait apraxia. Urinary incontinence may occur in the early stages. Changes in mood and behavior are common. Frontal lobe abnormalities are common including personality changes, loss of drive, difficulty in initiating activity or thoughts, and loss of insight (Ishii, Nishihara, & Imamura, 1986). As the disease progresses it may result in mutism and a parkinsonianlike state. Forgetfulness and mild confusion occur early. An amnestic syndrome is usually present but is typically less severe than that seen at comparable levels of dementia severity in AD (Bernard et al., 1992). Aphasia, apraxia, and neglect are not common. Roman (1987) notes that the dementia is of a "subcortical" pattern.

Recently, Bennett et al. (1990) have proposed standardized diagnostic criteria for BD. These include dementia, bilateral radiological abnormalities, and evidence of at least two of the following: vascular disease or a vascular risk factor, sign(s) of focal cerebrovascular disease, and signs of subcortical cerebral dysfunction. Although preliminary data on the diagnostic sensitivity and specificity of these criteria appear promising, prospective clinicopathological research is needed to verify and refine the criteria.

Neuropsychology of MID

Although the neurobehavioral consequences of discrete vascular lesions have been extensively studied, neuropsychological research on the vascular dementias has been sparse. A major problem has been the heterogeneity within the domain of vascular dementia. For the most part, clinical research has not differentiated among vascular dementia syndromes. As a result, few hard findings have emerged regarding characteristic neurobehavioral stigmata. A related problem has been the lack of generally accepted clinical and pathological diagnostic criteria alluded to above. On a more conceptual level, some have questioned whether MID, viewed as the cumulative effect of repeated infarction (Tatemichi, 1990), is a real, or at least usual, clinical entity (Brust, 1988). How many vascular events are necessary to produce a dementia syndrome? What evidence is there that these dementias actually progress? Should a patient with a single vascular lesion in the dominant hemisphere who is inattentive and globally aphasic be considered demented? On a methodological level, research comparing vascular dementia with other dementia syndromes has often failed to match on key variables like dementia severity, relied on outcome measures of doubtful relevance to dementia, or failed to document dementia within the sample of patients with vascular disease. Furthermore, most studies of MID do not differentiate among different forms of the disorder, making it difficult to generalize across studies. Despite these diagnostic, conceptual, and methodological problems, some interesting findings have begun to emerge from clinical research in this area.

The majority of studies have focused on general measures of intellect. The strategy has been to compare MID with AD to see what differences might exist between the two disorders. Perez and colleagues (Perez, Gay, & Taylor, 1975; Perez, Gay, Taylor, & Rivera, 1975; Perez, Rivera, et al., 1975; Perez, Stump, Gay, & Hart, 1976) used the Wechsler Adult Intelligence Scale (WAIS) and Wechsler Memory Scale (WMS) to compare MID and AD. They found that AD patients tend to have a greater degree of impairment than those with MID, performing more poorly on essentially all WAIS subtests. Brinkman, Largen, Cushman, Braun, and Block (1986) noted that Perez and colleagues failed to match their subjects on education or severity of dementia. The AD subjects were more educated but had lower Full Scale IQs, strongly suggesting that they were more severely demented than the MID patients.

Brinkman et al. (1986) selected their subjects to be matched for age, education, and severity of the dementia based on the WAIS Full Scale IQ and the WMS Memory Quotient (MQ). They then compared performance on subtests of the WAIS and WMS. No differences were found. Others have made similar observations using all or parts of the WAIS and WMS. Hier, Warrach, Gorelick, and Thomas (1989) found differences on Digit Span and Vocabulary and in verbal memory but no differences on Block Design or Information. Their subjects showed similar degrees of severity based on the Global Deterioration Scale (Reisberg, Ferris, deLeon, & Crook, 1982). These results suggest that when severity is taken into account, cognition, as measured by the WAIS and WMS, is equivalent between the two types of dementia.

A critical question becomes how much the WAIS and WMS are able to contribute to differential diagnosis. Fuld (1986) suggested that the profile of WAIS subtests may differentiate AD from other dementias. She identified the following profile:

$$A = (\text{Information} + \text{Vocabulary})/2$$
$$B = (\text{Similarities} + \text{Digit Span})/2$$
$$C = (\text{Digit Symbol} + \text{Block Design})/2$$
$$D = \text{Object Assembly}$$

Then $A > B > C <= D$ and $A > D$.

Ten of 17 probable AD patients met these criteria, whereas only 1 of 14 patients with other dementias fit the pattern. Brinkman and Braun (1984) found that 13 of 39 AD patients fit Fuld's profile, whereas only 2 of 23 MID patients had the pattern. The clinical utility of this profile is limited, however, since relatively few dementias of any type fit the profile.

The cardinal feature of AD is impaired episodic memory. Because much of the research on MID has used AD as a reference point, memory has been studied more extensively than other cognitive functions. To date, however, results of these studies have been mixed. In AD, the hippocampus, entorhinal cortex, and adjacent structures are preferentially affected, whereas this is not true in MID. One would expect, therefore, that episodic memory would be less impaired in MID than in AD at comparable levels of dementia severity. In two studies (Gainotti, Caltagirone, Masullo, & Miceli, 1980; Perez, Gay, et al., 1975), this hypothesis was supported, but the groups were not equated for dementia severity. In two negative studies that used the Buschke selective reminding paradigm as the key outcome measure, dementia was not adequately documented in one study (Loring, Meador, Mahurin, & Largen, 1986); in the other, the AD and MID groups were selected to have equivalent Wechsler MQs, thereby almost assuring a negative outcome (Brinkman et al., 1986). The best evidence in support of the hypothesis to date involves patients with putative BD. In one study (Bernard et al., 1992), verbal recognition memory was more defective in AD than in BD patients, whereas the groups, who were equivalent in dementia severity, did not differ on several measures of semantic memory. In another study from the same laboratory (Grosse, Gilley, Bernard, Wilson, & Bennett, 1991), AD and BD groups of equivalent dementia severity differed on two of three episodic memory measures in the expected direction. These latter studies were restricted to patients with mild dementia; it seems unlikely that AD-MID mnemonic differences will be observed in persons with more severe cognitive impairment. It remains to be seen whether these mnemonic differences will generalize to other forms of vascular dementia and, if so, what contribution they will make to differential diagnosis.

There has been little research on visuospatial/visuoconstructive ability in MID. Research using the Wechsler scales has not suggested preferential sparing or involvement of these abilities, although these studies cannot be considered definitive (Hier et al., 1989; Perez, Rivera, et al., 1975; Perez et al., 1976). More recently, Gainotti, Parlato, Monteleone, and Carlomagno (1992) suggest that selected qualitative signs of visual misperception are more characteristic in AD than in MID patients of equivalent dementia severity. Problem solving, abstraction, and concept formation, cognitive functions typically impaired with damage to prefrontal regions, are commonly compromised in MID. Neuropsychological research in this area has been sparse, however. Wolfe and colleagues (1990) found that patients with multiple subcortical lacunes showed deficits in shifting set, impaired executive functions on a verbal learning task, and decreased verbal fluency. Bernard et al. (1990) reported an isolated deficit on the Conceptualization subtest of the Mattis Dementia Rating Scale in BD patients relative to AD patients of equivalent dementia severity. Cummings (1991) has suggested that disturbed executive function is characteristic of subcortical cerebrovascular disease, which he attributes to lesions affecting dorsolateral frontal cortex, caudate nuclei, dorsomedial thalamic nuclei, and their interconnections. Executive dysfunction has not been well studied in neocortical MID.

The study of linguistic function in vascular dementia is complicated by the lack of accepted clinical diagnostic criteria. Thus, patients with lesions in Wernicke's or Broca's areas are often excluded from MID samples (e.g., Hier, Hagenlocker, & Shindler, 1985). Many such patients meet inclusion criteria specified, for example, by the IS (Hachinski et al., 1975) or DSM-III-R (American Psychiatric Association, 1987). Their exclusion would seem to rest on the important clinical distinction between aphasia and dementia. When aphasia is mild, this differentiation is often not problematic, but it can become quite difficult with more severe aphasia. Compounding the problem are the facts that most neuropsychological tests used to define dementia are linguistic and most aphasics, particularly those with posterior lesions, perform poorly on a wide range of neuropsychological tests. The exclusion of aphasia from the domain of MID creates awkward sampling problems for research in this area. For example, how severe must aphasia be to exclude a diagnosis of MID? Does a patient with MID who subsequently suffers a stroke in Wernicke's area no longer suffer from MID?

Given this problem with diagnostic classification, it is perhaps not surprising that linguistic function in MID has not been well characterized. When samples of MID (Fischer, Gatterer, Marterer, & Danielczyk, 1988) or BD (Bernard et al., 1990) are compared to AD patients of equivalent dementia severity, there are no apparent differences on measures of semantic processing (e.g., category fluency, letter fluency, visual confrontation naming). Since semantic/linguistic measures such as these appear to be especially good markers of dementia severity in AD (e.g., Kaszniak, Wilson, Fox, & Stebbins, 1986; Martin et al., 1987), the matching process may be obscuring subtle linguistic differences between AD and various forms of vascular dementia.

The prevalence of depression in AD and MID is uncertain. In addition to the use of selected samples, two problems in particular have beset research in this area. First, in some diagnostic classification systems, major depression serves to exclude a diagnosis of AD. Yet AD and depression are certainly not mutually exclusive disorders, and existing evidence does not suggest that depression influences the nature or course of the AD dementia (Lopez, Boller, Becker, Miller, & Reynolds, 1990; Drachman, O'Donnell, Lew, & Swearer, 1990). A second issue is how to ascertain information about depressive symptomatology in individuals with dementia that typically includes a dense anterograde amnesia. Current evidence suggests that, at least for AD, neither structured interview of the patient (Gilley et al., in press) nor self-report inventories (Gilley, Wilson, & Stebbins, 1992) are valid approaches. Structured interview of a knowledgeable informant, however, does appear to be a promising approach (Gilley & Wilson, 1991; Gilley et al., in press; Gilley, Bennett, Grosse, Wilson, & Fox, 1990).

With the above caveats in mind, current evidence does suggest a slightly increased rate of affective symptoms in MID compared to AD. Thus, Cummings, Miller, Hill, and Neshkes (1987) found depressive symptoms to be more common in their MID ($n = 15$) sample (60%; four with major depression) than in their AD ($n = 30$) sample (17%; none with major depression). Bucht, Adolfsson, and Winblad (1984) also found depressive symptoms to be increased in MID relative to AD. In a well-controlled study, Bernard et al. (1990) administered the 17-item

Hamilton Rating Scale (HRS) for depression (Hamilton, 1960) as a structured interview (Williams, 1988). The interview was conducted with the caregiver by individuals blinded to diagnosis and the study hypothesis. The subjects were patients with clinical diagnoses of AD ($n = 30$) or BD ($n = 11$) of equivalent age, education, and dementia severity. The mean HRS score in the BD group (9.9) was nearly twice that observed in the AD sample (4.7). Interestingly, the BD patients in this study were also rated as significantly more apathetic on the Rush Patient Behavior Checklist (Gilley, Wilson, Bennett, Bernard, & Fox, 1991), suggesting that depression in BD may be part of a "subcortical dementia" syndrome. Erkinjuntti, Ketonen, Sulkava, Vuorialho, and Palo (1987) did not observe affective differences in subcortical as compared to cortical forms of MID, however. Other forms of behavior disturbance have not been extensively studied in MID. Neither Cummings et al. (1987) nor Bernard et al. (1990) found an increased rate of delusional thinking or hallucinosis in MID or BD, respectively, as compared to AD.

In summary, it does appear that depression is more common in MID than in AD. The prevalence of depression is not known in either syndrome but appears relatively low compared to other neurodegenerative disorders (e.g., Parkinson's disease, Huntington's disease, multiple sclerosis). It remains to be seen whether depressive symptoms will prove useful in the differential diagnosis of MID.

Treatment

No current treatments have been shown to definitely improve the cognitive problems in patients with MID. There have been two main approaches to treatment. The first has been to identify and treat factors that can prevent development of stroke. There is considerable evidence that the incidence of stroke has been decreasing over the past 30 years (Garraway et al., 1979), presumably due to treatment and control of known risk factors for stroke. The second approach has been to develop treatments for those subjects who have developed MID.

There are a number of well-established risk factors for stroke. These include hypertension, cigarette smoking, hyperlipidemia (particularly cholesterol levels), diabetes mellitus, and ischemic heart disease. Hypertension has been the most important risk factor for stroke. Control of high blood pressure has played an important role in the decline of stroke over the past few decades. Smoking has an important role in affecting blood flow to the brain and in the development of atherosclerosis. Hypercholesterolemia is associated with increased risks of strokes as well as ischemic heart disease. Ischemic heart disease affects cerebral circulation directly through cardiac output and also from embolization, particularly in patients with atrial fibrillation. Atrial fibrillation is associated with a fivefold increased risk of cerebral infarction. Risk factor treatment appears to have a significant impact on the development of stroke and, by extension, of MID.

Meyer and colleagues have evaluated the effect of treating risk factors (hypertension) in patients with MID (Meyer, McClintic, Rogers, Sims, & Mortel, 1988). Using the CCSE to evaluate the extent of cognitive impairment, they reported that hypertensive subjects with MID had improvement in cognition, often into the normal range, with moderate control of systolic blood pressure (Meyer, Judd, Tawaklna, Rogers, & Mortel, 1986). When systolic blood pressure was in the 135- to 150-mm Hg range, performance on this global measure improved. If the systolic pressure was lower or higher, performance deteriorated. In the normotensive group, improved performance was associated with cessation of smoking. In a small study of randomized MID patients, it was found that daily aspirin improved cerebral blood flow and cognitive performance (Meyer, Rogers, McClintic, Mortel, & Lotfi, 1989). These studies are not definitive and need to be replicated and extended by other investigators. At present, their importance is to suggest that MID may be preventable, and if present, the dementia may be modifiable by treatment of risk factors for atherosclerotic diseases.

Disease Course

There is a surprising lack of longitudinal research on MID. Perhaps not surprisingly, existing data are not particularly consistent. Barclay, Zemcov, Blass, and Sansone (1985) observed similar rates of cognitive decline in AD and MID but increased mortality associated with MID. Hershey, Modic, Jaffe, and Greenough (1986) prospectively studied seven cases of vascular dementia with neurological evaluations and the CCSE (Jacobs et al., 1977), Functional Activities Questionnaire (FAS) (Pfeiffer et al., 1982), and the IS (Hachinski et al., 1975). Over half of their patients showed cognitive improvement over the first year of observation, a finding that is in sharp contrast to the relentless downhill course that characterizes AD. A recent study of a small cohort of patients with putative BD ($n = 13$) suggested a considerably reduced rate of annual cognitive decline ($M = 0.6$ Mini-Mental State Examination [MMSE] points $\pm$ 3.2) in comparison to AD patients ($n = 74$; $M = 3.9$ MMSE points $\pm$ 3.7), all followed for a minimum of 18 months (Bennett, Gilley, Wilson, & Fox, 1991). Clinical experience and indirect evidence from treatment studies (e.g., Meyer et al., 1989) suggest that many patients stabilize or improve cognitively. Indeed, stepwise deterioration and fluctuating course were thought to be so characteristic of MID that Hachinski and colleagues (1975) included them as items on the IS. At present, perhaps the most that can be said is that the course of cognitive decline in MID appears to differ from the relentless progression seen in AD. Indeed, it remains to be demonstrated that vascular disease can cause slowly progressive cognitive decline (Tatemichi, 1990). Binswanger's disease, the form of vascular dementia most likely to produce such a clinical picture, does not appear to do so (Bennett et al., 1991). Tatemichi (1990) has proposed that the course of cognitive change may prove to be the most useful and informative means of classifying vascular dementia syndromes. At present, clinicians are apt to minimize diagnostic error if they think of AD or mixed AD/MID when faced with steadily progressive cognitive deterioration.

Conclusion

The field of vascular dementia is currently in a state of flux. The diagnostic classification problems that have hampered clinical evaluation and research have led to new classification systems (Bennett et al., 1990; Chui et al., 1992; Roman et al., in press). The new systems have not solved the classification problems, but, importantly, they have recognized the heterogeneity within vascular dementia, capitalized on recent radiological advances, and, to some degree, confronted the difficult issue of establishing a causal connection between dementia and stroke. These systems should provide helpful guidance for clinicians; their impact on longitudinal clinicopathological research is apt to be even more profound. Such research is needed to identify the various forms of vascular dementia, their course and consequences, and the neural mechanisms responsible for the dementia. Neuropsychological knowledge of vascular dementia is a reflection of the current state of the field. The most informative neuropsychological research has been conducted on well-defined subtypes of vascular dementia (e.g., lacunar state, BD). Although sweeping generalizations about these dementias are not possible at present, the good news is that the new classification systems offer exciting opportunities for neuropsychological research in the next decade. This research is likely to sharpen differential diagnosis, clarify the temporal courses of different vascular and mixed dementia syndromes, identify factors that may modify that course, and provide insight into the pathophysiological basis of these dementia syndromes.

References

Alzheimer, A. (1902). Die seelenstorungen auf arteriosklerotischer grundlage. *Allqemeine Zeitschrift für Psychiatrie und Psychischgerichtliche Medizin*, 59, 695–711.

American Heart Association. (1988). Stroke statistics from the American Heart Association. *Stroke*, 19, 547.

American Psychiatric Association. (1987). *Diagnostic and statistical manual of mental disorders* (3rd ed., rev.). Washington, DC: Author.

Babikian, V., & Ropper, A. H. (1987). Binswanger's disease: A review. *Stroke*, 18, 2–12.

Barclay, L. L., Zemcov, A., Blass, J. P., & Sansone, J. (1985). Survival in Alzheimer's disease and vascular dementias. *Neurology*, 35, 834–840.

Bennett, D. A., Charletta, D., Gilley, D. W., Cochran, E., & Hayes, K. (1991). Clinical correlates of high signal lesions on MRI in pathologically proven Alzheimer's disease. *Neurology*, 41 (1), 407.

Bennett, D. A., Gilley, D. W., Wilson, R. S., & Fox, J. H. (1991). Rate of cognitive decline in Binswanger's disease vs. Alzheimer's disease with and without white matter lesions. *Annals of Neurology*, 30, 250.

Bennett, D. A., Wilson, R. S., Gilley, D. W., & Fox, J. H. (1990). Clinical diagnosis of Binswanger's disease. *Journal of Neurology, Neurosurgery and Psychiatry*, 53, 961–965.

Benson, D. F. (1979). *Aphasia, alexia, and agraphia*. New York: Churchill Livingstone.

Benson, D. F., Cummings, J. L., & Tsai, S. Y. (1982). Angular gyrus syndrome simulating Alzheimer's disease. *Archives of Neurology*, 39, 616–620.

Benson, D. F., Kuhl, D. E., Hawkins, R. A., Phelps, M. R., Cummings, J. L., & Tsai, S. Y. (1983). The fluorodeoxyglucose 18F scan in Alzheimer's disease and multi-infarct dementia. *Archives of Neurology*, 40, 711–714.

Bernard, B. A., Wilson, R. S., Gilley, D. W., Bennett, D. A., Waters, W. F., & Fox, J. H. (1992). Memory failure in Binswanger's disease and Alzheimer's disease. *The Clinical Neuropsychologist*, 6, 230–240.

Bernard, B. A., Wilson, R. S., Gilley, D. W., Grosse, D. A., Bennett, D. A., Whalen, M. E., & Fox, J. H. (1990). Performance of patients with BD and AD on the Mattis dementia rating scale. *Journal of Clinical and Experimental Neuropsychology*, 12, 22.

Binswanger, O. (1894). Die abgrenzung des allgemeinen progressiven paralyses. (Referate erstattet auf der Jahresversammlung des Vereins Deutscher Irrenärtzte zu Dresden am 20 September, 1894). *Berliner Klinische Wochenschrift, 31,* 1103–1105, 1137–1139, 1180–1186.

Brinkman, S. D., & Braun, P. (1984). Classification of dementia patients by a WAIS profile related to central cholinergic deficiencies. *Journal of Clinical Neuropsychology, 6,* 393–400.

Brinkman, S. D., Largen, J. W., Jr., Cushman, L., Braun, P. R., & Block, R. (1986). Clinical validators: Alzheimer's disease and multi-infarct dementia. In L. W. Poon (Ed.), *Handbook for clinical memory assessment of older adults.* Washington, DC: American Psychological Association.

Brun, A., & Englund, E. (1986). A white matter disorder in dementia of the Alzheimer type: A pathoanatomical study. *Annals of Neurology, 19,* 253–262.

Brust, J. C. M. (1988). Vascular dementia is overdiagnosed. *Archives of Neurology, 45,* 799–801.

Bucht, G., Adolfsson, R., & Winblad, B. (1984). Dementia of the Alzheimer type and multi-infarct dementia: A clinical description and diagnostic problems. *Journal of the American Geriatrics Society, 32,* 491–498.

Chui, H. C. (1989). Dementia: A review emphasizing clinicopathologic correlation and brain-behavior relationship. *Archives of Neurology, 46,* 806–814.

Chui, H. C., Victoroff, J. I., Margolin, D., Jagust, W., Shankle, R., & Katzman, R. (1992). Criteria for the diagnosis of ischemic vascular dementia proposed by the State of California Alzheimer's Disease Diagnostic and Treatment Centers. *Neurology, 42,* 473–480.

Cummings, J. L. (1991). Subcortical dementia as a manifestation of cerebrovascular disease. *NINDS/AIREN International Workshop on Vascular Dementia.* Workshop conducted at Bethesda, MD, April 19–21, 1991.

Cummings, J. L., & Benson, D. F. (1983). *Dementia—a clinical approach.* Boston: Butterworth's.

Cummings, J. L., Miller, B., Hill, M. A., & Neshkes, R. (1987). Neuropsychiatric aspects of multi-infarct dementia and dementia of the Alzheimer type. *Archives of Neurology, 44,* 389–393.

DeReuck, J., Crevitis, L., Deconster, S., Sieben, B., & Vander Becken, H. (1980). Pathogenesis of Binswanger's chronic progressive subcortical encephalopathy. *Neurology, 30,* 920–928.

Drachman, D. A., O'Donnell, B. F., Lew, R. A., & Swearer, J. M. (1990). The prognosis in Alzheimer's disease—'how far' rather than 'how fast' best predicts the course. *Archives of Neurology, 47,* 851–856.

Erkinjuntti, T. (1987). Types of multi-infarct dementia. *Acta Neurologica Scandinavica, 75,* 391–399.

Erkinjuntti, T., Ketonen, L., Sulkava, R., Vuorialho, M., & Palo, J. (1987). CT in the differential diagnosis between Alzheimer's disease and vascular dementia. *Acta Neurologica Scandinavica, 75,* 262–270.

Fischer, P., Gatterer, G., Marterer, A., & Danielczyk, W. (1988). Nonspecificity of semantic impairment in dementia of Alzheimer's type. *Archives of Neurology, 45,* 1341–1343.

Fisher, C. M. (1982). Lacunar strokes and infarcts: A review. *Neurology, 32,* 871–876.

Folstein, M., Anthony, J. C., Parhad, I., Duffy, B., & Gruenberg, E. M. (1985). The meaning of cognitive impairment in the elderly. *Journal of the American Geriatrics Society, 33,* 228–235.

Fuld, P. A. (1986). Pathological and chemical validation of behavioral features of Alzheimer's disease. In L. W. Poon et al. (Eds.), *Clinical memory assessment of older adults* (pp. 302–306). New York: American Psychological Association.

Fuster, J. (1980). *The prefrontal cortex: Anatomy, physiology, and neuropsychology of the frontal lobe*. New York: Raven Press.

Gainotti, G., Caltagirone, C., Masullo, C., & Miceli, G. (1980). Patterns of neuropsychologic impairment in various diagnostic groups of dementia. In L. Amaducci, A. N. Davis, & P. Antuono (Eds.), *Aging: Vol. 13. Aging of the brain and dementia* (pp. 245–250). New York: Raven Press.

Gainotti, G., Parlato, V., Monteleone, D., & Carlomagno, S. (1992). Neuropsychological markers of dementia on visual-spatial tasks: A comparison between Alzheimer's type and vascular forms of dementia. *Journal of Clinical and Experimental Neuropsychology, 14*(2), 239–252.

Garraway, W. M., Whisnant, J. P., Furlan, A. J., Phillips, L. H., Kurland, L. T., & O'Fallon, W. M. (1979). The declining incidence of stroke. *New England Journal of Medicine, 300*, 449–452.

Gilley, D. W., Bennett, D. A., Grosse, D. A., Wilson, R. S., & Fox, J. H. (1990). Risk factors and clinical features associated with depression in Alzheimer's disease. *Neurology, 40*, (Suppl. 1), 447.

Gilley, D. W., & Wilson, R. S. (1991). Nuisance parameters in the assessment of noncognitive manifestations of dementia. *Psychology and Aging, 6*, 528–532.

Gilley, D. W., Wilson, R. S., Bennett, D. A., Bernard, B. A., & Fox, J. H. (1991). Predictors of behavioral disturbance in Alzheimer's disease. *Journal of Gerontology: Psychological Sciences, 46*, 362–371.

Gilley, D. W., Wilson, R. S., Grosse, D. A., Harrison, D. W., Goetz, C. G., & Tanner, C. M. (in press). Impact of Alzheimer's-type dementia and information source on the assessment of depression. *Psychology and Aging*.

Gilley, D. W., Wilson, R. S., & Stebbins, G. T. (1992). Validity of the Geriatric Depression Scale in Alzheimer's disease. *Journal of Clinical and Experimental Neuropsychology, 14*(1), 20.

Ginsberg, M. D., Hedley-Whyte, E. T., & Richardson, E. P., Jr. (1976). Hypoxic-ischemic leukoencephalopathy in man. *Archives of Neurology, 33*, 5–14.

Grosse, D. A., Gilley, D. W., Bernard, B. A., Wilson, R. S., & Bennett, D. A. (1991). Semantic and episodic memory in Binswanger's versus Alzheimer's disease. *Journal of Clinical and Experimental Neuropsychology, 13*, 70.

Haase, G. R. (1977). Diseases presenting as dementia. In C. E. Wells (Ed.), *Dementia* (2nd ed., pp. 27–67). Philadelphia: F. A. Davis Company.

Hachinski, V. C., Iliff, L. D., Zilhka, E., Duboulay, G. H., McAllister, V. L., Marshall, J., Russell, R. W. R., & Symon, L. (1975). Cerebral blood flow in dementia. *Archives of Neurology, 32*, 632–637.

Hachinski, V. C., Lassen, N. A., & Marshall, J. (1974). Multi-infarct dementia a cause of mental deterioration in the elderly. *Lancet, 2*, 207–209.

Hachinski, V. C., Potter, P., & Merskey, H. (1987). Leuko-araiosis. *Archives of Neurology, 44*, 21–23.

Hamilton, M. (1960). A rating scale for depression. *Journal of Neurology, Neurosurgery and Psychiatry, 23*, 56–61.

Hershey, L. A., Modic, M. T., Jaffe, D. F., & Greenough, P. G. (1986). Natural history of the vascular dementias: A prospective study of seven cases. *Canadian Journal of Neurological Sciences, 13*, 559–565.

Hier, D. B., Hagenlocker, K., & Shindler, A. G. (1985). Language disintegration in dementia: Effects of etiology and severity. *Brain and Language, 25*, 117–133.

Hier, D. B., Warrach, J. D., Gorelick, P. B., & Thomas, J. (1989). Predictors of survival in clinically diagnosed Alzheimer's disease and multi-infarct dementia. *Archives of Neurology, 46*, 1213–1216.

Huang, K., Wu, L., & Luo, Y. (1985). Binswanger's disease: Progressive subcortical encephalopathy or multi-infarct dementia? *Canadian Journal of Neurological Sciences*, *12*, 88–94.

Ishii, N., Nishihara, Y., & Imamura, T. (1986). Why do frontal lobe symptoms predominate in vascular dementia with lacunes? *Neurology*, *36*, 340–345.

Jacobs, J. W., Bernhard, M. R., Delgado, A., & Strain, J. J. (1977). Screening for organic mental syndromes in medically ill. *Annals of Internal Medicine*, *86*, 40–45.

Jagust, W. J., Budinger, T. F., & Reed, B. R. (1987). The diagnosis of dementia with single photon emission computed tomography. *Archives of Neurology*, *44*, 258–262.

Joynt, R. (1988). Vascular dementia: Too much, or too little? *Neurology*, *45*, 801.

Kase, C. (1986). "Multi-infarct" dementia: A real entity? *Journal of the American Geriatrics Society*, *34*, 482–484.

Kase, C. S., Wolf, P. A., Bachman, D. L., Linn, R. T., & Cupples, L. A. (1989). Dementia and stroke: The Framingham study. In M. D. Ginsberg & W. D. Dietrich (Eds.), *Cerebrovascular diseases. 16th Research (Princeton) Conference* (pp. 193–198). New York: Raven Press.

Kaszniak, A. W., Wilson, R. S., Fox, J. H., & Stebbins, G. T. (1986). Cognitive assessment in Alzheimer's disease: Cross-sectional and longitudinal perspectives. *Canadian Journal of Neurological Science*, *13*, 420–423.

Katzman, R. (1983). Vascular disease and dementia. In M. D. Yahr (Ed.), *H. Houston Merritt memorial volume* (pp. 153–176). New York: Raven Press.

Kinkel, W. R., Jacobs, L., Polachine, I., Bates, V., & Heffner, R. R., Jr. (1985). Subcortical arteriosclerotic encephalopathy (Binswanger's disease) computed tomographic, nuclear magnetic resonance, and clinical correlations. *Archives of Neurology*, *42*, 951–959.

Kuhl, D. E., Metter, E. J., & Riege, W. H. (1985). Patterns of cerebral glucose utilization in depression, multiple infarct dementia, and Alzheimer's disease. In L. Sokologg (Ed.), *Brain imaging and brain function*. New York: Raven Press.

Ladurner, G., Iliff, L. D., & Lechner, H. (1982). Clinical factors associated with dementia in ischemic stroke. *Journal of Neurology, Neurosurgery and Psychiatry*, *45*, 97–101.

Liston, E. H., & LaRue, A. (1983). Clinical differentiation of primary degenerative and multi-infarct dementia: A critical review of the evidence. Part II: Pathological studies. *Biological Psychiatry*, *18*, 1467–1484.

Loeb, C., Gandolfo, C., & Bino, G. (1988). Intellectual impairment and cerebral lesions in multiple cerebral infarcts—a clinical computed tomography study. *Stroke*, *19*, 560–565.

Lopez, O. L., Boller, F., Becker, J. T., Miller, M., & Reynolds, C. F., III. (1990). Alzheimer's disease and depression: Neuropsychological impairment and progression of the illness. *American Journal of Psychiatry*, *147*, 855–860.

Loring, D. W., Meador, K. J., Mahurin, R. K., & Largen, J. W. (1986). Neuropsychological performance in dementia of the Alzheimer type and multi-infarct dementia. *Archives of Clinical Neuropsychology*, *1*, 335–340.

Luria, A. R., & Hutton, J. T. (1977). A modern assessment of the basic forms of aphasia. *Brain and Language*, *4*, 129–151.

Marie, P. (1901). Des foyers lacunaires de desintegration et de differents autres etats cavitaire du cerveau. *Revue de Medicine*, *21*, 281–298.

Martin, E. M., Wilson, R. S., Penn, R. D., Fox, J. H., Clasen, R. A., & Savoy, S. M. (1987). Cortical biopsy results in Alzheimer disease: Correlation with cognitive deficits. *Neurology*, *37*, 1201–1204.

Metter, E. J. (1985). *Speech disorders: Clinical evaluation and diagnosis*. New York: Spectrum.

Metter, E. J., Mazziotta, J. C., Itabashi, H. H., Mankovich, N. J., Phelps, M. E., & Kuhl,

D. E. (1985). Comparison of glucose metabolism, x-ray CT, and postmortem data in a patient with multiple cerebral infarcts. *Neurology, 35*, 1695–1701.

Meyer, J. S., Judd, B. W., Tawaklna, T., Rogers, R. L., & Mortel, K. F. (1986). Improved cognition after control of risk factors for multi-infarct dementia. *Journal of the American Medical Association, 256*, 2203–2209.

Meyer, J. S., McClintic, K. L., Rogers, R. L., Sims, P., & Mortel, K. F. (1988). Aetiological considerations and risk factors for multi-infarct dementia. *Journal of Neurology, Neurosurgery and Psychiatry, 51*, 1489–1497.

Meyer, J. S., Rogers, R. L., McClintic, K., Mortel, K. F., & Lotfi, J. (1989). Randomized clinical trial of daily aspirin therapy in multi-infarct dementia—a pilot study. *Journal of the American Geriatrics Society, 37*, 549–555.

Meyer, J. S., Rogers, R. L., Judd, B. W., Mortel, K. F., & Sims, P. (1988). Cognition and cerebral blood flow fluctuate together in multi-infarct dementia. *Stroke, 19*, 163–169.

Molsa, P. K., Marttila, R. J., & Rinne, U. K. (1982). Epidemiology of dementia in a Finnish population. *Acta Neurologica Scandinavica, 86*, 541–552.

Molsa, P. K., Paljarvi, L., Rinne, J. O., Rinne, U. K., & Sako, E. (1985). Validity of clinical diagnosis in dementia: A prospective clinicopathological study. *Journal of Neurology, Neurosurgery and Psychiatry, 48*, 1085–1090.

O'Brien, M. D. (1988). Vascular dementia is underdiagnosed. *Archives of Neurology, 45*, 797–798.

Perez, F. I., Gay, J. R. A., & Taylor, R. L. (1975). WAIS performance of neurologically impaired age. *Psychological Reports, 37*, 1043–1047.

Perez, F. I., Gay, J. R. A., Taylor, R. L., & Rivera, V. M. (1975). Patterns of memory performance in the neurologically impaired age. *Canadian Journal of Neurological Sciences, 1*, 347–355.

Perez, F. I., Rivera, V. M., Meyer, J. S., Gay, J. R. A., Taylor, R. L., & Mathew, N. T. (1975). Analysis of intellectual and cognitive performance in patients with multi-infarct dementia, vertebrobasilar insufficiency with dementia, and Alzheimer's disease. *Journal of Neurology, Neurosurgery and Psychiatry, 38*, 533–540.

Perez, F. I., Stump, D. A., Gay, J. R. A., & Hart, V. R. (1976). Intellectual performance in multi-infarct dementia and Alzheimer's disease—a replication study. *Canadian Journal of Neurological Sciences, 3*, 181–187.

Pfeiffer, R. I., Kurosaki, T. T., Harrah, C. H., Jr., Chance, J. M., & Filos, S. (1982). Measurement of functional activities in older adults in the community. *Journal of Gerontology, 37*, 323–329.

Reisberg, B., Ferris, S. H., deLeon, M. J., & Crook, T. (1982). The Global Deterioration Scale for the assessment of primary degenerative dementia. *American Journal of Psychiatry, 139*, 1136–1139.

Rogers, R. L., Meyer, J. S., Mortel, K. F., Mahurin, R. K., & Judd, B. W. (1986). Decreased cerebral blood flow precedes multi-infarct dementia, but follows senile dementia of Alzheimer's type. *Neurology, 36*, 1–6.

Roman, G. C. (1985). Lacunar dementia. In J. T. Hutton & A. D. Kenny (Eds.), *Senile dementia of the Alzheimer type* (pp. 131–151). New York: Alan R. Liss.

Roman, G. C. (1987). Senile dementia of the Binswanger type, a vascular form of dementia in the elderly. *Journal of the American Medical Association, 258*, 1782–1788.

Roman, G. C., Tatemichi, T. K., Erkinjuntti, T., Cummings, J. L., Masdeu, J. C., Garcia, J. H., Armaducci, L., Orgogozo, J.-M., Brun, A., Hofman, A., Chui, H. C., Moody, D. M., O'Brien, M. D., Yamaguchi, T., Grafman, J., Drayer, B. P., Bennett, D. A., Fisher, M., Ogata, J., Kokmen, E., Bermejo, F., Wolf, P. A., Gorelick, P. B., Bick, K. L., Pajeau, A., Bell, M. A., DeCarli, C., Culebras, A., Korczyn, A. D., Bogousslavsky, J., Hartmann, A., & Scheinberg, P. (in press). Vascular dementia: Diagnostic criteria for research studies. Report of the NINDS-AIREN International Work Group. *Neurology*.

Rosen, W. G., Terry, R. D., Fuld, P. A., Katzman, R., & Peck, A. (1980). Pathological verification of ischemic score differentiation of dementia. *Annals of Neurology, 7,* 486–488.

Strub, R. L., & Black, F. W. (1977). *The Mental Status Examination in Neurology*. Philadelphia: F. A. Davis Company.

Stuss, D. T., & Benson, D. F. (1986). *The frontal lobes* (pp. 59–61). New York: Raven Press.

Tatemichi, T. K. (1990). How acute brain failure becomes chronic. A view of the mechanisms of dementia related to stroke. *Neurology, 40,* 1652–1659.

Tatemichi, T. K. (1991). Cerebrovascular disease and dementia: Epidemiology, classification, and therapy. *NINDS/AIREN International Workshop on Vascular Dementia*. Workshop conducted at Bethesda, MD, April 19–21, 1991.

Tatemichi, T. K., Foulkes, M. A., Mohr, J. P., Hewitt, J. R., Hier, D. B., Price, T. R., & Wolf, P. A. (1990). Dementia in stroke survivors in the Stroke Data Bank cohort: Prevalence, incidence, risk factors, and computed tomographic findings. *Stroke, 21,* 858–866.

Thal, L. J., Grundman, M., & Klauber, M. R. (1988). Dementia: Characteristics of a referral population and factors associated with progression. *Neurology, 38,* 1083–1090.

Tomlinson, B. E., Blessed, G., & Roth, M. (1970). Observations on the brains of demented old people. *Journal of Neurological Science, 11,* 205–242.

Ulrich, J., Probst, A., & Wuest, M. (1986). The brain diseases causing senile dementia—a morphological study on 54 consecutive autopsy cases. *Journal of Neurology, 233,* 118–122.

Williams, J. (1988). A structured interview guide for the Hamilton Depression Rating Scale. *Archives of General Psychiatry, 45,* 742–747.

Winocur, G. (1984). Memory localization in the brain. In L. Squire & N. Butters (Eds.), *Neuropsychology of memory*. New York: Guilford Press.

Wolfe, N., Linn, R., Babikian, V. L., Knoefel, J. E., & Albert, M. L. (1990). Frontal systems impairment following multiple lacunar infarcts. *Archives of Neurology, 47,* 129–132.

15

White Matter Dementias

Stephen M. Rao

In recent years considerable attention has been devoted to subtyping dementing illnesses. One such classification schema posits a distinction between cortical and subcortical dementias (Albert, 1978; Cummings & Benson, 1984; Cummings, 1990). Alzheimer's and Pick's diseases are frequently cited as prototypes of cortical dementia, whereas Huntington's and Parkinson's diseases are viewed as "typical" subcortical dementias. The distinction is based not only on relative differences in the location of the neuropathology, but also on the pattern of neuropsychological deficits observed in these dementia subtypes. According to this schema, cortical dementias result in dramatic losses in intelligence, resulting from amnesia, aphasia, agnosia, and apraxia. In contrast, subcortical dementias are characterized by a relative preservation of intelligence and language in the context of problems with forgetfulness (due to retrieval failure rather than deficits in storage or encoding); slowed mental processing speed; and impairments in conceptual reasoning, sustained attention, and visuospatial processing.

These dementia subtypes are based on clinical and pathological observations of patients with primary disease of *gray matter* structures. It is not clear whether the subcortical dementia classification also applies to dementias that primarily involve the cerebral white matter (a partial list is presented in Table 15.1). Interest in *white matter* dementias has grown because of a relatively new imaging technology (i.e., magnetic resonance imaging [MRI]), that provides exquisite anatomic detail of regions of demyelination within the cerebral white matter.

TABLE 15.1.   Examples of Conditions Affecting Cerebral White Matter

Multiple sclerosis
Vascular (Binswanger's disease, leukoaraiosis)
AIDS dementia
Normal-pressure hydrocephalus
Progressive multifocal leukoencephalopathy
Alcoholic dementia
Marchiafava-Bignami disease
Toluene abuse
Closed head injury

Note: AIDS = acquired immunodeficiency syndrome.

438

In our previous writings we (Rao, 1986; Rao, 1990) have suggested that the pattern of dementia observed in patients with multiple sclerosis (MS), the most common white matter disease, is similar to that described in gray matter subcortical dementias. Other investigators, however, have suggested that white matter dementias possess unique neurobehavioral features (Filley, Franklin, Heaton, & Rosenberg, 1989).

In this chapter, we will examine whether white matter dementia should be viewed as a distinct and separate entity from subcortical dementia. The review will concentrate on studies of MS patients, because this illness is the best studied of the white matter dementias from a neuropsychological perspective. We will also review data regarding the neurobehavioral correlates of white matter lesions in patients with hypertensive disease. Finally, we will speculate regarding possible mechanisms by which white matter disease affects behavior. It should be noted that several diseases that can produce white matter dementia syndromes, such as acquired immunodeficiency syndrome (AIDS), alcoholism, closed head injury, and cerebrovascular disease, are discussed elsewhere in this volume.

Multiple Sclerosis

Disease Background

The clinical presentation in MS is highly variable owing to the nearly random distribution of demyelinating lesions scattered throughout the central nervous system (CNS) white matter. Whereas some degree of cognitive dysfunction occurs in approximately 40% to 60% of MS patients (Peyser, Rao, LaRocca, & Kaplan, 1990; Rao, Leo, Bernardin, & Unverzagt, 1991), the disease is rarely diagnosed on the basis of neurobehavioral symptoms. Motor weakness and ataxia, fatigue, spasticity, optic neuritis, diplopia, numbness, paresthesia, pain, and bowel/bladder dysfunction are some of the more common clinical symptoms. The diagnosis is generally based on well-defined criteria applied to information derived from the neurological examination and various laboratory studies, such as MRI, spinal fluid examinations, and evoked potentials (Sibley, 1990).

Most MS patients experience their first symptoms between the ages of 20 and 45, with the mean age of symptom onset between 29 and 33 (Matthews, Acheson, Batchelor, & Weller, 1985). Prevalence in the United States is approximately 60/100,000 (Baum & Rothschild, 1981; Kurtzke, 1984), making it the most common nontraumatic disabling neurological illness affecting young and middle-aged adults (Johnson et al., 1979). Prevalence rates generally increase with increasing latitudes away from the equator (Baum & Rothschild, 1981). The prevalence of MS is 1.5 to 1.9 times more common in females than males, and the rate among whites is nearly twice that among nonwhites (Baum & Rothschild, 1981). While the exact cause of MS is unknown, there is strong evidence that abnormal immune responses are important in the pathogenesis of MS (Iivanainen, 1981). It is also widely believed that genetic factors as well as early exposure to an environmental agent may play important roles (McDonald, 1986; McKhann, 1982).

The course of the disease is highly variable, ranging from benign (i.e., a few clinical exacerbations followed by nearly complete remission of symptoms) to severe (i.e., frequent clinical exacerbations with accumulating neurological deficit or chronic progressive deterioration). In the vast majority of cases the disease does not shorten lifespan (Kurtzke et al., 1970). Very little information is known regarding the natural history of dementia in MS. Cross-sectional neuropsychological studies have generally not found a relationship between cognitive test performance and length of illness (Ivnik, 1978a; Marsh, 1980; Rao, Hammeke, McQuillen, Khatri, & Lloyd, 1984). Results of longitudinal studies (Canter, 1951; Fink & Houser, 1966; Ivnik, 1978b) have produced equivocal results, but have been criticized because of numerous methodological shortcomings (i.e., small sample size, inadequate controls, and brief retest intervals). A recent study suggests that, on the average, the progression of cognitive deficits may be relatively slow in MS patients (Jennekens-Schinkel, Laboyrie, Lanser, & Van der Velde, 1990).

Dementia in MS patients can have a negative impact on social functioning. In a recently completed study at our medical center, we (Rao, Leo, Ellington, et al., 1991) found that MS patients with cognitive dysfunction were less likely to be employed, required greater personal assistance, and were less likely to engage in social activities than cognitively intact MS patients. These results could not be explained on the basis of group differences in physical disability, presence of affective disorder, or medication usage.

Dementia Features

In this section we will review the literature on the most common neurobehavioral abnormalities in MS. As is true of all symptoms of MS, considerable interpatient variability is observed with regard to dementia severity. As noted previously, the prevalence of cognitive dysfunction in MS ranges from 40% to 60%. Of the cognitively impaired patients, approximately 20% to 30% exhibit severe dementia (Rao et al., 1984). To illustrate the range of dementia severity in MS, we present in Table 15.2 the clinical, neuroimaging, and neuropsychological data obtained from three female patients with definite MS: one with little or no signs of dementia, one with mild to moderate cognitive dysfunction, and another with severe dementia. Throughout this section, we will refer to the results of the comprehensive neurobehavioral assessment presented in Table 15.2. Due to space limitations, it is not possible to present a complete description of the assessment procedures, although the reader may obtain this information from a previous paper (Rao, Leo, Haughton, St. Aubin-Faubert, & Bernardin, 1989). Impairment on a given neurobehavioral test was defined as performance less than the fifth percentile of a demographically matched normal control group ($N = 100$) (Rao, Leo, Bernardin, & Unverzagt, 1991).

MRI Findings

Pathological studies indicate that virtually all definite MS patients have cerebral white matter lesions at autopsy (Brownell & Hughes, 1962; Lumsden, 1970; Barnard & Triggs, 1974). Atrophy of the corpus callosum (Barnard & Triggs, 1974) and enlargement of the ventricles (Brownell & Hughes, 1962; Lumsden, 1970) are also common. Studies from our center (Rao, Leo, Haughton, et al., 1989) and from others (Franklin, Heaton, Nelson, Filley, & Seibert, 1988; Huber et al., 1987; Medaer et al., 1987; Reischies, Baum, Brau, Hedde, & Schwindt, 1988; Brainin

TABLE 15.2.   Examples of MS Patients with Minimal (D.A.),
Mild/Moderate (R.W.), and Severe (D.R.)
Neurobehavioral Impairment

	Patient		
	D.A.	R.W.	D.R.
Demographic and Illness Characteristics			
Age	33	48	56
Education	12	14	12
Sex	F	F	F
Handedness	R	L	R
Estimated VIQ (Barona et al., 1984)	104	110	101
MS duration (years)	10	6	16
Kurtzke EDSS (10)	6.0	6.0	6.5
MRI Findings			
Total lesion area (cm²)	20.9	67.4	115.2
Ventricular-brain ratio	.014	.055	.101
Size of the corpus callosum (cm²)	5.7	5.1	0.1
Neuropsychological Test Findings			
Mini-Mental State Examination	30	30	28
Verbal Intelligence (WAIS-R)	101	101	84[a]
Information (age-corrected scores)	7	10	8
Digit Span	12	9	8
Vocabulary	12	10	7[a]
Arithmetic	11	8	5[a]
Comprehension	11	11	8
Similarities	11	12	8
Memory			
Selective Reminding Test:			
Long-term storage (144)	105	61[a]	32[a]
Consistent long-term retrieval (144)	67	36[a]	0[a]
Recognition (24)	24	23	19[a]
Story Recall Test:			
Total recall (23)	12	11	7[a]
Delayed recall (23)	7	7	4[a]
7/24 Spatial Recall Test:			
Total recall (35)	33	31	20[a]
Controlled Oral Word Association Test			
Total words generated	53	28	22[a]
Abstract/Conceptual Reasoning			
Wisconsin Card Sorting Test:			
Categories completed (6)	6	0[a]	0[a]
Perseverative responses	15	88[a]	124[a]
Booklet Category Test:			
Total errors (208)	58	99	128[a]
Raven Progressive Matrices:			
Number correct (60)	51	37	13[a]
Speed of Information Processing			
Sternberg High Speed Scanning Task:			
Scan rate (msec per digit)	61	54	254[a]
Paced Auditory Serial Addition Test:			
Easy—number correct (60)	57	22[a]	NA
Hard—number correct (60)	36	13[a]	NA
Stroop Interference Test:			
Color/word—word condition (sec)	54	104	135[a]
Reaction Time:			
Complex—simple RT (msec)	201	120	764[a]

Continued

TABLE 15.2.   (*Continued*)

	Patient		
	D.A.	R.W.	D.R.
Language			
Abbreviated Boston Naming Test:			
Total correct (15)	15	15	9[a]
Oral Comprehension:			
Total correct (15)	12	9	9
Visuospatial Skills			
Hooper Visual Organization Test:			
Total correct (30)	27	28	14[a]
Judgment of Line Orientation Test:			
Total correct (35)	29	16[a]	11[a]
Facial Recognition Test:			
Total correct (58)	50	47	33[a]
Visual Form Discrimination Test:			
Total correct (32)	32	22[a]	19[a]
Interhemispheric Communication			
Verbal Dichotic Listening Task:			
Right ear (% correct)	53	67	60
Left ear (% correct)	53	50	30
Difference in % accuracy	0	17	30[a]
Object Naming Latency Task:			
Right visual field (msec)	771	878	997
Left visual field (msec)	792	929	1201
% difference in reaction time	3	6	19[a]
Personality			
Zung Depression Scale (80)	42[a]	32	29
State-Trait Anxiety Inventory:			
State (80)	28	23	26
Trait (80)	35	37	34
Katz Adjustment Scale:			
Withdrawal (24)	9	11	15[a]
Confusion (12)	3	3	5[a]
Helplessness (16)	5	4	9[a]

[a]Score exceeds the fifth percentile of a demographically matched normalcontrol group (*N* = 100).

Note: Numbers in parentheses refer to maximum scores for each scale; MS = multiple sclerosis; VIQ = Verbal IQ; EDSS = Expanded Disability Status Scale; MRI = magnetic resonance imaging; WAIS-R = Wechsler Adult Intelligence Scale-Revised; NA = not administered; RT = reaction time.

et al., 1988; Callanan, Logsdail, Ron, & Warrington, 1989; Anzola et al., 1990) have found robust correlations between cognitive test performance and various MRI indices of cerebral disease activity, such as total lesion area, size of the lateral and third ventricles, and size of the corpus callosum. In contrast, our attempts to relate the location of cerebral lesions to specific patterns of cognitive test performance have not met with success (Rao, Connolly, Haughton, and Leo, in preparation). We will speculate on the reasons for these negative findings in a later section.

All three of the MS patients presented in Table 15.2 had cerebral white matter involvement on MRI, although to varying degrees, as shown in Figure 15.1. Note

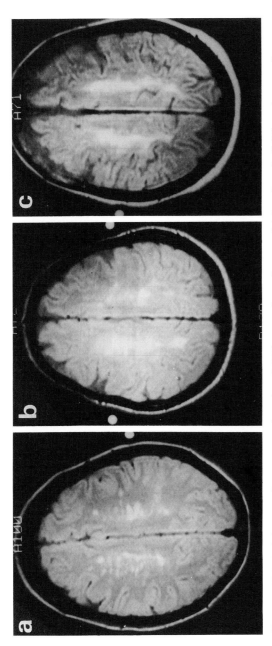

FIGURE 15.1 Axial magnetic resonance imaging (MRI) scans from three multiple sclerosis (MS) patients at the level just superior to the lateral ventricles. Note that Patient D.A. (a), who has no or minimal cognitive involvement, has small, discrete lesions. In contrast, Patients R.W. (b) and D.R. (c), who have mild to moderate and severe cognitive impairment, respectively, have large confluent lesions that involve large areas of the periventricular white matter.

that patient D.A. has multiple, small, well-defined lesions, whereas patients R.W. and D.R. have larger, irregular lesions formed from the coalescence of smaller lesions. For each of these patients, total lesion area, ventricular-brain ratio (a measure of ventricular dilatation), and size of the corpus callosum were measured using software routines on our MRI scanner (Rao, Leo, Haughton, et al., 1989) (see Table 15.2). The quantitative measure of lesion area indicated that patients R.W. and D.R. had three and six times the amount of lesion area, respectively, as patient D.A. This index generally corresponds with the overall severity of cognitive dysfunction. Furthermore, age-inappropriate ventricular enlargement is observed in D.R. and particularly in R.W., as reflected in the relatively large ventricular-brain ratios. Finally, D.R.'s midsaggital MRI scan revealed only a small ribbon of callosal tissue, the significance of which will be discussed below in relation to her performance on measures of interhemispheric communication.

Intelligence

As a group, MS patients display relatively small declines on standardized measures of intelligence (Rao, 1986). On the Wechsler scales, the Performance IQ (PIQ) score is typically 7 to 10 points less than the Verbal IQ (VIQ). As we have noted previously (Rao, 1986), it is not clear whether this VIQ-PIQ difference represents a true decline in nonverbal problem solving or is an artifact caused by noncognitive deficits in motor slowing and incoordination. These motor impairments may interfere with the rapid manipulation of test materials resulting in lowered PIQ scores. Whereas modifications to the administration procedures have been proposed for the assessment of MS patients (Peyser et al., 1990), we prefer not to administer the Performance subtests in favor of spatial reasoning tasks that do not involve fine motor speed and coordination (e.g., Raven's Standard Progressive Matrices).

Of the three MS patients presented in Table 15.2, all were estimated to have premorbid VIQs in the 101 to 110 range based on demographic variables (e.g., education, premorbid occupation) (Barona, Reynolds, & Chastain, 1984). Whereas all three patients obtained VIQ scores less than their premorbid estimates, the difference between expected and actual VIQs was relatively small for patients D.A. and R.W. (three to nine points), but was more than 1 standard deviation (17 points) for patient D.R.

Memory

Memory deficits have been extensively studied in MS patients and have been reviewed elsewhere (Grafman, Rao, & Litvan, 1990). Briefly, controlled investigations indicate that secondary (long-term) memory is impaired primarily due to an inability to spontaneously retrieve previously learned information (Beatty & Gange, 1977; Beatty, Goodkin, Monson, Beatty, & Hertsgaard, 1988; Fischer, 1988; Heaton, Nelson, Thompson, Burks, & Franklin, 1985; Jambor, 1969; Minden, Moes, Orav, Kaplan, & Reich, 1990; Rao et al., 1984; Rao, Leo, & St. Aubin-Faubert, 1989; Vowels, 1979). Performance on measures of verbal spontaneity, like the Controlled Oral Word Association Test (COWAT), is frequently correlated with deficits on list learning tests, providing additional support for a semantic retrieval deficit in MS patients. Recognition memory is normal or less impaired than retrieval (Caine, Bamford, Schiffer, Shoulson, & Levy, 1986; Carroll, Gates, & Roldan, 1984; Rao et al., 1984), suggesting relatively intact encoding and storage mechanisms. Other studies (Beatty, Goodkin, Beatty, & Monson, 1989; Rao, Bernardin, Ellington, & Leo, 1990) indicate that MS patients demonstrate a normal buildup and release from proactive interference on the Wickens (1970) task, suggesting again that semantic encoding is intact. In a recently completed study, we (Grafman, Rao, Bernardin, & Leo, 1991) have shown that MS patients perform normally on automatic memory tests (e.g., estimating the frequency of stimulus presentation), but are impaired on tests requiring effort (e.g., free recall). These results suggest that central motivational factors may play a role in the memory retrieval problems of MS patients.

In contrast, MS patients perform normally on measures of primary (short-term) memory, such as digit span (Litvan, Grafman, Vendrel, & Martinez, 1988a,b; Heaton, Nelson, Thompson, Burks, & Franklin, 1985; Jambor, 1969; Rao, Hammeke, McQuillen, Khatri, & Lloyd, 1984; Vowels, 1979), the recency effect on list learning (Rao, Leo, & St. Aubin-Faubert, 1989), and the Brown-Peterson Interference task (Litvan et al., 1988a; Rao, Leo, & St. Aubin-Faubert, 1989), although a defect in working memory (i.e., the articulatory loop) has been suggested (Litvan et al., 1988b).

Implicit memory has also been examined in MS patients (Beatty & Monson, 1990; Beatty, Goodkin, Monson, & Beatty, 1990; Rao, Grafman, DiGiulio, Mittenberg, Bernardin, Leo, Unverzagt, and Luchetta, in press). These studies have found that MS patients perform normally on measures of semantic and lexical priming and on tests of motor (i.e., procedural) learning. Previous studies have suggested that priming is impaired in cortical dementias, but motor learning is intact, whereas the opposite pattern has been observed in subcortical dementias: intact priming and impaired motor learning (Salmon, Shimamura, Butters, & Smith, 1988; Heindel, Butters, & Salmon, 1988; Heindel, Salmon, Shults, Walicke, & Butters, 1989). It has been suggested that priming is disrupted by widespread cortical involvement, whereas impaired motor learning results from lesions involving the striatum (Heindel et al., 1989). If this explanation is correct, it is not surprising that a white matter disease like MS would have no effect on either type of implicit memory. These data provide some support for the argument that white matter dementias may be distinct from gray matter subcortical dementias.

Results of memory testing in Table 15.2 suggest that R.W.'s memory impairment is fairly specific, consisting of impairment on word list learning (Selective Reminding Test [SRT]) and verbal fluency (COWAT). She also has preserved recognition memory and intact recall of contextually meaningful verbal information (Story Recall). Patient D.R. has impaired recall and recognition memory, although the latter would appear to be less severely affected. D.R.'s memory deficit is also more global than R.W., because D.R. is also impaired on a measure of nonverbal learning (7/24 Test).

Abstract/Conceptual Reasoning

Multiple sclerosis patients perform poorly on measures of abstract/conceptual reasoning, like the Category Test (Heaton et al., 1985; Peyser et al., 1980; Reitan et al., 1971), Wisconsin Card Sorting Test (WCST) (Heaton et al., 1985; Rao et al., 1987), Grassi Block Substitution Test (Parsons et al., 1957), Levine Concept Formation task (Rao & Hammeke, 1984), and Weigl Sorting Test (Jambor, 1969). On sorting tasks, investigators have frequently noted that MS patients make an inordinate number of perseverative responses. Both R.W. and D.R. demonstrate a high number of perseverative responses on the WCST and make a large number of errors on the Booklet Category Test. D.R. also was significantly impaired on the Raven Progressive Matrices Test, which assesses complex visuospatial perception and reasoning.

Speed of Information Processing

It is commonly assumed that patients with subcortical dementias exhibit a slowing of information processing speed. Several studies (Rao, St. Aubin-Faubert, & Leo, 1989; Rao, Leo, Bernardin, & Unverzagt, 1991; Litvan et al., 1988a; van den Burg et al., 1987) have shown that MS patients are impaired on such diverse measures as the Sternberg High Speed Scanning Task, Paced Auditory Serial Addition Test (PASAT), Stroop Interference Test, and complex reaction time. In each of these studies an attempt was made to separate the relative contributions of motor speed from decision time.

These tests were also administered to the three MS patients. Patient D.R. demonstrated a profound slowing of mental processes, as evidenced by a more than fourfold increase in scanning rate on the Sternberg task and a four- to sixfold increase in decision time, measured by subtracting simple from complex reaction time. D.R. also demonstrated a slowing in her reading on an interference task (Stroop Test). She was unable to learn the instructions to the PASAT and was therefore not administered this task. However, whereas the PASAT may not be appropriate for severely impaired patients, it is particularly sensitive in detecting attentional disturbances in MS patients with milder degrees of cognitive impairment (Rao, Leo, Bernardin, & Unverzagt, 1991), such as R.W., who may perform normally on other mental processing tasks.

Language

Aphasic disorders are considered to be rare in subcortical dementias (Cummings & Benson, 1984). Clinical case reports (Olmos-Lau, Ginsberg, & Geller, 1977) would suggest that aphasia is also rare in MS, occurring only when acute demyelinating lesions extend into gray matter structures of the dominant cerebral hemisphere (Olmos-Lau et al., 1977; Friedman, Brem, & Mayeux, 1983). Whereas paraphasic disturbance is uncommon and repetition speech and comprehension are generally intact in MS, naming difficulties occur with some regularity (Drayer, 1988; Caine et al., 1986; Jambor, 1969; Rao, Leo, & St. Aubin-Faubert, 1989; van den Burg et al., 1987; Beatty & Monson, 1989). It is possible that the naming deficits result from a more general breakdown in linguistic retrieval processes (Beatty, Monson, & Goodkin, 1989). Naming deficits are only observed in patient D.R., whose dementia is rated as severe (see Table 15.2).

Visuospatial Skills

Visuospatial processes are frequently impaired in subcortical dementias (Cummings & Benson, 1984). Until recently, little information has been available pertaining to this cognitive domain in MS patients. Beatty et al. (1988) found that MS patients are impaired on Money's Road Map Test, a measure of visuospatial perception. In addition, we (Rao, Leo, Bernardin, & Unverzagt, 1991) have found that MS patients are impaired on the Hooper Visual Organization Test and on three Benton et al.'s tests: Judgment of Line Orientation, Facial Recognition, and Visual Form Discrimination. Table 15.2 indicates that patient D.R. is impaired on all four measures, whereas R.W. is impaired on two: Judgment of Line Orientation and Visual Form Discrimination.

Interhemispheric Communication

Two studies (Jacobson, Deppe, & Murray, 1983; Rubens, Froehling, Slater, & Anderson, 1985) have demonstrated that MS patients experience left ear suppression in reporting consonant-vowel syllables presented in a dichotic listening paradigm. These studies suggest that linguistic information, which is initially processed in the right hemisphere, does not effectively cross the corpus callosum for subsequent analysis by the language-dominant, left hemisphere. We hypothesized that disturbances in interhemispheric communication would only be seen in those MS patients with significant atrophy of the corpus callosum. This hypothesis was supported by data from both a dichotic listening task and a visual object naming latency task (Rao, Bernardin, et al., 1989). Specifically, we found that only those MS patients with corpus callosum atrophy exhibited an exaggerated right ear effect on dichotic listening and slower vocal reaction times to naming objects presented in their left visual field.

Significant atrophy of the corpus callosum is observed on the midsaggital MRI scan of D.R. (see corpus callosum area measurement in Table 15.2). In keeping with the results of the group study noted above, this patient demonstrated an exaggerated right ear advantage on the Verbal Dichotic Listening Task and was significantly faster in naming objects presented to her right visual field (Object Naming Latency Task). These findings would suggest that D.R. has decreased interhemispheric communication. These results could not be explained as the result of nonspecific effects of severe dementia, because one would expect an equivalent reduction in accuracy from both ears on dichotic listening or a similar degree of slowing in response to stimuli presented to either visual field.

Personality

The extensive literature on affective disturbance in MS patients has been reviewed elsewhere (Devins & Seland, 1987; Ron, 1986; Minden & Schiffer, 1990). Both unipolar and bipolar depression are more commonly observed in MS patients than in the general population (Schiffer & Babigian, 1984; Whitlock & Siskind, 1980; Joffe, Lippert, Gray, Sawa, & Horvath, 1987; Schiffer, 1987; Minden, Orav, & Reich, 1987; Berrios & Quemada, 1990). In general, severity of depression does not correlate with the severity of cognitive dysfunction (Rao, Leo, Ellington, et al., 1991) or cerebral lesion involvement (Rao, Leo, Bernardin, Ellington, & Haughton, unpublished manuscript). Less commonly, some MS patients experience apathy and euphoria (Surridge, 1969; Brown & Davis, 1922). The presence of euphoria has been associated with cognitive deficits and ventricular dilatation on computed tomography (CT) scan (Rabins et al., 1986; Rao & Glatt, 1987).

We administered both self-report (Zung Depression Scale, State-Trait Anxiety Inventory) and relative rating scales (Katz Adjustment Scale) to the three MS patients (see Table 15.2). Self-reported depression (Zung Depression Scale) was only observed in D.A., who was essentially intact on cognitive testing. Conversely, D.R., the patient with severe cognitive impairment and extensive cerebral involvement on MRI, reported little if any depression. None of the patients reported clinically meaningful levels of anxiety. Results of the self-report scales are in contrast to relative ratings, as determined from the Katz Adjustment Scale. Patient D.R. is perceived by close observers to be more withdrawn, confused, and helpless. We suspect that the social withdrawal and helplessness are the result of apathy, problems with forming intentions, and impaired executive functions rather than feelings of sadness, low self-esteem, or other symptoms of depression.

Summary

The research literature and the three cases presented above illustrate several key features of the dementia syndrome in MS. In the mild form of the dementia, MS patients may exhibit sporadic deficits on measures of effortful, explicit memory (i.e., free recall), sustained attention, conceptual reasoning, and visuospatial perception. More severely demented MS patients also exhibit a reduction in verbal intelligence, a slowing of mental processing speed, reduced interhemispheric communication, and naming disturbance, in addition to more pronounced deficits in visuospatial perception and conceptual reasoning. Unlike cortical dementias, such as Alzheimer's diseases, MS patients have normal or near normal recognition memory, intact encoding skills, and normal priming. However, MS patients also demonstrate normal motor skill learning, which is in contrast to findings from gray matter subcortical dementias, like Huntington's and Parkinson's diseases. It is of interest that human immunodeficiency virus (HIV)-positive patients with subcortical dementia resulting primarily from white matter involvement, also have normal motor skill learning (Jones & Tranel, 1991).

Two final comments should be made with regard to the dementia in MS. First, studies have shown that the Mini-Mental State Examination (MMSE) is a poor indicator of dementia in MS (Beatty & Goodkin, 1990; Rao, Leo, Bernardin, & Unverzagt, 1991). Indeed, our most severely demented MS patient (D.R.) obtained a 28 of 30 on this scale. The typical cutoff for patients with suspected Alzheimer's dementia is 23. We speculate that most MS patients perform normally on the MMSE because of their relatively preserved language functions and normal span memory. More sensitive methods for screening cognitive impairment in MS patients have recently been proposed (Rao, Leo, Bernardin, & Unverzagt, 1991).

Second, most studies have shown a poor correlation between neurological disease parameters and results of neuropsychological testing. The Kurtzke Expanded Disability Status Scale (EDSS) disability ratings of the three patients in Table 15.2 were similar, yet major differences in cognitive test performance were observed. Several studies (Marsh, 1980; Peyser et al., 1980; Rao et al., 1984; van den Burg et al., 1987) have shown that EDSS ratings are uncorrelated or minimally correlated with degree of cognitive dysfunction. Likewise, disease duration may be an imperfect predictor of cognitive test performance (Marsh, 1980; Rao et al., 1984; Ivnik, 1978a). Not surprisingly, patient R.W., who has had symptoms of the disease for 6 years, shows signs of cognitive impairment, whereas D.A., who has had the disease for 10 years, does not. Some patients experience neurobehavioral changes early in the disease (Bergin, 1957; Young, Saunders, & Ponsford, 1976), whereas others never develop such changes.

Leuko-Araiosis

As part of our MS research program at the Medical College of Wisconsin, we have been administering an extensive neuropsychological test battery and MRI scanning to healthy, normotensive, middle-aged adults, who have served as controls for our MS patients. Consistent with other studies (Fazekas, 1989; Jernigan, Press, & Hesselink, 1990), we (Rao, Mittenberg, Bernardin, Haughton, & Leo, 1989) have found that approximately 20% of our normal controls have hyperintensities in the periventricular white matter. These lesions have been called euphemistically unidentified bright objects (UBOs), or more formally, leuko-araiosis (thinning of the white matter) (Hachinski, Potter, & Merskey, 1987). Studies have shown that the prevalence of leuko-araiosis increases with age, cardiovascular risk factors (e.g., hypertension), and cerebrovascular risk factors (Gerard & Weisberg, 1986; Awad, Spetzler, Hodak, Awad, & Carey, 1986; Brant-Zawadzki et al., 1985; Inzitari et al., 1987; George et al., 1986; Bradley, Waluch, Brant-Zawadzki, Yadley, & Wycoff, 1984). Roman (1987) has suggested that leuko-araiosis may represent the initial stages of a vascular dementia. Specifically, he suggested that Binswanger's disease, a white matter dementia, is not as uncommon as has been suggested in the literature and that there is a continuum of cognitive impairment depending on the severity of leuko-araiosis.

We (Rao, Mittenberg, et al., 1989) initially set out to determine the neuropsychological significance of leuko-araiosis in our normotensive sample by comparing subjects with and without leuko-araiosis using the same battery of neuropsychological tests as described in Table 15.2. No meaningful differences in cognitive abilities were observed between the two groups.

In a more recent study, we (Bernardin, Rao, Haughton, Yetkin, & Ellington, 1991) compared hypertensive patients with and without leuko-araiosis on a neuropsychological test battery. We excluded hypertensives with infarcts on MRI or a history of cerebrovascular disease (e.g., transient ischemic attacks). As expected, almost twice as many hypertensives (38%) had leuko-araiosis on their MRI scans as normotensives. Our results indicated that hypertensive patients with leuko-araiosis were no different from hypertensive patients without leuko-araiosis on neuropsychological testing. Thus our results do not support Roman's hypothesis that leuko-araiosis is a marker of early dementia.

To summarize, normotensive and hypertensive individuals with incidental white matter lesions (leuko-araiosis) perform normally on the same neuropsychological test battery that has been shown to be sensitive to the cognitive deficits of MS patients. It should be acknowledged that the total lesion area of the normotensive and hypertensive leuko-araiosis groups were significantly smaller than that of our MS patients. The mean total lesion area for MS patients was approximately 22 cm^2, whereas the lesion area for individuals with leuko-araiosis is less than 5 cm^2.

Treatment of White Matter Dementias

Little research has been devoted to the treatment of cognitive dysfunction in white matter dementias. Whereas considerable efforts have been expended to develop cognitive retraining programs for patients with stroke and closed head trauma (Ben-Yishay & Diller, 1983), no studies have evaluated retraining procedures in MS patients. This is somewhat surprising given the relatively high prevalence of MS (Johnson et al., 1979) and the impact of cognitive dysfunction on employment and social functioning (Rao et al., 1991). In our clinical practice, we have observed that MS patients with mild to moderate memory disturbance benefit from the use of environmental aids, such as notebooks, diaries, and calendars.

Using a pharmacological approach, we (Leo & Rao, 1988) reported a double-blind, placebo-controlled, crossover study of intravenous physostigmine, an ace-tylcholinesterase inhibitor, as a treatment for memory loss in four MS patients. Patients receiving physostigmine had better scores on a measure of recent memory functioning (i.e. the SRT, Buschke, 1973), than while receiving placebo. As a follow-up to this study, we (Unverzagt, Rao, & Antuono, 1991) recently completed a double-blind, placebo-controlled, crossover, long-term (1 month) study of oral physostigmine administered to 10 memory-impaired MS patients. As in the previous intravenous study, patients exhibited improvement on the SRT, but neither the patient nor their family members observed a change in everyday memory functioning.

Clearly, the development and testing of novel treatments for the cognitive problems of patients with MS and other white matter dementias should be a priority for future studies.

Conclusions

With the exception of subtle differences in performance on implicit memory tests, the pattern of cognitive deficits in MS is remarkably similar to that observed in gray matter subcortical dementias. Thus the use of a separate term to describe dementias of white matter may be somewhat premature.

The neurobehavioral findings from MS patients and individuals with leuko-araiosis would suggest that the severity of cognitive dysfunction is directly proportional to the total area, rather than the location, of cerebral white matter lesions. This implies that there may be a critical threshold that must be passed before cognitive deficits appear. We speculate that white matter lesions do not interfere with mental operations that involve highly focal cortical processes, such as syntax and comprehension, no matter how great the amount of cerebral white matter involved. In contrast, cortical processes that involve the integration of multiple cortical zones, such as memory retrieval and sustained attention, are more vulnerable to interference. However, cognitive functions are not disrupted in mildly involved cases due to redundancy of neural circuitry. Only when a critical mass of white matter tissue is involved do we begin to see cognitive impairments. Future clinicopathological studies with other white matter dementias (e.g., AIDS, Binswanger's disease) are needed to test the correctness of these speculations.

Acknowledgments

The author's research cited in this chapter was supported in part by a Research Career Development Award (K04 NS01055) and a Research Grant (R01 NS22128) from the National Institute of Neurological Disorders and Stroke and Research Grants (RG2206-A-3, RG2028-A-2) from the National Multiple Sclerosis Society.

References

Albert, M. L. (1978). Subcortical dementia. In R. Katzman, R. D. Terry, & K. L. Bick (Eds.), *Alzheimer's disease: Senile dementia and related disorders* (pp. 173–179). New York: Raven Press.

Anzola, G. P., Bevilacqua, L., Cappa, S. F., Capra, R., Faglia, L., Farina, E., Frisoni, G., Mariani, C., Pasolini, M. P., & Vignolo, L. A. (1990). Neuropsychological assessment in patients with relapsing-remitting multiple sclerosis and mild functional impairment: Correlation with magnetic resonance imaging. *Journal of Neurology, Neurosurgery and Psychiatry, 53*, 142–145.

Awad, I. A., Spetzler, R. F., Hodak, J. A., Awad, C. A., & Carey, R. (1986). Incidental subcortical lesions identified on magnetic resonance imaging in the elderly. I. Correlation with age and cerebrovascular risk factors. *Stroke, 17*, 1084–1089.

Barnard, R. O., & Triggs, M. (1974). Corpus callosum in multiple sclerosis. *Journal of Neurology, Neurosurgery and Psychiatry, 37*, 1259–1264.

Barona, A., Reynolds, C. R., & Chastain, R. (1984). A demographically based index of premorbid intelligence for the WAIS-R. *Journal of Consulting and Clinical Psychology, 52*, 885–887.

Baum, H. M., & Rothschild, B. B. (1981). The incidence and prevalence of reported multiple sclerosis. *Annals of Neurology, 10*, 420–428.

Beatty, P. A., & Gange, J. J. (1977). Neuropsychological aspects of multiple sclerosis. *Journal of Nervous and Mental Disease, 164*, 42–50.

Beatty, W. W., & Goodkin, D. E. (1990). Screening for cognitive impairment in multiple sclerosis: An evaluation of the Mini-Mental State Exam. *Archives of Neurology, 47*, 297–301.

Beatty, W. W., Goodkin, D. E., Beatty, P. A., & Monson, N. (1989). Frontal lobe dysfunction and memory impairment in patients with chronic progressive multiple sclerosis. *Brain and Cognition, 11*, 73–86.

Beatty, W. W., Goodkin, D. E., Monson, N., & Beatty, P. A. (1990). Implicit learning in patients with chronic progressive multiple sclerosis. *International Journal of Clinical Neuropsychology, 12*, 166–172.

Beatty, W. W., Goodkin, D. E., Monson, N., Beatty, P. A., & Hertsgaard, D. (1988). Anterograde and retrograde amnesia in patients with chronic progressive multiple sclerosis. *Archives of Neurology, 45*, 611–619.

Beatty, W. W., & Monson, N. (1989). Lexical processing in Parkinson's disease and multiple sclerosis. *Journal of Geriatric Psychiatry and Neurology, 2*, 145–152.

Beatty, W. W., & Monson, N. (1990). Semantic priming in multiple sclerosis. *Bulletin of the Psychonomic Society, 28*, 397–400.

Beatty, W. W., Monson, N., & Goodkin, D. E. (1989). Access to semantic memory in Parkinson's disease and multiple sclerosis. *Journal of Geriatric Psychiatry and Neurology, 2*, 153–162.

Ben-Yishay, Y., & Diller, L. (1983). Cognitive rehabilitation. In M. Rosenthal, E. R. Griffith, M. R. Bond, & J. D. Miller (Eds.), *Rehabilitation of the head injured adult* (pp. 367–380). Philadelphia: F. A. Davis Company.

Bergin, J. D. (1957). Rapidly progressing dementia in disseminated sclerosis. *Journal of Neurology, Neurosurgery and Psychiatry, 20*, 285–292.

Bernardin, L. J., Rao, S. M., Haughton, V. M., Yetkin, Z. F., & Ellington, L. A. (1991).

Neuropsychological significance of leuko-araiosis in a hypertensive population [Abstract]. *Journal of Clinical and Experimental Neuropsychology, 13*, 59.

Berrios, G. E., & Quemada, J. I. (1990). Depressive illness in multiple sclerosis. Clinical and theoretical aspects of the association. *British Journal of Psychiatry, 156*, 10–16.

Bradley, W. G., Waluch, V., Brant-Zawadzki, M., Yadley, R. A., & Wycoff, R. R. (1984). Patchy, periventricular white matter lesions in the elderly: A common observation during NMR imaging. *Noninvasive Medical Imaging, 1*, 35–41.

Brainin, M., Goldenberg, G., Ahlers, C., Reisner, T., Neuhold, A., & Deecke, L. (1988). Structural brain correlates of anterograde memory deficits in multiple sclerosis. *Journal of Neurology, 235*, 362–365.

Brant-Zawadzki, M., Fein, G., Van Dyke, C., Kiernan, R., Davenport, L., & deGroot, J. (1985). MR imaging of the aging brain: Patchy white-matter lesions and dementia. *American Journal of Neuroradiology, 6*, 675–682.

Brown, S., & Davis, T. K. (1922). The mental symptoms of multiple sclerosis. *Archives of Neurology and Psychiatry, 7*, 629–634.

Brownell, B., & Hughes, J. F. (1962). The distribution of plaques in the cerebrum in multiple sclerosis. *Journal of Neurology, Neurosurgery and Psychiatry, 25*, 315–320.

Buschke, H. (1973). Selective reminding for analysis of memory and learning. *Journal of Verbal Learning and Verbal Behavior, 12*, 543–550.

Caine, E. D., Bamford, K. A., Schiffer, R. B., Shoulson, I., & Levy, S. (1986). A controlled neuropsychological comparison of Huntington's disease and multiple sclerosis. *Archives of Neurology, 43*, 249–254.

Callanan, M. M., Logsdail, S. J., Ron, M. A., & Warrington, E. K. (1989). Cognitive impairment in patients with clinically isolated lesions of the type seen in multiple sclerosis: A psychometric and MRI study. *Brain, 112*, 361–374.

Canter, A. H. (1951). Direct and indirect measures of psychological deficit in multiple sclerosis. *Journal of General Psychology, 44*, 3–50.

Carroll, M., Gates, R., & Roldan, F. (1984). Memory impairment in multiple sclerosis. *Neuropsychologia, 22*, 297–302.

Cummings, J. L. (1990). *Subcortical dementia*. New York: Oxford University Press.

Cummings, J. L., & Benson, D. F. (1984). Subcortical dementia: Review of an emerging concept. *Archives of Neurology, 41*, 874–879.

Devins, G. M., & Seland, T. P. (1987). Emotional impact of multiple sclerosis: Recent findings and suggestions for future research. *Psychological Bulletin, 101*, 363–375.

Drayer, B. P. (1988). Imaging of the aging brain. Part II. Pathologic conditions. *Radiology, 166*, 797–806.

Fazekas, F. (1989). Magnetic resonance signal abnormalities in asymptomatic individuals: Their incidence and functional correlates. *European Neurology, 29*, 164–168.

Filley, C. M., Franklin, G. M., Heaton, R. K., & Rosenberg, N. L. (1989). White matter dementia: Clinical disorders and implications. *Neuropsychiatry, Neuropsychology, and Behavioral Neurology, 1*, 239–254.

Fink, S. L., & Houser, H. B. (1966). An investigation of physical and intellectual impairment changes in multiple sclerosis. *Archives of Physical Medicine and Rehabilitation, 47*, 56–61.

Fischer, J. S. (1988). Using the Wechsler Memory Scale-Revised to detect and characterize memory deficits in multiple sclerosis. *The Clinical Neuropsychologist, 2*, 149–172.

Franklin, G. M., Heaton, R. K., Nelson, L. M., Filley, C. M., & Seibert, C. (1988). Correlation of neuropsychological and MRI findings in chronic/progressive multiple sclerosis. *Neurology, 38*, 1826–1829.

Friedman, J. H., Brem, H., & Mayeux, R. (1983). Global aphasia in multiple sclerosis. *Annals of Neurology, 13*, 222–223.

George, A. E., de Leon, M. J., Kalnin, A., Rosner, L., Goodgold, A., & Chase, N. (1986).

Leukoencephalopathy in normal and pathologic aging: 2. MRI of brain lucencies. *American Journal of Neuroradiology, 7*, 567–570.

Gerard, G., & Weisberg, L. A. (1986). MRI periventricular lesions in adults. *Neurology, 36*, 998–1001.

Grafman, J., Rao, S. M., Bernardin, L., & Leo, G. J. (1991). Automatic memory processes in patients with multiple sclerosis. *Archives of Neurology, 48*, 1072–1075.

Grafman, J., Rao, S. M., & Litvan, I. (1990). Disorders of memory. In S. M. Rao (Ed.), *Neurobehavioral aspects of multiple sclerosis* (pp. 102–117). New York: Oxford University Press.

Hachinski, V. C., Potter, P., & Merskey, H. (1987). Leuko-araiosis. *Archives of Neurology, 44*, 21–23.

Heaton, R. K., Nelson, L. M., Thompson, D. S., Burks, J. S., & Franklin, G. M. (1985). Neuropsychological findings in relapsing-remitting and chronic-progressive multiple sclerosis. *Journal of Consulting and Clinical Psychology, 53*, 103–110.

Heindel, W. C., Butters, N., & Salmon, D. P. (1988). Impaired learning of a motor skill in patients with Huntington's disease. *Behavioral Neuroscience, 102*, 141–147.

Heindel, W. C., Salmon, D. P., Shults, C. W., Walicke, P. A., & Butters, N. (1989). Neuropsychological evidence for multiple implicit memory systems: A comparison of Alzheimer's, Huntington's, and Parkinson's disease patients. *Journal of Neuroscience, 9*, 582–587.

Huber, S. J., Paulson, G. W., Shuttleworth, E. C., Chakeres, D., Clapp, L. E., Pakalnis, A., Weiss, K., & Rammohan, K. (1987). Magnetic resonance imaging correlates of dementia in multiple sclerosis. *Archives of Neurology, 44*, 732–736.

Iivanainen, M. V. (1981). The significance of abnormal immune responses in patients with multiple sclerosis. *Journal of Neuroimmunology, 1*, 141–172.

Inzitari, D., Diaz, F., Fox, A., Hachinski, V. C., Steingart, A., Lau, C., Donald, A., Wade, J., Mulic, H., & Merksey, H. (1987). Vascular risk factors and leuko-araiosis. *Archives of Neurology, 44*, 42–47.

Ivnik, R. J. (1978a). Neuropsychological test performance as a function of the duration of MS-related symptomatology. *Journal of Clinical Psychiatry, 39*, 304–307.

Ivnik, R. J. (1978b). Neuropsychological stability in multiple sclerosis. *Journal of Consulting and Clinical Psychology, 46*, 913–923.

Jacobson, J. T., Deppe, U., & Murray, T. J. (1983). Dichotic paradigms in multiple sclerosis. *Eye and Hearing, 4*, 311–317.

Jambor, K. L. (1969). Cognitive functioning in multiple sclerosis. *British Journal of Psychiatry, 115*, 765–775.

Jennekens-Schinkel, A., Laboyrie, P. M., Lanser, J. B. K., & Van der Velde, E. A. (1990). Cognition in patients with multiple sclerosis. After four years. *Journal of the Neurological Sciences, 99*, 229–247.

Jernigan, T. L., Press, G. A., & Hesselink, J. R. (1990). Methods for measuring brain morphologic features on magnetic resonance images: Validation and normal aging. *Archives of Neurology, 47*, 27–32.

Joffe, R. T., Lippert, G. P., Gray, T. A., Sawa, G., & Horvath, Z. (1987). Mood disorder and multiple sclerosis. *Archives of Neurology, 44*, 376–378.

Johnson, R. T., Katzman, R., McGeer, E., Price, D., Shooter, E., & Silberberg, D. (1979). *Report of the panel on inflammatory, demyelinating and degenerative diseases* (Report No. 79-1916). Washington, DC: U.S. Department of Health.

Jones, R. D., & Tranel, D. (1991). Preservation of procedural memory in HIV-positive patients with subcortical dementia [Abstract]. *Journal of Clinical and Experimental Neuropsychology, 13*, 74.

Kurtzke, J. F. (1984). Neuroepidemiology. *Annals of Neurology, 16*, 265–277.

Kurtzke, J. F., Beebe, G. W., Nagler, B., Nefzger, M. D., Auth, T. L., & Kurland, L. T.

(1970). Studies on the natural history of multiple sclerosis. V. Long-term survival in young men. *Archives of Neurology, 22*, 215–225.

Leo, G. J., & Rao, S. M. (1988). Effects of intravenous physostigmine and lecithin on memory loss in multiple sclerosis: Report of a pilot study. *Journal of Neurologic Rehabilitation, 2*, 123–129.

Litvan, I., Grafman, J., Vendrell, P., & Martinez, J. M. (1988a). Slowed information processing in multiple sclerosis. *Archives of Neurology, 45*, 281–285.

Litvan, I., Grafman, J., Vendrell, P., Martinez, J. M., Junque, C., Vendrell, J. M., & Barraquer-Bordas, J. L. (1988b). Multiple memory deficits in patients with multiple sclerosis: Exploring the working memory system. *Archives of Neurology, 45*, 607–610.

Lumsden, C. E. (1970). The neuropathology of multiple sclerosis. In P. J. Vinken & G. W. Bruyn (Eds.), *Handbook of clinical neurology: Vol. 9. Multiple sclerosis and other demyelinating diseases* (pp. 217–309). New York: American Elsevier.

Marsh, G. (1980). Disability and intellectual function in multiple sclerosis. *Journal of Nervous and Mental Disease, 168*, 758–762.

Matthews, W. B., Acheson, E. D., Batchelor, J. R., & Weller, R. O. (1985). *McAlpine's multiple sclerosis.* New York: Churchill Livingstone.

McDonald, W. I. (1986). The mystery of the origin of multiple sclerosis. *Journal of Neurology, Neurosurgery and Psychiatry, 49*, 113–123.

McKhann, G. M. (1982). Multiple sclerosis. *Annual Review of Neuroscience, 5*, 219–239.

Medaer, R., Nelissen, E., Appel, B., Swerts, M., Geutjens, J., & Callaert, H. (1987). Magnetic resonance imaging and cognitive functioning in multiple sclerosis. *Journal of Neurology, 235*, 86–89.

Minden, S. L., Moes, E. J., Orav, J., Kaplan, E., & Reich, P. (1990). Memory impairment in multiple sclerosis. *Journal of Clinical and Experimental Neuropsychology, 12*, 566–586.

Minden, S. L., Orav, J., & Reich, P. (1987). Depression in multiple sclerosis. *General Hospital Psychiatry, 9*, 426–434.

Minden, S. L., & Schiffer, R. B. (1990). Affective disorders in multiple sclerosis: Review and recommendations for clinical research. *Archives of Neurology, 47*, 98–104.

Olmos-Lau, N., Ginsberg, M. D., & Geller, J. B. (1977). Aphasia in multiple sclerosis. *Neurology, 27*, 623–626.

Parsons, O. A., Stewart, K. D., & Arenberg, D. (1957). Impairment of abstracting ability in multiple sclerosis. *Journal of Nervous and Mental Disease, 125*, 221–225.

Peyser, J. M., Edwards, K. R., Poser, C. M., & Filskov, S. B. (1980). Cognitive function in patients with multiple sclerosis. *Archives of Neurology, 37*, 577–579.

Peyser, J. M., Rao, S. M., LaRocca, N. G., & Kaplan, E. (1990). Guidelines for neuropsychological research in multiple sclerosis. *Archives of Neurology, 47*, 94–97.

Rabins, P. V., Brooks, B. R., O'Donnell, P., Pearlson, G. D., Moberg, P., Jubelt, B., Coyle, P., Dalos, N., & Folstein, M. F. (1986). Structural brain correlates of emotional disorder in multiple sclerosis. *Brain, 109*, 585–597.

Rao, S. M. (1986). Neuropsychology of multiple sclerosis: A critical review. *Journal of Clinical and Experimental Neuropsychology, 8*, 503–542.

Rao, S. M. (1990). Multiple sclerosis. In J. L. Cummings (Ed.), *Subcortical dementia* (pp. 164–180). New York: Oxford University Press.

Rao, S. M., Bernardin, L., Ellington, L., & Leo, G. J. (1990). Memory loss in patients with multiple sclerosis: The role of semantic encoding [Abstract]. *Journal of Clinical and Experimental Neuropsychology, 12*, 74.

Rao, S. M., Bernardin, L., Leo, G. J., Ellington, L., Ryan, S. B., & Burg, L. S. (1989). Cerebral disconnection in multiple sclerosis: Relationship to atrophy of the corpus callosum. *Archives of Neurology, 46*, 918–920.

Rao, S. M., & Glatt, S. L. (1987). Association of euphoria and ventricular enlargement in multiple sclerosis [Abstract]. *Neurology, 37*(Suppl. 1), 181.

Rao, S. M., Grafman, J., DiGiulio, D., Mittenberg, W., Bernardin, L., Leo, G. J., Unverzagt, F., & Luchetta, T. (in press). Memory, dysfunction in multiple sclerosis: Its relation to working memory, semantic encoding, and implicit learning. *Neuropsychology*.

Rao, S. M., & Hammeke, T. A. (1984). Hypothesis testing in patients with chronic progressive multiple sclerosis. *Brain and Cognition, 3*, 94–104.

Rao, S. M., Hammeke, T. A., McQuillen, M. P., Khatri, B. O., & Lloyd, D. (1984). Memory disturbance in chronic progressive multiple sclerosis. *Archives of Neurology, 41*, 625–631.

Rao, S. M., Hammeke, T. A., & Speech, T. J. (1987). Wisconsin Card Sorting Test performance in relapsing-remitting and chronic-progressive multiple sclerosis. *Journal of Consulting and Clinical Psychology, 55*, 263–265.

Rao, S. M., Leo, G. J., Bernardin, L., & Unverzagt, F. (1991). Cognitive dysfunction in multiple sclerosis: I. Frequency, patterns, and prediction. *Neurology, 41*, 685–691.

Rao, S. M., Leo, G. J., Ellington, L., Nauertz, T., Bernardin, L., & Unverzagt, F. (1991). Cognitive dysfunction in multiple sclerosis: II. Impact on social functioning. *Neurology, 41*, 692–696.

Rao, S. M., Leo, G. J., Haughton, V. M., St. Aubin-Faubert, P., & Bernardin, L. (1989). Correlation of magnetic resonance imaging with neuropsychological testing in multiple sclerosis. *Neurology, 39*, 161–166.

Rao, S. M., Leo, G. J., & St. Aubin-Faubert, P. (1989). On the nature of memory disturbance in multiple sclerosis. *Journal of Clinical and Experimental Neuropsychology, 11*, 699–712.

Rao, S. M., Mittenberg, W., Bernardin, L., Haughton, V., & Leo, G. J. (1989). Neuropsychological test findings in subjects with leuko-araiosis. *Archives of Neurology, 46*, 40–44.

Rao, S. M., St. Aubin-Faubert, P., & Leo, G. J. (1989). Information processing speed in patients with multiple sclerosis. *Journal of Clinical and Experimental Neuropsychology, 11*, 471–477.

Reischies, F. M., Baum, K., Brau, H., Hedde, J. P., & Schwindt, G. (1988). Cerebral magnetic resonance imaging findings in multiple sclerosis: Relation to disturbance of affect, drive, and cognition. *Archives of Neurology, 45*, 1114–1116.

Reitan, R. M., Reed, J. C., & Dyken, M. (1971). Cognitive, psychomotor, and motor correlates of multiple sclerosis. *Journal of Nervous and Mental Disease, 153*, 218–224.

Roman, G. C. (1987). Senile dementia of the Binswanger type: A vascular form of dementia in the elderly. *Journal of the American Medical Association, 258*, 1782–1788.

Ron, M. A. (1986). Multiple sclerosis: Psychiatric and psychometric abnormalities. *Journal of Psychosomatic Research, 30*, 3–11.

Rubens, A. B., Froehling, B., Slater, G., & Anderson, D. (1985). Left ear suppression on verbal dichotic tests in patients with multiple sclerosis. *Annals of Neurology, 18*, 459–463.

Salmon, D. P., Shimamura, A. P., Butters, N., & Smith, S. (1988). Lexical and semantic priming deficits in patients with Alzheimer's disease. *Journal of Clinical and Experimental Neuropsychology, 10*, 477–494.

Schiffer, R. B. (1987). The spectrum of depression in multiple sclerosis: An approach for clinical management. *Archives of Neurology, 44*, 596–599.

Schiffer, R. B., & Babigian, H. M. (1984). Behavioral disorders in multiple sclerosis, temporal lobe epilepsy, and amyotrophic lateral sclerosis: An epidemiological study. *Archives of Neurology, 41*, 1067–1069.

Sibley, W. A. (1990). Diagnosis and course of multiple sclerosis. In S. M. Rao (Ed.), *Neurobehavioral aspects of multiple sclerosis* (pp. 5–14). New York: Oxford University Press.

Surridge, D. (1969). An investigation into some aspects of multiple sclerosis. *British Journal of Psychiatry, 115*, 749–764.

Unverzagt, F. W., Rao, S. M., & Antuono, P. G. (1991). Oral physostigmine in the treatment of memory loss in multiple sclerosis (MS) [Abstract]. *Journal of Clinical and Experimental Neuropsychology, 13*, 74.

van den Burg, W., van Zomeren, A. H., Minderhoud, J. M., Prange, A. J. A., & Meijer, N. S. A. (1987). Cognitive impairment in patients with multiple sclerosis and mild physical disability. *Archives of Neurology, 44*, 494–501.

Vowels, L. M. (1979). Memory impairment in multiple sclerosis. In M. Molloy, G. V. Stanley, & K. W. Walsh (Eds.), *Brain impairment: Proceedings of the 1978 Brain Impairment Workshop* (pp. 10–22). Melbourne, Australia: University of Melbourne.

Whitlock, F. A., & Siskind, M. M. (1980). Depression as a major symptom of multiple sclerosis. *Journal of Neurology, Neurosurgery and Psychiatry, 43*, 861–865.

Wickens, D. D. (1970). Encoding categories of words: An empirical approach to meaning. *Psychological Review, 77*, 1–15.

Young, A. C., Saunders, J., & Ponsford, J. R. (1976). Mental change as an early feature of multiple sclerosis. *Journal of Neurology, Neurosurgery and Psychiatry, 39*, 1008–1013.

PART III

BRAIN IMAGING

16

Positron Emission Tomography in Alzheimer's Disease

RANDOLPH W. PARKS, JAMES V. HAXBY,
AND CHERYL L. GRADY

Alzheimer's disease (AD) is a progressive brain disease that principally affects memory and higher cognitive function. Relating the neuropsychological symptoms of dementia of the Alzheimer type (DAT) to the distribution of neuropathological changes, however, has been problematic. Because the disease is progressive, most patients become severely demented before they die. The neuropathological basis for the more selective cognitive impairments of earlier stages of DAT, therefore, was usually a matter of speculation. The general pattern of neuropsychological symptoms associated with DAT could be accounted for, in a global manner, by the distribution of neuropsychological changes. Neuropsychologically, memory and higher cognitive functions, such as attention to complex sets, naming, and visuo-spatial construction (Becker, Huff, Nebes, Holland, & Boller, 1988; Cummings, Benson, Hill, & Read, 1985; Grady, Haxby, Horwitz, Sundaram, et al., 1988; Haxby et al., 1986; Haxby et al., 1990; Haxby, Grady, Koss et al., 1988; Martin et al., 1986), are disproportionately impaired; whereas focal, sensory, and motor neurological symptoms are usually absent. The neuropathology of AD selectively affects the association cortices (Gruenthal, 1926; Jamada & Mehraein, 1968; Kemper, 1984), the hippocampus and amygdala (Ball, 1976; Jamada & Mehraein, 1968), and subcortical and brainstem nuclei that project to the neocortex (Bondareff, Mountjoy, & Roth, 1982; Whitehouse et al., 1982; Yamamoto & Hirano, 1985); whereas the primary sensory and motor cortices, the basal ganglia, the thalamus, and the cerebellum are wholly or relatively spared (Gruenthal, 1926; Jamada & Mehraein, 1968; Kemper, 1984). Relations associating specific impairments of memory, attention, language, and visuospatial function with neuropathological changes in specific brain regions, however, have been elusive. Even when inter-individual variations in the distribution of neuropathological changes have been observed, they tended to be discounted. Gruenthal (1926), for example, noted substantial variations in the distributions of both senile plaques and neurofibrillary tangles, but concluded nonetheless that specific symptoms were an expression of the overall severity of damage and were not related to the site of the most severe neuropathology.

The development of methods for obtaining in vivo images of brain structure—computed tomography (CT) and, later, magnetic resonance imaging (MRI)—has also done little to further understanding of the biological basis for the cognitive impairments in DAT. Neuronal loss and atrophy are prominent features of AD, but the distribution of atrophic changes is difficult to discern in structural brain images. Moreover, atrophic changes in the early stages of DAT may be too slight to distinguish patients with DAT from age-matched controls (Creasey, Schwartz, Frederickson, Haxby, & Rapoport, 1986).

A second revolution in in vivo brain imaging, however, has made it possible to investigate brain-behavior relations in patients with DAT by developing methods for functional brain imaging. Functional brain imaging is based on methods for measuring the local concentrations of radioactive isotopes. By labeling compounds of interest with isotopes, the local concentration of the isotope becomes an index of the local rate for a physiological process. Most functional brain imaging studies have examined indices of oxidative metabolism—namely, blood flow, oxygen consumption, and glucose consumption (Ober, Reed, & Jagust, 1992; Pritchard & Brass, 1992). However, methods have also been developed for measuring other physiological parameters such as receptor densities and uptake of precursors for neurotransmitter synthesis (Parks, Loewenstein, & Chang, 1988).

Early methods of functional brain imaging produced nontomographic images of activity over the cortical surface based on radiation measured by multiple detectors placed over the surface of the scalp. Tomographic functional brain imaging, which allows the construction of cross-sectional images, can now be accomplished with two techniques, single photon emission computed tomography (SPECT) and positron emission tomography (PET). Like nontomographic surface imaging, SPECT detects single events with surface detectors, but the detectors are shielded to be more directionally specific, allowing tomographic image reconstruction. Positron emission tomography detects pairs of gamma rays emitted in opposite directions by positron-electron annihilations. Simultaneous detection of gamma rays by a pair of detectors localizes the annihilation event, and hence the original isotope, to a narrow, cylindrical volume connecting those detectors. Positron emission tomography is clearly the best method for functional brain imaging, but is significantly more expensive than nontomographic and SPECT imaging. Spatial resolution is higher than in SPECT and is more uniform across the image. Moreover, the method is quantitative, allowing measurement in physiologically meaningful units. SPECT, however, is significantly less expensive, making it possible to give more investigators access to functional brain imaging.

Functional brain imaging has been used extensively to study the distribution of disease-related alterations of brain function in patients with DAT. These studies, conducted by multiple, independent research groups, have generated a remarkably consistent account of the regions most likely to demonstrate reduced cerebral metabolism. Functional brain imaging has made it possible, for the first time, to investigate which regions demonstrate dysfunction in the early stages of DAT and to investigate how the distribution of disease-related reductions of cerebral metabolism evolves as the disease progresses. Functional brain imaging has also forced a clear awareness of the heterogeneity of DAT (Grady, Haxby, Horwitz, Sundaram, et al., 1988; Grady, Haxby, Horwitz, et al., 1990; Haxby, Duara, Grady, Rapoport, & Cutler, 1985; Haxby et al., 1990; Haxby, Grady, Koss, et al., 1988; Martin et

al., 1986). The distribution of disease-related reductions of cerebral metabolism have been found to vary markedly among patients, and these variations in metabolic patterns are related to variations in the patterns of neuropsychological impairment.

This chapter will review studies that have used functional brain imaging to investigate regional brain dysfunction in patients with DAT. This review will focus primarily on the extensive literature on PET studies of resting state cerebral metabolism. First, the patterns of disease-related reductions of cerebral metabolism that are observed in patients with DAT will be described. Second, cross-sectional and longitudinal studies of how the distribution of disease-related alteration of brain function change as the disease progresses will be reviewed. Third, studies of the relation between patterns of hypometabolism and patterns of neuropsychological impairment will be examined. Fourth, recent studies on patients with DAT will be reviewed that have examined the capacity of specific cortical regions to increase their rates of activity during the performance of selected cognitive tasks. Finally, we will briefly review differential diagnostic issues with PET scanning.

Patterns of Hypometabolism in Patients with DAT

Positron emission tomography studies of resting state regional cerebral metabolic rates for glucose (rCMRglc) and oxygen (rCMRO$_2$) in patients with DAT have shown that some brain structures are most likely to demonstrate reduced metabolic rates; namely, the association areas of the neocortex. Other brain structures consistently demonstrate relative sparing (e.g., the primary sensory and motor cortices, the basal ganglia, the thalamus, and the cerebellum). The distribution of metabolic reductions in the vulnerable regions, however, can vary markedly from patient to patient. Some of this interindividual variability can be attributed to overall severity of dementia. In more mildly demented patients, the region most likely to demonstrate the reduced metabolism is the parietal association cortex. Marked reductions of frontal association cortex metabolism are more often observed in patients with moderate to severe DAT. Most interindividual variability, however, is independent of disease severity. Across all disease severities, reductions of regional cerebral metabolism are often asymmetric, and the within-hemisphere distribution of hypometabolic regions can vary as well.

Selective Involvement of the Association Neocortices

Positron emission tomography studies of resting state rCMRglc and rCMRO$_2$ in patients with DAT have consistently found the largest reductions are in the association areas of the neocortex. Metabolic rates in the primary sensory and motor cortices, the basal ganglia, the thalamus, and the cerebellum have been found to be unaffected in DAT, when measured with low and midresolution tomographs (Duara et al., 1986; Haxby, Grady, Koss, et al., 1988; Kessler, Herholz, Grond, & Heiss, 1991; Kuhl, Metter, & Riege, 1985), or significantly less affected than are the association cortices, when measured with high-resolution tomographs (Kumar et al., 1991; McGeer et al., 1990). Figure 16.1 (see color plate) shows an extreme example of the selective involvement of the association cortices in a patient with severe DAT. All association cortices in this patient demonstrated marked

hypometabolism, allowing easy identification of the relatively spared primary pre-central and postcentral cortex, visual cortex, and auditory cortex, as well as the relatively spared basal ganglia and thalamus. Table 16.1 contains a summary of PET studies of resting state cerebral metabolism in patients with DAT. As can be seen in the table, high-resolution and low-resolution PET studies generated equivalent estimates of the size of primary cortex metabolic reductions. The high-resolution PET studies found these reductions to be significant because methodological improvements had substantially reduced interindividual variability in estimated rCMRglc values. In addition to improved spatial resolution, which leads to reduced partial-volume errors, improved methods for correcting attenuation of radiation counts—namely, the use of transmission scans to measure radiation attenuation in each individual subject—have substantially reduced measurement error.

Multiple studies (Table 16.1) have consistently shown that of the association cortices, the parietal lobe demonstrates the largest reductions of rCMR in patients with DAT relative to controls, especially in patients with only mild dementia. Estimates of parietal association cortex metabolic reductions in patients with mild to moderate DAT range from 23% to 39%, temporal association cortex metabolic reductions range from 15% to 30%, and frontal association cortex metabolic reductions range from 15% to 21%. Association cortex metabolic reductions are greater in patients with more severe DAT, as are primary somatosensory, motor, and visual cortex metabolic reductions. In patients with severe DAT, parietal association cortex metabolic reductions range from 40% to 54%, frontal association cortex metabolic reductions range from 26% to 43%, and temporal association cortex metabolic reductions range from 26% to 46%. In a small number of studies separate measures of primary visual cortex rCMRglc and occipital association cortex rCMRglc are reported and consistently show greater reductions in the association regions of the occipital lobe (Kuhl et al., 1985; Kumar et al., 1991). In the frontal association cortex, larger metabolic reductions tend to be found in premotor cortex than in more anterior prefrontal cortex (Haxby, Grady, Koss, et al., 1988; Kuhl et al., 1985; Kumar et al., 1991).

The selectively greater involvement of the association neocortices in DAT can also be illustrated by directly comparing association cortex rCMRglc and rCMRglc in less affected regions. These comparisons are usually accomplished by calculating ratios between metabolic rates for each individual patient. Because metabolic rates in different brain regions are often highly correlated, these ratios usually have substantially smaller variances than do the regional metabolic rates, especially in earlier studies using low-resolution tomographs and estimated attenuation correction. For example, in one study (Haxby, Grady, Koss, et al., 1988) the coefficient of variation (SD/M) for parietal rCMRglc in controls was 29%. By contrast, the coefficient of variation for the ratio of parietal to sensorimotor cortex was 6%. Consequently, the difference between controls and mildly impaired patients with DAT, expressed in control standard deviations, was 0.9 standard deviation for parietal rCMRglc and 2.4 standard deviation for parietal:sensorimotor ratios. The introduction of high-resolution tomographs and improved methods for attenuation correction have reduced, but not eliminated, the statistical advantage of these ratios for detecting significant regional abnormalities in patients with DAT (Kumar et al., 1991; Salerno et al., 1991).

TABLE 16.1. Reductions of Resting State Regional Cerebral Metabolism in Patients with Dementia of the Alzheimer Type (DAT) Expressed as Percentage of Control Values

Study	N Controls	N Patients	Dementia Severity	Frontal (%)	Sensorimotor (%)	Parietal (%)	Temporal (%)	Occipital (%)
Mild to moderate dementia								
Frackowiak et al., 1981[a]	14	7	Mild–Moderate	−15[b]		−25	−23	−11[c]
Foster et al., 1984	8	7	Mild	−19		−39	−27	−31[d]
Haxby et al., 1988	31	10	Mild	−20[e]		−27	−30	−22[c]
Haxby et al., 1988	31	14	Moderate	−21[e]	−11	−23	−16	−5[c]
Kessler et al., 1991	21	9	Mild–Moderate	−15[e]	−10	−19[g]	−15	−8[f]
Kumar et al., 1991	30	17	Mild	−20[e]	0	−25	−20	−13[f]
Kumar et al., 1991	30	19	Moderate	−28[e]	−13	−35	−26	−13[f]
All dementia severities								
Friedland et al., 1983	7	17	Mild–severe			−27[g]		
Ferris et al., 1983	13–21	15–22	Mild–severe		−24		−28	−21
McGeer et al., 1986	11	14	Mild–severe	−23[b]	−14	−20	−32	−18[h]
Akiyama et al., 1989	9	26	Mild–severe	−29[b]	−16	−22	−34	
Severe dementia								
Frackowiak et al., 1981[a]	14	6	Severe	−40[b]		−40	−26	−24[c]
Benson et al., 1983	16	8	Severe	−42	−36	−46		−36
Foster et al., 1984	8	8	Severe	−26		−42	−33	−36[d]
Kuhl et al., 1985	6	6	Severe	−37[i]	−27	−54	−32	−29[f]
Haxby et al., 1988	31	8	Severe	−43[e]	−26	−45	−34	−16[c]
Kumar et al., 1991	30	11	Severe	−45	−30	−52	−46	−35[f]

[a] rCMRO$_2$.
[b] Prefrontal cortex.
[c] Medial occipital cortex.
[d] Lateral occipital cortex.
[e] Premotor cortex.
[f] Calcarine cortex.
[g] Parietal and temporal cortex.
[h] Medial and lateral occipital cortex.
[i] Superior frontal cortex.

Variable Patterns of Association Cortex Metabolic Reductions

Although the association cortices are consistently shown to be most vulnerable to disease-related metabolic reductions in DAT, the pattern of reductions in the association regions of the right and left frontal, parietal, and temporal lobes can vary markedly from patient to patient. This interindividual heterogeneity was first demonstrated as increased right-left asymmetry of rCMRglc (Duara et al., 1986; Friedland, Budinger, Koss et al., 1985; Haxby et al., 1985; Kessler et al., 1991; Kuhl et al., 1985; McGeer et al., 1986; Figures 16.2 (see color plate) and 16.3). The increase in metabolic asymmetry is greater in the association cortices than in the primary sensorimotor cortices (Haxby et al., 1985; Haxby et al., 1990; Kumar et al., 1991; Loewenstein et al., 1989; McGeer et al., 1986), corroborating the selective involvement of the association cortices (see Figure 2.2). Primary visual cortex has shown no increase in asymmetry of rCMRglc in some reports (Haxby et al., 1985; Haxby et al., 1990; Loewenstein et al., 1989), but has been shown to be asymmetric in others (Kumar et al., 1991; McGeer et al., 1990; McGeer et al., 1986). Asymmetry of rCMRglc in the basal ganglia and thalamus has been shown to be significantly increased in patients with DAT relative to controls (Kumar et al., 1991; Loewenstein et al., 1989; McGeer et al., 1990). In the only study that divided patients according to dementia severity, asymmetry of rCMRglc in the basal ganglia and thalamus was not significantly increased in patients with mild and moderate dementia (Kumar et al., 1991). Increased asymmetry of rCMRglc indi-

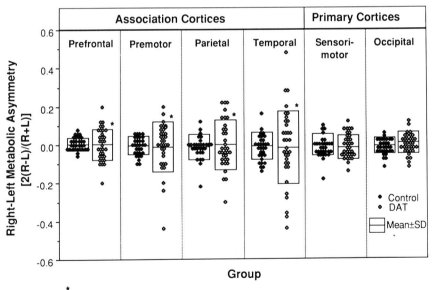

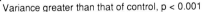
Variance greater than that of control, p < 0.001

FIGURE 16.3. Scatterplot of right-left asymmetries of glucose (rCMRglc) in four association cortical regions and two primary cortical regions for 33 patients with mild to severe dementia of the Alzheimer type (DAT) and 31 age-matched controls. Greater variance of asymmetries in the association regions, with no change in mean asymmetries, demonstrates the variable distribution of association cortex rCMRglc reductions in patients with DAT. (From Haxby et al., 1990).

cates that association cortex metabolic reductions, although usually bilateral, are often more severe in one hemisphere than in the other. In most studies, the right and the left sides are equally likely to demonstrate disproportionate hypometabolism (Duara et al., 1986; Friedland et al., 1985; Haxby et al., 1985; Haxby et al., 1990; Kuhl et al., 1985; Kumar et al., 1991; McGeer et al., 1990; McGeer et al., 1986). Two studies of older patients, however, found that more patients demonstrated predominant left-sided hypometabolism than predominant right-sided hypometabolism (Koss, Friedland, Ober, & Jagust, 1985; Loewenstein et al., 1989), although another study of older patients found no such directional preference (Grady, Haxby, Horwitz, Berg, & Rapoport, 1988).

Similar interindividual heterogeneity in the within-hemisphere distribution of association cortex metabolic reductions has also been demonstrated (Grady, Haxby, Schapiro, et al., 1990; Haxby, Grady, Koss, et al., 1988). Ratios of parietal to frontal association cortex rCMRglc demonstrate increased variance in patients with DAT relative to controls (Haxby, Grady, Koss, et al., 1988). Significant increases in the variance of frontal-temporal ratios as well as of frontal-parietal ratios can also be demonstrated in data reported by McGeer et al. (1990), although these investigators did not themselves test for inequality of variances.

In a search for other variations in the pattern of rCMRglc reductions in patients with DAT, Grady, Haxby, Schapiro, et al. (1990) performed a principal component analysis of rCMRglc values, obtained with a high-resolution PET scanner, in a group of 33 patients with mild to severe DAT. Using a Q-component analysis to examine correlations between subjects (rather than between regions), four orthogonal subgroups could be identified. The largest subgroup (45%) demonstrated what is now considered the classic pattern of rCMRglc reductions in patients with DAT—namely, reductions in the superior and inferior parietal lobules and posterior temporal lobe. A second subgroup of patients (24%), however, showed reduced rCRMglc in the orbitofrontal and anterior cingulate gyri, with relatively spared parietal rCMRglc. The third subgroup (15%) demonstrated lower rCMRglc in the association areas of the left hemisphere as compared to the right. The fourth subgroup (15%) had marked reductions in frontal as well as parietal and temporal association regions. Patients with disproportionate right-sided hypometabolism did not form a subgroup of their own, but were mixed among patients with mostly parietotemporal rCMRglc reductions (Group 1) or with frontoparietotemporal rCMRglc reductions (Group 4). This analysis revealed a subgroup of patients that had not been identified previously—namely, patients with disproportionate hypometabolism in the orbitofrontal and anterior cingulate gyri. Because these patients form only a small minority of patients with DAT, disproportionate metabolic reductions in these regions had gone undetected. In fact, these regions tend to show relatively small metabolic reductions in mixed groups of patients with DAT (Haxby, Grady, Horwitz, et al., 1988; Kumar et al., 1991). Neuropathological follow-up of patients with these different patterns of cortical hypometabolism is needed to determine whether they all have AD or whether one or more groups may include patients with other neuropathologies, such as non-Alzheimer frontotemporal degeneration.

Diminished Interregional Correlations in Patients with DAT

Examination of correlations between regional metabolic rates provides another method for investigating brain metabolic patterns that addresses the functional interdependence of brain regions (Clark, Kessler, Buchsbaum, Margolin, & Holcomb, 1984; Horwitz, Duara, & Rapoport, 1984; Horwitz, Grady, Schlageter, Duara, & Rapoport, 1987; Metter, Riege, Kuhl, & Phelps, 1984). Because inter-subject differences in global metabolic rates can account for most of the between-subject variance for regional metabolic rates, correlational analysis of PET data usually uses indices of regional rCMRglc that factor out global CMRglc, either by dividing regional rates by the global rate or by calculating partial correlations. Large correlations between metabolic rates in two regions indicate a functional dependency exists between those regions in the physiological state under study, from which it has been inferred that they are functionally coupled (Horwitz et al., 1984). Indeed, in rats that had had interhemispheric connections surgically removed by section of the corpus callosum, correlations between rCMRglc values in homologous right and left hemisphere regions were consistently reduced (Soncrant, Horwitz, Holloway, & Rapoport, 1986).

Horwitz et al. (1987) found that the number of significant regional metabolic intercorrelations was reduced in patients with DAT relative to healthy, age-matched controls. The loss of significant correlations was most apparent for correlations between homologous right and left hemisphere regions and for correlations between parietal and frontal association cortical regions. These findings are consistent with the increases in metabolic right-left asymmetries and parietal-premotor discrepancies discussed above.

Longitudinal Changes in rCMRglc in Patients with DAT

Longitudinal studies of resting state regional brain metabolism in patients with DAT have shown that the metabolic abnormalities associated with DAT—namely, disproportionate reductions of association cortex rCMRglc—appear very early in the course of the disease and worsen with time, but the pattern of association cortex metabolic reductions in individual patients are relatively stable.

The resting state brain metabolic abnormalities associated with DAT have been observed in patients whose cognitive impairments were too mild to warrant a diagnosis of dementia (Grady, Haxby, Horwitz, Berg, Rapoport, 1988; Haxby et al., 1986; Haxby, Grady, Horwitz, et al., 1988; Haxby et al., 1990). These patients had significant impairment of memory but no significant impairments of nonmemory language and visuospatial functions. Thus, they were not demented and only had possible AD, not probable AD, according to the NINCDS-ADRDA diagnostic criteria (McKhann et al., 1984). Nonetheless, all but one individually demonstrated significant abnormalities of parietal, temporal, or frontal rCMRgcl, as indicated by abnormal ratios of association cortex rCMRglc to primary cortex rCMRglc or by abnormal asymmetry of rCMRglc. The one subject who did not have significantly abnormal rCMRglc at initial evaluation subsequently developed an abnormality of temporal rCMRglc that preceded the development of significant nonmemory neuropsychological impairments. These findings indicate that at least some patients with very early DAT are able to maintain neocortically mediated neuropsychological function despite significant physiological neocortical dysfunction.

Worsening metabolic abnormalities in patients with DAT are evident longitudinally as relatively greater reductions of association cortex rCMRglc as compared

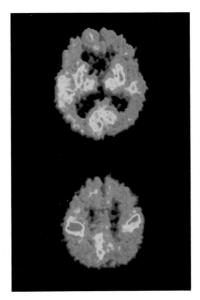

FIGURE 16.1. Positron emission tomography (PET) scan of resting state regional cerebral metabolic rates for glucose (rCMRglc) in a female patient with severe dementia of the Alzheimer type (DAT). Both cross-sectional images show markedly decreased metabolic rates in all association regions. The upper image shows relative preservation of rCMRglc in primary visual and auditory cortex, the basal ganglia, and the thalamus. The lower image shows relative preservation of rCMRglc in primary sensorimotor cortex.

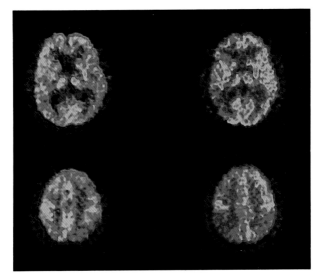

FIGURE 16.2. Positron emission tomography (PET) scans of resting state glucose (rCMRglc) in two patients with moderate dementia of the Alzheimer type (DAT). Both scans demonstrate right-left asymmetry of rCMRglc reductions. The patient on the left had greater rCMRglc reductions on the right as compared to the left. The patient on the right had greater rCMRglc reductions on the left as compared to the right. Note symmetry of rCMRglc in primary sensorimotor cortex and in the basal ganglia and thalamus.

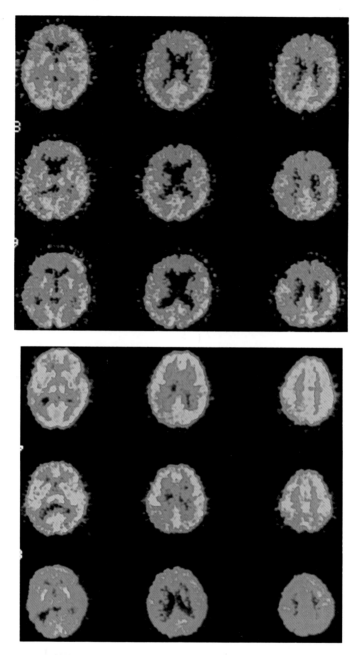

FIGURE 16.5. Longitudinal positron emission tomography (PET) studies of resting state glucose (rCMRglc) in two patients with moderate to severe dementia of the Alzheimer type (DAT). The patient in the upper panel initially demonstrated a relatively discrete focus of hypometabolism in the left frontal association cortex. This region continued to be the most hypometabolic on subsequent scans, but regions of hypometabolism in right frontal and left posterior association cortex also became evident. The patient in the lower panel initially demonstrated disproportionate hypometabolism in the left posterior association cortices. Subsequent scans demonstrate continued disproportionate hypometabolism in these regions, with general worsening of metabolic abnormality and dementia severity.

to reductions of primary cortex and subcortical rCMRglc. McGeer et al. (1990) obtained repeat PET scans on 13 patients with DAT with a mean follow-up interval of 15 months. When subcortical nuclei were excluded from analysis, 12 of the 13 patients individually demonstrated significant reductions of metabolic rates. The regions that demonstrated the greatest differences between controls and patients at the first scan also demonstrated the greatest reductions longitudinally. The regions demonstrating the greatest longitudinal change were association cortices in the parietal, temporal, and frontal lobes of both hemispheres. Salerno et al. (1991) obtained three to four PET studies in 10 patients with DAT, with a mean interval between first and last scan of 29 months. In this sample, absolute metabolic rates in only two regions, left premotor and prefrontal cortex, demonstrated significant change over time. Ratios of association cortex to primary cortex rCMRglc, however, demonstrated a more widespread distribution of worsening metabolic abnormality. Parietal:sensorimotor rCMRglc ratios demonstrated significant change in both hemispheres. Left hemisphere prefrontal:sensorimotor, premotor:sensorimotor, and temporal:calcarine rCMRglc ratios also declined significantly. The superiority of metabolic ratios over absolute metabolic rates for demonstrating change longitudinally in Salerno et al.'s (1991) study was due to the reduction of variance these ratios afforded. Worsening metabolic abnormality was most consistently demonstrated by a global index that contrasted association cortex rCMRglc in the parietal and premotor cortices to primary cortex rCMRglc in the sensorimotor and calcarine cortices. The ratio of these metabolic rates demonstrated a mean annual change of 6%, indicating that the annual percentage decrease in the association cortices was greater by 6% than the percentage decrease in the primary cortices.

The relative distribution of association cortex metabolic reductions tends to be relatively stable in patients with DAT. This stability of pattern has been repeatedly demonstrated as significant correlations between initial and follow-up association cortex asymmetries and ratios. In a sample of 15 patients with DAT with a mean follow-up interval of 15 months, Grady, Haxby, Schlageter, Berg, & Rapoport (1986) showed that right-left asymmetries from initial and follow-up scans were significantly correlated. In a further report on the same sample (Haxby et al., 1990), stability of right-left asymmetries was examined in 11 patients with initially mild DAT over a mean follow-up interval of 26 months. Initial and follow-up asymmetries in the parietal, temporal, and prefrontal association cortices were significantly correlated. This stability of right-left metabolic asymmetry is illustrated in Figure 16.4. This graph shows parietal metabolic asymmetries from 37 PET scans in 11 patients. The stability of these asymmetries is evident both in the relative magnitudes of asymmetries (absolute values) and in the directions of the asymmetries. Not a single patient changed direction of asymmetry over multiple repeated scans.

The stability of right-left metabolic asymmetries was demonstrated in a new sample of patients in the study of Salerno et al. (1991). Salerno et al.'s (1991) PET data were obtained with a high-resolution scanner (Scanditronix PC1024-7B with in-plane resolution of 6 mm, full width at half maximum), as compared to the earlier studies that used a low-resolution scanner (ECAT II). This sample of patients included three patients who had been included in the earlier reports by Grady et al. (1986), Haxby, Grady, Koss, et al. (1988), and Haxby et al. (1990). Correlations

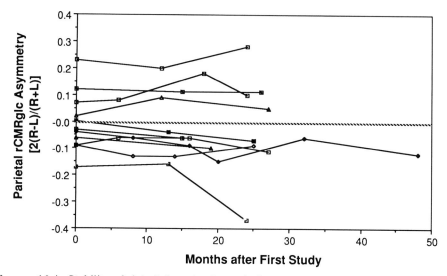

FIGURE 16.4. Stability of right-left parietal metabolic asymmetries in 11 patients with dementia of the Alzheimer type (DAT). All patients had mild DAT when first studied. Mean follow-up duration is 26 months. Note that no patient changed the direction of asymmetry. (From Haxby et al., 1990)

between initial and follow-up right-left rCMRglc asymmetries were significant in parietal, premotor, and prefrontal cortices. By contrast, one other study that examined right-left metabolic asymmetries longitudinally in patients with DAT failed to demonstrate stability (Jagust, Friedland, Budinger, Koss, & Ober, 1988). This study, however, had a smaller sample of patients ($N = 6$).

The within-hemisphere distribution of association cortex demonstrates a similar stability in individual patients (Haxby, Grady, Koss et al., 1988; McGeer et al., 1990; Salerno et al., 1991). Haxby, Grady, Koss, et al. (1988) examined stability of parietal:frontal rCMRglc ratios in 20 patients with mild to severe DAT over a mean follow-up interval of 19 months. Parietal:premotor and parietal:prefrontal ratios in both hemispheres were stable over time, as demonstrated by significant correlations between initial and follow-up ratios. Salerno et al.'s (1991) longitudinal study with a high-resolution scanner has shown a similar stability of frontal:parietal rCMRglc ratios. McGeer et al. (1990) examined stability of indices that contrasted frontal to parietal rCMRglc and that contrasted frontal to temporal rCMRglc in 13 patients with DAT. Both contrasts were highly stable, as demonstrated by highly significant correlations between initial and follow-up values ($r = .96$, and $r = .94$, for frontal-parietal and frontal-temporal contrasts, respectively).

McGeer et al. (1990) also obtained right-left rCMRglc asymmetries on the patients with DAT they studied longitudinally. They examined whether regions that demonstrated the greatest asymmetry in the initial scan of an individual patient continued to demonstrate the greatest asymmetry at follow-up. For each individual patient, they calculated the correlation between the nondirectional, absolute values of regional asymmetries from their first and second scans. Of 13 patients, 9 were found to have significant correlations. Because this analysis included regions that are relatively spared and, consequently, are less likely to be metabolically asymmetric, the significance of their result may simply reflect the continued differences between spared and affected regions. Because their analysis used absolute asymmetries, which do not reflect the direction of asymmetry, their results do not address the directional stability of metabolic asymmetries. Finally, because this analysis only examined correlations within individual patients, it did not address the stability of interindividual differences in the pattern of association cortex rCMRglc reductions.

To illustrate the longitudinal stability of individual patterns of association cortex metabolic reductions in patients with DAT, resting state PET scans from two patients with DAT are shown in Figure 16.5 (see color plate). These scans were obtained with a high-resolution scanner. These patients were part of the sample reported by Salerno et al. (1991) and Kumar et al. (1991). In the initial scan of Patient 1, a relatively discrete area of hypometabolism in left anterior association cortex can be seen, as compared to metabolism in the left posterior and right hemisphere association cortices. Disproportionate left frontal hypometabolism is evident on subsequent scans, obtained 1 and 2 years after the initial scan, although later scans demonstrate increasing involvement of right anterior and left posterior association regions. By contrast, Patient 2 had disproportionate hypometabolism in left posterior association cortex. Again, subsequent scans obtained 1 and 2 years after the initial scan demonstrate the same general pattern, with increasing involvement of other regions. These scans demonstrate that the patterns of metabolic reductions that distinguish individual patients from each other are easily discerned and, like fingerprints, characterize the patients for periods of at least 2 to 3 years.

Neuropsychological Correlates of Cerebral Metabolic Reductions in DAT

Analyses of the relationship between cerebral metabolic abnormalities, as reflected in indices calculated from PET or SPECT studies, and the severity of dementia have generally produced significant, although not very strong, correlations. The relationship is always in the expected direction, greater metabolic reductions in the association cortices being associated with greater cognitive impairment. Stronger relationships have been found between the pattern of association cortex metabolic reductions and the pattern of neuropsychological impairments. Again, the regions demonstrating disproportionately severe hypometabolism in a given patient are associated with greater impairment of cognitive functions associated with those regions, as compared to cognitive functions associated with less affected brain regions. Longitudinal studies of patients with DAT have shown that rate of change in overall severity can vary markedly among patients. In intermediate stages of DAT, the pattern of impairments—namely, the discrepancies between disproportionately affected functions and relatively less affected functions—can be relatively stable over periods of 1 to 3 years, despite worsening severity of dementia. Longitudinal studies of the relationship between cerebral metabolism and neuropsychological function have shown that the rate of change in overall severity is strongly related to the rate of change in the severity of the metabolic abnormality, as indexed by the discrepancy between association and primary cortex rCMRglc.

Relations with Severity of Impairment

In studies that have divided their patients into subgroups based on severity of dementia, the more severely demented patients have consistently demonstrated both greater reductions of absolute cortical metabolic rates (see Table 16.1; Foster et al., 1984; Frackowiak et al., 1981; Haxby, Grady, Koss, et al., 1988; Kumar et al., 1991) and greater abnormalities of indices that contrast association cortex metabolic rates to primary cortex metabolic rates (Haxby, Grady, Koss, et al., 1988; Kumar et al., 1991). When metabolic indices and neuropsychological measures of dementia severity are treated as continuous variables, they are generally found to be correlated. Foster et al. (1984) found no relation between overall cortical rCMRglc and two commonly used measures of dementia severity (Mattis Dementia Rating Scale [DRS], Mattis, 1976 and Wechsler Adult Intelligence Scale [WAIS] Full Scale IQ, Wechsler, 1955) but did find a significant relation with reaction time. Interestingly, Stern, Alexander, Prohounik, & Mayeux (1992) discovered an inverse relationship between education and parietotemporal perfusion deficits in AD patients. Frackowiak et al. (1981) found $rCMRO_2$ was significantly correlated with dementia severity in a mixed group of patients with vascular dementia and DAT. Haxby, Grady, Koss, et al. (1988) found significant correlations between three measures of dementia severity (Mini-Mental State Examination [MMSE], Folstein, Folstein, & Mchugh, 1975, DRS, WAIS IQ) and indices of parietal and premotor rCMRglc. Ratios of association cortex rCMRglc to sensorimotor cortex rCMRglc tended to demonstrate significant correlations more often than did the absolute metabolic rates in these association cortices. Kessler et al. (1991) found that another measure of overall dementia severity was significantly correlated with rCMRglc in parietal and temporal association cortices but not with rCMRglc in primary sensorimotor cortex.

Correlations Between Metabolic Patterns and Neuropsychological Patterns

Patients with DAT have heterogeneous patterns of association cortex rCMRglc reductions, and this heterogeneity is reflected in variable patterns of neuropsychological impairments. The most straightforward method for investigation of relationships between metabolic patterns and patterns of neuropsychological impairments was developed by Haxby et al. (1985). Metabolic patterns were indexed as pairwise discrepancies between selected association cortical regions. Between-hemisphere patterns were indexed as metabolic asymmetries; within-hemisphere patterns as ratios. Neuropsychological patterns were indexed as analogous pairwise discrepancies between selected neuropsychological tests of functions associated with the cortical regions being compared. Because neuropsychological tests, unlike rCMRglc, have uncertain scaling properties, comparison of two neuropsychological tests may be accomplished by a nonparametric transformation of test scores. Patient test scores were transformed to ranks. The difference between ranks for scores on two tests was used as the index of neuropsychological discrepancy. For example, a patient may have had the fifth best score (of 30 patients) on a test of visuospatial construction, but the 15th score on a test of verbal comprehension. That patients visuospatial-verbal discrepancy index, therefore, would be -10. That score would indicate that, relative to other patients with DAT, that patient had disproportionately more impairment on a test of verbal comprehension relative to impairment on a test of visuospatial construction. A correlation between this neuropsychological discrepancy index and the asymmetry between metabolic rates in right and left hemisphere parietal association cortex would indicate that disproportionate hypometabolism on the right, as compared to the left, was associated with disproportionate visuospatial impairment, as compared to verbal impairment.

Both metabolic and neuropsychological pattern indices demonstrate substantial intersubject heterogeneity over a wide range of dementia severities (Grady, Haxby, Horwitz, Sundaram, et al., 1988; Grady et al., 1986; Haxby et al., 1986; Haxby et al., 1990; Haxby, Grady, Koss, et al., 1988). Consequently, a mildly demented patient with disproportionate right-sided hypometabolism may have no verbal impairment and only a mild visuospatial construction apraxia. A moderately to severely demented patient with disproportionate right-sided hypometabolism, on the other hand, may have a marked verbal impairment but an even more profound visuospatial impairment. Both patients would demonstrate the expected correspondence between metabolic and neuropsychological patterns. The correlation between the metabolic pattern index—namely, rCMRglc asymmetry—and a single test score, however, could be zero because the metabolic pattern index is unrelated or only weakly related to overall dementia severity, whereas a single test score is strongly related to overall dementia severity. Because DAT is a gradually progressive illness, all samples of patients with DAT have variable levels of overall dementia severity. These differences in overall dementia severity must be factored out to detect the relationships between metabolic patterns and corresponding patterns of neuropsychological impairments. The use of neuropsychological discrepancy indices, rather than single test scores, successfully factors out dementia severity.

Metabolic pattern indices or right-left metabolic asymmetries and parietal-frontal discrepancies have consistently been shown to be significantly correlated with corresponding neuropsychological discrepancies. Right-left metabolic asymmetries in the parietal, frontal, and temporal cortices have consistently been found to be significantly correlated with visuospatial-verbal neuropsychological discrepancies in patients with moderate DAT (Figure 16.6 and Table 16.2) (Grady, Haxby, Horwitz, Sundaram, et al., 1988; Grady et al., 1986; Haxby et al., 1985; Haxby et al., 1986; Haxby et al., 1990). Patients with mild DAT, however, do not generally demonstrate these relationships, presumably because many of these patients have minimal or absent impairment of verbal and visuospatial functions. Similarly, parietal-frontal rCMRglc ratios have been shown to be correlated with patterns of neuropsychological impairments in patients with moderate but not mild DAT (Haxby, Grady, Koss, et al., 1988). Disproportionate frontal hypometabolism was associated with disproportionate impairment on a test of verbal fluency (FAS serial naming, Benton & Hansher, 1976) and disproportionate slowing on a test of attention to a simple set (Trail-Making Test, Trail A, Reitan, 1958). Disproportionate parietal hypometabolism was associated with disproportionate impairment on tests of verbal comprehension (Whitehouse's Syntax Comprehension Test, Haxby et al., 1985); calculations (WAIS Arithmetic, Wechsler, 1955); visuospatial construction (Extended Range Drawing Test, Haxby et al., 1985); and immediate visuospatial memory span (Block Tapping Span, Milner, 1971).

These correlations between metabolic and neuropsychological patterns were

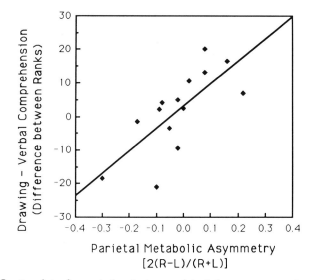

FIGURE 16.6. Scatterplot of correlation between right-left asymmetry of resting state glucose (rCMRglc) in parietal association cortex and the discrepancy between impairments of visuospatial construction and verbal comprehension. Patients were moderately demented. Patients in the upper right quadrant had lower left than right parietal metabolism and disproportionate impairment of verbal as compared to visuospatial function. (Data from Haxby et al., 1990)

initially demonstrated in a sample of moderately demented patients participating in the Laboratory of Neurosciences, National Institute on Aging (LNS/NIA) longitudinal study of DAT. Subsequently, these results have been validated in two independent samples of patients participating in the same study.

The patients in the LNS/NIA study who initially had mild DAT demonstrated no significant correlations between metabolic and neuropsychological patterns (Grady, Haxby, Horwitz, Sundaram, et al., 1988; Haxby et al., 1986; Haxby et al., 1990; Haxby, Grady, Koss, et al., 1988). These patients have been studied longitudinally. The patients who initially had no nonmemory language and visuospatial impairments subsequently developed significant impairments on some tests of those functions. The direction of metabolic asymmetries measured at their initial evaluation tended to predict whether they first developed significant verbal or visuospatial impairments (Grady, Haxby, Horwitz, Sundaram, et al., 1988). After an average follow-up duration of 26 months, the full group of initially mildly demented patients was found to have significant correlations between right-left metabolic asymmetries and visuospatial-verbal neuropsychological discrepancies (Table 16.2; Haxby et al., 1990).

In a later analysis of PET data obtained with a high-resolution PET scanner, Grady, Haxby, Schapiro, et al. (1990) divided a sample of patients with DAT, the majority of whom were not part of the sample in earlier analyses, in four subgroups based on metabolic pattern (see above). These subgroups had significantly different patterns of neuropsychological impairments. Patients in Subgroup 1, who showed the classic pattern of metabolic reductions in parietal and temporal association cortices, served as the basis of comparison for examining the neuropsychological

TABLE 16.2. Spearman Correlations Between Right-Left Metabolic Asymmetries and Visuospatial-Verbal Neuropsychological Discrepancies in Controls, Patients with Moderate DAT, and Patients with Initially Mild DAT at Initial Evaluation at Last Evaluation after a Mean Follow-up Duration of 26 Months

Neuropsychological Discrepancy[a]	Metabolic Asymmetry	Controls (N = 15 to 29)	Moderate DAT (N = 13)	Mild DAT (N = 10)	
				Initial	Follow-up
WAIS PDQ vs. VDQ	Prefrontal	−0.11	0.62*	0.01	0.47
	Premotor	−0.16	0.54	−0.13	0.46
	Parietal	−0.15	0.49	−0.15	0.36
	Temporal	0.28	0.44	0.02	0.38
WAIS PDQ vs. MDQ	Prefrontal	−0.07	0.45	0.04	0.78**
	Premotor	−0.06	0.51	−0.09	0.67*
	Parietal	0.02	0.65*	−0.16	0.50
	Temporal	0.03	0.42	0.04	0.59
Drawing vs. Comprehension	Prefrontal	−0.10	0.76**	0.04	0.38
	Premotor	−0.33	0.76**	−0.15	0.44
	Parietal	0.00	0.79**	0.04	0.23
	Temporal	0.12	0.53	−0.24	0.17
Verbal vs. Visual Recall	Prefrontal	−0.30	0.49	−0.22	0.44
	Premotor	−0.39	0.55*	−0.21	0.41
	Parietal	−0.40	0.69**	−0.16	0.68*
	Temporal	−0.17	0.48	−0.18	0.71*

[a]WAIS = Wechsler Adult Intelligence Scale; PDQ = Perceptual Organization Deviation Quotient; VDQ = Verbal Comprehension Deviation Quotient; MDQ = Memory and Freedom from Distractibility Deviation Quotient; Drawing = Extended Range Drawing Test; Comprehension-Syntax Comprehension Test, Verbal; and Visual Recall = Wechsler Memory Scale Logical Memory and Visual Reproduction subtests.
*p < .05. ** p < .01.
Note: From Haxby et al. (1990).

patterns demonstrated by patients in other groups. Patients in Subgroup 3, who demonstrated lower rCMRglc in the association areas of the left hemisphere as compared to the right, had greater verbal than visuospatial impairments as compared to Subgroup 1. Patients in Subgroup 2, who showed reduced rCMRglc in the orbitofrontal and anterior cingulate gyri with relatively spared parietal rCMRglc, had greater impairment on a test of verbal fluency as compared to impairment on a test of immediate visuospatial memory span.

Thus, in the LNS/NIA longitudinal study of DAT, variations in the pattern of association cortex metabolic reductions were found to be related to variable patterns of neuropsychological impairments in three separate samples of patients using two different methods of analysis. These results are further corroborated by the findings of Foster et al. (1984) and Martin et al. (1986). They found that DAT patients with predominant word-finding deficits had lower left than right rCMRglc values in perisylvian cortex and DAT patients with predominant visuospatial construction apraxia and lower right than left rCMRglc values in parietal cortex.

Analyses of correlations between single test scores and metabolic rates for single regions or metabolic pattern indices have yielded less consistent results. This inconsistency of results may be the result of not factoring out interindividual differences in overall dementia severity, as discussed previously. Friedland et al. (1985) and Koss et al. (1985) found that patients with lower right than left hemisphere (rCMRglc had greater impairment on tests of visuospatial construction, and patients with lower left than right frontal rCMRglc had greater language deficits. Mann, Mohr, Gearing, & Chase (1992) investigated whether a more rapidly deteriorating group of DAT patients had a different metabolic and cognitive pattern of deficits than a slow progression group. They found that patients with relatively fast progression had significantly greater hypometabolism frontally. Interestingly, the rapid progression group had significantly greater impairment in executive functions (verbal fluency, Benton & Hamsher, 1976; Mental Control subtest, Wechsler Memory Scale, 1945; and Ego State Inventory, McCarley, 1975) attributed to the frontal lobe. Parks, Cassens, et al. (1990) investigated Shipley Test (Shipley, 1940) performance correlations between rCMRglc and DAT patients. The subjects were from a larger group of DAT patients with predominant left hemisphere metabolic dysfunction (Loewenstein et al., 1989). The Shipley Abstraction and Vocabulary subtests were impaired in DAT patients and these tests were significantly correlated with the area of the left hemisphere that demonstrated the greatest hypometabolism (i.e., the left frontal region). On the other hand, McGeer et al. (1990) failed to find such a clear pattern of results. In a large sample of patients of all dementia severities, they calculated the correlations of single neuropsychological test scores, on the one hand; with metabolic rates for individual regions, metabolic asymmetries, frontal-parietal metabolic discrepancies, and frontal-temporal metabolic discrepancies, on the other. Although they found that higher metabolic rates were generally associated with better neuropsychological test scores, they found no evidence that the pattern of metabolic reductions was associated with the pattern of neuropsychological impairment. This negative finding may possibly be attributable to their use of single neuropsychological test scores rather than discrepancies between selected pairs of test scores. They did find that patients with metabolic asymmetries indicating disproportionate left-sided hypometabolism had lower scores on almost all neuropsychological tests, including some nonverbal tests. These results suggest that left lower rather than right metabolic asymmetries were associated with greater overall dementia severity in their sample of patients.

McGeer et al. (1990) did not examine any correlations between metabolic and neuropsychological patterns, nor did they subdivide their sample by overall dementia severity. As discussed above, the most consistent correlations between metabolic and neuropsychological impairments were found in the LNS/NIA study when neuropsychological test scores were converted to discrepancy indices, which factor out interindividual differences in overall dementia severity or premorbid ability. Moreover, metabolic and neuropsychological patterns were correlated only for patients in intermediate stages of the illness, after the development of significant impairments of nonmemory language and visuospatial functions and before dementia became so severe as to obscure any pattern of relative strengths and weaknesses.

Correlations Between Longitudinal Metabolic and Neuropsychological Changes

As discussed in previous sections, the pattern of association cortex metabolic reductions tends to be a relatively stable feature of individual patients for at least 2 to 3 years (Grady et al., 1986; Haxby et al., 1990; Haxby, Grady, Koss, et al., 1988; McGeer et al., 1990; Salerno et al., 1991). Similarly, the neuropsychological patterns, as indexed by neuropsychological discrepancies, also tend to be stable despite worsening of overall level of dementia (Grady et al., 1986; Haxby, Grady, Koss et al., 1988; Salerno et al., 1991). In very early DAT, the association cortex metabolic abnormalities appear before the appearance of demonstrable neocortically mediated language and visuospatial impairments (Grady, Haxby, Horwitz, Sundaram, et al., 1988; Haxby et al., 1986; Haxby et al., 1990; Haxby, Grady, Koss, et al., 1988). When language and visuospatial impairments develop subsequently, they tend to be correlated with the regions demonstrating disproportionate hypometabolism at previous evaluations (Grady, Haxby, Horwitz, Sundaram, et al., 1988; Haxby et al., 1990).

Two studies have examined whether the rate of change in metabolic indices is related to rates of change in neuropsychological measures (McGeer et al., 1990; Salerno et al., 1991). Longitudinal study of changes in neuropsychological function have found that the rate of overall cognitive decline varies markedly among patients (Haxby, Raffaele, Gillette, Schapiro, & Rapoport, 1992; Katzman et al., 1988; Salmon, Thal, Butters, & Heindel, 1990). In the LNS/NIA longitudinal study of DAT, there was a fourfold difference between the slowest and fastest rates of decline. The pattern of neuropsychological impairments, on the other hand, tends to be relatively stable in patients with moderate DAT—those functions showing disproportionate impairment continue to show the greatest impairment, relative to other functions, at follow-up (Grady et al., 1986; Haxby, Grady, Koss, et al., 1988; Salerno et al., 1991).

McGeer et al. (1990) had repeat scans on 13 patients with DAT with an average interscan interval of 15 months. They found that overall change in rCMRglc rates were uncorrelated with overall change in psychological tests scores. They also examined whether rate of change in single test scores, on the one hand, was related to rate of change in rCMRglc for individual regions or for frontal-parietal or frontal-temporal metabolic discrepancies and found no relation.

Salerno et al. (1991) had three to four scans on each of 10 patients, with an average interscan interval of 29 months. They derived a single index of DAT-related metabolic abnormality. This index was the ratio of bilateral parietal and premotor association cortex rCMRglc to bilateral sensorimotor and calcarine primary cortex rCMRglc. This index reduced both interindividual and intraindividual variance (see discussion above) and, by sampling both posterior and anterior association cortices, was more likely to reflect the metabolic abnormality found in most patients with DAT. As discussed above, this index most consistently demonstrated worsening metabolic abnormality for all patients. The rate of change in this index was also highly correlated with rate of change on two standard neuropsychological measures of overall dementia severity, the Mattis Dementia Rating Scale ($r = .75$, $p < .01$) (Mattis, 1976) and the Wechsler Adult Intelligence Scale Full Scale IQ ($r = .67$, $p < .05$) (Wechsler, 1955). Rates of change in metabolic patterns and rates of change in neuropsychological discrepancies, however, were mostly uncorrelated. The discrepancy between the findings of McGeer et al. (1990) and Salerno et al. (1991) can be attributed to two methodological improvements. First, instead of analyzing change in mean absolute rCMRglc values, Salerno et al. (1991) derived an index that reduced both interindividual and intraindividual variance. Second, Salerno et al. (1991) examined change over a follow-up period twice as long with three to four evaluations per patient instead of two. Increasing the follow-up interval and the number of evaluations significantly decreases the error of estimates of change. For example, by doubling the follow-up interval, the error associated with change estimates is halved. This reduction in error variance associated with estimating rates of change, associated with the use of a theoretically motivated and less variable index of DAT-related metabolic abnormality, can account for the ability of Salerno et al. (1991) to detect a relation between rate of progression of metabolic abnormality and rate of progression of dementia. The lack of correlation between rates of change in metabolic and neuropsychological pattern indices suggests that, because of the longitudinal stability of these measures, any real changes in their values may be too small to be detected above the error variance associated with change estimates.

Regional Brain Metabolism or Blood Flow During Cognitive Activity in DAT

In contrast to the consistency of results from studies of resting state regional cerebral metabolism in patients with DAT, the small number of studies that have measured rCMRglc or rCBF while DAT patients performed cognitive tasks have produced inconsistent results (Duara, Barker, Pascal, Loewenstein, & Boothe, 1990; Duara, Loewenstein, & Barker, 1990; Grady et al., 1991; Kessler et al., 1991). In part, these inconsistencies may be due to differences in the PET, cognitive, and image analysis methods employed. Most studies have measured rCMRglc using the PET-fluorodeoxyglucose (FDG) method while subjects performed cognitive tasks (Duara, Barker, Pascal, Loewenstein, & Boothe, 1990; Duara, Loewenstein, & Barker, 1990; Kessler et al., 1991). This method integrates activity over a relatively long period of time (30–40 minutes), requiring cognitive tasks on which consistent performance can be maintained for that duration. Using PET to measure rCBF during cognitive activity, using ^{15}O-labeled compounds, such as water, on the other hand, integrates activity over a much shorter period of time (40 seconds–4 minutes), with briefer intervals between scans (12 minutes), allowing more flexibility in the design of cognitive tasks (Grady et al., 1992). The shorter interval between scans allows the use of head movement restraint devices, making it possible to compare activation and control scans on a pixel-by-pixel basis and allowing more precise delineation of the regions activated by a given control task. Although algorithms have been developed that allow pixel-by-pixel comparison of scans obtained during different sessions (Lee, Berger, & Mintun, 1991; Mintun & Lee, 1990), these methods have not been applied to PET activation studies of patients with DAT.

Duara and his associates (Duara, Loewenstein, & Barker, 1990) investigated the effects of a verbal fluency test adapted for PET (Parks et al., 1988). Elderly normal subjects demonstrated a 21.4% global increase in CMRglc during verbal fluency test performance and the AD subjects showed an increase of 8%, as compared to resting state metabolism. When the verbal fluency test was performed in AD patients, there was no evidence of regional activation, but only decreases in bilateral occipital rCMRglc. The data suggested that there was an overall increase in the AD patients' metabolism in the anterior brain region and lack of activation in the posterior brain area, which may explain the decreased occipital rCMRglc.

Duara and his colleagues (Duara, Barker, Pascal, Loewenstein, & Boothe,

1990; Duara, Loewenstein, & Barker, 1990) have examined within-subject changes in rCMRglc associated with the performance of a complex task, Reading Memory Passages, that involves both reading and recall. This task was associated with activation of primary and association visual areas in the occipital lobe. Patients with DAT demonstrated activations of these regions that were equivalent to those seen in elderly controls. These researchers concluded that patients with DAT show metabolic increases associated with cognitive activity in association cortices that are hypometabolic at rest, suggesting that neuronal number and connectivity is spared in primary and association visual cortex. Their task, however, failed to activate association areas in the parietal and temporal lobes, regions that demonstrate the most consistent and largest reductions in resting state metabolism.

In a similar study of changes in rCMRglc associated with a complex task, Kessler et al. (1991) found that patients with DAT demonstrated a significantly smaller activation of global cerebral metabolism. In this study, subjects performed a recognition memory task (continuous visual recognition). In an attempt to equate performance of patients and controls, different versions were administered. The easier version had less abstract memoranda (figures, words, and letter strings) and tested retention over briefer intervals. Nonetheless, patient performances, as indexed by d', were inferior to those of controls. In controls, this task was associated with a large global increase in CMRglc of 21%. The largest activation was in the primary visual cortex (40%). Patients with DAT demonstrated a significantly smaller global increase in CMRglc (5.7%), but the regional pattern of changes in rCMRglc in patients and controls did not differ. In the one study by Duara, Loewenstein, & Barker (1990) in which intersubject comparisons were made (Reading Memory Passages) no significant differences in global CMRglc increases were found.

Grady et al. (1991) have examined changes in rCBF associated with performance of a visual discrimination task, face matching, in controls and in patients with mild and moderate DAT (Figure 16.7). Unlike the previous studies, that of Grady, Haxby, Horwitz, et al. (1990) compared rCBF during the face matching task to rCBF during a sensorimotor control task, thus factoring out activation in primary cortices and focusing the analysis on activations in association cortices. The studies of Duara, Barker, et al. (1990), Duara, Loewenstein, & Barker (1990), and Kessler et al. (1991) compared rCMRglc during cognitive activity to resting state rCMRglc. Consequently, the patterns of metabolic increases tended to be dominated by primary cortex activations. Performance of the face matching task has been associated with discrete activations of extrastriate visual cortices in occipital association and occipitotemporal cortices (Haxby et al., 1991). Additionally, old controls are found to demonstrate some activation of an extrastriate region in superior parietal cortex during this face matching task, an area that was only activated by a spatial vision task, location matching, in young subjects (Grady, Haxby, Horwitz, et al., 1990; Haxby et al., 1991). Patients with DAT demonstrated increases of occipital association and occipitotemporal rCBF during the performance of this task that were equivalent to those demonstrated in age-matched controls. Both absolute rCBF and normalized rCBF demonstrated equivalence of rCBF increases. Like the old controls, patients with DAT also demonstrated some activation of superior parietal rCBF. In addition, the patients demonstrated a significant increase in right premotor rCBF, a region that was not activated in controls.

The results of Grady et al. (1991) suggest that in patients with mild DAT, the

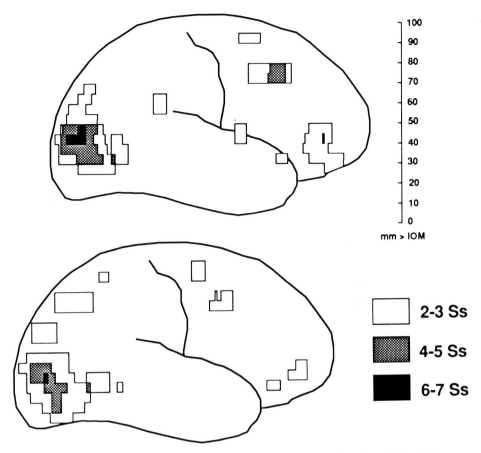

FIGURE 16.7. Right hemisphere regions demonstrating increased regional blood flow
during a face matching task as compared to during a sensorimotor control task in eight
healthy, age-matched controls and seven patients with mild and moderate dementia of
the Alzheimer type (DAT). Areas showing 30% increase in blood flow in 12 contiguous
pixels (48 mm²) in at least two subjects are depicted. Shading indicates the number of
subjects with overlapping blood flow increases. DAT patients and controls demonstrated
equivalent blood flow increases in right and left occipital association and occipitotemporal
cortices. DAT patients also demonstrated increased blood flow in right premotor cortex.
(Data from Grady et al., 1991)

mechanism for recruiting extrastriate visual cortical areas for cognitive processing
remains intact, even though the function of these regions has been affected by the
disease, as evidenced by resting state hypometabolism. This conclusion is in agreement with that of Duara, Barker, et al., (1990) and Duara, Loewenstein, & Barker
(1990). The results suggest further that both aging and DAT are associated with
the recruitment of additional regions for the performance of these tasks. In aging,
extrastriate regions in the more superior, spatial visual processing pathway are
recruited. In DAT, these spatial visual processing regions and right premotor cortex
are recruited. These additional activations may reflect mechanisms that compensate
for decreased visual perceptual efficiency in older and demented subjects. Alter-

natively, they may reflect a disorganization of cerebral activation that may underlie, at least in part, age-related and dementia-related decrements in visual perceptual ability.

Kessler et al.'s (1991) finding of lesser increases in absolute rCMRglc during cognitive activity disagrees with the findings of Duara, Barker, et al. (1990), Duara, Loewenstein, & Barker (1990), and Grady et al. (1991). Because Kessler et al. (1991) attempted, unsuccessfully, to equate the performance of controls and patients with DAT, they gave different tests to these two groups. Duara, Barker, et al. (1990), Duara, Loewenstein, & Barker (1990), and Grady et al. (1991) gave the same tasks to controls and patients with DAT. In the Duara, Barker, et al. (1990) and Duara, Loewenstein, & Barker (1990) study, a memory task was employed, presumably leading to substantial performance differences between controls and patients. In the Grady et al. (1991) study, a simple face matching test was employed, resulting in equivalent mean accuracies and response times for patients and controls, although patients had more variable response times. The discrepancy between these studies may be related to the differences in task difficulties and subject performances. The interaction between task difficulty, performance, and rCBF or rCMRglc increases is not well understood and requires further study to make interpretation of group differences in rCBF or rCMRglc activations possible.

Differential Diagnosis

Positron emission tomography studies of subjects with dementias usually show a distinctive pattern of metabolic hypometabolism relative to other cortical regions (Parks, Dodril, et al., 1990). In this section we briefly describe PET studies in several types of dementia.

Pseudodementia patients with concomitant depression sometimes present behavioral and neuropsychological impairments that are difficult to distinguish from DAT. One study showed pseudodementia patients (Baxter et al., 1989) often exhibit prefrontal instead of the DAT's temporal and parietal lower cerebral blood flow. However, the prefrontal cerebral blood flow in pseudodementia patients increased with treatment. Lower radiopharmaceutical prefrontal abnormalities are also found in PET scans of Pick's disease (Kamo et al., 1987; Salmon et al., 1988) and dementia of the frontal lobe type (Neary, Snowden, & Northen, 1988). Progressive supranuclear palsy (PSP) patients have very impaired frontal hypometabolism, but proportionally more premotor deficits in PSP separate this patient group from Pick's disease and dementia of the frontal lobe type (Goffinet et al., 1989). Multi-infarct dementia (MID) patients present with a random constellation of metabolic deficits (Benson et al., 1982). Kuhl et al. (1985) showed that MID patients had focal metabolic deficiencies scattered throughout the cortex, white matter, thalamus, caudate, and cerebellum. Whereas PET missed the smaller lacunar infarcts, ratios of parietal and caudate-thalamus metabolism distinguished DAT from MID and normal individuals. A recent study that compared DAT, MID and elderly controls found that metabolism in the basal ganglia, thalamus, and cerebellum was reduced significantly in patients with MID only (Mielke, Herholz, Grond, Kessler, & Heiss, 1992). Normal-pressure hydrocephalus patients do not show focal deficits

in metabolism, but rather global lower glucose metabolism (Jagust, Friedland, & Budinger, 1985).

The pattern of metabolic abnormality in Huntington's disease (HD) generally consists of lower metabolism in the area of the caudate (Berent et al., 1988; Kuhl et al., 1982; Hayden, Martin, & Stoessl, 1986). The regional glucose metabolism is related to deficits in neuropsychological test performance (Berent et al., 1988). Positron emission tomography studies have been inconsistent with respect to subjects at risk for HD. Mazziotta et al. (1987) found lower metabolism in the caudate in at-risk HD subjects, whereas Young et al. (1987) using different subjects did not find lower metabolism. These inconsistencies may be due in part to subject selection criteria and differences in PET slice data analysis. In a PET study of high-risk HD subjects in which the genetic deoxyribonucleic acid (DNA) polymorphic marker (Gusella et al., 1983) was available for some presymptomatic individuals, Hayden et al. (1987) found lower caudate metabolism. The metabolic abnormalities were evident in only three out of eight subjects. It is clear that those HD subjects who already exhibit the behavioral spasmodic, involuntary movements have abnormal caudate metabolism; however, the utility of predicting presymptomatic high- or low-risk HD subjects with PET remains unclear.

Summary

The development of methods for functional brain imaging has made it possible to study the distribution of disease-related impairments in the brain of patients with DAT at all stages of the illness, and to relate that distribution to neuropsychological impairments.

Multiple studies of resting state regional brain metabolism in patients with DAT have consistently demonstrated that the association cortices demonstrate the greatest metabolic reductions with relative sparing of the primary cortices, cerebellum, basal ganglia, and thalamus. Of the association cortices, those of the parietal lobe tend to be hypometabolic in the largest number of patients, show the largest metabolic reductions, and the first to demonstrate hypometabolism in patients with mild DAT.

The distribution of association cortex metabolic reductions can vary markedly among patients. Metabolic reductions in homologous association cortices of the right and left hemispheres are often asymmetric. Within the cerebral hemispheres, the relative severities of hypometabolism in the parietal, temporal, and frontal lobes can vary markedly. The distribution of hypometabolic brain regions in an individual patient tends to be stable over periods of at least 2 to 3 years. As dementia severity worsens, the severity of metabolic abnormalities also worsens, but the regions originally demonstrating disproportionate hypometabolism tend to continue to be the most hypometabolic.

The severity of metabolic reductions in the association cortices tends to be significantly correlated with overall dementia severity. Moreover, the pattern of metabolic reductions tends to be significantly correlated with the pattern of neuropsychological impairments. These correlations are usually found in patients with moderate dementia, however. Presumably, patients with mild DAT have not developed severe enough impairments of nonmemory language and visuospatial func-

tions to allow a clear pattern of disproportionate impairment and relative sparing to emerge. Test scores in patients with mild DAT may also still reflect premorbid patterns of strengths and weaknesses that are unrelated to the distribution of disease-related alterations in brain function. In severe DAT, dementia may be more global, and any residual patterns of disproportionate impairments may be obscured by floor effects.

At least one study has shown that the rate of change in the severity of these metabolic reductions is correlated with the rate at which the cognitive symptoms of dementia worsen (Salerno et al., 1991). Changes in the distribution of metabolic reductions, however, have not been shown to be related to changes in the pattern of neuropsychological impairments. This latter finding probably reflects the relative longitudinal stability of the distribution of metabolic reductions in patients with DAT.

Patients with very early DAT demonstrate significant abnormalities of resting state metabolism in the same association regions that are hypometabolic in patients with more advanced DAT. These patients have impairments of memory but no significant impairments of nonmemory language and visuospatial functions. The distribution of hypometabolism in individual patients tends to predict which nonmemory neuropsychological functions will first demonstrate significant impairment. These results suggest that patients with very early DAT are able to maintain neocortically mediated cognitive functions at premorbid levels despite some physiological impairment of the neocortex. The appearance of nonmemory language and visuospatial impairments, therefore, signals the depletion of a reserve functional capacity that had been diminishing for an undetermined period of time.

The small number of PET studies that have examined regional cerebral metabolism or blood flow in patients with DAT during cognitive activity have not yet produced a consistent account. The three studies reviewed here all showed that the change in relative blood flow or metabolism (regional values normalized to whole brain rates) associated with cognitive activity were equivalent for patients and controls. They differed, however, on whether the increment in absolute metabolic or blood flow rates were the same in patients and controls. Factors that may influence the capacity to increase local and global metabolic and blood flow rates to perform a cognitive activity include the nature of the cognitive function, the difficulty of the task, the effort evinced by the subject, and dementia severity. Differences in any of these factors may account for the discrepant findings. More research is needed to understand how these factors interact.

A comparison of Alzheimer PET studies as a whole show a consistent pattern of parietal metabolism deficits that is not typical of other dementias. Pick's disease, dementia of the frontal lobe, and progressive supranuclear palsy patients exhibit deficits in frontal areas of PET scans; however, progressive supranuclear palsy has more premotor than prefrontal involvement. Multi-infarct dementia patients demonstrate random scattered metabolic deficits, whereas Huntington's patients show lower caudate metabolism. Normal-pressure hydrocephalus subjects display lower overall glucose metabolism. In a review of PET's clinical role, Brooks (1991) suggested that PET can help characterize the type of dementia when clinical assessment and structural imaging remains unclear. In a stronger statement from a report of the Therapeutics and Technology Assessment Subcommittee of the American Academy of Neurology (1991), members indicated that PET procedures with

glucose metabolism or cerebral blood flow were a "safe and efficacious diagnostic clinical technique" (p. 166) for differential diagnosis of dementia. They further indicated PET was "at least, complementary to, and often unique rather than redundant with, structural imaging and EEG" (p. 166). Another member of the committee (Powers, Berg, Perlmutter, & Raichle, 1991) said that the clinical application of PET was overstated and premature. As clinical researchers we do view PET a useful tool, but always within the context of a full clinical workup (e.g., neuropsychological assessment, history, laboratory studies, etc.).

Positron emission tomography will enable researchers to generate new hypotheses about the proportional contribution of many neural networks in the brain (Parks, Lowenstein, Dodrill, et al., 1988; Parks, Crockett, & McGeer, 1989; Parks, et al., 1991; Petersen, Fox, Posner, Mintun, & Raichle, 1988; Squire et al., 1992). Tracers with short half-lives now allow subjects to receive five or more scans during short periods of time. This methodology will allow scientists to hierarchically subtract one scan from another in order to determine which features of the activation procedures are critical to producing changes in tracer distribution (Horwitz et al., 1992; Parks, Crockett, Tuokko, et al., 1989; Posner, Petersen, Fox, & Raichle, 1988).

Functional brain imaging during cognitive activation may allow closer examination of how neural systems are differentially affected by AD. The studies reviewed above tend to show preservation of the ability to alter regional patterns of activity to perform some cognitive activities. These results suggest that whereas mechanisms associated with maintaining resting state activity levels in the association cortices are affected early in the disease, mechanisms associated with recruiting an association cortical region for cognitive activity are less affected, even though the actual performance of that cognitive activity may be impaired. Thus, neural mechanisms that influence the same cortical region may be differentially affected by AD. Cognitive activation studies may provide a means for acquiring a deeper understanding of how AD affects local cortical function.

References

Ball, M. J. (1976). Neurofibrillary tangles and the pathogenesis of dementia: A quantitative study. *Neuropathology and Applied Neurobiology*, *2*, 395–410.

Baxter, L. R., Schwartz, J. M., Phelps, M. E., Mazziotta, J. C., Guze, B. H., Selin, C. E., Gerner, R. H., & Sumida, R. M. (1989). Reduction of prefrontal cortex glucose metabolism common to three types of depression. *Archives of General Psychiatry*, *46*, 243–250.

Becker, J. J., Huff, F. J., Nebes, R. D., Holland, A., & Boller, F. (1988). Neuropsychological function in Alzheimer's disease: Pattern of impairment and rates of progression. *Archives of Neurology*, *45*, 263–268.

Benson, F. D. (1982). The use of positron emission tomography scanning techniques in the diagnosis of Alzheimer's disease. In S. Corkin (Ed.), *Alzheimer's Disease: Vol. 19. A report of progress* (pp. 79–82). New York: Raven Press.

Benton, A. L., & Hansher, K. D. (1976). *Multilingual examination*. Iowa City, IA: University of Iowa.

Berent, S., Giordani, B., Lehtinen, S., Markel, D., Penny, J. B., Buchtel, H. A., Starosta-Rubinstein, S., Hichwa, R., & Young, A. B. (1988). Positron emission tomographic

scan investigations of Huntington's disease: Cerebral metabolic correlates of cognitive function. *Annals of Neurology, 23*, 541–546.

Bondareff, W., Mountjoy, C. Q., & Roth, M. (1982). Loss of neurones of adrenergic projection to cerebral cortex (nucleus locus coeruleus) in senile dementia. *Neurology, 32*, 164–169.

Brooks, D. J. (1991). PET: Its clinical role in neurology. *Journal of Neurology, Neurosurgery and Psychiatry, 54*, 1–5.

Clark, C. M., Kessler, R., Buchsbaum, M. S., Margolin, R. A., & Holcomb, H. H. (1984). Correlational methods for determining regional coupling of cerebral glucose metabolism. A pilot study. *Biological Psychiatry, 19*, 663–678.

Creasey, H., Schwartz, M., Frederickson, H., Haxby, J. V., & Rapoport, S. I. (1986). Quantitative computed tomography in dementia of the Alzheimer type. *Neurology, 36*, 1563–1568.

Cummings, J., Benson, D. F., Hill, M. A., & Read, S. (1985). Aphasia in dementia of the Alzheimer type. *Neurology, 35*, 394–397.

Duara, R., Barker, W., Pascal, S., Loewenstein, D., & Boothe, T. (1990). Behavioral activation PET studies in normal aging and Alzheimer's disease. *Journal of Nuclear Medicine, 31*, 730.

Duara, R., Grady, C. L., Haxby, J. V., Sundaram, M., Cutler, N. R., Heston, L., Moore, A. M., Schlageter, N. L., Larson, S., & Rapoport, S. I. (1986). Positron emission tomography in Alzheimer's disease. *Neurology, 36*, 879–887.

Duara, R., Loewenstein, D., & Barker, W. W. (1990). Utilization of behavioral activation paradigms for positron emission tomography studies in normal young and elderly subjects and in dementia. In R. Duara (Ed.), *Positron emission tomography in dementia* (pp. 131–148). New York: Wiley-Liss.

Folstein, M. F., Folstein, S. E., & Mchugh, P. R. (1975). Mini Mental State Examination. *Journal of Psychiatric Research, 12*, 189–198.

Foster, N. L., Chase, T. N., Mansi, L., Brooks, R., Fedio, P., Patronas, N. J., & DiChiro, G. (1984). Cortical abnormalities in Alzheimer's disease. *Annals of Neurology, 16*, 649–654.

Frackowiak, R. S. J., Pozzilli, C., Legg, N. J., Du Boulay, G. H., Marshall, J., Lenzi, G. L., & Jones, T. (1981). Regional cerebral oxygen supply and utilization in dementia. A clinical and physiological study with oxygen-15 and positron tomography. *Brain, 104*, 753–778.

Friedland, R. P., Budinger, T. F., Koss, E., & Ober, B. A. (1985). Alzheimer's disease: Anterior-posterior and lateral hemispheric metabolic alterations in cortical glucose utilization. *Neuroscience Letters, 53*, 235–240.

Goffinet, A. M., De Volder, A. G., Gillian, C., Rectem, D., Bol, A., Michel, C., Cogneau, M., Labar, D., & Laterre, C. (1989) Positron emission tomography demonstrates frontal lobe hypometabolism in progressive supranuclear palsy. *Annals of Neurology, 25*, 131–139.

Grady, C. L., Haxby, J. V., Horwitz, B., Berg, G., & Rapoport, S. I. (1988). Neuropsychological and cerebral metabolic function in early vs. late onset dementia of the Alzheimer type. *Neuropsychologia, 25*, 807–816.

Grady, C. L., Haxby, J. V., Horwitz, B., Schapiro, M. B., Rapoport, S. I., Ungerleider, L. G., Mishkin, M., Carson, R. E., & Herscovitch, P. (1992). Dissociation of object and spatial vision in human extrastriate cortex: Age-related changes in activation of regional cerebral blood flow measured with [^{15}O] water and positron emission tomography. *Journal of Cognitive Neuroscience, 4*, 23–34.

Grady, C. L., Haxby, J. V., Horwitz, B., Schapiro, M. B., Salerno, J., Gonzalez, A., & Rapoport, S. I. (1991). Activation of anterior and posterior extrastriate cortex during

face perception in patients with dementia. *Journal of Cerebral Blood Flow and Metabolism, 11* (Suppl. 2), S382.

Grady, C. L., Haxby, J. V., Horwitz, B., Schapiro, M. B., Ungerleider, L. G., Mishkin, M., Carson, R. E., Herscovitch, P., & Rapoport, S. I. (1990). Changes in regional cerebral blood flow (rCBF) demonstrate separate visual pathways for object discrimination and spatial location. *Journal of Clinical and Experimental Neuropsychology, 12,* 93.

Grady, C. L., Haxby, J. V., Horwitz, B., Sundaram, M., Berg, G., Schapiro, M., Friedland, R. P., & Rapoport, S. I. (1988). A longitudinal study of the early neuropsychological and cerebral metabolic changes in dementia of the Alzheimer type. *Journal of Clinical and Experimental Neuropsychology, 10,* 576–596.

Grady, C. L., Haxby, J. V., Schapiro, M. B., Gonzalez-Aviles, A., Kumar, A., Ball, M. J., Heston, L., & Rapoport, S. I. (1990). Subgroups in dementia of the Alzheimer type identified using positron emission tomography. *Journal of Neuropsychiatry and Clinical Neurosciences, 2,* 1–12.

Grady, C. L., Haxby, J. V., Schlageter, N. L., Berg, G., & Rapoport, S. I. (1986). Stability of metabolic and neuropsychological asymmetries in dementia of the Alzheimer type. *Neurology, 36,* 1390–1392.

Gruenthal, E. (1926). Ueber die Alzheimersche Krankheit: Eine histopathologische-klinische Studie. *Zentralblatt der Gesamte Neurologie und Psychiatrie, 101,* 128–157.

Gusella, J., Wexler, N., Conneally, P., Naylor, S., Anderson, M., Tanzi, R., Watkins, P., Ottina, K., Wallace, M., Sakaguchi, A., Young, A., Shoulson, I., Bonilla, E., Martin, J. (1983). A polymorphic DNA marker genetically linked to Huntington's disease. *Nature, 306,* 234–238.

Haxby, J. V., Duara, R., Grady, C. L., Rapoport, S. I., & Cutler, N. R. (1985). Relations between neuropsychological and cerebral metabolic asymmetries in early Alzheimer's disease. *Journal of Cerebral Blood Flow and Metabolism, 5,* 193–200.

Haxby, J. V., Grady, C. L., Duara, R., Schlageter, N. L., Berg, G., & Rapoport, S. I. (1986). Neocortical metabolic abnormalities precede non-memory cognitive deficits in early Alzheimer-type dementia. *Archives of Neurology, 43,* 882–885.

Haxby, J. V., Grady, C. L., Horwitz, B., Schapiro, M. B., Carson, R. E., Ungerleider, L. G., Mishkin, M., Herscovitch, P., Friedland, R. P., & Rapoport, S. I. (1988). Mapping of two visual pathways in man with regional cerebral blood flow (rCBF) as measured by positron emission tomography (PET) and $H_{215}O$. *Abstracts Society for Neuroscience, 14,* 750.

Haxby, J. V., Grady, C. L., Horwitz, B., Ungerleider, L. G., Mishkin, M., Carson, R. E., Herscovitch, P., Schapiro, M. B., & Rapoport, S. I. (1991). Dissociation of spatial and object visual processing pathways in human extrastriate cortex. *Proceedings of the National Academy of Science of the United States of America, 88,* 1621–1625.

Haxby, J. V., Grady, C. L., Koss, E., Horwitz, B., Heston, L. L., Schapiro, M. B., Friedland, R. P., & Rapoport, S. I. (1990). Longitudinal study of cerebral metabolic asymmetries and associated neuropsychological patterns in early dementia of the Alzheimer type. *Archives of Neurology, 47,* 753–760.

Haxby, J. V., Grady, C. L., Koss, E., Horwitz, B., Schapiro, M. B., Friedland, R. P., & Rapoport, S. I. (1988). Heterogeneous anterior-posterior metabolic patterns in Alzheimer's type dementia. *Neurology, 38,* 1853–1863.

Haxby, J. V., Raffaele, K., Gillette, J., Schapiro, M. B., & Rapoport, S. I. (1992). Individual trajectories of decline in patients with dementia of the Alzheimer type. *Journal of Clinical and Experimental Neuropsychology, 14,* 575–592.

Hayden, M., Martin, W., & Stoessl, A. (1986). Positron emission tomography in the early diagnosis of Huntington's disease. *Neurology, 36,* 888–894.

Hayden, M., Hewitt, J., Stoessl, A., Clark, C., Ammann, W., & Martin, W. (1987). The combined use of positron emission tomography and DNA polymorphisms for pre-clinical detection of Huntington's disease. *Neurology, 37*, 1441–1447.

Horwitz, B., Duara, R., & Rapoport, S. I. (1984). Intercorrelations of glucose metabolic rates between brain regions: Application to healthy males in a state of reduced sensory input. *Journal of Cerebral Blood Flow and Metabolism, 4*, 484–499.

Horwitz, B., Grady, C. L., Haxby, J. V., Schapiro, M. B., Rapoport, S. I., Ungerleider, L. G., & Mishkin, M. (1992). Functional associations among human posterior ex-trastriate brain regions during object and spatial vision. *Journal of Cognitive Neuroscience, 4*, 311–322.

Horwitz, B., Grady, C. L., Schlageter, N. L., Duara, R., & Rapoport, S. I. (1987). Inter-correlations of regional cerebral glucose metabolic rates in Alzheimer's disease. *Brain Research, 407*, 294–306.

Jagust, W. J., Friedland, R. P., & Budinger, T. F. (1985). Positron emission tomography with 18-F fluorodeoxyglucose differentiates normal pressure hydrocephalus from Alz-heimer type dementia. *Journal of Neurology, Neurosurgery and Psychiatry, 48*, 1091–1096.

Jagust, W. J., Friedland, R. P., Budinger, T. F., Koss, E., & Ober, B. (1988). Longitudinal studies of regional cerebral metabolism in Alzheimer's disease. *Neurology, 38*, 909–912.

Jamada, M., & Mehraein, P. (1968). Verteilungsmuster der senilen Veraenderungen im Gehirn. *Archiv fur Psychiatrie und Nervenkrankheiten, 211*, 308–324.

Kamo, H., McGeer, P. L., Harrop, R., McGeer, E. G., Calne, D. B., Martin, M. D., & Pate, B. D. (1987). Positron emission tomography and histopathology in Pick's dis-ease. *Neurology, 37*, 439–445.

Katzman, R., Brown, T., Thal, L. J., Fuld, P. A., Aronson, M., Butters, N., Klauber, M. R., Wiederholt, W., Pay, M., Renbing, X., Ooi, W. L., Hofstetter, R., & Terry, R. D. (1988). Comparison of rate of annual change of mental status score in four independent studies of patients with Alzheimer's disease. *Annals of Neurology, 24*, 384–389.

Kemper, T. (1984). Neuroanatomical and neuropathological changes in normal aging and in dementia. In M. Albert (Ed.), *Clinical neurology of aging* (pp. 9–52). New York: Oxford University Press.

Kessler, J., Herholz, K., Grond, M., & Heiss, W.-D. (1991). Impaired metabolic activation in Alzheimer's disease: A PET study during continuous visual recognition. *Neuro-psychologia, 29*, 229–243.

Koss, E., Friedland, R. P., Ober, B. A., & Jagust, W. J. (1985). Differences in lateral hemispheric asymmetries of glucose utilization between early- and late-onset Alz-heimer type dementia. *American Journal of Psychiatry, 142*, 638–640.

Kuhl, D. E., Metter, E. J., & Riege, W. H. (1985). Patterns of cerebral glucose utilization in depression, multiple infarct dementia, and Alzheimer's disease. In L. Sokoloff (Ed.), *Brain imaging and brain function* (pp. 211–226). New York: Raven Press.

Kuhl, D., Phelps, M., Markham, C., Metter, E., Riege, W., & Winter, J. (1982). Cerebral metabolism and atrophy in Huntington's disease determined by 18 FDG and com-puted tomographic scan. *Annals of Neurology, 12*, 424–434.

Kumar, A., Schapiro, M. B., Grady, C. L., Haxby, J. V., Wagner, E., Salerno, J., Friedland, R. P., & Rapoport, S. I. (1991). High-resolution PET studies in Alzheimer's disease. *Neuropsychopharmacology, 4*, 35–46.

Lee, K. S., Berger, K. L., & Mintun, M. A. (1991). Mathematical registration of PET images enhances detection of neural activation foci by subtraction image analysis. *Journal of Cerebral Blood Flow and Metabolism, 11* (Suppl. 2), S557.

Loewenstein, D. A., Barker, W. W., Chang, J.-Y., Apicella, A., Yoshii, F., Kothari, P.,

Levin, B., & Duara, R. (1989). Predominant left hemisphere metabolic dysfunction in dementia. *Archives of Neurology, 46,* 146–152.

Mann, U. M., Mohr, E., Gearing, M., & Chase, T. N. (1992). Heterogeneity in Alzheimer's disease: Progression rate segregated by distinct neuropsychological and metabolic profiles. *Journal of Neurology, Neurosurgery, and Psychiatry, 55,* 956–959.

Martin, A., Brouwers, P., Lalonde, F., Cox, C., Teleska, P., Fedio, P., Foster, N. L., & Chase, T. N. (1986). Towards a behavioral typology of Alzheimer's disease. *Journal of Clinical and Experimental Neuropsychology, 8,* 594–610.

Mattis, S. (1976). Mental status examination for organic mental syndrome in the elderly patient. In L. Bellack & T. B. Karasu (Ed.), *Geriatric psychiatry* (pp. 77–121). New York: Grune & Stratton.

Mazziotta, J., Phelps, M., Phal, J., Huang, S., Baxter, L., Riege, W., Hoffman, J., Kuhl, D., Lanto, A., Wapenski, J., & Markham, C. (1987). Reduced cerebral glucose metabolism in asymptomatic subjects at risk for Huntington's disease. *New England Journal of Medicine, 316,* 357–362.

McGeer, E. G., Peppard, R. P., McGeer, P. L., Tuokko, H., Crockett, D., Parks, R., Akiyama, H., Calne, D. B., Beattie, B. L., & Harrop, R. (1990). 18 Fluorodeoxyglucose positron emission tomography studies in presumed Alzheimer cases, including 13 serial scans. *Canadian Journal of Neurological Sciences, 17,* 1–11.

McGeer, P. L., Kamo, H., Harrop, R., Li, D. K. B., Tuokko, H., McGeer, E. G., Adam, M. J., Ammann, W., Beattie, B. L., Calne, D. B., Martin, W. R. W., Pate, B. D., Rogers, J. G., Ruth, T. J., Sayre, C. I., & Stoessl, A. J. (1986). Positron emission tomography in patients with clinically diagnosed Alzheimer's disease. *Canadian Medical Association Journal, 134,* 597–607.

McKhann, G., Drachman, D., Folstein, M., Katzman, R., Price, D., & Stadlan, E. M. (1984). Clinical diagnosis of Alzheimer's disease: Report of the NINCDS-ADRDA work group under the auspices of Department of Health and Human Services task force on Alzheimer's disease. *Neurology, 34,* 939–944.

Metter, E. J., Riege, W. H., Kuhl, D. E., & Phelps, M. E. (1984). Cerebral metabolic relationships for selected brain regions in healthy adults. *Journal of Cerebral Blood Flow and Metabolism, 4,* 1–7.

Mielke, R., Herholz, K., Grond, M., Kessler, J., & Heiss, W.-D. (1992). Severity of vascular dementia is related to volume of metabolically impaired tissue. *Archives of Neurology, 49,* 909–913.

Milner, B. (1971). Interhemispheric differences in the localization of psychological process in man. *British Medical Bulletin, 27,* 272–277.

Mintun, M. A., & Lee, K. S. (1990). *Journal of Nuclear Medicine, 31,* 816.

Neary, D., Snowden, J. S., & Northen, B. (1988). Dementia of frontal lobe type. *Journal of Neurology, Neurosurgery and Psychiatry, 51,* 353–361.

Ober, B. A., Reed, B. R., & Jagust, W. J. (1992). Neuroimaging and cognitive function. In D. I. Margolin (Ed.), *Cognitive neuropsychology in clinical practice* (pp. 495–531). New York: Oxford University Press.

Parks, R. W., Long, D. L., Levine, D. S., Crockett, D. J., Dalton, I. E., Zec, R. F., Colburn, K. L., Siler, G., Nelson, M. E., Bower, J. M., Becker, R. E., McGeer, E. G., & McGeer, P. L. (1991). Parallel distributed processing and neural networks: Origins, methodology and cognitive functions. *International Journal of Neuroscience, 60,* 195–214.

Parks, R., Cassens, G., Crockett, D. J., Herrera, J. A., Latterner, R., Lorenzo, G., Carner, R., & Dodrill, K. L. (1990). Correlation of performance on the Shipley Institute of Living Scale with regional cerebral glucose metabolism as measured by positron emission tomography dementia. *International Journal of Clinical Neuropsychology, 12,* 14–19.

Parks, R. W., Dodrill, K. L., Bennett, B. A., Crockett, D. J., Hurwitz, T. A., McGeer, P. L., & McGeer, E. G. (1990). Positron emission tomography and neuropsychological studies in dementia. In R. E. Becker & E. Giacobini (Eds.), *Alzheimer therapy: Early diagnosis* (pp. 315–327). New York: Taylor & Francis.

Parks, R. W., Crockett, D. J., & McGeer, P. L. (1989). Systems model of cortical organization: Positron emission tomography and neuropsychological test performance. *Archives of Clinical Neuropsychology, 4*, 335–349.

Parks, R. W., Crockett, D. J., Tuokko, H., Beattie, B. L., Ashford, J. W., Coburn, K. L., Zec, R. F., Becker, R. E., McGeer, P. L., & McGeer, E. G. (1989). Neuropsychological "systems efficiency" and positron emission tomography. *Journal of Neuropsychiatry and Clinical Neurosciences, 1*, 269–282.

Parks, R. W., Loewenstein, D., Dodrill, K. L., Barker, W. W., Yoshii, F., Chang, J. Y., Emran, A., Apicella, A., Sheramata, W. A., & Duara, R. (1988). Cerebral metabolic effects of a verbal fluency test in normal subjects: A PET scan study. *Journal of Clinical and Experimental Neuropsychology, 10*, 565–575.

Parks, R. W., Loewenstein, D. A., & Chang, J. (1988). Brain imaging: Positron emission tomography and cognitive functioning. In J. M. Williams & C. J. Long (Eds.), *Cognitive approaches to neuropsychology* (pp. 189–210). New York: Plenum Press.

Petersen, S. E., Fox, P. T., Posner, M. I., Mintun, M., & Raichle, M. E. (1988). Positron emission tomographic studies of the cortical anatomy of single-word processing. *Nature, 331*, 585–589.

Posner, M. I., Petersen, S. E., Fox, P. T., & Raichle, M. E. (1988). Localization of cognitive operations in the human brain. *Science, 240*, 1627–1631.

Powers, W. J., Berg, L., Perlmutter, J. S., & Raichle, M. E. (1991). Technology assessment revisited: Does positron emission tomography have proven clinical efficacy? *Neurology, 41*, 1339–1340.

Pritchard, J., & Brass, L. (1992). New anatomical and functional imaging methods. *Annals of Neurology, 32*, 395–400.

Reitan, R. M. (1958). Validity of the Trail Making Test as an indicator of organic brain damage. *Perceptual and Motor Skills, 8*, 271–276.

Salerno, J. A., Haxby, J. V., Grady, C. L., Gonzalez-Aviles, A., Rapoport, S. I., & Schapiro, M. B. (1991). Correlation of change in cerebral glucose utilization with cognitive decline in dementia of the Alzheimer type. *Program for the 48th Annual Meeting of the American Geriatrics Society, 34*.

Salmon, D. P., Thal, L. J., Butters, N., & Heindel, W. C. (1990). Longitudinal evaluation of dementia of the Alzheimer type: A comparison of three standardized mental status examinations. *Neurology, 40*, 1225–1230.

Salmon, E., Maquet, P., Sadzot, B., Dive, D., Degueldre, C., von Frenckel, R., & Franck, G. (1988). Positron emission tomography in Alzheimer's and Pick's disease. *Journal of Neurology, 235*, S1.

Shipley, W. C. (1940). A self-administering scale for measuring intellectual impairment and deterioration. *Journal of Psychology, 9*, 371–377.

Soncrant, T. T., Horwitz, B., Holloway, H. W., & Rapoport, S. I. (1986). The pattern of functional coupling of brain regions in the awake rat. *Brain Research, 369*, 1–11.

Squire, L. R., Ojemann, J. G., Miezin, F. M., Petersen, S. E., Videen, T. O., & Raichle, M. E. (1992). Activation of hippocampus in normal humans: A functional anatomical study of memory. *Proceedings of the National Academy of Science of the United States of America, 89*, 1837–1841.

Stern, Y., Alexander, G., Prohounik, I., & Mayeux, R. (1992). Inverse relationship between education and parietotemporal perfusion deficit in Alzheimer's disease. *Annals of Neurology, 32*, 371–375.

Therapeutics and Technology Assessment Subcommittee of the American Academy of Neurology. (1991). Assessment: Positron emission tomography. *Neurology, 41*, 163–167.

Wechsler, D. A. (1955). *Wechsler Adult Intelligence Scale*. New York: Psychological Corporation.

Whitehouse, P. J., Price, D. L., Struble, R. G., Clark, A. W., Coyle, J. T., & DeLong, M. R. (1982). Alzheimer's disease and senile dementia: Loss of neurons in the basal forebrain. *Science, 215*, 1237–1239.

Yamamoto, T., & Hirano, A. (1985). Nucleus raphe dorsalis in Alzheimer's disease: Neurofibrillary tangles and loss of large neurons. *Annals of Neurology, 17*, 573–577.

Young, A. B., Penney, J. B., Starosta-Subinstein, S., Markel, D., Berent, S., Rothley, J., Betley, A., & Hichwa, R. (1987). Normal caudate glucose metabolism in persons at risk for Huntington's disease. *Archives of Neurology, 44*, 254–257.

17

Single Photon Emission Computed Tomography and Applications to Dementia

RONALD S. TIKOFSKY, ROBERT S. HELLMAN, AND
RANDOLPH W. PARKS

Abnormalities of regional cerebral blood flow (rCBF) and metabolism have been demonstrated in many forms of dementia using positron emission tomography (PET) as discussed in the preceding section. Positron emission tomography imaging is highly regarded, but currently, due to its expense, it is not widely available for patient care. There is an alternative to PET—single photon emission computed tomography (SPECT)—that utilizes equipment that is typically found in many nuclear medicine departments. In PET, cross-sectional images are built up from pairs of simultaneously detected photons (Parks, Lowenstein, Dodrill, et al., 1988; Parks, Crockett, Tuokko, et al., 1989). These are known to be 180 degrees apart as they result from the annihilation of positrons (Parks, Crockett, & McGeer, 1989; Parks, Loewenstein, & Chang, 1988). Due to the administered radiopharmaceutical in SPECT, cross-sectional images are built up by measuring the incident angle as well as the amount and distribution of single photons (Tikofsky, Hellman, Antuono, & Saxena, 1990).

With modern gamma cameras, and Food and Drug Administration (FDA)-approved radiopharmaceuticals, it is possible, using SPECT, to perform functional brain imaging studies on dementia patients that are comparable to those obtained with PET. For SPECT, either a general purpose single detector rotating gamma camera (which can also be used for nontomographic imaging) or a dedicated multidetector special purpose tomographic gamma camera can be used (Devous, 1989). Like PET systems, dedicated multidetector systems are as yet not widely available. Image detail (resolution) with SPECT rCBF radiopharmaceuticals is usually poorer than that achieved with PET. However, newly introduced dedicated SPECT head imaging units can yield images with resolution ranges between 0.7 and 1.1 cm.

SPECT Limitations

It is necessary to recognize other limitations of SPECT methodology for functional brain imaging. One such limitation is that single photon radiotracers are not easily attached to physiological agents without affecting their localization. This has limited the presently available tracers to xenon-133, I-123 iodoamphetamine (IMP), and Tc-99m HMPAO (HMPAO), which measure rCBF. These agents have been selected because their lipophilic nature allows them to cross the blood-brain barrier. Xenon-133 rapidly washes out from the brain, but measurement of this washout allows for noninvasive absolute quantitation of rCBF. This is the only single photon agent that allows noninvasive absolute quantitation of rCBF. I-123 IMP passes the blood-brain barrier and is retained by nonspecific receptors. Tc-99m HMPAO similarly crosses the blood-brain barrier, but is retained by a metabolic change to a nonlipophilic secondary product. The differential retention mechanisms have imaging implications (not appropriate for discussion in this review), but in general, regional retention is proportional to rCBF. Measurement of only rCBF is not a severe limitation for studies of dementia. Although in instances of acute stroke there is an uncoupling between regional cerebral blood flow and metabolism, in demented subjects there is no significant mismatch (Frackowiak et al., 1981). Thus, for the study of dementia, examination of rCBF with SPECT is sufficient, and detailed knowledge of regional metabolism may not be necessary.

SPECT rCBF Methodology

SPECT rCBF evaluation for dementia can be performed using quantitative studies with a noninvasive inhalation xenon-133 technique (Obrist, Chivian, Cronqvist, & Ingvar, 1970; Ingvar, 1975; Ingvar & Lassen, 1979; Bonte, Ross, Chehabi, & Devous, 1986). Because of the lower energy photons, for which scatter and attenuation are more severe, this becomes a lower resolution study than that obtained with SPECT studies using IMP (SPECT/IMP) or HMPAO (SPECT/HMPAO). Imaging of demented patients with SPECT using these agents have produced results similar to those obtained with PET. In addition to providing noninvasive absolute quantitation inhalation, xenon-133 allows for rapid and repeated studies. However, it is sometimes more difficult to use this procedure with patients who have poor comprehension and agitation. In addition, xenon-133 studies require specialized detectors, which yield only limited tomographic levels.

In our laboratory, SPECT rCBF studies were initially performed using a single-headed rotating gamma camera (Hellman & Collier, 1988; Van Heertum & Tikofsky, 1989; Tikofsky, Hellman, Antuono, & Saxena, 1990). We are presently using a multidetector instrument (NeuroCam, GE Medical Systems, Milwaukee, WI). Time for imaging varies as a function of radiopharmaceutical, dose administered, patient tolerance, and imaging instrument, varying between 15 and 45 minutes. For agitated patients, a shorter imaging time of 15 to 20 minutes can provide sufficient data, although image detail may be sacrificed. This does not include the time needed for the tracer to localize following intravenous injection of IMP or HMPAO. Mild sedation at the time of imaging can be used in conjunction with HMPAO. Tomographic images are reconstructed from the acquired data and displayed in the transaxial, coronal, and sagittal planes for interpretation.

Normal SPECT Image Characteristics

An appreciation of normal SPECT image appearance is helpful, because these images are not morphological representations of the brain as seen with computed tomography (CT) or magnetic resonance imaging (MRI). Rather, what is portrayed is the amount of agent, or tracer, that is deposited in the grey and white matter, reflecting regional cerebral blood flow. Figure 17.1A, B, C presents a typical set of images in all three planes (transaxial, coronal, and sagittal) for a normal subject, imaged with the standard Medical College of Wisconsin protocol using IMP (Hellman & Collier, 1988; Tikofsky et al., 1990). SPECT/HMPAO images with a multi-detector system are shown in Figure 17.2A, B, C. The cerebral cortex is characterized by a ribbon of grey covering the circumference of the brain on the transaxial slices. The occipital regions tend to be darker, representing more tracer deposition if the images are obtained with the eyes open. Hemispheric tracer deposition is symmetrical, although locally there will be minor asymmetries.

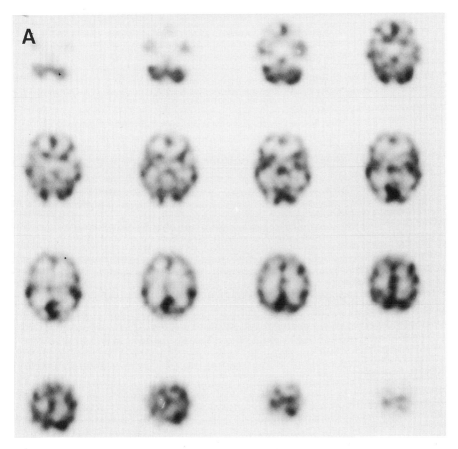

FIGURE 17.1. 123-Iodoamphetamine (IMP) images obtained with single detector rotating gamma camera system. (*A*) Normal IMP transverse images. These 8-mm thick tomograms demonstrate right-to-left hemispheric symmetry. Greatest uptake is observed in deep gray matter structures and the cortex. The distribution of activity in the cortex follows gyral architecture. Because the subject's eyes were open, prominent uptake is present in the visual cortex. (*B*) Normal IMP coronal images. 8-mm thick tomograms from frontal to occipital lobes. (*C*) Normal IMP sagittal images. 8-mm thick tomograms from the lateral surface of the right hemisphere through the midline to the lateral surface of the left hemisphere. *Figure continues.*

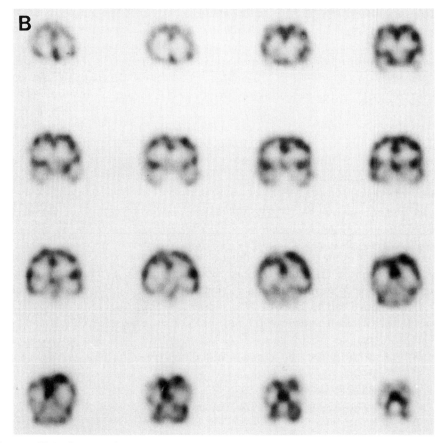

FIGURE 17.1. *Continued*

The density or darkness of the ribbon reflects the amount of tracer taken up by a particular region of cortex. With the newer imaging instruments it is possible to better identify structures such as the caudate nucleus, putamen, or thalamus (Figure 17.2A). The cerebellum shows a large amount of tracer uptake. This is because there is no significant difference between normal and demented subjects who have no evidence of cerebrovascular lesions. The ventricular system is not clearly demarcated from white matter because there is low tracer uptake in white matter due to white matter's low rCBF.

The coronal images (Figures 17.1B, 17.2B) go from frontal to occipital lobes. As in the transaxial images, the sensory motor cortex, basal ganglia, temporal lobes, parietal regions and cerebellum may be identified. Coronal images can be useful in identifying mesial temporal lobe deficits in Alzheimer's disease (AD) (Tikofsky, Harsch, Goldstein, Collier, & Hellman, 1987; Antuono, Tikofsky, Hellman, & Saxena, 1990). The abbreviation AD will be used to represent both early stage (onset before age 65) Alzheimer's disease, and late-stage Alzheimer's disease (onset after age 65), often referred to as senile dementia of the Alzheimer's type (SDAT).

Sagittal images (Figures 17.1C, 17.2C) go from the lateral surface of the right hemisphere through midline out to the lateral surface of the left hemisphere. The frontal, tip of the temporal lobe, sensory motor cortex (large arrows), parietal

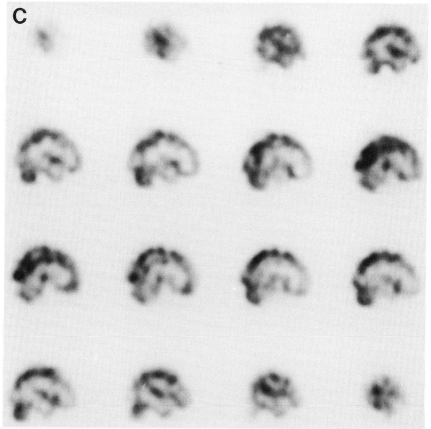

FIGURE 17.1. *Continued*

cortex (small arrows), occipital lobes, and cerebellum regions are identified. Sagittal images can be useful in identifying rCBF deficits due to middle cerebral artery lesions, and preservation of the sensory-motor regions in AD.

SPECT Image Interpretation Applied to Dementia

Three abnormal SPECT/IMP or SPECT/HMPAO patterns can be described: absent tracer uptake, reduced but not absent tracer uptake, and increased tracer uptake when compared to known normal appearance. Figure 17.3A, B, and C illustrate these patterns in the transaxial plane. For dementia, reduced but not absent uptake is the most common pattern. In moderate to severe AD there is often bilaterally reduced but not absent uptake in the temporoparietal (TP) and/or frontal regions (Figure 17.4) (Antuono et al., 1990). Absent uptake suggests cerebrovascular disease or multi-infarct dementia (MID). Increased uptake in demented subjects is unlikely unless there is an associated seizure disorder.

Examination of the AD images in Figure 17.4 show relatively symmetrical changes in both hemispheres. Differences in the amount of decreased uptake may reflect the variation in types of cognitive impairment presented by the patient.

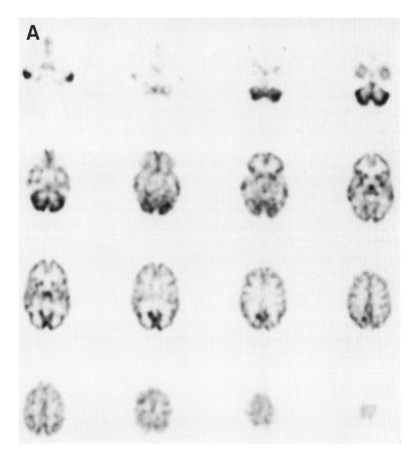

FIGURE 17.2. Tc-99m-hexamethylpropylenamine oxime (HMPAO) images obtained with multi-detector rotating gamma camera system (*A*) Normal HMPAO transverse images. Note that these 8-mm thick tomograms show similar tracer distribution as that noted in Figure 17.1. However, greater image detail than Figure 17.1 is noted due to use of the multi-detector instrument. Even in the case of use of a single detector system, there is usually greater detail seen in HMPAO images compared to IMP images. This is because larger amounts of the radio-tracer (Tc-99m)HMPAO are administered than for the radio-tracer (123I)IMP. (*B*) Normal HMPAO coronal images. 8-mm thick tomograms from frontal to occipital lobes. (*C*) Normal HMPAO sagittal images. 8-mm thick tomograms from the lateral surface of the right hemisphere through the midline to the lateral surface of the left hemisphere. *Figure continues*.

Reduced uptake is more frequently observed in the frontal lobes as cognitive function declines in AD. Whereas the typical pattern for AD is symmetric hypoperfusion, focal asymmetric areas of reduced tracer uptake are seen in AD patients who present with focal signs. It has been our experience that patients who initially present with prominent visual agnosia or progressive language deterioration show consistent reductions in tracer activity in the right parieto-occipital regions and left frontal lobe respectively.

    Vascular dementias are the second most common type of dementia. Approximately 20% of patients with occlusion of the middle cerebral artery will present with symptoms of dementia. Many of these patients will show areas of reduced

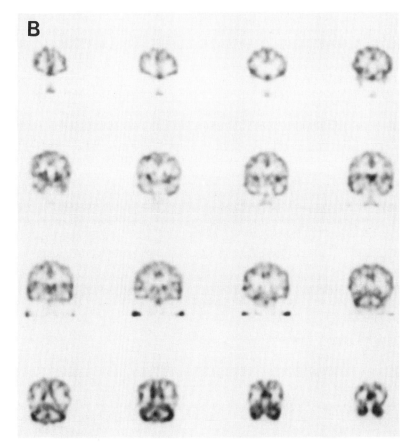

FIGURE 17.2. *Continued*

tracer uptake larger than the size of the infarct seen on CT or MRI (Seiderer et al., 1989). This finding suggests a dysfunctional region of the brain, which may represent cerebral diaschisis secondary to the infarct visualized with high-resolution anatomic imaging. Among the vascular dementias, MID may be difficult to distinguish from AD. In particular, the presence of a stroke does not preclude the possibility of AD. SPECT studies on patients with MID (Figure 17.5) will usually show two or more asymmetric perfusion deficits without the biparietal defects typically associated with AD. This can be helpful in clarifying the diagnosis when evidence from CT, MRI, or angiography does not correlate with ischemia scores used to establish a diagnosis of MID, or in the case of rapid onset of neurological symptoms with stepwise progression.

SPECT rCBF Imaging in Dementia

Xenon-133 Brain Imaging and Dementia

Chronologically, the earliest work with functional brain imaging for dementia used xenon-133 with multiple probe detectors. A significant relationship between mean

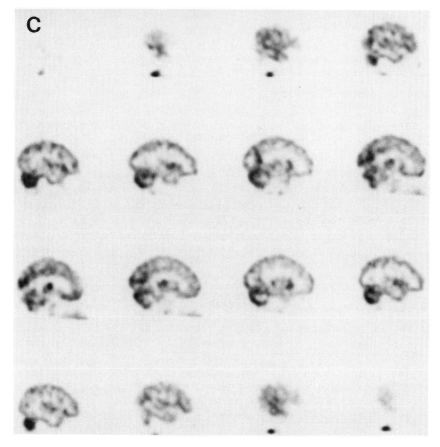

FIGURE 17.2. *Continued*

cerebral blood flow and cognitive impairment in dementia was first reported in
1951 (Freyhan, Woodford, & Kety, 1951). Lassen's results (Lassen, Feinberg, &
Lane, 1960) using xenon-133 suggested that the relationship between cognitive
deterioration and alterations in blood flow were best seen in the dominant hemisphere based on measures of average hemispheric blood flow. Gustafson and Risberg (1974) studied 50 demented patients (presenile and senile types) and demonstrated that those with longstanding dementia and severe impairment of cognitive
function had significantly decreased postrolandic cerebral blood flow. This was not
true in the earlier stages of the disease where the symptoms reflected primarily
affective personality changes. Ingvar (1975) cited the work of Hagberg and Ingvar
(1976), which demonstrated that various symptom complexes seen in presenile
dementia were related to reduced rCBF: limited dementia with only reduced memory has flow reduction in the temporal regions; with general cognitive loss and
impairment of verbal function, there is lower overall mean flow and some rCBF
reduction in temporal lobes; the most severely impaired patients showed marked
reduction in flow levels, particularly in the region of the occipitoparietotemporal
regions. He also showed that a reasoning task (Raven's matrices), with these
patients, produced an effect quite different from that seen in neurologically intact

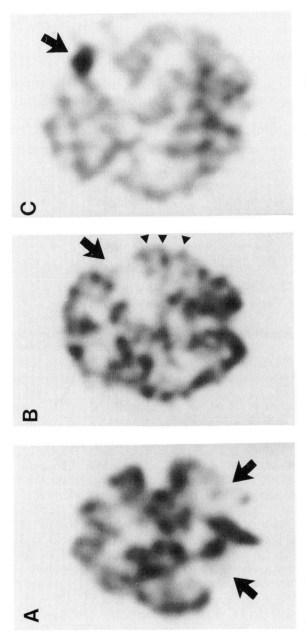

FIGURE 17.3. Patterns of abnormal tracer uptake. Tc-99m-hexamethylpropylenamine oxime (HMPAO) images obtained with multi-detector rotating gamma camera system. (*A*) Arrows indicate regions of absent tracer uptake in the right and left posterior temporal lobes. (*B*) Single arrow indicates absent tracer uptake in the tip of the left temporal lobe. Arrowheads indicate region of decreased tracer uptake in the left mid-temporal lobe region (compared to the analogous regions of the right hemisphere). (*C*) Arrow indicates a region of increased tracer uptake in the left frontal lobe. This image was photographed at lesser intensity in order to best demonstrate the region of hyperperfusion.

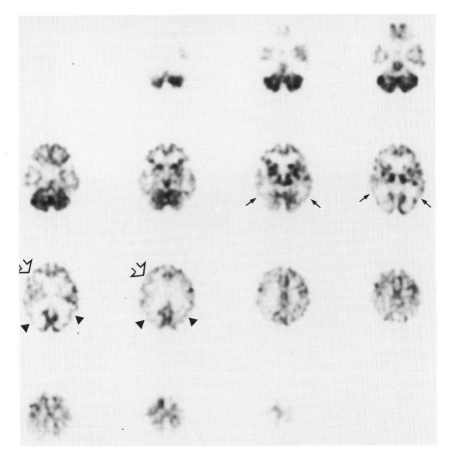

FIGURE 17.4. Subject with severe dementia of the Alzheimer's type. Tranverse
tomograms obtained with HMPAO and multi-detector SPECT system demonstrate
significant bi-hemispheric reductions of tracer uptake in the temporal (single arrows) and
parietal (arrowheads) areas. Right hemisphere involvement is greater than that of the
left; there is also a region of reduced tracer uptake in the right frontal area (open arrow).

patients. This is probably reflecting an inability to activate association cortex during
mental effort.

Risberg and Gustafson (1983) found significant differences in rCBF patterns
for Pick's disease (PD), AD, and MID when compared to normal controls or
depressed patients matched for age. Pick's disease subjects showed decreased rCBF
in the prerolandic frontal regions, whereas AD subjects showed rCBF decrease in
posterior regions. Late-onset (after age 65) dementia subjects showed more decreases in frontal lobe rCBF than those with early onset. For both groups, flow
was relatively well preserved in the motor strip, frontotemporal, and occipital
regions. The MID patients presented with heterogeneous and nonsystematic rCBF
abnormalities. In patients with small or deep lacunar infarcts, rCBF could fall
within normal limits. Evidence of left-right rCBF asymmetries corresponded to
more advanced disease. For 33 of their 50 patients for whom autopsy information
was available, there was good agreement with diagnosis of type of dementia and
neuropathological diagnosis.

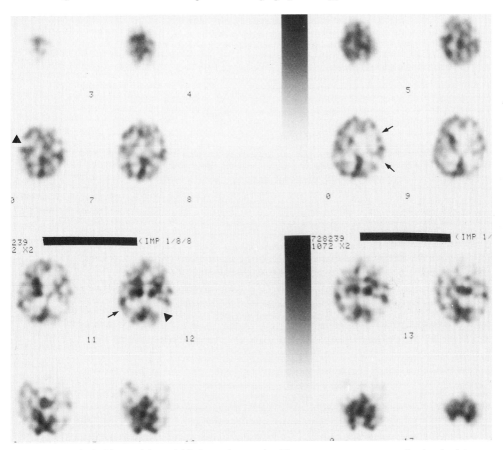

FIGURE 17.5. Subject with multi-infarct dementia. Transverse tomograms obtained with IMP and single detector SPECT system demonstrate scattered regions of decreased uptake (left frontal and parietal regions, right temporal lobe) and absent uptake in the left temporo-parietal and the right frontal regions. Regions of decreased uptake are indicated with single arrows. Region of absent uptake is indicated with arrowhead.

In a recent review of brain imaging in AD, Smith and Prohovnik (1987) summarized the findings of xenon-133 imaging in AD since 1984. They point out that these rCBF studies "were the first to consistently demonstrate global and focal deficits in AD correlated with clinical findings and validated by neuropathological evidence" (p. 135). In a later rCBF study in which 36 AD patients and 12 elderly controls were compared, Prohovnik and associates (1988) found that whole brain perfusion was significantly lower in the AD group. Interestingly, discriminant analysis was able to separate both groups with 90% accuracy. Parietotemporal regions were found to be disproportionately lower in the AD group, but relatively higher than control subject rCBF values in the perirolandic and occipital regions. Thus, the work with xenon-133 laid the foundation for the future development of SPECT using alternative radiopharmaceuticals to study dementia.

Two important studies were reported by Bonte and his colleagues investigating dementia with SPECT/xenon-133 with and without acetazolamide. In 1986, Bonte et al. (1986) studied 37 demented patients using inhalation and washout xenon-133 SPECT: 19 of 37 had AD, five had vascular types of dementia, one had Pick's disease, one had a temporal lobe tumor, six could not be scanned due to poor subject cooperation, and five had normal scans. The most frequent rCBF deficit was found in the posterior temporal areas. The rCBF reductions were usually symmetrical, but when asymmetrical, they tended to be worse in the left hemisphere. In more severe dementia, flow reductions are often seen in the parietal and occipital regions. Only occasional frontal lobe changes were observed. They suggested that quantitated xenon rCBF data (and the use of rCBF ratios) were useful for measuring changes in flow that are related to AD.

In 1989, Bonte et al. (1989) studied xenon-133 rCBF changes from baseline following intravenous administration of 1 g of the drug acetazolamide (ACZ) in patients with cerebrovascular disease (CVD) ($n = 16$), AD ($n = 35$), and normal controls ($n = 15$). Acetazolamide is a carbonic anhydrase inhibitor that indirectly produces dilatation of the cerebral microvasculator by elevating intracerebral carbon dioxide. Thus, the drug-induced changes in rCBF from baseline are a measure of vascular reactivity. Bonte, Devous, Weiner, Tinter, & Hom (1990) examined the ratio of rCBF in multiple regions of interest (ROIs) to the whole brain flow (ROI:WBF) for AD and CVD subjects to determine the number of ROI:WBF values greater than 2 standard deviations and greater than 4 standard deviations below the mean determined for controls. In pre-ACZ study, no significant difference was found between AD and CVD patients when only ratios greater than 2 standard deviations were considered. When AD and CVD patients were compared with respect to ratios greater than 4 standard deviations below expected norms, the difference between groups was significant. In 280 pre-ACZ regions, seven were greater than 4 standard deviations in the AD sample; and in 128 pre-ACZ regions, 12 were greater than 4 standard deviations below the normal means for CVD patients. There was a significant increase in rCBF between the pre-ACZ to post-ACZ conditions for AD patients, but not for the CVD patients. When the ROIs greater than 4 standard deviations below the expected norm were examined, there were sharp differences in response between AD and CVD patients. For the AD patients, the number of ROIs greater than 4 standard deviations dropped from seven to four, but for the CVD patients the number rose from 12 to 17. Bonte et al. (1989) assert that the vasculature in low-flow areas seen in AD can behave in a relatively normal fashion. In AD patients who have superimposed CVD, where both conditions are contributing to the patient's clinical presentation, lack of a post-ACZ rCBF response may be useful in establishing whether a regional deficit is due to CVD or AD.

SPECT Studies of Dementia with IMP

Cohen and his colleagues (Cohen et al., 1983; Cohen et al., 1984; Cohen et al., 1986) and Gemmell and colleagues (Gemmell et al., 1984) were among the first to report that SPECT/IMP brain imaging could be used to differentiate between demented and normal subjects, and that AD could be distinguished from MID. The number of patients in these studies was small ($N \leq 14$). No statistical treatment of the data was reported. They describe similar patterns of reduced rCBF bilaterally in the parietal lobes as characteristic of AD, but no specific pattern of SPECT/

IMP abnormality associated with MID. Cohen, however, suggests that multiple asymmetrical defects are present in MID. Cohen et al. (1984) asserted that patients with advanced AD showed a pattern of decreased bilateral parieto-occipital tracer uptake, which had been previously reported for PET and xenon-133. For Cohen et al. (1984), this late AD pattern clearly distinguished normals and MID patients. However, early AD patients could not easily be differentiated from normals or MID.

Wellman et al. (1985), using the radiopharmaceutical I-123 HIPDM, studied 25 patients with a clinical diagnosis of dementia. I-123 HIPDM localizes in the brain in a manner similar to that of IMP. They found that about half the AD patients had SPECT findings similar to those expected for MID (multiple asymmetric defects). The MRI studies of these patients showed multiple white matter lesions that correlated with the cortical findings seen with SPECT. A subcortical dementia such as Binswanger's was considered to be the likely etiology for these findings.

Derousene, Rancurel, Le Poncin Lafitte, Rapin, and Lassen (1985) challenged the studies that suggested that SPECT/IMP brain imaging had good specificity for discriminating AD from MID. Their 10 AD patients had great variability of rCBF abnormalities. The expected bilateral parietotemporal rCBF defect was found in only five cases. The others showed marked asymmetrical defects of the fronto-parietal regions, or diffuse subcortical defects. However, they reported a relationship between the severity of clinical symptoms and biparietal defects. This controversy concerning the ability of functional brain imaging to differentiate AD from other forms of dementia, particularly MID, is still to be resolved with SPECT.

These early studies lack both large samples and accurate classification of the patient samples. Little effort was made to correlate findings with specific neurological or neuropsychological test findings. Samples were not stratified on the basis of time since onset or severity of impairment.

Hellman et al. (1990) reported on visual grading of SPECT/IMP images for 24 patients with symptoms of dementia with no attempt to differentiate among types of dementia. Significant correlations were obtained between regions judged to be poorly perfused and specific neuropsychological deficits. Some of these correlations were: visual memory and right parietotemporal; block design and right and left parietotemporal, right and left parietal, right and left occipital; verbal fluency and left parietofrontal. These findings suggest that it is the relationship between specific neuropsychological deficit and region of reduced uptake rather than type of dementia that is critical to understanding the cognitive changes seen in dementia. A potential problem in the Hellman et al. (1990) study was that it employed qualitative rather than quantitative grading of images. Therefore, the interrater agreement for grading rCBF deficits was examined by Tikofsky et al. (1990). High rater reliability was obtained for distinguishing normals from demented subjects. There is greater disagreement among raters in identifying specific regions of rCBF deficit.

A reproducible method of quantitation not based on visual grading can help lessen the problem of rater disagreement. Johnson, Mueller, Walshe, English, and Holman, (1985) and Johnson, Mueller, Walshe, English, and Holman, (1988) report one of the first efforts to quantitate SPECT/IMP data obtained from 17 AD-type patients at least 3 years after onset. The ratio of tracer uptake of eight cortical regions to cerebellar uptake was determined. The ratio of parietal to cerebellar ratio for AD patients was reduced as compared to normal age-matched controls. Jagust, Budinger, and Reed, (1987) used a somewhat different method of quantitation for evaluating differences between AD subjects ($n = 9$), normals ($n = 5$), and MID subjects ($n = 2$). They used the ratio of the left and right temporoparietal regions (TP) against the whole tomographic slice (WTS). Statistically significant differences were found between AD and normals, and AD and MID subjects, but not for MID versus controls. The authors also report a significant correlation between Mini-Mental State Examination (MMSE) questionnaire score and the TP:WTS ratio. Significant correlations between MMSE score and quantitated regional tracer uptake ratios were also reported by Johnson et al. (1988, 1990) and Hellman et al. (1989). They found that as severity of dementia increased, the regional uptake ratios in multiple regions (frontal, parietal, posterior temporal, and occipital) decreased.

The studies discussed above focused on quantitative differences between AD and normals, and not between AD and other forms of dementia. Sharp et al. (1986) used DSM criteria and Hachinski Ischemic Scale (IS) score to classify 47 demented patients. Of the 47, 14 had AD; 13, MID; 11, alcoholic cortical atrophy; five, Korsakoff's syndrome; and four, Huntington's chorea. State of cognitive deterioration was assessed using a neuropsychological battery and the data were summarized on a four-point scale to reflect severity of impairment. Sharp et al. (1986) determined the ratio of SPECT/IMP uptake in five hemispheric cortical regions to the analogous region in the opposite hemisphere. The SPECT/IMP studies of the five normal subjects showed no evidence of reduced tracer uptake. A total of 47 regions showed reduction greater than 10% for the 14 AD patients as compared to normals. All 14 AD subjects had a significant bilateral reduction of tracer deposition in the temporoparietooccipital (TPO) areas. Twelve of the 14 AD subjects had other abnormalities, predominantly in the posterior frontal regions. No characteristic pattern was described for the MID subjects. Alcoholics had an irregular distribution of tracer uptake and no regions of focal abnormality.

Persons with human immunodeficiency virus (HIV) may present with cognitive changes that are characteristic of dementia. Masdeu et al. (1991) retrospectively studied 32 patients with HIV encephalopathy and cognitive changes with IMP rCBF/SPECT. They examined the effects of azidothymidine (AZT) in ameliorating the cognitive deficits and whether reduction of symptoms correlated with changes in rCBF/SPECT IMP findings in a subset of this group. Areas of multifocal cortical and subcortical hypoperfusion that may be characteristic of HIV dementia were described. Repeat rCBF/SPECT examinations showed a reduction of hypoperfusion in patients who responded well to AZT treatment, but the CT examinations were unchanged. These findings are in general agreement with those for other rCBF/SPECT and PET studies summarized by Kramer and Sanger (1990).

SPECT Studies of Dementia with HMPAO

Prior to 1986, all SPECT functional brain imaging dementia studies used either xenon-133, I-123 IMP, or HIPDM. Beginning with 1986, a new imaging agent, Tc-99m HMPAO, became available for SPECT brain imaging. It was expected that imaging with this agent in the demented population would yield results similar to those obtained with SPECT/IMP.

Neary et al. (1987) studied 41 patients with a history of progressive cognitive deterioration of at least 1 year's duration. Twenty-three met the usual criteria for probable AD; the remaining 18 subjects showed either frontal lobe dementia or progressive supranuclear palsy. Fourteen of their AD subjects had images with reduced uptake of HMPAO in the posterior regions of both hemispheres. This was also seen for two patients classified as non-AD frontal lobe dementia. None of the patients with supranuclear palsy demonstrated this deficit. The differences between AD and non-AD groups were statistically significant. In addition, AD posterior hemisphere rCBF deficits were significantly related to impairment of percepto-spatial performance. Only three of the AD patients showed unilateral posterior rCBF deficits, but seemed not to be related to language or perceptospatial impairment. Bilaterally reduced tracer uptake in the anterior frontal regions was seen in seven of nine patients classified as non-AD frontal lobe dementia, in seven of eight supranuclear palsy patients, and in only three of the AD subjects. There are also AD patients in this series where there were unilateral rCBF changes in the frontal regions.

Smith and Prohovnik (1987) and Gemmell et al. (1987) reported results from SPECT/HMPAO studies on the same group of 27 demented patients, 17 diagnosed as AD and 10 as MID. Four observers used visual grading to evaluate rCBF deficits in 10 areas, five per hemisphere. Gross level of cognitive impairment for each patient was estimated using a five-point scale derived from the administration of an extensive neuropsychological battery. Magnetic resonance imaging studies showed significant atrophy for all 27 subjects and infarction in 5 of the 10 MID patients. No focal MRI abnormalities were observed for the AD subjects. HMPAO deficits were more frequently observed in these 10 regions for AD than for MID patients. For example, bilateral perfusion deficits in the TPO region were reported for 13 of the 17 AD patients, but for only two MID patients. Frontal lobe deficits accompanied the TPO changes in 10 of the 17 AD patients. Smith, Gemmell, and Sharp (1987) note for MID patients there is a poor match between perfusion defects seen with SPECT/HMPAO and the infarcts seen with MRI or CT. The MID images range from normal to generalized low cerebral tracer uptake with some regions of low uptake that do match MRI- or CT-demonstrated infarcts.

Perani et al. (1988) were among the first to report quantitative SPECT/HMPAO data for dementia. Regions of interest were drawn over the cortical regions to yield 16 sets of values reflecting relative perfusion in each hemisphere. Activity in the cerebellum was used as a reference, so that cortical to cerebellar ratios could be calculated for each ROI. Significant differences were reported between normal controls ($n = 16$) and patients who met the criteria for probable AD ($n = 16$). In-slice and between-slice regional differences were reported along with demonstrable interactions between regions and group. Perfusion asymmetries were found for 14 of 16 AD patients. No consistent pattern of correlations between neuropsychological test performance and perfusion asymmetries were reported. Perani et al. (1988) suggest that hemispheric asymmetries may be related to subtypes of AD, especially in its early stages. This is in contrast to SPECT/IMP rCBF findings where regional deficits correlated with impaired performance on some neuropsychological tasks (Hellman et al., 1990; Tikofsky et al., 1991a).

In an HMPAO study of 23 mild to moderate AD patients, neuropsychological tests such as confrontation naming, apraxia, and semantic memory showed a positive correlation between frontal, inferior parietal, and superior temporal regions, but not with the remainder of regions (Goldenberg, Podreka, Suess, & Deecke, 1989). The authors suggested that these findings were consistent with AD abnormalities predominantly found in the association cortex. Results were less unequivocal with respect to hemispheric asymmetry. The latter inconsistent findings were hypothesized to be as a consequence of extended cortical systems that modulated the sequels of localized brain damage.

Another HMPAO study that compared 26 moderate to severe AD patients to 10 elderly controls found that the bilateral temporal cortex demonstrated the lowest rCBF (Montaldi et al., 1990). Whereas AD subjects exhibited significant correlations between neuropsychological tests of language and praxis and regions of interest, no correlations were found with memory tests. This lack of correlations with regions of interest and memory tests was attributed to a marked floor-effect of memory test performance in AD patients.

Burns, Philpot, Costa, Ell, and Levy (1989) used a method similar to Johnson et al. (1985, 1988) except that it used HMPAO instead of IMP to compare AD patients to normals. The cortical:cerebellar HMPAO ratios were correlated with measures of cognitive function. The AD patients had significantly lower tracer uptake bilaterally in the temporal and posterior parietal lobes than normal. The AD patients with apraxia and aphasia had the lowest tracer uptake in these regions. Age of onset was positively correlated with decreased activity in the left posterior parietal region, but negatively correlated with the right medial temporal region. Time since onset was positively correlated with left lateral temporal activity. There were also specific hemispheric relations between test variables (e.g., language dysfunction and left frontal, lateral temporal, and posterior parietal cortical: cerebellum ratios). Such findings with HMPAO and similar results reported by Hellman et al. (1990) with IMP suggest that it is possible to more precisely relate specific changes in cognitive function to specific regions of rCBF deficits.

Bartolini, Gasparetto, and Loeb (1990) examined the validity of SPECT/HMPAO for the differential diagnosis of dementia. Eighteen patients who met criteria for MID, and 22 for AD, had SPECT/HMPAO examinations. They were compared to 22 age-matched controls. Visually, SPECT was positive in 15 of 18 MID cases, and for 12 of the 15 there were discrepancies between SPECT findings and CT. Computed tomography showed no focal abnormalities in AD, and atrophy was seen in only 8 of the 22 AD cases. Quantitative differences between controls, MID, and AD subjects were evaluated with regional left:right hemisphere, and cortical: cerebellar HMPAO uptake ratios. No specific patterns were reported for the MID patients. Using left:right hemisphere ratios, a normal SPECT/HMPAO pattern was found in 7, asymmetrical uptake in 9, and bilateral symmetric decreased uptake in the posterior region for 6 of the 22 AD cases. Using cortical:cerebellar ratios, Bartolini et al. (1990) found it difficult to separate controls from ADs because of the wide overlap. This is in contrast to the findings of Hellman et al. (1989) with SPECT/IMP. Bartolini et al. (1990) believe that whereas SPECT/HMPAO may be useful in differentiating MID from AD, it may lead to misinterpretations when applied to an unselected population of patients.

Relative quantitation of regional left:right hemisphere SPECT/HMPAO uptake was also studied by Pizzolato, Dam, Ferlin, & Battistin, (1990) in 45 subjects (11 controls, 19 AD, and 15 MID). A predominant number of AD subjects showed parietotemporal reductions in uptake, and there was a significant correlation between parietal perfusion indices and cognitive impairment. In more advanced AD subjects, other uptake deficits were observed in temporal and frontal regions. Hemispheric asymmetries were seen in 10% of the AD cases as compared to controls. In MID subjects, images showed more diffuse and patchy patterns, and did not typically demonstrate the parietal deficits seen in AD.

Results of dementia studies using HMPAO confirm the findings obtained with SPECT/IMP. Both imaging agents permit a discrimination between demented patients and normals, but the differentiation between AD and MID is less clear. The choice of SPECT/HMPAO or SPECT/IMP will depend in part on physician preference, instrumentation available, patient condition, and availability of the radiopharmaceutical.

In a recent abstract, Bonte et al., 1990 compared xenon-133 and HMPAO in two groups of demented patients. Xenon-133 was used to study prospectively 119 demented patients (90, AD) and 47 patients (36, AD) with HMPAO. Using xenon-133, sensitivity for AD was 88% and specificity was 76%. Using HMPAO, the sensitivity for AD was 81% and specificity was 64%. There was no difference in either sensitivity or specificity with regard to AD between agents. Although more structural detail was apparent in HMPAO images, this afforded no benefit compared to xenon-133 SPECT studies for the diagnosis of AD.

The role of SPECT imaging for the detection of early onset of dementia remains to be determined. Cappa et al. (1990) tried to address this issue using SPECT/HMPAO. They compared 16 patients with a clinical diagnosis of mild to moderate AD (average time since onset of 20.9 months) with 16 age-matched controls. Regional:cerebellar HMPAO uptake ratios and left:right regional ratios were determined. As is the case with more severe dementia, the most significant rCBF reductions in uptake were found in the frontal and posterior TP regions bilaterally. Fourteen of their 16 AD patients had hemispheric asymmetries of relative perfusion that exceeded the normal range. A weakness of their study was that it did not address the issue of whether patients with early signs of dementia (vs. mild to moderate AD) would have rCBF changes to suggest AD.

Holman et al. (1992) addressed the issue of whether patterns derived from rCBF/SPECT HMPAO studies have predictive value for the presence of AD. They studied 132 consecutive patients with memory or cognitive difficulties referred for rCBF/SPECT scans. After an average of 10.1 months clinical follow-up, 52 had a confirmed diagnosis of AD. When there were bilateral TP defects, the probability of AD was 82%; with this pattern and additional defects the AD probability was 77%. The predictive value for AD declined with other patterns: 57% with unilateral TP defects; 43% with only frontal defects; and 18% with other large defects. No predictive value was found for AD in the presence of multiple small-cortical rCBF defects.

Activation studies have been described with rCBF/SPECT (Tikofsky & Hellman, 1991; George et al., 1991) but none with demented patients. Tikofsky, Hellman, Antuono, Hoffman, Krasnow, et al. (1991b) report on a pilot study using HMPAO in conjunction with the Boston Naming Test (BNT). They identified hemispheric differences between no BNT (baseline) and BNT, and a differential hemispheric response to BNT activation as a function of cumulative BNT score. Comparison of baseline to activation rCBF studies may aid in differentiating among patients with AD.

Conclusions

Based on the research to date it is clear that SPECT brain imaging is capable of reliably distinguishing normals from persons suffering from moderate and severe dementia. The degree and locus of altered rCBF are probably related to the type and severity of the cognitive decline associated with dementia (Jagust, Reed, Seab, & Budinger, 1990; Montaldi et al., 1990; Waldemar, Andersen, & Lassen, 1990; Waldemar, Paulson, & Lassen, 1990). With present SPECT instrumentation, problems exist in detecting the less severe alterations in rCBF that might be seen in early dementia. In general there appears a distinct biparietal-temporal reduction of rCBF in AD in the regions where PET and postmortem changes are observed. Conflicting evidence in the literature suggests a probable overlap in rCBF deficits for AD, MID, and other forms of dementia. Resolution of this issue may require SPECT imaging of factors such as receptor uptake 3-quinuclidinyl-4-iodobenzilate labeled with iodine 123 (QNB) (Holman et al., 1985; Weinberger et al., 1990), or response to cognitive stimulation (Tikofsky et al., 1991b). Discrimination of dementia type is a problem for PET as well, requiring measurement of factors other than rCBF and metabolism (Hellman et al., 1989). This poses a significant challenge to researchers in both SPECT and PET. However, both SPECT and PET already provide the quantitative means to assess regional effects of pharmacological therapies on dementia (Parks, Crockett, Manji, & Ammann, 1992; Parks et al., 1990). On the basis of the findings reported, there is every reason to expect that SPECT and rCBF imaging will make a significant contribution to our understanding of the perplexing problem of dementia.

References

Antuono, P. G., Tikofsky, R. S., Hellman, R. S., & Saxena, V. K. (1990). Single photon emission computed tomography (SPECT) in the evaluation of the dementias. *Mind, 4*, 6–8.

Bartolini, A., Gasparetto, B., & Loeb, C. (1990). Assessment of SPECT features in the differential diagnosis between degenerative and multiinfarct dementia. In L. Battistin & F. Gerstenbrand (Eds.), *Aging and dementia: New trends in diagnosis and therapy* (pp. 441–438). New York: Wiley-Liss.

Bonte, F. J., Devous, M. D., Sr., Reisch, J. S., Ajmani, A. K., Weiner, M. F., Hom, J., & Tintner, R. (1989). The effect of Acetazolamide on regional cerebral blood flow in patients with Alzheimer's disease or stroke as measured by single photon emission computed tomography. *Investigative Radiology, 24*, 99–103.

Bonte, F. J., Devous, M. D., Sr., Weiner, M. F., Tinter, R., & Hom, J. (1990). Performance comparison of Xe-133 and Tc-99m HM-PAO SPECT in patients with dementia. *Journal of Nuclear Medicine, 31*, (Abstract No. 99), 730.

Bonte, F. J., Ross, E. D., Chehabi, H. H., & Devous, M. D., Sr. (1986). SPECT study of regional cerebral blood flow in Alzheimer disease. *Journal of Nuclear Medicine, 10*, 579–584.

Burns, A., Philpot, M. P., Costa, D. C., Ell, P. J., Levy, R. (1989). *Journal of Neurology, Neurosurgery and Psychiatry, 52*, 248–253.

Cappa, S., Fieschi, C., Perani, D., Di Piero, V., Passafiume, D., Vallar, G., Fazio, F., & Lenzi, G. L. (1990). Neuropsychological correlates of SPECT findings in the early phase in dementia. In L. Battistin & F. Gerstenbrand (Eds.), *Aging and dementia: New trends in diagnosis and therapy* (pp. 397–404). New York: Wiley-Liss.

Cohen, M. B., Graham, L. S., Lake, R., Metter, E. J., Fitten, J., Kulkarni, M., Severin, R., Yamada, L., Chang, C. C., Woodruff, N., & Kling, A. S. (1986). Diagnosis of Alzheimer's disease and multiple infarct dementia by tomographic imaging of iodine-123 IMP. *Journal of Nuclear Medicine, 27*, 769–774.

Cohen, M. B., Graham, L. S., Lake, R., Metter, E. J., Kulkarni, M., Kling, A. S., Yamada, L., & Fitten, J. (1984). SPECT imaging I-123 IMP in dementia. *Clinical Nuclear Medicine, 9* (Suppl. 9S), 30.

Cohen, M. B., Metter, E. J., Graham, L. S., Wasterlain, C., Spolter, L., Lake, R. R., Rose, G., Yamada, L., & Chang, C. C. (1983). Differential diagnosis of dementia with "pure" I-123 iodoamphetamine and a clinical camera. *Journal of Nuclear Medicine, 24*, 106,

Derousene, C., Rancurel, G., Le Poncin Lafitte, M., Rapin, J. R., & Lassen, N. A. (1985). Variability of cerebral blood flow defects in Alzheimer's disease on [123]Iodo-isopropyl-amphetamine and single photon emission tomography [Letter to the editor]. *Lancet 1*, 1282.

Devous, M. D., Sr. (1989). Imaging brain function by single-photon emission computer tomography. In N. C. Andreasen (Ed.), *Brain imaging: Applications in psychiatry* (pp. 147–234). Washington, DC: American Psychiatric Press.

Frackowiak, R. S. J., Pozzilli, C., Legg, N. J., DuBoulay, G. H., Marshal, J., Lenzi, G. L., & Jones, T. (1981). Regional cerebral oxygen supply and utilization in dementia. A clinical and physiological study with oxygen-15 and positron tomography. *Brain, 104*, 753–778.

Freyhan, F. A., Woodford, R. B., & Kety, S. S. (1951). Cerebral blood flow and metabolism in psychosis of senility. *Journal of Nervous and Mental Diseases, 113*, 449–456.

Gemmell, H. G., Sharp, P. F., Besson, J. A. O., Crawford, J. R., Ebmeier, K. P., Davidson, J., & Smith, F. W. (1987). Differential diagnosis in dementia using the cerebral flow agent ^{99m}Tc HM-PAO: A SPECT study. *Journal of Computer Assisted Tomography, 11* (3), 398–402.

Gemmell, H. G., Sharp, P. F., Evans, N. T. S., Besson, J. A. O., Lyall, D., & Smith, F. W. (1984). Single photon emission tomography with ^{123}I-isopropylamphetamine in Alzheimer's disease and multi-infarct dementia [Letter to the editor]. *Lancet 2*, 1348.

George, M. S., Ring, H. A., Costa, D. C., Ell, P. J., Kouris, K., & Jarritt, P. H. (1991). *Neuroactivation and Neuroimaging with SPET*. London: Springer-Verlag.

Goldenberg, G., Podreka, I., Suess, E., & Deecke, L. (1989). The cerebral localization neuropsychological impairment in Alzheimer's disease: A SPECT study. *Journal of Neurology, 236*, 131–138.

Gustafson, L., & Risberg, J. (1974). Regional cerebral blood flow related to psychiatric symptoms in dementia with onset in the presenile period. *Acta Psychiatrica Scandinavica, 50*, 516–538.

Hagberg, B., & Ingvar, D. H. (1976). Cognitive reduction in presenile dementia related to regional abnormalities of cerebral blood flow. *British Journal of Psychiatry, 128*, 209–222.

Hellman, R. S., Antuono, P. G., Tikofsky, R. S., Rao, S. M., Krasnow, A. Z., Collier, B. D., Hoffmann, R. G., & Wainwright, P. (1990). Correlation between regional reductions in cerebral blood flow (SPECT/IMP) and neuropsychological test scores in dementia patients. *Journal of Nuclear Medicine, 31*, (Abstract No. 100), 731.

Hellman, R. S., & Collier, B. D. (1988). Single photon emission computed tomography: A clinical experience. In L. M. Freeman & H. S. Weissman (Eds.), *Nuclear medicine annual 1987* (pp. 51–101). New York: Raven Press.

Hellman, R. S., Tikofsky, R. S., Collier, B. D., Hoffmann, R. G., Palmer, D. W., Glatt, S. L., Antuono, P. G., Isitman, A. T., & Papke, R. A. (1989). Alzheimer disease: Quantitative analysis of I-123-iodamphetamine SPECT brain imaging. *Radiology, 172*, 183–188.

Holman, B. L., Gibson, R. E., Hill, T. C., Eckelman, W. C., Albert, M., & Reba, R. C. (1985). Muscarinic acetylcholine receptors in Alzheimer's disease: In vivo imaging with iodine 123-labeled 3-quinuclidinyl-4-iodoabenzilate and emission tomography. *Journal of the American Medical Association, 254*, 3063–3066.

Holman, B. L., Johnson, K. A., Gerada, B., Carvalho, P. A., & Satlin, A. (1992). The scintigraphic appearance of Alzheimer's disease: A prospective study using technetium-99m-HMPAO SPECT. *Journal of Nuclear Medicine, 33*, 181–185.

Ingvar, D. H. (1975). Brain work in presenile dementia and in chronic schizophrenia. In D. H. Ingvar & N. A. Lassen (Eds.) *Brain work: The coupling of function, metabolism and blood flow in the brain* (pp. 478–492). Copenhagen: Muksgaard.

Ingvar, D. H., & Lassen, N. A. (1979). Activity distribution in the cerebral cortex in organic dementia as revealed by measurements of regional cerebral blood flow. In F. Hoffmeister & C. Muller (Eds.), *Brain function in old age: evaluation of changes and disorders* (pp. 268–277). Berlin: Springer-Verlag.

Jagust, W. J., Budinger, T. F., & Reed, B. R. (1987). The diagnosis of dementia with single photon emission computed tomography. *Archives of Neurology, 44*, 258–262.

Jagust, W. J., Reed, B. R., Seab, J. P., & Budinger, T. F. (1990). Age at onset and single-photon emission computed tomographic patterns of regional cerebral blood flow. *Archives of Neurology, 47*, 628–633.

Johnson, K. A., Holman, B. L., Rosen, J., Nagel, J. S., English, R. J., & Growden, J. H. (1990). Iofetamine I 123 single photon emission computed tomography is accurate in the diagnosis of Alzheimer's disease. *Archives of Internal Medicine, 150*, 752–756.

Johnson, K. A., Mueller, S. T., Walshe, T. M., English, R. J., & Holman, B. L. (1985). Cerebral perfusion imaging in Alzheimer's disease with SPECT and I-123 IMP. *Neurology, 35* (Suppl. 1, Abstract No. PP242), 235.

Johnson, K. A., Mueller, S. T., Walshe, T. M., English, R. J., & Holman, B. L. (1988). Single photon emission computed tomography in Alzheimer's disease: Abnormal iofetamine I 123 uptake reflects dementia severity. *Archives of Neurology, 45*, 392–396.

Kramer, E. J., & Sanger, J. J. (1990). Brain imaging in acquired immunodeficiency syndrome dementia complex. *Seminars in Nuclear Medicine, 20*, 353–363.

Lassen, N. A., Feinberg, I., & Lane, M. H. (1960). Bilateral studies of cerebral oxygen uptake in young and aged normal subjects and in patients with organic dementia. *Journal of Clinical Investigation, 39*, 491–500.

Masdeu, J. C., Yudd, A., Van Heertum, R. L., Grundman, M., Hriso, E. , O'Connell, R. A., Luck, D., Camli, U., & King, L. N. (1991). Single-photon emission computed tomography in human immunodeficiency virus encephalopathy: A preliminary report. *Journal of Nuclear Medicine, 32*, 1471–1475.

Montaldi, D., Brooks, D. N., McColl, J. H., Wyper, D., Patterson, J., Barron, E., & McCulloch, J. (1990). Measurements of regional cerebral blood flow and cognitive performance in Alzheimer's disease. *Journal of Neurology, Neurosurgery and Psychiatry, 53*, 33–38.

Neary, D., Snowden, J. S., Shields, R. A., Burjan, A. W. I., Northern, B., Macdermott,

N., Prescott, M. C., & Testa, H. J. (1987). Single photon emission tomography using ⁹⁹ᵐTc-HM-PAO in the investigation of dementia. *Journal of Neurology, Neurosurgery and Psychiatry, 50*, 1101–1109.

Obrist, W. E., Chivian, E., Cronqvist, S., & Ingvar, D. (1970). Regional cerebral blood flow in senile and presenile dementia. *Neurology, 20*, 315–322.

Parks, R. W., Crockett, D. J., Manji, H. K., & Ammann, W. (1992). Assessment of bromocriptine intervention for the treatment of frontal lobe syndrome: A case study. *The Journal of Neuropsychiatry and Clinical Neurosciences, 4*, 109–111.

Parks, R. W., Crockett, D. J., & McGeer, P. L. (1989). Systems model of cortical organization: Positron emission tomography and neuropsychological test performance. *Archives of Clinical Neuropsychology, 4*, 335–349.

Parks, R. W., Crockett, D. J., Tuokko, H., Beattie, B. L., Ashford, J. W., Coburn, K. L., Zec, R. F., Becker, R. E., McGeer, P. L., & McGeer, E. G. (1989). Neuropsychological "systems efficiency" and positron emission tomography. *Journal of Neuropsychiatry and Clinical Neurosciences, 1*, 269–282.

Parks, R. W., Dodrill, K. L., Bennett, B. A., Crockett, D. J., Hurwitz, T. A., McGeer, P. L., & McGeer, E. G. (1990). Positron emission tomography and neuropsychological studies in dementia. In R. E. Becker & E. Giacobini (Eds.), *Alzheimer therapy: Early diagnosis* (pp. 315–327). New York: Taylor & Francis.

Parks, R. W., Loewenstein, D. A., & Chang, J. (1988). Brain imaging: Positron emission tomography and cognitive functioning. In J. M. Williams & C. J. Long (Eds.), *Cognitive approaches to neuropsychology* (pp. 189–210). New York: Plenum Press.

Parks, R. W., Loewenstein, D., Dodrill, K. L., Barker, W. W., Yoshii, F., Chang, J. Y., Emran, A., Apicella, A., Sheramata, W. A., & Duara, R. (1988). Cerebral metabolic effects of a verbal fluency test in normal subjects: A PET scan study. *Journal of Clinical and Experimental Neuropsychology, 10*, 565–575.

Perani, D., Di Piero, V., Vallar, G., Cappa, S., Messa, G. B., Berti, A., Passafiume, D., Scarlato, G., Gerundini, P., Lenzi, G. L., & Fazio, F. (1988). Technetium-99m HM-PAO SPECT study of regional cerebral perfusion in early Alzheimer's disease. *Journal of Nuclear Medicine, 29*, 1507–1514.

Pizzolato, G., Dam, M., Ferlin, G., & Battistin, L. (1990). Qualitative and quantitative SPECT findings in primitive and secondary dementia. In L. Battistin & F. Gerstenbrand (Eds.), *Aging and dementia: New trends in diagnosis and therapy* (pp. 441–438). New York: Wiley-Liss.

Prohovnik, I., Mayeux, R., Sackeim, H. A., Smith, G., Stern, Y., & Alderson, P. O. (1988). Cerebral perfusion as a diagnostic marker of early Alzheimer's disease. *Neurology, 38*, 931–937.

Risberg, J., & Gustafson, L. (1983). ¹³³Xe cerebral blood flow in dementia and in neuropsychiatry research. In P. L. Magistretti (Ed.), *Functional radionuclide imaging of the brain* (pp. 151–159). New York: Raven Press.

Sharp, P., Gemmell, H., Cherryman, G., Besson, J., Crawford, J., & Smith, F. (1986). Application of iodine-123-labeled isopropylamphetamine to the study of dementia. *Journal of Nuclear Medicine, 27*, 761–768.

Seiderer, M., Krappel, W., Moser, E., Hahn, D., Schmiedek, P., Buell, U., Kirsch, C., & Lissner, J. (1989). Detection and quantification of chronic cerebrovascular disease: Comparison of MR imaging, SPECT, and CT. *Radiology, 170*, 545–548.

Smith, F. W., Gemmell, H. G., & Sharp, P. F. (1987). The use of ⁹⁹Tᵐ-HM-PAO for the diagnosis of dementia. *Nuclear Medicine Communications, 8*, 525–533.

Smith, G., & Prohovnik, I. (1987). Brain imaging in Alzheimer's disease. In J. Wade, S. Kneˇevi , V. A. Maximilian, Z. Mubrin, & I. Prohovnik (Eds.), *Impact of functional imaging in neurology and psychiatry* (pp. 127–144). London: John Libbey & Company.

Tikofsky, R. S., & Hellman, R. S. (1991). Brain single photon emission computed tomography: Newer activation and intervention studies. *Seminars in Nuclear Medicine, 21*, 40–57.

Tikofsky, R. S., Harsch, H. H., Goldstein, M. D., Collier, B. D., & Hellman, R. S. (1987). CT, magnetic resonance imaging, and SPECT iodine-123 iodoamphetamine imaging of a patient with progressive cognitive deterioration. *Clinical Nuclear Medicine, 12*, 463–465.

Tikofsky, R. S., Hellman, R. S., Antuono, P. A., Hoffmann, R. A., Hammeke, T. A., Kir, K. M., Onsel, C., Krasnow, A. Z., Collier, B. D., Voslar, A. M., & Wainwright, P. (1991a). Quantitated SPECT/IMP and neuropsychological performance in dementia, *Journal of Nuclear Medicine, 32* (Abstract No. 142), 942.

Tikofsky, R. S., Hellman, R. S., Antuono, P. A., Hoffmann, R. A., Krasnow, A. Z., & Collier, B. D. (1991b). Boston naming test (BNT) enhanced quantitative SPECT HMPAO in Alzheimer's disease. *Radiology, 181P* (Abstract No. 486), 174.

Tikofsky, R. S., Hellman, R. S., Antuono, P., & Saxena, V. K. (1990). Understanding single photon emission computed tomography (SPECT) brain imaging. *Mind, 4*, 3–5.

Tikofsky, R. S., Hellman, R. S., Hoffmann, R. G., Antuono, P. G., Krasnow, A. Z., & Collier, B. D. (1990). Reliability of interrater interpretation of global and regional pathology for SPECT/IMP brain imaging. *European Journal of Nuclear Medicine, 16* (Abstract No. 665), 518.

Van Heertum, R. L., & Tikofsky, R. S. (1989). *Advances in cerebral SPECT imaging: An atlas and guideline for practitioners*. New York: Trivirum.

Waldemar, G., Anderson, A. R., & Lassen, N. A. (1990). TC-99m-HM-PAO in diagnosis of Alzheimer's disease by gamma tomography (SPECT). In L. Battisin & F. Gerstenbrand (Eds.), *Aging brain and dementia: New trends in diagnosis and therapy* (pp. 405–416) New York: Wiley-Liss.

Waldemar, G., Paulson, O. B., & Lassen, N. A. (1990). Brain imaging with SPECT in Alzheimer's disease. In S. I. Rapoport, H. Petit, D. Leys, & Y. Christen (Eds.), *Imaging, cerebral topography and Alzheimer's disease* (pp. 139–144) New York: Springer-Verlag.

Wellman, H. N., Gilmore, R., Hendrie, H., Mock, R., Kapuscinski, A., Appledorn, C. R., & Krepshaw, J. (1985). Dual head HIPDM SPECT imaging in the differential diagnosis of dementia with MR and CT correlation. *Journal of Nuclear Medicine, 26* (Abstract No. 450), 106.

Weinberger, D. R., Mann, U., Gibson, R. E., Coppola, R., Jones, D. W., Braun, A. R., Berman, K. F., Sunderland, T., Reba, R. C., & Chase, T. N. (1990). Cerebral muscarinic receptors in primary degenerative dementia as evaluated by SPECT with iodine-123-labeled QNB. In R. J. Wurtman et al. (Eds.), *Advances in neurology. Vol. 51: Alzheimer's disease* (pp. 147–150). New York: Raven Press.

18

Electrophysiological Indexes of Cortical Deterioration and Cognitive Impairment in Dementia

KERRY L. COBURN, RANDOLPH W. PARKS, AND
WALTER S. PRITCHARD

Measurements of electrical activity of the cerebral cortex (electrocortical activity) in the form of electroencephalograms (EEGs) or event-related potentials (ERPs) reflect information processing on a millisecond time scale in populations of cortical neurons and are the only means widely available for objectively monitoring cortical functioning in real time. It is perhaps to be expected that electrocortical activity will be altered in dementia, where pathological processes affect large areas of the cortex with devastating neuropsychological consequences. Altered EEGs in dementia have been reported for six decades, but until recently such reports have been necessarily qualitative and descriptive due to limitations in instrumentation and analysis procedures. These limitations are being overcome, and recent quantitative analytical EEG investigations suggest that both differential clinical diagnosis and basic research will benefit greatly. Late endogenous (cognitive) ERP components such as the P300 have been studied extensively in dementia. Because thorough reviews of this literature appear regularly, it will simply be noted here that increased P300 latency increases and, to a lesser extent, reduced amplitude are reliably found in dementias stemming from a wide variety of etiologies. A less well known literature addresses dementia-related changes in a subclass of ERPs, the sensory evoked potentials (EPs). Visual EPs are altered in at least some forms of dementia, and converging evidence from several fields suggest that the alteration may be specific to the cortical cholinergic deterioration of Alzheimer's disease (AD). Here limitations tend to be methodological rather than technological and very rapid progress is to be expected over the next few years.

EEG Changes in Aging and Dementia

Electroencephalographic changes in normal aging and dementia remain largely qualitative, descriptive, and even speculative despite six decades of investigation.

Until recently, EEG studies relied entirely on qualitative "visual analysis" of the ink-written EEG record, comparing it to an undefined "mental template" of normal activity. Although the EEG changes during aging, qualitative visual analysis has not allowed either normal age-related changes or the borderline with (often subtle) additional changes stemming from dementia to be established quantitatively. Despite these shortcomings, most studies suggest alterations in some forms of dementia similar to those seen during normal aging, but beyond the age-normal range.

The better studies (e.g., Soininen, Partanen, Helkala, & Riekkinen, 1982) have accomplished this using visual analysis of the ink-written traces by a reader blind to diagnosis, with ordinal ratings of specific EEG features and statistical analysis of obtained results. More recent quantitative work (e.g., Pentila, Partanen, Soininen, & Riekkinen, 1985) employing at least limited computer-assisted digital frequency analysis has generally confirmed the visually analyzed results.

EEG Changes in Normal Aging

In normal aging, most studies find increased diffuse activity in the delta (0–4 Hz) and theta (4–8 Hz) bands, with localized theta increases over the frontal and temporal lobes, variable slowing of the alpha rhythm (8–12 Hz), reduced alpha power, and increased beta (>12 Hz) activity (Busse, Barnes, Friedman, & Kelty, 1956; Celesia, 1986; Chatrian & Lairy, 1976; Levy, 1975; Obrist, 1976; Shearer, Emmerson, & Dustman, 1989; Thompson, 1976; Torres, Faoro, Loewenson, & Johnson, 1983).

The bilateral delta and theta increases described in normal aging have a frontal distribution with occasional involvement of central and temporal regions (Torres et al., 1983); unilateral increases are most frequently seen over the left anterior temporal area (Fenton, 1986; see Torres et al., 1983 for large normative study). Slow-wave increases do not seem to be related to decreased blood flow in normal aging (Libow, Obrist, & Sokoloff, 1971; Obrist et al., 1963). However, a large quantitative study (Duffy, 1985; Duffy, Albert, & McAnulty, 1984) of very carefully screened (hyperhealthy) elderly subjects suggested that the increased delta and theta generally ascribed to normal aging may be due to subclinical pathologies in putatively healthy elderly individuals. A similar lack of significant differences between young and elderly normals has been reported in other digitally analyzed EEG studies (Breslay, Starr, Sicotte, Higa, and Buchsbaum, 1989; Pentila et al., 1985), although the sample sizes have been small; it is questionable whether the lack of a significant difference is evidence of absence or simply absence of evidence.

The question of alpha slowing in normal aging has been addressed at considerable length (Celesia, 1986; Duffy et al., 1984; Hubbard, Sunde, & Goldensohn, 1976; Katz & Horowitz, 1982; Prinz, Peskind, et al., 1982; Prinz & Vitiello, 1989; Torres et al., 1983). When it is found (e.g., Wang & Busse, 1969), the slowing appears to be minimal (approximately 0.25–1.0 Hz) though statistically significant.

Increased beta activity in normal aging is not a universal finding (Matejcek, 1980), but is generally characterized as broad band (14–30 Hz) and tends to be most prevalent over central regions (Busse & Obrist, 1963; Gibbs & Gibbs, 1950). It may diminish greatly after age 80 (Fenton, 1986). Increased beta without increased slow activity was found among the hyperhealthy elderly subjects studied by Duffy et al. (1984) and Williamson et al. (1990). The latter found cognitive performance to correlate with frontal beta even after controlling for age, education, occupation, and medication. Five subjects showing early signs of intellectual decline all had marked reductions of frontal beta, suggesting that this may be an early indication of intellectual loss.

EEG Changes in AD

Fenton (1986) credits Hans Berger for the first description of EEG abnormalities associated with histologically confirmed AD in 1932. Even in early stages of the disorder it is rare to find a normal clinical EEG in a confirmed AD patient (Gordon & Sim, 1967; Johannesson, Hagberg, Gustafson, & Ingvar, 1979; Letemendia & Pampiglione, 1958; Soininen et al., 1982; Swain, 1959). Fenton (1986) puts the figure at less than 5%. This figure is somewhat misleading, however, since among 67 patients meeting DSM-III (American Psychiatric Association, 1980) criteria for dementia and NINCDS-ADRDA criteria for probable AD, Erkinjuntti et al. (1988) found clinically normal EEGs in 21% and noted up to 48% normal EEGs in other studies. Faught and Harrell (1990) have reported normal clinical EEGs in 17 of 45 AD patients (38%).

Mild AD patients as a group differ significantly from age-equivalent normal controls on a wide range of clinically described EEG measures (Soininen et al., 1982), and abnormalities increase with the clinical progression of dementia (Gordon, 1968; Johannesson, Brun, Gustafson, & Ingvar, 1977; Verma, Greiffenstein, Verma, King, & Caldwell, 1987; however, see Rae-Grant et al., 1986 for important exceptions). Quantitative studies confirm increased delta and theta (Figure 18.1) with decreased beta in AD patients compared to age-equivalent healthy controls (Brenner et al., 1986; Breslay et al., 1989; Duffy et al., 1984; Faught & Harrell, 1990; Gustafson et al., 1987; Ihl, Eilles, et al., 1989; Ihl, Maurer, Dierks, Frich, & Perisic, 1989; Iznak & Chayanov, 1990; Rice et al., 1990; Visser, Van Tilburg, Hooijer, Jonker, & De Rijke, 1985; see Markand, 1986 for review), and like EEG abnormalities in general, the distribution (Rice et al., 1990) and proportion of excess slow activity increase with disease severity (Coben, Danziger, & Storandt, 1985; Pentila et al., 1985; Primavera, Novello, Finocchi, Canevari, & Corsello, 1990). Beta has been reported to shift from an occipitoparietotemporal topographic distribution to a flatter, more frontal distribution with increasing disease severity (Ihl, Maurer, et al., 1989), a change that parallels greater temporoparietal than frontal decreases in blood flow assessed by single photon emission computed tomography (SPECT) (Ihl, Eilles, et al., 1989). Increased theta and decreased beta are seen in even mildly demented AD patients (Coben, Danziger, & Berg, 1983; Coben, Danziger, & Hughes, 1983; Coben, Chi, Snyder, & Storandt, 1990; Isse, Uchiyama, Tanaka, Kuroda, & Kojima, 1990) and may be the first EEG signs of the disorder.

Although alpha changes in normal aging are a matter of dispute, AD is reliably accompanied by decreased alpha (both decreased amplitude and a decrease in the frequency of the alpha peak; Obrist, 1978; Prinz & Vitiello, 1989; Prinz, Peskind, et al., 1982; Prinz, Vitaliano, et al., 1982; Soininen et al., 1982). Some investigators report alpha changes to be the earliest EEG manifestations of AD, preceding theta and beta changes (Gordon, 1968), although the issue is not settled. Comparison of AD patients showing normal alpha with those whose alpha is diminished or

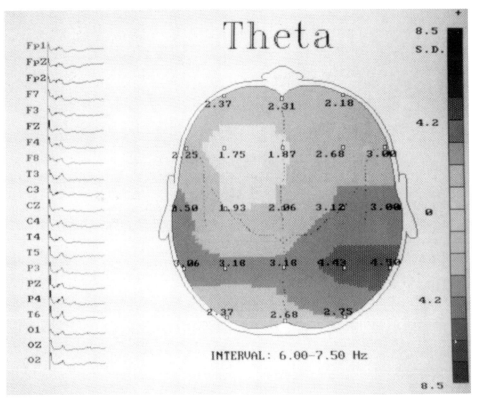

FIGURE 18.1. Topographic distribution of increased 6.0- to 7.5-Hz theta activity in Alzheimer's disease (AD). Mapped Z scores of the mean of 24 probable AD patients versus 12 age-equivalent healthy controls show significantly (Z > 3) to very significantly (Z > 4) increased theta over parietal and temporal regions bilaterally, and extending into frontal and central areas on the right (From Coburn, unpublished data).

absent (Sheridan, Sato, Foster, Bruno, Cox, Fedio, & Chase, 1988) finds parietal lobe hypometabolism measured by positron emission tomography (PET) and decreased performance IQ (measured by Wechsler Adult Intelligence Scale [WAIS]) in the latter group.

It has been reported widely that in AD (but perhaps not other dementing disorders; Johannesson et al., 1979) theta and finally delta increase in parallel with increasing degrees of intellectual impairment (Frey & Sjögren, 1959; Gueguen et al., 1990; Gordon & Sim, 1967; McAdam & McClatchey, 1952; McAdam & Robinson, 1957; Merskey et al., 1980; Mundy-Castle, Hurst, Beerstecher, & Prinsloo, 1954; Obrist, 1976; Obrist, Busse, Eisdorfer, & Kleemeier, 1962; Rae-Grant et al., 1987; Roberts, McGeorg, & Gaird, 1978; Soininen et al., 1982). Increased delta is characteristic of advanced AD, appearing in the most severe cases as bilateral bursts over temporal and frontal regions (Isse et al., 1990; Obrist, 1978; Pentila et al., 1985; Stigsby, 1988) and correlating with intellectual deterioration, morphometric measures of hippocampal neuronal loss and granulovacuolar degeneration (Rae-Grant et al., 1987), brainstem changes (Johannesson et al., 1977), and the number of senile plaques and tangle formations at autopsy (Muller & Schwartz, 1978).

During photic driving, AD patients do not show the normal peaks related to the driving frequency and its harmonics. Neither is alpha band power related systematically to the driving frequency, and the normal broad-based peak at 10 Hz is absent (Politoff, 1990).

Presenile Versus Senile Onset

Duffy et al. (1984) found significant EEG differences between patients having presenile and senile onset of AD symptoms. Although both groups manifested marked increases in delta and theta, these increases differed in topographic distribution. In presenile onset patients, the increases were most prominent over mid- and posterior-temporal regions, whereas in senile onset patients they had a frontal and anterior-temporal distribution. Duffy (1985) hypothesized that this difference suggested two possibilities: either presenile and senile onset reflect different disease entities, or there is a marked disease-age interaction in AD patients. The frontal EEG abnormalities in senile onset patients may underlie their relatively greater prominence of frontal lobe neurological signs, whereas the temporal distribution in presenile patients may underlie their relative prominence of memory dysfunction. Iznak and Chayanov (1990) found a greater slowing of posterior alpha and, in contrast to Duffy, a larger increase in diffuse delta and theta activity in younger (64.5 years) than in older (79.5 years) AD patients.

EEG Changes in Multi-Infarct Dementia

Unlike AD, both the EEG changes and the dementia in multi-infarct dementia (MID) tend to be of sudden onset and either nonprogressive or progressive in a stepwise manner. As expected with localized lesions, focal increases in slow activity (Roberts, McGeorg, & Gaird, 1978) and increased asymmetries in general (Soininen et al., 1982) are more pronounced in MID than in AD. Erkinjuntti et al. (1988) found clinically normal EEGs in only 1% of 77 MID patients, but noted rates as high as 41% in other studies. Most reports find groups of AD and MID patients to be distinguishable statistically on the basis of asymmetric (usually focal) slowing with intact alpha, but for individual patients the distinction is not sufficiently reliable to allow differential diagnosis on the basis of EEG alone.

Some quantitative EEG investigations do not find frequency domain differences between AD and MID patients (Erkinjuntti et al., 1988; Leuchter, Spar, Walter, and Weiner, 1987) or those with vascular dementia (Erkinjuntti et al., 1988), although again sample sizes tend to be small. In all groups, delta and theta increased and alpha decreased in parallel with the severity of dementia. Other studies do find differences. For example, Kong, Yiu, Su, Liu, and Chu (1990) found the mean frequency of the EEG to be slower in AD patients than in MID patients, with both being slower than controls. Alzheimer's disease patients also displayed less relative alpha power and greater relative delta power than MID patients, who did not differ from controls in this regard. In contrast, Saletu et al. (1988) reported greater delta and theta, a slower dominant alpha frequency, and less beta in MID patients than age-equivalent AD patients. Capitalizing on the focal nature of MID abnormalities, Saletu et al. (1988) further found the difference between the maximum and minimum power values from their 17-electrode topographic array to be a good discriminator of MID versus AD. Finally, in contrast to the abnormalities reported for AD patients, reviewed above, Politoff (1990) reported no EEG changes in MID patients relative to controls during photic driving.

EEG Changes in Other Dementias

Vascular dementia has been associated with a clinically normal EEG in 20% of 45 cases; in cases where abnormal EEGs were found, vascular dementia was indistinguishable from MID or AD on the basis of qualitative and limited quantitative EEG criteria (Erkinjuntti et al., 1988). However, Iznak and Chayanov (1990) reported greater alpha slowing in AD patients than in age-matched vascular dementia patients or normals.

Of the other primary dementing disorders Jakob-Creutzfeldt disease is recognizable by the presence of highly distinctive generalized quasi-periodic sharp complexes that appear in 70% or more of the patients as the disease progresses (Burger, Rowan, & Goldensohn, 1972; Kuroiwa & Celesia, 1980). Pick's disease is associated with a clinically normal EEG in approximately 50% of the cases (Fenton, 1986), with nonfocal frontotemporal slowing in the rest that does not progress with serial recordings. However, digital analysis of clinically normal patient records has shown them to differ significantly from those of healthy controls (Stigsby, 1988; Stigsby, Johannesson, & Ingvar, 1981). The delta and theta increases in Pick's disease are not as pronounced, and alpha activity tends to be much better preserved than in AD.

Subcortical Versus Cortical Dementias

Qualitative EEG differences between cortical and subcortical dementias (Albert, Feldman, & Willis, 1974) were addressed by Verma et al. (1987). Among 15 cortical dementia patients (13, AD; 2, Pick's) clinically normal or mildly abnormal EEGs were found in only three (evidently including both Pick's), whereas among 15 subcortical dementia patients (five normal-pressure hydrocephalus; three each, Huntington's, progressive supranuclear palsy, and lacunar state; one Parkinson's) matched for age and severity of dementia, normal or mildly abnormal EEGs were found in 14. Among the Pick's and all subcortical dementia patients, the progression of EEG abnormalities lagged behind that of clinical symptoms, whereas the two increased in parallel among AD patients.

Similarly, Kong et al. (1990) found that unlike AD and MID, the mean EEG frequency is not slowed relative to controls in subcortical arteriosclerotic encephalopathy with accompanying dementia. Neither MID nor arteriosclerotic patients manifested the changes in relative delta and relative alpha power that were seen in AD.

Visual EP (VEP) Changes in Aging and Dementia

Like the EEG, VEPs change slowly with normal aging and here too careful comparison with age-matched controls has revealed VEP changes in dementia beyond the age-normal range. While VEP studies tend to be much better analyzed than are EEG studies, and while they show larger effects of dementia, major limitations are apparent in the composition of patient and control groups. However, it appears that a specific pattern of VEP changes may be characteristic of AD and related to its underlying cortical pathology.

Although its importance has been largely overlooked until recently, it has been known for at least a quarter century that VEPs are altered in at least some forms of dementia in the elderly. Straumanis, Shagass, & Schwartz (1965) first noted that while the early waves of the flash VEP (FVEP) such as the P1 are of the normal latency, the middle and late waves such as the P2 are delayed in elderly demented patients compared to either young or elderly normal controls. The amount of delay increases with wave number and is much larger than the small delays seen with normal aging. This finding of normal early FVEP components (<100 msec) with significantly slowed later components in dementia has been confirmed by subsequent investigators (e.g., Coburn, Ashford, & Moreno, 1991; Harding, Wright, & Orwin, 1985; Laurian, Gaillard, & Wertheimer, 1982; Visser et al., 1976; Wright, Harding, & Orwin, 1986), and by a meta-analytic review of published studies (Pollock et al., 1989). The P2 delay is greater in longer duration (6 years) groups than in shorter duration (2 years) groups (Harding, Wright, & Orwin, 1985), and within individual patients the delay increases progressively over time, paralleling the worsening clinical condition (Orwin, Wright, Harding, Rowan, & Rolfe, 1986; Parks et al., 1991).

In his original paper, Straumanis et al. (1965) suggested that the normal P1 latency in dementia implies intact information transmission to the cortex (see also Cignak, 1961; Vaughan, 1966), whereas the delay of later waves implies alterations in subsequent information processing. As a general procedure applicable across laboratories, use of the P1 as an index of information arrival at the cortex can be problematic; this component is often not prominent in young normal adults and only develops with anticholinergic medication or advancing age. Even in elderly individuals the P1 may not be apparent, and its detection depends critically on the recording montage employed. As an alternative, Wright, Harding, & Orwin (1984) used the P100 component of the pattern reversal VEP (PRVEP) to index the arrival and initial processing of visual information at the cortex. (For historical reasons FVEP components are generally designated by the polarity-wave number convention such as P1 and P2 whereas PRVEP components are designated using the more current polarity-latency convention such as P100. For clarity and consistency with existing literature both conventions are retained here.) Like the P1, the P100 is generated in the visual system's primary projection area (Jeffreys & Axford, 1972; Michael & Halliday, 1971); the P2 appears to be generated in a separate cortical association area (Darcy, Ary, & Fender, 1980; Whittaker & Siegfried, 1983). The P100 is a sensitive indicator of pathologies afferent to and including primary visual cortex, but is insensitive to even widespread cortical lesions sparing this area (Blumhardt & Halliday, 1981). P100 is an easily measured, highly reproducible PRVEP component that is reliably present at all ages and its intersubject variability is less than that of the P1 over the entire age span (Halliday, 1982). P100 latency is only slightly affected by normal aging and is age-normal in primary dementia (Coben, Danzinger, & Hughes, 1983; Coburn et al., 1991; Harding et al., 1985; Wright et al., 1984; Wright et al., 1986). As with the P1, a normal latency P100 implies that retinogeniculostriate projection pathways are functionally intact; visual information reaches the occipital cortex at the normal time and is not delayed as in multiple sclerosis (MS) and some cases of MID. When both PRVEPs and FVEPs are recorded in elderly demented patients, the most commonly reported findings are a normal P100 and P1 coupled with a delayed P2 (Coburn et al., 1991; Doggett, Harding, & Orwin, 1981; Harding, Doggett, Orwin, & Smith, 1981; Harding et al., 1985; Orwin et al., 1986; Wright et al., 1984, 1986). Computations of interpeak latency differences between P1 and P2 or between P100 and P2 components as simple metrics of cortical processing (Wright et al., 1984) yield results virtually identical to raw P2 latencies; the P2 delay in dementia can be accounted for by a deterioration of some stage of information processing after the initial arrival of afferent information at primary visual cortex (Coburn et al., 1991). According to Wright et al. (1984, 1986) the slowing of the P2 with preservation of the P100 occurs only in primary dementia and is not found in age-equivalent patient groups suffering from affective disorder or cerebral atrophy without dementia, and is not an effect of medication (Cosi et al., 1982; Harding et al., 1985). In this laboratory, a selectively delayed P2 has been used as evidence of AD in the presence of vascular lesions (Parks et al., 1991).

Whereas the distinction of demented patients from nondemented controls is important, the crucial clinical differentiation is between groups of demented patients whose symptoms stem from different etiologies. Until recently, studies addressing VEP changes in dementia have not examined distinctions between different diagnostic subgroups; demented patients characterized by a variety of diagnostic systems have been compared exclusively to nondemented patients or normals. For example, Straumanis et al. (1965) based their findings on patients with chronic brain syndrome, whereas Wright et al. (1984, 1986) and Harding et al. (1985) studied patients suffering from primary presenile dementia within which they included senile dementia, Huntington's disease, and Pick's disease, as well as AD. Even when the specific diagnosis of AD is used (Harding, Wright, Orwin, & Smith, 1984), it is unclear whether these patients would meet current NINCDS-ADRDA criteria for probable AD (McKhann et al., 1984). Assuming that the majority of demented patients in these studies would today be classified as probable AD, it was until recently an open question whether the selective P2 delay is a specific feature of AD or a more general characteristic of dementia.

Recently, this laboratory compared probable AD patients to other clinically demented patients whose symptoms arose from non-AD etiologies, and to healthy elderly controls (Coburn et al., 1991). The selective P2 delay was found only in the probable AD group (Figure 18.2). Clinically demented patients with etiologies other than AD were indistinguishable from normals, suggesting that the selective P2 delay is a specific feature of AD. Identical results were found when visual global field power was analyzed rather than VEP voltages (Coburn, Ashford, & Moreno, in press), showing that the delayed P2 reflects an actual electrocortical change rather than being the result of technical recording factors. Furthermore, there is reason to believe that the P2 delay may stem from the cortical cholinergic deterioration in AD.

The selectively delayed P2 is unusual, because most pathologies affecting FVEP components cause amplitude reductions rather than latency increases, and a delayed FVEP usually reflects a pathology so severe that the PRVEP is also strongly affected

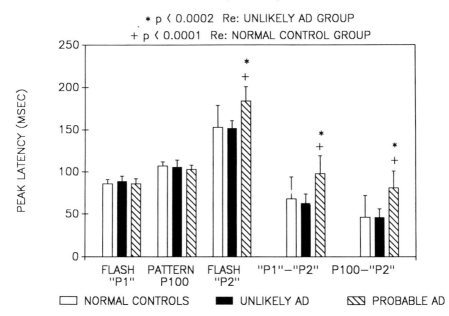

FIGURE 18.2. Selectively delayed P2 component in Alzheimer's disease (AD). Latencies of pattern reversal P100 and flash P2 components from probable AD and unlikely AD demented patients and age-equivalent healthy controls show significantly increased P2 latencies only among probable AD patients (From Coburn et al., 1991. Reprinted with permission).

(Halliday & Mushin, 1980; Harding, 1977; Wright et al., 1984). The selective P2 slowing in AD implies that some cortical process is affected after the initial response of the primary projection area. It is a general finding of PET (Benson, 1983; Benson et al., 1983; Cutler, 1988; Duara et al., 1986; Foster et al., 1983; Foster et al., 1984; Foster, Chase, Patronas, Gillespie, & Fedio, 1986; Small et al., 1989), SPECT (Gemmell et al., 1984; Johnson et al., 1988), and histological studies (Brun & Gustafson, 1976; Sim, 1979) that the cortical pathology in AD tends to affect association areas maximally while leaving primary projection areas relatively spared. In the visual system the number of neurofibrillary tangles is low in primary projection area 17 but increases 20-fold in adjacent association area 18 and doubles again in association area 20 (Lewis, Campbell, Terry, & Morrison, 1987); the regional and laminar distributions of these tangles imply deterioration of cortico-cortical projections. Decreased metabolism of these areas in AD patients correlates with impaired visuospatial performance (Foster et al., 1983, 1986). Also, visual association areas have decreased choline acetyltransferase (ChAT)-activity (Proctor et al., 1988) and decreased acetylcholine and nicotine binding (Whitehouse et al., 1986) in AD. The P2 delay may be a reflection of the magnitude of AD pathology in visual association cortex and may be specifically related to the cholinergic deficit. This suggestion is strengthened by the finding of Bajalan, Wright, and Van Der Vliet (1986) and in this laboratory (Figure 18.3A) that it can be reproduced in young nondemented subjects by anticholinergic medication. Even in the severely compromised cholinergic systems of AD patients, cholinergic and anticholinergic

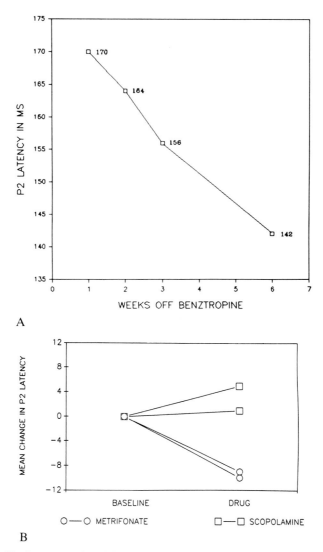

FIGURE 18.3. Cholinergic and anticholinergic medication effects on P2 latency. (A) P2 latency from a young nondemented subject after cholinergic suppression by benztropine is increased into the range characteristic of Alzheimer's disease (AD) (neither P1 nor P100 latencies are affected), but over the 6 weeks following drug termination P2 latencies return to the age-normal range. (B) P2 latencies from three probable AD patients show minimal additional increases after cholinergic suppression by scopolamine, but are decreased toward the normal range after cholinergic stimulation by metrifonate (From Coburn, unpublished pilot data).

medications produce small changes in P2 latency in the predicted directions (Figure 18.3B).

It is presently unclear whether VEP effects precede the onset of clinical symptoms. Coben, Danziger, & Hughes (1983) studied a group of 40 subjects with mild AD living in the community compared to healthy controls individually matched for age, sex, socioeconomic status, and race. Late PRVEP components (>150 msec) were delayed, whereas the FVEP P2 and other late components showed only nonsignificant slowing, suggesting that the latency increases may foreshadow the onset of clinical symptoms. More work in this area is urgently needed.

If the delayed P2 is specific to AD it may provide several unique clinical contributions. It may be the only objective physiological stigmatum of the disease that can be examined noninvasively in the full spectrum of the potential AD population. It may also provide a useful measure for determining progression of the disease within individual patients. Both of these contributions may aid clinical diagnosis. Finally, the P2 may be a useful objective measure for determining the effects of acute or chronic therapeutic interventions at the level of the cortical substrate.

Limiting Factors

Applications of computer-based frequency analysis to EEGs have been of limited usefulness due largely to technological constraints. Until recently, practical limitations restricted analysis to only a small number of channels (usually one to four) and there has been an unfortunate tendency to compensate for this channel limitation by using a bipolar recording montage. Because the bipolar montage used with differential amplifiers rejects common mode activity and generates a signal proportional to the voltage difference between two electrodes (overlying two active brain regions), the output signal is necessarily equivocal, being influenced by the frequency, amplitude, and phase relationships between the neuronal populations underlying the two electrode sites. The ambiguity introduced into the data makes it impossible to specify with any degree of certainty what changes are occurring and where those changes may be taking place.

Similarly, the common practice of recording VEPs from only a small number of scalp sites rather than employing the full International 10–20 System electrode array discards regional information and invites contamination from a wide variety of artifactual sources (Coburn & Moreno, 1988). Identification criteria or procedures are rarely specified for the measurement of VEP components, but the variety of component latencies and polarities described suggests that electrode montage may account for some of the discrepancies in the literature. Authors confronted with ambiguous or uninterpretable components in their VEP waveforms (e.g., Wright et al., 1986) may choose to drop potentially valuable data from analysis. This problem is compounded in some studies (e.g., Coben, Danziger, & Hughes, 1983; Pollock et al., 1989; Straumanis et al., 1965) by the use of estimated rather than measured electrode positions. An original prospective study reported in Pollock et al. (1989) found a significant P100 delay for AD patients compared to age-matched controls but no significant difference in the P2 despite the use of a one-tailed test. The authors themselves attributed their anomalous results to methodological factors.

Impact of New Technology and Methods

The technological picture has been changed dramatically in the past decade by three factors: powerful and inexpensive microcomputers, fast and efficient algorithms for frequency and statistical analysis, and interpolation-based topographic mapping routines. This combination now allows the simultaneous recording and digitization of EEG and EP data from a large number of sites (typically 16–32) on the head, very rapid EEG frequency analysis, and the mapping of results top-ographically on a computer-generated representation of the cerebral cortex. Top-ographic mapping can also be used to display the results of statistical analyses to assess their regional distributions. It is now possible to map the entire convexity of the cerebral cortex in terms of its regional frequency and amplitude character-istics, and more importantly, to map the anatomical distribution of statistically significant differences between patient and control groups. The equipment nec-essary to do this has only recently become available, and serious application of such devices to the study of AD has barely begun.

EEG Chaos, Information Processing Load, and Dementia

In addition to improvements in instrumentation, there have been recent advances in the mathematical models used to describe and analyze brain electrical activity. A very recent approach that may have important applications to dementia is chaos analysis. Traditionally modeled as a mixture of periodic components, random noise, and artifact, the EEG can also be viewed as a process manifesting deterministic chaos; the EEG may be governed by only a few variables interacting nonlinearly to produce a rapid loss of predictability and a seemingly random time series. Despite this temporal unpredictability, the asymptotic behavior of such systems is attracted toward a finite region of state space having a fractal geometry, with the trajectory of the system through this region of state space never exactly repeating. The existence of such strange attractors in state space is the hallmark of dissipative chaotic systems.

The important dependent variable for EEG studies is the dimensional com-plexity (DCx) of the attractor (see Pritchard & Duke, 1992, in press; Pritchard, Duke, & Coburn, 1991a, for discussion). Very low DCx estimates are found during the 3-Hz spikes and waves of a petit mal epileptic seizure and during the terminal stages of Jakob-Creutzfeldt disease, and increasingly higher DCx's during stage IV sleep (characterized by 3- to 4-Hz slow waves), stage II sleep (characterized by 12- to 14-Hz sleep spindles; Babloyantz, Salazar, & Nicolis, 1985; Babloyantz & Des-texhe, 1986, 1988), and rapid eye movement (REM) sleep (characterized by high-frequency desynchronized activity; Mayer-Kress & Layne, 1987). A low DCx during wakeful eyes-closed (EC) resting conditions (where synchronized EEG alpha is expected) is increased during the EEG desynchronization of medium anesthesia (Layne, Mayer-Kress, & Holfuss, 1986), but progressively decreased in parallel with EEG slowing during deeper levels of anesthesia (Watt & Hameroff, 1987).

In awake subjects under EC resting conditions, the DCx of occipital EEG is low, probably due to synchronized alpha, but rises when the eyes are opened (EO) and alpha blocks (Dvorak, Siska, Wackermann, Hrudova, & Dostalek, 1986; Mayer-Kress & Layne, 1987; Pritchard & Duke, 1992; Pritchard, Duke, & Coburn, 1991a, 1991b) or when cognitive tasks such as serial sevens (Rapp et al., 1985, 1989), serial 13s (Dvorak et al., 1986), two-digit additions (Nan & Jinghua, 1988), word association, abstraction, verbal memory, or visual memory (Mayer-Kress & Layne, 1987) are imposed.

A topographic mapping study (Pritchard, Duke, and Coburn, 1991b) found a correspondence between regional distributions of EEG frequencies and DCx, with lower DCx values over posterior regions where the synchronized medium frequency alpha rhythm was most prominent and progressively higher values over more anterior regions where less synchronized higher EEG frequencies predominated (Figure 18.4). The highest DCx values were found at midtemporal sites where high-frequency muscle tension artifact (Coburn & Moreno, 1988) was apparent in the EEG data. Digital filtering to remove high-frequency activity reduced DCx, with the greatest reduction over the midtemporal areas.

From these reports it appears that DCx is related (though indirectly) to EEG frequency composition. In states where low frequencies predominate and are widespread across the scalp (deep anesthesia, petit mal seizures, stage IV sleep) DCx estimates are particularly low, but increase under conditions and at scalp sites where midrange EEG frequencies predominate (stage II sleep, EC resting wakefulness, posterior sites) and are particularly high under conditions and at scalp sites where high frequencies predominate (cognitive tasks, EO resting, REM sleep, anterior and midtemporal sites). At all scalp sites DCx is reduced when high frequencies are selectively filtered from the EEG, but this effect is most pronounced at sites where high frequencies predominate.

Functionally, DCx may relate to processing load because it increases from nondreaming to dreaming sleep, from EC no-task to EC cognitive task, and from EC to EO conditions (Mayer-Kress & Layne, 1987). The processing load interpretation is particularly inviting for the effect of eye opening, because the DCx reduction is most pronounced over occipital regions of the cortex, which mediate visual perception (Pritchard, Duke, & Coburn, 1991a).

Of particular importance with regard to dementia, DCx parallels the declines in processing capabilities occurring with aging and in AD (Rapp et al., 1985; Zec, 1990). A topographic mapping study (Pritchard, Duke, and Coburn, 1991b; Pritchard, Duke, Coburn, & Robinson, 1992) compared young and elderly healthy

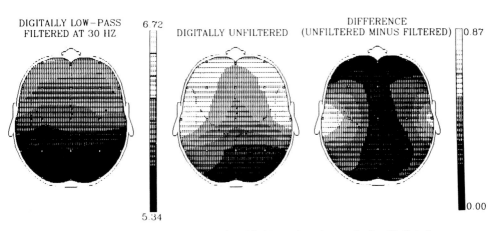

FIGURE 18.4. Electroencephalographic (EEG) dimensional complexity (DCx): locus × filter interaction. Topographic distribution of DCx in young normals shows regional variations related to the frequency composition of the EEG (From Pritchard et al., 1991a. Reprinted with permission).

subjects and elderly AD patients. Whereas DCx showed significant regional differences across scalp sites for all groups (reflecting the relatively lower DCx over
posterior sites), the interaction between condition (EC or EO) and scalp site was
lost among the elderly, and both this interaction and the main effect of condition
were lost among the demented (Figure 18.5). These results were replicated very
recently in a larger sample (Pritchard, Duke, Moore, Tucker, & Coburn, 1992)
and imply that while different brain regions continue to show characteristic patterns
of DCx, the dynamic responsivity to changing processing loads is reduced in normal
aging and lost in AD.

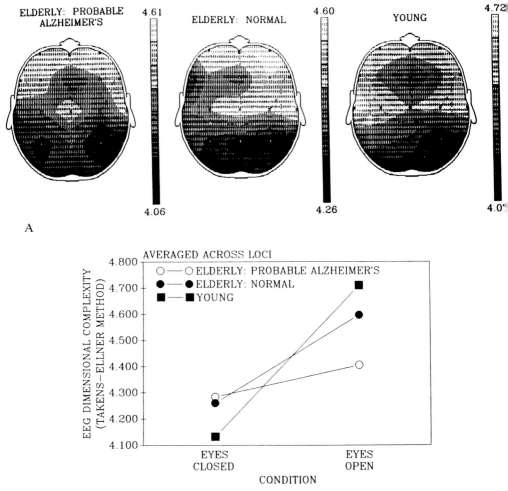

A

B

FIGURE 18.5. Electroencephalographic (EEG) dimensional complexity (DCx): aging and
Alzheimer's disease effects. (A) DCx varies systematically across the head in all groups
under resting conditions (average of eyes-open and eyes-closed conditions). (B) Eye
opening greatly increases DCx in young normals but the effect is reduced in elderly
normals and lost in AD patients, reflecting a loss of dynamic responsivity in the latter
group (From Pritchard et al., 1991b. Reprinted with permission).

There is also an intriguing suggestion that DCx under EC no-task conditions may reflect the processing load of a preceding cognitive task. Pritchard & Duke (1992) found that EC no-task DCx declines over successive trials. Rapp et al. (1989) alternated between no-task and two arithmetic task trials and found that compared to an initial no-task EC trial, successive EC trials following task trials had higher DCx's. Although the results are confounded by a failure to counterbalance the order in which easy (serial 2 additions) and difficult (serial 7 subtractions) tasks were administered, one interpretation is that a "trace" of the processing load carries over into the DCx of the succeeding no-task condition.

Summary and Conclusions

Most of the commonly encountered dementias are accompanied by EEG abnormalities of various types. In general these abnormalities are much more severe in cortical than in subcortical dementias, and in the former their regional distribution roughly parallels the distribution of pathological changes. In AD the changes take the form of increased slow activity (delta, theta) and decreased faster activity (alpha, beta), and the severity of these changes parallels the severity of dementia. Unfortunately this means that the EEG shows the least change early in the course of the illness when differential diagnosis is most problematic. Although at present EEG changes are not sufficiently reliable to be pathognomic of AD, they are pathognomic of Jakob-Creutzfeldt dementia and can be very useful in screening out other causes. This situation is likely to improve as quantitative methods of analysis replace the current qualitative methods in clinical EEG laboratories allowing better delineation of normal limits as a function of age and an improved characterization of the constellation of changes occurring in specific diseases. The impact of a new analysis method such as deterministic chaos is more difficult to predict. Chaos offers a fundamentally new way of looking at brain activity and processing load. Chaos analysis of the EEG shows large changes with normal aging and additional large changes with AD, but there is presently not enough information to judge its clinical utility.

The VEP changes in AD are very well documented and are closely linked to histological and biochemical changes in the occipital lobes. More fragmentary data link VEP changes to the cholinergic deterioration occurring in AD and suggest that the changes may not be found in other forms of dementia. If these suggestions are borne out, they offer both a powerful tool for differential diagnosis within the dementias and also an index of the effectiveness of treatments aimed at restoring cholinergic function at the level of the cortical substrate.

References

Albert, M. L., Feldman, R. G., & Willis, A. L. (1974). The 'subcortical dementia' of progressive supranuclear palsy. *Journal of Neurology, Neurosurgery and Psychiatry*, *37*, 121–130.

American Psychiatric Association. (1980). *Diagnostic and statistical manual of mental disorders*, (*3rd ed.*) Washington, DC: Author.

Babloyantz, A., & Destexhe, A. (1988). The Creutzfeldt-Jakob disease in the hierarchy of chaotic attractors. In M. Markus, S. Muller, & G. Nicolis (Eds.), *From chemical to biological organization* (pp. 307–316). New York: Springer-Verlag.

Babloyantz, A., & Destexhe, A. (1986). Low-dimensional chaos in an instance of epilepsy. *Proceedings of the National Academy of Sciences of the United States of America, 83,* 3513–3517.

Babloyantz, A., Salazar, J. M., & Nicolis, C. (1985). Evidence of chaotic dynamics of brain activity during the sleep cycle. *Physics Letters, 111A,* 152–156.

Bajalan, A. A. A., Wright, C. E., & Van Der Vliet, V. J. (1986). Changes in the human visual evoked potential caused by the anticholinergic agent hyoscine hydrobromide: Comparison with results in Alzheimer's disease. *Journal of Neurology, Neurosurgery and Psychiatry, 49,* 175–182.

Benson, D. F. (1983). Alterations in glucose metabolism in Alzheimer's disease. In *Banbury report 15: Biological aspects of Alzheimer's disease* (pp. 309–315). New York: Cold Spring Harbor Laboratory.

Benson, D. F., Kuhl, D. E., Hawkins, R. A., Phelps, M. E., Cummings, J. L., & Tsai, S. Y. (1983). The fluorodeoxyglucose 18F scan in Alzheimer's disease and multi-infarct dementia. *Archives of Neurology, 40,* 711–714.

Blumhardt, L. D., & Halliday, A. M. (1981). Cortical abnormalities and the visual evoked response. *Documenta Ophthalmologica Proceeding Series, 27,* 347–365.

Brenner, R. P., Ulrich, R. F., Spiker, D. G., Sclabassi, R. J., Reynolds, C. F., III, Marin, R. S., & Boller, F. (1986). Computerized EEG spectral analysis in elderly normal, demented and depressed subjects. *Electroencephalography and Clinical Neurophysiology, 64,* 483–492.

Breslay, J., Starr, A., Sicotte, N., Higa, J., & Buchsbaum, M. S. (1989). Topographic EEG changes with normal aging and SDAT. *Electroencephalography and Clinical Neurophysiology, 72,* 281–289.

Brun, A., & Gustafson, L. (1976). Distribution of cerebral degeneration in Alzheimer's disease. *Archives of Psychiatry and Neurological Science, 223,* 15–33.

Burger, L. J., Rowan, J., & Goldensohn, E. (1972). Creutzfeldt-Jakob disease. *Archives of Neurology, 26,* 428–433.

Busse, E. W., & Obrist, W. D. (1963). Significance of focal encephalographic changes in the elderly. *Postgraduate Medicine, 34,* 179–182.

Busse, E. W., Barnes, R. H., Friedman, E. L., & Kelty, E. J. (1956). Psychological functioning of aged individuals with normal and abnormal electroencephalograms. I. A study of non-hospitalized community volunteers. *Journal of Nervous and Mental Disease, 124,* 135–141.

Celesia, G. G. (1986). EEG and event-related potentials in aging and dementia. *Journal of Clinical Neurophysiology, 3,* 99–111.

Chatrian, G. E., & Lairy, G. C. (1976). Problems of aging. In A. Remond (Ed.), *Handbook of electroencephalography and Clinical Neurophysiology* (Vol. 6A, pp. 275–292). Amsterdam: Elsevier.

Ciganek, L. (1961). The EEG response (evoked potential) to light stimulus in man. *Electroencephalography and Clinical Neurophysiology, 13,* 165–172.

Coben, L. A., Danziger, W. L., & Berg, L. (1983). Frequency analysis of the resting awake EEG in mild senile dementia of Alzheimer type. *Electroencephalography and Clinical Neurophysiology, 55,* 372–380.

Coben, L. A., Danziger, W. L., & Hughes, C. P. (1983). Visual evoked potentials in mild senile dementia of Alzheimer type. *Electroencephalography and Clinical Neurophysiology, 55,* 121–130.

Coben, L. A., Danziger, W. L., & Storandt, M. (1985). A longitudinal EEG study of mild senile dementia of Alzheimer type: Changes at 1 year and at 2.5 years. *Electroencephalography and Clinical Neurophysiology*, *61*, 101–112.

Coben, L. A., Chi, D., Snyder, A. Z., & Storandt, M. (1990). Replication of a study of frequency analysis of the resting awake EEG in mild probable Alzheimer disease. *Electroencephalography and Clinical Neurophysiology*, *75*, 148–154.

Coburn, K. L., & Moreno, M. A. (1988). Facts and artifacts in brain electrical activity mapping. *Brain Topography*, *1*(1), 37–45.

Coburn, K. L., Ashford, J. W., & Moreno, M. A. (1991). Visual evoked potentials in dementia: Selective delay of flash P2 in probable Alzheimer's disease. *Journal of Neuropsychiatry and Clinical Neurosciences*, *3*, 431–435.

Coburn, K. L., Ashford, J. W., & Moreno, M. A. (in press). Delayed late component of visual global field power in probable Alzheimer's disease. *Journal of Geriatric Psychiatry and Neurology*.

Cosi, V., Vitelli, E., Gozzoli, A., Corono, M., Ceroni, M., & Callieco, R. (1982). Visual evoked potentials in aging of the brain. In J. Courgon, F. Mauguiere, & M. Revol. (Eds.), *Clinical applications of evoked potentials in neurology* (pp. 109–115). New York: Raven Press.

Cutler, N. R. (1988). Cognitive and brain imaging measures of Alzheimer's disease. *Neurobiology of Aging*, *9*, 92–94.

Darcy, T. M., Ary, J. P., & Fender, D. H. (1980). Spatiotemporal visually evoked scalp potentials in response to partial-field patterned stimulation. *Electroencephalography and Clinical Neurophysiology*, *50*, 348–355.

Doggett, C. E., Harding, G. F. A., & Orwin, A. (1981). Flash and pattern evoked potentials in patients with presenile dementia [Abstract]. *Electroencephalography and Clinical Neurophysiology*, *52*, 100P.

Duara, R., Grady, C., Haxby, J., Sundaram, B. E. S., Cutler, N. R., Heston, L., Moore, A., Schlageter, N., Larson, S., & Rapoport, S. I. (1986). Positron emission tomography in Alzheimer's disease. *Neurology*, *36*, 879–887.

Duffy, F. H. (1985). The BEAM method of neurophysiological diagnosis. In F. Nottebohm (Ed.), *Hope for a new neurology* (ANYAS Vol. 457, pp. 19–34). New York: New York Academy of Sciences.

Duffy, F. H., Albert, M. S., & McAnulty, G. (1984). Brain electrical activity in patients with presenile and senile dementia of the Alzheimer type. *Annals of Neurology*, *16*, 439–448.

Dvorak, I., Siska, J., Wackermann, J., Hrudova, L., & Dostalek, C. (1986). Evidence for interpretation of the EEG as a deterministic chaotic process with a low dimension. *Activitas Nervosa Superior*, *28*, 228–231.

Erkinjuntti, T., Larsen, T., Sulkava, R., Ketonen, L., Laaksonen, R., & Palo, J. (1988). EEG in the differential diagnosis between Alzheimer's disease and vascular dementia. *Acta Neurologica Scandinavica*, *77*, 36–43.

Faught, E., & Harrell, L. (1990). The theta/beta ratio in Alzheimer's disease. *Electroencephalography and Clinical Neurophysiology*, *76*, 85P.

Fenton, G. W. (1986). Electrophysiology of Alzheimer's disease. *British Medical Bulletin*, *42*, 29–33.

Foster, N. L., Chase, T. N., Fedio, P., Patronas, N. J., Brooks, R., & Di Chiro, G. (1983). Alzheimer's disease: Focal cortical changes shown by positron emission tomography. *Neurology*, *33*, 961–965.

Foster, N. L., Chase, T. N., Mansi, L., Brooks, R., Fedio, P., Patronas, N. J., & Di Chiro, G. (1984). Cortical abnormalities in Alzheimer's disease. *Annals of Neurology*, *16*, 649–654.

Foster, N. L., Chase, T. N., Patronas, N. J., Gillespie, M. M., & Fedio, P. (1986). Cerebral mapping of apraxia in Alzheimer's disease by positron emission tomography. *Archives of Neurology*, *19*, 139–143.

Frey, T. S., & Sjögren, H. (1959). The electroencephalogram in elderly persons suffering from neuropsychiatric disorders. *Acta Psychiatrica Scandinavica*, *34*, 38–45.

Gemmell, H. G., Sharp, P. F., Evans, N. T. S., Besson, J. A. O., Lyall, D., & Smith, F. W. (1984). Single photon emission tomography with 123 I-isopropylamphetamine in Alzheimer's disease and multi-infarct dementia. *Lancet*, *2*, 1348.

Gibbs, A. A., & Gibbs, E. L. (1950). *Atlas of electroencephalography*. Vol. 1: *Methodology and controls*. Cambridge, MA: Addison-Wesley.

Gordon, E. B. (1968). Serial electroencephalographic studies in presenile dementia. *British Journal of Psychiatry*, *144*, 799–780.

Gordon, E. B., & Sim, M. (1967). The EEG in presenile dementia. *Journal of Neurology, Neurosurgery and Psychiatry*, *30*, 285–291.

Gueguen, B., Derouesne, C., Ancri, D., Gasnault, J., Kalafat, M., Bourdel, M. C., Guillou, S., & Plancon, D. (1990). Computerized EEG, in dementia of the Alzheimer type (DAT): Diagnosis at early stage, subgroup determination and prediction of the rate of progression. *Electroencephalography and Clinical Neurophysiology*, *75*, S52–S53.

Gustafson, L., Edvinsson, L., Dahlgren, N., Hagberg, B., Risberg, J., Rosen, I., & Ferno, H. (1987). Intravenous physostigmine treatment of Alzheimer's disease evaluated by psychometric testing, regional cerebral blood flow (rCBF) measurement, and EEG. *Psychopharmacology*, *93*, 31–35.

Halliday, A. M. (Ed.). (1982). *Evoked potentials in clinical testing*. London: Churchill Livingstone.

Halliday, A. M., & Mushin, J. (1980). The visual evoked potential in neuro-ophthalmology. *International Journal of Ophthalmological Clinics*, *20*, 155–185.

Harding, G. F. A. (1977). The use of the visual evoked potential to flash stimuli in the diagnosis of visual defects. In Desmedt, J. E. (Ed.), *Visual evoked potentials in man: New developments* (pp. 500–508). Oxford: Clarendon Press.

Harding, G. F. A., Wright, C. E., & Orwin, A. (1985). Primary presenile dementia: The use of the visual evoked potential as a diagnostic indicator. *British Journal of Psychiatry*, *147*, 532–539.

Harding, G. F. A., Doggett, C. E., Orwin, A., & Smith, E. J. (1981). Visual evoked potentials in presenile dementia. *Documenta Ophthalmologica Proceeding Series*, *27*, 193–202.

Harding, G. F. A., Wright, C. E., Orwin, A., & Smith, E. J. (1984). The visual evoked potential in Alzheimer's disease. In R. H. Nodar & C. Barber (Eds.), *Evoked potentials II: The second international evoked potential symposium* (pp. 473–479). Boston: Butterworth's.

Hubbard, O., Sunde, D., & Goldensohn, E. S. (1976). The EEG in centenarians. *Electroencephalography and Clinical Neurophysiology*, *40*, 407–417.

Ihl, R., Eilles, C., Frich, L., Maurer, K., Dierks, T., & Perisic, I. (1989). Electrical brain activity and cerebral blood flow in dementia of the Alzheimer type. *Journal of Psychiatric Residency*, *29*, 449–452.

Ihl, R., Maurer, K., Dierks, R., Frich, L., & Perisic, I. (1989). Staging in dementia of the Alzheimer type: Topography of electrical brain activity reflects the severity of the disease. *Journal of Psychiatric Residency*, *29*, 399–401.

Isse, K., Uchiyama, M., Tanaka, K., Kuroda, A., & Kojima, T. (1990). A quantitative EEG study of Alzheimer type dementia. *Electroencephalography and Clinical Neurophysiology*, *75*, S65.

Iznak, A. F., & Chayanov, N. V. (1990). EEG mapping in elderly patients with various types of dementia. *Brain Topography*, *3*, 296–297.

Jeffreys, D. A., & Axford, J. G. (1972). Source locations of pattern-specific components of human visual evoked potentials. I. Component of striate cortical origin. *Experimental Brain Research, 16*, 1–21.

Johannesson, G., Brun, A., Gustafson, I., & Ingvar, D. H. (1977). EEG in presenile dementia related to cerebral blood flow and autopsy findings. *Acta Neurologica Scandinavica, 56*, 89–103.

Johannesson, G., Hagberg, B., Gustafson, I., & Ingvar, D. H. (1979). EEG and cognitive impairment in presenile dementia. *Acta Neurologica Scandinavica, 59*, 225–240.

Johnson, K. A., Holman, L., Mueller, S. P., Rosen, T. J., English, R., Nagel, J. S., & Growdon, J. H. (1988). Single photon emission computed tomography in Alzheimer's disease. Abnormal iofetamine I 123 uptake reflects dementia severity. *Archives of Neurology, 45*, 392–396.

Katz, R. I., & Horowitz, G. R. (1982). Electroencephalogram in the septuagenarian: Studies in a normal geriatric population. *Journal of the American Geriatrics Society, 3*, 273–275.

Kong, K.-W., Yiu, C.-H., Su, M.-S., Liu, H.-C., & Chu, F.-L. (1990). Quantitative EEG in the differential diagnosis between Alzheimer's disease and vascular dementia. *Brain Topography, 3*, 251–252.

Kuroiwa, Y., & Celesia, G. (1980). Clinical significance of periodic EEG patterns. *Archives of Neurology, 37*, 15–20.

Laurian, S., Gaillard, J.-M., & Wertheimer, J. (1982). Evoked potentials in the assessment of brain function in senile dementia. In J. Courjon, F. Mauguiere, & M. Revol (Eds.), *Clinical applications of evoked potentials in neurology* (pp. 287–293). New York: Raven Press.

Layne, S. P., Mayer-Kress, G., & Holfuss, J. (1986). Problems associated with dimensional analysis of electroencephalogram data. In G. Mayer-Kress (Ed.), *Dimensions and entropies in chaotic systems* (pp. 246–256). New York: Springer-Verlag.

Letemendia, F., & Pampiglione, G. (1958). Clinical and electroencephalographic observations in Alzheimer's disease. *Journal of Neurology, Neurosurgery, and Psychiatry, 21*, 167–172.

Leuchter, A. F., Spar, J. E., Walter, D. O., & Weiner, H. (1987). Electroencephalographic spectra and coherence in the diagnosis of Alzheimer's-type and multi-infarct dementia. *Archives of General Psychiatry, 44*, 993–998.

Levy, R. (1975). The neurophysiology of dementia. *British Journal of Psychiatry, 9*, 119–123.

Lewis, D. A., Campbell, M. J., Terry, R. D., & Morrison, J. H. (1987). Laminar and regional distributions of neurofibrillary tangles and neuritic plaques in Alzheimer's disease: A quantitative study of visual and auditory cortices. *Journal of Neuroscience, 7*, 1799–1808.

Libow, L. S., Obrist, W. D., & Sokoloff, L. (1971). Cerebral circulatory and electroencephalographic changes in elderly men. In S. Granick & R. D. Patterson (Eds.), *Human aging II* (pp. 41–41). Rockville, MD: DHEW Publication.

Markand, O. N. (1986). Electroencephalogram in dementia. *American Journal of EEG Technology, 26*, 3–17.

Matejcek, M. (1980). Cortical correlates of vigilance regulation and their use in evaluating effects of treatment. In M. Goldstein (Ed.), *Ergot compounds and brain function: Neuroendocrine and neuropsychiatric aspects* (pp. 339–349). New York, Raven Press.

Mayer-Kress, G., & Layne, S. P. (1987). Dimensionality of the human electroencephalogram. In S. H. Koslow (Ed.), *Perspectives in biological dynamics and theoretical medicine* (pp. 62–87). New York: New York Academy of Sciences.

McAdam, W., & McClatchey, W. T. (1952). The electroencephalogram in aged patients of a mental hospital. *Journal of Mental Sciences, 98*, 711–715.

McAdam, W., & Robinson, R. A. (1957). Senile intellectual deterioration and the electroencephalogram: A quantitative correlation. *Journal of Mental Sciences, 103*, 819–825.

McKhann, G., Drachman, D., Folstein, M., Katzman, R., Price, D., & Stadlan, E. (1984). Clinical diagnosis of Alzheimer's disease. *Neurology, 34*, 939–944.

Merskey, H., Ball, M. J., Blume, W. T., Fox, A. J., Fox, H., Hersch, E. L., Kral, V. A., & Palmer, R. B. (1980). Relationships between psychological measurements and cerebral organic changes in Alzheimer's disease. *Canadian Journal of Neurological Sciences, 7*, 45–49.

Michael, W. F., & Halliday, A. M. (1971). Differences between the occipital distribution of upper and lower field pattern-evoked responses in man. *Brain Research, 32*, 311–324.

Muller, H. F., & Schwartz, G. (1978). Electroencephalograms and autopsy findings in geropsychiatry. *Journal of Geronotology, 33*, 504–513.

Mundy-Castle, A. C., Hurst, L. A., Beerstecher, D. M., & Prinsloo, T. (1954). The electroencephalogram in the senile psychoses. *Electroencephalography and Clinical Neurophysiology, 6*, 245–252.

Nan, X., & Jinghua, X. (1988). The fractal dimension of the EEG as a physical measure of conscious human brain activities. *Bulletin of Mathematical Biology, 50*, 559–565.

Obrist, W. D. (1976). Problems of aging. In A. Remond (Ed.), *Handbook of electroencephalography and clinical neurophysiology* (Vol. 6, Part A, pp. 275–292) Amsterdam: Elsevier.

Obrist, W. D. (1978). Electroencephalography in aging and dementia. Alzheimer's disease: Senile dementia and related disorders. In R. Katzman, R. D. Terry, & K. L. Bick (Eds.), *Aging*, (Vol. 7, pp. 227–231). New York: Raven Press.

Obrist, W. D., Busse, E. W., Eisdorfer, C., & Kleemeier, R. W. (1962). Relation of the electroencephalogram to intellectual function in senescence. *Journal of Gerontology, 17*, 197–206.

Obrist, W. D., Sokoloff, L., Lassen, N. A., Lane, M. H., Butler, R. N., & Feinberg, I. (1963). Relation of EEG to cerebral blood flow and metabolism in old age. *Electroencephalography and Clinical Neurophysiology, 15*, 610–619.

Orwin, A., Wright, C. E., Harding, G. F. A., Rowan, D. C., & Rolfe, E. B. (1986). Serial visual evoked potential recordings in Alzheimer's disease. *British Medical Journal, 293*, 9–10.

Parks, R. W., Zec, R. F., Kuhn, M., Vicari, S., Feldman, E., Coburn, K. L., Ashford, J. W., Crockett, D. J., Moreno, M. A., & Rashid, A. (1991). Electrocortical mapping, MRI, and neuropsychological measures: Evidence of Alzheimer's disease in the presence of vascular lesions. *Archives of Clinical Neuropsychology, 6*, 393–408.

Pentila, M., Partanen, J. V., Soininen, H., & Riekkinen, P. J. (1985). Quantitative analysis of occipital EEG in different stages of Alzheimer's disease. *Electroencephalography and Clinical Neurophysiology, 60*, 1–6.

Pollock, V. E., Schneider, L. S., Chui, H. C., Henderson, V., Zemansky, M., & Sloane, R. B. (1989). Visual evoked potentials in dementia: A meta-analysis and empirical study of Alzheimer's disease patients. *Biological Psychiatry, 25*, 1003–1013.

Politoff, A. L. (1990). EEG background activation in Alzheimer's disease. *Electroencephalography and Clinical Neurophysiology, 76*, 80P.

Primavera, A., Novello, P., Finocchi, C., Canevari, E., & Corsello, L. (1990). Correlation between Min-Mental State Examination and quantitative electroencephalography in senile dementia of the Alzheimer type. *Neuropsychobiology, 23*, 74–78.

Prinz, P. N., & Vitiello, M. V. (1989). Dominant occipital (alpha) rhythm frequency in early stage Alzheimer's disease and depression. *Electroencephalography and Clinical Neurophysiology, 73*, 427–432.

Prinz, P. N., Peskind, E., Vitaliano, P., Raskind, M., Eisdorfer, C., Zemcuznikov, N., &

Gerber, C. (1982). Changes in the sleep and waking EEG in non-demented and demented elderly. *Journal of the American Geriatrics Society*, *30*, 86–93.

Prinz, P., Vitaliano, P., Vitiello, M., Bokan, J., Raskind, M., & Gerber, C. (1982). Sleep EEG and mental function changes in mild, moderate, and severe dementia of the Alzheimer's type. *Neurobiology of Aging*, *3*, 361–370.

Pritchard, W. S., & Duke, D. W. (1992). Dimensional analysis of no-task human EEG using the Grassberger-Procaccia method. *Psychophysiology*, *2*, 182–192.

Pritchard, W. S., & Duke, D. W. (in press). Measuring chaos in the brain: A tutorial review of nonlinear dynamical EEG analysis. *International Journal of Neuroscience*.

Pritchard, W. S., Duke, D. W., & Coburn, K. L. (1991a). Dimensional analysis of topographic EEG: some methodological considerations. In D. W. Duke & W. S. Pritchard (Eds.), *Measuring chaos in the human brain* (pp. 181–198). Singapore: World Scientific.

Pritchard, W. S., Duke, D. W., & Coburn, K. L. (1991b). Altered EEG dynamical responsivity associated with normal aging and Alzheimer's disease. *Dementia*, *2*, 102–105.

Pritchard, W. S., Duke, D. W., Coburn, K. L., & Robinson, J. H. (1992). Nonlinear dynamical EEG analysis applied to nicotine psychopharmacology and Alzheimer's disease. In P. Lippiello, A. Collins, J. Gray, & J. Robinson (Eds.), *The biology of nicotine* (pp. 195–214). New York: Raven Press.

Pritchard, W. S., Duke, D. W., Moore, N. C., Tucker, K. A., & Coburn, K. L. (1992). Altered dynamical responsivity associated with probable Alzheimer's disease: Replication and extension. *EEG/Chaos Newsletter*, *3*(1), 5–6.

Proctor, A. W., Lowe, S. L., Palmer, A. M., Francis, P. T., Esiri, M. M., Stratmann, G. C., Najlerahim, A., Patel, A. J., Hunt, A., & Bowen, D. M. (1988). Topographical distribution of neurochemical changes in Alzheimer's disease. *Journal of Neurological Science*, *84*, 125–140.

Rae-Grant, A. D., Blume, W. T., Lau, K., Fisman, M., Hachinski, V., & Merskey, H. (1986). The EEG in Alzheimer's type dementia: Lack of progression with sequential studies. *Canadian Journal of Neurological Sciences*, *13*, 407–409.

Rae-Grant, D., Blume, W., Lau, C., Hachinski, V. C., Fisman, M., & Merskey, H. (1987). The electroencephalogram in Alzheimer-type dementia. *Archives of Neurology*, *44*, 50–54.

Rapp, P. E., Bashore, T. R., Martinerie, J. M., Albano, A. M., Zimmerman, I. D., & Mees, A. I. (1989). Dynamics of brain electrical activity. *Brain Topography*, *2*, 99–118.

Rapp, P. E., Zimmerman, I. D., Albano, A. M., dee Guzman, G. C., Greenbaum, N. N., & Bashore, T. R. (1985). Experimental studies of chaotic neural behavior: Cellular activity and electroencephalographic signals. In H. G. Othmer (Ed.), *Nonlinear oscillations in chemistry and biology* (pp. 175–197). New York: Springer-Verlag.

Rice, D. M., Buchsbaum, M. S., Starr, A., Auslander, L., Hagman, J., & Evans, W. J. (1990). Abnormal EEG slow activity in left temporal areas in senile dementia of the Alzheimer type. *Journal of Gerontology Medical Sciences*, *45*, M145–M151.

Roberts, M. A., McGeorg, A. P., & Gaird, F. I. (1978). Electroencephalography and computerized tomography in vascular and nonvascular dementia. *Journal of Neurology, Neurosurgery and Psychiatry*, *41*, 903–906.

Saletu, B., Anderer, P., Paulus, E., Grunberger, J., Wicke, L., Neuhold, A., Fischhof, P. K., Litschauer, G., Wagner, G., Hatzinger, R., & Dittrich, R. (1988). EEG brain mapping in SDAT and MID patients before and during placebo and xantinolnicotinate therapy: Reference considerations. In D. Samson-Dollfus, J. D. Guieu, J. Gotman, & P. Etevenon (Eds.), *Statistics and topography in quantitative EEG* (pp. 251–275). New York: Elsevier.

Shearer, D. E., Emmerson, R. Y., & Dustman, R. E. (1989). EEG relationships to neural aging in the elderly: Overview and bibliography. *American Journal of EEG Technology, 29*, 43–63.

Sheridan, P. H., Sato, S., Foster, N., Bruno, G., Cox, C., Fedio, P., & Chase, T. N. (1988). Relation of EEG alpha background to parietal lobe function in Alzheimer's disease as measured by positron emission tomography and psychometry. *Neurology, 38*, 747–750.

Sim, M. (1979). Early diagnosis of Alzheimer's disease. In A. I. M. Glen & L. J. Whalley (Eds.), *Alzheimer's disease* (pp. 78–85). London: Churchill Livingstone.

Small, G. W., Kuhl, D. E., Riege, W. H., Fujikawa, D. G., Ashford, J. W., Metter, J., & Mazziota, J. C. (1989). Cerebral glucose metabolic patterns in Alzheimer's disease. *Archives of General Psychiatry, 46*, 527–532.

Soininen, H., Partanen, V. J., Helkala, E.-L., & Riekkinen, P. J. (1982). EEG findings in senile dementia and normal aging. *Acta Neurologica Scandinavica, 65*, 59–70.

Stigsby, B. (1988). Dementias (Alzheimer's and Pick's disease): Dysfunctional and structural changes. *American Journal of EEG Technology, 28*, 83–97.

Stigsby, B., Johannesson, G., & Ingvar, D. H. (1981). Regional EEG analysis and regional cerebral blood flow in Alzheimer's and Pick's disease. *Electroencephalography and Clinical Neurophysiology, 51*, 537–547.

Straumanis, J. J., Shagass, C., & Schwartz, M. (1965). Visually evoked cerebral response changes associated with chronic brain syndromes and aging. *Journal of Gerontology, 20*, 498–506.

Swain, J. M. (1959). Electroencephalographic abnormalities in presenile atrophy. *Neurology (Minneapolis), 9*, 722–727.

Thompson, L. W. (1976). Cerebral blood flow, EEG, and behavior in aging. In R. D. Terry & S. Gershon (Eds.), *Neurobiology of aging* (pp. 103–119). New York: Raven Press.

Torres, F., Faoro, A., Loewenson, R., & Johnson, E. (1983). The electroencephalogram of elderly subjects revisited. *Electroencephalography and Clinical Neurophysiology, 56*, 391–398.

Vaughn, H. G. (1966). The perceptual and physiologic significance of visual evoked responses recorded from the scalp in man. In H. M. Burian & J. H. Jocabson (Eds.), *Clinical electroretinography* (pp. 203–223). Oxford: Pergamon Press.

Verma, N. P., Greiffenstein, M. F., Verma, N., King, S. D., & Caldwell, D. L. (1987). Electrophysiologic validation of two categories of dementias—cortical and subcortical. *Clinical Electroencephalography, 18*(1), 26–33.

Visser, S. L., Stam, F. C., Van Tilburg, W., Op Den Velde, W., Blom, J. L., & De Rijke, W. (1976). Visual evoked response in senile and presenile dementia. *Electroencephalography and Clinical Neurophysiology, 40*, 385–392.

Visser, S. L., Van Tilburg, W., Hooijer, C., Jonker, C., & De Rijke, W. (1985). Visual evoked potentials (VEP's) in senile dementia (Alzheimer type) and in non-organic behavioural disorders in the elderly: Comparison with EEG parameters. *Electroencephalography and Clinical Neurophysiology, 60*, 115–121.

Wang, H. S., & Busse, E. W. (1969). EEG of healthy old persons—a longitudinal study. I. Dominant background activity and occipital rhythm. *Journal of Gerontology, 24*, 419–426.

Watt, R. C., & Hameroff, S. R. (1987). Phase space analysis of human EEG during general anesthesia. In S. H. Koslow (Ed.), *Perspectives in biological dynamics and theoretical medicine* (pp. 286–288). New York: New York Academy of Sciences.

Whitehouse, P. J., Martino, A. M., Antuono, P. G., Lowenstein, P. R., Coyle, J. T., Price, D. L., & Keller, K. J. (1986). Nicotinic acetylcholine binding sites in Alzheimer's disease. *Brain Research, 371*, 146–151.

Whittaker, S. G., & Siegfried, J. B. (1983). Origin of wavelets in the visual evoked potential. *Electroencephalography and Clinical Neurophysiology, 55*, 91–101.

Williamson, P. C., Merskey, H., Morrison, S., Rabheru, K., Fox, H., Wands, K., Wong, C., & Hachinski, V. (1990). Quantitative electroencephalographic correlates of cognitive decline in normal elderly subjects. *Archives of Neurology, 47*(11), 1185–1188.

Wright, C. E., Harding, G. F. A., & Orwin, A. (1984). Presenile dementia—the use of the flash and pattern VEP in diagnosis. *Electroencephalography and Clinical Neurophysiology, 57*, 405–415.

Wright, C. E., Harding, G. F. A., & Orwin, A. (1986). The flash and pattern VEP as a diagnostic indicator of dementia. *Documenta Ophthalmologica, 62*, 89–96.

Zec, R. F. (1990). Neuropsychology: Normal aging vs. early AD. In R. E. Becker & E. Giacobini (Eds.), *Alzheimer disease: Current research and early diagnosis* (pp. 105–117). New York: Taylor & Francis.

19

Computed Tomography and Magnetic Resonance Imaging

DALE A. CHARLETTA, DAVID A. BENNETT,
AND ROBERT S. WILSON

The ability of computed tomography and magnetic resonance imaging (MRI) scanners to noninvasively image the brain has directly influenced the clinical management of patients with several adult-onset dementing illnesses. Morphological imaging may demonstrate potentially treatable causes of dementia in a significant portion of persons referred to tertiary care clinics for evaluation of cognitive impairment (Bennett & Evans, 1992). Therefore, most authorities recommend neuroimaging as part of the routine diagnostic evaluation for dementia (Katzman, 1990). In this chapter, a brief introduction to the basic concepts underlying computed tomography (CT) and MRI will precede a more detailed discussion of the diagnostic utility of these procedures in specific dementing diseases.

Computed Tomography

Computed tomography involves the serial X-ray irradiation of an axial slice of tissue from multiple angles. Photons are absorbed as a function of the average electron density of tissue within a voxel (volume element). As the flux of photons exits the tissue at various angles, they are recorded by an arc of detectors that relay the information to a digital computer for image reconstruction. The CT image is thus roughly equivalent to a plain radiograph of a slab of tissue. Two major factors limit the utility of CT in the evaluation of dementia patients, however. Foremost is a physical limitation of CT scanning, termed *Hounsfield artifact*, which refers to a hardening of the X-ray beam by the calvarium (decreasing the average photon wavelength). The result is an artifactual increase in the density of the adjacent brain parenchyma and streak-like artifacts that obscure the anatomy of the posterior and middle fossae and the cerebral convexities. These artifacts limit the use of CT for morphometry of temporal lobe structures and cortical sulci, important areas in the evaluation of patients with dementia.

A second limitation of CT is the relative lack of contrast between cerebral gray and white matter. Although pathological processes that markedly alter the radiopacity of brain parenchyma such as infarct, abscess, tumor, and edema are readily detected by CT, more subtle pathology, such as myelin pallor and low-grade gliomas, is not as easily demonstrated.

On the other hand, CT can accurately discriminate between the different densities of the brain and cerebrospinal fluid (CSF), thereby providing an effective means of assessing ventricular volume. In addition, modern scanners require less than 1 second to acquire the data for each slice. Although patient motion during scan acquisition causes artifacts, which degrade image quality, this difficulty can often be overcome by having individual CT slices repeated by the technologist.

Magnetic Resonance Imaging

After CT, neuroimaging experienced a quantum leap forward when MRI scanners became commercially available. Unlike CT, which relies on ionizing radiation, MRI scanners image the human body by using advanced mathematics to calculate the signal intensity of radiofrequency waveforms emitted by paramagnetic nuclear dipoles placed in superconducting magnets. These waveforms are related to inherent spin-lattice (T1) and spin-spin (T2) relaxation times in each voxel of tissue, and are localized in space to produce an image. Magnetic resonance imaging is unaffected by many of the artifacts that plague CT images. For example, the absence of beam-hardening artifact permits the accurate portrayal of brain anatomy in the posterior fossa and middle cranial fossae and in the cerebral cortex adjacent to the calvarium.

Another advantage of MRI over CT is its sensitivity to differences in tissue composition, which is one to two orders of magnitude greater than CT. Brain gray and white matter are easily distinguished on the basis of differing myelin and water content. The water content of normal gray and white matter is 82% and 70%, respectively (Brant-Zawadzki, 1988). Pathological processes that alter the normal water or myelin content of tissue result in striking changes in MRI signal intensity. Processes that increase the water content of brain parenchyma (i.e., encephalomalacia, vasogenic edema from neoplasm or inflammation, cytotoxic edema from infarction, dilatation of perivascular CSF [Virchow-Robin] spaces) or alter the myelin content and/or structure of white matter (i.e., demyelination, dysmyelination) are, therefore, better demonstrated by MRI than CT (Bradley, Waluch, Brant-Zawadzki, Yadley, & Wycoff, 1984). An increase in interstitial water is manifested by increased signal intensity on T2-weighted (long TR, long TE) images (Brant-Zawadzki, 1988). Unfortunately, MRI images currently take longer to acquire than comparable CT slices, on the order of 3 minutes longer for a series of T1-weighted and 8 minutes longer for T2-weighted spin-echo scans. The patient must remain motionless in a confined space for the duration of the scan. This severely limits the utility of MRI scanning in unsedated patients with advanced dementia. Unlike CT, MRI slices cannot be viewed during acquisition. The recent development of echo-planar scanning techniques promises slice acquisition times on the order of 20 to 50 ms, which is much faster than most current CT scanners. These techniques require costly hardware and software upgrades, however, and will not be available on all scanners.

Alzheimer's Disease

Macroscopically, several atrophic changes can be discerned in the brains of persons dying with Alzheimer's disease (AD) (Figure 19.1 A, B) relative to the nondemented elderly (Creasey & Rapoport, 1985). Brain weight is reduced approximately 100 g from the third to eighth decade for both males and females (Dekaban & Sadowsky, 1978). There is a further reduction in brain weight of about 100 g in persons with AD (Terry, Peck, DeTeresa, Schechter, & Horoupian, 1981). Morphologically, this reduction in brain weight is reflected in gyral atrophy and ventricular dilatation. Pathological studies have demonstrated increased third, lateral, and total (Hubbard & Anderson, 1981) ventricular volume with advancing age.

Because both agonal state and postmortem fixation can alter brain volume, gyral atrophy and ventricular dilatation may be more reliably estimated from antemortem CT or MRI (Earnest, Heaton, Wilkinson, & Manke, 1979; Gyldensted, 1977; Huckman, Fox, & Topel, 1975; Hughes & Gado, 1981; Ito, Hatazawa, Yamaura, & Matsuzawa, 1981; Jernigan, Press, & Hesselink, 1990; Laffey, Peyster, Nathan, Haskin, & McGinley, 1984; LeMay, 1984; Wippold, Gado, Morris, Duchek, & Grant, 1991). Efforts to find a morphometric correlate to a diagnosis of AD have concentrated primarily on the interfaces between brain and CSF: gyral atrophy, ventricular dilatation, and selective atrophy (Sandor et al., 1992). More recently, white matter changes have come under increasing scrutiny (Shah et al., 1991; Coffey et al., 1992).

Gyral Atrophy

Cross-sectional studies suggest that gyral atrophy begins at age 40 and increases thereafter (Gyldensted, 1977; Huckman et al., 1975; Coffey et al., 1992). The degree of gyral atrophy is not, however, diagnostic of AD (Wilson, Fox, Huckman, Bacon, & Lobick, 1982). Quantitating sulcal size with CT (the initial work in this area preceded the advent of MRI) is technically difficult. Because most sulci are located immediately adjacent to the calvarium, image quality is degraded due to beam-hardening artifact. In addition, the small size of the cortical sulci makes them vulnerable to partial volume effects. For example, if a sulcus occupies only a portion of a voxel's volume, the overall radiopacity of the voxel will represent a weighted average of the radiopacities and volumes of the various structures that comprise the voxel. The voxel's total attenuation may thus be closer to that of brain parenchyma or calvarium than to CSF, causing the voxel to be excluded from the collection of voxels assigned to the sulci. Some studies have attempted to compensate for partial volume effects by calculating weighted volumes for voxels that have attenuation values intermediate between CSF and brain parenchyma. These technical difficulties have impeded precise quantification of sulcal volume. In fact, semiquantitative evaluations by experienced neuroradiologists appear to be as accurate as morphometry for the evaluation of sulcal volume (Coffey et al., 1992; LeMay et al., 1986).

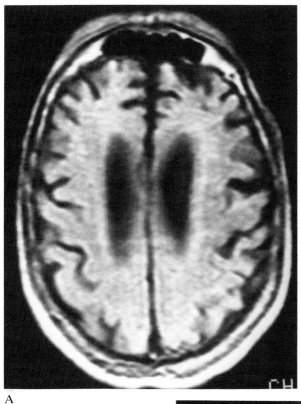

A

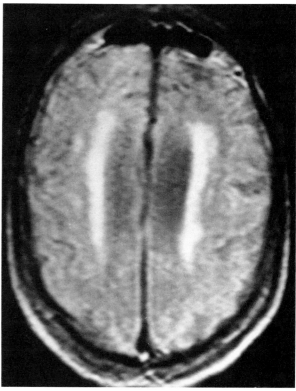

FIGURE 19.1. A 73-year-old
male with pathology-proven
Alzheimer's disease. (*A*)
Axial T1-weighted (TR, 1000;
TE, 30) spin-echo scan
demonstrates prominence of
cortical sulci and lateral
ventricles. (*B*) Matching
proton-density weighted (TR,
1900; TE, 50) scan shows a
thick periventricular band of
high signal intensity. A few
foci exhibiting similar signal
are present in the subcortical
white matter.

B

Ventricular Size

The lateral ventricles, therefore, have been found to be more amenable to morphometric analyses. Initially, linear measurements of ventricular width were compiled (Albert, Naeser, Levine, & Garvey, 1984; Brinkman, Sarwar, Levin, & Morris, 1981; deLeon et al., 1980; Drayer, Heyman, Wilkinson, Barrett, & Weinberg, 1985; Gomori, Steiner, Melamed, & Cooper, 1984; Gyldensted, 1977; Huckman et al., 1975; Hughes & Gado, 1981). These were later accompanied by linear measurements of calvarial size to compensate for variations in cranial vault capacity (deLeon et al., 1989; Ford & Winter, 1981; Wilson et al., 1982). Ventricular dilatation is consistently seen in cross-sectional studies of normal aging (Gyldensted, 1977; Huckman et al., 1975; Coffey et al., 1992). Although ventricular size is increased in AD relative to age-matched normal controls, this is not a reliable diagnostic sign (Damasio et al., 1983; deLeon et al., 1980; Drayer et al., 1985; Eslinger, Damasio, Graff-Radford, & Damasio, 1984; Fox, Topel, & Huckman, 1975; Gado et al., 1982; Huckman et al., 1975; Soininen, Partanen, Puranen, & Reikkinen, 1982; Wilson et al., 1982). Patterns of ventricular dilatation such as selective dilatation of the third ventricle or temporal horns of the lateral ventricles have been suggested to be more specific for AD (Kido et al., 1989). There appears to be a weak correlation between linear planimetric measures of ventricular width and dementia severity, but this association is often not observed if the range of dementia severity is restricted by eliminating normal controls from the sample (deLeon et al., 1980; Drayer et al., 1985; Kaszniak, Garron, Fox, Bergen, & Huckman, 1979; Pearlson & Tune, 1986; Wilson et al., 1982).

Ventricular Volume

As more sophisticated image processing hardware and software became available, efforts shifted to direct measurement of ventricular volume (Penn, Belanger, & Yasnoff, 1978). This technique typically involves "tracing" the ventricular contour on each brain image by using a light pen, trackball, digitizing tablet, or density-contour-following software (Damasio et al., 1983; Kaye, DeCarli, Luxenberg, & Rapoport, 1992; Ito et al., 1981; Yerby, Sundsten, Larson, Wu, & Sumi, 1985; Schwartz et al., 1985). The ventricular area for each slice is multiplied by the known slice thickness to yield the ventricular volume for the slice. Total ventricular volume is then determined by simply adding the volumetric measurements of each slice. The parenchymal volume can be calculated in a similar fashion (deLeon et al., 1989; Wippold et al., 1991). More recently, semiautomated computerized methods of morphometric analysis have been developed using three-dimensional reconstructions (Damasio & Frank, 1992; Filipek et al., 1989). Despite these technical advances, ventricular volume has only a slightly more robust correlation with dementia severity than linear or planimetric measures (Bigler, Hubler, Cullum, & Turkheimer, 1985; Gado et al., 1982; Naugle, Cullum, Bigler, & Massman, 1985).

Hippocampal Imaging

More sophisticated techniques of volume quantification have recently been applied to MRI images. In addition to correlating AD with ventricular area and volume, correlations have also been demonstrated with selective atrophy of key structures that are consistently involved in the pathology of AD (Coffey et al., 1992). Efforts have been aimed at quantitating selective atrophy of the hippocampi in AD (Jack, Petersen, O'Brien, & Tangalos, 1992; Kesslak, Nalcioglu, & Cotman, 1991; Press, Amaral, & Squire, 1989; Seab et al., 1988; Van Hoesen, Hyman, & Damasio, 1991). The hippocampi are located in the mesial temporal lobe adjacent to the anterior horn of the lateral ventricle. They are almost invariably involved in the pathology of AD (Ball, 1977), and can easily be visualized with MRI images obtained in the coronal plane (Kesslak et al., 1991; Squire, Amaral, & Press, 1990). Computed tomography is inadequate for visualization of the hippocampi because it is prone to artifact in the floor of the middle cranial fossa where the hippocampus resides (Jack et al., 1988; Jack et al., 1992; Naaidich et al., 1987). Although hippocampal imaging has already proven useful in evaluating amnesic patients (deToledo-Morrell, Morrell, Charletta, McNally, & Ristanovic, 1991), there has been insufficient research to date to evaluate its diagnostic utility in AD and other dementia syndromes.

Longitudinal Studies

The overlap between ventricular size in normals and those with AD limits the diagnostic utility of a single brain scan. The rate of ventricular dilatation as determined by serial scans, however, may correlate better with progressive cognitive dysfunction (Brinkman & Largen, 1984; DeCarli, Kaye, Horwitz, & Rapoport, 1990; Gado, Danziger, Chi, Hughes, & Coben, 1983; Luxenberg, Haxby, Creasey, Sundaram, & Rapoport, 1987). Longitudinal CT data with concomitant neuropsychological testing suggests that the progression of atrophic changes may be diagnostic of dementia (Bird, Levy, & Jacoby, 1986; deLeon et al., 1989). In these cases, however, neuropsychological test performance appears to be a more reliable indicator of dementia. Nonetheless, for research purposes, longitudinal scans may provide insight into the pathoanatomic progression of AD (Bird et al., 1986; deLeon et al., 1989; Brinkman & Largen, 1984; Wippold et al., 1991).

White Matter Changes

Postmortem studies suggest that in both healthy elderly and persons with AD, ventricular dilatation results primarily from atrophy of subcortical white matter (de la Monte, 1989; Henderson, Tomlinson, & Gibson, 1980; Miller, Alston, & Corsellis, 1980; Terry et al., 1981) with little to no change in the cortical width. These macroscopic atrophic changes can be grossly visualized with neuroimaging. Early studies using CT reported global decreases in the average brain radiodensity of the subcortical white matter (Hounsfield units) (Naeser, Gebhardt, & Levine, 1980) or loss of gray-white matter discriminability (George, deLeon, Ferris, & Kricheff, 1981). Later studies, however, have failed to replicate these findings (Gado et al., 1983; Wilson et al., 1982).

More recently, white matter lesions on MRI and leuko-araiosis on brain CT (Hachinski, Potter, & Merskey, 1987) have attracted considerable attention. Some investigators have suggested that the white matter lesions may be related to AD (Brun & Englund, 1986). They are a common finding in the elderly, however

(Drayer, 1988; Leys et al., 1990; Zimmerman, Fleming, Lee, Saint-Louis, & Deck, 1986). Despite numerous investigations over the past several years, the etiology and significance of white matter lesions remain controversial (see below).

Several studies have attempted to correlate the extent of white matter lesions with the severity of cognitive dysfunction, with mixed results (Aharon-Peretz, Cummings, & Hill, 1988; Bennett, Gilley, Wilson, Fox, & Huckman, 1992; Harrell et al., 1991; Johnson et al., 1987; Kertesz, Polk, & Carr, 1990; Mirsen et al., 1991; Rao et al., 1989; Steingart et al., 1987; Zubenko et al., 1990). Although controversial (Hunt et al., 1989), it appears that white matter may contribute to cognitive dysfunction in healthy elderly persons (Austrom et al., 1990; Boone, Miller, Lesser, et al., 1992; Steingart et al., 1987), these data suggest that the contribution of white matter lesions to cognitive dysfunction in persons with AD is relatively small (Bennett, Gilley, et al., 1992). The true significance of white matter lesions is uncertain, however, and pathological studies suggest that they can signify a range of phenomenon (see below).

Vascular Dementia

The area of vascular dementia includes all dementia syndromes resulting from ischemic, anoxic or hypoxic brain damage (Hachinski, 1990; Loeb, 1990). It includes, therefore, a quite heterogeneous group of conditions. Early research efforts concentrated on defining the arteriosclerotic dementias. More recently, however, researchers have stressed the heterogeneity within the vascular dementias and the need to develop differential pathological and clinical diagnostic criteria for each (see chapter 14) (Bennett, Wilson, Gilley, & Fox, 1990; Chui et al., 1992; Tatemichi, 1990). For conceptual purposes, this chapter will address two types of vascular dementia: (a) the classic cortical arteriosclerotic vascular dementia often termed *multi-infarct dementia* (MID) and (b) the prototype subcortical vascular dementia, Binswanger's disease.

Multi-Infarct Dementia

The concept of MID suggests that one type of vascular dementia is due to the combined effects of multiple, discrete cerebral infarctions (Hachinski, Lassen, & Marshall, 1974). Computed tomography and MRI scans in these persons should demonstrate, by definition, at least two lesions. An early clinicopathological study of arteriosclerotic dementia suggested that at least 50 ml, and perhaps 100 ml, of infarcted tissue was necessary to account for a vascular dementia (Tomlinson, Blessed, & Roth, 1968, 1970). Although some quantitative studies suggest that in persons with vascular disease, dementia is associated with a greater volume of white matter lesions (Liu et al., 1992), volume of infarction, however, has never been required for the diagnosis of vascular dementia (Erkinjuntti & Sulkava, 1991). More recent studies, in fact, have emphasized the importance of the location of vascular lesions in determining whether a dementia is of vascular origin. For example, some evidence suggests that bilateral strokes (Ladurner, Iliff, & Lechner, 1982), left-hemisphere strokes (Liu et al., 1992), or thalamic involvement (Loeb,

1990) may be crucial to the development of a dementia syndrome. Unfortunately, specific radiological criteria for the diagnosis of MID do not yet exist.

Binswanger's Disease

Binswanger's disease is a relatively rare dementing illness thought to result from the cumulative effects of multiple subcortical complete and incomplete infarctions and "ischemic demyelination" (Babikian & Ropper, 1987; Bennett et al., 1990; Caplan & Schoene, 1978; Roman, 1987). These white matter lesions are easily visualized on both CT and MRI, although the latter is more sensitive (Johnson et al., 1987; Kinkel, Jacobs, Polachini, Bates, & Heffner, 1985). Figure 19.2 shows an example of these radiological abnormalities as visualized on MRI. Although these white matter lesions were initially thought to be diagnostic of Binswanger's disease, they have been variously associated with age, vascular risk factors, functional impairment, cognitive dysfunction, and AD (Awad, Spetzler, Hodak, Awad, & Carey, 1986; Inzitari et al., 1987; Kertesz et al., 1988; Leys et al., 1991; Masdeu et al., 1989; van Swieten et al., 1991). Furthermore, radiological-pathological studies demonstrate that several pathological entities, including infarction, incomplete infarction, demyelination, gliosis, and dilated perivascular spaces, may all have a similar radiological appearance (Awad, Johnson, Spetzler, & Hodak, 1986; Ball, 1989; Braffman et al., 1988a, 1988b; Brun & Englund, 1986; Grafton et al., 1991; Hwier et al., 1989; Jungreis, Kanal, Hirsch, Martinez, Moossy, 1988).

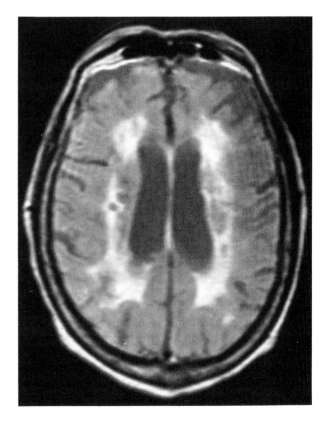

FIGURE 19.2. This spin-density weighted spin-echo magnetic resonance (MR) scan (TR, 2200; TE, 50) of an 80-year-old female with dementia reveals high-signal-intensity changes involving the periventricular white matter consistent with ischemic demyelination associated with Binswanger's disease.

The increased sensitivity of MRI to white matter changes (Ajax et al., 1986; Bradley et al., 1984; Brown, Hesselink, & Rothrock, 1988; Erkinjuntti et al., 1989; Hachinski et al., 1987) relative to CT comes at the expense of decreased specificity. Many white matter lesions visualized on MRI cannot be located at later postmortem examination. In fact, recent radiological-pathological studies demonstrate that many demented persons with white matter lesions have AD at autopsy (Bennett, Charletta, Gilley, Cochran, & Hayes, 1991; Janota, Mirsen, Hachinski, Lee, & Merskey, 1989). Radiological-pathological studies suggest that most dilated perivascular spaces are less than 2 × 2 mm (Braffman, Grossman, et al., 1988). It is important to realize, therefore, that simply demonstrating an "abnormal" brain scan does not demonstrate that a dementia is of vascular origin (Janota et al., 1989). Many persons with AD will have CT and MRI scans indistinguishable from persons with vascular dementia (Bennett, Gilley, et al., 1992; Janota et al., 1989; Leys et al., 1991). Recently developed diagnostic criteria for Binswanger's disease have incorporated these observations (Bennett et al., 1990; Chui et al., 1992).

Pick's Disease

Pick's disease is a degenerative dementia of unknown etiology. Clinically similar cases called lobar dementia or dementia of the frontal lobe type (see Chapter 8) may or may not have the same etiology. Selective atrophy of the frontal and parietal lobes is characteristic of Pick's disease. The disease has been suggested by CT or MRI scans that demonstrate dilatation of the sylvian fissures and the frontal horns of the lateral ventricles and marked gyral atrophy predominantly involving the frontal and temporal lobes (Cummings & Duchen, 1981; Wechsler, Verity, Rosenchein, Fried, & Scheibel, 1982; McGreachie, Flemming, Sharer, & Hyman, 1979). Figure 19.3 shows MR images from a pathologically verified case of Pick's disease.

Huntington's Disease

Huntington's disease is an autosomal dominant neurodegenerative dementing disease with complete penetrance. On gross pathological examination of the brain there is obvious atrophy of the caudate nucleus, in addition to generalized cerebral atrophy. The CT and MRI scans reveal dilatation of the frontal horns of the lateral ventricles and marked atrophy of the caudate nuclei (Terrence, Delaney, & Alberts, 1977), in addition to the less specific finding of cerebral atrophy.

Creutzfeldt-Jakob Disease

There are at least three human spongiform encephalopathies: Creutzfeldt-Jakob disease (CJD), Gerstmann-Straussler-Scheinker disease (GSS), and kuru. There is no classic CT or MRI appearance corresponding to a diagnosis of Creutzfeldt-Jakob disease. Many patients have generalized atrophy (Galves & Cartier, 1984; Kavanen et al., 1985), which may be accompanied by either increased (Gertz,

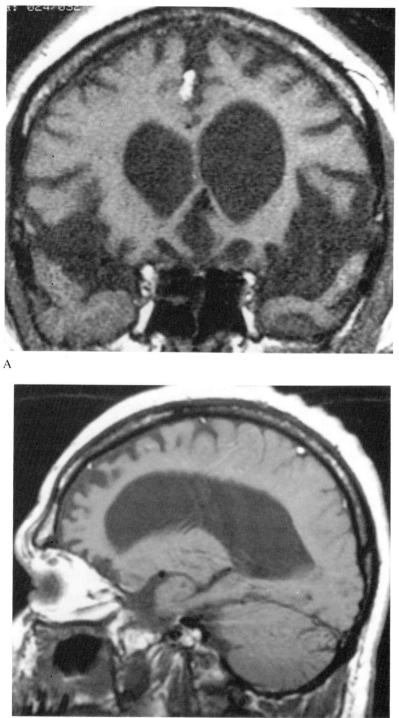

A

B

FIGURE 19.3. This 65-year-old male had progressive dementia secondary to pathology-proven Pick's disease. (A) Coronal T1-weighted (TR, 400; TE, 17) spin-echo image demonstrates severe dilation of ventricles, interhemispheric fissure, sylvian fissures, and cortical sulci. (B) Parasagittal T1-weighted (TR, 600; TE, 19) image through the left lateral ventricle reveals that the cortical atrophy selectively involves the frontal and temporal lobes to a greater extent than the parietal or occipital lobes.

Henks, & Cervos-Navarro, 1988; Milton, Atlas, Lavi, & Mollman, 1991) or decreased (Farlow et al., 1989) signal intensities in the basal ganglia. In some cases, serial scans have demonstrated progressive cortical sulcal and ventricular enlargement over several months (Rao, Brennan, & Garcia, 1977), a pattern distinctly unusual for AD.

Parkinson's Disease

The prevalence of dementia accompanying Parkinson's disease (PD) is estimated at about 10% (Mayeux et al., 1988), with an estimated overall incidence rate of nearly 70 per 1000 person-years (Mayeux et al., 1990). In many, but not all cases, this is due to the coexistence of PD with AD (Bennett, Stebbins, et al., in press). In general, persons with PD who become demented are elderly.

Ventricle size in demented persons with PD is increased relative to age-matched nondemented persons with PD (Sroka, Elizan, Yahr, Burger, & Mendoza, 1981). Unfortunately, there was no AD control group. It is unclear whether persons with PD without dementia have more atrophy than age-matched controls (Adam et al., 1983; Huber, Paulson, Shuttleworth, & Chakeres, 1988; Steiner, Gomori, & Melamed, 1985). Characteristic changes on high field-strength MRI have also been reported in PD (Braffman, Grossman, et al., 1988). Low signal changes occur in the putamen and caudate nuclei and the substantia nigra on T2-weighted images, reflecting the paramagnetic properties of the increased iron concentration in these locations (Drayer et al., 1986). Another finding is "smudging" of the pars reticulata of the substantia nigra on T2-weighted images, which may also represent excessive iron deposition. Newer "low flip-angle" or "gradient recall" pulse sequences are particularly susceptible to magnetic field inhomogeneity caused by iron (Braffman, Grossman, et al., 1988). High field-strength magnets also accentuate the effects of iron (Drayer, Burger, et al., 1986). Finally, there have been several reports of selective atrophy of the pars compacta of the substantia nigra detected with MRI (Duguid, De La Paz, & DeGroot, 1986; Doraiswamy et al., 1991; Huber, Chakeres, Paulson, & Khanna, 1990). Unfortunately, these findings are not specific enough for a diagnostic test for PD, and they do not correlate with either dementia severity or motoric dysfunction. Progressive supranuclear palsy (PSP), a variant of PD, is characterized by midbrain, pontine, and cerebellar atrophy (Ambrosetto, Michelucci, Forti, & Tassinari, 1984; Haldeman, Goldman, Hyde, & Pribram, 1981; Geremia & Huckman, 1990).

Mass Lesions

Intracranial mass lesions are uncommon, potentially treatable causes of dementia. Neoplastic, hemorrhagic, and infectious processes may produce mass lesions of sufficient size to cause dementia. Primary brain tumors affecting the elderly population include meningioma, glioma, and primary central nervous system (CNS) lymphoma. Slower growing meningiomas and low-grade astrocytomas produce a slower onset of clinical symptoms that may stimulate other forms of dementia such as AD. Meningiomas have a characteristic extra-axial location, although a small

percentage have an ependymal origin. They are usually uniformly dense on preinfusion CT scans, due to the presence of psammomatous calcifications. They enhance uniformly and intensely after contrast administration. On MRI scans, meningiomas may be isointense to normal brain on preinfusion T1 and T2-weighted sequences. Associated edema, when present, produces a region of high signal intensity on T2-weighted images.

Gliomas

Cerebral gliomas have a varied appearance depending on histology and grade. Low-grade astrocytomas are usually low-attenuation on preinfusion CT, exhibit no enhancement (although the pilocytic variety may contain an enhancing mural nodule), and produce little surrounding low-attenuation edema. They may contain dense foci of calcification. Low-grade astrocytomas are typically low-signal on T1-weighted images (T1WI), and high signal on T2-weighted image (T2WI). High-grade astrocytomas (glioblastoma multiforme) are usually low-attenuation on CT scans relative to normal white matter, and low-T1/high-T2 signal intensity MRI scans. They tend to spread along white matter fiber tracts, including the commisural and projectional tracts (which do not permit the spread of edema). Many exhibit contrast enhancement, which characteristically has an undulating "garland" shape.

Oligodendrogliomas

Oligodendrogliomas are particularly prone to calcify (up to 90%) (Vonofakos, Marcu, & Hacker, 1979), often in a dense "popcorn" pattern.

CNS Lymphoma

Primary CNS lymphoma is usually hyperdense on CT scans relative to normal gray matter. There is usually no central necrosis. On MRI scans, primary CNS lymphoma is usually hypointense on T1-weighted images and hyperintense on T2-weighted scans. There may or may not be associated contrast enhancement on CT and MRI. These lesions have a predilection for the deep midline parenchyma, periventricular white matter, and corpus callosum. They are multiple in 50% of cases (Pagani, Libshitz, Wallace, & Hayman, 1981).

Secondary CNS lymphoma usually spreads along the leptomeninges. It is difficult to image by CT due to the relative insensitivity of CT for displaying structures adjacent to the inner table of the calvarium. Contrast-enhanced MRI usually reveals intense meningeal enhancement.

Metastatic Tumor

Metastatic tumors in brain parenchyma usually arise from lung and breast primary tumors, with colon, melanocyte, and thyroid primaries less common. Unlike primary brain tumors, metastases are typically multiple, well defined, spherically shaped, and originate near the gray-white matter junction. Large metastases usually necrose centrally.

Most metastases, high-grade gliomas, and large meningiomas are accompanied

by a "vasogenic" pattern of white matter edema that typically spreads along associative white matter fiber tracts, limited by subcortical U fibers, commisural and projectional fiber tracts. Edema is easily detected on CT scans as a region of low attenuation, and on MRI scans as an area of high signal intensity on T2WI. The edema arises from breakdown of the blood-brain barrier. This phenomenon also permits contrast material to egress from the intravascular space to interstitial space, causing enhancement. An alternative mechanism of enhancement is the inherent high vascularity of the neoplasm itself. CT and MRI are thus very sensitive for detection of neoplastic processes that may cause dementia, with gadolinium-DTPA-enhanced MRI scans being more sensitive by virtue of the ability of MRI to image the cerebral convexities and posterior fossa. This is particularly useful for demonstrating meningeal carcinomatosis as shown in Figure 19.4. Overall, gadolinium-DTPA-enhanced MRI is the procedure of choice for detection of brain neoplasm (Breger et al., 1987; Russell et al., 1987; Stack, Antoun, Jenkins, Metcalfe, & Isherwood, 1988).

Trauma

Trauma can lead to dementia via several mechanisms detectable by neuroimaging scans. Hematomas occurring in the brain parenchyma, epidural, or subdural spaces

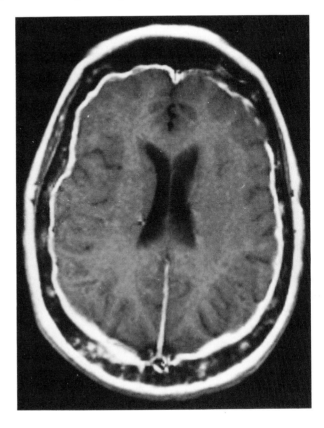

FIGURE 19.4. Progressive adult-onset dementia in this 64-year-old female with breast carcinoma was proven by this gadolinium-DTPA-enhanced T1-weighted (TR, 550; TE, 20) spin-echo scan to be caused by meningeal carcinomatosis, most likely a direct extension from multiple calvarial metastases.

may attain enough mass to impair cognition. Axonal shearing injuries can cause profound neurological deficits despite often minimal foci of high signal on T2WI.

Subarachnoid Hemorrhage

Subarachnoid hemorrhage may result in hydrocephalus (and thus dementia) by interfering with CSF absorption by arachnoid granulations. Subarachnoid blood is best detected by CT, where it becomes manifest by increased density of the cisterns, ventricles, and/or cortical sulci. These structures normally are less radiopaque than brain parenchyma. When blood is mixed with the CSF, the opacity of CSF increases, becoming isodense or hyperdense relative to normal brain parenchyma. The diagnosis of hydrocephalus requires imaging of the ventricular system (see below), which can be accomplished by CT or MRI.

Subdural Hematoma

Chronic subdural hematomas may have a slowly progressive clinical picture of dementia, unlike intracerebral and epidural hemorrhages, which tend to have a more acute onset. Acutely, subdural hematomas are usually crescent shaped, convex outward, and concave inward. They are usually located adjacent to the inner table of calvarium, but may lie adjacent to the falx or tentorium. They are usually surrounded by a collagenous capsule that contains friable neovascularity. As the hemoglobin molecules are broken down by proteolytic enzymes, water is drawn in across the osmotic gradient. This process expands the hematoma and causes traction on the capsule, which is prone to bleeding, completing a vicious cycle. Chronic subdural hematomas may be biconvex, therefore, due to this osmotic expansion. Computed tomographic scans often reveal the extracerebral collections with enhancing peripheral membranes. The density of any hematoma decreases over time, from an initial value higher than normal gray matter, to an "isodense" phase during which they may be difficult to detect, and finally to a "hypodense" phase. Figure 19.5 shows an example of chronic subdural hematoma seen on CT. Small subdural and epidural hematomas may be difficult to detect by CT due to beam-hardening artifact, which limits resolution of the cerebral convexities, as described above. Magnetic resonance imaging is especially sensitive for detection of subacute subdural, epidural, and intracerebral collections of blood (Zimmerman et al., 1986). Not only is MRI better for evaluation of the convexities in general, but methemoglobin (a product of hemoglobin catabolism) is paramagnetic (Ebisu, Narues, Horikawa, Tanaka, & Higuchi, 1989; Gomori, Grossman, & Goldberg, 1985) and, therefore, acts as a natural contrast material. As methemoglobin is further catabolized to hemosiderin, the MRI signal intensity decreases to a level below that of normal brain parenchyma and thus appears black on T1WI and even more so on T2WI images.

Shearing

Traumatic axonal shearing, or diffuse axonal injury (DAI), is difficult to detect by CT. When severe, it becomes manifest as multiple foci of low attenuation in the subcortical and pericallosal white matter. Magnetic resonance imaging has proven

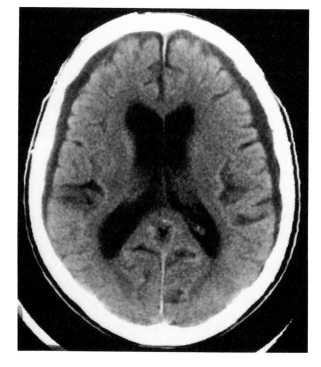

FIGURE 19.5. This 78-year-old male experienced a gradual onset of dementia. Preinfusion computed tomography (CT) scan demonstrates bilateral chronic subdural hematomas. Note the lack of shift of midline structures resulting from "balance" of volume between the two blood collections. The attenuation of chronic subdural hematomas is less than that on normal brain parenchyma.

to be much more sensitive for revealing shearing injuries. Magnetic resonance shows multiple elliptical foci of high T2 signal intensity (Gentry, Godersky, & Thompson, 1988).

Acquired Immune Deficiency Virus

The human immunodeficiency virus (HIV) is neurotropic and is found in the brain and spinal cord in about half of patients at autopsy (see Chapter 5). Rapidly progressive cerebral and cerebellar atrophy is typical. Later in the course of the disease, white matter changes become manifest. These changes vary from diffuse, patchy increased signal to multifocal lesions on T2WI. White matter lesions usually appear later in the disease course (Post et al., 1988). The diffuse pattern of white matter abnormality may represent actual HIV infection, whereas the pattern of multiple discrete foci of increased signal on T2WI may be indicative of progressive multifocal leukoencephalopathy (PML) (Olsen, Longo, Mills, & Norman, 1988). Progressive multifocal leukoencephalopathy is caused by papovaviruses JC and SV40. The CT and MRI findings are nonspecific. The CT scans reveal patchy areas of low attenuation within white matter (Guilleux, Steiner, & Young, 1986). These foci are usually asymmetric. They become confluent as they enlarge. On MRI, which is much more sensitive, the affected areas exhibit low and high signal on T1WI and T2WI, respectively. There is usually little or no mass effect. The cortical surface is usually not involved, and enhancement rarely occurs.

Patients with acquired immune deficiency syndrome (AIDS) are also predisposed to developing CNS lymphoma (usually primary, originating in white matter),

Kaposi's sarcoma, glioma, other viral infections such as cytomegalovirus (CMV) and herpes simplex, tuberculosis, and toxoplasmosis. Lymphoma and glioma were discussed earlier. Cytomegalovirus infection in immunocompromised adults rarely leads to necrotizing encephalitis and ependymitis (Post, Hensley, Moskowitz, & Fishl, 1986). T2-weighted images reveal periventricular high-signal-intensity lesions that are thick or nodular. Enhancement may also occur. The appearance is similar to that of CNS lymphoma.

Hydrocephalic Dementia

Hydrocephalus refers to ventriculomegaly secondary to altered CSF flow dynamics. The term *ex vacuo hydrocephalus* was once commonly used to refer to ventriculomegaly secondary to loss of adjacent brain parenchyma from atrophy, infarction, or other causes of encephalomalacia. Since there is no underlying alteration in CSF flow dynamics, however, this term is misleading and is therefore falling out of favor. Hydrocephalus may be subdivided into normal-pressure and obstructive varieties. Figure 19.6 shows an example of obstructive hydrocephalus visualized on CT.

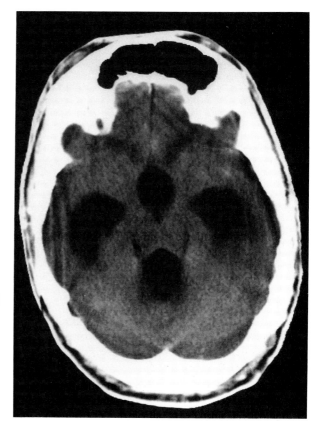

FIGURE 19.6. Noninfused computed tomography (CT) scan of an 18-year-old male with dementia demonstrates striking enlargement of the third, fourth, and lateral ventricles caused by hydrocephalus. Cerebrospinal fluid was obstructed by neurofibrosarcoma metastasis. Unlike the ventricular dilation that occurs with atrophy, the cortical sulci and cerebral fissures are smaller than normal in hydrocephalus.

Normal-Pressure Hydrocephalus

Hydrocephalus from any cause can produce dementia. The term *normal-pressure hydrocephalus* (NPH) is often reserved for cases of slowly progressive symptomatic hydrocephalus (see Chapter 10) (Anderson, 1986). Despite numerous publications, the diagnosis and prognosis of NPH remain an enigma (Vanneste & van Acker, 1990; Vanneste, Augustijn, Dirven, Tan & Goedhart, 1992). To date, there is no accepted classic CT or MRI finding that predicts a good response to CSF shunting.

Normal-pressure hydrocephalus involves enlargement of the ventricles without physical obstruction within the ventricular system. There is an interruption of CSF flow at the level of the cisterns and/or arachnoid villi. Normal-pressure hydrocephalus may result from fibrotic scarring of the leptomeninges resulting from subarachnoid hemorrhage or meningitis, or from infiltration of the leptomeninges by metastatic disease. Both CT and MRI will demonstrate ventricular enlargement that is disproportionate to the size of the cortical sulci. There may be periventricular interstitial edema secondary to transependymal migration of CSF. The edema will appear as a zone of decreased density on CT scans, and low-T1/high-T2 signal intensity on MRI.

The relationship between vascular disease and hydrocephalus remains an area of debate that has a profound impact on the diagnosis of NPH (Gallassi et al., 1991). Specifically, the relationship between white matter changes and Binswanger's disease and NPH remains unclear (George, 1991; Roman, 1991): patients with Binswanger's disease typically have large ventricles (Caplan & Schoene, 1978) and patients with NPH often have extensive white matter lesions.

It is important to remember that ventricular dilatation is also seen in AD, predominantly the result of white matter atrophy. Therefore, it is not uncommon for patients with typical AD to show ventricular dilatation that is disproportionate to the degree of sulcal atrophy (Ford & Winter, 1981), although this remains controversial (Arai et al., 1983).

Dysmyelinating Disease

Multiple Sclerosis

Multiple sclerosis (MS) is clinically characterized by multiple neurological deficits separated in time and space (see Chapter 15). Oligoclonal bands may be detected on CSF analysis. Evoked potential studies are frequently abnormal. Imaging studies are particularly useful to help establish the diagnosis. Chronic MS may result in dementia. Computed tomography is somewhat insensitive to the changes of early MS. "Hot" plaques undergoing active inflammation may enhance with contrast, particularly on double-dose-delayed CT. The chronic atrophic changes of MS and the low-attenuation changes in the white matter that accompany chronic demyelination may also be demonstrated on CT. The diagnosis of MS was one of the early success stories of MRI due to its sensitivity to MS plaques. These lesions occur in the periventricular white matter in about half of cases. Other common locations include the brainstem, spinal cord, periaqueductal region, and floor of the fourth ventricle. The cord is occasionally involved without concomitant brain lesions. The middle cerebellar peduncles are also a common site. No location is spared, however, including the basal ganglia, thalami, and cerebral cortex. The lesions are best demonstrated on *proton-density* weighted images (long TR, short TE). As with CT, contrast enhancement occasionally occurs in the acute phase. The lesions are usually ovoid and, when periventricular, are oriented perpendicular to the ventricular surface, which reflects the perivenular involvement demonstrated pathologically. "Giant" MS plaques may also occur and masquerade as other entities such as neoplasms and abscesses. Chronic plaques tend to have lower signal on T1WI than normal white matter (and lower than leuko-araiosis changes, for that matter). Like CT, MR will demonstrate the atrophy that accompanies chronic MS. The midsagittal plane is particularly helpful for evaluating atrophy of the corpus callosum, which occurs late in MS.

Leukodystrophies

The leukodystrophies, or dysmyelinating diseases, result from enzyme deficiencies that cause the production of abnormal myelin or poor myelin development (Canavan's disease, Krabbe's disease, metachromatic leukodystrophy, adrenoleukodystrophy, Alexander's disease). These diseases lead to mental retardation, usually in the first decade of life. Because they are not usually considered in the setting of adult-onset dementia, they are beyond the scope of this chapter.

Lipidoses

Abnormal sphingolipid metabolism also usually becomes clinically evident early in life and is thus not a part of the picture of adult-onset dementia. Examples include Tay-Sachs, Gaucher's, Neimann-Pick, Fabry's disease, and ceroid lipofuscinosis. Magnetic resonance imaging findings usually reflect basal ganglia ischemia (high signal on T2WI). Fabry's disease occasionally becomes manifest in the second or third decade of life. Small basal ganglia infarcts occur early. Late in the disease, high signal involves the periventricular white matter on T2WI. The adult form of Gaucher's disease has similar features: atrophy, infarction, and rarely, hemorrhage.

Alcohol Dementia

Chronic alcohol abuse leads to dementia via a presumed direct cytotoxic effect. The CT and MRI manifestations include atrophy, with particular involvement of the superior cerebellar vermis and frontotemporal regions (Fox, Ramsey, Huckman, & Proske, 1976; Koller et al., 1981). This atrophy may be reversible following treatment. The general imaging appearance of atrophy (prominence of ventricles, sulci, and cisterns) has already been described. Alcoholism may also cause infarcts, particularly following drinking binges (Hillbom & Kaste, 1981). Central pontine myelinolysis sometimes follows prolonged intoxication. Patients typically present with hyponatremia that is too rapidly overcorrected, causing osmotic shock to the brainstem. The CT and MRI reveal corresponding abnormalities (Rosenbloom et al., 1984). Marchiafava-Bignami disease is a rare result of alcohol abuse. Originally described in Italian males drinking red wine, it is now understood to be a more general, if uncommon, outcome of alcoholism. Clinically, hemiparesis, dementia, seizures, and coma may occur. The CT findings include atrophy of the corpus callosum and cerebral cortex. Magnetic resonance imaging additionally reveals linear high signal on T2WI in the corpus callosum (Holland, 1987) and often white matter lesions in the periventricular and subcortical regions.

Future Directions

Rapid advances in imaging technology brought about by concomitant break-throughs in physics, engineering, mathematics, and chemistry continue to pro-foundly affect the diagnosis and treatment of patients with dementia. Computed tomography scanners continue to improve in scan time with subsecond slice acquisition now routine. Research continues on monochromatic X-ray lasers, which may provide images similar to CT but with increased spatial resolution and de-creased patient radiation dose. Magnetic resonance technology continues to pro-gress after 10 years of clinical use. Promising new techniques such as the echo planar pulse sequence are enabling near-real-time scan acquisition times on the order of tens of milliseconds. Early research combining these new pulse sequences with bolus intravenous gadolinium-DTPA is enabling regional cerebral blood vol-ume mapping in response to visual task activation. Other functional mapping studies are sure to follow. Perfusion imaging techniques currently enable static images of very acute infarcts. Researchers are currently working out the details of dynamic MRI of CSF flow, which promises to augment the diagnosis of normal-pressure hydrocephalus. Magnetic resonance angiography continues to improve in spatial resolution. Faster scanning techniques are ameliorating problems from turbulent blood flow. The spatial resolution of magnetic resonance angiography is approach-ing that of intra-arterial digital subtraction angiography (IA-DSA). Conventional arteriography remains the "gold standard" for diagnosis of subtle vascular pa-thology such as aneurysms and arteriovenous malformations, and will be required for interventional neuroradiology techniques (such as embolization of arteriovenous fistulae and aneurysms) well into the future. New digital subtraction angiography equipment continues to improve in spatial and contrast resolution. Matrix sizes of 1024×1024 are now commonplace. Future 2048×2048 matrices will make conventional cut-film arteriography obsolete.

Work is progressing on techniques for manipulating digital image data using computer workstations. It should become easier to correlate MRI, CT, magne-toencephalography (MEG), PET, and SPECT images as techniques to accomplish this move from the laboratory to clinical use. Three-dimensional graphics work-stations can now be connected directly to scanners to enable precise measurement of neuroanatomic structures. It remains to be seen how this capability will affect the routine workup of patients with Alzheimer's disease and other dementias.

References

Adam, P., Fabre, N., Guell, A., Bessoles, G., Roulleau, J., & Bes, A. (1983). Cortical atrophy in Parkinson disease: Correlation between clinical and CT findings with special emphasis on prefrontal atrophy. *American Journal of Neuroradiology, 4*, 442–445.

Aharon-Peretz, J., Cummings, J. L., & Hill, M. A. (1988). Vascular dementia and dementia of the Alzheimer type. *Archives of Neurology, 45*, 719–721.

Ajax, A. E., deLeon, M. J., Kalnin, A., Rosner, L., Goodgold, A., & Chase, N. (1986). Leukoencephalopathy in normal and pathologic aging: 2. MRI of brain lucencies. *American Journal of Neuroradiology, 7*, 567–570.

Albert, M., Naeser, M. A., Levine, H. L., & Garvey, A. J. (1984). Ventricular size in patients with presenile dementia of the Alzheimer's type. *Archives of Neurology, 41*, 1258–1263.

Ambrosetto, P., Michelucci, R., Forti, A., & Tassinari, C. A. (1984). CT findings in progressive supranuclear palsy. *Journal of Computer Assisted Tomography, 8*(3), 406–409.

Anderson, M. (1986). Normal pressure hydrocephalus. *British Medical Journal, 293*, 837–838.

Arai, H., Kobayashi, K., Ikeda, K., Nagao, Y., Ogihara, R., & Kosaka, K. (1983). A computed tomography study of Alzheimer's disease. *Journal of Neurology, 229*, 69–77.

Austrom, M. G., Thompson, R. F., Jr., Hendrie, H. C., Norton, J., Farlow, M. R., Edwards, M. K., & Dean, R. (1990). Foci of increased T-2 signal intensity in MR images of healthy elderly subjects. A follow-up study. *Journal of the American Geriatric Society, 38*, 1133–1138.

Awad, I. A., Spetzler, R. F., Hodak, J. A., Awad, C. A., & Carey, R. (1986). Incidental subcortical lesions identified on magnetic resonance imaging in the elderly. I. Correlation with age and cerebrovascular risk factors. *Stroke, 17*, 1084–1089.

Awad, I. A., Johnson, P. C., Spetzler, R. F., & Hodak, J. A. (1986). Incidental subcortical lesions identified on magnetic resonance imaging in the elderly. II. Postmortem pathological correlations. *Stroke, 17*, 1090–1097.

Babikian, V., & Ropper, A. H. (1987). Binswanger's disease: A review. *Stroke, 18*,(1), 2–12.

Ball, M. J. (1977). Neuronal loss, neurofibrillary tangles and granulovacuolar degeneration in the hippocampus with ageing and dementia. A quantitative study. *Acta Neuropathology (Berlin), 37*, 111–118.

Ball, M. J. (1989). "Leukoaraiosis" explained. *Lancet, 1*, 612–613.

Bennett, D. A., Charletta, D., Gilley, D. W., Cochran, E., & Hayes, K. (1991). Clinical correlates of high signal lesions on magnetic resonance imaging in pathologically proven Alzheimer's disease. *Neurology, 41*(Suppl.1), 407.

Bennett, D. A., & Evans, D. A. (1992). Alzheimer's disease. *Disease-a-Month, 38*, 1–64.

Bennett, D. A., Gilley, D. W., Wilson, R. S., Fox, J. H., & Huckman, M. S. (1992), Clinical correlates of white matter hyperintensities in Alzheimer's disease. *Journal of Neurology, 239*, 186–190.

Bennett, D. A., Stebbins, G., Gilley, D. W., & Goetz, C. G. (in press), Parkinson's disease. In J. C. Morris (Ed.), *Handbook of dementing illnesses*. New York: Marcel Dekker.

Bennett, D. A., Wilson, R. S., Gilley, D. W., & Fox, J. H. (1990). Clinical diagnosis of Binswanger's disease. *Journal of Neurology, Neurosurgery and Psychiatry, 53*, 961–965.

Bigler, E. D., Hubler, D. W., Cullum, C. M., & Turkheimer, E. (1985). Intellectual and memory impairment in dementia. Computerized axial tomography volume correlations. *Journal of Nervous and Mental Disorders, 173*, 347–362.

Bird, J. M., Levy, R., & Jacoby, R. J. (1986). Computed tomography in the elderly: Changes over time in a normal population. *British Journal of Psychiatry, 148*, 80–85.

Boone, K. B., Miller, B. L., Lesser, I. M., Mehringer, C. M., Hill- Gutierrez, E., Goldberg, M. A., Berman, N. G. (1992). Neuropsychological correlates of white-matter lesions in healthy elderly subjects. *Archives of Neurology, 49*, 549–554.

Bradley, W. G., Waluch, V., Brant-Zawadzki, M., Yadley, R. A., & Wycoff, R. R. (1984). Patchy, periventricular white matter lesions in the elderly: A common observation during NMR imaging. *Noninvasive Medical Imaging, 1*(1), 35–41.

Braffman, B., Grossman, R., Goldberg, H., Stern, M., Hurtig, H., Hackney, D., Bilaniuk, L., & Zimmerman, R. (1988). MR imaging of Parkinson disease with spin-echo and gradient-echo sequences. *American Journal of Neuroradiology, 9*, 1093.

Braffman, B. H., Zimmerman, R. A., Trojanowski, J. Q., Gonatas, N. K., Hickey, W. F., & Schlaepfer, W. W. (1988a). Brain MR: Pathologic correlation with gross and histopathology. 1. Lacunar infarction and Virchow-Robin spaces. *American Journal of Radiology, 151*, 551–558.

Braffman, B. H., Zimmerman, R. A., Trojanowski, J. Q., Gonatas, N. K., Hickey, W. F., & Schlaepfer, W. W. (1988b). Brain MR: Pathologic correlation with gross and histopathology. 2. Hyperintense white-matter foci in the elderly. *American Journal of Radiology, 151*, 559–566.

Brant-Zawadzki, M. (1988). MR imaging of the brain. *Radiology, 166*(1), 1–10.

Breger, R. K., Papke, R. A., Pojunas, K. W., Williams, A., Papke, R., Haughton, V., & Daniels, D. (1987). Benign extraaxial tumors: Contrast enhancement with Gd-DTPA. *Radiology, 163*, 427.

Brinkman, S. D., & Largen, J. W., Jr. (1984). Changes in brain ventricular size with repeated CAT scans in suspected Alzheimer's disease. *American Journal of Psychiatry, 141*(1), 81–83.

Brinkman, S. D., Sarwar, M. A., Levin, H. S., & Morris, H. H., III (1981). Quantitative indexes of computed tomography in dementia and normal aging. *Radiology, 138*, 89–92.

Brown, J. J., Hesselink, J. R., & Rothrock, J. F. (1988). MR and CT of lacunar infarcts. *American Journal of Radiology, 151*, 367–372.

Brun, A., & Englund, E. (1986). A white matter disorder in dementia of the Alzheimer type: A pathoanatomical study. *Annals of Neurology, 19*, 253–262.

Caplan, L. R., & Schoene, W. C. (1978). Clinical features of subcortical arteriosclerotic encephalopathy (Binswanger's disease). *Neurology, 28*, 1206–1215.

Chui, H. C., Victoroff, J. I., Margolin, D., Jagust, W., Shankle, R., & Katzman, R. (1992). Criteria for the diagnosis of ischemic vascular dementia proposed by the State of California Alzheimer's disease diagnostic and treatment centers. *Neurology, 42*, 473–480.

Coffey, C. E., Wilkinson, W. E., Parashos, I. A., Soady, S. A. R., Sullivan, R. J., Patterson, L. J., Figiel, G. S., Webb, M. C., Spritzer, C. E., & Djang, W. T. (1992). Quantitative cerebral anatomy of the aging human brain: A cross-sectional study using magnetic resonance imaging. *Neurology, 42*, 524–536.

Creasey, H., & Rapoport, S. I. (1985). The aging human brain. *Annals of Neurology, 17*, 2–10.

Cummings, J. L., & Duchen, L. W. (1981). The Klüver-Bucy syndrome in Pick disease. *Neurology, 38*, 680–684.

Damasio, H., Eslinger, P., Damasio, A. R., Rizzo, M., Huang, H. K., & Demeter, S. (1983). Quantitative computed tomographic analysis in the diagnosis of dementia. *Archives of Neurology, 40*, 715–719.

Damasio, H., & Frank, R. (1992). Three-dimensional in vivo mapping of brain lesions in humans. *Archives of Neurology, 49*, 137–143.

DeCarli, C., Kaye, J., Horwitz, B., & Rapoport, S. (1990). Critical analysis of the use of computer-assisted transverse axial tomography to study human brain in aging and dementia of the Alzheimer type. *Neurology, 40*, 872–883.

Dekaban, A. S., & Sadowsky, B. S. (1978). Changes in brain weights during the span of human life: Relation of brain weights to body heights and body weights. *Annals of Neurology, 4*, 345–356.

de la Monte, S. M. (1989). Quantitation of cerebral atrophy in preclinical and end-stage Alzheimer's disease. *Annals of Neurology, 25*, 450–459.

deLeon, M. J., Ferris, S. H., George, A. E., Reisberg, B., Kricheff, I. I., & Gershon, S. (1980). Computed tomography evaluations of brain-behavior relationships in senile dementia of the Alzheimer's type. *Neurobiology of Aging, 1*, 69–79.

deLeon, M. J., George, A. E., Reisberg, B., Ferris, S. H., Kluger, A., Stylopoulos, L. A., Miller, J. D., La Regina, M. E., Chen, C., & Cohen, J. (1989). Alzheimer's disease: Longitudinal CT studies of ventricular change. *American Journal of Neuroradiology, 10*, 371–376.

deToledo-Morrell, L., Morrell, F., Charletta, D., McNally, T., & Ristanovic, R. (1991). Detection of hippocampal functional pathology with long-latency evoked potentials generated in the context of mnemonic demand [Abstract]. *Epilepsia, 32*, 94.

Doraiswamy, P. M., Shah, S. A., Husain, M. M., Escalona, P. R., McDonald, W. M., Figiel, G. S., & Krishnan, K. R. R. (1991). Magnetic resonance evaluation of the midbrain in Parkinson's disease. *Archives of Neurology, 48*, 360.

Drayer, B. P. (1988). Imaging of the aging brain. Part II: Pathologic conditions. *Radiology, 166*, 797–806.

Drayer, B., Olanow, W., Burger, P., Johnson, G. A., Herfkens, R., & Reiderer, S. (1986). Parkinson plus syndrome: Diagnosis using high field MR imaging of brain iron. *Radiology, 159*, 493–498.

Drayer, B., Burger, P., Darwin, R., Riederer, S., Herfkens, R., & Johnson, G. (1986). Magnetic resonance imaging of brain iron. *American Journal of Neuroradiology, 7*, 373.

Drayer, B. P., Heyman, A., Wilkinson, W., Barrett, L., & Weinberg, T. (1985). Early-onset Alzheimer's disease: An analysis of CT findings. *Annals of Neurology, 17*, 407–410.

Duguid, J. R., De La Paz, R., & DeGroot, J. (1986). Magnetic resonance imaging of the midbrain in Parkinson's disease. *Annals of Neurology, 20*, 744–747.

Earnest, M. P., Heaton, R. K., Wilkinson, W. E., & Manke, W. F. (1979). Cortical atrophy, ventricular enlargement and intellectual impairment in the aged. *Neurology, 29*, 1138–1143.

Ebisu, T., Narues, S., Horikawa, Y., Tanaka, C., & Higuchi, T. (1989). Nonacute subdural hematoma: Fundamental interpretation if MR images based on biochemical and in vitro MR analysis. *Radiology, 171*, 449–453.

Erkinjuntti, T., & Sulkava, R. (1991). Diagnosis of multi- infarct dementia. *Alzheimer's Disease and Associated Disorders, 5*(2), 112–121.

Erkinjuntti, T., Sulkava, R., Palo, J., & Ketonen, L. (1989). White matter low attenuation on CT in Alzheimer's disease. *Archives of Gerontological Geriatrics, 8*, 95–104.

Eslinger, P. J., Damasio, H., Graff-Radford, N., & Damasio, A. R. (1984). Examining the relationship between computed tomography and neuropsychological measures in normal and demented elderly. *Journal of Neurology, Neurosurgery and Psychiatry, 74*, 1319–1325.

Farlow, M. R., Yee, R. D., Dlouhy, S. R., Conneally, P. M., Azzarelli, B., & Ghetti, B. (1989). Gerstmann-Straussler-Scheinker disease. I. Extending the clinical spectrum. *Neurology, 39*, 1446–1452.

Filipek, P. A., Kennedy, D. N., Caviness, V. S., Rossnick, S. L., Spraggins, T. A., & Starewicz, P. M. (1989). Magnetic resonance imaging-based brain morphometry: Development and application to normal subjects. *Annals of Neurology, 25*, 61–67.

Ford, C. V., & Winter, J. (1981). Computerized axial tomograms and dementia in elderly patients. *Journal of Gerontology, 36*, 164–169.

Fox, J. H., Ramsey, R. G., Huckman, M. S., & Proske, A. E. (1976). Cerebral ventricular enlargement: Chronic alcoholics examined by computerized tomography. *Journal of the American Medical Association, 236,* 365.

Fox, J. H., Topel, J. L., & Huckman, M. S. (1975). Use of computerized tomography in senile dementia. *Journal of Neurology, Neurosurgery and Psychiatry, 39,* 948–953.

Gado, M., Danziger, W. L., Chi, D., Hughes, C. P., & Coben, L. A. (1983). Brain parenchymal density measurements by CT in demented subjects and normal controls. *Radiology, 147,* 703–710.

Gado, M., Hughes, C. P., Danziger, W., Chi, D., Jost, G., & Berg, L. (1982). Volumetric measurements of the cerebrospinal fluid spaces in demented subjects and controls. *Radiology, 144,* 535–538.

Gallassi, R., Morreale, A., Montagna, P., Sacquegna, T., DiSarro, R., & Lugaresi, E. (1991). Binswanger's disease and normal-pressure hydrocephalus: Clinical and neuropsychological comparison. *Archives of Neurology, 48,* 1156–1159.

Galves, S., & Cartier, L. (1984). Computer tomography findings in 15 cases of Creutzfeldt-Jakob disease with histological verification. *Journal of Neurology, Neurosurgery and Psychiatry, 47,* 1244–1246.

Gentry, L. R., Godersky, J. C., & Thompson, B. (1988). MR imaging of head trauma: Review of the distribution and radiopathologic features of traumatic lesions. *American Journal of Neuroradiology, 9,* 101–110.

George, A. E. (1991). Chronic communicating hydrocephalus and periventricular white matter disease: A debate with regard to cause and effect. *American Journal of Neuroradiology, 12,* 42–44.

George, A. E., deLeon, M. J., Ferris, S. H., & Kricheff, I. I. (1981). Parenchymal CT correlates of senile dementia (Alzheimer disease): Loss of gray-white matter discriminability. *American Journal of Neuroradiology, 2,* 205–213.

Geremia, G. K., & Huckman, M. S. (1990). Degenerative diseases of the cerebral hemispheres, brainstem, and cerebellum. *Radiology: Diagnosis, Imaging, Intervention.* (Vol. 3, chap. 39, p. 9). Philadelphia: J. B. Lippincott Company.

Gertz, H. J., Henks, H., & Cervos-Navarro, J. C. (1988). Creutzfeldt-Jakob disease: Correlation of MRI and neuropathologic findings. *Neurology, 38,* 1481–1482.

Gomori, J. M., Grossman, R. I., & Goldberg, H. I. (1985). Intracranial hematomas: Imaging by high-field MR. *Radiology, 157,* 87–93.

Gomori, J. M., Steiner, I., Melamed, E., & Cooper, G. (1984). The assessment of changes in brain volume using combined linear measurements: A CT-scan study. *Neuroradiology, 26,* 21–24.

Goto, K., Ishii, N., & Fukasawa, H. (1981). A clinical, neuropathological, and CT study. *Radiology, 141,* 678–695.

Grafton, S. T., Sumi, S. M., Stimac, G. K., Alvord, E. C., Shan, C., & Nochlin, D. (1991). Comparisons of postmortem magnetic resonance imaging and neuropathologic findings in the cerebral white matter. *Archives of Neurology, 48,* 293–298.

Guilleux, M-H., Steiner, R. E., & Young, I. R. (1986). MR imaging in progressive multifocal leukoencephalopathy. *American Journal of Neuroradiology, 7,* 1033–1035.

Gyldensted, C. (1977). Measurements of the normal ventricular system and hemispheric sulci of 100 adults with computed tomography. *Neuroradiology, 14,* 201–204.

Hachinski, V. C. (1990). The decline and resurgence of vascular dementia. *Canadian Medical Association Journal, 142,* 107–111.

Hachinski, V. C., Lassen, N. A., & Marshall, J. (1974). Multi-infarct dementia: A cause of mental deterioration in the elderly. *Lancet, 2,* 207–209.

Hachinski, V. C., Potter, P., & Merskey, H. (1987). Leuko-araiosis. *Archives of Neurology, 44,* 21–23.

Haldeman, S., Goldman, J. W., Hyde, J., & Pribram, H. F. W. (1981). Progressive supranuclear palsy, computed tomography and response to antiparkinsonian drugs. *Neurology, 31*, 442–445.

Harrell, L. E., Duvall, E., Folks, D. G., Duke, L., Bartolucci, A., Conboy, T., Callaway, R., & Kerns, D. (1991). The relationship of high-intensity signals on magnetic resonance images to cognitive and psychiatric state in Alzheimer's disease. *Archives of Neurology, 48*, 1136–1140.

Henderson, G., Tomlinson, B. E., & Gibson, P. H. (1980). Cell counts in human cerebral cortex in normal adults throughout life using an image analysing computer. *Journal of Neurological Sciences, 46*, 113–136.

Hillbom, M., & Kaste, M. (1981). Ethanol intoxication: A risk factor for ischemic brain infarction in adolecscents and young adults. *Stroke, 12*, 422.

Holland, B. A. (1987). Diseases of white matter. In M. Brant-Zawadzki & D. Norman (Eds.), *Magnetic resonance imaging of the central nervous system* (chap. 16). New York: Raven Press.

Hubbard, M., & Anderson, J. M. (1981). Age, senile dementia and ventricular enlargement. *Journal of Neurology, Neurosurgery and Psychiatry, 44*, 631–635.

Huber, S. J., Chakeres, D. W., Paulson, G. W., & Khanna, R. (1990). Magnetic resonance imaging in Parkinson's disease. *Archives of Neurology, 47*, 735–737.

Huber, S. J., Paulson, G. W., Shuttleworth, E. C., & Chakeres, D. (1988). Magnetic resonance imaging is nonspecific to dementia in Parkinson's disease [Abstract]. *Neurology*, (Suppl. 1) *38*, 329.

Huckman, M. S., Fox, J. H., & Topel, J. (1975). The validity of criteria for the evaluation of cerebral atrophy by computed tomography. *Radiology, 116*, 85–92.

Hughes, C. H., & Gado, M. (1981). Computed tomography and aging of the brain. *Radiology, 139*, 391–396.

Hunt, A. L., Orrison, W. W., Yeo, R. A., Haaland, K. Y., Rhyne, R. L., Garry, P. J., & Rosenberg, G. A. (1989). Clinical significance of MRI white matter lesions in the elderly. *Neurology, 39*, 1470–1474.

Hwier, L. A., Bauer, C. J., Schwartz, L., Zimmerman, R. D., Morgello, S., & Deck, M. D. F. (1989). Large Virchow-Robin spaces: MR-clinical correlation. *American Journal of Neuroradiology, 10*, 929–936.

Inzitari, D., Diaz, F., Fox, A., Hachinski, V. C., Steingart, A., Lau, C., Donald, A., Wade, J., Mulic, H., Merskey, H. (1987). Vascular risk factors and Leuko-araiosis. *Archives of Neurology, 44*, 42–47.

Ito, M., Hatazawa, J., Yamaura, H., & Matsuzawa, T. (1981). Age-related brain atrophy and mental deterioration—a study with computed tomography. *British Journal of Radiology, 54*, 384–390.

Jack, C. R., Gehring, D. G., Sharbrough, F. W., et al. (1988). Temporal lobe volume measurement from MR images: Accuracy and left-right asymmetry in normal persons. *Journal of Computer Assisted Tomography, 12*, 21–29.

Jack, C. R., Petersen, R. C., O'Brien, P. C., & Tangalos, E. G. (1992). MR-based hippocampal volumetry in the diagnosis of Alzheimer's disease. *Neurology, 42*, 183–188.

Janota, I., Mirsen, T. R., Hachinski, V. C., Lee, D. H., & Merskey, H. (1989). Neuropathologic correlates of leuko-araiosis. *Archives of Neurology, 46*, 1124–1128.

Jernigan, T. J., Press, G. A., & Hesselink, J. R. (1990). Methods for measuring brain morphologic features on magnetic resonance images. *Archives of Neurology, 47*, 27–32.

Johnson, K. A., Davis, K. R., Buonanno, S., Brady, T. J., Rosen, J., & Growdon, J. H. (1987). Comparison of magnetic resonance and roentgen ray computed tomography in dementia. *Archives of Neurology, 44*, 1075–1080.

Jungreis, C. A., Kanal, E., Hirsch, W. L., Martinez, A. J., & Moossy, J. (1988). Normal perivascular spaces mimicking lacunar infarction: MR imaging. *Radiology, 69*, 101–104.

Kaszniak, A. W., Garron, D. C., Fox, J. H., Bergen, D., & Huckman, M. (1979). Cerebral atrophy, EEG slowing, age, education and cognitive functioning in suspected dementia. *Neurology, 49*, 1273–1279.

Katzman, R. (1990). Should a major neuroimaging procedure (CT or MRI) be required in the workup of dementia? An affirmative view. *Journal of Family Practice, 31*, 401–405.

Kavanen, J., Haltia, M., Erkinjuntti, T., Sulkava, R., Ketonen, L., & Sipponen, J. (1985). Cerebral MR and CT imaging in Creutzfeldt-Jakob disease. *Journal of Computer Assisted Tomography, 9*, 125–128.

Kaye, J. A., DeCarli, C., Luxenberg, J. S., Rapoport, S. I. (1992). The significance of age-related enlargement of the cerebral ventricles in healthy men and women measured by quantitative computed x-ray tomography. *Journal of the American Geriatrics Society, 40*, 225–231.

Kertesz, A., Black, S. E., Tokar, G., Benke, T., Carr, T., & Nicholson, L. (1988). Periventricular and subcortical hyperintensities on magnetic resonance imaging: Rims, caps, and unidentified bright objects. *Archives of Neurology, 45*, 404–408.

Kertesz, A., Polk, M., & Carr, T. (1990). Cognition and white matter changes on magnetic resonance imaging in dementia. *Archives of Neurology, 47*, 387–391.

Kesslak, J. P., Nalcioglu, O., & Cotman, C. W. (1991). Quantification of magnetic resonance scans for hippocampal and parahippocampal atrophy in Alzheimer's disease. *Neurology, 41*, 51–54.

Kido, D. K., Caine, E. D., LeMay, M., Ekholm, S., Booth, H., & Panzer, R. (1989). Temporal lobe atrophy in patients with Alzheimer disease: a CT study. *American Journal of Neuroradiology, 10*, 551.

Kinkel, W. R., Jacobs, L., Polachini, I., Bates, V., & Heffner, R. R., Jr. (1985). Subcortical arteriosclerotic encephalopathy (Binswanger's disease). Computed tomographic, nuclear magnetic resonance, and clinical correlations. *Archives of Neurology, 42*, 951–959.

Koller, W. C., Glatt, S. L., Fox, J. H., Kaszniak, A. W., Wilson, R. S., & Huckman, M. S. (1981). Cerebellar atrophy: Relationship to aging and cerebral atrophy. *Neurology, 31*, 1486.

Ladurner, G., Iliff, L. D., & Lechner, H. (1982). Clinical factors associated with dementia in ischemic stroke. *Journal of Neurology, Neurosurgery and Psychiatry, 45*, 97–101.

Laffey, P. A., Peyster, R. G., Nathan, R., Haskin, M. E., & McGinley, J. A. (1984). Computed tomography and aging: Results in a normal elderly population. *Neuroradiology, 26*, 273–278.

LeMay, M. (1984). Radiologic changes of the aging brain and skull. *American Journal of Neuroradiology, 143*, 383–389.

LeMay, M., Stafford, J. L., Sandor, T., Albert, M., Haykal, H., & Samani, A. (1986). Statistical assessment of perceptual CT scan ratings in patients with Alzheimer type dementia. *Journal of Computer Assisted Tomography, 10*(5), 802–809.

Leys, D., Pruvo, J. P., Parent, M., Delacourte, A., Petit, H., Vermersch, P., Rapoport, A., Soetaert, G., Steinling, M., & Clarisse, J. (1991). Could wallerian degeneration contribute to "leuko-araiosis" in subjects free of any vascular disorder? *Journal of Neurology, Neurosurgery and Psychiatry, 54*, 46–50.

Leys, D., Soetaert, G., Petit, H., Fauquett, A., Pruvo, J. P., & Steinling, M. (1990). Periventricular and white matter magnetic resonance imaging hyperintensities do not differ between Alzheimer's disease and normal aging. *Archives of Neurology, 47*, 524–527.

Liu, C. K., Miller, B. L., Cummings, J. L., Mehringer, C. M., Goldberg, M. A., Howng,

S. L., & Benson, D. F. (1992). A quantitative MRI study of vascular dementia. *Neurology, 42*, 138–143.

Loeb, C. (1990). Vascular dementia. *Dementia, 1*, 175–184.

Luxenberg, J. S., Haxby, J. V., Creasey, H., Sundaram, M., & Rapoport, S. I. (1987). Rate of ventricular enlargement in dementia of the Alzheimer type correlates with rate of neuropsychological deterioration. *Neurology, 37*, 1135–1140.

McGreachie, R. E., Flemming, J. O., Sharer, R., & Hyman, R. A. (1979). Diagnosis of Pick's disease by computed tomography. *Journal of Computer Assisted Tomography, 23*, 111.

Masdeu, J. C., Wolfson, L., Lantos, G., Armerman, P., Tobin, J. N., Grober, E., & Whipple, R. (1989). Brain white-matter changes in the elderly prone to falling. *Archives of Neurology, 46*, 1292–1296.

Mayeux, R., Chen, J., Mirabello, E., Marder, K., Bell, K., Dooneief, G., Cote, L., & Stern, V. (1990). An estimate of the incidence of dementia in idiopathic Parkinson's disease. *Neurology, 40*, 1513–1517.

Mayeux, R., Stern, Y., Rosenstein, R., Marder, K., Hauser, A., Cote, L., & Fahn, S. (1988). An estimate of the prevalence of dementia in idiopathic Parkinson's disease. *Archives of Neurology, 45*, 260–262.

Miller, A. K. H., Alston, R. L., & Corsellis, J. A. N. (1980). Variations with age in the volumes of grey and white matter in the cerebral hemispheres of man: Measurements with an image analyser. *Neuropathology and Applied Neurobiology, 6*, 119–132.

Milton, W. J., Atlas, S. W., Lavi, E., Mollman, J. E. (1991). Magnetic resonance imaging of Creutzfeldt-Jacob disease. *Annals of Neurology, 29*, 438–440.

Mirsen, T. R., Lee, D. H., Wong, C. J., Diaz, J. F., Fox, A. J., Hachinski, V. C., & Merskey, H. (1991). Clinical correlates of white-matter changes on magnetic resonance imaging scans of the brain. *Archives of Neurology, 48*, 1015–1021.

Naaidich, T. P., Daniels, D. L., Haughton, V. M., Williams, A., Pojunas, K., & Palacios, E. (1987). Hippocampal formation and related structures of the limbic lobe: Anatomic-MR correlation. Part I. Surface features and coronal sections. *Radiology, 162*, 747–754.

Naeser, M. A., Gebhardt, C., & Levine, H. L. (1980). Decreased computerized tomography numbers in patients with presenile dementia. *Archives of Neurology, 37*, 401–409.

Naugle, R. I., Cullum, C. M., Bigler, E. D., & Massman, P. J. (1985). Neuropsychological and computerized axial tomography volume characteristics of empirically derived dementia subgroups. *Journal of Nervous and Mental Disorders, 173*, 596–604.

Olsen, W. L., Longo, F. M., Mills, C. M., & Norman, D. (1988). White matter disease in AIDS: Findings at MR imaging. *Radiology, 169*, 445–448.

Pagani, J. J., Libshitz, H. I., Wallace, S., & Hayman, L. A. (1981). Central nervous system leukemia and lymphoma: Computed tomographic manifestations. *American Journal of Neuroradiology, 2*, 397–403.

Pearlson, G. E., & Tune, L. E. (1986). Cerebral ventricular size and cerebrospinal fluid acetylcholinesterase levels in senile dementia of the Alzheimer type. *Psychiatry Research, 17*, 23–29.

Penn, R. D., Belanger, M. G., & Yasnoff, W. A. (1978). Ventricular volume in man computed from CAT scans. *Annals of Neurology, 3*, 216–223.

Post, M. J. D., Hensley, G. T., Moskowitz, L. B., & Fishl, M. (1986). Cytomegalic inclusion virus encephalitis in patients with AIDS: CT, clinical, and pathological correlation. *American Journal of Neuroradiology, 7*, 275–280.

Post, M. J. D., Tate, L. G., Quencer, R. M., Hensley, G. T., Berger, J. R., Sheremata, W. A., & Maul, G. (1988). CT, MR and pathology in HIV encephalitis and meningitis. *American Journal of Neuroradiology, 9*, 469–476.

Press, G. A., Amaral, D. G., & Squire, L. R. (1989). Hippocampal abnormalities in amnesic patients revealed by high-resolution magnetic resonance imaging. *Nature, 341*, 54–57.

Rao, K., Brennan, T. G., & Garcia, J. H. (1977). Computed tomography in the diagnosis of Creutzfeldt-Jakob disease. *Journal of Computer Assisted Tomography, 1*, 211.

Rao, S. M., Mittenberg, W., Bernardin, L., Haughton, V., & Leo, G. J. (1989). Neuropsychological test findings in subjects with leukoaraiosis. *Archives of Neurology, 46*, 40–44.

Roman, G. C. (1987). Senile dementia of the Binswanger type. A vascular form of dementia in the elderly. *Journal of the American Medical Association, 258*(13), 1782–1788.

Roman, G. C. (1991). White matter lesions and normal-pressure hydrocephalus: Binswanger's disease of Hakim syndrome? *American Journal of Neuroradiology, 12*, 40–41.

Rosenbloom, S., Buchalz, D., Kuman, A., Kaplan, R., Moses, H., & Rosenbaum, A. (1984). Evaluation of central pontine myelinolysis on CT. *American Journal of Neuroradiology, 5*, 110.

Russell, E. J., Geremia, G. K., Johnson, C. E., Huckman, M. S., Ramsey, R. G., Washburn-Bleck, J., Turner, D. A., & Norusis, M. (1987). Multiple cerebral metastases: Detectability with Gd-DTPA-enhanced MR imaging. *Radiology, 165*, 609.

Sandor, T., Jolesz, F., Tieman, J., Kikinis, R., Jones, K., & Albert, M. (1992). Comparative analysis of computed tomographic and magnetic resonance imaging scans in Alzheimer patients and controls. *Archives of Neurology, 49*, 381–384.

Scheinberg, P. (1988). Dementia due to vascular disease—a multifactorial disorder. *Stroke, 19*, 1291–1299.

Schwartz, M., Creasey, H., Grady, C. L., Deleo, J. M., Frederickson, H. A., Cutler, N. R., & Rapoport, S. I. (1985). Computed tomographic analysis brain morphometrics in 30 healthy men, aged 21 to 81 years. *Annals of Neurology, 17*, 146–157.

Seab, J. P., Jagust, W. J., Wong, S. T. S., Roos, M. S., Reed, B. R., & Budinger, T. F. (1988). Quantitative NMR measurements of hippocampal atrophy in Alzheimer's disease. *Magnetic Resonance Medicine, 8*, 200–208.

Shah, S. A., Doraiswamy, P. M., Husain, M. M., Figiel, G. S., Boyko, O. B., McDonald, W. M., Ellinwood, E. H., & Krishnan, K. R. R. (1991). Assessment of posterior fossa structures with midsagittal MRI: The effects of age. *Neurobiology of Aging, 12*(4), 371–374.

Soininen, H., Partanen, J. V., Puranen, M., & Reikkinen, P. J. (1982). EEG and computed tomography in the investigation of patients with senile dementia. *Journal of Neurology, Neurosurgery and Psychiatry, 45*, 711–714.

Squire, L. R., Amaral, D. G., & Press, G. A. (1990). Magnetic resonance imaging of the hippocampal formation and mammillary nuclei distinguish medial temporal lobe and diencephalic amensia. *Journal of Neuroscience, 10*(9), 3106–3117.

Sroka, H., Elizan, T. S., Yahr, M. D., Burger, A., & Mendoza, M. R. (1981). Organic mental syndrome and confusion states in Parkinson's disease. Relationship to computerized tomographic signs of cerebral atrophy. *Archives of Neurology, 28*, 339–342.

Stack, J. P., Antoun, N. M., Jenkins, J. P. R., Metcalfe, R., & Isherwood, I. (1988). Gadolinium-DTPA as a contrast agent in magnetic resonance imaging of the brain. *Neuroradiology, 30*, 145.

Steiner, A., Gomori, J. M., & Melamed E. (1985). Features of brain atrophy in Parkinson's disease. *Neuroradiology, 27*, 158–160.

Steingart, A., Hachinski, V. C., Lau, C., Fox, A., Diaz, F., Cape, R., Lee, D., Initari, D., & Merskey, H. (1987). Cognitive and neurologic findings in demented patients with diffuse white matter lucencies on computed tomographic scan (leuko-araiosis). *Archives of Neurology, 44*, 32–35.

Sze, G., de Armond, S. J., Brant-Zawadzki, M., Davis, R. L., Norman, D., & Newton,

T. H. (1986). Foci of MRI signal (pseudo lesions) anterior to the frontal horns: Histologic correlations of a normal finding. *American Journal of Neuroradiology, 7,* 381–387.

Tatemichi, T. K. (1990). How acute brain failure becomes chronic. A view of the mechanisms of dementia related to stroke. *Neurology, 40,* 1652–1659.

Terrence, C. F., Delaney, J. F., & Alberts, M. C. (1977). Computed tomography for Huntington's disease. *Neuroradiology, 13,* 173.

Terry, R. D., Peck, A., DeTeresa, R., Schechter, R., & Horoupian, D. S. (1981). Some morphometric aspects of the brain in senile dementia of the Alzheimer type. *Annals of Neurology, 10,* 184–192.

Tomlinson, B. E., Blessed, G., & Roth, M. (1968). Observations on the brains of non-demented old people. *Journal of Neurological Sciences, 7,* 331–356.

Tomlinson, B. E., Blessed, G., & Roth, M. (1970). Observations on the brains of demented old people. *Journal of Neurological Sciences, 11,* 205–242.

Van Hoesen, G. W., Hyman, B. T., & Damasio, A. R. (1991). Entorhinal cortex pathology in Alzheimer's disease. *Hippocampus 1*(1), 1–8.

van Swieten, J. C., Geyskes, G. G., Derix, M. M. A., Peeck, B. M., Ramos, L. M. P., van Latum, J. C., & van Gijn, J. (1991). Hypertension in the elderly is associated with white matter lesions and cognitive decline. *Annals of Neurology, 30,* 825–830.

Vanneste, J., Augustijn, P., Dirven, C., Tan, W. F., & Goedhart, Z. D. (1992). Shunting normal-pressure hydrocephalus: Do the benefits outweigh the risks? *Neurology, 42,* 54–59.

Vanneste, J., & van Acker, R. (1990). Normal pressure hydrocephalus: Did publications alter management? *Journal of Neurology, Neurosurgery and Psychiatry, 53,* 564–568.

Vaughn, G. M., Bradley, W. G., Marshall, C. E., Bhoopat, T., & Rhodes, R. (1988). Deep white matter infarction: Correlation of MR imaging and histopathologic findings. *Radiology, 167,* 517–522.

Vonofakos, D., Marcu, H., & Hacker, H. (1979). Oligodendrogliomas: CT patterns with emphasis on features indicating malignancy. *Journal of Computer Assisted Tomography, 3,* 783–788.

Wechsler, A. F., Verity, M. A., Rosenchein, S., Fried, I., & Scheibel, A. B. (1982). Pick's disease: A clinical, computed tomographic, and histologic study with Golgi impregnation observations. *Archives of Neurology, 39,* 287–290.

Wilson, R. S., Fox, J. H., Huckman, M. S., Bacon, L. D., & Lobick, J. J. (1982). Computed tomography in dementia. *Neurology, 32,* 1054–1057.

Wippold, F. J., Gado, M. H., Morris, J. C., Duchek, J. M., & Grant E. A. (1991). Senile dementia and healthy aging: A longitudinal CT study. *Radiology, 179,* 215–219.

Yerby, M. S., Sundsten, J. W., Larson, E. B., Wu, S. A., & Sumi, S. M. (1985). A new method of measuring brain atrophy: The effect of aging in its application for diagnosing dementia. *Neurology, 35,* 1316–1320.

Zimmerman, R. A., Bilaniuk, L. T., Hackney, D. B., Goldberg, H. I., & Grossman, R. I. (1986). Head injury: Early results of comparing CT and high-field MR. *American Journal of Neuroradiology, 7,* 757–764.

Zimmerman, R. D., Fleming, C. A., Lee, B. C. P., Saint-Louis, L. A., & Deck, M. D. F. (1986). Periventricular hyperintensity as seen by magnetic resonance: Prevalence and significance. *American Journal of Neuroradiology, 7,* 13–20.

Zubenko, G. S., Sullivan, S., Nelson, J. P., Belle, S. H., Huff, F. J., & Wolf, G. L. (1990). Brain imaging abnormalities in mental disorders in late life. *Archives of Neurology, 47,* 1107–1111.

PART IV

MANAGEMENT OF ALZHEIMER'S PATIENTS

20

Psychosocial Evaluation and Management of the Alzheimer's Patient

HOLLY TUOKKO

The purpose of this chapter is to describe the role of psychosocial evaluation in the clinical assessment of individuals with Alzheimer's disease (AD) and related disorders. Although neuropsychological evaluation of individuals with AD and related disorders is perhaps most often concerned with diagnostic issues, information derived from neuropsychological evaluation can potentially be of value in managing and planning care for the demented individual. In both contexts, the evaluation of psychosocial functioning is crucial.

According to the currently available diagnostic criteria (DSM-III-R, American Psychiatric Association [APA], 1987; ICD-10, World Health Organization [WHO], 1988), dementia is defined by a decline in memory and other cognitive functions in comparison to the individual's previous level of functioning. It is determined by a history of decline in performance and from abnormalities noted on clinical examination and neuropsychological assessment. In addition, the diagnostic criteria for dementia emphasize that the decline in cognitive functions leads to "impaired functioning in daily living" (WHO, 1988) or that this decline "significantly interferes with work or usual social activities or relationships with others" (APA, 1987). Although interviewing an informant is recommended, little other guidance is given as to methods for evaluating and documenting deficits in everyday or psychosocial functioning (APA, 1987). A clear understanding of the nature, extent, and sequence of the emergence of psychosocial deficits is needed to address the diagnostic issues and may also contribute to the differential diagnosis between dementias of different etiologies.

It is generally agreed that the earliest symptoms in most patients with AD are cognitive (e.g., failing memory, visuospatial disorders, and language deficits, most notably word finding and other deficiencies in verbal expression). Yet at least superficial social functioning tends to remain remarkably well preserved early in the course of the disease. In contrast, it has been noted (Neary, Snowden, Northen, & Goulding, 1988; Gustafson, 1987) that the early features of dementia of the frontal lobe type tend to be characterized by social breakdown and marked personality change with inappropriate affect and lack of concern. The early features associated with this disorder included neglect of hygiene and personal responsibilities. Behavior was described as rigid, inflexible, and socially inappropriate. Disturbance of cognitive functions was described as variable or not prominent early in the course. Similarly, early marked personality changes that impact on social functioning may be seen in patients with Huntington's disease well before the onset of the movement disorder or cognitive impairment (Lishman, 1978).

Neuropsychological assessments tend to focus on the clarification of the cognitive functioning of the affected individual. Psychosocial functioning involves the interaction between characteristics of the individual and the social environment in which the individual functions. By developing an understanding of the individual's environmental situation, the neuropsychologist can potentially provide valuable information for guiding the management and care of dementia victims. The vast majority of individuals with dementia are cared for by family members in the community, and, thus, issues related to the caregiver and the impact of caregiving arise as central environmental issues.

Evaluation

The concept of psychosocial functioning is broad and may include all aspects of cognitive, behavioral, social, and functional competence. However, for the purpose of this chapter, discussion will be limited to the evaluation of functional competence or the ability to engage in activities necessary for independent functioning. Comprehensive measures designed to address the multiple domains associated with overall psychosocial functioning have been developed (e.g., Lawton, Moss, Fulcomer, & Kleban, 1982; Duke University Center for the Study of Aging, 1978; Linn & Linn, 1984) for use in studies of normal aging. The length and focus of these measures would typically preclude their use as routine clinical tools; hence, they will not be discussed in this chapter.

Activities of Daily Living

Perhaps the most commonly utilized measures of psychosocial functioning are those assessing basic *activities of daily living* (ADL). These instruments typically focus on the domain of physical self-maintenance skills (e.g., toileting, dressing, eating habits, bathing, ambulation, and grooming) rated along ordinal scales. Many ADL measures have been developed, although their psychometric properties often remain unspecified. Examples of two of the more thoroughly researched instruments are the Physical Self-Maintenance Scale (PSMS) (Lawton & Brody, 1969) and the Rapid Disability Rating Scale (RDRS-2) (Linn, 1967; Linn & Linn, 1982). The PSMS was designed to coordinate observations in the areas of toileting, eating, dressing, grooming, ambulation, and bathing by having the caregivers provide ratings along five levels of functioning ranging from "completely independent" to "dependent." The RDRS-2 includes areas of physical functioning beyond the usual components of ADL scales. Areas covered by the RDRS-2 include eating, walking, mobility, bathing, dressing, toileting, grooming, and adaptive tasks (managing money/possessions; telephoning; and buying items such as newspapers, toilet articles, and snacks). Additional areas assessed by the RDRS-2 include items re-flecting degree of disability (i.e., communication, hearing, sight, diet, incontinence, and medications) and degree of special problems (i.e., mental confusion, uncoop-erativeness, and depression). Each item of the instrument is rated along a four-point scale in terms of the amount of assistance or degree of disability evidenced by the patient.

The major limitation to the use of ADL measures in the evaluation of AD is that very little disability of this type is revealed even in moderately impaired community dwelling AD patients (Teri, Borson, Kiyak, & Yamagishi, 1989). It has been concluded (Linn & Linn, 1981) that these measures are most appropriate for use with hospitalized patients.

Instrumental Activities of Daily Living

A second group of measures addresses the more complex skills associated with self-maintenance, or *instrumental activities of daily living* (IADL). The most widely used measure of this type is the Instrumental Activities of Daily Living Scale (Lawton & Brody, 1969). Ratings are made along scales varying in length from three to five points, reflecting varying degrees of competence in the following areas: ability to use a telephone, shopping, food preparation, housekeeping, laundry, mode of transportation, responsibility for own medication, and ability to handle finances. In contrast to the ADL measures, IADL instruments tend to be less applicable to institutionalized patients, because often the institution performs the functions assessed by these scales. Thus, IADL activities focus on abilities in which nonperformance is likely to signal a degree of impairment that would demand intervention by others, making them particularly useful for assessment of com-munity dwellers. Of interest, Teri et al. (1989) found that moderately impaired community dwelling AD patients were usually able to perform these tasks as well as ADL tasks. However, a significant association between age and instrumental skills ($r = .28, p < .01$) was observed, despite the finding that the older patients were not more cognitively impaired than the younger ones. It was hypothesized that decreased health or increased physical disability associated with increasing age may have contributed to this finding.

An alternative approach to the use of ordinal scales completed with information provided by caregivers is to examine functional abilities directly by having patients perform actual tasks. The Performance Activities of Daily Living Scale is an in-strument that focuses on rudimentary skills of primary interest in institutional settings (Kuriansky & Gurland, 1976). The Direct Assessment of Functional Status (DAFS) (Lowenstein et al., 1989) was specifically designed to be sensitive to subtle changes in higher order functional abilities that may occur in the incipient phases of AD and other dementias. The behavioral domains assessed by the DAFS include time orientation, communication abilities, transportation, financial skills, shopping skills, eating skills, and dressing/grooming skills. The items and subscales of the DAFS were constructed in a hierarchical fashion to reflect higher or lower order skills in keeping with the functional model described by Reisberg et al. (1984) and Reisberg, Ferris, and Franssen (1985). Although measures of this type circumvent the difficulties associated with relying either on self-reports of patients, or, more often, accounts of caregivers, the ability to perform a task in an artificial situation may not generalize to everyday life. A demented individual may be able to perform tasks such as meal preparation or shopping on direct request or prompting, but fail to do so in the course of their everyday lives due to apathy, lack of awareness, or failures in memory functioning. It has been suggested (Linn & Linn, 1984) that the use of rating scales may be the preferred means of obtaining estimates characterizing the individual's actual daily behavior.

Other Activities of Daily Living

The concept of psychosocial functioning includes many forms of behavior not addressed by the measures discussed. Relatively sophisticated or complex psychosocial skills are difficult to assess and may be overlooked during a routine evaluation of an individual's functional status. However, when working with dementia victims, clinicians may find themselves in the position of providing judgments as to an individual's competence to handle finances without supervision, to make decisions in the workplace, or to drive a vehicle. These judgments may play a major role in legal proceedings such as guardianship for persons and property or may carry legal responsibilities for the clinician. For example, in many jurisdictions, physicians and psychologists are required to report to the local licensing authority patients whose conditions might affect their ability to drive. The more prominent legal responsibility of physicians and psychologists revolves around the duty to warn patients of foreseeable danger to themselves and others should they continue to drive in the presence of a condition known to have the potential to impair driving ability. Decisions in recent cases in the United States have found physicians liable for failing to warn their patients of foreseeable danger while operating a motor vehicle when suffering from disorders such as congestive heart failure, history of stroke, and epilepsy (Coopersmith, Korner-Bitensky, & Mayo, 1989). Even in the absence of a specific legal requirement, there exists an ethical obligation to act responsibly with respect both to the patient and society. Yet, only recently has the relationship between the presence and severity of dementia of the Alzheimer type (DAT) and functional ability to drive a vehicle safely been examined (Donnelly & Karlinsky, 1990).

At a certain point in the course of a dementia, there is little doubt that there is clear and foreseeable danger to self and others should a severely demented individual attempt to drive. However, there is little to guide decisions when individuals are in the earlier stages of a dementing disorder. Friedland et al. (1988) studied 30 patients with DAT and 30 healthy age-matched control subjects. They found that 47% of the dementia patients had been involved in an automobile crash in the 5 years preceding the study, whereas only 10% of the controls had had accidents in this time period. Of the 19 patients who had stopped driving, only eight had done so without the occurrence of an accident. The occurrence of crashes was not related to duration or severity of dementia. Lucas-Blaustein, Filipp, Dungan, and Tune (1988) reported that 30% of a diagnostically heterogeneous sample of 53 dementia patients had at least one accident since the onset of symptoms, and another 11% were reported to have "caused" others to have accidents. Sixteen of the 53 dementia cases (31%) were still driving at the time of the study. Fourteen of these individuals continued to drive alone and 10 continued to drive at night. However, the majority of these 14 cases were considered to be safe drivers by their caregivers. It was also noted that most of these individuals only drove in their own neighborhood and tended to drive slower than the speed limit. Each of these studies gathered the driving information by administering questionnaires to the patient's caregiver. Tallman, Tuokko, Weir, and Beattie (1990) examined the driving records spanning a 5-year period for 165 community dwelling individuals with diagnoses of dementia. A control group, matched for age, gender, and location of residence (e.g., rural vs. urban) was generated from the data base containing a 5-year driving record for all licensed drivers in the province of British Columbia, Canada: 23% of the dementia cases had been involved in an accident in the past 5-year period, whereas 13.33% of the control sample had been involved in accidents. From these studies, it seems clear that drivers with diagnoses of dementia are involved in more traffic accidents than cognitively intact older drivers or a random sample of age- and gender-matched individuals.

Although these studies suggest a problem with driving exists, they tell us little about the nature of the problem. Traffic accidents are semirandom events that are relatively rare and difficult to predict. In order to better understand the effects of cognitive impairment on the aged driver and to create the basis for responsible intervention, information concerning the actual driving behavior of these individuals is needed. Yet, Friedland et al. (1988) conclude:

> Although the incidence of crashes is lower in the early years of the disease, our data show there is no period of disease during which driving is safe. Neither the duration of the disease nor overall dementia severity can be used to predict which DAT patients can safely drive . . . We recommend that patients with the diagnosis of DAT not drive a motor vehicle. (p. 785)

In a companion editorial, Drachman (1988) argues that it is a mistake to categorically prohibit all DAT patients from driving under all circumstances. In so doing, he draws attention to the social consequences of such action and argues that the diagnostic issues surrounding AD are still evolving. A definitive diagnosis requires brain tissue confirmation and the clinical diagnosis of dementia, and AD is encumbered by issues concerning accurate early diagnosis and heterogeneity of clinical presentation in terms of rate of progression and manifestation of behavioral and cognitive deficits. Drachman (1988) suggests that there is a need to accurately evaluate functions that are necessary for competent driving, noting that limitations of driving privileges should be based on demonstration of impaired driving competence rather than the suspicion of the presence of a dementing disorder. Until some useful guidelines emerge from appropriate research, clinicians need to be aware of the potential for occurrence of driving difficulties and the procedures for obtaining formal driving evaluation through the appropriate government transportation authorities (Donnelly & Karlinsky, 1990).

As is evident from this discussion on driving, guidelines and procedures for evaluating an individual's competence to engage in a specific higher order psychosocial task are limited. As with driving, studies examining the relationships between cognitive functioning and competence to perform other higher order psychosocial tasks in dementia victims are beginning to emerge. An appreciation of the complexities of these relationships, particularly early in the course of a dementing process, is needed if clinicians are to make responsible recommendations concerning individuals' specific behavioral competencies.

Relationships between cognition and everyday functioning

Although it has been suggested that deterioration in behavioral, cognitive, and psychosocial functions are interdependent and follow an orderly progression (Reisberg, Ferris, DeLeon, & Crook, 1982), few studies have examined these relationships. Weintraub, Baratz, and Mesulam (1982) reported on two case studies of demented individuals who showed marked discrepancies between the extent of the cognitive deficits and the degree of impairment in daily living activities. In addition to noting that the extent of involvement of cognitive functions may not reflect the person's functional capacity at home, they observed that the pattern of impairment in both spheres of behavior appeared to parallel each other. That is, a person with pronounced memory impairment relative to other cognitive deficits also showed deficits in everyday functioning reflective of the underlying memory impairment. Similarly, Henderson, Mack, and Williams (1989) found that measures of memory and visuoconstructive functions but not disease severity, attention, or language emerged as predictors of spatial disorientation in everyday functioning as reported by caregivers. Vitaliano, Breen, Albert, Russo, and Prinz (1984) examined the degree to which five measures of cognition (attention, calculation, recognition memory, recall, and orientation) could predict three classes of functional competence (recreation, communication, and maintenance). They found that it was possible to predict functional competence from a knowledge of attention and memory deficits. Teri et al. (1989) examined the relationships between measures of behavior, cognition, and ADL performance. Level of behavior disturbance was largely unrelated to performance on the Dementia Rating Scale (DRS), a measure of cognitive functioning, or the Instrumental Activities of Daily Living and Self-Care Skills, a measure assessing both IADL and ADL. Overall level of cognitive impairment was associated with poor performance of IADL. The two subscales of the DRS that correlated significantly with IADL scores were Initiation/Perseveration and Memory. These studies lend support to the contention that cognitive and functional abilities are interdependent and begin to address specific interrelationships.

Another approach to examining the interdependence between cognitive and psychosocial skills is to compare the relative patterns of impairment across different functional domains. Multidimensional rating scales such as the Clinical Dementia Rating Scale (CDR) (Hughes, Berg, Danziger, Coben, & Martin, 1982) permit this type of examination. The CDR consists of six cognitive and behavioral categories: Memory, Orientation, Judgment and Problem Solving, Community Affairs, Home and Hobbies, and Personal Care. Ratings of healthy (CDR 0), questionable (CDR 0.5), mild (CDR 1), moderate (CDR 2), and severe (CDR 3) are assigned from extensive information obtained from a collateral informant and psychometric assessment of the patient. A global severity rating is then determined by applying criteria to the scores obtained on each dimension (Berg, 1988). It is apparent from the criteria for determining the global rating that, between domains, scores for an individual may vary.

The Functional Rating Scale (FRS) (Crockett, Tuokko, Koch, & Parks, 1989;

Tuokko & Crockett, 1991), a derivative of the CDR, contains two additional domains: Language and Affect (see Table 20.1). The Language domain characterizes the communication skills of the patient, taking into account receptive and expressive language skills. The Affect domain refers to changes in mood or personality (e.g., increased irritability, aggressiveness, anxiety, agitation) with impaired contact with reality (i.e., prominent hallucinations or delusions) as an endpoint (severe impairment). These two domains were included because they are extremely important factors to be considered in management planning. Each domain is rated from healthy (1) to severe impairment (5).

In the Clinic for Alzheimer Disease and Related Disorders at the University Hospital-UBC Site, Vancouver, Canada, an outpatient diagnostic setting, the FRS is completed for each patient by a multidisciplinary team including a geriatrician/internist, psychiatrist, social worker, neuropsychologist, speech pathologist, and neurologist. Each team member assesses the patient and interviews a collateral informant, usually a friend or family member. The team comes to a consensus for each rating of the FRS using all information obtained. Diagnoses are made by the team in accordance with the DSM-III-R criteria for dementia and the NINCDS-ADRDA (McKhann et al., 1984) criteria for AD. Patients who do not meet the standard criteria for dementia (Not Demented) include those with Memory scores of 1 or 2. The sum of the ratings on the FRS is used to define levels of severity: Mild, FRS = 16–24; Moderate, FRS = 25–32; and Severe, FRS = 33–40.

The FRS ratings for 496 patients diagnosed as Not Demented or Probable-AD were tabulated and the Probable-AD group was classified with respect to level of severity. The FRS ratings for the Probable-AD group were also reclassified according to the CDR criteria to determine correspondence between the two scales (see Table 20.2). These results indicated that, on average, the groups resulting from the CDR classifications were modestly more impaired with a broader range of FRS scores than the groups resulting from the FRS classifications.

To examine the relative patterns of impairment for each level of severity, the percentage of cases assigned each rating in each severity domain of the FRS is shown in Tables 20.3 and 20.4. The majority of ratings in each domain for the Not Demented group reflected no or questionable impairment. The notable exception is the rating for Affect, which may reflect a high incidence of mood disorder in this group. The mildly impaired Probable-AD group showed a dispersion of scores within each domain, with the largest percentages for most individual domains falling at the Mild level of impairment. Of note is the finding that 93.8% of the cases were able to perform Personal Care tasks adequately. Personal Care continued to be relatively preserved in relation to other psychosocial domains for the moderately impaired group. The severely impaired Probable-AD group continued to show some dispersion of scores. These findings illustrate that individual cases may vary with respect to level of impairment in different functional domains even within the same severity level.

To determine the correspondence between the FRS levels of severity and other measures of cognitive and psychosocial functioning, the neuropsychological test performance of the Not Demented, Mild, Moderate, and Severe Probable-AD patients was examined in relation to the performance of 76 volunteers recruited from senior citizen's activity groups in the community. Each person in the normal elderly (NE) sample was judged suitable for inclusion on the basis of interview

TABLE 20.1. Functional Rating Scale

	Healthy (1)	Questionable (2)	Mild (3)	Moderate (4)	Severe (5)
Memory	No deficit, or inconsistent forgetfulness evident only on clinical interview	Variable symptoms reported by patient or relative, seemingly unrelated to level of functioning	Memory losses which interfere with daily living, more apparent for recent events	Moderate memory loss, only highly learned material retained, new material rapidly lost	Severe memory loss, unable to recall relevant aspects of current life, very sketchy recall of past life
Social/Community and Occupational	Neither patient nor relative aware of any deficit	Variable levels of functioning reported by patient or relatives, no objective evidence of deficits in employment or social situations	Patient or relative aware of decreased performance in demanding employment or social settings, appears normal to casual inspection	Patient or relative aware of ongoing deterioration, does not appear normal to objective observer, unable to perform job, little independent functioning outside home	Marked impairment of social functioning, no independent functioning outside home
Home and Hobbies	No changes noted by patient or relative	Slightly decreased involvement in household tasks and hobbies	Engages in social activities in the home but definite impairment on some household tasks, some complicated hobbies and interests abandoned	Only simple chores/ hobbies preserved, most complicated hobbies/interests abandoned	No independent involvement in home or hobbies

Personal Care	Fully capable of self-care	Occasional problems with self-care reported by patient/relatives or observed	Needs prompting to complete tasks adequately (i.e., dressing, feeding, hygiene)	Requires supervision in dressing, feeding, hygiene, and keeping track of personal effects	Needs constant supervision and assistance with feeding, dressing, or hygiene
Language Skills	No disturbance of language reported by patient or relative	Subjective complaint or relative reports of language deficits, usually limited to word finding or naming	Patient or relative reports variable disturbances in such skills as articulation or naming, occasional language impairment evident during examination	Patient or relative reports consistent language disturbance, language disturbance evident on examination	Severe impairment of receptive and/or expressive language, production of unintelligible speech
Problem Solving and Reasoning	Solves everyday problems adequately	Variable impairment of problem solving, similarities, differences	Difficulty in handling complex problems	Marked impairment on complex problem-solving tasks	Unable to solve problems at any level, trial-and-error behavior often observed
Affect	No change in affect reported by patient or relative	Appropriate concern with respect to symptomatology	Infrequent changes in affect (e.g., irritability) reported by patient or relative, would appear normal to objective observer	Frequent changes in affect reported by patient or relative, noticeable to objective observer	Sustained alterations of affect, impaired contact with reality observed or reported
Orientation	Fully oriented	Occasional difficulties with time relationships	Marked difficulty with time relationships	Usually disoriented to time and often to place	Oriented only to person or not at all

TABLE 20.2.   Comparison of Clinical Dementia Rating (CDR) and Functional
Rating Scale (FRS) scores

Functional Rating Scale	Clinical Dementia Rating				
	0	0.5	1	2	3
	(N = 10)	(N = 164)	(N = 164)	(N = 112)	(N = 46)
M	11.6	16.4	22.3	30.5	38.0
SD	(2.7)	(3.3)	(4.3)	(3.1)	(2.0)

TABLE 20.3.   Percentage of Not Demented and Mild Probable AD Cases Assigned
Each Rating on the FRS

FRS	Not Demented					Mild				
	1	2	3	4	5	1	2	3	4	5
Memory	12.4	57.5	26.3	3.8	0	0	0	52.6	47.4	0
Social/Occupational	9.7	44.6	41.9	3.8	0	0	6.2	83.5	10.3	0
Home/Hobbies	27.4	45.2	23.1	3.8	0.5	4.1	29.9	54.6	11.3	0
Personal Care	79.6	18.3	1.1	0.5	0.5	62.9	30.9	6.2	0	0
Language	48.9	41.4	8.1	1.1	0.5	25.8	28.9	40.2	5.2	0
Problem Solving	40.3	43.5	14.5	1.6	0	7.2	27.8	43.3	19.6	2.1
Affect	7.5	24.2	22.6	43.5	2.2	8.2	13.4	48.5	23.7	6.2
Orientation	71.0	24.7	4.3	0	0	12.4	39.2	32.0	16.5	0

Note: AD = Alzheimer's disease; FRS = Functional Rating Scale.

TABLE 20.4.   Percentage of Moderate and Severe Probable AD Cases Assigned
Each Rating on the FRS

FRS	Moderate					Severe				
	1	2	3	4	5	1	2	3	4	5
Memory	0	0	9.6	77.2	13.2	0	0	0	9.1	90.9
Social/Occupational	0	0	29.4	69.9	0.7	0	0	0	44.2	55.8
Home/Hobbies	0	3.7	40.4	52.9	2.9	0	0	3.9	45.5	50.6
Personal Care	16.2	32.4	34.6	16.9	0	0	0	15.6	42.9	41.6
Language	7.4	16.9	31.6	41.9	2.2	1.3	1.3	5.2	36.4	55.8
Problem Solving	0	4.4	24.3	57.4	14.0	0	0	2.6	15.6	81.8
Affect	5.1	2.9	36.8	36.8	18.4	1.3	0	15.6	29.9	53.2
Orientation	0.7	5.9	19.9	64.7	8.8	0	0	0	19.5	80.5

Note: AD = Alzheimer's disease; FRS = Functional Rating Scale.

and medical questionnaire material. None of the individuals included were receiving institutional or home care services, had a history of treatment for psychiatric or neurological conditions, or were less than 50 years of age. Each patient was administered the Information, Similarities, Digit Span, Block Design, and Digit Symbol subtests from the Wechsler Adult Intelligence Scale-Revised (WAIS-R) (Wechsler, 1981); the Multifocus Assessment Scale (MAS) (Coval, Crockett, Holliday, & Koch, 1985); item 227 (Visual Memory) from the Luria Nebraska Neuropsychological Battery (LNNB) (Golden, Hammeke, & Purisch, 1980) modified to include copy and 5-minute delayed recall components; Cued Recall Procedure for Memory Assessment (Buschke, 1984; Tuokko & Crockett, 1989; Tuokko, Vernon-Wilkinson,

Weir, & Beattie, 1991); Controlled Word Association Test (CWAT) (Benton, 1968); and measures of finger tapping speed and grip strength. The MAS is composed of eight subtests assessing rudimentary social skills (Social Behavior); rudimentary auditory and visual receptive language skills (Auditory Receptive Language, Visual Receptive Language); orientation to time, place, and personally relevant information (Mental Status and Orientation); life satisfaction (Mood); rudimentary expressive language skills (Expressive Language); and accessibility to testing (Accessibility). The Social Behavior, Expressive Language, and Accessibility subscales provide ratings of the observed behavior during testing. The remaining subscales are performance-based measures. The Present Functioning Questionnaire (PFQ) is administered as a structured interview with a collaborative informant, usually a close family member (Crockett et al., 1989; Tuokko & Crockett, 1991). This measure was constructed to reflect problems encountered in everyday functioning as identified in the research literature on aging for use with an outpatient population suspected of dementia. The 65 items of the PFQ are arranged into the problem areas of Personality, Everyday Tasks, Language Skills, Memory Functions, and Self-Care Functions. Care is taken to pursue areas in which a problem (i.e., change in behavior) has been identified by determining when the symptom first became apparent, how frequently the problem arises, and how the problem impacts on the care of the individual. In this manner, it is possible to obtain information pertinent to the developmental sequence of symptoms as well as the severity of disruption caused by the problem.

Table 20.5 contains the means and standard deviations obtained for the NE sample and each of the patient groups. Test scores falling more than 2 standard deviations below the means obtained by the NE sample are indicated to illustrate the emergence of deficits across the levels of severity. However, it must be noted that the NE sample, like many volunteer samples, is relatively well educated. Thus, using the scores obtained for this sample on some of the measures (e.g., WAIS-R subtests) for comparison purposes may result in the overidentification of deficits. Bearing this in mind, examination of Table 20.3 suggests that the Not Demented group shows minimal impairment even though family members reported problems in the areas of Memory, Everyday Tasks, and Language. The Mild group shows pervasive problems on measures of memory and the emergence of problem-solving difficulties. Deficits on measures of language functioning and more pervasive difficulties on problem-solving measures emerge. All measures, with the exception of grip strength, show defective performances for the Severe group. Problems reported by collaborative informants increase within each problem area and in the number of problem areas identified across levels of severity.

These examinations of the FRS illustrate the evolution of deficits in the cognitive and psychosocial functioning of AD patients over the course of the disease and indicate that there may be marked differences in the types of problems manifest between individuals within the same global level of severity. The identified interrelationships between cognitive and psychosocial functioning and differences between individuals serve as a basis for formulating appropriate management strategies for AD patients. However, other factors such as environmental demands may impact on the functioning of individuals. For example, persons primarily engaged in routine, overlearned tasks may continue to function relatively independently well into the course of a dementing illness, whereas difficulty performing in a highly

TABLE 20.5. Means (*M*) and Standard Deviations (*SD*) of Neuropsychological Measures for Normal Elderly (NE), Not Demented (ND), Mild, Moderate, and Severe Probable AD Patients

									Probable Alzheimer Disease					
	NE (N = 76)		*ND* (N = 186)		*Mild* (N = 97)		*Moderate* (N = 136)		*Severe* (N = 77)	
Memory										
WAIS-R										
Information	13.0	(2.4)	9.9	(3.4)	*7.2	(2.7)	*4.8	(2.6)	*1.6	(1.7)
Digit Span	12.8	(3.0)	10.5	(3.2)	9.0	(2.7)	*6.4	(2.8)	*3.3	(3.4)
MAS										
Mental Status	9.9	(0.1)	*9.5	(1.4)	*7.1	(2.3)	*4.3	(2.4)	*1.1	(1.4)
Orientation	9.9	(0.1)	*9.6	(1.3)	*8.2	(1.6)	*6.4	(1.9)	*2.5	(2.4)
LNNB										
Immediate	4.2	(0.8)	3.7	(1.1)	*2.3	(1.2)	*1.6	(1.1)	*0.5	(0.8)
Delay	4.7	(0.6)	4.1	(0.9)	2.4	(1.3)	1.4	(1.4)	0.3	(0.7)
Cued Recall[a]										
Immediate	8.4	(1.8)	6.5	(2.5)	*2.7	(2.1)	*1.7	(1.9)	*0.1	(0.3)
Retrieval	27.7	(4.6)	21.9	(7.4)	*10.0	(5.6)	*7.1	(5.2)	*1.2	(1.9)
Acquisition	35.9	(0.4)	*34.4	(3.4)	*27.3	(6.7)	*21.0	(9.3)	*5.8	(9.3)
Retention	11.9	(0.2)	12.0	(5.7)	*8.6	(3.2)	*6.5	(3.7)	*1.2	(2.6)
Language										
MAS										
Auditory receptive language	7.5	(0.8)	7.7	(0.7)	7.4	(1.1)	6.9	(1.4)	*3.9	(2.7)
Visual receptive language	8.9	(0.5)	8.7	(0.7)	8.5	(0.9)	*6.9	(1.9)	*2.9	(3.1)
Expressive language	3.0	(0.0)	*2.9	(0.3)	*2.8	(0.4)	*2.5	(0.7)	*1.4	(0.9)
CWAT	38.6	(12.2)	29.9	(13.0)	24.6	(11.4)	14.9	(9.8)	*4.3	(5.8)
Problem solving										
WAIS-R										
Similarities	14.3	(2.6)	10.6	(3.4)	*7.8	(3.2)	*5.7	(2.8)	*2.3	(2.5)
Block Design	13.4	(3.1)	10.3	(3.1)	7.6	(3.4)	*4.9	(3.1)	*2.4	(2.3)
Digit Symbol[b]	14.9	(2.7)	*8.7	(2.9)	*6.5	(2.9)	*4.1	(3.1)	*1.3	(1.5)

Measure					
Motor					
Tapping					
Right	46.7 (8.9)	40.2 (11.5)	40.9 (10.9)	33.9 (12.8)	*20.7 (18.9)
Left	41.4 (8.5)	37.4 (10.8)	37.4 (9.7)	32.5 (11.7)	*20.1 (18.3)
Grip					
Right	31.1 (12.3)	28.5 (10.9)	24.7 (11.1)	22.1 (12.0)	15.9 (12.8)
Left	28.3 (11.1)	26.1 (10.9)	22.5 (10.5)	19.7 (11.9)	14.5 (11.5)
LNNB					
Copy	4.9 (0.2)	4.9 (0.3)	4.9 (0.5)	*4.1 (1.1)	*2.2 (2.2)
Executive					
MAS					
Social behavior	11.0 (0.0)	*10.9 (0.3)	*10.8 (0.6)	*10.8 (0.6)	*9.2 (2.7)
Mood	9.0 (4.7)	3.9 (7.2)	6.5 (5.9)	6.4 (5.9)	6.3 (6.2)
Accessibility	9.8 (0.3)	9.8 (0.6)	9.5 (0.8)	9.0 (1.1)	*7.0 (2.3)
Present functioning questionnaire					
Personality	1.5 (2.0)	4.4 (3.1)	*4.6 (2.7)	*6.3 (2.9)	*7.5 (3.5)
Everyday	0.3 (0.9)	*2.2 (2.3)	*4.3 (2.6)	*7.2 (2.5)	*9.3 (2.5)
Language	0.2 (0.9)	*1.7 (1.9)	*2.1 (1.9)	*3.5 (2.1)	*5.3 (1.9)
Memory	0.9 (1.8)	*5.5 (5.2)	*8.5 (2.9)	*10.0 (2.6)	*11.2 (2.1)
Self-care	0.1 (0.4)	0.3 (0.9)	0.5 (1.1)	*1.6 (1.8)	*6.3 (3.6)
Total	2.9 (4.8)	*13.5 (8.2)	*19.5 (6.9)	*28.5 (7.0)	*39.4 (9.3)
Other					
Age	69.4 (8.6)	65.9 (11.1)	70.5 (8.4)	71.8 (7.9)	71.1 (8.8)
Education	13.2 (3.5)	11.8 (3.2)	11.7 (3.3)	10.4 (3.3)	12.4 (8.0)
FRS Total	8.4 (1.0)	15.8 (3.2)	21.3 (2.1)	28.1 (2.3)	36.6 (2.5)

[a] N = 157, Not Demented; N = 80, Mild; N = 45, Severe.

[b] N = 121, Not Demented; N = 52, Mild; N = 86, Moderate; N = 28, Severe.

*> 2 SD below M of normal elderly sample.

Note: WAIS-R = Wechsler Adult Intelligence Scale-Revised; MAS = Multifocus Assessment Scale; LNNB = Luria Nebraska Neuropsychological Battery; CWAT = Controlled Word Association Test; FRS = Functional Rating Scale; AD = Alzheimer's disease.

demanding occupation may be one of the first indications of the onset of cognitive impairment. Thus, an important part of psychosocial evaluation when management is of particular concern includes understanding the environmental context of the AD patient.

Management

The neuropsychological approach to the assessment of individuals with AD and related disorders tends to focus on the identification and characterization of cognitive impairments. This information can be valuable, not only for diagnostic purposes, but for guiding the management and care of dementia victims when supplemented with an understanding of psychosocial functioning or how the individual interacts with environment. The vast majority of individuals with dementia are cared for by family members in the community. Care is most often provided in the home environment for two reasons: (a) typically, families are reluctant to relinquish the care of their loved one to others; and (b) the cost of long-term institutionalization is very high. Hence, the family and the impact of dementia on the family need to be considered as environmental components.

Alzheimer's Disease and Caregivers

Rabins, Mace, and Lucas (1982) conducted a study to identify behaviors exhibited by dementia patients that led families to seek assistance. The families of 55 dementia patients were asked an open-ended question to identify the "biggest problem" in patient care. Twenty-two different problems were reported—50% or more of the respondents identified the following problems: memory disturbance, catastrophic reactions, demanding/critical behavior, night wandering, hiding things, communication difficulties, suspiciousness, making accusations, meals, daytime wandering, and bathing. The problem identified as the "most serious" included physical violence, memory disturbance, incontinence, catastrophic reactions, hitting, making accusations, and suspiciousness. Sanford (1975) had caregivers indicate the incidence of behavior problems on a checklist and then note which problems would need to be alleviated to establish a tolerable situation in the home. Sleep disturbance, fecal incontinence, general immobility, and dangerous behavior were least well tolerated. Using a sample of 214 caregivers, Gilleard, Belford, Gilleard, Whittick, and Geldhill (1984) found the need for constant supervision, proneness to fall, incontinence, night-time wandering, and the inability of dementia patients to engage in meaningful activities on their own initiative were perceived as major problems.

The impact of behavioral problems on the health and well-being of the caregivers has also been investigated. In a large-scale community based study (Deimling & Bass, 1984), "disruptive behaviors" such as striking a family member, swearing, disrupting meals; and "poor social functioning" such as uncooperativeness, withdrawal, and isolation were significantly associated with poor family relationships and caregiver stress, even when the level of patient cognitive impairment was controlled. Many additional factors have been investigated (e.g., Morris, Morris, & Britton, 1988; Baumgarten, 1989) that may affect the coping ability of the

caregiver, including their attributions and coping strategies, the quality of the caregiver's relationship with the demented individual, and the family and social context. These studies highlight the need to consider the characteristics and concerns of the caregivers when formulating care plans for patients. Other studies (e.g., Colerick & George, 1986; Zarit, Todd, & Zarit, 1986) suggest that the decision to institutionalize may be more related to the caregiver's ability to cope than to the symptoms exhibited by the demented individual. Thus, if it is a public health goal to maintain dementia patients in the community as long as possible, the provision of community based programs or services designed to relieve caregiving strain is of utmost importance.

Advice for Caregivers

The major needs and problems of family caregivers were documented since 1978 from a statewide family caregiver support program conducted in California (Friss, 1990). It was indicated that the provision of information, advice, and referral was the primary need of families. One of the most important contributions the neuropsychologist can make to the management and care of demented individuals is the provision of information to help families understand previously inexplicable behavior and difficulties in terms of brain-behavior relationships. This can be done by demonstrating areas of impaired performance and illustrating strategies for circumventing deficits. Clearly, more research is needed examining the relationships between cognitive and social functioning and, as yet, little information is available that clearly specifies the "fit" between patterns of cognitive deficits and behavioral interventions that optimize patient functioning. However, an understanding of the patient's cognitive strengths and weaknesses can provide a basis for the development of possible strategies for modifying patient behavior and the action of caregivers (Zarit & Zarit, 1983). Alzheimer's disease patients may vary greatly in terms of their patterns of abilities, as well as the requirements of their daily lives or other factors (e.g., past experiences, social support systems, financial resources, etc.). Hence, strategies for managing behavior may vary considerably from case to case. Follow-up evaluations of the patient are helpful for monitoring the disorder and modifying management strategies as problems emerge and subside.

One initial approach to determining appropriate management strategies is to examine the types of deficits manifest. Management strategies specific to deficits in each cognitive or social domain can then be generated. To illustrate, some strategies and techniques for managing the AD patient will be described in the context of the psychosocial domains of the FRS.

Memory

Very early in the course of AD, the evident memory impairment may be a circumscribed retrieval deficit with acquisition and retention of material remaining intact. The provision of cues in the environment (e.g., calendar in visible place, message pad and pen by telephone, wearing name tags) may be sufficient to support retrieval. Similarly, in conversation the provision of cues or framing information so as to promote recognition may prove useful. As memory problems become more pervasive, affecting acquisition and retention, strengthening the initial encoding of new information through repetition may prove useful. Experimental studies have shown that having an AD patient observe a task being performed, verbalizing the sequence of steps needed to perform the task, and imitating the performance of the task results in superior recall of the task than providing any one of these procedures alone (Gallie, Graf, & Tuokko, 1990).

"Social and Occupational Effects" or "Concerns"

Although the social skills of AD patients tend to remain relatively intact well into the course of the disease, embarrassment or insecurity resulting from memory and other cognitive deficits may result in social withdrawal or increasing irritability in social settings. A nonjudgmental, supportive social environment may help to alleviate some of the fears of the AD patient. Engaging in an activity with one other individual within the context of a larger social gathering may also allow the AD patient to be actively involved without becoming overwhelmed by the demands of the environment. The increasing social demands of the AD patient may become taxing for the caregiver (e.g., "He follows me around all day like a puppy!"). Alzheimer's disease patients may be reluctant to leave the familiar surroundings of their own home or stay with someone other than the primary caregiver. However, for the benefit of both the primary caregiver and the AD patient, adjustment to involvement in an activity center outside the home or having help come into the home can be made with continued support and reassurance.

Home and Hobbies

Early in the course of the disease, the most common problems in the home may involve the operation of appliances and the accomplishment of complex household chores or hobbies. Some of these difficulties can be circumvented by simplifying the task (e.g., revert to simpler or pre-prepared meals; hand-wash dishes instead of using dishwasher) but guidance or assistance may be required where this type of simplification is untenable. This guidance may take the form of breaking down complex tasks into steps and providing prompts to complete each step in the sequence. For example, setting the table may be accomplished by first handing the plates to the AD patient and indicating where they are to be placed. Subsequent trips to the table may be made to add each piece of the setting. The AD patients who maintained complex hobbies such as knitting, crocheting, woodworking, or model building may continue their involvement by using simpler patterns or attempting smaller projects. As the disease progresses, safety in the home is of increasing concern. Fire hazards such as the stove, irons, kettles and cigarette smoking are of particular concern, but there are many other potential hazards in the home for the cognitively impaired. Some precautions which may prove useful include the following:

1. Removal of stove switch knobs or fuses or turning off the gas under the stove when there is no supervision in the kitchen.
2. Using a kettle that whistles or an electric kettle with an automatic shutoff.
3. Installing safety latches on cupboards that contain dangerous substances.
4. Removing the sink stopper to avoid overflow accidents.
5. Lowering the hot water heater temperature and covering hot water pipes to avoid burns or scalds.
6. Marking sliding glass doors with decorative tape or decals.

7. Demarking the edge of steps, bathtub, or countertops with tape or paint of contrasting color.

8. Placing locks on doors or windows where they cannot be seen, or in unusual places.

9. Adding a thermostat lock.

10. Ensuring that floor (i.e., surface, rug, or matting) is not slippery or easily tripped over and does not create frightening reflections.

11. Putting out of view potentially dangerous objects such as power tools, scissors, knives, liquor, firearms, lighters, matches, and fragile glassware.

Personal Care

Personal care typically remains relatively preserved until well into the course of the disease. However, problems with dressing, eating, grooming, and toileting, when they emerge, can be very difficult for caregivers to manage. Problems with dressing are usually noted first. The AD patient may have difficulty selecting appropriate clothing or may be content to wear the same clothes day after day, failing to recognize the need for laundering. Keeping only seasonal clothes in the closet or providing a limited selection of outfits may alleviate some of the problems encountered in choosing clothing. Purchasing duplicate sets of the same clothes and rotating them may allow the AD patient the comfort of wearing clean familiar clothing. Some personal care problems occurring relatively early in the course (e.g., urinating in an inappropriate location; eating food off only one side of the plate) may be due to spatial disorientation or poor visuospatial processing. Providing a sign or symbol designating the bathroom may be of assistance in some cases. Leaving the light on in the bathroom at night may help the AD patient find their way to the correct location. Coloring the water in the toilet bowl may also assist in identifying the proper location to urinate within the bathroom. Turning the plate occasionally during the meal may assist the patient in locating the food. Many people have well-developed lifelong personal care routines, and maintenance of these routines may foster continued independent functioning. As the disease progresses, problems emerge in all aspects of personal care. Initially, prompting may be sufficient to maintain the behavior. At later stages, it becomes necessary to break tasks into more manageable units for the patient and prompt or assist at each step. For example, early in the course of the disease a reminder to brush teeth may be adequate. Later, it may be necessary to place toothpaste on the brush and hand it to the patient. At a later stage, it may be necessary to begin the brushing movement with the patient's hand before the task is engaged in.

Problem Solving and Reasoning

Problem solving and reasoning difficulties may be manifest in many ways and may often be apparent early in the course of the disease. For people who are still in the workforce at the onset of the disease, the initial signs of deterioration often emerge in the workplace due to the complexity of many job situations. Disturbances in functioning may become readily apparent when complex tasks such as managing finances, completing tax returns, or planning and arranging meetings or trips are undertaken. Alzheimer's disease patients show increasing difficulty comprehending abstract concepts as the disease progresses. Time concepts lose their meaning and unfamiliar or unexpected situations are dealt with in a trial-and-error fashion. Here again, tasks can be broken down into simple components for the AD patient, but assistance may be required with complex decision making. Arrangement for power of attorney or committeeship may need to be made to ensure that the AD patient is not in jeopardy.

Language Skills

Disturbances in receptive and expressive language typically evolve gradually over the course of the disease. Early in the course, subtle language-related deficits may be manifest with careful testing, but may not be readily apparent to family members. Slowness in word finding may be evident, or the AD patient may circumlocute to arrive eventually at the correct response. Responses may be vague or only tangentially related to questions asked due to incomplete comprehension. Reading may be well maintained, but comprehension of what is read may be impaired. Paraphasic errors occurring in conversation may or may not be self-corrected. In the later stages of AD, verbal output may remain fluent but lack content and/or consist primarily of jargon. Particularly in the early stages, it is not uncommon for families to underestimate the language disturbance of the AD patients. It is often assumed that if patients can read out loud, they also comprehend what is read, or that if patients provide responses, they understood the question. Although communication disorders themselves are often not treatable in AD, families may be taught techniques to improve communication (Bayles & Kasniak, 1987). Clarifying for the family the types of language problems experienced by the AD patient and illustrating techniques for improving communication can assist families in caring for the AD patient. Suggestions for improving communication between the caregiver and the AD patient may include the following: use familiar, concrete terms; use direct statements; be literal (i.e., avoid metaphors and analogies); choose simple, relevant topics; replace pronouns (e.g., he, she) with proper nouns (e.g., Mary, Dr. Jones); break long sentences into shorter ones; revise and restate the misunderstood; allow more time for responses; and be attentive to body language and establish eye contact. It is important to establish reliable yes/no responses to assist communication with severely impaired patients.

Affect

Changes in mood or affect of AD patients is not uncommon and can be of great concern to the caregiver. Increasing irritability, anxiety, depression, emotional lability, aggressiveness, and suspiciousness are some of the more common problems faced by the caregiver. In the case of severe behavior disturbance, medical intervention (e.g., antidepressant, antipsychotic medication) may be required. However, the side effects of medications can be detrimental to patient functioning and need to be closely monitored. Often, environmental manipulations can be used instead to reduce behavioral disturbance. For example, the frequency and impact of catastrophic reactions can often be lessened by teaching the family to avoid confrontations with the patient by using distraction or approaching the situation in another manner. It is important for caregivers to stay calm because anxiety or aggressiveness on their part may heighten the reaction of the AD patient. Identifying the source or stimulus evoking the behavior may lead to a simple, practical solution. For example, increased irritability may be a sign of physical pain or may be a reaction to events happening around the patient. Alzheimer's disease patients may hallucinate or misinterpret their environment and become agitated in response. Adequate lighting, particularly in the evening, can reduce misinterpretations of shadows or forms. The television and mirrors may be sources of confusion for the AD patient. If the AD patient does not seem frightened or bothered by a delusion, hallucination, or misinterpretation of the environment, ignoring it may be the best approach. In other situations, it may be necessary to cover mirrors or remove objects that create concern on the part of the AD patient. False accusations (e.g., infidelity of spouse) may be hurtful to caregivers who, in response, argue or try to reason with the AD patient. Such accusations may be expressions of fear by the AD patient and reassurance may help to alleviate these fears (e.g., that the spouse may abandon the AD patient for someone else).

Orientation

Disorientation to time may be apparent relatively early in the course of the disease. Appointments may be missed or there may be confusion as to the date, day of the week, month, or year. The patient may also become confused regarding time of day. Although this type of disorientation may be viewed as part of the more pervasive memory problems, appreciation of the concepts of time may also be disturbed. The use of calendars and talking clocks may assist in providing time context for the AD patient. Disorientation with respect to place or how to find one's way around familiar locations may emerge as the disease progresses. Ensuring that the AD patient carries proper identification is crucial if there is a chance that they may become lost. Firmly secured bracelets that carry a contact telephone number or other pertinent information can be obtained. As noted earlier, symbols or labels placed in highly visible locations may assist with spatial orientation (e.g., familiar objects or pictures placed on the patient's door). Demarcation of areas with lights or contrasting colors may also assist in this regard (e.g., light in bathroom at night).

Resources

In addition to contributing to the consultation/planning process in this manner, the clinician may direct caregivers to other available resources.

1. Many reference materials are available for the caregivers to provide them with background information and suggest alternative strategies for coping with behavior change. These include: *The 36 Hour Day: A Family Guide for Caring for Persons with Alzheimer Disease, Related Dementing Illness and Memory Loss in Later Life* (Mace & Rabins, 1981); *Alzheimer's Disease: A Guide for Families* (Powell & Courtice, 1983); *A Guide to Alzheimer's Disease for Family, Spouse and Friends* (Reisberg, 1983); *Dementia: A Practical Guide to Alzheimer's Disease and Related Illness* (Heston & White, 1984); and *Once I Have Had My Tea: A Guide to Understanding and Caring for Memory-Impaired Elderly* (Hladik, 1982).

2. Alzheimer support groups established across North America are probably the most readily accessible educational resource for caregivers of dementia patients. Gonyea (1989), in Boston, evaluated the strengths and weaknesses of 301 Alzheimer support groups. The findings revealed that these groups primarily provide educational and peer support. Involvement in peer support groups offers the family members the opportunity to ventilate their feelings and discuss problems with others who share the caregiving experience. In addition, the Alzheimer's societies and

associations across North America serve as excellent resource centers for educational materials (e.g., family care guides, instructive videotapes).

3. As noted earlier, living with a cognitively impaired individual may have a major impact on the health and well-being of the caregiver. The long-term management of the patient is, to a large extent, dependent on the strength of the social support network. Thus, it is important for caregivers to attend to their own needs as well as those of the AD patient. However, all too often caregivers overlook their own physical and emotional needs. Isolation, feelings of guilt, grief over the losses associated with AD, and chronic fatigue are all common experiences for caregivers. To ensure that the AD patient is receiving the best possible care, it is important for caregivers to maintain realistic expectations for themselves, the AD patient, and others around them. This may involve seeking assistance from other family members, friends, or community resources. It is necessary for the caregiver to try to get enough rest, exercise, and time to themselves if they are to effectively cope with the demands of providing care. The impact of family dynamics may emerge as an issue in the development of a support network for the caregiver. Counseling may help caregivers and/or other members of the support network to adjust to and cope with the ever-changing demands of caring for the AD patient.

4. Various services may be available in the community to assist family members in caring for a dementia patient at home. Although not available in all communities, some of the more commonly utilized services include homemaker services, home delivered meals, adult day center programs, transportation services, and respite care. Utilization of available services allows the family to have time away from the caregiving situation and provides relief from day-to-day demands.

5. In some instances, the need for institutionalization will emerge as being in the best interest of the patient and the caregiver. The decisions to institutionalize and locate a suitable placement are often very difficult tasks for families. Assisting families in these decisions may require much care, understanding, and effort. The sense of guilt felt by families may be lessened by continued support and encouragement to remain actively involved in patient care.

The provision of behavioral management services within care facilities is a relatively new and increasingly visible focus of the neuropsychologist's study of dementia. Although many of the problems encountered in patient/caregiver interactions parallel those encountered in the home by families, new issues centering around adjustment to and management within an institutional environment are emerging (e.g., the need for special units designed for the AD patient) (Goldman & Lazarus, 1988). Specific assessment techniques for use in the formulation of effective interventions within care facilities are being developed (e.g., Coval et al., 1985; Montgomery, 1989) and may provide new insights into strategies for care of persons with dementia and, specifically, of AD patients.

Summary

In conclusion, understanding the psychosocial functioning of the individual with dementia, or the interaction between the person and the environment, is of utmost importance for both diagnostic and care-planning purposes. Although it is often assumed that performance on cognitive tasks offers an adequate estimation of functioning in daily-living activities, little research has addressed this assumption. There is reason to believe that the relationships between cognitive functioning and performance of everyday tasks may vary in relation to stage of dementia, pattern of cognitive deficits/strengths, and the nature of the everyday task itself. Characteristics of the environment in which the individual functions may also play a major role. Continued research is needed to clarify these psychosocial relationships in our endeavor to maximize the level of independent functioning and quality of life for AD patients and their caregivers. In the meantime, practical suggestions for managing the behavior of the AD patient are available through many sources and agencies. Providing information concerning the nature of the disease, strategies and techniques for managing behavior, and the needs of caregivers to families of AD patients is an important first step in this direction.

References

American Psychiatric Association. (1987). *Diagnostic and statistical manual of mental disorders* (3rd ed., rev.) Washington, DC: Author.

Baumgarten, M. (1989). The health of persons giving care to the demented elderly: A critical review of the literature. *Journal of Clinical Epidemiology, 42*(12), 1137–1148.

Bayles, K., & Kasniak, A. W. (1987). *Communication and cognition in normal aging and dementia.* Boston: College Hill Press, Brown and Co.

Benton, A. L. (1968). Differential behavioral effects in frontal lobe disease. *Neuropsychologia, 6*, 53–60.

Berg, L. (1988). Clinical Dementia Rating (CDR). *Psychopharmacology Bulletin, 24*(4), 637–639.

Buschke, H. (1984). Cued recall in amnesia. *Journal of Clinical Neuropsychology, 6*(4), 433–440.

Colerick, E. J., & George, L. K. (1986). Predictors of institutionalization among caregivers of patient's with Alzheimer's disease. *Journal of the American Geriatrics Society, 34*(7), 493–498.

Coopersmith, H. G., Korner-Bitensky, N., & Mayo, N. E. (1989). Determining medical fitness to drive: Physician's responsibilities in Canada. *Canadian Medical Association Journal, 140*, 375–378.

Coval, M., Crockett, D., Holliday, S., & Koch, W. (1985). A Multifocus Assessment Scale for use with frail elderly populations. *Canadian Journal of Aging, 4*(2), 101–109.

Crockett, D., Tuokko, H., Koch, W., & Parks, R. (1989). The assessment of everyday functioning using the Present Functioning Questionnaire and the Functional Rating Scale. *Clinical Gerontologist, 8*(3), 3–25.

Deimling, G. T., & Bass, D. M. (1984). *Mental status among the elderly: Effect of spouse and adult-child caregivers.* Presented at the Gerontological Society, San Antonio, TX.

Donnelly, R., & Karlinsky, H. (1990). The impact of Alzheimer's disease on driving ability: A review. *Journal of Geriatric Psychiatry and Neurology, 3*, 67–72.

Drachman, D. A. (1988). Who may drive? Who may not? Who shall decide? *Annals of Neurology, 24*(6), 787–788.

Duke University Center for the Study of Aging. (1978). Multidimensional functional assessment: the OARS methodology. Durham, NC: Duke University Press.

Friedland, R. P., Koss, E., Kumar, A., Gaine, S., Metzler, D., Haxby, J. V., & Moore, A. (1988). Motor vehicle crashes in dementia of the Alzheimer type. *Annals of Neurology, 24*, 782–786.

Friss, L. (1990). A model state-level approach to family survival for caregivers of brain-impaired adults. *Gerontologist, 30*(1), 121–125.

Gallie, K., Graf, P., & Tuokko, H. (1990). Study strategies and their ability to offset memory losses caused by Alzheimer disease [Special edition/newsletter]. *Canadian Association on Gerontology, 17*, 32.

Gilleard, C. J., Belford, H., Gilleard, E., Whittick, J. E., & Geldhill, K. (1984). Emotional distress among supporters of the elderly mentally infirm. *British Journal of Psychiatry, 145*, 172–177.

Golden, C. J., Hammeke, T. A., & Purisch, A. D. (1980). *Luria-Nebraska Neuropsychological Battery*. Los Angeles: Western Psychological Services.

Goldman, L. S., & Lazarus, L. W. (1988). Assessment of memory and dementia in the nursing home. *Clinics in Geriatric Medicine, 4*, 589–600.

Gonyea, J. G. (1989). Alzheimer's disease support groups: An analysis of structure, format and perceived benefits. *Social Work in Health Care, 14*(1), 61–72.

Gustafson, L. (1987). Frontal lobe degeneration of the non-Alzheimer type. II. Clinical picture and differential diagnosis. *Archives of Gerontology and Geriatrics, 6*, 209–223.

Henderson, V. W., Mack, W., & Williams, B. W. (1989). Spatial disorientation in Alzheimer's disease. *Archives of Neurology, 46*, 391–394.

Heston, L., & White, J. (1984). *Dementia: A practical guide to Alzheimer's disease and related illness*. New York: W. H. Freeman.

Hladik, P. (1982). *Once I have had my tea: A guide to understanding and caring for memory-impaired elderly*. Syracuse: Author.

Hughes, C. P., Berg, L., Danziger, W. L., Coben, L. A., & Martin, R. L. (1984). A new clinical scale for staging dementia. *British Journal of Psychiatry, 140*, 566–572.

Kuriansky, J. B., & Gurland, B. (1976). Performance test of activities of daily living. *International Journal of Aging and Human Development, 7*, 343–352.

Lawton, M. P., & Brody, E. M. (1969). Assessment of older people: Self-maintaining and instrumental activities of daily living. *Gerontologist, 9*, 179–186.

Lawton, M. P., Moss, M., Fulcomer, M., & Kleban, M. H. (1982). A research and service-oriented multi-level assessment instrument. *Journal of Gerontology, 37*, 91–99.

Linn, M. S. (1967). A rapid disability rating scale. *Journal of the American Geriatrics Society, 15*, 211–214.

Linn, M. W., & Linn, B. S. (1981). Problems in assessing response to treatment in the elderly by physical and social function. *Psychopharmacology Bulletin, 17*(4), 74–81.

Linn, M. W., & Linn, B. S. (1982). The Rapid Disability Rating Scale-2. *Journal of the American Geriatrics Society, 30*, 378–382.

Linn, M. W., & Linn, B. S. (1984). Self-Evaluation of Life (SELF) scale: A short comprehensive self-report of health for the elderly. *Journal of Gerontology, 39*, 603–612.

Lishman, W. A. (1978). *Organic psychiatry*. Oxford: Blackwell.

Lowenstein, D. A., Amigo, E., Duara, R., Guterman, A., Hurwitz, D., Berkowitz, N., Wilkie, F., Weinberg, G., Black, B., Gittelman, B., & Eisdorfer, C. (1989). A new scale for the assessment of functional status in Alzheimer's disease and related disorders. *Journal of Gerontology: Psychological Sciences, 44*(4), 114–121.

Lucas-Blaustein, M. J., Filipp, L., Dungan, C., & Tune, L. (1988). Driving in patients with dementia. *Journal of the American Geriatrics Society, 36*, 1087–1091.

Mace, N. L., & Rabins, P. V. (1981). *The 36 hour day: A family guide to coping for persons with Alzheimer's disease and related dementing illnesses and memory loss in later life*. Baltimore: Johns Hopkins University Press.

McKhann, G., Drachman, D., Folstein, M., Katzman, R., Price, D., & Stadlan, E. M. (1984). Clinical diagnosis of Alzheimer's disease: Report of the NINCDS-ADRDA work group under the auspices of Department of Health and Human Services task force on Alzheimer's disease. *Neurology, 34,* 939–944.

Montgomery, K. (1989). *A problem behaviour assessment tool for long-term care.* Presented at the 17th annual meeting of the International Neuropsychological Society, Vancouver, British Columbia, Canada.

Morris, R. G., Morris, L. W., & Britton, P. G. (1988). Factors affecting the emotional well-being of the caregivers of dementia sufferers. *British Journal of Psychiatry, 153,* 147–156.

Neary, D., Snowden, J. S., Northen, B., & Goulding, P. (1988). Dementia of the frontal lobe type. *Journal of Neurology, Neurosurgery and Psychiatry, 51,* 353–361.

Powell, L. S., & Courtice, K. (1983). *Alzheimer's disease: A guide for families.* Reading, MA: Addison Wesley.

Rabins, P. V., Mace, N. L., & Lucas, M. J. (1982). The impact of dementia on the family. *Journal of the American Medical Association, 248*(3), 333–335.

Reisberg, B., Ferris, S. H., DeLeon, M. J., & Crook, T. (1982). The Global Deterioration Scale for assessment of primary degenerative dementia. *American Journal of Psychiatry, 139,* 1136–1139.

Reisberg, B. (1983). *A guide to Alzheimer's disease for family, spouse and friends.* New York: The Free Press.

Reisberg, B., Ferris, S. H., Armand, R., DeLeon, M. J., Schneck, M. K., Buttinger, C., & Bornstein, J. (1984). Functional staging of dementia of the Alzheimer type. *Annals of the New York Academy of Sciences, 435,* 481–483.

Reisberg, B., Ferris, S. H., & Franssen, E. (1985). An ordinal functional assessment tool for Alzheimer's type dementia. *Hospital and Community Psychiatry, 36,* 593–595.

Sanford, J. R. A. (1975). Tolerance of debility in elderly dependents by supporters at home: Its significance for hospital practice. *British Medical Journal, 3,* 471–475.

Tallman, K., Tuokko, H., Weir, J., & Beattie, B. L. (1990). Driving records of patients referred to a dementia clinic [Special edition/newsletter]. *Canadian Association on Gerontology, 17,* 43.

Teri, L., Borson, S., Kiyak, H. A., & Yamagishi, M. (1989). Behavioral disturbance, cognitive dysfunction and functional skill. *Journal of the American Geriatrics Society, 37,* 109–116.

Tuokko, H., & Crockett, D. (1989). Cued recall and memory disorders in dementia. *Journal of Clinical and Experimental Neuropsychology, 11*(2), 278–294.

Tuokko, H., & Crockett, D. (1991). Assessment of everyday functioning in normal and malignant memory disordered elderly. In D. Tupper & K. Cicerone (Eds.), *The neuropsychology of everyday life: Issues in development and rehabilitation* (pp. 135–182). Boston: Kluwer Academic Publishers.

Tuokko, H., Vernon-Wilkinson, R., Weir, J., & Beattie, B. L. (1991). Cued recall and early identification of dementia. *Journal of Clinical and Experimental Neuropsychology, 13*(6), 871–879.

Vitaliano, P. P., Breen, A. R., Albert, M. S., Russo, J., & Prinz, P. N. (1984). Memory, attention and functional status in community-residing Alzheimer type dementia patients and optimally healthy aged individuals. *Journal of Gerontology, 39*(1), 58–64.

Wechsler, D. (1981). *Wechsler Adult Intelligence Scale-Revised manual.* New York: Psychological Corporation.

Weintraub, S., Baratz, R., & Mesulam, M-M. (1982). Daily living activities in the assessment of dementia. In S. Corkin et al. (Eds.), *Alzheimer's disease: A report of progress (Aging, Vol. 19)* (pp. 189–192). New York: Raven Press.

World Health Organization. (1988). *Mental, behavioural and developmental disorders: Diagnostic criteria for research in accordance with the tenth revision of the international classification of diseases.* Geneva: Author.

Zarit, S. H., & Zarit, J. M. (1983). Cognitive impairment. In P. M. Lewinsohn & L. Teri (Eds.), *Clinical geropsychology: New directions in assessment and treatment.* New York: Pergamon Press.

Zarit, S. H., Todd, P. A., & Zarit, J. (1986). Subjective burden of husbands and wives as caregivers: A longitudinal study. *Gerontologist, 26,* 260–266.

21

Pharmacological Treatment in Alzheimer's Disease

J. Wesson Ashford and Ronald F. Zec

Proposed pharmacological treatments for Alzheimer's disease (AD) have been derived from the emerging knowledge about neurotransmitter systems affected by AD. The cortical neurons affected include glutamatergic and somatostatin/gamma-aminobutyric acid (GABA)ergic neurons, whereas the cortical projection neurons affected belong mainly to the nucleus basalis of Meynert cholinergic system, the norepinephrine system of the rostral locus ceruleus, and the serotonin system of the rostral raphe nuclei (Perry, 1987). It is important to consider what common factor could link these diverse systems, and the most likely factor is their involvement in memory function (Ashford & Jarvik, 1985; Ashford, Kolm, Colliver, Bekian, & Hsu, 1989; Butcher & Woolf, 1989; DiPatre, 1991). There is no known approach to preventing, halting, or even slowing the progression of the AD process or the consequent neuronal loss and dementia. One possible pathogenesis is the accumulation in the brain of the abnormal protein amyloid. If amyloid deposition is shown to be pathogenic, then drugs that interfere with amyloid deposition may be able to alter the course of the disease. Until a pathogenic mechanism is identified or a drug is demonstrated to slow the progression of AD, pharmacotherapeutic attempts will probably be limited to palliation of the cognitive impairment. However, at this time, many of the noncognitive psychiatric symptoms, which are common in AD and other dementias, are treatable.

In AD there has recently been considerable investigation of whether neurotransmitter enhancement therapy, mostly cholinergic, might ameliorate the dementia symptoms. There have been some reports of statistically significant positive effects, but no large study has yet demonstrated any clinically significant improvement of the core dementia symptoms—impairment of memory and other cognitive functions. However, many of the other psychiatric symptoms and behavioral disruptions commonly found in AD patients resemble those of other psychiatric disorders (Burns, Jacoby, & Levy, 1990). Specific psychiatric difficulties such as depression, psychosis, agitation, sleep dysregulation, and several other behavioral disorders are common in AD and other demented patients, and these symptoms do respond to treatment. Furthermore, certain types of dementia can be caused by several other diseases that are treatable. In some cases, the actual cause of the dementia can be corrected. Therefore, some of these dementias are reversible, while in other cases, the dementia progression can be slowed or halted (Besdine et al., 1980).

This chapter addresses the medical and pharmacological management of AD patients. We initially discuss the diagnostic factors that can cause or exacerbate dementia and that may respond to specific treatment. We then review the history of nonspecific treatments for improving dementia. This leads to discussion of research into the treatment of the memory loss, the predominant feature of dementia (American Psychiatric Association [APA], 1987). Specific practical issues in management of the psychiatric symptoms common in dementia patients are outlined. The final point is the issue of whether the underlying AD pathological process can be directly halted in the future.

BASIC MEDICAL EVALUATION AND TREATMENT

When patients present with memory problems, they should receive a complete dementia evaluation (Wells, 1977). This evaluation begins with a history and physical exam. Before instituting pharmacological treatments, electrocardiograph (ECG), chest radiograph, and other routine laboratory tests (Table 21.1) must also be

TABLE 21.1.   Basic Medical Evaluation

Medical history
Physical examination, neurological examination
Mental status examination
  Mini-Mental State Examination (Folstein et al., 1975; Ashford et al., 1992)
Neuropsychological testing
Electrocardiogram
Chest radiograph
Routine urinalysis
Blood tests
  Complete blood count
  Serological test for syphilis
  Serological test for HIV if a risk-factor is present
  Chemistry panel
    Electrolytes (Na, K, Cl, CO_2, Ca, Mg)
    Liver function tests (bilirubin, enzymes, ammonia)
    Kidney function tests (BUN, creatinine)
    Lipid panel (cholesterol, triglycerides)
    Thyroid panel (T_3, T_4, TSH)
  Vitamin B_{12}, folate levels
Magnetic resonance image of brain
Electroencephalogram
Others if indicated
  Computed Tomography scan of brain
  Skull radiograph
  Isotope cysternography
  Drug screen and drug levels

Note: HIV = human immunodeficiency virus; BUN = blood urea nitrogen; T_3 = triiodoth-yronine; T_4 = thyroxine; TSH = thyroid-stimulating hormone.
Source: Adapted from Wells, 1977

obtained, both in consideration of the increased incidence of medical problems in the elderly and the sensitivity of elderly patients to medication. The specific purposes of this evaluation are:

> 1. To diagnose significant medical conditions that might contribute to the cognitive impairment, including an inventory of recent and current pharmacological treatments.
> 2. To define the basis of the cognitive impairment, including the likelihood of AD and other causes of dementia, treatable and untreatable.
> 3. To determine the severity of the dementia (Ashford et al., 1992).

A complete dementia evaluation is widely considered to be a necessary first step in the management of the demented patient.

Hypertension

The significant medical problem most commonly encountered in the demented patient is hypertension, affecting about 50% of the population at age 60 years. Hypertension is the most common risk factor for stroke and hence, multi-infarct dementia. Furthermore, multi-infarct dementia frequently co-occurs with AD (Tomlinson, Blessed, & Roth, 1970). Several medications used to treat hypertension can have an adverse effect on mental function, particularly those with effects on catecholamines, such as alpha-methyldopa and propranolol. The newer beta-blockers cross the blood-brain barrier more slowly, and may variably affect cognitive function (Palac et al., 1990). Peripherally active agents, including the smooth muscle relaxers, calcium channel blockers, and angiotensin-converting enzyme (ACE) inhibitors, so far, appear to be better for the demented patients, and agents from the latter two groups are under scrutiny as possible cognition enhancers (Ban et al., 1990; Deyo, Straube, & Disterhoft, 1989; Ferris, 1990; Sandin, Jasmin, & Levere, 1990). A few psychologically active medications, such as amphetamines or methylphenidate, will raise blood pressure, and thus should be considered carefully before they are used in elderly patients. Many medications, including neuroleptics and tricyclic antidepressants, will lower blood pressure, and thus can be used cautiously in hypertensive patients, adjusting the antihypertensive medication according to shifts in blood pressure. Antihypertensives and all types of tranquilizers also increase the risk of falling in the elderly (Buchner & Larson, 1987; Sorock & Shimkin, 1988).

Medications

The second significant medical issue to consider in evaluating demented patients is their medication. Elderly patients have a variety of common medical ailments and are prescribed an average of seven medications by the time they are 70 years old (Kumar, Salama, Desai, & Kumar, 1988). Many of these medications are psychoactive (Salzman & Van Der Kolk, 1980). Many medications can disrupt cognitive function in elderly individuals who are less able to tolerate certain medications than are younger individuals (Table 21.2).

Normal elderly individuals are sensitive to anticholinergic actions (Table 21.3)

TABLE 21.2. Prescribed Drugs that can Interfere with Cognition

Antihypertensives:
  Alpha-methyldopa, propranolol
Anticholinergics:
  Belladonna alkaloids
    Scopolamine, atropine (e.g., preanesthetic)
  Antispasmodics
    Propantheline, dicyclomine (Donnatal)
  Antidepressants (especially amitriptyline, Richelson, 1990a),
  Neuroleptics (especially thioridazine, Richelson, 1990b),
  Antiparkinsonian agents
    Benztropine, trihexyphenidyl
Antihistaminics:
  H2—for ulcers
    Cimetidine, ranitidine, famotidine, diphenhydramine
GABA agonists:
  Barbiturate receptor agonists
    Barbiturates, diphenylhydantoin, carbamazepine
  Benzodiazepine receptor agonists
    Diazepam, alprazolam, triazolam, temazepam, oxazepam, lorazepam, clonazepam,
      possibly ethanol
  Direct agonists
    Baclofen, valproic acid

TABLE 21.3. Anticholinergic Side Effects

Central
  Failure to consolidate memory
  Sedation, drowsiness, fatigue
  Confusion
  Speech disturbance
  Hallucinations, delirium
  Coma
Peripheral
  Change in heart rate (slow → fast)
  Dryness of the mouth, thirst, difficulty swallowing
  Pupillary dilation, blurred vision
  Attack or exacerbation of narrow-angle glaucoma
  Inhibition of sweating; dry, hot skin
  Constipation
  Difficulty urinating

and can be cognitively impaired by these medications (Miller et al., 1988). Several medications with anticholinergic side effects have commonly been given to the elderly. Central cholinergic function is already significantly impaired in AD patients, and they are accordingly more sensitive to the memory disrupting side effects of anticholinergic drugs (Sunderland, Tariot, et al., 1987).

Patients with ulcers or other stomach problems are frequently given histamine receptor (H_2) blockers (cimetidine, ranitidine, and famotidine), which can adversely affect mental function. This effect is more common in elderly patients with renal or hepatic dysfunction (Lesser, Miller, Boone, & Lowe, 1987; Henann, Carpenter, & Janda, 1988; Lipsy, Fennerty, & Fagan, 1990). There is no evidence that antacids adversely affect mental function (Heyman et al., 1984; Graves et al., 1990), except where blood aluminum levels are directly associated with cognitive dysfunction in patients with kidney problems on dialysis (Salusky, Foley, Nelson, & Goodman, 1991).

Frequently, an attempt to treat an agitated patient with a "minor tranquilizer" will lead to a patient receiving a GABA-agonist medication. GABA agonists include direct GABA-receptor agonists (e.g., baclofen, valproic acid), barbiturate-receptor agonists (e.g., barbiturates, phenytoin, carbamazepine), and benzodiazepine-receptor agonists (e.g., diazepam, alprazolam, triazolam, temazepam, oxazepam, lorazepam, clonazepam, and possibly ethanol). GABA is the primary inhibitory neurotransmitter in the brain and is associated with anxiety reduction, seizure threshold elevation, sedation, and muscle relaxation (Zorumski & Isenberg, 1991). Many studies have shown that GABA agonists interfere with memory (Scharf, 1987; Ghonheim & Mewalt, 1990) and are thus generally contraindicated in patients with memory problems.

Pharmacotherapy for Treatable Dementias

The elderly frequently have medical problems, several of which can impair cognitive function. Therefore, it is crucial to determine whether there are any underlying factors, such as thyroid disease or vitamin deficiency, which might be a cause or contributing factor of a patient's dementia. Additionally, these other conditions can coexist with AD. Therefore, any medical abnormalities should be identified and further evaluated (Besdine et al., 1980). Accordingly, any significant medical condition (e.g., urinary tract infection, Parkinson's disease, and even visual and hearing difficulties) should be appropriately treated to reduce excess disability in these patients.

Several types of dementia other than AD may respond to specific treatment. The second most common cause of dementia is multiple vascular infarcts, often due to small thromboses. The presence of vascular insults to the brain can be sensitively detected by a magnetic resonance imaging (MRI) scan of the head, although the presence of punctate changes neither proves that vascular changes have caused the dementia nor eliminates the possibility of AD. The best approach to the possibility of cerebrovascular disease is to take the same approach that cardiologists recommend for cardiovascular disease (Table 21.4). This approach includes alterations of diet, increased exercise, weight loss, elimination of exposure to tobacco products, and rigorous control of blood pressure below 140/90. Antiplatelet therapy is recommended; for example, one half aspirin tablet per day (Grotta, 1987), but other regimens are under development (Hass et al., 1989). Stringent management of blood cholesterol and other lipids is also important (Brown et al., 1990; Roussouw, Lewis, Path, & Rifkind, 1990; Zimetbaum, Frishman, & Aronson, 1991). Hypertension itself can be related to cognitive dysfunction (Wilkie & Eisdorfer, 1971), although diastolic pressure should not be pushed below 80 (Meyer, Judd, Tawaklna, Rogers, & Mortel, 1986; Tjoa & Kaplan, 1990; Fletcher & Balpott, 1982).

Alcoholism is the third most common cause of dementia (Wells, 1977). Concentrations of alcohol associated with inebriation probably do not directly kill brain cells (alcohol-induced GABA agonism or *N*-methyl-D-aspartate [NMDA]-gluta-

TABLE 21.4. Preventive Therapy for Vascular Disease

1. Low cholesterol diet (low saturated fats; high monounsaturated fats, as found in olive oil, peanut oil, canola oil, deep-sea fish)
2. Exercise, as tolerated
3. Weight loss in overweight individuals
4. Avoidance of tobacco products, second-hand smoke, nicotine
5. Rigorous blood-pressure control below 140/90
6. Antiplatelet therapy (one half aspirin per day)
7. Management of blood cholesterol (diet, medication, monitoring)

mate receptor antagonism might even be protective [Olney, 1988]). However, chronic, heavy alcohol use can induce cerebral atrophy, possibly due to prolonged neuronal inhibition, with resultant diminishment of cognitive function. Alcoholism can be associated with dietary deficits and can lead to thiamine deficiency and Wernicke-Korsakoff encephalopathy. Intoxication frequently leads to accidents involving head trauma, which itself can induce cognitive dysfunction. Also, alcohol withdrawal increases the excitability of neurons, predisposing to seizures and the induction of hypoxic and excitotoxic brain damage. Alcohol-induced liver disease can also lead to hepatic encephalopathy. (Alcoholic brain disease discussed in Greenfield's *Neuropathology*, 1984; see also Brierley & Graham, 1984.) Treatment of alcoholic dementia should involve efforts to eliminate access to alcohol, improve diet, and provide vitamin supplementation. Abstinence has been shown by several studies to lead to some reversal of alcohol-related cerebral atrophy.

Depression or related psychological states can also mimic dementia (McAllister, 1983). In any case where psychogenic dementia is suspected, a psychiatric evaluation must be conducted. Whenever clinically significant depression is associated with cognitive impairment, the depression should be vigorously treated, regardless of whether the depression is secondary to the dementia or the dementia is secondary to the depression. The first step in treating depressed patients with cognitive impairment is antidepressant pharmacotherapy. Electroconvulsive therapy (ECT) should be considered in cases resistant to pharmacological treatment. Supportive therapy, particularly for the family, should be conducted, but is of minimal direct benefit if the patient cannot consolidate new information. Because dementia secondary to depression can easily be missed, all patients should be evaluated for depressive features.

Another cause of dementia is Parkinson's disease. This disease frequently co-occurs with AD (Boller, Mizutani, Roessmann, & Gambetti, 1980; de la Monte, Wells, Hedley-Whyte, & Growdon, 1989). Treatment of the parkinsonian symptoms may be accompanied by an improvement of cognition.

Other causes of dementia are less frequent, but some of these diseases can be selectively treated and result in improved cognitive function. The most dramatic improvements occur with surgical removal of a benign brain tumor (1% of all dementias). Specific infections, including neurosyphilis, may also improve with treatment. Failure in specific organs (e.g., thyroid, heart, liver, kidney) can also cause dementia that reverses when the dysfunction of that organ is corrected. Even electrolyte imbalance reversal can improve cognition. Pernicious anemia can cause a dementia that can improve with vitamin B_{12} treatment (Wells, 1977).

Biological Issues Relevant to Treating Dementia Patients

Before considering the variety of psychological symptoms of demented patients that can be treated by conventional therapies, it is important to recognize the neuronal disruptions that cause the dementia of AD and the related disorders. The most marked deficit in AD as well as epileptic, hypoxic, hypoglycemic, and Wernicke-Korsakoff varieties of memory disorder is in the medial temporal lobe structures, the hippocampus and the amygdala (Brierly & Graham, 1984; Brun, 1983; Hirano & Zimmerman, 1962; Hyman, Van Hoesen, Damasio, & Barnes, 1984). A major deficit in the Alzheimer brain involves the cholinergic neurons projecting from the nucleus basalis of Meynert to the association cortices. This deficit is associated with a loss of nicotinic receptors more clearly than muscarinic receptors. The norepinephrine neurons of the locus ceruleus are affected variably (Bondareff & Mountjoy, 1986), as are the serotonin neurons of the rostral raphe nuclei (Palmer et al., 1987). It is essential to consider these possible neurotransmitter deficiencies when selecting pharmacological agents for treating psychological disruption in a demented patient. Attempts to directly augment these neurotransmitter deficits have been the principal approach to pharmacotherapy for AD.

Still, no single neurotransmitter or other unique brain factor has yet been linked to the cause of AD. However, control of the excitability of certain neurons, especially the systems involving the voltage-dependent NMDA-glutamate receptor calcium channel, may play a key role in AD (Greenamyre et al., 1988). This excitability seems to be modulated by all of the above neurotransmitters as well as other glutamate receptors and GABA (Palmer & Gershon, 1990). Central somatostatin function is also reduced in AD (Beal, Mazurek, Svendsen, Bird, & Martin, 1986; Sunderland, Rubinow, et al., 1987), but the role of this neurotransmitter has not yet been established. Until more is known about how the rate of AD progression is modulated, all medications should be used sparingly in Alzheimer patients except in carefully monitored research settings.

Treating the Memory Problems of Alzheimer's Disease

Based on the demonstrations of dramatic deficits in cholinergic function in the cortex, nucleus basalis of Meynert, and basal ganglia in AD patients (Bartus, Dean, Beer, & Lippa, 1982), there have been numerous efforts to augment the function of the cholinergic activity in demented patients. Early efforts focused on physostigmine, with mixed results (Ashford, Soldinger, Schaeffer, Cochran, & Jarvik, 1981; Jorm, 1986; Gustafson et al., 1987). With careful administration of a single oral dose, a maximum benefit is achieved at a plasma cholinesterase inhibition of 15% (Kumar et al., 1988; Sherman et al., 1988). However, this maximum benefit is only about a 5% improvement in memory, which is less than the daily fluctuation for Alzheimer patients. Given the risks and side effects of the anticholinesterase drugs, this mode of therapy has not yet proven to be clinically useful (Jenike, Albert, Heller, Gunther, & Goff 1990; Kumar & Calache, 1991). Lecithin (phosphatidylcholine), a natural source of the choline that is required for acetylcholine synthesis and whose abundance influences the rate of acetylcholine production, has also been widely tested, with no clear beneficial effects (Little, Levy, Chuaqi-Kidd, & Hand, 1985). Citicoline, a drug acting on phosphatidylcholine biosynthesis, showed a preliminary beneficial effect (Suryani, Adnjana, & Jensen, 1988). Direct stimulation of acetylcholine receptors by injecting bethanechol intrathecally was thought to hold promise (Harbaugh, Roberts, Coombs, Saunders, & Reeder, 1984), but has not proven to be useful (Penn, Martin, Wilson, Fox, & Savoy, 1988; Read et al., 1990). Injecting other substances by the intrathecal route remains a promising approach (Wilson & Martin, 1988). Muscarinic stimulation using arecoline (Tariot, Cohen, et al., 1988), oxotremorine (Davis et al., 1987), or other agents (Bruno, Mohr, Gillespie, Fedio, & Chase, 1986; Mouradian, Mohr, Williams, & Chase,

1988) produces considerable side effects without a clear benefit for memory in demented patients. Nicotinic-receptor stimulation with nicotine has also produced mixed results (Newhouse et al., 1988; Sahakian, Jones, Levy, Gray, & Warburton, 1989; Jones, Levy, & Sahakian, 1990).

The enhancement of the activity of naturally produced and released acetylcholine by blocking central acetylcholinesterase remains the most compelling approach (Becker & Giacobini, 1988; Ashford, Sherman, & Kumar, 1989). The essential question is whether long-term cholinesterase inhibition can upregulate and activate central nicotinic receptors (Bhat, Turner, Marks, & Collins, 1990). Recent trials have suggested that long-term (over 9 months) physostigmine might slightly retard the progression of AD (Jenike, Albert, Baer, 1990). Tetrahydroaminoacridine (THA) produced beneficial effects in AD patients in an initial study (Summers, Majovski, Marsh, Tachiki, & Kling, 1986). Numerous large-scale trials to replicate the early success of this drug have not demonstrated clear positive effects (Gauthier et al., 1990; Eagger, Levy, & Sahakian, 1991). However, the question of some subtle benefit remains. The Food and Drug Administration (FDA) has approved the use of this drug as a treatment for AD only for humanitarian purposes as of the end of 1991, due to the lack of clear evidence for a clinical benefit. THA also has significant liver toxic effects (Ashford, Sherman, & Kumar, 1989). Other agents in this class may be more beneficial while producing less toxicity. For example, metrifonate has produced some improvement of cognitive function with only minor side effects (Becker et al., 1990). In the case of metrifonate, a maximum benefit of 10% improvement of memory is achieved at a reticulocyte cholinesterase inhibition of 45%, although even this effect has not yet been shown to be clinically efficacious.

Whereas cholinergic agents have been studied most closely for an effect on memory, they may have a nonspecific effect on functioning. Assessment of claims of improvement on any type of behavior is difficult because of alternative explanations: the cholinergic agent could improve general cortical cholinergic function, or act in the basal ganglia to produce a neuroleptic effect, thus improving function by decreasing agitation. Recently, there has been interest in nerve growth factor (NGF) as an agent to help cholinergic neurons to survive (Hefti & Weiner, 1986), but such neuronal stimulation could possibly make AD progress more rapidly (Butcher & Woolf, 1989).

Several studies have targeted other neurotransmitters, but no significant successes have yet been demonstrated. Many older studies of stimulants, including amphetamines, which augment catecholamine activity, have failed to show an improvement of memory (Drachman, 1977). More recent studies on Alzheimer patients with more selective catecholaminergic drugs have also been unsuccessful (Mohr et al., 1989; Schlegel et al., 1989). Zimelidine, a serotonin re-uptake blocker, did not measurably improve memory in AD patients (Cutler et al., 1985). The agent Gerovital H3 is not generally considered to have a beneficial effect on memory, but a possible monoamine oxidase inhibitory effect may contribute to some general sense of well-being (Olsen, Bank, & Jarvik, 1978). The use of a monoamine oxidase (MAO) type B inhibitor (selegiline) to enhance the function of serotonin and norepinephrine has shown initial promise (Tariot et al., 1987; Monteverde, Gnemmi, Rossi, & Monteverde, 1990). Somatostatin is another agent that could be targeted, but replacement therapy requires intraventricular administration (Wilson & Martin, 1988). Targeting opiate systems for blockade with naloxone also was unsuccessful in ameliorating cognitive impairments in AD patients (Tariot, Gross, et al., 1988; Henderson et al., 1989).

A fundamental difficulty in considering neurotransmitter-augmenting strategies in treating AD is that this approach cannot ameliorate structural damage. For example, damage to the medial temporal lobe structures may be so severe as to supersede any possibility of a pharmacological benefit once those changes have occurred.

Treatable Psychiatric Symptoms Frequently Associated with Dementia

Clinicians have identified a broad range of psychological symptoms that are related to specific psychiatric disorders such as depression or schizophrenia. When symptoms common to other psychiatric disorders occur in the demented patient, their neural basis is no more clear than it is in the other psychiatric disorders. However, it is easy to conjecture that depressive symptoms in a demented patient could be related to Alzheimer-based disruptions of serotonergic or catecholaminergic systems. Similarly, psychotic symptoms could be related to disruption of these systems or acetylcholine, dopamine, or glutamate systems. Pharmacological agents affecting each of these systems have been implicated in the induction of psychosis or delirium. Whereas any psychiatric symptom can occur in a demented patient, certain symptoms are more frequent in patients with AD (Merriam, Aronson, Gaston, Wey, & Katz, 1988; Teri, Larson, & Reifler, 1988; Wragg & Jeste, 1989): depression (Fischer, Simanyi, & Danielczyk, 1990), psychosis (Burns et al., 1990), and sleep disorder (Ballinger, Reid, & Heather, 1982). These symptoms are usually amenable to the same pharmacological treatments used to treat these symptoms when associated with other psychiatric disorders, although the treatments must be tailored for this population (Winograd & Jarvik, 1986). The most difficult symptoms in demented patients for families to deal with tend to be disorders of behavior including agitation and aggression. When pharmacological treatments directed at specific psychiatric symptoms have failed, the clinician must address the difficult task of treating disruptive behavior (see Chapter 20).

Depression

Depending on the criteria, depression occurs somewhere between rarely and frequently in demented patients. The literature has attributed considerable importance to distinguishing these secondary depressive symptoms from a primary depression presenting as a dementia (Fischer et al., 1990). In most cases of depression, symptoms such as dysthymia, apathy, or anergy are apparent (Ballinger et al., 1982). The difficult cases are those of primary depression presenting as dementia in which the depressive symptoms are not obvious (McAllister, 1983). The difficulty in recognizing depression is one of the most compelling arguments for psychiatrists to evaluate all dementia cases. Many physicians have difficulty even considering the possibility that psychiatric disorders might be present. If it is not possible to obtain an evaluation by a qualified geriatric or neuropsychiatrist, there are several rating scales (e.g., Hamilton Depression Scale [Hamilton, 1960]; Geriatric Depression Scale [Yesavage et al., 1983]) that can serve as a guide to detecting the presence of depression.

There are many factors that predispose demented patients to developing depressive symptoms or a full depression (Kral, 1983). First, the stress of knowing that one's memory is no longer functioning could induce an adjustment reaction. As normal event stresses occur, the demented patient will be less able to cope, and these events will serve as stressors capable of inducing depression. A major biological consideration is that the norepinephrine and serotonin systems are affected by AD, and these systems are also implicated in depression, suggesting a direct link between AD and the development of depression. Furthermore, a considerable literature has suggested that depression, possibly related to disruption of norepinephrine and/or serotonin systems, might directly cause dementia, a state termed *pseudodementia* or *depression-associated dementia*. (However, depression-associated dementia is associated with apathy, unresponsiveness, and memory retrieval problems rather than selective impairment of memory encoding.) Consequently, the causes of concurrent dementia and depressive symptoms are potentially confounded. Regardless of the cause of depression, patients with dementia who have depressive symptoms should be treated with antidepressant therapy. In most cases, the depression will improve with therapy, but the dementia will remain unchanged or improve only slightly (Reifler, Larson, Teri, & Poulsen, 1986). Thus, the major diagnostic issue—distinguishing dementia from depression—should be resolved by vigorously treating the depressive symptoms.

Antidepressant medications have clearly established efficacy in geriatric and demented patients (Reifler et al., 1989). However, the art in prescribing these medications is predicting which medication would be best for a particular patient. The factors to be considered are the nature of the depression (agitated, retarded), desired secondary effects (tranquilization, sedation), and unwanted side effects such as daytime sedation, agitation, orthostatic hypotension (Neshkes et al., 1985), and undesirable anticholinergic effects including memory disruption and constipation. No one medication has yet demonstrated a specificity for a particular variety of depression, but therapeutic dose is inversely related to the potency of monoamine re-uptake blockade. Cortically projecting serotonin and norepinephrine neurons are disrupted by AD, but no method, using either neurotransmitter information or symptom clustering, has been demonstrated to be successful for predicting antidepressant efficacy in the depression associated with AD. However, because of the impairment of particular cholinergic systems in AD and the sensitivity of these patients to anticholinergic effects, drugs with even moderate anticholinergic effects (Richelson, 1990a) should be avoided. On this basis, trazodone has been a particularly useful drug for treating demented patients with depression (Gerner, Estabrook, Steuer, & Jarvik, 1980; Spar & LaRue, 1990). Trazodone also has mild calming effects, and can usefully be given at night to help sleep. But trazodone can cause postural hypotension (dizziness) and does not have strong potency for treating difficult cases. It has minimal cardiac toxicity. Because of their low anticholinergic side effects, fluoxetine, desipramine, and nortriptyline (Kumar, Smith, Reed, & Leelavathi, 1987) are also useful. There are no reports on the efficacy of the new drug bupropion, but it has minimal effects on cardiac output (Roose et al., 1991). Blood levels can be checked to be sure that an adequate dose is being administered.

In treatment-resistant cases, MAO inhibitors may also be useful (Ashford & Ford, 1979), but the diet must be reliably monitored and the patient must be carefully checked for postural hypotension. The new selective MAO type B inhibitor, selegiline, may be very useful because of its lack of side effects (Tariot et al., 1987; Mann et al., 1989). Monoamine oxidase inhibitors might also benefit cognitive function (Monteverde et al., 1990). Stimulants, e.g., methylphenidate (Ritalin), amphetamine, are also helpful on occasion, especially in the presence of behavioral retardation or excessive sleepiness.

Dosing of all drugs given to the elderly must be done cautiously, especially antidepressants: "start low and go slow" (Table 21.5).

Treatment with ECT has been controversial, especially in the demented patient. A fundamental issue is that in the past, ECT has been associated with memory impairment. However, with modern methods, including anesthesia, avoidance of anticholinergic premedications, hyperoxygenation of the patient before, during, and after the treatment, and brief pulse treatment, there may be less postictal confusion and long-term disruption of memory (Devanand, Verma, Tirumalasetti, & Sackeim, 1991). The advantage of unilateral treatment remains controversial; while it might cause less memory impairment, it may also be less therapeutically effective. When there is an adequate cardiovascular reserve, ECT rapidly and safely improves depression in a large portion of the cases. If there are cardiovascular problems, the plans for managing post-ECT tachycardia, hypertension, and agitation should be carefully planned before proceeding with treatment. Because hypertension is so frequent and can be so severe following ECT, ECT is contraindicated in patients with strokes, aneurysms, or a history of transient ischemic attacks. Electroconvulsive therapy can also help movement disorders, including parkinsonism (Douyon, Serby, Klutchko, & Rotrosen, 1989), which are common in the elderly. However, the only way to be truly convinced of the potential benefit of ECT is to see a severely demented patient with some depressive features unresponsive to antidepressant medication return to a high level of normal functioning after only four treatments.

Psychosis

Psychotic symptoms are among the most disturbing features of dementia. Psychotic symptoms are common (Ballinger et al., 1982); can occur early in the illness (Rubin

TABLE 21.5.   Psychiatric Medications of Use in Demented Patients

Generic Medication	Common Trade Name	Indication	Starting Dose	High Dose
Trazodone	Desyrel	Agitated	25–50 mg	300 mg
Fluoxetine	Prozac	Severe	20 mg	40 mg
Desipramine	Norpramine	Retardated	25 mg	150 mg
Nortriptyline	Pamelor	Vegetative	25 mg	150 mg
Bupropion	Wellbutrin	Side-effect sensitivity	100 mg	300 mg
Sertraline	Zoloft	Few side effects	50 mg	100 mg
Nardil	Nardil	Last choice	15 mg	60 mg
Selegiline	Deprenyl	Resistant	10 mg	20 mg

Note: Since these drugs have minimal anticholinergic side effects, they are not considered to have adverse effects on cognition.

& Kinscherf, 1989); and usually involve delusions, hallucinations, or misidentifications (Burns et al., 1990). Persecutory delusions, such as delusion of theft, are particularly common. The psychosis of AD has a different character from that of schizophrenia. The first-rank psychotic symptoms such as thought broadcasting or delusions of possession are not seen in the Alzheimer patient. Rather, three types of symptoms seem to occur: (a) those that may be derived from a failed memory without the realization that memory has failed ("I don't remember misplacing my keys, so someone must have stolen them"); (b) those that could be a manifestation of selective, critical isolation (seeing people in the room who are not there); and (c) those related to disruption of cortical organization, such as Capgras' syndrome (the belief that significant others have been replaced by impostors, a problem frequently attributable to damage of the right temporal lobe facial recognition region [Kumar, 1986]).

Psychotic symptoms are frequently treated successfully. Whereas several articles have debated and reviewed the merit of neuroleptics in the treatment of agitation in demented patients (Rosen, Bohon, & Gershon, 1990; Raskind, Risse, & Lampe, 1987; Satlin & Cole, 1988; Sunderland & Silver, 1988), these medications can control psychotic symptoms in about 80% of the patients (Smith, Taylor, & Linkous, 1974). However, considerable caution must be used in treating elderly patients with neuroleptics (Salzman, 1982).

High-potency neuroleptics are preferred because of their low anticholinergic side-effect profile (Richelson, 1990b), and the least anticholinergic of these, haloperidol, has been shown at least equal in efficacy to thioridazine for treating demented patients with psychosis (Smith et al., 1974); and thioridazine, with its strong anticholinergic side-effect profile, is more likely to induce cognitive dysfunction (Steele, Lucas, & Tune, 1986). Various high-potency neuroleptics have side-effect profiles that are not significantly different and have similar therapeutic efficacy (Lovett et al., 1987). These neuroleptics must be used carefully because of their high potency and long half-life. These drugs are frequently disliked by family members because if first prescribed in excessive doses, these drugs will cause severe parkinsonian symptoms. With a half-life of weeks, these drugs can slowly build up to toxic levels without the caregivers perceiving the problem. These drugs are also highly associated with falls, probably because they slow motor responsiveness, and some have peripheral alpha$_2$-adrenergic-blocking side effects that can cause postural hypotension. But if used in very low doses (e.g., haloperidol, 0.5 mg at bedtime, but rarely exceeding 2 mg/day), they are effective agents for controlling psychotic symptoms in afflicted patients (Steinhart, 1983). Haloperidol can also be administered intramuscularly in the decanoate form once per month, but again, in very low doses (5–20 mg/month). The new medication, clozapine, may cause difficulties in demented patients because of its strong anticholinergic side effects (Richelson, 1990b), but it may be useful in patients with parkinsonian symptoms (Pfeiffer, Kang, Graber, Hofman, & Wilson, 1990).

Behavior Disorders, Agitation, and Aggression

About 20% of demented patients with psychotic symptoms do not respond to neuroleptic medication. Often, these patients are agitated, disruptive or aggressive, become a major management problem, and require a creative approach (Risse &

Barnes, 1986; Salzman, 1987; Maletta, 1990). In some cases, treatment with a sedating antidepressant such as trazodone, possibly in combination with a neuroleptic, is helpful. In the past, many difficult demented patients were given GABA-agonist medications (particularly diazepam [Valium]) in large doses. In fact, many nursing home patients used to be treated with progressively larger doses that were accompanied by considerable sedation, impairment of cognitive function, and rebound agitation. Therefore, GABA agonists are now generally avoided in the treatment of dementia patients. One exception is carbamazepine, which is useful in controlling aggressive behavior in demented patients (Gleason & Schneider, 1990). Valproic acid could similarly be considered. Also, propranolol may be an effective agent in controlling disruptive behavior (Weiler, Mungas, & Bernick, 1988). A newer drug, buspirone, has efficacy as an anxiolytic and does not impair memory or cause confusion (Hart, Colenda, & Hamer, 1991). Buspirone has shown some promise in relieving agitation in dementia patients. In fact, aggressive or impulsive patients may respond well to serotonergic agents such as trazodone (Desyrel), buspirone (Buspar), or fluoxetine (Prozac) (Sobin, Schneider, & McDermott, 1989). Lithium can have adverse side effects in AD patients (Kelwala, Pomara, Stanley, Sitaram, & Gershon, 1984) and should be reserved for patients with a bipolar disorder history and manic symptoms that have responded to lithium in the past (Satlin & Cole, 1988). A last resort because of its anticholinergic side effects is the use of diphenhydramine (Benadryl) for "management problems." At late stages of the disease, patients occasionally become difficult to control, and at that time, nonspecific treatments need to be considered.

Another problem is "sundowning." Some patients, perhaps because of less illumination in their environment, because of circadian rhythm problems, or because of fatigue, become agitated and confused toward the end of the day. Sundowning should first be treated with environmental modifications (e.g., improved room lighting, increasing familiarity, and stabilizing the daily routine). Sleep rhythm disruption may also contribute to this problem and should be addressed.

Sleep Disorders

Insomnia is a symptom that occurs in a high proportion of dementia patients and can be very disruptive to the social environment, whether the patient is living with the family or in a nursing home. Lack of adequate rest may also contribute to the patient's agitation and confusion. The sleep disorder of AD is characterized better as a loss of circadian rhythm than as an insomnia or hypersomnia (Prinz et al., 1982; Prinz, Vitiello, Raskind, & Thorpy, 1990). Alzheimer patients frequently have interrupted sleep at night and take naps during the day. This loss of the normal diurnal rhythm may be due to dysfunction of basal forebrain circadian rhythm modulators adjacent to the nucleus basalis of Meynert. However, sleep disorders need not be treated unless they are disruptive to the patient's milieu. Sleeplessness becomes a major problem when the patient is keeping others awake at night, at risk for wandering, or exhibiting dangerous behaviors.

In all cases, when considering treating sleep disorders, it is important to first consider the psychosocial framework. The patient's day should be active, stimulating, and include plenty of exercise. Caffeine and nicotine should be avoided. The sleeping area should be quiet and free of distractions. Having the light off may help promote sleep in some patients, whereas having the light on may reduce confusion in others. Sleep hygiene is the first recommended approach to handling sleep disorders in the demented patient. Drugs should generally be avoided because of the possibility that they can exacerbate confusion.

Pharmacological treatment of sleep disorders in the demented patient begins with considering whether depression or psychotic symptoms underlie the sleep problem. The sleep problems of depressed patients respond well to trazodone (Mouret, Lemoine, Minuit, Benkelfat, & Renardet, 1988). Antipsychotic (neuroleptic) therapy can help the agitated or psychotic patient to sleep, and in cases where this is a problem in the evening, the whole medication dose can be given at bedtime. In the past, L-tryptophan had been advocated by many clinicians as an active hypnotic. L-Tryptophan is the natural precursor of serotonin, whose modulation is important in sleep (Hartmann, 1977). L-Tryptophan tablets were withdrawn from the market in 1989 because of the eosinophilia-myalgia syndrome associated with their use. However, this syndrome has now been linked to the use of genetically engineered bacteria by one Japanese firm in the manufacturing of this otherwise harmless amino acid (Belongia et al., 1990; Sakimoto, 1990). Whether the FDA allows L-tryptophan to be returned to the market as a prescription drug may depend on whether it can be shown to have a beneficial effect in carefully controlled studies.

If antidepressants or antipsychotics are not helpful to restore an acceptable sleep pattern, the next agent to consider is diphenhydramine, the most widely used over-the-counter sleeping aid in the country. Whereas diphenhydramine has memory disruptive anticholinergic side effects, these side effects rarely cause a problem the next day. GABA agonists should be avoided as outlined above. In extreme circumstances, where a potent sleeping pill is made necessary by medical or social circumstances, triazolam is the most rapid and effective agent available, and is largely metabolized by the next day so that a minimal degree of further memory impairment is caused. The dose of triazolam should be half of that given to young adults (Greenblat et al., 1991). Temazepam is a secondary, slightly more slowly metabolized drug.

Developmental History of Treatments for Dementia

Past treatments for dementia were developed on the basis of a variety of conceptualizations. When dementia was considered to be related to hardening of the arteries of the brain, strategies were developed to increase blood flow to the brain. Cyclospasmol and Hydergine were considered to relax cerebral arteries and increase blood flow. This view changed in the light of data indicating that many demented patients have normal cerebral arteries and that the decrease of blood flow to the AD brain is a secondary event due to decreased metabolism. Hydergine was then investigated as a drug that might enhance cerebral metabolism. Although Hydergine at one time led drug sales in the world, the most recent studies dispute that it has any beneficial effect (Thompson et al., 1990). Other drugs such as caffeine and amphetamines have been tested as stimulants that might reverse dementia. Whereas no study has shown stimulants to improve memory or stop the AD process, these agents may improve daytime function in selected patients. Similarly, nootropic agents such as piracetam have been studied for their potential to enhance metabolism and improve memory. Some studies of piracetam and lecithin have produced some beneficial effects (Friedman et al., 1981; Samorajski, Vroulis, & Smith, 1985), but this approach has not been substantiated. Direct treatment of the reported AD-related deficit in membrane fluidity with S-adenosyl-L-methionine produced no symptomatic improvement (Cohen, Satlin, & Zubenko, 1988).

There have been hundreds of millions of dollars invested in the testing and advertising of agents for their ability to improve cognition. Furthermore, there is a wide range of drugs currently in clinical trials to determine their effectiveness in treating AD (Cooper, 1991; Ferris, 1990). The testing of these agents is itself difficult, easily leading to results that can be misinterpreted as indicating that a drug is useful (Isaacs, 1979; Jarvik et al., 1990). Many drugs have been shown to enhance memory in animals, but failed to produce any beneficial effect in humans. A major problem is that when many tests are given, the probability of a positive result is increased. Thus, when many tests are being applied to many drugs, more rigorous criteria must be used to judge a result as positive. The essential question is whether a drug has a clinically significant effect, rather than merely a statistically significant effect in one isolated study. However, the ultimate issue is whether the AD process can be slowed or halted. So far, there is no accepted evidence that any intervention has been able to influence the course of AD.

In understanding dementia as a clinical syndrome, it is apparent that regardless of the cause, there is considerable similarity between symptoms. The primary symptom of dementia is impairment of memory, particularly the retention of new information. Memory involves many brain systems. One of the most vulnerable systems is the CA1 pyramidal neuron group of the hippocampus. The CA1 system is disrupted by several processes including Wernicke-Korsakoff syndrome, hypoxia, hypoglycemia, epilepsy, and AD (Brierly & Graham, 1984). The basis for this selective vulnerability is thought to be the heavy metabolic load for continuously constructing new memory connections. This load requires a large resource of thiamine (Cavanaugh, 1984) and a high brain concentration of NMDA-glutamate receptors (Cotman et al., 1989). The high concentration of NMDA-glutamate receptors would predispose these cells to one form of excitotoxicity (Olney, 1969, 1988). Other systems also subserve memory, such as the cholinergic system that includes the nucleus basalis of Meynert neurons. This cholinergic system is disrupted in the dementia of Alzheimer disease, alcoholism, and Parkinson's disease (Arendt, Bigl, Arendt, & Tennstedt, 1983). Norepinephrine systems (Stein & Wise, 1969) and serotonin systems (Kandel & Schwartz, 1982) have also been related to certain aspects of memory and both are disrupted in AD. Consequently, the site of the AD attack is most likely to be a fundamental memory mechanism. The NMDA-glutamate receptor (Greenamyre et al., 1988; Greenamyre & Young, 1989) or intrinsic neuronal processes activated by this receptor may be the site of that attack.

Dementia involves not only memory dysfunction but impairment of other higher cortical functions. However, it is possible that many of the ancillary symptoms of AD are due to disruptions of the episodic and semantic memory neural substrates subserving these functions. Accordingly, the current conceptualization driving the search for the cause of AD is the structure of brain memory formation at the synaptic level (Terry et al., 1991). In the search for understanding AD, two basic neural abnormalities have been discovered: (a) the excessive phosphorylation of the microtubule-associated protein-tau (MAP-t); and (b) the aberrant cleavage of the preamyloid protein to produce amyloid. Both of these processes seem to be part of natural mechanisms associated with the architectural adjustment of neuronal processes to form new memories. It is not known how both processes become disrupted, but one possibility is that a cellular protease gets out of control (Carrell, 1988) in vulnerable cells in response to certain stresses. The responsible stresses may be as diverse as trauma, blood-brain barrier leaks, nutritional deficiencies, or social changes. Such stresses will directly impact those neurons that are responsible for generating new connections (i.e., neurons involved in forming new memories). Neurons requiring the most plasticity (rearrangement of axonal and dendritic connections) seem to be particularly vulnerable to developing AD pathology.

New treatment strategies are focusing on basic mechanisms of neural plasticity. For example, a protease inhibitor may stop the progression of the disease by slowing the phosphorylation of MAP-t and the abnormal cleavage of the preamyloid protein. Another strategy considers the voltage-dependent calcium channel of the NMDA-glutamate receptor, which may be a primary controller of cell branching (Brewer & Cotman, 1989). Aluminum ions, similar in size to calcium ions, may slip into the neuron through this calcium channel and disrupt neurofilaments. This issue of whether aluminum plays a role in the development of AD has remained controversial (Crapper McLachlan, 1986; Bertholf, 1987; Zatta, Giordano, Corain, & Bombi, 1988; Edwardson & Candy, 1989). Aluminum chelation therapies have been tried, although not with clear success (Cardelli, Russell, Bagne, & Pomara, 1985; Kruck, Fischer, & McLachlan, 1990; Crapper McLachlan, et al., 1991). Furthermore, fluoride may protect against AD by keeping aluminum ions out of the body (Still & Kelley, 1980). Alternatively, directly dampening the activity of this calcium channel with its natural inhibitors, Mg^{++} and Zn^{++}, might also be able to halt the disease progression. It is hoped that the understanding of these mechanisms will lead to the developments of interventions that will protect neurons from undergoing these disastrous changes.

Future Prospects for the Treatment of Alzheimer's Disease

There continues to be hope that the basis of AD will be understood, and that understanding will lead to a direct treatment or prevention of this disease. To approach a treatment, it is first necessary to understand why certain neurochemical systems are disrupted by the disease. Most therapeutic strategies directed at treating a disease process either prevent the effect of the causative agent (e.g., aspirin for prevention of multiple small strokes) or decrease the vulnerability of the cells at risk (thiamine for alcoholic dementia). Whereas treatments of the past were found by trial and error, modern treatment strategies are developed by understanding systems and how these systems are disrupted by disease processes.

Addendum

In March 1993, an advisory committee to the Food and Drug Administration (FDA) recommended that the agency approve the marketing of Cognex (tacrine hydrochloride) for use in the treatment of the symptoms of Alzheimer's disease (FDA T93-13, 1993). The committee cited two recently published placebo-controlled studies (Davis et al., 1992; Farlow et al., 1993) which demonstrated that tacrine provides a clinically meaningful improvement in the symptoms of some Alzheimer's patients. The committee concluded, however, that the studies do not provide evidence that the drug alters the progression of the disease. A final decision about approval of the drug has not been made by the FDA as of April 1993.

References

American Psychiatric Association. (1987). *Diagnostic and statistical manual of mental disorders* (3rd ed., rev.). Washington, DC: American Psychiatric Association.

Arendt, T., Bigl, V., Arendt, A., & Tennstedt, A. (1983). Loss of neurons in the nucleus basalis of Meynert in Alzheimer's disease, paralysis agitans and Korsakoff's disease. *Acta Neuropathology (Berlin)*, *61*, 101–108.

Ashford, J. W., & Ford, C. V. (1979). Use of MAO inhibitors in elderly patients. *American Journal of Psychiatry*, *136*, 1466–1467.

Ashford, J. W., & Jarvik, L. (1985). Alzheimer's disease: Does neuron plasticity predispose to axonal neurofibrillary degeneration? *New England Journal of Medicine*, *313*, 388–389.

Ashford, J. W., Kolm, P., Colliver, J. A., Bekian, C., & Hsu, L. N. (1989). Alzheimer patient evaluation and the Mini-Mental State: Item characteristic curve analysis. *Journal of Gerontology: Psychological Sciences*, *44*, 139–146.

Ashford, J. W., Kumar, V., Barringer, M., Becker, M., Bice, J., Ryan, N., & Vicari, S. (1992). Assessing Alzheimer severity with a global clinical scale. *International Psychogeriatrics*, *4*, 55–74.

Ashford, J. W., Sherman, K. A., & Kumar, V. (1989). Advances in Alzheimer therapy: Cholinesterase inhibitors. *Neurobiology of Aging*, *10*, 99–105.

Ashford, J. W., Soldinger, S., Schaeffer, J., Cochran, L., & Jarvik, L. F. (1981). Physostigmine and its effects on six patients with dementia. *American Journal of Psychiatry*, *138*, 829–830.

Ballinger, B. R., Reid, A. H., & Heather, B. B. (1982). Cluster analysis of symptoms in elderly demented patients. *British Journal of Psychiatry*, *140*, 257–262.

Ban, T. A., Morey, L., Aguglia, E., Azzarelli, O., Balsano, F., Marigliano, V., Caglieris, N., Sterlicchio, M., Capurso, A., Tomasi, N. A., Crepaldi, G., Volpe, D., Palmieri, G., Ambrosi, G., Polli, E., Cortellaro, M., Zanussi, C., & Froldi, M. (1990). Nimodipine in the treatment of old age dementias. *Progress in Neuro-Psychopharmacology and Biological Psychiatry*, *14*, 525–551.

Bartus, R. T., Dean, R. L., Beer, B., & Lippa, A. S. (1982). The cholinergic hypothesis of geriatric memory dysfunction. *Science*, *217*, 408–471.

Beal, M. F., Mazurek, M. F., Svendsen, C. N., Bird, E. D., & Martin, J. B. (1986). Widespread reduction of somatostatin-like immunoreactivity in the cerebral cortex in Alzheimer's disease. *Annals of Neurology*, *20*, 489–495.

Becker, R. E., Colliver, J., Elble, R., Feldman, E., Giacobini, E., Kumar, V., Markwell, S., Moriearty, P., Parks, R., Shillcutt, S. D., Unni, L., Vicari, S., Womack, C., & Zec, R. F. (1990). Effects of metrifonate, a long-acting cholinesterase inhibitor, in Alzheimer disease: Report of an open trial. *Drug Development Research*, *19*, 425–434.

Becker, R. E., & Giacobini, E. (1988). Mechanisms of cholinesterase inhibition in senile dementia of the Alzheimer type: Clinical, pharmacological, and therapeutic aspects. *Drug Development Research*, *12*, 163–195.

Belongia, E. A., Hedberg, C. W., Gleich, G. J., White, K. E., Mayeno, A. N., Loegering,

D. A., Dunnette, S. L., Pirie, P. L., MacDonald, K. L., & Osterholm, M. T. (1990). An investigation of the cause of the eosinophilia-myalgia syndrome associated with tryptophan use. *New England Journal of Medicine, 323*, 359–365.

Bertholf, R. L. (1987). Aluminum and Alzheimer's disease: Perspectives for a cytoskeletal mechanism. *Critical Reviews of Clinical Laboratory Science, 25*, 195–210.

Besdine, R. W., Brody, J. A., Butler, R. N., Duncan, L. E., Jarvik, L., & Libow, L. (1980). Senility reconsidered: Treatment possibilities for mental impairment in the elderly. *Journal of the American Medical Association, 244*, 259–263.

Bhat, R. V., Turner, S. L., Marks, M. J., & Collins, A. C. (1990). Selective changes in sensitivity to cholinergic agonists and receptor changes elicited by continuous physostigmine infusion. *Journal of Pharmacology and Experimental Therapeutics, 255*, 187–196.

Boller, F., Mizutani, T., Roessmann, U., & Gambetti, P. (1980). Parkinson disease, dementia, and Alzheimer disease: Clinicopathological correlations. *Annals of Neurology, 7*, 329–335.

Bondareff, W., & Mountjoy, C. Q. (1986). Number of neurons in nucleus locus ceruleus in demented and non-demented patients: Rapid estimation and correlated parameters. *Neurobiology of Aging, 7*, 297–300.

Brewer, G. J., & Cotman, C. W. (1989). NMDA receptor regulation of neuronal morphology in cultured hippocampal neurons. *Neuroscience Letters, 99*, 268–273.

Brierly, J. B., & Graham, D. I. (1984). Hypoxia and vascular disorders of the central nervous system. In J. H. Adams, J. A. N. Corsellis, & L. W. Duchen (Eds.), *Greenfield's neuropathology* (pp. 125–207). New York: Wiley.

Brown, G., Albers, J. J., Fisher, L. D., Schaefer, S. M., Lin, J. T., Kaplan, C., Zhao, X. Q., Bisson, B. D., Fitzpatrick, V. F., & Dodge, H. T. (1990). Regression of coronary artery disease as a result of intensive lipid-lowering therapy in men with high levels of apolipoprotein B. *New England Journal of Medicine, 323*, 1289–1298.

Brun, A. (1983). An overview of light and electron microscopic changes. In B. Reisberg (Ed.), *Alzheimer's disease: The standard reference* (pp. 37–47). New York: The Free Press.

Bruno, G., Mohr, E., Gillespie, M., Fedio, P., & Chase, T. N. (1986). Muscarinic agonist therapy of Alzheimer's disease: A clinical trial of RS-86. *Archives of Neurology, 43*, 659–661.

Buchner, D. M., & Larson, E. B. (1987). Falls and fractures in patients with Alzheimer-type dementia. *Journal of the American Medical Association, 257*, 1492–1495.

Burns, A., Jacoby, R., & Levy, R. (1990). Psychiatric phenomena in Alzheimer's disease. I, II, III, IV. *British Journal of Psychiatry, 157*, 72–94.

Butcher, L. L., & Woolf, N. J. (1989). Neurotropic agents may exacerbate the pathologic cascade of Alzheimer's disease. *Neurobiology of Aging, 10*, 557–570.

Cardelli, M. B., Russell, M., Bagne, C. A., & Pomara, N. (1985). Chelation therapy: Unproved modality in the treatment of Alzheimer-type dementia. *Journal of the American Geriatrics Society, 33*, 548–551.

Carrell, R. W. (1988). Alzheimer's disease: Enter a protease inhibitor. *Nature, 331*, 478–479.

Cavanaugh, J. B. (1984). The problems of neurons with long axons. *Lancet, 1*, 1284–1287.

Cohen, B. M., Satlin, A., & Zubenko, G. S. (1988). S-Adenosyl-L-methionine in the treatment of Alzheimer's disease. *Journal of Clinical Psychopharmacology, 8*, 43–47.

Cooper, J. K. (1991). Drug treatment of Alzheimer's disease. *Archives of Internal Medicine, 151*, 245–249.

Cotman, C. W., Bridges, R. J., Taube, J. S., Clark, A. S., Geddes, J. W., & Monaghan, D. T. (1989). The role of the NMDA receptor in central nervous system plasticity and pathology. *Journal of NIH Research, 1*, 65–74.

Crapper McLachlan, D. R. (1986). Aluminum and Alzheimer's disease. *Neurobiology of Aging*, 7, 525–532.

Crapper McLachlan, D. R., Dalton, A. J., Kruck, T. P. A., Bell, M. Y., Smith, W. L., Kalow, W., & Andrews, D. F. (1991). Intramuscular deferoxamine in the patients with Alzheimer's disease. *Lancet*, 337, 1304–1308.

Cutler, N. R., Haxby, J., Kay, A. D., Narang, P. K., Lesko, L. J., Costa, J. L., Ninos, M., Linnoila, M., Potter, W. Z., Renfrew, J. W., & Moore, A. M. (1985). Evaluation of zimeldine in Alzheimer's disease: Cognitive and biochemical measures. *Archives of Neurology*, 42, 744–748.

Davis, K. L., et al. (1992). A double-blind, placebo-controlled multicenter study of tacrine for Alzheimer's disease. *New England Journal of Medicine*, 327, 1253–1259.

Davis, K. L., Hollander, E., Davidson, M., Davis, B. M., Mohs, R. C., & Horvath, T. B. (1987). Induction of depression with oxotremorine in patients with Alzheimer's disease. *American Journal of Psychiatry*, 144, 468–471.

de la Monte, S. M., Wells, S. E., Hedley-Whyte, E. T., & Growdon, J. H. (1989). Neuropathological distinction between Parkinson's dementia and Parkinson's plus Alzheimer's disease. *Annals of Neurology*, 26, 309–320.

Devanand, D. P., Verma, A. K., Tirumalasetti, F., & Sackeim, H. A. (1991). Absence of cognitive impairment after more than 100 lifetime ECT treatments. *American Journal of Psychiatry*, 148, 929–932.

Deyo, R. A., Straube, K. T., & Disterhoft, J. F. (1989). Nimodipine facilitates associative learning in aging rabbits. *Science*, 243, 809–811.

DiPatre, P. L. (1991). Cytoskeletal alterations might account for the phylogenetic vulnerability of the human brain to Alzheimer's disease. *Medical Hypotheses*, 34, 165–170.

Douyon, R., Serby, M., Klutchko, B., & Rotrosen, J. (1989). ECT and Parkinson's disease revisited: A "naturalistic" study. *American Journal of Psychiatry*, 146, 1451–1455.

Drachman, D. A. (1977). Memory and cognitive function in man: Does the cholinergic system have a specific role? *Neurology*, 27, 783–790.

Eagger, S. A., Levy, R., & Sahakian, B. J. (1991). Tacrine in Alzheimer's disease. *Lancet*, 337, 989–992.

FDA T93-13, March 18, 1993. Advisory Committee Recommends Approval of Cognex. Food and Drug Administration, U.S. Department of Health and Human Services, Public Health Service, Rockville, Maryland.

Farlow, M., et al. (1993). A controlled trial of tacrine in Alzheimer's disease. *Journal of the American Medical Association*, 268, 2523–2529.

Ferris, S. H. (1990). Therapeutic strategies in dementia disorders. *Acta Neurologica Scandinavica* (Suppl.), 129, 23–26.

Fischer, P., Simanyi, M., & Danielczyk, W. (1990). Depression in dementia of the Alzheimer type and in multi-infarct dementia. *American Journal of Psychiatry*, 147, 1484–1487.

Folstein, M. F., Folstein, S. E., & McHugh, P. R. (1975). "Mini-Mental State": A practical method for grading the cognitive state of the patients for the clinician. *Journal of Psychiatry Research*, 12, 189–198.

Friedman, E., Sherman, K. A., Ferris, S. H., Reisberg, B., Bartus, R. T., & Schneck, M. K. (1981). Clinical response to choline plus piracetam in senile dementia: Relation to red-cell choline levels. *New England Journal of Medicine*, 304, 1490–1491.

Gauthier, S., Bouchard, R., Lamontagne, A., Baily, P., Bergman, H., Ratner, J., Tesfaye, Y., Saint-Martin, M., Bacher, Y., Carrier, L., Charbonneau, R., Clarfield, A. M., Collier, B., Dastoor, D., Gauthier, L., Germain, M., Kissel, C., Krieger, M., Kushnir, S., Masson, H., Morin, J., Nair, V., Neirinck, L., & Suissa, S. (1990). Tetrahydroaminoacridine-lecithin combination treatment in patients with intermediate-stage Alzheimer's disease: Results of a Canadian double-blind, crossover, multicenter study. *New England Journal of Medicine*, 322, 1272–1276.

Gerner, R., Estabrook, W., Steuer, J., & Jarvik, L. (1980). Treatment of geriatric depression with trazodone, imipramine, and placebo: A double-blind study. *Journal of Clinical Psychiatry*, *41*, 216–220.

Ghoneim, M. M., & Mewaldt, S. P. (1990). Benzodiazepines and human memory: A review. *Anesthesiology*, *72*, 926–938.

Gleason, R. P., & Schneider, L. S. (1990). Carbamazepine treatment of agitation in Alzheimer's outpatients refractory to neuroleptics. *Journal of Clinical Psychiatry*, *51*, 115–118.

Graves, A. B., White, E., Koepsell, T. D., Reifler, B. V., Van Belle, G., & Larson, E. B. (1990). The association between aluminum-containing products and Alzheimer's disease. *Journal of Clinical Epidemiology*, *43*, 35–44.

Greenamyre, J. T., Maragos, W. F., Albin, R. L., Penney, J. B., & Young, A. B. (1988). Glutamate transmission and toxicity in Alzheimer's disease. *Progress in Neuro-Psychopharmacology and Biological Psychiatry*, *12*, 421–430.

Greenamyre, J. T., & Young, A. B. (1989). Excitatory amino acids and Alzheimer's disease. *Neurobiology of Aging*, *10*, 593–602.

Greenblat, D. J., Harmatz, J. S., Shapiro, L., Engelhardt, N., Gouthro, T. A., & Shader, R. I. (1991). Sensitivity to triazolam in the elderly. *New England Journal of Medicine*, *324*, 1691–1698.

Grotta, J. C. (1987). Current medical and surgical therapy for cerebrovascular disease. *New England Journal of Medicine*, *317*, 1505–1516.

Gustafson, L., Edvinsson, L., Dahlgren, N., Hagberg, B., Risberg, J., Rosen, I., & Ferno, H. (1987). Intravenous physostigmine treatment of Alzheimer's disease evaluated by psychometric testing, regional cerebral blood flow (rCBF) measurement, and EEG. *Psychopharmacology*, *93*, 31–35.

Hamilton, M. (1960). A rating scale for depression. *Journal of Neurology, Neurosurgery and Psychiatry*, *23*, 56–62.

Harbaugh, R. E., Roberts, D. W., Coombs, D. W., Saunders, R. L., & Reeder, T. M. (1984). Preliminary report: Intracranial cholinergic drug infusion in patients with Alzheimer's disease. *Neurosurgery*, *15*, 514–518.

Hart, R. P., Colenda, C. C., & Hamer, R. M. (1991). Effects of buspirone and alprazolam on the cognitive performance of normal elderly subjects. *American Journal of Psychiatry*, *148*, 73–77.

Hartmann, E. (1977). L-Tryptophan: A rational hypnotic with clinical potential. *American Journal of Psychiatry*, *134*, 366–370.

Hass, W. K., Easton, J. D., Adams, H. P., Pryse-Phillips, W., Molony, B. A., Anderson, S., & Kamm, B., for the Ticlopidine Aspirin Stroke Study Group (1989). A randomized trial comparing ticlopidine hydrochloride with aspirin for the prevention of stroke in high-risk patients. *New England Journal of Medicine*, *321*, 501–507.

Hefti, F., & Weiner, W. J. (1986). Nerve growth factor and Alzheimer's disease. *Annals of Neurology*, *20*, 275–281.

Henann, N. E., Carpenter, D. U., & Janda, S. M. (1988). Famotidine-associated mental confusion in elderly patients. *Drug Intelligence and Clinical Pharmacy*, *22*, 976–978.

Henderson, V. W., Roberts, E., Wimer, C., Bardolph, E. L., Chui, H. C., Damasio, A. R., Eslinger, P. J., Folstein, M. F., Schneider, L. S., Teng, E. L., Tune, L. E., Weiner, L. P., & Whitehouse, P. J. (1989). Multicenter trial of naloxone in Alzheimer's disease. *Annals of Neurology*, *25*, 404–406.

Heyman, A., Wilkinson, W. E., Stafford, J. A., Helms, M. J., Sigmon, A. H., & Weinberg, T. (1984). Alzheimer's disease: A study of epidemiological aspects. *Annals of Neurology*, *15*, 335–341.

Hirano, A., & Zimmerman, H. M. (1962). Alzheimer's neurofibrillary changes. *Archives of Neurology*, *7*, 227–242.

Hyman, B. T., Van Hoesen, G. W., Damasio, A. R., & Barnes, C. L. (1984). Alzheimer's disease: Cell-specific pathology isolates the hippocampal formation. *Science, 225,* 1168–1170.

Isaacs, B. (1979). The evaluation of drugs in Alzheimer's disease. *Age and Ageing, 8,* 1–7.

Jarvik, L. F., Berg, L., Bartus, R., Heston, L., Leith, N., Phelps, C., Shader, R., & Whitehouse, P. (1990). Clinical drug trials in Alzheimer disease: What are some of the Issues? *Alzheimer Disease and Associated Disorders, An International Journal, 4,* 193–202.

Jenike, M. A., Albert, M. S., Heller, H., Gunther, J., & Goff, D. (1990). Oral physostigmine treatment for patients with presenile and senile dementia of the Alzheimer's type: A double-blind placebo-controlled trial. *Journal of Clinical Psychiatry, 51,* 3–7.

Jenike, M. A., Albert, M. S., & Baer, L. (1990). Oral physostigmine as treatment for dementia of the Alzheimer type: A long term outpatient trial. *Alzheimer Disease and Associated Disorders, An International Journal, 4,* 226–231.

Jones, G., Levy, R., & Sahakian, B. (1990). Nicotine and Alzheimer's disease. *British Journal of Psychiatry, 156,* 280–281.

Jorm, A. F. (1986). Effects of cholinergic enhancement therapies on memory function in Alzheimer's disease: A meta-analysis of the literature. *Australian and New Zealand Journal of Medicine, 20,* 237–240.

Kandel, E. R., & Schwartz, J. H. (1982). Molecular biology of learning: Modulation of transmitter release. *Science, 218,* 433–443.

Kelwala, S., Pomara, N., Stanley, M., Sitaram, N., & Gershon, S. (1984). Lithium-induced accentuation of extrapyramidal symptoms in individuals with Alzheimer's disease. *Journal of Clinical Psychiatry, 45,* 342–344.

Kral, V. A. (1983). The relationship between senile dementia (Alzheimer type) and depression. *Canadian Journal of Psychiatry, 28,* 304–306.

Kruck, T. P. A., Fisher, E. A., & McLachlan, D. R. C. (1990). Suppression of deferoxamine mesylate treatment-induced side effects by coadministration of isoniazid in a patient with Alzheimer's disease subject to aluminum removal by ion-specific chelation. *Clinical Pharmacology and Therapeutics, 48,* 439–446.

Kumar, V. (1986). Capgras' syndrome in a demented patient. *British Journal of Psychiatry, 150,* 251.

Kumar, V., Salama, A. A., Desai, B., & Kumar, N. (1988). A community survey: Drug prescribing in dementia and in the normal elderly. *American Journal of Alzheimer's Disease and Related Disorders and Research, 3,* 16–20.

Kumar, V., Smith, R. C., Reed, K., & Leelavathi, D. E. (1987). Plasma levels and effects of nortriptyline in geriatric depressed patients. *Acta Psychiatrica Scandinavica, 75,* 20–28.

Kumar, V., Smith, R. C., Sherman, K. A., Ashford, W., Murphy, J., Giacobini, E., & Colliver, J. (1988). Cortisol responses to cholinergic drugs in Alzheimer's disease. *International Journal of Clinical Pharmacology, Therapy, and Toxicology, 26,* 471–476.

Kumar, V., & Calache, M. (1991). Treatment of Alzheimer's disease with cholinergic drugs. *International Journal of Clinical Pharmacology, Therapy, and Toxicology, 29,* 23–37.

Lesser, I. M., Miller, B. L., Boone, K., & Lowe, C. (1987). Delusions in a patient treated with histamine H_2 receptor antagonists. *Psychosomatics, 28,* 501–502.

Lipsy, R. J., Fennerty, B., & Fagan, T. C. (1990). Clinical review of histamine-2 receptor antagonists. *Archives of Internal Medicine, 150,* 745–751.

Little, A., Levy, R., Chuaqi-Kidd, P., & Hand, D. (1985). A double-blind, placebo controlled trial of high-dose lecithin in Alzheimer's disease. *Journal of Neurology, Neurosurgery and Psychiatry, 48,* 736–742.

Lovett, W. C., Stokes, D. K., Taylor, L. B., Young, M. L., Free, S. M., & Phelan, D. G. (1987). Management of behavioral symptoms in disturbed elderly patients: Comparison of trifluoperazine and haloperidol. *Journal of Clinical Psychiatry*, *48*, 234–236.

Maletta, G. J. (1990). Pharmacologic treatment and management of the aggressive demented patient. *Psychiatric Annals*, *20*, 446–55.

Mann, J. J., Aarons, S. F., Wilner, P. J., Keilp, J. G., Sweeney, J. A., Pearlstein, T., Frances, A. J., Kocsis, J. H., & Brown, R. P. (1989). A controlled study of the antidepressant efficacy and side effects of (-)-deprenyl. *Archives of General Psychiatry*, *46*, 45–50.

McAllister, T. W. (1983). Overview: Pseudodementia. *American Journal of Psychiatry*, *140*, 528–533.

Merriam, A. E., Aronson, M. K., Gaston, P., Wey, S. L., & Katz, I. (1988). The psychiatric symptoms of Alzheimer's disease. *Journal of the American Geriatrics Society*, *36*, 7–12.

Meyer, J. S., Judd, B. W., Tawaklna, T., Rogers, R. L., & Mortel, K. F. (1986). Improved cognition after control of risk factors for multi-infarct dementia. *Journal of the American Medical Association*, *256*, 2203–2209.

Miller, P. S., Richardson, J. S., Jyu, C. A., Lemay, J. S., Hiscock, M., & Keegan, D. L. (1988). Association of low serum anticholinergic levels and cognitive impairment in elderly presurgical patients. *American Journal of Psychiatry*, *145*, 342–345.

Mohr, E., Schlegel, J., Fabbrini, G., Williams, J., Mouradian, M., Mann, U. M., Claus, J. J., Fedio, P., & Chase, T. N. (1989). Clonidine treatment of Alzheimer's disease. *Archives of Neurology*, *46*, 376–378.

Monteverde, A., Gnemmi, P., Rossi, F., & Monteverde, A. (1990). Seleginine in the treatment of mild to moderate Alzheimer-type dementia. *Clinical Therapeutics*, *12*, 315.

Mouradian, M. M., Mohr, E., Williams, J. A., & Chase, T. N. (1988). No response to high-dose muscarinic agonist therapy in Alzheimer's disease. *Neurology*, *38*, 606–608.

Mouret, J., Lemoine, P., Minuit, M. P., Benkelfat, C., & Renardet, M. (1988). Effects of trazodone on the sleep of depressed subjects—a polygraphic study. *Psychopharmacology*, *95*, S37–S43.

Neshkes, R. E., Gerner, R., Jarvik, L. F., Mintz, J., Joseph, J., Linde, S., Aldrich, J., Conolly, M. E., Rosen, R., & Hill, M. (1985). Orthostatic effect of imipramine and doxepin in depressed geriatric outpatients. *Journal of Clinical Psychopharmacology*, *5*, 102–106.

Newhouse, P. A., Sunderland, T., Tariot, P. N., Blumhardt, C. L., Weingartner, H., Mellow, A., & Murphy, D. L. (1988). Intravenous nicotine in Alzheimer's disease: a pilot study. *Psychopharmacology*, *95*, 171–175.

Olney, J. W. (1969). Brain lesions, obesity, and other disturbances in mice treated with monosodium glutamate. *Science*, *164*, 719–721.

Olney, J. W. (1988). Revelations in excitotoxicology: What next? *Frontiers in Excitatory Amino Acid Research*, 589–596.

Olsen, E. J., Bank, L., & Jarvik, L. F. (1978). Gerovital-H3: A clinical trial as an antidepressant. *Journal of Gerontology*, *33*, 514–520.

Palac, D. M., Cornish, R. D., McDonald, W. J., Middaugh, D. A., Howieson, D., & Bagby, S. P. (1990). Cognitive function in hypertensives treated with atenolol or propranolol. *Journal of General Internal Medicine*, *5*, 310–318.

Palmer, A. M., Francis, P. T., Benton, J. S., Sims, N. R., Mann, D. M. A., Neary, D., Snowden, J. S., & Bowen, D. M. (1987). Presynaptic serotonergic dysfunction in patients with Alzheimer's disease. *Journal of Neurochemistry*, *48*, 8–15.

Palmer, A. M., & Gershon, S. (1990). Is the neuronal basis of Alzheimer's disease cholinergic or glutamatergic? *Federation of American Societies for Experimental Biology, 4,* 2745–2752.

Penn, R. D., Martin, E. M., Wilson, R. S., Fox, J. H., & Savoy, S. M. (1988). Intraventricular bethanechol infusion for Alzheimer's disease: Results of double-blind and escalating-dose trials. *Neurology, 38,* 219–222.

Perry, E. K. (1987). Cortical neurotransmitter chemistry in Alzheimer's disease. In H. Y. Meltzer (Ed.), *Psychopharmacology: The third generation of progress* (pp. 887–895). New York: Raven Press.

Pfeiffer, R. F., Kang, J., Graber, B., Hofman, R., & Wilson, J. (1990). Clozapine for psychosis in Parkinson's disease. *Movement Disorders, 5,* 239–242.

Prinz, P. N., Peskind, E. R., Vitaliano, P. P., Raskind, M. A., Eisdorfer, C., Zemcuznikov, N., & Gerber, C. J. (1982). Changes in the sleep and waking EEG's of nondemented and demented elderly subjects. *Journal of the American Geriatrics Society, 30,* 86–93.

Prinz, P. N., Vitiello, M. V., Raskind, M. A., & Thorpy, M. J. (1990). Geriatrics: Sleep disorders and aging. *New England Journal of Medicine, 323,* 520–526.

Raskind, M. A., Risse, S. C., & Lampe, T. H. (1987). Dementia and antipsychotic drugs. *Journal of Clinical Psychiatry, 48,* 16–18.

Read, S. L., Frazee, J., Shapira, J., Smith, C., Cummings, J. L., & Tomiyasu, U. (1990). Intracerebroventricular bethanechol for Alzheimer's disease: Variable dose-related responses. *Archives of Neurology, 47,* 1025–1030.

Reifler, B. V., Larson, E., Teri, L., & Poulsen, M. (1986). Dementia of the Alzheimer's type and depression. *Journal of the American Geriatrics Society, 34,* 855–859.

Reifler, B. V., Teri, L., Raskind, M., Veith, R., Barnes, R., White, E., & McLean, P. (1989). Double-blind trial of imipramine in Alzheimer's disease patients with and without depression. *American Journal of Psychiatry, 146,* 45–49.

Richelson, E. (1990a). Antidepressants and brain neurochemistry. *Mayo Clinic Proceedings, 65,* 1227–1236.

Richelson, E. (1990b). Psychopharmacology of schizophrenia: Past, present, and future. *Psychiatric Annals, 20,* 640–644.

Risse, S. C., & Barnes, R. (1986). Pharmacologic treatment of agitation associated with dementia. *Journal of the American Geriatrics Society, 34,* 368–376.

Roose, S. P., Dalack, G. W., Glassman, A. H., Woodring, S., Walsh, B. T., & Giardina, E. G. V. (1991). Cardiovascular effects of bupropion in depressed patients with heart disease. *American Journal of Psychiatry, 148,* 512–516.

Rosen, J., Bohon, S., & Gershon, S. (1990). Antipsychotics in the elderly. *Acta Psychiatrica Scandinavica, 358,* 170–175.

Roussouw, J. E., Lewis, B., Path, F. R. C., & Rifkind, B. M. (1990). The value of lowering cholesterol after myocardial infarction. *New England Journal of Medicine, 323,* 1112–1119.

Rubin, E. H., & Kinscherf, D. A. (1989). Psychopathology of very mild dementia of the Alzheimer type. *American Journal of Psychiatry, 146,* 1017–1021.

Sahakian, B., Jones, G., Levy, R., Gray, J., & Warburton, D. (1989). The effects of nicotine on attention, information processing, and short-term memory in patients with dementia of the Alzheimer type. *British Journal of Psychiatry, 154,* 797–800.

Sakimoto, K. (1990). The cause of the eosinophilia-myalgia syndrome associated with tryptophan use. *New England Journal of Medicine, 323,* 992–993.

Salusky, I. B., Foley, J., Nelson, P., & Goodman, W. G. (1991). Aluminum accumulation during treatment with aluminum hydroxide and dialysis in children and young adults with chronic renal disease. *New England Journal of Medicine, 324,* 527–531.

Salzman, C. (1982). A primer on geriatric psychopharmacology. *American Journal of Psychiatry, 139,* 67–74.

Salzman, C. (1987). Treatment of the elderly agitated patient. *Journal of Clinical Psychiatry*, *48*, 19–22.

Salzman, C., & Van Der Kolk, B. (1980). Psychotropic drug prescriptions for elderly patients in a general hospital. *Journal of the American Geriatrics Society*, *28*, 18–22.

Samorajski, T., Vroulis, G. A., & Smith, R. C. (1985). Piracetam plus lecithin trials in senile dementia of the Alzheimer type. *Annals of the New York Academy of Sciences*, *444*, 478–481.

Sandin, M., Jasmin, S., & Levere, T. E. (1990). Aging and cognition: Facilitation of recent memory in aged nonhuman primates by nimodipine. *Neurobiology of Aging*, *11*, 573–575.

Satlin, A., & Cole, J. O. (1988). Psychopharmacologic interventions. In L. F. Jarvik & C. H. Winograd (Eds.), *Treatments for the Alzheimer patient: The long haul* (pp. 59–79). New York: Springer.

Scharf, M. B. (1987). Clinical commentary: Benzodiazepine-induced amnesia [Monograph]. *Journal of Clinical Psychiatry*, *5*, 3.

Schlegel, J., Mohr, E., Williams, J., Mann, U., Gearing, M., & Chase, T. N. (1989). Guanfacine treatment of Alzheimer's disease. *Clinical Neuropharmacology*, *12*, 124–128.

Sherman, K. A., Kumar, V., Ashford, J. W., Murphy, J. W., Elble, R. J., & Giacobini, E. (1988). Effect of oral physostigmine in senile dementia patients: Utility of blood cholinesterase inhibition and neuroendocrine responses to define pharmacokinetics and pharmacodynamics. In R. Strong, W. G. Wood, & W. J. Burke (Eds.), *Aging, Vol. 3. Central nervous system disorders of aging: Clinical interventions and research* (pp. 71–90). New York: Raven Press.

Smith, G. R., Taylor, C. W., & Linkous, P. (1974). Haloperidol versus thioridazine for the treatment of psychogeriatric patients: A double-blind clinical trial. *Psychosomatics*, *15*, 134–138.

Sobin, P., Schneider, L., & McDermott, H. (1989). Fluoxetine in the treatment of agitated dementia. *American Journal of Psychiatry*, *146*, 1636.

Sorock, G. S., & Shimkin, E. E. (1988). Benzodiazepine sedatives and the risk of falling in a community-dwelling elderly cohort. *Archives of Internal Medicine*, *148*, 2441–2444.

Spar, J. E., & LaRue, A. (1990). *Concise guide to geriatric psychiatry*. Washington, DC: American Psychiatric Press.

Steele, C., Lucas, M. J., & Tune, L. (1986). Haloperidol versus thioridazine in the treatment of behavioral symptoms in senile dementia of the Alzheimer's type: Preliminary findings. *Journal of Clinical Psychiatry*, *47*, 310–312.

Stein, L., & Wise, C. D. (1969). Release of norepinephrine from hypothalamus and amygdala by rewarding medial forebrain bundle stimulation and amphetamine. *Journal of Comparative and Physiological Psychology*, *67*, 189–198.

Steinhart, M. J. (1983). The use of haloperidol in geriatric patients with organic mental disorder. *Current Therapeutic Research*, *33*, 132–142.

Still, C. N., & Kelley, P. (1980). On the incidence of primary degenerative dementia vs. water fluoride content in South Carolina. *Neurotoxicology*, *1*, 125–131.

Summers, W. K., Majovski, L. V., Marsh, G. M., Tachiki, K., & Kling, A. (1986). Oral tetrahydroaminoacridine in long-term treatment of senile dementia, Alzheimer type. *New England Journal of Medicine 315*, 1241–1245.

Sunderland, T., Rubinow, D. R., Tariot, P. N., Cohen, R. M., Newhouse, P. A., Mellow, A. M., Mueller, E. A., & Murphy, D. L. (1987). CSF somatostatin in patients with Alzheimer's disease, older depressed patients, and age-matched control subjects. *American Journal of Psychiatry*, *144*, 1313–1316.

Sunderland, T., & Silver, M. A. (1988). Neuroleptics in the treatment of dementia. *International Journal of Geriatric Psychiatry*, *3*, 79–88.

Sunderland, T., Tariot, P. N., Cohen, R. M., Weingartner, H., Mueller, E. A., III, & Murphy, D. L. (1987). Anticholinergic sensitivity in patients with dementia of the Alzheimer type and age-matched controls. *Archives of General Psychiatry*, *44*, 418–426.

Suryani, L. K., Adnjana, T. A. K., & Jensen, G. D. (1988). Citicoline treatment of memory deficits in elderly people. *International Journal of Geriatric Psychiatry*, *3*, 235–236.

Tariot, P. N., Cohen, R. M., Sunderland, T., Newhouse, P. A., Yount, D., Mellow, A. M., Weingartner, H., Mueller, E. A., & Murphy, D. L. (1987). L-deprenyl in Alzheimer's disease. *Archives of General Psychiatry*, *44*, 427–433.

Tariot, P. N., Cohen, R. M., Welkowitz, J. A., Sunderland, T., Newhouse, P. A., Murphy, D. L., & Weingartner, H. (1988). Multiple-dose arecoline infusions in Alzheimer's disease. *Archives of General Psychiatry*, *45*, 901–905.

Tariot, P. N., Gross, M., Sunderland, T., Cohen, M. R., Weingartner, H., Murphy, D. L., & Cohen, R. M. (1988). High-dose naloxone in older normal subjects: Implications for Alzheimer's disease. *Journal of the American Geriatrics Society*, *36*, 681–686.

Teri, L., Larsen, E. B., & Reifler, B. V. (1988). Behavioral disturbance in dementia of the Alzheimer's type. *Journal of the American Geriatrics Society*, *36*, 1–6.

Terry, R. D., Masliah, E., Salmon, D. P., Butters, N., DeTeresa, R., Hill, R., Hansen, L. A., & Katzman, R. (1991). Physical basis of cognitive alterations in Alzheimer's disease: Synapse loss is the major correlate of cognitive impairment. *Annals of Neurology*, *30*, 572–580.

Thompson, T. L., Filley, C. M., Mitchell, W. D., Culig, K. M., LoVerde, M., & Byyny, R. L. (1990). Lack of efficacy of hydergine in patients with Alzheimer's disease. *New England Journal of Medicine*, *323*, 445–448.

Tjoa, H. I., & Kaplan, N. M. (1990). Treatment of hypertension in the elderly. *Journal of the American Medical Association*, *264*, 1015–1018.

Tomlinson, B. E., Blessed, G., & Roth, M. (1970). Observations on the brains of demented old people. *Journal of the Neurological Sciences*, *11*, 205–242.

Weiler, P. G., Mungas, D., & Bernick, C. (1988). Propranolol for the control of disruptive behavior in senile dementia. *Journal of Geriatric Psychiatry and Neurology*, *1*, 226–230.

Wells, C. E. (1977). *Dementia*. Philadelphia: F. A. Davis Company.

Wilkie, F., & Eisdorfer, C. (1971). Intelligence and blood pressure in the aged. *Science*, *172*, 959–962.

Wilson, R. S., & Martin, E. M. (1988). New intrathecal drugs in Alzheimer's disease and psychometric testing. *Annals of the New York Academy of Sciences*, *531*, 180–186.

Winograd, C. H., & Jarvik, L. F. (1986). Physician management of the demented patient. *Journal of the American Geriatrics Society*, *34*, 295–308.

Wragg, R. E., & Jeste, D. V. (1989). Overview of depression and psychosis in Alzheimer's disease. *American Journal of Psychiatry*, *146*, 577–587.

Yesavage, J. A., Brink, T. L., Rose, T. L., Lum, O., Huang, V., Adey, M., & Leirer, V. O. (1983). Development and validation of a geriatric depression screening scale: A preliminary report. *Journal of Psychiatric Research*, *17*, 37–49.

Zatta, P., Giordano, R., Corain, B., & Bombi, G. G. (1988). Alzheimer dementia and the aluminum hypothesis. *Medical Hypotheses*, *26*, 139–142.

Zimetbaum, P., Frishman, W., & Aronson, M. (1991). Lipids, vascular disease, and dementia with advancing age: Epidemiological considerations. *Archives of Internal Medicine*, *151*, 240–244.

Zorumski, C. F., & Isenberg, K. E. (1991). Insights into the structure and function of GABA-benzodiazepine receptors: Ion channels and psychiatry. *American Journal of Psychiatry*, *148*, 162–173.

22

Legal, Financial, and Ethical Issues in Alzheimer's Disease and Other Dementias

William H. Overman and Alan Stoudemire

Modern medicine has made significant strides in improving the care and treatment in physical and mental disorders. Statistics reveal the impact of these advances on life expectancy and in population demographics. Currently, the single fastest growing segment of the American population is the over-100 age group. It is estimated that within less than three decades, the 65-plus population will constitute as much as one third of the total population of the United States.

As the population lives longer, there will be a concomitant increase in the complexity of issues faced by the medical profession. Patients will be more subject to chronic debilitating illnesses with both physical and mental complications, and as a result, new dilemmas are emerging. This chapter will address several of these practical concerns as they relate to legal, financial, and ethics issues faced by Alzheimer disease patients and their families (see also Overman & Stoudemire, 1988).

Legal, Financial, and Ethical Issues of Aging

The educational needs for all professions involved in the care of the elderly are changing as society struggles to cope with mounting demands placed upon it by a growing elderly population. These needs should incorporate a wide range of issues applicable to aging into academic and continuing education programs. Professionals in medicine, law, and allied health professions should be trained to recognize the special needs of the aging population, which include the following:

Personal autonomy.
Adapting to physical limitations.
Planning for possible mental or physical incapacity and the potential need for long-term care.
Understanding medical health insurance programs and addressing the lack of financial aid for long-term care.
Identifying integrated and interdisciplinary approaches to health care.

Long-recognized issues, such as a patient's consent to receive treatment, the process of informed consent, a patient's right to withhold treatment, and autonomy in assessment of patient competence to make decisions, have taken on new importance and urgency. Furthermore, as health care costs have rapidly risen, increased attention is focused on many long-term health care issues. Particular attention is given to sufferers of Alzheimer's disease because research indicates that many elderly individuals suffer from some form of dementia. Some controversial issues, with broad consequences, have raised ethical questions on the meaning of life, the quality of life, right to life, prolonging life for its own sake, as well as legal questions of guardianship, durable power of attorney, living wills, durable medical powers of attorney, and the preservation and protection of finances. The hefty costs of medical care, long-term care insurance (its availability, limitations, benefits, and costs), Medicaid (planning and qualifying) and its future, community services, as well as alternatives to private residential living are just some of the financial concerns of families with victims of Alzheimer's disease.

Addressing many of these issues in any given case requires a multidisciplinary approach. A team of experts on a hospital staff might include a physician, attorney, psychologist, social worker, and a financial planner. At the earliest indications of Alzheimer's disease, the family should seek professional advice from an attorney and financial adviser in making important legal and financial arrangements for the future. The remainder of this chapter will address relevant legal and financial issues.

Informed Consent

Informed consent is a legal concept derived from English common law; patients are given the right to decide independently whether they will receive any or a particular form of medical care, and what that care will consist of. The rule of consent requires that the patient give permission to the physician before rendering a treatment. Informed consent requires that the patient's permission be based on a reasonable or appropriate explanation of the proposed treatment (*Schloendorff v. Society of New York Hospital*, 1914; *Meretsky v. Ellenby*, 1979; *Pugsley v. Privette*, 1980). In recent years the courts have found that patients must also be advised of the risks they incur if treatment is declined. This corollary to informed consent is often referred to as *informed refusal* (*Truman v. Thomas*, 1980; *Crisher v. Spak*, 1983).

Consent is informed, however, only if the subject is mentally capable or "competent," has been provided with enough information to reach an informed or knowledgeable decision, and has not been coerced (Macdonald, Meyer, & Essig, 1986; *Kaimowitz v. Michigan*, 1974; Mills & Daniels, 1987). Competency is legally assessed at different levels in different situations. Clinicians may perform a mental status examination and a neuropsychological assessment and form an opinion on a patient's ability to make a reasoned judgment about a particular matter. However, the patient's actual competency is determined by the court (Mills & Daniels, 1987; Roth, Meisel, & Lidz, 1977; Applebaum & Roth, 1981; Mills, 1985). Most courts apply a standard concerning the patient's ability to make a reasonable decision in legally deciding how much information a physician is required to release. This is reflected in the trend toward the "patient's rights" approach to the issue of informed consent, as represented by the language that appears in the American Hospital Association Statement on a Patient's Bill of Rights (1973):

> The patient has the right to receive from his physician information necessary to give informed consent prior to the start of any procedure and/or treatment. Except in emergencies, such information for informed consent should include but not necessarily be limited to the specific procedure and/or treatment, the medically significant risks involved, and the probable duration of incapacitation. Where medically significant alternatives for care or treatment exist, or when the patient requests information concerning medical alternatives, the patient has the right to such information. The patient also has the right to know the name of the person responsible for the procedure and/or treatment.

Alzheimer's disease patients may be competent in the early stages of the disorder, but competency will inevitably deteriorate as the disease progresses. Thus competency must be assessed before making medical, legal, or financial decisions. In this regard, the Uniform Probate Code prefers the term *incapacity* to describe "incompetency," and defines an incapacitated person as

> "any person who is impaired by reason of mental illness, mental deficiency, physical illness or disability, advanced age, chronic use of drugs, chronic intoxication, or other cause (except minority) to the extent that he lacks sufficient understanding or capacity to make or communicate responsible decisions concerning his person." (Uniform Probate Code, 1969)

In certain emergency situations, medical decisions may need to be made for the mentally incompetent dementia patient. If emergency treatment is needed, then the doctrine of "implied consent" may be invoked (Mills & Daniels, 1987). This doctrine allows the physician to evaluate and treat the emergency condition against the apparent will of the patient, but is circumscribed by the legal requirement that *if* the patient is unconscious or otherwise unable to provide informed consent, the physician has a duty to attempt to contact the patient's family or guardian.

If a medical situation that is not an emergency involves an incompetent patient requiring medical care, a second opinion may be obtained. Legal consultation from the hospital may be secured to guide legal decisions and legal proceedings, if necessary, particularly if life-support systems or resuscitation procedures are involved. State statutes govern the legality of spouses, parents, siblings, children, and common-law spouses to act on behalf of incompetent adult patients in medical matters. As these statutes are continuously evolving in this regard, it may be advisable to conduct formal legal proceedings to determine the eligibility of family members to provide consent for the incompetent patient. If deemed necessary, emergency guardianship arrangements are normally possible in most states within 5 to 7 days. If there is no available family member to serve as a guardian, a court will appoint one.

Guidelines for Planning

Planning will allow patients to exercise their own rights and make their own decisions. The process should begin with the execution of four legal documents: a living will; a durable medical power of attorney; a durable financial power of attorney; and a will. These documents should be coordinated with financial and medical planning, enlisting the assistance of qualified legal and medical professionals. The documents will ensure that a patient's directives will be carried out over the course of his lifetime, and will enable his health care providers to offer treatment with a minimum of legal and financial complications.

The Living Will

Unfortunately, this document has a misleading name; it concerns both a patient's right to die and the implementation of life-support systems. In some states, this document is called a "natural death directive." The living will deals with the sensitive issue of withholding life support, a matter that first appeared before the U.S. Supreme Court in the *Cruzan* case (which will be examined in detail below; *Cruzan v. Missouri*, 1990). The living will is not available in every state, although many states recognize it as a legal document. Specific wording and terms of drafting the living will also vary by state. Usually, the intention of the living will is to express a person's desire not to be kept alive artificially, and to legally protect the physician to whom it is presented as he is legally responsible for withholding or disconnecting the patient's life support. The physician's diagnosis must adhere to at least some of the following conditions before a living will can be enforced: terminal illness is a requirement, as are intolerable pain, permanent coma, a persistent vegetative state, and a substantial loss in quality of life. The physician must consult with the patient's family, but neither the physician nor family may ignore the directives as stated in the living will. If the physician does not respect the wishes of the patient as set forth, he faces severe legal penalties.

In some states, a living will is called a "durable medical power of attorney." This document typically encompasses a broader range of medical issues than does the living will. Because many states limit the use of the living will to terminal illnesses or conditions, and prohibit the disconnection of nutrition/hydration devices by invoking a living will, legislatures are now recognizing the durable medical power of attorney as a specific legal document.

Durability

A "durable" power of attorney specifically states that the document "survives" the subsequent incapacity of the person who signs it. If such a statement is not included in the document, the old common law could apply, and the power of attorney could expire when the signatory is later incapacitated.

The Durable Medical Power of Attorney

The document referred to as the durable medical power of attorney enables competent individuals to make their own decisions and incorporate into a document their own beliefs concerning health-care preferences before they succumb to illness. The document can specify the provision or withholding of specific types of treatment, and the withholding, connecting, and disconnecting of life-support systems. The presence of a valid durable medical power of attorney prevents courts from depriving a patient of his basic civil rights, as could happen under guardian stewardship. Furthermore, without such a document, a guardian sometimes has to obtain a court order to secure legal authority to make many medical decisions, including those which may seek the termination of the patient's life. The durable medical power of attorney assumes additional importance as our society wrestles with the "right to die" issue. The *Cruzan* case provides a good study of this issue and several related questions: Does a patient really have the "right" to die? Does the patient or his family have the "right" to artificially sustain life or to withdraw life support? What is "death with dignity?"

For 4 years, from 1986 to 1990, Nancy Cruzan was kept alive by feeding tubes in a skilled care facility, where an attending neurosurgeon described her as living in a "persistent vegetative state." While she exhibited motor reflexes, she manifested no indications of significant cognitive function, and was in this condition with no signs of improvement since her arrival in 1986. Advised that their daughter would never improve, and feeling that she was actually dead, Nancy Cruzan's parents went to court to get an order to have the feeding tubes removed. The Missouri Supreme Court rejected their petition, ruling that if a patient is incapacitated and cannot make his own medical decisions (specifically pertaining to life-support systems), no other individual has the legal authority to make these decisions on the patient's behalf. The court further held that oral statements about life-support systems made to others by a patient are not legally binding. The court denied Nancy Cruzan's parents' request on the basis that they had not proven Nancy Cruzan's desires concerning life support. The parents took their case to the U.S. Supreme Court. In its decision rendered June 23, 1990 in the *Cruzan* case (*Cruzan v. Missouri*, 1990), the Supreme Court effectively enhanced the importance of the durable medical power of attorney. Justice Brennan stated, "Nancy Cruzan is entitled to choose to die with dignity" (*Cruzan v. Missouri*, 1990, p. 4926). The Supreme Court's decision was based on the constitutional right of each person to "self-determination;" that is, the right to decide what will or will not be done to them. However, the court went on to say that each state must set its own standards for decisions regarding life-support systems for incapacitated persons. The establishment of these standards would have to be mandated by legislation or by court decision.

The Supreme Court's ruling has effectively placed severe limits on a family's authority to make decisions like the designation of an incapacitated individual as a "do not resuscitate," as well as a family's authority to make a decision regarding the use, withholding, or disconnection of life support systems. Therefore, a patient would be well advised to create both a living will and a durable medical power of attorney if he wants to designate someone to be able to make medical decisions for him when he cannot do so. The U.S. Congress passed the Patient Self-Determination Act (Omnibus Budget Reconciliation Act, 1990) on November 5, 1990 to respond to the precedent set by the *Cruzan* decision of an incapacitated patient lying in a persistent vegetative state, incapable of making a decision as to their welfare, but considered "self-determining" and therefore rendering any outside legal authority invalid. The Act requires care facilities that participate in the Medicare and Medicaid programs to provide written information to all patients about the availability of advance directives.

Guardianship of Adults

Guardianship (or in some states, conservatorship) is a legal relationship that somewhat resembles that of parent and child. The guardian is appointed to administer the affairs of the ward (the individual who needs assistance). This relationship is termed *fiduciary*, which demands the highest degree of responsibility on the part of the guardian. A guardian can make decisions concerning the ward or his property. A conservator, however, can normally handle only the property of the incapacitated person.

The proceedings to establish either type of relationship are held in what is the equivalent of a probate court; here, formally, the guardian or conservator is given authority to act on behalf of the ward and thereafter is accountable for each and every action he takes. Guardianship normally terminates only with the death of the ward, although a proceeding can be filed in probate court if the guardian wishes to resign.

If the guardian handles the ward's property, the guardian must file a bond. Generally, the ward's income can be used for the maintenance of the ward and for certain other lawful expenses. The guardian cannot sell any of the ward's property without an order from the probate court. The guardian must also file an annual expense and balance report with the court. In general, guardianship deprives the ward of many fundamental constitutional and civil rights, and tends to publicly label the ward as incapacitated or incompetent.

Application for Guardianship

A typical permanent guardianship procedure requires 5 to 7 weeks to process, although a probate court will consider emergency applications. The application follows a standard legal format and is filed in the probate court of the county in which the ward resides. The probate court reviews the application, which requires information pertaining to the exact circumstances of the proposed ward, including why guardianship is required. As the court reviews the application, the ward is notified that the process of application is taking place. In addition, the ward is told that he will be evaluated by a court-appointed physician or psychologist, and of the right to retain legal counsel. Such counsel will be appointed by the court if the proposed ward cannot afford one. An evaluator visits the proposed ward and prepares a written report for the court. If the evaluator considers a guardianship necessary, a hearing is held at the probate court. At the hearing, which may assume the format of a jury trial, the standards of competency and incompetency discussed above are applied by the court. If the court determines that a guardianship is necessary, the court declares the proposed ward to be an "incapacitated adult," and appoints a guardian. The appointee may be an individual of the ward's choosing, often a friend or relative, or if no elected person is acceptable or available, the court can make a selection. A court may appoint a representative of a public social service agency like a state department for family services as a guardian of the person, and a financial institution to be a guardian of property. Recently, guardianship procedures and laws have come under scrutiny, and have been made more restrictive. The Uniform Probate Code now requires that the ward be of a certain "advanced age." Of concern are ethical issues governing autonomy and protection of the right to self-determination.

Alternatives to Guardianship

Most professionals in the field of aging believe that less restrictive alternatives to guardianship should be employed where possible. These include joint ownership of property, gifting, representative payee arrangements, the durable (financial) power of attorney, and trust agreements.

Joint Ownership of Property

A trusted relative or friend of an elderly individual may become co-owner of real estate and securities to provide assistance in making bank deposits, writing checks, or paying bills, by signing his own name to such transactions. Disadvantages of this concept are the possibility of the co-owner legally absconding with the primary owner's assets on the authority of his own signature, the fact that all real estate transactions require both parties' written consent, and the reality of all assets becoming the property of the co-owner upon the original owner's death, bypassing the will. The addition of another person to the title of real estate without the right of survivorship does not allow that person's interest to remain in effect after the death of the original owner, but if the second person preceded the original owner in death, his share of the property goes to his estate. Therefore, the original owner could find himself forced out of his own home because of problems in the second person's estate.

Gifting

Gifting property is a potentially valuable planning tool, with advantages and drawbacks. The person making the gift may enjoy the process, and may help protect and preserve his property when he faces chronic illness or the prospects of long-term care. However, once given away, the giver loses all control over the gifted property, including legal claims in the event of a financial emergency. Another issue is raised if the recipient is trusted to return the gift to the giver if needed, but the recipient dies. Furthermore, the recipient could use the gift in ways not intended by the giver.

Representative Payee Arrangements

If a person receives income from Social Security, a railroad pension, or the Veterans Administration, he may need assistance in handling these benefits. The agency paying the benefits can appoint a person (the *representative payee*) to receive and handle those benefits for the beneficiary. The proposed representative payee must apply to the benefits agency and demonstrate that he is the primary caregiver of the beneficiary, has a continuous relationship with him, that the beneficiary cannot manage his own funds, and that the application has a strong concern for the beneficiary's welfare. The payee must later account to the agency for the proper handling of the benefits. A beneficiary doesn't have to be legally incompetent, and the payee can be a different person than a court-appointed guardian. The representative payee arrangement can be terminated by the beneficiary, frequently with a doctor's statement showing capability, or if the beneficiary can demonstrate to the agency that the payee has misused the benefits or otherwise doesn't have the best interests of the beneficiary in mind.

The Durable (Financial) Power of Attorney

The durable financial power of attorney is the most frequently used alternative to guardianship or conservatorship. The signatory keeps his basic civil rights, can revoke the document while competent, and makes his own decisions. The arrangement pertains exclusively to matters of business and finance, and names the specific person or persons the individual desires to manage his affairs. The document, used in transactions with banks, stock brokerage firms, government agencies, and pension funds, can include specific checks and balances on the agent's authority.

Trust Agreements

A trust is more formal than a power of attorney and provides additional protections. It is frequently used as part of a general estate plan and when tax planning is an issue. The creation of a trust requires the creation of a trust agreement or declaration of trust, and the transfer of property to the trust. The property in the trust is then handled by the person or persons (trustees) named by the donor. A trust is like an "artificial person" in that it must have its own tax identification numbers, and file federal and state tax returns annually. The donor specifies exactly which powers and authorities are to be given to the trustee(s), and designates the beneficiaries. The donor may be the trustee, and can be the beneficiary. The trust can be revocable by the donor and can expire at the donor's death. The property in the trust can either be passed through the donor's will, or be distributed outside the estate if designated by the trust agreement.

Recently, trusts gained popularity as a means of qualifying the donor for governmental assistance like Medicaid. This practice was abused, and the Medicaid law was changed to eliminate the establishment of "Medicaid qualifying trusts" unless very specific provisions are included in the trust agreement; provisions most people find unacceptable.

Financial Planning and Medicaid

Financial issues are particularly important to Alzheimer's disease patients and their caregivers. The likely prospect of long-term care is expensive. Without effective financial planning, the patient, his spouse, and family may be impoverished by costs of the patient's care.

An option available through the private insurance industry is long-term care insurance ("nursing home" insurance). The coverage offered under many long-term policies excludes Alzheimer's disease and other dementias by considering them a form of mental illness rather than organic or cognitive disorders. Other policies might only pay for "convalescent" care and will therefore not cover Alzheimer's disease because it is chronic by nature. Long-term care policies must be reviewed carefully prior to consideration.

Medicaid, an amendment to the Social Security program utilizing state-administered federal funds, is the only financial option for patients in the United States without the means or foresight to have made other plans. To qualify for Medicaid benefits, the patient must be impoverished.

In 1988, the Medicare/Medicaid laws were amended with the addition of the Medicare Catastrophic Coverage Act (MCCA, 1988). The MCCA has had a fundamental impact on our national health care policy and on the private insurance industry. Strong public opposition to MCCA prompted its repeal in November, 1989; however, the Medicaid portion was left intact by the U.S. Senate. Two sections of MCCA have impacted Medicaid qualification planning. One is the section "Protection of Income and Resources of Couple for Maintenance" (MCCA, 1988), which applies to every nursing home admission made on or after September 30, 1989. It theoretically provides an income and asset "allowance" which will allow the "healthy" spouse to live in the community without needing welfare benefits. The other section is the "Thirty Month Transfer Penalty Rule," which applies to any transfers made on or after July 1, 1988. This new rule replaced the previous "Two Year Transfer Rule." The "look-back" or disallowance period for income/asset transfers was increased from 2 years to 30 months. A mandatory penalty for certain transfers made during the "look-back" period was also created. The transfers which are penalized are those made (a) for less than fair-market value, and (b) within the 30 months immediately preceding entry into a nursing home (not application for Medicaid assistance). The maximum penalty period is capped at 30 months of mandatory ineligibility for Medicaid benefits.

The Will (Last Will and Testament)

A will is a legal construct which designates its testator's (the individual making the will) disposition of assets, or estate, upon his death. A will should be established early in life, or upon accumulation of a significant number of assets, and revised as changes in economic status, designated guardians of children, and beneficiaries occur.

A will should be written, and made voluntarily without coercion. The testator may be an Alzheimer's patient and may execute a valid will if he has the requisite legal capacity to do so. Some patients may execute a valid will during a legally recognized "lucid interval."

As wills are prepared, a couple is likely to make "mirror" declarations, in which each spouse leaves everything to the other with the provision that if the other spouse precedes the first in death, everything goes to the children. If one of the couple requires long-term care, and the healthy spouse dies first, the inheritance to the invalid spouse may increase his resources beyond Medicaid eligibility limits. This situation would require the designation of a guardian to manage the invalid spouse's assets, which would then be spent on the cost of his care. The desire of the couple to see that their children receive their estate would be defeated. Planning by qualified financial and legal counsel can ensure that some assets are inherited by trustworthy persons who will use them to pay for items not covered by Medicaid, and to improve the quality of the patient's life during his final years.

Conclusions

Because physicians, neuropsychologists, and social workers will generally be the first professionals to have contact with patients, they are best able to influence the patients and their families to initiate financial planning. As soon as a diagnosis of Alzheimer's disease or other dementia is made or suspected, the explanation of certain aspects of the disease will help the family understand the need for immediate and long-range planning, utilizing the professional expertise of attorneys and financial counselors. This will help diminish the enormous emotional and financial burden that Alzheimer's disease and other dementias present for the patient and their family.

References

American Hospital Association Statement on a Patient's Bill of Rights. (1973). *Hospitals, 47*, 41.

Applebaum, P. S., & Roth, L. H. (1981). Clinical issues in the assessment of competency. *American Journal of Psychiatry, 138*, 1462–1467.

Cobbs v. Grant, 8 Cal. 3d 229, 502 P. 2d 1, 104 Cal. Rptr. 505 (1972).

Crisher v. Spak, 122 Misc. 2d 355, 471 N.Y.S. 2d 741 (1983).

Cruzan, Nancy Beth, by her Parents and Co-Guardian, Lester L. Cruzan, et ux., Petitioners v. Director, Missouri Department of Health, et al. (No. 88-1503, June 25, 1990; 58LW 4916).

Cruzan, Nancy Beth, Lester, L., & Joyce Cruzan, Petitioners v. David B. Mouton, esq., and Thad C. McCanse, esq., Co-Guardians ad litems, Estate No. CV384-9P, Cir. Ct. Jasper County, Missouri (Probate Div., Dec. 14, 1990).

Kaimowitz v. Michigan Department of Mental Health Div. No. 73-91434-A W., Cir. Ct., Wayne County, Mich. (1973), abstracted in 13 *Criminal Law Rep.* 2452, reprinted in *Law, Psychiatry and the Mental Health System*, by Brooks, A. D. (1974). New York: Little, Brown.

Macdonald, M. G., Meyer, K. C., & Essig, B. (1986). *Health care law: A practical guide.* New York: Matthew Bender.

Medicare Catastrophic Coverage Act. (1988). Public Law 100-360, § 303(a), 42 U.S.C. § 1396a.

Meretsky v. Ellenby, 370 So. 2d 1222, Fla. Dist. Ct. App. (1979).

Mills, M. J. (1985). Legal issues in psychiatric treatment. *Psychiatric Medicine, 2*, 245–261.

Mills, M. J., & Daniels, M. L. (1987). Medical-legal issues. In A. Stoudemire & B. S. Fogel (Eds.), *Principles of medical psychiatry* (pp. 463–476). Orlando, FL: Grune & Stratton.

Omnibus Budget Reconciliation Act, §§ 4206 & 4751 (1990).

Overman, W., & Stoudemire, A. (1988). Guidelines for legal and financial counseling of Alzheimer's disease patients and their families. *American Journal of Psychiatry, 145*, 1495–1500.

Pugsley v. Privette, 220 Va. 892, 263 S.E. 2d 69 (1980).

Roth, L. H., Meisel, A., & Lidz, C. W. (1977). Tests of competency to consent to treatment. *American Journal of Psychiatry, 134*, 279–284.

Schloendorff v. Society of New York Hospital, 211 N.Y. 125, 105 N.E. 92 (1914).

Truman v. Thomas, 27 Cal. 3d 285, 611 P.2d 902, 165 Cal. Rptr. 308 (1980).

Uniform Probate Code, § 5-101(1), Adopted by National Conference of Commissioners on Uniform Laws (American Bar Association, Aug., 1969).

Author Index

Note: Italicized numbers represent the page on which the complete reference appears.

Test Index

Note: Page numbers followed by t indicate tables.

Subject Index

Note: Page numbers followed by t indicate tables; those followed by f refer to figures.